GENERAL PSYCHOLOGY SERIES
EDITORS
Arnold P. Goldstein, Syracuse University
Leonard Krasner, Stanford University & SUNY at Stony Brook

HANDBOOK OF CHILD AND ADOLESCENT ASSESSMENT
(Vol. 167)

Titles of Related Interest

Bellack/Hersen BEHAVIORAL ASSESSMENT: A Practical Handbook, Third Edition

Dana MULTICULTURAL ASSESSMENT PERSPECTIVES FOR PROFESSIONAL PSYCHOLOGY

Golden CLINICAL INTERPRETATION OF OBJECTIVE PSYCHOLOGICAL TESTS, Second Edition

Goldstein/Hersen HANDBOOK OF PSYCHOLOGICAL ASSESSMENT, Second Edition

Hersen/Bellack DICTIONARY OF BEHAVIORAL ASSESSMENT TECHNIQUES

Johnson/Goldman DEVELOPMENTAL ASSESSMENT IN CLINICAL CHILD PSYCHOLOGY: A Handbook

Kellerman/Burry HANDBOOK OF PSYCHODIAGNOSTIC TESTING: The Analysis of Personality in the Psychological Report, Second Edition

Kratochwill/Morris THE PRACTICE OF CHILD THERAPY, Second Edition

Matson/Ollendick ENHANCING CHILDREN'S SOCIAL SKILLS: Assessment and Training

Meyer THE CLINICIAN'S HANDBOOK: Integrated Diagnostics, Assessment, and Intervention in Adult and Adolescent Psychopathology, Third Edition

Oster/Caro/Eagen/Lillo ASSESSING ADOLESCENTS

Teglasi CLINICAL USE OF STORY TELLING: Emphasizing the T.A.T. with Children and Adolescents

HANDBOOK OF CHILD AND ADOLESCENT ASSESSMENT

Edited by

THOMAS H. OLLENDICK
Virginia Polytechnic Institute and State University

MICHEL HERSEN
Nova University

ALLYN AND BACON
Boston • London • Toronto • Sydney • Tokyo • Singapore

Copyright © 1993 by Allyn and Bacon
A Division of Simon & Schuster, Inc.
160 Gould Street
Needham Heights, MA 02194

All rights reserved. No part of the material protected by this copyright notice may be reproduced or utilized in any form or by any means, electronic or mechanical, including photocopying, recording, or by any information storage and retrieval system, without the written permission of the copyright owner.

Library of Congress Cataloging-in-Publication Data

Handbook of child and adolescent assessment / edited by Thomas H. Ollendick, Michel Hersen.
    p. 528 cm. — (General psychology series : 167)
  Includes indexes.
  ISBN 0-205-14592-2
  1. Children—Medical examinations. 2. Behavioral assessment of children. 3. Children—Psychological testing. 4. Mental illness--Diagnosis. I. Ollendick, Thomas H. II. Hersen, Michel.
III. Series.
RJ50.H36 1991
618.92′0075—dc20   90-49071
                                                              CIP

ISBN 0-205-14592-2
H45925

Printed in the United States of America

10 9 8 7 6 5 4 3 2 1   96 95 94 93 92

**To Our Children Who Are Rapidly Becoming,
Or Already Have Become, Adolescents**

**Laurie and Katie
and
Jonathan and Nathaniel**

CONTENTS

Preface   xi

PART I. FUNDAMENTAL ISSUES

1.	Child and Adolescent Behavioral Assessment	Thomas H. Ollendick Michel Hersen	3
2.	Developmental Considerations in Child Assessment	William Yule	15
3.	Diagnostic Issues in Child Assessment	Helen Orvaschel Paul Ambrosini Harris Rabinovich	26
4.	Neurological Assessment	Janet B. Teodori	41
5.	Ethical Issues in the Psychological Assessment of Children	Gerald P. Koocher	51

PART II. SPECIFIC ASSESSMENT STRATEGIES

6.	Interviewing	Kay Hodges Janice Zeman	65

7.	Checklists and Rating Scales	John Piacentini	82
8.	Self-Report Methodology	William M. Reynolds	98
9.	Self-Monitoring	Edward S. Shapiro Christine L. Cole	124
10.	Direct Observation	Billy A. Barrios	140
11.	Peer-Referenced Assessment Strategies	Frank M. Gresham Steven G. Little	165
12.	Physiological Assessment	Neville J. King	180
13.	Intellectual and Achievement Testing	Alan S. Kaufman Toshinori Ishikuma	192
14.	Neuropsychological Assessment	Gregory T. Slomka Ralph E. Tarter	208
15.	Projective Techniques	A. J Finch, Jr. Ronald W. Belter	224

PART III. ASSESSMENT OF SPECIFIC POPULATIONS

16.	Anxiety Disorders	Cyd C. Strauss	239
17.	Depression	John F. Curry W. Edward Craighead	251
18.	Attention Deficit Hyperactivity Disorder	Mark D. Rapport	269
19.	Conduct Disorder	Alan E. Kazdin	292
20.	Tics and Tourette's Disorder	Floyd R. Sallee	311
21.	Mental Retardation	Michael G. Aman David Hammer Johannes Rojahn	321
22.	Pervasive Developmental Disorders	Lee M. Marcus Eric Schopler	346
23.	Obesity	William G. Johnson Linda K. Hinkle	364
24.	Eating Disorders	David M. Garner Peggy Parker	384
25.	Headaches	Donald A. Williamson Suzanne M. Savin David H. Gleaves	400

26.	Pain	Dennis C. Russo Beate M. Lehn Charles B. Berde	413
27.	Physical Abuse and Neglect	Robert T. Ammerman	439

Afterword — 455

Author Index — 457

Subject Index — 489

About the Editors and Contributors — 501

PREFACE

In this multiauthored handbook, we explore the principles and procedures of child and adolescent assessment. Using our earlier volume, *Child Behavioral Assessment* (Pergamon Press, 1984), as a springboard, we extend our coverage to adolescence and suggest that *all* assessment practices—behavioral and nonbehavioral—be guided by a set of principles that will lead to a set of developmentally sensitive and empirically validated procedures. Toward this end, we define assessment as an *exploratory, hypothesis-testing process in which a range of developmentally sensitive and empirically validated procedures is used to understand a given child, group, or social ecology and to formulate and evaluate specific intervention procedures*. Recent advances have shown the viability of this multimethod approach in providing a complete picture of the child or adolescent and the context in which his or her problematic behavior occurs and in which it can be altered. Still, much remains to be learned, and the field of child and adolescent assessment can be said to be in its own state of childhood or adolescence.

Attention to these developments has guided us in the selection of contributors and topics of this volume. All contributors are practicing clinicians in the field of child and adolescent assessment and treatment and are highly aware of the importance of development and growth as they relate to the assessment and treatment of youth. In addition, all contributors are empirically minded and active researchers; consequently, the chapters are current, data-bound, and clinically useful.

The volume is organized in three parts: fundamental issues, specific assessment strategies, and the assessment of specific populations. In the first part, conceptual, developmental, diagnostic, and ethical issues are explored in detail. The purpose of this section is to provide a basis for the various assessment procedures that follow. In the second part, specific assessment procedures that comprise the multimethod approach are described. Procedures illustrated range from structured interviews to direct behavioral observations to projective tests. For each procedure, issues related to reliability, validity, and clinical utility are addressed. In the third section, this assessment process is illustrated for diverse psychiatric and pediatric populations, including those with anxiety disorders, depression, attention deficit-hyperactivitiy disorder, conduct disorder, tics and Tourette disorders, mental retardation, pervasive developmental disorders, obesity, anorexia, headache, pediatric pain, and child abuse and neglect. In this section, careful attention to psychometric and developmental issues is afforded and case illustrations are highlighted. Finally, we provide a brief commentary on the future of child and adolescent assessment. All in all, the handbook is intended to be a source book for advanced undergraduate students, graduate students, and mental health professionals working with children and adolescents.

In an undertaking such as this, many persons are to be acknowledged. Among the foremost are the contributors, whose expertise and dedication to the project will become readily evident to the reader. Without them, up-to-date scholarly coverage of the various topics would not have been possible. We would also like to acknowledge our good friend Jerome B. Frank and the other professionals at Pergamon Press whose encouragement, support, and patience have been welcomed. They have been most helpful in bringing the project to fruition. In addition, we would like to thank two persons who have assisted us with secretarial and technical matters and provided the necessary day-to-day support for our efforts on this project and others: Cynthia Koziol and Mary Newell. Although they have worked behind the scenes, their presence has been felt and is appreciated. Finally, we extend our warm thanks and appreciation to our spouses and children, who have supported us in less tangible but nonetheless invaluable ways. To them we dedicate this effort.

Thomas H. Ollendick
Blacksburg, Virginia
Michel Hersen
Fort Lauderdale, Florida

PART I

FUNDAMENTAL ISSUES

EDITORS' COMMENTS

It is of interest that the assessment of children and adolescents has only recently kept pace with the evaluation of their adult counterparts. Although in the last 10 years increased attention has been accorded to both the assessment and treatment of childhood and adolescent disorders, it is with the advent of the *Diagnostic and Statistical Manual of Mental Disorders,* Third Edition (DSM-III) in 1980 that full justice to childhood psychiatric diagnosis was achieved. Indeed, the number of childhood categories in DSM-III is considerably greater than in DSM-II (second edition), when such classification initially was given short shrift. Earlier in the 1960s and 1970s child behavior therapists had carefully pinpointed many of the behaviors that are now subsumed under the DSM-III and DSM-III-R (revised) categories. Also contributing to the reliable and valid assessment of childhood psychopathology are the carefully designed semistructured and structured interview schedules developed within the last decade. But here too, these have succeeded their counterparts originally intended for use with adult patients. Nonetheless, the situation is vastly improved now over the views held at the beginning of the century that children were "miniature adults." Indeed, the chapters in this section in particular, and throughout the book in general, clearly reflect the importance of developmental features in making accurate appraisals of childhood and adolescent psychopathology. Sensitivity to such variables by necessity has a marked effect on the nature and type of assessment devices used, as well as the particular content of the questions posed.

In Part I of this book some of the fundamental issues in this area are outlined in the first five chapters. In chapter 1, Ollendick and Hersen consider the salient principles and procedures involved in the evaluation of children and adolescents. Underscored is the multimethod approach that involves behavioral interviews, self-reports, self-monitoring, other reports, standardized testing, and behavioral observation (both in vivo and of the analogue variety). In chapter 2, Yule focuses on the critical importance of developmental considerations in childhood assessment. In so doing, Yule shows how a developmentally accurate appraisal will lead to treatment that is geared at the appropriate level for the child. In chapter 3, Orvaschel, Ambrosini, and Rabinovich document improvements in the current nosological scheme. However, they clearly point to the research that remains to be carried out, especially as to the specific relationship of etiology and particular prevention and treatment strategies. In chapter 4, Teodori emphasizes the importance of the medical evaluation (especially the neurological assessment) with respect to a comprehensive picture of the child. As a number of behavioral anomalies are due to a neurological etiology, it is important to obtain a complete medical history bolstered by a physical examination and relevant laboratory tests. Finally, in chapter 5, Koocher considers the numerous ethical issues faced by the psychological assessor of children. Presented are examples of ethical problems and ethical violations, questions of test bias, and issues of user competence. Guiding ethical principles are based on the American Psychological Association's *Standards of Educational and Psychological Testing*.

CHAPTER 1

CHILD AND ADOLESCENT BEHAVIORAL ASSESSMENT

Thomas H. Ollendick
Michel Hersen

The assessment of child and adolescent behavior disorders is of relatively recent origin. Behavior disorders in youths, though occasionally acknowledged before the twentieth century, received little concerted attention. Up to that time, the disorders of children and adolescents were viewed no differently from those of adults. In all likelihood, this state of affairs resulted from the prevailing viewpoint of youths as miniature adults. In general, they were viewed as small versions of adults, evincing problems similar to adults and benefiting from reasoned advice much like their adult counterparts (cf. Aries, 1962; Brown, 1939; Rie, 1971).

By contrast, the twentieth century has witnessed extensive study of "childhood" and "adolescence" and the behavior disorders associated with these periods of development. In recent years, emergence of the field of "developmental psychopathology" (Achenbach, 1982; Sroufe & Rutter, 1984) has helped guide efforts to understand, assess, and treat the many disorders of childhood and adolescence. Just how useful these new developments will be, however, is not completely known at this time. However, advances have been made, and our understanding of child and adolescent behavior disorders has been enriched greatly (Mash & Terdal, 1989; Ollendick & Hersen, 1989).

Within this stream of events, the behavioral assessment and treatment of disorders in children and adolescents evolved. Although application of behavioral principles to the treatment of child and adolescent behavior problems has a rich tradition (e.g., Holmes, 1936; Jones, 1924; Watson & Rayner, 1920), behavioral assessment of these disorders has lagged significantly behind and has received less attention in the intervening years. Two primary themes characterized early developments in child and adolescent behavioral assessment: (1) adherence to an operant perspective that placed considerable emphasis on observable events, current behavior, the situational determinants of behavior, and intraindividual comparisons (Bijou & Peterson, 1971; Mash & Terdal, 1981), and (2) a lack of attention to normal developmental processes and normative comparisons that would have permitted specific child and adolescent behaviors to be compared to appropriate reference groups (Ciminero & Drabman, 1977; Evans & Nelson, 1977; Ollendick & Hersen, 1984). Although the early work in child and adolescent behavioral assessment had a number of shortcomings, it did provide the necessary impetus for an *empirical,* functional approach.

In our introductory chapter, we briefly examine the foundations of child and adolescent behavioral assessment and explore its theoretical underpinnings. In so doing, we endeavor to provide a broader context in which child and adolescent behavioral assessment can be viewed as an empirically based, developmentally sensitive, multimethod approach. It should be stated from the outset, however, that child and adolescent behavioral assessment is much more than a collection of techniques, such as self-monitoring or behavioral observation. Rather, it entails a set of problem-solving strategies that are designed to provide a complete picture of the child or adolescent (Mash & Terdal, 1981; Ollendick & Hersen, 1984). In the remaining chapters of the *Handbook,* this approach is developed in greater detail. In addition, a variety of assessment strategies are described and then applied to specific disorders of childhood and adolescence. Throughout, integrated assessment and treatment are detailed, and sensitive issues related to ethical concerns in child and adolescent behavior assessment are explored.

CHILD AND ADOLESCENT BEHAVIORAL ASSESSMENT

Psychological assessment has been defined as the "systematic use of a variety of special techniques in order to better *understand* a given individual, group, or social ecology" (McReynolds, 1968, p. 2, emphasis added). From a traditional perspective, such a notion of assessment has led to the search for underlying personality characteristics or traits that are "responsible for" or causal of current functioning. In contrast, psychological assessment from a behavioral perspective has been directed toward a description of current behavior and a specification of organismic and environmental conditions that occasion and maintain it. In short, behavioral assessment has led to the search for antecedent and consequent events of behavior, rather than underlying causes.

Excellent reviews of the major conceptual differences between psychological assessment from traditional and behavioral perspectives have been presented elsewhere (e.g., Goldfried & Kent, 1972; Kanfer & Saslow, 1969). Briefly, three major distinctions have been offered. First, differences have been noted in the underlying assumptions about what constitutes "personality." In the traditional approach, psychological traits or personality characteristics are assumed to produce consistency in behavior that is stable and exists independently of situational variation ("personologism"). However, from a behavioral perspective, greater emphasis is placed on the behavior itself, and temporal and cross-situational consistency in behavior is not necessarily expected. Rather, behavior is viewed as a result of current environmental factors ("situationalism") or of current environmental factors interacting with organismic factors ("interactionism"). Thus, the current environment is stressed more in behavioral assessment than in traditional assessment. The focus of assessment is what the child or adolescent *does* in a given situation rather than what he or she *has* (Mischel, 1973). Second, differences have been noted in the specification and selection of test items. In the traditional approach, test items are selected on the basis of a priori theoretical assumptions about the role of personality variables in behavior. In the behavioral approach, on the other hand, items are selected on the basis of how well they represent specific stimulus situations associated with behavior. Hence, for example, behavioral assessment of oppositional behavior might involve observation of the child or adolescent in varying situations (e.g., home, school, clinic) and determining the frequency, intensity, or duration of the targeted behaviors in those situations rather than measuring a hypothetical construct such as "hostility toward mother," which in turn is thought to be causative of oppositional, defiant behavior. Third, basic differences exist in the level of inference and subsequent interpretation of test responses. In traditional assessment, a child's response is viewed as a "sign" or indirect manifestation of underlying personality traits such as "hostility," as described in the preceding example. In contrast, interpretation of test responses in behavioral assessment is based on a low level of inference and involves a "sampling" approach.

As described by Goldfried and Kent (1972), the behavioral approach requires that the specific behaviors sampled in the test comprise a subset of the actual behaviors to be targeted for change. Such similarity between test responses and criterion measures of behavior is one of the most important and distinguishing characteristics of child and adolescent behavioral assessment.

Early distinctions between traditional and behavioral assessment have proven heuristic in highlighting basic differences in both the purposes and methods of assessment. Furthermore, they have been instrumental in focusing child and adolescent behavioral assessment more directly on "target behaviors" and the events that precede and follow these behaviors. Accurate observation and recording of target behaviors remain the hallmark of behavioral assessment and the benchmark by which other methods can be evaluated (Gelfand & Hartmann, 1975; Mash & Terdal, 1981; Ollendick & Hersen, 1984; Sulzer-Azaroff & Mayer, 1977).

As behavioral approaches with children and adolescents evolved from sole reliance on basic operant procedures to those incorporating cognitive and self-control procedures, the methods of assessment—though not the purposes—also changed. In this process, specification of target behaviors has been widened to include evaluation of cognitions and affect, as well as large-scale social systems that affect the child or adolescent and his or her family (Mash & Terdal, 1981, 1989). Furthermore, the important role of affect and cognition in mediating behavior change, at least for some children and adolescents, has been acknowledged (e.g., Kendall, 1987; Kendall & Hollon, 1980; Leitenberg, Yost, & Carroll-Wilson, 1986; Meichenbaum, 1977). Similarly, the notion that children and adolescents are active arrangers and determiners of their environment, rather than simply passive responders, has become widely accepted (e.g., Bandura, 1969, 1977; Mischel, 1973, 1979). These recent developments expand the scope of behavioral assessment to include broader and richer contexts in which ecological, social, cultural, and developmental influences on behavior can be examined more productively. In 1981, Mash and Terdal described child behavioral assessment as "a range of deliberate problem-solving strategies for understanding children and childhood disorders" (p. 8). By extension, child *and* adolescent behavioral assessment can be viewed along similar lines (Ollendick & Hersen, 1984). The outcome of these problem-solving strategies is to provide a "picture" of the child or adolescent that is informative, accurate, and useful in both the understanding and modification of diverse psychological disorders.

Explicit in this view of behavioral assessment is the notion that multiple assessment strategies are useful in advancing our understanding of psychological disorders and in formulating and evaluating viable treatment strategies. Assessment methods, including the clinical interview, self-monitoring, behavioral observation, standardized testing, rating forms from significant others (e.g., peers, parents, and teachers), and self-report measures may all be worthwhile and even desirable. For that matter, the use of traditional personality tests and projective techniques might also be useful. Given our current state of knowledge in this area or, perhaps more accurately, our lack thereof, this position appears defensible so long as the individual strategies themselves have been validated empirically (Hersen & Bellack, 1976; Mash & Terdal, 1989; Ollendick & Hersen, 1984). Inasmuch as individual assessment strategies are inadequate, the combination of them serves to compound rather than compensate for their inherent inadequacies. Thus, acceptability of a multiple assessment approach rests firmly on the availability of a range of psychometrically sound measures and the empirical demonstration of their additive utility (incremental validity). While superiority of a multiple assessment approach has not yet been demonstrated, it does appear to be clinically useful. Although advocating a multiple assessment approach, we are reminded of Evans's eloquent admonition: "Taking careful aim is still more important than the bore of the barrel or the gauge of the shot" (Evans, 1982, p. 124).

In summary, child and adolescent behavioral assessment can be described as an exploratory, hypothesis-testing process in which a range of specific procedures is used to understand a given individual, group, or social ecology and to formulate and evaluate specific intervention strategies (Ollendick & Hersen, 1984). Three primary characteristics guide the selection and use of specific procedures in behavioral assessment:

1. a multimethod approach that yields the best "picture" of the child or adolescent,
2. the selection of procedures that have been validated empirically, and
3. the sensitivity of the procedures to developmental and normative issues.

Of course, the exact procedures to be used depend heavily on the specific behavior problems and the social context in which the behavior problems occur. A simple "test battery" approach is not being recommended; rather, the careful selection of empirically validated and developmentally sensitive procedures is proposed.

CHARACTERISTICS OF CHILD AND ADOLESCENT BEHAVIORAL ASSESSMENT

Multimethod Approach

As we have noted, early child and adolescent behavioral assessment procedures were directed primarily toward identification of discrete and highly specific target behaviors and their controlling variables. Observable behaviors like hitting, tantrums, sitting in a chair, and eye contact were isolated for study and modification. While the importance of systematic assessment of discrete target behaviors should not be underestimated, more recent advances have incorporated a broader view of child behavior and its assessment (Mash & Terdal, 1981). This new view more clearly encompasses activities of the organism that mediate antecedent and consequent events, including physiological reactions, affective responses, and covert cognitions. Furthermore, it more clearly examines distal as well as proximal events that serve to affect child behavior.

Because Kanfer and Saslow's (1969) S-O-R-K-C model of assessment espouses a thorough analysis of both overt and covert behaviors and acknowledges that behavior is determined by a variety of events (including ecological, social, and cultural ones), we have found this approach useful in guiding the selection of child and adolescent behavioral assessment strategies. The S component refers to antecedent events and includes those internal or external stimulus events that are thought to be functionally related to the behavior in question. The O refers to the biological status of the organism (child or adolescent) and includes those variables (e.g., genetic, physiological, neurological, and biochemical) that constrain specific behaviors. Inclusion of the organism is particularly significant in child and adolescent behavioral assessment, because rapid developmental changes affect both the form and function of specific behaviors. R refers to observed (or reliably reported) behaviors and encompasses motor behavior, cognitive-verbal behavior, and physiological-emotional behavior (Lang, 1978). This is the response that is frequently targeted for change. From an expanded developmental-behavioral perspective, R allows for inclusion of cognitive events such as self-statements, expectancies, and plans as well as the developmental factors associated with these responses (Ollendick & King, 1991). K describes the schedules or contingency-related conditions and includes such variables as the frequency and timing of response outcomes. Examination of an individual's learning history, including the duration of specific behaviors, provides valuable information in this regard. Finally, C refers to the consequences of behavior, be they environmental or organismic. As noted by Mash and Terdal (1989), it is important to distinguish between events following a response that are functionally related in altering future probabilities and consequent events that are contiguous but that have not been shown to have response-controlling properties.

In the S-O-R-K-C model, a wide range of assessment strategies may be useful, including behavioral interviews, checklists, rating forms, standardized intellectual and personality instruments, self-reports, self-monitoring forms, and behavioral observations. Collectively, these sources of information generate a wealth of data regarding the child or adolescent, his or her behavior, and the context in which that behavior occurs.

Before examining the psychometric properties of these various sources, we would like to briefly describe the procedural steps in the S-O-R-K-C model of child and adolescent behavioral assessment. The first step involves an analysis of the presenting concerns and entails specification of behavioral excesses, deficits, and assets. As noted previously, these behaviors might include motor behaviors, cognitive-verbal behaviors, and physiological-affective behaviors. In the second step, a standard functional analysis of the identified behaviors is undertaken. Antecedent and consequent events, both proximal and distal, are determined. In this step, the probable consequences of behavior change for the child or adolescent and for those involved with him or her are also determined. That is, "an attempt is made to determine how the behavior is functional within the social milieu and what consequences might ensue if treatment is, or is not, successful" (Ollendick & Cerny, 1981, p. 29). A motivational analysis is undertaken in the third step to determine various incentives and aversive conditions that operate for the child or adolescent, both at the present time and from his or her learning history. In the fourth step, a developmental analysis of biological, cognitive, and social variables that affect current behavior is undertaken and the probable response to treatment is considered. For example, organic conditions (e.g., defective vision, glandular imbalances), cognitive limitations (e.g., intellectual ability, ability to generate and use self-statements), and socioeconomic variables (e.g., lower-class environment, paucity of environmental stimulation) that affect or interact with the problematic behaviors (and their resolution) are examined. In the fifth step, an analysis of the capacity for "self-control" is examined. Information in this regard is obtained most directly from an analysis of those situations in which the child or adolescent is able to control the problematic behavior and indirectly from specific self-report and other-report instruments. In the sixth step, interpersonal relationships are reviewed, with special emphasis upon peer and family relationships. This analysis provides the basis for identifying those relationships that have affected development of the problematic behavior and those social resources that might play a potentially significant role in treatment programming. In the final step, an analysis is made of the sociocultural-physical environment to determine whether treatment goals are congruent with the norms or expectations of the individual's particular background and current milieu.

Although assessment following the S-O-R-K-C model is time-consuming, the thoroughness of the approach and its incorporation of diverse multiple assessment methods make it especially attractive to us. However, we must remind the reader once again of Evans's (1982) admonition that errors in clinical judgment are not necessarily minimized by inclusion of many different methods. As also noted by Mash and Terdal (1981), an implicit danger in the multimethod approach is that it is reminiscent of the old, traditional "test battery" approach. In this approach, it is frequently assumed that the more information we have, the better we are able to understand and treat children and adolescents. Although there is considerable empirical support for the notion that different methods yield varied information, there is little available support for the hypothesis that such additional information leads to a "truer" or more useful understanding of the child or adolescent, or that more efficacious treatment necessarily follows. In this regard, it is important that child behavioral assessors "give some attention to the incremental validity associated with using multiple methods, in order to avoid the perpetration of potentially unnecessary and costly procedures" (Mash & Terdal, 1981, pp. 41–42). Incremental validity can be assessed by determining the relationship between the amount of information obtained and the degree of understanding that follows from such a comprehensive approach (e.g., Mash, 1979). Moreover, the treatment utility of this approach can be ascertained (Hayes, Nelson, & Jarrett, 1987). Treatment utility refers to the degree to which the assessment process is shown to contribute directly to beneficial treatment outcome. We might, for example, wish to examine the treatment utility of using direct behavioral observations to guide treatment planning above and beyond that provided by the self-reports of adolescents who are phobic of social encounters. All adolescents could be observed in a social situation and complete a self-report measure of fear; however, the behavioral observation for only half the adolescents could be made available for treatment planning. If the adolescents for whom the behavioral observations were made available improved more than those whose treatment plans were based solely on their self-report, then the treatment utility of behavioral observations would be established (for this problem with an individual of this age). In a similar fashion, treatment utility of interviews, role-plays, personality tests, and other devices could be evaluated (Hayes et al., 1987). Although the concept is a relatively new one, it shows considerable promise. We should not necessarily assume that "more" assessment is "better" assessment.

Empirically Validated Measures

Undoubtedly, a variety of factors enter into determining exactly which methods of assessment should be used. Among these are the nature of the target behaviors (e.g., self-statements, social skills, affective expression), characteristics of the child or adolescent (e.g., age, sex, cognitive skills, particular learning history), the referral source (e.g., parents, teachers, social workers, law enforcement officers), the assessment setting (e.g., home, school, clinic, institution), the sociocultural milieu (e.g., socioeconomic status, religious affiliation), and the specific purpose of assessment (e.g., diagnosis, placement, intervention, understanding). Regardless of the exact methods selected, however, it is essential that the chosen ones possess sound psychometric qualities. All too frequently, child and adolescent behavioral assessors have chosen or designed methods of convenience, without due regard for adequate standardization, reliability, validity, or clinical utility. With such an idiosyncratic approach, comparison across studies is made extremely difficult, and advancement of an assessment technology and an understanding of specific behavior disorders cannot be realized.

The role of conventional psychometric standards in evaluating the adequacy of child and adolescent behavioral assessment methods is highly controversial (e.g., Cone, 1987; Cone & Hawkins, 1977, Cone & Hoier, 1986). On the one hand, basic assumptions concerning the situational-specificity and temporal instability of behavior appear to defy the use of psychometric standards. For example, how can a self-report or role-play test of assertiveness designed to "sample" heterogeneous social situations (McFall, 1982; Ollendick, 1984; Scanlon & Ollendick, 1985) be expected to possess high internal consistency or good split-half reliability? Furthermore, how can such instruments be expected to possess concurrent validity when cross-situational variability is the norm rather than a reflection of invalid instruments? Such notions of reliability and validity are most appropriate to traitlike, nomothetic conceptions in which behavior is viewed as reasonably stable over time and relatively consistent across situations (Cone, 1987). On the other hand, if no two situations are exactly alike and there is no consistency in behavior over time, the prediction and generalizability of behavior become meaningless and impossible. Such an extreme idiographic stance precludes meaningful assessment, except of a particular behavior in a particular setting and at a particular point in time.

It appears to us that some child and adolescent behavioral assessors have misinterpreted Mischel's intent when he first stated that the focus of assessment from a behavioral perspective "shifts from describing situation-free people with broad trait adjectives to analyzing the specific interactions between conditions and the cognitions and behaviors of interest" (Mischel, 1973, p. 265). Mischel did not intend to do away with personality or its measurement: "My intentions . . . were not to undo personality but to defend individuality and the uniqueness of each person against what I saw as the then-prevalent form of clinical hostility: the tendency to use a few behavioral signs to categorize people enduringly into fixed slots on the assessor's favorite nomothetic trait dimensions and to assume that these slot positions were sufficiently informative to predict specific behavior and to make extensive decisions about a person's whole life" (Mischel, 1979, p. 740).

It is evident from these statements, as well as from other research findings (e.g., Gresham, 1982; Loeber, 1982; Ollendick, 1981), that we need not totally dismiss the notions of cross-situational and cross-temporal consistency of behavior. Although we cannot expect a high degree of congruence in behavior across diverse situations or over extended periods of time, we can expect a modicum of behavioral consistency across those situations that involve increasingly similar stimulus-and-response characteristics and which are temporarily related (Bem & Allen, 1974). Inasmuch as diverse methodologies (e.g., interviews, self-reports, other-reports) are used to assess various facets of behaviors under these conditions, a modest relationship among the various measures can be expected. In such circumstances, application of conventional psychometric standards to evaluation of child behavioral assessment strategies becomes less problematic and increasingly useful.

We must begin to develop standardized measures of child and adolescent behaviors that possess adequate test-retest reliability and criterion validity. Within the tenets of the behavioral perspective, attention to such considerations is both desirable and possible (e.g., Cone, 1977). Regardless of the assessment methods used, we must expect our measures to be consistent over time and to be related to one another (as long as they are obtained under similar stimulus situations and as long as change because of an intervention program or a normal developmental process has not occurred). Furthermore, under the same assumptions, we must expect our measures to be reasonably good predictors of subsequent behavior and adjustment (predictive validity). Such validity has already been demonstrated for certain classes of behavior with diverse measures like behavioral observation (e.g., Olweus, 1979), self-report (e.g., Ollendick, 1981), teacher ratings (e.g., Cown, Pederson, Babigian, Izzo, & Trost, 1973), and sociometric ratings (e.g., Hartup, Glazer, & Charlesworth, 1967). Furthermore, when these multiple measures have been used in the same studies, a moderate degree of both concurrent and predictive validity has been obtained, at least for socially dysfunctional behavior (e.g., Gresham, 1982; Ollendick, 1981).

It is not possible to delineate the many factors related to standardization, reliability, validity, and clinical utility for each method here. However, some of the more important considerations and issues are addressed in the chapters that follow in section 2. Attention to these psychometric qualities directly guided the selection of specific methods for this volume. In subsequent chapters, each method is described and their psychometric properties are reviewed. Before leaving this section, however, we must return briefly to the notion of multimethod assessment and the selection of specific methods to use. While a multimethod approach that is based on empirically validated instruments is recommended, it should be clear that it is not always possible or necessary to use all of the suggested methods. A "test battery" approach is not being recommended. The specific assessment devices to be used depend on a variety of factors, including the nature of the referral question and the personnel, time, and resources available to the child behavior assessor. Nonetheless, given the limitations of the various procedures, as well as the desirability of having a complete picture of the child or adolescent, we recommend that as many procedures as possible be used. Any one procedure, including direct behavioral observation, is not sufficient to meet the various assessment functions that are required for a thorough functional analysis of the child's behavior problems. The multimethod approach is not only helpful in assessing specific behaviors and in determining response to behavior change, but it may be useful in understanding child behavior disorders and in advancing our knowledge in this area of study.

Developmental and Normative Comparisons

Just as assessment procedures must be psychometrically sound and empirically validated, they must also be sensitive to developmental changes when used with children and adolescents (Edelbrock, 1984). Perhaps the most noteworthy characteristic of youth in general is developmental change (Ciminero & Drabman, 1977; Evans & Nelson, 1977; Mash & Terdal, 1981). Such change, whether it is based on hypothetical stages of cognitive or social development or empirically derived developmental norms, has clear implications for the selection of specific assessment methods and the evaluation of behavior change.

Age-related verbal and cognitive abilities directly affect the appropriateness of certain methods of assessment. Self-monitoring, for instance, requires the ability to compare one's own behavior against a standard and to accurately judge occurrence or nonoccurrence of targeted events and behaviors. Most children below 6 years of age lack the requisite ability to self-monitor and may not profit from such procedures. In fact, the limited research available suggests that self-monitoring may be counterproductive when used with such children, resulting in confusion and impaired performance (e.g., Higa, Thorp, & Calkins, 1979). These findings suggest that self-monitoring procedures are better suited for children who possess sufficient cognitive abilities to benefit from their use (Shapiro, 1984). In a similar vein, age-related variables constrain the use of certain self-report and sociometric measures with young children. It has often been noted that sociometric devices must be simplified and presented in pictorial form to children under 6 years of age (Hops & Lewin, 1984; McCandless & Marshall, 1957). The picture-form sociometric device provides the young child with a set of concrete, visual cues regarding the children to be rated and, of course, does not require him or her to read the names of the children being rated. The roster-and-rating method used so frequently with older children is simply not appropriate for younger children.

Similarly, self-report measures need to be carefully designed with the verbal and cognitive abilities of the young child in mind. Some time ago, one of the authors (Ollendick, 1983) undertook the revision and restandardization of the Fear Survey Schedule for Children (Scherer & Nakamura, 1968). This scale, while useful with older children, was found to be less reliable and valid with children under 8 years of age. Although younger children appeared to understand the fear-stimulus items, they were unable to grasp the notion of rating their fear on a 5-point scale. When a 3-point scale was used ("none," "some," or "a lot"), however, the children were able to reliably and validly rate their fear, as evidenced by good test-retest reliability and congruence with a behavioral measure of fear (Ollendick, 1983). Recently, this revised scale has been used to explore the generalizability of fear across cultural, age, and gender dimensions (Ollendick, King, & Frary, 1989; Ollendick & Yule, 1990).

Other methods of child behavioral assessment are not without their age-related constraints. Although untested at this time, it seems plausible that reactivity to behavioral observation may also be age related. For example, the social comparison literature suggests that as children become older, they compare and evaluate their own behavior against relevant social norms (e.g., Ollendick, Shapiro, & Barrett, 1982; Ruple, Parsons, & Ross, 1976). While an adult's presence might not serve as a cue for such an evaluative process with young children or, for that matter, with adolescents, it might be predicted to do so for the older child. Confirmation of this hypothesis awaits empirical verification, however.

In summary, age-related constraints are numerous and await clearer articulation and categorization. Until that occurs, it is imperative that child and adolescent behavioral assessors be aware of developmental considerations and constraints when selecting specific methods of assessment. Certain procedures are more appropriate for specific age groups and ability levels than others. The continued and indiscriminate use of developmentally insensitive instruments will fail to advance our understanding and subsequent modification of behavior disorders in children and adolescents.

Rapid and uneven changes associated with normal developmental processes and experiences also have implications for the selection of target behaviors and for evaluation of their change over time. In this regard, the development of normative information is invaluable. As noted by Mash and Terdal (1981), behavioral assessors have emphasized intraindividual comparisons and have given scant attention to normative comparisons. Normative comparisons provide information about the child or adolescent's behavior relative to the behavior of other youth in an appropriate reference group (e.g., age, sex, culture). While intraindividual comparisons examine an individual's behavior relative to his or her own baseline rate of behavior, they provide little information about the behavior with respect to that of a suitable reference group. Clearly, intraindividual comparisons are necessary; however, so too are normative comparisons if we wish to establish the social validity of our assessment and treatment efforts (Kazdin, 1977; Wolf, 1978).

Several studies have described "normal" age trends in specific child and adolescent behavior disorders. For example, specific fears and phobias have been shown to occur with regularity during the course of normal development. Most infants show a startlelike response to loss of support or to sudden and loud noises. Later, during the first year of life, babies evidence a fear of strangers in which they react with fearlike panic to unfamiliar people and unfamiliar situations. Fear of animals tend to appear between the ages of 2 and 3, while fear of the dark emerges between 3 and 4 years of age. School avoidance characteristically occurs upon entry into school (and upon subsequent changes in schools or grade levels), while evaluative fear and social fear develop during middle childhood and adolescence. Presence of such regularity in fears and phobias, of course, does not "explain" their occurrence. Undoubtedly, emerging cognitive abilities (e.g., Bauer, 1980) as well as common situational events (Miller, Barrett, & Hampe, 1974; Ollendick, 1979; Ollendick & Mayer, 1983) interact to occasion their presence. Furthermore, regularity in occurrence does not necessarily imply that such fears are transitory or not problematic to the child (Graziano, 1975). We know that persistent and excessive fears are present in 3 to 8 percent of children (Ollendick, 1979). Furthermore, we know that such fears are not transitory, as many fears persist into adulthood (e.g., Marks & Gelder, 1966), while other fears, such as school phobia, may serve as early precursors to agoraphobia in adults (Berg, 1976; Berg, Marks, McGuire, & Lipsedge, 1974; Ollendick & Huntzinger, 1990).

While caution must be excercised in the blind use of developmental norms, as previously stated, they do provide good "markers" for target selection and behavior change. For example, a child whose fear of the dark is evident at 10 years of age is clearly exhibiting deviant behavior from a normative standpoint; on the other hand, the child who evinces fear of the dark at 4 years of age is not. Just as a 1-year-old child displays poor bowel control and a 5-year-old child frequently reverses the letters b, d, p, and q, so too might a child at 4 years of age display fear of the dark. Fear of the dark itself may not be unusual for this age; however, its intensity, duration, and persistence may be of concern. Similar conclusions have been offered about aggressive behavior (Olweus, 1979), withdrawn behavior (Furman, 1980), and cross-dressing behavior (Rekers, 1978) in children.

Thus, normative comparisons are most useful in the identification of behavioral excesses and deficits and in the evaluation of behavior change over time. To the extent that behaviors are not stable and that rapid and uneven developmental change characterizes child and adolescent behavior, behavioral assessors must be aware of the extent to which behavior change is a function of intervention and developmental change. The combined use of intraindividual and normative comparisons can assist in both of these endeavors.

Based on these characteristics, we put forth several generalizations regarding child and adolescent behavioral assessment:

1. Children and adolescents represent special populations. The automatic extension of adult behavioral assessment methods to children and adolescents is not warranted and often is inappropriate. Age-related variables affect the choice of methods as well as the procedures employed.
2. Given rapid developmental change in children and adolescents, normative comparisons are required to ensure that appropriate target behaviors are selected and that change in behavior is related to treatment, not to normal developmental change. Such comparisons require identification of suitable reference groups and information about the "natural" course of child and adolescent behavior problems.
3. Thorough child and adolescent behavioral assessment involves multiple targets of change, including overt behavior, affective states, and cognitions. Furthermore, such assessment entails determining the context (e.g., familial, social, cultural) in which the behavior occurs and the "function" that the targeted behaviors serve.
4. Given the wide range of targets for change, multimethod assessment is desirable and necessary. Multimethod assessment should not be viewed simply as a "test battery" approach; rather, methods should be selected on the basis of their appropriateness to the referral question. Regardless of

the measures used, they should be empirically validated and developmentally sensitive.

In the chapters that follow in section 2, this empirically based, developmentally anchored, multimethod approach is explicated in greater detail. A variety of methods are explored, and their relevance to child and adolescent behavioral assessment is described. In section 3, this approach is explicated with specific psychological disorders. Before moving to these sections, however, we shall briefly turn our attention to the role of the child and adolescent in behavioral assessment.

THE ROLE OF THE CHILD AND ADOLESCENT IN BEHAVIORAL ASSESSMENT

All too frequently, child and adolescent behavioral assessors have conceptualized youth and their disorders in a rather passive, static fashion. Tests are administered *to* youths, ratings are obtained *on* youths, and behaviors are observed *in* youths. This process relegates the child or adolescent to a role of passive responder, someone who is incapable of actively shaping and determining his or her environment. Rarely are the thoughts, feelings, perceptions, attributions, or expectations of the child or adolescent considered.

Although a thorough investigation of these organismic processes in children and adolescents and their effects on behavior have been explored only recently, they hold considerable promise in advancing our understanding of child and adolescent behavior and our prediction of behavior change. Illustratively, conceptions of behavioral disorders are a potentially relevant, if not critical, area of further study. To what causes do children attribute aggressive or withdrawn behavior in themselves or in their peers? Are there age-related trends in these attributions? Do causal attributions (as well as self-efficacy and outcome expectancies) interact with treatment efficacy? If so, do they interact differently for youths of different ages? The answers to these questions are of both theoretical interest and applied clinical significance.

A partial answer to these questions can be found in some early research efforts. For example, studies by Coie and Pennington (1976) and Dollinger, Thelen, and Walsh (1980) have shown that an interesting developmental trend exists in children's conceptions of child deviance and their attributions of its causes. Younger children conceive deviant behavior as that which is "different" from their own behavior or interests. Furthermore, younger children attribute the cause of such deviant behavior to external factors such as mean parents, a bad teacher, or "other kids." In contrast, older children and adolescents conceive of deviant behavior as that which deviates from some social norm. Moreover, they attribute the cause of deviant behavior to internal factors like "not having the ability" or "not trying hard enough." Interestingly, as a child matures into later adolescence, both conceptions and attributions approximate those held by adults (e.g., Compas, Friedland-Bandes, Bastien, & Adelman, 1981). What are the practical implications of these rapidly changing conceptions and attributions? The elucidation of these phenomena with children, adolescents, and parents in a clinical context seems especially critical, because observations made by parents (or teachers) invariably precipitate clinical intervention. Consider the 8-year-old child who is brought to the clinic by his parents because he is inattentive in school, displays disruptive behavior, and is receiving low grades. The child, as well as his peers, perceive the problem as an external one—one demanding clear environmental change. However, the parents and teachers perceive the child's problems as a lack of "self-control" and that he "just has to try harder" and everything will work out. While adults and children are perceiving the situation differently, they both may be perceiving it correctly. Both sets of perceptions and attributions must be clarified and considered in the assessment, treatment, and evaluation aspects of child and adolescent behavior therapy.

Other research has shown that treatment procedures may have differential effects depending on children's causal attributions. For instance, Bugental, Whalen, and Henker (1977) compared a self-instructional package to a contingent social reinforcement program with medicated and unmedicated hyperactive boys. The self-instruction program was most effective for unmedicated boys who were internal in their locus of control attributions. On the other hand, the social reinforcement program worked best for unmedicated boys who reported an external locus of control. From a similar perspective, Ollendick, Elliot, and Matson (1980) showed that self-reported locus of control was related to success of behavioral contracting and token economy programs with adjudicated male delinquents. The extension of Bandura's (1977) notion of self-efficacy to children would also probably prove productive in this regard. In this connection, we have developed measures of self-efficacy and outcome expectancy for children's social skills. In our initial efforts, we have found these measures to be related to the presence of specific behavioral and cognitive skills and to be predictive of differential change following cognitive restructuring or behavioral interventions (Ollendick, 1982; Ollendick & Schmidt, 1987). Although considerably more research must be performed, such attributional and expectancy constructs appear to be of heuristic value in planning and implementing specific intervention strategies.

Thus, while this area of research is just now evolving, we view it as one of the most important developments in child behavioral assessment. Much remains to be learned; much is likely to be gained.

SUMMARY

In this introductory chapter, we have attempted to elucidate some of the most important principles and procedures of child and adolescent behavioral assessment. We have described child and adolescent behavioral assessment as an empirically based, developmentally sensitive, multimethod approach in which a range of specific procedures are used to *understand* a given child (adolescent), group, or social ecology. We also argue that child and adolescent behavioral assessment is an exploratory, hypothesis-testing process in which a wide range of information is reviewed to obtain a complete "picture" of the child or adolescent and the meaningful contexts in which his or her behavior occurs. From this standpoint, a wide range of methods is not only necessary, but desirable; these methods include behavioral interviews, self-reports, self-monitoring, other-reports, standardized instruments, and behavioral observations.

We have also noted that the incremental validity of this approach is in need of verification and that important issues related to rapid changes in development in children need to be considered when using this approach. Nonetheless, at this state of our knowledge, such an approach is not only heuristic, but it also appears warranted. Advancement in this area of research and clinical practice demands concerted effort and systematic attention. In particular, the role of the child and adolescent in the behavioral assessment paradigm is likely to continue to be a most important area of investigation.

REFERENCES

Achenbach, T. M. (1982). *Developmental psychopathology* (2nd ed.). New York: John Wiley & Sons.

Aries, P. (1962). *Centuries of childhood*. New York: Vintage Books.

Bandura, A. (1969). *Principles of behavior modification*. New York: Holt, Rinehart, & Winston.

Bandura, A. (1977). Self-efficacy: Toward a unifying theory of behavioral change. *Psychological Review, 84*, 191–215.

Bauer, D. (1980). Childhood fears in developmental perspective. In L. Hersov & I. Berg (Eds.), *Out of school*. New York: John Wiley & Sons.

Bem, D. J., & Allen, A. (1974). On predicting some of the people some of the time: The search for cross-situational consistencies in behavior. *Psychological Review, 81*, 506–520.

Berg, I. (1976). School phobia in the children of agoraphobic women. *British Journal of Psychiatry, 128*, 86–89.

Berg, I., Marks, I., McGuire, R., & Lipsedge, M. (1974). School phobias and agoraphobia. *Psychological Medicine, 4*, 428–434.

Bijou, S. W., & Peterson, R. F. (1971). The psychological assessment of children: A functional analysis. In P. McReynolds (Ed.), *Advances in psychological assessment* (Vol. 2). Palo Alto, CA: Science and Behavior Books.

Brown, F. J. (1939). *The sociology of childhood*. Englewood Cliffs, NJ: Prentice-Hall.

Bugental, B. D., Whalen, C. K., & Henker, B. (1977). Causal attributions of hyperactive children and motivational assumptions of two behavior-change approaches: Evidence for an interactionist position. *Child Development, 48*, 874–884.

Ciminero, A. R., & Drabman, R. S. (1977). Current developments in the behavioral assessment of children. In B. B. Lahey and A. E. Kazdin (Eds.), *Advances in clinical child psychology* (Vol. 1). New York: Plenum Press.

Coie, J. D., & Pennington, B. F. (1976). Children's perceptions of deviance and disorder. *Child Development, 47*, 407–413.

Compas, B. E., Friedland-Bandes, R., Bastien, R., & Adelman, H. S. (1981). Parent and child causal attributions related to the child's clinical problem. *Journal of Abnormal Child Psychology, 9*, 389–397.

Cone, J. D. (1977). The relevance of reliability and validity for behavioral assessment. *Behavior Therapy, 8*, 411–426.

Cone, J. D. (1987). Behavioral assessment with children and adolescents. In M. Hersen & V. B. Van Hasselt (Eds.), *Behavior therapy with children and adolescents: A clinical approach*. New York: John Wiley & Sons.

Cone, J. D., & Hawkins, R. P. (Eds.), (1977). *Behavioral assessment: New directions in clinical psychology*. New York: Brunner/Mazel.

Cone, J. D., & Hoier, T. S. (1986). Assessing children: The radical behavioral perspective. In R. J. Prinz (Ed.), *Advances in behavioral assessment of children and families* (Vol. 2). New York: JAI Press.

Cowen, E. L., Pederson, A., Babigian, H., Izzo, L. D., & Trost, M. A. (1973). Long-term follow-up of early detected vulnerable children. *Journal of Consulting and Clinical Psychology, 41,* 438–445.

Dollinger, S. J., Thelen, M. H., & Walsh, M. L. (1980). Children's conceptions of psychological problems. *Journal of Clinical Child Psychology, 9,* 191–194.

Edelbrock, C. S. (1984). Developmental considerations. In T. H. Ollendick & M. Hersen (Eds.), *Child behavioral assessment: Principles and procedures.* New York: Pergamon Press.

Evans, I. M. (1982). Review of Nay's *Multimethod clinical assessment. Behavioral Assessment, 4,* 121–124.

Evans, I. M., & Nelson, R. O. (1977). Assessment of child behavior problems. In A. R. Ciminero, K. S. Calhoun, & H. E. Adams (Eds.), *Handbook of behavioral assessment.* New York: Wiley-Interscience.

Furman, W. (1980). Promoting social development: Developmental implications for treatment. In B. B. Lahey & A. E. Kazdin, *Advances in clinical child psychology* (Vol. 3). New York: Plenum Press.

Gelfand, D., & Hartmann, D. P. (1975). *Child behavior analysis and therapy.* New York: Pergamon Press.

Goldfried, M. R., & Kent, R. N. (1972). Traditional versus behavioral personality assessment: A comparison of methodological and theoretical assumptions. *Psychological Bulletin, 77,* 409–420.

Graziano, A. M. (1975). *Behavior therapy with children* (Vol. 2). Chicago, Aldine.

Gresham, F. M. (1982). Social interactions as predictors of children's likability and friendship patterns: A multiple regression analysis. *Journal of Behavioral Assessment, 4,* 39–54.

Hartup, W. W., Glazer, J. A., & Charlesworth, R. (1967). Peer reinforcement and sociometric status. *Child Development, 38,* 1017–1024.

Hayes, S. C., Nelson, R. O., & Jarrett, R. B. (1987). The treatment utility of assessment. *American Psychologist, 42,* 963–974.

Hersen, M., & Bellack, A. S. (1976). *Behavioral assessment: A practical handbook.* New York: Pergamon Press.

Higa, W. R., Thorp, R. G., Calkins, R. P. (1979). Developmental verbal control of behavior: Implications for self-instructional training. *Journal of Experimental Child Psychology, 26,* 489–497.

Holmes, F. B. (1936). An experimental investigation of a method of overcoming children's fears. *Child Development, 7,* 6–30.

Hops, H., & Lewin, L. (1984). Peer sociometric forms. In T. H. Ollendick & M. Hersen (Eds.), *Child behavioral assessment: Principles and procedures.* New York: Pergamon Press.

Jones, M. C. (1924). The elimination of children's fears. *Journal of Experimental Psychology, 7,* 382–390.

Kanfer, F. H., & Saslow, G. (1969). Behavioral diagnosis. In C. M. Franks (Ed.), *Behavior therapy: Appraisal and status.* New York: McGraw-Hill.

Kazdin, A. E. (1977). Assessing the clinical or applied importance of behavior change through social validation. *Behavior Modification, 1,* 427–452.

Kendall, P. C. (1987). Ahead to basics: Assessments with children and families. *Behavioral Assessment, 9,* 321–332.

Kendall, P. C., & Hollon, S. D. (Eds.), (1980). *Cognitive-behavioral intervention: Assessment methods.* New York: Academic Press.

Lang, P. J. (1978). Fear reduction and fear behavior: Problems in treating a construct. In J. M. Shlien (Ed.), *Research in psychotherapy* (Vol. 3), Washington, DC: American Psychological Association.

Leitenberg, H., Yost, L. W., & Carroll-Wilson, M. (1986). Negative cognitive errors in children: Questionnaire development, normative data, and comparisons between children with and without self-reported symptoms of depression, low self-esteem, and evaluation anxiety. *Journal of Consulting and Clinical Psychology, 54,* 528–536.

Loeber, R. (1982). The stability of antisocial and delinquent child behavior: A review. *Child Development, 53,* 1431–1446.

Marks, I. M., & Gelder, M. G. (1966). Different ages of onset in varieties of phobia. *American Journal of Psychiatry, 123,* 218–221.

Mash, E. J. (1979). What is behavioral assessment? *Behavioral Assessment, 1,* 23–29.

Mash, E. J., & Terdal, L. G. (1981). Behavioral assessment of childhood disturbance. In E. J. Mash & L. G. Terdal (Eds.), *Behavioral assessment of childhood disorders.* New York: Guilford Press.

Mash, E. J., & Terdal, L. G. (1989). Behavioral assessment of childhood disturbance. In E. J. Mash & L. G. Terdal (Eds.), *Behavioral assessment of childhood disorders* (2nd ed.). New York: Guilford Press.

McCandless, B. R., & Marshall, H. R. (1957). A picture sociometric technique for preschool children and its relation to teacher judgment of friendship. *Child Development, 28,* 139–148.

McFall, R. M. (1982). A review and reformulation of the concept of social skills. *Behavioral Assessment, 4,* 1–33.

McReynolds, P. (1968). *Advances in psychological assessment* (Vol. 1). Palo Alto, CA: Science and Behavior Books.

Meichenbaum, D. H. (1977). *Cognitive-behavior modification.* New York: Plenum Press.

Miller, L. C., Barrett, C. L., & Hampe, E. (1974). Phobias of childhood in a prescientific era. In A. Davids (Ed.), *Child personality and psychopathology: Current topics.* New York: John Wiley & Sons.

Mischel, W. (1973). Toward a cognitive social learning reconceptualization of personality. *Psychological Review, 80,* 252–283.

Mischel, W. (1979). On the interface of cognition and personality: Beyond the person-situation debate. *American Psychologist, 34,* 740–754.

Ollendick, T. H. (1979). Fear reduction techniques with

children. In M. Hersen, R. M. Eisler, & P. M. Miller (Eds.), *Progress in behavior modification* (Vol. 8). New York: Academic Press.

Ollendick, T. H. (1981). Assessment of social interaction skills in school children. *Behavioral Counseling Quarterly, 1*, 227–243.

Ollendick T. H. (1982). The Self-Efficacy Questionnaire for Children's Social Skills. Unpublished manuscript. Virginia Polytechnic Institute and State University, Blacksburg, Virginia.

Ollendick, T. H. (1983). Reliability and Validity of the Revised Fear Survey Schedule for Children (FSSC-R). *Behaviour Research and Therapy, 21*(6), 685–692.

Ollendick, T. H. (1984). Development and validation of the Children's Assertiveness Inventory. *Child and Family Behavior Therapy, 5*(3), 1–15.

Ollendick, T. H., & Cerny, J. A. (1981). *Clinical behavior therapy with children*. New York: Plenum Press.

Ollendick, T. H., Elliott, W. R., & Matson, J. L. (1980). Locus of control as related to effectiveness in a behavior modification program for juvenile delinquents. *Journal of Behavior Therapy and Experimental Psychiatry, 11*, 259–262.

Ollendick, T. H., & Herson, M. (Eds.), (1983). *Handbook of child psychopathology*. New York: Plenum Press.

Ollendick, T. H., & Hersen, M. (Eds.), (1984). *Child behavioral assessment: Principles and procedures*. New York: Pergamon Press.

Ollendick, T. H., & Hersen, M. (Eds.), (1989). *Handbook of child psychopathology* (2nd ed.). New York: Plenum Press.

Ollendick, T. H., & Huntzinger, R. M. (1990). Separation anxiety disorders in children. In M. Hersen & C. G. Last (Eds.), *Handbook of child and adult psychopathology: A longitudinal perspective*. New York: Pergamon Press.

Ollendick, T. H., & King, N. J. (1991). Developmental factors in child behavioral assessment. In P. R. Martin (Ed.), *Handbook of behavior therapy and psychological science: An integrative approach* (pp. 57–72). New York: Pergamon Press.

Ollendick, T. H., King, N. J., & Frary, P. B. (1989). Fears in children and adolescents: Reliability and generalizability across gender, age, and nationality. *Behaviour Research and Therapy, 27*, 19–26.

Ollendick, T. H., & Mayer, J. (1983). School phobia. In S. M. Turner (Ed.), *Behavioral treatment and anxiety disorders*. New York: Plenum Press.

Ollendick, T. H., & Schmidt, C. R. (1987). Social learning constructs in the prediction of peer interaction. *Journal of Clinical Child Psychology, 16*, 80–97.

Ollendick, T. H., Shapiro, E. S., & Barrett, R. P. (1982). Effects of vicarious reinforcement in normal and severely disturbed children. *Journal of Consulting and Clinical Psychology, 50*, 63–70.

Ollendick, T. H., & Yule, W. (1990). Depression in British and American children and its relationship to anxiety and fear. *Journal of Consulting and Clinical Psychology, 58*(1), 126–129.

Olweus, D. (1979). Stability of aggresive reaction patterns in males: A review. *Psychological Bulletin, 86*, 852–875.

Rekers, G. A. (1978). Sexual problems: Behavior modification. In B. B. Wolman (Ed.), *Handbook of treatment of mental disorders in childhood and adolescence*. Englewood Cliffs, NJ: Prentice-Hall.

Rie, H. E. (Ed.), (1971). *Perspectives in child psychopathology*. Chicago: Aldine-Atherton.

Ruple, D. N., Parsons, J. E., & Ross, J. (1976). Self-evaluative responses of children in an achievement setting. *Child Development, 47*, 990–997.

Scanlon, E. M., & Ollendick, T. H. (1985). Assertiveness in children: The reliability and validity of three self-report measures. *Child and Family Behavior Therapy, 7*, 9–22.

Scherer, M. W., & Nakamura, C. Y. (1968). A fear survey schedule for children (FSS-FC): An analytic comparison with manifest anxiety (CMAS). *Behavior Research and Therapy, 6*, 173–182.

Shapiro, E. S. (1984). Self-monitoring procedures. In T. H. Ollendick & M. Hersen (Eds.), *Child behavioral assessment: Principles and procedures*. New York: Pergamon Press.

Sroufe, L. A., & Rutter, M. (1984). The domain of developmental psychopathology. *Child Development, 55*, 17–29.

Sulzer-Azaroff, B., & Mayer, G. R. (1977). *Applying behavior analysis procedures with children and youth*. New York: Holt, Rinehart, & Winston.

Watson, J. B., & Rayner, R. (1920). Conditioned emotional reactions. *Journal of Experimental Psychology, 3*, 1–14.

Wolf, M. M. (1978). Social validity: The case for subjective measurement or how behavior analysis is finding its heart. *Journal of Applied Behavior Analysis, 11*, 203–214.

CHAPTER 2

DEVELOPMENTAL CONSIDERATIONS IN CHILD ASSESSMENT

William Yule

INTRODUCTION

Behavior therapy and behavior modification have transformed the ways in which children's behavioral and emotional problems have been treated. Along with this welcome revolution have come improvements in the ways in which presenting problems have been assessed. To begin with, assessment concentrated on objective descriptions of the presenting problem and attempted to isolate contemporaneous setting events and consequences (Bijou & Baer, 1961). The valuable *A-B-C* of functional analysis came to the fore, and great emphasis was paid to direct observation and reports of observable behaviors (Gelfand & Hartmann, 1975).

For a time, it almost looked as if children did not think or feel, and the younger the child, the less likely was he or she to be asked his or her view of the presenting problem. This tendency to ignore the child's own account of what was happening also stemmed from a different tradition (paradoxically, from the psychoanalytic tradition, in which direct questioning was often eschewed in favor of indirect measures such as projective tests and interpretation of play or drawings).

It has long been recognized that there are major differences between working with children and working with adults (Yule, 1977). Children rarely refer themselves for treatment, and one usually must try to make sense of complaints and worries about the child's behavior that are expressed by adults such as parents, teachers, or other caretakers. Not surprisingly, this difficulty has led behavioral assessors to call for more objective descriptions of presenting problems and to investigate the surprising lack of agreement that sometimes exists between adult reporters (Rutter, Tizard, & Whitmore, 1970).

The major difference between working with children and working with adults is that children are rapidly developing, and somehow this has to be taken into account both in assessment and in treatment. This necessity has long been recognized (Ollendick & King, 1991), but the problem is how to do it effectively. The purpose of this chapter is to define what is meant by "developmental perspective" and to examine how that can and should influence the assessment of children's problems. To do this, we consider some of the advances made in the past decade in the emerging field of "developmental psychopathology," and we examine some of the central questions addressed in this literature and considering the implications for assessment.

Other writers on this topic (Edelbrock, 1984; Ollendick & King, 1991) have contrasted the nomothetic and idiographic approaches to assessment. These approaches are not incompatible, but each addresses different questions that are relevant to assessment. The utility of behavior rating schedules in assessment is examined from a developmental perspective. The place of psychometric assessment of cognitive ability and academic attainment as part of a comprehensive assessment of children's problems is also considered.

ASSESSMENT

Assessment is not and should not be merely the application of available tools or techniques. Assessment should always be undertaken for a stated purpose, and that will, to a large extent, determine what is relevant. A proper, broadly based functional analysis of the presenting problem should lead to a fuller understanding of how the problem arose, how it is maintained, and what interventions are most appropriate. This implies that the therapist has a good awareness of the range of acceptable and normal adjustments given the social circumstances in which the child is placed.

When a parent brings a child in for help, the first question to be considered is "What is the complaint?" Is the complainant's view of the referral problem complete, or does the clinician view things differently after a full description and history have been elicited? Even if the referrer and the clinician agree about the nature of the presenting problem, is it indeed a problem? To answer these questions satisfactorily, the clinician needs a good grounding in normal child development and developmental psychopathology.

The clinician needs to have a sophisticated mixture of normative and idiographic approaches to assessment. Within certain limits, a nomothetic, normative approach helps answer the question "What is wrong?" in the sense of "Compared with other children of this age and from comparable sociocultural backgrounds, is the behavior complained of deviant in any way?" Then the behavioral assessment goes much further and asks how that is functionally related to the child's effective social environment.

With greater use of screening schedules of symptom or behavior checklists (Barkley, 1988) and of standardized interview protocols (Edelbrock & Costello, 1988), much of the art of guesswork in deciding what constitutes a problem will be reduced, but one is still left demanding a formulation, or functional analysis, which illuminates an understanding of the nature of the problem and suggests what to do about it.

In other words, as is discussed in more detail in the following paragraphs, when deciding whether a behavior is deviant, one is not merely asking whether it occurs in the general population at an abnormally low rate. This is using the concept of abnormality in a narrow, statistical way. The real question for the clinician is whether the behavior is interfering with the child's development or causing difficulties for the family or society. This involves making social judgments tempered by an understanding of child development.

It might be very rare to find a child with a fear of seeing a stork fly overhead. Before undertaking any functional analysis (or psychodynamic interpretation), one would want to know whether that rare fear resulted in any avoidant or other behaviors that had a negative impact on the child's development. How handicapping is the behavior? At the other end of the frequency distribution, temper tantrums are very common, especially in preschool children. Indeed, if children do not try to assert themselves against parental authority, one might wonder whether there is something wrong—are parents using discipline that is too harsh? The point is that even though temper tantrums are so common as to be a normal part of development, parents must still react to them and deal with them. Why? Because failure to do so results in the child's not being properly socialized (Patterson, 1982). The decision on when to intervene is made not on the basis of the frequency of occurrence of the behavior but on the basis of our understanding of the significance of that behavior for future development.

A DEVELOPMENTAL PERSPECTIVE

Consider the following scenario: You are told that a child bursts into uncontrollable tears on being separated from the parents in the waiting room. Your trainee asks you if this is abnormal. Is this separation anxiety? Being an experienced clinician, you reply, "It depends"; it depends on the age of the child. In most instances, it is normal for a child 3 to 5 years of age to show reluctance to separate from his or her parents and being asked to accompany a stranger, particularly in a strange place. Indeed, if a child of this age does *not* show discomfort at separation, one begins to suspect the quality of the attachment. On the other hand, if the girl is 15 years old, one would definitely regard crying on separating as abnormal.

Adolescents of that age should be able to negotiate such a separation with reasonable confidence. You feel pleased with yourself that you have just illustrated the value of a developmental perspective in assessing the significance of a piece of behavior. Then your trainee says that he omitted to say that he was not referring to behavior in a psychology waiting room, but in a dentist's waiting room, and was it not normal for a 15-year-old to show anxiety in that setting!

This example is given to illustrate the point that while age is indeed a major factor in determining the significance we attach to any presenting behavior, the social circumstances must also be considered. Behavior does not exist in a vacuum. That is why most child behavior therapists find a broad-based social learning theory (Bandura, 1973) the most useful framework for understanding problems and suggesting solutions. Such a theory emphasizes the interaction between characteristics of the child and factors in the effective social environment.

So where does developmental theory come into this? Indeed, what is "development"? I must confess a distrust of those who claim to know about "developmental theory." In my view, there is no such theory—at least not one overarching theory that can usefully inform us about how children develop. Rather, there is a bewildering set of minimodels and minitheories, each trying to deal with changes in children's functioning either at different periods in their lives or in different psychological functions such as perception, language, and memory. By and large, the different theories seem to ignore each other's work—and many also seem keener on theories than on data that might disprove the theories.

Thus, Piaget's theories predominantly address how children develop a cognitive understanding of their world. His views on "stages" are so well known that many people assume that they are "true." And yet, his work was developed outside the mainstream of child development theory and paid scant attention to other psychological methodologies or findings. His was a biological view of development, and his cross-sectional methodology emphasized the separation between the stages he posited. Staats (1971) argued that most of the phenomena described by Piaget and his followers could be interpreted within a social learning framework that instead emphasized the continuity of development across stages.

Other theorists, such as Kohlberg, followed the Piagetian tradition when examining how children judge normal dilemmas. Again, discrete stages are posited and are all too often uncritically accepted. It is often not acknowledged that this stage theory differs from Piaget's in that the different forms of reasoning can coexist. It is also overlooked that the way in which children (or adults, for that matter) judge an ethical dilemma does not necessarily determine how they behave. It is not the case that the older we are, the wiser we behave.

A third set of stage theories are those of Freud dealing with psychosexual development. Children are seen as passively passing through stages, their development being impeded by obstacles or even regressing in the face of trauma. This view owes more to literature than to science, and the evidence on children's psychosexual development clearly shows that whatever Freud was unaware of during the "latency" period, children are certainly far from inactive (Rutter, 1980).

Apart from being "stage" theories, these three sets of influential theories really have very little in common. The psychological mechanisms determining growth of cognitive understanding bear little relationship to any supposedly underlying socioemotional behavior. None of the theories takes into account all of the work done in perceptual development, language development, development of peer relationships, development during adolescence, and so on. They pay little attention to the work in individual differences in personality or temperament, or to biological development generally.

This is not the place to attempt a synthesis of all these bodies of knowledge. There is no one theory of development to guide us in assessment. Rather, we need to be aware of many different bodies of knowledge, and to realize that some are better substantiated than others.

We also need to be aware of the changing views of the child as an actor in development. Even 25 years ago, the predominant, or certainly a very influential, view was that development was largely biologically determined. Such a view was anathema to the new theorists of behavior modification and behavior therapy. It seemed too pessimistic. By ignoring the biological basis of behavior and seeking explanations solely in the here-and-now influences on behavior, they undoubtedly broke through to a much more optimistic era of interventions.

Simultaneously, child developmentalists were recognizing the contributions the child brought to all aspects of development. Soon, the tabula rasa model was discarded in favor of viewing the child as an active participant in development. The direction of influence was not all one way: The child helped shape the environment. Thus, parents react to individual differences in children. Different children "call out" different responses from their social environment. As parents have known all along, children do have different temperaments from birth, and these shape how they develop (Berger, 1985).

The implications of this for child assessment are many. For example, it implies that we must begin to take into account a child's temperament or personality when planning treatment (Berger, 1985; Keogh, 1982). It has long been known that children who are extremely introverted react differently to praise and punishment than children who are extremely extroverted (Eysenck & Eysenck, 1969; Keogh, 1982). They respond to different teaching styles in the classroom. Surely these differences need to be accomodated in setting up an individual treatment program.

With young infants, it can be very reassuring to a parent to be told that anyone would find their unpredictable child difficult to rear. It can boost parental self-confidence to be told (when true) that their parenting style is perfectly adequate for most children—just not effective with this particular one. This reassurance can dramatically alter the way such a parent participates in a parent training program.

All this is not to say that stage theories carry no implications for child assessment. Far from it. It is very helpful to remember that young children think and reason about their worlds differently from older children. This has to be borne in mind when interviewing children, when trying to elicit their own understanding of their problem, and equally, when giving them instructions, feedback, or explanations. However, it must also be emphasized that the "stages" should only be regarded as rough guidelines. We know that there are such wide individual differences in the rate at which children develop that we should never make assumptions about the individual child from knowing only his or her chronological age.

There is scant literature on children's concepts and understanding of death (Childers and Wimmer, 1971; Koocher, 1974; Wolff, 1969). It is reasonably consistent in concluding that it is not until around the age of 10 or 11 that *most* children appreciate that death is both universal and irreversible. This knowledge is essential for all who are working with children who are dying or bereaved. It helps explain why some younger children show an almost casual, matter-of-fact interest in death of a loved one and are less upset by it than adults (Wolff, 1969). But it would be wrong to assume that all younger children fail to have an adult appreciation of the significance of death, and indeed a few children as young as 4 years old have been found to have quite mature understanding. Knowledge of the broad outline of the development of the conceptualization of death helps clinicians formulate their questions, but the onus must always be to check whether or not the particular child conforms to the average. When in doubt, it is always useful to ask children to repeat or rephrase their own understanding; in that way, many misunderstandings can be revealed.

DEVELOPMENTAL PSYCHOPATHOLOGY

The past decade has witnessed the emergence of a new subspecialty: developmental psychopathology (Cicchetti, 1984; Sroufe & Rutter, 1984). It aims to heal a rift that occurred, especially in North America, between academic and clinical child psychology. It focuses on both development and psychopathology. "The developmental psychopathologist is concerned with the origins and time course of a given disorder, its varying manifestations with development, its precursors and sequelae, and its relation to nondisordered patterns of behavior" (Sroufe & Rutter, 1984, p. 18). Developmental psychopathologists, like social learning theorists, look to normal development to illuminate pathological development. They are interested in continuities and changes in behavior across time. This fits in well with the tradition of risk research (Garmezy, 1974) and attempts to answer questions not only about why some children are more vulnerable than others, but also about what protective factors operate to lessen the impact of stressors. If we knew more about protective factors, we could do more with treatment and prevention.

As noted previously, there is no one general theory of child development. Sroufe and Rutter (1984), following Santostefano (1978), articulate several propositions that are broadly agreed across many theories.

Holism

"... the meaning of behavior can only be determined within the total psychological context" (Sroufe & Rutter, 1984, p. 20). As shown earlier, the meaning of crying depends in part on the immediate social demands placed on the child. This principle states that the behavior also needs to be evaluated in its broader psychological context. One simply cannot judge the significance of a behavior on the basis of its physical, stimulus properties.

Directedness

Children are not passive reactors to the demands of the environment. Development consists of a reorganization of previous elements, skills, and behavior, not just a linear addition of skills.

Differentiation of Modes and Goals

Over time, children's reactions to their environment become both more flexible and increasingly complex in organization. Thus, one sign of pathology is for children to get stuck in a particular way of trying to solve a problem.

Mobility of Behavioral Functions

Earlier behavior becomes integrated into later patterns, and ". . . the individual does not operate only in terms of behaviors that define a single stage. Especially in periods of stress, early modes of functioning may become manifest" (Sroufe & Rutter, 1984, p. 21). In other words, under stress, those patterns of behavior that have most recently become integrated into the child's repertoire are most susceptible of disruption. This is very different from the unsatisfactory concept of "regression" in that all the skills achieved remain available in the child's repertoire; some earlier ones also manifest at times of stress.

The Problem of Continuity and Change

Above all, development is seen as lawful, even though we are still far from understanding the processes involved in these laws. Sroufe and Rutter (1984) emphasize: "The continuity lies not in isomorphic behaviors over time but in lawful relations to later behavior, however complex the links" (p. 21). One is reminded here of the search for correlates between early behavior and later adjustment that, on the whole, proved fruitless until Thomas, Chess, and Birch (1968), in their New York Longitudinal Study, recast the net and looked for continuities in *style* of behavior (temperament) rather than continuities of content per se.

It is now recognized that there are many complex ways in which child behavior is related to later and even adult adjustment (Rutter, 1983). One of the most powerful predictors of later adult psychopathology is inadequate peer relations. As Sroufe and Rutter (1984) point out, this relationship may be due to two interacting reasons: (1) Poor peer relations are signs of failure to adapt during childhood, and that failure persists; (2) social support later on acts as a buffer against adult stressors.

Clearly, this view of development, with its implications for psychopathology, is far removed from the lessons learned in the Skinner box. And yet these models must be integrated into the ways that child therapists assess children's problems if we are to provide the best advice possible. As noted earlier, I find no difficulty in accommodating the notion of a biological basis for behavior and the notion of the child as an active participant interacting with his or her soical environment within a broad social learning framework (Yule, 1978; Bandura, 1973). Understanding how a problem has arisen may provide useful guidance on what aspects to focus on, but the treatment will still focus on the present. There will be implications for maintaining gains and preventing future problems, as well as implications for preventing such problems arising in other children.

The implications of developmental psychopathology also affect child assessment indirectly, insofar as they affect the ways in which we classify children's disorders. In addition to the World Health Organization's International Classification of Diseases, which all governments have agreed to use to report on the pattern of disorders in different countries, the American Psychiatric Association has produced its own *Diagnostic and Statistical Manual,* now in its third, revised edition. Critics of both ICD-9 and DSM-III-R are agreed that while they help to improve communication between therapists and researchers, they are still too adult oriented and pay insufficient attention to developmental aspects of disorders (Yule, 1981; Rutter and Shaffer, 1980; Cantwell, 1988).

Garber (1984) makes the point that children differ from adults in cognition, language, physiology, and emotions. "Such maturational differences may impact children's abilities to experience or express certain affects, cognitions and behaviors, and thus the manner in which symptoms are expressed may differ over the course of development" (p. 32). In my own recent work on the effects of major disasters on children's adjustment, it became clear that children as young as 8 years old showed most of the symptoms of posttraumatic stress disorder (PTSD)—with unpleasant intrusive thoughts, poor concentration, and sleep disorders predominating (Yule & Williams, 1990; Yule, 1989). DSM-III-R, while admitting that PTSD might occur in children, was far from explicit in how it might manifest. Many adolescents found it very hard to discuss the disaster with their parents and indulged in frantic socializing to avoid such discussions. Objectively, their social contacts increased; subjectively, they were suffering. Indeed, only by asking the children explicitly about their thoughts and feelings could one elicit the symptomatology that was missed by broad-spectrum health-screening questionnaires. Preschool children reacted with more repetitive play and drawing than did older children, but even the younger children experienced very disturbing, intrusive thoughts about the disaster. Again, only careful interviewing elicited these phenomena. The moral of this is that the clinician working with young children must bear in mind that children differ in their level of understanding and in their ability to express themselves, and they must carefully cross-check what the child is feeling before embarking on any treatment program.

Garber also notes that some disorders, such as mental handicap and autism, first manifest in childhood and persist into adulthood. Others, such as encopresis or enuresis manifest in childhood but rarely persist into adulthood. Some, such as anorexia and bulimia, are more typical of adolescence. Suicide, although rare before puberty, is rapidly becoming the commonest cause of death in adolescence, and peaks in old age. Major depression and schizophrenia are rare in childhood. There is greater evidence for continuity of such disorders as psychopathy and psychoses than for neuroses. "Most children with emotional problems grow up to be substantially normal, although compared to controls, children with emotional problems are twice as likely to have psychiatric problems in adult life" (p. 33). Garber argues that originally, much of the interest in helping children was to prevent adult disorders, and that is laudable. However, ". . . it is not necessary for a disorder to persist into adulthood in order for it to be considered a valid disorder in its own right" (p. 33).

Thus, encopresis is a difficult problem for many parents and children to cope with. Yet, apart from those with a severe mental handicap, few adults suffer from encopresis (Bellman, 1966; Doleys, Schwartz, & Ciminero, 1981). The implication is that the disorder clears up spontaneously, but surely no one would argue that this recovery should not be speeded up by effective behavioral intervention (Doleys, Schwartz, & Ciminero, 1981).

Enuresis is another predominantly developmental disorder that draws attention to another important consideration in assessment—sex differences. Enuresis is universal initially. Bladder control is gradually gained in the preschool years, with girls gaining control earlier than boys (Shaffer, 1985). Enuretic boys in their middle years of schooling are no more likely to have a psychiatric disorder than their peers without enuresis, but those girls who are enuretic are much more likely to have a psychiatric disorder (Rutter, Yule, & Graham, 1973). In this instance, the same behavior—loss of bladder control—has a different significance if it occurs in a boy than in a girl.

IMPLICATIONS FOR BEHAVIORAL ASSESSMENT

So how can one integrate some of these findings and ideas into glood clinical practice? First, such a developmental perspective argues strongly against assessing or treating any piece of behavior in isolation. One needs to have a sophisticated understanding about how the behavior fits in with the child's overall adjustment.

Second, although not yet fully articulated in ways that are easily operationalized, future assessments will need to focus more on patterns of adjustment, their flexibility and adaptability, than on isolated symptoms.

Third, where isolated symptoms are presented for assessment, their significance, deviance, or abnormality need to be evaluated against a complex set of developmental norms as well as environmental demands. By this is meant that some isolated behaviors will be seen to be sufficiently distressing as to warrant immediate intervention, irrespective of their long-term prognosis; some will be judged as not particularly handicapping currently, but because of their implications for later adjustment will require intervention; some will be regarded as of little consequence either now or in the future and therefore will not be treated.

Fourth, the views of the child need to be given greater consideration. The best way of finding these out is to ask. As Garber (1984) puts it, "Historically one informant often overlooked in the assessment of children has been the child himself. Despite their cognitive and linguistic limitations, however, children are becoming a more integral part of the assessment and classification process . . ." (p. 44).

The Use of Screening Questionnaires

As child assessment has progressed, greater use has been made of behavior rating scales completed by parents, teachers, and, occasionally, the children themselves (Barkley, 1988). Undoubtedly, the better constructed modern instruments can assist in assessment, but I emphasize *can assist*. Such instruments are a help in systematically asking about various behaviors, but they are no substitute for clinicians' exercising their informed judgment.

Among the best known and most widely used behavior rating scales are, in Britain, the Rutter Behavior Rating Scales (B-Scale) for completion by Parents and Teachers (Rutter, 1967; Rutter, Tizard, & Whitmore, 1970); and in the United States, the Child Behavior Checklist (CBCL) (Achenbach & Edelbrock, 1983). Both have been used extensively in epidemiological studies and subjected to sophisticated psychometric analyses. Both have been widely translated and standardized in different languages and in different countries.

Basically, both sets of scales ask informants to rate descriptions of behavior on 3-point scales and then scores are summated over the items. Each scale has a number of subscales, and each identifies one group of anxiety/neurotic/internalizing symptoms and another group of conduct disorder/antisocial/externalizing symptoms. The CBCL asks parents to rate 118 items; Rutter's B-Scale asks teachers to rate 26 items. Children scoring above empirically determined levels are regarded as showing deviant behavior or as having a high risk of showing a psychiatric disorder.

These scales do what they were originally intended to do well. That is, in large populations they quickly screen out those children at highest risk of having the commonest broad type of psychiatric disorder, namely neurotic and antisocial disorders. What they cannot do so well is to differentiate among subtypes of these broad groups of disorders. Moreover, they cannot identify rare disorders such as autisim or PTSD.

From the enormous data bases now built up on such scales, as well as on more specific instruments as the Fear Survey Schedule for Children Revised (Ollendick, 1983; Ollendick, King, & Frary, 1989; Ollendick, Yule, & Ollier, 1991) different proportions of children are reported, or report themselves, to have particular behaviors at different ages. Sex differences are also quickly apparent. Such data are invaluable in judging the statistical rarity or abnormality of a behavior. However, items that were endorsed by only a very small percentage of children were eliminated during the course of the development of the scales.

Looking at the age trends is informative but potentially misleading. While it is clear, for example, that the proportion of children reported as enuretic declines with age, this pattern does not tell us the probability of a particular child at one point in time gaining continence by any particular later point. This is because the data are cross-sectional rather than longitudinal. They do not allow us to calculate how many children at point 1 remain incontinent at point 2; how many gained continence by time 2; nor how many were dry at time 1 but became incontinent by time 2. Cross-sectional data are useful for assessing the rarity of occurrence of a problem and for giving a general guide to developmental patterns, but they are insufficiently detailed to permit the judgment of the probability of recovery in a given time.

As Garber (1984) notes, most epidemiological studies since the 1950s have found that ". . . the average child exhibits a few symptoms of many types of devaint behavior, but less frequently shows a large number of symptoms from any one disorder" (p. 35). This, of course, is the main justification for using behavior rating scales and summing scores over disparate symptoms. Knowing that most children will endorse a large number and a wide range of fears is helpful when the significance of the fears presented by a child are assessed in a clinic. However, a child may also present with a highly specific, circumscribed, but nevertheless very handicapping fear (McGrath, Tsui, Humphries, & Yule, 1989). As with all presenting problems, one has to obtain information about the intensity, duration, and frequency and to judge the severity so determined against what is developmentally normal for a child coming from that particular sociocultural background.

Part of the problem of judging the significance of behaviors in context is that children's behavior is usually situation specific. When it was first noted (e.g., in the early 1960s in the Isle of Wight epidemiological studies [Rutter, Tizard, & Whitmore, 1970]) that parents and teachers identified *different* children as deviant on rating scales, the findings were greeted with surprise. Who was "telling the truth"? Which informant's views should be given priority in deciding whether the child "really" had a problem? These questions were based on the old-fashioned assumption rooted in 1950s personality theories that children bring similar behavioral tendencies to bear in all situations. Now it is recognized that children adapt their behavior to the differing demands of different social situations, and this fits much more comfortably with a social learning theory formulation of children's development. In the minority of cases in which parents and teachers agree that children's behavior is deviant, as in the case of pervasive overactivity (Schachar, Rutter, & Smith, 1981), then one is usually dealing with a more serious disorder.

A final limitation to the use of general screening questionnaires must be emphasized. They were never intended to be used as definitive diagnostic instruments nor to act as criteria against which to assess the effectiveness of intervention. Nor were they designed to identify psychopathology that was not recognized at the time the scales were developed. This last statement seems obvious, but, for example, the Rutter Scales were used by McFarlane, Policansky, and Irwin (1987) in their studies of the effects of Australian bush fires on children and by Galante and Foa (1986) in their studies of the effects of the Italian earthquakes of November 23, 1980.

McFarlane et al. (1987) found that parents reported more pathology than teachers in the first few months. Teachers were reluctant to participate in follow-up studies because they did not want to upset the children (although how completing a questionnaire in private is even known to the child is not clear), but those who did not cooperate endorsed more items at follow-up. However, when children are asked directly about their subjective distress following disasters, much more psychopathology is recorded (Yule & Williams, 1990). This disparity illustrates that the scales should not be used for purposes for which they were not developed and, again, emphasizes the point that if you want to know how children feel, ask them!

Age-Related Problems

Both epidemiological and developmental data help in drawing attention to the sorts of problems most common or most characteristic at particular ages. Table 2–1, adapted from Sroufe and Rutter (1984), Garber (1984), and other sources, lists important developmental tasks and issues alongside common pathology. The implication of this information is that if a child of a particular age is referred, one should quickly check out whether any of the other problems are present as well as check on how well the child is negotiating the salient developmental tasks.

Table 2–1 is not intended to be a comprehensive schema, and clearly there are problems with it. For instance, is the fear of strangers that marks the 8- to-10-month object permanence stage the same as "separation anxiety" as manifested then or later, at entry to school at age 5 years? Is insecure attachment, as determined by an artificial "strange situations" task, the same as the sort of attachment and emotional problems shown by children who have multiple caretakers? Our loose usage of such terms is potentially confusing, but the issues they address are important for healthy child development.

It has long been recognized that depression and suicide are very rare in prepubertal children (Rutter, Izard, & Read, 1986; Shaffer, 1986). Garber (1984) suggests that both depend on a particular level of cognitive development—sense of self, ability to appreciate the future, ability to understand death fully. Kovacs (1986) argues that it is unlikely that children younger than 6 or 7 can reliably report on their own thought processes and think clearly about the future. However, after that age, she argues that much can be gained by direct interviews of children about their mood and functioning.

Cognitive Level

Many of the examples just given have directly or indirectly referred to the child's level of cognitive development. At one time, psychologists took pride in their ability to assess a child's level of cognitive ability and his or her educational attainment. The past two decades have seen this practice fall into disuse. By virtue of its often being omitted, it would sometimes appear as if child therapists ignored IQ in assessing children's difficulties. Let me briefly argue why I believe this would be a mistake.

First, we know from epidemiological studies (Rutter, Tizard, & Whitmore, 1970) that educational failure and emotional or behavioral problems overlap. If intelligence and educational attainment are not assessed together, important competencies that may be contributing to presenting problems will be overlooked.

Second, with younger children especially, it is vital to have an accurate estimate of level of language development as well as general cognitive functioning. All too often, one sees children who have severe language problems failing to cope with the demands of their social environments and then presenting with oppositional behavior. Sadly, in my experience, social services departments, which are responsible for placing children with foster parents or for adoption often fail to inquire into the child's level of cognitive development. It is then frustrating to witness a social worker explaining a complex set of relationships to a child who cannot understand and so does not benefit from the explanations given.

Behavior therapists, too, are guilty of forgetting that children have to meet the cognitive demands of school. There are many papers describing the application of behavior modification to classroom management, but there are few examples of people considering whether children are placed in the correct class, whether the curriculum is appropriate, and so on (Berger, 1982; Berger, Yule, & Wigley, 1987).

Table 2-1. Age, Developmental Issues, and Psychopathology

AGE	DEVELOPMENTAL ISSUES	DEVELOPMENTAL TASK/PROCESS	PSYCHOPATHOLOGY
0–1	Biological regulation Harmonious dyadic interaction Formation of an effective attachment relationship	Object permanancy	Sleep disturbance Feeding difficulty Separation anxiety
1–2.5	Exploration and mastery of the object world (caretaker as secure base) Responding to external control of impulses		Separation anxiety Temper tantrums
3–5	Flexible self-control; self-reliance identification and gender concepts establishing effective peer contacts	Moral development Perspective taking Empathy	Conduct disorder— Undersocialized Aggressive
6–12	Social understanding (equity, fairness) Gender constancy—Same-sex friendships School adjustment Sense of industry and competence	Peer relationships Friendship pattern	Schizoid disorder
13+	Formal operations in thinking (ability to judge own thinking) Beginning heterosexual relationships Emancipation	Concept of death Time perspective Differentiation of self	Suicide
	Identity	Self-esteem	Depression

Blagg's (1987) description of his rapid treatment of school refusal emphasizes the need to consider the educational ability and the suitability of school placement. It must also be remembered that gifted children who are understimulated can also present with behavior problems in class.

SUMMARY

The field of developmental psychopathology is rapidly expanding, and behavior therapists working with children must continue to act as applied scientists and incorporate the new findings into their repertoire. Children are important sources of information and should not be ignored. This emphasis on interviewing children about their problems is to be welcomed, but the emerging trend of developing standardized interview schedules is less welcome.

One has to remember the purposes for which standardized interviews, like behavior rating scales, are developed. In many cases, they are developed for use in large-scale epidemiological studies in which it is vital to obtain comparable information from all informants. But sometimes they are also developed in a very simplified form so that minimally trained interviewers can use them. Sometimes the interviews are merely reworkings of the symptoms mentioned in DSM-III-R, and, as noted earlier, there is nothing magical about these results of committee deliberations. No child therapist should feel constrained to stick to any interview developed by a committee, but should remain true to the spirit of intensive investigation of the single case that has been the hallmark of behavior therapy over the years.

Because interviewing is recommended more and more often, one should think carefully about the developmental aspects of how children report on their own inner experiences. Ollendick and King (1991) note that interviewing will be a less useful source of data in younger children, and Kovacs (1986) comments that while it is useful to ask children about their mood and functioning, children below the age of 6 or 7 have difficulty in commenting on their own thought processes. This, of course, ties in with the well-known concept of when children can cognitively decenter, but there are very wide individual differences in when children achieve these skills. The rule should be that one should always ask the child, but the weight given to the child's view will depend on your assessment of his or her cognitive development.

Behavior therapists have always adjusted their assessment and treatment approaches to the developmental level of the child, but they have not often written about this. Thus, direct observation is clearly very important when assessing the problems of preverbal children. With young children 4 to 10 years of age, simple family points systems are invaluable as a tool in child management, but older children regard this as "babyish." After 10 years, reciprocal and mediated contracting comes to the fore in modifying many behavioral problems.

Early writers on the treatment of children's phobias reported on the difficulties that children had in learning to relax and to control their imaginations, and so more active, in vivo treatments were recommended for children than for adults. Experience over the years has shown that young children can be taught to relax as therapists develop better techniques, but there are still problems in getting very young children to reliably report on their subjective distress, to make fine discriminations about progress or about constructing hierarchies, so more use is still made of in vivo methods in which direct observation of discomfort replaces subjective reports.

Techniques of cognitive self-control of behavior clearly must take on board a developmental perspective. Again, this is implicit in many early writings and in the manner in which responsibility for control of behavior is gradually passed from external controls to internal ones, as when token programs are gradually faded out. What is needed is much more empirical and experimental work to determine the influences of cognitive and socioemotional development on the success of different types of intervention.

There is a tension—and I hope it is a constructive one—between traditional behavioral approaches to assessment and treatment and the burgeoning findings from developmental psychopathology. Many of these findings come from studies of groups of children and, as always, the therapist working with the individual child has to be aware of the findings and judge the extent to which they apply to the particular child. Thus, in conducting a behavioral assessment, one has to have a wide knowledge of normal child development, or developmental psychopathology, and of their associated normative findings; but in the end one has to undertake an idiographic, functional analysis of the problem being presented if the child is to receive the best help available.

REFERENCES

Achenbach, T. M., & Edelbrock, C. S. (1983). *Manual for the Child Behavior Checklist and Revised Child Behavior Profile*. Burlington, VT: T. A. Achenbach.

Bandura, A. (1973). *Agression: A social learning analysis*. London: Prentice-Hall.

Barkley, R. A. (1988). Child behavior rating scales and checklists. In M. Rutter, A. H. Tuma, & I. S. Lann (Eds.), *Assessment and diagnosis in child psychopathology* (pp. 113–155). London: David Fulton Publishers.

Bellman, M. (1966). Studies on encopresis. *Acta Paediatrica Scandinavica* (Supplement No. 70).

Berger, M. (1982). Applied behavior analysis in education: A critical assessment and some implications for training teachers. *Educational Psychology, 2*, 289–300.

Berger, M. (1985). Temperament and individual differences. In M. Rutter & L. Hersov (Eds.), *Child and adolescent psychiatry: Modern approaches* (2nd ed.) (pp. 3–16). Oxford: Blackwell Scientific Publications.

Berger, M., Yule, W., & Wigley, V. (1987). The Teacher-Child Interaction Programme (TCIP): Implementing behavioral programs with troublesome individual children in the primary school. In K. Wheldall (Ed.), *The Behaviourist in the classroom* (pp. 90–111). London: Allen and Unwin.

Bijou, S. W., & Baer, D. M. (1961). *Child development. I: A systematic and empirical theory*. New York: Appleton-Century-Crofts.

Blagg, N. (1987). *School phobia and its treatment*. London: Croom Helm.

Cantwell, D. P. (1988). DSM-III studies. In M. Rutter, A. H. Tuma, & I. S. Lann (Eds.), *Assessment and diagnosis in child psychopathology* (pp. 3–36). London: David Fulton Publishers.

Childers, P., & Wimmer, M. (1971). The concept of death in early childhood. *Child Development, 42*, 1299–1301.

Cicchetti, D. (1984). The emergence of developmental psychopathology. *Child Development, 55*, 1–7.

Doleys, D. M., Schwartz, M. S., & Ciminero, A. R. (1981). Elimination problems; Enuresis and encopresis. In E. J. Mash & L. G. Terdal (Eds.), *Behavioral assessment of childhood disorders* (pp. 679–710). New York: Guilford Pres.

Edelbrock, C. (1984). Developmental considerations. In T. H. Ollendick & M. Hersen (Eds.), *Child behavioral assessment: Principles and procedures* (pp. 20–37). New York: Pergammon Press.

Edelbrock, C., & Costello, A. J. (1988). Structured psychiatric interviews for children. In M. Rutter, A. H. Tuma, & I. S. Lann (Eds.), *Assessment and diagnosis in child psychopathology* (pp. 87–112). London: David Fulton Publishers.

Eysenck, H. J., & Eysenck, S. B. G. (1969). *Personality structures and measurement*. London: Routledge and Kegan Paul.

Galante, R., & Foa, D. (1986). An epidemiological study of psychic trauma and treatment effectiveness after a natural disaster. *Journal of the American Academy of Child and Adolescent Psychiatry, 25*, 357–363.

Garber, J. (1984). Classification of childhood psychopathology: A developmental perspective. *Child Development, 55*, 30–48.

Garmezy, N. (1974). Children at risk: The search for the

antecedents of schizophrenia. I: Conceptual models and research methods. *Schizophrenia Bulletin, 8,* 14–90.

Gelfand, D. M., & Hartmann, D. P. (1975). *Child behavior analysis and therapy.* New York: Pergamon.

Keogh, B. K. (1982). Children's temperament and teachers' decisions. In R. Porter & G. M. Collins (Eds.), *Temperamental differences in infants and young children* (pp. 269–278). London: Pitman.

Koocher, G. P. (1974). Talking with children about death. *American Journal of Orthopsychiatry, 44,* 404–411.

Kovacs, M. (1986). A developmental perspective on methods and measures in the assessment of depressive disorders: The clinical interview. In M. Rutter, C, Izard, & P. Read (Eds.), *Depression in young people: Developmental and clinical perspectives* (pp. 435–465). New York: Guilford Press.

McFarlane, A. C., Policansky, S., & Irwin, C. P. (1987). A longitudinal study of the psychological morbidity in children due to a natural disaster. *Psychological Medicine, 17,* 727–738.

McGrath, T., Tsui, E., Humphries, S., & Yule, W. (1989). Successful treatment of a noise phobia in a nine-year-old girl with systematic desensitization in vivo. *Behavioural Approaches with Children, 13,* 143–150.

Ollendick, T. H. (1983). Reliability and validity of the revised Fear Survey Schedule for Children (FSSC-R). *Behavior Research and Therapy, 21,* 685–692.

Ollendick, T. H. & King, N. J. (1991). Developmental factors in child behavioral assessment. In P. Martin (Ed.), *Scientific foun... tions of behavior therapy.* New York: Pergamon.

Ollendick, T. H., King, N. J., & Frary, R. B. (1989). Fears in children and adolescents: Reliability and generalizability across gender, age, and nationality. *Behavior Research and Therapy, 27,* 19–26.

Ollendick, T. H., Yule, W., & Ollier, K. (1991). Fears in British children and their relationship to manifest anxiety and depression. *Journal of Child Psychology and Psychiatry, 32,* 321–331.

Patterson, G. R. (1982). *Coercive family process.* Eugene, OR: Castalia Publishing.

Rutter, M. (1967). A children's behavior questionnaire for completion by teachers: Preliminary findings. *Journal of Child Psychology and Psychiatry, 8,* 1–11.

Rutter, M. (1980). Psychosexual development. In M. Rutter (Ed.), *Scientific foundations of developmental psychiatry* (pp. 322–339). London Heinemann Medical.

Rutter, M. (1983). Continuities and discontinuities in socio-emotional development: Empirical and conceptual perspectives. In R. Harmon & R. Emde (Eds.), *Continuities and discontinuities in development.* New York: Plenum Press.

Rutter, M., Izard, C. E., & Read, P. B. (Eds.) (1986). *Depression in young people: Developmental and clinical perspectives.* New York: Guilford Press.

Rutter, M., & Shaffer, D. (1980). A step forward or back in terms of the classification of child psychiatric disorders? *Journal of the American Academy of Child Psychiatry, 19,* 371–394.

Rutter, M., Tizard, J., & Whitmore, K. (Eds.) (1970). *Education, health, and behaviour.* London: Longmans.

Rutter, M., Yule, W., & Graham, P. J. (1973). Enuresis and behavioral deviance: Some epidemiological considerations. In I. Kolvin, R. McKeith, & S. R. Meadows (Eds.), *Bladder control and enuresis.* Clinics in developmental medicine, Nos. 48/49 (pp. 137–147). London: Heinemann Medical/Spastics International Medical Publications.

Santostefano, S. (1978). *A biodevelopmental approach to clinical child psychology.* New York: John Wiley & Sons.

Schachar, R., Rutter, M., & Smith, A. (1981). The characteristics of situationally and pervasively hyperative children: Implications for syndrome definition. *Journal of Child Psychology and Psychiatry, 22,* 375–392.

Shaffer, D. (1985). Enuresis. In M. Rutter & L. Hersov (Eds.), *Child and adolescent psychiatry: Modern approaches* (2nd ed.) (pp. 465–481). Oxford: Blackwell Scientific Publications.

Shafer, D. (1986). Developmental factors in child and adolescent suicide. In M. Rutter, C. E. Izard, & P. B. Read (Eds.), *Depression in young people: Clinical and developmental perspectives* (pp. 383–396). New York: Guilford Press.

Sroufe, L. A., & Rutter, M. (1984). The domain of developmental psychopathology. *Child Development, 55,* 17–29.

Staats, A. W. (1971). *Child learning, intelligence and personality: Principles of a behavioral interactions approach.* New York: Harper & Row.

Thomas, A., Chess, S., & Birch, H. G. (1968). *Temperament and behavior disorders in children.* London: University of London Press.

Wolff, S. (1969). *Children under stress.* London: Allen Lane, Penguin Press.

Yule, W. (1977). Behavioural approaches to treatment. In M. Rutter & L. Hersov (Eds.), *Child psychiatry: Modern approaches.* Oxford: Blackwell Scientific Publications.

Yule, W. (1978). Behavioural treatment of conduct disorder. In L. A. Hersov, M. Berger, & D. Shaffer (Eds.), *Aggression and anti-social behaviour in childhood and adolescence* (pp. 115–141). Oxford: Pergamon Press.

Yule, W. (1981). The epidemiology of child psychopathology. In B. B. Lahey & A. E. Kazdin (Eds.), *Advances in clinical child psychology* (Vol. 4) (pp. 1–51). New York: Plenum.

Yule, W. (1989). The effects of disasters on children. *Newsletter of the Association for Child Psychology and Psychiatry, 11,* 3–6.

Yule, W. & Williams, R. (1990). Post-traumatic stress reactions in children. *Journal of Traumatic Stress, 3,* 279–295.

CHAPTER 3

DIAGNOSTIC ISSUES IN CHILD ASSESSMENT

Helen Orvaschel
Paul Ambrosini
Harris Rabinovich

Diagnostic assessment of child psychopathology is a complex undertaking. It is complex, in part, because of its dependence on the status of the classification system available. The system of classification in current use is more specific and descriptive than its predecessors, but diagnostic validity and reliability remain problematic. The multifaceted nature of child and adolescent assessment must take many issues into account, including developmental considerations, multiple informants, diagnostic continuity and stability, and comorbidity of disorders. This chapter addresses several of these variables as they pertain to the establishment and undertaking of psychiatric morbidity in children.

DIAGNOSTIC VALIDITY AND RELIABILITY

We begin our review of diagnostic issues in child assessment with a general discussion of the validity and reliability of the current system of classification.

Validity refers to the extent to which something measures what it purports to measure. An example of this is the ability of an achievement test to measure academic performance. If the test provided an accurate reflection of academic performance, we would consider it a valid measure of achievement. *Reliability* refers to the consistency with which something is measured. Giving the achievement test at two different times, by two different administrators, or in two different forms should yield similar results. This would provide evidence of reliability. Clearly, there are several types of validity and reliability.

Given the current descriptive, atheoretical diagnostic system in psychiatry, the issue of diagnostic validity has reemerged and taken on new importance. Historically, the concept of multiple mental disorders with separate etiologies, natural histories, and treatments is derived from the classic views of Kraepelin (1919) and Bleuler (1950). Similar approaches had considerable success earlier in the twentieth century, with the identification of the spirochete as the etiolog-

---

This work was supported, in part, by a W. T. Grant Foundation Scholar Award, No. 8308700.

ical agent in syphilis (Merritt, Adams, & Solomon, 1946) and the recognition of niacin deficiency as the etiologic agent in pellagra (Spies, 1955).

The Kraepelin and Bleuler approaches to classification were abandoned for many years in favor of a nosology based on Freudian and other psychological theories. Dissatisfaction with these theoretical approaches was widespread, however, and many scientists continued to advocate etiologically based categories of disorder. Still others argued that psychiatric disorders have multifactorial causation and could not be categorized on the basis of unique etiologies. In any case, little is known about the etiology of psychiatric disorders, multifactorial or otherwise. Current systems are phenomenologically or descriptively based rather than etiologically or theoretically based.

In the absence of an etiologic basis, alternative methods for achieving diagnostic validity in psychiatry were proposed by Robins and Guze (1970). These included clinical description, laboratory study, exclusion of other disorders, follow-up study, and family study. These methods correspond roughly to face, concurrent, discriminant, predictive, and descriptive types of validity. Robins and Guze's (1970) proposal suggested that the validity of a diagnostic category can be measured by the degree to which it can be coherently described, associated with laboratory findings, delimited from other categories of disorder, predictive of course and outcome, and distinguished by unique family patterns.

Robins and Guze (1970) applied their method of validity to the diagnosis of schizophrenia as it was described at the time. They noted that the category contained good prognosis and poor prognosis "schizophrenias," which differed in their patterns of familial aggregation. The poor prognosis schizophrenics had higher prevalence rates of schizophrenia among their first-degree relatives, while the good prognosis schizophrenics had higher prevalence rates of affective disorders among their first degree relatives. They concluded that the category of schizophrenia described at that time contained at least two different diagnostic entities. These methods of diagnostic validity were extended to other disorders and led to the development of explicit symptom and behavioral diagnostic criteria (Feighner, Robins, Guze, Winokur et al., 1972).

Some of the diagnostic validation methods proposed by Robins and Guze have been criticized and are not without problems. While prediction is an important aspect of validity, a single disorder may have different outcomes because of a variety of environmental and constitutional variables. How does the clinician distinguish between differing outcomes of the same disorder and differing outcomes delineating separate disorders? In psychiatry, laboratory studies have been disappointing and have not achieved the sensitivity and specificity needed to aid in the definition or validation of diagnoses. Similarly, pharmacological response has been proposed as a diagnostic validator, but current psychopharmacology is too nonspecific to be diagnostically useful. Alternative components of diagnostic validity have been discussed (Spitzer & Williams, 1980), but they remain to be more fully explored.

Despite problems, the power of the Robins and Guze method lies in its iterative application. When applied iteratively, the proposed diagnostic validators should enable scientists to modify and refine diagnoses to more homogeneous and clinically meaningful categories of disorder. This is similar to approximation techniques in mathematics, in which solutions to equations depend on parameters or sets of parameters. Initially, the values of the parameters are "guessed at" or approximated. When solutions match, the parameters have been guessed correctly; when they do not, the degree and direction of mismatch suggest how to adjust the parameters. For psychiatric disorders, an iterative application of desciption, laboratory study, familial aggregation, and the like should eventually provide distinct disorders linked to specific etiologies.

Do the diagnoses used in child assessment identify children with a disorder that has a common etiology and pathophysiology? The answer to this question is not yet known. There are multiple aims of diagnostic systems, and these include scientific study, communication between practitioners, and treatment selection. The purpose of our current DSM system (APA, 1987) appears to be communication primarily, with scientific study a secondary goal. Given how little is known about psychopathological disorders in children, the DSM-III-R had little empirical data upon which to establish categories. In fact, the current classification system may have most value as a means of communication, making the system's reliability a greater focus than its validity.

There are numerous measures of diagnostic reliability, including interrater, test-retest, and internal consistency. Information and criteria variance contribute to diagnostic unreliability (Spitzer, Endicott, & Robins, 1978), as does informant variance (for children), discussed elsewhere in this chapter. There are many who believe that criteria variance was minimized through the development of specified diagnostic criteria. While specified criteria are helpful, operational criteria would be far better. For child categories in particular, the need for operational criteria are critical to the establishment of reliability.

The range and extent of normal behavior is less well defined for children than for adults, largely because of constant developmental changes. How short does an attention span have to be to be considered short? How much distractibility is clinically significant? How much activity is too much, and at what age? In a similar vein, how long does a depressed child have to be depressed to be considered symptomatic, and what are the expected behavioral manifestations? Temper tantrums in a preschooler may be within normal limits, but they may be indistinguishable from psychomotor agitation and irritability. The list of examples could go on.

The problems in understanding, interpreting, and ultimately operationalizing child behaviors are difficult but not insurmountable. The DSM system is a categorical approach derived from a series of clinical impressions thought to represent discrete psychopathological entities. Help in eventually operationalizing child behaviors may ultimately come from an alternative classification system, the dimensional approach. This approach uses statistical operations to classify symptoms and children. One criticism of the dimensional approach has been that the nature of the analytic methods can influence the classification of patients (Pfohl & Andreasen, 1978). Despite this and other problems, the dimensional approach to classification may provide relevant normative data needed to operationalize some of the diagnostic criteria currently in DSM-III-R. In addition, the dimensional approach offers an alternative diagnostic validator against which to compare current DSM categorical systems and has yielded many interesting findings (Achenbach, 1985).

FAMILY PSYCHIATRIC HISTORY

Family psychiatric history refers generally to the rate of specific psychiatric disorders in the biological relatives of an index case or proband. As previously discussed, such data have been used in efforts to validate diagnostic categories, as well as to examine patterns of genetic and environmental transmission (Andreasen et al., 1986). Morbid risk rates in parents and other relatives provide essential information about potential genetic and nongenetic risk factors for child psychopathology. Familial morbidity data may aid the clinician in differential diagnosis, have implications for treatment, and provide important insights into family interaction.

The etiology of most psychiatric disorders will probably require consideration of genetic and environmental risk factors (Kendler & Earls, 1986). Since the family is viewed as the focal point of a child's life, it is not surprising that the determination of psychiatric disorder in the family is an important aspect in the assessment of child psychopathology. While the role of family environment has long been viewed as essential to our understanding of child psychiatric illness, support for the role of genetics has a more recent history.

Much of the work in psychiatric genetics began with schizophrenia. The risk of schizophrenia was found to be 10 times higher in the biological offspring of schizophrenic parents than in those without schizophrenic parents. This increased risk remained the same even if the child was reared from birth by nonschizophrenic parents (Kety, Rosenthal, Wender, Schulsinger, & Jacobsen, 1975). Clearly, such data implicated a genetic liability and led to research efforts with children to identify precursors and premorbid indicators of vulnerability to illness (Erlenmeyer-Kimling, Cornblatt, & Golden, 1983).

Similar work on the familial aggregation of affective disorders began to emerge in the 1970s (Gershon, Bunney, Leckman et al., 1976). Studies reported higher rates of unipolar depression in the families of depressed probands and higher rates of bipolar disorder in the families of manic probands (Gershon, Hamovit, Guroff et al., 1982; Weissman, Gershon, Kidd et al., 1984). These initiatives led investigators to extend research to children and adolescents and focused attention on their risk for affective disorders.

Strober and Carlson (1982) reported on clinical and genetic predictors of bipolar disorder in adolescents. They found even higher rates of familial mania in their adolescent-onset bipolar patients than had been previously reported for adult bipolar probands. Similarly, children with early-onset depression have been found to have higher rates of unipolar depression in relatives than children without an early-onset disorder (Orvaschel, 1990). Such data are consistent with a hypothesized association between early-onset illness and increased familial loading.

The role of genetics has been implicated in many other psychiatric disorders, including panic disorder (Crowe, Noyes, Pauls, & Slyman, 1983), Tourette's syndrome, and obsessive-compulsive disorder (Pauls, Towbin, Leckman, Zahner, & Cohen, 1986). Furthermore, Last and Strauss (1990) found that children with separation-anxiety disorder who exhibited school refusal had mothers with higher rates of school refusal histories than a comparison group. Familial aggregation has also been reported for childhood attention-deficit disorder (Biederman, Munir, Knee, Habelow, Armentano, Autor, Hoge, & Waternaux, 1986).

While the literature cited thus far is not intended as a comprehensive review of psychiatric genetics, it does emphasize the importance of family psychiatric history in the diagnostic assessment of child psychopathology. There is evidence that some diagnoses "breed true," suggesting the transmission of specific psychiatric disorders rather than the transmission of general pathology. This assumption is supported by the increased familial morbidity of bipolar disorder in manic probands, with no parallel increase in familial schizophrenia. Similarly, unipolar probands do not have higher rates of schizophrenia or bipolar disorder in their families, but they do have familial aggregation of unipolar disorder.

Family psychiatric history data are beginning to identify children at increased risk for specific disorders. These data are also providing information on age of onset probabilities and, in some cases, medication selection (e.g., contraindications of tricyclics for those with a family history of bipolar disorder, as well as the dangers of stimulants for those with a family history of Tourette's syndrome). While no specific mode of transmission has been unequivocally identified for any of the psychiatric disorders, genetic-linkage studies are clearly progressing in that direction. When success in this area is achieved, the implications for early intervention and true primary prevention efforts will be challenging indeed.

DIAGNOSTIC STABILITY

Another criterion proposed for the validity of a classification system is the stability of the identified categories of disorder. Longitudinal and follow-up data provide information on natural history, prognosis, and predictive validity, and contribute to our understanding of the continuities and discontinuities between child and adult psychopathology. While we still lack a wealth of research on the stability of child diagnoses across the age span, some recent reports are available in the literature. A review of this literature provides important information but also raises questions about our use and understanding of the term *diagnostic stability*.

The classic study by Robins (1974) reported the 30-year follow-up of clinically referred children and nonreferred controls. She found that children referred for antisocial behavior had an extremely high prevalence (45%) of adult antisocial behavior when compared with controls (4%). Robins also noted a relationship between the severity of child antisocial behavior and adult adjustment. This study provided the strongest support to date of the stability and continuity of childhood conduct disorder and its predictive power for adult antisocial behavior.

In contrast to the findings by Robins, a longitudinal study reported by Vaillant and Schnurr (1988) provided a more equivocal picture of psychiatric stability. Their 45-year prospective study of male subjects did find a relationship between affective disorder, alcoholism, and poor late midlife adjustment. However, they reported also finding significant discontinuity in life-span mental health. Only 8.5% of the 188 men in the sample remained consistently in the top quartile of adjustment, while 5.3% fell consistently in the bottom quartile. Forty-one percent of the sample were described as psychiatrically impaired at different points over time, but not consistently so. This sample was comprised initially of male college sophomores selected because they showed no signs of physical or mental illness in their freshman year. Yet a high proportion of these normal, healthy men (46.3%) showed evidence of psychiatric impairment or disorder at one or more points of their life.

Zeitlin (1986) examined psychopathology longitudinally, in a study of the relationship between child and adult psychiatric disorder. He identified persons who had attended the Maudsley Children's Department before age 16 and who had also attended the Maudsley as an adult. He compared these index cases to adult Maudsley patients with no childhood treatment history and child Maudsley patients with no adult treatment history. Zeitlin reported many significant symptom continuities from childhood to adulthood, including obsessions (72%), aggression (38%), depression (85%), anxiety (74%), and phobias (42%).

While these data appear to provide evidence for continuities in psychopathology, the retrospective view is again more equivocal. For example, of those who had anxiety disorders as children, 73.5% had anxiety as an adult, but 50% of adult anxiety disorder patients had no childhood history. Similarly, while an association was found between child and adult depression, most adult depressives did not have childhood depression histories. These data support the need for both prospective and retrospective examination of behavioral continuity questions. They also indicate that the childhood onset of a disorder is a risk factor for adult psychopathology, but that this risk factor is neither necessary nor sufficient for subsequent (adult) psychiatric disorder.

The three studies just discussed represent long-term longitudinal research. Several reports are now available on follow-ups of shorter duration that investigate the course and stability of child psychiatric disorders. Cantwell and Baker (1989) examined the psychiatric stability of 151 children who had initially presented to a speech-and-hearing clinic. Their 4- to 5-year follow-up found that children with pervasive development disorder (PDD) and children with attention deficit disorder with hyperactivity (ADDH) manifested the most diagnostic stability (100% and 80%, respectively). Separation-anxiety disorder (SAD) had a high rate of recovery (44%) and a low rate of stability (11%), with the remaining cases receiving other diagnoses. Overanxious disorder (OAD) had a fair rate of recovery (25%) and low stability (25%), as did affective disorders (29% recovery, 29% stability), with remaining cases receiving other, mostly emotional disorder diagnoses. Adjustment disorders tended to be particularly unstable, with none receiving the same diagnosis at follow-up. Cases of adjustment disorder with depressed mood were all found to be recovered at time 2. In contrast to ADDH, attention deficit disorder (ADD) without hyperactivity had no diagnostic stability. Twenty percent were considered recovered at time 2, and the remaining cases received other diagnoses.

While these data have implications for diagnostic reliability and validity, the definition of stability should be examined before conclusions are drawn. In the Cantwell and Baker presentation, a diagnosis was considered stable if a child carried the same diagnostic label at time 2 as assigned at time 1. Therefore, categories of disorder with a chronic course such as PDD and ADDH should show high stability according to this definition and, in fact, did just that. The poor showing of ADD without hyperactivity brings into question the usefulness and validity of this subclassification. On the other hand, SAD, OAD, and affective disorders are episodic in nature and should not be expected to remain constant over a 4- to 5-year period. Forty-four percent of SAD children were well at follow-up, which suggests that this disorder may indeed be of shorter duration and unknown prognostic significance. OAD and depression had lower rates of full recovery than did SAD, and many children carried other diagnoses at time 2. This fact does not invalidate their diagnostic status at time 1. It may simply confirm the episodic nature of these disorders and suggests that such children are at increased risk for other, additional disorders over time.

Kovacs et al. (1984a) provide more specific data on the course and stability of childhood affective disorders. They reported on 65 children who met criteria for major depression (MDD), dysthymic disorder (DD), or adjustment disorder with depressed mood (ADDM). Recovery rates for these children varied as a function of their specific diagnostic subclassification. ADDM children made the fastest recovery, with 90% well within 9 months; recovery for MDD children was 92% at 18 months; recovery for DD children was 89% at 72 months. They noted, too, that an early age of onset was associated with a more protracted illness for the MDD and DD cases only.

In a subsequent report, Kovacs et al. (1984b) examined recurrence risk for these children. Again, ADDM children did well, with this diagnosis showing no predictive risk for MDD. For children with an intake diagnosis of MDD, 40% of those who had recovered had a second episode of MDD within 2 years. For children with DD, 69% had an episode of MDD within 5 years of their onset of DD. These data indicate diagnostic stability for MDD and DD, as well as a relationship between the two categories of affective disorder. However, the diagnosis of ADDM again shows a short-term, self-remitting course with little prognostic significance for risk of more compelling psychopathology. The stability of MDD and DD lies, in part, in their ability to predict recurrence risk for the same or a related disorder.

While additional prospective and follow-up studies of specific categories of child disorders are now available in the literature (Loeber, 1982; Kandel & Davies, 1986; Clarizio, 1989), the material presented thus far provides important insights on the issue of stability and its meaning for child psychopathology. Stability can be assessed in the short term or over long periods of time. Truly short-term stability (1 week to 1 month) may be viewed as equivalent to diagnostic reliability. The examination of a more lengthy duration of stability can provide information on rates of recovery, remission, recurrence, episodicity, or chronicity. A life-span perspective will add to our knowledge of behavioral continuities, long-term outcome, and the function of early-onset disorders as risk factors for adult psychiatric morbidity.

The data examined above also indicated that our view of behavioral continuity can be altered as a function of the prospective or retrospective design of the research. The early onset of a major affective disorder does appear to confer added risk for adult affective illness, but current data suggest that most depressed adults lack childhood depression histories. The contrary is true for childhood conduct disorder

(CD) and its relationship to adult antisocial behavior (ASP; Antisocial Personality). While a substantial proportion of childhood CDs remit, very few adult ASPs lack a childhood history. Both affective disorders and CD confer risk for adult psychopathology, but their meaning is different. The data for CD and ASP suggest a continuity in the relationship of these two diagnoses, such that ASP is the adult outcome of childhood CD. This is not the case for affective disorders. Although a depressed child may be at increased risk for depression as an adult when compared with a nondepressed child, adult depressives more often lack this childhood history. Perhaps for the affective disorders, child and adult onsets represent different illnesses (biologically or genetically), or a more severe form of the same underlying illness; but the adult disorder is not simply the natural outcome of the child disorder.

Finally, it should be emphasized that psychiatric disorders cannot be viewed unidimensionally, and their stability must be weighed in light of their chronic or episodic course. A child diagnosed as autistic or mentally retarded at age 5 should continue to meet criteria for these diagnoses at ages 10, 15, and 20. However, this outcome is highly unlikely for 5-year-old children diagnosed with SAD or MDD. The SAD children should be recovered by age 10 and may show little or no additional psychopathology at ages 15 and 20. The MDD children should be recovered in part, but with many children continuing to manifest recurring episodes of the same or a related affective illness, and others showing evidence of additional or alternate forms of psychopathology throughout the age span. Diagnostic stability is not a unitary concept and an individual may vary with respect to his or her psychiatric health or illness throughout the life span. This is no more likely to invalidate a psychiatric diagnosis than is the waxing and waning of episodic physical illnesses. Without appropriate consideration of the chronic or episodic nature of a diagnosis, our understanding of stability and disorder outcome data may be subject to misinterpretation. These data should be viewed in terms of the knowledge we gain about risk for psychopathology or behavioral continuity rather than simply diagnostic validity.

COMORBIDITY

A complicating factor in child assessment and diagnostic validity is comorbidity. Nosological comorbidity is the co-occurrence of two or more disorders in the same individual at a level greater than would be expected by chance. Comorbidity has implications for differential diagnosis, treatment, and prognosis. The increasing interest in psychiatric comorbidity emerged more forcefully as a direct consequence of the current psychiatric nosological frame of reference and the nonhierarchial, nonetiological, categorial approach introduced by DSM-III (APA, 1980). In addition, the use of structured and semistructured psychiatric interview schedules greatly increased awareness of the comorbid phenomenon for psychiatric disorders first appearing in childhood and adolescence.

The predominant nosological system in current use is the categorical approach, which gained major prominence with the introduction of specified diagnostic criteria systems such as the Feighner Criteria (Feighner, Robins, Guze, Woodruff et al., 1972), the Research Diagnostic Criteria (Spitzer, Endicott, & Robins, 1978), and the DSM-III (American Psychiatric Association, 1980) schemes. The impetus for the use of specified criteria systems was, in part, to improve diagnostic reliability and validity (Cloninger, 1989; Robins & Guze, 1970). An alternate nosological strategy is the dimensional approach. This approach stresses the use of descriptive or empirically derived factors or clusters to characterize a disorder (Paykel, 1982). In child psychiatric nosology, the Child Behavior Checklist (Achenbach & Edelbrock, 1983) is a prime example of this classificatory approach. However, this orientation makes it difficult to explore the relationship among dimensions, as one is still left not knowing if mixed dimensions represent entities in themselves or the co-occurrence of more than one dimension (Paykel, 1982; Zeitlin, 1986). However, the categorical approach also does not ensure an accurate understanding of overlapping syndromes or comorbidity.

Factors other than classification orientation also impinge on the issue of comorbidity. These include developmental issues, age effects, subject sampling, methods of diagnostic assessment, and hierarchial diagnosing (i.e., establishing primacy of one comorbid disorder over other co-occurring illnesses). Numerous studies have reported on the frequency of comorbid psychiatric diagnoses in children and adolescents on general inpatient units or outpatient services, in specialty outpatient clinics, or in nonpsychiatric community-based populations.

It is quite clear from the existing literature that comorbidity is the rule rather than the exception. However, comorbid disorders are much more likely in patient samples, because children with multiple problems are more likely to be referred (Werry, Reeves, & Elkind, 1987). The corollary of this suggests that comorbid rates in community and probability samples will be lower. The published literature on comorbidity in childrean and adolescents, however, is not always comparable across studies because of several compounding methodological differences. These factors include the following: (a) Researchers study only a limited age span; (b) different diagnostic instruments generate different rates of disorder; (c) diagnostic distinctions are not always maintained, so that subtypes of anxiety, behavior, or affective disorders may be combined for analyses; (d) symptom rather than syndrome comorbidity is analyzed; (e) the rules to distinguish primacy of co-occurring disorders remain uncertain, or there is a lack of evidence to determine which behavioral constellation should have priority; and (f) the stability of the diagnostic picture can change quite rapidly.

A review of current comorbidity data is provided, with a focus on categorical rather than dimensional diagnosis. All the studies selected utilized a structured (i.e., DISC) or semistructured (K-SADS, SCID, ISC) interview to establish diagnoses (see chapter 6). Comorbid rates are listed in Table 3-1 and tabulated to highlight the specific comorbid frequencies in commonly diagnosed affective, anxiety, and behavioral disorders. The figures represent current as opposed to lifetime comorbidity, as has been reported in other studies (Munir, Biederman, & Knee, 1987).

In the category of affective disorders, one quarter of prepubertal major depressives have coexisting dysthymia (or double depression). The rates of comorbidity for major depressive disorder (MDD) and the anxiety disorders are as follows: avoidant disorder

Table 3-1a. Studies of Comorbidity: The Affective Disorders

	PATIENT CHARACTERISTICS			COMORBID AFFECTIVE DISORDERS (%)[a]		
	SOURCE	AGE	N	MDD	DD	BP
Affective						
Major Depression						
Kovacs et al. (1988, 1989)	outpt	8–14	62		25.8	
Geller et al. (1985)	outpt	5–12	36			
		12–16	23			
Marriage et al. (1986)	mixed	8–17	12			
Ryan et al. (1987)	outpt	9.6[b]	92			4.2
		14.7[b]	95			4.4
Haley et al. (1988)	inpt	15[b]	33			
Ambrosini et al. (1988)	outpt	6–12	45			
		13–18	73			
Dysthymia						
Marriage et al. (1986)	mixed	8–17	12			
Kovacs et al. (1988)	outpt	8–14	39			
Anxiety						
Overanxious						
Last et al. (1987)	outpt	5–18	47	34.0	8.5	
Separation Anxiety						
Last et al. (1987)	outpt	5–18	43	32.6	4.7	
Panic Disorder						
Alessi et al. (1987)	inpt	Adol	10	50.0	20.0[c]	20.0
Obsessive-Compulsive						
Swedo et al. (1988)	NIMH	2–16[d]	69	24.6		
Flamant et al. (1988)	epi	14–18	18	16.7	5.6	
Substance Abuse						
DeMilio (1989)	inpt	14–18	57	35.1	10.5	

[a] MDD: major depressive disorder; DD: dysthymic disorder; BP: bipolar
[b] Mean.
[c] Minor depression.
[d] Age of onset.

(AD), 2.2% to 9.6%; panic disorder (PAN), 4.4%; overanxious disorder (OAD), 17.7% to 64.4%; separation-anxiety disorder (SAD), 6.9% to 86.1%; phobic disorder (PD), 5.5% to 45.3%; and obsessive-compulsive disorder (OCD), 6.7% to 10.9%. Some co-occurrence of disorders can be expected, in part as a function of the independent prevalence of each disorder in the population. Therefore, it is not surprising that the highest rates of comorbidity between MDD and the anxiety disorders are for OAD, SAD, and PD, given the higher population prevalence of these three disorders (Anderson, Williams, McGee, & Silva, 1987; Bird et al., 1988; Costello, Costello, Edelbrock, Burns, Dulcan, Brent, & Hidalgo, 1988; DeMilio, 1989).

The co-occurrence of behavioral disorders in children and adolescents with MDD reveals a wide range (8.3%–45.5%) for conduct disorder (CD), with the highest rate reported for an inpatient sample. Attention deficit disorder (ADD) co-occurred more frequently in prepubertal MDD than adolescent MDD (28.4% vs. 8.2%) and oppositional disorder (OD) followed a similar trend (88.9% vs. 50.7%).

In those subjects identified as anxiety disordered, one third to one half of those with OAD, SAD, or PAN had a comorbid MDD; the rate in OCD patients was only 16.7% to 24.6%. Co-occurring anxiety disorders in those with anxiety diagnoses appear to follow the same trends seen in MDD. The rates are highest for the three most common syndromes (OAD, SAD, and PD).

Table 3-1b. Studies of Comorbidity: The Anxiety Disorders

	PATIENT CHARACTERISTICS			COMORBID ANXIETY DISORDERS (%)[a]					
	SOURCE	AGE	N	AD	OAD	SAD	PD	PAN	OCD
Affective									
Major Depression									
Kovacs et al. (1988, 1989)	outpt	8–14	62		17.7	38.7			
Geller et al. (1985)	outpt	5–12	36			86.1			
		12–16	23			47.8			
Marriage et al. (1986)	mixed	8–17	12						
Ryan et al. (1987)	outpt	9.6[b]	92		20.7	57.9	45.3		10.5
		14.7[b]	95		19.6	37.0	27.2		10.9
Haley et al. (1988)	inpt	15[b]	33			15.2			
Ambrosini et al. (1988)	outpt	6–12	45	2.2	64.4	44.4	20.0	4.4	6.7
		13–18	73	9.6	61.6	6.9	5.5		9.6
Dysthymia									
Marriage et al. (1986)	mixed	8–17	12		23.1	30.8		5.1	2.6
Kovacs et al. (1988)	outpt	8–14	39						
Anxiety									
Overanxious									
Last et al. (1987)	outpt	5–18	47	14.9		44.7	31.9[c]	8.5	6.4
Separation Anxiety									
Last et al. (1987)	outpt	5–18	43	11.6	48.8		9.3[c]		2.3
Panic Disorder:									
Alessi et al. (1987)	inpt	Adol	10				−10.0		
Obsessive-Compulsive									
Swedo et al. (1988)	NIMH	2–16[d]	69		15.9	7.3	17.4		
Flament et al. (1988)	epi	14–18	18		16.7		11.1		
Substance Abuse									
DeMilio (1989)	inpt	14–18	57	7.0[e]					

[a] AD: avoidant disorder; OAD: overanxious disorder; SAD: separation anxiety disorder; PD: phobic disorder; PAN: panic disorder; OCD: obsessive-compulsive disorder
[b] Mean.
[c] Simple phobia, social phobia & agoraphobia.
[d] Age of onset.
[e] Avoidant personality & social phobia.

PD rates seem somewhat lower in those with SAD (9.3%), and comorbid anxiety rates in OCD are generally lower than in those with SAD and OAD.

Co-occurring behavioral disorders in those with anxiety diagnoses follow the trends seen in those diagnosed with MDD, with the ordering of highest to lowest frequency being OD, ADD, and CD. However, OD co-occurs at a much lower rate with anxiety disorders than with MDD.

In substance abusing (SAB) adolescent inpatients, 35.1% had co-occurring MDD, while 14% and 42.1% had co-occurring ADD or CD, respectively. However, a report by DeMilio (1989) noted an 18% rate of transient MDD, which cleared within three weeks of hospitalization; 16% of these inpatients had features suggesting personality disorder.

Although several trends can be gleaned from this compilation of data, the comorbid frequency rates listed in Table 3-1 must be interpreted cautiously. For example, in Last, Hersen, Kazdin, Finkelstein, and Strauss' (1987) sample of 69 anxious children and adolescents, almost one third ($n = 23$) had a diagnosis of MDD. Of these 23 subjects, 61% and 70%, respectively, had either co-occurring OAD or SAD. This same group also looked at comorbidity in the same diagnostic population but classified their anxiety disorders on a primary-secondary basis, thereby altering their rates of comorbidity (Last, Strauss, & Francis, 1987).

The co-occurrence rates, however, need to be interpreted in some meaningful way so that substantive questions can be answered. In this vein, Kovacs, Gatsonis, Paulauskas, and Richards (1989) reported that comorbid anxiety disorders did not affect the length of the index episode in those with primary MDD, DD, or adjustment disorder with depressed mood. However, it lengthened the index MDD episode in those with secondary MDD, while shortening the episode in those with secondary MDD and dysthymia. There was also evidence suggesting that comorbid anxiety disorders may lengthen the interval before the next MDD. A co-occurring conduct disorder, however, did not affect the length of the index episode of MDD nor alter the length of the symptom-free interval until the next episode of MDD (Kovacs, Paulauskas, Gatsonis, & Richards, 1988).

Ambrosini and Metz (1988) assessed, with the K-SADS-III-R, 118 MDD children and adolescents and 85 nondepressed anxiety disordered youngsters attending the same specialty clinic. They noted that while SAD and PD were more common in prepubertal MDD than in adolescent MDD, neither syndromes were significantly associated with prepubertal MDD. Rather, it became apparent that SAD and PD were simply more common in prepubertal children in general, since nondepressed prepubertal children had the same rates of SAD and PD as the prepubertal depressed sample. However, this is not the case for OAD, whose comorbidity was significantly higher in both adolescent (61.6%) and prepubertal (64.4%) MDD, compared to their age-matched nondepressed psychiatric controls (38% and 30%, respectively). This suggests that of all the anxiety disorders, only OAD significantly co-occurred in child and adolescent MDD patients. One explanation of this finding may be the overlap in criteria for the two disorders. Four of the seven symptoms for OAD (brooding; negative self-image; excessive reassurance, demanding, clinging; and somatic complaints) are within the RDC domain for minor depression. Such a finding also parallels the large co-occurrence of generalized anxiety disorder in adult MDD reported by Breslau and Davis (1985).

Although there remain many pitfalls in the theoretical underpinnings of the comorbid concept for psychiatric disorders, its occurrence is commonplace. Its significance remains as a factor in directing choice and formulation of treatment planning, treatment response, morbidity, and subsequent prognosis. Finally, understanding comorbidity clearly will increase our knowledge of psychopathology beyond the specific nature of the comorbid disorders.

INFORMANT VARIANCE

Psychiatric assessment of children and adolescents by its very nature demands that information be obtained from multiple sources. Although use of specified diagnostic criteria and structured interviews has improved diagnostic reliability, informant disagreements on symptoms and complaints remain problematic. This dilemma expands as additional informants are recruited to report their views of a child's problems. Poor agreement between informants does not necessarily imply that information from any one individual is invalid. Children, parents, and teachers have different areas of concern (Kashani, Orvaschel, Burk, & Reid, 1985) and some symptoms may be situation-dependent (Achenbach, McConaughy, & Howell, 1987). A basic understanding of parent-child agreement and consistency among informants is necessary for the clinician as well as for the researcher.

Numerous studies have analyzed parent-child agreement in various clinic settings using different

Table 3-1c. Studies of Comorbidity: Other Disorders

	PATIENT CHARACTERISTICS			COMORBID OTHER DISORDERS (%)[a]				
	SOURCE	AGE	N	AN/BN	SAB	OD	ADD	CD
Affective								
Major Depression								
Kovacs et al. (1988, 1989)	outpt	8–14	62					14.5
Geller et al. (1985)	outpt	5–12	36					11.1
		12–16	23					34.8
Marriage et al. (1986)	mixed	8–17	12					8.3
Ryan et al. (1987)	outpt	9.6[b]	92					15.8
		14.7[b]	95					10.9
Haley et al. (1988)	inpt	15[b]	33	12.1				45.5
Ambrosini et al. (1988)	outpt	6–12	45			88.9	28.9	11.1
		13–18	73			50.7	8.2	17.8
Dysthymia								
Marriage et al. (1986)	mixed	8–17	12					47.6
Kovacs et al. (1988)	outpt	8–14	39					15.4
Anxiety								
Overanxious								
Last et al. (1987)	outpt	5–18	47			14.9	19.2	4.3
Separation Anxiety								
Last et al. (1987)	outpt	5–18	43			20.9	23.3	4.7
Panic Disorder								
Alessi et al. (1987)	inpt	Adol	10	10.0		—		
Obsessive-Compulsive								
Swedo et al. (1988)	NIMH	2–16[d]	69		5.8	10.1	10.1	7.3
Flament et al. (1988)	epi	14–18	18	16.7			11.1	
Substance Abuse								
DeMilio (1989)	inpt	14–18	57				14.0	42.1

[a] AN/BN: anorexia/bulimia nervosa; SAB: substance abuse; OD: oppositional disorder; ADD: attention deficit disorder; CD: conduct disorder.
[b] Mean.
[d] Age of onset.

diagnostic interviews or symptomatic rating scales. Agreement data have also been looked at in pathologic and normal samples. As a rule, all studies find some significant level of agreement, but the magnitude of the agreement is modest at best. This finding, however, is not unexpected, because a similar phenomenon occurs in adult populations when ascertaining rates of psychopathology in families of psychiatric probands. Essentially, it has been clearly shown that rates of disorder are lower when using a family history approach (i.e., obtaining diagnostic information from informants) than when using the family study method (i.e., obtaining diagnostic information from direct interview) (Andreasen, Rice, Endicott, Reich, & Coryell, 1986; Orvaschel, Thompson, Belanger, Prusoff, & Kidd, 1982; Thompson, Orvaschel, Prusoff, & Kidd, 1982; Werry, Methuen, Fitzpatrick, & Dixon, 1983). Some investigators view the parental report as a subset of the child's report (Weissman, Wikramaratne, Warner, John, Prusoff, Merikangas, & Gammon, 1987). However, data on informant agreement have identified a number of variables that influence concordance rates. These variables include assessment methodology, symptom content, patient characteristics, and reporter characteristics.

Assessment Methodology

Several investigators report equivocal parent-child agreement data using structured (Edelbrock, Costello, Dulcan, Conover, & Kala, 1986; Herjanic, 1982; Kashani et al., 1985; Welner, Reich, Herjanic, Jung,

& Amado, 1987) or semistructured (Chambers, Puig-Antich, Hirsch, Paez, Ambrosini, Tabrizi, & Davies, 1985; Geller, Nelson, & Warham, 1988; Ivens & Rehm, 1988; Weissman et al., 1987) interviews, self-report (Moretti, Fine, Haley, & Marriage, 1985; Weissman, Orvaschel, & Padian, 1980) or parent and clinician rating instruments (Kazdin, French, Unis, & Esveldt-Dawson, 1983; Mokros, Poznanski, Grossman, & Freeman, 1987). Rates of diagnostic agreement, corrected for chance, are generally significant but quite scattered in both normal and pathologic samples. For example, correlations between parent and child depression ratings are quite variable (Kazdin et al., 1983; Mokros et al., 1987). The clinical consequence of these discrepancies is exhibited by the finding that parental ratings of severity of their children's depression do not discriminate among inpatient or outpatient child psychiatric subjects with different diagnoses (Moretti et al., 1985). Highly structured interviews have been reported to have low reliability with children under 10 (Edelbrock, 1985) and, at times, elicit inconsistent and misinterpreted responses across the age span (Breslau, 1987). Yet, even semistructured interviews show low parent-child agreement, because informants focus on different symptom constellations or lack information on the presence or absence of certain symptoms.

Symptom Content

Since the time of Herjanic, Herjanic, Brown, and Wheatt's (1975) report, which found that parent-child agreement was dependent on symptom content, other investigators have replicated and expanded these findings. Essentially, agreement between informants is best for concrete, observable, severe, and unambiguous symptoms (Herjanic, 1982). From a clinical perspective, these data suggest that parents report more behavioral and conduct problems with children, while children report more affective and neurotic problems (Edelbrock et al., 1986). Only alcohol and drug abuse did not fit this internalizing-externalizing pattern (Edelbrock et al., 1986). Children report these behaviors more often than parents, probably because parents lack the necessary information. Angold, Weissman, John, Merikangas, Prusoff, Wickramaratne, Gammon, and Warner (1987), in an interesting analysis of parent and child reports of affective symptoms, noted that parents were unlikely to report symptoms not reported by their children. Therefore, parent reports of children's affective symptomatology have good specificity but poor sensitivity, confirming the need to obtain this information directly from the child (Orvaschel, Weissman, Padian, & Lowe, 1981).

Patient Characteristics

Not only is parent-child agreement related to symptom content, but interactional effects exist for age, sex, symptom clusters, and diagnoses. While neither Edelbrock et al. (1986) nor Herjanic et al. (1975) found significant differences in parent-child agreement as a function of age, the magnitude of the parent-child differences were larger for the younger children. On the other hand, Achenbach et al. (1987) reported greater consistency of ratings between different informants and the reports by the 6- to 11-year-old cohort compared to the reports by adolescents. This greater agreement was not large and was specific to undercontrolled (externalizing) vs. overcontrolled (internalizing) behaviors. However, when assessing stability of reports, there appeared to be higher reliability from parents of younger children than from the parents of older children, whereas the converse is true for children (i.e., the reliability of children's reports improves with age) (Edelbrock, 1985). Weissman et al. (1987) particularly noted interaction effects for age, sex, and diagnosis when they analyzed the discrepancies between parent and child reporting. After the age of 15, girls' self-reports of depression increased considerably compared to those of boys, and thus mother and daughter diagnostic disagreement far exceeded those reported by mothers and sons.

Reporter Characteristics

Achenbach et al. (1987) reported that informant-child agreement was low regardless of whether the reporter was the mother, father, teacher, or mental health worker. There did appear to be more consistency between informants who have similar roles with the child and higher correlations among various measures of psychopathology when completed by the same informant (Weissman et al., 1980). However, there were minimal correlations between mothers' and fathers' reports of their children's symptomatology (Kazdin et al., 1983).

Parental mental status may also affect parents' and children's reports. Morretti et al. (1985) and Breslau, Davis, and Prabucki (1988) noted that parents who had significant depressive symptomatology or depressive disorder rated their children high not only on depressive symptoms, but in all symptom domains. Breslau noted also that children of depressed mothers reported more depressive symptomatology than did children of nondepressed parents, suggesting perhaps a truly higher symptom prevalence.

In summary, agreement between informants and child reports are generally modest to low. Nevertheless, these various informants may still be viewed as reliable reporters. Lower agreement has been noted with more highly structured interviews, in which clarification of potentially ambiguous questions is not usually permitted. Children seem to be better reporters about internal states, while parents and teachers are better on externalizing behaviors. However, parents' reliability of reporting is best for younger children, while older children are more reliable reporters about themselves than are their parents. Those informants observing a child in more similar situations will be more consistent in their reporting. Also, an informant's own psychiatric status may bias reporting such that more dysfunctional behaviors are endorsed. The clinician and researcher must be cognizant of such constraints on the reliability of information, so that these parameters may become as much a part of the assessment process as eliciting information and listening empathically.

SUMMARY

Despite many improvements in diagnostic classification, many diagnostic assessment issues remain unresolved. If the goal of our science is to identify the etiology of child psychopathology and to develop specifically targeted interventions and strategies of prevention, we clearly have a long road to travel. The issues we included in our review were selected because they lack resolution, are the focus of current research, and are likely to be provocative. They are all important considerations in the assessment of child and adolescent psychopathology because they focus on how we are to understand and integrate the information we collect. As data are generated on these issues, we should begin to fill in the nosologic puzzle of child psychopathology.

REFERENCES

Achenbach, T. M. (1985). *Assessment and taxonomy of child and adolescent psychopathology*. Beverly Hills: Sage.

Achenbach, T. M., & Edelbrock, C. S. (1983). *Manual for the child behavior checklist and revised child behavior profile*. Burlington, VT.

Achenbach, T. M., McConaughy, S. H., & Howell, C. T. (1987). Child/adolescent behavioral and emotional problems: Implications of cross-informant correlations for situational specificity. *Psychological Bulletin, 101*, 213–232.

Alessi, N. E., Robbins, D. R., & Dilsaver, S. C. (1987). Panic and depressive disorders among psychiatrically hospitalized adolescents. *Psychiatry Research, 20*, 275–283.

Ambrosini, P. J., & Metz, C. (1988). Clinical and biological correlates of depression in children and adolescents. Presented at Henry Ford Hospital, Detroit, MI.

American Psychiatric Association. (1980). *Diagnostic and statistical manual of mental disorders, third edition*. Washington, DC: Author.

American Psychiatric Association. (1987). *Diagnostic and statistical manual of mental disorders, third edition, revised*. Washington, DC: Author.

Anderson, J. C., Williams, S., McGee, R., & Silva, P. A. (1987). DSM-III disorders in preadolescent children. *Archives of General Psychiatry, 44*, 69–76.

Andreasen, N. C., (1982). Concepts, diagnosis and classification. In E. S. Paykel, (Ed.), *Handbook of affective disorders* (pp. 27–29). New York: Guilford Press.

Andreasen, N. C., Rice, J., Endicott, J., Reich, T., & Coryell, W. (1986). The family history approach to diagnosis: How useful is it? *Archives of General Psychiatry, 43*, 421–429.

Angold, A., Weissman, M. M., John, K., Merikangas, K. R., Prusoff, B. A., Wickramaratne, P., Gammon, G. D., & Warner, V. (1987). Parent and child reports of depressive symptoms in children at low and high risk of depression. *Journal of Child Psychology and Psychiatry, 28*, 901–915.

Biederman, J., Munir, K. A., Knee, D., Habelow, W., Armentano, M., Autor, S., Hoge, S. K., & Waternaux, C. (1986). A family prevalence study of probands with attention deficit disorder and normal controls. *Journal of Psychiatric Research, 20*, 263–274.

Bird, H. R., Canino, G., Rubio-Stipec, M., Gould, M. S., Ribera, J., Sesman, M., Woodbury, M., Huertas-Goldman, S., Pagan, A., Sanchez-Lacay, A., & Moscosa, M. (1988). Estimates of the prevalence of childhood maladjustment in a community survey in Puerto Rico. *Archives of General Psychiatry, 45*, 1120–1126.

Bleuler, E. (1950). *Dementia Praecox or the Group of Schizophrenias*, (Translated J. Zinkin). New York: International Universities Press.

Breslau, N. (1987). Inquiring about the bizarre: False positives in diagnostic interview schedule for children (DISC) ascertainment of obsessions, compulsions, and psychotic symptoms. *Journal of American Academy of Child and Adolescent Psychiatry, 26*, 639–644.

Breslau, N., & Davis, G. C. (1985). Further evidence on the doubtful validity of generalized anxiety disorders. *Psychiatry Review, 16*, 177–179.

Breslau, N., Davis, G. C., & Prabucki, K. (1988). Depressed mothers as informants in family history research—Are they accurate? *Psychiatry Research, 24,* 345–359.

Cantwell, D. P., & Baker, L. (1989). Stability and natural history of DSM-III childhood diagnoses. *Journal of American Academy of Child and Adolescent Psychiatry, 28,* 691–700.

Chambers, W. J., Puig-Antich, J., Hirsch, M., Paez, R., Ambrosini, P. J., Tabrizi, M. A., & Davies, M. (1985). The assessment of affective disorders in children and adolescents by semistructured interview. *Archives of General Psychiatry, 42,* 696–702.

Clarizio, H. (1989). Continuity in childhood depression. *Adolescence, 24,* 253–267.

Cloninger, C. R. (1989). Establishment of diagnostic validity in psychiatric illness: Robins and Guze's methods revisited. In L. N. Robins and J. E. Barrett (Eds.), *The Validity of Psychiatric Diagnosis,* (pp. 9–18). New York: Raven Press.

Costello, E. J., Costello, A. J., Edelbrock, C., Burns, B. J., Dulcan, M. K., Brent, D., & Hidalgo, J. (1988). Psychiatric disorders in pediatric primary care. *Archives of General Psychiatry, 45,* 1107–1116.

Crowe, R. R., Noyes, R., Pauls, D. L., & Slyman, D. (1983). A family study of panic disorder. *Archives of General Psychiatry, 40,* 1065–1069.

DeMilio, L. (1989). Psychiatric syndromes in adolescent substance abusers. *American Journal of Psychiatry, 146,* 1212–1214.

Edelbrock, C. (1985). Age differences in the reliability of the psychiatric interview of the child. In: *Child Development,* (pp. 265–275), Society for Research in Child Development, Inc.

Edelbrock, C., Costello, A. J., Dulcan, M. K., Conover, N. C., & Kala, R. (1986). Parent-child agreement on child psychiatric symptoms assessed via structured interview. *Journal of Child Psychology and Psychiatry, 27,* 181–190.

Erlenmeyer-Kimling, L., Cornblatt, B., & Golden, R. R. (1983). Early indicators of vulnerability to schizophrenia in children at high genetic risk. In: S. B. Guze, F. J. Earls, & J. E. Barrett (Eds.). *Childhood Psychopathology and Development,* (pp. 247–264). New York: Raven Press.

Feighner, J. P., Robins, E., Guze, S. B., Winokur, G., Woodruff, R. A., & Munoz, R. (1972). *Archives of General Psychiatry, 26,* 168–171.

Feighner, J. P., Robins, E., Guze, S. B., Woodruff, R. A., Winokur, G., & Munoz, R. (1972). Diagnostic criteria for use in psychiatric research. *Archives of General Psychiatry, 26,* 57–63.

Flamant, M. E., Whitaker, A., Rapoport, J. L., Davies, M., Berg, C. Z., Kalikow, K., Sceery, W., & Shaffer, D. (1988). Obsessive compulsive disorder in adolescence: An epidemiological study. *Journal of American Academy of Child and Adolescent Psychiatry, 27,* 764–771.

Geller, B., Chestnut, E. C., Miller, M. D., Price, D. T., & Yates, E. (1985). Preliminary data on DSM-III associated features of major depressive disorder in children and adolescents. *American Journal of Psychiatry, 142,* 643–644.

Geller, B., Nelson, K. A., & Warham, J. E. (1988). Research assessment of depression and suicidal behavior utilizing the Kiddie-Schizophrenia and Affective Disorders Schedule. *Advances in Adolescent Mental Health, 3,* 209–218.

Gershon, E. S., Bunney, W. E. Jr., Leckman, J. F., Van Eerdewegh, M., & DeBauche, B. A. (1976). The inheritance of affective disorders: A review of the data and hypotheses. *Behavior Genetics, 6,* 227, 261.

Gershon, E. S., Hamovit, J., Guroff, J. J., Dibble, E., Leckman, J. F., Sceery, W., Targum, S. D., Nurnberger, J. I., Golden, L. R., & Bunney, E. E. (1982). A family study of schizoaffective, bipolar I, bipolar II, unipolar, and normal control probands. *Archives of General Psychiatry, 39,* 1157–1167.

Haley, G. M. T., Fine, S., & Marriage, K. (1988). Psychotic features in adolescents with major depression. *Journal of American Academy of Child and Adolescent Psychiatry, 27,* 489–493.

Herjanic, B. (1982). Development of a structured psychiatric interview for children: Agreement between child and parent on individual symptoms. *Journal of Abnormal Child Psychology, 10,* 307–324.

Herjanic, B., Herjanic, M., Brown, F., & Wheatt, T. (1975). Are children reliable reporters? *Journal of Abnormal Child Psychology, 3,* 41–48.

Ivens, C., & Rehm, L. P. (1988). Assessment of childhood depression: Correspondence between reports by child, mother, and father. *Journal of American Academy of Child and Adolescent Psychiatry, 27,* 738–741.

Kandel, D. B., & Davies, M. (1986). Adult sequelae of adolescent depressive symptoms. *Archives of General Psychiatry, 43,* 255–262.

Kashani, J. H., Orvaschel, H., Burk, J. P., & Reid, J. C. (1985). Informant variance: The issue of parent-child disagreement. *Journal of American Academy of Child Psychiatry, 24,* 437–441.

Kazdin, A. E., French, N. H., Unis, A. S., & Esveldt-Dawson, K. (1983). Assessment of childhood depression: Correspondence of child and parent ratings. *Journal of American Academy of Child Psychiatry, 22,* 157–164.

Kendler, K. S., & Earls, L. J. (1986). Models of the joint effect of genotype and environment on liability to psychiatric illness. *American Journal of Psychiatry, 143,* 279–289.

Kety, S. S., Rosenthal, D., Wender, P. H., Schulsinger, F., & Jacobsen, B. (1975). Mental illness in the biological and adoptive families of adopted individuals who have become schizophrenic: A preliminary report based on psychiatric interviews. In R. R. Fieve, D. Rosenthal, & H. Brill (Eds.), *Genetic research in psychiatry,* (pp. 147–165). Baltimore: Johns Hopkins University Press.

Kovacs, M., Feinberg, T. L., Crouse-Novak, M. A., Paulauskas, S. L., & Finkelstein, R. (1984a). Depressive disorders in childhood. I. A longitudinal prospective study of characteristics and recovery. *Archives of General Psychiatry, 41*, 229–237.

Kovacs, M., Feinberg, T. L., Crouse-Novak, M.A., Paulauskas, S. L., Pollock, M., & Finkelstein, R. (1984b). Depressive disorders in childhood. II. A longitudinal study of the risk for a subsequent major depression. *Archives of General Psychiatry, 41*, 643–649.

Kovacs, M., Gatsonis, C., Paulauskas, S. L., & Richards, C. (1989). Depressive disorder in childhood. IV. A longitudinal study of comorbidity with risk for anxiety disorders. *Archives of General Psychiatry, 46*, 776–782.

Kovacs, M., Paulauskas, S., Gatsonis, C., & Richards, C. (1988). Depressive disorders in childhood. III. A longitudinal study of comorbidity with and risk for conduct disorders. *Journal of Affective Disorders*, 205–217.

Kraepelin, E. (1919). *Signs of Mental Disorder Alienist and Neurologist, 40*, 85.

Last, C. G., Hersen, M., Kazdin, A. E., Finkelstein, R., & Strauss, C. C. (1987). Comparison of DSM-III separation anxiety and overanxious disorders: Demographic characters and patterns of comorbidity. *Journal of American Academy of Child and Adolescent Psychiatry, 26*, 527–531.

Last, C. G., & Strauss, C. C. (1990). School refusal in anxiety-disordered children and adolescents. *Journal of American Academy of Child and Adolescent Psychiatry, 29*, 31–35.

Last, C. G., Strauss, C. C., & Francis, G. (1987). Comorbidity among childhood anxiety disorders. *Journal of Nervous and Mental Disorders, 175*, 725–730.

Loeber, R. (1982). The stability of antisocial and delinquent child behavior: A review. *Child Development, 53*, 1431–1446.

Marriage, K., Fine, S., Moretti, M., & Haley, G. (1986). Relationship between depression and conduct disorder in children and adolescents. *Journal of American Academy of Child and Adolescent Psychiatry, 25*, 687–691.

Merritt, H. H., Adams, R. D., & Solomon, H. C. (1946). *Neurosyphilis*. New York: Oxford University Press.

Mokros, H. B., Poznanski, E., Grossman, J. A., & Freeman, L. N. (1987). A comparison of child and parent ratings of depression for normal and clinically referred children. *Journal of Child Psychology and Psychiatry, 28*, 613–627.

Moretti, M. M., Fine, S., Haley, G., & Marriage, K. (1985). Childhood and adolescent depression: Child-report versus parent-report information. *Journal of American Academy of Child Psychology, 24*, 298–302.

Munir, M. B., Biederman, M., & Knee, D. (1987). Psychiatric comorbidity in patients with attention deficit disorder: A controlled study. *Journal of Academy of Child and Adolescent Psychiatry, 26*, 844–848.

Orvaschel, H. Early onset psychiatric disorder in high risk children (1990). *Journal of American Academy of Child and Adolescent Psychiatry, 29*, 184–188.

Orvaschel, H., Thompson, W. D., Belanger, A., Prusoff, B., & Kidd, K. K. (1982). Comparison of the family history method to direct interview: Factors affecting the diagnosis of depression. *Journal of Affective Disorders, 4*, 49–59.

Orvaschel, H., Weissman, M. M., Padian, N., & Lowe, T. (1981). Assessing psychopathology in children of psychiatrically disturbed parents: A pilot study. *Journal of American Academy of Child Psychiatry, 20*, 112–122.

Pauls, D. L., Towbin, K. E., Leckman, J. F., Zahner, G. E. P., & Cohen, D. J. (1986). Gilles de la Tourette's Syndrome and obsessive-compulsive disorder: Evidence supporting a genetic relationship. *Archives of General Psychiatry, 43*, 1180–1182.

Paykel, E. S. (1982). *Handbook of Affective Disorders*, (pp.27–29). New York: Guilford Press.

Pfohl, B. & Andreasen, N. C. (1978). Development of classification systems in psychiatry. *Comprehensive Psychiatry, 19*, 197–207.

Robins, L. N. (1974). *Deviant children grown up*. New York: Robert E. Krieger.

Robins, E., & Guze, S. B. (1970). Establishment of diagnostic validity in psychiatric illness: Its application to schizophrenia. *American Journal of Psychiatry, 126(7)*, 107–111.

Ryan, N., Puig-Antich, J., Ambrosini, P., Rabinovich, H., Robinson, D., Nelson, B., & Iyenger, S. (1987). The clinical picture of major depression in children and adolescents. *Archives of General Psychiatry, 44*, 854–861.

Spies, T. (1955). Nutrition and disease, pellagrous psychosis. *Postgraduate Medical Journal, 17*, 70.

Spitzer, R. L., Endicott, J., & Robins, E. (1978). Research Diagnostic Criteria. *Archives of General Psychiatry, 35*, 773–782.

Spitzer, R. L., & Williams, J. B. W. (1980). Classification of mental disorders and DSM-III. In H. Kaplan, A. M. Freedman, & B. J. Sadock (Eds.) *Comprehensive textbook of psychiatry, Vol. 4*, (pp. 1035–1072). Baltimore: Williams & Wilkens.

Strober, M. & Carlson, G. (1982). Bipolar illness of adolescents with major depression: Clinical, genetic, and psychopharmalogic predictors in a three-to-four year prospective follow-up investigation. *Archives of General Psychiatry, 39*, 549–555.

Swedo, S. S., & Rapoport, J. L. (1988). Phenomenology and differential diagnosis in obsessive-compulsive disorder in children and adolescents. In: J. L. Rapoport, (Ed.), *Obsessive-compulsive disorder in children and adolescents* (pp. 13–32). Washington, DC: APA Press.

Thompson, W. D., Orvaschel, H., Prusoff, B., & Kidd, K. K. (1982). An evaluation of the family history method for ascertaining psychiatric disorder. *Archives of General Psychiatry, 39*, 53–58.

Vaillant, G. E., & Schnurr, P. (1988). What is a case? A 45-year study of psychiatric impairment with a college sample selected for mental health. *Archives of General Psychiatry, 45*, 313–319.

Weissman, M. M., Gershon, E. S., Kidd, K. K., Prusoff, B. A., Leckman, J. F., Dibble, E., Hamovit, J., Thompson, W. D., Pauls, D. L., & Guroff, J. J. (1984). Psychiatric disorder in relatives of probands with affective disorders: The Yale-NIMH collaborative family study. *Archives of General Psychiatry, 41*, 13–21.

Weissman, M. M., Orvaschel, H., & Padian, N. (1980). Children's symptom and social functioning self-report scales. *Journal of Nervous and Mental Disorders, 168*, 736–740.

Weissman, M. M., Wickramaratne, P., Warner, V., John, K., Prusoff, B. A., Merikangas, K. R., & Gammon, G. D. (1987). Assessing psychiatric disorders in children. *Archives of General Psychiatry, 44*, 747–753.

Welner, Z., Reich, W., Herjanic, B., Jung, K. G., & Amado, H. (1987). Reliability, validity, and parent-child agreement studies of the diagnostic interview for children and adolescents (DICA). *Journal of American Academy of Child and Adolescent Psychiatry, 26*, 649–653.

Werry, J. S., Methven, R. J., Fitzpatrick, J., & Dixon, H. (1983). The interrater reliability of DSM III in children. *Journal of Abnormal Psychology, 11*, 341–354.

Werry, J. S., Reeves, J. C., & Elkind, G. S. (1987). Attention deficit, conduct, oppositional, and anxiety disorders in children: I. A review of research on differentiating characteristics. *Journal of American Academy of Child and Adolescent Psychiatry, 26*, 133–143.

Zeitlin, H. (1986). *The natural history of psychiatric disorder in children*. Maudsley Monographs No. 29, Oxford University Press.

CHAPTER 4

NEUROLOGICAL ASSESSMENT

Janet B. Teodori

When children are assessed by a neurologist for developmental problems, the evaluation includes a medical history and a physical exam and may require laboratory tests. The history is detailed and includes that of the present illness and past medical problems. The history of the present illness is a careful description by the child or the child's caretakers of this problem that led to their seeking neurological consultation. In the setting of our discussion, this is generally a problem related to the child's development, such as, "Johnny is 5 and still doesn't speak," "Susan is 3 and has not yet learned to walk correctly," or "Anthony used to smile and babble, but he no longer does so." Before problems can be identified, each of these situations requires a review of the child's performance, a record of when and how the problem first became apparent, and a description of how things have progressed since the problem was first identified. A careful medical history provides the rest of the data needed to understand the course of events.

The medical history includes birth history, developmental history, school history, IQ test results, social history, nutritional history, history of exposure to chemicals or toxins, history of other family illnesses, other medical illnesses, medications, hospitalizations, surgery, and a review of systems that inquires about all other aspects of the child's physical functioning. Based on this information, a picture of the overall course of the child's health and development can be ascertained. A physical exam is then conducted. This includes a general physical exam as well as a detailed neurological evaluation. As part of the general physical exam, the child's height, weight, and head circumference are measured and plotted on a growth chart. These measurements show how the child's physical growth compares to that of other children of his or her age. Blood pressure, heart rate, respiration rate, and temperature are also measured. Then, a general description of the child's physical appearance and behavior is recorded. Physical appearance is described, with special attention given to facial features, skin, spine, and extremities. When these parts of the child are examined, one looks for signs suggestive of abnormal formation of body parts. Such signs include epicanthal folds, downward- or upward-slanting eyes, abnormal formation of the ears, syndactyly, polydactyly, scoliosis, and hyper- or hypopigmented skin lesions. General aspects of descriptions of the child's behavior are also carefully recorded. The child's ability to attend to the tasks presented by the examiner, and his or her mood and ability to respond to conversation and play should be noted. Following this, physical exam of ears, nose, throat, heart, lungs, abdomen, genitals, and extremities is performed.

The neurological exam consists of several parts: mental status, gait and station, cranial nerves, motor, sensory, and cerebellar (Adams & Victor, 1981) tests. In the mental status part of the examination, specific information about the child's cognitive functioning is evaluated. This includes aspects of receptive and expressive speech, general knowledge, memory, calculation, drawing, right or left preference and discrimination, ability to utilize objects, and the ability to perform ideomotor activity. The ability to perform one- two- and three-step commands and to recognize body parts should be tested. Each of these tests must be evaluated in terms of the expected performance for a child of that age. This information can be obtained from multiple sources.

The subsequent sections of the neurologic examination are to evaluate other areas of neurological function, including the upper motor neuron pathways, the brainstem, the cerebellum, the spinal cord, peripheral nerves, and muscles. The first section frequently considered is gait and station. In this part of the examination, observation of the patient's stance when erect and gait while walking, running, walking on toes, walking on heels, tandem walking, and stair climbing is described. Inability to walk unassisted is also recorded.

The next section is the cranial nerve examination. The cranial nerves originate from the brainstem. The cranial nerves examined involve smell, vision, eye movements, facial sensation, facial movement, hearing, palatal movement and tongue movement, taste, and shoulder elevation. An examination for strabismus is also conducted, and the neurologist uses an ophthalmoscope to visualize the interior of the eye. Isolated abnormalities or patterns of abnormalities may be helpful in identifying for the neurologist a particular disease or disease process.

The next section involves the motor exam. In this part of the examination, muscle bulk and consistency are ascertained by palpation. Tone, which is assessed by passive movement of the extremities, is examined for signs of spasticity or hypotonicity. Range of movement is also noted at this time, and the examiner looks particularly for the presence of contractures. Deep tendon reflexes are elicited by the use of a reflex hammer. Here the examiner is looking for the presence of hyperactive reflexes, which may be seen in spasticity, or hypoactive reflexes, which may be seen in other neuromuscular diseases. One also tests for the presence of clonus, which is a repetitive beating at the ankle or knee joint in response to physical stimulation and may be a sign of spasticity. A normal downward or abnormal upward response of the toes is also sought by physical stimulation at the sole of the foot. The abnormal upward toe response is referred to as the Babinski sign and may represent a sign of spasticity. Strength is then tested in all muscle groups. The presence of involuntary abnormal movements is also recorded in the motor exam section. These are described in detail in terms of both quality and quantity. Tics, choreiform movements, and tremors are often mentioned in this section.

The next section is coordination or cerebellar functions. The presence of ataxia, dysmetria, nystagmus, tremor, or dysarthria may be commented upon in this section. Particular tests are performed to elicit these findings. Also, the ability to perform rapid, alternating movements is examined. Children who are "clumsy" may have abnormalities in this area without other neurological abnormalities.

The last section is the sensory exam, which includes evaluation of both cortical and peripheral sensory function. Peripheral sensory function involves discrimination of touch, pin, temperature, vibration, and position. Cortical sensory function includes discrimination of localization of touch, simultaneous stimulation on two sides of the body, graphaesthesia (the ability to recognize written symbols on the hand), and stereognosis (the ability to recognize objects when placed in the hand without visual cues). The ability to perform these tests is also dependent on the child's developmental level and general ability to attend.

Once the neurological examination has been completed, the data can be used in conjunction with the history to formulate a differential diagnosis. A primary objective of child assessment is to ensure that his or her development is progressing normally. If it is not, then using data gleaned from the history and physical examination, one may propose explanations for why the child's development is abnormal. This may then lead to laboratory evaluations to prove or disprove one's impressions. A general screening test battery for a child who is not developmentally normal would include a CT scan, an EEG, a urine test for inborn errors of metabolism, and chromosomal analysis. Other tests may be added when looking for specific neurological disorders. Some of these are discussed in the following sections.

PATTERNS OF DEVELOPMENT

Normally, development progresses in a forward direction and a rate characteristic for the child's age. The stages of development and developmental milestones attained by children at various ages have been described in multiple sources. When considering the developmental progress of a particular child, one must first, of course, objectively describe his or her skills in various areas, and then secondarily, consider what factors may play a role in the progress. Although certain children show variability in their development, with perhaps particular areas of well-advanced skills and other areas of relatively slower developmental performance, the examiner should take note when any or all developmental skills fall below what is outlined as a normal limit for that child's age. For example, if a child does not walk or talk by the age of 2 years, one must first consider the possible physical explanations by thorough evaluation of overall intellectual and motor function, speech, and hearing. Only after these sources of dysfunction are eliminated should one consider psychosocial or other causes of failure to progress. When evaluating a child's developmental progress, another warning sign may be elicited in the history (i.e., a child who has developed normally to a certain age and then has begun to lose skills). Unless this is associated with a particular physical injury or illness, it a red flag of progressive neurological dysfunction that needs careful consideration.

When therapists encounter children who do not appear to be progressing at the expected rate for their age, or who are reported to be losing skills, an underlying neurological disorder should be considered. In this chapter, we discuss neurological disorders associated with delays in development and those associated with loss of developmental milestones. Neurologists refer to the former disorders as static encephalopathy and the latter disorders as progressive encephalopathy.

Static Encephalopathy

Static encephalopathy is a term used to describe a condition in children in which their developmental skills continue to progress, but at a rate slower than the normal limit for their age. Certain neurological disorders are characterized by static encephalopathy. Many of these are congenital or hereditary in nature, but others may be acquired either in utero, during the birth process, or later during infancy or childhood. A list of hereditary or congenital neurological disorders include chromosomal abnormalities, such as Down syndrome, Fragile X syndrome, Turner's syndrome, and Noonan's syndrome. Also included are brain malformations, such as holoprosencephaly, microcephaly, macrocephaly, porencephaly, and agenesis of the corpus callosum. Acquired disorders may be divided into those acquired in utero, such as infection and fetal drug exposure, and those acquired postnatally or perinatally. Neurological insults that may be acquired perinataly—that is, during the birth process or shortly thereafter—include asphyxia, infection, and intraventricular hemorrhage. Neurological insult occurring during infancy and childhood include infection, head injury, and Reye's syndrome among others. In the following sections, we discuss some of these disorders.

Chromosomal Disorders

The chromosomal disorders that affect the nervous system also affect other parts of the body, so that particular physical characteristics typical of each may be sought on physical exam. Down syndrome is perhaps the most common and best known chromosomal abnormality (Smith, 1982c). It consists of an abnormal state in which three, rather than two, number 21 chromosomes exist in the individual cells of the body. Thus, the other name for Down syndrome is trisomy 21. Characteristic physical features include hypotonia with open mouth and protruding tongue, mental deficiency, small head size, upslanting palpebral fissures, small nose with low nasal bridge, epicanthal folds, Brushfield spots on the iris, small teeth, short neck, short fingers, a simian crease on the hands, structural heart anomalies, loose redundant skin at the neck, and a relatively small penis in males. Other abnormalities may be found. The IQ in children is generally below 50. Severe congenital heart defects may be a major cause of mortality. Diagnosis of Down syndrome can be made by inspection of physical features and confirmed by chromosomal studies. These studies may show one of three types of abnormalities: The first is the complete trisomy 21, in which every cell has three chromosomes number 21; the second is a mosaic of cells with trisomy 21 and normal chromosomal number; the third is a chromosomal translocation, which may be inherited from a parent carrier (Smith, 1982c). The degree of intellectual ability appears to be least impaired in the mosaic variety of Down syndrome.

The Fragile X syndrome (Opitz, 1984) is an X-linked recessive syndrome caused by a constriction in the X chromosome at band XQ27. Because of its recessive X-linked nature, the full phenotype occurs in males only. Physically, these males have a long face with prominent forehead, prominent large chin, and flattened midface area. Testicular enlargement is common in late adolescent and adult men. Mental retardation is moderate in males with the full syndrome, although there may be mild mental retardation in a female who is heterozygous for the X-linked abnormality. Proof of the diagnosis is obtained by special chromosomal analysis, which must be particularly requested at the time of chromosomal testing.

Malformations of the Brain

Disorders of the developing nervous system are divided into three basic types: disorders of induction, proliferation, and migration (Menkes, 1985). All defects caused by one of these processes occur during a particular part of fetal growth when that process is dominant in brain development. For example, defects of induction occur during the first month of gestation, when the neural tube forms. The neural tube later develops to become the brain, brainstem, and spinal cord. Relatively common problems such as spina bifida occur during the induction period. A more devastating form of induction malformation is anencephaly, where no brain forms at all because of failure of the anterior neural tube to close. Holoprosencephaly, an induction disorder in which the brain fails to form completely into the normal two hemispheric pattern, may present in variable degrees of severity. It may be present as a relatively mild defect, such as with agenesis of the corpus callosum, where perhaps only subtle learning disabilities occur, or as a more severe defect with minimal functional brain tissue. Often, presence of holoprosencephaly can be suspected by observing facial anomalies in a child. Such anomalies are closely set eyes, cleft lip and palate, and absence of the nasal filtrum or nasal septum.

Disorders of migration and proliferation occur during the second through the seventh months of gestation. These include microgyria, macrogyria, lissencephaly, microcephaly, and macrocephaly. The first three refer to abnormalities of the normal brain gyral pattern, with gyri being too small, too large, or absent in these disorders, respectively. Microcephaly results from an inadequate number of neurons in the brain itself, and where it is present, gyria abnormalities also can be found. Macrocephaly can result from an abnormally high proliferation of brain cells. Children with any of these disorders have mental retardation to varying degrees, often have seizures, and have spasticity as well. Children with these disorders tend to have head circumferences that remain small for age over the years, except in the case of macrocephaly, where the head circumference is large for the given age.

When a head circumference begins to enlarge at a rate faster than that expected for a child of the same age, a progressive intercranial lesion should be suspected, rather than one of these congenital defects as we have discussed. In any case, abnormalities of head size, either too large or too small, should be referred to a neurologist for evaluation.

Congenital Infection

Cytomegalovirus and toxoplasmosis are among the more common of the so-called congenital infection syndromes. These syndromes have much in common clinically. The newborn suffering with the diseases in utero may be born with small birthweight, skin rash, enlarged liver and spleen, jaundice, microcephaly, and retinal abnormalities. They may also have hypotonia and seizures and will evidence developmental delay (Fenichel, 1985).

Diagnosis may be made by the presence of the clinical syndrome, the occurrence of elevated serum immunoglobulins, which suggest fetal infection, and the presence of intracranial calcifications, which may be seen on CT scan.

Treatment is available only for toxoplasmosis. Pyrimethamine and sulfadiazine may be given for 3-week periods three to four times during the first year of life (Fenichel, 1985).

Fetal Exposure to Drugs

Certain drugs taken during pregnancy can have an adverse effect on fetal development. The fetus is particularly susceptible to drugs during the first trimester, when active brain and other organ formation is occurring. Two drugs that are known to have considerable negative impact on fetal development are hydantoin (Smith, 1982a) and alcohol (Smith, 1982b). Both of these may cause physical changes in the baby, as well as intellectual difficulties. The physical findings in both instances may include growth deficiency, a broad flat nasal bridge, small distal phalanges in hands and feet, and short upturned nose. Children with the fetal hydantoin syndrome may also have ocular hypertelorism. The fetal alcohol syndrome often produces children who have a long, smooth philtrum and a thin, smooth upper lip. In addition to mild mental deficiency, children with fetal alcohol exposure may show a behavioral pattern of irritability as infants and hyperactivity as children.

Diagnosis can be made through obtaining a history of alcohol or hydantoin ingestion during pregnancy, particularly during the first trimester, and identifying the presence of physical anomalies and intellectual impairment as just described.

The only treatment of these conditions is prevention.

Perinatal Asphyxia

During the birth process, babies may experience complications that lead to oxygen deprivation to the brain. There are a variety of causes of this sort of injury; among them are fetal sedation secondary to drugs given to the mother during pregnancy, ruptured placenta or umbilical cord, knotted umbilical cord, and conditions during which the mother herself suffers from decreased blood profusion. Apgar scores at birth perhaps are the best predictor of brain damage. An Apgar score is a summation of from zero to two points given for each of five categories. The categories are color, respiration, muscle tone, reflex irritability, and heart rate. A maximum score of 10 can be obtained by a newborn when all of these categories are optimal. Apgar scores are given at 1, 5, and 10 minutes of age. When an Apgar score is 3 or less at 10 minutes of age, it predicts a 68 percent chance of death during the first year of life. Of the survivors, 12½ percent will be neurologically damaged. An Apgar score of less than 6 at 5 minutes correlates with a three times greater risk of neurological abnormalities at 1 year than in the normal population (Menkes, 1985).

Intraventricular Hemorrhage

Intraventricular hemorrhage (Fenichel, 1985) may occur in a full-term or premature infant; when it occurs in a full-term infant, it typically originates in the choroid plexus. This is a structure within the ventricular cavities that is highly vascular and is the area where cerebrospinal fluid is produced. Hemorrhages of the choroid plexus are frequently spontaneous (i.e., without a precipitating cause). If there are no other complications, the children may well develop neurologically intact. Intraventricular hemorrhage in the premature infant is graded in severity from 1 to 4, depending on the location of the hemorrhage in the brain and the amount of ventricular enlargement.

Unless overriding complications occur, grades 1 and 2 frequently result in no neurological deficit in the child. Grades 3 and 4 intraventricular hemorrhage are more likely to result in ultimate handicap, however.

The diagnosis of intraventricular hemorrhage in a newborn is usually suspected when there is a clinical change, often occurring as either apnea or seizures. An ultrasound or CT scan are the diagnostic tests of choice to confirm the presence of such a hemorrhage.

Treatment of the intraventricular hemorrhage itself is not performed. However, when a complication such as hydrocephalus occurs, neurosurgical treatment with an intraventricular shunt may become necessary.

Infection

Postnatally acquired infection of the central nervous system is referred to as either encephalitis or meningitis. *Encephalitis* implies that the infection involves the tissues of the brain itself, whereas *meningitis* refers to infection of the tissues which surround the brain, the meninges. Most commonly, the infective agents are viral or bacterial. However, other infective agents may also be involved; these include parasites, fungus, protozoa, rickettsia, or tuberculin bacilli (Bell & McCormick, 1981). Whatever the infective agent, both meningitis and encephalitis can cause permanent neurological deficits and even death. Much depends on the particular agent involved and the degree of illness in the particular patient.

Among the bacterial causes of meningitis, hemophilus influenza, pneumococcal and meningococcal infections can be quite devastating. Death or mild to sever neurological deficits are not an uncommon outcome. Hearing loss or deafness, visual loss, seizures, mental retardation, and motor disturbances can also occur in a significant percentage (Bell & McCormick, 1981). Early rapid treatment improves outcome substantially.

Viral causes of meningitis are usually without sequelae. However, when a virus infects the brain itself, as in encephalitis, significant impairment or death can occur (Bell & McCormick, 1981). Herpes virus causes encephalitis and produces an illness that is often very severe, with fever, vomiting, headache, and focal neurological deficits. These can include weakness, seizures, speech loss, and cranial nerve dysfunction, among others.

The diagnosis of herpes virus encephalitis can be confirmed by brain biopsy; however, generally the clinical scenario is sufficient to suggest the diagnosis and allow for institution of treatment. In addition to the clinical picture, abnormal EEG patterns in the temporal lobe of the brain and abnormalities on the CT scan in the temporal lobe lend further support to the diagnosis (Bell & McCormick, 1981).

Treatment generally consists of the drug Acyclovir. However, recovery of the patients is often incomplete despite adequate treatment.

Reye's Syndrome

Reye's syndrome (Menkes, 1985) is presumably related to a systemic viral illness and specifically results from dysfunction of mitochondria, which are small intracellular organelles. In the past, an association between the use of salicylates during a viral illness and the occurrence of Reye's syndrome had been observed. Since salicylates use has decreased for treatment of viral illnesses in children, so has the incidence of Reye's syndrome decreased.

Neurologic dysfunction occurs secondary to raised intracranial pressure, which results primarily from brain swelling. Neurologic dysfunction is the main symptom of this illness. Four stages of the illness have been identified, and these tend to follow each other successively as the illness worsens over a 24- to 48-hour period (Dezanteux, Dinswiddle, Helms, & Matthew, 1986). Stages 1 and 2 generally consist of confusion, lethargy, vomiting, agitation, and delirium. Stages 3 and 4 consist of markedly decreased responsiveness to the environment or coma, abnormal posturing of the extremities, described as decorticate or decerebrate, and prominent EEG abnormalities. Children who progress only to stage 1 or 2 of the illness often recover completely. However, children whose illness progresses to stages 3 and 4 are likely to have some residual neurological impairment.

A diagnosis may be made by correlation of the clinical scenario with laboratory findings from blood samples, and examination of the EEG. There is no specific treatment for the disease itself; however, symptoms of the disease, such as raised intracranial pressure, may be treated in an intensive care unit. Outcome is generally a function of the stage to which the disease progresses, or the occurrence of additional complications.

Progressive Encephalopathy

These disorders are associated with the loss of developmentally acquired skills. They may appear at various times, but typically the child's development is normal until the onset of the neurological disorder. At that time, skill acquisition begins to plateau, and then previously acquired skills start to be lost. There are a vast number of disorders in this category. For a therapist or a physician who is planning to refer a child to a pediatric neurologist, it is not necessary to make a particular diagnosis, but it may be critically important to recognize that a progressive encephalopathy of some form is taking hold. This can be done when taking a patient's developmental history by ascertaining from the parents or caretakers of the child that there has been a significant loss of skills in which he or she previously had been competent. Examples of this in a history might include a child who said several words and then lost the ability to say those words, a child who was actively learning to walk and now shows little ability for gross physical activity, or a child who smiled readily and was receptive to others and who now seems withdrawn and apathetic. Of course, there may be other factors involved in precipitating a particular developmental change in a child; however, at noting the loss of previously acquired developmental milestones, a red flag should always be raised in the therapist's mind of a possible progressive encephalopathy disorder.

Metabolic Disease

A large number of disorders in the progressive encephalopathy category are called metabolic disorders. In general, these disorders reflect an abnormality in an enzymatic step that is responsible for degradation or synthesis of cellular constituents. Metabolic disorders may be the result of abnormal metabolism of amino acids, sugars, mucopolysaccharides, mucolipidoses, gangliosidoses, or long-chain fatty acids. As far as the nervous system is concerned, some of these disorders affect primarily the gray matter of the brain and spinal cord, others affect primarily white matter, while others affect both gray and white matter. The gray matter is the part of the nervous system where the neurons themselves are located. White matter surrounds the long processes of the neurons, as they reach from one part of the nervous system to another. Disorders involving primarily white matter may present with early loss of reflexes or atrophic changes in the optic disc. Some metabolic disturbances affect other parts of the body as well as the nervous system. Sometimes they produce enlargement or dysfunction of internal organs, such as the liver, spleen, or heart, or abnormalities of the skin or bones. Therefore, when one examines children with progressive encephalopathy, one must look for physical signs in the rest of the body, as well as carefully examining the nervous system.

Aminoacidurias

Aminoacidurias are disorders of amino acid metabolism in the body. Because of particular enzyme defects, necessary amino acids are not formed in the body and abnormal accumulations of intermediary amino acids occur. There are many amino acid disorders; some are relatively common, like phenylketonuria, and some are very rare. The major amino acid disorders include phenylketonuria, maple syrup urine disease, and homocystinuria.

Phenylketonuria. Phenylketonuria (Levy, 1986) is an inherited metabolic disease of the nervous system resulting from a deficiency in phenylalanine hydroxylase, which converts phenylalanine to tyrosine. It is inherited as an autosomal recessive condition. Although the children are physically normal at birth, they soon develop stigmata of the disease, with vomiting, irritability, developmental delay, dry rough eczematoid skin, and a musty odor. Typically, the children have blond hair and blue eyes. They may be microcephalic. IQs are generally less than 80, except in a small percentage of patients.

Laboratory testing reveals specific abnormalities: Brain wave abnormalities can be seen on EEG, and abnormal phenylalanine levels can be detected by a blood test. Neonatal screening is routinely performed for this disease.

These children may be treated with a special diet containing low levels of phenylalanine. If started early in life, this diet may curtail some of the disability associated with the disease.

Homocystinuria. Homocystinuria is inherited as an autosomal recessive condition. Although three different enzyme defects may produce the syndrome of homocystinuria, the efficiency of the enzyme cystathionine-beta-synthase is most associated with mental retardation. Other findings in these children can include stroke due to thromboembolism, lens dislocation, and osteoporosis with secondary scoliosis. The children frequently become tall and thin as they reach puberty.

Laboratory diagnosis can be performed by a urine test to detect homocystine. When a newborn screening is performed, a blood test is used to detect an intermediary (methionine) in the blood.

Treatment may be undertaken by special diet, which carefully modifies amino acid intake. Some patients may be responsive to supplementary vitamins, specifically pyrodoxine and folate. With early treatment, some of the disability, especially mental retardation, may be prevented.

Maple Syrup Urine Disease. Maple syrup urine disease is so named because of the maple syrup smell that is characteristic of the child's urine. The disease may be manifest in three forms: classic, intermittent, and mild. Relative deficiencies of the branch ketoacid dehydrogenase result in these three variations. The mild form may present only with progressive mental retardation.

Diagnosis can be made by examining blood and urine specimens for the abnormal presence of branch chain keto acids. Treatment is conducted by giving thiamine, a vitamin, and a protein-restricted diet. Treatment may modify, although not fully reverse, the course of the illness.

Urea Cycle Disorders

This group of six disorders reflect enzyme deficiencies in the pathway of urea metabolism (Batshaw, 1984). Most become manifest in the newborn or during infancy as a severe illness, which is often fatal; however, partial enzymatic defects also occur, and some children may present with mental retardation alone or milder neurologic symptoms. This can occur with citrullinemina, ornithine transcarbamylase deficiency, arginosuccinic aciduria, and hyperarginemia.

The classic clinical picture of these disorders is a patient with mental retardation and seizures who has intermittent attacks of vomiting and ataxia that occasionally progress to stupor or coma. Attacks are associated with elevated serum ammonia levels. These episodes may be triggered by infection or increased protein consumption.

Chronic treatment can be given with dietary protein restriction and amino acid supplementation. Acute treatment may be given to the symptomatic child confined in a hospital. In general, these disorders are quite rare and difficult to treat. A few centers in the country specialize in the treatment of urea cycle disorders. Treatment ameliorates but does not fully reverse the course of the illness (Batshaw et al., 1982).

Mucopolysaccharidosis

These disorders result from enzymatic block in the breakdown of complicated carbohydrates. Generally, organ systems in addition to the central nervous system are affected. Hunter's syndrome (Type II mucopolysaccharidosis) presents in early childhood with hepatosplenomegaly, mental retardation, and skeletal abnormalities. Sanfilippo disease (Type III mucopolysaccharidosis) may present with dementia, hearing and visual loss, seizures, and bone and joint abnormalities (Rapin, 1970a, 1970b).

Diagnosis may be made by urine analysis for metabolic byproducts, or by skin biopsy. No treatment is available.

Neurocutaneous Syndromes

Tuberous Sclerosis. Tuberous sclerosis (Koch & Friedman, 1981) is generally inherited in an autosomal dominant pattern. Individuals with this disorder have a wide variation in their degree of impairment. Often an infant will present with developmental delay, and after the diagnosis of tuberous sclerosis is made in the infant, it is found that a parent or grandparent also has the disorder. Characteristic physical signs can be found on examination of the skin. These include hypopigmented spots, ashleaf spots (which are the shape of ash leaves and can be found on the back), shagreen patches (raised and palpable), adenoma sebaceum (fibromatous lesions that appear across the nose and cheek), and periungal fibromas (which occur around the base of the nail bed). Other physical signs may be detected by ophthalmologic examination of the eye. In the interior of the eye may be seen white plaques that are quite distinctive. These children are also susceptible to tumors of the eye, as well as of the heart, brain, and kidney. Patients who show mental retardation are also likely to have seizures.

Diagnosis may be made by examination of the skin with ultraviolet light, fundoscopic examination of the eye, CT scan of the brain, and kidney and cardiac ultrasound examinations.

Other than treatment for seizure control, there is no treatment of the condition itself. Because of the inherited pattern, genetic counseling is suggested.

Neurofibromatosis. Neurofibromatosis is inherited in an autosomal dominant pattern. In this disorder there is wide variation in the clinical expression of illness. Additionally, there are two forms. One is called the central form (Kanter et al., 1980), in which patients develop tumors of the acoustic nerve in adult life. The other is the peripheral form; this more common form is characterized by multiple hyperpigmented spots and superficial neurofibromas. A pathognomonic sign of neurofibromatosis is freckling in the underarm (Riccardi, 1982).

Clinically, these patients may have seizures, learning disabilities, and mental retardation, as well as peripheral nerve disorders related to the neurofibromas. These patients also have a relatively high incidence of central nervous system tumors. The patients with the central disorder present with hearing loss. Diagnosis must be made clinically or on the basis of CT scan of the brain. There is no curative treatment for this disorder. Problems such as seizures or tumors that may be caused by the disorder are treated symptomatically.

Disorders of White Matter

This category includes six diseases in which white matter only is involved: these include Alexander's disease, Canavan's disease, Pelizaeus-Merzbacher disease, Krabbe disease, adrenoleukodystrophy, and metachromatic leukodystrophy. These disorders are generally transmitted in a recessive pattern; however, Pelizaeus-Merzbacher Disease is an X-linked recessive disorder, with only males being affected. Each of these disorders has variable clinical presentations and severity. In general, when the disorder presents early in life, it is more severe. Histologically, all these disorders show demyelinization or loss of white matter. However, Alexander's and Canavan's diseases affect only the central nervous system, whereas the others may affect the brain, spinal chord, and peripheral nerves. In general, these disorders present with disturbance of gait, pathologic reflexes, and optic atrophy, as well as mental regression with loss of developmental milestones. Diagnosis can be made by determination of abnormal enzyme concentrations or activity, or the accumulation of abnormal byproducts that result from the faulty metabolism. CT scan of the brain or MRI may also be helpful in making the diagnosis (Fenichel, 1988).

These disorders are not treatable.

Disorders of Gray Matter

Rett Syndrome

Rett syndrome (Hagberg et al., 1983) is an idiopathic disorder that occurs in females. It has been associated with an abnormality on the X chromosome in certain cases. Girls who have previously been normal begin to show signs of developmental regression usually during the second year of life. In addition to loss of language skills, there is a characteristic loss of the ability to purposefully use one's hands. This generally has occurred by the age of 3, and the children wring their hands in stereotypic fashion. As the illness progresses, children eventually become ataxic with subsequent loss of the ability to walk, and they become microcephalic with loss of appropriate head growth. Many children also develop seizures.

Diagnosis is made clinically on the basis of history and physical exam. Treatment is not available except for treatment of the seizures.

Mitochondrial Encephalopathies

These disorders result from dysfunction of mitochondria, which are small intracellular organelles (Driscoll, Larsen, & Gruber, 1987). The faulty metabolism that results from their dysfunction leads to mental retardation with dementia, myopathy, seizures, and eye movement abnormalities.

Diagnosis can be made by determination of serum lactate and muscle biopsy. No treatment is available to reverse the underlying defect, but symptomatic treatment is available for some patients.

Neuronal Ceroid Lipofuscinosis

These disorders (Rapin, 1970b) are often rapidly progressive disorders, with dementia, myoclonus, refractory seizures, and muscular degeneration. Pathologically, one sees accumulation of a fatty substance, ceroid, in neurons, resulting in their dysfunction and subsequent death.

Diagnosis can be made with electron microscopy of a skin biopsy specimen. No treatment is available for the underlying disorder, and seizures are treated with difficulty.

SUMMARY

In summary, the neurological assessment of children is comprehensive and requires a patient history and physical exam as well as laboratory tests. One of the most important facts to be learned from the history is whether the child's development is progressing forward at the expected rate. Failures of normal development due to delay or regression are described as static or progressive encephalopathy. A number of different disease entities may produce each of these patterns. A differential diagnosis can be formulated by consideration of all features in the history and physical exam. Laboratory tests may be used to further clarify the diagnosis. Consultation with a pediatric neurologist should be sought in evaluation of a child with static or progressive encephalopathy.

REFERENCES

Adams, R. D., & Victor, M. (1981). *Principles of neurology* (2nd ed.). New York: McGraw-Hill.

Batshw, M. L. (1984). Hyperammonemic. *Current Problems in Pediatrics, 11*, 18–37.

Batshaw, M. L., Brusilow, S., Waber, L., Blom, W., Brubakk, A. M., Burton, B. K., Cann, H. M., Kerr, D., Mamunes, P., Matalon, R., Myerberg, D., & Schafer, I. A. (1982). Treatment of inborn errors of urea synthesis. *New England Journal of Medicine, 306*, 1387–1392.

Bell, W. E., & McCormick, W. F. (1981). *Neurologic infections in children.* Philadelphia: W. B. Saunders Company.

Dezanteux, C. A., Dinswiddle, R., Helms, P., & Matthew, D. J. (1986). Recognition and early management of Reyes syndrome. *Archives of Diseases in Childhood, 61*, 647–651.

Driscoll, P. F., Larsen, P. D., Gruber, A. B. (1987). MELAS syndrome. *Archives of Neurology, 44*, 971–973.

Fenichel, G. M. (1985). *Neonatal neurology.* New York: Churchill Livingstone, Inc.

Fenichel, G. M. (1988). *Clinical pediatric neurology: A signs and symptoms approach* (pp. 118–146). Philadelphia: W. B. Saunders.

Hagberg, B., Aicardi, J., Karin, D., & Ramos, O. (1983). A progressive syndrome of autism, dementia, ataxia, and loss of purposeful hand use in girls: Retts syndrome—Report of 35 cases. *Annals of Neurology, 14*, 471.

Kanter, W. R., Eldridge, R., Fabricant, R., Allen J. C., & Koerber T. (1980). Central neurofibromatosis with bilateral acoustic neuroma: Genetic, clinical and biochemital distinctions from peripheral neurofibromatosis. *Neurology, 30*, 851.

Koch, R., & Friedman, E. G. (1981). Accuracy of newborn screening programs for phenylketonoria. *Journal of Pediatrics, 98*, 267–269.

Levy, H. L. (1986). Phenylketonuria—1986. *Pediatrics in Review, 7*, 269–275.

Menkes, J. H. (1985). *Textbook of child neurology (3rd ed.).* Philadelphia: Lea & Febiger.

Opitz, J. M. (1984). *X-linked mental retardation.* New York: Alan R. Liss.

Rapin, I. (1970a). Progressive genetic-metabolic diseases of the central nervous system in children. *Pediatric Annals, May*, 11–12.

Rapin, I. (1970b). Progressive genetic-metabolic diseases of the central nervous system in children. *Pediatric Annals, May*, 18–20.

Riccardi, V. M. (1982). The multiple forms of childhood neurofibromatosis. *Pediatrics Review, 3*, 293.

Smith, D. W. (1982a). Fetal hydantoin syndrome. In D. W. Smith, *Recognizable patterns of human malformation: Genetic, embryologic and clinical aspects* (pp. 414–417). Philadelphia: W. B. Saunders.

Smith, D. W. (1982b). Fetal alchohol syndrome. In D. W. Smith, *Recognizable patterns of human malformation: Genetic, embryologic and clinical aspects* (pp. 411–413). Philadelphia: W. B. Saunders.

Smith, D. W. (1982c). Genetics, genetic counseling, and prevention via early fetal recognition. In D. W. Smith, *Recognizable patterns of human malformation: Genetic, embryologic and clinical aspects* (pp. 565–566). Philadelphia: W. B. Saunders.

CHAPTER 5

ETHICAL ISSUES IN THE PSYCHOLOGICAL ASSESSMENT OF CHILDREN

Gerald P. Koocher

Children were among the first beneficiaries of psychological assessment and probably also among the first victims of its misuse. An important historical watershed event in the history of psychology and education occurred in 1904 when public school administrators in Paris, France sought the help of Alfred Binet to assist them in dealing with the large number of "nonlearners" in their classrooms. The authorities sought to develop special schools where such children would not be held to the standard academic curriculum. Well aware of potential teacher biases in making assignment decisions of this sort, they asked Binet, a prominent French psychologist, to help them in developing a scientific means of separating the "dull and feebleminded" children from the others. Out of perceived practical necessity, the original Binet scales for assessing intelligence and the concept of an IQ (i.e., intelligence quotient) were born. The instrument first published in 1905 began the application of standardized psychological assessment of children.

Crossing the oceans took more time in those days, but by the end of World War I, America had fully caught on to the utility of such assessment tools. In the autumn of 1922, a young American reporter for *The New Republic* magazine named Walter Lippman began a critical series of articles commenting on trends in the application of "Mr. Binet's test" to the English-speaking world. Long before most of today's clinical psychologists were born, young Mr. Lippman cautioned that "great mischief" might result if society came to believe that such tests ". . . constitute a sort of last judgment on the child's capacity . . ." (Lippman, 1922, p. 297). Although psychologists are now considerably more attuned to the potential hazards he envisioned, significant difficulties of the sort he described still persist today.

Ethical problems in psychological assessment may arise in many ways. There may be difficulties in the basic science underlying the instrument or assessment procedure (i.e., the construction, validity, or reliability of the tool or technique), the manner in which the test is administered, the competence of the test user, or biases built into the structure of the test. Other problems may involve professional standards in the use and application of such tools, including the specific purpose to which the data are put, the issue of informed consent by test takers or their surrogates, handling of obsolete test data, and the release of raw test data to others. Increasingly, psychologists are also discovering that they may be liable to suit for *loss in evaluation* when they negligently make assessment errors that result in some loss or damages to clients. Much of this chapter focuses on school-related issues simply because the educational system has been the most frequent user of psychological assessment techniques with children since Binet began his work for the public schools of Paris. Because tests are often used in schools and other agencies serving children and because of the powerful impact that test results may have in children's lives, limiting the misuse or abuse of these techniques is especially important.

BASIC PSYCHOMETRIC CONCEPTS

Key Psychometric Terms

Although this chapter is no substitute for formal coursework in psychological assessment and test construction, it seems appropriate to summarize briefly a few important concepts that are often central to ethical complaints regarding the assessment of children. With apologies to those thoroughly familiar with measurement techniques, these key concepts include *reliability*, *validity*, *sources of error*, and the *standard error of measurement*.

Reliability is that property of the test that assures repeatable results. A reliable instrument measures whatever attribute it assesses dependably over time and across populations. Tests of stable human attributes should have a high test-retest reliability. For example, if a ninth-grade student earns a certain score on a French vocabulary test on Friday, that same student should earn a similar score on readministration of the same test the following Monday, other things being held equal (e.g., if no special studying or presentation of additional material occurred over the weekend). Likewise, the test should yield similar scores for people of similar French vocabulary ability when tested under similar conditions, whether or not they differ on other extraneous characteristics such as age, sex, or race. If any given test does not measure something reliably, it is invalid and useless, since one could never know whether differences in scores were related to the skill or trait being assessed or to the unreliability of the tool.

Validity refers to the idea of whether an otherwise reliable test actually gauges what it is supposed to measure. As noted above, a test cannot possibly be valid if it is unreliable. On the other hand, a test can yield highly reliable scores that are not a valid assessment of what the test purports to measure. For example, we could design a highly reliable means to measure children's foot sizes, but could not reasonably claim that the resulting FSQ (i.e., Foot Size Quotient) is a valid indicator of childhood depression. To do so, we would have to provide evidence of a relationship between the FSQ and depression. Those who develop, publish, and market tests are responsible for proving that a particular instrument is appropriately validated for its recommended uses. Validity may be considered from several different perspectives, as summarized in the following paragraphs.

Content validity is the simplest type of validity to conceptualize. It is sometimes called *face validity*, because the test items or data to be collected are deemed valid indicators of the behavior to be measured simply by looking at them (i.e., on their face). A test item that clearly samples behavior from the domain of interest is said to have content validity. For example, a sixth-grade math test should contain problems or calculations that are taught in the sixth grade. The tasks should be related to the ability or trait we wish to measure.

Construct validity refers to the degree to which a test's scores can be used to infer individual differences associated with some hypothetical construct (Green, 1981; Guion, 1974). However, even the most basic assertions regarding the very existence of some hypothetical constructs can be a controversial matter (e.g., constructs such as ego strength, penis envy, or even intelligence have been the objects of such controversy). One result is that tests purporting to measure such constructs are often controversial themselves. A classic example of questionable construct validity in a test designed for administration to children is the *Blacky Pictures* (Blum, 1950). Administration of the test requires displaying a series of cartoon pictures featuring a dog named Blacky and members of his or her family depicting various behaviors illustrative of Freudian constructs such as oral aggression, autoeroticism, anal rage, and castration anxiety. Obviously, the demand characteristics of the stimuli evoke certain types of responses. Psychologists who adhere to a single-minded psychoanalytic perspective might be expected to assert that responses to these test stimuli provide proof of the construct's validity and proceed to make personality interpretations based on that assumption. A behaviorally oriented colleague would find such an inference laughable and discount the Freudian constructs as not being directly observable in behavior. The burden of establishing whether a test measures a given construct as claimed in its test manual or advertising falls to the test developer. Clinicians using such tools, however, must also be prepared to defend their choice of instruments and assessments based on such data.

Criterion-related validity refers to whether a particular test's outcome is related to other criteria in either predictive or concurrent fashion. For example, do Scholastic Aptitude Test scores obtained during high school predict grades during the freshman year of college? Do IQ scores on a newly developed test of intelligence correlate well with scores of the same children on an existing well-standardized test of intelligence? These two questions illustrate the points of predictive and concurrent validity respectively.

Sources of error are factors that cause variations in test scores and result in inaccurate measurement. These may arise in many different ways to affect test scores. One child may have come to school hungry on the day of the test. Another might be highly motivated to please the examiner, while many of her classmates could not care less. Still another child might be feeling ill or nervous or might be very familiar with some of the tasks on a given test. The significance of any particular source of error depends on the specific use of the test and the life context of the specific individual who took it. One reason for studying the reliability of a test is to locate and estimate the magnitude of the errors of measurement that might affect it. Any given test has many sources of *standard error*, and the user is responsible for becoming familiar with these and considering them in light of the comparisons to be made. A *standard error of measurement* is a score interval or range of scores that, given certain assumptions, has a certain probability of including any individual test taker's true score.

Examples of Ethical Problems Linked to Poor Psychometrics

Failure to understand the standard error of measurement was illustrated by a psychologist who tested an 8-year-old developmentally delayed child and obtained WISC-R (Wechsler Intelligence Scale for Children - Revised) Verbal and Performance IQ scores 4 to 5 points higher than the previous testing results. The psychologist told the child's parents that this was a sign that their child "could be making intellectual progress." The psychologist apparently did not understand the basic concept of standard error. In reality the scores were well within the normal test-retest reliability range, meaning that the standard error built into the test could fully account for the difference in scores. The parents were dangerously and cruelly misled by the psychologist's incorrect comments.

Using tests for purposes for which they were not properly validated is another aspect of psychometric impropriety. A psychologist administered the Rorschach Inkblots to a 12-year-old child and later testified in court that the results of the Rorschach showed there was a "50% probability the child will suffer a personality disorder, if forced to continue residing with the mother." This "expert opinion" is inexcusable and dangerous both from a scientific perspective and in terms of the impact it may have on the parties involved if a judge were to base a decision on it. The Rorschach Inkblots have never been validated for use in child-custody decision making. In addition, there is no basis for drawing conclusions about future personality development and the mother's role in it from a single set of test data collected from the child. Finally, the 50% probability cited by the psychologist is the product of her own imagination, although she presents it in a manner that implies that it has some empirical validity. She might as well suggest the judge flip a coin to decide the issue.

Another psychologist developed a "new psychological test for children" that might well have been termed the Detrimental School Function Test (DSFT). The DSFT was a collection of test items loosely adapted or pirated from several existing instruments. The psychologist published and marketed the test as a means of evaluating children's learning skills, based on "expected norms" he extrapolated from other test manuals. He has not attempted the expensive and time-consuming task of standardizing the DSFT on a representative sample of children. This psychologist may well be violating copyright law in the development of his "new test," because he draws heavily on copyrighted test material without proper consent. Beyond that, however, he has apparently set up a potentially confusing situation in which children may be evaluated by a totally bogus set of norms. He has adopted a strategy of test development that ignores all basic principles of validity documentation. Because trained psychologists are likely to recognize these problems, one must also question the target audience for the new test. One suspects he may hope to market it to pediatricians or other professionals not trained in psychometrics and probably too naive to see the problems. This could make matters worse, because the unsophisticated users might then mislead others, and so on.

REVISED STANDARDS

Those interested in ethical issues associated with the psychological testing of children will certainly want to become familiar with the revised *Standards for Educational and Psychological Testing*, authored jointly by the American Educational Research Association, American Psychological Association, and National Council on Measurement in Education (1985). Besides reviewing basic technical standards for test construction and professional standards for test use, this reference volume provides detailed guidelines for consideration when assessing children in schools, linguistic minorities, and handicapped persons. Among the key principles detailed in these *Standards* are assumptions that those who give and interpret the tests are trained to understand and adhere to administration and scoring procedures, interpret test results, and conform to accepted practices concerning safeguarding confidential materials and timely reporting of the test results.

Standard Operating Procedures

The principal value of psychological tests derives from the fact that they prescribe a means for collecting and analyzing a standardized slice of human behavior. Basic rules for test administration and scoring must be carefully followed to be sure that the sampling and examination of the behavior in question are comparable across different occasions and with diverse people. Reference manuals with detailed instructions and norms must be made available by the test publisher for this purpose.

Examples of Ethical Violations of Standard Operational Procedures

The test manual for the Childhood Reading Achievement Profile, developed by an educational psychologist, provides information on converting raw scores to age and grade equivalents, but contains no information on the sample population used in establishing the norms such as geographic distribution, socioeconomic status, ethnic or racial composition, or similar demographic variables. The test manual described here is simply inadequate. Users have no access to information that is critical to interpreting test scores. The omission of such data effectively voids any potential application of the test, even if it is valid and reliable. As matters stand, there is no basis for test users to conclude that the sample of children to be tested reasonably resembles the population for which norms exist.

The parents of a second-grade pupil became aware that she was having problems in school and asked for a conference with the principal to arrange for legally mandated help. Anxious to collect some data before the parent conference, the principal ordered the child to sit with a fourth-grade class where group-administered intelligence tests were being administered. When the child's scores were compared to second-grade norms, they were low, and the principal advised the parents that their child had intellectual deficits. Usual procedures were substantially violated here. The child was removed from her classroom without any preparation and placed with an unfamiliar group of children (most likely in a desk too large for her size). She was asked to participate in a procedure that was not explained to her in advance. She may have felt badly about not doing well in school and might perceive this treatment as a punishment. She was most likely at a substantial emotional disadvantage in this context. Even if we assume that the test was reliable and that the administration of it described here was valid, it would be inappropriate to base a significant conclusion about any child's ability solely on a paper-and-pencil test. The primary ethical problem here was undertaking an assessment in circumstances in which the child's psychosocial environment had been disrupted, while not making any efforts to help her to adjust. The best approach would have been to schedule the assessment with sufficient time to provide the child an explanation and then to test her with a group of peers. Alternatively, an assessment could be undertaken by an individual examiner who could take the time to form rapport with the child and make individual behavioral observations. In any case, the test results should be interpreted only by someone knowledgeable about the test and only in the context of what is otherwise known about her (i.e., her family and school history, health, general behavior).

When a small-town mental health clinic was flooded, many of the psychological testing supplies were damaged. To save money, the executive director told his staff to photocopy test forms and cut out pieces of cardboard to replace waterlogged puzzle parts, rather than to purchase new supplies. One can be sympathetic about the flood or the limited budget of the agency, but neither justifies violation of copyright laws, as would be the case in photocopying official test record booklets. More troubling, however, is the plan to make new test kit pieces from cardboard cutouts. The test norms were developed using certain standard test stimuli. Handcrafting new puzzle parts alters the standardized stimuli and has an unpredictable impact on the test results, invalidating them for direct comparison with scores obtained with a standard set of test materials.

Test Bias

The issue of test bias has been the focus of considerable public attention and debate. The term itself has many complex aspects. It may manifest itself as a function of a skill or trait being measured, a statistical phenomenon, a selection model, a problem with test-item content, a matter of overinterpretation, a use of improper criteria, or even a problem in the environment where the testing took place. In an overview of the scholarly research on test bias, Cole (1981) argues that the basic issue in the matter of test bias is simply a question of validity. She distinguishes between whether a test is valid for some specific purpose, and whether it ought to be used (even if valid). The use of tests per se has served as a lightning rod or a focal point of anger related to more broad and difficult social questions. In such a context, testing itself never provides all the answers. Problems that have been associated with psychological testing, such as inappropriate labeling of children and self-fulfilling prophecies linked to teacher expectancy are more appropriately viewed as the result of uninformed or unethical test users, rather than poor tests (Hobbs, 1975). Answers to complex social problems can rarely be found with a psychological test. The test data may provide clues, suggest directions, or document progress, but the benefits or drawbacks are the products of human interpretation.

In the case of *Larry P. v. Riles* (1979), a federal court prohibited the use of standardized intelligence tests as a means of identifying educable mentally retarded (EMR) black children or for placing such children in EMR classes. The genesis of this case was the fact that black children were disproportionately overrepresented in such classes at the northern California school district in question and that the primary basis for such placement in the district at that time was such tests (Lambert, 1981). Attorneys for the children argued that the test items were drawn from white, middle-class culture, that whites had more advantages and opportunities than blacks, and that language used by black children may not correspond to that used in the test. In addition, they noted that the motivation of the black children to perform on the tests may have been adversely influenced by the race of the examiners, who were mostly white, and that the number of blacks in the standardization sample was very low.

The type of problem demonstrated here is essentially a validity issue. That is to say, the test was being used for making a type of discrimination or judgment for which it was neither intended nor validated. Using a single psychometric instrument as the sole or primary criterion in making critical educational or other life decisions fails to consider each individual as a whole being in a specific life context. As such, this use of a test suggests unethical assessment practices.

In *PASE v. Hannon* (1980), a different federal court in Illinois reached the opposite decision from its West Coast counterpart in the *Larry P.* case. Continued use of psychological tests in educational decision making was permitted. This contrast is of interest because many of the same psychological experts testified in both cases, both cases were under active judicial review simultaneously, and the outcomes were quite different. One might be tempted to read these cases as contrast or contradiction in the legal system. It is more likely that the contrasting opinions are best regarded as context specific. That is, the court was most likely convinced that use of the psychometric tools in Illinois was more appropriate to the context than was the use of the same instruments by the psychologists in the San Francisco school district. Because two different judges and sets of facts were involved, however, a definitive conclusion on this point is impossible. In addition, many of the school personnel conducting the assessments in the Illinois case were people of color themselves, perhaps lending credibility to their denial that no inappropriate discrimination occurred. The point to be made is that the clinician who becomes involved in testing that is to be used for critical decision making bears an especially heavy ethical burden to ensure that the data are applied in an appropriate scientific context that does not unfairly discriminate against any individual being assessed.

As an aside, it is somewhat ironic that the judge in the *PASE* case permitted the questions and keyed answers to standardized IQ tests to become a part of the public record. The court obviously had little concern for the matter of test security. The Committee on Psychological Tests and Assessments of the American Psychological Association is currently at work on special guidelines in the face of increasing demands by courts across the nation for disclosure of responses to particular test items.

User Competence

Who is qualified to purchase, administer, and interpret a psychological test to be used with children? This is not a simple question when applied to those who assess adults, but when children are the objects of the evaluation the matter becomes even more complex. At the simplest level, user competence may refer to the ability of an individual examiner to administer and score a particular instrument in a manner that yields a valid test protocol. More important, however, is the ability to interpret the meaning of the test results for the particular individual being tested in the context of that person's life circumstances.

A wide variety of tests is available for use with infants, toddlers, and older children, but these are not generally taught in graduate programs where most clinical or counseling psychologists are trained. Such programs have traditionally focused the bulk of their psychometric coursework and practica on the testing of adult clients. In addition, the behavior of children has a wider normal range of variation than that of adults. Establishing the proper rapport with children is more time consuming, and understanding the difference between a response that means "I don't know the answer" and "I'm not going to cooperate with you" or "I know, but I won't tell" takes a special awareness of child development and an understanding of children. The pace of the assessment interview and the need for the examiner to work actively to engage the client is often more variable and demanding than with adult clients.

The role of the test-publishing companies in the determination of user competence is a "sometimes" issue. Most reputable companies classify their products into usage categories and seek to establish at least minimal user qualification before a sale. Such companies are, however, not in the credentialing business and are more concerned about making profits on the sales of their products than on the impossible task of preventing all possible unauthorized uses. Determination of user qualifications usually means requiring that the party placing the order be either a member of the American Psychological Association or a licensed psychologist. Not all licensed psychologists and not all APA members are qualified to use psychological tests, let alone test children. In addition, even those test publishers that do specify user qualifications for purchase by individuals (as opposed to institutional buyers) may ignore their own stated policy when shipping in response to institutional purchase orders from large hospitals or school systems. We must conclude that there are no assurances that the sale of psychological tests is restricted to qualified users and that, as a result, many people who obtain and administer such tests may not be technically qualified to do so.

Examples of User Competence Issues

A supervisor in an APA-approved internship program was assigned to work with a trainee who had little experience in child work. The trainee was assigned to assess a toddler, although he was unfamiliar with the particular test instruments that would be needed to adequately evaluate a child of that age. He mentioned his reservations to the supervisor, who told him to "read the test manual and practice the items and go to it." The trainee has a difficult situation on his hands. He is more sensitive to the ethical problems involved in inadequate test-user competence and more aware of his own limitations than is his supervisor. At the same time, however, the trainee wants to be seen as a good student by his supervisor and is under some pressure to ignore his sense of what is in the patient's best interests in this particular case. In the ideal circumstance, the trainee could approach the supervisor and reframe the concern as an ethical dilemma for him: "I feel uneasy about testing this child without first being checked out more thoroughly on this instrument. I'm afraid that it would be unethical of me to undertake the assessment without some help." This type of approach highlights the problem without attributing blame to the supervisor. If the supervisor ignores or trivializes this request, the trainee may decide to seek counsel from other colleagues on site or from the training director at his university. One only hopes he will not give in to the pressure to undertake an assignment he cannot adequately complete without additional training or supervisory support.

A psychologist with a large consulting practice that involves considerable psychological testing makes heavy use of assistants. After meeting a child briefly, the psychologist usually leaves the youngster in the hands of an assistant, who administers the appropriate instruments, scores them, and drafts several descriptive paragraphs. The psychologist subsequently edits the materials into a psychological evaluation report to which he signs only his own name. This model for conducting child assessments is not entirely ethically appropriate. The psychologist is obviously being assisted by a more junior person in a substantial manner but is producing reports that are signed in a manner that might mislead readers into concluding that he was the sole evaluator of the child. If the assistant is properly trained, supervised, and authorized under state law to perform the functions described, the use of an assistant in this context is not unethical. The ethical problem is that of fairly and accurately representing for readers of the report and for third-party payers (e.g., insurance companies) who personally conducted the evaluation. In addition, the psychologist would be expected to review the test data and discuss the child's examination behavior with the assistant in order to fully grasp the context before preparing the report. One would want to know more about these details before rendering final judgment on the propriety of the psychologist's behavior.

In an effort to "streamline and economize," the head of psychological services of a regional school district has purchased a variety of psychological testing software packages that can be used on the desktop microcomputers in each of the school buildings. Some of the software packages are intended to administer psychological tests to children who sit at the terminal alone. Other programs generate psychological evaluation reports based on intelligence test subtest scores computed by psychometricians in the school system. The numbers are punched in, and a finished report prints out. The program head is very proud of bringing her department into the "computer age." These plans raise many significant ethical questions. Although it is not unusual to have adult clients enter responses to test items on a computer keyboard as these are displayed on a monitor screen, it is another matter entirely to leave a child to perform such tasks unsupervised. Without taking the child's attention span, fine-motor coordination, and reading abilities into consideration, it is not possible to determine how valid or reliable the test data obtained by these means might be. Although there are many software programs that generate reports based on simple data entry, these reports generally fall into two categories: data summaries and interpretive reports. The data summaries present scores, averages, ratios, graphs, and so on. The interpretive reports generally produce narrative or descriptive paragraphs composed by mechanical means, but often sounding as though they may have been written by a clinician. When generated by software produced by reputable firms, these reports include a printed warning that the data can be interpreted only by a trained clinician. One difficulty is that this statement may be absent or ignored. Many psychologists believe that interpretive reports should be generated in a manner that precludes their use without reformulation or refinement by a well-trained clinician. The psychologist's planned use of the new technology does not seem to give adequate consideration to these points. It would be well for her to review the *Guidelines for Computer-Based Tests and Interpretations* prepared by the APA's Committee on Professional Standards and Committee on Psychological Tests and Assessments (1986).

SOME CONSEQUENCES OF ADVOCACY AGAINST MISUSE OF TESTS

Conscientious psychologists occasionally find themselves in the unenviable position of having to advocate for clients in matters involving misuse or psychological test data or techniques. Such advocacy is especially painful because it involves pointing out problems often caused by other colleagues or their assessment methods. At the same time, however, psychologists are better equipped by training and experience to recognize and properly criticize such abuses. Nonetheless, the personal costs of such advocacy can be significant.

The potential adverse consequences of such advocacy are well illustrated by the case of a psychologist in private practice, who was asked by the parents of a child who was experiencing school problems to undertake an evaluation. When the child recognized some of the standardized test items, the psychologist inquired and discovered that another psychologist who worked within the school system had begun a similar evaluation a few days earlier without the parent's knowledge or consent. The psychologist retained by the parents attempted collegial consultation with her school-based colleague and met with only limited cooperation. She soon discovered that the school psychologist had made some significant errors in his assessment procedures and the school system, relying in part on his work, was refusing services to which the child seemed entitled under state and federal law. Unable to resolve the matter informally, she filed complaints against the psychologist and the municipality with agencies of the state and federal government. A variety of counterparges were then filed by the school system's psychologist against her with licensing and ethics boards, while rumors were spread in the community that she was emotionally unstable. Her well-intentioned efforts in support of her client ended up subjecting her to considerable personal distress, despite the appropriateness of her cause and her efforts.

Another case of the same genre involved Muriel

Forrest, a master's-level school psychologist, who had an unblemished record in a dozen years of service to the Edgemont Union Free School District. In the face of increasing special education costs, she was prohibited by her superiors from conducting full and comprehensive evaluations, discussing the results of her evaluations, denominating specific handicapping conditions of the children she assessed, or making recommendations for appropriate services and programs for handicapped children. When she refused to go along with these prohibitions, her reports were rewritten, she was chastised for criticizing the school system's policy, and her contract was ultimately terminated in a manner that allowed her only five days' notice to prepare rebuttal before recommendation of termination (Bersoff, 1980; *Forrest v. Ansbach*, 1980).

Although both of these cases revolve around misguided assessment strategies (one by an unnamed school psychologist and the other dictated by Edgemont Union Free School District), both also illustrate some of the hazards of attempting to be a strong child advocate or whistle blower in the public arena. Although the first psychologist discussed in this category was eventually successful in having the proper services provided to her client, assorted complaints filed against her before licensing or ethics panels persisted for many months and were not disposed of before she incurred considerable legal expenses and great personal aggravation. In addition, she had no real means of addressing the rumors that had been started about her "emotional instability." These unfounded aspersions had a significant adverse effect on her private practice.

The unnamed psychologist lost some clients and Muriel Forrest lost her job without redress. In an amicus brief filed jointly on Muriel Forrest's behalf by the American, New York, and Westchester County Psychological Associations, Bersoff (1980) concludes

> ... the only permissible inference which may be drawn from the failure of (the school system) to renew (Ms. Forrest's) contract considering her splendid record of over a dozen years is that they objected to her activities devoted to advocating, supporting, and enforcing the civil rights of handicapped children and their parents. (p.41)

Nevertheless, Ms. Forrest's appeal for reinstatement was ultimately lost some 4 years after her firing on a procedural technicality. Unfortunately, being right and ethically correct does not always guarantee a desirable outcome.

Consent

Psychological assessment should not be undertaken without the informed consent of the person being evaluated. When the client is a child, a parent or guardian should be asked for formal permission on behalf of the child. The process of obtaining permission should provide the adults making the decision with all the information that might reasonably be expected to influence their decision in consideration of the child's best interests.

Two case examples on this point illustrate the issues. In the first case, all the students in grades 3, 5, and 7 at the South Middle School were given the National Scholastic Achievement Test to assess their progress midway through the school year. No advance notice was given to the children or their families, nor was specific permission to test the children obtained from their families.

The second case involves a 10-year-old boy who had a significant behavior problem and also seemed to be falling behind in his schoolwork. In an effort to assess psychological aspects of the situation and provide appropriate interventions, the school principal asked the psychologist assigned to the school to conduct a full assessment of the child on an urgent basis. Neither the principal nor the psychologist sought formal permission from the boy's family before beginning the process.

The testing undertaken in both of these cases may seem relatively benign, but that does not excuse the failure to seek permission in the 10-year-old's case or to give adequate notice (and the opportunity to express concerns) in the case of the group test administration at the middle school. Although routine school achievement testing is not very invasive, parents have the right to be informed both of the testing and of the results. In some school systems with a history of discrimination against people of color or inappropriate use of test data (see, for example, the case of *Larry P. v. Riles* discussed earlier in this chapter), parents or the psychological consultants may want to monitor the testing and use of results closely. When individualized assessment is recommended for a child, both federal and many state laws combine to dictate parental involvement and consent before initiating the assessment. Seeing the 10-year-old boy without his parents' consent could possibly result in formal charges being filed against both the psychologist and the school system. In both situations, however, it is in the best interests of the schools to maintain a cooperative and nonadversarial relationship with parents. It is far wiser to provide abundant information and seek permission routinely, rather than to have to undo the damage caused by failure to use a thoughtful approach. Psychologists may be helpful in making this point to school administrators who may inadvertently overlook it.

Obsolescence of Test Data

Psychologists are obligated to purge obsolete test data from files of their private patients. When psychologists are employees of hospitals, clinics, or other agencies, they are obliged to work with the record-keeping staff at those agencies to see that obsolete materials are not kept on file in a manner that could possibly lead to their misuse. This is a particularly important issue when children who may be the objects of psychological assessment early in their development have long outgrown the problems that led to the evaluation. The data yielded in most child assessments will have little relevance many years later.

Consider the case of the 6-year-old child who was evaluated with a full psychological battery of cognitive and projective tests at the Community Child Guidance Center because of school adjustment problems in first grade. More than a dozen years have passed since that time, and the raw test data remain in the case file on the child in the guidance center's record room. At the age of 20, he enlists in the military. Subsequently access to his files is sought by official personnel evaluating him for security clearance.

Although some psychologists might have an intellectual curiosity about the 20-year-old, no one could argue with any form of scientific validity that cognitive, visual-motor, or projective test data collected at age 6 are in any way relevant to his current appropriateness for military security clearance. Perhaps if he had been tested routinely in longitudinal fashion for several years, some useful information might exist. Such compilations of data over time on a single child are rare in clinical practice. If any data on clients such as this one do exist, someone may someday want to come looking for them. Providing obsolete data in such circumstances is a double disservice. It is a disservice to the client, since it is not valid for any important purpose and could ultimately be used to his disadvantage. For similar reasons, providing such data to other agencies, even with the client's consent, is a disservice because they might be led to believe that they have information with some valid present meaning. The most appropriate course of action would be to routinely cull files of such information (e.g., raw test data or protocols and obsolete reports). The definition of obsolescence should be made in consideration of the age of the client at the time, the nature of the problem, and the current context. Particular exceptions would be in cases in which litigation based on issues at the time of the assessment is still pending (e.g., a lawsuit for damages suffered following a head injury) or when longitudinal test data are necessary to document changes associated with a progressive medical condition.

Who Owns the Data?

Psychologists are often asked to release copies of raw test data. The actual test protocols are generally the property of the individual practitioner or agency where the assessment was done, much as case notes or medical records would be. Unlike more general notes or records, however, raw test data and test protocols are specialized information that cannot readily be understood or interpreted by people without specialized training. The ethical propriety of supplying copyrighted or limited-circulation material depends on purposes for which the data are sought and on the qualifications of intended recipients.

Consider the case of the psychologist who receives insistent telephone calls from the father of a child she had tested a few weeks earlier. The parent had read her report and disagrees with several of her conclusions and recommendations. He demands that she provide him with copies of the raw data and test protocols. "After all," he notes, "I paid for the testing and I have a right to my child's records."

This parent's demand presents several ethical problems. To begin with, some of the test protocols may be copyrighted with distribution to the general public prohibited (e.g., IQ test record blanks). In addition, the raw data collected during assessment sessions often contain casual observations, marginal comments, or other working notes of a speculative nature that were never intended for public disclosure. Similarly, some data or comments may be elicited from the child that may be confidential or otherwise ought not to be reported directly to people who are not trained to consider it in context (e.g., a response to a projective test stimulus card in which the "child in the story" says or does something unpleasant to or about the "parent in the story"). Considerable specialized training is required to administer and interpret psychological tests.

The parent's demand for the data may reflect

inadequate explanation or discussion of the test results by the psychologist, and in that sense might have been preventable. If she had met with the parents in advance to discuss the ground rules for providing feedback before undertaking the evaluation or had met with the parents following the evaluation to review her findings and answer their questions in person, the demand for the data might have been forestalled. Even at this point, an offer to review the findings might address the parent's real needs. I also recommend providing parents with a copy of the actual test report. In many states, parents have full access to their child's formal medical records by law. Even when parental access is not guaranteed by law, one should assume that a parent with legal custody will at some point have access to the report. It is much better for them to have it handed to them by the author with the chance to ask questions, than to see it later without benefit of interpretation.

On occasions when a parent continues to insist on copies of raw data or test protocols, despite appropriate efforts to address their questions and concerns, one should attempt to ascertain the reason for the request. If, for example, the goal is to provide information that would be helpful to a colleague, such as a psychologist treating the child who has been tested, the intent may be quite appropriate. I advise giving the following explanation in any case:

> Although my formal report is a part of your child's record and you are welcome to a copy of it, the notes I take and test forms I complete during the course of my evaluation are working notes. These are not a finished product and even the actual test responses could not be effectively interpreted without specialized training. Although I would be glad to share specific test response data with another qualified professional of your choosing, it would be unethical for me to provide these materials to untrained people.

The preamble to *Principle 8* on assessment techniques of the *Ethical Principles of Psychologists* states that psychologists "guard against the misuse of assessment results," and Section F of the same principle notes that psychologists "do not encourage or promote" the use of such materials by "inappropriately trained or otherwise unqualified persons." The best route to provide the data to another person the insistent parent might select would be first to secure a written release and to telephone the intended recipient to determine the person's needs (i.e., which data are desired) and qualifications to interpret that data. If specific scores or responses are needed, this fact can be more easily determined.

It is not unusual to hear accounts of clinicians who, angry about unpaid bills, refuse to release test data or reports. Consider the following case. A psychologist completed a child assessment 3 months ago and finished the testing report promptly. He filed a claim with the client's insurance company and, after some inquiries, has been advised by the claims department that payment was made directly to the subscriber. The psychologist then receives a signed release of information from the child's school seeking a copy of the report to use in educational planning. While the report is of valid interest to the school, the psychologist telephones the parents, who assure him that "the check is in the mail." The psychologist tells them that his report will be in the mail as soon as the check arrives and otherwise will be withheld.

Here, the psychologist is obviously holding the report hostage in an effort to collect his fee. No matter how reprehensible the parents may be in withholding the insurance money they have already collected, and no matter how recalcitrant they or any other client may be in paying a bill, the psychologist's behavior is unethical. It is never proper to withhold information to the detriment of a client because of an unpaid bill. The psychologist would be within his rights to request payment at the time service is rendered (i.e., the day of the appointment) or to use appropriate legal means (e.g., small claims court) to collect a legitimate debt, but he should not use his report for retaliatory purposes or as a means to force payment.

GUIDING PRINCIPLES

When developing, administering, or interpreting psychological assessment tools, psychologists must exercise caution to ensure that the *Standards for Educational and Psychological Testing* are followed:

- Adhere to copyright rules and respect the legitimate proprietary rights of test developers and publishers.
- Be certain that reports or conclusions based on test results are reported accurately and in a manner that can be understood by the intended audience.
- Take care to avoid making (or permitting others to make) decisions based on test data that are inconsistent with the normative base or usual intended uses of the instrument as described in the test manual.
- Do not use test instruments you have not been trained to administer and interpret, and do not permit people working under your supervision to do so.
- Do not undertake psychological assessment of a

child without the consent of that child's parent or legal guardian.
- Remove obsolete raw test data from your own clinical files on a routine basis. If employed by a private institution or agency, encourage the appropriate authorities at that facility to cull obsolete data from their files on a similar basis.
- Upon receipt of proper written consent, psychologists should be willing to release copies of raw test data to other mental health professionals, so long as the intended recipient is trained to score and interpret such data. Although many different mental health professionals may make good use of psychological test results in their care of clients, not all are trained to make sense of the raw data.

Psychologists should never withold assessment reports or data needed for clinical assessment, treatment planning, or educational program design because a bill has not been paid. Financial considerations should not hinder meeting the psychological needs of the client.

REFERENCES

American Educational Research Association, American Psychological Association, and National Council on Measurement in Education (1985). *Standards for educational and psychological testing.* Washington, DC: American Psychological Association.

American Psychological Association. (1986). *Guidelines for computer-based tests and interpretations.* Washington, DC: Author.

Bersoff, D. N. (1980). *Brief for amici curiae in the Matter of Muriel Forrest v. Gordon M. Ambach.* Washington, DC: American Psychological Association.

Blum, G. (1950). *The Blacky Pictures.* New York: Psychological Corporation.

Cole, N. S. (1981). Bias in testing. *American Psychologist, 36,* 1067–1077.

Forrest v. Ansbach, 436 N.Y.S. 2d 119 (1980).

Green, B. F. (1981). A primer of testing. *American Psychologist, 36,* 1001–1011.

Guion, R. M. (1974). Open a new window: Validities and values in psychological measurement. *American Psychologist, 28,* 287–296.

Hobbs, N. (Ed.) (1975). *Issues in the classification of children* (2 Vols.). San Francisco: Jossey-Bass.

Lambert, N. M. (1981). Psychological evidence in Larry P. versus Wilson Riles. *American Psychologist, 36,* 937–952.

Larry P. v. Riles, 343 F. Supp. 1306 N.D. Cal. 1972. (preliminary injunction), *affirmed,* 502 F. 2d 963 (9th Cir. 1974), opinion issued No. C-71-2270 RFP (N.D. Cal. October 16, 1979).

Lippman, W. (1922). The abuse of tests. *The New Republic,* November 15, 1922, 297–298.

PASE v. Hannon, 506 F. Supp. 831, N.D. Ill. (1980).

PART II

SPECIFIC ASSESSMENT STRATEGIES

EDITORS' COMMENTS

Psychological assessment has been described as the systematic use of a variety of special techniques to better understand a given individual, group, or social ecology. In chapter 1, we elaborated on this definition and suggested that psychological assessment should also assist us in the selection and evaluation of intervention strategies. With both of these objectives in mind, we reasoned that a multimethod approach that is empirically validated and developmentally sensitive ought to be used in order to obtain an accurate and comprehensive "picture" of the child or adolescent.

In part II, our contributors explore the empirical and developmental features of a wide variety of procedures including structured interviews, checklists and rating forms, self-report measures, self-monitoring, direct behavioral observation, sociometric ratings, physiological assessment, intellectual and achievement testing, neuropsychological assessment and, finally, projective assessment. Of course, neither we nor the contributors would argue that *each* of these procedures is necessary in any one instance. We are not suggesting a "test battery" approach; rather, we are proposing that specific strategies be drawn from this array of procedures. Of course, the exact procedures to be used will depend on the referral questions and the resources of the clinician and researcher.

In the chapters that follow, the principles underlying these specific and sometimes diverse procedures are explored, and illustrative test materials are presented. In selecting procedures for this section, we deliberately sought out those assessment strategies that are used frequently in clinical settings *and* that possessed some empirical support for their use with children and adolescents of varying ages. As the reader will quickly see, however, the level of empirical support and the appropriateness of these various strategies differ. Some are empirically valid and developmentally sensitive; others are less so. It has been our goal to present widely diverse but frequently used procedures and to examine their empirical and developmental status for children and adolescents.

CHAPTER 6

INTERVIEWING

Kay Hodges
Janice Zeman

Structured and semistructured interviews have become an integral part of clinical and research work with children and adolescents. In clinical practice, clinicians have increasingly looked to the child as an informant. In research protocols, there is increasing consensus that it is important to interview the child, and for the preadolescent child, also the parent. The impetus for these changes appears to derive in part to the development of psychometrically sounder methods for assessing children, which was in turn facilitated by the operationalization of diagnoses in the third edition of the *Diagnostic and Statistical Manual* (DSM-III) (American Psychiatric Association, 1980).

These developments have permitted researchers to accumulate knowledge about child psychopathology in a more systematic and efficient fashion. Within clinical settings, concern about legal vulnerability has led some clinicians to conduct interviews that are comprehensive. In this chapter, five of the most widely used structured and semistructured interviews are described, and relevant psychometric data are presented. For clinicians or researchers interested in less structured approaches, the literature on diagnostic play interviews provides guidelines for interviewing children (Greenspan, 1981; Lourie & Rieger, 1974; Simmons, 1974).

OVERVIEW OF INTERVIEWS

Several child interviews were developed simultaneously, following the lead of researchers in the adult literature. From 1975 to 1980, four interviews were independently developed, including the Diagnostic Interview for Children and Adolescents (DICA) (Herjanic, Herjanic, Brown, & Wheatt, 1975), the Schedule for Affective Disorders and Schizophrenia for School Aged Children (K-SADS) (Puig-Antich & Chambers, 1978), the Child Assessment Schedule (CAS) (Hodges & Fitch, 1979), and the Interview Schedule for Children (ISC) (Kovacs, 1983). The K-SADS was modeled after the adult interview developed by researchers at Columbia University, the Schedule for Affective Disorders and Schizophrenia (SADS) (Endicott & Spitzer, 1978). The DICA was modeled after the predecessors of the Diagnostic Interview Schedule (DIS) (Robins, Helzer, Croughan, & Ratcliff, 1981), developed by researchers at the Washington University School of Medicine. The CAS was modeled after a traditional child clinical interview, rather than an existing adult research interview. The ISC was developed by Kovacs and her colleagues (Kovacs, 1983) for their longitudinal study with depressed children. Thus, the K-SADS and the

ISC were originally developed to study depression in children, while the CAS and the DICA were designed for more general research purposes in child clinical settings.

In an effort to generate an interview for epidemiological research, the National Institute of Mental Health (NIMH) sponsored the development of a child interview to parallel the DIS. This effort yielded the Diagnostic Interview Schedule for Children (DISC), which was developed under an NIMH grant awarded to Costello and his colleagues (A. J. Costello, Edelbrock, Dulcan, Kalas, & Klaric, 1984). The psychometric results generated on the DIS were sufficiently disappointing to necessitate continued efforts to improve it. These efforts generated the DISC-2 (Shaffer et al., 1988), a precursor to the DISC-R (Shaffer, Fisher, Piacentini, Schwab-Stone, & Wicks, 1989).

These interviews are quite similar in their key features, yet each has unique characteristics. Each interview consists mostly of a series of questions the examiner asks the child. After listening to the child's responses to each inquiry, the examiner scores the relevant interview items. The response formats are either categorical (i.e., yes, no, sometimes), as is the case for the CAS, DICA, and the DISC, or ratings of degree or severity (e.g., 0 to 8), as employed for the ISC and the K-SADS. While the administration time varies considerably depending on the patient characteristics and the specific interview, interviewing a child seldom takes less than an hour and can be lengthier. All of the interviews have a parallel parent version that asks the parent about the child's symptomatology. All are reported as employable with youth aged 8 to 16, with some claiming to be appropriate for children as young as 6. However, examination of the interviews reveals that they obviously differ in appropriateness for use with preadolescent children. Also, not all of them have research data supporting the reliability of the interview when used with younger children.

Each of the interviews makes diagnostic determinations according to the revised version of DSM III (DSM III-R) (American Psychiatric Association, 1987). With the exception of the ISC, all of the interviews can be used to determine the major disorders of childhood, including conduct disorder, attention deficit-hyperactivity disorder, oppositional-defiant disorder, major depressive episode, dysthymia, separation anxiety, overanxious disorder, phobias, obsessive-compulsive disorder, encopresis, enuresis, and possible psychosis (i.e., screening questions). Some of the interviews (i.e., DICA, DISC, K-SADS) generate diagnostic information for disorders that are rare in the general population and in younger children (e.g., mania, eating disorders), but are more common in late adolescence and among adolescent psychiatric inpatients. The ISC has an addenda that can be used to inquire about these less common diagnoses, and a similar approach has been applied with the CAS. There is obviously a tradeoff, because the more inclusive the interview, the more difficult it is for younger children and the less applicable for the less disturbed.

While all of the interviews generate diagnoses, the CAS and the DISC have also been used to generate scale scores, reflecting the number of diagnostically keyed items that were endorsed for each diagnosis. Three of the interviews (i.e., CAS, ISC, K-SADS) are more typically used in a semistructured fashion. The CAS has many open-ended questions. The authors of the ISC and K-SADS specifically instruct users to modify the interview as needed. For all three of these interviews, the examiner is to score the intent of the child's responses, not the child's verbatim *yes* or *no* answers. Interviewers should be clinicians who are especially knowledgeable about diagnostic issues with children. Furthermore, the authors of the ISC and K-SADS state that the same person should interview both the parent and the child, with the parent being interviewed first. The diagnoses are based on both interviews as well as on any other available information. In fact, in Kovacs' application of the ISC, diagnoses were based on all available information and were verified by consensus among the team of research clinical interviewers (Kovacs et al., 1984). While this same procedure can be used for the other three interviews, this has been a decision left up to the researchers. In regard to generating diagnoses, the CAS, DICA, and DISC have computer algorithm scoring programs available.

With the exception of the CAS, the interviews are primarily organized around symptom clusters, corresponding to the diagnostic entities. In contrast, the CAS was designed to be similar to a traditional clinical interview (i.e., inquiry is organized around topics such as school, friends, hobbies, family, etc.). Only about half of the CAS items are diagnostically keyed, with the remainder reflecting adjustment concerns across various life spheres. The CAS generates scale scores for these thematic sections, called "content scales."

Which interview is best? These is no "best" interview. Rather, several factors should be considered in choosing an interview, including (a) the setting in which the work is to take place, (b) the question of interest to the researcher or clinician, and (c) the degree to which the psychometric data available on the measure is generalizable to the specific application. In regard to the latter, the question is whether reliability and validity have been demonstrated for the specific population and for the outcome variables being generated (i.e., diagnosis, scale scores).

OVERVIEW OF PSYCHOMETRIC ISSUES

When interviews are used for research purposes, they should meet the same standards of reliability and validity as other assessment measures. However, several conditions make the psychometric study of structured interviews more complicated than is typically the case in instrument development. Validation of a structured interview is the validation of the assessment itself, not the diagnostic nosology it utilizes (Spitzer, 1983). Unfortunately, the diagnostic criteria, as operationalized in DSM-III, are still in the preliminary stages of being validated. In actuality, the validation of the interview procedure and of the diagnostic criteria are confounded in most of the current work.

A second complication is that there is no "gold standard" by which to compare the measures for purposes of validation. Previously it was hoped that parental reports could serve as such a standard. However, poor concordance has been consistently demonstrated between child report and that of other informants, including parents, clinicians, and teachers, across a variety of instruments (Achenbach, McConaughy & Howell, 1987).

A third dilemma is that children are developmentally immature and, as a consequence, lower levels of reliability estimates can be anticipated, and perhaps, less valid self-reports as well (see Kovacs, 1986, for a review).

In the discussion that follows, the interviews are reviewed (in alphabetical order), with an emphasis on data relevant to reliability and validity. These interviews are almost always used to comment on type of disorder or symptoms, not just on the presence or absence of any disorder. Thus, the data are reviewed from that perspective. Emphasis will be placed on data specific to each of four major diagnostic categories, including attention deficit disorder (ADD), conduct disorder, depression (i.e., major depressive episode or dysthymia), and anxiety disorders (i.e., overanxious or separation-anxiety disorder). Since all the studies cited here were begun before the revised DSM-III was finalized, the diagnoses referred to are DSM-III. Additionally, the review is restricted to studies that (a) generate data on the child version of the interviews, (b) primarily address psychometric issues, and (c) for reliability studies, those interrater studies that also include a test-retest component. Data on interviews administered to the child instead of the parent are not comparable. For example, much higher test-retest reliabilities have been generated for interviews administered to parents than to children (see Edelbrock, Costello, Dulcan, Kalas, & Conover, 1985). Following a precedent set by Edelbrock and Costello (1988), concordance between parent and child will be conceptualized as interinformant reliability.

The statistic typically used in determining diagnostic concordance is the kappa statistic (κ) (Bartko & Carpenter, 1976). There is no clear consensus on the interpretation of kappa. In this review, the guidelines proposed by Landis and Koch (1977), and utilized by Shaffer et al. (1988) will be used (i.e., excellent reliability indicated by κ greater than .75; good by κ between .59 and .75; fair by κ between .40 and .58; and poor by κ less than .40). Because kappa is sensitive to base rates of the disorder, caution should be exercised in comparing values across studies (Robins, 1985). Agreement for continuous scores (i.e., scales) is quantified by the Pearson r correlation of Intraclass Correlation Coefficient (ICC) (Bartko & Carpenter, 1976). Effect size of correlational data follows guidelines provided by Cohen (1988) (i.e., small, .10; medium, .30; and high, .50 or greater). For test-retest data, a correlation of .70 or above is considered good.

Caution should be exercised in directly comparing findings across studies because of the varying conditions under which studies are conducted. For example, Cohen, O'Connor, Lewis, Velez, and Malachowski (1987) discuss various factors that probably affect the degree of diagnostic agreement. Following their example, Table 6-1 presents our view of factors that appear to influence diagnostic agreement, including design of the study, subject characteristics, interviewers' familiarity with each other, characteristics of the information sources, and characteristics of the diagnostic process. These conditions are commented on in the tables that summarize study findings. For each interview, data are presented separately for diagnostic concordance (i.e., agreement on presence or absence of diagnosis) and for agreement on symptom scores composed of diagnostic items. For the sake

Table 6-1. Factors Influencing Diagnostic Agreement

FACTORS	HYPOTHESIZED HIGHER AGREEMENT	HYPOTHESIZED LOWER AGREEMENT
Design factors		
Interview interval	1 to 2 days	2 to 3 weeks or longer
Independence of interviewers	Same interview for subject, or interviewers have knowledge of each other's interview	Interviewers blind to each other's interview
Subject characteristics		
Type of sample	Referred to specialized clinic	Heterogeneous population
Age of child	Early school-aged	Adolescents
Interviewer characteristics		
Interviewers' familiarity with each other	Clinicians share the same framework, work together	Clinicians not trained together nor worked together
Training level of interviewer[a]	Mental health clinician	Lay interviewer
Characteristics of information source		
Area of life information sampled from	Same	Different sampling
Informant	Same	Different
Characteristics of diagnostic process		
Symptom type	Observable, concrete	Less observable, less specific
Diagnostic specificity	Not specific to diagnosis, large groupings of diagnostic categories	Specific to diagnoses and subtypes of diagnoses
Strictness to which diagnostic criteria are applied	Allow leeway (e.g., duration or presence of a symptom)	Strict application of diagnostic criteria
Number of diagnoses permitted[b]	Primary diagnoses given	No limit of diagnoses and no hierarchial exclusions
Diagnostic method[b] (assuming structured interview given)	Clinician involvement (esp. if trained together)	Computer generated
Impairment criteria or "caseness" determined by clinician	Clinician involved in determining impairment	Presence or absence of diagnosis used as only criteria

[a] Data not consistently supportive of conclusion
[b] The conditions that lead to high or low agreement for these factors appear less clear than for the other factors. Other variables appear to be relevant.

of brevity, reliability findings are summarized in Tables 6-2 and 6-3 for diagnoses and in Tables 6-4 and 6-5 for symptom scales. For both diagnoses and scales, studies that assess test-retest and interrater reliability (see Tables 6-2 and 6-4) and those that determine parent-child interinformant reliability (Tables 6-3 and 6-5) are summarized.

CAS

The development of the CAS has evolved through three versions. The original CAS, dated 1978, is the least structured and is useful for younger children (i.e., 5 to 7 years old). While the CAS was originally designed to be used primarily with children aged 7 to 12 years old, the most recent version, dated 1986, has been successfully used with adolescents (e.g., Kashani, Orvaschel, Rosenberg, & Reid, 1989).

The CAS is theoretically organized around 11 topic areas: school, friends, activities and hobbies, family, fears, worries and anxieties, self-image, mood (especially sadness), somatic concerns, physical complaints, expression of anger, and reality testing symptomatology. Diagnostically related items are embedded within these content areas. The relationship between the content scales and the diagnostic items are outlined in Hodges and Saunders (1989).

The CAS has three sections to the interview: content area questions, onset and duration questions, and interviewer observational judgments. Quantitative scale scores are generated for the total interview, for the diagnostically related symptom scales, and for the

Table 6–2. Reliability of Diagnostic Concordance for Child Interviews: Test-Retest and Interrater Studies

INTERVIEW AND REFERENCE	SAMPLE[a]			KAPPAS FOR DIAGNOSES[b]				SPECIAL CONDITIONS DX PROCEDURE & RETEST INTERVALS
	N	TYPE	AGE	CONDUCT DISORDER	DEPRESSION	ANXIETY	ADD	
CAS Hodges, Cools, & McKnew (1989)	32	Inpt	6–12 $M=9$	.71	.83	.72	.43	Computer $M=9$ days
DICA Welner et al. (1987)	27	Inpt	7–17 $M=12$	1.00	.90	.76	1.00	Clinical 1–7 Days
DISC—Mild/Moderate Criteria Costello et al. (1984)	242	Psych ref	6–18	.44	DE .44 DY .47	OV .28 SA .39	.21	Computer $M=12$ Days
DISC—Severe Criteria Costello et al. (1984)	242	Psych ref	6–18	.47	DE .36	OV .34 SA .38	.21	Computer $M=12$ Days
DISC-2 Shaffer et al. (1988)	74	Psych pts	11–17 $M=13$	.55	DE .63	SA .72	.48	Computer 1–3 Weeks
ISC Last (1987)	65	Anx dx	5–18	.86	DE .84 DY .66	.84	.86	Clinical Approx. 2 Hrs.

[a] Inpt = psychiatric inpatients; Psych ref = Psychiatric referrals; Off = offspring; Al = alcoholics; Dep = depressed; Anx = anxiety disordered; Ped = pediatric; Fam = families

[b] For depression, includes major depression (DE), and dysthymia (DY), and for anxiety, include overanxious disorder (OV) and separation anxiety (SA). Subtype data are presented when data for both combined are not provided. GAD = generalized anxiety disorder; ADD = attention deficit disorder. Data for ADD with hyperactivity are given if available (to approximate DSM-III-R).

Table 6-3. Reliability of Diagnostic Concordance for Child Interviews: Interinformant (parent/child) Studies

INTERVIEW AND REFERENCE	SAMPLE[a]		AGE	KAPPAS FOR DIAGNOSES[b]				CONDITIONS
	N	TYPE		CONDUCT DISORDER	DEPRESSION	ANXIETY	ADD	DX PROCEDURE & CONCORDANCE CRITERIA
DICA Reich et al. (1982)	307	Psych ref & ped pts	6-16	.37	.36	—	—	Computer
Welner et al. (1987)	(See Table 6-2)			.80	.63	—	.66	Clinical; Ignored Duration; ±1 Symptom
Earls, Reich et al. (1988)	55 fam	Off al & controls	6-17 $M=12$	.50	.17	.11	.41	Computer
Sylvester et al. (1988)	53 fam	Off dep, off anx & controls	7-17	.17 (CD or OP)	DE .11	.17	.42	Internal Scoring System
DISC—Mild/ Moderate Criteria Costello et al. (1984)	(See Table 6-2)		6-18	.32	DE .14 DY .16	OV .02 SA .15	.03	Computer
DISC—Severe Criteria Costello et al. (1984)	(See Table 6-2)		6-18	.28	DE .08 DY .05	OV .04 SA .07	.04	Computer
DISC-2 Shaffer et al. (1988)	(See Table 6-2)		11-17 $M=13$	.31	<.40	.15	-.10	Computer

[a] Inpt = psychiatric inpatients; Psych ref = Psychiatric referrals; Off = offspring; Al = alcoholics; Dep = depressed; Anx = anxiety disordered; Ped = pediatric; Fam = families
[b] For depression, includes major depression (DE), and dysthymia (DY), and for anxiety, include overanxious disorder (OV) and separation anxiety (SA). Subtype data are presented when data for both combined are not provided. GAD = generalized anxiety disorder; ADD = attention deficit disorder. Data for ADD with hyperactivity are given if available (to approximate DSM-III-R).

Table 6–4. Reliability of Symptom Scores for Child Interviews: Test-Retest and Interrater Studies

INTERVIEW AND REFERENCE	SAMPLE[a]			CORRELATIONS FOR SCALES[b]					SPECIAL CONDITIONS
	N	TYPE	AGE	TOTAL SCORE	CONDUCT DISORDER SCALE	DEPRESSION SCALE	ANXIETY SCALE	ADD SCALE	DX PROCEDURE & RETEST INTERVALS
CAS Hodges, Cools, & McKnew (1989)	32	Inpt	6–12 M = 9	.89	.75	DE .89 DY .86	OV .80 SA .66	.89	Computer M = 9 days
DISC Edelbrock et al. (1985)	70	Psych ref	6–8	.39	.58	.30	.49	.61	Computer M = 12 days
	87	Psych ref	9–13	.55	.73	.53	.54	.66	M = 12 days
	85	Psych ref	14–18	.81	.77	.81	.77	.73	Computer M = 12 days
K-SADS Apter et al. (1989)	70	Inpt	11–18 M = 16	—	ICC = .96	ICC = .72	—	—	Clinical; used other info; only 1 dx given; 1 week interval

Note: All values in chart are Pearson correlations (r) except for intraclass correlations (ICC), which are so indicated.
[a]Inpt = psychiatric inpatients; Psych ref = Psychiatric referrals; Off = offspring; Al = alcoholics; Dep = depressed; Anx = anxiety disordered; Ped = pediatric; Fam = families
[b]For depression, includes major depression (DE), and dysthymia (DY), and for anxiety, include overanxious disorder (OV) and separation anxiety (SA). Subtype data are presented when data for both combined are not provided. GAD = generalized anxiety disorder; ADD = attention deficit disorder. Data for ADD with hyperactivity are given if available (to approximate DSM-III-R).

Table 6-5. Reliability of Symptom Scores for Child Interview: Interinformant (parent/child) Studies

INTERVIEW AND REFERENCE	SAMPLE[a]			CORRELATIONS FOR SCALES[b]					SPECIAL CONDITIONS
	N	TYPE	AGE	TOTAL SCORE	CONDUCT DISORDER	DEPRESSION	ANXIETY	ADD	DX PROCEDURE
CAS Hodges, Gordon et al. (in press)	48	Inpt	6-12 M = 10	.41	.63	DE .46 DY .47	OV .12 SA .26	.47	Computer
DICA Earls, Smith et al. (1988)	55 fam	Off al & controls	6-17 M = 12	.38	—	—	.18	—	Internal Scoring System
DISC Edelbrock et al. (1986)	70	Psych ref	6-8	.09	.26	−.08	.10	.10	Computer
	87	Psych ref	9-13	.10	.53	.30	.13	.34	Computer
	85	Psych ref	14-18	.29	.51	.32	.36	.20	Computer
K-SADS Apter et al. (1989)	(See Table 6-4)		11-18 M = 16	ICC = .75	ICC = .62	ICC = .35 (GAD)	—	—	Clinical; used other info; only 1 dx given

Note: All values in chart are Pearson correlations (r) except for intraclass correlations (ICC), which are so indicated.
[a] Inpt = psychiatric inpatients; Psych ref = Psychiatric referrals; Off = offspring; Al = alcoholics; Dep = depressed; Anx = anxiety disordered; Ped = pediatric; Fam = families
[b] For depression, includes major depression (DE) and dysthymia (DY), and for anxiety, include overanxious disorder (OV) and separation anxiety (SA). Subtype data are presented when data for both combined are not provided. GAD = generalized anxiety disorder; ADD = attention deficit disorder. Data for ADD with hyperactivity are given if available (to approximate DSM-III-R).

11 content areas just listed. Detailed scoring guidelines to aid in establishing interrated reliability are available (Hodges, 1983).

Diagnoses

A reliability study with preadolescent children by Hodges, Cools, and McKnew (1989) yielded kappa values in the excellent range for "any depression" disorder and in the good range for conduct disorder and "any anxiety" disorder (see Table 6-2). ADD was characterized by a fair kappa value. Diagnoses were computer generated and based only on child report. Additionally, internal consistency data for a psychiatric sample generated satisfactory alpha values for conduct disorder, depression, anxiety, and ADD, with all being .80 or above (Hodges, Saunders, Kashani, Hamlett, & Thompson, in press). An inter-interview diagnostic concordance study comparing the CAS and the K-SADS found good concordance for conduct disorder ($\kappa = .63$) and depression ($\kappa = .61$) and fair for anxiety ($\kappa = .54$). Poor concordance was observed for ADD ($\kappa = .39$) (Hodges, McKnew, Burbach, & Roebuck, 1987), unless information from a school questionnaire was included.

A study by Hodges (1990) with preadolescent psychiatric patients yielded data relevant to both convergent and discriminant validity. Depressed children, as diagnosed by the CAS, scored higher than the nondepressed on the Children's Depression Inventory (CDI) (Kovacs, 1983). As expected, there was no difference observed for the conduct versus nonconduct disordered and the anxiety versus the nonanxiety disordered children. Also, the anxiety disordered children scored higher than the nonanxiety children on the Trait scale of the State-Trait Anxiety Inventory for Children (STAIC) (Spielberger, 1973). As hypothesized, no difference was found between the conduct and nonconduct disordered and the depressed and the nondepressed groups on this measure.

Symptom Scores

The test-retest study by Hodges, Cools, and McKnew (1989) also evaluated the reliability of the symptom scores. The correlations were significant and satisfactory for total score, conduct disorder, depression, anxiety, and ADD (see Table 6-4). T-tests on symptoms at time 1 and time 2 revealed no significant differences on any symptom scales.

Hodges, Gordon, and Lennon (1990) conducted a parent-child, interinformant reliability study on the same sample of subjects. Significant correlations between child and parent scores were observed for the total score, conduct disorder, depression (both major depressive episode and dysthymia), and attention deficit disorder. All of these correlations were of medium or large effect size (see Table 6-5). However, nonsignificant correlations were observed for the anxiety symptom scales.

Evidence of contrast group validity is offered by a study in which psychiatric inpatients, outpatients, and normal controls were compared (Hodges, Kline, Stern et al., 1982). Inpatients scored significantly higher than controls on the total score for the interview, conduct disorder, depression, and ADD. For anxiety, inpatients scored higher than both outpatients and controls. Sixty-six percent of the sample was correctly classified as either inpatient, outpatient or control.

The CAS child interview has been compared to other measures assessing parent or clinician view of the child's symptomatology. Hodges et al. (1982) found significant correlations, between the corresponding scales on the CAS and the Child Behavior Checklist (CBCL) (Achenbach & Edelbrock, 1983), including total score ($r = .57$), conduct disorder ($r = .50$), and depression ($r = .51$). In an epidemiological study conducted in Holland by Verhulst, Althaus, and Berden (1987), the total score on the CAS was found to correlate significantly ($r = .58$) with the total score on the Rutter-Graham parent interview (Richman, Stevenson, & Graham, 1982). In the same study, the correspondence between the child's score on the CAS and global psychiatric rating was also high ($r = .64$).

The CAS symptom scales also have been compared to the child's report on questionnaires. The STAIC correlated significantly with the CAS anxiety symptom scale ($r = .54$) as did the CDI with the CAS depression symptom scale ($r = .53$).

Content Scales

The reliability of the 11 content areas has been reported in the same studies that assessed reliability of the symptom scales (Hodges & Cools, 1990; Hodges, Gordon, & Lennon, 1990). Evidence of contrast group validity for the symptom scales was also provided in the previously mentioned study by Hodges, Kline, Stern, Cytryn, & McKnew (1982). Evidence of contrast group validity was provided by a discriminant analysis conducted in the Dutch epidemiological study (Verhulst et al., 1987). Seventy-six percent of the children were correctly classified by the CAS symptom scales. The morbidity criterion was determined as disturbed versus nondisturbed, made by a psychiatrist who used the Graham-Rutter interview with the parents as the source of information. Three content scales (i.e., friends, family, and worries) were found to reduce lambda significantly.

Remarks

There has been a systematic attempt to study the psychometric properties of the CAS, with an emphasis on child report by preadolescent children. These studies suggest that for conduct disorder and depression, there is evidence of reliability and validity for diagnostic determinations as well as symptom scale scores. The validity data includes contrast group validity and concordance with another interview, with parental report, and with child's self-report on questionnaires. For ADD, the symptom scale score appears to be reliable, but not so for diagnosis. The data for anxiety disorders is more uneven, although the symptom score for all anxiety symptoms was found to be reliable. Additionally, the psychometric data on the total score for the interview and for the content area scales appear favorable. Both have been used to assess symptom change and to discriminate disturbed from nondisturbed children. The CAS appears to be particularly useful for studying target populations that are younger (preadolescents and early adolescents) and that vary from healthy to disturbed. The total symptom score and the CAS content scales have also been used to assess change in symptomatology (Runyon et al., 1988; Bousha, 1985).

DICA

Earlier research on the DICA was conducted with the first version of the DICA dated 1969 (Welner, Reich, Herjanic, Jung, & Amado, 1987). The diagnoses were based on the International Classification of Psychiatric Disorders as well as the Feighner et al. (1972) criteria. A revised version of the DICA was developed in 1981 and included the DSM-III diagnoses. Recently, the DICA was further revised to incorporate DSM-III-R criteria (i.e., DICA-R). The DICA-R has three versions: children aged 6–12, adolescents aged 13–17, and parents. However, no psychometric data are available on this version (Reich & Welner, 1988).

Diagnoses

In a test-retest, interrater reliability study, Welner et al. (1987) reported excellent kappa values for conduct disorder, ADD, "any depression" disorder, and "any anxiety" disorder (see Table 6-2). However, it is not clear to what extent clinical judgment was involved. The authors note that the coding of all the lay interviewers was carefully checked by two psychiatrists, and diagnoses were made using the coding guide prepared in the interview according to DSM-III criteria (Welner et al., 1987).

Interinformant reliability for the presence or absence of diagnosis has been generated by four studies. In Welner et al. (1987), data on parent-child concordance were also generated. However, concordance was not based on strict adherence of DSM-III. Only the symptoms were attended to, with duration information ignored. In addition, the diagnoses were considered concordant if they were off by one symptom. The values obtained were excellent for conduct disorder and in the good range for depression and ADD (Table 6-3). No data relevant to anxiety were reported. These results were considered to be an improvement over previous parent-child concordance findings in which the kappa values for conduct disorder and depression were both in the poor range (Reich, Herjanic, Welner, & Gandhy, 1982). Two other studies that have calculated parent-child concordance have found very poor concordance for "any depression" and "any anxiety" diagnoses (Earls, Reich, Jung, & Cloninger, 1988; Sylvester, Hyde, & Reichler, 1987). Also, in the Sylvester et al. (1987) study, poor concordance for behavioral disorders, which included conduct disorder and oppositional disorder, was also observed (Table 6-3).

In regard to validity, there are three relevant studies. In Kashani and Orvaschel (1988), anxious adolescents reported more anxiety and hostility on a self-report measure than did nonanxious adolescents. However, the diagnosis of anxiety was based not only on the presence of DSM-III diagnosis, as reported by the adolescents, but also on determination of "caseness" by a reviewing psychiatrist who used the parent version of the DICA to assess degree of dysfunction and the need for treatment. Agreement between DICA diagnoses and chart diagnosis was determined by Welner et al. (1987). The kappas were in the fair range (.43–.52) except for anxiety disorder, which was poor ($\kappa = .03$). In Sylvester et al. (1987), diagnostic concordance between the DICA diagnosis and the Personality Inventory for Children (PIC) (Lacher & Gdowski, 1979) was determined, using a t-score of 65 or greater on the corresponding scale as a cutoff score for the PIC. All the kappas were in the range of poor reliability ($\kappa = .11–.30$).

Symptom Scores

In Earls, Smith, Reich, and Jung (1988), interinformant reliability between parent and child was computed for two symptom scores. The correlation between the total scores for the parent and child was moderate ($r = .38$; $p < .03$); however, the correlation for anxiety items was nonsignificant ($r = .18$).

Remarks

At the level of broad diagnostic categories (i.e., "any anxiety"), test-retest reliability for the four major categories has been demonstrated. However, this has been restricted to the research team in St. Louis. There is evidence across studies of parent-child concordance for conduct disorder and attention deficit disorder. There is evidence of validity by way of agreement with chart diagnosis, except for anxiety disorder. There is no evidence to support reliability or validity of symptom scores.

DISC

Diagnoses

As can be seen from Table 6-2, the test-retest reliability generated from the original study on the DISC (Costello et al., 1984) was fair for conduct disorder and depression and poor for anxiety and ADD. Altering the computer algorithm to reduce the number of diagnoses (referred to as *severe criteria*) worsened matters, with only conduct disorder being reliable. Because much of the subsequent work with the DISC used these two algorithms, an explanation about how they were generated is in order. The original computer algorithm for DSM-III appeared to result in an unduly high proportion of children meeting criteria, and subsequently was labeled *mild/moderate criteria*. To make a more restrictive set of criteria, which was termed *severe criteria*, the following solution was generated: DSM-III criteria were met as defined by the computer algorithm, and the total number of symptoms included in the criteria for the disorder exceeded an arbitrary cutoff point, chosen so that the number diagnosed by this method then approximated the number diagnosed by the clinicians in the study (Costello et al., 1984).

Diagnostic agreement between parent and child interviews was also generated by Costello et al. (1984). As can be seen from Table 3, all the kappa values were in the poor range for both criteria.

Contrast group validity was examined in a study by Costello, Edelbrock, and Costello (1985), who matched 40 children making routine pediatric visits to 40 children (aged 7 to 11) in the original Costello et al. (1984) sample of psychiatric referrals. Sensitivity (i.e., percentage of ill cases correctly identified) and specificity (i.e., percentage of well cases correctly identified) was determined. For the moderate criteria, sensitivity was 95% and specificity was 25%; for the severe criteria, the sensitivity was 45% and the specificity was 80%. Thus, for the computer-generated diagnoses based on DSM-III, three fourths of the pediatric patients received diagnoses, whereas when more stringent criteria were used, less than half of the psychiatric children were identified as ill.

Costello and her colleagues (Costello, Edelbrock, Costello, Dulcan, & Brent, 1986) conducted a large two-stage study in which 300 children enrolled in an HMO, aged 7 to 11, were interviewed. Agreement of presence of any diagnosis between DISC computer-generated diagnoses and clinician-determined diagnoses was poor ($\kappa = .23$), as was the case for the same comparison to diagnoses made by the child's pediatrician ($\kappa = .04$ for emotional diagnoses and ($\kappa = .13$ for behavioral diagnoses).

A recent study by Weinstein, Stone, Noam, Grimes, & Schwab-Stone (1989) with a sample of adolescent psychiatric inpatients determined diagnostic concordance between computer-generated DISC diagnoses and clinician diagnoses on admission. They found poor concordance across all four diagnostic categories, with κ ranging from .03 to .09.

Reliability findings are also available for the DISC-2, a revised version of the DISC, which has been field tested with a primarily adolescent sample (Shaffer et al., 1988). Test-retest reliability yielded kappa values in the fair range or better, although neither dysthymia nor overanxious disorder was studied (see Table 6-2). Interinformant reliability between the child and parent versions were poor across all diagnoses (see Table 6-3).

Diagnostic concordance was also assessed between DISC-2 computer-generated diagnoses and two variations of clinician-determined diagnoses made after administering an alternate semistructured interview (i.e., one diagnosis was strictly guided by DSM-III criteria and the other was not). Diagnostic concordance with the DSM-III-guided clinician diagnosis was poor for all diagnoses except ADD ($k = .48$). For the comparison to the other clinician-determined diagnosis, concordance was poor except for depression ($\kappa = .57$).

Symptom Scores

Edelbrock et al. (1985) reported on test-retest reliability for symptom scores for the sample studied in Costello et al. (1984). In Table 43 in Edelbrock et al. (1985), correlations are provided for each group studied (i.e., 6–9, 10–13, and 14–18). Satisfactory correlations were observed for all the diagnostic categories for the oldest group of children (14 to 18 years old) and for conduct disorder for the 10- to-13-year-old group.

Parent-child agreement for the Costello et al. (1984) sample is present in Table 53 (Edelbrock, Costello, Dulcan, Conover, & Kala, 1986). For the youngest children (6–8 years), nonsignificant results were observed for all diagnoses. For the 9- to-13-year-old group, a large effect was found for conduct disorder and medium effects for ADD and depression. For the oldest group (14–18 years old), a large effect was observed for conduct disorder, and medium effects for depression and "any anxiety" disorder. The correlations were nonsignificant for the total symptom score, until the age of 14 years. Additionally, the parent-child agreement was very poor ($r = .17$ for total sample) for the symptoms relevant to diagnoses of anxiety, depression, and phobias, whereas the agreement was large ($r = .51$ for the total sample) for behavioral conduct symptoms.

Contrast group validity is presented in the study cited above by Costello, Edelbrock & Costello (1985). The psychiatric-referred patients reported significantly more symptoms than their pediatric controls for all four diagnostic groups and for the total symptom score. However, parent-child concordance, assessed by the correlation between the total symptom score on the DISC and the total CBCL behavior problem score, was less favorable ($r = .14$ for the psychiatric group and $r = .29$ for pediatric group).

Remarks

The DISC is a highly structured interview that was designed to be used by lay interviewers in epidemiological studies. Thus far, the efforts to develop such an instrument have been disappointing. The reliability data suggest that it could be appropriate for use with adolescents, or with older children, primarily to assess conduct disorders. There is no evidence of validity for diagnostic utility, as assessed by correspondence to clinician or pediatrician judgments, or by ability to discriminate disturbed from nondisturbed children. DISC symptom scores are useful in differentiating disturbed and nonreferred samples. The available test-retest reliability on the revised DISC represents an improvement. However, it may not be superior if the comparison were restricted to the adolescents in the original DISC sample. Also, testing of children younger than 11 has not been undertaken with the revised DISC, and thus, at this time it is recommended only for adolescents (P. Fisher, personal communication, October, 1989).

ISC

The format of the ISC is briefly described, because it differs from the format of the other interviews. There are core symptoms that assess depression in depth, questions evaluating mental status, two items about dating and sexual behaviors, behavioral observations related to displays of psychopathology, and the interviewer's impressions of the child. There are also provisions made for the interviewer to note duration of symptoms. Most of the coding consists of severity ratings. Addenda are available to assess additional diagnoses; however, psychometric data on the addenda have not been reported.

Data by Individual Symptom

In Kovacs (1983), parent-child agreement was assessed, with a sample of 75 who were participants in a longitudinal study of depression. Pearson r's were generated for each symptom. The mean correlation for the content areas ranged from .32 to .79. Less agreement was noted for items which reflect more internalized, subjective phenomenon.

Diagnoses Based on Both Child and Parent Interviews

Test-retest reliability was assessed by Last and her colleagues (Last, 1987; Last, Hersen, Kazdin, Finkelstein, & Strauss, 1987) for a sample of 65 outpatients referred to an anxiety disorders clinic. The test-retest interval was notably short; the two interviews were accomplished on the same day (i.e., morning and afternoon). The kappa values were in the excellent range, except for dysthymia, which was fair. They were as follows: ADD, .86; conduct disorder, .86; "any anxiety" disorder, .84, major depression, .84, and dysthymia, .66 (Last, 1987). These data are not directly comparable to previously reported data because the diagnoses were not generated by child interview only. Furthermore, as pointed out by Last (1987), these results may not be generalizable to other applications given that a number of factors may have enhanced agreement. These factors include (a) a very short test-retest interval; (b) potential interviewer bias given that the interviewers knew that the subjects were recruited for an anxiety disorders study; (c) use of the same two interviewers who were professionally familiar with each other; and (d) generation of diagnoses based on clinical impression.

Remarks

There is limited psychometric data on the ISC. In part, this is probably because the instrument was developed to be used by a group of experienced clinicians to assess presence and change in depressive symptoms in children and adolescents. The only reported reliability data that reflect on specific diagnoses is that proved by Last (1987), which may likely not be generalizable.

There is no formal validity data. However, the ISC has proven to be a valuable research interview in the projects conducted at the Western Psychiatric Institute and Clinics; one by Kovacs and colleagues on depression and another by Last and colleagues on anxiety in youth. Inasmuch as these projects are generating valuable data, it reflects very well on the ISC. However, the results of these studies do not contribute formally to the psychometric data base on the ISC, because they are exploring previously uninvestigated areas. Thus, the findings cannot serve as a "gold standard." Kovacs (1985) points out that the ISC may be most valuable to researchers who need the flexibility offered by the semistructured approach and who desire to use individual symptom ratings to determine diagnoses for the purpose of selecting cases.

K-SADS

There are two versions of the K-SADS: the epidemiological version (K-SADS-E), which was designed to record past and current episodes of disorder, and the present episode version (K-SADS-P), which inquires about current disorders. After a brief, unstructured discussion to establish rapport, the inquiries are organized around major diagnostic categories. In the E version, for each question, the examiner indicates whether the symptom is present currently and whether it was present in the past. Thus, in essence it involves asking and rating each question twice. For the P version, most items are also asked about and rated twice; the first rating records the symptom severity at its worst during the present episode of the illness (or the previous 12 months, whichever is shorter), and the second records the information for the last week. Thus, when the K-SADS is used to assess change, only the last week rating is used. The developers recommend that both the epidemiological and present episode versions be given in assessing clinical samples because the epidemiological version does not assess levels of symptom severity. The K-SADS has been revised numerous times, with the most recent version (i.e., K-SADS-IIIR) (Ambrosini, 1986) being the fourth revision.

In using the P version of the K-SADS, the examiner makes four ratings for each item: child's report for worst time and last week; mother's report for both time periods, and then a "summary" rating for each time period. Summary ratings are based on all available sources of information about the child, not just the interviews (Ambrosini, 1986).

Diagnosis Based on Both Child and Parent Interviews

Test-retest reliability was determined for diagnoses and for symptom scales in a study by Chambers et al. (1985) of 52 children aged 6 to 17. Because the examiner interviewed both the child and parent and made diagnoses based on all available information, these findings are not comparable to the other studies cited. The kappa values were in the good range for nonmajor depressive disorders ($\kappa = .70$) and for conduct disorder ($\kappa = .63$); fair for major depressive episode ($\kappa = .54$); and poor for anxiety disorder ($\kappa = .24$).

Diagnostic concordance has been studied by Carlson, Kashani, Thomas, Vaidya, and Daniel (1987), by Cohen, O'Connor, Lewis, Velez, and Malachowski (1987), and Hodges et al. (1987), as reported previously. In Carlson et al. (1987), the K-SADS conducted on admission to an inpatient unit was compared to a best estimate diagnosis based on chart review at discharge. For the K-SADS, an experienced child psychiatrist generated diagnoses based on an integration of all available information and after having interviewed both the child and the parent. The kappas were in the (a) poor range for overanxious disorder (κ = .35); (b) fair range for separation anxiety (κ = .44), "any depression disorder" (κ = .58), and for ADD (κ = .56), and (c) good range for conduct disorder (κ = .69). Both the K-SADS rater and the clinician who conducted the chart review may have been highly influenced by the admission and referral records, to which both had access. In Cohen et al. (1987), all kappa values for diagnostic agreement between the K-SADS and the DISC (including both mild and severe diagnostic criteria) were poor (κ < .40).

Symptom Scores

Ambrosini, Metz, Prabucki, & Lee (1989) determined internal consistency for the K-SADS-IIIR over six scoring time frames (i.e., two time periods for child, mother, and summary ratings). For ADD, anxiety disorders, and major depressive episode, good values were obtained (i.e., all .75 or greater). In the Chambers et al. (1985) study, test-retest correlations were determined for scales of symptoms recommended for the adult SADS. Only two of the scales correspond to the major diagnostic categories reviewed in this chapter: depressed mood (ranging from 2 to 17 items) and conduct disorder (composed of 18 items). Good test-retest reliability was observed for depression (r ranging from .67 to .81) and for conduct disorder (r = .74). Test-retest reliability for the anxiety scale, which was formed from a composite of summary ratings for various anxiety diagnoses, was poor (r = .41). Internal consistency was good for depression (alpha ranging from .68 to .84) and for conduct disorder (alpha = .86) but poor for anxiety (alpha = .39).

Interinformant, parent-child reliability of the K-SADS-E was the focus of a study by Angold et al. (1987). The same examiner interviewed the child and the parent. Data was presented only for the depressive symptoms. The authors note striking levels of disagreement, despite the fact that the interviewer of the child was not blind to the parents' responses. Of 21 symptoms, only 4 had kappa values above .40, and they were all in the fair range.

In a study by Apter, Orvaschel, Laseg, Moses, and Tyano (1989) with an Israeli adolescent inpatient population, diagnostic agreement on symptom scales was determined for test-retest and interinformant (i.e., mother-child) reliability. Correlations were good for the two scales relevant to this review; for depressed mood and thoughts, ICC = .72 and for conduct disorder ICC = .96. Mother-child agreement was also good for these two scales: ICC = .62 for depression and ICC = .75 for conduct disorder. It is noteworthy that the mother-child agreement for generalized anxiety disorder was poor (ICC = .35), as has typically been the case for anxiety diagnoses. Apparently all interviewers reviewed material from the referral source and emergency room prior to conducting the interviews. If this were the case, they may have been similarly influenced by this information.

Remarks

Very few data are available about the psychometric qualities of children's report on the K-SADS. With the exception of the Apter et al. (1989) study, the mother and child were interviewed by the same person; the interview of the child took place with foreknowledge of parental report; the interviewer had access to other information on the child (e.g., referral information, chart data) before the interview; and diagnoses were made based on the clinician's judgment, using all sources of information. All of these conditions, while laudable from a clinical perspective, preclude learning about the psychometric properties of the child's report and also leave open the possibility of shared interviewer bias, based on the perspective of the child given in the information from other sources. This is particularly worrisome given evidence of poor concordance between parent and child observed by Angold et al. (1987) for depressive symptoms.

In any case, the reliability data for the K-SADS, as it is typically administered, indicates that depression and conduct disorder data are satisfactory, for both diagnosis and the symptom scales. However, the comparable data for anxiety have been unacceptably low (Chambers et al., 1985; Apter et al., 1989).

There is a paucity of formal validity studies with the K-SADS. However, as with the ISC, the K-SADS has been used productively to study childhood and adolescent depression. As with the ISC, this is problematic from the perspective that the instrument is being used to study an area about which very little is known. This is especially the case when the findings are negative as has been observed for some of the biologically oriented studies on childhood depression (e.g., sleep pattern, cortisol secretion, and responsivity to antidepressant medication) (see Puig-Antich [1986] and Rutter [1988] for reviews).

SUMMARY

Semistructured and structured interviews have proven to be very useful in both research and clinical applications. They certainly represent a major improvement over clinician judgment (i.e., without the benefit of an interview format), because of the reduction in information variance. Overall, use of these interviews does not appear to decrease diagnostic validity. Moreover, across studies there appears to be increased comparability of diagnostic classifications.

As for the individual interviews, each is in need of further psychometric improvement. The existing data suggest that they differ in the degree to which they are applicable across different ages, symptom/diagnosis type, and sample type (i.e., subject characteristics). In particular, more research is needed on the child's ability to self-report, uncontaminated by parental report, as has also been emphasized by others (Angold et al., 1987; Rutter, 1988). After further study, perhaps the interviews can be modified to be even more appropriate to the developmental limitations of children. Additionally, there are remaining questions about whether reliability and validity is systematically influenced by the degree of structure in the interview format and by the level of professional training of the interviewer. Each of these questions is legitimately related to the procedural validity (Spitzer, 1983) of the interviews.

The results of the studies reviewed in this chapter raise additional questions related to broader issues in child psychopathology. While a detailed discussion of them is beyond the scope of this chapter (see Hodges & Cools, 1990), it is apparent that the most critical issues are related to diagnostic or criterion validity. They include (a) the adequacy of the diagnostic criteria for the major diagnoses as well as subtypes, especially for the anxiety disorders, (b) the need for specific impairment criteria for each diagnosis, in addition to the diagnostic criteria that are currently in DSM-III-R (i.e., determination of "caseness"); (c) the method of generating diagnoses (i.e., strictness of applying diagnostic criteria, as reflected in computer versus clinician generated diagnoses); and (d) the development of guidelines for integrating information from various informants.

Research findings in these related areas will permit better evaluation of the interview method for obtaining self-report information from children. Hopefully, this will lead to improved interview procedures and will further our goal of developing a better understanding of the concerns and problems experienced by children.

REFERENCES

Achenbach, T. M., & Edelbrock, C. (1983). *Manual for the Child Behavior Checklist and Revised Child Behavior Profile*. Burlington, CT: Queen City Printers.

Achenbach, T. M., McConaughy, S., & Howell, C. (1987). Child/adolescent behavioral and emotional problems: Implications of cross informant correlations for situational specificity. *Psychological Bulletin, 101*, 213–232.

Ambrosini, P. J. (Ed.). (1986). *Schedule for Affective Disorders and Schizophrenia for School Age Children (6–18 yrs) (K-SADS-IIIR)*. Unpublished manuscript.

Ambrosini, P. J., Metz, C., Prabucki, K., & Lee, J. (1989). Video tape reliability of the third revised edition of the K-SADS. *Journal of the American Academy of Child and Adolescent Psychology, 28*, 723–728.

American Psychiatric Association. (1968). *Diagnostic and statistical manual of mental disorders* (2nd ed.). Washington, DC: Author.

American Psychiatric Association. (1980) *Diagnostic and statistical manual of mental disorders* (3rd ed.). Washington, DC: Author.

American Psychiatric Association. (1987) *Diagnostic and statistical manual of mental disorders* (3rd ed. rev.). Washington, DC: Author.

Angold, A., Weismann, M. M., John, K., Merikangas, K. R., Prusoff, B. A., Wickramaratne, P., Gammon, G. D., & Warner, V. (1987). Parent and child reports of depressive symptoms in children at low and high risk of depression. *Journal of Child Psychology and Psychiatry, 28*, 901–915.

Apter, A., Orvaschel, H., Laseg, M., Moses, T., & Tyano, S. (1989). Psychometric properties of the K-SADS-P in an Israeli adolescent inpatient population. *American Journal of Child and Adolescent Psychiatry, 28*, 61–65.

Bartko, J. J., & Carpenter, W. T., Jr. (1976). On the methods and theory of reliability. *Journal of Nervous and Mental Disease, 163*, 307–317.

Bousha, D. M. (1985). *A controlled investigation of therapeutic focus in limit-setting insight-oriented psychotherapy with acting-out children*. Unpublished doctoral dissertation, University of Rochester, Rochester, N.Y.

Carlson, G., Kashani, J., Thomas, M., Vaidya, A., & Daniel, A. (1987). Comparison of two structured interviews on a psychiatrically hospitalized population of children. *Journal of the American Academy of Child and Adolescent Psychiatry, 26*, 645–648.

Chambers, W. J., Puig-Antich, J., Hirsch, M., Paez, P.,

Ambrosini, P. J., Tabrizi, M. A., & Davies, M. (1985). The assessment of affective disorders in children and adolescents by semi-structured interview: Test-retest reliability of the Schedule for Affective Disorders and Schizophrenia for School Age Children, Present Episode Version. *Archives of General Psychiatry, 42*, 696–702.

Cohen, J. (1988). *Statistical power analysis for the behavioral sciences* (2nd ed.). Hillsdale, NJ: Lawrence Erlbaum Associates.

Cohen, P., O'Connor, P., Lewis, S., Velez, C., & Malachowski, B. (1987). Comparison of DISC and K-SADS-P interviews of an epidemiological sample of children. *Journal of the American Academy of Child and Adolescent Psychiatry, 26*, 662–667.

Costello, A. J., Edelbrock, L. S., Dulcan, M. K., Kalas, R., & Klaric, S. H. (1984). *Report on the NIMH Diagnostic Interview Schedule for Children (DISC)*. Washington, DC: National Institute of Mental Health.

Costello, E. J., Edelbrock, C., Costello, A., Dulcan, M., & Brent, D. (1986). *The diagnosis and management of psychopathology in children in an organized primary healthcare setting* (Final Report on No. 278-83-0006 [DB]). Washington, DC: National Institute of Mental Health.

Costello, E. J., Edelbrock, C. S., Costello, A. J. (1985). Validity of the NIMH diagnostic interview schedule for children: A comparison between psychiatric and pediatric referrals. *Journal of Abnormal Child Psychology, 13*, 579–595.

Earls, F., Reich, W., Jung, K. G., & Cloninger, C. R. (1988). Psychopathology in children of alcoholic and antisocial parents. *Alcoholism: Clinical and Experimental Research, 12*, 481–487.

Earls, F., Smith, E., Reich, W., & Jung, K. (1988). Investigating psychopathological consequences of a disaster in children: A pilot study incorporating a structured diagnostic interview. *Journal of the American Academy of Child and Adolescent Psychiatry, 27*, 90–95.

Edelbrock, C., & Costello, A. J. (1988). Structured psychiatric interviews for children. In M. Rutter, A. H Tuma, & I. S. Lann (Eds.), *Assessment and diagnosis in child psychopathology* (pp. 87–112). New York: Guilford Press.

Edelbrock, C., Costello, A. J., Dulcan, M. K., Conover, N. C., & Kala, R. (1986). Parent-child agreement on child psychiatric symptoms assessed via structured interview. *Journal of Child Psychology and Psychiatry, 27*, 181–190.

Edelbrock, C., Costello, A. J., Dulcan, M., Kalas,l R., & Conover, N. C. (1985). Age difference in the reliability of the psychiatric interview of the child. *Child Development, 56*, 265–275.

Endicott, J., & Spitzer, R. L. (1978). A diagnostic interview: The Schedule for Affective Disorders and Schizophrenia. *Archives of General Psychiatry, 35*, 837–844.

Feighner, J., Robins, E., Guze, S., Woodruff, R., Winokur, G., & Munoz, R. (1972). Diagnostic criteria for use in psychiatric research. *Archives of General Psychiatry, 26*, 57–63.

Greenspan, S. I. (1981). *The clinical interview of the child*. New York: McGraw Hill.

Herjanic, B., Herjanic, M., Brown, R., & Wheatt, T. (1975). Are children reliable reporters? *Journal of Abnormal Child Psychology, 3*, 41–48.

Hodges, K. (1983). *Guidelines to aid in establishing interrater reliability with the Child Assessment Schedule*. Unpublished manuscript.

Hodges, K. (1990). Depression and anxiety in children: A comparison of self-report questionnaires to clinical interview. *Psychological Assessment: A Journal of Consulting and Clinical Psychology, 2*, 376–381.

Hodges, K., & Cools, J. (1990). Structured diagnostic interviews. In A. M. LaGreca (Ed.), *Through the eyes of the child: Obtaining self-report from children and adolescents* (pp. 109–149). Boston, MA: Allyn and Bacon.

Hodges, K., Cools, J., & McKnew, D. (1989). Test-retest reliability of a clinical research interview for children: The Child Assessment Schedule (CAS). *Psychological Assessment: A Journal of Consulting and Clinical Psychology, 1*, 317–322.

Hodges, V. K., & Fitch, P. (1979). *Development of a mental status examination interview for children*. Paper presented at the meeting of the Missouri Psychological Association, Kansas City, MO.

Hodges, K., Gordon, Y., & Lennon, M. (1990). Parent-child agreement on symptoms assessed via a clinical research interview for children: The Child Assessment Schedule (CAS). *Journal of Child Psychology and Psychiatry, 31*, 427–436.

Hodges, K., Kline, J., Stern, L., Cytryn, L., & McKnew, D. (1982). The development of a child assessment schedule for research and clinical use. *Journal of Abnormal Child Psychology, 10*, 173–189.

Hodges, K., McKnew, D., Burbach, D. J., & Roebuck, L. (1987). Diagnostic concordance between the Child Assessment Schedule (CAS) and the Schedule for Affective Disorders and Schizophrenia for School-Age Children (K-SADS) in an outpatient sample using lay interviewers. *Journal of the American Academy of Child and Adolescent Psychiatry, 26*, 654–661.

Hodges, K., & Saunders, W. (1989). Internal consistency of a diagnostic interview for children: The Child Assessment Schedule. *Journal of Abnormal Child Psychology, 17*, 691–701.

Hodges, K., Saunders, W., Kashani, J., Hamlett, K., & Thompson, R. (in press). Internal consistency of DSM-III diagnoses using symptom scales of the Child Assessment Schedule (CAS). *Journal of the American Academy of Child and Adolescent Psychiatry*.

Kashani, J., & Orvaschel, H. (1988). Anxiety disorders in mid-adolescents: A community sample. *American Journal of Psychiatry, 145*, 960–964.

Kashani, J., Orvaschel, H., Rosenberg, T., & Reid, J. (1989). Psychopathology among a community sample of children and adolescents: A developmental perspective. *Journal of the American Academy of Child and Adolescent Psychiatry, 28,* 701–706.

Kovacs, M. (1983). *The Interview Schedule for Children (ISC): ISC Interrater and parent-child agreement.* Unpublished manuscript.

Kovacs, M. (1985). The Interview Schedule for Children (ISC). *Psychopharmacology Bulletin, 21,* 991–994.

Kovacs, M. (1986). A developmental perspective on methods and measures in the assessment of depressive disorders: The clinical interview. In M. Rutter, C. E. Tizard, & P. B. Read (Eds.), *Depression in young people: Clinical and developmental perspectives* (pp. 435–465). New York: Guilford Press.

Kovacs, M., Feinberg, T. L., Crouse-Novak, M. A., Paulauskas, S. L., Pollock, M., & Finkelstein, R. (1984). Depressive disorders in childhood: II. A longitudinal study of the risk for a subsequent major depression. *Archives of General Psychiatry, 41,* 643–649.

Lachar, D., & Gdowski, C. L. (1979). *Actuarial assessment of child and adolescent personality: An interpretive guide for the Personality Inventory for Children Profile.* Los Angeles: Western Psychological Services.

Landis, J. R., & Koch, G. G. (1977). The measurement of observer agreement for categorical data. *Biometrics, 33,* 159–174.

Last, C. G. (1987). Developmental considerations. In C. G. Last & M. Hersen (Eds.), *Issues in diagnostic research* (pp. 201–216). New York: Plenum Press.

Last, C., Hersen, M., Kazdin, A., Finkelstein, R., & Strauss, C. (1987). Comparison of DSM-III separation anxiety and overanxious disorders: Demographic characteristics and patterns of comorbidity. *American Academy of Child and Adolescent Psychiatry, 26,* 527–531.

Lourie, R., & Rieger, R. E. (1974). Psychiatric and psychological examination of children. In S. Arieti (Ed.), *American handbook of psychiatry* (Vol. 2, pp. 3–36). New York: Basic Books.

Orvaschel, H., Puig-Antich, J. (1987). *Schedule for Affective Disorder and Schizophrenia for School-Age Children, Epidemiological Version (K-SADS-E).* Unpublished manuscript.

Puig-Antich, J. (1986). Psychobiological markers: Effects of age and puberty. In M. Rutter, C. E. Izard, & P. B. Read (Eds.), *Depression in young people: Developmental and clinical perspectives* (pp. 341–381). New York: Guilford Press.

Puig-Antich, J., & Chambers, W. (1978). *The Schedule for Affective Disorders and Schizophrenia for School-Age Children (Kiddie-SADS).* New York: New York State Psychiatric Institute.

Reich, W., Herjanic, B., Welner, Z., & Gandhy, P. R. (1982). Development of a structured psychiatric interview for children: Agreement in diagnosis comparing child and parent interviews. *Journal of Abnormal Child Psychology, 10,* 325–336.

Reich, W., & Welner, Z. (1988). *Diagnostic Interview for Children and Adolescents.* Unpublished manuscript. Washington University School of Medicine, St. Louis.

Richman, N., Stevenson, J., & Graham, P. J. (1982). *Pre-school to school: A behavioral study.* London: Academic Press.

Robins, L. (1985). Epidemiology: Reflections on testing the validity of psychiatric interviews. *Archives of General Psychiatry, 42,* 918–924.

Robins, L., Helzer, J., Croughan, J., & Ratcliff, K. (1981). National Institute of Mental Health diagnostic interview schedule: Its history, characteristics, and validity. *Archives of General Psychiatry, 38,* 381–389.

Runyon, D. K., Everson, M., Edelsohn, G. A., Hunter, W., & Coulter, M. (1988). Impact of legal intervention on sexually abused children. *Journal of Pediatrics, 113,* 647–653.

Rutter, M. (1988). Depressive disorders. In M. Rutter, A. H Tuma, & I. S. Lann (Eds.), *Assessment and diagnosis in child psychopathology* (pp. 347–376). New York: Guilford Press.

Shaffer, D., Fisher, P., Piacentini, J., Schwab-Stone, M., & Wicks, J. (1989). *Diagnostic Interview Schedule for Children (DISC-2C). Child Version.* Unpublished manuscript.

Shaffer, D., Schwab-Stone, M., Fisher, P., Davies, M., Piacentini, J., & Gioia, P. (1988). *Results of a field trial and proposals for a new instrument (DISC-R).* Washington, DC: National Institute of Mental Health (Grant Nos. MH 36971 & MH CRC 30906-10).

Simmons, J. E. (1974). *Psychiatric examination of children.* Philadelphia: Lea and Febiger.

Spielberger, C. D. (1973). *Preliminary manual for the State-Trait Anxiety Inventory for Children.* Palo Alto, California: Consulting Psychologists Press.

Spitzer, R. (1983). Psychiatric diagnosis: Are clinicians still necessary? *Comprehensive Psychiatry, 24,* 399–411.

Sylvester, C., Hyde, T., & Reichler, R. (1987). The Diagnostic Interview for Children and Personality Inventory for Children in studies of children at risk for anxiety disorders or depression. Journal of the *American Academy of Child and Adolescent Psychiatry, 26,* 668–675.

Verhulst, F. C., Althaus, M., & Berden, G. (1987). The Child Assessment Schedule: Parent-Child agreement and validity measures. *Journal of Child Psychology and Psychiatry, 28,* 455–466.

Weinstein, S. R., Stone, K., Noam, G. G., Grimes, K., & Schwab-Stone, M. (1989). Comparison of DISC with clinicians' DSM-III diagnoses in psychiatric inpatients. *Journal of the American Academy of Child and Adolescent Psychiatry, 28,* 53–60.

Welner, Z., Reich, W., Herjanic, B., Jung, K. G., & Amado, H. (1987). Reliability, validity, and parent-child agreement studies of the Diagnostic Interview for Children and Adolescents (DICA). *Journal of the American Academy of Child and Adolescent Psychiatry, 26,* 649–653.

CHAPTER 7

CHECKLISTS AND RATING SCALES

John Piacentini

The use of rating scales and checklists in the assessment of child and adolescent behavior problems has become increasingly popular over the last several years. As opposed to self-report measures or direct observations, informant ratings allow for the collection of relevant information from those individuals most likely to initiate referrals and follow-through on treatment for their behavior-disordered children. Although behavior ratings can be collected from almost any person familiar with the child (including mental health workers, teaching aides, coaches, siblings and classmates), by far the most common informants are parents and teachers. Many researchers and clinicians feel that parents are the most important source of information regarding children's behavior problems because they have the greatest familiarity with their child's behavior across the largest number of settings (Achenbach & Edelbrock, 1978; Mash & Terdal, 1988). On the other hand, most teachers have had a much wider exposure to normative child behavior and are therefore better equipped to identify behavioral deviance in a given youngster. According to McMahon (1984) the importance of parental reports may tend to decline, and that of teachers may increase as the child grows older and enters school.

ADVANTAGES OF RATING SCALES

The advantages associated with the use of rating scales and checklists are several and have been elucidated by a number of writers, such as Barkley (1987), Beck (1988), and Edelbrock (1987, 1988). First, rating scales provide a standardized format for the collection of data, ensuring systematic and comprehensive coverage of the behaviors in question. This structured format also serves to reduce the subjectivity inherent in informant judgments of deviant child behaviors and to increase reliability. Second, rating scales draw on the informant's past experience with the child across numerous situations and circumstances. By drawing on the raters' cumulative experience, day-to-day variability is minimized, allowing a more stable and reliable description of the child's behavior to emerge. Third, rating scales are efficient, easy, and economical to use in terms of both the actual cost and the time needed to complete and score the ratings, and interpret the results. Fourth, these measures allow for the collection of data regarding potentially rare, yet salient behaviors (e.g., firesetting, suicidal gestures) that are unlikely to be picked up by direct observational methods. Fifth, rating scales exist in a number of different formats and for a wide variety of topic areas, and so an appropriate scale can be found for almost any need. Broad-band scales (e.g., the Child Behavior Checklist; Achenbach & Edelbrock, 1983) can be used to provide a broad overview of the child's social, behavioral, and emotional functioning, while other scales (e.g., the Conners Parent and Teacher Rating Scales; Goyette, Conners & Ulrich, 1978) are designed to provide a more in-depth examination of specific disorders or problem areas. Finally, rating scales provide quantifiable information regarding the presence, frequency, and severity of both specific behaviors and global attributes. Scales that have been adequately normed allow for the statistical determination of the age appropriateness or relative deviance of the reported behaviors.

Given their ease of use and ability to provide quantitative information, it is not surprising that the utility of child behavior rating scales has been demonstrated for a number of applications in both clinical and research settings. Clinically, rating scales are ideally suited for use as initial screening measures for new referrals, because they allow for the efficient collection of quantifiable data regarding the severity and general nature of the referred child's problems and the degree to which these problems impair the child and warrant intervention. These measures can also play an important role, perhaps adjunctive, in diagnostic formulation and treatment selection by providing information related to the pervasiveness of symptoms across different settings and the degree of deviance of these behaviors. Repeated administration of rating scales can be used to monitor treatment response and provide indications for modifying treatment if the goals of the intervention are not being met.

Rating scales have shown research utility for both epidemiologic and clinical studies. Broad-band checklists have been used as primary assessment measures in large-scale single-stage population surveys and as efficient screening instruments in multi-stage surveys to identify high-risk subjects for in-depth follow-up evaluations. Parent and teacher ratings have also been used to develop dimensionally based classification systems of child psychopathology and to ensure homogeneous samples for descriptive, etiologic, and treatment studies for a number of childhood disorders.

ASSUMPTIONS UNDERLYING USE

According to Cairns and Green (1979) the rater's task is to assign the child or adolescent a place on the psychological or behavioral dimensions of interest based upon the rater's social judgment regarding the intensity, quality, or frequency, or a combination of these characteristics of the child's behavior. Cairns and Green outlined several assumptions underlying the rater's ability to complete this task. The rater is assumed to possess a shared understanding with the investigator or other raters of both the attribute or construct to be rated and also which of the individual's behaviors reflect that attribute. The rater is also assumed to possess the ability to detect information relevant to the attribute of interest in the stream of daily life activities of the person being rated and to share with other raters the same underlying "scale" on which the attribute will be rated.

However, a number of variables can affect the degree to which these assumptions hold true. First, several characteristics of both the informant and the child have been shown to influence behavior ratings. As will be shown, these characteristics—which include child and informant gender and symptomatology and social desirability—can affect not only the absolute level of ratings but also the degree of agreement across different raters. In addition, ratings of child behavior can be influenced by the rater's degree of familiarity with both the child and his or her environment and the rating process in general. Finally, children's behavior can be highly variable across situations and over time, and this variability can also affect informant ratings. One of the most consistent findings in child behavior assessment research is the fact that raters who observe subjects in similar settings (i.e., teachers and teaching aides or mothers and fathers) tend to have significantly higher rates of agreement than do informants who observe and rate children under different conditions (cf., Achenbach, McConaughy & Howell, 1987). The inability of rating scales to take into account the situational or contextual variability of a child's behavior is one of the more commonly cited criticisms of these measures (Mash & Terdal, 1988). In an attempt to address this criticism, Barkley (1981a, 1981b; Barkley & Edelbrock, 1986) has developed parallel home and school questionnaires that, instead of assessing specific problem behaviors, assess specific situations in which problem behaviors may occur.

In addition to these intrapersonal and situational factors, the accuracy and consistency of ratings can also be influenced by characteristics of the rating scale itself. One such characteristic is the time frame of the rating scale, which may span less than 1 day to several months or more. While the most commonly specified time frames range between 1 week and 1 month, many scales do not indicate any fixed period of time on which the ratings are to be based, leaving individual raters to determine this important parameter on their own. The number of response options and the type of anchor points are also important determinants of agreement across raters. Although vague, imprecise anchor points (e.g., never, sometimes, often) can be interpreted quite diversely by different raters, which may lead to increased response variability, overly precise descriptors tend to decrease reliability and validity (Conners, 1973; Edelbrock, 1988). Other factors influencing response variation include individual item specificity, questionnaire scope and length, and factor construction techniques (Barkley, 1987; Edelbrock, 1988).

PSYCHOMETRIC CONSIDERATIONS

Many early behaviorists downplayed the importance of reliability and validity as criteria for the development and selection of behavioral assessment measures. This opposition to the use of psychometric criteria was largely based on the inability to reconcile the notion that behavior is situationally determined, with the psychometric concepts of stability across situations and over time (Marsh & Terdal, 1988). In recent years, however, psychometric performance has become increasingly accepted as an important consideration for instrument development and selection (O'Leary & Johnson, 1986). While the psychometric properties of individual instruments are presented in the following review of specific rating scales, it is useful to discuss a number of general issues related to the reliability and validity of these measures.

Reliability

Three types of reliability should be considered when discussing behavioral rating scales: test-retest, internal consistency, and interrater. Test-retest reliability is the stability of ratings over time and is measured by the degree of correlation between scores collected across multiple assessments. While most rating scales possess good to excellent test-retest reliability ($r \geq .80$) over short retest intervals (i.e., 1 month or less), (Achenbach & Edelbrock, 1978; Edelbrock, 1988), longer retest intervals generally result in lower test-retest reliability. One explanation for this decreased reliability over time is the observation that subsequent administrations of many rating scales yield lower scores than the initial assessment (Achenbach & Edelbrock, 1978; Werry & Sprague, 1974). Possible causes for this attenuation effect have been described, including practice effects, reactivity, the episodic nature of some childhood disorders, and statistical regression (McMahon, 1984; Milich, Roberts, Loney & Caputo, 1980). In addition to shorter retest intervals, other factors have been shown to positively affect test-retest reliability, including well-defined anchor points, more than two response options, and well-trained raters (O'Leary & Johnson, 1979).

Internal consistency is the homogeneity of the rating scale or the extent to which scale items measure the same phenomenon. Although there are several available methods for determining internal consistency, two of the most commonly used are split-half reliability and coefficient alpha. Split-half reliability is calculated by dividing the scale into two subscales (usually odd items versus even items) and then determining the correlation between the subscale scores. Coefficient alpha refers to the mean correlation between all possible splittings of the rating scale (Cronbach, 1951). Measures designed to assess discrete syndromes or unitary phenomena are expected to have high internal consistency. For multifactorial scales or scales covering a wide variety of behaviors, however, internal consistency is necessarily lower (Nay, 1979). All else being equal, longer rating scales have higher internal consistency than those with fewer items (Anastasi, 1976).

Interrater Agreement

As mentioned earlier, interrater reliability is dependent upon many factors, including the degree of similarity of the situations in which the child is being rates (i.e., home vs. school) and the rater's familiarity with the child and experience with the measures being used. In general, agreement between mothers and fathers tends to be moderately high, while that between parents and teachers is usually much lower (Achenbach, McConaughy, & Howell, 1987; Garrison and Earls, 1985; Schaughency & Lahey, 1985). However, as Jensen, Traylor, Xenakis, & Davis (1988) note, the relatively strong correlations between mother and father ratings should not be taken as a measure of good interparent agreement, for several reasons. These include the fact that most of the reported reliability estimates do not take into account error variance between parents and thus may be spuriously high. Jensen, Traylor, Xenakis & Davis (1988) also questioned the use of the reliability coefficient as a measure of interrater agreement, because this statistic is dependent on the relative rank ordering, but not actual magnitude, of scores. This criticism becomes especially relevant in light of the fact that mothers are more likely to give higher ratings to their children than are fathers (Achenbach & Edelbrock, 1983; Jensen, Traylor, Xenakis, & Davis 1988; Mash & Johnston, 1983).

Several studies have identified additional child and rater characteristics that may affect agreement between raters. Mothers with higher levels of emotional and psychological distress have been found to view their children as more disturbed (Jensen, Xenakis, Davis, & DeGroot, 1988; Piacentini, Lahey, Frick, Patake, & Christ, 1988; Rickard, Forehand, Wells, Greist, & McMahon, 1981; Schaughency & Lahey, 1985), while marital discord has also been tied to bias in maternal ratings of child behavior problems, at least as compared to teacher ratings (Emery & O'Leary, 1984). The rated child's gender and type of symptoms and family status have all been shown to influence discrepancy levels between adult raters (for a review, see Jensen, Xenakis, Davis, & DeGroot, 1988).

Studies examining the correspondence between parent ratings and child self-reports have also found low levels of correlation, with children reporting lower symptom levels than their parents (Achenbach *et al.*, 1987; Kazdin, Esveldt-Dawson, Unis, & Rancurello, 1983; Kazdin, French & Unis, 1983; Kazdin, French, Unis, & Esveldt-Dawson, 1983). While several factors, including the child's age, gender, type of symptoms, family size, and family stress, have been tentatively shown to influence parent-child agreement in a nonclinical sample (Jensen, Traylor, Xenakis, & Davis 1988; Jensen, Xenakis, Davis, & DeGroot, 1988), replication of these results in clinic samples is still needed.

Validity

As noted by Edelbrock (1987), the questionable reliability and validity of child psychiatric diagnoses as a standard measure of child psychopathology has hampered validation studies of behavioral assessment measures, including rating scales and checklists. For this reason, the validity of a given behavioral measure must be established on the basis of its cumulative performance against multiple validating criteria. There are several types of validity pertinent to rating scales. The most important include content, construct, and criterion-related validity. Content validity measures the degree to which the rating scale items cover a representative sample of the behavior domain to be measured (Anastasi, 1976). Adequate content validity is usually ensured by deriving items from diagnostic criteria or clinical correlates of the disorder of interest or from careful evaluations of children with the disorder (Kazdin & Petti, 1982). Although ensuring adequate content validity is an important first step in instrument development, not all measures are equally successful in achieving this goal. For example, although many rating scales are available that reportedly measure conduct disorder, the items comprising many of these scales show only minimal to moderate correspondence to accepted diagnostic criteria for this disorder (e.g., DSM-III-R, American Psychiatric Association, 1987). Instead the majority of these scales consist primarily of items assessing behaviors such as argumentativeness, noncompliance, irritability, and disruptiveness, and as such, would be more accurately described as measures of oppositional behavior.

More recently, a handful of scales have been developed that contain items corresponding directly to DSM-III or DSM-III-R diagnostic criteria for childhood disorders, including the SNAP Rating Scale for hyperactivity (Atkins, Pelham, & Licht, 1985), the New York Disruptive Behavior Scales (Piacentini, Abikoff, Guardino, Klass, & Klein, 1989), and the Gadow-Sprafkin Stony Brook Child Psychiatric Checklist (Gadow & Sprafkin, 1987). While the initial results suggest that scales such as these may offer enhanced clinical and research utility, continued psychometric and normative work remains to be done before they can be established for general use.

A second type of validity is construct validity, or the extent to which the scale measures the psychological concept or construct of interest (e.g., self-esteem, depression, hyperactivity). Construct validity is assessed by examining the relationship between scale scores and scores on other instruments measuring the same construct. Finally, criterion-related validity measures the extent to which rating scale scores are related to independent measures (e.g., criteria) of the behaviors the scale is intended to cover. Criterion-related validity encompasses a number of different types of validity, depending upon both the valence and temporal relationship between the instrument being tested and the criterion or criteria of interest. Predictive validity is a measure of how well scale scores are able to predict some future salient outcome, while concurrent validity indicates the degree to which scale scores correlate with criterion measures administered at approximately the same time. Concurrent validity can be subdivided further into convergent validity (the extent to which the scale correlates with measures with which it should correlate) and discriminant validity (the extent to which the scale does not correlate with measures with which it should not correlate). For example, a depression rating scale would be expected to be highly correlated with other measures of depression but have low correlations with measures of other disorders, such as hyperactivity. Campbell and Fiske (1959) proposed the multitrait-multimethod matrix to systematically examine convergent and discriminant validity. This method also allows one to examine the influence of method type on the level of agreement between measures.

Several criteria have been used in the validation of behavior rating scales, including clinic-referral status, diagnosis, direct observation, and scores on other rating scales. While most rating scales show highly significant levels of statistical discrimination between groups of normal and disturbed children (Edelbrock, 1987), the degree of overlap between these two groups is often relatively high. For example, Achenbach and Edelbrock (1981) examined the effect of different cutoff points for the Child Behavior Checklist (CBCL) (Achenbach, 1978) on screening efficiency and found misclassification rates between referred and nonreferred children ranging from 9% to 30%, depending on the method used. Several scales have also been shown to discriminate between diagnostic subgroups of children (Edelbrock, Costello, & Kessler, 1984; Kazdin, Esveldt-Dawson, Unis, & Rancurello, 1983; Kazdin & Heidish, 1984; Werry, Sprague, & Cohen, 1975). Again, however, the degree of misclassification is often not addressed and can be significant. Lahey, McBurnett, Piacentini, Hartdagen, Walker, Frick, and Hynd (1987) examined the degree of agreement between the diagnostic classification of attention deficit disorder with hyperactivity (ADDH) based solely on established cutoff scores for each of four (two parent and two teacher) commonly used hyperactivity rating scales and classification based on comprehensive clinical diagnostic assessments, and found misclassification rates for the four rating scales ranging from 25% to 30%. Similarly, Ullman, Sleator, & Sprague (1985a) compared scores on the Conners Abbreviated Teacher Rating Scale (ATRS) (Conners, 1973) for an unselected sample of children and for a sample of children referred to a clinic for possible hyperactivity and found a 31.5% rate of overlap between the two groups of those scoring above the recommended cutoff score of 15.

Validation studies utilizing direct behavioral observations have also found significant correlations between observed behavior and rating scale scores (Kazdin, Esveldt-Dawson, & Loar, 1983; Rapoport & Benoit, 1975; Reed & Edelbrock, 1983). However, the degree of correlation is dependent on a number of factors, including the extent of overlap between rating scale items and the behaviors being observed, the raters' experience with deviant child behavior, and the similarity between the setting and structure of the observation session and the context in which the rater usually sees the child. While most direct observations focus on discrete behaviors occurring over a short interval, behavior ratings typically reflect a more global perspective occurring over a longer period of time. For example, in contrast to teacher ratings of hyperactivity, a number of studies have found that parent ratings correlate poorly with observational measures of activity, distractibility, and inattention (Barkley & Ullman, 1975; Rapoport & Benoit, 1975), perhaps because of the greater similarity of the observation setting to the child's classroom than to his or her home, and because of the teacher's greater familiarity with what constitutes deviant behavior.

While the above review has identified psychometric weaknesses associated with child behavior rating scales, including relatively low levels of both cross-situational agreement and discriminant validity, to a certain degree these weaknesses are a result of both the situational nature of the phenomena being assessed and the lack of well-established, standardized validation criteria.

REVIEW OF INDIVIDUAL RATING SCALES

Hundreds of informant rating scales covering a wide range of child behavior problems exist, and many new scales are published each year. The following review of individual rating scales is, by necessity, selective. The measures discussed were chosen on the basis of the frequency of use, psychometric strength, and demonstrated or potential levels of clinical and research utility.

Broad-Band Scales

Revised Behavior Problem Checklist

The original Behavior Problem Checklist (BPC) (Peterson, 1961; Quay, 1977; Quay & Peterson, 1979) was one of the first standardized rating scales for child psychopathology. The BPC consists of 55 items, rated 0 (not at all), 1 (mild problem), or 2 (severe problem), comprising four empirically derived factors: Conduct Problems, Personality Problems, Inadequate-Immature, and Socialized Delinquency. No time frame on which the ratings are to be based is specified. More than 100 published studies exist attesting to the basic validity of the BPC factors, the discriminant validity of the scale, and the sensitivity of the scale to a wide variety of treatment effects (Quay, 1977).

The Revised Behavior Problem Checklist (RBPC) (Quay & Peterson, 1983, 1987) resulted from a major 1980 revision of the BPC that was undertaken to improve the measurement of broad-band dimensions of child psychopathology without compromising the simplicity and usability of the scale (Quay & Peterson, 1983). The initial step in the revision process consisted of increasing the item pool to 150 items, the majority of which were derived from more than 40 factor analytic studies of childhood disorders. Some of these additional items were rewritten BPC items, whereas other were new. Factor analysis of the enlarged item pool replicated the original four BPC factors and identified two new minor factors, labeled Psychotic Behavior and Motor Excess. The elimination of 73 items adversely affecting internal consistency or having high loadings on more than one factor resulted in the incorporation of 77 scorable items into the RBPC. Twelve additional items not scored and not related to any of the above six factors were also added, resulting in a final scale length of 89 items. Limited norms for the RBPC are available for both nonreferred samples and several subsamples of children with specific learning or behavioral handicaps (Aman, Werry, Fitzpatrick, Lowe, & Waters, 1983; Quay & Peterson, 1983, 1987).

The initial results regarding the reliability of the RBPC suggest that the revisions were successful (Quay & Peterson, 1983). Two-month test-retest reliability determined from teacher ratings of 149 students in grades 1 through 6 ranged from .49 (Socialized Aggression) to .83 (Attention Problem-Immaturity), while internal consistency for the six factors ranged from .68 to .95 across six separate samples. Interrater agreement is also good, ranging from .52 to .85 for teachers and from .55 to .93 for parents (Quay & Peterson, 1983). While the validity of the RBPC has not yet been studied as extensively as that of the earlier version, initial results are also promising. Not surprisingly, RBPC scale scores are highly correlated with corresponding BPC factors. Perhaps the most impressive property of the RBPC, however, is its construct validity. Because the items for the scale were gathered from an exhaustive review of the literature, the scale content and factor structure truly represent a consensus about what is known about the dimensions of maladaptive child behavior (Lahey & Piacentini, 1985). The scale has been shown to discriminate between referred and nonreferred samples (Aman & Werry, 1984; Quay & Peterson, 1983) and between different diagnostic subgroups of hyperactive children as well (Lahey, Schaughency, Frame, & Strauss, 1985; Lahey, Schaughency, Strauss, & Frame, 1984). Separate subscales have also been found to correlate in the expected directions with intelligence, academic achievement, direct observations of behavior, and peer nominations (Hagborg, 1990; Quay & Peterson, 1983, 1987). While the results of preliminary psychometric investigations are impressive, the absence of more representative norms limits the utility of the RBPC for classification and screening purposes.

Child Behavior Checklist

The parent and teacher versions of the Child Behavior Checklist (CBCL) (Achenbach, 1978; Achenbach & Edelbrock, 1979; Edelbrock & Achenbach, 1984) were developed to cover a broad range of childhood behavior problems. Relatively unique among informant rating scales, the CBCL also contains items covering several positive attributes related to academic and social competency. The parent CBCL consists of 118 items rated on a scale of 0 (not true), 1 (sometimes true), 2 (very true), which covers specific behavior problems and 20 social competency items. Responses are scored on the Child Behavior Profile, which is used to generate percentile scores and t-scores for the several subscales making up the scale. Social competency items are summed across three a priori subscales, labeled Activities, Social, and School, while the rest of the items load onto empirically derived behavior problem scales. Normative data were collected on a randomly selected stratified sample of 1,300 children from the Greater Washington, D.C. area who had not received mental health services in the preceding year (Achenbach & Edelbrock, 1981). To reflect the finding of significant differences in item prevalence and factor structure as a function of age and gender, six different Child Behavior Profiles were developed to provide separate norms for boys and girls at each of three different age ranges (4–5, 6–11, and 12–16) (Achenbach and Edelbrock (1981, 1983). Each behavior profile is composed of eight or nine narrow-band factors grouped under one of two broad-band syndromes labeled Externalizing and Internalizing (see Table 7-1).

Good to excellent reliability has been reported for the parent CBCL. Achenbach and Edelbrock (1981, 1983) reported 1-week test-retest reliability of .95 for behavior problem and .99 for social competence total scale scores, while 3-month reliability ranged from .84 to .97 for the same scales, respectively. High levels of interparent agreement (.99 for behavior problems and .98 for social competence) were also described by these authors for a sample of 168 clinic children. Much lower levels of mother-father agreement were reported by Garrison and Earls (1985), who found Pearson correlations of .47 for social competence, .52 for behavior problems, .56 for the externalizing sum, and .40 for the internalizing sum, in a sample of normal 6- and 7-year-olds. Correlations for individual narrow-band factors ranged from .08 (Somatic Complaints) to .58 (Aggressive, Delinquent) for boys and from −.11 (Sex Problems) to .66 (Somatic Complaints) for girls. Validity studies of the CBCL have also yielded generally favorable results. Significant correlations between CBCL factor scores and scores on corresponding factors from other established measures, including the Conners Parent Rating Scale, the RBPC, and the Diagnostic Interview Schedule for Children (Achenbach & Edelbrock, 1983; Costello & Edelbrock, 1985; Mash & Johnston, 1983) have been used to demonstrate good concurrent validity, while the scale has also been shown to discriminate between clinic and normal children as well as children within different diagnostic subgroups (Achenbach & Edelbrock, 1981, 1983; Hodges, Kline, Stern, Cytryn, & McKnew, 1982).

The teacher version of the CBCL, or Teacher Report Form (TRF) (Achenbach & Edelbrock, 1986; Edelbrock & Achenbach, 1984) is similar to the parent CBCL in both content and format, except that items

Table 7-1. Factor Structure of the Child Behavior Checklist by Age and Gender

GROUP	INTERNALIZING SYNDROMES	MIXED SYNDROMES	EXTERNALIZING SYNDROMES
Boys aged 4-5	Social withdrawal Depressed Immature Somatic complaints	Sex problems	Schizoid Aggressive Delinquent
Girls aged 4-5	Somatic complaints Depressed Schizoid or anxious Social withdrawal	Obesity	Aggressive Sex problems Hyperactive
Boys aged 6-11	Schizoid or Anxious Depressed Uncommunicative Obsessive-Compulsive Somatic Complaints	Social withdrawal	Hyperactive Aggressive Delinquent
Girls aged 6-11	Depressed Social withdrawal Somatic withdrawal Schizoid-obsessive		Hyperactive Sex problems Delinquent Aggressive
Boys aged 12-16	Somatic complaints Schizoid Uncommunicative Immature Obsessive-compulsive	Hostile withdrawal	Delinquent Aggressive Hyperactive
Girls aged 12-16	Anxious-obsessive Somatic complaints Schizoid Depressed withdrawal	Immature-hyperactive	Delinquent Aggressive Cruel

covering behaviors occurring outside the school setting (e.g., bedwetting, nightmares) were eliminated, and items more pertinent to school (e.g., disruptive in class, messy work) were added. In addition, the competence scale of the TRF contains items targeting academic performance, classroom behavior, and school placement. Overall, the item contents of the CBCL and TRF are approximately 80% similar. Separate norms are available for boys and girls aged 6–11 and 12–16. Similar to the parent CBCL, the Teacher Profiles were developed from a large representative sample ($n = 1100$) of nonreferred children and reflect different factor structures for each age by gender combination.

Average test-retest reliabilities for the behavior problem scales of TRF are satisfactory, ranging from .74 to .96 (mean = .89), over a 1-week interval, while 2- and 4-month retest intervals yielded reliabilities of .77 and .64, respectively (Edelbrock & Achenbach, 1984). Edelbrock, Greenbaum, and Conover (1985) reported an average 1-week test-retest reliability for the adaptive functioning scales of .91. Because of its more recent development, fewer validity studies exist for the TRF than for the parent CBCL. However, those studies that are available are generally positive. Edelbrock et al. (1985) reported strong correlations between TRF externalizing factor scores and scores on corresponding Conners Teacher Rating Scale factors. TRF scores have also been shown to correlate with classroom observations (Kazdin, Esveldt-Dawson, & Loar, 1983; Reed & Edelbrock, 1983) and clinician evaluations (Garrison & Earls, 1985) and to discriminate clinic-referred from nonreferred children, hyperactive from nonhyperactive disturbed children, and learning-disordered from emotionally disturbed children (Edelbrock & Achenbach, 1984; Edelbrock, Costello, & Kessler, 1984; Harris, King, Reifler, & Rosenberg, 1984).

Overall, both parent and teacher versions of the CBCL possess impressive psychometric characteristics, and research based on these scales has contributed a great deal to the development of a dimensional typology of childhood psychopathology. The CBCL and TRF are currently the most commonly used screening instruments for epidemiologic studies of childhood disorders and are being used with increasing frequency for a variety of clinical purposes as well. However, the fact that different factor structures are available for different ages limits the utility of these scales for longitudinal research or long-term clinical follow-up.

Narrow-Band Scales

Conners Rating Scales

The Conners Parent and Teacher Rating Scales are among the most commonly used measures by both researchers and clinicians for the assessment of childhood hyperactivity (Rosenberg & Beck, 1986). The Conners scales were originally developed to provide a method for the systematic identification of children with hyperactivity and to serve as standardized outcome measures for psychopharmacological treatment studies of this disorder. Before describing the Conners scales further, it is important to note that several different versions of both the parent and teacher scales exist and a number of different factor structures and norms have also been published. In addition, some versions of the questionnaires contain minor variations in the number of items or item wordings and do not correspond to any of the available factor structures or norms. The resulting confusion on the part of both researchers and clinicians who use these scales or attempt to generalize results across multiple research reports has led some to argue that the use of the Conners scales as research instruments should be reconsidered (Ullman et al., 1985a).

Conners Parent Rating Scale

The original Conners Parent Rating Scale (CPRS) (Conners, 1973) consists of 93 items rated on a 0–3 scale and subgrouped into 25 a priori clusters, including problems of eating, problems of sleeping, muscular tension, restlessness, temper, problems in school, stealing, perfectionism, and additional problems. A 73-item version of the CPRS has also been described (Conners, 1970). In a reanalysis of Conner's (1970) original data, Conners and Blouin (1980) presented normative data for the CPRS and reported an eight-factor solution for the questionnaire. These eight factors were labeled Conduct Disorder, Fearful-Anxious, Restless-Disorganized, Learning Problem-Immature, Psychosomatic, Obsessional, Antisocial, and Hyperactive-Immature. Conners and Barkley (1985) presented a slightly different version of the 93-item parent scale, the Parent Symptom Questionnaire (PSQ) and also described an eight-factor solution based on an analysis of 683 clinic outpatients and normal children. However, the factor names were slightly different from those described by Conners and Blouin, and it is not clear which version of the scale was used for the latter factor analysis. In an overview of commonly used rating scales for childhood hyperactivity, Edelbrock and Rancurello (1985) refer to a five-factor solution for the 73-item version of the CPRS based on 316 clinically referred children. Adequate test-retest reliability and internal consistency have been demonstrated for a slightly modified version of the CPRS by Glow (Glow, 1983; Glow, Glow, & Rump, 1982), who also provided norms for this version based on 1,919 Australian youngsters (Glow, 1981). The scale has shown good concurrent and discriminant validity (Mash & Johnston, 1983; Ross & Ross, 1982; Weissman, Orvaschel, & Padian, 1980), although at least one study has found an unacceptably high misclassification rate when children are identified as hyperactive on the basis of this scale alone (Lahey et al., 1987). The CPRS has also demonstrated utility as an outcome measure in a variety of treatment studies of hyperactive children (cf., Barkley, 1977), although, as mentioned earlier, a strong practice effect has been reported for the scale (Werry & Sprague, 1974), with scores tending to decrease between first and second administrations. Persons wishing to use this scale as a treatment outcome measure should plan at least two baseline administrations before beginning treatment (Conners & Barkley, 1985).

The CPRS was revised and restandardized by Goyette, Conners, and Ulrich (1978). Items with low factor loadings in previous factor analyses or highly similar or redundant to other items were eliminated, combined with other items, or reworded, resulting in the elimination of 45 items. A factor analysis for the new 48-item scale based on a mixed sample of 570 children yielded six factors corresponding closely to the first six factors of the original scale, which they labeled Conduct Problem I (oppositional, aggressive), Learning Problems, Psychosomatic, Impulsive-Hyperactive, Conduct Problem II (steals, emotionally labile), and Anxiety. Goyette et al. (1978) provided age by gender norms broken down into 3-year intervals from ages 3 to 17 based on the same sample and reported mean interparent correlations for each factor ranging from .46 (Psychosomatic) to .57 (Conduct Problem) with a mean correlation of .51. Test-retest reliability has not been reported, although the CPRS-R may be prone to the same practice effects characteristic of the earlier version. While the validity of the CPRS-R has not been as extensively studied as that of the original scale, given the similarity of the items and the factor structure between the two scales, it would be expected that the findings from the earlier scale, at least regarding the externalizing factors, are somewhat generalizable to the revised version (Barkley, 1977). Given the greater comprehensiveness and more extensive validation of the CPRS as compared to the CPRS-R, Conners and Barkley (1985) recommend that the earlier version be used preferentially over the CPRS-R, although the brevity and more extensive norms of the latter version may make it the scale of choice in certain situations.

Conners Teacher Rating Scale

The original Conners Teacher Rating Scale (CTRS) (Conners, 1969) consists of 39 items scored on the same 0–3 scale as the parent versions. While several different factor structures and associated norms have been published, Conners recommends that those reported by Trites, Blouin, and Laprade (1982) and based on 9,583 Canadian schoolchildren be used. Trites et al. (1982) identified six factors labeled Hyperactivity, Conduct Disorder, Emotional-Overindulgent, Anxious-Passive, Asocial, and Daydreams/Attendance Problem and provided norms broken down by gender for each age between 4 and 12 years old. Trites et al. (1982) reported internal consistencies (Cronbach's alpha) for these factors ranging from .94 (Hyperactivity) to .61 (Daydreams/Attendance Problems). Test-retest reliability for the CTRS has been good ranging from .72 to .92 at 1 month (Conners, 1973) and from .35 to .57 at one year (Trites, Blouin, Ferguson, & Lynch, 1981). Teacher-teacher, teacher-classroom observer, and interparent agreement has been adequate, while parent-teacher agreement has been much lower (Glow, 1981; Kazdin, Esveldt-Dawson, & Loar, 1983; Trites et al. 1982). Extensive data on the validity of the CTRS exists (Barkley, 1987; Klee & Garfinkle, 1983; Kupietz, Bialer, & Winsburg, 1972; Lahey, Green, & Forehand, 1980; Trites & Laprade, 1983), and the scale has demonstrated sensitivity to treatment effects in a variety of studies of children with hyperactivity (Barkley, 1977; Conners, 1969). As previously mentioned, because of the number of similar, yet slightly different, versions of the CTRS being used, caution must be used when scoring and interpreting this scale.

The CTRS underwent revision and restandardization concurrently with the CPRS (Goyette et al., 1978). The revised scale (CTRS-R) consists of 28 items loading on three factors (Conduct Problem, Hyperactivity, and Inattentive-Passive). As can be seen, most items assessing internalizing and other nondisruptive behaviors were eliminated in the revision. Similar to the CPRS-R, separate norms are available by gender for ages 3 to 17. One-week test-retest reliability for the total scale score was .96 and ranged from .88 (Inattentive-Passive) to .95 (Conduct Disorder, Hyperactivity) for individual factors (Edelbrock, Greenbaum, & Conover, 1985). Goyette et al. (1978) reported moderate levels of parent-teacher agreement at the factor level with correlations of .33 for Conduct Problem (Parent and Teacher scales), .36 for Impulsive-Hyperactive (P) and Hyperactivity (T), and .45 for Learning Problem (P) and Inattentive-Passive (T). While the validity of the CTRS-R has not been assessed nearly as extensively as that of the original scale, criterion-related validity, including convergent and discriminant validity, has been demonstrated by Edelbrock et al. (1985).

Conners Abbreviated Rating Scale

An abbreviated scale (alternatively called the Hyperkinesis Index; the Conners Abbreviated Parent-Teacher Questionnaire [CAPTQ]; or the Conners Abbreviated Symptom Questionnaire [ASQ]), for use with both parents and teachers was developed by Conners (1973), who selected the 10 items with the highest factor loadings on the original teacher scale. While this scale has been construed as a measure of hyperactivity and has been extensively used as an entrance criterion as a measure of hyperactivity and has been extensively used as an entrance criterion for psychopharmacological treatment studies of this disorder, because it was derived from all the CTRS factors and not just the Hyperactivity factor, it is actually a broad-based measure of psychopathology (Conners & Barkley, 1985). Since the abbreviated scale contains items assessing aggression, overactivity, and inattention, the use of this scale as a selection criterion in research settings will lead to the formation of inappropriately heterogeneous groups. Further complicating the picture is the fact that several different versions of this scale exist leading to the scoring and interpretation problems already described. If this scale is to be used, Conners recommends that the Goyette et al. (1978) norms be used. To overcome the problems inherent in the abbreviated scale, Loney and Milich (1981) developed the Iowa Conners. This 10-item scale, which is scored in similar fashion to the CTRS, consists of the five items from the Conduct Disorder factor and the five items from the Hyperactivity factor, which load the highest on their respective factors but do not load on the other factor. The five items from each factor are scored separately and are supposed to yield purely aggressive (high aggression factor scores, low hyperactivity factor scores), purely hyperactive (low aggression factor scores, high hyperactivity factor scores), or mixed (high scores on both factors) subjects. To date, only limited data are available concerning the reliability and validity (Langhorne & Loney, 1979) of this measure.

ADD-H Comprehensive Teacher Rating Scale (ACTeRS)

The ACTeRS (Ullman, Sleator, & Sprague, 1984a) is a 24-item teacher rating scale scored on a 5-point scale from 1 (almost never) to 5 (almost always). Similar to the Conners scales, the ACTeRS was developed to aid in the diagnosis of children with hyperactivity and the monitoring of response to psychopharmacologic treatments (Ullman, Sleator & Sprague, 1985b). The ACTeRS consists of four subscales (Attention, Hyperactivity, Social, and Oppositional), which were identified through factor analysis. Raw scores for each factor are coded on separate profile sheets for boys and girls that yield percentile scores. These percentile scores are based on ratings of 1,347 nonreferred kindergarten through fifth graders (653 girls, 694 boys), but are not broken down by age (Ullman, Sleator, & Sprague, 1984a). The profile sheets are somewhat confusing to interpret, as increased deviance is indicated by higher percentile scores for the Hyperactivity and Oppositional factors, but lower percentile scores for the Attention and Sociability factors. Norms derived from clinical samples are not available; however, the authors assert that scores falling at or below the 10th percentile on the Attention factor can be considered as confirmatory evidence for a diagnosis of hyperactivity (Ullman et al., 1985b).

Since it is a relatively new scale, few published reports regarding the psychometric properties of the ACTeRS are available. Ullman et al. (1985b) reported that high levels of internal consistency and interrater agreement, along with the factor purity of the items, make the scale a valuable assessment tool for hyperactivity research. Barkley (1977) cites unpublished data from the scale authors indicating moderate to good levels of test-retest and interrater reliability and internal consistency. The scale has also been reported to discriminate hyperactive from both normal (Ullman, Sleator, & Sprague, 1984b) and depressed (Pataki, Carlson, & Rapport, 1989) children and to be sensitive to psychopharmacological treatment effects (Pataki et al., 1989; Ullman & Sleator, 1985). While

Eyberg Child Behavior Inventory

The Eyberg Child Behavior Inventory (ECBI) (Eyberg & Ross, 1978) is described by the authors as a comprehensive, behaviorally specific instrument for the assessment by parents of conduct disorders in children between the ages of 2 and 17. To ensure adequate content validity of the inventory, the 36 items making up the ECBI were compiled from case records of children with conduct problems to reflect the most common problem behaviors reported by the children's parents. Each item is rated on two dimensions, a seven-point frequency scale (1=never, 7=always), and a yes-no scale on which the parent indicates whether or not the behavior is a problem. The two summary scores, i.e., Total Intensity Score and Total Problem Score, are derived by summing the frequency and problem behavior ratings, respectively. Norms for the ECBI were collected on 512 pediatric referrals ranging in age from 2 to 12 years (Robinson, Eyberg, & Ross, 1980) and a smaller, less representative sample of 102 13- to 16-year-olds (Eyberg & Robinson, 1983). Robinson et al. (1980) reported 3-week test-retest reliabilities of .86 for the Intensity Score and .88 for the Problem Score. Internal consistency (split-half correlations) were .95 and .94 for the Intensity and Problem scores, respectively. Good interparent agreement in a small sample of adolescents was reported by Eyberg and Robinson (1983). Regarding discriminant validity, the scale has been shown to differentiate between normal and behavior-problem youngsters in both prepubertal (Eyberg & Ross, 1978) and adolescent (Eyberg & Robinson, 1983) samples. Robinson et al. (1980) reported a high correlation between Problem and Intensity scores ($r = .75$), indicating that to a large degree these subscales are measuring the same thing and thus, may be redundant.

A companion teacher instrument, the Sutter-Eyberg School Behavior Inventory (SESBI) (Sutter & Eyberg, 1984), has recently been developed. While the format and many of the items are identical to those in the ECBI, several new items were developed on the basis of a chart review of the most common teacher complaints of referred children. Although Funderburke and Eyberg (1989) reported adequate reliability and validity for the SESBI, these results were collected on a small sample of 3- to 5-year-old children only. No published reports supporting the use of this scale in older children could be located.

Children's Depression Inventory (Parent Version)

The Children's Depression Inventory (CDI-C) (Kovacs, 1981) is one of the most commonly used self-report rating scales in the study of child and adolescent depression. More recently, a parent version of this instrument, the CDI-P, has been developed. No specific reference exists for the CDI-P; instead, several similar versions appear to have been deveoped simultaneously by a number of childhood depression researchers, most notably Kazdin and his colleagues (Kazdin, Esveldt-Dawson, Unis, & Rancurello, 1983; Kazdin, French, & Unis, 1983; Kazdin, French, Unis, & Esveldt-Dawson, 1983). Similar to the child version, the CDI-P consists of 27 items assessing affective, cognitive and behavioral symptoms of depression. Each item consists of three statements (rated 0, 1, or 2) describing the symptom, and the parent is asked to select the statement most descriptive of their child during the past two weeks. Kazdin, French, Unis, & Esveldt-Dawson (1983) examined 6-week test-retest reliability for the CDI-P in a sample of 5- to 13- year-old child psychiatric inpatients, and reported reliability coefficients of .61 for mothers and .54 for fathers (as compared to .50 for the children, themselves). Complicating the interpretation of these results, however, is the fact that, overall, the severity of the children's depression decreased significantly over the retest interval, although for the CDI only the difference on maternal ratings reached significance. Wierzbicki (1987) examined the psychometric properties of the CDI-P as completed by mothers in a nonclinical sample and reported a 1-month test-retest reliability of .75, split-half (odd-even) reliability of .74, and a Cronbach's alpha coefficient of .85. This is only slightly lower than the internal consistencies (Cronbach's alpha) reported by Kazdin, French, and Unis (1983) of .83 for mothers and .85 for fathers. Mother-father agreement for the scale has generally been moderate to good, averaging .64 across three inpatient studies (Kazdin, Esveldt-Dawson, Unis, & Rancurello, 1983; Kazdin, French & Unis, 1983; Kazdin, French, Unis, & Esveldt-Dawson, 1983). Reports of parent-child agreement have been much more variable ranging from −.03 to .74 in inpatient samples (Kazdin, Esveldt-Dawson, Unis, & Rancurello, 1983; Kazdin, French, & Unis, 1983; Kazdin, French, Unis, & Esveldt-Dawson, 1983; Romano & Nelson, 1988) and from .59 to .66 in an outpatient sample (Wierzbicki, 1987). The CDI-P possesses good concurrent validity, as it has been shown to correlate moderately well with a number of other depression measures (Kazdin, French, & Unis, 1983; Romano & Nelson, 1988; Wierzbicki, 1987). Investigations of discriminant validity have been more troublesome, however, as the scale has been show to discriminate depressed from normal but not from other psychiatrically disturbed children (Romano & Nelson, 1988).

Matson Evaluation of Social Skills (MESSY)

The Matson Evaluation of Social Skills with Youngsters (MESSY) (Matson, Rotatori, & Helsel, 1983) is a 64-item scale designed to identify deficiencies in children's social functioning and monitor treatment outcome following participation in social skills training programs. While the scale can be completed by either teachers or parents, norms are available only for teachers. A parallel 62-item children's self-report version is also available. Items for the MESSY were designed to cover a broad range of verbal and nonverbal socially facilitative and nonfacilitative behaviors and are scored on a 1 (not at all) to 5 (very much) Likert-type scale. Teacher norms are based on ratings of 322 nonreferred school children who ranged in age from 4 to 18 years. Factor analysis identified two factors labeled Inappropriate Assertiveness/Impulsiveness and Appropriate Social Skills. While the limited validity studies available for the Teacher-MESSY have generally been favorable (Helsel & Matson, 1984; Raymond & Matson, 1989), additional psychometric studies and clinical norms are needed. Nevertheless, the MESSY has been an important step in the development of standardized, empirically based social skills assessment measures.

SUMMARY

This review has described a number of issues and assumptions related to the use of informant checklists and rating scales. Several advantages and uses of rating scales were presented, as were a number of potential limitations, including the failure of most scales to take relevant contextual or situational factors into account. Almost all of the measures described were shown to possess adequate reliability and validity; however, several of the scales require the collection of additional normative data. In addition, most of the best standardized narrow-band informant scales were primarily designed to cover one specific dimension of childhood psychopathology (e.g., hyperactivity) while coverage of the remaining dimensions, especially the internalizing disorders such as anxiety and depression is extremely limited. The development of standardized informant reports for the anxiety and depressive disorders is extremely important, especially in light of the recent descriptive and treatment efforts in this area (cf., Klein & Last, 1989). Given the many advantages associated with the use of informant rating scales, these measures should be considered valuable components of any standard research or clinical assessment of child behavior problems in that they provide a fast, efficient, and reliable method of collecting information for a variety of purposes. However, when using informant rating scales, care must be taken to gather information from as many different sources as possible, and the use of these measures as the sole or primary source of data to generate diagnoses of child psychopathology should be avoided.

REFERENCES

Achenbach, T. M. (1978). The Child Behavior Profile: I. Boys aged 6–11. *Journal of Consulting and Clinical Psychology, 46*, 478–488.

Achenbach, T. M., & Edelbrock, C. S. (1978). The classification of child psychopathology: A review and analysis of empirical efforts. *Psychological Bulletin, 85*, 1275–1301.

Achenbach, T. M., & Edelbrock, C. S. (1979). The Child Behavior Profile: II. Boys aged 12-16 and girls aged 6-11 and 12-16. *Journal of Consulting and Clinical Psychology, 47*, 223–233.

Achenbach, T. M., & Edelbrock, C. S. (1981). Behavioral problems and competencies reported by parents of normal and disturbed children aged four through sixteen. *Monographs of the Society for Research in Child Development, 46* (No. 188).

Achenbach, T. M., & Edelbrock, C. S. (1983). *Manual for the Child Behavior Checklist and Revised Child Behavior Profile*. Burlington, VT.: Author.

Achenbach, T. M., & Edelbrock, C. S. (1986). *Manual for the teacher version of the Child Behavior Checklist and Child Behavior Profile*. Burlington, VT.: Author.

Achenbach, T. M., McConaughy, S. H., & Howell, C. T. (1987). Child/adolescent behavioral and emotional problems: Implications of cross-informant correlations for situational specificity. *Psychological Bulletin, 101*, 213–232.

Aman, M. D., & Werry, J. S. (1984). The Revised Behavior Problem Checklist in clinic attenders and nonattenders:

Age and sex effects. *Journal of Clinical Child Psychology, 13,* 237–242.

Aman, M. D., Werry, J. S., Fitzpatrick, J., Lowe, M., & Waters, J. (1983). Factor structure and norms for the Revised Behavior Problem Checklist on New Zealand children. *Australian and New Zealand Journal of Psychiatry, 17,* 354–360.

American Psychiatric Association. (1987). *Diagnostic and statistical manual of mental disorders* (3rd. ed., revised). Washington, D.C.: Author.

Anastasi, A. (1976). *Psychological Testing* (4th ed.). New York: Macmillan.

Atkins, M. S., Pelham, W. E., & Licht, M. H. (1985). A comparison of objective classroom measures and teacher ratings of attention deficit disorder. *Journal of Abnormal Child Psychology, 13,* 155–167.

Barkley, R. A. (1977). A review of stimulant drug research with hyperactive children. *Journal of Child Psychology and Psychiatry, 18,* 137–165.

Barkley, R. A. (1981a). Hyperactivity. In E. Mash & L. Terdal (Eds.), *Behavioral assessment of childhood disorders.* New York: Guilford Press.

Barkley, R. A. (1981b). *Hyperactive children: A handbook for diagnosis and treatment.* New York: Guilford Press.

Barkley, R. A. (1987). Child behavior rating scales and checklists. In M. Rutter, A. H. Tuma & I. S. Lann (eds.), *Assessment and diagnosis in child psychopathology* (pp. 113–155). New York: Guilford Press.

Barkley, R. A., & Edelbrock, C. S. (1986). Assessing situational variation in children's problem behaviors: The home and school situations questionnaires. In R. Prinz (Ed.), *Advances in behavioral assessment of children and families.* Greenwich, CT: JAI Press.

Barkley, R. A., & Ullman, D. G. (1975). A comparison of objective measures of activity and distractibility in hyperactive and nonhyperactive children. *Journal of Abnormal Child Psychology, 3,* 231–244.

Beck, S. (1988). Questionnaires and Checklists. In C. L. Frame & J. L. Matson (Eds.), *Handbook of assessment in childhood psychopathology* (pp. 79–106). New York: Plenum Press.

Cairns, R. B., & Green, J. A. (1979). How to assess personality and social patterns: Observations or ratings? In R. B. Cairns (Ed.), *The analysis of social interactions* (pp. 209–226). Hillsdale, NJ.: Lawrence Erlbaum Associates.

Campbell, D. T., & Fiske, D. W. (1959). Convergent and discriminant validation by the multitrait-multimethod matrix. *Psychological Bulletin, 56,* 81–105.

Conners, C. K. (1969). A teacher rating scale for use in drug studies with children. *American Journal of Psychiatry, 126,* 884–888.

Conners, C. K. (1970). Symptom patterns in hyperkinetic, neurotic, and normal children. *Child Development, 41,* 667–682.

Conners, C. K. (1973). Rating scales for use in drug studies with children. *Psychopharmacology Bulletin* [Special issue, Pharmacotherapy of children], 24–84.

Conners, C. K., & Barkley, R. A. (1985). Rating scales and checklists for child psychopharmacology. *Psychopharmacology Bulletin* [Special issue, Rating scales and assessment instruments for use in pediatric psychopharmacology research], *21,* 809–815.

Conners, C. K., & Blouin, A. G. (1980). *Hyperkinetic syndrome and psychopathology in children.* Paper presented at the meeting of the American Psychological Association, Montreal.

Costello, E. J., & Edelbrock, C. S. (1985). Detection of psychiatric disorders in pediatric primary care: A preliminary report. *Journal of the American Academy of Child Psychiatry, 24,* 771–774.

Cronbach, L. J. (1951). Coefficient Alpha and the internal structure of tests. *Psychometrika, 16,* 297–334.

Edelbrock, C. S. (1987). Psychometric research on children and adolescents. In C. G. Last & M. Hersen (Eds.), *Issues in diagnostic research* (pp. 219–240). New York: Plenum Press.

Edelbrock, C. S. (1988). Informant reports. In E. S. Shapiro & T. R. Kratchowill (Eds.), *Behavioral assessment in schools: Conceptual foundations and practical applications* (pp. 351–383). New York: Guilford Press.

Edelbrock, C. S., & Achenbach, T. M. (1984). The teacher version of the Child Behavior Checklist: I. Boys aged 6–11. *Journal of Consulting and Clinical Psychology, 52,* 207–217.

Edelbrock, C. S., Costello, A. J., & Kessler, M. K. (1984). Emprical corroboration of Attention Deficit Disorder. *Journal of the American Academy of Child Psychiatry, 23,* 285–290.

Edelbrock, C. S., Greenbaum, R., & Conover, N. C. (1985). Reliability and concurrent relations between the teacher version of the Child Behavior Profile and the Conners Revised Teacher Rating Scale. *Journal of Abnormal Child Psychology, 13,* 295–304.

Edelbrock, C. S., & Rancurello, M. D. (1985). Childhood hyperactivity: An overview of rating scales and their applications. *Clinical Psychology Review, 5,* 429–445.

Emery, R. E. & O'Leary, K. D. (1984). Marital discord and child behavior problems in a nonclinic sample. *Journal of Abnormal Child Psychology, 12,* 411–420.

Eyberg, S. M., & Robinson, E. A. (1983). Conduct problem behavior: Standardization of a behavioral rating scale with adolescents. *Journal of Clinical Child Psychology, 12,* 347–354.

Eyberg, S. M., & Ross, A. W. (1978). Assessment of child behavior problems: The validation of a new inventory. *Journal of Clinical Child Psychology, 7,* 113–116.

Funderburke, B. W., & Eyberg, S. M. (1989). Psychometric characteristics of the Sutter-Eyberg Student Behavior Inventory: A school behavior rating scale for use with preschool children. *Behavioral Assessment, 11,* 297–313.

Gadow, K. D., & Sprafkin, J. (1987). *Stony Brook Child Psychiatric Checklist—3R.* Department of Psychiatry and Behavioral Science, State University of New York at Stony Brook.

Garrison, W. T., & Earls, F. (1985). The Child Behavior Checklist as a screening instrument for young children. *Journal of the American Academy of Child Psychiatry, 24*, 76–80.

Glow, R. A. (1981). Cross-validity and normative data on the Conners Parent and Teacher Rating Scales. In K. Gadow & J. Loney (Eds.), *Psychosocial aspects of drug treatment for hyperactivity*. Boulder, CO: Westview Press.

Glow, R. A., Glow, P. H., & Rump, E. E. (1982). The stability of child behavior disorders: A one-year test-retest study of the Adelaid versions of the Conners Teacher and Parent Rating Scales. *Journal of Abnormal Child Psychology, 10*, 33–60.

Goyette, C. H., Conners, C. K., & Ulrich, R. F. (1978). Normative data on the Revised Conners Parent and Teacher Rating Scales. *Journal of Abnormal Child Psychology, 6*, 221–236.

Hagborg, W. J. (1990). The Revised Behavior Problem Checklist and severely emotionally disturbed adolescents: Relationship to intelligence, academic achievement, and sociometric ratings. *Journal of Abnormal Child Psychology, 18*, 47–53.

Harris, J. C., King, S. L., Reifler, J. P., & Rosenberg, L. A. (1984). Emotional and learning disorders in 6–12 year-old boys attending special schools. *Journal of the American Academy of Child Psychiatry, 23*, 431–437.

Helsel, W. J., & Matson, J. L. (1984). The assessment of depression in children: The internal structure of the Child Depression Inventory (CDI). *Behaviour Research and Therapy, 22*, 289–298.

Hodges, K., Kline, L., Stern, L., Cytryn, L., & McKnew, D. (1982). The development of a child assessment interview for research and clinical use. *Journal of Abnormal Child Psychology, 10*, 173–189.

Jensen, P. S., Traylor, J., Xenakis, S. N., & Davis, H. (1988). Child psychopathology rating scales and interrater agreement: I. Parents' gender and psychiatric symptoms. *Journal of the American Academy of Child Psychiatry, 27*, 442–450.

Jensen, P. S., Xenakis, S. N., Davis, H., & DeGroot, J. (1988). Child psychopathology rating scales and interrater agreement: II. Child and family characteristics. *Journal of the American Academy of Child Psychiatry, 27*, 451–461.

Kazdin, A. E., Esveldt-Dawson, K., & Loar, L. (1983). Correspondence of teacher ratings an direct observations of classroom behavior of psychiatric inpatient children. *Journal of Abnormal Child Psychology, 11*, 549–564.

Kazdin, A. E., Esveldt-Dawson, K., Unis, A. S., & Rancurello, M. D. (1983). Child and parent evaluations of depression and aggression in psychiatric inpatient children. *Journal of Abnormal Child Psychology, 11*, 401–413.

Kazdin, A. E., French, N. H., & Unis, A. S. (1983). Child, mother, and father evaluations of depression in psychiatric inpatient children. *Journal of Abnormal Child Psychology, 11*, 167–180.

Kazdin, A. E., French, N. H., Unis, A. S., & Esveldt-Dawson, K. (1983). Assessment of childhood depression: Correspondence of child and parent ratings. *Journal of the American Academy of Child Psychiatry, 22*, 157–164.

Kazdin, A. E., & Heidish, I. E. (1984). Convergence of clinically derived diagnoses and parent checklists among inpatient children. *Journal of Abnormal Child Psychology, 12*, 421–436.

Kazdin, A. E., & Petti, T. A. (1982). Self-report and interview measures of child and adolescent depression. *Journal of Child Psychology and Psychiatry, 23*, 437–457.

Klee, S. H., & Garfinkle, B. D. (1983). The computerized continuous performance task: A new measure of inattention. *Journal of Abnormal Child Psychology, 11*, 487–496.

Klein, R. G., & Last, C. (1989). *Anxiety disorders in children*. Newbury Park, CA: Sage Publications.

Kovacs, M. (1981). Rating scales to assess depression in school-aged children. *Acta Paedopsychiatrica, 46*, 305–315.

Kupietz, S., Bialer, I. & Winsburg, B. (1972). A behavior rating scale for assessing improvement in behaviorally deviant children: A preliminary investigation. *American Journal of Psychiatry, 128*, 1432–1436.

Lahey, B. B., Green, K. D., & Forehand, R. (1980). On the independence of ratings of hyperactivity, conduct problems, and attention deficits in children. *Journal of Consulting and Clinical Psychology, 48*, 566–574.

Lahey, B. B., McBurnett, K., Piacentini, J. C., Hartdagen, S., Walker, J., Frick, P. J., & Hynd, G. W. (1987). Agreement of parent and teacher rating scales with comprehensive clinical assessments of Attention Deficit Disorder with Hyperactivity. *Journal of Psychopathology and Behavioral Assessment, 5*, 429–439.

Lahey, B. B., & Piacentini, J. C. (1985). An evaluation of the Quay-Peterson Revised Behavior Problem Checklist. *Journal of School Psychology, 23*, 285–289.

Lahey, B. B., Schaughency, E. A., Frame, C. L., & Strauss, C. C. (1985). Teacher ratings of attention problems in children experimentally defined as exhibiting attention deficit disorder with and without hyperactivity. *Journal of the American Academy of Child Psychiatry, 24*, 613–616.

Lahey, B. B., Schaughency, E. A., Strauss, C. C., & Frame, C. L. (1984). Are attention deficit disorders with and without hyperactivity similar or dissimilar disorders? *Journal of the American Academy of Child Psychiatry, 23*, 302–309.

Langhorne, J. E., & Loney, J. (1979). A four-fold model for subgrouping the Hyperkinetic/MBD syndrome. *Child Psychiatry and Human Development, 9*, 153–159.

Loney, J., & Milich, R. S. (1981). Hyperactivity, inattention, and aggression in clinical practice. In M. Wolraich & D. K. Routh (Eds.), *Advances in behavioral pediatrics* (Vol. 2). Greenwich, CT: JAI Press.

Mash, E. J., & Johnston, C. L. (1983). Parental perceptions

of child behavior problems, parenting self-esteem, and mothers' reported stress in younger and older hyperactive and normal children. *Journal of Consulting and Clinical Psychology, 51,* 68–99.

Mash, E. J., & Terdal, L. G. (1988). Behavioral assessment of child and family disturbance. In E. J. Mash & L. G. Terdal (Eds.), *Behavioral assessment of childhood disorders* (2nd ed.). New York: Guilford Press.

Matson, J. L., & Rotatori, A. F., & Helsel, W. J. (1983). Development of a rating scale to measure social skills in children: The Matson Evaluation of Social Skills with Youngsters (MESSY). *Behaviour Research and Therapy, 21,* 335–340.

McMahon, R. J. (1984). Behavioral checklists and rating scales. In T. H. Ollendick & M. Hersen (Eds.), *Child behavioral assessment: Principles and procedures* (pp. 80–105). New York: Pergamon Press.

Milich, R., Roberts, M. A., Loney, J., & Caputo, J. (1980) Differentiating practice effects and statistical regression on the Conners Hyperkinesis Index. *Journal of Abnormal Child Psychology, 8,* 549–552.

Nay, W. R. (1979). *Multimethod clinical assessment.* New York: Gardner Press.

O'Leary, K. D., & Johnson, S. B. (1979). Psychological assessment. In H. C. Quay & J. S. Werry (Eds.), *Psychopathological disorders of childhood* (2nd ed.). New York: John Wiley & Sons.

O'Leary, K. D., & Johnson, S. B. (1986). Assessment and assessment of change. In H. C. Quay & J. S. Werry (Eds.), *Psychopathological disorders of childhood* (3rd ed.). New York: Wiley.

Pataki, C. S., Carlson, G. C., & Rapport, M. D. (1989). Psychopharmacologic treatment of children with attentional and mood disorders: Effects of behavior and mood. *Scientific Proceedings of the Annual Meeting of the American Academy of Child and Adolescent Psychiatry, 5,* 37–38.

Peterson, D. R. (1961). Behavior problems of middle childhood. *Journal of Consulting Psychology, 25,* 205–209.

Piacentini, J. C., Abikoff, H. A., Guardino, M., Klass, E., & Klein, R. G. (1989). Teacher Ratings of DSM-III-R Disruptive Behavior Disorders: Prevalence in a normative sample. *Scientific Proceedings of the Annual Meeting of the American Academy of Child and Adolescent Psychiatry, 5,* 81–82.

Piacentini, J. C., Lahey, B. B., Frick, P., Pataki, C. S., & Christ, M. A. (1988). Comparison of mother- and teacher-identified hyperactive children. *Scientific Proceedings of the Annual Meeting of the American Academy of Child and Adolescent Psychiatry, 4,* 67.

Quay, H. C. (1977). Measuring dimensions of deviant behavior: The Behavior Problem Checklist. *Journal of Abnormal Child Psychology, 5,* 277–287.

Quay, H. C., & Peterson, D. R. (1979). *Manual for the Behavior Problem Checklist.* Privately printed.

Quay, H. C., & Peterson, D. R. (1983). *Interim manual for the Revised Behavior Problem Checklist.* Coral Gables, FL: Author.

Quay, H. C., & Peterson, D. R. (1987). *Manual for the Revised Behavior Problem Checklist.* Coral Gables, FL: Author.

Rapoport, J. L., & Benoit, M. (1975). The relation of direct home observations to the clinic evaluation of hyperactive school age boys. *Journal of Child Psychology and Psychiatry 16,* 141–147.

Raymond, K. I., & Matson, J. L. (1989). Social skills in the hearing impaired. *Journal of Clinical Child Psychology, 18,* 247–258.

Reed, M. L., & Edelbrock, C. S. (1983). Reliability and validity of the Direct Observation Form of the Child Behavior Checklist. *Journal of Abnormal Child Psychology, 11,* 521–530.

Rickard, K. M., Forehand, R., Wells, K. C., Greist, D. L., & McMahon, R. J. (1981). Factors in the referral of children for behavioral treatment: A comparison of mothers of clinic-referred deviant, clinic-referred non-deviant, and nonclinical children. *Behaviour Research and Therapy, 19,* 201–205.

Robinson, E. A., Eyberg, S. M., & Ross, A. W. (1980). The standardization of an inventory of child conduct problem behaviors. *Journal of Clinical Child Psychology, 9,* 22–28.

Romano, B. A., & Nelson, R. O. (1988). Discriminant and concurrent validity of measures of children's depression. *Journal of Clinical Child Psychology, 17,* 255–259.

Rosenberg, R. P., & Beck, S. (1986). Preferred assessment methods and treatment modalities for hyperactive children among clinical child and school psychologists. *Journal of Clinical Child Psychology, 15,* 142–147.

Ross, D. M., & Ross, S. A. (1982). *Hyperactivity: Current issues, research, and theory* (2nd ed.). New York: John Wiley & Sons.

Schaughency, E. A., & Lahey, B. B. (1985). Mothers' and fathers' perceptions of child deviance: Roles of child behavior, parental depression, and marital satisfaction. *Journal of Consulting and Clinical Psychology, 53,* 718–723.

Sutter, J., & Eyberg, S. M. (1984). *Sutter-Eyberg Student Behavior Inventory.* (Available from Sheila Eyberg, Department of Clinical and Health Psychology, University of Florida, Gainesville, FL, 32610).

Trites, R. L., Blouin, A. G., Ferguson, H., & Lynch, G. W. (1981). The Conners Teacher Rating Scale: An epidemiological inter-rater reliability and follow-up investigation. In K. Gadow & J. Loney (Eds.), *Psychosocial aspects of drug treatment for hyperactivity.* Boulder, CO: Westview Press.

Trites, R. L., Blouin, A. G., & Laprade, K. (1982). Factor analysis of Conners Teacher Rating Scale based on a large normative sample. *Journal of Consulting and Clinical Psychology, 50,* 615–623.

Trites, R. L., & Laprade, K. (1983). Evidence for an independent syndrome of hyperactivity. *Journal of Child Psychology and Psychiatry, 24,* 573–586.

Ullman, R. K., Sleator, E. K. (1985). ADD children: Which

children are helped by stimulants. *Clinical Pediatrics, 24,* 547–551.

Ullman, R. K., Sleator, E. K., & Sprague, R. L. (1984a). A new rating scale for diagnosis and monitoring of ADD children. *Psychopharmacology Bulletin, 20,* 160–164.

Ullman, R. K., Sleator, E. K., & Sprague, R. L. (1984b). ADD children: Who is referred from the schools? *Psychopharmacology Bulletin, 20,* 308–312.

Ullman, R. K., Sleator, E. K., & Sprague, R. L. (1985a). A change of mind: The Conners Abbreviated Rating Scales reconsidered. *Journal of Abnormal Child Psychology, 13,* 553–565.

Ullman, R. K., Sleator, E. K., & Sprague, R. L. (1985b). Introduction to the use of ACTeRS. *Psychopharmacology Bulletin* [Special issue, Rating scales and assessment instruments for use in pediatric psychopharmacology research], *21,* 915–920.

Weissman, M. M., Orvaschel, H., & Padian, N. (1980). Children's symptom and social functioning self-report scales: Comparison of mothers' and children's reports. *Journal of Nervous and Mental Disorders, 168,* 736–740.

Werry, J. S., & Sprague, R. L. (1974). Methylphenidate in children-effect of dosage. *Australian and New Zealand Journal of Psychiatry, 8,* 9–19.

Werry, J. S., Sprague, R. L., & Cohen, M. N. (1975). Conners' Teacher Rating Scale for use in drug studies with children: An empirical study. *Journal of Abnormal Child Psychology, 3,* 217–229.

Wierzbicki, M. (1987). A parent form of the Children's Depression Inventory: Reliability and validity in nonclinical populations. *Journal of Clinical Psychology, 43,* 390–397.

CHAPTER 8

SELF-REPORT METHODOLOGY

William M. Reynolds

INTRODUCTION

The assessment of personality, affect, attitudes, character, values, attributions, temperament, emotion, cognitive styles, behavior, and other psychological and personological aspects of children and adolescents represent an important domain of research and clinical practice. Self-report has traditionally been the primary method for the assessment of personality (Angleitner & Wiggins, 1986), as well as for a number of internalizing aspects of the individual. These latter include characteristics such as depression, anxiety, loneliness, self-concept, and other dimensions of the self that involve subjective feelings and self-evaluation. Self-report procedures have been used with children and adolescents to assess a wide range of personal characteristics. Self-report, as a method of appraisal of the emotional status or state of a child or adolescent, provides a unique perspective and information about the youngster. Many aspects of one's psychological state are, to an extent, subjective or constitute a domain for which self-report is the primary modality. For instance, the assessment of self-concept is, at a basic level, a youngster's report of his or her self-evaluation or perception of competence.

This chapter focuses on self-report as an assessment strategy with children and adolescents. Although many self-report inventories and scales developed specifically for adults have been used with young people, for the most part, these measures will not be discussed in this chapter. Because many self-report scales and inventories are described in detail in later sections of this book, no attempt will be made to provide in-depth descriptions of the many self-report measures developed over the past two decades, let alone the last 60 years.

This chapter provides a broad perspective on the use of self-report as a method of assessment with children and adolescents. This examination includes a brief historical review, considerations of the characteristics and use of self-report, and an overview of domains for which self-report measures have been developed. The intent of this chapter is to provide a foundation for the understanding of self-report as an assessment methodology with children and adolescents.

SELF-REPORT AS AN ASSESSMENT METHODOLOGY

What constitutes the description of a measure as a self-report assessment devise? Broadly defined, self-report involves the direct response of an individual to some form of stimuli (Sundberg & Reynolds, in progress). Within this global perspective, we may view many cognitive as well as projective assessment techniques as self-report methodologies. For example, self-monitoring of behaviors or cognitions (e.g., thought sampling) within an assessment or treatment program can be considered a form of guided self-report that typically focuses on a limited number of behaviors or cognitions, sampled in one or more environments, and reported on over a specified time period. Differences in classes of self-report methods occur as a function of level of stimuli structure and ambiguity, as well as level of inference specific to the response as a sign, sample, or correlate of individual characteristics.

If we define self-report to include all manner of assessment that utilizes a direct response by the subject, within a natural or controlled setting, with or without stimuli (structured or unstructured), a tremendous number of assessment procedures come to mind. Objective personality tests are typically viewed as the prototypic example of self-report methodology. Clinical interviews, whether they are structured, semistructured, or unstructured, are also examples of self-report methods. Likewise, most projective techniques may be viewed as utilizing self-report as a basic assessment modality. A major differentiation among these procedures is the degree of inference placed on the subject's report by the evaluator as well as the extent to which a theoretical model is used in the interpretation of responses. Theoretical perspectives on personality and psychopathology have driven the development of a number of projective methods, from the well-known work of Henry Murray to the once well-known, now somewhat obscure, work of Lipot Szondi. While greater objectivity has been realized in the scoring of projective assessment procedures (e.g., Exner & Weiner, 1982), interpretation is, in most cases, largely based on dynamic interpretation of scores as "signs" of underlying psychological processes and pathologies. This sign approach has been used extensively in psychological assessment. The view of responses to objective tests (including self-report) as signs and samples of behavior is not new and has been discussed for many years (e.g., Loevinger, 1957). There are numerous issues specific to the viability and utility of self-report as a general assessment methodology, as well as related topics such as the stability of personality (e.g., Epstein, 1979). Unfortunately, space limitations preclude a formal delineation and discussion of these important and sometimes controversial perspectives.

Within the scope of this chapter, the more common conceptualization of self-report as a method that requires an individual to respond to a set of structured verbal or written statements or questions is used. Questions or statements may require a response indicative of the individual's self-evaluation of mental state (e.g., "I feel sad"); their agreement or disagreement with a particular statement, perspective, or belief (e.g., "Good kids are sometimes punished"); or require the respondent to choose between two or more fixed choices that are specific to the respondent (e.g., [a] "I like to go to movies with friends," [b] "I like to read," [c] "I like to play sports"). Self-report measures demonstrate a wide range of response formats, types of options, and response perspectives (e.g., assessment of one's likes or dislikes, agreement or disagreement, true or false about self, feel or do not feel, etc.). This chapter focuses on what has become the traditional perspective of self-report assessment: the paper-and-pencil questionnaire.

The use of self-reports of children and adolescents for the assessment of affective and behavioral characteristics is not new. In the 1920s and 1930s, a number of multidimensional self-report measures of adjustment and temperament for children and adolescents were developed. A major force in the field of psychology during this period was the mental hygiene movement, which had a particular impact on the study of children's mental health. This movement provided impetus for the development of self-report measures of child personality and adjustment for use by psychologists, teachers, and other mental health professionals. To a large extent, these precursors to contemporary measures have been discarded and, for the most part, have faded from current thought.

As will be shown, the perspectives that the development of child self-report measures began in the 1950s or 1960s as a response to declining interest in projective measures (La Greca, 1990) or are a relatively recent development or emphasis (Beck, 1987; Beitchman & Corradini, 1988; Stone & Lemanek, 1990) fail to acknowledge the very rich history of self-report measures designed to assess child and adolescent personality. Although there appears to be an increased interest in child and adolescent self-report, this is not a new assessment focus. It is likely that this renewed interest in self-report measures is in part a reaction to the limitations of behavioral assessment, the recognition of cognitions as important components for understanding the individual (Reynolds & Stark, 1983), along with the contemporary focus of psychologists on internalizing disorders of childhood and adolescence (Reynolds, 1990a). The following brief, historical perspective on the development of self-report measures designed for use with children and adolescents is provided as a way to illustrate a sample of what we may have forgotten or what has past out of the literature over the past half-century.

HISTORICAL EXCURSION

As noted earlier, the use of self-report measures with children and adolescents is not a recent development in psychology. A historical survey of self-report measures developed specifically for use with young people suggests that this methodology has been actively employed for the past 60 years, with numerous tests, scales, and inventories developed since the 1930s. Thus, self-report as an assessment strategy coincides with projective tests in its initial clinical and research applications with children and adolescents.

An examination of early child and adolescent self-report measures suggests clinical interests across numerous content domains. As is described below, many of the areas assessed one-half century ago are consistent with domains evaluated by contemporary self-report measures. For instance, Carl Rogers in 1931 (Rogers, 1931a, 1931b) developed the Test of Personality Adjustment for children ages 9 through 13 years. This measure provided scores on 4 scales—personal inferiority, social maladjustment, family maladjustment, daydreaming—and a total score. With separate answer booklets for boys and for girls, and a manual with limited (by today's standards) psychometric information, this test was used in research and clinical practice for more than 30 years, with normative revisions suggested in 1958 (Burchinal, Gardner, & Hawkes, 1958). In 1961, the title of this measure was changed to the Personality Adjustment Inventory, along with four wording changes made to items and a revised introduction in the manual. Although some scales on this measure, such as daydreaming, may appear somewhat antiquated, others, such as those focusing on social maladjustment and family maladjustment, are similar in assessment focus to contemporary child and adolescent measures.

Prior to Roger's work in this area, Ellen Mathews (1923) modified Woodworth's Personal Data Sheet, the latter generally viewed as one of the first objective personality scales. Published by the Stoelting Company, the Woodward-Mathews Personal Data Sheet consisted of 75 items using a *yes-no* response format. The basic focus of this scale was as a measure of "emotional stability" of children aged 9 through 19 years. Of some interest is the fact that this measure came out around the time of extensive European emigration into the United States; thus we find the development of norms for a range of "special groups," including Italian and Jewish children, orphans, mentally retarded youngsters, and various groups of "delinquent" children. From an examination of research from that period, this test appears to have been used as a general measure of "neurotic" characteristics. Slawson (1926), using this scale with a large sample study of incarcerated delinquents in New York, found that more than 84% of delinquents scored above the mean of nondelinquent, normal children reported by Mathews. Likewise, Courthial (1931) found delinquent adolescent girls significantly higher on neurotic symptoms on the Woodward-Mathews than a nondelinquent control group.

Cady (1923) also modified Woodward's Personal Data Sheet in a study of delinquent boys 12 to 14 years of age. Barbara Burks (1928) used the Cady modification of the Personal Data Sheet in her classic nature-nurture study of 214 children adopted before the age of 12 months and 105 children living with their own parents. Thus, as with early intelligence tests, a major impetus in the design and use of early child and adolescent personality tests was the assessment of individuals who were culturally different or who differed from the mainstream of society.

In 1934, Pintner, a pioneer in the area of performance-based measures of intelligence, (e.g., Pintner & Patterson, 1917), and colleagues (Pintner, Maller, Forlano, & Axelrod, 1934, 1935) developed the Pupil Portraits test as a measure of adjustment of children in grades 4 through 8. This 100-item measure was available in two alternate forms (a rarity for personality measures) and was standardized on more than 3,000 children with separate norms for boys and girls. Although basically a self-report measure, it can be considered somewhat of a semiprojective (or objective-projective) in that the examinee responds to items that consist of positive and negative statements describing children, (i.e., "This child thinks his friends do not care much for him"), a procedure similar to that used by Adkins and Ballif (1973) in their measure (Animal Crackers) of achievement motivation in young children. Item content on the Pupil Portraits reflect subscales specific to the relationship of the child to school environment, teacher, classmates, himself or herself, and home and family.

Several years later, Pintner, Loftus, Forlano, and Alster (1937) developed what we would view as a traditional objective paper-and-pencil measure of personality for use with children. Consisting of 105 items, the Aspects of Personality Inventory (API) assessed dimensions of ascendant-submissive behavior (e.g., "I don't mind when other children get ahead of me in line"), extrovert-introvert behavior (e.g., "I keep quiet when I am with other people"), and emotional stability (e.g., "I often feel sick when I have to go to school"). Many of the items on this scale are remarkably similar to those found on contemporary child self-report measures. In their article on the reliability of the API, Pintner and Forlano (1938) report relatively low split-half reliabilities for ascendent-submissive and extrovert-introvert scales, and high reliabilities (.80s and .90s) for the emotional stability scale.

Brown, in 1935, published the Personality Inventory for Children, a personality inventory of adjustment in children in grades 4 through 9. Originating from his dissertation at Ohio State University in 1933 and described in 1934, the PIC was published by The Psychological Corporation in 1935 to assess "psychoneurotic" characteristics of children and young adolescents. Consisting of 80 items and normed on 2,748 children 9 through 14 years of age, the revised PIC provided scores on youngsters' personality in the areas of home, school, physical symptoms, insecurity, and irritability. It is interesting to note that Carl Rogers (then a professor at Ohio State University) in his 1941 review of this measure, begins by stating: "It is difficult to know the purpose of this carelessly devised inventory" (p. 84). As readers of test reviews may gather, not much has changed in the nature of test reviews by authors of competing or similar measures.

The Baxter Child Personality Test by Edna Baxter (1937) provided parallel child and mother report inventories, each consisting of 92 questions. Designed for use with children 4 to 13 years of age, this measure assessed 23 different traits (e.g., friendliness, compliance, cheerfulness, respect, courtesy, tidiness, self-control, courage, concentration, grace, etc.). It is interesting that Baxter found a correlation of .82 between the mother and child report scales.

In 1939, Tiegs, Clark, and Thorpe, published the California Test of Personality (CTP) (by the old California Test Bureau, later to become CTB/McGraw-Hill, and more recently, CTB/Mcmillan/McGraw-Hill). Various forms of this measure were developed for use with children in grades 4 through high school age, with later forms developed for younger children down to kindergarten age. The original form of the CTP consisted of scales of self-reliance, sense of personal worth, sense of personal freedom, sense of belonging, withdrawing tendencies, nervous symptoms, social standards, social skills, antisocial tendencies, family relations, school relations, community relations, and several subtotal and total adjustment scores. Over the years, the CTP has been used extensively in schools and in research, with numerous revisions undertaken by the publisher. As recently as 1981, Goh, Teslow, and Fuller reported that in a national sample of 274 practicing school psychologists, the CTP was the third most often used self-report personality inventory, behind self-concept scales and the MMPI.

The 1930s also saw the development of self-report personality measures designed for use with adolescents as well as adults. The venerable Adjustment Inventory by Hugh Bell was developed in 1934 and included a form for high school and college students. The high school form provided scores on four scales: home, health, social, and emotional. The student form of the Adjustment Inventory was revised in 1962 and included six subscales: home, health, submissiveness, emotionality, hostility, and masculinity. Bell also developed the School Inventory in 1937, which was more of a global assessment of high school students' (grades 10 to 12) attitudes toward school, teachers, and so on. With poor norms and little rationale for items and assessment focus, this measure did not match the success of the Adjustment Inventory. Along with Bell's Adjustment Inventory, Robert Bernreuter's Personality Inventory, designed for use with high school students and adults, was also a popular inventory before the MMPI and in the early days of its use. Developed as his dissertation at Stanford University in 1931, the Personality Inventory provided scores specific to neurotic tendency, self-sufficiency, introversion-extraversion, dominance-submission, self-confidence, and sociability (the latter two subscales developed by John Flanagan). With separate norms for high school students, the Personality Inventory was extensively used in research. In 1935, Ewina Cowan and colleagues developed the Cowan Adolescent Personality Schedule, which yielded scores on nine scales, measuring fear, family emotion, family authority, inferiority, nonfamily authority, responsibility, escapes, neurotic, and compensation. This scale was also perceived as a measure for the diagnosis of psychological problems of adolescents (Brigden, 1939).

The Personal Index was developed by Loofbourow and Keys in 1933 for boys in junior high school grades 7 through 9. Originally consisting of eight tests, the final form of the PI consisted of four distinct scales with different response formats, and included scales of false vocabulary, social attitudes, courtesy, and adjustment questionnaire. Many of the scales and items were adapted from existing instruments. The Personal Index was somewhat unique in that it included a validity index, in the False Vocabulary scale, which was specific to the assessment of dissimulation tendencies (falsification, overly positive self-report). Viewed as a measure of "overstatement," this scale required the subject to mark the words known to him or her, with a number of "false" words (e.g., "simmuck") included on the list. The Adjustment Questionnaire component of the Personal Index consisted of 90 *yes-no* questions (e.g., "Do you ever wish that you were dead?") and came closest to a traditional self-report inventory. The authors provided validity evidence that included contrasted groups validity (normal boys versus problem behavior youth) and acceptable levels of reliability.

An interesting (albeit somewhat strange) measure, the Personality Quotient Test, was developed by Henry Link in 1936a and revised and published by The Psychological Corporation in 1938 for use with adolescents in junior and senior high school. This measure, also known as the PQ Test, attempted to capitalize on the widespread acceptance of the IQ score by providing a PQ (Personality Quotient) score. Link was active in describing his scale in professional publications as well as the popular press of the time. The latter is illustrated by his 1936b article "Personality Can Be Acquired," which appeared in *Readers Digest*. A combination of open-ended questions and 150 item self-report questionnaire, the PQ Test provided scores on dimensions of extroversion, social aggressiveness, self-determination, economic self-determination, and adjustment to the opposite sex. All items were scored for extroversion and a number of items for the remaining "sub-traits," as Link referred to the other subscales. Thus, most items overlapped on two or more subscales. In his original article, Link (1936a) provides some enlightening perspectives on personality development in youngsters. For example, Link notes that the item specific to social dancing "is also one of the items contributing the most heavily toward personality" (p. 533). Other "highly significant" items according to Link included such critical items (with apologies to L. Goldberg, 1974) as "Do you go to Sunday School?" and "When you have two things to do, one you like and one you dislike, do you generally do the thing you don't like first?" Although the notion of the PQ as a metric similar to the IQ did not succeed, the current use of standard scores with two standard deviations above the mean as clinically relevant is conceptually similar to this perspective.

The 1940s brought the initial development of the Child Personality Scale by Mary Amatora Tschechtelin (1944), which was formally published 7 years later (Amatora, 1951). Although not a great measure, nor one that generated much research beyond a dozen or so journal articles by its author, this scale is noteworthy in that it was designed to incorporate ratings on 22 dimensions by teachers, peers, and self-ratings. Thus, the Child Personality Scale presented a multimethod assessment approach to the assessment of children's personality. To judge by an examination of the 22 dimensions (each rated on a 10-point scale), this measure provided more of an assessment of personality and behavior than pathology, as illustrated by ratings of sociability, popularity, courtesy, cooperation, generosity, persistence, patience, thoughtfulness, sense of humor, and dependability. A slightly modified form of this scale was later known as the Personality Rating Scale. This form of tripartite assessment methodology has reemerged (e.g., teacher-parent-self; teacher-peer-self; teacher-parent-peer), with some authors viewing this approach as new or novel.

In the 1940s, interest in temperament, combined with developments in factor analysis, resulted in a number of temperament and personality inventories. Guilford and Martin (1943) developed the Guilford-Martin Inventory of Factors for adolescents in grades 10 and above, and adults, which included scales of general activity, ascendance-submission, masculinity-feminity, inferiority feelings, and nervousness. This was revised and expanded by Guilford and Zimmerman in 1949 as the Guilford-Zimmerman Temperament Survey, for youngsters in grade 9 and above, with 10 scales of temperament and personality. Louis Thurstone (1949) developed the Thurstone Temperament Schedule (TTS) for use with adolescents in grades 9 and above, and with adults. The TTS consisted of 140 items, using a *yes, no*, or *?* response format, and produced scores on seven temperament scales—Active, Vigorous, Impulsive, Dominant, Stable, Sociable, and Reflective—with 20 items per scale.

In the late 1940s, Remmers, Shimberg, and Drunker (1949) developed the SRA Youth Inventory for youngsters in grades 7 through 12, with scores provided on scales of school, future, myself, people, home, dates and sex, health, general and basic difficulty. Several years later Remmers and Bauernfeind (1951) developed the SRA Junior Inventory for grades 4 through 8, assessing five of the Youth Inventory scales. Both of these tests were somewhat revised and came out under a new publisher (Scholastic Testing Service) as the STS Youth Inventory and STS Junior Inventory. Revisions included deletion of scales and items of a perceived personal nature (e.g., dates and sex).

The 1950s witnessed the development of numerous inventories (and constructs) by Raymond B. Cattell and colleagues at the Institute for Personality and Ability Testing (IPAT). Most of these measures were designed for junior and senior high school students and adults and included the IPAT Neurotic Personality Factor Test, IPAT Contact Personality Factor Test, IPAT Anxiety Scale, Children's Personality Questionnaire, Early School Personality Questionnaire, and the IPAT High School Personality Questionnaire (HSPQ; previously the Junior Personality Quiz). The HSPQ was designed to measure 14 personality dimensions in youngsters ages 12 to 18 years and continues to be used today. A very interesting derivation measure by Cattell was the IPAT Music Preference Test of Personality developed in 1953 and designed for children ages 6 and above and adults. This measure provided 11 scores (in the Cattellian bipolar tradition) such as adjustment vs. frustrated emotionality, resilience vs. withdrawn schizothymia, anxiety and concern vs. paranoid imperiousness, and so on. What makes this measure rather unique as a self-report inventory is its format and materials. On this measure, personality traits of children were assessed by youngsters' responses (like, dislike, indifferent) to 100 15-to-20-second piano renditions (items) of muscial scores (e.g., the "Prelude to Tristan and Isolde"). Items along with instructions were on a phonograph record. Apart from youngsters' enjoyment of Wagner, the basic premise of this measure appears to be that certain music appeals to various moods, the latter of which are associate with different personality traits.

An interesting (although somewhat unusual) study of personality in 11-year-olds by Cattell and Gruen (1955) examined a battery of 142 tests and indices (only 128 were administered to all subjects) in a sample of 184 children. Testing involved approximately 8 hours of group and individual assessment! Factor analytic procedures produced significant factor loadings from 104 variables on 16 factors. The tests included self-report, or, as Cattell refers to questionnaire measures, *Q-data;* behavioral, physiological and projective assessment procedures (non-self-report) referred to as *OT* or objective test data; and behavioral ratings or life records of behavior (*BR* or *LR* data) based on direct performance or observations. Initial measures included such diverse tasks as "Low Shock Suggestibility," "Impairment of Hidden Finger Maze by Shock," "Willingness to Believe Strange Facts," "Preference for Neatness," "Excess of Hardheaded or Cynical/Oversentimental Attitudes," and various reaction time procedures, to name a few of the measures in this battery.

The results of the study just reported were coalesced into an 18-factor test battery called the Objective-Analytic Personality Test Battery and published by Cattell and colleagues in 1955. This test, designed for children ages 11 through 16 and for adults, included a battery of performance tests (e.g., flicker fusion, estimation of time, color-form sorting, esthetic sense in color, and readiness to act out animal sounds (among others). These measures were proposed to measure 18 personality factors. If we settle somewhere between this latter test and the HSPQ for the number of factors, we end up with the Sixteen Personality Factor Questionnaire (16 PFQ) (Cattell, Eber, & Tatsuoka, 1970), probably best known of the Cattell et al. measures, developed in the early 1950s, and designed for ages 16 and older. Although these tests were quite varied in scope and meaningfulness, there is no doubt that Cattell has had a tremendous impact on the assessment of personality as well as intelligence (he was a leader in the development of culture-fair intelligence tests) in children, adolescents, and adults. It is also interesting to note that 50 years ago, Cattell (then G. Stanley Hall Professor at Clark University), in his 1941 review of the Student Form of Bell's Adjustment Inventory, begins by stating: "To the writing of inventories there is no end, and one would think that today a very potent excuse would be necessary for putting a new one on the market" (p. 51).

A number of personality inventories developed for adults in the 1940s and 1950s continue to be used with adolescents in clinical and research settings. Best known are the Minnesota Multiphasic Personality Inventory (MMPI) (Hathaway & McKinley, 1940) and the California Psychological Inventory (CPI) (Gough, 1957). The past decade has seen a renewed interest in the use of the MMPI with adolescents. Several investigators, such as Archer (Archer, 1984; 1987; Archer, Pancoast, & Klinefelter, 1989; Archer, White, & Orvin, 1979) and Colligan (Colligan &

Offord, 1986) have examined the efficacy of new adolescent norms for the MMPI. Although designed primarily for use with adults, the MMPI has been used with children as young as age 12 (Marks, Seeman, & Haller, 1974).

The self-report measures for children and adolescents noted above are not inclusive of all the scales and inventories developed during the first half of the century. Many of the earlier inventories and scales can be criticized on the basis of psychometric standards, such as reliability, validity, and norms. However, as will be shown below, these criticisms are not unique to early personality measures.

The historical synopsis presented above suggests a number of interesting commonalities between these early measures and contemporary trends in child and adolescent assessment. The role of the family as exemplified in aspects of family maladjustment and discord, the assessment of temperament, assessment of internalizing problems such as withdrawal, perceptions of social competence and self-esteem or personal self-worth; and the assessment of the child from a multi-informant perspective (e.g., self, peer, teacher, parent, observer), are all examples of contemporary trends in assessment that can be traced to much earlier measures.

What can be deduced from this brief historical illustration of child and adolescent self-report measures? It is clear that beginning in the 1920s and 1930s a major focus in personality assessment was on the development and publication of self-report measures for children and adolescents. These measures were typically multidimensional in nature, usually consisting of from four to nine subscales. In addition, measures were designed for different populations, such as clinic-referred, school-based, and delinquent. Although some tests and items appear naive by today's standards, others are similar to items found on present-day self-report measures.

ISSUES AND ASSUMPTIONS IN THE USE OF SELF-REPORT BY CHILDREN AND ADOLESCENTS

Numerous issues relate either directly or indirectly to the use of self-report methodology for the evaluation of personality and affect in children. Many of these issues are specific to whether children are competent reporters of their feelings and behaviors. Adolescents are generally viewed as competent to deal with the task demands of self-report measures, including many developed and used with adults. However, attention to such features as reading level, psychosocial maturity to understand and deal with scale content, differences in endorsement proportions, and experiential factors make the direct utilization of adult measures with adolescents a potentially less-than-reasonable proposition. Unless formal evaluation of scale psychometric utility, scale content, and construct viability has been established with young persons, adult measures should be used with caution or not at all. Furthermore, because of differences in base rates for certain psychopathologies as well as developmental and environmental differences, adult norms or cutoff scores should not be used with adolescents unless empirical evidence suggests their utility and validity.

Within the traditional model of self-report as a response to structured statements on paper-and-pencil or similar-format questionnaires, self-report may be viewed as the reporting of one's attitudes or mental states. Thus, individuals are given the task demand of accessing their own mental state or self-representation and providing a report according to a prescribed response format. The degree to which a person can given an accurate report of his or her own mental state may be influenced by a number of conditions. Wilson (1985) delineated four conditions that may foster or hinder accurate access to mental states: motivated self-deception, effects of self-analysis (i.e., self-reflection), incorrect adoption of feeling rules (such as convincing oneself that he or she feels happy when in fact the opposite is true), and the amount and accessibility of processing preceding attitudes. Most of the data for these influences on an individual's accessibility to mental states is derived from adult self-attribution literature. However, it is clear that such conditions are equally salient for the use of self-report measures with children and adolescents.

Developmental Issues

A multitude of developmental aspects are important to consider when utilizing self-report with young children. Very few measures are designed for use with children below the age of 7 years. There are several reasons for the limited number of self-report measures for preschool and early-school-age children. Linguistic competence is clearly an important prerequisite. To deal with this issue, most measures for young children are individually administered and often utilize pictorial representations as a response format.

Developmental issues include the child's self-awareness and ability to differentiate between emotions, as well as understanding that different, sometimes seemingly opposite, emotions can occur concurrently. Harter (1986), integrating the work of Fisher (1980) and Selman (1980) with her own developmental research, has described a cognitive-developmental perspective on the development of emotional understanding in children. Research generally supports hierarchical-developmental levels of children's understanding of their feelings, although mental age may also be a factor, with brighter children often demonstrating increased self-awareness of their feelings (Carroll & Steward, 1984). This is an important domain of study, because the ability to accurately differentiate emotions is a key component in providing valid self-report data.

Inherent in the use of self-report with children and adolescents is the expectation that the youngster is capable of reliable self-monitoring of the domain of behavior, affect, cognitions, feelings, and so on, evaluated by the measure in question. This ability to accurately self-monitor may be viewed as a developmental phenomena. While data suggest that young children can be taught to accurately self-monitor overt behaviors, their ability to self-monitor thoughts, feelings, and other covert internalized phenomena is a reasonable question that goes beyond the mechanical concerns of reading ability and comprehension level. Furthermore, for some problem domains, impairment in the youngster's ability to accurately self-monitor certain symptoms may itself be consistent with the disorder, such as in the case of depression. This is also related to children's metacognitive ability (Flavell, 1977), and in particular, metacognitions of emotion. Meichenbaum, Burland, Gruson, and Cameron (1985) have provided a useful discussion of metacognitive assessment of children by the use of self-report (primarily interview) methods.

The many developmental issues related to the use of self-report methods with children go beyond the scope of this chapter. Stone and Lemanek (1990) have provided a cogent, in-depth description and discussion of developmental issues related to the use of self-report with children. Also relevant is the notion that control-related beliefs are developmental in their origin, and that these beliefs in conjunction with changes in social situations may influence the expression of emotional problems in youngsters. Rothbaum and Weisz (1989) have done an excellent job in organizing and presenting this latter perspective.

Social Desirability

Social desirability and other forms of dissimulation and response styles have been extensively studied in adults and, to a limited extent, in children and adolescents. Although several measures of social desirability have been developed for use with children (e.g., Crandall, Crandall, & Katkovsky; 1965; Crandall, 1966; Ford & Rubin, 1970), youngsters appear to be relatively good (i.e., nondissimulating) respondents to self-report inventories. There are a number of potential confounds in the application of social desirability questionnaires as a direct measure of dissimulation on other self-report measures. For instance, responses to social desirability measures have been interpreted as the personality characteristic of need for approval (Crowne, 1979; Crowne & Marlowe, 1964). In addition, individual difference variables may confound scores on some measures. Mabe and Treiber (1989) found that mental age demonstrated a moderately high correlation with the Children's Social Desirability Questionnaire (Crandall et al. 1965) in a sample of 75 inpatient children from ages 6 to 16. Children with younger mental ages gave higher socially desirable responses on this measure.

Self-Disclosure

The willingness of a youngster to self-disclose information about self, family, or others has not been actively researched. For most research purposes, self-disclosure is probably not a major concern, given potential anonymity, group testing, and the perceived outcome of the report. However, in some clinical settings, the youngster's willingness to report potentially negative information may be an issue. For instance, in doing research on suicidal ideation in adolescents who have recently attempted suicide, some hospitalized youngsters report low levels of ideation and, when queried, indicate their belief that if they respond that they continue to think about suicide they will not be discharged. Although the majority of youngsters report continued clinical levels of suicidal ideation after their attempt, this example illustrates how situational factors may limit or result in a lack of self-disclosure.

Psychometric Qualities

Psychometric characteristics, such as reliability, validity, and normative information are standard features and requirements for psychological tests and measures. Such information is essential for the determination of the utility of a self-report measure for research and clinical practice. A major focus of assessment is the documentation of the effectiveness of therapy (Sundberg, Snowden, & Reynolds, 1978). Thus, it is critical that we use measures that demonstrate high levels of reliability and validity. The interpretation of reliability and validity coefficients is, to an extent, a function of the specific construct assessed, the nature of the instrument, the subjects, and the assessment situation. For instance, we may expect a trait measure, such as a self-concept scale or locus of control questionnaire, to demonstrate relatively high test-retest reliability over a 1- or 2-month time period. On the other hand, we may expect that a state-specific measure, such as a loneliness or depression inventory, will demonstrate lower test-retest reliability estimates due to natural changes over time. However, when examining internal consistency of a measure, we must be realistic as to whether we can consider a scale useful when 25 percent or more of the score is error variance (i.e., a reliability coefficient of less than .75).

Beyond the traditional interpretation of reliability and validity, psychometric indices, such as internal consistency (item homogeneity), can also provide an examination of the extent to which youth, and in particular young children, are able to provide consistent responses to self-report items. This also provides insight into the validity of the construct with young children. Many of the measures for children are based on measures or constructs that were developed with adults. The degree to which these constructs are valid and similar entities in children is often overlooked. For instance, perception of internal-external control of reinforcement (locus of control) has been assessed in children, adolescent, and adults, and is—rightly or wrongly—generally viewed as similar across developmental levels. However, a striking trend in internal consistency can be observed as a function of age. Research with younger children generally finds low internal consistency, with reliability coefficients so low as to suggest that much of the resultant score is error variance. One interpretation of this may be that generalized expectancies for control, as well as other attributional styles, are developmental in nature and are not well developed in young children.

Another important psychometric characteristic often overlooked or inadequately addressed is that of normative information. Norms are basic for the interpretability of scores on a measure. Key features of norms are representativeness and recency. Norms should be representative of the population and, in general, should be stratified or differentiated on those variables (e.g., sex, age) for which meaningful differences in scores are found. A caveat to the latter statement is the development of norms for clinical phenomena such as depression or anxiety. For some clinical disorders or problems, we generally consider the severity of symptoms as the primary feature. As an example, we generally find girls demonstrating higher scores than boys on depression measures. While separate norms for males and females may provide some additional information, the critical issue is not whether the individual is male or female, but the absolute magnitude of the score. To suggest that a score above a critical level for boys is not critical for girls, because difference bases rates ignore the reality that both boys and girls manifesting that level of symptom severity may be depressed. The same applies whether we are using raw scores, percentiles, standard scores, or other indices.

The clinical interpretation of norms becomes complex when we recognize across different domains of personality and problem behaviors, the variability in the distributions of constructs, as well as differences in base rates. Statistical procedures used to develop standard score norms generally assume a reasonable degree of normality of raw score distribution. For many clinical disorders, raw score distributions on self-report and other-report measures are quite skewed and far from normal. Furthermore, in the case of multidimensional measures, developers may apply the same selection ratio (such as a t-score of 70) to a range of problem behaviors that demonstrate different base rates.

OVERVIEW OF CHILD AND ADOLESCENT SELF-REPORT MEASURES

The section that follows provides a brief overview of a range of self-report measures used with children and adolescents. While by no means exhaustive of contemporary self-report scales, the measures noted below illustrate assessment procedures across a number of domains of personality, affect, attributions, and behaviors. Because of space limitations, the focus here is on bandwidth coverage, rather than fidelity in descriptions of measures. Greater emphasis is placed on single domain (unidimensional) rather than multidimensional measures, although examples of the latter are noted at the end of this chapter.

For the most part, self-report measures designed for

use with children have focused on more internalizing features, and less so on overt, externalizing problems. There are a few exceptions to this. Humphrey (1982) developed a self-report measure of self-control behavior for young children, the Children's Perceived Self-Control Scale (CPSCS). This dichotomous-format, 11-item scale was designed to assess behavioral aspects of children's self-control in the classroom. Humphrey (1982) reported a test-retest reliability of .71 for this measure, while Reynolds and Stark (1985) reported an internal consistency reliability of .61. Although the latter study found minimal relationship between children's reports on the CPSCS and their performance on the Matching Familiar Figures Test (Kagan, Rosman, Day, Albert, & Phillips, 1964), significant relationships ($rs = .31$ to .50) were observed between the CPSCS and teacher's reports of children's behavior on several formal self-control rating scales.

Self-report has also been the mainstay for the assessment of a number of overt problem behaviors in adolescence. A number of investigators (e.g., Atwood, Gold, & Taylor, 1989; Donovan, Jessor, & Costa, 1988; Jessor & Jessor, 1977; Newcomb & Bentler, 1988) have utilized self-report methodology for the evaluation of such externalizing problems as alcohol and drug use, delinquency, and sexual behavior. Other researchers have focused on individual personality characteristics, such as adolescent narcissism. An example of the latter are the two measures Pseudoautonomy and Peer-Group Dependence, developed by Lapan and Patton (1986), based on Kohut's psychology of the self. For the most part, these measures are not reviewed here.

Another domain of note is the use of self-report measures of major and minor stressful life events with children and adolescents. Scales developed by Compas, Davis, Forsythe, and Wagner (1987), Johnson (1986), and Swearingen and Cohen (1985) are illustrations of some of the measures recently developed to assess stressors in young people. Also related to this domain are measures designed to assess specific stressors. For instance, Kurdek and Berg (1987) reported on the psychometric characteristics of the Children's Beliefs About Parental Divorce Scale (CBAPS), a 36-item self-report measure that provides scores on dimensions of peer ridicule and avoidance, paternal blame, fear of abandonment, maternal blame, hope of reunification, and self-blame. Similarly, the assessment of youngsters' perceptions of the family, most often as a source of stress or dysfunction, has generated a host of self-report measures (e.g., McCubbin & Thompson, 1987; Moos & Moos, 1981; Olson, Portner, & Lavee, 1985), and represents an interesting domain of self-report methodology, albeit one that goes beyond the scope of this chapter. An excellent description and discussion of family assessment methods, including child self-report measures, has been provide by Jacob and Tennenbaum (1988).

A SELECTION OF CHILD AND ADOLESCENT SELF-REPORT MEASURES

This section describes a wide range of domains that have utilized child and adolescent self-report as an assessment methodology. As previously noted, many of these domains tend to be specific to internalizing problems or characteristics, or focus on cognitive components of externalizing or more generalized problems such as anger. Other evaluation domains are specific to personality and beliefs about the individual and the environment. Although not exhaustive, this section does illustrate the many formal applications of self-report methods with children and adolescents.

Achievement Motivation

A number of self-report measures of achievement motivation have been developed for use with children and adolescents. Adkins and Ballif (1973) developed Animal Crackers as a measure of achievement motivation in kindergarten and first-grade children. Animal Crackers (a revised form of the earlier Gumpgookies; Adkins & Ballif, 1970) consists of 60 items and yields subscale scores of school enjoyment, purposiveness, self-confidence, instrumental activity, and self-evaluation, as well as a total score. Items are presented to children as pairs of animals on a printed booklet, and an examiner describes alternative behaviors for each animal in the pair. The response format requires the child to fill in the circle under the animal that is most like the child. For example, item 15 reads: "This pony wants to come to school tomorrow. This pony want to stay at home tomorrow." (Hint: do not give this test on Fridays.) The authors report high internal consistency reliability for the total test score, while Reynolds and Downing (1982) found low to moderate reliabilities for the subscales.

The Children's Academic Intrinsic Motivation Inventory (CAIMI) by Gottfried (1985, 1986) is a 122-item measure providing scores of intrinsic motivation specific to reading, math, social studies, science, and general orientation to school. Designed for use with youngsters in grades 4 through 8, the CAIMI has demonstrated high levels of internal consistency reliability and moderate test-retest reliability over a 2-month period.

Alcoholism

In recent years, researchers have begun to focus on the formal assessment of drinking behavior and attitudes of young people. A measure specific to psychological and social domains of adolescent drinking behavior is the Adolescent Drinking Index (ADI) (Harrell & Wirtz, 1989a, 1989b). The ADI consists of 24 items and provides a total score and subscales of self-medicated drinking and rebellious behavior related to drinking. The authors report high reliability for the ADI with school-based and clinical samples.

The Alcohol Expectancy Questionnaire-Adolescent Form (AEQ-A) by Goldman, Brown, and Christiansen is a 90-item, true-false measure that provides scores on subscales of the following: alcohol is a powerful agent, alcohol can enhance or impede social behavior, alcohol improves cognitive and motor functioning, alcohol enhances sexuality, alcohol leads to deteriorated cognitive and behavioral functioning, alcohol increases arousal, and alcohol promotes relaxation. As can be seen from the subscales, this measure is quite specific to expectancies adolescents may have regarding the use and effects of alcohol. In a longitudinal study of 637 adolescents, Christiansen, Smith, Roehling, and Goldman (1989) reported internal consistency reliability estimates ranging from .77 to .86 for the AEQ-A subscales.

Anger, Assertiveness, and Aggression

Several measures have been developed to assess aggression, anger, and assertiveness in children. Some of these measures have focused on children's social behaviors and aspects of social skills (e.g., assertiveness), while others have dealt with more clinical problem behaviors (e.g., anger management). Finch and Rogers (1984) reported on the Children's Inventory of Anger (CIA) (Nelson & Finch, 1978) an inventory designed to assess anger control problems in clinic and school-based samples of children in grades 3 through 8. The CIA consists of 71 items and uses a 4-point response format consisting of four stick-figure faces drawn with facial expressions demonstrating a range of anger. Numerical ratings and verbal responses associated with levels of anger accompany each figure. Finch and Rogers report on a series of studies demonstrating high internal consistency and test-retest reliability, as well as construct and criterion-related validity for the CIA with normal and emotionally disturbed children.

Spielberger (1988) recently developed the State-Trait Anger Expression Inventory (STAXI) as a measure of the experience and expression of anger in adolescents and adults. Spielberger differentiates anger from hostility and aggression and provides a conceptual basis for the state versus trait anger distinction. Consisting of 44 items rated on a 4-point Likert-type scale, the STAXI provides scores on six scales (State Anger, Trait Anger, Anger-in, Anger-out, Anger Control, and Anger Expression). Norms for adolescents are based on 2,469 youngsters in junior and senior high schools. The author reports internal consistency reliabilities of .82 to .90 for the State and Trait Anger scales for adolescent males and females.

A number of related dimensions of externalizing behaviors and emotion are measured by the Children's Action Tendency Scale (CATS), a 30-item (a 39-item version was also developed) forced-choice instrument designed by Deluty (1979) to provide scores on aggressiveness, assertiveness, and submission in children in grades 3 through 6. Although relatively modest split-half reliabilities were reported, the author notes that the CATS is not a trait measure, but a reflection of respondents' probable behavior in conflict situations.

The Children's Assertive Behavior Scale (CABS) by Michelson and Wood (1982) is a 27-item self-report measure of assertive behavior in children in fourth through sixth grades. Based on a behavioral-analytic test development procedure, the items on the CABS present youngsters with a 5-point range of responses, varying from very passive (-2) to very aggressive ($+2$), with an assertive response as the midpoint (0). Michelson and Wood, in their development article (1982) and in a number of paper presentations and unpublished manuscripts report adequate validity and relatively high test-retest reliability ($r_{tt} = .87$, over 4 weeks) for the CABS. The degree to which the response format represents a continuum may be debated, and there appears to be room for error in the interpretation of summed scores. Wojnilower and Gross (1984) summed the absolute scores on the CABS items to arrive at a total score. One must wonder whether a youngster with a high aggressive score and one with a high passive score demonstrate the same level of nonassertiveness. Likewise, a simple summation of the negative and positive weights would suggest that a youngster who demonstrates some very passive along with very aggressive responses would have the same score as a youngster who consistently demonstrates assertive responses.

Ollendick (1984) devloped the Children's Assertiveness Inventory (CAI), a 14-item *yes-no* format measure for the assessment of assertiveness in children 6 to 12 years of age. Ollendick and colleagues (Ollendick, 1981, 1984; Scanlon & Ollendick, 1985) report relatively low internal consistency but moderate (r_{tt} = .76) test-retest reliability. Because of the limited number of items and dichotomous response format, the low internal consistency with young children is not an unusual finding. The level of test-retest reliability is supportive of this measure, as well as suggestive of the reliability of children's reports of assertiveness.

Anxiety and Related Disorders

Anxiety and related disorders represents a broad clinical domain of child and adolescent problems. Within this domain we may include a range of measures dealing with anxiety of perceived components of anxiety, as well as other clinical problems such as fears, phobias, obsessions, and compulsions. A number of newer measures have focused on cognitions of youngsters either by the rating of preidentified cognitive statement or the use of thought-sampling or think-aloud procedures.

Individual scales for the assessment of anxiety in children have been in existence for nearly 40 years. One of the first measures to be used in clinical and research studies was the Children's Manifest Anxiety Scale, a measure of generalized anxiety by Castenada, McCandless, and Palermo (1956). Shortly thereafter, interest in situation-specific (state) forms of anxiety emerged as illustrated by the Test Anxiety Scale for Children by Sarason, Davidson, Lighthall, Waite, and Ruebush (1960). Recent measures have generally followed one of these paths, assessing a generalized domain of anxiety (as a general trait) or a situation-task specific (state) form of anxiety.

There has also been a recent trend toward the development of measures to differentiate within-subject as well as domain-specific aspects of anxiety in children. For instance, Zatz and Chassin (1983) reported on a measure of test-anxious cognition, the Children's Cognitive Assessment Questionnaire, a 40-item measure assessing domains of positive and negative evaluation, and on- and off-task cognitions. The development of domain-specific aspect of anxiety can be seen in the Social Anxiety Scale for Children (SASC) by La Greca, Dandes, Wick, Shaw, and Stone (1988). Consisting of 10 items, the SASC focuses on anxiety in children specific to peer and social relations. Designed for use with children in grades 2 through 6, the SASC provides scores on subscales of fear of negative evaluation and social avoidance and distress. The subscales, as might be inferred from the low number of items, demonstrate moderate levels of reliability.

Other investigators have attempted to differentiate between components of anxiety response. As examples, the Cognitive and Somatic Trait Anxiety Inventory and Cognitive and Somatic State Anxiety Inventory (Fox & Houston, 1983), are 24- and 27-item scales, respectively, designed to evaluate cognitive and somatic components of generalized (i.e., trait) and situation-specific (i.e., state) anxiety in children. To describe the ever-increasing number of new child self-report measures of anxiety and related disorders is beyond the scope of this chapter. A few of the more commonly used scales are noted below.

The State-Trait Anxiety Inventory for Children (STAIC) was developed by Spielberger, Edwards, Montuori, and Lushene (1973) to measure state and trait components of anxiety in children ages 9 through 12 years of age. Each subscale consists of 20 items using either a three-alternative or 3-point rating scale. The authors report moderate levels of test-retest reliability and somewhat higher internal consistency reliability. Finch, Montgomery, and Deardorff (1974) found relatively low test-retest reliability for the STAIC in a sample of emotionally disturbed children. Papay and Spielberger (1986) reported on the use of the STAIC with young children in kindergarten through second grade, with low to moderate internal consistency reliabilities for individual administration (r_α = .71 and .76) of the trait and state scales, respectively.

The Children's Manifest Anxiety Scale was revised by Reynolds and Richmond in 1978. The Revised Children's Manifest Anxiety Scale (RCMAS) for youngsters ages 6 through 19 years, consists of 28 content and 9 lie-scale items, and uses a *yes-no* response format. All items on the RCMAS are keyed in the *yes* direction. Reynolds and Richmond (1985) report internal consistency for the RCMAS of .82 for the standardization sample and Reynolds, Anderson, and Bartell (1985) found an internal consistency reliability coefficient of .88 in a sample of 166 children.

A brief measure of anxiety in children ages 5 through 12 years is the Child Anxiety Scale (CAS) by Gillis (1980). Consisting of 20 items and normed on

2,105 children, the CAS is orally administered, with children marking their responses on a red or blue circle next to each item number on an answer sheet. An examination of item content suggests that many of the items may reflect content other that anxiety (a criticism common to many anxiety scale). For instance, items of the CAS deal with such content as "Are you lucky?" "Do you feel cheerful and happy most of the time?" "Are other children nice to you?" "Can other people do things better than you?" "Do people think you are bad?" "Are you pretty good at most things?" and so on.

In recent years, a renewed clinical and research interest in obsessive-compulsive disorders in children and adolescents has emerged (Johnston & March, in press). Consistent with this is the development of measures specific to the assessment of this disorder in youngsters. The Leyton Obsessional Inventory—Child Version is a downward revision of an adult inventory for use with children and adolescents (Berg, Rapoport, & Flament, 1986). The original child version was designed as a 44-item card sort and provided scores specific to the number of symptoms present as well as scores specific to the interference and resistance of symptoms present. Initial data suggested high reliability and contrasted groups validity between OCD and normal controls. Flament et al. (1985) found the 44-item LOI-CV sensitive to treatment outcome. A 20-item paper-and-pencil survey form of the LOI-CV was reported on by Berg et al. (1988), using a *yes-no* format to identify symptoms, with the *yes* symptoms rated on a four-point scale of interference. Psychometric data from a large-scale epidemiological study of adolescents suggests that the 20-item form demonstrated reasonably good reliability and validity for use in research as well as clinical applications (Berg et al., 1988; Flament et al., 1988).

In addition to the assessment of anxiety in children, an area of active study since the 1920s has been fears and phobias in young persons, with self-report used as a major assessment methodology. Most self-report measures of children's fears require the child to provide a rating of their fear across a range of situations (items). Inventories may be general and evaluate a wide range of potentially fearful situations or stimuli, or they may be specific, such as fear inventories dealing with medical procedures (e.g., hospitals, dental procedures, etc.). The use of thermometer-type devices on which children report their level of fear have also been used as a self-report method for the evaluation of specific fears and situations.

The original 80-item version of the Fear Survey Schedule for Children (FSSC) by Scherer and Nakamura (1968) was revised by a number of investigations, including Rydall and Dietiker (1979) and Ollendick (1983). The Children's Fear Survey Schedule (CFSS) by Rydall and Dietiker represents a shortened version of the FSSC. Consisting of 48 specific fears, the CFSS uses a 3-point response scale, as opposed to the 5-point scale, the FSSC. The Fear Survey Schedule for Children-Revised (FSSC-R) by Ollendick consists of the 80 items of the FSSC but uses a revised three-point response format. Ollendick (1983) reports high levels of internal consistency and short-term test-retest reliability for this revised measure. The Louisville Fear Survey Schedule by Miller, Barrett, Hampe, and Noble (1972) provides for child self-report as well as parent report of severity of fear in 81 situations. Designed for use with children ages 4 to 18, there is minimal psychometric data on the child report format of this scale.

Last (in press), in reviewing several of the commonly used self-report measures of anxiety in children, notes that some self-report measures are poor in discriminating between children with various anxiety disorders and controls. Furthermore, research suggests that when youngsters with both anxiety *and* depressive disorders are compared to only anxious and control children, differences in self-reported anxiety appear and suggest potential confounds in what these measure are evaluating (Strauss, Last, Hersen, & Kazdin, 1988). Finch, Lipovsky, and Casat (1989) have provided a cogent review of this issue and the notion that self-report measures of anxiety (as well as depression) may be assessing a generalized construct of negative affectivity.

Depression and Related Domains

Assessment represents a key link in the identification of depression in children and adolescents as well as a means for determining the efficacy of treatment (Reynolds, 1990b). The assessment of depression in young persons has become a multimethod extravaganza with the availability of different measures, using different sources of information (e.g., parent, child, teacher, peer) and different response formats (e.g., self-report versus clinical interview). What has emerged is a diverse set of procedures, with the majority of research finding minimal concordance across sources (raters), but relatively high within-rater relationships (Reynolds, in press a). The assessment of the depth or severity of depressive symptoms, using paper-and-pencil measures, does provide useful information as to the subjective level of depressive symptomatology experienced by the youngster. With regard to internalizing problems such as depression, children have been found to be reasonably reliable reporters (Reynolds & Graves, 1989).

A number of self-report measures for the evaluation of depressive symptomatology in children and adolescents have been developed over the past decade. Three measures are described in this chapter, all of which have been used by various investigators as outcome measures in the demonstration of treatment efficacy (e.g., Kahn, Kehle, Jenson, & Clark, 1990; Reynolds & Coats, 1986; Stark, Reynolds, & Kaslow, 1987). The Children's Depression Inventory by Kovacs (CDI) (Kovacs, 1979; 1981) has been the most frequently used measure of depression in research investigations with children. The CDI is a 27-item three-alternative forced-choice measure. For each item, the child selects the symptom level that best characterizes how he or she is feeling. There is a large amount of research on the CDI, with studies typically reporting internal consistency reliability coefficients in the mid to upper .80s (e.g., Nelson, Politano, Finch, Wendel, & Mayhall, 1987), and somewhat lower test-retest reliability coefficients depending on the interval between testings (e.g., Kovacs, 1981, 1983; Smucker, Craighead, Craighead, & Green, 1986).

Although not designed as a diagnostic measure, the CDI is useful in assessing the severity of depressive symptomatology in children. One question on the clinical use of the CDI is what cutoff score represents a clinically relevant level of depressive symptoms? Kovacs (1983) suggests that a cutoff score of 13 be used to delineate a clinical level of depression, although this score will overidentify a significant number of nondepressed youngsters. Overall, the CDI is a useful self-report measure of depression in children, although the lack of a test manual, normative information, and guidelines for interpretation of scores limits the clinical use of this scale.

The Reynolds Child Depression Scale (RCDS) (Reynolds, 1989a), previously called the Child Depression Scale (e.g., Bartell & Reynolds, 1986; Reynolds et al., 1985; Stark et al., 1987), is a brief, 30-item self-report measure of depressive symptomatology in children ages 8 through 12 years. The RCDS consists of 29 items that utilize a 4-point Likert-type response format, and one item for which the response format is five smiley-type faces ranging from happy to sad.

Normative information based on over 1,600 children representing heterogeneous ethnic and socioeconomic backgrounds is reported in a detailed manual, along with procedures for administration, scoring and interpretation, and extensive data on reliability and validity. Internal consistency reliability for the total standardization sample was .90. Reynolds and Graves (1989) reported a test-retest reliability coefficient of .85 for the RCDS using a 4-week interval between testing with an ethnically diverse sample of 220 children from grades 3 through 6. Validity data are presented in the form of high correlations with other self-report and clinical interview measures of childhood depression, as well as content validity, factor analysis, discriminant validity and clinical utility (Reynolds, 1989b).

Reynolds Adolescent Depression Scale

The Reynolds Adolescent Depression Scale (RADS) (Reynolds, 1986, 1987a) is a 30-item, paper-and-pencil self-report measure of depression designed for use with adolescents ages 13 through 19 years. The RADS uses a 4-point response format with items worded at a third-grade reading level. Item content includes somatic, motivational, cognitive, mood, and vegetative components of depression. The RADS manual reports data on more than 11,000 adolescents from the midwestern, southeastern, and western portions of the United States. For screening and clinical applications, a cutoff score has been validated to designate a clinically relevant level of symptom severity. Internal consistency reliability estimates have been uniformly high (ranging from .92 to .96) with different samples of normal and depressed adolescents ranging in size from 126 to 2,240 (Reynolds, 1987a; 1989c; Reynolds & Miller, 1989). Test-retest reliability with a 6-week interval between testings was .80 with a sample of 104 adolescents. Reynolds and Miller (1985) report an internal consistency reliability coefficient of .87 for the RADS with a sample of adolescents with mild mental retardation.

Several studies have established the validity of the RADS using bivariate and multivariate procedures to examine relationships with other depression scales and measures of related constructs (Reynolds, 1985; 1987a; 1989c). The RADS has been found to be highly correlated with other self-report measures of depression (r's ranging from .70 to .89). A correlation of .83 was found between the RADS and the Hamilton Depression Rating Scale (Hamilton, 1960) with a sample of 111 adolescents, substantiating criterion-related validity.

The Suicidal Ideation Questionnaire (SIQ) (Reynolds, 1987b) is a measure designed to evaluate domains of suicidal ideation manifested by adolescents and young adults. There are two adolescent forms of the SIQ. A 30-item form, referred to as the SIQ, is designed for use with older adolescents in grades 10 to 12, and young adults. A 15-item form, the SIQ-JR, is designed for use with younger adolescents in grades 7 to 9. The SIQ manual (Reynolds, 1988a) presents data suggesting high reliability (r_α = .97 for the SIQ and .94 for the SIQ-JR), and evidence of content and construct validity. King, Raskin, Gdowski, Butkus, and Opipari (1990) found that the SIQ differentiated between adolescent girls with a recent suicide attempt and those without a history of suicide attempts. Reynolds (1990c) reported correlations of .62 and .68 between the Suicidal Behaviors Interview (Reynolds, in press b), a semi-structured clinical interview of suicidal behaviors, and the SIQ and SIQ-JR, respectively. A 25-item adult form of the SIQ has recently been developed (Reynolds, in press c) which has demonstrated high reliability in college students, normal, and clinical samples of adults (Reynolds, 1991; Reynolds, Kobak, & Greist, 1990).

Hopelessness, as characterized by a negative view of the future, is conceptually related to the domains of depression and suicidal behaviors. Kazdin and colleagues (Kazdin, French, Unis, Esveldt-Dawson, & Sherick, 1983; Kazdin, Colbus, & Rodgers, 1986) have developed the Hopelessness Scale for Children (HSC), a 17-item dichotomous (T/F) format measure for children ages 6 through 13 years. Initial reliability of this measure was moderate (r_α = .75). Subsequently, Kazdin, Rodgers, and Colbus (1986) reported an internal consistency reliability of .97, although a 6-week test-retest resulted in a substantially lower reliability coefficient (r_{tt} = .52). They also report data supporting the concurrent validity of this measure.

A dimension of depression, that of anhedonia, as operationalized by reduced capacity to experience pleasure and diminished interest in previously reinforcing activities, has recently been the focus of scale development. Kazdin (1989) has reported on the development of the Pleasure Scale for Children, a self-report measure of anhedonia for children ages 6 through 13 years. Consisting of 39 items and using a 3-point response format, the Pleasure scale demonstrated high internal consistency reliability in the development sample of 232 inpatient children. Kazdin also provides extensive evidence for the validity of this scale.

Eating Disorders

Several measures specific to research on eating disorders have been developed over the past 15 years, most focusing on adolescent and adult populations. Some of these measures focus on psychological characteristics of persons with eating disorders, while other measures are specific to clinical symptoms of eating disorders. The Eating Disorders Inventory developed by Garner and colleagues (Garner & Olmstead, 1984; Garner, Olmstead, & Polivy, 1983) consists of 64 items and provides scores on eight subscales: drive for thinness, bulimia, body dissatisfaction, ineffectiveness, perfectionism, interpersonal distrust, interoceptive awareness, and maturity fears. With norms based on 981 high school girls, and various samples of college students and clinical patients, the EDI is designed to assess psychological and behavioral characteristics found in individuals with eating disorders.

A measure specific to clinical symptoms of anorexia and bulimia in adolescents is the Anorexia-Bulimia Inventory (ABI) by Stein and Brinza (1989). The ABI consists of 186 items and provides subscales specific to anorexia and bulimia and other problem behaviors related or sometimes found to coexist with eating disorders. Other scales such as the Eating Attitudes Test (EAT) (Garner & Garfinkel, 1979; Garner, Olmsted, Bohr, & Garfinkel, 1982) and the Bulimia Test (BULIT) (Smith & Thelen, 1984) developed for use with college students and adults have been used with adolescents (e.g., Attie & Brooks-Gunn, 1989; Stein & Brinza, 1989).

Pain and Health-Related Somatic Symptoms

A number of investigators have investigated aspects of children's health-related behaviors and somatic concerns using self-report methods. In particular, pain in children is often assessed using self-report (beyond asking the age-old question: Does it hurt?). This is an important application of self-report methodology, given the clinical importance of understanding when a child is experiencing pain as well as the intensity of pain. A recent study by Zeltzer, LeBaron, Richie, Reed, Schoolfield, and Prihoda (1988) examined children's ability to quantify somatic symptoms of nausea and vomiting in samples of normal children and children with cancer ages 6 to 11 years of age, and adults. Using vignettes and two 10-point scales assessing time and bother, the latter using faces of children showing different levels of distress, the authors conclude that children are competent reporters of somatic complaints. LeBaron and Zeltzer (1984) also used a series of five hand-drawn faces to assess self-reported pain and anxiety in a sample of child and adolescent cancer patients.

Belter, McIntosh, Finch, and Saylor (1988), in a study of young children ages 3 to 6 years, used the faces scale of LeBaron and Zeltzer (1984) along with several other pain scales including the "pain thermometer" and the "Oucher" scale. The authors reported moderate levels of reliability and high intercorrelations among the measures. Given the young ages of the subjects, the results of this study support the use of self-report pain measures with children.

Locus of Control

Assessment of children's perception of control of reinforcement has been an area of active study for the past 25 years across a wide range of clinical and nonclinical populations (e.g., Finch, Pezzuti, & Nelson, 1975; Linn & Hodge, 1982) and outcomes (e.g., Messer, 1972). One of the first children's locus of control measures was the Bialer-Cromwell Children's Locus of Control Scale by Bialer (1961). Consisting of 23 items using a *yes-no* response format, this scale has been used with nonretarded and children with mental retardation.

One of the best known locus of control measures for children is the Intellectual Achievement Responsibility Questionnaire (IAR) by Crandall, Katkovsky, and Crandall (1965) for use with youngsters 8 through 18 years of age. The IAR consists of 34 items and uses a two-alternative forced-choice format. The IAR has been used extensively with children and adolescents as a self-report measure of locus of control for achievmenet-related beliefs and in research on learned helplessness as exemplified by the systematic studies in the 1970s by Dweck and colleagues (e.g., Diener & Dweck, 1978; Dweck, 1975). In a review of research on the IAR, Crandall (1978) reported that there appear to be a number of historical changes in children's internal perceptions when comparing children in the 1960s to those in the 1970s. One issue specific to this scale is the low reliability of the subscales reported by the authors and other investigators (e.g., Reynolds & Miller, 1989). As will be shown, low reliability is a problem of many locus of control and attributional style measures design for use with children.

A well-known scale for children is the Children's Nowicki-Strickland Internal-External Control Scale (CNS-IE) (Nowicki & Strickland, 1973), a 40-item *yes-no*-format measure for children in grades 3 through 12. The authors report somewhat low to moderate internal consistency reliability, with coefficients showing a trend for higher reliability in the older subjects. Test-retest reliability is relatively low for a measure assessing a "trait" type construct. Although somewhat weak psychometrically, the CNS-IE is one of the "better" locus of control scales for children.

Two scales for the assessment of locus of control in young children have been developed. Nowicki and Duke (1974) constructed a measure consisting of 26 items using a cartoon format and referred to as the Preschool and Primary Nowicki-Strickland Internal-External Control Scale (PPNS-IE). The PPNS-IE was designed for use with children 4 through 8 years of age. Reliability data (test-retest) is provided only for 7-year-old children. An examination of the item-total scale correlations for younger (5- and 6-year-olds) and older (7- and 8-year-olds) children suggests some difference in responses between younger and older children on this measure. Most of the item-total scale correlations were low, with some negative item-total correlations reported. Research generally finds low internal consistency reliability for this measure (Herzbergen, Linney, Seidman, & Rapoport, 1979), although this problem is nearly universal with locus of control measures for young children.

The Stanford Preschool Internal-External Scale (SPIES) by Mischel, Zeiss, and Zeiss (1974) was developed to measure young children's expectancies about whether events occur as a consequence of their own action or from external forces. Consisting of 14 forced-choice items and differentiated by subscales for positive and negative events, the SPIES demonstrates very low internal consistency reliabilities.

A recent measure of children's perceptions of control of reinforcement is Connell's (1985) Multidimensional Measure of Children's Perceptions of Control, a 48-item self-report scale designed for children in grades 3 through 9. The MMCPC provides scores along three domains: Domain of control (cognitive, social, physical, and general); Source of control (internal, powerful others, unknown control), and Outcome (success, failure). Items are scored on a 4-point scale. Subscales consist of relatively few items, and internal consistency reliabilities tend to be low to moderate. This measure is well conceived in terms of contemporary theoretical perspectives on perceptions of control, although the low reliabilities, in part due to the few items on each subscale, detract from the overall utility of this measure.

A measure related to the general domain of attributions for success and failure within academic domains is the Mastery Orientation Inventory (MOI) (Reynolds & Miller, 1989; in press), a 40-item self-report measure of adolescents' learned helplessness in academic situations. In a series of studies reported by Reynolds & Miller (1989), the MOI demonstrated high levels of internal consistency reliability ($r_\alpha = .92$ to $.95$) and moderate test-retest reliability over a 12-week period ($r_{tt} = .77$). Validity evidence in the form of correlations with measures of depression, locus of control, and teachers' behavioral ratings of adolescents' helplessness is provided by the authors.

Loneliness

Loneliness is a domain for which the individual's subjective feelings may best be assessed by self-report. A number of researchers (e.g., Moore & Schultz, 1983; Reynolds, 1987a; 1985) have used the revised UCLA Loneliness Scale (Russell, Peplau, & Curtona, 1980), a 20-item self-report measure of loneliness with adolescents. Asher, Hymel, and Renshaw (1984) developed a 16-item self-report loneliness (and social dissatisfaction) scale for children in the third through sixth grades. The authors reported high internal consistency reliability ($r_\alpha = .90$) with a sample of 506 children. This measure was later modified by Asher and Wheeler (1985), who reported the same level of reliability as that found with the original scale.

Self-Concept

Self-concept in children and adolescents is a domain clearly defined by the use of self-report measures. Over the years, numerous measures of self-concept for children have been developed. Those presented here are a few of the many measures and represent a range of formats and construct specificity.

The Piers-Harris Children's Self-Concept Scale (Piers, 1984) is a frequently used measure of self-concept in children. Developed for use with youngsters ages 8 through 18 years, the Piers-Harris consists of 80 items with a *yes-no* response format. Overall internal consistency reliability tends to be high (around .90). A number of subscales demonstrating substantially lower reliabilities are suggested in the Piers-Harris manual.

The Coopersmith Self-Esteem Inventory (SEI) (Coopersmith, 1959, 1967) consists of 58 short statements requiring a "like me" or "unlike me" response, with 8 of the items constituting a lie scale. Coopersmith (1967) and others (e.g., Spatz & Johnson, 1973) report adequate reliability coefficients (>.80). A 25-item short form (Form B) developed by Coopersmith has also been used in research investigations, and demonstrates reasonable reliability (Reynolds et al., 1985).

Harter has developed several measures that fall within the general domain of self-concept but are somewhat more specific to the construct of perceived competence within a model of effectance motivation (Harter, 1978, 1990). Harter (1982) developed the Perceived Competency Scale for Children (PCSC) as a measure of self-worth with subscales of cognitive, social, physical, and general self-worth. A downward extension of this scale for young children using a pictorial response format was reported by Harter and Pike (1984). Harter (1988) also developed an upward extension of this measure, the Self-Perception Profile for Adolescents, which assesses eight domains: scholastic competence, social acceptance, athletic competence, physical appearance, job competence, romantic appeal, behavioral conduct, and close friendship, as well as a global self-worth score. In developing these measures, Harter has done a nice job in the integration of theory, developmental issues, and test construction.

The Offer Self-Image Questionnaire for Adolescents by Offer, Ostrov, and Howard (1981, 1984) is a 130-item measure assessing domains of psychological self, social self, family self, sexual self, and coping self. Across these five aspects of self, standard scores on 11 subscales are obtained and include impulse control, emotional tone, body and self-image, social relationships, morals, vocational-educational goals, sexual attitudes, family relations, mastery of external world, psychopathology, and superior adjustment. Offer and colleagues have used this measure in an extensive line of research on adolescents and changes in adolescent self-image.

A brief and noteworthy measure of global self-esteem in adolescents is the Rosenberg Self-Esteem Scale (RSES) (Rosenberg, 1965). Consisting of 10 items using a 4-point response format, the RSES was originally designed to be scored as a Guttman scale, although most researchers have used it as a Likert-type scale by summing responses to all items. The RSES has demonstrated reasonably high reliabilities ($r_\alpha s$ = .80s) across a range of studies. The brevity of this measure, along with the strong psychometric characteristics and theoretical foundation provided by Rosenberg (1965), supports its use as a measure of global self-esteem, particularly in research applications.

Reynolds (in press, d) developed the Academic Self-Concept Scale—High School Version, a 15-item downward revision of the Academic Self-Concept Scale (Reynolds, 1988b). Designed to measure an academic facet of self-concept consistent with the model of self-concept presented by Shavelson, Hubner, and Stanton (1976), the ASCS-HS has demonstrated high reliability ($r_\alpha s$ = .88 to .89) and validity as shown by correlations with the RSES (rs = .65 to .74) and high school grades (rs = .55 to .58) with large samples of adolescents (ns ranging from 753 to 1,054) (Reynolds, 1985).

Related to the general domain of self-concept is the construct of self-efficacy. While a number of investigators have developed study-specific measures of self-efficacy, a few researchers have focused on the development of self-efficacy scales, with documentation of reliability and validity. Based on Bandura's (1977) general conceptualization of self-efficacy, Wheeler and Ladd (1982) developed the Children's Self-Efficacy for Peer Interaction Scale (CSPI) to assess social self-efficacy (positive peer interactions) in third- through fifth-grade children. Consisting of 22 statements describing social situations, the response format requires the youngster to respond either "HARD," "hard," "easy," or "EASY" to each statement (e.g., "A kid is yelling at you. Telling the kid to stop is———for you"). Ten of the items deal with nonconflict situations and 12 are specific to conflict situations. The authors present reasonable evidence for the reliability and validity of this measure.

BROAD-BANDWIDTH MEASURES FOR THE ASSESSMENT OF CHILD AND ADOLESCENT PERSONALITY, PSYCHOPATHOLOGY, AND PROBLEM BEHAVIORS

In addition to the many single domain self-report measures, some of which were described previously, a number of multidimensional self-report measures of psychopathology and personality have been developed for use with children and adolescents. As noted at the beginning of this chapter, there is a long history to the development of such measures for young persons. Both the MMPI and CPI continue to be used with youngsters, particularly adolescents. Another measure, the Eysenck Personality Inventory was revised as the Eysenck Personality Questionnaire (Eysenck & Eysenck, 1975), the junior form of this measure is designed for use with youngsters aged 7 through 15 years. Likewise, the High School Personality Questionnaire with a revised manual (HSPQ) (Cattell, Cattell, & Johns, 1984), continues to be used with adolescents. There are four forms of the HSPQ, although Form A, with norms based on more than 7,000 adolescents, may be the most viable from a norm-referenced perspective. In recent years, a number of multidimensional measures have been developed, several of which are briefly noted below.

Beitchman, Raman, Carlson, Clegg, and Kruidenier (1985) developed the Children's Self-Report Psychiatric Rating Scale (also referred to as the Children's Self-Report Scale: CSRS), a 55-item self-report measure that yields scores on dimensions of conduct problems, lie-immaturity, positive self-peer, worry, negative peer, antisocial-permissive, sensitive-emotional, and positive family factors. Designed to be used with children aged 6 through 13 years, Beitchman, Kruidenier, and Clegg (1987) report on the efficacy of the CSRS for differentiating between clinical (defined as conduct disordered, neurotic, and mixed) and normal children.

The Child Rating Scale (CRS) by Hightower et al. (1987) is a relatively brief measure, assessing four domains of social-emotional adjustment. Consisting of 35 items using a 3-point response format, the CRS assesses children's self-report on rule compliance/acting out, anxiety/withdrawal, interpersonal social skills, and self-confidence subscales. The initial development article, with samples of more than 2,000 children in grades 1 through 6, suggests that the CRS is a reliable and valid measure of socioemotional characteristics of children.

Millon and colleagues developed the Millon Adolescent Personality Inventory (MAPI) (Millon, Green, & Meagher, 1982), a 150-item true-false measure of dimensions of personality style, expressed concerns, and behavioral correlates. Scores are provided on 20 subscales, 8 specific to personality style, 8 assessing expressed concerns, and 4 dealing with behavioral correlates. Internal consistency reliabilities for the scales range from .67 to .84, with a median reliability of .76. Given the ratio of items to subscales, there is substantial item overlap across subscales, and for some subscales there is over 50 percent item overlap.

The Youth Self-Report (YSR) by Achenbach and Edelbrock (1987) is a 102-item inventory that follows in the factor analytic/taxonomic footsteps of the Child Behavior Checklist. Designed for use with youngsters 11 through 18 years of age, the YSR items are simple statements (e.g., "I cry a lot") to which the youngster responds "not true," "somewhat or sometimes true," or "very true or often true." Youngsters are asked to respond to the statement as it "describes you now or within the past 6 months." As with other measures by Achenbach, different sets of subscores are derived for boys and girls, with different items found on subscales of the same syndrome description for boys and girls. The authors report adequate short-term test retest reliability.

The Adolescent Psychopathology Scale by Reynolds (in press e) focuses on formal dimensions of psychopathology delineated by the Diagnostic and Statistical Manual of Mental Disorders—3rd ed. revised (DSM-IIIR; American Psychiatric Association, 1987). With scores on both Axis I (psychopathology: e.g., major depression, conduct disorder, panic disorder, anorexia nervosa, bulimia nervosa, schizophrenia, adjustment disorder, avoidant—overanxious disorder, somatization disorder, psychoactive substance abuse, oppositional defiant disorder, etc.) and Axis II (personality: e.g., borderline personality disorder, avoidant personality disorder, schizotypal personality disorder, etc.) disorders, as well as content scales (e.g., self-concept, introversion, aggression, suicide, etc.), the APS provides a systematic evaluation of multiple problem domains of adolescents. Initial investigations (Reynolds, 1990d) suggest that the APS demonstrates high reliability with clinic (range of internal consistency reliability = .78 to .95) and school-based (internal consistency reliability range = .75 to .94) samples.

SUMMARY

Self-report assessment of children and adolescents represents a rich source of information. As indicated in this chapter, self-report has been a methodology for the assessment of personality in children since the 1920s. The self-report measures noted and described in this chapter are not presented as either the best or the worst of child and adolescent measures. Rather, these measures are presented as illustrations of the many domains and forms of child and adolescent self-report. For the most part, these measures demonstrate accept-able levels of psychometric integrity and clinical utility. However, when one surveys the myriad of self-report, as well as parent, teacher, and peer report measures, the words of the late Oscar K. Buros, while a bit harsh, still appear to be valid: "At least half of the tests currently on the market should never have been published. Exaggerated, false, or unsubstantiated claims are the rule rather than the exception" (pp. xxvii-xxviii).

Within the past decade, studies examining characteristics of children from multiple respondent perspectives have generally found minimal concordance across raters (e.g., Achenbach, McConaughy & Howell, 1987). Numerous reasons for such variation in reports have been presented, although most contemporary perspectives view the report of the child as an important source of information. Realistically, no self-report measure is perfect. Some measures are better than others, and some children are better than other children in reporting their own behaviors, feelings, emotional states, and beliefs. The same may be said for other reporters, whether they are parents, teachers, peers, or observers. The use of child and adolescent self-report should be tempered by the developmental level of the youngster, the specific domain that is assessed, the psychometric adequacy of the measure, and the availability and utility of other sources of information.

REFERENCES

Achenbach, T. M., & Edelbrock, C. (1987). *Manual for the youth self-report and profile*. Burlington, VT: University of Vermont.

Achenbach, T. M., McConaughy, S. H., & Howell, C. T. (1987). Child/adolescent behavioral and emotional problems: Implications of cross-informant correlations for situational specificity. *Psychological Bulletin, 101*, 213–232.

Adkins, D. C., & Ballif, B. L. (1970). Factors of motivation in young children: Theoretical and empirical. *Educational Perspectives, 9*, 7–11.

Adkins, D., & Ballif, B. (1973). *Animal crackers: A test of motivation to achieve*. Monterey, CA: CTB/McGraw-Hill.

Amatora, M. (1951). *Child personality scale*. Cincinnati, OH: C. A. Gregory.

American Psychiatric Association (1987). *Diagnostic and statistical manual of mental disorders—(3rd ed. rev.)*, Washington, D. C.: Author.

Angleitner, A., & Wiggins, J. S. (1986). Introduction. In A. Angleitner and J. S. Wiggins (Eds.). *Personality assessment via questionnaires: Current issues in theory and measurement*. (pp. 1–3). Berlin: Springer-Verlag.

Archer, R. P. (1984). Use of the MMPI with adolescents: A review of salient issues. *Clinical Psychology Review, 4,* 241–251.

Archer, R. P. (1987). *Using the MMPI with adolescents.* Hillsdale, NJ: Lawrence Erlbaum Associates.

Archer, R. P., Pancoast, D. L., & Klinefelter, D. (1989). A comparison of MMPI code types produced by traditional and recent adolescent norms. *Psychological Assessment: A Journal of Consulting and Clinical Assessment, 1,* 23–29.

Archer, R. P., White, J. L., & Orvin, G. H. (1979). MMPI characteristics and correlates among adolescent psychiatric inpatients. *Journal of Clinical Psychology, 35,* 498–504.

Asher, S. R., Hymel, S., & Renshaw, P. D. (1984). Loneliness in children. *Child Development, 55,* 1456–1464.

Asher, S. R., & Wheeler, V. A. (1985). Children's loneliness: A comparison of rejected and neglected peer status. *Journal of Consulting and Clinical Psychology, 53,* 500–505.

Attie, I., & Brooks-Gunn, J. (1989). Development of eating problems in adolescent girls: A longitudinal study. *Developmental Psychology, 25,* 70–79.

Atwood, R., Gold, M., & Taylor, R. (1989). Two types of delinquents and their institutional adjustment. *Journal of Consulting and Clinical Psychology, 57,* 68–75.

Bandura, A. (1977). Self-efficacy: Toward a unifying theory of behavior change. *Psychological Review, 84,* 191–215.

Bartell, N. P., & Reynolds, W. M. (1986) Depression and self-esteem in academically gifted and nongifted children: A comparison study. *Journal of School Psychology, 24,* 55–61.

Baxter, E. D. (1937). The Baxter Child Personality Test. *Journal of Applied Psychology, 21,* 410–430.

Beck, S. (1987). Questionnaires and checklists. In C. L. Frame & J. L. Matson (Eds.), *Handbook of assessment in childhood psychopathology* (pp. 79–106). New York: Plenum Press.

Beitchman, J. H., & Corradini, A. (1988). Self-report measures for use with children: A review and comment. *Journal of Clinical Psychology, 44,* 477–490.

Beitchman, J. H., Kruidenier, B., & Clegg, M. (1987). The Children's Self-Report Rating Scale: Screening accuracy and predictive power reconsidered. *Journal of the American Association of Child and Adolescent Psychiatry, 26,* 49–52.

Beitchman, J. H., Raman, S., Carlson, S., Clegg, M., & Kruidenier, B. (1985). The development and validation of the Children's Self-Report Psychiatric Rating Scale. *Journal of the American Association of Child and Adolescent Psychiatry, 24,* 413–428.

Bell, H. M. (1934). *The adjustment inventory: Student form.* Stanford, CA: Stanford University Press. [Later Published by Consulting Psychologists Press].

Bell, H. M. (1937). *School inventory.* Stanford, CA: Stanford University Press.

Belter, R. W., McIntosh, J. A., Finch, A. J., & Saylor, C. F. (1988). Preschoolers' ability to differentiate levels of pain: Relative efficacy of three self-report measures. *Journal of Clinical Child Psychology, 17,* 329–335.

Berg, C. J., Rapoport, J. L., & Flament, M. F. (1986). The Leyton Obsessional Inventory-Child Version. *Journal of the American Academy of Child and Adolescent Psychiatry, 25,* 84–91.

Berg, C. J., Whitaker, A., Davies, M., et al. (1988). The survey form of the Leyton Obsessional Inventory-Child Version: Norms from the epidemiologic study. *Journal of the American Academy of Child and Adolescent Psychiatry, 27,* 759–763.

Bernreuter, R. G. (1931). *Personality inventory.* Stanford, CA: Stanford University Press. [Later published by Consulting Psychologists Press].

Bialer, I. (1961) Conceptualization of success and failure in mentally retarded and normal children. *Journal of Personality, 29,* 303–320.

Brigden, R. L. (1939). The Cowan Adolescent Personality Schedule: Its function in psychological diagnosis. *American Journal of Medical Jurisprudence, 2,* 97–99.

Brown, F. (1934). A psychoneurotic inventory for children between nine and fourteen years of age. *Journal of Applied Psychology, 18,* 566–577.

Brown, F. (1935). *Personality Inventory for Children.* New York: The Psychological Corporation. [Later published as the *Brown Personality Inventory for Children* by the Public School Publishing Co., Cincinnati, OH].

Burchinal, L. G., Gardner, B., & Hawkes, G. R. (1958). A suggested revision of norms for the Rogers Test of Personality Adjustment. *Child Development, 29,* 135–139.

Burks, B. S. (1928). The relative influence of nature and nurture upon mental development. *27th Yearbook, National Society for the Study of Education,* Part I. (pp. 219–316). Chicago: University of Chicago Press.

Buros, O. K. (Ed.) (1972). *The seventh mental measurements yearbook* (Vol 1). Highland Park, NJ: Gryphon Press.

Cady, V. M. (1923). The estimation of juvenile incorrigibility. *Journal of Delinquency Monographs, 2.*

Carroll, J. J., & Steward, M. S. (1984). The role of cognitive development in children's understandings of their own feelings. *Child Development, 55,* 1486–1492.

Castenada, A., McCandless, B. R., & Palermo, D. S. (1956). The children's form of the Manifest Anxiety Scale. *Child Development, 27,* 317–326.

Cattell, R. B. (1941). Review of the Adjustment Inventory: Student Form. In O. K. Buros (Ed.). *The nineteen forty mental measurements yearbook* (pp. 51). Highland Park, NJ: Mental Measurements Yearbook.

Cattell, R. B., Cattell, M. D., & Johns, E. (1984). *Manual and norms for the high school personality questionnaire.*

Champaign, IL: Institute for Personality and Ability Testing.
Cattell, R. B., Cogan, E. A., Gruen, W., & Husek, T. (1955). *Objective-analytic personality test battery*. Champaign, IL: Institute for Personality and Ability Testing.
Cattell, R. B., Eber, H. W., & Tatsuoka, M. M. (1970). *Handbook for the sixteen personality factor questionnaire (16 PF)*. Champaign, IL: Institute for Personality and Ability Testing.
Cattell, R. B., & Gruen, W. (1955). The primary personality factors in 11-year-old children by objective tests. *Journal of Personality, 23*, 460–478.
Christiansen, B. A., Smith, G. T., Roehling, P. V., & Goldman, M. S. (1989). Using alcohol expectancies to predict adolescent drinking behavior after one year. *Journal of Consulting and Clinical Psychology, 57*, 93–99.
Colligan, R. C., & Offord, K. P. (1986, April). *The MMPI and adolescents of the 80's: A critique*. Paper presented at the Annual Meeting, National Association of School Psychologists.
Compas, B. E., Davis, G. E., Forsythe, C. J., & Wagner, B. M. (1987). Assessment of major and daily stressful events during adolescence: The Adolescent Perceived Events Scale. *Journal of Consulting and Clinical Psychology, 55*, 534–541.
Coopersmith, S. (1959). A method for determining types of self-esteem. *Journal of Abnormal and Social Psychology, 59*, 87–94.
Coopersmith, S. (1967). *The antecedents of self-esteem*. San Francisco, CA: Freeman.
Cornell, E. L., & Coxe, W. W. (1934). *A performance ability scale: Examination manual*. Yonkers, NY: World Book Company.
Connell, J. P. (1985). A new multidimensional measure of children's perceptions of control. *Child Development, 56*, 1018–1041.
Courthial, A. (1931). Emotional differences of delinquent and non-delinquent girls of normal intelligence. *Archives Psychology, 133*.
Cowan, E. A., McClellan, M. C., Pratt, B. M., & Skaer, M. (1935). An adolescent personality schedule. *Child Development, 6*, 77–87.
Crandall, V. C. (1966). Personality characteristics and social and achievement behaviors associated with children's social desirability response tendencies. *Journal of Personality and Social Psychology, 4*, 477–486.
Crandall, V. C. (1978, August). *New developments with the Intellectual Achievement Responsibility Scale*. Paper presented at the Annual Meeting, American Psychological Association, Toronto.
Crandall, V. C., Crandall, V. J., & Katkovsky, W. (1965). A children's social desirability questionnaire. *Journal of Consulting Psychology, 29*, 27–36.
Crandall, V. C., Katkovsky, W., & Crandall, V. J. (1965). Children's belief in their own control of reinforcements in intellectual achievement situations. *Child Development, 36*, 91–109.
Crowne, D. P. (1979). *The experimental study of personality*. Hillsdale, NJ: Lawrence Erlbaum Associates.
Crowne, D. P., & Marlowe, D. (1964). *The approval motive: Studies in evaluative dependence*. New York: Wiley.
Deluty, R. H. (1979). Children's Action Tendency Scale: A self-report measure of aggressiveness, assertiveness, and submissiveness in children. *Journal of Consulting and Clinical Psychology, 47*, 1061–1071.
Diener, C. I., & Dweck, C. S. (1978). An analysis of learned helplessness: Continuous changes in performance, strategy, and achievement cognitions following failure. *Journal of Personality and Social Psychology, 36*, 451–462.
Donovan, J. E., Jessor, R., & Costa, F. M. (1988). Syndrome of problem behavior in adolescence: A replication. *Journal of Consulting and Clinical Psychology, 56*, 762–765.
Dweck, C. S. (1975). The role of expectations and attributions in the alleviation of learned helplessness. *Journal of Personality and Social Psychology, 31*, 674–685.
Epstein, S. (1979). The stability of behavior: I. On predicting most of the people much of the time. *Journal of Personality and Social Psychology, 37*, 1097–1126.
Exner, J. E., & Weiner, I. B. (1982). *The Rorschach: A comprehensive system, Volume 3: Assessment of children and adolescents*. New York: John Wiley & Sons.
Eysenck, H. J., & Eysenck, S. B. G. (1975). *Eysenck personality questionnaire*. San Diego: Educational and Industrial Testing Service.
Finch, A. J., Lipovsky, J. A., & Casat, C. D. (1989). Anxiety and depression in children and adolescents: Negative affectivity or separate constructs? In P. C. Kendall and D. Watson (Eds.), *Anxiety and depression: Distinctive and overlapping features* (pp. 171–202). San Diego: Academic Press.
Finch, A. J., Montgomery, L. E., & Deardorff, P. (1974). Reliability of State-Trait Anxiety with emotionally disturbed children. *Journal of Abnormal Child Psychology, 2*, 67–69.
Finch, A. J., Pezzuti, K. A., & Nelson, W. M. (1975). Locus of control and academic achievement in emotionally disturbed children. *Journal of Consulting and Clinical Psychology, 43*, 103.
Finch, A. J., & Rogers, T. R. (1984). Self-report instruments. In T. H. Ollendick & M. Hersen (Eds.), *Child behavioral assessment: Principles and procedures*. (pp. 106–123). New York: Pergamon.
Fisher, K. W. (1980). A theory of cognitive development: The control and construction of hierarchies of skills. *Psychological Review, 87*, 477–531.
Flament, M. F., Rapoport, J. L., Berg, C. J., Sceery, W., Kilts, C., Mellstrom, B., & Linnoila, M. (1985). Clomipramine treatment of childhood obsessive-compulsive disorder. *Archives of General Psychiatry, 42*, 977–983.
Flament, M. F., Whitaker, A., Rapoport, J., et al., (1988).

Obsessive-compulsive disorder in adolescence: An epidemiologic study. *Journal of the American Academy of Child and Adolescent Psychiatry, 27*, 764–771.

Flavell, J. H. (1977). *Cognitive development.* Englewood Cliffs, NJ: Prentice-Hall.

Ford, L. H., & Rubin, B. M. (1970). A social desirability questionnaire for young children. *Journal of Consulting and Clinical Psychology, 35*, 195–204.

Fox, J. E., & Houston, B. K. (1983). Distinguishing between cognitive and somatic trait and state anxiety in children. *Journal of Personality and Social Psychology, 45*, 862–870.

Garner, D. M., & Garfinkel, P. E. (1979). The Eating Attitudes Test: An index of the symptoms of anorexia nervosa. *Psychological Medicine, 9*, 273–279.

Garner, D. M., & Olmsted, M. P. (1984). *Eating disorder inventory manual.* Odessa, FL: Psychological Assessment Resources.

Garner, D. M., Olmsted, M. P., Bohr, Y., & Garfinkel, P. E. (1982). The Eating Attitudes Test: Psychometric features and clinical correlates. *Psychological Medicine, 12*, 871–878.

Garner, D. M., Olmsted, M. P., & Polivy, J. (1983). *Eating disorder inventory* Odessa, FL: Psychological Assessment Resources.

Gillis, J. S. (1980). *Child anxiety scale manual.* Champaign, IL: Institute for Personality and Ability Testing.

Goh, D. S., Teslow, C. J., & Fuller, G. B. (1981). The practice of psychological assessment among school psychologists. *Professional Psychology, 12*, 696–706.

Goldberg, L. R. (1974). Objective diagnostic tests and measures. *Annual Review of Psychology, 25*, 343–366.

Gottfried, A. E. (1985). Academic intrinsic motivation in elementary and junior high school students. *Journal of Educational Psychology, 77*, 631–635.

Gottfried, A. E. (1986). *Children's academic intrinsic motivation inventory.* Odessa, FL: Psychological Assessment Resources.

Gough, H. G. (1957). *California psychological inventory manual.* Palo Alto, CA: Consulting Psychologists Press.

Guilford, J. P., & Martin, H. G. (1943). *Guilford-martin inventory of factors.* Beverly Hills, CA: Sheridan Supply Co.

Guilford, J. P., & Zimmerman, W. S. (1949). *Guilford-Zimmerman temperament survey.* Beverly Hills, CA: Sheridan Supply Co.

Hamilton, M. (1960). A rating scale for depression. *Journal of Neurology, Neurosurgery, and Psychiatry, 23*, 56–62.

Harrell, A. V., & Wirtz, P. W. (1989a). Screening for adolescent problem drinking: Validation of a multidimensional instrument for case identification. *Psychological Assessment: A Journal of Consulting and Clinical Psychology, 1*, 61–63.

Harrell, A. V., & Wirtz, P. W. (1989b). *Adolescent drinking index: Professional manual.* Odessa, FL: Psychological Assessment Resources.

Harter, S. (1978). Effectance motivation reconsidered: Toward a developmental model. *Human Development, 21*, 34–64.

Harter, S. (1982). The perceived competency scale for children. *Child Development, 53*, 87–97.

Harter, S. (1986). Cognitive-developmental processes in the integration of concepts about emotions and the self. *Social Cognition, 4*, 119–151.

Harter, S. (1988). *Manual for the self-perception profile for adolescents.* Denver: University of Denver.

Harter, S. (1990). Issues in the assessment of the self-concept of children and adolescents. In A. M. La Greca (Ed.) *Through the eyes of the child: Obtaining self-reports from children and adolescents* (pp. 292–325). Boston: Allyn and Bacon.

Harter, S., & Pike, R. (1984). The pictorial scale of perceived competence and social acceptance for young children. *Child Development, 55*, 1969–1982.

Hathaway, S. R., & McKinley, J. D. (1940). A multiphasic personality schedule: I. Construction of the schedule. *Journal of Psychology, 10*, 249–254.

Herzbergen, S. D., Linney, J. A., Seidman, E., & Rapoport, J. (1979). Preschool and Primary Locus of Control Scale: Is it ready for use? *Developmental Psychology, 15*, 320–324.

Hightower, A. D., Cowen, E. L., Spinell, A. P., Lotyczewski, B. S., Guare, J. C., Rohrbeck, C. A., & Brown, L. P. (1987). The Child Rating Scale: The development and psychometric refinement of a socioemotional self-rating scale for young school children. *School Psychology Review, 16*, 239–255.

Humphrey, L. L. (1982). Children's and teacher's perspectives on children's self-control: The development of two rating scales. *Journal of Consulting and Clinical Psychology, 50*, 624–633.

Jacob, T., & Tennenbaum, D. L. (1988). Family assessment methods. In M. Rutter, A. H. Tuma, and I. S. Lann (Eds.) *Assessment and diagnosis in child psychopathology* (pp. 196–231). New York: Guilford Press.

Jessor, R., & Jessor, S. L. (1977). *Problem behavior and psychosocial development: A longitudinal study of youth.* New York: Academic Press.

Johnson, J. H. (1986). *Life events as stressors in childhood and adolescence.* Newbury Park, CA: Sage Publications.

Johnston, H. F., & March, J. S. (in press). Obsessive-compulsive disorder in children and adolescents. In W. M. Reynolds (Ed.), *Internalizing disorders in children and adolescents.* New York: John Wiley & Sons.

Kagan, J., Rosman, B. L., Day, D., Albert, J., & Phillips, W. (1964). Information in the child: Significance of analytic and reflective attitudes. *Psychological Monographs, 78*, (I, Whole No. 578).

Kahn, J. S., Kehle, T. J., Jenson, W. R., & Clark, E. (1990). Comparison of cognitive-behavioral, relaxation, and self-modeling interventions for depression among middle-school students. *School Psychology Review, 19*, 196–211.

Kazdin, A. E. (1989). Evaluation of the Pleasure Scale in the assessment of anhedonia in children. *Journal of the American Academy of Child and Adolescent Psychiatry, 28*, 364–372.

Kazdin, A. E., Colbus, D., & Rodgers, A. (1986). Assessment of depression and diagnosis of depressive disorder among psychiatrically disturbed children. *Journal of Abnormal Child Psychology, 14*, 499–515.

Kazdin, A. E., French, N. H., Unis, A. S., Esveldt-Dawson, K., & Sherick, R. B. (1983). Hopelessness, depression, and suicidal intent among psychiatrically disturbed inpatient children. *Journal of Consulting and Clinical Psychology, 51*, 504–510.

Kazdin, A. E., Rodgers, A. & Colbus, D. (1986). The Hopelessness Scale for Children: Psychometric characteristics and concurrent validity. *Journal of Consulting and Clinical Psychology, 54*, 241–245.

King, C. A., Raskin, A., Gdowski, C. L., Butkus, M., & Opipari, L. (1990). Psychosocial factors associated with urban adolescent female suicide attempts. *Journal of the American Academy of Child and Adolescent Psychiatry, 29*, 289–294.

Kovacs, M. (1979). *Children's depression inventory*, University of Pittsburgh School of Medicine. Author.

Kovacs, M. (1981). Rating scales to assess depression in school-aged children. *Acta Paedopsychiatrica, 46*, 305–315.

Kovacs, M. (1983). *The Children's Depression Inventory: A self-rating scale for school-aged youngsters*. Unpublished manuscript.

Kurdek, L. A., & Berg, B. (1987). Children's Beliefs About Parental Divorce Scale: Psychometric characteristics and concurrent validity. *Journal of Consulting and Clinical Psychology, 55*, 712–718.

La Greca, A. M. (1990). Issues and perspectives on the child assessment process. In A. M. La Greca (Ed.), *Through the eyes of the child: Obtaining self-reports from children and adolescents*. (pp. 3–17). Boston: Allyn and Bacon.

La Greca, A. M., Dandes, S. K., Wick, P., Shaw, K., & Stone, W. L. (1988). Development of the Social Anxiety Scale for Children: Reliability and concurrent validity. *Journal of Clinical Child Psychology, 17*, 84–91.

Lapan, R., & Patton, M. J. (1986). Self-psychology and the adolescent process: Measures of pseudoautonomy and peer-group dependence. *Journal of Counseling Psychology, 33*, 136–142.

Last, C. G. (in press). Anxiety disorders in childhood and adolescence. In W. M. Reynolds (Ed.), *Internalizing disorders in children and adolescents*. New York: John Wiley & Sons.

LeBaron, S., & Zeltzer, L. (1984). Assessment of acute pain and anxiety in children and adolescents by self-reports, observer reports, and a behavior checklist. *Journal of Consulting and Clinical Psychology, 52*, 729–738.

Link, H. C. (1936a). A test of four personality traits of adolescents. *Journal of Applied Psychology, 20*, 527–534.

Link, H. C. (1936b). Personality can be acquired. *Readers Digest, 29* (12), 1–4.

Link, H. C. (1938). *Personality quotient test*. New York: Psychological Corporation.

Linn, R. T., & Hodge, G. K. (1982). Locus of control in childhood hyperactivity. *Journal of Consulting and Clinical Psychology, 50*, 592–593.

Loevinger, J. (1957). Objective tests as instruments of psychological theory. *Psychological Reports, 3*, 635–694.

Loofbourow, G. C., & Keys, N. (1933). A group test of problem behavior tendencies in junior high school boys. *Journal of Educational Psychology, 9*, 641–653.

Mabe, P. A., & Treiber, F. A. (1989). Social desirability response tendencies in psychiatric inpatient children. *Journal of Clinical Psychology, 45*, 194–201.

Marks, P. A., Seeman, W., & Haller, D. L. (1974). *The actuarial use of the MMPI with adolescents and adults*. Baltimore: Williams and Wilkins.

Mathews, E. (1923). A study of emotional stability in children. *Journal of Delinquency, 8*, 1–40.

McCubbin, H. I., & Thompson, A. I. (Eds.) (1987). *Family assessment inventories for research and practice*. Madison: University of Wisconsin Press.

Meichenbaum, D., Burland, S., Gruson, L., & Cameron, R. (1985). Metacognitive assessment. In S. R. Yussen (Ed.), *The growth of reflection in children*, (pp. 3–30). Orlando, FL: Academic Press.

Messer, S. B. (1972). The relation of internal-external control to academic performance. *Child Development, 43*, 1456–1462.

Michelson, L., & Wood, R. (1982). Development and psychometric properties of the Children's Assertive Behavior Scale. *Journal of Behavioral Assessment, 4*, 3–13.

Miller, L. C., Barrett, C. L., Hampe, E., & Noble, H. (1972). Factor structure of childhood fears. *Journal of Consulting and Clinical Psychology, 39*, 264–268.

Millon, T., Green, C. J., & Meagher, R. B. (1982). *Millon adolescent personality inventory manual*. Minneapolis, MN: National Computer Systems.

Mischel, W., Zeiss, R., & Zeiss, A. (1974). Internal-external control and persistence: Validation and implications of the Stanford Preschool Internal-External Scale. *Journal of Personality and Social Psychology, 29*, 265–278.

Moore, D., & Schultz, N. R. (1983). Loneliness at adolescence: Correlates, attributions, and coping. *Journal of Youth and Adolescence, 12*, 95–100.

Moos, R. H., & Moos, B. S. (1981). *Family environment scale manual*. Palo Alto, CA: Consulting Psychologists Press.

Nelson, W. M., & Finch, A. J. (1978). *The children's inventory of anger*. Unpublished manuscript. Cincinnati: Xavier University.

Nelson, W. M., Politano, P. M., Finch, A. J., Wendel, N., & Mayhall, C. (1987). Children's Depression Inventory:

Normative data and utility with emotionally disturbed children. *Journal of the American Academy of Child and Adolescent Psychiatry, 26,* 43–48.

Newcomb, M. D. & Bentler, P. M. (1988). *Consequences of adolescent drug use: Impact on the lives of young adults.* Newbury Park: Sage Publications.

Nowicki, S., & Duke, M. P. (1974). A preschool and primary internal-external control scale. *Developmental Psychology, 10,* 874–880.

Nowicki, S., & Strickland, B. R. (1973). A locus of control scale for children. Journal of Consulting and Clinical Psychology, 40, 148–155.

Offer, D., Ostrov, E., & Howard, K. I. (1981). *The adolescent: A psychological self-portrait.* New York: Basic Books.

Offer, D., Ostrov, E., & Howard, K. I. (Eds.). (1984). *Patterns of adolescent self-image.* San Francisco: Jossey-Bass.

Ollendick, T. H. (1981) Assessment of social interaction skills in school children. *Behavioral Counseling Quarterly, 1,* 227–243.

Ollendick, T. H. (1983). Reliability and validity of the Revised Fear Survey Schedule for Children (FSSC-R). *Behaviour Research and Therapy, 21,* 685–692.

Ollendick, T. H. (1984). Development and validation of the Children's Assertiveness Inventory. *Child Behavior Therapy, 5,* 1–15.

Olson, D. H., Portner, J., Lavee, Y. (1985). *Family adaptability and cohesion evaluation scales III.* St. Paul, MN: Family Social Sciences, University of Minnesota.

Papay, J. P., & Spielberger, C. D. (1986). Assessment of anxiety and achievement in kindergarten and first- and second-grade children. *Journal of Abnormal Child Psychology, 14,* 279–286.

Piaget, J. (1981). *Intelligence and affectivity: Their relationship during child development.* Palo Alto, CA: Annual Reviews.

Piers, E. V. (1984). *Piers-Harris children's self-concept scale: Revised manual.* Los Angeles: Western Psychological Services.

Pintner, R., & Forlano, G. (1938). Four retests of a personality inventory. *Journal of Educational Psychology, 29,* 93–100.

Pintner, R., Loftus, J. J., Forlano, G., & Alster, B. (1937). *Aspects of personality.* Yonkers, NY: World Book Co.

Pintner, R., Maller, J. B., Forlano, G., & Axelrod, H. C. (1934). *Pupil portraits.* New York: Bureau of Publications, Teachers College, Columbia University.

Pintner, R., Maller, J. B., Forlano, G., & Axelrod, H. C. (1935). The measurement of pupil adjustment. *Journal of Educational Research, 28,* 334–348.

Pintner, R., & Paterson, D. G. (1917). *A scale of performance tests.* New York: Appleton & Company.

Remmers, H. H., & Bauernfeind, R. H. (1951). *SRA junior inventory.* Chicago: Science Research Associates.

Remmers, H. H., & Shimberg, B., & Drucker, A. J. (1949). *SRA youth inventory.* Chicago: Science Research Associates.

Reynolds, C. R., & Richmond, B. O. (1978). What I Think and Feel: A revised measure of children's manifest anxiety. *Journal of Abnormal Child Psychology, 6,* 271–280.

Reynolds, C. R., & Richmond, B. O. (1985). *Revised Children's Manifest Anxiety Scale Manual.* Los Angeles: Western Psychological Services.

Reynolds, W. M. (1985, March). *Development and validation of a scale to measure depression in adolescents.* Paper presented at the Annual Meeting of the Society for Personality Assessment, Berkeley, Calif.

Reynolds, W. M. (1986). *Reynolds adolescent depression scale.* Odessa, FL: Psychological Assessment Resources.

Reynolds, W. M. (1987a). *Reynolds adolescent depression scale: Professional Manual.* Odessa, FL: Psychological Assessment Resources.

Reynolds, W. M. (1987b). *Suicidal ideation questionnaire.* Odessa, FL: Psychological Assessment Resources.

Reynolds, W. M. (1988a). *Suicidal ideation questionnaire: Professional Manual.* Odessa, FL: Psychological Assessment Resources.

Reynolds, W. M. (1988b). Measurement of academic self-concept in college students. *Journal of Personality Assessment, 52,* 223–240.

Reynolds, W. M. (1989a). *Reynolds child depression scale.* Odessa, FL: Psychological Assessment Resources.

Reynolds, W. M. (1989b). *Reynolds child depression scale: Professional Manual.* Odessa, FL: Psychological Assessment Resources.

Reynolds, W. M. (1989c). Suicidal ideation and depression in adolescents: Assessment and research. In P. F. Lovibond and P. Wilson (Eds.), *Clinical and abnormal psychology,* (pp. 125–135). Amsterdam: Elsevier Science Publishers.

Reynolds, W. M. (1990a). Introduction to the nature and study of internalizing disorders in children and adolescents. *School Psychology Review, 19,* 137–141.

Reynolds, W. M. (1990b). Depression in children and adolescents: Nature, diagnosis, assessment, and treatment. *School Psychology Review, 19,* 158–173.

Reynolds, W. M. (1990c). Development of a semi-structured clinical interview for suicidal behaviors in adolescents. *Psychological Assessment: A Journal of Consulting and Clinical Psychology. 3,*

Reynolds, W. M. (1990d). *Initial reliability of the Adolescent Psychopathology Scale with clinic and school-based samples.* Unpublished manuscript. Madison: University of Wisconsin.

Reynolds, W. M. (1991). Psychometric characteristics of the Adult Suicidal Ideation Questionnaire in college students. *Journal of Personality Assessment, 56,* 289–307.

Reynolds, W. M. (in press a). Depressive disorders in children and adolescents. In W. M. Reynolds (Ed.)

Internalizing disorders in children and adolescents. New York: John Wiley & Sons.

Reynolds, W. M. (in press b). *Suicidal behaviors interview.* Odessa, FL: Psychological Assessment Resources.

Reynolds, W. M. (in press c). *Adult suicidal ideation questionnaire.* Odessa, FL: Psychological Assessment Resources.

Reynolds, W. M. (in press d). *Academic Self-Concept Scale—High School Version.* Odessa, FL: Psychological Assessment Resources.

Reynolds, W. M. (in press e). *Adolescent Psychopathology Scale.* Odessa, FL: Psychological Assessment Resources.

Reynolds, W. M., Anderson, G. & Bartell, N. (1985). Measuring depression in children: A multimethod assessment investigation. *Journal of Abnormal Child Psychology, 13,* 513–526.

Reynolds, W. M., & Coats, K. I. (1986). A comparison of cognitive-behavioral therapy and relaxation training for the treatment of depression in adolescents. *Journal of Consulting and Clinical Psychology, 54,* 653–660.

Reynolds, W. M., & Downing, M. (1982, March). *Can we measure achievement motivation in young children?* Paper presented at the Annual Meeting, American Educational Research Association, New York City.

Reynolds, W. M. & Graves, A. (1989). Reliability of children's reports of depressive symptomatology. *Journal of Abnormal Child Psychology. 17,* 647–655.

Reynolds, W. M., Kobak, K., & Greist, J. H. (1990, August). *Suicidal ideation in outpatients with major depression, anxiety disorders, and nonpsychiatric controls.* Paper presented at the Annual Meeting, American Psychological Association. Boston.

Reynolds, W. M., & Miller, K. L. (1985). Depression and learned helplessness in mentally retarded and nonretarded adolescents: An initial investigation. *Applied Research in Mental Retardation, 6,* 295–307.

Reynolds, W. M., & Miller, K. L. (1989). Assessment of adolescents' learned helplessness in achievement situations. *Journal of Personality Assessment, 53,* 211–228.

Reynolds, W. M., & Miller, K. L. (in press). *Mastery orientation inventory.* Odessa, FL: Psychological Assessment Resources.

Reynolds, W. M. & Stark, K. D. (1983). Cognitive behavior modification: The clinical application of cognitive strategies. In M. Pressley & J. R. Levin (Eds.) *Cognitive strategy research: Psychological foundations* (pp. 221–266). New York: Springer-Verlag.

Reynolds, W. M., & Stark, K. D., (1985). Self-control in children: A multimethod examination of treatment outcome measures. *Journal of Abnormal Child Psychology, 14,* 13–23.

Rogers, C. (1931a). *Test of personality adjustment.* New York: Association Press.

Rogers, C. R. (1931b). Measuring personality adjustment in children nine to thirteen years of age. *Teachers College Contributions to Education, Whole No. 458.*

Rogers, C. R. (1941). Review of the Personality Inventory for Children. In O. K. Buros (Ed.). *The nineteen forty mental measurements yearbook.* (pp. 84). Highland Park, NJ: Mental Measurements Yearbook.

Rosenberg, M. (1965). *Society and adolescent self-image.* Princeton, NJ: Princeton University Press.

Rothbaum, F., & Weisz, J. R. (1989). *Child psychopathology and the quest for control.* Newbury Park, CA: Sage Publications.

Russell, D., Peplau, L. A., & Curtona, C. E. (1980). The revised UCLA Loneliness Scale: Concurrent and discriminant validity evidence. *Journal of Personality and Social Psychology, 39,* 471–480.

Rydall, M. R., & Dietiker, K. E. (1979). Reliability and clinical validity of the Children's Fear Survey Schedule. *Journal of Behavior Therapy and Experimental Psychiatry, 19,* 303–310.

Sarason, S. B., Davidson, K. S., Lighthall, F. F., Waite, R. R., & Ruebush, B. K. (1960). *Anxiety in elementary school children.* New York: John Wiley & Sons.

Scanlon, E. M., & Ollendick, T. H. (1985). Children's assertive behavior: The reliability and validity of three self-report measures. *Child and Family Behavior Therapy, 7,* 9–21.

Scherer, M. W., & Nakamura, C. Y. (1968). A fear survey schedule for children (FSS-FC): A factor analytic comparison with manifest anxiety. *Behavior Research and Therapy, 6,* 173–182.

Selman, R. L. (1980). *The growth of interpersonal understanding: Developmental and clinical analyses.* New York: Academic Press.

Shavelson, R. J., Hubner, J. J., & Stanton, G. C., (1976). Self-concept: Validation of construct interpretations. *Review of Educational Research, 46,* 407–441.

Slawson, J. (1926). *The delinquent boy.* Boston: Badger.

Smith, M. C., & Thelen, M. H. (1984). Development and validation of a test for bulimia. *Journal of Consulting and Clinical Psychology, 52,* 863–872.

Smucker, M. R., Craighead, W. E., Craighead, L. W., & Green, B. J. (1986). Normative and reliability data for the Children's Depression Inventory. *Journal of Abnormal Child Psychology, 14,* 25–39.

Spatz, K. C., & Johnston, J. O. (1973). Internal consistency of the Coopersmith Self-Esteem Inventory. *Educational and Psychological Measurement, 33,* 875–876.

Spielberger, C. D. (1988). *State-Trait Anger Expression Inventory: Professional Manual.* Odessa, FL: Psychological Assessment Resources.

Spielberger, C. D., Edwards, C. D., Montuori, J., & Lushene, R. (1973). *State-trait anxiety inventory for children.* Palo Alto: CA: Consulting Psychologists Press.

Stark, K. D., Reynolds, W. M., & Kaslow, N. J. (1987). A comparison of the relative efficacy of self-control therapy and behavioral problem-solving therapy for depression in children. *Journal of Abnormal Child Psychology, 15,* 91–113.

Stein, D. M., & Brinza, S. R. (1989). Bulimia: Prevalence

estimates in female junior high and high school students. *Journal of Clinical Child Psychology, 18,* 206–213.

Stone, W. L., & Lemanek, K. L. (1990). Developmental issues in children's self-reports. In A. M. LaGreca (Ed.), *Through the eyes of the child: Obtaining self-reports from children and adolescents.* (pp. 18–56). Boston: Allyn and Bacon.

Strauss, C. C., Last, C. G., Hersen,M., & Kazdin, A. E. (1988). Association between anxiety and depression in children and adolescents with anxiety disorders. *Journal of Abnormal Child Psychology, 16,* 57–68.

Sundberg, N. D., & Reynolds, W. M. (in progress). *Assessment of persons* (2nd ed.). Englewood Cliffs, NJ: Prentice Hall.

Sundberg, N. D., Snowden, L. R., & Reynolds, W. M. (1978). Toward assessment of personal competence and incompetence in life situations. *Annual Review of Psychology, 29,* 179–221.

Swearingen, E. M., & Cohen, L. H. (1985). Measurement of adolescents' life events: The Junior High School Life Experiences Survey. *American Journal of Community Psychology, 13,* 69–85.

Thurstone, L. L. (1949). *Thurstone temperament schedule.* Chicago: Science Research Associates.

Tiegs, E. W., Clark, W. W., & Thorpe, L. P. (1939). *California test of personality: A profile of personal and social adjustment.* Los Angeles: California Test Bureau.

Tschechtelin, M. A. (1944). Comparability of child and adult personality rating scales. *Journal of Educational Psychology, 35,* 309–313.

Wheeler, V. A., & Ladd, G. W. (1982). Assessment of children's self-efficacy for social interactions with peers. *Developmental Psychology, 18,* 795–805.

Wilson, T. D. (1985). Strangers to ourselves: The origins and accuracy of beliefs about one's own mental states. In J. H. Harvey and G. Weary (Eds.), *Attributions: Basic issues and applications.* (pp. 9–36). Orlando, FL: Academic Press.

Wojnilower, D. A., & Gross, A. M. (1984). Assertive behavior and likeability in elementary school boys. *Child and Family Behavior Therapy, 6* (4), 57–70.

Zatz, S., & Chassin, L. (1983). Cognitions of test-anxious children. *Journal of Consulting and Clinical Psychology, 51,* 526–534.

Zeltzer, L. K., LeBaron, S., Richie, D. M., Reed, D., Schoolfield, J., & Prihoda, T. J. (1988). Can children understand and use a rating scale to quantify somatic symptoms? Assessment of nausea and vomiting as a model. *Journal of Consulting and Clinical Psychology, 56,* 567–572.

CHAPTER 9

SELF-MONITORING

Edward S. Shapiro
Christine L. Cole

Self-monitoring, self-recording, self-observation, and self-assessment all refer to the systematic observation and recording of one's own behavior. As an assessment procedure, self-monitoring may be an effective method for gathering information on specific child behaviors. This may be one aspect of a pretreatment behavior analysis to determine an appropriate target behavior, gather baseline data on the frequency of a target behavior, or obtain information on the antecedents and consequences of a target behavior. Self-monitoring may also be used on an ongoing basis as a means of evaluating the effects of an intervention procedure. However, as discussed later, there are limitations on its routine use as a data collection procedure.

In addition to being useful for assessment purposes, self-monitoring may also serve as a means for behavior change. Numerous studies have demonstrated that the activity of self-monitoring may result in reactive effects, or changes in the behavior being monitored (e.g., Blick & Test, 1987; Kapadia & Fantuzzo, 1988a; McCurdy & Shapiro, 1988). Not only does self-monitoring often change behavior, but the change is almost always in the desired direction. Although reactivity does not always result from self-monitoring (e.g., Fixsen, Phillips, & Wolf, 1972; Shapiro & Ackerman, 1983), behavior change does occur with sufficient regularity that it may interfere with the use of self-monitoring for assessment purposes.

METHODOLOGY OF SELF-MONITORING

Types of Behaviors Self-Monitored

Behaviors self-monitored by children or adolescents can vary across numerous dimensions. These include objectivity, complexity, and number of behaviors.

Objectivity

Behaviors chosen for self-monitoring can be those that are observable by individuals themselves or others such as on-task behavior, calling-out, or completed work assignments. Additionally, those events that are part of subjective, private experiences such as negative self-statements, urges to talk during discussion, or thoughts of self-destruction, can also be targets for self-monitoring. Occurrence of observable behaviors can be easily verified through observations by independent recorders. Those events that are covert cannot be confirmed except through inferences from one's observable behavior. Although the degree of reliability with these less observable responses is always questionable, use of such self-reported behavior is important in understanding the origins and maintenance of specific behavioral patterns.

Complexity

Behaviors targeted for self-monitoring may range from simple, discrete events such as single hand raises or number of tasks completed through more complex chains of responses, which might include antecedents and consequences of behavior. For example, a student with difficulties in heterosexual relationships could be asked to record the events surrounding an anticipated approach to a member of the opposite sex. These events would include self-talk, thoughts, feelings, and other covert responses. Additionally, the student could record outcomes of the interaction.

Number of Behaviors

Self-monitoring may involve assessing and recording single or multiple responses. For example, following a written language assignment, a student may be asked to monitor the number of words written, number of words spelled correctly, number of correct punctuations marks, number of correct capitalizations, and so forth. Similarly, during a self-instruction program, a student may have a checklist of items to self-monitor related to following instructional commands during task completion.

Two other dimensions that are important to consider in selecting behaviors to be self-monitored are the timing and schedule of recording. Behaviors can be recorded immediately after their occurrence or after some delay (such as the end of class, the period, or school day). Likewise, use of event recording (each instance of behavior is noted) or a partial interval time sampling method (occurrence within interval regardless of frequency) could be employed. Results from each of these approaches to recording data can potentially affect the outcome. However, equally important are the potential practical considerations one must give in setting up a recording system that carefully matches the available resources.

Types of Data Collected

Frequency Counting

Probably the simplest and most common method for collecting self-monitored data is to have individuals record the occurrence of specified target behaviors. These behaviors are summed over the entire time that the behavior is to be observed and are usually reported as a frequency (of time) or rate. For example, Piersel (1985) instructed an adolescent to record on a prepared form the completion of academic assignments as they were placed in a teacher's desk. Ollendick (1981) taught two boys to use a wrist counter to record each occurrence of nervous tics.

Time Sampling

Another procedure commonly used in observational data collection involves dividing the observational period into equal units of time and recording presence or absence of the targeted behavior during each of the separate intervals. Under partial interval sampling, the entire interval is recorded as behavior present following any single occurrence of the behavior. Whole interval sampling requires the behavior to be present throughout the entire interval for the interval to be recorded as behavior present. Finally, momentary time sampling specifies presence or absence of behavior only at a specific moment in time (usually the beginning of the interval), with any subsequent occurrence of the behavior between observation intervals ignored.

Each of these method of time sampling can be easily applied within a self-monitoring format. For example, Sugai and Rowe (1984) instructed a 15-year-old male with mild retardation to self-monitor in-seat behavior at the end of a 10-minute interval. Shapiro, McGonigle, and Ollendick (1980) employed a common variation of time sampling in self-monitoring research. Children were instructed to record, at the moment they heard a tone played at variable intervals, whether or not they were on task. A less precise time sampling procedure was employed by McLaughlin (1984), in which students were instructed to record the presence or absence of studying "whenever they thought about it."

Narrative Descriptions

Another form of self-monitoring requires individuals to provide written logs or descriptions of events. These are often useful in the early stages of selecting target behaviors and offer information helpful to the clinician in possibly understanding variables playing important roles in the development and maintenance of problem behaviors. At times, these descriptions may be prompted by having individuals write the thoughts preceding and following the occurrence of the self-monitored behavior or events.

Devices Used for Self-Monitoring

The methods used for collecting data through self-monitoring are very simple. Most commonly, different versions of paper-and-pencil tests are employed. For example, McLaughlin, Burgess, and Sackville-West (1982) used a sheet with 50 small squares. Children were instructed to mark a "+" or "−" at each designated interval based upon their judgment of whether they were or were not on task. Shapiro et al. (1980) had a teacher place gummed stars on a sheet with 15 squares contingent on attending behavior present as the end of each work interval sounded. Figure 9-1 provides illustrations of various types of paper-and-pencil recording devices.

Mechanical devices are also popular in self-monitoring programs. These can include golf counters, wrist counters, industrial response counters, or any device capable of tracking discrete behaviors. For example, Mace, Shapiro, West, Campbell, and Altman (1986), working with adults with moderate to severe mental retardation who were unable to count accurately, created a device to assist clients in counting completed work samples. Each time the individuals finished assembling the required items in a bag, they were taught to place a ring on a wooden dowel rod. The rod was marked to indicate the criterion number of completed items necessary to earn the identified rewards. Likewise, Shapiro, Browder, and D'Huyvetters (1984), working with autistic children who did not possess counting skills, created a board on which students learned to place coins upon completion of each assigned worksheet. Completion of the board signaled meeting the criterion for selecting reinforcers.

Considerations for Self-Monitoring with Children

Self-monitoring procedures have been employed across a wide range of populations of children and adolescents (Gardner & Cole, 1988). Although the process and procedures employed when using self-monitoring do not vary across populations, there are some important issues that should be considered when children or adolescents are self-monitoring. First, individuals who are engaging in self-monitoring must be clear about the behaviors targeted for recording. With young children especially, ongoing visual reminders of the target behaviors may be necessary. Kunzelmann (1970) has recommended using simple stick-figure drawings that demonstrate the correct behaviors to be self-monitored. These *countoons* can provide ongoing reminders to students of the behaviors that are supposed to be self-monitored.

Another important consideration in using self-monitoring with children is the degree to which a child feels uncomfortable with the task of self-monitoring. Although some children are excited by and welcome the opportunity to engage in a self-monitoring procedure that may be visible to their peers, others may feel embarrassed by the task and may be less likely to engage in accurate or effective self-monitoring. Clinicians should carefully discuss and explore the child's feelings about using these procedures and may need to make the self-monitoring activities less obvious to peers when the situation warrants such action.

A further consideration when using self-monitoring with children or adolescents is that the target behaviors and procedures employed for monitoring are age appropriate. Clearly, it may be inappropriate to ask an adolescent to keep track of attending behavior by playing an auditory signal that is loud enough to be heard by other members of their class and having them record presence or absence on a recording sheet. Similarly, it may be impossible for young elementary-age students to accurately report their thoughts or urges to call out.

SELF-MONITORING AS AN ASSESSMENT PROCEDURE

As an assessment procedure, self-monitoring can serve to help in selecting target behaviors for intervention as well as provide a means of monitoring the response during baseline or intervention phases. The key issues when using self-monitoring for assessment surround accuracy of the self-monitoring process.

Procedures for Determining Accuracy

Several procedures have been employed for determining accuracy of self-monitored responses. Nelson (1977) noted that the most commonly used procedure was to compare self-recordings with those made simultaneously with an external observer. Shapiro

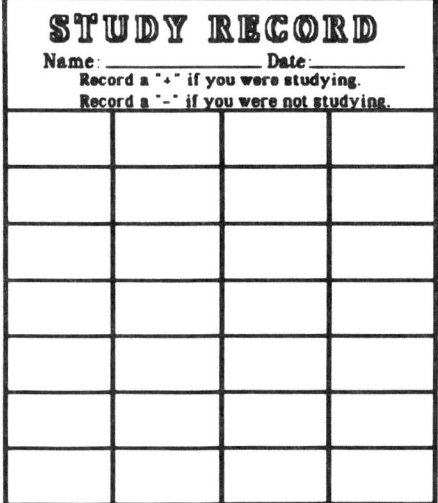
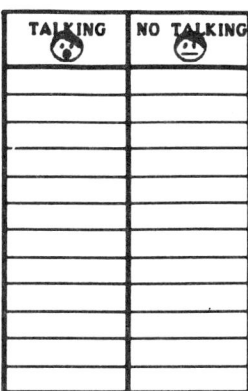
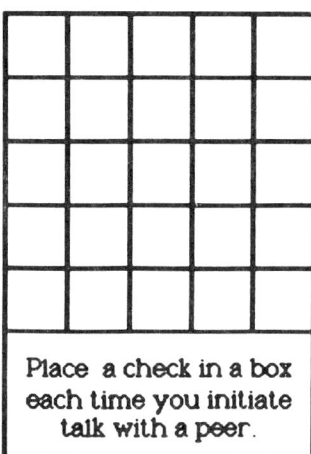

Figure 9-1. Various types of pencil-and-paper self-recording forms. From Gardner & Cole (1988). Reproduced with permission.

(1984) suggested a variation of this procedure by having the self-recorded data compared to a specific criterion that can be directly verified, such as a permanent product measure. For example, Piersel (1985) examined the accuracy of a student's self-recording of the completion of assignments by comparing the data with teacher-completed records. Shapiro and Ackerman (1983) had persons with mental retardation compare their self-recorded record of completed units of work with a count of the actual number of units finished.

An additional method for determining accuracy of self-monitoring involves comparing self-recorded data with data obtained through a mechanical counting device. For example, Mahoney, Moore, Wade, and Moura (1973) determined accuracy by comparing student answers that were automatically recorded by a teaching machine with the students' own recording.

When self-monitored responses involve discrete, observable events, such procedures for collecting accuracy of self-monitoring data are straightforward. However, when self-monitoring involves the evaluation of covert responses such as thoughts or feelings, accuracy of self-monitoring can be assessed only indirectly by examining the anticipated outcomes of the self-monitoring process. For example, accuracy of self-monitoring for a student who is instructed to monitor study time may indirectly be assessed by noting changes on actual test scores. Accuracy for a depressed adolescent who is told to self-monitor destructive thoughts may have to be evaluated by the number of emergency phone calls or contacts made over time. Clearly, it is virtually impossible to obtain external validation of the accuracy of the self-monitoring for such behaviors.

One very important methodological issue related to self-monitoring accuracy is the distinction between observer accuracy and observer agreement (Johnson & Bolstad, 1973; Nelson, 1977). Observer accuracy is determined by comparing performance with an existing and verifiable criterion. In contrast, observer agreement involves comparing self-recordings with those made by an independent observer. Most of the research on self-monitoring has provided examinations of observer accuracy, but few have established levels of observer agreement. For example, a student asked to self-monitor work completion may "forget" on one occasion to mark a recording sheet but remember at some later time. If one compares the self-monitored results with the actual work completion as recorded by the teacher, it may appear that the student was self-monitoring accurately. In reality, the student may have failed to follow the steps prescribed in the self-monitoring procedure. To truly assess observer accuracy, one would need to observe individuals engaging in self-monitoring and determine whether or not they actually made the self-monitored response at each moment the response was supposed to occur. Thus, with our example student who was supposed to self-record task completion when each worksheet was finished, observer accuracy of self-monitoring would be determined by having the observer note whether the student actually made the required self-monitored response each time a worksheet was finished.

Another important point related to determining the accuracy of self-monitoring is making sure that children or adolescents are actually making discriminations between correct and incorrect instances of a target response. For instance, if students are told to monitor whether they are or are not working at a given signal, accuracy of self-monitoring should be determined by observing whether students record "working" or "not working" consistent with their self-observed behavior versus always self-recording the same response (e.g., "working") regardless of their behavior. A student observed to not make the discrimination between instances and non-instances of the target behavior clearly requires specific training before one can assess whether he or she is self-monitoring accurately.

Variables Affecting Accuracy of Self-Monitoring

Numerous studies have shown that children and adolescents of varying populations are capable of accurate self-monitoring (e.g., Howell, Rueda, & Rutherford, 1983; Litrownik, Freitas, & Franzini, 1978; Rhode, Morgan, & Young, 1983). However, some studies have reported low or inconsistent accuracy across students. For example, Nelson, Hay, Devany, and Koslow-Green (1980) found student accuracy in an elementary classroom to range from .51 to .79. Shapiro et al. (1984) found a wide range of self-monitoring accuracy across a group of severely multihandicapped students. Similarly, Shapiro et al. (1980) noted some severely handicapped students who never achieved beyond a 50% level of self-monitored accuracy across the entire study.

In general, studies that have examined self-monitoring accuracy of children and adolescents appear to be equivocal. Although accuracy is reported to be very high in some studies, it is found to be low in others. Furthermore, within the same study with individuals displaying common behavioral, cognitive, and emotional characteristics, accuracy of self-monitoring may vary widely. A number of factors that may partially account for this variability have been noted.

Awareness of Accuracy Assessment

When students are aware that their self-monitored behavior is being checked, they are more likely to show highly levels of accuracy. For example, Rhode et al. (1983) taught students to subjectively rate their academic and behavioral responding during 15-minute intervals of an independent work period. Students initially earned bonus points by accurately matching their teachers' rating, which was obtained simultaneously with their self-monitored ratings. Rhode et al. (1983) found that after the matching procedure was faded, students tended to rate themselves less accurately. By instituting "surprise" match periods during which the teacher unexpectedly required students to match teacher ratings to earn points, they were able to maintain high levels of accuracy throughout the remainder of their study.

Training and Reinforcement for Accurate Self-Monitoring

Not surprisingly, accuracy of self-monitoring can greatly increase when students are trained to self-monitor accurately. For example, Shapiro et al. (1980) found that simply instructing students to engage in self-monitoring procedures resulted in only modest improvements in classroom on-task behavior and self-monitoring accuracy among a group of students with moderate to severe handicaps. As soon as training in self-monitoring was instituted, significant improvements in accuracy and on-task behavior were noted. Nelson, Lipinski, and Boykin (1978) found that adolescents with mental retardation who were trained in self-recording of appropriate verbalizations from videotape and regular classroom experiences exhibited significantly more accurate self-monitoring than those given only minimal instruction.

Again not surprisingly, providing contingent reward for accurate self-monitoring can increase the accuracy of self-monitored responses. For example, Robertson, Simon, Pachman, and Drabman (1979) found that self-monitoring accuracy, which was increased initially by earning points contingent on matching the external evaluation of the teacher, could be systematically faded where students maintain high levels of accuracy without the presence of external monitoring.

Valence of Target Behavior

Another variable that may influence the accuracy of self-monitoring is the valence of the behavior being recorded. Kanfer (1977) speculated that the self-monitoring of an undesirable behavior may result in covert aversive responses that may result in the person's not attending to occurrences of the behavior and producing inaccurate self-monitored data. Nelson, Hay, Hay, and Carstens (1977) found such effects with teachers instructed to self-record classroom verbalizations. Accuracy of self-monitoring was found to be greater for positive verbalizations than for negative verbalizations. However, some studies have not clearly supported these results (e.g., Litrownik & Freitas, 1980).

Nature of the Recording Device

Given that some devices used for self-monitoring are quite obtrusive and others somewhat subtle, different self-monitoring devices may lead to differential accuracy of self-recording. For example, Nelson et al. (1978) found that handheld counters resulted in slightly more accurate self-monitoring than belt-worn counters among adolescents with mental retardation. Although there are little data to support this notion, it seems logical that devices used with children that rely less on memory are likely to result in more accurate self-monitoring.

Other Variables Affecting Accuracy

Several other variables have been identified as having potential effects on self-monitoring accuracy. For example, the nature of the behavior being recorded (Lipinski & Nelson, 1974), the requirement to perform other behavior simultaneously with self-recording (Epstein, Webster, & Miller, 1975), and the schedule of self-monitoring (Frederiksen, Epstein, & Kosevsky, 1975) have all been found to be related to accuracy of self-monitoring.

Conclusions

When self-monitoring is being employed as an assessment procedure, one major concern must be related to accuracy of the self-monitoring response. After all, unless one is judged to be self-monitoring accurately, it is impossible to conclude that the obtained data are reliable. Indeed, accuracy of self-monitoring can be viewed as a check of treatment integrity (or in this case, assessment integrity). As with any intervention procedure, it has become increasingly important to determine the validity and reliability of the application of the independent variable to determine whether the observed outcomes on behavior can be attributed to the implementation of this procedure.

SELF-MONITORING AS A TREATMENT PROCEDURE

The primary concern when self-monitoring is employed as an intervention procedure rather than as an assessment device is the change in responding that can occur simply as a result of the monitoring process itself. This effect, known as reactivity, has been the subject of extensive discussion and investigation (e.g., Gardner & Cole, 1988; Haynes, 1978; Nelson, 1977, 1981; Shapiro, 1984). Studies of reactivity in self-monitoring with children and adolescents have included a wide range of school-based behaviors such as on-task behavior (e.g., Hallahan, Lloyd, Kneedler, & Marshall, 1982), completion of work assignments (e.g., Piersel, 1985), out-of-seat behavior (Sugai & Rowe, 1984), nervous tics (Ollendick, 1981), and appropriate classroom conversation (Nelson et al. 1978). It is important to note, however, that self-monitoring, when used alone, has not always resulted in behavior changes (e.g., Ballard & Glynn, 1975; Howell et al., 1983; Shapiro & Ackerman, 1983). Because reactivity of self-monitoring has been difficult to predict, several investigators have offered hypotheses regarding why reactivity occurs.

Explanations of Reactivity in Self-Monitoring

Two basic theoretical explanations for reactivity have been offered. Kanfer (1970, 1977), emphasizing covert variables, suggests that the process of self-monitoring is presumed to have covert motivational properties that either increase or reduce the strength of the preceding self-recorded behavior. Thus, the process of self-assessment and self-recording leads to a self-evaluation, which may be self-reinforcing. It is, then, the combined properties of the self-monitoring process, along with its concomitant self-evaluation, that results in behavior change and the observed reactivity.

Rachlin (1974) suggested an alternative hypothesis emphasizing that the self-recording of a response may serve as a cue, reminding the person of the typical external consequences applied to the target response. Nelson and Hayes (1981) extended this view beyond the self-recording process and suggested that the entire self-monitoring procedure, including therapist instruction, training in self-monitoring, the self-recording device, feedback from others, the occurrence of the target behavior, and the self-recorded response, act to cue the person regarding the anticipated environmental consequences to follow.

Although these theoretical explanations offer potential heuristics for future research, only a few studies have offered empirical support for either position (e.g., Mace & Kratochwill, 1985; Nelson & Hayes, 1981). Gardner and Cole (1988) have suggested that these explanations may indeed not be incompatible with each other, and that both may work in concert to produce reactive effects.

Variables Affecting Reactivity of Self-Monitoring

Regardless of the reasons underlying the occurrence of reactivity in self-monitoring, several variables have been identified that may enhance or diminish the likelihood of reactive effects. Specifically, these variables include (a) valence of the target behavior, (b) presence and nature of the recording device, (c) goals, reinforcement, and feedback, (d) timing of self-recording, (e) training in accurate self-monitoring, and (f) reinforcement for accurate self-monitoring.

Valence of Target Behavior

Kanfer (1970) hypothesized that self-monitoring would typically increase responses when the behavior being monitored is considered to be positive or desirable by the person and would likewise decrease responses that are negative or undesirable. Broden, Hall, and Mitts (1971), in one of the first investigations of self-monitoring, found that an adolescent instructed to self-monitor periods of study behavior (desirable response) showed substantial increases in responding and that another student instructed to self-monitor talking out in class (undesirable response) showed concomitant decreases in this behavior. Others (e.g., Litrownik & Freitas, 1980) have found stronger effects when positive behaviors are self-monitored as opposed to negative behaviors. Few studies have clearly demonstrated whether reactive effects tend to occur more often with positively than with negatively valenced behaviors. Intuitively, however, it does seem that drawing attention to negatively valenced behaviors may have some aversive consequences and, while potentially leading to reactive reductions of undesirable responses, may not concomitantly increase more desirable behaviors. In contrast, targeting positively valenced responses may lead to increases in desired, prosocial behavior and decreases in undesirable, negative behavior.

Presence and Nature of the Recording Device

Simply the presence or absence of a recording device may result in reactive effects. Piersel (1985) found that the critical variable in obtaining reactivity in a third-grade boy instructed to self-record assignment completion was the presence of a recording sheet. Likewise, the more obtrusive the recording device, the stronger the potential for reactive effects (Nelson et al., 1978). In general, however, there have been few studies specifically manipulating the type of recording device.

Motivation for Behavior Change

The degree to which children or adolescents wish to alter their behavior may play an important role in the strength of the reactive response to self-monitoring. These effects have been most clearly documented in studies of adult smoking behavior in which the willingness to reduce smoking was the most critical factor in producing reactivity to self-monitoring (McFall, 1970; McFall & Hammen, 1971). With children, Piersel (1985) found that self-monitoring was more reactive for those students who wanted to increase their rate of school work completion than those who did not. Although difficult to measure objectively, it does seem that student self-report regarding desirability of a specific behavior would play an important role in predicting the potential impact of self-monitoring on that behavior.

Goals, Reinforcement, and Feedback

Setting specific performance goals can clearly result in differential responding of children and adolescents (e.g., Spates & Kanfer, 1977). However, goal setting alone may not substantially alter performance without concomitant monitoring of performance toward that goals (Sagotsky, Patterson, & Lepper, 1978). Significant attention is needed to assess the impact of goal setting on reactive self-monitoring, given the recent interest and outcome on the use of formative evaluation in education (e.g., Fuchs, Fuchs, & Hamlett, 1989). Whether this remains as a critical and necessary variable in the self-monitoring process is unknown and should be the subject of future investigations.

Timing of Self-Recording

The strength of reactivity can be partially predicted by the delay between when a self-monitored response occurs and its subsequent self-recording. It would be anticipated that long delays between the behavioral occurrence and its recording would result in less reactivity. Although these findings have been supported in studies with adults (e.g., Bellack, Rozensky, & Schwartz, 1974; Rozensky, 1974), Nelson, Hay, Devany, and Koslow-Green (1980) found self-monitoring to be unaffected by a substantial delay in the recording of classroom verbalizations. Clearly, more research is needed before this hypothesis is dismissed.

Training in Accurate Recording

As with self-monitoring accuracy, reactivity of self-monitoring may be influenced by training individuals in the process of accurate recording. Shapiro et al. (1980) found more reactive effects in children with mental retardation when they were provided specific training in the self-observation and self-recording components of self-monitoring as compared to when they were provided only minimal instructions in the process. Others (e.g., Nelson et al., 1978; Shapiro et al., 1984) have found that training in accurate self-monitoring affected the reactivity of some individuals but not others.

Conclusions

When self-monitoring is employed as an intervention procedure, the primary concern is to maximize the potential for reactive effects. Many variables appear to be related to these effects, in particular, selecting students motivated to change their behavior, targeting positive or desirable responses in contrast to undesirable behaviors, providing training in accurate self-monitoring, setting goals, and providing reinforcement and feedback contingent on responding. It is important to note, however, that reactive effects of self-monitoring appear to be idiosyncratic and often unpredictable. Although one would like to accurately predict the occurrence of reactive effects, this appears to be most difficult. Perhaps a more pragmatic approach to using self-monitoring as an intervention is to recognize that, given the simplicity of the procedure, it may be a "first step" in the remediation sequence, moving to more intrusive and elaborate interventions only when self-monitoring fails to show reactivity.

RELATIONSHIP BETWEEN ACCURACY AND REACTIVITY

An important issue related to self-monitoring concerns the nature of the relationship between the accuracy of self-monitoring and its reactivity. Studies examining this relationship have shown mixed results. Interestingly, there have been several investigations in which children and adolescents with poor accuracy of self-monitoring have still displayed significant improvements in desired behaviors (e.g., Shapiro et al., 1980; Shapiro et al., 1984). Peterson, House, and Alford (1975) have argued that some minimal level of accuracy must be present to achieve any reactive self-monitoring. Indeed, it seems difficult to say that self-monitoring has even occurred if one cannot document better than chance levels of self-monitoring accuracy.

One potential explanation for the failure of studies to demonstrate that accurate self-monitoring is related to reactivity may be the way that self-monitoring accuracy is measured. If self-monitoring has the anticipated effects, overt self-monitoring of responses should gradually fade to more covert efforts. Thus, although students initially may remember to record each completed assignment as instructed, they may gradually "forget" to make the overt recording but still covertly note their work completion. The resulting data show inaccurate self-monitoring. One way to partially account for these findings is for investigators to routinely include data substantiating the training of accurate self-monitoring to a criterion. Once the criterion is obtained, subsequent accuracy checks could be made by instructing students to "remember to record on your data sheets as I told you before" and determine for that session whether accuracy is maintained.

APPLICATIONS OF SELF-MONITORING WITH CHILDREN AND YOUTH

Self-Monitoring of Academic Behaviors

Self-monitoring frequently has been used to modify the academic behaviors of children and adolescents. For example, students have been taught to self-monitor their on-task behavior, academic productivity, and academic accuracy.

On-Task Behavior

Self-monitoring of attention, or on-task behavior, has frequently involved a procedure whereby students periodically ask themselves, "Am I paying attention?" Children may be cued to self-monitor by an audio tone or physical gesture from the teacher, or they may simply be instructed to record whenever they think of it. Several studies have demonstrated the utility of self-monitoring of attention with various child populations. Hughes and Hendrickson (1987) evaluated the use of self-monitoring of attention with entire classes of regular education students. Self-monitoring was found to increase on-task behavior during independent seatwork with both at-risk and nonrisk elementary students.

Blick and Test (1987) evaluated the effects of self-monitoring on-task performance with 12 mildly handicapped (9 learning disabled, 2 educable mentally handicapped, and 1 emotionally handicapped) high-school students. Students were taught to self-monitor on-task behavior first in the presence of audible cues (a tape with a verbal cue to "record" or a chime that sounded at regular intervals) and later independently as audible cues were faded. Results indicated that all students' on-task behavior increased to an acceptable level during self-monitoring intervention. With the exception of two students, subjects' on-task behavior maintained in the absence of audible cues. Consistent with previous research (Hallahan & Sapona, 1983; Rhode, Morgan, & Young, 1983), the most accurate recorders were on-task more often than their less accurate counterparts.

Self-monitoring of attention has also been used with students who are labeled behavior disordered (e.g., McLaughlin, 1983; McLaughlin, Krappman, & Welsh, 1985; McLaughlin & Truhlicka, 1983). In the McLaughlin (1983) study, for example, three male elementary students were taught to self-monitor on-task behavior "when they remembered to do so" during the first 30 minutes of spelling, handwriting, and math periods. Results indicated increased on-task behavior for each student in each academic subject with self-monitoring. On-task remained at acceptable levels at follow-up 90, 180, 280, and 330 days later. With self-monitoring of attention, academic accuracy also increased in handwriting and math for each student. However, for one student, a 12% decrease was noted in spelling.

Kapadia and Fantuzzo (1988b) designed a prompting ribbon to help more severely disabled children visually monitor time and thus increase their sustained attention to academic tasks. Three children with developmental disabilities and severe behavior problems self-monitored their on-task behavior using this "linear timer," a motorized red and green ribbon. At the beginning of each trial, only the green portion of the ribbon was visible to the subject. As the interval progressed, the red portion of the ribbon became more visible until finally the ribbon itself stopped and a light went on indicating the end of the interval. Results indicated increased sustained attention to criterion levels with teacher-administered and later self-administered reinforcement. Additionally, during the final 6 days of the study, children continued to use these procedures in maintaining target levels of sustained attention without adult instructions or reinforcement.

Hallahan and colleagues have conducted a series of self-monitoring studies with children labeled learning disabled (e.g., Hallahan, Lloyd, Kneedler, & Marshall, 1982; Hallahan, Lloyd, Kosiewicz, Kauffman, & Graves, 1979; Hallahan, Marshall, & Lloyd, 1981; Lloyd, Hallahan, Kosiewicz, & Kneedler, 1982; Rooney, Polloway, & Hallahan, 1985). Generally these researchers used the procedure involving a tape-recorded beep at random intervals to cue students to ask themselves, "Am I paying attention? (The interested reader is referred to reviews by Hallahan and Sapona [1983] and Snider [1987].) According to their findings, self-monitoring of attention leads to increases in on-task behavior of these children. The cue (tone) to self-monitor and the recording response appeared to be necessary elements in the procedure, while external reinforcers did not. Of those studies that evaluated academic productivity, a majority demonstrated improved but inconsistent results.

Related to the question of whether accuracy influences the reactivity of self-monitoring attention, Hallahan et al. (1981) found that when self-monitoring was inaccurate, on-task behavior did not improve in children with learning disabilities. However, after students were provided 1 day of corrective feedback for inaccurate recording, their on-task behavior increased. Results of a subsequent investigation by Rooney, Hallahan, and Lloyd (1984) suggest that it may be consistency in self-recording, rather than accuracy, that is the important issue. In this study, when students were reinforced for correct use of the procedure (i.e., recording a number of responses consistent with the number of recorded beeps, without regard for accuracy), greater gains in on-task behavior were observed than when they were not reinforced.

Academic Productivity

Self-monitoring has also been shown to enhance academic productivity in students with a variety of characteristics. Studwell and Moxley (1984) evaluated the use of self-monitoring by kindergarten children of progress in skills targeted across the curriculum (e.g., *ABC*s, rhyming, address, numerals, left versus right, etc.). Children's records and chosen papers were placed on public display. Results showed that the rate of children's achievement of these skills increased dramatically when the children began to keep and display their own records. In addition, accuracy of self-monitoring was found to be 100%; no disagreements were reported between what the teachers and the children recorded.

Reiter, Mabee, and McLaughlin (1985) evaluated the use of self-monitoring with a 7½-year-old second grader labeled learning disabled. The study was located in a resource classroom during daily 30-minute sessions. The student was given a small notebook containing a list of assignments (and pictures beside each). She was instructed to give herself a "+" for each assignment she completed and a "−" for those she did not complete. At the end of 30 minutes, she counted the number of pluses and minuses and recorded the totals. Data indicated that self-monitoring increased on-task behavior and decreased time required to complete daily assignments in this subject.

Wall (1982) evaluated the relative effects of self-monitoring and self-reinforcement on children's academic test performance. Subjects were 85 fourth-grade students from four public school classes. Classes were randomly assigned to conditions with or without self-monitoring and self-reinforcement. Tests in history, Spanish, and reading comprehension were given regularly. The self-monitoring group checked their answers and self-recorded their number correct on a cumulative record sheet. These students were noncontingently given 900 points at the end of the third session. The self-reinforcement procedure involved students self-awarding up to 300 points at the end of each of the three contingency sessions on the basis of what they thought they had earned. Results showed that self-reinforcement with or without self-monitoring was significantly more effective in increasing test scores than self-monitoring or no monitoring. Children who self-monitored did not increase their test performance over time and did not score differently from children who did not self-monitor. However, while children's self-monitoring was not reactive, it was highly accurate and therefore potentially useful for assessment purposes.

Kapadia and Fantuzzo (1988a) compared the relative effectiveness of teacher-administered assessment and reinforcement with self-assessment and self-administered reinforcement on spelling performance of children with learning handicaps. Although both the teacher- and self-administered interventions resulted in gains in spelling performance, self-administered procedures produced greater gains that were maintained at a higher level after treatment was withdrawn. Concurrent increases in the untreated on-task behavior were found, but no increases were obtained in arithmetic performance.

Finally, Harris (1986) evaluated the differential effects of self-monitoring attentional behavior and self-monitoring spelling performance on on-task behavior and academic response rate in four children with learning disabilities and attentional problems. Results showed similar increases in on-task behavior during both self-monitoring of attention and self-monitoring of productivity for all subjects. However, results were less clear for academic response rate, with self-monitoring of productivity showing a superior effect over that observed during self-monitoring of attention for one subject, an equivalent effect for one subject, and less clear effects for two subjects. The author noted that differences between the two self-monitoring conditions included the following:

1. Self-monitoring on-task may be more intrusive and more time-consuming (although Hallahan et al. [1983] reported that subjects do not find it highly intrusive or time-consuming).
2. Self-monitoring of productivity involved a self-graphing component, whereas self-monitoring of attention did not.

Academic Accuracy

A few studies have examined the effects of self-monitoring on students' academic accuracy (e.g., number of correct answers to problems or test questions). McLaughlin, Burgess, and Sackville-West (1982) compared the effects of self-monitoring and self-monitoring plus matching on the percentage of correct responses in reading workbooks of six students with behavioral handicaps. Each student was instructed to mark a "+" when studying and a "−" when not studying at random intervals determined by each individual student. The self-monitoring plus matching condition was identical except that all students had to match the teacher's records within one score to earn 20 points in the ongoing token program. Results showed that, although the percentage of problems correct increased over baseline levels for all students with the implementation of self-monitoring, self-monitoring plus matching was more effective than self-monitoring alone. Self-monitoring accuracy was higher during the self-monitoring plus matching condition for each of the six students. Finally, the academic accuracy of those students who experienced the self-monitoring plus matching condition last maintained at higher levels at follow-up than those students who experienced the self-monitoring alone condition last. As suggested by the authors, these findings may indicate that accurate self-monitoring is required before maintenance of behavior change can occur at high levels.

Roberts and Nelson (1982) examined the differential effectiveness of self-monitoring correctness of answers to arithmetic problems (academic accuracy) and self-monitoring on-task behavior with three third-grade boys. Results showed, first, that self-monitoring academic accuracy or on-task behavior increased on-task behavior for all three subjects. Second, self-monitoring increased rate of completion (academic productivity) of arithmetic problems for two of the three subjects; there were no differences in rate between self-monitoring conditions (on-task vs. academic accuracy) for either of these subjects. Third, self-monitoring did not have consistent effects on correctness of attempted arithmetic problems (academic accuracy) as a function of whether on-task behavior or academic accuracy was self-monitored. Thus, the findings of this study indicate that "self-monitoring may be a useful intervention tool in classroom settings to increase on-task behavior and academic response rate, but not to increase academic response accuracy" (p. 117).

Finally, Rooney et al. (1985) investigated the efficacy of self-monitoring attention and self-monitoring academic accuracy with low-functioning students in a learning disabilities (LD) class. Results showed that the self-monitoring of attention increased attention in two of the four subjects. The combination of both procedures was effective for all four subjects in increasing on-task behavior and for three of the four subjects in increasing accurate responses in an arithmetic task.

Self-Monitoring of Social Behaviors

In addition to providing a useful tool for influencing academic responding, self-monitoring has also been shown to provide effective intervention for children's social behaviors. Studies that have investigated self-monitoring of disruptive behavior, inappropriate verbalizations, and social skills are described.

Disruptive Behavior

Christie, Hiss, and Lozanoff (1984) taught children labeled as hyperactive to self-record a variety of appropriate and inappropriate social and academic behaviors (i.e., inattention, out-of-seat or off-task, aggression, emotional outbursts, disruptive noise, attention solicitation, talking, and on-task or attention). The self-monitoring procedure involved the teacher signaling children (either verbally or with a nonverbal gesture) at intervals of time that were convenient for the teacher (approximately every 15 minutes) to record their own behavior. Results showed that the signaled self-recording produced decreases in inattentive and inappropriate classroom behavior, and increased on-task behavior for all subjects.

In a study by Sugai and Rowe (1984), self-monitoring was used to effectively decrease the out-of-seat behavior of a 15-year-old male labeled educable mentally handicapped. Self-recording was associated with significant decreases in the percentage of intervals of inappropriate out-of-seat behavior in the absence of systematic consequences for in-seat and out-of-seat behavior. The author commented that "It is unknown if improved in-seat behavior resulted in greater opportunities for engagement in desirable academic and social behaviors which, in turn, would be expected to increase the likelihood of reinforcement from the teacher" (p. 26).

Fowler (1986) used a self-monitoring procedure to maintain decreases in disruptive behavior observed using a peer-monitoring procedure in a special kindergarten class. Improvements achieved during the peer-monitoring procedure were maintained, for the most part, during the self-monitoring procedure.

Using a slightly different type of self-monitoring procedure, Kehle, Clark, Jenson, and Wampold (1986) had elementary schoolchildren with behavior disorders view an 11-minute, edited videotape of themselves behaving in an appropriate manner (i.e., all disruptive behaviors were deleted). Results showed that the percentage of disruptive classroom behaviors were dramatically reduced and maintained at a 6-week follow-up.

McCurdy and Shapiro (1988) partially replicated and extended the Kehle et al. (1986) study with five elementary students with behavior disorders. In this study, students were shown an edited videotape either of themselves or of a peer behaving in an appropriate manner. Results were idiosyncratic but provided some support for the use of this type of self-observation procedure with some students.

Inappropriate Verbalizations

Nelson et al. (1980) studied various aspects of self-monitoring appropriate and inappropriate verbalizations in three separate experiments. In the first experiment, elementary schoolchildren self-monitored either appropriate or inappropriate verbalizations either before or after their occurrences. Although self-monitoring produced behavior change for some children, it neither consistently increased appropriate verbalizations nor consistently decreased inappropriate verbalizations as had been expected. Self-monitoring before or after the occurrence of verbalizations did not differentially affect self-monitoring of either appropriate or inappropriate verbalizations.

In the second experiment, two second-grade children self-monitored appropriate and inappropriate verbalizations in two classes, whereas in two other classes, the entire class was trained to self-monitor. Also, in one self-monitoring condition, the self-recording sheet was clearly visible on top of the students' desks, whereas in the other self-monitoring condition, the device was kept beneath the desktop when not in use. The authors found that self-monitoring did not consistently decrease inappropriate verbalizations nor consistently increase appropriate verbalizations or hand-raising. More subtle effects from the obtrusiveness of the self-recording sheet could not be determined.

In the third experiment, 12 children were selected by their teachers as exhibiting high-freqeuncy inappropriate classroom verbalizations. The children were instructed to self-monitor either appropriate or inappropriate verbalizations. Self-monitoring appropriate verbalizations increased these responses for third graders but not for fifth graders. Self-monitoring inappropriate verbalizations decreased these responses for fifth graders but increased them for first graders.

Overall, the findings of the Nelson et al. (1980) study suggest the following:

1. Although self-monitoring produced behavior changes for some children, it neither consistently increased the frequency of appropriate verbalizations nor consistently decreased the frequency of inappropriate verbalizations.
2. Children generally self-monitored appropriate verbalizations more accurately than inappropriate verbalizations (with the exception of first graders).
3. No consistent over- or underestimations of appropriate or inappropriate verbalizations were observed.

Social Skills

Self-monitoring has been used to facilitate maintenance and generalization of positive effects observed during social skills training. For example, Kiburz, Miller, and Morrow (1984) found that self-monitoring enhanced the effects of social skills training of greeting and thanking skills. Treatment effects were further enhanced by adding a reinforcement component.

In another study, Kelly et al. (1983) used self-monitoring to facilitate generalization of behavior change produced by social skills training with four adolescents attending vocational classes in a residential treatment program. Although social skills training resulted in rapid acquisition of appropriate responses to a supervisor's instructions, there was no generalization of the behavior change to the vocational training setting. When subjects were taught to self-monitor their responses to instructions in the vocational training setting, appropriate responses in that setting quickly increased.

Finally, Gajar, Schloss, Schloss, and Thompson (1984) used self-monitoring and feedback to modify the conversational skills of youths who had suffered head traumas. The two subjects were taught to self-monitor positive or negative conversational behaviors. Results indicated an increased percentage of appropriate responding with self-monitoring. As both procedures were effective, a clear statement of the relative effectiveness of each could not be made.

SUMMARY

Self-monitoring has widespread applicability as both an assessment and intervention procedure. During the past decade, it has become a standard technique for use with children and adolescents exhibiting behavior problems in school, home, clinical, and institutional settings. In designing a self-monitoring program, a number of factors must be considered, including the type of behavior to be self-monitored, the type of data to be collected, and the device to be used for self-monitoring. In addition, there are special considerations for self-monitoring by children.

When self-monitoring is used primarily as an assessment procedure, the key issues are those surrounding accuracy of the self-monitoring process. Accuracy of self-monitoring must be established prior to concluding that the obtained data are reliable. A number of factors were discussed to maximize accuracy of self-monitoring. When employed as an intervention procedure, the major issue surrounding self-monitoring is reactivity, or behavior change that occurs simply as a result of the act of self-monitoring. The primary goal is to maximize the potential for reactive effects through attention to a number of variables discussed.

Although research has demonstrated the usefulness of self-monitoring with children and adolescents who have a variety of handicapping conditions in various settings, several questions remain. Despite the wide-ranging effectiveness, many of the critical factors involved in both the accuracy and reactivity of self-monitoring have not been isolated. While a large number of variables related to the issues of reactivity and accuracy have been investigated with adult populations, research on these variables with children has been much more limited. Results of studies in which adult populations were used may not be generalizable to children. Furthermore, consistency of results are lacking in use with children with specific problem characteristics. Until such issues are addressed, it will be difficult to identify aspects of self-monitoring that are critical to achieving accurate assessment or maximum reactivity in programs with children and adolescents.

REFERENCES

Ballard, K. D., & Glynn, T. (1975). Behavioral self-management in story writing with elementary school children. *Journal of Applied Behavior Analysis, 8,* 387–398.

Bellack, A. S., Rozensky, R., & Schwartz, J. A. (1974). A comparison of two forms of self-monitoring in a behavioral weight control program. *Behavior Therapy, 5,* 523–530.

Blick, D. W., & Test, D. W. (1987). Effects of self-recording on high-school students' on-task behavior. *Learning Disabilities Quarterly, 10,* 203–213.

Broden, M., Hall, R. V., & Mitts, B. (1971). The effect of self-recording on the classroom behavior of two 8th grade students. *Journal of Applied Behavior Analysis, 4,* 191–199.

Christie, D. J., Hiss, M., Lozanoff, B. (1984). Modification of inattentive classroom behavior: Hyperactive children's use of self-recording with teacher guidance. *Behavior Modification, 8,* 391–406.

Epstein, L. H., Webster, J. S., & Miller, P. M. (1975). Accuracy and controlling effects of self-monitoring as a function of concurrent responding and reinforcement. *Behavior Therapy, 6,* 654–666.

Fixsen, D. L., Phillips, E. L., & Wolf, M. M. (1972). Achievement place: The reliability of self-reporting and peer-reporting and their effects on behavior. *Journal of Applied Behavior Analysis, 5,* 19–30.

Fowler, S. A. (1986). Peer-monitoring and self-monitoring: Alternative to traditional teacher management. *Exceptional Children, 52,* 573–581.

Frederiksen, L. W., Epstein, L. H., & Kosevsky, B. P. (1975). Reliability and controlling effects of three procedures for self-monitoring smoking. *Psychological Record, 25,* 255–264.

Fuchs, L. S., & Fuchs, D., & Hamlett, C. L. (1989). Effects of alternative goal structures within curriculum-based measurement. *Exceptional Children, 55,* 429–439.

Gajar, A., Schloss, P. J., Schloss, C. N., & Thompson, C. K. (1984). Effects of feedback and self-monitoring on head trauma youths' conversation skills. *Journal of Applied Behavior Analysis, 17,* 353–358.

Gardner, W. I., & Cole, C. L. (1988). Self-monitoring procedures. In E. S. Shapiro & T. R. Kratochwill (Eds.), *Behavioral assessment in schools: Conceptual foundations and practical applications.* (pp. 206–242). New York: Guilford Press.

Hallahan, D. P., Lloyd, J. W., Kneedler, R. D., & Marshall, K. J. (1982). A comparison of the effects of self versus teacher assessment of on-task behavior. *Behavior Therapy, 13,* 715–723.

Hallahan, D. P. Lloyd, J. W., Kosiewicz, M. M., Kauffman, J. M., & Graves, A. W. (1979). Self-monitoring of attention as a treatment for a learning disabled boy's off-task behavior. *Learning Disability Quarterly, 2,* 24–32.

Hallahan, D. P., Marshall, K. J., & Lloyd, J. W. (1981). Self-recording during group instruction: Effects on attention to task. *Learning Disability Quarterly, 4,* 407–413.

Hallahan, D. P., & Sapona, R. (1983). Self-monitoring of attention with learning-disabled children: Past research and current issues. *Journal of Learning Disabilities, 16,* 616–620.

Harris, K. R. (1986). Self-monitoring of attentional behavior versus self-monitoring of productivity: Effects on on-task behavior and academic response rate among learning disabled children. *Journal of Applied Behavior Analysis, 19,* 417–423.

Haynes, S. N. (1978). *Principles of behavioral assessment.* New York: Gardner Press.

Howell, K. W., Rueda, R., & Rutherford, R. B. (1983). A procedure for teaching self-recording to moderately retarded students. *Psychology in the Schools, 20,* 202–209.

Hughes, C. A., & Hendrickson, J. M. (1987). Self-monitoring with at-risk students in the regular class setting. *Education and Treatment of Children. 10,* 225–236.

Johnson, S. M., & Bolstad, O. D. (1973). Methodological issues in naturalistic observation: Some problems and solutions for field research. In L. A. Hamerlynck, L. C. Handy, & E. J. Mash (Eds.), *Behavior change: Methodology, concepts, and practice* (pp. 7–67). Champaign, IL: Research Press.

Kanfer, F. H. (1970). Self-monitoring: Methodological limitations and clinical applications. *Journal of Consulting and Clinical Psychology, 35,* 143–152.

Kanfer, F. H. (1977). The many faces of self-control. In R. B. Stuart (Ed.), *Behavioral self-management: Strategies, techniques, and outcomes* (pp. 1–48). New York: Bruner/Mazel.

Kapadia, E. S., & Fantuzzo, J. W. (1988a). Effects of teacher- and self-administered procedures on the spelling performance of learning-handicapped children. *Journal of School Psychology, 26,* 49–58.

Kapadia, S., & Fantuzzo, J. W. (1988b). Training children with developmental disabilities and severe behavior problems to use self-management procedures to sustain attention to preacademic/academic tasks. *Education and Training in Mental Retardation, 23,* 59–69.

Kehle, T. J., Clark, E., Jenson, W. R., & Wampold, B. E. (1986). Effectiveness of self-observation with behavior disordered elementary school children. *School Psychology Review, 15,* 289–295.

Kelly, W. J., Salzberg, C. L., Levy, S. M., Warrenteltz, R. B., Adams, T. W., Crouse, T. R., & Beegle, G. P. (1983). The effects of role-playing and self-monitoring on the generalization of vocational social skills by behaviorally disordered adolescents. *Behavioral Disorders, 9,* 27–35.

Kiburz, C. S., Miller, S. R., & Morrow, L. W. (1984). Structured learning using self-monitoring to promote maintenance and generalization of social skills across settings for a behaviorally disordered adolescent. *Behavioral Disorders, 10,* 47–55.

Kunzelmann, H. D. (Ed.) (1970). *Precision teaching.* Seattle, WA: Special Child Publications.

Lipinski, D. P., & Nelson, R. O. (1974). The reactivity and unreliability of self-recording. *Journal of Consulting and Clinical Psychology, 42,* 118–123.

Litrownik, A. J., & Freitas, J. L. (1980). Self-monitoring in moderately retarded adolescents. *Behavior Therapy, 11,* 245–258.

Litrownik, A. J., Freitas, J., & Franzini, L. (1978). Self-regulation in mentally retarded children: Assessment and training of self-monitoring skills. *American Journal of Mental Deficiency, 82,* 499–506.

Lloyd, J. W. Hallahan, D. P. Kosiewicz, M. M., & Kneedler, R. D. (1982). Reactive effects of self-assessment and self-recording on attention to task and academic productivity. *Learning Disability Quarterly, 5,* 216–227.

Mace, F. C., & Kratochwill, T. R. (1985). Theories of reactivity in self-monitoring: A comparison of cognitive-behavioral and operant models. *Behavior Modification, 9,* 323–344.

Mace, F. C., Shapiro, E. S., West, B. J., Campbell, C., & Altman, J. (1986). The role of reinforcement in reactive self-monitoring. *Applied Research in Mental Retardation, 7,* 315–327.

Mahoney, M. J., Moore, B. S., Wade, T. C., & Moura, N. G. M. (1973). The effects of continuous and intermittent self-monitoring on academic behavior. *Journal of Consulting and Clinical Psychology, 41,* 65–69.

McCurdy, B. L., & Shapiro, E. S. (1988). Self-observation and the reduction of inappropriate classroom behavior. *Journal of School Psychology, 26,* 371–378.

McFall, R. M. (1970). Effects of self-monitoring on normal smoking behavior. *Journal of Consulting and Clinical Psychology, 35,* 135–142.

McFall, R. M., & Hammen, C. L. (1971). Motivation, structure, and self-monitoring: The role of specific factors in smoking reduction. *Journal of Consulting and Clinical Psychology, 37,* 80–86.

McLaughlin, T. F. (1983). Effects of self-recording for

on-task and academic responding: A long term analysis. *Journal of Special Education Technology, 6*(3), 5–12.

McLaughlin, T. F. (1984). A comparison of self-recording and self-recording plus consequences of on-task and assignment completion. *Contemporary Educational Psychology, 9,* 185–192.

McLaughlin, T. F., Burgess, N., & Sackville-West, L. (1982). Effects of self-recording and self-recording + matching on academic performance. *Child Behavior Therapy, 3*(2/3), 17–27.

McLaughlin, T. F., Krappman, V. F., & Welsh, J. M. (1985). The effects of self-recording for on-task behavior of behaviorally disordered special education students. *Remedial and Special Education, 6*(4), 42–45.

McLaughlin, T. F., & Truhlicka, M. (1983). Effects on academic performance of self-recording and self-recording and matching with behaviorally disordered students: A replication. *Behavioral Engineering, 8*(2), 69–74.

Nelson, R. O. (1977). Assessment and therapeutic functions of self-monitoring. In M. Hersen, R. M. Eisler, & P. M. Miller (Eds.), *Progress in behavior modification* (Vol. 5, pp. 263–308). New York: Academic Press.

Nelson, R. O. (1981). Theoretical explanations for self-monitoring. *Behavior Modification, 5,* 3–14.

Nelson, R. O., Hay, L. R., Devany, J., & Koslow-Green, L. (1980). The reactivity and accuracy of children's self-monitoring: Three experiments. *Child Behavior Therapy, 2*(3), 1–24.

Nelson, R. O., Hay, L. R., Hay, W. M., & Carstens, C. B. (1977). The reactivity and accuracy of teachers' self-monitoring of positive and negative classroom verbalizations. *Behavior Therapy, 8,* 972–985.

Nelson, R. O., & Hayes, S. C. (1981). Theoretical explanations of reactivity in self-monitoring. *Behavior Modification, 5,* 3–14.

Nelson, R. O., Lipinski, D. P., & Boykin, R. A. (1978). The effects of self-recorders' training and the obtrusiveness of the self-monitoring device on the accuracy and reactivity of self-monitoring. *Behavior Therapy, 9,* 200–208.

Ollendick, T. H. (1981). Self-monitoring and self-administered overcorrection: The modification of nervous tics in children. *Behavior Modification, 5,* 75–84.

Peterson, G. L., House, A., & Alford, H. F. (March, 1975). Self-monitoring: Accuracy and reactivity in patients' recording of their clinically targeted behavior. Paper presented at the meeting of the Southeastern Psychological Association, Atlanta.

Piersel, W. C. (1985). Self-observation and completion of school assignments: The influence of a physical recording device and expectancy characteristics. *Psychology in the Schools, 22,* 331–336.

Rachlin, H. (1974). Self-control. *Behaviorism, 2,* 94–107.

Reiter, S. M., Mabee, W. S., & McLaughlin, T. F. (1985). Self-monitoring: Effects for on-task and time to complete assignments. *Remedial and Special Education, 6*(1), 50–51.

Rhode, G., Morgan, D. P., & Young, K. R. (1983). Generalization and maintenance of treatment gains of behaviorally handicapped students from resource rooms to regular classrooms using self-evaluation procedures. *Journal of Applied Behavior Analysis, 16,* 171–188.

Roberts, R. N., & Nelson, R. O. (1982). The effects of self-monitoring on children's classroom behavior. *Child Behavior Therapy, 3*(2/3), 105–120.

Robertson, S. J., Simon, S. J., Pachman, J. S., & Drabman, R. S. (1979). Self-control and generalization procedures in a classroom of disruptive retarded children. *Child Behavior Therapy, 1,* 347–362.

Rooney, K. J., Hallahan, D. P., & Lloyd, J. W. (1984). Self-recording of attention by learning disabled students in the regular classroom. *Journal of Learning Disabilities, 17,* 360–363.

Rooney, K., Polloway, E. A., & Hallahan, D. P. (1985). The use of self-monitoring procedures with low IQ learning disabled students. *Journal of Learning Disabilities, 18,* 384–389.

Rozensky, R. H. (1974). The effect of timing of self-monitoring behavior on reducing cigarette consumption. *Journal of Behavior Therapy and Experimental Psychiatry, 5,* 301–303.

Sagotsky, G., Patterson, G. J., & Lepper, M. R. (1978). Training children's self-control: A field experiment in self-monitoring and goal-setting in the classroom. *Journal of Experimental Child Psychology, 25,* 242–253.

Shapiro, E. S. (1984). Self-monitoring procedures. In T. H. Ollendick & M. Hersen (Eds.), *Child behavioral assessment: Principles and procedures* (pp. 148–165). New York: Pergamon Press.

Shapiro, E. S., & Ackerman, A. (1983). Increasing productivity rates in adult mentally retarded clients: The failure of self-monitoring. *Applied Research in Mental Retardation, 4,* 163–181.

Shapiro, E. S., Browder, D. M., & D'Huyvetters, K. K. (1984). Increasing academic productivity of severely, mild-handicapped children with self-management: Idiosyncratic effects. *Analysis and Intervention in Developmental Disabilities, 4,* 171–181.

Shapiro, E. S., McGonigle, J. J., & Ollendick, T. H. (1980). An analysis of self-assessment and self-reinforcement in a self-managed token economy with mentally retarded children. *Applied Research in Mental Retardation, 1,* 227–240.

Snider, V. (1987). Use of self-monitoring of attention with LD students: Research and application. *Learning Disability Quarterly, 10,* 139–151.

Spates, C. R., & Kanfer, F. H. (1977). Self-monitoring, self-evaluation, and self-reinforcement in children's learning: A test of a multistage self-regulation model. *Behavior Therapy, 8,* 9–16.

Studwell, P., & Moxley, R. (1984). Self-recording in kindergarten: A study in naturalistic evaluation. *Psychology in the Schools, 21,* 450–456.

Sugai, G., & Rowe, P. (1984). The effect of self-recording on out-of-seat behavior of an EMR student. *Education and Training of the Mentally Retarded, 19,* 23–28.

Wall, S. M. (1982). Effects of systematic self-monitoring and self-reinforcement in children's management of test performances. *The Journal of Psychology, 111,* 129–136.

Workman, E. A., Helton, G. B., Watson, P. J. (1982). Self-monitoring effects in a four-year-old child: An ecological behavior analysis. *Journal of School Psychology, 20,* 57–64.

CHAPTER 10

DIRECT OBSERVATION

Billy A. Barrios

The measurement of child and adolescent disorders may take many different forms (e.g., Mash & Terdal, 1988; Ollendick & Hersen, 1984; Quay & Werry, 1979). Fortunately, the many different forms fall neatly into one of four categories: interviews and questionnaires, checklists and inventories, participant and nonparticipant observation, and bioelectric and mechanical recording. No one of the four general methods of measurement is inherently superior to any of the others; nor is any one of the four general methods of measurement completely independent of any of the others (e.g., Foster, Bell-Dolan, & Burge, 1988; Hartmann & Wood, 1982; Jacobson, 1985a, 1985b). All, in fact, are needed to establish the significance and worth of one another—a point oftentimes overlooked by the proponents of any one particular form of assessment.

This chapter focuses on the assessment method of participant and nonparticipant (i.e., direct) observation. It is a method that has been much described, discussed, and debated (e.g., Cone & Foster, 1982; Foster & Cone, 1980; Gottman, 1985; Hartmann, 1982; Jacobson, 1985a, 1985b; Kazdin, 1981; Weiss & Froham, 1985). It is also a method that has yet to be presented from the perspective of developmental psychopathology. The purpose of this chapter is to provide just such a presentation. Specifically, we describe and discuss the very distinctive steps involved in the construction, implementation, interpretation, and evaluation of an observational system for the assessment of a child and adolescent disorder. We also offer some simple guidelines for the selection of an observational system and for the improvement of our observational systems. We begin our presentation, though, with a brief description of the major aims of the assessment of child and adolescent disorders, because such aims are the sole reasons for direct observational systems to exist.

AIMS

The aim of all clinical assessment is to assist in the understanding and treating of the problem condition of the client (e.g., Barrios, 1988; Barrios & Hartmann, 1986; Cronbach, 1960; Mash & Terdal, 1988). In essence, this translates into helping us make several critical decisions and take several critical steps regarding the client. The first of these is diagnosing or classifying the performance pattern of the child or adolescent; the second is determining whether or not the performance pattern constitutes a problem; and the third is deciding whether or not to treat the problematic or nonproblematic condition. If treatment is judged to be in order, then four other key decisions and actions come into play. The first of these is identifying the instigating and maintaining agents of the performance pattern; the second is selecting an appropriate intervention for the condition; the third is evaluating the effectiveness of the treatment; and the fourth is altering the intervention in light of the evaluation of its effectiveness.

In the abstract, we look to observational data for guidance in arriving at each one of these pressing and pivotal decisions and associated actions. In practice, though, we tend to draw upon observational data for only two of them: the identification of the instigating and maintaining factors of the child's condition and the evaluation of treatment outcome. We do so because these are the two purposes for which direct observation appears to be best suited. We are allowed more time to perform these two activities and are granted more assistance to perform them than we are the other activities. We need such time and assistance to use an observational system and for an observational system to be of use to us—a matter that will become most evident when we discuss the elements and mechanics of direct observation. The quickness with which we are called upon to provide a diagnosis or designate a condition as a problem simply does not allow for the use of an observational system. Neither does the isolation in which we are called upon to assess and intervene with a child or adolescent. Again, why this is so will become most clear when we detail the elements and mechanics of direct observation.

DEFINITION

All clinical assessment is simply a set of rules and operations for quantifying the performance of the client (e.g., Hartmann & Wood, 1982; Nunnally, 1978). The rules specify the domain of content of interest, the nature of the testing situation, the collection of test responses, and the scoring of test responses. The method of direct observation differs from other methods of clinical assessment in two important respects: the domain of content of interest is limited to objective behavior and the collection of information on the objective behavior of interest is done by human observers (e.g., Barton & Ascione, 1984; Cairns & Green, 1979).

By definition, then, an observational system is a set of rules and operations for gathering information on objective client behavior through the use of human observers. The exact rules and activities of a system, though, are arrived at by decision. That is, we, the system developer, decide what behaviors of the client are to be observed, who is to observe them, and when and where the observations are to be done. Furthermore, we decide on how the observations are to be conducted and noted and how the recordings are to be combined into scores. All of these decisions are based upon one or more of the following: theory, consensus, evidence, experience, and intuition. And the wisdom of all of these decisions in large part determines the worth of the observational system.

In the next section, we discuss in depth each of the aforementioned decisions or steps involved in the development of an observational system for a child or adolescent disorder. In particular, we cite the many different considerations that enter into each decision or step and the many different options that apply to each decision or step.

CONSTRUCTION

As previously stated, there are four basic steps in the construction of an observational system: specifying the behaviors of interest, defining the assessment situation, delineating the data collection, and developing the scoring key. Germane to the completion of each of these is a host of theories and concepts and findings known collectively as developmental considerations (e.g., Edelbrock, 1984; Garber, 1984; Kazdin, 1989; Kendall, Lerner, & Craighead, 1984).

Developmental Considerations

In the construction of an observational scheme for a child or adolescent disorder, there are two tendencies we would do well to resist and three phenomena we would do well to attend to. The former are adultomorphism and the developmental uniformity myth; the latter are developmental symptom substitution, comorbidity, and contextual control. By adultomorphism is meant the tendency to view disorders of childhood and adolescence as identical in makeup to the disorders of adulthood; thus, the same terms and definitions and measures that are used for the disorders of adulthood are seen as appropriate for use with the disorders of childhood and adolescence (Phillips, Draguns, & Bartlett, 1975). To date, much evidence argues against this view of children as miniature adults (cf. Garber, 1984). Many of the discrete behaviors said to compose the disorders of adulthood have not been detected in children and adolescents; and many of the discrete problem behaviors of childhood and adolescence have not been manifested in their exact form into adulthood. Such discontinuity argues strongly against the casual application of adult definitions and instruments to the direct observation of children and adolescents.

Another tendency that we would do well to withstand is the developmental uniformity myth (Kendall et al., 1984; Kendall & Williams, 1986). An extension of the patient uniformity myth in psychotherapy research (Kiesler, 1966), the developmental uniformity myth is the notion that all children are alike and thus can all be assessed with the same instruments and can all be treated with the same interventions. As the name indicates, such a notion is a myth. Children of differing ages and genders do indeed vary from one another in a number of important respects. For example, they vary in terms of attention span and language ability and behavioral repertoire; they vary in terms of the types of behaviors they exhibit, the frequency with which they exhibit them, and the seriousness with which they are viewed by the adult community (e.g., Barrios & Hartmann, 1988; Rodriguez, Rodriguez, & Eisenberg, 1959; Rutter, 1972, 1980; Schectman, 1970). Knowledge of these and other age and sex trends is most valuable in the construction of an appropriate observational system for a child of a particular age and gender.

Sensitivity to three other phenomena is also helpful. The first of these is developmental symptom substitution—the replacement of one problem behavior by another with an increase in age (Levitt, 1971). Though not well researched, the phenomenon is well borne out by our experiences with children and adolescents (Kazdin, 1989). For example, children who at an early age taunt other children often do not do so at a later age, but instead physically attack them. Such changes in the form of the problem obviously complicate the assessment of the child over time. Another little-researched but often cited phenomenon is that of comorbidity—the presence of two or more distinct disorders at any one time (Kazdin, 1989). For example, a child may display within roughly the same time frame two constellations of behaviors, each distinct from the other and each denoted by a different disorder label (e.g., anxiety and depression). Such complexity in the performance picture of the child poses serious challenges for direct observation (e.g., the tracking of both constellations simultaneously may be unfeasible, the presence of one constellation may interfere with the tracking of the other). And finally there is the well-documented phenomenon of contextual control—the influence of the situation over responding. While this is true for both adults and children, we have tended to be more mindful of such influence in our assessment of the problem behaviors of the former than in our assessment of the problem behaviors of the latter (Garber, 1984). For example, in many of our assessments of the problem behaviors of children, a key aspect of the environmental context is missing: the persons who found the behaviors of the child objectionable and who referred the child for treatment. Since such persons are part of the context in which the behavior occurs, they may influence the occurrence of the behavior; thus, they should be included as part of the assessment situation for that behavior (e.g., Patterson, 1964, 1977).

As a whole, these developmental considerations alert us to the unique and dynamic nature of child and adolescent behavior. And in doing so, they come to form a list of do's and don'ts in the direct observation of child and adolescent disorders. In short, we don't automatically apply the models and definitions and measures of adult disorders to the measurement of child and adolescent disorders, as such models and definitions and measures may not be at all fitting. Furthermore, we don't automatically employ the same definitions and instruments in the assessment of all children, as children of varying age and gender may vary greatly in what they are capable of and in what adults find acceptable and unacceptable from them. Instead, what we do is develop definitions and instruments that acknowledge and accommodate the unique and changing and complex nature of child and adolescent behavior. That is, we do take into account age, gender, and context in our development and employment of an observational system for a child or adolescent disorder. Exactly when and how we do so is touched upon in the following paragraphs.

Specifying the Domain

The first step in constructing an observational scheme is specifying the domain of content of interest. Typically we do so by breaking the step down into three parts: (1) sketching the window of observation, (2) defining the behavior(s) of interest, and (3) identifying the dimensions of interest. In sketching the window of observation, we establish both the scope of assessment and the boundaries of a problem condition. The window we draw can be of one of three types: the symptom, the syndrome, or the system. In the window of the symptom, the problem condition or disorder is framed in terms of a single, isolated behavior, and assessment is focused on the observation of that single, isolated behavior. Much of the work of child behavior modifiers, with its emphasis on a discrete target behavior, offers examples aplenty of this type of window (e.g., Gelfand & Hartmann, 1984; Marholin, 1978; Ross, 1981).

With the window of the syndrome, the problem condition is broadened to a constellation of behaviors that have been formally hypothesized or informally observed or empirically demonstrated to go together. Assessment, then, is concerned with the observation of these individual but interrelated behaviors. Much of the work of mainstream child psychotherapists, with its use of clinically derived or empirically derived diagnostic schemes, provides examples of this type of window (e.g., Mash & Barkley, 1989; Ollendick, 1986).

And finally there is the window of the system. The disorder is traced in terms of the behavior of both the child and the social unit of which he or she is a member (e.g., family, school class, play group); assessment is devoted to the observation of the actions and interactions of the child and the other members of the social unit. Much of the work of family therapists furnishes examples of this type of window (e.g., Alexander & Parsons, 1982; Foster & Robin, 1989; Patterson, 1982, 1986).

Each window has certain attractive and unattractive features. Most appealing about the window of the symptom is its simplicity. Limiting a problem condition to a single, isolated behavior greatly simplifies and speeds up the construction of an observational system. Such simplicity, though, hardly ever covers all of the concerns of a parent or teacher or child; thus, such a window is hardly ever considered to be of adequate content coverage (Mash, 1985). The window of the syndrome allows for greater coverage of the concerns of a parent or teacher or child, and as such, it has the advantage of greater content coverage than the window of the symptom. With this increased coverage, though, come increased complexity and time in putting together an adequate observational system. And even with this increased coverage, the window still does not encompass many of the contextual features that many of us think are instrumental in the problem behaviors of the child (e.g., the behavior of the parent). The latter is not true of the window of the system. Broad in scope, the window of the system allows for the observation of both the child and the context. With so broad a scope, though, there is always the very real danger of the window buckling under its own weight (e.g., the number of persons being tracked, the number of behaviors being observed).

Whatever the size of the window we sketch, we must next define the behaviors that fall within the window. In other words, we must compose operational definitions for the behaviors of interest. Ideally, we seek to put together definitions that are objective, understandable, and sure (Hawkins & Dobes, 1977). An objective definition is one that refers only to directly observable features of the performance of interest; an understandable definition is one that is couched in plain and simple language; and a sure definition is one that calls for little or no inference. The more objective and understandable and sure a definition is, the more likely is the definition to be used in a consistent fashion by two or more observers (Gelfand & Hartmann, 1984; Hawkins & Dobes, 1977). And as we will see in a later section of this chapter, consistent use of a definition by two or more observers is one of the main determinants of the soundness and usefulness of an observational system.

Arriving at the desired definitions is generally a four-part process: researching, writing, reviewing, and revising. In researching, we comb the literature for definitions of the behaviors of interest, and we canvass key adults in the child's environment for their definitions of the behaviors of interest. From these oftentimes loose and abstruse descriptions, we compose definitions that are more to our liking. That is, we develop definitions that are of the desired form (i.e., objective, understandable, and sure) and content (i.e., the view of the behaviors of interest shared by us, our colleagues, and key adults). Having developed such definitions, we have knowledgeable persons examine them for their appropriateness and prospective observers examine them for their clarity. If they are found lacking, they are revised; and if they are not, they are field-tested. In field testing, we send two naive observers with only definitions in hand out into a classroom or a home or a clinic. And we use the agreement in what they report seeing as an indication of the adequacy of the definitions (e.g., Hartmann & Wood, 1982; Hawkins & Dobes, 1977). High agreement suggests that we are ready to move on to the next step in the construction process; low agreement suggests the need for revision and repeated field testing.

The behaviors we select for observation can vary along any of the following dimensions: frequency, latency, duration, intensity, and direction (Gelfand & Hartmann, 1984). Thus, in specifying the domain of content, it is critical that we specify which of the five response dimensions are of interest to us. That is, it is essential that we identify which dimensions of which behaviors we will be tracking. Typically, we base our selection on three factors: the availability of recording devices, the ostensible nature of the behavior, and the developmental status of the child (e.g., Barrios & Hartmann, 1988; Barton & Ascione, 1984; Hartmann & Wood, 1982). Certain response dimensions of latency and duration both call for the use of a timing device such as a stopwatch. Having such a device permits the measurement of the two dimensions; not having such a device precludes the measurement of the two dimensions. Whether or not a response dimension is selected for observation, then, depends in part on whether or not we have the necessary equipment. We say "in part," for if we base our decision solely on the availability of devices, we are basing our decision simply on convenience. That is not an acceptable reason to us or to the rest of the professional community.

The obvious nature of the behavior of interest also plays a role in the selection process. The selection process is straightforward when the response dimensions of significance are self-evident; the selection process is involved when the response dimensions of significance are obscure. The "behaviors" of attention and compliance are two examples of the former; the "behaviors" of shyness and belligerence are two examples of the latter. Duration is an obvious response dimension of interest for attention, frequency an obvious response dimension of interest for compliance. The response dimensions of interest for shyness and belligerence, though, are not so clear-cut. For behaviors such as these, the developmental status of the child carries much weight in the selection process.

The developmental status of the child is determined by comparing his or her behavior to the behavior deemed acceptable for a child of his or her age and gender and physical condition. Dimensions along which the behavior of the child differs from this standard of acceptability are dimensions we may wish to target for observation. Take, for example, the behavior of crying when teased by one's siblings or peers. For a 4-year-old, the dimension of duration is more likely to differ from the standard than the dimension of frequency is, as most 4-year-olds will display some sniveling upon being teased. Thus for a 4-year-old, we are more likely to select duration than frequency as a dimension of interest. The situation is reversed for a 12-year-old. For a 12-year-old, the dimension of frequency is most likely to stand out from the standard, as most 12-year-olds will not shed a tear upon being teased. Thus for a 12-year-old, we are most likely to target frequency as the dimension to observe.

In principle, we would be wise to let the developmental status of the child be our sole guide in the selection of dimensions to observe, for doing so would ensure the tracking of the most pertinent response dimensions. In practice, though, we have very few opportunities to follow this principle, for we have very few formal standards of acceptability for most of the behaviors we wish to observe. Obviously, this is a situation that needs to be rectified. Correction, though, will be a long time coming. In the interim, then, we may wish to draw upon informal templates of acceptability for guidance—templates based on our clinical experience, our concepts of normality, and our conversations with parents, teachers, and other child care providers. And we may wish to use these templates in conjunction with information on the availability of recording devices and the ostensible nature of the behavior of interest.

Selecting the Setting

Having selected the behaviors to be observed, the next step in the construction process is selecting the setting in which said behaviors are to be observed. In general, three considerations enter into the selection of an observation setting: the relevance of the stimulus situation, the salience of the stimulus situation, and the consistency of the stimulus situation (e.g., Foster et al., 1988; Hartmann & Wood, 1982; Nay, 1979). All three are attended to, for all three are critical to the soundness of the observational measures. This becomes most apparent when we remind ourselves of the fact that an observation setting is simply a test, a collection of tasks or items or stimuli for assessing a behavior of interest (Green, 1981). In putting together a paper-and-pencil test, great care is taken in selecting items that are relevant to the response in question and presenting said items such that they are salient to the subject in question. Moreover, great pains are taken to standardize the presentation of items so that reliable measurement of the response can be achieved. The same great care must be exercised in selecting an observation setting.

Both reason and research enter into our appraisal of the relevance of a stimulus situation. Research is used to identify the stimuli that reliably evoke the response of interest. And reason is used to determine the similarity between these evocative stimuli and the stimulus situation. Rarely, though, do we have a good fix on these specific evocative stimuli. Instead, what we have is a good grasp of the general features of the naturalistic setting in which the response occurs. That being the case, we usually determine the relevance of a stimulus situation by comparing it to the naturalistic setting.

With this criterion in mind, two studies illustrate two observation settings of differing degrees of relevance (Van Hasselt, Hersen, Bellack, Rosenblum, & Lamparski, 1979; Wine, 1979). In the Van Hasselt et al. (1979) study, an 11-year-old boy was observed for anxious behavior in relation to school examinations. The observations were made in a clinic room, where the child sat alone at a table with a memory drum atop it. A list of seven letters was presented on the drum and the child was asked to anticipate correctly each letter on the list. In the Wine (1979) study, several fourth-graders were also observed for anxious behavior regarding school examinations. These observations, however, were made in the children's customary classroom, with the customary teacher and customary seating. The children were informed that a very difficult exam would be administered. Similar in focus, the two studies are strikingly dissimilar in the situations in which the observations were done. The stimulus situation in the Van Hasselt et al. (1979) study bears little resemblance to the naturalistic setting, whereas the stimulus situation in the Wine (1979) study bears much resemblance to the naturalistic setting. Were we to have to choose between the two, we would certainly choose the latter, for the latter is much more relevant as an observation setting than the former.

To repeat, we wish to select a relevant, salient, and consistent stimulus situation as an observation setting. That is, we wish to select a stimulus situation that is similar in nature to the naturalistic setting, in both its foreground and background features. And we wish to select a stimulus situation in which the key foreground features are both prominent and robust. By prominent, we mean conspicuous enough to capture the child's attention; and by robust, we mean intense enough to occasion the behavior of interest. As an example of the former, consider two situations for observing a child's compliance to parental requests. In one situation, parental requests are made in the absence of any extraneous noise such as the television or radio or stereo blaring. In the other situation, parental requests are made in the midst of such noise and commotion. Clearly the child has a better chance of hearing the parent's commands in the first situation than in the second situation; thus, clearly the first situation is more salient than the second situation in terms of the presentation of key stimulus features. As an example of the other aspect of robustness, consider two situations for observing a child's fear of spiders and snakes. In the first situation, the child is seated at a table onto which a live spider and live snake are placed. In the other situation, the child is seated at a table, onto which a plastic spider and plastic snake are placed. Clearly the first situation is more likely to provoke a response on the part of the child than is the second situation; thus, clearly the first situation is more robust than the second situation in terms of the presentation of key stimulus features.

Finally, we wish to select a stimulus situation that is consistent across all measurement occasions, as such consistency is called for in standardized assessment. In other words, we would like an observation setting in which the child is exposed to the same events on each measurement occasion. Such consistency may be inherent to the situation or may need to be imposed onto it. Take, for example, the case in which we have two 4-year-olds, both of whom are anxious when separated from their mother. One of the 4-year-olds attends a preschool program and thus is separated from his mother at the same time and in the same way 5 days a week. The other 4-year-old attends no type of preschool or day care program, but instead simply spends most of his time at home close to his mother. The predictability of the first child's life circumstances lends itself well to the standardized assessment of separation from the mother, whereas the unpredictability of the second child's life circumstances does not. For the standardized assessment of the second child's reaction to separation from the mother, some type of structure would need to be imposed.

As our discussion reveals, selecting an observation setting can oftentimes turn into creating an observation setting. If relevant stimuli vary in number and intensity and duration from one occasion to the next, then steps must be taken to ensure invariance along these dimensions from one measurement occasion to the next. If relevant stimuli appear with such irregularity as to prohibit careful assessment, then steps must be taken to ensure reliable presentation of relevant stimuli so as to permit careful assessment. Selecting an observation setting, in essence, translates into securing a standardized assessment situation, one that is appropriate for the behavior of interest of the child of interest. The natural environment may at times provide us with such a situation. When, however, it does not, our task is to create one.

Collecting the Observations

Having identified a setting for our observations, the next step is to develop a protocol for collecting our observations. The protocol details the scheduling of observations and the recording of observations. In the scheduling of observations, the number and duration of the sessions are specified, as are the length and sequence of the observing and reporting intervals. In the recording of observations, the system of notation and documentation of observations is specified, as is the system of compilation and storage of observations. In the following paragraphs, we discuss some of the factors that influence the determination of each of these facets.

The number of observation sessions we choose to conduct depends primarily on the nature of the stimulus situation. If the stimulus situation occurs infrequently, then the number of observation sessions will equal the number of stimulus appearances, as carrying out observations with each stimulus occurrence will be a fairly simple matter. A medical examination or a school examination is an example of such a stimulus situation. If, however, the stimulus situation occurs often, then the number of observation sessions will be some portion of the stimulus appearances, as carrying out observations on all stimulus occasions will be an impossible matter. Parental requests or peer conflicts are an example of such a stimulus situation. In this case, the number of observation sessions to conduct becomes purely a sampling matter—how many sessions are needed to adequately represent performance across all stimulus occasions? Three considerations guide us in determining the number of observation sessions needed: the frequency of the behavior of interest, the stability of the behavior of interest, and the complexity of the behavior of interest (Haynes, 1978). Frequent behaviors are more likely to be observed from one session to the next than are infrequent behaviors; thus, frequent behaviors require fewer sessions for a representative sample than do infrequent behaviors. The same is true of stable and unstable behaviors. Stable behaviors are more likely to appear from one session to the next than are unstable behaviors; thus, stable behaviors call for fewer sessions for a representative sample than do unstable behaviors. This is also the case for simple and complex behaviors. Simple behaviors are more likely to be noted upon their occurrence than are complex behaviors; thus, simple behaviors need fewer sessions for a representative sample than do complex behaviors.

Three issues also figure into our determination of the duration of an individual observation session: the duration of the stimulus situation, the dependability of the behavioral sample, and the demands of the data-collection procedure. Ideally, we would like for the observation session to be of the same length as the stimulus situation, as such correspondence would ensure complete coverage of said occasion. However, this is not always possible. There are some stimulus situations that are of too great a length to monitor throughout. As such, the duration of the observation session must be some portion of the duration of the stimulus situation. The question is, what portion of the stimulus situation do we monitor for a representative sample of the performance of interest? Again, we look to the nature of the behavior of interest for assistance in answering this particular sampling question. Infrequent, unstable, and complex behaviors all require longer periods of monitoring for a representative sample than do frequent, stable, and simple behaviors. And they do so for all of the reasons previously cited. Thus, the frequency, stability, and complexity of the behavior of interest are all major determinants of the length of an individual observation session.

There is one other important consideration in our determination of the length of a session: the demands placed upon our observers. When these demands are high, such as the monitoring of multiple behaviors on the part of multiple persons, session length is best kept short; however, when the demands placed upon our observers are low, such as the monitoring of a single behavior on the part of a single person, session length can be drawn out. The reason for this is that with high demands comes the high risk of observer fatigue and frustration, and with the high risk of observer fatigue and frustration comes the high risk of deterioration in the quality of observations. We would like to avoid all of this at all costs. Thus, we take into consideration the demands of the data-collection procedure in our determination of the length of our observation sessions.

Once we have decided on a timeframe for an individual observation session, we must decide on a timetable for observing and reporting. That is, we must partition the session into intervals for observing the behavior of interest and reporting on what we have witnessed. And we must specify the length and arrangement of these intervals. We do so primarily on the basis of the response dimension of interest (e.g.,

Foster et al., 1988; Gelfand & Hartmann, 1984; Kazdin, 1981). In the following paragraphs, we describe the four most common timetables for observing and reporting.

Continuous recording takes the form of concurrent intervals of observing and reporting. That is, there is virtually no lapse between our observing of a behavior and our reporting of that observation. Continuous recording or real-time observation is best employed when the behaviors of interest are numerous, when the persons of interest are numerous, or both (Hartmann & Wood, 1982). To be more specific, continuous recording or real-time observation is best employed when the several behaviors of interest are abrupt in onset and termination and when the dimensions of interest are frequency and duration. In that way, continuous recording allows us to capture a sequence of different behaviors by the same person or an exchange of different behaviors by different persons. Difficulties with this timetable arise, though, when the behaviors of interest or the persons of interest are too many to monitor with precision or when the onset and termination of the behaviors are too indistinct.

Event recording is similar in form to that of continuous recording, in that both timetables involve concurrent intervals of observing and reporting. The former differs from the latter, though, in terms of being restricted to the response dimension of frequency. In event recording, we simply note the appearance of a behavior as it occurs, letting little time elapse between our observation of the onset of the behavior and our registration of said observation (Kelly, 1977; Wright, 1960). Event recording appears best suited, then, for study of behaviors that are discrete in nature—discrete in onset and discrete in incidence. Problems with the timetable arise when there is some uncertainty as to what constitutes the initiation of the behavior or what differentiates one occurrence of the behavior from the next.

Scan recording consists of successive, nonoverlapping intervals of observing and reporting (Hartmann & Wood, 1982). During the observing period, we survey the environment for the presence of the behaviors of interest; and during the reporting period, we make note of what we have observed. This type of arrangement is best used when the behaviors of interest are numerous, the persons of interest are numerous, and the response dimension of interest is duration. In terms of the behaviors of interest, the most appropriate for tracking via scan recording are those that are simple and salient. We encounter difficulties with this type of timetable when the behaviors of interest are too many or too complex or too subtle to monitor with continuous precision.

Interval recording also takes the form of successive, nonoverlapping intervals of observing and reporting (Kelly, 1977). During the observing period, we watch for the occurrence of the behaviors of interest for the entire interval or for some portion of the interval; and during the reporting period, we note whether or not the behaviors were present throughout the observation interval or through some critical portion of it (Powell, Martindale, & Kulp, 1975). Both forms of interval recording are most often used when the response dimensions of interest are frequency and duration. And both forms of interval recording are fraught with difficulties (e.g., Powell et al., 1975; Powell, Martindale, Kulp, Martindale, & Bauman, 1977; Powell & Rockinson, 1978; Repp, Roberts, Slack, Repp, & Berkler, 1976). The main weakness is the tendency to overestimate or underestimate the frequency or duration of the behaviors of interest.

All four types of timetables are used in conjunction with a coding and collection procedure—a system for alerting one to the behaviors of interest, for making note of the appearance of the behaviors of interest, and for gathering up the notations of one's observations (e.g., Barton & Ascione, 1984; Foster et al., 1988). Having selected a timetable, then, the next step in the development of an observation system is the development of a coding and collection procedure. In essence, this is a three-part process: the creation of a behavioral code, the creation of a coding sheet, and the establishment of a mechanism for data deposit and retrieval.

A behavioral code is simply a set of symbols or shorthand labels for the behaviors of interest. In putting together such a set, we strive for certain features. First, we wish to keep the set to a manageable number of symbols or labels—a number that neither overwhelms nor insults our observers. Second, we wish to have symbols or labels that are concise, descriptive, and distinct. That is, we wish to have symbols or labels that are easily memorized, easily distinguished from one another, and easily transferred to a recording sheet.

A recording sheet is simply a form for documenting our observations of the behaviors of interest. This form may either complicate or facilitate the conscientious monitoring of the behaviors of interest. We hope for the latter. In developing a recording sheet, we strive for the following features: First, we seek a simple form, one that is void of all extraneous detail and distraction. Second, we aim for a form that has a clear layout, one in which there is no confusion as to what markings go where on the sheet. And third, we desire a form that is convenient and compatible, one that allows for a smooth, ongoing sequence of surveying, recognizing, and recording.

To this sequence of surveying, recognizing, and recording, we must add the activities of depositing, collecting, and storing. In other words, we must set up some steps for gathering up and safeguarding the completed recording sheets. We do so with certain aims in mind. First and foremost, we wish to uphold the client's rights to privacy and confidentiality. That is, we wish to protect all completed recording sheets from theft or loss or unauthorized release. Second, we wish to have the exchange of completed recording sheets be as easy as possible. That is, we want both the deposit of the completed recording sheets by the observers and the collection of these completed sheets by the investigators to be convenient.

Scoring the Responses

Once collected, our observations must be organized into some sort of manageable and meaningful form. Thus, the next step in the construction of an observation system is the development of a scoring key, a set of rules for organizing our observations into a manageable and meaningful numerical form. The development of a scoring key centers on four issues. The first of these is whether to treat the separate behaviors of interest as individual entities or to combine the separate behaviors of interest into one or more larger response units. In other words, the first decision in the development of a scoring key is whether or not to create one or more behavioral clusters (e.g., Haynes, 1986). Such a decision, of course, does not have to be made when there is only a single response of interest (e.g., when the window of observation is that of the symptom). Rare, though, are the problem conditions of a child or an adolescent that can be captured adequately by a single, isolated response.

If we elect to group individual responses into one or more behavioral composites, we must then decide on a plan for the combining of said responses. In general, we have two alternatives to choose from. One is to assign equal importance or weight to all of the responses in the formation of a composite score (e.g., Giebehain & Barrios, 1986; Melamed & Siegel, 1975; Wine, 1979). The other alternative is to assign differential importance or weight to the different responses in the formation of a composite score (e.g., Jay, Ozolins, Elliott, & Caldwell, 1983; Melamed, Hawes, Heiby, & Glick, 1975).

The plan we choose will to a large extent depend upon two other considerations. One is the need to develop a scoring key that is age appropriate; the other is the need to develop a scoring key that is gender appropriate. As mentioned earlier, considerable evidence points to differences both between and within age groups in the composition of certain problem conditions (e.g., Barrios & Hartmann, 1988; Kazdin, 1989; Kendall et al., 1984). Given such differences, the aim is to design a scoring key that is in accord with the response makeup of the problem condition of interest for both the age group of interest and the gender of interest.

Selecting the Observers

The final step in the construction of a direct observation system is the selecting of observers—the persons who will be entrusted with observing and recording the behaviors of interest. This selecting of observers is a most critical step in the construction process, for much of the success of our direct observation system hinges upon how well these persons meet our trust. That is, much of the success of our direct observation system rests upon how faithfully our observers follow our code and scheme for tracking the behaviors of interest.

At present, the literature offers little guidance in the selection of observers. That is, the literature tells us little about the type of person in whom we would do well to place our trust. The reason it does so is because little investigation into the characteristics of the good observer has been done. The reasons for little investigation into the characteristics of the good observer are two. One is the longstanding belief that good observers are akin to good artists: They are born, not made (Boice, 1983). And like the talents of good artists, the talents of good observers are and always will be very much a mystery. The other reason is the contemporary belief that good observers are akin to good machines: They are made and maintained, not born and blessed. And like the performance of a good machine, the performance of a good observer is and always will be very much a function of care and conditions—the care taken to properly train an observer and the conditions chosen to properly monitor an observer.

Our belief is that the truth lies somewhere in between these two extreme positions. Thus, we believe it is wise to be somewhat selective in whom we entrust the observing and recording of the behaviors of interest. But as mentioned before, we find little in the literature in the way of data-base recommendations as to whom to select as an observer. Fortunately, we do find much in the literature in the way of speculation as to what type of person we might wish to select as an observer. Specifically, we find much speculation in the literature as to what type of developmental, motivational, intellectual, and sensory-perceptual characteristics might make for a good observer (cf. Boice, 1983). Thus, the literature offers much from which we can fashion a tentative framework for selecting observers.

Among the major developmental characteristics thought to make for a good observer are maturity, emotional stability, empathy, and honesty (e.g., Allport, 1937; Hartmann & Wood, 1982; Taft, 1955). And among the major motivational characteristics put forth as important are dedication, commitment, enthusiasm, patience, and perseverance (e.g., Dancer, Braukmann, Schumaker, Kirigin, Willner, & Wolf, 1978; Guttman, Spector, Sigal, Rakoff, & Epstein, 1971; Knapp, 1978; Yarrow & Waxler, 1979). Most often added to this list are the intellectual characteristics of meticulousness, insightfulness, and detachedness and the sensory-perceptual characteristics of attentiveness, receptiveness, and discrimination (e.g., Allport, 1937; Knapp, 1978; Yarrow & Waxler, 1979). On the surface, all of these appear to be reasonable criteria upon which to choose observers. Our hope is that systematic research will lead to a shortening of the list, which in turn will lead to a shortening of the time needed to complete this step in the construction of a direct observation system.

Convenience and inconspicuousness have also been suggested as good bases for selecting observers. From this has come the recommendation that peers and parents and siblings serve as our observers (e.g., Foster et al., 1988; Haynes & Horn, 1982). We have certain reservations about the wisdom of this recommendation. Much of the literature on parent training points out that many parents have difficulty carrying out many of the assignments of the training program, one assignment being the monitoring of their child's behavior (cf. O'Dell, 1986). Preconceptions, expections, and mood fluctuations have all been found to interfere with compliance and completion of the training program (cf. O'Dell, 1986). Therefore, we find it safe to assume that many parents will have much difficulty faithfully following our code and scheme for tracking the behaviors of interest. Moreover, we find it safe to assume that peers and siblings will experience even more difficulty faithfully following our code and scheme for tracking the behaviors of interest, as they tend to be less capable and concerned than are parents. This is not to say that we do not ever see ourselves as having peers or parents or siblings as observers, for we do. We see ourselves, though, being most selective when choosing which peers and parents and siblings serve as our observers. And we see ourselves as basing our selection on the characteristics just cited.

IMPLEMENTATION

There are three basic steps in the implementation of our direct observation system: (a) gaining permission from the relevant parties, (b) training and monitoring the observers, and (c) troubleshooting breakdowns in the faithful tracking of the behaviors of interest. The former is concerned with ethical matters, the latter two with technical matters. All are discussed in detail in the following paragraphs.

Gaining Permission

The observation system we develop will in all cases call for tracking and recording certain behaviors of the child and in many cases will call for the tracking and recording of certain behaviors of both the child and certain others such as the parents or teachers or classmates. Whatever the case may be, our observation system will constitute an intrusion upon the lives of these people, and thus, calls for permission from these people for the implementation of said system (Barton & Ascione, 1984; Kazdin, 1981). Soliciting and securing permission to observe entails a listing on our part of the behaviors we wish to observe, the persons we wish to do the observing, and the settings in which we want the observing to be done. Soliciting and securing permission to observe will also require a listing on our part of the possible risks and benefits associated with being observed, as well as the precise steps being planned to ensure the privacy and safety of the observations collected. An obvious risk the person runs in being observed is being singled out as a person with a problem, and an obvious benefit the person may receive in being observed is a richer understanding of the behaviors of interest (Barrios & O'Dell, 1989). These and other risks and benefits of being observed must be made known to those persons whose permission we seek.

As mentioned previously, the person whose permission we seek will depend largely upon the scope of our observational system. That is to say, it will depend largely on the type of window we sketch: the symptom, the syndrome, or the system. The person whose permission we seek will also be determined by whose cooperation we need to carry out our direct observational system. For example, our system for tracking and recording the classroom behavior of a child may not call for the monitoring of the behavior of the teacher. It may, however, necessitate the assistance of the teacher, and thus, it may require our gaining consent and cooperation of said teacher. Finally, the person whose permission we seek will also be a function of the maturity level of the persons we aim to observe. Most children in most instances will not be considered mature enough to offer informed consent to being observed. In these instances, then, approval must be sought from the children's parents or legal guardians. In those instances, though, in which the child qualifies as a mature minor, we advise gaining the approval of both the child and his or her parent or guardian.

With securing permission to observe comes sensitizing all or almost all the relevant persons to their being observed. And with such sensitization may come changes in the way these persons act during the periods during which they are being watched (cf. Harris & Lahey, 1982a, 1982b; Haynes & Horn, 1982; Wasik & Loven, 1980). In turn, such observations may give rise to erroneous conclusions and actions regarding the behaviors of interest. To circumvent these potential problems, some have suggested bypassing the step of consent to observe, either entirely or in part. Others have suggested carrying out our observations in less conspicuous, more surreptitious ways. And still others have suggested doing away with human observers entirely and replacing them with mechanical surveillance devices. To all of these suggestions we have serious ethical, practical, or philosophical objections. Skipping over our receiving permission to observe goes against the grain of our professional code of conduct and against the grain of an open and honest therapeutic relationship; carrying out our observations in a more covert fashion does not seem possible in most situations without greatly complicating our assessment scheme; and replacing our human observers with recording machines serves only to distance us further from the subject matter we hope to understand—an issue we discuss further in the final section of this chapter.

At this time, the approach we recommend to handling the possible reactive effects of being observed is twofold. First, we recommend that all of us participate in some way in the systematic study of the effects of being observed, as such study will lead to specification of which behaviors by whom in what settings are affected in what ways by awareness of the act of being observed. And second, we recommend making certain adjustments in the way we introduce our observers into certain situations and in the length of time in which we keep them there. The exact nature of these situations and the adjustments is touched upon in the following paragraphs.

Training and Monitoring Observers

Over the last 60 years, several sets of guidelines for training and monitoring observers have been developed and disseminated (e.g., Arrington, 1932; Foster et al., 1988; Hartmann & Wood, 1982; Johnson & Bolstad, 1973; Kent & Foster, 1977). In essence, they all reduce to six basic steps, all of which are listed in Table 10-1 and described in the following paragraphs.

The first step in the training and monitoring of our observers is *orientation*. Specifically, this entails communicating to our observers the importance of assessment in the understanding and treating of child and adolescent disorders. Furthermore, it entails emphasizing to our observers the importance of objective assessment in these two endeavors. Combined, these two messages alert our observers to the integral role they will play in understanding and treating the behaviors of interest.

During this first phase, we also inform our observers of the expectations and responsibilities that come with the role they are being asked to play. That is, we tell them of the need for independent, unbiased, and faithful recording of the behaviors of interest. We tell them that if they confer with one another in their recordings of the behaviors of interest, they will seriously undermine the veridicality and utility of said recordings; we tell them that if they form active hypotheses about the behaviors of interest, they run the risk of being influenced by the hypotheses in their recording of the behaviors of interest (e.g., Kent, O'Leary, Diament, & Dietz, 1974; Shuller & McNamara, 1976). We tell them that if they deviate from the scheme for observing and recording the behaviors of interest, they will distort the meaning of the scores based upon their recordings (e.g., Kent et al., 1974; Wildman, Erickson, & Kent, 1975). Finally, we inform our observers of the need to keep confidential the identity of the persons of interest and the recordings of the behaviors of interest.

The second step in the training and monitoring of our observers is *education,* the purpose of which is to familiarize our observers with the response definitions of and recording scheme for the behaviors of interest.

Table 10-1. Common Steps in the Training and Monitoring of Observers

STEP	DESCRIPTION
Orientation	Informing observers of the importance of objective assessment in the understanding and treating of childhood disorders. Informing observers of their duties and responsibilities, in particular their independent, unbiased, and faithful recording of the behaviors of interest.
Education	Instructing observers in the response definitions and recording scheme through the use of written materials, filmed illustrations, and live demonstrations.
Evaluation	Assessment of observers' knowledge of the response definitions, coding system, and recording scheme through the use of written and oral examinations. Representation of materials until observers are thoroughly acquainted with all aspects of tracking and recording of the behaviors of interest.
Application	Graduated implementation of the observation system across a range of situations, beginning with analog ones and ending with actual setting of interest. Transition from one situation to the next contingent upon observers achieving a criterion level of agreement and accuracy.
Recalibration	Assessment of the accuracy and agreement of observers' recordings in the setting of interest. Identification and correction of any breakdowns in the fidelity of observers' recordings.
Termination	Questioning observers as to the merits of the observation system. Informing observers of their contributions to the understanding and treating of the behaviors of interest. Reminding observers of the need to maintain confidentiality.

This we do by presenting written descriptions, filmed depictions, and live demonstrations of the response definitions of the behaviors of interest and by allowing ample time for our observers to read and review each of these descriptions, depictions, and demonstrations. A similar tack is taken to acquaint our observers with the coding system and recording scheme for observing and noting the behaviors of interest.

In the third step, *evaluation,* we quiz our observers on their knowledge of the response definitions, the coding system, and the recording scheme (e.g., Bertucci, Huston, & Perloff, 1974). As a rule, we accept nothing less than perfection on these written and oral examinations. Consequently, when errors are committed, we take sufficient time to review those aspects of our direct observation system that our observers have failed to grasp. Then we retest our observers on their knowledge of said aspects. We repeat this sequence of testing, reviewing, and retesting until all of our observers are cognizant of all response definitions, behavioral codes, and recording steps.

Also being evaluated during this phase of observer training and monitoring are our response definitions, coding system, and recording scheme. For in testing our observers for their comprehension of these aspects of our direct observation system, we are in some sense testing for the adequacy of these aspects—the clarity of the response definitions, the simplicity of the behavioral codes, and the feasibility of the recording steps. An important element of this phase of observer training is soliciting and considering feedback from our observers on the clarity of our response definitions, the simplicity of our behavioral codes, and the feasibility of our recording steps.

Once all of our observers have passed all of our tests, the next phase of their training is *application.* As the title suggests, this phase involves having our observers carry out our scheme for tracking and recording the behaviors of interest over a series of situations, beginning with analog ones and ending with the actual one. Movement of our observers from one situation to the next is contingent upon achieving some criterion level of agreement and accuracy.

The aim here is to make certain that our observers are proficient in the use of our observation system before they begin tracking and recording the behaviors of interest in the situation of interest. To this end, we make a point of including analog situations that offer rich and realistic representations of the performance of interest (e.g., Kent & Foster, 1977; Nay, 1979). What is more, we overtrain our observers in these analog situations so that the sequence of tracking and recording the behaviors of interest becomes well ingrained (e.g., Kazdin, 1977; Wildman & Erickson, 1977).

Proficiency of recording in analog situations does not, however, guarantee proficiency of recording in the actual situation of interest. Therefore, certain additional steps are taken to ensure faithful application of our direct observation system in the situation of interest. The first of these is gradually introducing our observers to the actual setting. The thinking here is that slow entry into the actual situation will allow our observers to become accustomed to the setting and will allow persons in the setting to become accustomed to our observers (Hartmann & Wood, 1982). The second step is providing our observers with ongoing feedback as they begin tracking and recording the behaviors of interest in the actual situation. Specifically, we provide them with feedback concerning the accuracy of their observations, then feedback concerning the agreement between their observations. We do so in that order because accurate recordings are what we seek foremost from our observers and because doing so helps promote accurate recording on the part of our observers (DeMaster, Reid, & Twentyman, 1977). We remind our observers of their duties and responsibilities—the independent, unbiased, and faithful recording of the behaviors of interest. And we inform our observers that we will be either continuously or periodically checking the accuracy and agreement of their observations for as long as they are tracking and recording the behaviors of interest.

As just mentioned, the gradual introduction of our observers to the actual setting is thought to serve a twofold purpose: to allow our observers to become accustomed to being in the situation and to allow the persons in the situation to become accustomed to being observed. And as mentioned earlier, the latter is of great concern to us as we do not wish for our persons of interest in the situation of interest to act differently by virtue of their being observed. How gradual, then, must our introduction of our observers to the actual setting be in order for our persons of interest to not be affected by the presence of said observers? Research to date does not spell out for us a specific timetable for getting our subjects accustomed to being observed. Research to date does, however, suggest to us what types of subjects might require a lengthier timetable for getting accustomed to being observed than other types do. Specifically, studies show older children being more affected than younger children to the act of being observed, weaker responses being more affected than stronger responses to the act of being observed, and socially sensitive behaviors being more affected than socially innocuous behaviors to the act of being observed (Haynes & Horn, 1982; Mash & Hedley, 1975; Wasik & Loven, 1980). All of this suggests that we would be wise to allow more time for habituation to our observers the older are the persons we wish to observe, the weaker are the responses of these persons we wish to observe, and the ruder are the behaviors of these persons we wish to observe.

Recalibration is the fifth step in the training and monitoring of our observers. And the aim of this step is to maintain reliable and accurate recording on the part of observers. For once observers have been introduced into the actual setting and are tracking and recording the behaviors of interest as we would like for them to, we would like to make certain that they continue to do so throughout their time in said setting. To do so, we assess the recordings of observers for their accuracy and agreement, on either an ongoing or an intermittent basis. Such assessments allow us to detect whether or not our observers are deviating from the response definitions we have put forth, whether or not our observers are disagreeing with one another in what they are witnessing, or both. Furthermore, such assessments allow us to take corrective action in the event of deviations or disagreements or both. Such assessments also serve as opportunities to remind our observers of the integral role they play in our understanding and treating the behaviors of interest, reminders that may serve to renew and reinforce commitment and dedication on the part of our observers.

The need for these checks on the accuracy and agreement of our observers' recordings is well documented. When left to their own devices, observers tend to stray from the response definitions they have been asked to follow (e.g., Kent et al., 1974; Wildman et al., 1975). And when asked to observe for an extended period of time, they have a tendency to become careless and lackadaisical in their recording of the behaviors of interest (e.g., Wasik & Loven, 1980). Our checking on the accuracy and agreement of our observers' recordings is our way, then, of fighting these two tendencies.

In assessing the recordings of our observers for their accuracy and agreement, we follow several guidelines. First, we alert our observers to the fact that we will be carrying out these assessments. We do not, however, alert our observers as to exactly when these assessments will be carried out. In this way, our observers are kept somewhat in the dark—aware that we will be checking up on their performance, unaware as to when these checks will occur. And it is such partial awareness on the part of our observers that best promotes faithful and dependable tracking and recording of the behaviors of interest (e.g., Kent, Kanowitz, O'Leary, & Cheiken, 1977; Romanczyk, Kent, Diament, & O'Leary, 1973). Second, we examine the recordings of our observers first for their accuracy and then for their agreement. Assessing for accuracy may take any of the following forms: retesting our observers on the response definitions and recording scheme, comparing the recordings of our observers to those of some mechanical device, comparing the recordings of our observers to some permanent product of the behaviors of interest, or comparing the recordings of our observers to those of calibrator observers on some criterion sample of the behaviors of interest (cf. Foster & Cone, 1980). Assessing for agreement may also take many different forms. Specifically, assessing for agreement may call for computing any one of a number of different indices of correspondence between our observers' recordings (cf. Hartmann, 1977; Hartmann & Wood, 1982). Whatever form our assessment of the accuracy and agreement of observers' recordings may take, we make a point of assessing them in that order. For in doing so, we reiterate and reinforce the message that it is accurate tracking and recording of the behaviors of interest we seek most from our observers. And we render it more likely that our observers will supply us with what we seek (e.g., DeMaster et al., 1977; Hartmann & Wood, 1982). Third, we correct for any breakdowns in the accuracy and agreement of our observers' recordings. We do so by first identifying the source of a breakdown, then by taking sensible steps to remove the identified source of the breakdown. A general plan that we follow for pinpointing and correcting breakdowns is described in the upcoming section on troubleshooting. And fourth, we praise our observers for their efforts and we remind our observers of their importance to understanding and treating the behaviors of interest. In essence, we express our appreciation to our observers. Such displays of appreciation are indeed warranted. And such displays of appreciation may serve to maintain the motivation and dedication of our observers to faithful tracking of the behaviors of interest.

The final step in the training and monitoring of our observers is *termination*—a step we carry out once observers have done all that we have asked of them. In other words, the step of termination begins when the tracking and recording of the behaviors of interest come to an end. Specifically, the aims of the step are fivefold. First, we wish to question our observers on a host of issues regarding our direct observation system—for example, the clarity and comprehensiveness of the response definitions, the simplicity and distinctiveness of the behavioral codes, the utility and representativeness of the recording scheme. Second, we wish to brief our observers on the insights and decisions we derived from their observations—for example, the identification of maintaining variables, the selection of an intervention, the determination of the effectiveness of the intervention. Third, we wish to remind our observers of the continuing need to respect the rights of confidentiality and privacy of the persons of interest—for example, to not disclose the names of the persons of interest to anyone, to not reveal the nature of the behaviors of interest to anyone, to not divulge any of the clinical decisions and actions to anyone. Fourth, we wish to thank our observers for their invaluable contributions to our understanding and treating the behaviors of interest—for example, their assistance in identifying the instigating and maintaining factors behind the behaviors of interest, their assistance in selecting a sensible and feasible intervention for the behaviors of interest, their assistance in determining the effectiveness of said intervention for the behaviors of interest. And finally, we wish to dismiss but not forget our observers. For we may wish to call upon our observers in the event we want additional recordings of the behaviors of interest among new persons of interest. In fact, all that we have said to this point in the chapter points to our wanting the same observers collecting any new or additional recordings for us. For all that we have said to this point in the chapter points to the job of being an observer as being difficult and demanding. To be exact, the job of observer calls for knowledge, objectivity, concentration, discipline, and consistency. None of it comes easily. All of it comes in part through much training and practice. Cognizant of all of this, we do not dismiss and dispose of our observers; we retain and reemploy our observers whenever the need for further recording of the behaviors of interest arises.

Troubleshooting

Though we take great pains to promote faithful tracking and recording of the behaviors of interest, breakdowns in tracking and recording do occur. Our task, then, is to locate the source of these breakdowns and to reinstate faithful tracking and recording of the behaviors of interest on the part of our observers. A listing of the most common reasons and remedies for inaccuracies and inconsistencies in the recordings of observers is provided in Table 10-2.

Table 10-2. Guidelines for Troubleshooting Breakdowns in a Direct Observation System

SOURCE	DESCRIPTION
Definitions	Lack of clear, specific, or credible response definitions may lead to breakdowns in faithful tracking and recording of the behaviors of interest. Remedy may be to put forth more concrete and precise response definitions, with more distinct boundaries and apt labels.
Demands	Behaviors of interest may be too numerous or too complex to permit faithful tracking and recording. Or behavioral code may be too complex or the observational period too long to permit faithful tracking and recording. Remedy may be to reduce the number of behaviors of interest, reduce the complexity of the behavioral code, or reduce the duration of the observation period.
Distractions	External and internal events that compete with the behaviors of interest for the observers' attention may lead to breakdowns in faithful tracking and recording. Remedy may be to impose greater structure onto the observation setting or to alter the observers' placement in said setting or to replace the observer with a more attentive one.
Discontent	Mistreatment of observers may lead to breakdowns in faithful tracking and recording. Remedy may be to accord greater respect, appreciation, and praise to observers.

In our efforts to pinpoint the source of a breakdown in observers' recordings, we begin with the most obvious candidates—the *definitions* of the behaviors of interest and the *demands* of the recording scheme. We examine the response definitions of the behaviors of interest for their clarity and specificity and credibility. And we revise our definitions accordingly, thoroughly retraining our observers in the use of these revised definitions. Deciding whether or not our definitions are wanting in clarity, specificity, and credibility is a four-step process. The first step is a rational inspection on our part of these three features of our response definitions. The second and third steps are rational inspections on the part of our colleagues and our observers of the same three dimensions of the same definitions. The fourth step is an integration of the views of all three parties and a determination of the adequacy of the definitions in terms of each one of the three dimensions. Revising our definitions with respect to their clarity or specificity or credibility calls for a similar four-step process. In the first step, we identify words that might render our definitions more concrete and precise; we identify examples that might delineate the boundaries of our definitions with more exactness; and we identify labels that might denote the response elements of our definitions with more trustworthiness. In the second and third steps, our colleagues and our observers identify words, examples, and labels that they believe might serve these same functions. In the fourth step, we assimilate all of these suggestions and arrive at a set of revised definitions that we hope will be clearer, more specific, and more credible than the original set. Acquainting and training our observers in the use of these revised definitions follows the same series of steps as the one carried out in the acquainting and training of our observers in the use of the original definitions (e.g., orientation, education, evaluation, application).

As mentioned previously, the demands of the recording scheme are another likely reason for any breakdowns in the accuracy and agreement of our observers' recordings. These demands of our recording scheme take three forms: the number and complexity of the behaviors that our observers are asked to keep track of, the complexity of the code that our observers are asked to note their observations in, and the duration of the period that our observers are asked to track and record the behaviors of interest. Deciding whether or not these three type of demands are too great to permit faithful tracking and recording is a four-step process—a process similar to the one for deciding whether or not our response definitions are wanting in clarity, specificity, or credibility. The first three steps call for a rational appraisal of the demands of our recording scheme by us, our colleagues, and our observers. The fourth step calls for an integration of the three appraisals and a determination of the reasonableness of each type of demand. Reducing the demands of our recording scheme may take any of the following forms: decreasing the number of behaviors to be tracked, simplifying the nature of the behaviors to be tracked, simplifying the code for noting observations, decreasing the duration of the observation period, or some combination of the above. Deciding which of these actions to take is a consensual process much like the one for revising our response definitions. That is, we and our colleagues and our observers each identify ways in which we would like to see the demands of the recording scheme reduced. And from these three lists, a shared strategy is identified and implemented. Our revised and, we hope, more reasonable recording scheme is then taught to our observers in the same manner as our original recording scheme was taught.

Distraction and *discontent* are two other forces that may undermine the fidelity and integrity of our observers's recordings. Less obvious than difficulties with the definitions of our behaviors of interest and the demands of our recording scheme, distraction and discontent may be far more insidious and ruinous. As such, these two forces deserve careful consideration.

The many events that vie with the behaviors of interest for our observers' attention are of two types: external and internal. Examples of the former are noise and commotion; examples of the latter are worries and troubles. When too numerous or too intense, events of each type may distract our observers from the task at hand, which in turn may lead to breakdowns in the faithfulness of their tracking and recording of the behaviors of interest.

Detecting and addressing external distractors is far more straightforward than detecting and addressing internal distractors. In the former, we and our colleagues and observers scan the recording situation for features and events that may draw our observers' attention away from the features and events of interest. We next compile a list of strategies for reducing or eliminating these possible distractors, select the most sensible and feasible ones from the list, and implement and evaluate these strategies. For example, our inspection of the recording situation may reveal that frequent announcements over the school's public address system interferes with picking up the verbal behavior of the child of interest. Rectifying this matter may take the form of having the principal refrain from making such announcements while observations are being made or having our observers situated closer to the child so that the child's voice is heard over such announcements.

To detect and address internal distractors, a similar set of steps is involved. We and our colleagues and observers examine our observers for any features or sensations that may interfere with their performing the task at hand. We do this through questioning, probing, and observing—questioning and probing our observers about their physical state, emotional state, and life situation; watching our observers for telltale signs of distress, discomfort, and preoccupation. Once possible distractors are identified, possible solutions are generated, with the most reasonable and feasible of the strategies implemented and evaluated. For example, conversations with our observers may point to our observers being overextended. That is, our observers may be entering into far too many commitments and taking on far too many responsibilities in their lives than they can possibly honor and handle. As a result, they find their mind wandering to these other commitments and responsibilities when their mind is to be on the task of tracking and recording the behaviors of interest. To remedy this situation, we might ask our observers to let go of some of these other commitments and responsibilities, or we might let go of these observers and replace them with others who have fewer activities competing for their time, attention, and energy.

Observer discontent is a particular type of internal distractor that may arise from any of the following: unpleasant and unprofessional interactions between us and our observers, unpleasant and unprofessional interactions between fellow observers, and unpleasant and unprofessional interactions between our observers and ancillary others such as parents or teachers of the child of interest. To wit, observer discontent is likely to occur whenever our observers are treated in an abusive, harsh, or disrespectful manner. Checking for observer discontent consists of assessing the quality of observers' relationship with us, with one another, and with ancillary others. We do this by questioning the parties in each of the relationships and by observing how the parties relate to one another. Correcting for observer discontent may consist of changing certain ways in which the parties respond to one another, clarifying certain ways in which the parties misunderstand one another or both. For example, an examination of our interactions with observers might reveal that we are much too free in our criticism of our observers and much too frugal in our praise of them. As such, our observers feel unappreciated by us and feel animosity towards us. To reverse this situation, we might be more generous in our praise of our observers or more judicious in our criticism of them or both.

INTERPRETATION

Having gathered all the observations we wish on all the behaviors of interest, we must next make sense out of these observations. As we did with the tasks before, we approach this task in a stepwise fashion. First, we determine whether or not to believe our observations. Second, we compare our set of observations to some other set of observations. On the bases of these two steps, we decide what is to be done next with respect to the behaviors of interest.

Determining whether or not to believe the recordings of our observers entails computing one of two indices: an index of the accuracy of our observers' recordings or an index of the consistency of our observers' recordings. As mentioned earlier, determining the accuracy of our observers' recording first entails establishing an objective criterion for the behaviors of interest (e.g., Foster & Cone, 1980). Such a criterion might be a permanent product of the behaviors of interest or a mechanical record of the behaviors of interest or a concomitant recording of the behaviors of interest by expert observers. Whatever the standard we erect, we check the recordings of our observers against it and compute a quantitative index of the degree of match. At present, there are some 20 different statistics for indexing the accuracy of our observers' recordings—the 20 different statistics varying in terms of the types of data for which they are suited, the ease with which they are computed, the degree to which they are congruent with other statistics and practices of the field of measurement (e.g., Berk, 1979; Frick & Semmel, 1978; Tinsley & Weiss, 1975). To aid us in selecting the most appropriate index for our particular needs and our particular data set, we draw upon one of the many sets of guidelines that have been put forth (e.g., Gelfand & Hartmann, 1984; Hartmann, 1977; Hartmann & Wood, 1982).

In lieu of an objective, credible criterion for the behaviors of interest, determining the credibility of our observers' recordings reduces to determining the consistency of said recordings. Though not synonymous with accuracy, consistency provides us with indirect support for the veridicality of our observers' recordings and allows us to ascribe further meaning to our observers' recordings. Determining the consistency of our observers' recordings consists of comparing the recordings of one observer to the corresponding ones of the other observer and computing a quantitative index of the degree of correspondence. As is the case for the accuracy of our observers' recordings, there are many different statistics for indexing the consistency of our observers' recordings (e.g., Berk, 1979; Frick & Semmel, 1978; Tinsley & Weiss, 1975). Fortunately, there are also many sets of decision rules that we can look to for guidance in selecting the most suitable statistic for our specific needs and our specific data set (e.g., Gelfand & Hartmann, 1984; Hartmann, 1977; Hartmann & Wood, 1982).

Convinced of the soundness of our observers' recordings, we must next ascribe meaning to the scores. We do this by placing our set of observations against the backdrop of some other set of observations and ascertaining the degree of match. In general, this backdrop takes one of three forms: a subset of the observations of the behaviors of interest for the persons of interest, a set of observations of criterion performance for the behaviors of interest, or a set of observations of the behaviors of interests for persons of a suitable reference group (Barrios, 1988).

The first type of backdrop is known as the client-referenced approach to data interpretation, the second as the criterion-referenced approach to data interpretation, and the third as the norm-referenced approach to data interpretation. In the client-referenced approach, we may place the posttreatment observations of the behaviors of interest against the pretreatment observations of the behaviors of interest, and, on the basis of how well they match up, decide whether to denote the former as improvements. We may then place the follow-up observations of the behaviors of interest against the posttreatment observations of the behaviors of interest, and, on the basis of how well they match up, decide whether to denote the former as maintenance of said improvements. Whatever the arrangement, what is critical is that we are using a subset of our recordings to derive meaning for some other subset of our recordings.

In the criterion-referenced approach, observations of standard performance for the behaviors of interest serve as the backdrop for our recordings. This standard may be for what is acceptable performance with respect to the behaviors of interest or for what is unacceptable performance with respect to the behaviors of interest. If the former is the case, the competency of our client's performance is reflected in how well it measures up to this standard. If the latter is the case, the problem status of our client's performance is reflected in how well it measures up to this standard. Whatever the case, what is critical is that the criterion be appropriate for our persons of interest—appropriate in terms of age and gender.

The same is true for the norm-referenced approach. In this approach, we place our observations of our client's performance against those of a suitable reference group's performance. If we find the performance of our client falling far short of the performance of the reference group, we may designate the former as lacking. Or if we find the performance of our client exceeding the performance of the reference group, we may designate the former as excelling. What is critical here is that we have appropriate persons serving as the reference group—appropriate in terms of age and gender for our persons of interest.

Additional meanings may be ascribed to our recordings through more direct means. Specifically, this entails empirically determining the correspondence between our measures and those of other behaviors of interest. To guide us in this process, we draw upon one of three models: the psychometric model, the generalizability model, or the accuracy model. In the following paragraphs, the terminology and techniques of each are discussed.

The *psychometric model* is the dominant framework for establishing the meaning of psychological measures (e.g., Anastasi, 1988; Barrios, 1988; Nunnally, 1978). In essence, the model guides us in determining the reliability and validity of our measures—reliability being the consistency of our recordings across conditions in which they are purported to be the same, validity being the correspondence of our recordings with other measures that are purported to be either related or unrelated. Since there are various conditions across which our recordings are expected to be constant and various other measures to which our recordings are expected to be related or unrelated, there are various types of reliability and validity, each different type of reliability and validity denoting a different type of meaning.

In the direct observation of child and adolescent disorders, we are primarily interested in the consistency of our recordings across different observers and across different occasions. Thus, we are primarily interested in determining the interobserver reliability and temporal stability of our recordings (Barrios & Hartmann, 1986). With respect to the validity of our measures, we are most concerned with the correspondence of our recordings to those other measures of the same disorder of interest. We are also most concerned with the correspondence of our recordings of the person of interest in the setting of interest with those of the person of interest in other settings, the correspondence of our recordings of the person of interest with those of persons of different race and gender, and the correspondence of our recordings with those of persons of different age. Thus, we are most interested in determining the convergent validity, ecological validity, population validity, and temporal validity of our recordings (e.g., Barrios & Hartmann, 1988; Messick, 1980). Such determinations are made through the use of the class of statistics known as correlational techniques (e.g., Anastasi, 1988; Nunnally, 1978).

In the *generalizability model,* we ascribe meaning to our recordings by identifying the conditions across which we can safely generalize recordings (Cronbach, Gleser, Nanda, & Rajaratnam, 1972). With regard to the assessment of child and adolescent disorders, we are most interested in determining the degree to which we can generalize from the recordings of one of our behaviors of interest to the recordings of another of our behaviors of interest. What is more, we are interested in determining the degree to which we can generalize from the recordings of one observer to those of another observer, from the recordings of the behaviors of interest in one setting to those of the behaviors of interest in another setting, and from the recordings of the behaviors of interest on one occasion to those of the behaviors of interest on another occasion. In other words, we are most intent on determining the response generality, observer generality, setting generality, and time generality of our recordings (Cone, 1978). We do so through the use of analysis of variance techniques (Brennan, 1983; Cronbach et al., 1972).

In the *accuracy model,* ascribing meaning to our recordings is a twofold process (Cone, 1981). First, we compare our recordings to an independent, incontrovertible index of the behaviors of interest. Second, we combine these comparisons across certain conditions of interest. Among the conditions of chief interest to us are time, setting, method, and response-relation (Cone, 1981). That is, we wish to determine the accuracy of our recordings across different occasions and different settings. We also wish to determine the accuracy of our recordings of the behaviors of interest across other recordings of the same behaviors collected through different methods. And last, we wish to determine the accuracy of our recordings of purported relationships between the behaviors of interest and other behaviors. To repeat, to do so we must first compare the recordings against some agreed-upon, objective standard. For the conditions of occasions, settings, and methods, only one such standard is needed, as the same behaviors are tracked across all three conditions. For the condition of response-relation, however, as many different standards are needed as there are different groups of behaviors that are being tracked and that are purported to be related to one another. To quantify and combine these comparisons, we compute a series of simple percentage agreement statistics (Cone, 1981).

In sum, the construction, implementation, and interpretation of a direct observation system can be seen as a long series of decisions and actions. We begin with a specifying of the problem space and end with an assigning of meaning to our recordings. And in between, we perform a whole host of tasks ranging from selecting a setting for our observations to monitoring the performance of our observers. A complete listing of the steps involved in constructing, implementing, and interpreting a direct observation system is provided in Table 10-3.

SELECTION

Many are the times we will opt to adopt an available direct observation system rather than develop our own direct observation system. Our reasons for doing so will be basically twofold: convenience and contribution. As we have seen, putting together a direct observation system is a costly and time-consuming undertaking. When possible, then, it is much more convenient and economical for us to adopt an existing

Table 10-3. Decision Steps in the Construction, Implementation, and Interpretation of a Direct Observation System

STEP	DECISION
Specifying the domain	One must sketch a window of observation of either a symptom or a syndrome or a system. One must select response dimensions for each of the behaviors of interest. And one must compose an objective, understandable, and sure definition for each of the behaviors of interest.
Selecting the setting	One must select a relevant, salient, and stable stimulus situation as an observation setting.
Collecting the observations	One must specify the number, duration, and sequence of observing and recording periods. One must develop a manageable and meaningful set of symbols for the behaviors of interest. One must develop a clear and convenient form for recording observations of the behaviors of interest. And one must develop a safe procedure for depositing, collecting, and storing these completed forms.
Scoring the responses	One must develop rules for organizing the observations into manageable and meaningful numerical units. And such rules must yield scores that are age appropriate and sex appropriate.
Selecting the observers	One must choose persons who will faithfully follow the code and scheme for tracking and recording the behaviors of interest.
Gaining permission	One must gain permission to observe from all relevant parties. And one must garner permission from all parties whose cooperation is needed to carry out the observations.
Training and monitoring observers	One must orient observers to the importance of the task at hand and educate them as to response definitions and recording scheme. One must test their knowledge of said definitions and scheme, then have them carry out said scheme in the actual setting of interest. Finally, one must monitor the accuracy and agreement of the observers' recordings.
Troubleshooting breakdowns	One must identify the source of any breakdowns in faithful tracking and recording of the behaviors of interest. Then one must eliminate said source so as to restore faithful tracking and recording of the behaviors of interest.
Interpreting the data	One must compute indices of the accuracy and agreement of the observers' recordings. One must place these recordings against one of three backdrops: a subset of said recordings, recordings of criterion performance, or recordings of a suitable reference group. One must ascribe further meaning to the data through the use of one of three models: psychometric model, generalizability model, or accuracy model.

system for the tracking and recording of behaviors of interest rather than make our own. It is also more constructive. For when we employ an existing system, we contribute to the knowledge base of that system. That is, we add to the meaning that can be ascribed to recordings obtained from the system.

At present, we suffer from no shortage of instruments for the direct observation of child and adolescent disorders. For example, for the assessment of fears and anxieties alone, we have more than 50 different systems to choose from (Barrios & Hartmann, 1988). We do, however, suffer from a shortage of guidelines for selecting the system most suitable for our specific needs and purposes. In the following paragraphs, we offer a provisional framework for the selection of a direct observational system.

Eight major considerations enter into the selection of a direct observation system for use in the assessment of a child or adolescent disorder. The first of these is *nomen*—the name by which an instrument is known. Ideally, we would like to use an instrument whose title contains the common term for the behaviors of interest. In doing so, we both promote and practice the use of precise language in our assessment and communication of the behaviors of interest. To do contrary, to use instruments with vague and ambiguous titles, is to create confusion and doubt in our minds and in the minds of others as to what is being assessed. To avoid such confusion and doubt, we therefore seek instruments with titles that are exact and that match the accepted term for the behaviors of interest.

The second consideration in choosing an instrument is the size and scope of the *window* of observation. As mentioned earlier in the making of a direct observation system, phenomenon of interest may take one of three general forms: discrete responses on the part of the person of interest (i.e., symptom), clusters of responses on the part of the person of interest (i.e., syndrome), or collections of responses on the part of the person of interest and other relevant persons (i.e., system). The window through which we watch the phenomenon of interest can be of one of three general sizes, the smallest being the symptom, the intermediate being the syndrome, and the largest being the system. The bigger the window, the busier we will tend to be. For the bigger the window, the greater will be the number of persons and behaviors being tracked and recorded. We strive, then, to select instruments with windows that match our potential for tracking and recording and our purposes for assessing the person of interest.

All direct observation systems are developed with certain persons in mind. That is, all direct observation systems are developed for the study of persons of certain age, sex, race, or culture. These systems may not be suitable for use with persons of differing age, sex, race, or culture, unless, of course, they have been shown to be so. *Subjects,* then, is the third factor that we take into account in our selection of a direct observation system. For we too have certain persons of certain age, sex, race, or culture whom we wish to study. So, we wish to select instruments that are tried and true for the subjects of our study.

All direct observation systems are also developed with a certain situation in mind. That is, all direct observation systems are developed for use in a particular context. Typically, the context is of one of three types: the natural environment, an artificial environment that simulates the natural environment, or an analog environment that approximates the natural environment to some degree. Aside from varying along the dimension of naturalism, the three contexts vary along the dimension of control and structure. Direct observation systems for use in the natural environment typically do not call for a great deal of experimental control and structure, whereas direct observation systems for use in an artificial environment that simulates the natural one typically do call for a great deal of experimental control and structure. For in the latter, considerable control and structure are needed to create and duplicate the actual stimulus conditions that give rise to the behaviors of interest. Such control and structure are generally not needed for systems used in an analog situation, as the aim of such systems is not to duplicate the actual stimulus conditions that give rise to the behaviors of interest, but merely to approximate those conditions. Thus, direct observation systems for use in analog environments typically call for an intermediate degree of experimental control and structure. *Setting,* then, is the fourth factor that enters into our selection of a direct observation system. Because we will have access to only certain types of situations in our study of the person of interest, we wish to select instruments that have been developed and approved for use in said types of situations. And because we will be able to wield only a certain amount of control and structure over the testing situation, we wish to select instruments that are compatible with the amount of control and structure.

The fifth consideration in selecting a direct observation system is *observers*—the persons entrusted with carrying out the recording scheme. With all direct observation systems, these are persons who are selected and trained and monitored in a certain manner. For example, they may be selected for certain characteristics such as age and experience and dependability, as these may be characteristics that have been shown to relate to faithful tracking and recording of the behaviors of interest; they may be trained for a certain duration to a certain criterion, as such a duration and criterion may have been shown to lead to faithful tracking and recording of the behaviors of interest; and they may be monitored according to a certain timetable, as such a timetable may have been shown to maintain faithful tracking and recording of the behaviors of interest. Obviously, we wish to choose for use only those instruments that we can implement with precision. That is, we wish to choose for use only those instruments whose selection, training, and monitoring of observers is commensurate with what we are able to offer in the way of observer selection, training, and monitoring.

The type of *scoring* key that comes with an instrument is the sixth consideration in our selection of a direct observation system. Most instruments reduce recordings of the behaviors of interest in one of two ways: they combine the recordings so as to yield a score for each of the behaviors of interest or they combine the recordings so as to yield a single score for the behaviors of interest as a whole. The latter combine the recordings in one of two ways: They assign equal importance to the individual behaviors in the formation of a composite score, or they assign differential importance to the individual behaviors in the formation of a composite score. That is, they compute either an unweighted or a weighted summary score for the behaviors of interest as a whole. Ideally, we would like to choose for use an instrument whose scoring is compatible with the window and the subjects of our study. That is, we would like for the scores derived from the instrument to be of the same size as the window chosen for observation—the symptom, the syndrome, or the system. What is more, we would like the scores derived from the instrument to be suitable for the subjects chosen for study—their age, gender, race, and culture.

All available instruments for direct observation of child and adolescent disorders come with not only a key for scoring of one's recordings but also a key for interpreting of one's recordings. That is, they all come with a recommended backdrop and established network of relationships. Sensible selection of a direct observation system, then, calls for careful consideration of an instrument's backdrop and network. As mentioned earlier, this backdrop may take one of three forms: the previous or desired performance of the person of interest, criterion performance for the behaviors of interest for the person of interest, or normative performance for the behaviors of interest for the person of interest. Each of the three different types of backdrops allows for three different types of comparisons. Crucial, then, in the selection of a direct observation system is choosing an instrument that allows for the comparison of interest.

More often than not, though, we will be wanting to do more than compare our recordings to some other recordings (i.e., backdrop). To be exact, more often than not, we will be wanting to generalize from our recordings to some other recordings. The extent to which we can safely do so will be a function of the instrument's established network of relationships. As mentioned earlier, there are three main maps that are used to trace a measure's network of relationships to other measures: the psychometric model, the generalizability model, and the accuracy model. The three models differ from one another in the techniques they use to trace a measure's relationships with other measures and in the terms they use to denote the relationships. These differences, though, are of little concern to us in the selection of an instrument for use. What is of concern is the exact nature of the network of relationships that has been traced. For in selecting a direct observation system for use, we wish to choose an instrument whose established network of relationships includes the relationships of interest to us—the generalizations we wish to make on the bases of our recordings.

In sum, selecting a direct observation system to meet one's specific needs, resources, and purposes is a not-so-simple affair. The several factors cited above must be weighed and integrated. And this weighing and integrating must lead to the identification of the most appropriate instrument. A restatement of the eight most serious considerations in the selection of a direct observation system is provided in Table 10-4.

SUMMARY

In closing, we would like to share some of our general observations regarding the current status and future trends in the direct behavioral observation of child and adolescent disorders. And we would like to put forth some general recommendations regarding the future use of direct behavioral observation in the assessment of child and adolescent disorders. As for current practice, there is no question that the construction, implementation, and interpretation of a direct

Table 10-4. Considerations in the Selection of a Direct Observation System

CONSIDERATION	DESCRIPTION
Nomen	One would like an instrument whose name captures the behaviors of interest and matches the accepted term for said behaviors.
Window	One would like an instrument whose window of observation allows for the tracking and recording of all behaviors of interest on the part of all persons of interest.
Subjects	One would like an instrument that has been proven appropriate for use with the persons of interest.
Setting	One would like an instrument whose testing situation is compatible with the control and structure one can exert.
Observers	One would like an instrument whose recommended method of selecting, training, and monitoring observers is compatible with what one can offer in the way of observer selecting, training, and monitoring.
Scoring key	One would like an instrument whose scoring key yields units compatible with one's window of observation and suitable for one's subjects of observation.
Backdrop	One would like an instrument for which there is a backdrop that allows one to make the comparison of interest.
Network	One would like an instrument whose empirical network of relationships permits the generalization of interest.

observation system is a complex and costly affair. And as a result of this complexity and costliness, direct observation is rapidly becoming the measurement method of the specialist.

Some degree of specialization is, of course, needed to perform and to improve upon any type of work. Overspecialization, though, leads to an unhealthy separation between production and application. To be specific, overspecialization creates a huge division between those of us who devise and revise direct observation systems (i.e., the measurement specialist) and those of us who desire to use them as aids in the treatment of child and adolescent disorders (i.e., the clinical practitioner).

Guided by the metaphor of the camera, today's specialist appears intent on developing more and more sophisticated direct observation systems that rely upon more and more technical equipment and expertise. Today's specialist appears bent on widening the gap between the creation of direct observation systems and the wide-scale application of such systems.

To reverse this problematic trend, we recommend replacing the metaphor of the camera with the metaphor of the window. As a guiding metaphor, the window has a number of distinct advantages over the camera. First, the metaphor of the window is more likely than the metaphor of the camera to preserve and promote the human element in direct behavioral observation. That is, the metaphor of the window is more likely than the metaphor of the camera to uphold and enhance the definition of the method as one of a human observer watching a human subject. Second, the metaphor of the window is more likely than the metaphor of the camera to foster a close familiarity between scientist and subject. The reason for this is that the former is more likely to have the scientist immediately involved in the tracking and recording of the subject. Third, the metaphor of the window holds greater promise than the metaphor of the camera in focusing much-needed attention to the issue of scale in the direct observation of child and adolescent disorders. Here the reason is that the metaphor of the camera leads us to believe that there are no limits to the number of persons and the number of behaviors we might track, whereas the metaphor of the window makes us most mindful of the very real limits to the number of persons and the number of behaviors we might track with precision. And fourth, the metaphor of the window holds greater promise than the metaphor of the camera in promoting and supporting simplicity. With the metaphor of the camera, we are most enamored of the technical aspects of our direct observation system; whereas with the metaphor of the window, we are most interested in the functional aspects of our direct observation system—the primary ones being utility and practicality. Thus, as a whole, the metaphor of the window appears to be more conducive to the practice of good science than the metaphor of the camera.

Our hope is that the measurement method of direct

observation survives and thrives in the years ahead. Toward this end, we have delineated the major steps involved in the construction, implementation, and interpretation of a direct observation system; we have described a provisional framework for the selection of a direct observation system; and we have proposed a metaphor to guide us in the development and evaluation of a direct observation system. Thus, we hope that this chapter will prove to be of some service to those interested in and committed to direct observation of child and adolescent disorders.

REFERENCES

Alexander, J., & Parsons, B. V. (1982). *Functional family therapy*. Monterey, CA: Brooks/Cole.

Allport, G. W. (1937). *Personality*. New York: Holt, Rinehart & Winston.

Anastasi, A. (1988). *Psychological testing* (6th ed.). New York: Macmillan.

Arrington, R. E. (1932). Interrelations in the behavior of young children, *Child Development Monographs*, No. 8.

Barrios, B. A. (1988). On the changing nature of behavioral assessment. In A. S. Bellack & M. Hersen (Eds.), *Behavioral assessment: A practical handbook* (3rd ed., pp. 3–41). New York: Pergamon Press.

Barrios, B. A., & Hartmann, D. P. (1986). The contribution of traditional assessment: Concepts, issues, and methodologies. In R. O. Nelson & S. C. Hayes (Eds.), *Conceptual foundations of behavioral assessment* (pp. 81–110). New York: Guilford Press.

Barrios, B. A., & Hartmann, D. P. (1988). Fears and anxieties. In E. J. Mash & L. G. Terdal (Eds.), *Behavioral assessment of childhood disorders* (2nd ed., pp. 196–262). New York: Guilford Press.

Barrios, B. A., & O'Dell, S. L. (1989). Fears and anxieties. In E. J. Mash & R. A. Barkley (Eds.), *Treatment of childhood disorders* (pp. 167–221). New York: Guilford Press.

Barton, E. J., & Ascione, F. R. (1984). Direct observation. In T. H. Ollendick & M. Hersen (Eds.), *Child behavioral assessment: Principles and procedures* (pp. 166–194). New York: Pergamon Press.

Berk, R. A. (1979). Generalizability of behavioral observations: A clarification of interobserver agreement and interobserver reliability. *American Journal of Mental Deficiency, 83*, 460–472.

Bertucci, M., Huston, M., & Perloff, E. (1974). Comparative study of progress notes using problem-oriented and traditional methods of charting. *Nursing Research, 23*, 351–354.

Boice, R. (1983). Observational skills. *Psychological Bulletin, 93*, 3–29.

Brennan, R. L. (1983). *Elements of generalizability theory*. Iowa City: ACT Publications.

Cairns, R. B., & Green, J. A. (1979). How to assess personality and social patterns: Observations or ratings. In R. B. Cairns (Ed.), *The analysis of social interactions*. Hillsdale, NJ: Lawrence Erlbaum Associates.

Cone, J. D. (1978). The behavioral assessment grid (BAG): A conceptual framework and taxonomy. *Behavior Therapy, 9*, 882–888.

Cone, J. D. (1981). Psychometric considerations. In M. Hersen & A. S. Bellack (Eds.), *Behavioral assessment: A practical handbook* (2nd ed., pp. 36–68). New York: Pergamon Press.

Cone, J. D., & Foster, S. L. (1982). Direct observation in clinical psychology. In J. N. Butcher & P. C. Kendall (Eds.), *Handbook of research methods in clinical psychology*. New York: John Wiley & Sons.

Cronbach, L. J. (1960). *Essentials of psychological testing* (2nd ed.). New York: Harper & Row.

Cronbach, L. J., Gleser, G. C., Nanda, H., & Rajaratnam, N. (1972). *The dependability of behavioral measurements*. New York: John Wiley & Sons.

Dancer, D. D., Braukmann, C. J., Schumaker, J. B., Kirgin, K. A., Willner, A. G., & Wolf, M. M. (1978). The training and validation of behavior observation and description skills. *Behavior Modification, 2*, 113–134.

DeMaster, B., Reid, J., & Twentyman, C. (1977). The effects of different amounts of feedback on observer's reliability. *Behavior Therapy, 8*, 317–329.

Edelbrock, C. (1984). Developmental considerations. In T. H. Ollendick & M. Hersen (Eds.), *Child behavioral assessment: Principles and procedures* (pp. 20–37). New York: Pergamon Press.

Foster, S. L., Bell-Dolan, D. J., & Burge, D. A. (1988). Behavioral observation. In A. S. Bellack & M. Hersen (Eds.), *Behavioral assessment: A practical handbook* (3rd ed., pp. 119–160). New York: Pergamon Press.

Foster, S. L., & Cone, J. D. (1980). Current issues in direct observation. *Behavioral Assessment, 2*, 313–338.

Foster, S. L., & Robin, A. L. (1989). Parent-adolescent conflict. In E. J. Mash & R. A. Barkley (Eds.), *Treatment of childhood disorders* (pp. 493–528). New York: Guilford Press.

Frick, T., & Semmel, M. I. (1978). Observer agreement and reliabilities of classroom observational measures. *Review of Educational Research, 48*, 157–184.

Garber, J. (1984). Classification of childhood psychopathology: A developmental perspective. *Child Development, 55*, 30–48.

Gelfand, D. M., & Hartmann, D. P. (1984). *Child behavior: Analysis and therapy* (2nd ed.). New York: Pergamon Press.

Giebenhain, J., & Barrios, B. A. (1986, November). *Multichannel assessment of children's fears*. Paper presented at the meeting of the Association for Advancement of Behavior Therapy, Chicago.

Gottman, J. M. (1985). Observational measures of behavior therapy outcome: A reply to Jacobson. *Behavioral Assessment, 7*, 317–322.

Green, B. F. (1981). A primer of testing. *American Psychologist, 36,* 1001–1011.
Guttman, H. A., Spector, R. M., Sigal, J. J., Rakoff, V., & Epstein, W. B. (1971). Reliability of coding affective communications in family therapy sessions: Problems of measurement and interpretation. *Journal of Consulting and Clinical Psychology, 37,* 397–402.
Harris, F. C., & Lahey, B. B. (1982a). Subject reactivity in direct observational assessment: A review and critical analysis. *Clinical Psychology Review, 2,* 523–538.
Harris, F. C., & Lahey, B. B. (1982b). Recording system bias in direct observational methodology: A review and critical analysis of factors causing inaccurate coding behavior. *Clinical Psychology Review, 2,* 539–556.
Hartmann, D. P. (1977). Considerations in the choice of interobserver reliability estimates. *Journal of Applied Behavior Analysis, 10,* 103–116.
Hartmann, D. P. (Ed.). (1982). *New directions for methodology of social and behavioral science: Using observers to study behavior.* San Francisco: Jossey-Bass.
Hartmann, D. P., & Wood, D. D. (1982). Observational methods. In A. S. Bellack, M. Hersen, & A. E. Kazdin (Eds.), *International handbook of behavior modification and therapy* (pp. 109–138). New York: Plenum Press.
Hawkins, R. P., Dobes, R. W. (1977). Behavioral definitions in applied behavior analysis: Explicit or implicit. In B. C. Etzel, J. M. LeBlanc, & D. M. Baer (Eds.), *New developments in behavioral research: Theory, method and application.* Hillsdale, NJ: Lawrence Erlbaum Associates.
Haynes, S. N. (1978). *Principles of behavioral assessment.* New York: Gardner Press.
Haynes, S. N. (1986). Assessing intervention outcome. In R. O. Nelson & S. C. Hayes (Eds.), *Conceptual foundations of behavioral assessment* (pp. 386–429). New York: Guilford Press.
Haynes, S. N., & Horn, W. F. (1982). Reactivity in behavioral observation: A review. *Behavioral Assessment, 4,* 369–385.
Jacobson, N. S. (1985a). The role of observational measures in behavior therapy outcome research. *Behavioral Assessment, 7,* 297–308.
Jacobson, N. S. (1985b). Uses versus abuses of observational measures. *Behavioral Assessment, 7,* 323–330.
Jay, S. M., Ozolins, M., Elliott, C., & Caldwell, S. (1983). Assessment of children's distress during painful medical procedures. *Journal of Health Psychology, 2,* 133–147.
Johnson, S. M., & Bolstad, O. D. (1973). Methodological issues in naturalistic observation: Some problems and solutions for field research. In L. A. Hamerlynck, L. C. Handy, E. J. Mash (Eds.), *Behavior change: Methodology, concepts, and practice.* Champaign, IL: Research Press.
Kazdin, A. E. (1977). Artifact, bias, and complexity of assessment: The ABCs of reliability. *Journal of Applied Behavior Analysis, 10,* 141–150.
Kazdin, A. E. (1981). Behavioral observation. In M. Hersen & A. S. Bellack (Eds.), *Behavioral assessment: A practical handbook* (2nd ed., pp. 101–124). New York: Pergamon Press.
Kazdin, A. E. (1989). Developmental psychopathology: Current research, issues, and direction. *American Psychologist, 44,* 180–187.
Kelly, M. B. (1977). A review of the observational data-collection and reliability procedures reported in the *Journal of Applied Behavior Analysis. Journal of Applied Behavior Analysis, 10,* 97–101.
Kendall, P. C., Lerner, R. M., & Craighead, W. E. (1984). Human development and intervention in childhood psychopathology. *Child Development, 55,* 71–82.
Kendall, P. C., & Williams, C. L. (1986). Therapy with adolescents: Treating the "marginal man." *Behavior Therapy, 17,* 522–537.
Kent, R. N., & Foster, S. L. (1977). Direct observational procedures: Methodological issues in naturalistic settings. In A. R. Ciminero, K. S. Calhoun, & H. E. Adams (Eds.), *Handbook of behavioral assessment* (pp. 279–328). New York: Wiley.
Kent, R. N., Kanowitz, J., O'Leary, K. D., & Cheiken, M. (1977). Observer reliability as a function of circumstances of assessment. *Journal of Applied Behavior Analysis, 10,* 317–324.
Kent, R. N., O'Leary, K. D., Diament, C., & Dietz, A. (1974). Expectation biases in observational evaluation of therapeutic change. *Journal of Consulting and Clinical Psychology, 42,* 774–780.
Kiesler, D. J. (1966). Some myths of psychotherapy research and the search for a paradigm. *Psychological Bulletin, 65,* 110–136.
Knapp, M. L. (1978). *Nonverbal communication in human interaction.* New York: Holt, Rinehart & Winston.
Levitt, E. E. (1971). Research on psychotherapy with children. In S. L. Garfield & A. E. Bergin (Eds.), *Handbook of psychotherapy and behavior change: An empirical analysis* (pp. 474–494). New York: John Wiley & Sons.
Mahrolin, D. (Ed.). (1978). *Child behavior therapy.* New York: Gardner Press.
Mash, E. J. (1985). Some comments on target behavior selection in behavior therapy. *Behavioral Assessment, 7,* 63–78.
Mash, E. J., & Barkley, R. A. (Eds.). (1989). *Treatment of childhood disorders.* New York: Guilford Press.
Mash, E. J., & Hedley, J. (1975). Effect of observer as a function of prior history of social interaction. *Perceptual and Motor Skills, 40,* 659–669.
Mash, E. J., & Terdal, L. G. (Eds.). (1988). *Behavioral assessment of childhood disorders* (2nd ed.). New York: Guilford Press.
Melamed, B. G., Hawes, R. R., Heiby, E., & Glick, J. (1975). Use of filmed modeling to reduce uncooperative behavior of children during dental treatment. *Journal of Dental Research, 54,* 757–801.
Melamed, B. G., Siegel, L. J. (1975). Reduction of anxiety in children facing hospitalization and surgery by use of

filmed modeling. *Journal of Consulting and Clinical Psychology, 43,* 511–521.

Messick, S. (1980). Test validity and the ethics of assessment. *American Psychologist, 35,* 1012–1027.

Nay, W. R. (1979). *Multimethod clinical assessment.* New York: Gardner Press.

Nunnally, J. (1978). *Psychometric theory* (2nd ed.). New York: McGraw-Hill.

O'Dell, S. L. (1986). Progress in parent training. In M. Hersen, R. M. Eisler, & P. M. Miller (Eds.), *Progress in behavior modification* (Vol. 17, pp. 57–108). New York: Academic Press.

Ollendick, T. H. (1986). Behavior therapy with children and adolescents. In S. L. Garfield & A. E. Bergin (Eds.), *Handbook of psychotherapy and behavior change* (3rd ed., pp. 565–624). New York: John Wiley & Sons.

Ollendick, T. H., & Hersen, M. (Eds.). (1984). *Child behavioral assessment: Principles and procedures.* New York: Pergamon Press.

Patterson, G. R. (1964). An empirical approach to the classification of disturbed children. *Journal of Clinical Psychology, 20,* 326–337.

Patterson, G. R. (1977). Accelerating stimuli for two classes of coercive behaviors. *Journal of Abnormal Child Psychology, 5,* 335–350.

Patterson, G. R. (1982). *Coercive family process.* Eugene, OR: Castalia.

Patterson, G. R. (1986). Performance models for antisocial boys. *American Psychologist, 41,* 432–444.

Phillips, L., Draguns, J. G., & Bartlett, D. P. (1975). Classification of behavior disorders. In N. Hobbs (Ed.), *Issues in the classification of children.* San Francisco: Jossey-Bass.

Powell, J., Martindale, A., & Kulp, S. (1975). An evaluation of time-sample measures of behavior. *Journal of Applied Behavior Analysis, 8,* 463–469.

Powell, J., Martindale, B., Kulp, S., Martindale, A., & Bauman, R. (1977). Taking a closer look: Time sampling and measurement error. *Journal of Applied Behavior Analysis, 10,* 325–332.

Powell, J., & Rockinson, R. (1978). On the instability of interval time sampling to reflect frequency of occurrence data. *Journal of Applied Behavior Analysis, 11,* 531–532.

Quay, H. C., & Werry, J. S. (Eds.). (1979). *Psychopathological disorders of childhood* (2nd ed.). New York: John Wiley & Sons.

Repp, A. C., Roberts, D. M., Slack, D. L., Repp, C. F., & Berkler, M. S. (1976). A comparison of frequency, interval, and time-sampling methods of data collection. *Journal of Applied Behavior Analysis, 9,* 501–508.

Rodriguez, A., Rodriguez, M., & Eisenberg, L. (1959). The outcome of school phobia: A follow-up study based on 41 cases. *American Journal of Psychiatry, 116,* 540–544.

Romanczyk, R. G., Kent, R. N., Diament, C., & O'Leary, K. D. (1973). Measuring the reliability of observational data: A reactive process. *Journal of Applied Behavior Analysis, 6,* 175–186.

Ross, A. O. (1981). *Child behavior therapy: Principles, procedures and empirical basis.* New York: John Wiley & Sons.

Rutter, M. (1972). Relationship between child and adult psychiatric disorders. *Acta Psychiatrica Scandinavica, 48,* 3–21.

Rutter, M. (Ed.). (1980). *Scientific foundations of developmental psychiatry.* London: Heinemann.

Schectman, A. (1970). Psychiatric symptoms observed in normal and disturbed children. *Journal of Clinical Psychology, 26,* 38–41.

Shuller, D. Y., & McNamara, J. R. (1976). Expectancy factors in behavioral observation. *Behavior Therapy, 7,* 519–527.

Taft, R. (1955). The ability to judge people. *Psychological Bulletin, 52,* 1–23.

Tinsley, H. E. A., & Weiss, D. J. (1975). Interrater reliability and agreement of subjective judgments. *Journal of Counseling Psychology, 22,* 358–376.

Van Hasselt, V. B., Hersen, M., Bellack, A. S., Rosenblum, N. D., & Lamparski, D. (1979). Tripartite assessment of the effects of systematic desensitization on a multi-phobic child: An experimental analysis. *Journal of Behavior Therapy and Experimental Psychiatry, 10,* 51–55.

Wasik, B. H., & Loven, M. D. (1980). Classroom observational data: Sources of inaccuracy and proposed solutions. *Behavioral Assessment, 2,* 211–227.

Weiss, R. L., & Froham, P. E. (1985). Behavioral observation as outcome measures: Not through a glass darkly. *Behavioral Assessment, 7,* 309–316.

Wildman, B. G., & Erickson, M. T. (1977). Methodological problems in behavioral observation. In J. D. Cone & R. P. Hawkins (Eds.), *Behavioral assessment: New directions in clinical psychology.* New York: Brunner/Mazel.

Wildman, B. G., Erickson, M. T., & Kent, R. N. (1975). The effect of two training procedures on observer agreement and variability of behavior ratings. *Child Development, 46,* 520–524.

Wine, J. D. (1979). Test anxiety and evaluation threat: Children's behavior in the classroom. *Journal of Abnormal Child Psychology, 7,* 45–59.

Wright, H. F. (1960). Observational child study. In P. Mussen (Ed.), *Handbook of research methods in child development.* New York: John Wiley & Sons.

Yarrow, M. R., & Waxler, C. Z. (1979). Observing interaction: A confrontation with methodology. In R. B. Cairns (Ed.), *The analysis of social interactions.* Hillsdale, NJ: Lawrence Erlbaum Associates.

CHAPTER 11

PEER-REFERENCED ASSESSMENT STRATEGIES

Frank M. Gresham
Steven G. Little

Interest in the assessment and training of social skills for children and adolescents has increased astronomically over the past 5 years. It is fair to say that *social skills* is the current zeitgeist in applied psychology, special education, and other mental health professions. Paralleling this interest in social skills has been the development of assessment methodologies designed to accurately identify children in need of social skills training (SST), to monitor the progress of SST, and to evaluate the outcomes of SST programs (Gresham & Elliott, 1990).

PEER-REFERENCED ASSESSMENT STRATEGIES

This chapter focuses on a key construct in social skills: the degree to which a child's peers perceive the child's behavior or accept the child into the peer group. Peers are in a unique position to judge a child's social behavior and represent a critical source of assessment information. We present a comprehensive review of the peer-referenced assessment literature, including psychometric characteristics, correlates of peer-referenced assessments, classification of sociometric types, and ethical issues in peer-referenced assessment.

DEFINITIONS OF PEER-REFERENCED ASSESSMENT

Peer-referenced assessment (PRA) is a broad term describing a collection of techniques designed to measure either the attraction among members of a specific group or the specific behaviors, traits, or roles of persons in a specific social group. Asher and Hymel (1981) made an important distinction between sociometric assessment and peer assessment. Sociometrics measure the degree to which children are liked or disliked by peers, whereas peer assessments measure specific characteristics or behaviors of children in social groups. Distinctions between sociometric and peer assessments are important, because interpretations of research findings can be confusing by failing to differentiate these separate methodologies (Asher & Hymel, 1981; Dygdon, 1988).

Peer-referenced assessment, which includes both sociometrics and peer assessment, has one common element: The information provided is collected from one's peers. Unlike tests, behavior rating scales, direct observations, and role-play measures, peer-referenced assessments are based on data collected from a relatively large number of persons. These data, in turn, are averaged, weighted, or transformed to calculate scores along various dimensions of sociometric status or social behavior functioning. Information provided by peers cannot be obtained from other sources and therefore represents valuable data regarding a child's social competence.

Purpose and Uses

The primary purpose of peer-referenced assessment is to obtain a reliable and valid measure of peer perceptions of a child or a child's behavior. This information can be used in a number of ways, depending on the reason for conducting the assessment. One, PRAs have been used extensively in research as independent or predictor and dependent or criterion variables. Some researchers have used PRA data to study the behavioral correlates of sociometric status (Coie, 1985; Dygdon, Conger, & Keane, 1987; Gelb & Jacobson, 1988; Gresham, 1982). Other researchers have used PRA strategies to investigate the dimensions of children's social behavior (Pekarik, Prinz, Liebert, Weintraub, & Neale, 1976). Still others have used PRA data as dependent or outcome variables in social skills training programs (Gresham & Nagle, 1980; La Greca & Santogrossi, 1980; Ladd, 1985; Oden & Asher, 1977).

Two, PRA strategies have been used to study characteristics of specific clinical populations. For example, Asarnow (1988) studied likability, peer acceptance, and peer rejection in a sample of psychiatrically disturbed (depressed, conduct disordered, and attention deficit disorder with hyperactivity) children. Lefkowitz and Testiny (1980) used PRA to study behavioral characteristics of depressed children, and Strauss, Lahey, Frick, Frame, and Hynd (1988) have used PRA to study peer social status of children with anxiety disorders. Whelan and Henker (1984) reviewed several studies investigating the sociometric status of children classified as hyperactive. The majority of studies in this area have used sociometric status or peer assessment data as dependent or criterion variables rather than as independent or predictor variables. An exception to this can be found in a study conducted by Altmann and Gotlib (1988) in which children were classified as depressed on the basis of the *Peer Nomination Inventory of Depression* (PNID) (Lefkowitz & Testiny, 1980).

PRA also has been used extensively in educational research, particularly special education research, to study peer social status and social behavior functioning of various mildly handicapped groups. Gresham and Reschly (1987) used both peer assessment and sociometric data in a comparison between learning-disabled and non-learning-disabled children. Other authors have compared mildly mentally retarded to nonretarded children (Morrison, 1981) and emotionally disturbed to nondisturbed children (Gresham & Reschly, 1988; Hersh & Walker, 1983).

Special education application of PRA has focused on comparing the sociometric status of mainstreamed mildly handicapped students to those of nonhandicapped peers. A number of reviews have shown that mainstreamed mildly handicapped children have lower sociometric status than their nonhandicapped peers (Gottlieb, 1981; Gresham, 1982; Madden & Slavin, 1983). Several researchers have attempted to discover "causal" factors related to poor peer acceptance of mildly handicapped children using PRA strategies (Gottlieb, Semmel, & Veldman, 1978; Morrison, MacMillan, & Forness, 1983).

In summary, PRA has many applications in psychological and educational research. Its uses include identifying subtypes of sociometric status, defining clinical populations, selecting children or adolescents for social skills training, gauging the outcomes of social skills training programs, measuring the social status of mildly handicapped children in mainstreamed classrooms, and predicting long-term adjustment in longitudinal research (Asher, 1985; Coie, 1985; Gresham, 1982; Ladd, 1985; Parker & Asher, 1987).

DEFINITIONS OF SOCIAL COMPETENCE

PRA strategies have figured prominently into most definitions of social competence. Social competence, however, has been a rather difficult construct to define. A major task facing researchers and practitioners in the future will be to agree on a working definition of social competence (social skills).

There are a number of well-known definitions of social competence in the literature. McFall (1982) distinguished between social competence and social skill. In his model, *social competence* represents evaluative judgments that a given behavioral performance was adequate. Competence can be used to judge past performances or to predict future performances. *Social skills* are specific behaviors required to perform a social task in a competent manner. Social skills are situationally specific behaviors that lead to judgments of competence by significant others.

Writing out of a developmental perspective, Ladd and Mize (1983) defined social skills as the ability to organize thoughts and actions into an integrated behavioral pattern toward socially or culturally acceptable goals. This definition also implies that persons continually assess and modify goal-directed behaviors to increase the probability of achieving one's social goals.

Foster and Ritchey (1979) used more of an applied behavior analytic definition by defining social skills as situationally specific behaviors that maximize the probability of producing, maintaining, or enhancing positive effects for an individual. Libet and Lewinsohn (1973) used a similar definition by viewing social skills as behaviors that are positively or negatively reinforced and not emitting behaviors that are punished or extinguished by others.

A final definition of social skills has been termed a *social validity* definition. According to this definition, social skills are situationally specific behaviors that predict important social outcomes for children and youth (Gresham, 1983; 1986). Important social outcomes include, but are not limited to, peer acceptance, acceptance by significant adults (e.g., parents and teachers), academic achievement, feelings of self-efficacy or self-esteem, and absence of psychopathology. This definition also states that important social outcomes vary as a function of developmental level. For example, important social outcomes for preschoolers differ from important social outcomes for adolescents. A similar logic has been applied to the conception of adaptive behavior over the past 30 years (Reschly & Gresham, 1988).

The focus of this chapter is to discuss how PRA can be used to operationalize the socially important outcome of peer acceptance. Given the numerous variations of PRA and the multidetermined nature of scores of PRA measures, the meaning of validity of these measures becomes paramount. An overview of validity in PRA is presented in the following section. Specific studies attesting to the validity of PRA methods is presented in a latter section.

VARIATIONS IN PEER-REFERENCED ASSESSMENT

Although all peer-referenced strategies involve having members of a group "judge" other group members on some dimensions (Kane & Lawler, 1978), methods of peer evaluations vary in the procedures they employ and in the information they provide. For example, Kane and Lawler (1978) identify three categories of peer-based procedures: nomination procedures, rating procedures, and ranking procedures. Expanding on these, McConnell and Odom (1986) discuss five methodologies: peer nominations, peer ratings, paired comparison, peer assessment, and "mixed" assessments. The following section is organized following McConnell and Odom's methodological categories.

Peer Nominations

Originally developed by Moreno in 1934, peer nomination is probably the most frequently used sociometric technique (Asher & Hymel, 1981). The general procedure involves asking children in a classroom to select one or more children who fit certain criteria (e.g., most liked, best friend, preferred playmate). Negative evaluations are sometimes also requested. For example, Coie and Kupersmidt (1983) asked children to select, from a roster of classmates, the three they liked the best and the three they liked the least. The measure of social status a child receives using this method is usually just the sum of the child's nominations.

Although this procedure is very simple and straightforward, several variations on the basic procedure have been employed. One variation involves allowing the rater either a fixed or an unlimited number of peer nominations. In a fixed-choice procedure, the tester specifies the number of choices each child is asked to make. For example, Gresham (1981) asked third- and fourth-grade children to nominate three classmates who were their best friends. In an unlimited-choice procedure, children are allowed to nominate as many peers as they would like.

Weighting systems have also been used in an attempt to gather more accurate information. Instead of having raters simply list their nominations in any order, they are requested to rank order the nominations along the dimension being assessed. This allows a more precise measurement of sociometric status by assigning higher values to those children nominated first relative to later selections. When using this type of procedure, however, it is critical for raters to know that the order of nominations is important in providing the ratings. The use of a weighting system, however, may make little difference. Research comparing weighted versus unweighted procedures have resulted in relatively high correlations (Gottman, 1977; Foster

& Ritchey, 1985), indicating that weighting may make little difference in interpretation (Foster, Bell-Dolan, & Berler, 1986).

Another variation on peer nominations involves using multiple criteria instead of a single criterion in an attempt to improve the reliability and validity of results. For multiple criteria to increase the strength of ratings, however, it is important that the same general attribute be measured. This is especially important in light of evidence indicating that children may have differential preferences for peers they would like to work with and play with (Asher & Hymel, 1981).

A final variation of peer nominations involves presenting pictures of classmates from which each rater selects a finite number of liked and disliked classmates (Moore & Updegraff, 1964). This technique may prove to be particularly useful when working with a preschool or developmentally delayed population, because it removes both memory and writing components.

Peer Ratings

Peer rating measures (Roistacher, 1974; Singleton & Asher, 1977; Thompson & Powell, 1951) require raters to rate, on a Likert-type scale, each member of a peer group along certain dimensions (e.g., how much they like or dislike the child; desirability as a playmate or workmate). The general procedure involves giving raters a class roster and instructing them to rate each classmate on the same rating scale. The ratings for each classmate are then summed for each individual, and an overall social status score is derived.

Variations on this procedure most frequently involve changes in number of points along the continuum. Scales have ranged from 2 points (Odom & DuBose, 1981) to 7 points (Roistacher, 1974). Graphics have replaced numbers in a variation sometimes used with younger children. For example, Asher, Singleton, Tinsley, and Hymel (1979) provided preschool children with pictures of peer group members and asked the children to rate each with a happy, neutral, or sad face, depending upon each classmate's desirability as a playmate. In another interesting variation, Pack and McCaffrey (1976) presented mentally retarded subjects with pictures of themselves and peers as well as drawings of tables and chairs. The subjects were asked to place photographs of those they would like to work with around the table with them. Tables closer and farther away were also presented to arrive a rating for each child.

In developing peer rating scales, it is important to specify the items clearly and concretely, preferably in behavioral terms. All raters should have the same understanding as to what each point on the rating scale means to ensure comparability among ratings. Therefore, if one is using a procedure such as the happy faces used by Asher et al. (1979), it may be advisable to discuss with the group the meaning of each rating prior to the actual rating process.

Paired Comparisons

The paired-comparison technique was originally used by Koch (1933) and involves respondents being presented with all possible pairs of names (or pictures) of peers. Specifically, all possible classmate dyads are created, and the rater is instructed to choose which of the two children he or she would choose on the relevant dimension (e.g., liked better, preferred playmate, etc.). The number of times an individual is chosen by his or her classmates is then computed to achieve the measure of social status.

This procedure has not been used as extensively as the two procedures previously discussed, possibly because of the time required to construct and administer it. For example, Koch (1933) took 3 months to complete an assessment of a preschool class. It does, however, appear to have adequate reliability and avoids the need for controversial negative ratings.

Peer Assessment

Although independent to and historically older than sociometrics (Gronlund, 1959), peer assessment is not frequently mentioned in conjunction with the sociometric techniques previously discussed. Although there are differences between the two methodologies, there is a tremendous overlap between the two (Asher & Hymel, 1981). With peer assessments, children are asked to rate others on variety of dimensions with the intent of rating the behavior of other children as opposed to their attraction toward others. This may involve an open-ended verbal or written description of peers or a more structured questionnaire or interview format designed to examine children's perceptions of peer behavior. Hartshorne, May, and Maller (1929) created the "Guess Who?" test in which each child in the class guesses who in the class fits a specific description. This procedure is probably the most frequently used structured peer assessment technique and has been revised and used extensively since the original work by Hartshorne et al. (1929).

Bower (1960) developed a variation of the "Guess

Who?" test called the Class Play technique. In this test, each child is asked to nominate classmates for roles in a class play. These roles can be either positive or negative. A final variation was developed by Shapiro and Sobel (1981) and is entitled the Shapiro Sociometric Role Assignment Test (SSRAT). This procedure involves having class members generate descriptions of classmates, rating them into positive, neutral, and negative categories, and then choosing a classmate who fits each description.

Mixed Assessments

As mentioned previously, there is a great deal of overlap between sociometric and peer assessment methodologies. Mixed assessment refers to these techniques. An example of a mixed assessment technique is the Pupil Evaluation Inventory (PEI) (Pekarik et al., 1976). The PEI is a 35-item questionnaire in which children consider each of their peers for nomination to items describing a wide spectrum of behaviors. Three factors emerged via factor analysis: likability (a sociometric factor), aggression, and withdrawal (both peer assessment factors). An abbreviated version of the PEI for preschool children, the Peer Perception Inventory (Milich, Landau, Kilby, & Whitten, 1982), contains 13 items and assesses popularity, rejection, aggression, hyperactivity, and sociability. Other examples of mixed techniques include the Friendship Rating Scale (Bailey & Pierce, 1975) and the Peer Nomination Inventory (Wiggins & Winder, 1961).

PSYCHOMETRIC CHARACTERISTICS

Reliability

Peer Nominations

Peer nominations are probably the most commonly used sociometric technique. One major asset of this technique, at least for elementary schoolchildren, is that nomination scores tend to have adequate reliability (Asher & Hymel, 1981; McConnell & Odom, 1986). The most frequently reported reliability measure is stability over time of frequency of nominations scores. Bonney (1943) examined stability of positive nomination scores with elementary school students over a 1-year period and found comparable reliabilities to achievement test scores (rs = .67 & .84, respectively). Busk, Ford, and Shulman (1973) reported 8-week test-retest reliabilities for positive nominations of .76 for fourth graders and .84 for sixth graders.

Roff, Sells, and Golden (1972) reported test-retest reliabilities over an extended period of time. Using elementary school students, they found correlations of .52 over a 1-year period and .42 over a 2-year period for positive nominations and .38 and .34 respectively, for negative evaluations. Northway (1969) also noticed a decrease in reliability coefficients as the time interval between testing increased and an increase in stability coefficients with age. This latter point is important, because only moderately high stability coefficients have been found with preschool children even when a picture nomination procedure was used (Asher & Hymel, 1981).

More recently, several authors have investigated stability of nominations as a function of the classification derived from the nominations. Dygdon and Conger (1987: cited in Dygdon, 1988) compared first graders' nominations of liked, disliked, and neglected peers at either 1½-to-2-week or 5-week intervals. Their results revealed stability coefficients of .76 for liked, .90 for disliked, and .60 for neglected at the 1½-to-2-week interval and correlations of .75 for liked, .66 for disliked, and .45 for neglected for the 5-week interval. Similar results were found by Newcomb and Bukowski (1984), who found many instances of change in group membership across assessment occasions. They recommended that classification systems not be used on the basis of only one assessment occasion. Across studies, it apppears that the "neglected" group is the most unstable.

Peer Ratings

When compared to nomination procedures, peer ratings tend to have higher test-retest reliability coefficients. The greater reliability of peer ratings is probably a result of the fact that the score any child receives is the average of the scores from a large number of children (the entire peer group) and thus, the rating of only a few classmates will have a minimal effect if there is relative consistency in ratings of the majority of class members. Nominations, on the other hand, are affected much more dramatically by the gain or loss of a single nomination.

Using third- and fourth-grade children, Oden and Asher (1977) found median test-retest correlation (6-week interval) of .82 for a "play with" scale, .84 for a "work with" scale, and .69 for a positive nomination measure. In a direct comparison of nomination and rating procedures, Thompson and Powell (1951) found consistently higher correlations for the rating procedure at 1 day, 1 week, and 5 weeks.

The superiority in stability of rating techniques is particularly evident in preschool and handicapped populations. Asher, Singleton, Tinsley, and Hymel (1979) had two classes of 4-year-olds respond to both nomination and rating formats at a 4-week interval. The stability coefficients for the rating procedure were higher in both classes (.81, .74) than for either positive (.56, .38) or negative (.42, given only in one class) nominations. Using a procedure similar to that of Asher and his colleagues, Odom and DuBose (1981) found a stability coefficient of .61 after a 1-month period with a handicapped preschool population.

Unfortunately, not all studies have demonstrated such high correlations. Rubin and Daniels-Beirness (1983) found a 1-year test-retest reliability of .48 for children tested in kindergarten and again in first grade on a 3-point rating scale. With 3-week intervals between assessments, Gresham (1981) found correlations of .30 between occasions 1 and 2, .59 between occasions 2 and 3, and .39 between occasions 1 and 3 for play ratings and .33, .63, and .20, respectively, for work ratings.

Paired Comparisons

Paired comparisons appear to be the most reliable sociometric measure (McConnel & Odom, 1986). Vaughn and Waters (1981) obtained test-retest correlations of .92 for a one-semester interval and .90 across an entire year for a preschool population. Cohen and Van Tassell (1978) examined the stability of an abbreviated paired-comparison technique for 3- and 4-year-olds. For 3-year-olds they report correlations of .62, .87, and .53 between occasions 1 and 2, 2 and 3, and 1 and 3, respectively. For 4-year-olds, they present a stability coefficient of .90.

Peer Assessment

Most peer assessment techniques have documented both test-retest and internal consistency reliabilities. The "Guess Who?" test reported a split-half reliability of .88 for a subset of the total test (Hartshorne et al. (1929). Milich et al. (1982) found a mean test-retest reliability of .78 for preschool children. The PEI was reported by its authors to have consistently high split-half and 2-week test-retest reliabilities for factor scores (Pekarik et al., 1976). Similar results were found in a more recent study using a 4-week interval (Johnston, Pelham, Crawford, & Atkins, 1988).

Conclusions

The main conclusion to be drawn regarding the reliability of peer-referenced assessments is "It depends." It depends on the techniques employed, the populations used, the number of criteria used, and the length of time between assessments. The variability among studies is dramatic, with many studies not reporting indices of reliability. McConnell and Odom (1986) reviewed 27 sociometric and peer assessment reliability studies and found that 11 studies made no mention of reliability. Of the remaining 16 studies, 13 investigated test-retest reliability with stability coefficients ranging from .10 to .98, with the majority of the stability coefficients in the .80s to .90s. Internal consistency was mentioned in six studies, with a range from .56 to .92. Variability in these reliability estimates makes it imperative that reliability be assessed each time sociometric techniques are used.

VALIDITY OF PEER-REFERENCED ASSESSMENT

Validity refers to the appropriateness, meaningfulness, and usefulness of specific inferences made from test scores (American Psychological Association, 1985). What is validated are the inferences drawn from test scores and not an assessment or measurement instrument, per se.

Although distinctions have been made among different types of validity (e.g., content, criterion-related), all forms of validity can be considered subsets of *construct validity* (Anastasi, 1988). Several types of data can provide evidence for construct validity, such as developmental changes, group differentiation, convergent-discriminant validity, internal consistency, correlations with other measures, and factor analyses. Perhaps the most useful way of viewing construct validity is in terms of a *nomological network*. Cronbach and Meehl (1955) suggested that the meaning of a construct can be made clear by placing the construct in a nomological network, which refers to a collection of interrelationships among many constructs. By demonstrating the relationships among similar and dissimilar constructs, knowledge is added about the construct of interest. Elaboration of a nomological network is accomplished by adding more observable behaviors to the network, resulting in less inference about the construct in question.

Dygdon (1988) argued that establishing the validity of PRA devices is difficult, because "appropriate" criterion measures are difficult to define. In her review, Dygdon maintained that peer judgments of social status or social behavior should not necessarily be expected to match or even correlate with other measures of social competence. We disagree with this logic. By adopting the notion of a nomological network, evidence for the validity of inferences drawn from PRA methods has been established. We know a great deal more about the nomological network surrounding PRA now than we did just 10 years ago. In other words, there are some clearly established, observable connections in the nomological network, thereby supporting the construct validity of PRA. We will review several lines of evidence attesting to the construct validity of PRA strategies in subsequent sections of this chapter.

Another type of validity that has significant implications for PRA is a nontraditional form of validity known in the behavioral literature as *social validity*. Wolf (1978) described social validity as occurring on three levels:

1. establishing the social significance of goals of behavior change programs,
2. establishing the social acceptability of methods to change behavior, and
3. establishing the social importance of effects produced by behavior change programs.

Social validity is important for PRA strategies, particularly in terms of social significance and social importance. First, many social skills training programs have used PRA to select children for treatment (see Coie, 1985; Gresham, 1986; Ladd, 1985). Various types of children have been selected on the basis of sociometric status such as poorly accepted, rejected, isolated, or controversial. Other social skills training programs have selected children on the basis of peer assessment strategies designed to measure aggression, social withdrawal, social anxiety, and attention deficits. Based on a number of studies, it appears that PRA methods identify children in need of social skills training and therefore have social validity according to a social significance criterion.

The social importance of PRA is evidenced also by its use as an outcome or dependent variable in many social skills training studies. That is, if social skills training is effective in changing social behavior, one would expect that these behavioral changes would make a socially important difference in how peers perceive the child's behavior and acceptance in the peer group. PRA seems like a natural outcome variable in social skills training studies, at least in terms of both face validity and social validity. McConnell and Odom (1986) cogently point out, however, that nonbehavioral factors (e.g., gender, race, physical attractiveness) can influence peer judgments, so that sole reliance on PRA as an outcome variable is ill-advised. We agree with this assessment and discuss the influence of nonbehavioral correlates of PRA in a subsequent section.

CORRELATES OF PEER-REFERENCED ASSESSMENT

A plethora of studies have investigated the correlates of PRA. Most of these studies have focused on identifying the correlates of sociometric status, although some studies have examined correlates of peer assessment measures (Asher & Hymel, 1981; McConnell & Odom, 1986). Correlates of PRA can be categorized into nonbehavioral and behavioral aspects of a child or the child's behavior. Nonbehavioral correlates are those factors that are not subject to direct intervention, such as gender, age, race, and name (McConnell & Odom, 1986). Behavioral correlates are under direct control of environmental variables and usually are more amenable to change (e.g., social knowledge, social skills, verbal skills). A brief discussion of these correlates is provided in the following sections.

Nonbehavioral Correlates

Several variables related to a child's standing on a PRA measure have little, if anything, to do with the child's behavior. For example, a child's gender influences sociometric ratings when cross-sex sociometrics are used (Asher & Hymel, 1981). That is, boys nominate girls less often than they nominate other boys for play or friendship nominations, and vice versa.

Physical attractiveness represents another variable influencing sociometric ratings of children, particularly for females. Vaughn and Langlois (1983) found that physical attractiveness was correlated with a paired-comparison sociometric. This correlation, however, was produced by the strong relationship between attractiveness and peer acceptance for females. Correlations between males' physical attractiveness and peer acceptance most often have been nonsignificant (Dion & Berscheid, 1974; McConnell & Odom, 1986; Vaughn & Langlois, 1983).

Other researchers have found relationships between children's names and sociometric status. Foster (1983) indicated that unusual or infrequent names are associated with lower sociometric status. McDavid and Harari (1966) showed that children with unusual names resulted in lower peer acceptance across a number of children's groups.

Relationships have been found between a child's race and acceptance in peer groups. Singleton and Asher (1979) found significant preferences for same-race peers (black versus white) in racially integrated schools. In addition, these same-race preferences tended to increase with age, especially for black children. Gresham and Reschly (1987) found an interaction between children's race (black versus white) and group membership as mildly handicapped or nonhandicapped. Using cross-race PRA methods (i.e., peer ratings and structured peer assessments), Gresham and Reschly showed that white, nonhandicapped students had higher peer acceptance scores than black, nonhandicapped students, whereas black, mildly handicapped students had higher acceptance scores than black, nonhandicapped students. This interaction was interpreted as reflecting greater discrepancies in academic achievement between white, nonhandicapped and mildly handicapped students relative to black, nonhandicapped and mildly handicapped students.

A final class of nonbehavioral variables influencing peer acceptance is setting variables in which PRA measures are collected. Perhaps the largest body of literature on this topic is in the special education literature that has investigated the sociometric status of mainstreamed handicapped children compared to nonhandicapped children. One of the most consistent findings in this literature is the lower sociometric status of mainstreamed handicapped children relative to their nonhandicapped peers (Asher & Taylor, 1981; Gresham, 1981, 1982; Madden & Slavin, 1983). Interpretations of this finding are difficult, because interactions between a child's handicapping condition, social behavior, teacher attitudes, and numerous unmeasured variables affect sociometric scores to an unknown degree.

Behavioral Correlates

Behavioral correlates of PRA have received the lion's share of research in the social competence assessment literature. Several researchers have found that popular children, as defined by sociometric assessment, engage in more social interactions than unpopular children. Direct observations of popular and unpopular children have demonstrated that the former group is more likely to contribute relevant conversation during play (Putallaz, 1983), engage in parallel functional play (Rubin & Daniels-Bierness, 1983), receive and initiate more social behavior judged to have positive affect (Dodge, 1983), and use effective peer group entry strategies (Dodge, Schlundt, Schocken, & Delugack, 1983). Furthermore, peer assessment data have shown that popular children are viewed as leaders and as being more cooperative than unpopular children when in familiar groups (Coie & Kupersmidt, 1983).

One of the most consistent findings in this area of research is that children classified as *rejected* display higher levels of aggressive or acting-out behavior than children not classified as rejected (Coie & Kupersmidt, 1983; Dodge, 1983; Ladd, 1981; Rubin, 1982). In contrast, children classified as *neglected* tend to exhibit behavioral characteristics typical in internalizing behavior disorders such as shy, anxious, and social withdrawn social behaviors (Coie, 1985).

In studies using teacher ratings and direct observations, rejected children also have been reported to display more inattentive, hyperactive, and disruptive behavior than other sociometric groups (Dodge et al., 1983; Green, Vosk, Forehand, & Beck, 1981; Vosk, Forehand, Parker, & Rickard, 1982). Rejected children receive more negative responses from peers than other children (Dodge, 1983; Gresham, 1982). The chance for receiving negative responses from peers is greater for the rejected children even when they emit the same behaviors as do popular children (Coie, 1985).

Children of low sociometric status have been reported to be poorer academic achievers relative to children who are average or above average in peer acceptance. Coie (1985) suggested, however, that the correlations between academic performance and social standing are between .20 and .40, suggesting that many children with problems in peer acceptance do not exhibit academic deficiencies. Generally, research has shown that children rated low in both social and academic areas were more disruptive and more aggressive and displayed more inappropriate social behavior than high achievers (Bursuck & Asher, 1986; Coie & Krehbiel, 1984; Krehbiel, 1983).

In a comprehensive investigation of behavioral correlates of sociometric status, Frentz, Gresham, and Elliott (in press) found that early adolescents classified as rejected tended to exhibit higher levels of conduct disorder, attention problems, and social withdrawal on the Revised Behavior Problem Checklist (Quay & Peterson, 1983) than children classified as popular. Also, rejected adolescents were rated by teachers as having poorer social skills, lower academic achievement, and less self-control than popular adolescents. No differences on the above measures were found between popular, neglected, and controversial sociometric status groups.

In summary, behavioral correlates of sociometric status and peer assessments suggest that children and adolescents who are actively rejected from the peer group display characteristics of externalizing behavior problems (e.g., fighting, aggressive behavior, disruptive behavior, hyperactive behavior) and lower levels of social skills than nonrejected groups. Children who are neglected or socially isolated tend to display characteristics of internalizing or overcontrolled behaviors such as shyness, anxiety, and social withdrawal. Although there have been many studies in the PRA literature using somewhat differing terminologies regarding sociometric status, the most consistent findings regarding behavioral correlates of sociometric status have been with children and adolescents classified as rejected, neglected, or popular.

CLASSIFICATION OF SOCIOMETRIC TYPES

Several systems exist for classifying children on the basis of sociometric assessment into sociometric subtypes. Differentiation of sociometric subtypes provides potentially useful information for selecting groups for social skills training, studying behavioral correlates of different sociometric statuses, and predicting outcomes for children with various sociometric groups.

Peery (1979) developed a classification system for preschoolers using positive and negative peer nominations. In this system, *social preference* and *social impact* are used to derive four sociometric subgroups. Social preference is defined as the difference between the number of positive and negative peer nominations, and social impact is defined as the sum of positive and negative peer nominations. In Peery's system, four sociometric subgroups are formed: *Isolated* (negative social preference and low social impact), *Rejected* (negative social preference and high social impact), *Amiable* (positive social preference and low social impact), and *Popular* (positive social preference and high social impact).

Peery's (1979) system was modified by Coie et al. (1982) and developed for elementary-age students. Coie et al. used standardized (z scores) rather than raw scores to calculate "liked most" and "liked least" scores, which are combined to form the dimensions of social preference and social impact. In this system, children in classrooms are asked to select from class rosters three peers they like most and three peers they like least. For each child, all nominations are summed to form like most (LM) and liked least (LL) scores, which are standardized within grades. These scores are used to calculate *social preference* (SP) and *social impact* (SI) scores. Social preference is defined as LM−LL, and social impact is defined as LM+LL. Based on combinations of these scores, five sociometric groups are formed: *Popular* (positive SP, high SI), *Rejected* (negative SP and high SI), Neglected (negative SP and low SI), *Controversial* (mixed SP and high SI), and *Average* (means of SP and SI dimensions).

To eliminate the use of negative peer nominations, Asher and Dodge (1986) used a combination of positive nominations and peer ratings to classify sociometric status groups. This procedure involved calculating LM scores as in the Coie et al. (1982) system and using ratings from a 5-point Likert-type scale to substitute for negative peer nominations. A rating of 1 on the Likert-type scale was equated with negative nominations, and these values were substituted into the Coie et al. (1982) formula. This system corresponds highly to the original method, with 91% of children being correctly classified as rejected. However, this system was only 53% accurate in classifying neglected children and even less accurate in classifying controversial children.

The Coie et al. (1982) system was criticized by Newcomb and Bukowski (1984), primarily on the grounds of standardizing nomination data. Newcomb and Bukowski argued that there is little evidence to suggest that nomination data are normally distributed, thereby making scores calculated from nominations misleading. These authors advocated using a probability level to determine what raw scores are at or below a given chance level based on group size and the number of nominations requested. Using this modification, rejected children have rare LL scores and LM scores at or below the mean, whereas popular children have rare LM scores and LL scores at or below the mean. Neglected children have rare SI scores, controversial children have rare LM and LL score, and average children have SI, LM, and LL scores at or above chance levels.

Comparisons among the Peery (1979), Coie et al.

(1982), and Newcomb and Bukowski (1984) systems showed that the Peery system could not classify 12%, the Coie et al. system could not classify 48%, and the Newcomb and Bukowski system could classify all subjects into the various sociometric subgroups. Using a 5-week test-retest interval, Newcomb and Bukowski found that the Peery system was least stable (agreement = 54%), followed by the Coie et al. system (agreement = 61%), and Newcomb and Bukowski system (agreement = 71%). In all systems, the neglected category was the least stable (28%, 33%, and 40%, respectively).

ETHICAL ISSUES IN PRA

Past discussions of PRA have not emphasized the potential of ethical concerns involved in collecting potentially sensitive assessment information from a child's peers. There are three areas of primary concern involving the use of PRA techniques:

1. parental permission,
2. child permission, and
3. use of negative peer nominations.

Each of these will be discussed in the following sections.

Parental Permission

Informed consent forms the basis of all ethical research with human subjects. Assessment techniques involving child participants require particular attention to the informed consent ethical principles. The general procedure followed when using child participants is to seek informed consent from parents for child participation. Little is known about the effects of informed consent on PRA. Wicker (1968) found that parents who are in professional or managerial occupations whose children have IQs above 100 are more likely to give consent for child participation in research projects than are parents in lower status occupations. Obviously, this affects the representativeness of a sample upon which PRA is based.

The meaning of informed consent for PRA is nebulous. For example, if a parent does not grant permission for a child to participate, does this mean that the child cannot provide a rating or nominations for peers, or does it mean that peers cannot provide rating or nominations for the target child? To date, there is no clear ethical answer to this question.

Another issue in PRA is whether or not parental consent is necessary. The majority of PRAs are conducted in school classrooms where numerous assessments are conducted daily by teachers who are constantly evaluating students' social or emotional and academic behaviors. It could be argued that PRA data constitute a part of normal pupil appraisal and, thus, parental consent is not imperative. To make this argument, however, it is essential to ensure confidentiality of assessment results and documentation of PRA as a minimal-risk procedure.

We recommend that results of PRAs be treated in the same manner as any other assessment procedure. PRA differs from individual assessment data, because the source of the data is the child's peers rather than the child. It is important to recognize that results of PRA procedures do not become part of the child's official school record unless there is a documented need for the PRA results.

Child Permission

Concerns similar to those of parental consent involve the role of the child in providing consent to participate in peer-referenced assessments. The major question one must ask is whether the child, considering the fact that he or she is a minor by law, is entitled to the same rights adults have for informed consent, or do we defer consent to the parents? This is a difficult question to answer and one for which there is no clear answer. It is probably advisable to obtain written consent from parents first, but in turn to allow the child the right to veto that consent. The one exception to this is if peer-referenced assessment strategies were part of a complete evaluation for the purpose of establishing a handicapping condition, in which case the right to a "free, appropriate, public education" may supersede the right to individual child consent.

Giving children the opportunity to refuse participation in peer-referenced assessments may bias assessment results. To date, research addressing this issue is minimal. It seems logical to assume, however, that refusal to participate is not a random process leading to a less-than-valid sociometric rating of the peer group. In a 1977 study with high school seniors, Lueptow, Mueller, Hammes, and Master (1977) found that nonconsenting students had lower intelligence test scores and grades than did consenting students. They also compared consent rates before and after the establishment of ethical guidelines and found a 100% consent rate when the project was presented as a requirement versus a voluntary consent rate of 69.7% and 42.4% for students 18 and over and younger than 18, respectively. In a more recent study comparing consenters and nonconsenters, Severson and Ary (1983) looked at self-reported alcohol, cigarette, and marijuana use among a group of seventh graders. Results indicated that both cigarette and marijuana smoking were related to consent rate, with smokers being more disproportionately represented than nonconsenters. It seems clear, then, that allowing children the opportunity to consent to participate may bias a sample and influence the validity of the results.

Use of Negative Peer Nominations

Possibly the most controversial aspect of peer-referenced assessment techniques is the use of negative nominations. As discussed in a previous section, peer nominations frequently involve children indicating those peer group members whom they do not like. The idea of having children elicit negative choices is sometimes disturbing to parents, teachers, and review committees. Opposition to negative ratings is based on the fear that it will lead to overt social rejection in the classroom as well as affective responses on the part of the child being rated (e.g., withdrawal, lower self-esteem).

Although a great deal of concern has been raised in the past, only one empirical study to date addresses this issue. Hayvren and Hymel (1984) asked two groups of preschool children to identify liked and disliked playmates and then observed their behavior 10 minutes after this assessment. One group was also observed 2 weeks before and 2 weeks after the assessment. Their results indicated that although some children did talk about the assessment at 10 minutes after assessment, the verbalizations were mainly concerning their choice of liked peers, or they made only general comments. No comments were made with regard to disliked peers. With regard to interactional behavior, the authors observed no differences in subjects' interaction patterns from the pretest to posttest.

It appears that negative peer nominations do not have the dire consequences predicted by some individuals. This is important in the use of sociometric measures, as research has consistently found that negative ratings are not simply the opposite of positive ones (Asher & Hymel, 1981). Using negative peer nominations allows distinctions between accepted and rejected peers as well as identification of neglected children (i.e., those who receive few, if any, positive or negative nominations). This distinction could not be made from positive nominations alone.

In spite of indications that negative nominations do not produce deleterious effects, there remains some hesitancy in using these procedures. As a result, some individuals have proposed alternate procedures to distinguish between neglected and rejected children. Ladd (1983) suggests having the teacher make the distinction between subtypes of unpopular children. Although this may be one alternative approach, data are needed on agreement rates between teacher classifications and peer nominations. This is especially important in light of Ladd's finding that teachers were less confident in their ability to identify neglected as opposed to rejected children.

Although it is important to acknowledge the concerns that individuals have raised concerning the ethics of using negative peer nominations, it appears that negative peer nominations are an appropriate and worthwhile technique to use in sociometric assessment. One should, however, be very careful to ensure the confidentiality of negative assessment data.

SUMMARY

There is much evidence to support the use of PRA in assessing social competence of children and adolescents. Our conception of the construct validity of PRA is based on the nomological network surrounding PRA strategies. Clearly, there are behavioral and nonbehavioral connections in this nomological network supporting the construct of peer social status. Perhaps more importantly, PRA has social validity in terms of selecting individuals for social skills training and documenting the effects of social skills training programs.

Given the wide variation in PRA methods, researchers and practitioners should be careful when selecting a given assessment strategy. Nominations, ratings, and peer assessment strategies may yield different information for different purposes with varying degrees of reliability and validity. Hopefully, this chapter has presented important features of each method to guide selection of a given assessment methodology.

Little has been written to date on the ethics of PRA. Unlike individual assessments, PRA has the potential of violating confidentiality principles by the "public" nature of these assessments. Procedural safeguards can be built into PRA to ensure that confidentiality is not violated and that potential deleterious side effects are minimized. Combined with other established methods for assessing social competence, PRA data provides a unique view of the behavioral and nonbehavioral effects a child has in a social environment.

REFERENCES

Altman, E., & Gotlib, I. (1988). The social behavior of depressed children: An observational study. *Journal of Abnormal Child Psychology, 16,* 29–44.

American Psychological Association (1985). *Standards for educational and psychological testing.* Washington, DC: Author.

American Psychological Association (1990). Ethical principles of psychologists. *American Psychologist, 45,* 390–395.

Anastasi, A. (1988). *Psychological testing* (6th ed.). New York: Macmillan.

Asarnow, J. (1988). Peer status and social competence in child psychiatric inpatients: A comparison of children with depressive, externalizing, and concurrent depressive and externalizing disorders. *Journal of Abnormal Child Psychology, 16,* 151–162.

Asher, S. (1985). An evolving paradigm in social skill training research with children. In B. Schneider, K. Rubin, & J. Ledingham (Eds.), *Children's peer relations: Issues in assessment and intervention* (pp. 157–171). New York: Springer-Verlag.

Asher, S., & Dodge K. (1986). Identifying children who are rejected by their peers. *Developmental Psychology, 22,* 444–449.

Asher, S. R., & Hymel, S. (1981). Children's social competence in peer relations: Sociometric and behavioral assessment. In J. D. Wine & M. D. Smye (Eds.), *Social competence.* New York: Guilford Press.

Asher, S. R., & Taylor, A. R. (1981). Social outcomes of mainstreaming: Sociometric assessment and beyond. *Exceptional Education Quarterly, 1,* 13–30.

Asher, S. R., Singleton, L. C., Tinsley, B. R., & Hymel, S. (1979). A reliable sociometric measure for preschool children. *Developmental Psychology, 15,* 443–444.

Bailey, J. A., & Pierce, K. A. (1975). The Friendship Rating Scale: A sociometric instrument. *Elementary School Guidance and Counseling, 9,* 218–225.

Bonney, M. E. (1943). The relative stability of social, intellectual, and academic status in grades II to IV, and the interrelationships between various forms of growth. *Journal of Educational Psychology, 34,* 88–102.

Bower, E. M. (1960). *Early identification of emotionally handicapped children in school.* Springfield, IL: Charles C Thomas.

Brown, L. L., & Hammill, D. D. (1983). *Behavior Rating Profile.* Austin, Texas: Pro-Ed.

Burns, E. (1974). Reliability and transitivity of pair-comparison sociometric responses of retarded and nonretarded subjects. *American Journal of Mental Deficiency, 78,* 482–485.

Bursuck, W. D., & Asher, S. R. (1986). The relationship between social competence and achievement in elementary school children. *Journal of Clinical Child Psychology, 15,* 41–49.

Busk, P. L., Ford, R. C., & Shulman, J. L. (1973). Stability of sociometric responses in classrooms. *The Journal of Genetic Psychology, 123,* 69–84.

Cohen, A. S., & Van Tassel, E. A. (1978). A comparison of partial and complete paired comparisons in sociometric measurement of preschool groups. *Applied Psychological Measurement, 2,* 31–40.

Coie, J. D. (1985). Fitting social skill intervention to the target group. In B. Schneider, K. Rubin, & J. Ledingham (Eds.), *Children's peer relations: Issues in assessment and intervention* (pp. 141–156). New York: Springer-Verlag.

Coie, J. D., & Krehbiel, G. (1984). Effects of academic tutoring on the social status of a low-achieving socially rejected child. *Child Development, 55,* 1465–1478.

Coie, J. D., & Kupersmidt, J. B. (1983). Behavioral analysis of emerging social status in boys' groups. *Child Development, 54,* 1400–1416.

Coie, J. D., Dodge, K. A., & Coppotelli, H. (1982). Dimensions and types of social status: A cross-age perspective. *Developmental Psychology, 18,* 557–570.

Cronbach, L. J., & Meehl, P. E. (1955). Construct validity in psychological tests. *Psychological Bulletin, 52,* 281–302.

Dion, K. K., & Bersheid, E. (1974). Physical attractiveness and peer perception among children. *Sociometry, 37,* 1–12.

Dodge, K. A. (1983). Behavioral antecedents of peer social status. *Child Development, 54,* 1386–1399.

Dodge, K. A., Schlundt, D. C., Schocken, I., & Delugack, J. D. (1983). Social competence and children's sociometric status: The role of peer group entry strategies. *Merrill-Palmer Quarterly, 29,* 309–336.

Dygdon, J. A. (1988). Peer-based assessment in the study of children's social competence and social skills. In M. Hersen, R. M. Eisler, & P. M. Miller (Eds.), *Progress in behavior modification.* Vol. 23. (pp. 165–207). Newbury Park, CA: Sage Publications.

Dygdon, J. A., Conger, A., & Keane, S. (1987). Behavioral correlates of social acceptance, rejection, and neglect in children: Peer perceptions. *Journal of Clinical Child Psychology, 16,* 2–8.

Foster, S. L. (1983, May). *The nature and recognition of stimulus cues in social situations.* Paper presented at the ninth annual meeting of the Association for Behavior Analysis.

Foster, S. L., & Ritchey, W. L. (1979). Issues in the assessment of social competence in children. *Journal of Applied Behavior Analysis, 12,* 625–638.

Foster, S. L., & Ritchey, W. L. (1985). Behavioral correlates of sociometric status for fourth-, fifth-, and sixth-grade children in two classroom situations. *Behavioral Assessment, 7,* 79–93.

Foster, S. L., Bell-Dolan, D., & Berler, E. S. (1986). Methodological issues in the use of sociometrics for selecting children for social skills research and training. In R. J. Prinz (Ed.), *Advances in behavioral assessment*

of children and families (Vol. 2, pp. 227–248). Greenwich, CT: JAI Press.
Frentz, C., Gresham, F. M., & Elliott, S. N. (in press). Popular, controversial, neglected, and rejected adolescents: Contrasts of social competence and achievement differences. *Journal of School Psychology*.
Gelb, R., & Jacobson, J. (1988). Popular and unpopular children's interactions during cooperative and competitive peer group activities. *Journal of Abnormal Child Psychology, 16*, 347–361.
Gottlieb, J. (1981). Mainstreaming: Fulfilling the promise. *American Journal of Mental Deficiency, 86*, 115–126.
Gottlieb, J., Semmel, M., & Veldman, D. (1978). Correlates of social status among mainstreamed mentally retarded children. *Journal of Educational Psychology, 70*, 396–405.
Gottman, J. M. (1977). Toward a definition of social isolation in children. *Child Development, 48*, 512–517.
Green, K. D., Vosk, B., Forehand, R., & Beck, S. (1981). An examination of differences among sociometrically identified accepted, rejected, and neglected children. *Child Study Journal, 11*, 117–124.
Gresham, F. M. (1981). Validity of social skills measures for assessing social competence in low status children: A multivariate investigation. *Developmental Psychology, 17*, 390–398.
Gresham, F. M. (1982). Misguided mainstreaming: The case for social skills training with handicapped children. *Exceptional Children, 48*, 420–433.
Gresham, F. M. (1983). Social validity in the assessment of children's social skills: Establishing standards for social competency. *Journal of Psychoeducational Assessment, 1*, 299–307.
Gresham, F. M. (1986). Conceptual issues in the assessment of social competence in children. In P. Strain, M. Guralnick, & H. Walker (Eds.), *Children's social behavior: Development, assessment, and modification* (pp. 143–179). Orlando, FL: Academic Press.
Gresham, F. M., & Elliott, S. N. (1990). *Social Skills Rating System*. Circle Pines, MN: AGS.
Gresham, F. M., & Nagle, R. J. (1980). Social skills training with children: Responsiveness to modeling and coaching as a function of peer orientation. *Journal of Consulting and Clinical Psychology, 48*, 718–729.
Gresham, F. M., & Reschley, D. J. (1988). Social skills and peer acceptance in the mildly handicapped. In T. Kratochwill (Ed.), *Advances in school psychology* (pp. 203–247). Hillsdale, NJ: Lawrence Erlbaum Associates.
Gresham, F. M., & Reschly, D. J. (1987). Sociometric differences between mildly handicapped and nonhandicapped black and white students. *Journal of Educational Psychology, 79*, 195–197.
Gronlund, N. E. (1959). *Sociometry in the classroom*. New York: Harper.
Hammill, D. D., Brown, L., & Bryant, B. R. (1989). *A consumer's guide to tests in print*. Austin, Texas: Pro-Ed.

Hartshorne, H., May, M. A., & Maller, J. B. (1929). *Studies in the nature of character. II. Studies in service and self-control*. New York: Macmillan.
Hayvren, M., & Hymel, S. (1984). Ethical issues in sociometric testing: Impact of sociometric measure on interaction behavior. *Developmental Psychology, 20*, 844–849.
Hersh, R. H., & Walker, H. M. (1983). Great expectations: Making schools effective for all students. *Policy Studies Review, 2*, 147–188.
Johnston, C., Pelham, W. E., Crawford, J. J., & Atkins, M. S. (1988). A psychometric study of positive and negative nominations and the Pupil Evaluation Inventory. *Journal of Abnormal Child Psychology, 16*, 617–626.
Kane, J. S., & Lawler, E. E. (1978). Three methods of peer assessment. *Psychological Bulletin, 85*, 555–586.
Koch, H. J. (1933). Popularity in preschool children: Some related factors and a technique for its measurement. *Child Development, 4*, 164–175.
Krehbiel, G. (1983). *Sociometric status and academic achievement-based differences in behavior and peer-assessed reputation*. Unpublished manuscript, Duke University.
Ladd, G. (1985). Documenting the effects of social skills training with children: Process and outcome assessment. In B. Schneider, K. Rubin, & J. Ledingham (Eds.), *Children's peer relations: Issues in assessment and intervention* (pp. 243–269). New York: Springer-Verlag.
Ladd, G. W. (1981). Effectiveness of a social learning method for enhancing children's social interaction and peer acceptance. *Child Development, 52*, 171–178.
Ladd, G. W. (1983). Social networks of popular, average, and rejected children in school settings. *Merrill-Palmer Quarterly, 29*, 283–307.
Ladd, G., & Mize, J. (1983). A cognitive-social learning model of social-skill training. *Psychological Review, 90*, 127–157.
LaGreca, A. M., & Santogrossi, D. (1980). Social skills training with elementary school students: A behavioral group approach. *Journal of Consulting and Clinical Psychology, 48*, 226–227.
Lefkowitz, M., & Testiny, E. (1980). Assessment of childhood depression. *Journal of Consulting and Clinical Psychology, 48*, 43–50.
Libert, J., & Lewinsohn, P. (1973). Concept of social skills with special reference to the behavior of depressed persons. *Journal of Consulting and Clinical Psychology, 40*, 304–312.
Lueptow, L., Mueller, S. A., Hammes, R. R., & Master, L. S. (1977). The impact of informed consent regulations on response rate and response bias. *Sociological Methods and Research, 6*, 183–203.
Madden, N. M., & Slavin, R. E. (1983). Mainstreaming students with mild handicaps: Academic and social outcomes. *Review of Educational Research, 53*, 519–569.
McConnell, S. R., & Odom, S. L. (1986). Sociometrics: Peer-referenced measures and the assessment of social

competence. In P. Strain, M. Guralnick, & H. Walker (Eds.), *Children's social behavior: Development, assessment, and modification.* Orlando, FL: Academic Press.

McDavid, J. W., & Harari, H. (1966). Stereotyping of names and popularity in gradeschool children. *Child Development, 37,* 453–459.

McFall, R. (1982). A review and reformulation of the concept of social skills. *Behavioral Assessment, 4,* 1–33.

Milich R., Landau, S., Kilby, G., & Whitten, P. (1982). Preschool peer perceptions of the behavior of hyperactive and aggressive children. *Journal of Abnormal Child Psychology, 10,* 497–510.

Moore, S. G., & Updegraff, R. (1964). Sociometric status of preschool children as related to age, sex, nuturance-giving and dependency. *Child Development, 35,* 519–524.

Moreno, J. L. (1934). *Who shall survive? A new approach to the problem of human interrelations.* New York: Beacon House.

Morrison, G., MacMillan, D., & Forness, S. (1983). Influences on the sociometric ratings of mildly handicapped children: A path analysis. *Journal of Educational Psychology, 75,* 63–74.

Morrison, G. M. (1981). Sociometric measurement: Methodological considerations of its use with mildly learning handicapped and nonhandicapped children. *Journal of Educational Psychology, 73,* 193–201.

Newcomb, A. F., & Bukowski, W. M. (1984). A longitudinal study of the utility of social preference and social impact sociometric classification schemes. *Child Development, 55,* 1434–1447.

Northway, M. L. (1969). The stability of young children's social relationships. *Educational Research, 11,* 54–57.

Oden, S., & Asher, S. (1977). Coaching children in social skills for friendship making. *Child Development, 48,* 496–506.

Odom, S. L., & DuBose, R. F. (1981). *Peer rating assessments of integrated preschool classes: Stability and concurrent validity of the measures and the efficacy of the peer model.* Paper presented at the National Convention for the Council for Exceptional Children, New York.

Pack, P. L., & McCaffrey, L. G. (1976). A sociometric technique for use with moderately or severely retarded persons. *Journal of Group Psychotherapy, Psychodrama, and Sociometry, 29,* 127–129.

Parker, J., & Asher, S. (1987). Peer relations and later personal adjustment: Are low-accepted children at risk? *Psychological Bulletin, 102,* 357–389.

Peery, J. C. (1979). Popular, amiable, isolated, rejected: A reconceptualization of sociometric status in preschool children. *Child Development, 50,* 1231–1234.

Pekarik, E. G., Prinz, R. J., Leibert, D. E., Weintraub, S., & Neale, J. M. (1976). The Pupil Evaluation Inventory: A sociometric technique for assessing children's social behavior. *Journal of Abnormal Child Psychology, 4,* 83–97.

Putallaz, M. (1983). Predicting children's sociometric status from their behavior. *Child Development, 54,* 1417–1426.

Quay, H. C., & Peterson, D. R. (1983). *Revised Behavior Problem Checklist.* Coral Gables, FL: Author. (University of Miami)

Reschly, D. J., & Gresham, F. M. (1988). Adaptive behavior and the mildly handicapped. In T. Kratochwill (Ed.), *Advances in school psychology* (pp. 249–282). Hillsdale, NJ: Lawrence Erlbaum.

Roff, M., Sells, B., & Golden, M. M. (1972). *Social adjustment and personality development in children.* Minneapolis: University of Minnesota Press.

Roistacher, R. C. (1974). A microeconomic model of sociometric choice. *Sociometry, 37,* 219–238.

Rubin, K. H. (1982). Non-social play in preschoolers: Necessary evil? *Child Development, 53,* 651–657.

Rubin, K. H. & Daniels-Beirness, T. (1983). Concurrent and predictive correlates of sociometric status in kindergarten and grade one children. *Merrill-Palmer Quarterly, 29,* 337–352.

Severson, H. H., & Ary, D. V. (1983). Sampling bias due to consent procedures with adolescents. *Addictive Behaviors, 8,* 433–437.

Shapiro, S. B., & Sobel, M. (1981). Two multinominal random sociometric voting models. *Journal of Educational Statistics, 6,* 287–310.

Singleton, L. C., & Asher, S. R. (1979). Peer preferences and social interaction among third-grade children in an integrated school district. *Journal of Educational Psychology, 69,* 330–336.

Strauss, C., Lahey, B., Frick, P., Frame, C., & Hynd, G. (1988). Peer social status of children with anxiety disorders. *Journal of Consulting and Clinical Psychology, 56,* 137–141.

Thompson, G. G., & Powell, M. (1951). An investigation of the rating-scale approach to the measurement of social status. *Educational and Psychological Measurement, 11,* 440–455.

Vaughn, B. E., & Langlois, J. H. (1983). Physical attractiveness as a correlate of peer status and social competence in preschool children. *Developmental Psychology, 19,* 561–567.

Vaughn, B. E., & Waters, E. (1981). Attention structure, sociometric status, and dominance: Interrelations, behavioral correlates, and relationships to social competence. *Developmental Psychology, 17,* 275–288.

Vosk, B., Forehand, R., Parker, J. B., & Rickard, K. (1982). A multimethod comparison of popular and unpopular children. *Developmental Psychology, 18,* 571–575.

Whalen, C., & Henker, B. (1984). Hyperactivity and attention deficit disorder: Expanding frontiers. *The Pediatric Clinics of North America, 31,* 397–427.

Wicker, A. W. (1968). Requirements for protecting privacy of human subjects: Some implications for generalization of research findings. *American Psychologist, 23,* 70–72.

Wiggins, J. S., & Winder, C. L. (1961). The Peer Nomination Inventory: An empirically derived sociometric measure of adjustment in preadolescent boys. *Psychological Reports, 9,* 643–677.

Willingham, W. W. (1959). On deriving standard scores for peer nominations with sub-groups of unequal size. *Psychological Reports, 5,* 397–403.

Wolf, M. M. (1978). Social validity: The case for subject measurement or how applied behavior analysis is finding its heart. *Journal of Applied Behavior Analysis, 11,* 203–214.

Zammuto, R. F., London, M., & Rowland, K. M. (1982). Organization and rater differences in performance appraisals. *Personnel Psychology, 35,* 643–658.

CHAPTER 12

PHYSIOLOGICAL ASSESSMENT

Neville J. King

Of all the domains of child assessment, one of the most challenging and rapidly growing is that of physiological assessment. However, the notion of physiological data contributing to the overall assessment of the child and helping in the design of effective treatments is by no means a recent development. As early as the 1920s, Mary Cover Jones recognized the significance of monitoring physiological responses (Jones, 1924). In her now classic case study of a young phobic boy, Jones found that the boy's blood pressure increased when he was exposed to a fear-eliciting stimulus. Thus, Jones concluded that "visceral arousal" was very much part of the child's fear response. On the basis of these findings, as well as behavioral observations, she developed a "deconditioning" program that was successful in alleviating the child of his phobic condition. However, since this early study, reports of physiological recordings have been sporadic in the clinical child literature. Thus, for many years, physiological data were of little interest compared to the more traditional sources of data such as the interview, self-report and psychological tests.

The resurgence of interest in physiological assessment that we are witnessing now can be attributed to several influences. "Organismic" factors (physiological and cognitive) play a key role in contemporary perspectives of behavioral assessment (e.g., Kanfer & Saslow, 1969; Lazarus, 1971; Molloy, 1984; Ollendick & Hersen, 1984). Focusing on anxiety and fears, for example, Lang (1977) has been a strong advocate of a tripartite analysis according to which aversive emotional states have subjective, visceral, and overt behavioral referents. Reflecting the influence of Lang and others, the preintervention assessment of anxiety-disordered children is comprehensive and cognizant of physiological measures (King, Hamilton, & Ollendick, 1988; Ollendick & Francis, 1988). Similarly, evaluations of fear-reduction programs entail measures reflective of these response systems or "channels" in children (Morris & Kratochwill, 1983).

Again illustrative of conceptual influences, the autonomic nervous system has been of interest to learning theorists for many years. In fact, operant conditioning procedures have been applied to responses mediated by the autonomic nervous system (Miller, 1969). Leaving aside the theoretical debate about the validity of such conditioning (Katkin & Murray, 1968), these efforts resulted in the development of a procedure that is commonly referred to as "biofeedback training." Popular in the treatment of many child disorders such as headaches and cerebral palsy (Varni, 1983), the aim of biofeedback training is to facilitate voluntary control or self-regulation over the targeted physiological response. However, the use of biofeedback once again calls for physiological assessment. Apart from the fact that the conditions under treatment may require medical and physiological assessment, biofeedback training is dependent on the monitoring of the targeted physiological response for its success. Recent decades have in fact seen many technological advances, such as physiological recording and computers, that have facilitated the growth of physiological assessment. With these kinds of conceptual and technological developments, it was inevitable that physiological assessment would become more prominent in child assessment.

It is now clear that the usefulness of physiological measures in the assessment of child disorders depends on several factors. Kallman and Feuerstein (1986) have noted three essential points. First, because of the complexity and expense of physiological recording instruments, physiological measures should provide information that cannot be obtained as efficiently by other means. In other words, consideration should be given to cost efficiency. Second, the physiological response should be uniquely related to the presenting disorder in such a way that the measure is of use in predicting and modifying behavior. In the clinic setting, for example, the physiological measure should contribute to the selection or implementation of an appropriate treatment strategy. Third, physiological measures must have an adequate degree of reliability and validity for their use. Thus, physiological assessment procedures should be empirically sound. In addition to the requirements outlined by Kallman and Feuerstein, physiological assessment must also be developmentally sensitive. The age of the subject has a bearing not only on the assessment procedure, but on the interpretation of data as well. Obviously, the physiological assessment of a child is markedly different from that of an adult. Furthermore, the physiological assessment of a 5-year-old is quite different from that of a 10-year-old and a 15-year-old. Above all, physiological data should be examined in conjunction with other sources of information. Certainly, physiological data are not regarded as superior merely because they are obtained through the use of "scientific" instruments. These features of physiological assessment are consistent with the contemporary approach to child assessment, which emphasizes multi-method assessment, reliability and validity of measures, and developmental sensitivity (Mash & Terdal, 1981; Ollendick & Hersen, 1984).

The aim of this chapter is to show how physiological assessment contributes to the overall assessment of child disorders. Following a brief examination of the instrumentation and measures used with children, we focus on developmental factors. Thus, attention is drawn to the importance of the child's behavior during assessment, as well as the influence of age on physiological responding. Consistent with an empirical approach to the assessment of child disorders, we also examine the reliability and validity of physiological assessment. A further objective is to illustrate the application of physiological assessment in clinical work and research, and to outline some of the major methodological and conceptual issues in these endeavors. However, biochemical assessment is not discussed (see review by Zeichner, 1987).

INSTRUMENTATION AND MEASURES

The instrumentation used in physiological assessment has been nicely reviewed by Sturgis and Gramling (1988). The physiograph is still the basic instrument used in physiological assessment. With this instrument it is possible to monitor otherwise covert physiological events. Sturgis and Gramling point out that the equipment of interest in physiological assessment typically includes (a) electrodes or transducers that detect the signal; (b) the physiograph itself; (c) output devices including penwriters and oscilloscopes; and (d) integraters and other means of quantifying the output. Regarding the detection of the physiological response, electrodes are used when the response of interest involves a bioelectric signal (e.g., muscle activity). Although needle electrodes are used for specialist purposes, most physiological recording with children relies on surface electrodes. Nearly all electrodes used today are made of silver-silver chloride disks encased in a plastic housing; skin contact is made through a paste or jellylike substance capable of conducting electrical activity. Transducers are used in physiological assessment when the response of interest is in the form of physical or mechanical energy (e.g., strain gauge strapped around chest to monitor respiratory activity).

In addition to the physiograph, a great deal of physiological instrumentation is also commercially available, such as that developed for biofeedback training. Although biofeedback instrumentation has simplified physiological monitoring, some have expressed doubts about the understanding and use of the measures that have been taken (Sturgis & Gramling, 1988). Of course, there are many other physiological instruments, including portable recorders and telemetric devices, all of which increase the range of options available to the clinician in the physiological assessment of child disorders. However, physiological assessment requires technological expertise in electrode placement, equipment operation, and data quantification.

The most common physiological measures taken with children reflect activity in the musculoskeletal system, cardiovascular system, electrodermal system, respiratory system, and central nervous system. Excellent discussions of these physiological responses, covering their anatomy, physiology and measurement, can be found in other sources (e.g., Kallman & Feuerstein, 1986; Sturgis & Gramling, 1988). In brief, musculoskeletal activity has been subjected to different measures over the years, although the electromyogram (EMG) is the most frequently used in the assessment of muscular tension. Strictly speaking, the EMG is a recording of electrical activity in the muscle from which the level of muscular activity is inferred (Goldstein, 1972; Nietzel, Bernstein, & Russell, 1988). The muscles most frequently assessed include the frontalis (located in the forehead), the trapezius muscle (located in the shoulders), and the brachioradialus muscles (located in the lower arms) (Hassett, 1978; Sturgis & Arena, 1984). Because of the influence of other muscles, authorities warn against assigning the muscle of origin to the EMG recording. Although we tend to speak of frontalis EMG in the assessment of children, for example, this degree of specificity probably cannot be justified (Stern, Ray, & Davis, 1980).

The most common measures of cardiovascular activity in children include heart rate, blood pressure, and vasomotor activity. Of these, heart rate is the most common, as it is easily monitored and is less sensitive to extraneous influences (Nietzel et al., 1988). The electrical impulses associated with the beating heart yield a distinctive pattern that is recorded as the electrocardiogram (ECG or EKG). Blood pressure is usually reported in terms of systolic and diastolic blood pressure (expressed in millimeters of mercury, i.e., mm Hg). Diastolic blood pressure represents the force of the blood flow at the time the cardiac muscles relax and is considered to be the more sensitive of the blood pressures in the assessment of children (Nietzel et al., 1988). Vasomotor activity has been divided into two components: blood volume and blood volume pulse. Whereas blood volume represents the absolute level of blood in the tissue, the blood volume pulse refers to blood flow through the tissue with each cardiac contraction (Kallman & Feuerstein, 1986). As sympathetic arousal produces peripheral vasoconstriction and a reduction in blood supply to the extremities, skin temperature is yet another measure of physiological arousal.

Measures of electrodermal activity are also frequently used in the physiological assessment of children; the two most common measures of electrodermal activity are skin conductance and its reciprocal, skin resistance (Zeichner, 1987). Innervated by the sympathetic nervous system, the sweat glands have a direct influence on skin conductance and skin resistance. More specifically, increases in sweating produce increased conductance (decreased resistance). Consequently, measures of electrodermal activity are believed to be useful indices of autonomic arousal in children. As noted by Nietzel et al. (1988), the changes that occur after the presentation of a stimulus are referred to as elicited or evoked responses. However, changes in skin conductance may also occur in the absence of any specific stimulus presentations. These changes are called spontaneous or nonspecific fluctuations. Although these are less marked than evoked responses, they are considered to be a relatively valid measure of arousal (Nietzel et al., 1988). As pointed out by Stern et al. (1980), physiological recordings in general can be differentiated in terms of spontaneous activity, tonic activity (i.e., resting or background level of activity), and phasic activity (i.e., discrete physiological responses that are elicited by specific stimuli).

The use of physiological instrumentation and the above measures assumes an understanding of some basic processes and principles in physiology. Foremost of these is habituation, which is evident in the physiological responding of children. Habituation refers to the cessation or diminution of responding that occurs to the repeated presentation of the same stimulus (Stern et al., 1980). Illustratively, the presentation of an anxiety-provoking slide to a child will usually elicit a marked change in heart rate that eventually disappears as the child becomes accustomed to the stimulus through repeated exposures. Habituation is influenced by a number of factors, particularly the intensity of the stimulus. Thus, a very intense stimulus will produce a slower rate of habituation. This process can also be inhibited if the child is engaged in some kind of cognitive or behavioral activity. However, habituation does not occur equally across physiological systems (Sturgis & Gramling, 1988). For example, finger-pulse volume and blood volume have been found to decrease across habituation trials among anxious subjects in the absence of changes in electrodermal activity (O'Gorman, 1983).

Also evident in physiological assessment are the orienting and defensive responses. The orienting response is sometimes referred to as the "What is it?" reflex. As noted by Lynn (1966), the orienting response is characterized by a number of physiological changes, including increased sensitivity of the sense organs, increased muscle tone, activation of the electroencephalogram, peripheral vasoconstriction, cephalic vasodilation, increased skin conductance, and respiratory changes. More threatening stimuli are liekly to elicit a defensive response. In contrast to the orienting response, this response pattern is marked by a turning away from the stimulus as well as decreased sensitivity of the sense organs, vasoconstriction in the periphery and in the head, and increased heart rate. As noted by Sturgis and Gramling (1988), the defensive response is often exhibited by phobic subjects towards anxiety-provoking stimuli (Lang, Melamed, & Hart, 1970; Fredrikson, 1981; Hare & Blevings, 1975). The orienting and defensive responses have also been compared in terms of habituation. Not surprisingly from a survival viewpoint, the orienting response habituates quite rapidly, whereas the defensive response habituates far more slowly (Stern et al., 1980).

Often referred to in physiological studies, the law of initial values holds that the magnitude of elicited physiological responses is partly determined by the prestimulus or baseline level of activity (Wilder, 1950). For example, a child with a relatively low tonic heart rate may find it difficult to produce further decreases through relaxation training, compared to a child with a much higher tonic heart rate. Although the law of initial values seems to apply to most cardiovascular and vasomotor responses, it does not appear to be operative in other physiological systems such as electrodermal responses (Sturgis & Gramling, 1988). Nonetheless, the law of initial values should be considered in the evaluation of children's physiological responses in assessment and treatment. Further information on these principles can be found in other texts (Greenfield & Sternbach, 1972; Hassett, 1978; Sturgis & Arena, 1984; Sturgis & Gramling, 1988).

DEVELOPMENTAL FACTORS

Given their physical and cognitive abilities, children should not be expected to act like miniature adults during physiological assessment. In the physiological assessment of children suffering from headaches, for example, Blanchard and Andrasik (1985) have observed that children often exhibit fear and apprehension about equipment. This is particularly true in the case of obtrusive instrumentation such as the physiograph. Quite understandable in terms of what research findings have revealed about the fears of children (King, Ollier, Iacuone, Schuster, Bays, Gullone, & Ollendick, 1989; Ollendick, King, & Frary, 1989), many youngsters feel vulnerable and express worries about physical danger and harm (e.g., from receiving an electric shock). Blanchard and Andrasik (1985) also point out that children have a reduced ability to comprehend the rationale of the assessment procedures. Another problem concerns the resistive behaviors that children sometimes display towards personnel responsible for the attachment and removal of electrodes and transducers. Although these procedures are harmless, the skin preparations and resulting sensations can be irritating for children.

The adaptation period is an important part of physiological assessment. Sturgis and Arena (1984) have noted that the adaptation period provides the subject an opportunity to become familiar with the setting and thus allows for the stabilizaton of the physiological response being measured (tonic or resting level). In a review of the little research that has addressed the adaptation period (e.g., Meyers & Craighead, 1978), Sturgis and Arena concluded that adaptation rates appear to be different across the various physiological systems. Thus, as a conservative estimate, they maintain that a 13-minute adaptation period should be planned. However, maintaining the cooperation of children for these extended durations in the laboratory can be problematic, as they are apt to produce boredom and restlessness.

To some extent at least, these difficulties can be anticipated by the clinician. Age-appropriate explanations of the equipment and the purpose of the visits should be offered to children before assessment. As suggested by Blanchard and Andrasik (1985), videotaped demonstrations and a tour of the facilities before assessment are helpful in this respect. Having parents participate in the assessment procedure, while the child observes, is also a useful strategy in alleviating anxiety and gaining the trust of the child. For Blanchard and Andrasik, even "humorous" references to electric chairs and electric shock are discouraged, with electrodes being referred to as "sensors" and "pick-ups." Sometimes less threatening and intrusive options are possible in physiological assessment. For example, Sharpley and his colleagues examined heart rate reactivity in children to academic tasks in school attended by the children (Sharpley, Parsons, &

Tillinh, 1989). In this study, heart rate was monitored by a photoelectric pulse transducer attached to the earlobe and coupled to a personal computer. Other less threatening physiological assessment procedures have also been reported. Representative of these is the Palmar Sweat Index. This particular measure is a quantification of the sweat gland activity of the hand and is obtained through an impression of the skin (Dabbs, Johnson, & Leventhal, 1968; Johnson & Dabbs, 1967; Lore, 1966). Although lacking the precision of the physiograph, it has proved to be a useful physiological measure in the assessment of transitory anxiety in children (e.g., Johnson & Stockdale, 1975; Melamed & Siegel, 1975). Nonetheless, for ethical reasons, as well as seeking explicit cooperation from the child, the subject must still be adequately informed about the physiological measure before assessment.

Of course, we must also consider the influence of developmental factors in physiological responding. Illustratively, the potency of developmental factors is evident in the cardiac and electrodermal responses of children. In relation to tonic heart rate in children, both heart rate and heart rate variability decrease with age (Shinebourne, 1974). Furthermore, developmental influences are evident in the cardiac reactivity of children, as shown by the well-known "visual cliff" studies. Infants around 6 to 7 months display overt fear behavior and distress when exposed to a simulated cliff (Gibson & Walk, 1960; Schwartz, Campos, & Baisel, 1973). Before this critical stage of perceptual-motor development, infants exhibit exploratory behavior and cardiac deceleration in the presence of the "cliff" (orienting response). In contrast, the older infants who have reached this stage of development, and are obviously upset by exposure to the simulated cliff, demonstrate cardiac acceleration (defensive response). Not surprisingly, developmental changes in the cardiovascular response system are associated with complex age-related functional and morphological changes (Porges & Fox, 1986). More extensive reviews of developmental trends in cardiac activity can be found in other sources (e.g., Graham & Clifton, 1974; Porges & Fox, 1986; Venables, 1980).

Although the literature on electrodermal activity in infants and children is somewhat conflicting, developmental factors appear to have a bearing on the tonic and phasic activity of this physiological system (Edelberg, 1972; Venables, 1980). In a large cross-sectional study of children on the island of Mauritius, Venables and his colleagues found that a peak value of conductance level was reached at about 5 years (Venables, 1980). Although the generalizability of these data are uncertain, they are reminiscent of an early report in which few adult subjects showed as conductance levels as high as those of infants (Jones, 1935). Regarding evoked electrodermal responses, Janes, Hesselbrock, and Stern (1978) found that younger children were more responsive than older children on a variety of electrodermal responses. These differences were evident in conditioning, habituation, and spontaneous activity between trials. Morrow, Boring, Keough, and Haesly (1960) studied skin resistance conditioning in three groups of subjects—children, young adults, and aged adults. Although all three groups exhibited conditioning, age differences were observed in the magnitude of the responses. Underlying these developmental shifts are a set of physical changes related to sweat gland density and functioning (Porges & Fox, 1986). In sum, developmental factors appear to exert a profound influence on the electrodermal activity of children (Edelberg, 1982; Porges & Fox, 1986; Venables, 1980).

As already implied, other subject variables may influence the physiological responses of children. In a study on racial differences in autonomic responses, Janes, Worland, and Stern (1976) found that black children were more responsive in a vasomotor measure whereas white children were more responsive in skin potential. These differences were explained in terms of possible greater hydration in the skin of black children. No differences emerged for heart rate between the two groups. In a subsequent study, however, Janes and her colleagues found fewer racial differences than expected in measures of electrodermal activity (Janes et al., 1978). As pointed out by Sturgis and Arena (1984), data on possible sex differences in physiological response patterns are scarce (e.g., Murphy, Alpert, Willey, & Somes, 1988). However, the phases of the menstrual cycle might be expected to influence the physiological responding of girls, particularly in view of the varying levels of estrogen and progesterone secreted into the body (Wineman, 1971).

Looking at this complex state of affairs, what conclusions are to be drawn for the purposes of child assessment? As noted by Porges and Fox (1986), early development is marked by the maturation of the peripheral physiological systems, which become more "integrated" with central control systems. During the later years of life, the physiological systems exhibit various levels of attenuated output and dysfunction. In other words, the effect of age is biphasic. Thus in physiological assessment, we should examine how far an aspect of autonomic reactivity may be limited by the child's physiological development before considering alternate interpretations (Venables, 1980). Unfortunately for the clinician, this is not always a straightforward exercise, as there are insufficient normative data on the physiological responses of children. Of course, age-related norms are available in certain areas, such as tonic heart rate (Shinebourne, 1974). However, physiologists themselves have confirmed the general dearth of normative data and have called for prospective, longitudinal investigations (Venables, 1980). In the meantime, clinicians are required to make judgments about physiological responses on the basis of what limited data are available.

RELIABILITY AND VALIDITY

In light of the above considerations, it is not surprising that reliability and validity are of major concern in the physiological assessment of children. As Kallman and Feuerstein (1986) have emphasized, changes in physiological recording may not always be attributable to psychobiologically relevant stimuli. These kinds of changes are sometimes referred to as *artifacts*. We have already noted the susceptibility of the child to respond behaviorally and physiologically to novel stimuli, and consequent need for adaptation periods and repeated assessments. However, many other artifacts need to be controlled to obtain satisfactory reliability and validity.

Movement artifacts are a particular concern in the assessment of children, as any shift to the interface between the subject and the electrode will produce an artifact in the physiological recording. Given the likelihood of some movement, it is recommended that the child be closely observed so that movements preceding changes in the physiological recording can be noted. Kallman and Feuerstein (1986) point out that, in the case of small bioelectric signals (i.e., EMG or EEG), movement artifacts become crucial. Even eye blinks will produce changes in the EEG or frontalis muscle tension recording.

Turning to other kinds of artifacts, it has been found that transient electrical fields interfere with physiological recordings. Electrical interference may arise from fluorescent lights, AC power outlets and electromechanical equipment. This artifact can be controlled through electrically shielding the physiological laboratory, filtering, or grounding the child (see Kallman & Feuerstein, 1986; Stern et al., 1980). Furthermore, noise, light, and other sensory stimuli affect the physiological responding of the child. Thus, attention should be given to ambient sensory levels during physiological assessment. The ideal assessment environment would be electrically shielded, temperature-controlled, sound-treated, and illuminated at a constant level within and between assessment sessions (Kallman & Feuerstein, 1986).

In a similar vein, Sturgis and Arena (1984) have cautioned that the reliability of physiological measures is affected by many factors. Focusing on test-retest reliability of physiological measures, these authors believe that we should expect some degree of change in physiological reactivity over time. Test-retest reliability of physiological measures has been examined in several investigations with adults. Recently, Waters and his colleagues examined the test-retest reliability of a number of physiological measures to anger imagery, aversive slides, and other assessment procedures (Waters, Williamson, Bernard, Blouin, & Faulstich, 1987). Significant but modest correlations were found for skin conductance level and response, skin temperature, respiration rate, heart rate, and systolic blood pressure. Absolute scores were more often stable than change scores. However, the reliability of physiological measures with children must be examined empirically rather than assumed on the basis of adult studies.

Of course, problems in reliability also set limits for the validity of these measures (Sturgis & Arena, 1984). Typically, the validity of a physiological measure is evaluated on the basis of how well it correlates with other measures of the same construct. In the presence of an anxiety-provoking stimulus, for example, a child might exhibit an elevation in heart rate. The validity of this measure is frequently gauged through comparison with changes on other indices of cardiovascular reactivity (Beidel, 1988). At first glance, we might also expect to find a relationship between physiological measures and other measures (cognitive and overt behavioral) of the child's anxiety.

On monitoring the pulse rate of high school and college students preceding a regular course examination, Morris and Liebert (1970) found that increases in pulse rate were directly proportional to test anxiety scores. Thus, the more anxious the students were about tests, the greater the increases in heart rate. In contrast to these findings, Kutina and Fischer (1977) examined the relationship between heart rate data and other measures of anxiety in children undergoing neutral and stressful situations. A correlation was found between heart rate and scores on the Children's Manifest Anxiety Scale (Castaneda, McCandless, &

Palermo, 1956). However, this involved a negative correlation with high anxiety scores being associated with low heart rate. Overall, the correlations between physiological measures and other measures are typically low to moderate in nature, and inconsistently reported from study to study (Johnson & Melamed, 1979). Obviously, it is imperative that we more fully understand these relationships and underlying processes. As we shall find, there are many complexities relating to the issue of validity (see section entitled "Response Fractionation"). Crucial as they are to the physiological assessment of child disorders, reliability and validity await fuller articulation and psychometric evaluation.

APPLICATIONS

Of much interest from a diagnostic viewpoint are the physiological characteristics of children evincing emotional or behavioral disorders. Hyperactivity has been of particular interest in terms of physiological assessment. In an early study, Satterfield and Dawson (1971) found a lower skin conductance level and fewer spontaneous fluctuations in the electrodermal activity of hyperactive children relative to controls. Howevver, subsequent investigations have failed to replicate this finding (see review by Hastings and Barkley, 1978), and it is now believed that there are no differences in autonomic resting levels between hyperactive and nonhyperactive children. However, it appears to be fairly well established that hyperactive children show a deficiency in autonomic responding during a variety of tasks (e.g., Satterfield & Dawson, 1971). Zeichner (1987) has noted that the extent of the observed autonomic changes appear to be contingent on task and stimulus characteristics. Notwithstanding these promising developments, a recent review underlines the complexity of the physiological findings on hyperactivity (Zahn, 1986). Suffice it to say that these investigations have not yet produced a physiological marker for the differential diagnosis of hyperactivity.

In contrast to hyperactivity, there are many child disorders that have not been examined as thoroughly in terms of their physiological characteristics. Representative of these are the anxiety disorders of children. In a very recent study, however, Beidel (1988) examined the cardiovascular responses of test-anxious and non-test-anxious children when engaging in two social-evaluative tasks. These tasks were a timed vocabulary test and an oral reading session. The anxious children displayed significantly higher heart rates on these tasks than their nonanxious peers; however, there were no differences between the groups on systolic and diastolic blood pressure. Some interesting observations were also made concerning habituation. Not unexpectedly, the heart rate of the nonanxious children declined during the tasks as the children adapted to them. In contrast, the test-anxious children maintained a constant heart rate elevation. In other words, habituation was not as evident for the anxious children as the nonanxious children. These results are helpful to our understanding of the physiological reactivity of anxious children. It is now imperative that such physiological investigations be carried out with children meeting DSM-III-R or ICD-10 criteria.

Physiological monitoring has proved to be quite valuable in the assessment and treatment of child disorders. Many uncontrolled case studies involving physiological recording have been reported (e.g., Braud, Lupin, & Braud, 1975; Danquah, 1974; Duckro, Purcell, Gregory, & Schultz, 1985; Lang & Melamed, 1969). Lang and Melamed were successful in their physiological assessment of a 9-month-old infant who had been hospitalized because of persistent vomiting and severe weight loss. Although extensive medical tests showed there was no organic basis to the infant's illness, his condition was life-threatening and therefore of considerable urgency. Following unsuccessful attempts at dietary changes and mechanical maneuvers to improve the feeding situation, an aversive conditioning procedure was recommended as a last resort.

The infant was assigned a private room and closely observed for 2 days during and after normal feeding periods, and was found to reliably regurgitate most of his food intake within 10 minutes of each feeding. In an attempt to obtain a clearer physiological picutre of the infant's response, EMG activity under the chin and at other sites was recorded on a physiograph. This strategy was successful in identifying changes to the normal response pattern that were associated with vomiting. Confirmed by the observations of a nurse, these changes were usually preceded by sucking behavior. After two days of monitoring, the conditioning procedures were commenced.

As vomiting and other responses could be reliably tracked on the physiograph, it was possible to intervene at the optimum point in the vomiting sequence. Mild electric shock was initiated at the first sign of reverse peristalsis, but not during the preceding sucking behavior, since the latter represented a normal response. Typically, the nurse would signal as soon as she considered an emesis was beginning. If EMG changes confirmed this judgment, then shock was applied. Occasionally, the EMG would initiate this sequence with the observational judgment following. This procedure succeeded in producing crying in the infant, a response that was incompatible with the onset of vomiting. Consequently, the infant's ruminative vomiting was brought under control within a few sessions. The cessation of vomiting was accompanied by weight gains, increased activity, and general responsiveness, resulting in the discharge of the child from the hospital. Thus, physiological monitoring helped to objectify the presenting disorder, and along with other sources of information, ensured that the shocks were administered in a scientifically and ethically appropriate manner.

Single-case experimental analyses have also included physiological measures (e.g., Cataldo, Bird, & Cunningham, 1978; Finley, Niman, Standley, & Wansley, 1977; Hampstead, 1979; Hughes, Henry, & Hughes, 1980; Van Hasselt, Hersen, Bellack, Rosenblum, & Lamparski, 1979). For example, Van Hasselt et al., (1979) used measures of cardiovascular reactivity in their assessment and treatment of an 11-year-old multiple phobic boy. As part of the initial assessment, the child was interviewed and completed a fear survey schedule for children that indicated three primary fears: blood, heights, and testtaking. The child's self-reported fears were corroborated by parents and teachers. Subsequent to the identification of the target phobias through self- and other-reports, they were assessed on motoric, physiological, and cognitive indexes. For example, the child's fear of blood was assessed by bringing a blood-soaked pillowcase progressively closer to him while seated until he signaled the termination of the test (motoric). In conjunction with such exposures, he was also required to assess his level of subjective fear (cognitive). Heart rate and finger pulse volume were also monitored during such exposures to ascertain his level of autonomic arousal (physiological).

Assessment data indicated that the child exhibited marked changes in the motoric, cognitive, and physiological channels for each of the phobias. Thus relaxation training and systematic desensitization were implemented to help the boy overcome his excessive fears. Consistent with multiple-baseline strategies, treatment was directed sequentially and cumulatively to the targeted fears. The assessment of the motoric, cognitive and physiological response systems continued independently of the child's treatment. On the basis of data derived from these "probe" sessions, it became apparent that the fear-reduction procedures were effective on motoric and cognitive measures. However, less substantial results were observed with regard to changes in physiological functioning. Except for heart rate changes in relation to his phobia of heights, reduction of fear as assessed by physiological indices did not coincide with the introduction of treatment. Nonetheless, all gains were maintained over 1-, 4-, and 6-month follow-up periods. As would be evident, this study is a nice illustration of physiological assessment as part of multimethod assessment. As a result of physiological monitoring over the treatment period and at the follow-ups, it was also possible to examine the relationship between the dependent variables.

Finally, more extensive between-group studies with children have frequently included measures of physiological responsiveness (e.g., Barabsz, 1973; Braud, 1978; Fassler, 1985; Guyer & Guyer, 1984; Melamed & Siegel, 1975; Zaichkowsky & Zaichkowsky, 1984). Illustratively, Braud has reported the use of physiological measures in a controlled evaluation of frontalis EMG-biofeedback training for hyperactive children. In this study, he compared the efficacies of biofeedback training and progressive relaxation relative to controls. Prior to treatment it was found that the hyperactive children exhibited significantly greater levels of frontalis EMG activity than nonhyperactive children. As well, no differences between medicated and nonmedicated hyperactive children were found on measures of frontalis EMG activity. These particular findings support the argument that hyperactive children are not only overactive but also overly tense. Thus, physiological assessment data proved useful in affirming an important assumption concerning the arousal-reduction interventions. Regarding the effectiveness of the interventions, both biofeedback training and progressive relaxation successfully produced a significant reduction in frontalis EMG activity compared to controls. The treatment groups also showed the lowest level of autonomic arousal as measured by peripheral temperature. As might be expected given the specificity of training, the children who received frontalis EMG-biofeedback training demonstrated a greater reduction in frontalis muscle tension than those children who underwent training in progressive relaxation. In addition to physiological changes, the interventions produced improvements on various other measures, particularly emotionality and aggression. Medicated and nonmedicated children showed equal ability to reduce tension levels, although the nonmedicated children showed significantly greater behavioral improvements.

While the capacity of hyperactive children to undertake physiological monitoring and biofeedback training might be questioned, the findings of this study affirm their abilities to participate in these procedures. Another feature of the study concerns the monitoring of two different physiological responses to gauge the arousal-reduction effects of the interventions. However, the evaluation of the interventions went beyond the physiological data in accord with the principle of multimethod assessment.

RESPONSE FRACTIONATION

The relationship between physiological measures and measures of activity in other channels (cognitive and overt behavioral) is characterized by a lack of significant covariation. These measures do not necessarily covary with changing environmental conditions, nor do they demonstrate similar effects from intervention (Haynes, 1978). Terms such as *desynchrony, asynchrony,* and *response fractionation* have been used to describe this lack of response covariation. This concept has been cogently argued in the general literature on behavioral assessment (e.g., Hodgson & Rachman, 1974; Lang, 1977; Haynes, 1978), and more recently articulated in relation to the assessment of child disorders (King et al., 1988; Mash & Terdal, 1981; Ollendick & Hersen, 1984).

Response fractionation is particularly evident in the outcomes of intervention with children. In the treatment of the multiphobic boy described in the previous section, Van Hasselt et al. (1979) found that physiological improvements were not as evident as gains on subjective and behavioral measures. On the other hand, children sometimes evince physiological changes in the absence of improvements on other criteria (e.g., Zaichkowsky & Zaichkowsky, 1984). Obviously, it cannot be assumed that treatment improvements in one response system imply improvements in the other response systems. Thus, the breadth of treatment improvements must be determined empirically. Of course, response fractionation is confounded by measurement issues. Quite simply, the low degree of correspondence among such measures may be due to methodological deficiencies (Papillo, Murphy, & Gorman, 1988). Although it is difficult to escape the overall conclusion that desynchrony exists, we should continue to refine the reliability and validity of our measures so that we can obtain a greater understanding of these complexities in child assessment.

In addition to the desynchrony between physiological measures and other measures of behavior, there is not always synchrony among different physiological measures when purporting to assess the same construct (Haynes, 1978). It will be recalled that in her physiological monitoring of test-anxious children during evaluative tasks, Beidel (1988) observed increases in heart rate but not for diastolic and systolic blood pressures. Yet, in another study on test-anxious children, Barabsz (1973) found that anxiety-provoking stiumli were more effective in eliciting changes in electrodermal activity than heart rate. Even under the same assessment conditions, children may also exhibit different response patterns. Illustratively, stressful stimuli may elicit mainly cardiac responses in some children, whereas other children may show greater responsibility on other physiological measures. These complexities in physiological responding are related to two well-known principles, namely, stimulus-response specificity and individual-response stereotypy (see Stern et al., 1980). In brief, these principles hold that reliable patterns of autonomic responses tend to be associated with specific stimuli and individuals (Haynes, 1978). The principle of autonomic balance is also of special relevance to individual differences in the physiological responding of children. Accordingly, some children display responses that reflect predominant sympathetic activation, whereas other children exhibit responses that reflect parasympathetic responsivity (Wenger, 1966). In light of these complexities, a range of physiological measures are preferred in the assessment of children (e.g., Hermecz & Melamed, 1984; Zaichkowsky & Zaichkowsky, 1984).

SUMMARY

Concern for physiological measures is consistent with contemporary conceptualizations of child assessment. Typically, "organismic" factors (physiological and cognitive) are central to the understanding of child disorders and their assessment. As well as these conceptual influences, technological developments have facilitated the growth of physiological assessment. Although the physiograph is the basic instrument used in physiological assessment, many other instruments have been developed, including biofeedback systems, portable recorders, and telemetric devices.

The most common physiological measures used in the assessment of child disorders include those representative of activity in the musculoskeletal system (e.g., frontalis EMG), cardiovascular system (e.g., heart rate, blood pressure and vasomotor activity) and electrodermal system (e.g., skin conductance and skin resistance). Of course, the clinician wishing to undertake physiological assessment with children must develop technological expertise concerning electrode placements, the operation of equipment, and data quantification. Furthermore, the clinician must have an understanding of basic physiological processes such as habituation and the law of initial values.

Developmental factors were found to be important in two ways. First, the behavior of children during assessment cannot be expected to be like that of adults. Many children require some "preparation," especially for assessment that involves obtrusive equipment and multiple recordings. Second, developmental factors have an influence on physiological responding as illustrated in relation to cardiovascular and electrodermal responses. Concern was also expressed about the dearth of normative data on children's physiological responses, as well for the reliability and validity of physiological assessment.

Physiological measures have proved useful in the assessment of child disorders as shown in case reports, single-subject experimental analyses, and group outcome comparisons. We found that physiological measures helped in the specification of the presenting disorder and also contributed to the selection and implementation of interventions. In addition, physiological measures have played a central role in the evaluation of treatment effectiveness. Perhaps the most serious concern for the clinician is the asynchrony between physiological, cognitive and overt behavioral measures. Furthermore, physiological measures are not always in synchrony when purporting to assess the same construct. Obviously the physiological assessment of child disorders involves many complexities, as do other domains of child assessment. Nonetheless, there can be little doubt as to the usefulness of physiological measures, provided they meet the criteria of multimethod assessment, developmental sensitivity, and reliability and validity.

REFERENCES

Barabasz, A. F. (1973). Group desensitization of test anxiety in elementary school. *Journal of Psychology, 83,* 295–301.

Beidel, D. (1988). Psychophysiological assessment of anxious emotional states in children. *Journal of Abnormal Psychology, 97,* 80–82.

Blanchard, E. B., & Andrasik, F. (1985). *Management of chronic headaches. A psychological approach.* New York: Pergamon Press.

Braud, L. W. (1978). The effects of frontal EMG biofeedback and progressive relaxation upon hyperactivity and its behavioral concomitants. *Biofeedback & Self-Regulation, 3,* 69–89.

Braud, L. W., Lupin, M. N., & Braud, W. G. (1975). The use of electromygraphic biofeedback in the control of hyperactivity. *Journal of Learning Disabilities, 8,* 420–425.

Castaneda, A., McCandless, B., & Palermo, D. (1956). The children's form of the Manifest Anxiety Scale. *Child Development, 27,* 317–326.

Cataldo, M. F., Bird, B., L., & Cunningham, C. E. (1978). Experimental analysis of EMG feedback in treating cerebral palsy. *Journal of Behavioral Medicine, 1,* 311–322.

Dabbs, J. M., Johnson, J. E., & Leventhal, H. (1968). Palmar sweating: A quick and simple measure. *Journal of Experimental Psychology, 78,* 347–350.

Danquah, S. A. (1974). The treatment of monosymptomatic phobia by systematic desensitization. *Psychopathologie Africaine, 10,* 115–120.

Duckro, P. N., Purcell, M., Gregory, J., & Schultz, K. (1985). Biofeedback for the treatment of oral incontinence in a child with ureterosigmoidostomy. *Biofeedback & Self-Regulation, 10,* 325–333.

Edelberg, R. (1972). Electrical activity of the skin. Its measurement and uses in psychophysiology. In N. S. Greenfield & R. A. Sternbach (Eds.), *Handbook of psychophysiology* (pp. 367–418). New York: Holt Rinehart & Winston.

Fassler, D. (1985). The fear of needles in children. *American Journal of Orthopsychiatry, 55,* 371–377.

Fredrikson, M. (1981). Orienting and defensive reactions to phobic and conditioned fear stimuli in phobics and normals. *Psychophysiology, 18,* 232–239.

Finley, W. W., Niman, C. A., Standley, J., & Wansley, R. A. (1977). Electrophysiologic behavior modification of frontal EMG in cerebral-palsied children. *Biofeedback & Self-Regulation, 2,* 59–79.

Gibson, E. J., & Walk, R. D. (1960). The "visual cliff". *Scientific American, 202,* 64–71.

Goldstein, I. B. (1972). Electromyography: A measure of skeletal muscle response. In N. S. Greenfield & R. A. Sternbach (Eds.), *Handbook of psychophysiology* (pp. 329–365). New York: Holt, Rinehart & Winston.

Graham, F. K., & Clifton, R. K. (1974). Heart rate change as a component of the orienting response. *Psychological Bulletin, 65,* 305–320.

Greenfield, N. S., & Sternbach, R. D. (Eds.). (1972). *Handbook of psychophysiology.* New York: Holt, Rinehart & Winston.

Guyer, N. P., & Guyer, C. G. (1984). Implementing relaxation training in counseling emotionally healthy adolescents. A comparison of three modes. *American Mental Health Counselors Association Journal, 6,* 79–87.

Hampstead, W. J. (1979). The effects of EMG-assisted

relaxation training with hyperkinetic children. A behavioral alternative. *Biofeedback & Self-Regulation, 4,* 113–125.

Hare, R. D., & Blevings, G. (1975). Defensive responses to phobic stimuli. *Biological Psychology, 3,* 1–13.

Hassett, J. (1978). *A primer of psychophysiology.* San Francisco: W. H. Freeman.

Hastings, J. E., & Barkley, R. A. (1978). A review of psychophysiological research with hyperkinetic children. *Journal of Abnormal Child Psychology,* 1978, *6,* 413–447.

Haynes, S. N. (1978). *Principles of behavioral assessment.* New York: Gardner Press.

Hermecz, D. A., & Melamed, B. G. (1984). The assessment of emotional training in fearful children. *Behavior Therapy, 15,* 156–172.

Hodgson, R., & Rachman, S. (1974). Desychrony in measures of fear. *Behaviour Research & Therapy, 12,* 319–326.

Hughes, H., Henry, D., & Hughes, A. (1980). The effect of frontal EMG biofeedback training on the behavior of children with activity-level problems. *Biofeedback & Self-Regulation, 5,* 207–219.

Janes, C. L., Hesselbrock, V., & Stern, J. A. (1978). Parental psychopathology, age and race as related to electrodermal activity of children. *Psychophysiology, 15,* 24–33.

Janes, C. L., Worland, J., & Stern, J. (1976). Skin potential and vasomotor responsiveness of black and white children. *Psychophysiology, 13,* 523–527.

Johnson, R., & Dabbs, J. M. (1967). Enumeration of active sweat glands: A simple physiological indicator of psychological changes. *Nursing Research, 16,* 273–276.

Johnson, P. A., & Stockdale, D. F. (1975). Effects of puppet therapy on palmar sweating of hospitalized children. *Johns Hopkins Medical Journal, 137,* 1–5.

Johnson, S. B.., & Melamed, B. G. (1979). The assessment and treatment of children's fears. In B. B. Lahey & A. E. Kazdin (Eds.), *Advances in clinical child psychology* (Vol. 2, pp. 107–139). New York: Plenum Press.

Jones, H. E. (1935). The galvanic skin reflex as related to overt emotional expression. *American Journal of Psychology, 47,* 241–251.

Jones, M. C. (1924). A laboratory study of fear: The case of Peter. *Journal of Genetic Psychology, 31,* 308–315.

Kallman, W. M., & Feuerstein, M. J. (1986). Psychophysiological procedures. In A. R. Ciminero, K. S. Calhoun, & H. E. Adams (Eds.), *Handbook of behavioral assessment* (3rd ed., pp. 325–350). New York: Wiley-Interscience.

Kanfer, F. H., & Saslow, G. (1969). Behavioral diagnosis. In C. M. Franks (Ed.), *Behavior therapy: Appraisal and status* (pp. 417–444). New York: McGraw-Hill.

Katkin, E. S., & Murray, E. N. (1968). Instrumental conditioning of autonomically mediated behavior: Theoretical and methodological issues. *Psychological Bulletin, 70,* 52–68.

King, N. J., Hamilton, D. I., & Ollendick, T. H. (1988). *Children's phobias: A behavioural perspective.* Chichester: Wiley.

King, N. J., Ollier, K., Iacuone, R., Schuster, S., Bays, K., Gullone, E., & Ollendick, T. H. (1989). Fears of children and adolescents: A cross-sectional Australian study using the Revised-Fear Survey Schedule for Children. *Journal of Child Psychology and Psychiatry.*

Kutina, J., & Fischer, J. (1977). Anxiety, heart rate and their interrelationship at mental stress in school children. *Activatas Nervosa Superior, 19,* 89–95.

Lang, P. (1977). Imagery in therapy: An information-processing analysis of fear. *Behavior Therapy, 8,* 862–886.

Lang, P., & Melamed, B. G. (1969). Case report: Avoidance condition therapy of an infant with chronic rumative vomiting. *Journal of Abnormal Psychology, 74,* 1–8.

Lang, P. J., Melamed, B. G., & Hart, J. (1970). A psychophysiological analysis of fear modification using an automated desensitization procedure. *Journal of Abnormal Psychology, 76,* 220–234.

Lazarus, A. A. (1971). *Behavior therapy and beyond.* New York: McGraw-Hill.

Lore, R. K. (1966). Palmar sweating and transitory anxiety in children. *Child Development, 37,* 116–124.

Lynn, R. (1966). *Attention, arousal and the orientation reaction.* Oxford: Pergamon Press.

Mash, E. J., & Terdal, L. G. (Eds.) (1981). *Behavioral assessment of childhood disorders.* New York: Guilford Press.

Melamed, B. G., & Siegel, L. J. (1975). Reduction of anxiety in children facing hospitalization and surgery by use of filmed modeling. *Journal of Consulting & Clinical Psychology, 43,* 511–521.

Meyers, A. W., & Craighead, W. E. (1978). Adaptation periods in clinical psychophysiological research. A recommendation. *Behavior Therapy, 9,* 355–362.

Miller, N. E. (1969). Learning of visceral and glandular responses. *Science, 163,* 434–445.

Molloy, G. (1984). A five factor framework for conceptualizing human behavior change: Old wine arranged in new casks. *Behaviour Change, 1,* 18–24.

Morris, L. W., & Liebert, R. M. (1970). Relationship of cognitive and emotional components of test anxiety to physiological arousal and academic performance. *Journal of Consulting & Clinical Psychology, 35,* 332–337.

Morrow, M. C., Boring, F. W., Keough, T. E., & Haesly, R. R. (1969). Differential GSR conditioning as a function of age. *Developmental Psychology, 1,* 299–302.

Murphy, J. K., Alpert, B. S., Willey, E. S., & Somes, G. S. (1988). Cardiovascular reactivity to psychological stress in healthy children. *Psychophysiology, 25,* 144–152.

Nietzel, M. T., Bernstein, D. A., & Russell, R. L. (1988). Assessment of anxiety and fear. In A. S. Bellack & M. Hersen (Eds.), *Behavioral assessment: A practical handbook.* (3rd ed., pp. 280–312). New York: Pergamon Press.

O'Gorman, J. G. (1983). Habituation and personality. In A. Gale & J. Edwards (Eds.), *Physiological correlates of human behavior, Volume 3, Individual differences and psychopathology* (pp. 45–61). London: Academic Press.

Ollendick, T. H. (1983). Reliability and validity of the revised Fear Survey Schedule for Children (FSSC-R). *Behaviour Research & Therapy, 21*, 685–692.

Ollendick, T. H., & Francis, G. (1988). Assessment and treatment of childhood phobias. *Behavior Modification, 12*, 165–204.

Ollendick, T. H., & Hersen, M. (Eds.) (1984). *Child behavioral assessment. Principles and procedures.* New York: Pergamon Press.

Ollendick, T. H., King, N. J., & Frary, R. (1989). Fears in children and adolescents: Reliability and generalizability across gender, age and nationality. *Behaviour Research & Therapy, 27*, 19–26.

Papillo, J. F., Murphy, P. M., & Gorman, J. M. (1988). Psychophysiology. In C. G. Last & M. Hersen (Eds.), *Handbook of anxiety disorders* (pp. 217–250). New York: Pergamon Press.

Porges, S. W., & Fox, N. A. (1986). Developmental psychophysiology. In M. G. H. Coles, E. Donchin, & S. W. Porges (Eds.), *Psychophysiology. Systems, process and applications* (pp. 611–625). New York: Guilford Press.

Ray, W. J., & Raczynski, J. M. (1981). Psychophysiological assessment. In M. Hersen & A. S. Bellack (Eds.), *Behavioral assessment. A practical handbook* (2nd ed., pp. 175–211). New York: Pergamon Press.

Satterfield, J. H., & Dawson, M. E. (1971). Electrodermal correlates of hyperactivity in children. *Psychophysiology, 8*, 191–197.

Schwartz, A. N., Campos, J. J., & Baisel, E. J. (1973). The visual cliff: Cardiac and behavioral responses on the deep and shallow sides at five and nine months of age. *Journal of Experimental Child Psychology, 35*, 86–99.

Sharpley, C. F., Parsons, G. M., & Tillinh, H. (1989). Children's heart rate reactivity responses to three school tasks. *Psychology in the Schools, 26*, 411–414.

Shinebourne, E. A. (1974). Growth and development of the cardiovascular system. In J. A. Davis & J. Dobbing (Eds.) *Scientific foundations of pediatrics* (pp. 198–213). London: Heinemann.

Stern, R. M., Ray, W. J., & Davis, C. M. (1980). *Psychophysiological recording.* New York: Oxford University Press.

Sturgis, E. T., & Arena, J. G. (1984). Psychophysiological assessment. In M. Hersen, A. S. Bellack, & P. M. Miller (Eds.), *Progress in behavior modification.* (Vol. 17, pp. 1–30). New York: Academic Press.

Sturgis, E. T., & Gramling, S. (1988). Psychophysiological assessment. In A. S. Bellack & M. Hersen (Eds.), *Behavioral assessment. A practical handbook* (3rd ed., pp. 213–251). New York: Pergamon Press.

Van Hasselt, V. B., Hersen, M., Bellack, A. S., Rosenblum, N. D., & Lamparski, D. (1979). Tripartite assessment of the effects of systematic desensitization in a multiphobic child: An experimental analysis. *Journal of Behavior Therapy & Experimental Psychiatry, 10*, 51–55.

Varni, J. W. (1983). *Clinical behavioral pediatrics. An interdisciplinary biobehavioral approach.* New York: Pergamon Press.

Venables, P. H. (1980). Autonomic reactivity. In M. Rutter (Ed.), *Scientific foundations of developmental psychiatry* (pp. 165–175). London: Heinemann.

Waters, W. F., Williamson, D. A., Bernard, B. A., Blouin, D. C., & Faulstich, M. E. (1987). Test-retest reliability of psychophysiological assessment. *Behaviour Research & Therapy, 25*, 213–221.

Wenger, M. A. (1966). Studies of autonomic balance: A summary. *Psychophysiology, 2*, 173–186.

Wilder, J. (1950). The law of initial value. *Psychosomatic Medicine, 12*, 392–400.

Wineman, E. W. (1971). Autonomic balance changes during the human menstrual cycle. *Psychophysiology, 8*, 1–6.

Zahn, T. P. (1986). Psychophysiological approaches to psychopathology. In M. G. H. Coles, E. Donchin, & S. W. Porges (Eds.), *Psychophysiology. Systems, processes and applications* (pp. 508–610). New York: Guilford Press.

Zahn T. P., Abate, F., Little, B. C., & Wender, P. H. (1975). Minimal brain dysfunction, stimulant drugs and autonomic nervous system activity. *Archives of General Psychiatry, 32*, 381–387.

Zaichkowsky, L. B., & Zaichkowsky, L. D. (1984). The effects of a school-based relaxation training program on fourth grade children. *Journal of Clinical Child Psychology, 13*, 81–85.

Zeichner, A. (1987). Neuropsychological, physiological and biochemical assessment. In C. L. Frame & J. L. Matson (Eds.), *Handbook of assessment in childhood psychopathology. Applied issues in differential diagnosis and treatment evaluation*, (pp. 107–129). New York: Plenum Press.

CHAPTER 13

INTELLECTUAL AND ACHIEVEMENT TESTING

Alan S. Kaufman
Toshinori Ishikuma

The purpose of this chapter is to provide a brief introduction to the assessment of intellectual functioning and academic achievement of children and adolescents through the use of individually administered standardized tests. While reviewing major intelligence and achievement tests that are frequently used by clinicians, this chapter provides a paradigm for "intelligent" testing to guide a practitioner's assessment techniques.

Typically, intelligence tests measure cognitive abilities that are broadly applicable to problem solving and that are good predictors of academic success in schools. Achievement tests assess knowledge and skills that are obtained through specific training or subjects in schools, typically in the domains of reading, mathematics, and spelling. It is important to note that both intelligence and achievement tests measure "developed abilities," or what the individual has learned (Anastasi, 1985). It is clear, then, that intelligence-achievement division should not be associated with an innate potential or environmental dichotomy; instead, both tests are measures of prior learning, which is a product of interactions between genetic and environmental factors (Kaufman, 1979). Furthermore, the intelligence-achievement distinction is often muddy, since popular tests within both domains include some tasks that are essentially the same (e.g., general information, arithmetic).

Clinicians use intelligence and achievement tests for a wide variety of purposes, including diagnosis of disability, educational or vocational training and placement, and educational or therapeutic planning. However, most of these uses really involve the clinical assessment of the child or adolescent, not just psychometric assessment, in that (1) testing sessions produce not only numbers but in-depth insight about the subject, and (2) "information derived from interviewing and from case histories is combined with test scores to build up an integrated picture of the individual" (Anastasi, 1985, p.xxiv). The integrated and thorough grasp of the individual can often lead clinicians to an appropriate remedial or therapeutic plan. Intellectual level can affect one's choice of therapeutic programs (Kaufman & Reynolds, 1984). For example, a 12-year-old with a verbal IQ of 120 on the WISC-R may appreciate active listening, whereas the 12-year-old with a Verbal IQ of 75 may be more responsive to play therapy.

To learn the proper administration and scoring procedures for individually administered tests and to develop a healthy respect for following standardized procedures require intense practice and clinical supervision. The principles and concepts developed in this chapter should help examiners to choose appropriate tests for their evaluation purposes and interpret the test results properly once they have mastered the technical skills of administration and scoring.

A PHILOSOPHY OF INTELLIGENT TESTING

Intelligent testing is a philosophy or paradigm of assessment widely practiced and best represented in Kaufman's (1979) book, *Intelligent Testing with the WISC-R*. Intelligent testing is an actuarially based clinical assessment, facilitated by the use of theories and research findings in psychology and education, whose main purpose is to derive an intervention to improve the life circumstances of the referred individual.

As any informed individual knows, use of intelligence tests remains controversial. On one side, there is a cry for the abolishment of all ability tests, and on the other side, psychologists must administer intelligence tests under unrealistic, rigid rules that overemphasize the role of the obtained global scores (Kaufman & Reynolds, 1984). Major legal cases concerning use of intelligence tests in schools differ on whether intelligence tests are fair (PASE case in Illinois) or unfair (the Larry P. Case in California); professionals continue to disagree (Kaufman & Harrison, 1986). It is likely that the future will continue to bring heated arguments about the use of intelligence tests and calls to ban them. It is equally likely that new and revised instruments will continue to be published. A middle ground is sorely needed. Tests must be preserved along with their accumulated clinical data and their influential place in the neurological, psychological, and educational literature. At the same time, knowledge of the weaknesses of tests should be realized (1) to improve testers' ability to interpret profiles of any test, and (2) to enable them to select supplementary tests and subtests so as to secure a thorough assessment of the intellectual abilities of any child or adolescent (Kaufman & Reynolds, 1984).

The following suggestions for using intelligence and achievement tests should help examiners become more "intelligent" testers.

1. *The primary focus of the evaluation is the referred individual, and the tests fade into the background as only vehicles to understanding*. Interpretation and communication of test results should be done in the context of referral reasons, the individual's background and environment assessment, and clinical observation. It is particularly important to view the individual in his or her cultural and linguistic background, given the fact that culturally and linguistically diverse (CLD) groups (Hispanics, African Americans, Native Americans, and Asian Americans) make up 20 percent of children under 17 in the United States and one third of all school-age children will fall into this category by the year 2000 (Miller, 1989). For example, a WISC-R Verbal IQ means different things if the child is an Anglo-American or Mexican American.

2. *The main purpose of assessment is to make recommendations for helpful interventions*. By using intelligence and achievement tests, clinicians should become more effective helping agents. The tests are "not instruments for labeling, placement in dead-end programs, or disillusionment on the part of eager caring teachers and parents" (Kaufman & Reynolds, 1984, p. 201). Therefore, global test scores are deemphasized; instead, practitioners should be flexible in interpreting the test profiles in light of a broad knowledge of theories in psychology and education, and with an eye toward intervention methods that research or clinical experience finds to be effective.

3. *Clinical skills are essential to intelligent administration and interpretation*. An individual evaluation is a type of human relationship in which the intelligent tester samples the individual's behavior under fixed experimental conditions. The samples of behavior are intended to be representative of the individual's intellectual or academic functioning, and to reveal aspects of his or her noncognitive functioning (e.g., motivation level, frustration tolerance). Establishing and maintaining rapport are most important; good examiners will respect the child or adolescent as a person and will convey that respect. Clinical observation of behavior during testing is critical to appropriately interpret test results; however, it is also important to observe the individual's behavior in other settings (e.g., the waiting room, playground, a classroom) to validate the generalizability of any inferences made on the basis of the behavior during testing (Kaufman & Reynolds, 1984).

4. *Knowledge and skill in psychometrics and measurement are requisite to intelligent testing*. The clinical evaluation of test performance should be guided by "careful analyses of the statistical properties of the test scores, the internal psychometric characteristics of the test, and the data regarding their relation-

ship to external factors" (Kaufman & Reynolds, 1984, p. 202).

5. *The intelligent tester is a scientist-practitioner.* The meaning of this suggestion is threefold: (a) Examiners should be knowledgeable about recent research findings on the psychometric properties (e.g., reliability and validity) of the new and different intelligence and achievement tests, to facilitate the choice of the appropriate ones for each individual; (b) examiners should assume the role of scientists and detectives and use tests as tools to develop hypotheses about the individual; and (c) examiners should strive to interpret the test results and make recommendations in light of theories and research findings in psychology and education.

Intelligence and achievement tests do not make decisions about the individual; people make decisions and we use tests to provide some of the information necessary for making decisions (Anastasi, 1988). The basic principle of testing is that the individual being evaluated has special needs, and it is the intelligent tester's job to help meet them (Kaufman & Harrison, 1986).

PSYCHOMETRIC PROPERTIES OF INDIVIDUAL INTELLIGENCE AND ACHIEVEMENT MEASURES

To be able to evaluate individual tests and choose an appropriate one for each assessment purpose, examiners need to examine psychometric properties of the scales. Standardization, reliability, and validity of tests are described briefly here.

This chapter focuses on norm-referenced tests that permit comparison of the individual's performance to that of individuals in a norm group. Today the major intelligence and achievement tests are developed from large, nationally stratified samples of individuals. Stratification variables should match U.S. Census figures as closely as possible on variables such as age, sex, race, socioeconomic status (parental occupation or education), geographic region, and community size (e.g., city or rural area). Such careful sampling is essential to ensure the stability and the generalizability of scores earned on norm-referenced tests (Kaufman & Reynolds, 1984).

Reliability is an index of accuracy of test scores and is a prerequisite to validity. The reliability of intelligence and achievement tests is usually reported in the form of internal consistency and test-retest coefficients. Standard errors of measurement (SEM), based on the reliability of the test, represent bands of error around scores with certain confidence level (e.g., 90%); SEMs should always be provided in test manuals. Examiners should always report test scores with an appropriate band of error as a caution against rigid use of cutoff scores for placement.

Validity refers to "the overall degree of justification for test interpretation and use" (Messick, 1980, p. 1014); it tells the degree to which an examiner's inferences based on test scores are justifiable. Typically, there are three categories of evidence to support such inferences from intelligence and achievement tests: content, criterion-related, and construct validity. The literature on the validity of the major intelligence measures is quite massive (Kaufman & Reynolds, 1984), while validity studies on achievement scales are much less impressive. To become more familiar with criteria for the evaluation of tests, practitioners should refer to *Standards for Educational and Psychological Testing* (AERA, APA, & NCME, 1985).

MAJOR CONTEMPORARY MEASURES OF INTELLIGENCE

Many intelligence scales are available, and several new tests are currently being developed, including the Kaufman Adolescent and Adult Intelligence Test (KAIT) (Kaufman & Kaufman, in press) and the Das/Naglieri Cognitive Assessment System (see Naglieri & Das, 1986). In the following sections, we review three of the most popular intelligence scales for children and adolescents: the Wechsler Intelligence Scale for Children-Revised (WISC-R) (Wechsler, 1974), the Kaufman Assessment Battery for Children (K-ABC) (Kaufman & Kaufman, 1983a), and the Stanford-Binet Intelligence Scale Fourth Edition (S-BIV; Thorndike, Hagen, & Sattler, 1986a). The K-ABC covers both intelligence and achievement.

Wechsler Intelligence Scale for Children-Revised (WISC-R)

The WISC-R, soon to be replaced by the WISC-III, is the most widely used instrument for assessing the intelligence of children and adolescents; it covers the 6-to-16-year age range and has been the subject of extensive research. The 12 WISC-R subtests (10 regular, 2 supplementary) are divided between the Verbal scale, which assesses verbal comprehension and expression, and the Performance scale, which measures nonverbal reasoning and visual-motor coordination. The Verbal subtests include Information, Similarities, Arithmetic, Vocabulary, Comprehension, and Digit Span (optional). The Performance subtests are Picture Completion, Picture Arrangement, Block Design, Object Assembly, Coding, and Mazes (optional).

Standardization and Norms

The WISC-R was standardized in the early 1970s on a representative, national sample of 2,200 children stratified to match U.S. Census figures on age, sex, race (white-nonwhite), occupation of head of household, urban-rural residence, and geographic region. Three deviation IQs are derived from the WISC-R: a Verbal IQ, a Performance IQ, and a summary or global Full Scale IQ. The three IQs are normalized standard scores with a mean of 100 and a standard deviation of 15. Performance on each subtest is expressed as a scaled score with a mean of 10 and a standard deviation of 3. The norms are good, but they have two major flaws: They fail to include a representative group of Hispanics, and they are out of date (about 20 years old).

Reliability and Validity

Internal consistency and stability of the WISC-R are excellent, and evidence in support of construct and criterion-related validity has been repeatedly reported (Kaufman, 1979; Sattler, 1988). Factor analysis of the WISC-R (e.g., Kaufman, 1975) typically supports that it measures g and three factors for normal and exceptional groups: Verbal Comprehension, Perceptual Organization, and Freedom from Distractibility. The Verbal Comprehension and Perceptual Organization factors correspond well to the WISC-R Verbal-Performance dichotomy, offering outstanding support for the validity of the WISC-R's Verbal and Performance constructs (Kaufman, Harrison, & Ittenbach, 1990).

Although less robust than the two major WISC-R dimensions, the Freedom from Distractibility factor (usually consisting of Arithmetic, Digit Span, and Coding) is also fairly stable and important for clinical interpretation of the WISC-R results. Consequently, testers should routinely administer the optional Digit Span subtest and not think of it as a supplement to the battery (Kaufman, 1979). The third WISC-R factor can be explained by either the noncognitive domain (attention span or anxiety) or the cognitive domain (sequential ability, symbolic skills, or short-term memory). Since high or low scores on this dimension will have different meanings for different children, testers have to use their clinical acumen to interpret the meaning of the score. Intelligent testers will routinely study the nature of the child's incorrect responses, his or her strategies for solving problems, relevant referral and background information, along with their clinical observations of the child's test behavior (Kaufman et al., 1990).

As factor-analytic research suggests, WISC-R interpretation should begin by examining the child's Full Scale IQ and the V-P discrepancy; only then should testers attempt to interpret fluctuations in the child's subtest profile. Kaufman et al. (1990) recommend the following rule of thumb to determine whether each subtest score differs significantly from the child's own mean score: ±3 points from the child's mean for all six Verbal subtests and Block Design, and ±4 points from the child's mean for the remaining five Performance subtests. The figures are different from ones suggested by Kaufman (1979), because of the need to take into account the effect of multiple comparisons (Silverstein, 1982).

Sizable V-P IQ discrepancies and considerable scaled-score ranges on the WISC-R ("scatter") are often considered to be unusual and indicate abnormality (Kaufman et al., 1990). However, one out of three normal children has a significantly V-P IQ discrepancy at the 5% level (12 or more points) (Kaufman, 1976b), and the average scaled-score range (highest minus lowest scaled score) for the Full Scale is a substantial seven points (±2) (Kaufman, 1976a). Representative research with learning-disabled and other kinds of exceptional children has produced similar findings, suggesting that previous stereotypes about the wide scatter in the Wechsler profiles of learning-disabled and emotionally disturbed individuals may be false (Kaufman et al., 1990). Statistical significance is important, but not sufficient. It is necessary to examine whether profile fluctuations are statistically significant (whether differences are "real" or merely due to chance), but it is also essential to know how prevalent these fluctuations are. Only when V-P IQ differences or scaled-score ranges are significant and rare (e.g., V-P differences of 28 or more points occur less than 2% of the time in the normal population), then the WISC-R profile can be used as one piece of evidence leading to a diagnosis of abnormal conditions such as neurological dysfunction. When WISC-R fluctuations cannot be considered unusual by any reasonable standard, significant V-P discrepancies and strengths or weaknesses in the subtest profile have no *diagnostic* significance; but they have *educational* significance, offering insight into the child's profile of abilities and forming the basis of potentially important remedial suggestions.

Evaluation

How well does the WISC-R measure the intelligence of culturally and linguistically diverse (CLD) children? The WISC-R has some unbiased qualities. Factor-analytic investigations with African Americans, Hispanics, and Native Americans (e.g., Juliano, Haddad, & Carroll, 1988) indicate that the WISC-R assesses the same three factors (abilities) for CLD groups as for whites. The predictive and concurrent validity data also indicate that WISC-R IQs are equally effective predictors of academic achievement for minorities and whites (e.g., Poteat, Wuensch, & Gregg, 1988). Also, the rank ordering of item difficulties on the WISC-R has been reported to be similar for CLD groups and whites (e.g., Sandoval, Zimmerman, & Woo-Sam, 1983). However, Flaugher (1978) described the intricacies of the test bias issue and advised test users not to settle on one operational definition of test bias. Many aspects of test bias are not easily solved by empirical indexes. For example, although the WISC-R measures a Verbal Comprehension factor with white and Hispanic children, the factor may mean different things: verbal intelligence for white children and proficiency in cognitive academic aspects of English as a second language for Hispanic children. Although some research has supported the validity of the WISC-R with CLD group children, the battery is not free from these biases. Intelligent testers should interpret the WISC-R results in the context of a child's cultural and linguistic environment and supplement the WISC-R with numerous additional measures.

One criticism of the WISC-R has been that the Verbal scale measures school achievement rather than intelligence (e.g., Feuerstein, 1979). Retarded children typically perform poorest on the three Verbal subtests in Bannatyne's "Acquired Knowledge" group (Information, Arithmetic, Vocabulary), and reading- and learning-disabled children score low on Information and Arithmetic. Consequently, depressed Verbal and Full Scale IQs may be a direct effect of poor school achievement (rather than a *cause* of the low achievement), therefore providing an incorrect estimate of children's "ability" or potential (Kaufman et al., 1990). Similar problems occur when the Verbal scale is given to children with limited English proficiency. The results should be interpreted in light of the child's level of acculturation and sociocultural factors (Valencia, 1983).

For a more detailed discussion of WISC-R interpretation, consult Kaufman (1979) and Sattler (1988). Recent reviews of research on the WISC-R are presented in Kaufman et al. (1990).

Kaufman Assessment Battery for Children (K-ABC)

Since the K-ABC was published, it has been the subject of extensive research. The K-ABC is designed to measure the intelligence and achievement of children 2½ through 12½ years of age. The K-ABC distinguishes intelligence from achievement much in the way Cattell and Horn (e.g., Horn & Cattell, 1966) theorized fluid and crystallized abilities. The K-ABC defines intelligence as the ability to mentally process information to solve unfamiliar problems (i.e., fluid abilities), while it defines achievement as acquired knowledge of facts and skills, often related to formal schooling (i.e., crystallized abilities). Intelligence is measured by two Mental Processing scales (Sequential and Simultaneous), which are combined to form a Mental Processing Composite; all processing scales are separate from the Achievement scale. The information processing model is based on a convergence of several cognitive and neuropsychological theories (Luria, 1966; Neisser, 1967; Sperry, 1968). Sequential processing focuses on the serial or temporal ordering of stimuli to solve problems, and simultaneous processing focuses on holistic, often visual, integration of stimuli to solve problems.

The 16 subtests of the K-ABC are Hand Movements, Number Recall, and Word Order (Sequential Processing); Magic Window, Face Recognition, Gestalt Closure, Triangles, Matrix Analogies, Spatial Memory, and Photo Series (Simultaneous Processing); and Expressive Vocabulary, Faces & Places, Arithmetic, Riddles, Reading/Decoding, and Reading/Understanding (Achievement). Children are given a fixed number of subtests (7 to 13) according to their chronological age. Administration of the complete K-ABC takes about 35 to 85 minutes, depending on the child's age.

The K-ABC yields standard scores on five global scales: Sequential Processing, Simultaneous Processing, Mental Processing Composite, Achievement, and Nonverbal (a special "short form" consisting of Sequential and Simultaneous subtests that do not require verbal directions or Verbal responses).

All Sequential and Simultaneous Processing subtests include an unscored sample and teaching items (first two scored items administered to each child). If the child fails a sample item or a teaching item, the tester teaches the task using alternative methods or wording (including a different language, if necessary) to ensure that the child understands the type of response expected.

Standardization and Norms

The K-ABC was standardized on a representative, national sample of 2,000 children, stratified to match U.S. Census figures on age, sex, parental education, ethnic group (white, African American, Hispanic, and other), geographic region, community size, and educational placement. The five global scales and the Achievement subtests of the K-ABC yield normalized standard score with a mean of 100 and a standard deviation of 15. The global intelligence score, analogous to the Full Scale IQ on the WISC-R, is the Mental Processing Composite (MPC) standard score. The Sequential and Simultaneous Processing subtests have scaled scores with a mean of 10 and a standard deviation of 3, like the WISC-R subtests.

Reliability and Validity

Reliabilities of the K-ABC are reasonably high (Mehrems, 1984). Criterion-related and construct validity of the K-ABC have been well supported by comparing the K-ABC to other intelligence and achievement tests. The K-ABC MPC correlates well with the WISC-R IQs (typically low to mid .70s) and the S-B IV Composite SAS (.80s), and significantly with the old Binet (.60s) for normal and exceptional children; yet the K-ABC contributes something new to the realm of intelligence assessment (Kamphaus & Reynolds, 1987). The MPC predicts academic achievement well; however, the K-ABC Achievement scale is a better predictor than the MPC or the WISC-R (e.g., Naglieri, 1985).

Factor-analytic investigations of the K-ABC have been conducted using the standardization sample and independent samples. Major findings are as follows. First, the K-ABC is a good measure of Spearman's g, and the Achievement subtests are among the highest measures of g (e.g., Jensen, 1984). This result suggests that Spearman's g might be better labeled "general achievement" than general intelligence (Kaufman, 1984a). Second, the structure of the K-ABC into Sequential Processing, Simultaneous Processing, and Achievement scales is typically supported for samples of normal and exceptional children (e.g., Kaufman & McLean, 1987). In some studies (Kaufman & McLean, 1986; Keith, Hood, Eberhart, & Pottebaum, 1985), a fourth, "Reading factor" (loaded by two Reading subtests) emerges for learning-disabled children that is separate from the Achievement factor. Kamphaus and Reynolds (1987) offered the following alternative norms for use with the K-ABC: a reading composite (a combination of the two Reading subtests), a verbal intelligence score (a combination of all Achievement subtests except the Reading subtests), and a global scale composite (a combination of Sequential and Simultaneous and the verbal intelligence composite). The alternative model should be used primarily when a specific child's performance cannot be adequately explained using the sequential, simultaneous, and achievement structure of the K-ABC (Kaufman & Kaufman, 1983b).

Because the K-ABC measures intelligence based on theory and research in neuropsychology, several studies have investigated neuropsychological aspects of the scale and provided encouraging support for the neuropsychological foundation of the battery; these studies also support the use of the K-ABC as an adjunct measure, to be administered along with neurological and neuropsychological tests. The K-ABC demonstrates a close relationship to the Luria-Nebraska Children's Battery (e.g., Snyder, Leark, Golden, Grove, & Allison, 1983). Studies on the K-ABC scores of children with neurological problems demonstrate the relationship of the Sequential Processing scale to left hemisphere impairment and of the Simultaneous Processing scale to right hemisphere impairment (e.g., Shapiro & Dotan, 1985).

Evaluation

The K-ABC has many strengths as a measure of intelligence and achievement of exceptional children (Kamphaus & Reynolds, 1987). For example, the K-ABC is useful for (a) determining ability and achievement discrepancies in the diagnosis of learning disabilities, because it includes separate conormed intelligence and achievement measures, (b) testing the relationship of intelligence to acculturation for some CLD group children such as Hispanics through the intelligence/achievement division (Fourquean, 1987), and (c) measuring the intelligence of children with limited English proficiency and those with hearing impairments through the standardized Nonverbal scale.

The K-ABC has some limitations: (a) The K-ABC does not measure well the intelligence of gifted children who are 11 or 12 years old because of lack of adequate "top" (Kaufman, 1984b); (b) The K-ABC does not measure oral expression well, especially the ability to express complex thoughts in one's own words; and (c) The Sequential Processing scale is composed only of short-term memory tests, and the Simultaneous Processing scale lacks a verbal task.

To become familiar with clinical use of the K-ABC, readers should consult *The K-ABC Interpretive Manual* (Kaufman & Kaufman, 1983b) and Kamphaus and Reynolds' (1987) text. Recent reviews of literature on the K-ABC can be found in Kaufman et al. (1990).

Stanford-Binet Intelligence Scale: Fourth Edition (S-BIV)

After Terman (1916) successfully adapted the Binet-Simon Scale of Intelligence to develop the Stanford-Binet for use with American children and adults, the scale was revised by Terman and Merrill in 1937 and 1960, and the 1960 revision (Form L-M) was renormed in 1972. S-BIV is significantly different from the earlier versions.

The S-BIV is based on a three-level hierarchical model of cognitive abilities, and it is normed for ages 2 to 23 years. The first level measures g, or general reasoning ability. The second level measures three dimensions: crystallized abilities (knowledge and skills acquired through experience), fluid-analytic abilities (acquisition and use of information to solve unfamiliar problems), and short-term memory. The first two dimensions are derived from Cattell and Horn's theory of intelligence (e.g., Horn & Cattell, 1966). At the third level, the crystallized abilities dimension is divided into verbal reasoning and quantitative reasoning scales, while the fluid-analytic abilities dimension consists of the abstract and visual reasoning scale. The three scales, along with short-term memory, constitute the four cognitive areas assessed by the S-BIV: Verbal Reasoning, Quantitative Reasoning, Abstract/Visual Reasoning, and Short-Term Memory. The four areas are represented by 15 separate subtests, although some subtests are designed for only a portion of the age range. The S-BIV authors dropped the age-scale format that defined the previous editions of the Binet; instead, they adapted the subtest format employed by the WISC-R and K-ABC, in which items of the same type are put together in a single subtest. The subtests are Vocabulary, Comprehension, Absurdities, and Verbal Relations (Verbal Reasoning Area); Quantitative, Number Series, and Equation Building (Quantitative Reasoning Area); Pattern Analysis, Copying, Matrices, and Paper Folding and Cutting (Abstract/Visual Reasoning Area); and Bead Memory, Memory for Sentences, Memory for Digits, and Memory for Objects (Short-Term Memory Area). The four areas are combined to form a composite of general intelligence.

The S-BIV uses an adaptive testing format. In stage 1, the tester administers a "routing" subtest: Vocabulary. The starting point on the routing subtest depends solely on the examinee's chronological age; however, performance on Vocabulary along with the individual's chronological age are used to determine the "entry level" for all remaining subtests. In stage 2, the tester establishes a basal level and a ceiling level for each subtest. The tester administers between 8 and 13 subtests, depending on the entry level. Administration time may range from 30 to 90 minutes after rapport has been established (Delaney & Hopkins, 1987), but it may be 2 hours with an adolescent (Sattler, 1988). Longer administration times are also common.

Standardization and Norms

The S-BIV was standardized on a national sample of 5,013 individuals between the ages of 2 and 23 years. The five stratification variables for the standardization sample were geographic region, community size, ethnic group, age, and sex. While socioeconomic status (SES) has been carefully controlled by major intelligence tests such as the WISC-R and K-ABC, this crucial variable was not adequately stratified for the S-BIV. As a result, the sample includes an unusual excess of children whose parents were from upper SES categories; the authors applied a weighting procedure to adjust the normative data. Therefore, an advantaged child was counted as a fraction of a case, while a child from less advantaged backgrounds was counted as more than one case. The adequacy of the weighting procedures was not discussed in the *Technical Manual* (Thorndike et al., 1986b) and is open to question (e.g., Reynolds, 1987; Spruill, 1987).

Raw scores on each of the 15 subtests are converted to Standard Age Scores (SAS), or normalized standard scores with a mean of 50 and a standard deviation of 8. The area scores and composite are expressed as an Area SAS and a Composite SAS, respectively, and have a mean of 100 and a standard deviation of 16. A Composite SAS is analogous to the Full-Scale IQ on the WISC-R or to the Mental Processing Composite on the K-ABC, although the latter two global scores have a standard deviation of 15 rather than the Binet's 16.

Reliability and Validity

Data on internal consistency of the S-BIV are reported in the *Technical Manual* (Thorndike et al., 1986b). Kuder-Richardson 20 reliability coefficients range from .95 to .99 for the Composite SAS, and from .80 to .97 for the Area SASs. All subtests except Memory for Objects (.66–.78) have excellent reliabilities (often in the .80s and .90s). To examine the construct validity of the S-BIV, factor analyses of the standardization sample have been conducted by using principal factor analysis (Reynolds, Kamphaus, & Rosenthal, 1988; Sattler, 1988) and confirmatory factor analysis techniques (Keith, Cool, Novak, White, & Pottebaum, 1988; Thorndike et al., 1986b). All studies have supported the authors' contention that the scale is a good measure of *g*. Keith et al. (1988) mildly supported a four-factor model of the scale for ages 7 and above; Thorndike et al. (1986b) supported the model only for ages 12 and above. Reynolds et al. (1988) and Sattler (1988) did not identify four factors for any age group. Therefore, one should refrain from interpreting the four Area SASs and should focus instead on the Composite SAS and on fluctuations in the subtest profile (Sattler, 1988).

The concurrent and construct validity of the S-BIV have been investigated by comparing the scale to other major intelligence tests, including Form L-M of the Stanford-Binet, WISC-R, WPPSI, WAIS-R, and the K-ABC (e.g., Carvajal, Gerber, Hewes, & Weaver, 1987; Hartwig, Sapp, & Clayton, 1987; Thorndike et al., 1986b). The median correlation of the Composite SAS and IQs measured by other tests in the studies reported by Thorndike et al. (1986b) is .80. In most of the studies, the S-BIV yielded lower (5 points or less) mean scores than did the criterion test. These studies support the validity of the Composite SAS. Yet, it is not clear how well the Composite SAS indicates the general ability of individuals with limited English proficiency (Cronbach, 1988).

Evaluation

The strengths of the S-BIV include the wide age range, the use of adaptive testing, the high quality of the individual subtests, and the impressive variety of tasks that comprise the battery. Additionally, many tasks include items that challenge bright children and adults. The scale measures the general intelligence level of individuals who are 23 years old or younger. However, the problem of inadequate standardization (Spruill, 1987) and failure of factor analysis to support the four hypothesized areas (Glutting, 1989) limit the use of the scale. Also, testers are given the freedom to administer fewer than the number of subtests that are intended for each age; the ability to arbitrarily select which subtests are given to a child increases the possibility of test abuse. Clearly, however, much more research is needed to understand the clinical utility of the fourth edition of the Stanford Binet.

MAJOR CONTEMPORARY MEASURES OF ACHIEVEMENT

There are two kinds of individual achievement tests: one for assessment of the individual's general educational development and one for diagnostic assessment of the focal area. The latter type includes the Woodcock Reading Mastery Test—Revised (WRAT-R) (Woodcock, 1987) and the KeyMath Revised: A Diagnostic Inventory of Essential Mathematics (Connolly, 1988). In subsequent sections, we will discuss three general, multisubtest scales of achievement that are frequently used by clinicians: Kaufman Test of Educational Achievement (K-TEA) (Kaufman & Kaufman, 1985a, 1985b). Peabody Individual Achievement Test—Revised (PIAT-R); (Markwardt, 1989), and Wide Range Achievement Test—Revised (WRAT-R) (Jastak & Wilkinson, 1984).

Kaufman Test of Educational Achievement (K-TEA)—Brief and Comprehensive Forms

The K-TEA is an individually administered achievement battery for students in grades 1 through 12 (ages 6 through 18). The K-TEA is available in two forms: one *Brief* for quick screening of school achievement and one *Comprehensive* for in-depth measurement of achievement, including assessment of strengths and weaknesses in very specific skills and processes. The Brief Form consists of Reading, Spelling, and Mathematics; the Comprehensive Form consists of Reading Decoding, Reading Comprehension, Mathematics Application, Mathematics Computation, and Spelling. The two forms do not overlap in item content and have separate manuals. Average testing time is about 30 minutes for the Brief Form and 55 to 65 minutes for the Composite Form, although testing times are considerably less for young school-age children. The K-TEA is easy to administer and objective to score (1 or 0).

Standardization and Norms

Two standardizations were conducted with the Comprehensive Form, permitting the development of separate norms for the fall ($n = 1,067$) and spring ($n = 1,409$). The Brief Form was normed in the fall on 589 individuals, who were also tested on the Comprehensive Form to allow for the application of the equipercentile equating procedure: The Brief Form was equated to the Comprehensive Form to permit construction of fall and spring norms for both versions of the K-TEA. Sample characteristics for both Forms provided a close match to Census figures on the stratification variables of grade, sex, geographic region, socioeconomic status (parental education), and race or ethnic group (white, African American, Hispanic, and other); age and education placement (regular and special education classes) were secondary stratification variables. Reynolds (1986a) pointed out that the K-TEA is "one of the best, most carefully standardized individual tests of achievement available" (p. 891). The Brief Form yields scores for each of the three subtests and a Battery Composite, while the Comprehensive Form provides scores for each of the five subtests and three global composites: Reading, Mathematics, and Total Battery. All subtest and composite scores are standard scores, with a mean of 100 and a standard deviation of 15, derivable from either grade-based or age-based norms.

Psychometric Properties

The internal consistency and test-retest reliability of the Comprehensive and Brief Forms are excellent (Lewandowski, 1986). Brief From subtests had average split-half reliability coefficients of .85–.91 across age and grade, along with similar stability coefficients. Comprehensive Form subtests had average split-half coefficients of .90–.95 and also had closely similar stability coefficients. The Brief Form Battery Composite had split-half and stability coefficients in the low to mid .90s; the three Comprehensive Form composites produced values of .93–.98. Comprehensive Form/Brief Form reliability was calculated by testing nearly 600 students in grades 1 through 12. The total battery composites correlated quite well with each other (.87 to .97). In general, the Brief Form is a reliable screening tool of achievement in Reading, Mathematics, and Spelling.

The K-ABC manuals provide considerable evidence of content, construct, and concurrent validity of the battery. Lewandowski (1986) praised the content validity of the K-TEA: "The five subtests have items drawn from curricula in the designated areas" (p. 260). The construct validity of the K-TEA is also impressive (Worthington, 1987): It is supported by developmental progression of raw scores and high correlations between subtest and Battery composite score. The concurrent validity of the Comprehensive Form and Brief Form were explored with individual and group measures of school achievement. In general, the correlations between the K-TEA and established tests of reading, spelling, and mathematics were high (Lewandowski, 1986). For example, the K-TEA Comprehensive Form Reading Decoding subtest correlated .84 with the PIAT Reading Recognition, while the K-TEA Mathematics Composite correlated .75 with the PIAT Mathematics. The K-TEA Battery Composite correlated very well (.86) with the PIAT Total. Correlations of the Brief Form with other tests provided similar results.

However, Lewandowski (1986) warned that the "only available information on validity is presented in the test manual" (p. 260). It is clear, then, that this limitation can be resolved only by time and future research (Lewandowski, 1986).

Evaluation

The K-TEA is not only a norm-referenced test (NRT), but also serves as a criterion-referenced test (CRT). It allows clinicians to find error patterns made by the child or adolescent in specific skills, operations, and processes. The error analysis enables teachers to "use the results from the K-TEA to address accurately the specific areas for remediation" (Roberts, 1989, p. 30). Other strengths of the K-TEA include (1) the availability of the Brief Form, a far superior instrument "to most on the market for quick assessment of skills" (Worthington, 1987, p. 326); (2) the providing of norms by grade and age for fall and spring test administrations (Lewandowski, 1986); (3) the providing of concise parent reports with bands of error clearly defined (Lewandowski, 1986; Radencich, 1986); and (4) the presentation of a useful interpretive scheme in the manuals (Reynolds, 1986a).

The weaknesses of the K-TEA are not major (Lewandowski, 1986), but include (a) lack of measures in writing, listening, and language arts (Reynolds, 1986a), and (b) limited floor for young school-age children, and limited ceiling for high-functioning adults (Lewandowski, 1986; Reynolds, 1986a).

The K-TEA has been reviewed very favorably. As Lewandowski (1986) pointed out, the K-TEA is "a state of the art test" (p. 260) and is clearly one of the best individually administered measures of achievement for students.

Peabody Individual Achievement Test—Revised (PIAT-R)

The PIAT-R is an updated, revised, and restandardized edition of the PIAT, which enjoyed fairly widespread use for children and adolescents. The PIAT-R, normed for grades K through 12 (ages 5 through 18), is composed of six subtests: five from the original PIAT (General Information, Reading Recognition, Reading Comprehension, Mathematics, and Spelling) and a new Written Expression subtest. On Reading Comprehension, Mathematics, and Spelling, the individual chooses one correct answer out of four. A Written Expression subtest includes two levels: Level I for kindergarten and first-grade children and Level II for students in grades 2 through 12. In Level I, the child demonstrates prewriting skills, such as copying letters and words from dictation, and in Level II the student writes a story in response to a picture prompt. When used with the WISC-R, clinicians must be aware of the substantial overlap between the PIAT-R's construct of achievement and Wechsler's construct of verbal intelligence; both include measures of arithmetic and general information.

Although the authors estimate 60 minutes for administering the whole battery, it may take more time because of an increase in the length of all subtests. Each subtest has exactly 16 more items than the old PIAT. Training Exercises are a set of three sample items at the beginning of each PIAT-R subtest, except Level II of Written Expression. Including Training Exercises helps younger or less experienced individuals understand what is required on that subtest. The PIAT-R is easy to administer, and except for the Written Expression subtest, is easy to score.

Standardization and Norms

The PIAT-R was standardized on 1,563 individuals between grades K and 12 (97 to 148 at each grade level) and age 5 through 18 years. The normative sample matched Census data closely on the four stratification variables: sex, geographic region, socioeconomic status (parental education), and race or ethnic group. The norms are provided by both age and grade (fall, winter, and spring administration). The PIAT-R yields standard scores with a mean of 100 and a standard deviation of 15 for each of the five old subtests and for three composites: Reading, Written Language (combining scores on Spelling and Written Expression), and Total Test (excluding Written Expression). Scores for Written Expression are stanines for both Level I and II, and norm-based developmental scaled scores (1 to 15) for Level II.

Reliability and Validity

One might be concerned with the reliability of the PIAT-R because of the chance factors at work in the three multiple-choice subtests. Reliability coefficients of the PIAT-R are presented in a number of ways in the manual. Split-half reliability coefficients for the five subtests (excluding Written Expression) and for the composites were outstanding: for ages 5 through 18 years, medians were .93 to .97 for the five subtests, .97 for Total Reading, and .99 for Total Test. The test-retest reliability data were good but not as exceptional as the split-half values. The median stability coefficients for the five regular subtests were excellent, averaging .90–.96 for eight age groups between 6 and 16 years (sample sizes of 23 to 39); however, they were inconsistent for Mathematics and Reading Comprehension. Values for these two subtests dipped as low as .65, with three of the eight coefficients for Mathematics falling below .80.

None of the reliability coefficients for the Written Expression subtest are very good. Interrater reliabilities for Level II ranged from .30 to .81 (median of .58) for one picture to prompt a story, and from .53 to .77 (median of .67) for the other picture prompt. Alternate "form" reliability coefficients for Level II with two prompts ranged from .44 to .61. Although values of coefficient alpha were higher, this technique is inappropriate when items are not experimentally independent (Kaufman, 1990).

Content and construct validity of the PIAT-R are discussed in the manual. Regarding content validity of the battery, the relevance and representativeness of the PIAT-R items to the content taught in the schools in the United States are well described. Three sources of evidence for construct validity are discussed in the manual: developmental changes in the means, correlations with other tests, and factor analysis. PIAT-R subtest and composite raw scores increase with grade level and age groups. The PPVT-R correlated .50 to .72 with the PIAT-R subtests. The manual's lack of correlation studies with other reading and mathematics tests is a flaw. The results of factor analysis are not satisfactory. They did not support the construct underlying the new Total Reading composite, as each

Reading task loaded highest on a different factor. Written Expression behaved differently from Spelling; thus, the construct underlying the Written Language Composite was not supported.

Evaluation

The strengths of the PIAT-R include excellent standardization sample, examiner-friendly format (easy to administer and score), and the manual's informative chapter on proper interpretation of test scores and of the resultant profile (Markwardt, 1989, Part III). The major weaknesses are (a) the multiple-choice format for three subtests (problematic stability coefficients indicate the existence of the problem), (b) Reading Comprehension's format, which depends on short-term memory (the printed sentence is removed from view when the student selects the picture that illustrates the sentence) as well as visual perception skills, and (c) the unimpressive psychometric properties of the new Written Expression subtest. Because the PIAT-R was just published, much research will help us understand the utility of the battery.

Wide Range Achievement Test—Revised (WRAT-R)

The WRAT-R, the sixth edition of the popular achievement test (first introduced in 1936), is composed of Level I (ages 5 through 11 years) and Level 2 (ages 12 through 74 years). The three WRAT-R subtests are Reading, Spelling, and Arithmetic. The WRAT-R was designed to measure academic codes that are needed to learn the basic skills of reading, spelling, and mathematics while eliminating the effects of comprehension, which involve deriving meaning from the codes (Jastak & Wilkinson, 1984). Thus, Reading measures only reading recognition, and Arithmetic assesses only computation.

The WRAT-R takes about 30 minutes to administer. However, administrative procedures are confusing (Reid, 1986). For example, the test is basically administered individually, but part of Spelling "may be given to larger groups" (Jastak & Wilkinson, 1984, p. 7).

Standardization and Norms

The WRAT-R was standardized on a large sample ($n = 5,600$; 200 per age groups from 5 through 74 years). Five stratification variables were used: age, sex, race (white and nonwhite), geographic region, and metropolitan versus nonmetropolitan residence. Nevertheless, the norms are very poor. The reviewers of the test pointed out the following problems: (a) the failure to supply the proportions of the standardization sample corresponding to each supposed stratification variable (Harrison, 1987), (b) the failure to use socio-economic status as a variable (Harrison, 1987), (c) collapsing all nonwhite racial groups into one category without providing a rationale (Clark, 1987; Reynolds, 1986b), and (d) serious distortion of the proportions by region in the sampling process (Clark, 1987; Reid, 1986).

The WRAT-R yields standard scores with a mean of 100 and a standard deviation of 15 for each of three subtests. However, standard scores are based only on ages. Because achievement tests are often given to children repeating grades or starting school later than usual, norms based on grade level should have been provided.

Reliability and Validity

The reliability and validity of the WRAT-R are poorly supported. Because the Rasch analysis was used in item selection, person separation indices and item separation indices were reported as evidence of internal consistency for the three subtests. Test users unfamiliar with the Rasch model experience difficulty evaluating these two indices (Reid, 1986). The failure to provide traditional internal-consistency data (e.g., split-half, alpha coefficients) is inexcusable (Reynolds, 1986b). Test-retest coefficients are reported, but they are useless because the authors of the WRAT-R failed to indicate the time interval (Harrison, 1987) and they did not provide the characteristics of the samples except for age.

Content validity is commonly used in evaluating achievement tests (Anastasi, 1988). However, the manual of the WRAT-R provide little information about the content validity, believing that "the content validity of the WRAT-R is apparent" (Jastak & Wilkinson, 1984, p. 62). A monograph entitled "content validity" by Jastak Associates (1987) addresses the issue: but they define the domain in Reading and Spelling as "every written word in the English language" (pp. 3–4) and the domain in Arithmetic as "all possible arithmetic calculation problems" (p. 5); thus, they fail to discuss the relevancy and representativeness of the WRAT-R items to the content taught in today's schools.

Construct validity is also scarcely reported in the manual (Reynolds, 1986b). Only two sources of evidence are addressed: internal consistency and increasing raw scores with age. However, the raw score means obtained by the standardization sample do not demonstrate a clear developmental progression (Harrison, 1987).

Regarding the evidence for concurrent validity, the manual primarily reports a summary of studies comparing the WRAT with other achievement tests (Harrison, 1987). A few recent studies investigated concurrent validity of the WRAT-R. Merrill (1985) found correlations of .70 to .85 for the corresponding subtests of the WRAT-R and Woodcock-Johnson Psycho-Educational Battery—Achievement. Jastak Associates (1985) report correlations from .37 to .72 for the WRAT-R subtests and WISC-R Verbal, Performance, and Full scales. Spruill and Beck (1986) found correlations of .47 to .71 for the WRAT-R subtests and the three WAIS-R IQ scales. In sum, information about construct and concurrent validity is very limited.

Evaluation

Because of poorly developed norms and poor psychometric properties, the WRAT-R should not be used for any reason. A quick assessment of achievement does not save time for clinicians in schools, because the results from the WRAT-R are misleading and confusing. Nonetheless, despite the strongly negative evaluations of reviewers over the years, the WRAT (and now WRAT-R) remains by far the individual achievement battery most often used in schools, clinics, and private practices.

CASE STUDY

The following case report provides an illustration of the intelligent testing approach. This particular report integrates the results from two major intelligence tests (WISC-R and K-ABC) and helps to illustrate the numbers of different aspects of the intelligent testing paradigm. Names, locations, and several other details in the report have been modified to ensure John's anonymity.

Psychoeducational Evaluation
Confidential
For Professional Use Only

NAME: John Johnson School: Center Elementary
C.A: 8-9 Grade: 2
Data of Testing: Nov. 9 Examiner: Jamey Roy

Tests Administered

Wechsler Intelligence Scale for Children—Revised (WISC-R) Kaufman Assessment Battery for Children (K-ABC)

Referral and Background Information

John was referred for testing by his teacher, who is concerned by his lack of progress in second grade and the extreme anxiety he exhibits when called upon to speak in class. He is in the average group in reading after having repeated first grade. He is repeating the same reader this year and there appears to be very little carryover. Skills development tests indicate specific problems with sequencing and drawing conclusions. His teacher reports seeing "concern in his eyes." He is reported to be quite artistic, aggressive with other kids, and "squirmy—off in his own world." The teacher indicated that he does not daydream when doing independent work, only when she is giving directions. Self-esteem is a concern of the parents as well as of his teacher. Mr. and Mrs. Johnson feel this may be caused in part by his repeating the first grade. John has two sisters, ages 6 and 14.

A review of the cumulative records indicate that all his teachers have been concerned not only about his reading but about his poor work habits and use of class time as well. He has participated in remedial reading programs the past 2 years, but with little reported success. His Stanford Achievement Test percentile ranks in May of this calendar year for reading, mathematics, and listening were 56, 30, and 38, respectively. The reading percentile showed an increase from the 25th percentile in May of 1987. Mathematics was not listed as a problem area on the referral or in past conference notes, and he is reported to be doing satisfactorily in the average group.

Appearance and Behavioral Characteristics

John is a handsome 8½-year-old Caucasian male with dark hair and brown eyes. He is neat in appearance and of average build. Rapport was easily established and maintained during the testing sessions. The examiner has had numerous occasions to interact with John and his entire class in group guidance sessions. He stated that he liked mathematics best and reading least of all his subjects. As an icebreaker and to get some indication of his feelings toward himself and his family, he was asked to draw his family. He spent 16 minutes absorbed in the task. His drawings were appropriate, but he erased many times, appearing to be quite perfectionistic.

John exhibited much more confidence on items that did not require him to give a verbal response. His body posture and facial expressions visibly altered when response requirements changed from a motor to a verbal one. He was quick to give up when verbal responses were called for, and he did not respond to encouragement. He seldom gave incorrect verbal responses; rather, he gave no responses. He was eager to attempt tasks requiring a motor response. He frequently asked for reinforcement in the form of questions such as, "Did I get it right?" "Are they in the right order?" and so on. The most verbalizing he did was on a task requiring him to complete some mazes. He encouraged himself on these and even displayed a sense of humor after attempting the last one by saying, "Whew! I sure hope there's no number 10."

Test Results and Interpretation

John was given the WISC-R and the K-ABC. On the WISC-R he obtained a Full Scale IQ of 93, placing him in the Average range of intellectual functioning and at the 32nd percentile for children his age. The chances are 90 percent that his true Full Scale IQ is in the 88–98 range. On the K-ABC he earned a Mental Processing Composite Standard Score (MPC) of 97±6 (with 90% confidence), which also places him in the Average range.

On the WISC-R, John's Performance IQ of 104±7 indicates average abilities when he expresses himself by manipulating nonverbal concrete materials, whereas his Verbal IQ of 86±6 reveals below-average abilities when he is required to give verbal responses to oral questions. On the K-ABC, John obtained an Achievement standard score of 88±4, indicating below-average success on tasks that rely heavily on acquired knowledge and school-related skills. This score is nine points lower than score on the MPC, supporting the low Verbal and high Performance profile on the WISC-R.

On the K-ABC, John obtained an average to high-average range score of 109±7 on the Simultaneous Processing Scale (73rd percentile), while receiving a well-below-average to below-average range score of 80±8 on the Sequential Processing Scale. (ninth percentile). This significant difference suggests much better functioning when integrating many stimuli at once than when manipulating one stimulus at a time in serial fashion. This pattern was also evidenced by the WISC-R. On both intelligence tests, John performed much better on tasks demanding usage of several stimuli, such as finding the missing part of a picture, assembling several identical triangles into an abstract pattern to match a model, and placing photographs of an event in chronological order (86th percentile on the average) than he did on tasks requiring sequential processing of information, such as repeating digits in the same order presented, touching a series of silhouettes of common objects in the same sequence as the examiner said the names of the objects, and performing a series of hand movements in the same sequence as the examiner performed them (17th percentile). Many of these tasks also indicate a weak, generalized short-term memory, as does a low score on a task asking him to rapidly copy abstract symbols paired with numbers. On this last task, John was unable to quickly memorize the pattern, although he could motorically reproduce the simple designs. John's weakness in sequential processing and short-term memory may be an answer to his poor math and listening scores on standardized achievement tests. In these testing sessions, he had a difficult time solving oral arithmetic problems with and without visual cues.

Virtually all of John's lower scores are greatly influenced by feelings of anxiety. This is certainly consistent with the "concern in his eyes" reported by the teacher and the behaviors observed by the examiner. John's high level of anxiety could well have depressed many of his scores.

Summary and Recommendations

John is an 8-year-old male who was referred for testing by his second-grade teacher, who is concerned by his lack of progress in second grade and the extreme anxiety he exhibits in class. He repeated first grade. He scored in the average range of intellectual functioning on both the WISC-R, with a Full Scale IQ of 93, and the K-ABC with an MPC of 97. John's ability to deal with verbal comprehension and school-related tasks, as shown with a Verbal IQ on the WISC-R of 86 and a K-ABC Achievement Standard Score of 88, are significantly lower than his ability to express his intelligence through manipulation of nonverbal concrete materials in a holistic manner. This is evidenced by his Performance IQ of 104 on the WISC-R and his Simultaneous Processing Standard Score of 109 on the K-ABC. His ability to deal with stimuli in a serial fashion is significantly below his simultaneous abilities and is shown in his Sequential Processing Standard Score of 80. John's feelings of anxiety are clearly evident through the testing sessions.

Recommendations are as follows:

1. Use teaching materials that John, a simultaneous learner, can see and manipulate. His performance is best when visual integration of stimuli is required and verbal responses are not demanded.

2. Keep instruction short and review instruction over time in an effort to accommodate his memory difficulty.

3. John's feelings of anxiety, especially toward verbalization, need to be addressed.
   a. The school counselor might wish to include him in some individual and group sessions to deal with his anxiety. Play therapy using sand and clay may be a good choice for him. In a group, demanding him to verbalize should be increased as gradually as possible.
   b. His teachers should be sensitive to his feelings and try to let his responses be as nonverbal as possible until he is more comfortable.
   c. Oral reading in class should be kept to a minimum.
   d. Praise of any verbal efforts should be low-key and sincere.

4. His academic progress should be closely monitored. If he does not begin to perform in a solidly average manner, he might need to be considered for some remedial help in a small group setting.

SUMMARY

Throughout this chapter, attempts were made to provide a model for the intelligent use and intelligent interpretation of tests of intelligence and academic achievement. This model demands a scientist-practitioner who can integrate his or her psychometric and statistic skill with a broad knowledge in psychology and education, and with clinical acumen. This approach is illustrated in the case of John, particularly the integration and cross-validation of data from both test batteries to support important hypotheses about John's functioning (i.e., High Performance-Low Verbal, and High Simultaneous-Low Sequential). The use of the model is most effective in the development of therapeutic and remedial hypotheses for children or adolescents experiencing a variety of cognitive or affective disorders (Kaufman & Reynolds, 1984).

Once individualized programs have been implemented, follow-up assessment and evaluation should be conducted to refine or change the programs, as the model recognizes the error inherent in dealing with psychological constructs and the complexities of individual human behaviors (Kaufman & Reynolds, 1984). Becoming an intelligent tester is challenging and difficult but greatly rewarding because examiners can be helping agents, to meet the individual's special needs and improve his or her life circumstances, rather than serving as a "classifier" who simply places a person in a special class and allows predictions of future failure to come true.

REFERENCES

American Educational Research Association, American Psychological Association, & National Council on Measurement in Education. (1985). *Standards for educational and psychological testing.* Washington, DC: American Psychological Association.

Anastasi, A. (1985). Mental measurement: Some emerging trends. In J. V. Mitchell (Ed.), *The ninth mental measurements yearbook* (pp. xxiii-xxix). Lincoln, NE: The Buros Institute of Mental Measurement, University of Nebraska Press.

Anastasi, A. (1988). *Psychological testing* (6th ed.). New York: Macmillan.

Carvajal, H., Gerber, J., Hewes, P., & Weaver, K. A. (1987). Correlations between scores on Stanford-BinetIV and Wechsler Adult Intelligence Scale—Revised. *Psychological Reports, 61,* 83–86.

Clark, E. (1987). Review of the Wide Range Achievement Test. In J. C. Conoley, J. J. Kramer, & J. V. Mitchell (Eds.), *The supplement to the ninth mental measurements yearbook* (pp. 240–242). Lincoln, NE: The Buros Institute of Mental Measurements, University of Nebraska Press.

Connolly, A. J. (1988). *Manual for KeyMath Revised: A Diagnostic Inventory of Essential Mathematics.* Circle Pines, MN: American Guidance Service.

Cronbach, L. J. (1988). Review of the Stanford-Binet Intelligence Scale, fourth edition. In J. C. Conoley, J. J. Kramer, & J. V. Mitchell (Eds.), *The supplement to the ninth mental measurements yearbook* (pp. 200–203). Lincoln, NE: The Buros Institute of Mental Measurements, University of Nebraska Press.

Delaney, E. A., & Hopkins, T. F. (1987). *Examiner's handbook: An expanded guide for fourth edition users.* Chicago: Riverside.

Feuerstein, R. F. (1979). *The dynamic assessment of retarded performance: The learning potential assessment device, theory, instruments, and techniques.* Baltimore, MD: University Park Press.

Flaugher, R. L. (1978). The many definitions of test bias. *American Psychologist, 33,* 671–679.

Fourqurean, J. M. (1987). A K-ABC and WISC-R comparison for Latino learning disabled children of limited English proficiency. *Journal of School Psychology, 25*, 15–21.

Glutting, J. J. (1989). Introduction to the structure and application of the Stanford-Binet Intelligence Scale—Fourth Edition. *Journal of School Psychology, 27*, 69–80.

Harrison, P. L. (1987). Review of the Wide Range Achievement Test. In J. C. Conoley, J. J. Kramer, & J. V. Mitchell (Eds.), *The supplement to the ninth mental measurements yearbook* (pp. 242–244). Lincoln, NB: The Buros Institute of Mental Measurements.

Hartwig, S. S., Sapp, G. L., & Clayton, G. A. (1987). Comparison of the Stanford-Binet Intelligence Scale: Form L-M and the Stanford-Binet Intelligence Scale Fourth Edition. *Psychological Reports, 60*, 1215–1218.

Horn, J. L., & Cattell, R. B. (1966). Refinement and test of the theory of fluid and crystallized intelligence. *Journal of Educational Psychology, 57*, 253–270.

Jastak Associates (1985). *WRAT-R/WISC-R correlations*. Wilmington, DE: Author.

Jastak Associates (1987). *WRAT-R monograph #1: Content validity*. Wilmington, DE: Author.

Jastak, S., & Wilkinson, G. S. (1984). *Wide Range Achievement Test—Revised*. Wilmington, DE: Jastak Associates.

Jensen, A. (1984). The black-white difference in the K-ABC: Implications for future tests. *Journal of Special Education, 18*(3), 377–408.

Juliano, J. M., Haddad, F. A., & Carroll, I. L. (1988). Three-year stability of WISC-R factor scores for black and white, female and male children classified as learning-disabled. *Journal of School Psychology, 26*, 317–325.

Kamphaus, R. W., & Reynolds, C. R. (1987). *Clinical and research applications of the K-ABC*. Circle Pines, MN: American Guidance Service.

Kaufman, A. S. (1975). Factor analysis of the WISC-R at eleven age levels between 6½ and 16½ years. *Journal of Consulting and Clinical psychology, 43*, 135–147.

Kaufman, A. S. (1976a). Do normal children have "flat" ability profiles? *Psychology in the Schools, 13*, 284–285.

Kaufman, A. S. (1976b). Verbal-Performance IQ discrepancies on the WISC-R. *Journal of Counsulting and Clinical Psychology, 44*, 739–744.

Kaufman, A. S. (1979). *Intelligent testing with the WISC-R*. New York: Wiley.

Kaufman, A. S. (1984a). K-ABC and controversy. *Journal of Special Education, 18*(3), 409–444.

Kaufman, A. S. (1984b). K-ABC and giftedness. *The Roeper Review, 7*, 83–88.

Kaufman, A. S. (1990). *Assessing adolescent and adult intelligence*. Boston: Allyn & Bacon.

Kaufman, A. S., & Harrison, P. L. (1986). Intelligence tests and gifted assessment: What are the positives? *Roeper Review, 8*, 154–159.

Kaufman, A. S., & Kaufman, N. L. (1983a). *K-ABC administration and scoring manual*. Circle Pines, MN: American Guidance Service.

Kaufman, A. S., & Kaufman, N. L. (1983b). *K-ABC interpretive manual*. Circle Pines, MN: American Guidance Service.

Kaufman, A. S., & Kaufman, N. L. (1985a). *Manual for the Kaufman Test of Educational Achievement (K-TEA) Brief Form*. Circle Pines, MN: American Guidance Service.

Kaufman, A. S., & Kaufman, N. L. (1985b). *Manual for the Kaufman Test of Educational Achievement (K-TEA) Comprehensive Form*. Circle Pines, MN: American Guidance Service.

Kaufman, A. S., & Kaufman, N. L. (in press). *Manual for the Kaufman Adolescent and Adult Intelligence Test (KAIT)*. Circle Pines, MN: American Guidance Service.

Kaufman, A. S., & McLean, J. E. (1986). K-ABC/WISC-R factor analysis for a learning disabled population. *Journal of Learning Disabilities, 19*(3), 145–153.

Kaufman, A. S., & McLean, J. E. (1987). Joint factor analysis of the K-ABC and WISC-R with normal children. *Journal of School Psychology, 25*, 105–108.

Kaufman, A. S., Harrison, P. L., & Ittenbach, R. F. (1990). Intelligence testing in the schools. In T. B. Gutkin & C. R. Reynolds (Eds.), *Handbook of school psychology* (2nd ed.). New York: John Wiley & Sons.

Kaufman, A. S., & Reynolds, C. R. (1984). Intellectual and academic acheivement tests. In T. H. Ollendick & M. Hersen (Eds.), *Child behavioral assessment: Principles and procedures* (pp. 195–220). New York: Pergamon Press.

Keith, T. Z., Cool, V. A., Novak, C. G., White, L. J., & Pottebaum, S. M. (1988). Confirmatory factor analysis of the Stanford-Binet fourth edition: Testing the theory-test match. *Journal of School Psychology, 26*, 253–274.

Keith, T. Z., Hood, C., Eberhart, S., & Pottebaum, S. M. (1985, April). *Factor structure of the K-ABC for referred school children*. Paper presented at the meeting of the National Association of School Psychologists, Las Vegas, NV.

Lewandowski, L. J. (1986). Kaufman Test of Educational Achievement. *Journal of Reading, 30*, 258–261.

Luria, A. R. (1966). *Higher cortical functions in man*. New York: Basic Books.

Markwardt, F. C. (1989). *Manual for the Peabody Individual Achievement Test—Revised (PIAT-R)*. Circle Pines, MN: American Guidance Service.

Mehrens, W. A. (1984). A critical analysis of the psychometric properties of the K-ABC. *The Journal of Special Education, 18*(3), 297–310.

Merrill, K. H. (1985). *Analysis: The new WRAT-R compared with Woodcock-Johnson achievement and WISC-R*. Unpublished manuscript, Mesa Public Schools, Mesa, AZ.

Messick, S. (1980). Test validity and the ethics of assessment. *American Psychologist, 35*, 1012–1027.

Miller, G. (1989). Foreward in J. T. Gibles, L. N. Huang, &

Associates (Ed.), *Children of color: Psychological interventions with minority youth* (pp. xi–xii). San Francisco, CA: Jossey-Bass.

Naglieri, J. A. (1985). Normal children's performance on the McCarthy Scales, Kaufman Assessment Battery, and Peabody Individual Achievement Test. *Journal of Psychoeducational Assessment, 3*, 123–129.

Naglieri, J. A., & Das, J. P. (1986, August). Validity of the Das/Naglieri Cognitive Assessment System, Experimental Version. In W. Strein (Chair), *School psychology: Research and practice*. Paper presented at the 94th annual meeting of the American Psychological Association, Washington, DC.

Neisser, U. (1967). *Cognitive psychology*. New York: Appleton-Century-Crofts.

Poteat, G. M., Wuensch, K. L., & Gregg, N. B. (1988). An investigation of differential prediction with the WISC-R. *Journal of School Psychology, 26*, 59–68.

Radencich, M. C. (1986). Kaufman Test of Educational Achievement. *Academic Therapy, 21*, 619–622.

Reid, N. (1986). Testing the test: Wide Range Achievement Test: 1984 Revised edition. *Journal of Counseling and Development, 64*, 538–539.

Reynolds, C. R. (1986a). Kaufman Test of Educational Achievement. In C. R. Reynolds & L. Mann (Eds.), *Encyclopedia of special education* (pp. 890–891). New York: John Wiley & Sons.

Reynolds, C. R. (1986b). Wide Range Achievement Test (WRAT-R), 1984 Edition. *Journal of Counseling and Development, 64*, 540–541.

Reynolds, C. R. (1987). Playing IQ roulette with the Stanford-Binet, 4th edition. *Measurement and Evaluation in Counseling and Development, 20*, 139–141.

Reynolds, C. R., Kamphaus, R. W., & Rosenthal, B. L. (1988). Factor analysis of the Stanford-Binet fourth edition for ages 2 years through 23 years. *Measurement and Evaluation in Counseling and Development, 21*, 52–63.

Roberts, F. (1989, December). Kaufman Test of Educational Achievement. *NASP Communique*, p. 30.

Sandoval, J., Zimmerman, I. L., & Woo-Sam, J. M. (1983). Cultural difference on WISC-R Verbal items. *Journal of School Psychology, 21*, 49–55.

Sattler, J. M. (1988). *Assessment of children* (3rd ed.). San Diego: Jerome M. Sattler.

Shapiro, E. G., & Dotan, N. (1985, October). *Neurological findings and the Kaufman Assessment Battery for Children*. Paper presented at the National Association of Neuropsychologists, Philadelphia, PA.

Silverstein, A. B. (1982). Pattern analysis as simultaneous statistical inference. *Journal of Consulting and Clinical Psychology, 50*, 234–240.

Snyder, T. J., Leark, R. A., Golden, C. J., Grove, T., & Allison, R. (1983, March). *Correlations of the K-ABC, WISC-R, and Luria-Nebraska Children's Battery for exceptional children*. Paper presented at the meeting of the National Association of School Psychologists, Detroit, MI.

Sperry, R. W. (1968). Hemisphere deconnection and utility in conscious awareness. *American Psychologist, 23*, 723–733.

Spruill, J. (1987). Stanford-Binet Intelligence Scale, fourth edition. In D. J. Keyser & R. C. Sweetland (Eds.), *Test Critiques: Volume VI* (pp. 544–559). Kansas City, MO: Test Corporation of America.

Spruill, J., & Beck, B. (1986). Relationship between the WAIS-R and Wide Range Achievement Test—Revised. *Educational and Psychological Measurement, 46*, 1037–1040.

Terman, L. M. (1916). *The measurement of intelligence*. Boston: Houghton-Mifflin.

Thorndike, R. L., Hagen, E. P., & Sattler, J. M. (1986a). *Guide for administering and scoring the fourth edition: Stanford Binet Intelligence Scale*. Chicago: Riverside.

Thorndike, R. L., Hagen, E. P., & Sattler, J. M. (1986b). *Technical manual for Standard-Binet Intelligence Scale: Fourth Edition*. Chicago: Riverside.

Valencia, R. R. (1983). Stability of the McCarthy Scales of Children's Abilities over a one-year period for Mexican-American children. *Psychology in the Schools, 20*, 29–34.

Wechsler, D. (1974). *Manual for Wechsler Intelligence Scale for Children—Revised*. San Antonio: The Psychological Corporation.

Woodcock, R. W. (1987). *Manual for Woodcock Reading Mastery Tests—Revised (WRMT-R)*. Circle Pines, MN: American Guidance Service.

Worthington, C. F. (1987). Kaufman Test of Educational Achievement, Comprehensive Form and Brief Form. *Journal of Counseling and Development, 65*, 325–327.

CHAPTER 14

NEUROPSYCHOLOGICAL ASSESSMENT

Gregory T. Slomka
Ralph E. Tarter

The primary aim of neuropsychological assessment is the investigation of the functional status of the brain by evaluation of performance on standardized psychometric tests. In such an investigation, a broad range of cognitive, perceptual, and psychomotor tests are typically administered to determine whether there is disruption of a specific neural system or whether there is generalized cerebral impairment.

Taylor (1990) associates the modern origins of clinical neuropsychology to research conducted by Lashley (1923) and Goldstein (1939). It emerged as a distinct discipline in the 1960s and presently is a recognized specialty. Qualified professionals are accorded diplomate status by the American Board of Professional Psychology. There are two major neuropsychology societies, and clinical neuropsychology is an established division of the American Psychological Association. Neuropsychological research methods are presently in the vanguard of procedures available for documenting brain-behavior relationships for a variety of neurological, psychiatric, and medical disorders.

The neuropsychological assessment of children is a complex undertaking. This is because inferences about disturbed brain integrity in children must be made in the context of brain development. Because neurodevelopmental maturation is not a linear process, this is especially difficult. Also, in contrast to the adult, where the emphasis is on the consequences of acquired cerebral damage, impairment in the child could be the result of either disturbed development, acquired injury, or both of these factors together as the cause of neurocognitive deficit. Hence, an understanding of the basis of performance impairment on neuropsychological tests in children has to be accomplished within a multifactorial framework that considers both intrinsic developmental factors as well as a myriad of extrinsic variables.

DISTINCTION BETWEEN PSYCHOMETRIC AND NEUROPSYCHOLOGICAL ASSESSMENT

A neuropsychological assessment is superficially similar to a standardized intelligence and academic achievement evaluation. Objective standardized tests are administered, and the results are interpreted according to how the child performs relative to the general population. This is generally referred to as a norm-referenced evaluation. The feature that distinguishes neuropsychological tests from psychometric tests, however, is its validity in permitting inferences about the functional status of the brain. By the analysis of performance on neuropsychological tests, it is possible to understand how the brain is functionally organized with respect to cognitive processes, as well as to infer the presence, severity, and location of a cerebral lesion (Rourke, Bakker, Fisk, Strang, 1983).

The traditional psychometric assessment of children typically relies on a battery of tests measuring academic achievement, intelligence, developmental maturity, and emotional adjustment. Commonly, inferences about cerebral integrity are drawn from such as assessment. For example, the WISC-R profile, consisting of such indices as the verbal-performance IQ discrepancy or variability among the subtest scores, is used to indicate whether there is brain injury or dysfunction. It is essential to be cognizant of the fact, however, that these psychometric procedures were neither initially designed nor subsequently validated to ascertain brain functional integrity. Hence, inferences about neuropsychological dysfunction using such tests are tenuous at best. When psychometric measures are complemented with neuropsychological tests, the data base from which to draw inferences is not only substantially expanded, but also the information obtained relates more closely to understanding the functional neurological status of the brain. Thus, whereas psychometric tests may assist in defining areas of deficit (e.g., visuospatial capacity, language capacity), neuropsychological tests are validated specifically to determine whether an impairment is indeed due to neurological or neurodevelopmental factors.

DISTINCTION BETWEEN CLINICAL NEUROLOGY AND CLINICAL NEUROPSYCHOLOGY

The neurological and neuropsychological examinations together comprise the basis to comprehensively evaluate the developing nervous system. Although the aims and methods are similar in some respects, there are a number of important distinguishing features between the clinical neurological and clinical neuropsychological examinations.

The neurological examination is oriented toward the evaluation of sensory, motor, and reflex functions. The typical pediatric examination consists primarily of general observation of the child, a brief evaluation of mental status, a systematic examination of the head and neck, and intensive evaluation of the cranial nerves, sensory-motor systems, and reflexes. Where there is suspicion of neurological pathology, biochemical and other neurodiagnostic studies are additionally conducted. These typically include neuroimaging techniques, such as nuclear magnetic resonance (MRI) or computerized axial tomography (CT) scans. Depending also on the specific type of pathology implicated, neuropsychological studies in the form of either an electroencephalogram or evoked potentials may also be conducted. Generally, neuroimaging procedures are recommended where there is suspicion of a mass lesion (e.g., tumor), whereas the EEG is most useful for detecting seizure disorders. The evoked potential evaluation is most sensitive to detecting dysfunction of the sensory and motor pathways. Together, clinical neurological, neuroradiological, and neurophysiological procedures are extremely sensitive for detecting the presence and location of cerebral lesions. On the other hand, their value for clarifying presence and severity of neurodevelopmental disorders is much more limited.

The neuropsychological examination assesses sensory and motor functions only to the degree that a disturbance may implicate a disruption of the higher cortical functions, such as perception and cognition. The major emphasis of the neuropsychological examination is thus the objective quantitative assessment of cognitive processes; therefore, the assessment is more concerned with elucidating the effects of cerebral lesions on behavioral capacity, and ultimately, psychosocial adjustment. Hence, whereas the neurological examination is directed primarily to delineating etiology or underlying pathophysiology, the neuropsychological evaluation is mainly concerned with determining the adaptive ramifications of the neuropathological condition. Because most developmental disabilities are not associated with structural brain lesions, but nonetheless occur in conjunction with a variety of cognitive deficits that interfere with adjustment potential, a neuropsychological assessment that focuses on the description of the outcome of cerebral dysfunction is thus extremely important with respect to implementing an effective program of rehabilitation.

It is important to recognize that neither the neurological nor the neuropsychological examination supplants the other. Furthermore, the neuropsychological assessment should not be employed to merely confirm a neurological diagnosis. Rather, by providing a quantitative and objective assessment of neurocognitive processes, a more integrated and comprehensive understanding of the child's problems can be obtained. In addition, it should be noted that neuropsychological testing can provide a baseline measure of functioning and monitor the course of neurological and developmental disorders, quantitate the rate of recovery from injury or disease, as well as to document the effectiveness of rehabilitation. To the extent that information accrued from a neuropsychological evalutation has direct practical implications by measuring the skills required for adaptive everyday living (e.g., learning, problem solving, psychomotor coordination), it is possible to identify the areas of adjustment failure caused by neurocognitive or developmental deficits and subsequently to implement targeted interventions to ameliorate or compensate for these deficiencies.

NEURODEVELOPMENTAL PERSPECTIVE

The neuropsychological evaluation of children presents a variety of demanding challenges. The clinican attempting to draw structure-function relationships must recognize the changing and immature status of the nervous system. Consequently, cognitive capacities are not fully formed and indeed may be organized differently in the brain of the child than in the brain of an adult. Moreover, the consequences of acquired brain damage not only covaries with locus and type of lesion, but also the age at which the lesion occurred. Also, the outcome of cerebral injury varies depending on the specific type of pathology interacting with the plasticity of the immature brain and the psychosocial environment that places a variety of expectancies and demands on the child. Not uncommonly, the ramifications of a cerebral lesion can remain difficult to detect until functional maturation of the brain is complete. In effect, this means that a child with handicapping neurocognitive deficits may not be recognized as having an impairment until late adolescence or early adulthood, at which time it may be too late to implement an effective intervention.

Early attempts at developing neuropsychological assessment procedures for children were directed to correlating the psychological impairment with gross morphological disturbances of the brain. This approach presumed that specific cognitive processes were localized in discrete brain regions and hence tests could be developed that reliably assess injury in these specific brain regions. It was also presumed that the models of brain functional organization, based on research conducted on adults, were generalizable to children. Both of these presumptions have since been proven to be incorrect.

To better understand the neuropsychological assessment process, the complexity of neurodevelopmental maturation must first be examined. This discussion will readily reveal why simple isomorphic relationships do not exist between brain morphology and behavior. A detailed overview of the mechanisms of brain maturation lies, however, outside the scope of this discussion. The following synopsis should nonetheless suffice to illustrate the general process of brain development. For a more detailed discussion of this topic, the reader is referred to Kolb and Fantie (1989), Rourke et al. (1983), Spreen, Tupper, Risser, Tuokko, and Edgell (1984), and Majovski (1989).

Brain maturation begins in the first trimester of embryonic development. The brain forms initially as a neural tube surrounding a single ventricle. By the fourth week of gestation, the forebrain, midbrain, and hindbrain begin to develop. Recognizable subcortical structures are developed by 12 weeks of gestation. By 20 weeks, or mid-gestation, all the neurons the brain will ever possess will have been produced. However, migration of neurons from the germinal matrix continues until after birth to culminate in the development of the association areas of the cortex.

The cortex consists of six layers with regionally specific cell differentiation. Specialized filaments known as radiolglial fibers originating in the ventricular zone provide a means to guide and direct neurons to their final location in the cortical mantle. As the cortex develops and thickens, sulci appear and the brain takes on its characteristic appearance. Accompanying this process of morphological development, the neuronal composition of the cortex becomes increasingly differentiated with respect to axonal and dendritic development. During the neuronal migration, the axons of the neurons develop to permit communication among cells. These axonal connections form a network of cortical and subcortical connections within and between the two cerebral hemispheres. Dendritic development tends to begin after neuronal migration has initiated and typically is a slower process than axonal development. Myelination of the neurons begins in the spinal cord around the third month of gestation. However, by the time of birth, only certain brain stem centers subserving neonatal reflexes are fully developed. It is important to note that the process of neuronal myelination continues up to late adolescence, with different cortical regions myelinating at different rates. Generally, however, the motor and sensory areas mature first, followed by the association areas.

Following birth, brain growth continues in a series of spurts. The increase in brain mass is not due, however, to any further neuronal propagation; this process was completed during gestation. Rather, the increase in brain mass is due largely to processes associated with dendritic arborization and myelination, glial cell development, and vascularization of the brain.

At maturity, the cortex in each hemisphere is similar yet distinguishable in gross anatomical appearance. The functional significance, if any, of these morphological differences, although a topic of fascination for over a century, still remains unknown.

Each cerebral hemisphere is demarcated into four lobes defined by somewhat general neuroanatomical reference points; these lobes are the frontal, temporal, parietal, and occipital. The right and left hemispheres are interconnected by white matter fiber tract systems that permit interhemispheric communication. Certain functional attributes can be imputed to each of these regions or lobes at maturity. The temporal lobe primarily subserves acoustic information processing, whereas the parietal and occipital lobes subserve mainly somesthetic and visual information processing, respectively. The frontal lobe, actually an association area of the limbic system, comprises about 30% of the brain mass. It has no specific sensory modality to subserve, but rather underlies the higher order cognitive processes and regulates goal-directed motivation as well as voluntary motor movement. Neurobehavioral relationships are generally not specified according to such specific anatomical representation but rather are conceptualized in the context of the whole cerebrum across anterior-posterior, left hemisphere-right hemisphere and cortical-subcortical axes.

The mature human brain is a complex electrochemical system consisting of approximately 10 billion neurons. It is capable of processing simultaneously 600 bits of information. It is completely dependent on other organ systems for maintaining its life-sustaining needs (e.g., energy, nutrition, oxygen) but ultimately controls all biological processes. From the standpoint of psychological processes, the brain, in addition to serving as the information-processing apparatus for the organism, in conjunction with the endocrine system (the primary means of chemical communication within the body), subserves and regulates motivation and emotion.

Genetic anomalies, exposure to teratogens in utero, and disease as well as trauma, are the most common factors causing neurological abnormalities during gestation. The outcomes may manifest as gross developmental malformations, such as spina bifida, microcephaly, or agenesis of specific cortical regions (see Caviness & Williams, 1979). The consequences of disordered embryogenesis need not, however, be as dramatic as these developmental anomalies. In more subtle outcomes, disturbances may be detectable only in the form of a developmental disability and without evidence of visible cerebral pathology. Significantly, Geschwind and Galaburda (1985, 1987) present evidence implicating defective neuronal migration and cell assembly in the left cerebral hemisphere as the neuropathological basis for a developmental reading disability. They conduct postmortem studies of a group of dyslexics and found a higher prevalence of defective neuronal aggregation (ectopias and dysplasias), an increased prevalence of arteriovenous malformation, in addition to generalized neurodevelopmental arrest in the left hemisphere of dyslexics compared to control children. In addition, they found that the Sylvian fissure was longer and that the planum temporal was smaller or absent in the left hemisphere than in the right hemisphere. This sheath of neurons at the juncture of the temporal, parietal, and occipital lobes underlies intersensory integration; a lesion in this area has long been known to result in a dyslexia along with other cognitive disturbances. Differences were also seen in the size of both the left frontal operculum and left occipital lobe compared to the homologous regions in the right hemisphere. These investigators interpreted their findings from a developmental perspective, hypothesizing that the longer time required for left hemisphere maturation increases its vulnerability to injury. For a more detailed discussion of the developmental correlates of lateralized cerebral dysfunction, the reader is referred to Molfese and Segalowitz (1988).

The causes for most developmental disorders from a pathophysiological perspective remain largely unknown (Caviness & Williams, 1979). The cellular processes involved in brain development are understood in only a rudimentary fashion. Nonetheless, it is critical to differentiate congenital lesions caused by abnormal development from acquired cerebral dysfunction reflecting the loss of previously acquired functioning.

In the case of acquired lesions, age of onset is perhaps the most critical factor affecting cognitive development. The neuropsychological effects of the lesion depend on large measure on the maturational stage of the brain region at the time of injury. At the cellular level, compensatory neuronal changes as a function of age vary following cerebral insult. Early injuries, for example, permit axonal collateral sprouting (Gall & Lynch, 1980). Compensatory sprouting of local projecting fibers can, to some degree, reestablish functions that are lost because of injury. The site of the lesion, its size, severity, and natural history, as well as the premorbid condition of the person and the interval between the occurrence of the lesion and neuropsychological testing must be known in order to fully explain the impact of the lesion or psychological functioning.

Early notions about the response of an immature brain to injury or disease suggested that, until the association networks subserving specific cognitive functions are developed, the young child's brain was essentially equipotential; that is, uncommited areas that were not injured could readily assume the impaired functions. The hemisphericity studies of St. James-Roberts (1979, 1981) and Dennis and Kohn (1975) found, for example, that reasonably competent language (typically a left hemisphere mediated function) could also be subserved in an isolated right hemisphere; however, subtle deficits in oral and written comprehension as well as verbal production were nonetheless present in affected individuals. Similarly, in an isolated left hemisphere, competent performance on visuospatial tasks (typically presumed to be a right hemisphere mediated function) could be demonstrated, but subtle deficits were nonetheless present. The conclusion to be drawn is that the immature brain is not completely equipotential with respect to its capacity to subserve the broad array of cognitive process required for adaptive functioning.

Differentiating the effects of any potential acquired cerebral dysfunction upon cognitive functioning is not as obvious as what may be implied from a model of simple structure-function relationships. Postnatal brain development occurs in spurts. Epochs of increased myelination and dendritic arborization occur, for example, at roughly the ages 3 to 10 months, 2 to 4 years, 6 to 8 years, 10 to 12 years, and 14 to 16 years (Epstein, 1978; 1979). These stepwise increments correlate to some degree with cognitive development. It is also interesting to note that these maturational epochs roughly correlate with Piaget's stages of cognitive development (Kolb & Fantie, 1989), although there is considerable interindividual variation in progression through these maturational stages.

Measuring higher cognitive functioning in children depends not only upon understanding the lengthy development of the central nervous system, but additionally requires knowledge of other factors, including genetic, medical, social, and environmental variables that can influence outcome. The neuropsychological assessment of children is thus complicated by the direct effects of an insult on neurodevelopment in relation to the ongoing process of psychosocial maturation. In tandem with greater neuronal differentiation and functional psychological organization, there occurs expansion of the individual's behavioral repertoire. With progressing development, certain behaviors are diminished or extinguished altogether, while more differentiated behaviors emerge. Deprivation or injury at any critical stage of neural or cognitive development can limit this process of behavior and differentiation. Rourke et al. (1983), summarizing Rudel's (1978) description of primary consequences of brain damage sustained in childhood, concluded that the effects of central nervous system (CNS) injury can (a) appear early and disappear as the result of compensation, (b) appear early and culminate in enduring deficit or (c) become apparent only at some later phase in development.

THE ASSESSMENT PROCESS

A neuropsychological assessment typically begins with the referral question. The purpose and appropriateness of the referral must be clear so that a determination can be made about whether a neuropsychological assessment is indeed necessary and appropriate.

Based on the information obtained from the referral, medical and psychosocial documentation, and informants (e.g., parents, teachers), a decision is made about the process and goals of the measurement. Two excellent structured interview schedules have been developed for this purpose by Gardner (1979) and Wilson (1986). In addition, brief checklists completed by the parents can also help characterize the youngster and provide information that will need to be considered in selecting the tests to be administered. For example, deficits in the child's attentional capacities, communication abilities, or susceptibility to fatigue because of illness of one kind or another are major factors that need to be ascertained before formal testing is initiated.

Neuropsychologists differ among themselves with respect to their utilization of the clinical and historical data base. For some, this information is used to develop hypotheses regarding the probable etiology of the child's disorder. For these practitioners, the assessment consists of an iterative process of hypothesis testing. Hence, as the evaluation proceeds, the test protocol is modified and adapted to the new information as it is accrued. Thus, the evaluation is driven by a series of hypotheses until the examiner is satisfied with having obtained an understanding of the child's problems. For other practitioners, the clinical data base is viewed as distinct from the objective testing. The information obtained from the referral source, interview, and elsewhere is interpreted in parallel to the assessment information at the end of the evaluation to yield an overall conclusion about the child's neurocognitive status. Neither of these two assessment strategies has been proven to be superior to the other. However, they do reflect marked differences in orientation to understanding brain-behavior relationships among neuropsychologists.

Assessment Parameters

Phases of Assessment

The comprehensive neuropsychological battery encompasses standardized and validated tests that can provide an objective and quantitiative assessment of sensory, motor, and cognitive functions. The product of the neuropsychological evaluation is a profile of scores documenting the child's neurocognitive strengths and weaknesses.

Prior to lengthy and labor-intensive testing, it is usually desirable to employ a short test battery of sensitive but nonspecific tests to determine whether a neurocognitive deficit is present or absent. If no impairment is detected, it may be advisable to terminate assessment at this juncture. However, where impairments are present, there is then justification to fully document the type and severity of deficits.

The second stage of the evaluation typically consists of a broad-based pandemic assessment. It is this phase of the assessment that identifies, with a high degree of specificity, the domains of neurocognitive impairment. Thus, the child's abilities and limitations across the multiple dimensions of cognitive functioning are elucidated at this stage of assessment.

Following documentation of selected impairment in neurocognitive functioning, it is generally desirable to administer specialized or modality-specific tests to more fully delineate the nature of the cognitive deficit. This is essential for devising a rehabilitation plan. Hence, if a deficit is found in a particular area (e.g., language, motor capacity), a specialized battery that comprehensively evaluates that specific neurocognitive domain should be administered.

In summary, a three-stage assessment procedure is recommended. Not only is this approach the most efficient strategy of assessment, but more importantly, it enables gathering in systematic fashion the information required for helping the child overcome the deficits.

Content

In composing a neuropsychological test battery, it is important to be cognizant of the fact that the larger the number of tests, the greater is the sensitivity and specificity of the battery for detecting both the presence and locus of a cerebral lesion. Thus, the protocol must be broad enough to ensure coverage of the wide array of cognitive processes. However, determining the composition of the assessment battery does not occur in vacuo. For example, constraints exist with respect to the duration of testing that is possible. Hence, the experience of the examiner, the nature of the child's problem requiring clarification, and the condition of the child undergoing the assessment all should influence the test components to be included in the neuropsychological battery. The point to be made is that administration of "canned" batteries in an inflexible manner and without regard to the overall clinical context does not constitute a skillful neuropsychological assessment.

Assessment Context

Practical considerations ultimately must guide the neuropsychological evaluation of children. Because of the child's handicapping developmental or neurological disorder, it may not be possible to conform exactly to standardized administration procedures. The examiner must nonetheless attempt to elicit optimal performance from the child. Hence, some latitude in test administration that is usually not possible in the traditional psychometric assessment is generally acceptable. Whereas every attempt is made to sustain the standardized conditions of test administration, it may thus be necessary, for example, to repeat and clarify instructions or even give demonstrations of the task requirements. Time constraints may also need to be relaxed to assess the child's capabilities independent of performance speed or efficiency.

The preschool child presents a special problem in neuropsychological assessment. There are only a few neuropsychological procedures specifically normed for use with this age group. Wilson (1986) identifies test appropriate for use with young children and provides recommendations as to how to design an appropriate battery. Although clinical inferences can be drawn from among a number of age-appropriate instruments that tap sensory-motor, language, and cognitive functioning, a framework for the integration of such diverse data has not yet been formally elucidated.

It is also imperative that adequate attention be given to "floor and ceiling" effects when testing children. It is sometimes necessary to use tests designed for age groups outside the limits of the original normative standardization to ensure adequate sampling of a specific behavioral or cognitive domain. This could, for example, require the utilization of the Memory scale from the McCarthy Scales of Childrens Abilities, an instrument normed on children aged 2½ to 8½ years when testing a severely compromised adolescent. Sattler (1988) has provided a number of useful examples of such downward extensions of traditional tests.

Stability of Neurocognitive Capacity

It is important to underscore the value of serial assessments to determine whether a change in status occurs in conjunction with chronological development. Serial evaluations not only enable charting the course of the child's neurocognitive development, but also enables quantitating the rate of improvement that occurs in tandem with treatment.

Assessment Strategy

In view of the practical need to conduct the examination as efficiently as possible, there are two general approaches that can be taken. Each has particular advantages, depending on the individual case and resources available to the examiner. The two approaches involve either the administration of a fixed or uniform battery to all cases or a flexible battery in which the particular tests administered are tailored to the predetermined needs of the child.

Two of the most representative examples of fixed batteries are the child and adolescent versions of the Halstead-Reitan Battery (Reitan, 1969; Reitan & Davison, 1974; Seltz & Reitan, 1979b) and the Luria Nebraska Battery for Children (Golden, 1986). Each of these batteries was originally developed for use with adults and subsequently was modified for the assessment of children. These two neuropsychological batteries will be discussed at length in the following section. However, their administration and the interpretation of the data obtained requires specialized training and substantial knowledge about the functional organization of the human brain.

The flexible battery, on the other hand, consists of an ad hoc compendium of tests designed to respond to the referral question. Although, these two approaches may superficially appear quite antagonistic, most clinicians typically employ a strategy combining a fixed-core battery in conjunction with a more variable flexible battery. The core battery administered first points to areas of strengths and weaknesses in the child that comprises the basis to administer other tests. A representative battery, for example, might include a core assessment consisting of several brief tests measuring perception, psychomotor skill, visuospatial capacity, attention, memory, and language. Not uncommonly, a standard intelligence test accompanied by an educational achievement test is included in the core assessment. As the evaluation unfolds, a complement of individualized neuropsychological tests are added that varies from child to child. Such an approach is consistent with the three-stage assessment model described above and also ensures comprehensive coverage of cognitive processes.

Extensive controversy surrounds the issue of whether the fixed or flexible battery approach to assessment is superior. No research has yet been conducted to empirically examine this issue, at least with respect to the relative impact of each approach on the ultimate clinical disposition and outcome of the child. Hence, the intense debate generated over this issue has been largely unproductive. This is perhaps because of the small number of neuropsychologists who conduct research on children as opposed to the increasing numbers who confine their activities to being practitioners.

Most importantly, a fixed-core battery offers the advantage of maintaining a uniform data base. This enables comparing the neurocognitive status among different disorders, especially where the conditions are rare or infrequent. Through such a systematic accumulation of standardized and uniform data, neuropsychologists can then learn about brain-behavior relationships in an organized manner. The two most common fixed batteries are the Halstead-Reitan and

Luria-Nebraska batteries. The Halstead-Reitan battery (HRB) consists of empirically derived tests that have been validated without a priori assumptions about how the brain is functionally organized. During the course of the developmental and standardization of this battery, tests were added and dropped based on their capacity to discriminate brain-damaged from non-brain-damaged persons. Although the tests are widely used for the assessment of children and adolescents, not all aspects of neurocognitive functioning are adequately assessed (e.g., learning, memory), and the tests themselves do not link closely to current understanding of the functional organization of cognitive capacities in the brain. Rather, a high degree of interpretative skill is required to relate the data obtained to the presence, location, and severity of cerebral lesions. In contrast, the Luria-Nebraska Neuropsychological Battery (LNNB) is composed of tests that putatively assess specific neural systems or cerebral regions. The validity of this battery is, therefore, ultimately based on the validity of the theory regarding brain functional organization; in this case, Luria's regional equipotential model of functional brain organization (Luria, 1966). Whether one battery is superior to the other with respect to improving the prognosis of the child has not yet been proven.

Employing an ad hoc or flexible battery of tests maximizes efficiency, because at each stage of the assessment the examiner determines whether and how to continue the evaluation to satisfy the objectives of the referral. The administration of tests that are not confined to preconceived protocols is necessary to address the idiosyncratic problems of each child. Perhaps more than any other criterion, however, the judgment, skill, and knowledge among neuropsychologists in selectively tailoring individualized batteries separates practitioners who fully understand neurobehavioral relationships from those who function as psychometricians.

Wilson (1986) and Tarter and Edwards (1986) describe a decision branching approach in which hypotheses are tested at each phase of the assessment to determine the next stage of evaluation. This approach necessarily requires a highly experienced examiner and may contribute to a biased evaluation contingent on the theoretical orientation of the particular practitioner. Another adverse consequence, especially for inexperienced neuropsychologists, is that certain aspects of neurocognitive impairment that are present may not be detected.

In summary, the neuropsychological evaluation typically consists of features of both the fixed and flexible types of batteries. To more fully elucidate the information that can be derived from a fixed-core assessment, or as discussed herein, phase two of the evaluation, the Halstead-Reitan and Luria Nebraska Batteries are discussed in more detail below. This aspect of the evaluation as previously noted is the most labor-intensive aspect of neuropsychological assessment.

THE CHILD AND ADOLESCENT VERSION OF THE HALSTEAD-REITAN NEUROPSYCHOLOGICAL BATTERIES

Two forms of the Halstead-Reitan battery are available for the assessment of children. These are the Halstead-Reitan Neuropsychological Test Battery, which is applicable for children between 9 and 14 years of age (Reitan & Davison, 1974) and the Reitan-Indiana Test Battery, which is applicable for children between 5 and 8 years of age (Reitan, 1969). These two test batteries comprise a downward extension and modification of the Halstead-Reitan Neuropsychological Battery used for the assessment of adults. Each battery is composed of a complement of tests that measure sensory or perceptual functioning, visuospatial capacity, psychomotor ability, abstracting capacity, language, attention, and certain aspects of memory. The battery is generally administered in conjunction with the Wechsler Intelligence Scale for Children and academic achievement tests. Significantly, the Reitan batteries are the most researched and validated method for determining the presence of brain damage or dysfunction. Numerous studies have documented the capacity of the tests in the battery to detect CNS disorder and also have been shown to be useful for describing and quantitating the abilities of normal children (Boll, 1974; Reitan, 1974; Tusushima & Towne, 1977; Seltz, 1981; Seltz & Reitan, 1979a; Nussbaum & Bigler, 1989).

Halstead-Reitan Battery for Children

The 9 to 14 age version of the Reitan battery most closely approximates the adult form. The major difference is that the tests for children have been truncated by removing the more difficult items applicable to adults. The battery consists of the following components:

Sensory and Perceptual Examination

This aspect of the assessment screens for tactile, auditory, and visual capacity. Unilateral and bilateral stimuli are presented in each modality to determine whether perceptual problems are present. With vision restricted, light touches are applied to each hand and to the side of the face. In addition, the examiner lightly rubs his or her fingertips behind each ear. This procedure is usually followed by an assessment of the visual fields by having the examiner display hand or finger movements to the subjects at eye level as well as above and below eye level in various positions of the visual field.

Tactile Finger Location

A light touch is applied to the tips of the child's fingers. The score is the number of identification errors. This test evaluates both attention and tactile localization on each side of the body.

Fingertip Number Writing

The digits 3, 4, 5, and 6 are drawn on the child's fingertips. The task demand for the child is to report the number being drawn on the fingertips without the opportunity to visually observe the experimenter performing the test. This test primarily evaluates presence of agnosia—that is, the incapacity to extrapolate meaning from tactile-sensory information (agraphesthesia).

Tactile Form Recognition

Without the opportunity for visual inspection, the child places one hand through an aperture in a vertically placed board. A plastic clip, having one of four geometric shapes, is then placed in the child's palm. The child is required to point with the other hand to the shape of the plastic chip displayed on the board. This test evaluates for the presence of an agnosia for shape (stereoagnosia). Total time recognition across trials as well as accuracy are scored.

Aphasia Screening Test

This test consists of 32 items measuring various aspects of linguistic ability, inlcuding naming ability, phrase repetition, oral comprehension as well as reading, spelling, and writing. In addition, arithmetic ability, visuomotor coordination, left-right orientation, and praxis abilities are assessed. Performance is scored using a method devised by Seltz and Reitan (1979b).

Seashore Rhythm Test

The child is orally presented 30 pairs of prerecorded rhythm patterns. The task demand is for the child to discriminate whether each rhythm pair is the same or different. Although primarily a test of nonverbal auditory discrimination capacity, the test also provides valuable information about attentional abilities. The number of correct responses is scored.

Trailmaking Tests

The task demand of the first part (Trails A) is similar to connect-the-dot games with which most children are familiar. The score is the time to complete the task. The second part (Trails B) requires the child to alternately connect sequenced numbers and letters (1-a; 2-b; etc.). This part of the test is scored for both time and number of errors. The Trailmaking test is a sensitive but nonspecific test of CNS disturbance. Optimal performance requires such capacities as visual scanning and tracking, motor sequencing, symbol recognition, and visuomotor speed.

Finger Tapping

With the palm flat and moving only the index finger, the child taps a manual telegraph key as quickly as possible for 10 seconds. The mean score across five trials with each hand is recorded. This task is a measure of simple motor speed.

Grip Strength

The child is required to squeeze a hand dynamometer as hard as possible to measure hand strength. The mean score, recorded in kilograms, is recorded for each hand across three trials. On both the finger tapping and grip strength tests, comparisons are made between levels of performance of the dominant and nondominant hands.

Category Test

This abstracting test requires the child to select from four alternatives the option that identifies or corresponds to a predetermined concept. At the end of the concept identification test, several items are repeated so as to evaluate memory capacity in a cursory fashion. The score is the total number of errors. This test taps higher level abstract conceptual skills and is sensitive to generalized cerebral dysfunction.

Tactual Performance Tests

While blindfolded, the child is required to place six geometric shaped blocks into a form board. The task is performed three times: with the preferred hand, with the nonpreferred hand, and, with both hands simultaneously. Following this procedure, the form board is removed, and the child is requested to draw as many of the shapes of the blocks as can be recalled as well as to localize their position in the form board. The time required to complete the three parts of the test as well as the accuracy of the drawings are scored. Overall, the scores indicate how well the child can analyze, integrate, and remember spatial information.

Speech Sounds Perception Test

A series of 30 phonemes are presented from a tape recording. The child is required to select the correct match from among four alternatives. This test evaluates the child's capacity to discriminate linguistic stimuli. The number of errors is scored.

Reitan-Indiana Battery for Children

This battery is applicable for children between 5 and 8 years of age. A number of the components included in the battery for older children have been modified for use with younger children. For example, the Category Test does not use Roman numerals. Color is the main stimulus. The finger tapping test employs an electric telegraph key with a much larger key surface to accommodate the more limited dexterity of the young child. Three of the tests included in the Halstead-Reitan Battery for Children (Speech Sounds, Seashore Rhythm, Trailmaking) are omitted. The following two tests are, however, unique to the Reitan-Indiana Battery.

Matching Test

This is a sequential motor task in which the child is required to touch a series of circles as quickly as possible in a specified order. The time to complete the sequence and the number of errors made are scored.

Color-Form Test

This task requires the child to alternate between touching shapes or colors that are on a stimulus board. This test measures cognitive flexibility and the capacity to inhibit a motor response. Time and errors are scored.

All of the other tests comprising the Reitan-Indiana Battery for Children are adapted variations of tests comprising the Halstead-Reitan Battery for Children.

Scoring and Interpretation of the Halstead-Reitan Batteries

Multiple indices of performance are recorded. Initially, performance on the various tests is scored and compared to normative standards (Knights & Norwood, 1980; Reed, Reitan, & Klove, 1965; Spreen & Gaddes, 1969). Scores exceeding two standard deviations below the population mean are defined as potentially pathognomonic. With regard to the use of cutoff scores, it should be cautioned that sole reliance on these indices can lead to a false positive conclusion about the presence of neurological disorder. Many factors besides cerebral disorder can cause failure on a test; thus using only cutoff scores can lead to erroneous conclusions.

Areas of strength and weakness are ascertained by examining the overall configuration of scores across all tests. This analysis of the child's performance is essential for making inferences about specific cerebral regions and neural systems that may be compromised. Decision rules have also been developed for inferring brain lesion localization based upon a combination of cutoff scores and total profile analysis. Seltz and Reitan (1979b), for example, propose a decision rule system in which raw scores are converted into ratings ranging from 0 (normal) to 3 (definitely abnormal). These authors were able to correctly classify 73% of a sample consisting of normal, learning-disabled, and brain-damaged children. After deleting the learning-disabled group, classification accuracy increased to 87%. However, as pointed out by Rourke et al. (1983) and Nussbaum and Bigler (1986), application of these types of actuarial decision rule systems may not be appropriate to the individual case and indeed may even lead to misclassification of the child if other sources of data are also not considered.

Pathognomonic signs provide additional valuable neuropsychological information. For example, imperception on one side of the body (hemineglect) is a very sensitive and specific sign for localizing a cerebral lesion to the parietal lobe. Other signs similarly contribute to the overall analysis of the child's performance. In summary, the conjoint use of multiple strategies of test data interpretation (normative comparisons, cutoff scores, profile analysis, and pathognomic signs) enables detection of the presence of focal and diffuse cerebral lesions as well as provides valuable information about the nature and severity of neurodevelopment disability.

Luria-Nebraska Neuropsychological Battery for Children: Description

The children's version of the Luria Neuropsychological Test Battery for Children consists of 149 items organized into 11 clinical scales:

1. Motor. This scale measures psychomotor speed, unilateral and bimanual coordination, ideomotor praxis, and constructional abilities.
2. Rhythm. The test items on this scale measure acoustic processing involving discrimination and reproduction of simple and complex stimuli. Like the Seashore Rhythm Test, selective attentional problems can also compromise performance.
3. Tactile. Tactile-haptic processing is evaluated using tasks measuring 2-point discrimination: point and pressure sensitivity and directional sense. Graphesthesia and stereognosis are also assessed.
4. Visual. The items comprising this scale document perceptual recognition and discrimination capacities as well as the ability to perform more complex visuospatial problem-solving tasks.
5. Receptive. These tests evaluate the child's capacity to discriminate phonemes in addition to the processing of grammatical and syntactical stimuli that are relevant to the assessment of linguistic comprehension.
6. Expression language. The motor aspects of language are evaluated by testing naming ability, repetition ability, and verbal fluency.
7. Writing ability. The analysis and synthesis of stimuli with respect to spelling ability are evaluated on this test as well as expositional skills and motor writing abilities.
8. Reading. Sound-symbol relationships are assessed along with the capacity to read and comprehend increasingly complex lexical material.
9. Arithmetic. The items comprising this scale assess the person's understanding of numerical concepts and documents arithmetic ability.
10. Memory. Immediate and short-term memory capacity for verbal and nonverbal information are evaluated by this scale.
11. Intelligence. This scale, sharing many of the features of the WISC-R subtests, provides a general measure of intelligence.

Administration of this battery is straightforward and can usually be accomplished in less than 90 minutes. Unlike the Halstead-Reitan Battery, components of which take more than 30 minutes to administer, none of the individual items within the Luria-Nebraska requires more than 3 minutes. Scoring of the item is based on a Likert scale of 0, 1, or 2 corresponding respectively to normal performance, one and two standard deviations below the mean.

Interpretation of the results of the assessment, as described by Golden (1989), combines quantitative and qualitative methods. Initially, screening for the presence or absence of brain damage is accomplished by determining the number of clinical scales in which the scores are elevated above a predetermined critical level. It has been found that where three or more scales are critically elevated, 75% to 85% of brain-damaged cases are correctly classified.

More clinically useful information is derived, however, from conducting a pattern analysis. Although the items in the battery are organized into 11 scales, there is substantial item overlap with respect to the underlying organization of these functional psychological capacities. For example, an attention deficit disorder could result in impairment on the rhythm, receptive language, and arithmetic scales, as well as cause impaired performance on other scales. Thus, it is essential to examine the configuration of impairment with respect to how performance on the various items aggregate between as well as among scales in order to fully specify the neurocognitive deficit. In addition to the above synthesis of the data, another method of interpretation involves documenting 60 attributes of test behavior and performance that can be incorporated into the interpretive process. Like the Halstead-Reitan Batteries, the combined use of quantitative and qualitative scoring systems enables multifactorial description of the presence and severity of cerebral dysfunction. The 286-item full Luria-Nebraska Battery is appropriate for administration to adolescents as young as 10 years of age. It shares similar profile characteristics but expands the number of tests to which the adolescent is exposed.

The current version of the Luria-Nebraska Neuropsychological Battery is undergoing revision. The revision, in process of development, will combine components of the current child and adult variations of this battery and thus will permit testing individuals ranging from young childhood through adulthood. A preliminary factor analysis of the revised Luria-Nebraska Neuropsychological Battery reveals 37 primary scales. While this is a rather large number of primary dimensions, it has the advantage of permitting a refined analysis of neurobehavioral functioning (Golden, 1989).

Remarks

The Halstead-Reitan and Luria-Nebraska neuropsychological batteries adapted for children have been proven valid for detecting the presence of brain damage. A comprehensive review of their clinical utility can be found in Hynd and Willis (1988). For additional discussions of their psychometric properties, the reader is also referred to Boll (1981), Lezak (1983), and Sattler (1988).

Research has not proven either neuropsychological battery to be superior over the other. Each battery has notable limitations. For example, the Halstead-Reitan batteries for children provide very limited coverage of language and memory processes. The Luria-Nebraska battery for children overly emphasizes linguistically mediated problem solving and only superficially evaluates visuospatial processes. Recognizing the shortcomings of each battery, it is thus frequently necessary to supplement these protocols with other measures, especially those that more definitely define general ability and levels of academic functioning. Hence, there frequently is the need to employ an individualized battery in conjunction with each of these core standard batteries. Moreover, neither battery can be used in an inflexible fashion without great risk for misinterpretation by practitioners who are unfamiliar with developmental and neuropsychological principles. Experience, combined with good judgment, is essential for conducting a comprehensive neuropsychological evaluation of children.

GOALS OF NEUROPSYCHOLOGICAL ASSESSMENT

The applications of neuropsychological testing in children has expanded significantly in the past decade beyond the traditional role of disability documentation or lesion specification. Increasingly, neuropsychological assessment techniques are being applied to children whose disabilities are not associated with known neuropathological processes (Taylor & Fletcher, 1990). Specifically, these procedures have proven useful for the assessment of learning disability, attention deficit disorder, as well as for chronic disease and psychiatric illness. Under these circumstances, the results of testing can enhance understanding of the functional and adaptive limitations of the child.

Psychoeducational Assessment

Hartlage and Telzrow (1984, 1986) have extensively examined the use of neuropsychological assessment procedures in the context of educational evaluations. They suggest an assessment strategy that combines the use of standard psychoeducational tests with several neuropsychological screening tests. In this manner, children can be readily identified who need a more extensive neuropsychological assessment. A typical battery consists of a standard test of intelligence (e.g., WISC-R), an educational achievement test (e.g., Peabody Individual Achievement Test), and several brief tests measuring receptive language (e.g., Peabody Picture Vocabulary Test), constructional ability (Developmental Test of Visuomotor Integration), psychomotor ability (Finger Tapping Test), and tactile sensory perception (Fingertip Number Writing).

While this is obviously a superficial assessment, Hartlage and Telzrow (1984) assert nonetheless that the major domains of neurocognitive functioning essential for general screening are covered. Moreover, and importantly, administration and interpretation of the data from such a battery is within the competency level of most practicing school psychologists. Recently, Telzrow (1989) has expanded on this general strategy to promote a flexible battery approach that is not only sensitive to detecting neurocognitive deficit but also can identify the specific nature of impairment and thus point to the areas of deficit requiring habilitation.

In summary, neuropsychological assessment in the school setting can be an important adjunct to traditional psychoeducational evaluation. The information obtained about a generalized or specific learning deficiency, particularly where there is evidence of a neurologically based developmental disability, has important ramifications for classroom placement as well as for early detection and amelioration of neurocognitive deficit.

Treatment Directed Neuropsychological Assessment

Rourke and colleagues (Rourke et al., 1983; Rourke, 1986) propose a treatment-directed assessment protocol. The end point of their extensive multistage assessment is to recommend a remedial plan based only in part on the identified deficits. In arriving at such recommendations, the neuropsychological data, medical findings, and psychosocial history and adjustment are synthesized into a comprehensive explanatory framework.

A major emphasis in this approach is to understand the effects of cerebral dysfunction or injury on the child's abilities over time. To this end, Rourke et al. (1983, 1986) advocate a comprehensive neuropsychological examination that consists of a fixed battery of Reitan measures accompanied by a variety of additional tests. From such an assessment protocol, deficits can ostensively be detected ranging from sensory-perceptual impairments to higher order cognitive disturbances.

Developmental Perspective in Assessment

Taylor and Fletcher (1990) describe a "biobehavioral systems" approach to neuropsychological assessment. Neurocognitive, environmental, and psychosocial variables are integrated to comprehensively explain the child's developmental progress. In addition to the information directly obtained from the testing, emphasis is placed upon findings accrued using observational techniques, informant reports of the child's behavior, as well as information documented in other clinical, educational, and laboratory assessments.

The ultimate goal of this type of assessment is to describe the structure and organization of abilities in the child at a particular point in time rather than to merely derive a differential diagnosis. Taylor, Fletcher, and Satz (1984) describe the four components of such as assessment. First, a core battery of standardized tests is used to identify the specific problem (e.g., learning disability, sensory or motor disorder, language deficit). Neurocognitive capacity is then further evaluated using a battery of neuropsychological tests deemed to be appropriate for the particular case. In this fashion, the major neurocognitive domains are covered. Importantly, these processes are evaluated with respect to how they compare to the child's general ability level. The third component of the evaluation consists of an assessment of emotional, motivational, and psychosocial factors that may contribute to the child's problems. Great importance is attached to the degree to which nonneurological factors could influence cognitive or neuropsychological performance. Finally, etiological parameters are identified that can further help explain the basis of the manifest disturbances; however, this aspect of the evaluation is not deemed to be central to the goals of a neuropsychological assessment. As noted by Fletcher (1988), the assessment strategy instead focuses on quantitating the child's ability. By emphasizing functional capacity and downplaying the importance of etiology (although recognizing the importance of this information), it is possible to delineate the child's cognitive strengths and weaknesses in the context of the overall psychosocial milieu. Interventions can then be implemented that are targeted to the child's specific needs within a developmental and psychosocial framework.

Remarks

The three assessment approaches described above are not mutually exclusive. All have in common the need to relate assessment to intervention, whether it be in an educational, treatment, or developmental framework. Thus, differences among the three approaches are not as much substantive as they reflect varying degrees of emphasis. Hence, for example, a school-based assessment places different demands upon the clinician than does a hospital-based assessment. The extent to which one approach may be superior to the others has not been empirically investigated. In all likelihood, no differences exist, since each approach assesses the same basic domains of neurocognitive functioning. Also, they all recognize the importance of the child's psychosocial circumstances as codeterminants of any manifest impairment. Finally, it should be noted that the current state of the field is such that there are a plethora of psychometric tests used to evaluate general ability level and to a lesser extent tests that have been developed that are specifically sensitive to identifying cerebral dysfunction. However, very little has been accomplished with respect to understanding how the information accrued from the evaluation can be utilized to develop effective habilitation programs. Indeed, the paucity of experimentation currently ongoing in the field of applied neurobehavioral rehabilitation with children is cause for alarm, and although there are variations among assessment strategies, there is no empirical basis indicating that any assessment approach will substantially improve the rehabilitative efforts applied to children determined to have neurocognitive impairments.

COVERAGE

Even though the strategy, context, and objectives of the neuropsychological evaluation may differ widely among practitioners, there is general consensus that the comprehensive evaluation should encompass the following neurocognitive domains.

Sensory-Perceptual Capacity

The results of the neuropsychological evaluation should inform about the presence of disturbance in the auditory, somesthetic, and visual systems. An attempt should also be made to differentiate deficits having a cerebral from a peripheral etiology. In addition, the child's capacity to integrate and appreciate the equivalence of information presented through the different modalities should be ascertained. Deficits identified in elementary sensory-perceptual functions are sure to affect higher level skills.

Language

Ultimately, communication capacity is perhaps the most important determinant of academic performance. Verbal-conceptual abilities are also critical determinants in higher level problem-solving skills and in general adaption. Orla and written comprehension and expressive abilities need to be elucidated that may implicate a deficit in reading (dyslexia), spelling (dysgraphia), or spoken communication (dysphasia). With respect to spoken language, differentiation needs to be made between the presence of a disorder of symbolic language processing (dysphasia) and an articulation disorder (e.g., dysarthria, stuttering).

Learning and Memory

Visual and auditory modalities need to be evaluated for both symbolic (language) and figural (visuospatial) stimuli. The rate of learning as well as short- and long-term memory-storage and retrieval capacities need to be described. Learning and memory processes are multifaceted; hence, impairments in one or more aspect can occur as a consequence of both developmental and acquired cerebral dysfunction.

Motor Capacity

Gross and fine motor control as well as strength using either hand needs to be evaluated. Ataxia, implicating a cerebellar disorder, should also be assessed. Psychomotor processes encompassing measures of tremor, eye-hand coordination, and sequential movement are essential components of the comprehensive evaluation.

Attention

The capacity to select, sustain, and shift attention are measurable when tests are used that require mental effort and persistence. Informant reporting as well as general observation of the child during the course of the evaluation can additionally provide important information about attentiveness and susceptability to distraction.

Visuospatial Capacity

The capacity to analyze and organize the perceptual field using recognition and constructional tests is closely linked to chronological development. Numerous tests are available that can provide information about the child's ability to synthesize stimulus elements into a gestalt, find the details in complex stimuli, and traverse motorically a visuospatial matrix (maze). Orientation of the body in space as well as the capacity to recognize the orientation of stimuli are especially important to evaluate. Localization of sound in space as well as the ability to recognize geometric shapes without the benefit of vision are also routine aspects of the neuropsychological evaluation.

Abstract Reasoning

Various tests are available to evaluate the child's capacity to learn as well as identify concepts. Tasks should be administered that examine the ability to exercise these higer order cognitive processes using both linguistic and figural stimuli.

Executive Processes

With increasing developmental maturity, the child should acquire the broad-based self-regulating capacities necessary for goal-directed behavior. These capacities include planning, self-monitoring, use of internal language mediation, motor control, and cognitively mediated goal-directed behavior. As can be seen, these processes overlap with several of the neurocognitive capacities described previously. They are included here as a separate category because together these processes characterize the individual's ability to employ cognitive strategies in an ongoing and adaptive manner.

Each of the above domains of assessment should be covered in the course of a comprehensive neuropsychological evaluation. The information obtained, regardless of tests used or the theoretical inclinations of the practitioner, enables understanding of the basis for any manifest cognitive disorder. For example, while a reading disability may be readily detected using any one of a variety of measures, the basis for this deficit requires analyzing the problem into its functional components. Hence, a reading problem can occur as the result of simply poor vision or be consequential to perceptual problems, visuomotor problems, or deficits related to linguistic information processing. The skill of the clinical neuropsychologist is graded not by the ability to give tests to detect impairment, but rather to extract the information from such tests to formulate an understanding of the basis of the impairment.

SUMMARY

The neuropsychological evaluation of children poses numerous challenges to the clinician. First, the competency of the practitioner requires knowledge of neurobiological maturation, brain-behavior relationships, developmental psychology, and the general field of neuropsychology. Second, the evaluation of children necessarily entails understanding the efficacy and appropriateness of the plethora treatments and rehabilitation procedures presently available. And third, the examination process itself requires skill, patience, and an ability to integrate a large amount of information such that a comprehensive understanding of the child is obtained in the context of his or her interactions with a psychosocial environment.

As can be seen from the discussion in this chapter, the fields of developmental and child neuropsychology are still young. Not surprisingly, there is little consensus regarding the strategies of conducting the evaluation. Moreover, the paucity of validated instrumentation and proven effective methods for remediation or rehabilitation is noteworthy. It is evident that there is an urgent need for systematic clinical research. With the increasing survival rates of children either born with or acquiring neurological impairment, there will be an accompanying need to provide these children with every opportunity to maximize their full potential. This effort is required for both social, altruistic, as well as economic reasons. Without doubt, the neuropsychological evaluation and rehabilitation of impaired children will increasingly figure more prominently in the health care delivery system.

REFERENCES

Boll, T. J. (1974). Behavioral correlates of cerebral damage in children age 9–14. In R. M. Reitan & L. A. Davison (Eds.), *Clinical neuropsychology: Current status and application*. Washington, DC: Winston.

Boll, T. J. (1981). The Halstead-Reitan neuropsychological battery. In S. Filskov & T. J. Boll (Eds.), *Handbook of clinical neuropsychology* (pp. 577–607). New York: Wiley-Interscience.

Caviness, V. S., & Williams, R. S. (1979). *Cellular pathology of developing human cortex*. Research publication of the Association for Research in Nervous and Mental Diseases, *57*, 69–98.

Dennis, M., & Kohn, B. (1975). Comprehension of syntax in infantic hemiplesics after hemidecortication. Left hemisphere superiority. *Brain and Language, 2*, 472–482.

Epstein, H. T. (1978). Growth spurts during brain development: Implications for educational policy and practice. In J. S. Chall & A. F. Mirsky (Eds.), *Education and the brain: The 77th yearbook of the National Society of the Study of Education (Part II)*. Chicago: University of Chicago Pres.

Epstein, H. T. (1979). Correlated brain and intelligence development in humans. In M. E. Hahn, C. Jensen, & B. C. Dudek (Eds.), *Development and evolution of brain size: Behavioral implications* (pp. 111–131). New York: Academic Press.

Fletcher, J. M. (1988). Brain-injured children. In E. J. Mash & L. G. Terdal (Eds.), *Behavioral assessment of childhood disorders* (Vol. 2). New York: Guilford Press.

Gall, C., & Lynch, G. (1980). *Neural development: I. Current topics in developmental biology, 15*, pp. 159–182). New York: Academic Press.

Gardner, R. A. (1979). *The objective diagnosis of minimal brain dysfunction*. Cresskill, NJ: Creative Therapeutics.

Geschwind, N., & Galaburda, A. M. (1985). Cerebral lateralization: Biological Mechanisms, associations and pathology: A hypothesis and program for research. *Archives of Neurology, 42*, 428–459.

Geschwind, N., & Galaburda, A. M. (1987). *Cerebral lateralization: Biological mechanisms, associations and pathology I*. Cambridge, MA: MIT Press.

Golden, C. J. (1986). *Manual for the Luria-Nebraska Neuropsychological Battery: Children, Revision*. Los Angeles, WPS.

Golden, C. J. (1989). The Nebraska Neuropsychological Children's Battery. In C. R. Reynolds & E. Fletcher-Janzen (Eds.), *Handbook of clinical neuropsychology*. New York: Plenum Press.

Goldstein, K. (1939). *The organism*. New York: American.

Hartlage, L. C., & Telzrow, C. F. (1984). Rehabilitation of persons with learning disabilities. *Journal of Rehabilitation, 50,* 31–34.

Hartlage, L. C., & Telzrow, C. F. (1986). *Neuropsychological assessment and intervention with children and adolescents.* Sarasota, FL: Professional Resources Exchange.

Hynd, G. W., & Willis, W. G. (1988). *Pediatric neuropsychology.* New York: Grune & Stratton.

Kolb, B., & Fantie, B. (1989). Development of the child's brain and behavior. In C. R. Reynolds & E. Gletcher-Janzen (Eds.), *Handbook of clinical child neuropsychology.* New York: Plenum Press.

Knights, R. M., & Norwood, J. A. (1980). *Revised Smooth normative Data on the Neuropsychological Test Battery for Children.* Ottawa: Knights Psychological Consultants.

Lashley, K. S. (1923). *Brain Mechanisms and Intelligence.* Chicago: University of Chicago Press.

Lezak, M. D. (1983). *Neuropsychological assessment* (2nd ed.). New York: Oxford University Press.

Majovski, L. V. (1989). Higher cortical function in children: A developmental perspective. In C. R. Reynolds & E. Fletcher-Janzen (Eds.), *Handbook of clinical child neuropsychology.* New York: Plenum Press.

Molfese, D. L., & Segalowitz, S. J. (1988). *Brain lateralization in children; Developmental implications.* New York: Guilford Press.

Nussbaum, N. L., & Bigler, E. D. (1986). Neuropsychological and behavioral profiles of empirically derived subgroups of learning disabled children. *International Journal of Clinical Neuropsychology, 8,* 82–89.

Nussbaum, N. L., & Bigler, E. D. (1989). Halstead-Reitan neuropsychological test batteries for children. In C. R. Reynolds & E. Fletcher-Janzen (Eds.), *Handbook of clinical child neuropsychology.* New York: Plenum.

Reed, H. B. C., Reitan, R. M., & Klove, H. (1965). Influence of cerebral lesions on psychological test performances of older children. *Journal of Consulting Psychology, 29,* 247–251.

Reitan, R. M. (1969). *Manual for administration of neuropsychological test batteries for adults and children.* Indianapolis, IN: Author.

Reitan, R. M. (1974). Psychological effects of cerebral lesions in children of early school age. In R. M. Reitan & L. A. Davison (Eds.), *Clinical neuropsychology: Current status and applications.* Washington, DC: Winston.

Reitan, R. M., & Davison, L. A. (Eds.) (1974). *Clinical neuropsychology: Current status and applications.* Washington, DC: Winston.

Rourke, R. P., Bakker, D. J., Fisk, J. L., & Strang, J. D. (1983). *Child neuropsychology: An introduction to theory, research, and practice.* New York: Guilford Press.

Rourke, B. P., Fisk, J. L., & Strang, J. D. (1986). *Neuropsychological assessment of children: A treatment oriented approach.* New York: Guilford Press.

Rudel, R. G. (1978). Neuroplasticity: Implications for development and education. In J. S. Chall & A. F. Mirsky (Eds.), *Education and the brain (Part II).* Chicago: University of Chicago Press.

Sattler, J. M. (1988). *Assessment of children* (3rd ed.). San Diego: Author.

Seltz, M., & Reitan, R. M. (1979a). Neuropsychological test performance of normal, learning-disabled and brain damaged older children. *Journal of Nervous and Mental Disease, 167,* 298–302.

Seltz, M., & Reitan, R. M. (1979b). Rules of neuropsychological diagnosis: Classification of brain function in older children. *Journal of Consulting and Clinical Psychology, 47,* 258–264.

Seltz, M. (1981). Halstead-Reitan neuropsychological test battery for children. In G. W. Hynd & J. E. Obrzut (Eds.), *Neuropsychological assessment and the school age child: Issues and procedures.* New York: Grune & Stratton.

Spreen, O., & Gaddes, W. (1969). Developmental norms for fifteen neuropsychological tests, ages 6–15. *Cortex, 5,* 171–191.

Spreen, O., Tupper, D., Risser, A., Tuokko, H., & Edgell, D. (1984). *Human developmental neuropsychology.* New York: Oxford University Press.

St. James-Roberts, I. (1979). Neurological plasticity, recovery from brain insult, and child development. In H. W. Reese & L. P. Lipsitt (Eds.), *Advances in child development and behavior* (pp. 254–319). New York: Academic Press.

St. James-Roberts, I. (1981). A reinterpretation of hemispherectomy data without functional plasticity of the brain. *Brain and Language, 13,* 21–52.

Tarter, R. E., & Edwards, K. L. (1986). Neuropsychological batteries. In T. Incagnoli, G. Goldstein and C. J. Golden (Eds.), *Clinical applications of neuropsychological test batteries.* New York: Plenum Press.

Taylor, H. G., Fletcher, J. M., & Satz, P. (1984). Neuropsychological assessment of children. In G. Goldstein & M. Hersen (Eds.), *Handbook of psychological assessment.* New York: Pergamon Press.

Taylor, H. G., & Fletcher, J. M. (1990). Neuropsychological assessment of children. In G. Goldstein & M. Hersen (Eds.), *Handbook of psychological assessment* (2nd ed.) (pp. 228–255). New York: Pergamon Press.

Telzrow, C. F. (1989). Neuropsychological applications of common educational and psychological tests. In C. R. Reynolds & E. Fletcher-Janzen (Eds.), *Handbook of clinical child neuropsychology.* New York: Plenum Press.

Tusushima, W. T., & Towne, W. S. (1977). Neuropsychological abilities of young children with questionable brain disorders. *Journal of Consulting and Clinical Psychology, 45,* 757–762.

Wilson, B. C. (1986). An approach to the neuropsychological assessment of the preschool child with developmental deficits. In S. B. Filskov & T. J. Boll (Eds.), *Handbook of clinical neuropsychology.* (Vol. 2). New York: John Wiley & Sons.

CHAPTER 15

PROJECTIVE TECHNIQUES

A. J Finch, Jr.
Ronald W. Belter

Projective techniques have become such an established part of psychological assessment that most classifications of personality tests begin with projective and objective techniques. Projective techniques are generally regarded as those tests in which the individual gives a response to an ambiguous stimulus, and this response provides the examiner with some unique understanding of the individual's deepest conflicts, needs, or personality dynamics.

The concept of projection was employed by Freud (1894) to describe a defensive process whereby the ego attempted to defend itself by attributing unacceptable impulses to the external world. Murray (1938) broadened Freud's concept of projection to include more than a defensive strategy. For Murray, projection referred to the fact that the individual tended to be influenced by his or her total experiences, including internal needs and past events, when responding to an ambiguous situation. As a result, when faced with a situation with considerable uncertainty, such as an ambiguous stimulus, the individual "projects" previous experiences and needs onto that situation. Frank (1939) formulated the concept of projection into the *projective hypothesis,* which was then applied to several psychological tests. Since the formulation of the projective hypothesis, the Rorschach, Thematic Apperception Test, human figure drawings, and several other, less structured tests have been traditionally classified as "projective tests."

With the return to a more objective era in psychology typified by the behavioral movement, projective techniques came to symbolize a set of tests that lacked reliability, validity, and scientific support. Consequently, many psychologists associated projective techniques with an unscientific past and became dogmatic in their rejection of such practices. Despite this rejection by a segment of psychology, projective techniques continue to be employed and appear to be enjoying a revival. In fact, Tuma and Pratt (1982) found that most clinical child psychologists use projective measures. The purpose of this chapter is to evaluate the current status of selected projective techniques and to describe the nature of research that is currently underway in the area. However, this chapter will not attempt to be exhaustive in its review. Each section provides a brief description of the instruments, discusses the difficulties in evaluating the reliability and validity of the measure, and attempts to outline directions for additional research.

APPERCEPTION TECHNIQUES

Apperception techniques are those testing situations in which the individual is presented a picture and is asked to make up a story about what is happening in it. The assumption is that the individual's response will reflect the needs, desires, and conflicts the individual is experiencing.

The first of the major apperception tests was the Thematic Apperception Test (TAT) (Murray, 1943). The TAT consists of 31 picture cards depicting dramatic events or critical situations. Most of the pictures contain at least one person with whom the individual can identify when telling a story. Among the cards, different sets have been specified for use with men, women, boys, and girls, as well as a set for all subjects. Most individuals administer about 10 cards to a subject despite Murray's original instruction to administer 20 cards in two separate sessions. The original instructions for children required the child to make up a story for each picture, including what happened before, what is happening now, what the people are thinking and feeling, and how it will end.

When the TAT was originally introduced, it was designed to be scored according to various presses and needs described in Murray's (1938) theory of personality. However, a major problem with the TAT has been the absence of a single scoring system that can be adopted for clinical and research purposes. This problem exists despite the availability of a variety of scoring systems in addition to Murray's (Arnold, 1949; Aron, 1949; Bellak, 1975; Dana, 1959; Fine, 1955; Henry, 1956; Holt, 1951; Pine, 1960; Rotter, 1946; Stein, 1955; Tomkins, 1947; Wyatt, 1947). Most individuals do not score the TAT in clinical use, but instead read the responses of the subjects to obtain an understanding of the individual's inner feelings; thus, the interpretation of the TAT is a clinical art form (Dana, 1985).

A major problem encountered when examining the literature on the TAT has been the many different combinations of cards that are possible. Despite several attempts to standardize the cards administered (Hartman, 1970), each clinician and researcher usually administers a unique subset of the 31 cards. In a recent paper, Keiser and Prather (1990) examined a 10-year period (1978–1988) of research with the TAT and found that most studies did not indicate which cards were employed. However, in those studies in which the cards employed were specified, only 1 of the 31 cards was common in those studies. The authors conlcude that there was such variability in the cards employed that it was impossible to generalize from one study to the next.

Despite these difficulties with methodology, there have been some successful scoring systems for measuring single characteristics such as hostility and aggression (Davids & Rosenblatt, 1958; Hafner & Kaplan, 1960), achievement (McClelland, Atkinson, Clark, & Lowell, 1953) and depression (Aaron, 1967). On the other hand, attempts to provide comprehensive scoring systems have been unsuccessful. For example, Neman and colleagues (Neman, Brown, & Sells, 1973; Neman, Neman, & Sells, 1974) attempted to develop an objective scoring system for the measurement of personality functioning. They collected data on a large national sample of children but concluded that the TAT was inappropriate for the assessment of personality functioning in children.

Given this state of affairs, it is easy to understand why questions of reliability and validity remain an issue with the TAT (Sharkey & Ritzler, 1985). This concern may explain the marked decrease in research conducted on the TAT in the 1970s and 1980s (Polyson, Norris, & Ott, 1985). However, this decreasing research is in contrast to the clinical use of the test, which appears to be holding constant (Lubin, Larsen, & Matarazzo, 1984).

In addition to the concerns about the reliability and validity of the TAT, numerous authors have suggested that the TAT tends to have a bias toward eliciting negative emotional themes (Garfield & Eron, 1948; Holmstrom, Silber, & Karp, 1990; Ritzler, Sharkey, & Chudy, 1980; Sharkey & Ritzler, 1985). These authors have contended that many of the TAT cards are gloomy and negative and consequently tend to result in the reporting of only negative feelings. Research with the TAT tends to support this contention. McArthur (1976) has demonstrated that the stimulus characteristics of the cards, not the unique personality characteristics of the child, are the primary determinants of the response.

One additional complaint is frequently voiced about the TAT. The actual pictures have become quite dated, and many appear to have limited relevance to everyday life. Because the pictures were produced in the 1930s, it is easy to understand why so many of the pictures seem outdated. Whether or not this has an effect on the nature of the response given by the subject has not been investigated, but anyone who has given the TAT to adolescents and children is familiar with their negative comments about the "old" pictures.

This accumulation of problems has resulted in the introduction of a variety of apperception measures as alternatives to the TAT. A complete review of these measures is beyond the scope of this chapter. Interested readers should see Obrzut and Boliek (1986) for a more detailed discussion of apperception tests. However, a brief overview of some of the other apperception measures is provided here.

Bellak and Bellak (1949) introduced the Children's Apperception Test for young children, which consists of 10 cards containing pictures of animals in various activities and interactions. Animals were employed rather than humans because it was believed that children would identify more readily with the animals. In addition, it was felt that they would elicit more projective material from the children, because there were fewer social restrictions on the behavior of cartoon animals. Whether children can identify with the animals or not and whether they will provide more projective material to the animal cards has been a point of debate. The CAT has been found to elicit longer responses from children than does the TAT (Myler, Rosenkrantz, & Holmes, 1972). However, Lawton (1966) found that the stories children provide in response to CAT cards with human characters are as meaningful as the ones they provide in response to the original ones with animals. As a result, the CAT is available in both animal and human forms.

Bellak (1975) has suggested that the analysis of the child's responses to the CAT should focus primarily on the content of responses with regard to the hero, his or her status, primary conflicts, and outcomes of the stories. Bellak's scoring system is more qualitative than quantitative and does not lend itself readily to research. Other scoring systems have been suggested, such as the one by Chandler, Shermis, and Lempert (1989), which focuses on the need-threat analysis of children's stories. This system appears to have some potential for research and clinical use. However, most of the scoring systems have poor reliability and questionable validity (Haworth, 1966), and most clinicians use the CAT in a subjective manner and do not score the responses at all.

McArthur and Roberts (1982) introduced the Roberts Apperception Test for Children (RATC) to assess children's perceptions of interpersonal situations, including their thoughts, concerns, conflicts, and coping styles. It was designed for children from 6 through 15 years of age. There are 27 stimulus cards, and the child is administered 16 of these with different cards for males and females. Each card depicts children in common situations, conflicts, and stressful situations. Scenes of parental affection and disagreement, aggressive situations, observations of nudity, and school and peer interactions are provided.

A scoring system is provided for measuring both adaptive and maladaptive functioning. The scoring system includes eight adaptive scales and five clinical scales. Three additional dimensions, called critical indicators, are also part of the scoring system. The authors report that critical indicators are rarely seen in well-adjusted children. Scores from the adaptive and clinical scales are converted into normalized t-scores according to the age of the child.

Interpretation of the RATC combines both qualitative and quantitative information. The qualitative interpretation is similar to Bellak's and looks for recurrent themes, typical defenses, the nature of interpersonal relations, and so forth. The quantitative information obtained from the RATC includes (1) sequential analysis of the individual profile scales and indicators, and (2) comparison of mean scale scores for the adaptive and clinical scales, (3) examination of interscale variability (i.e., scatter) and (4) use of the Interpersonal Matrix.

Reliability and validity data as reported by the authors appear to be good. Few normative data on 200 children are provided, and additional normative data seem to be needed, because the number of subjects at the various age levels is small. However, the RATC appears to be well designed and to hold potential for research and clinical assessment of children. Despite this potential, there needs to be a great deal of investigation of the reliability of the various scores and the validity of the constructs. To date, there has been only limited research interest in this potentially useful measure.

Karp, Holmstrom, and Silber (1989) have recently developed the Apperceptive Personality Test for adolescents and adults. This test was designed to address a number of the criticisms leveled at the TAT. First, the authors decided to limit the number of cards to eight and to administer all cards to all subjects. This decision was made to eliminate the problem with different studies employing different cards. In addition, the authors report that this number approximates the actual number of apperception cards employed by most clinicians and researchers. The pictures present a variety of males, females, young, and old individuals in ambiguous activities in familiar, everyday settings. In addition, various minority members are represented.

All eight APT cards are administered to each subject in a standard order, with the instructions similar to those of most apperception tests. The subject is asked to make up a story for each card, and each story is to have a beginning, a middle, and an ending or outcome. The subject is told that the story should be imaginative and should tell what each person is doing, thinking, and feeling. Immediately following the administration, the subject is given a questionnaire to complete about each picture.

The authors contend that a major difficulty with the TAT is the lack of a consistent scoring system. They believe that this difficulty arises in part because the examiner is required to make difficult judgments or interpretations about the verbalizations provided by the subject. To eliminate this problem, the authors developed the APT Questionnaire booklet, which consists of one sheet per card and a group of questions asking the subject to respond to a series of six questions about each story. According to Holmstrom, Silber, and Karp (1990) the various questions are concerned with the following issues:

1. The relationships between the characters.
2. The feelings or emotions of the characters.
3. The actions of each character.
4. Who the central figure is for each story.
5. The outcome of the story rated on a five-point scale ranging from *very happy or very successful* (5) to *very unhappy or very unsuccessful* (1).
6. Impressions of both story characters are described on seven-point rating scales using the following nine bipolar adjective pairs: smart-stupid, mean-kind, capable-inept, caring-indifferent, dishonest-honest, leader-follower, happy-sad, trustworthy-untrustworthy, and successful-unsuccessful (Holmstrom, Silber, Karp, 1990, p. 257).

The APT Questionnaire asks the subject to code the information directly from the story as the objective basis for the story. As a result, there is no need for judgment or interpretation on the part of the examiner. APT scoring is simplified through the selection of various subsets of variables, and a computer program is available to help score the responses. In addition, the examiner has the actual stories available for qualitative interpretation.

The test-retest reliability of the APT, determined for the various scoring categories, appears to be encouraging. In addition, initial investigations of validity appear to warrant further study. This measure has potential for both research and clinical work with adolescents. However, it has not been evaluated with children, and the reading level and format for answering questions may limit its usefulness with younger subjects. In addition, most of the work to date has been done with college students, and the effectiveness of this measure with patient populations has not been demonstrated.

There appears to be renewed interest in the area of apperception tests, and new measures are being developed to address the criticisms of traditional tests such as the TAT and CAT. Initial reports indicate that they may prove to be more reliable and valid than the earlier measures. However, whether or not these newer tests will enjoy the clinical popularity of these earlier tests will depend on their clinical utility and availability to the clinicians.

DRAWING TECHNIQUES

Children's drawings have a certain appeal that make them of considerable interest to people who work with children. One has only to walk through the hallways of most elementary schools to see drawings freely displayed on the walls and bulletin boards. Psychologists working with children have a similar fascination with their drawings. Goodenough (1926) reported on the usefulness of children's drawings as estimates of intellectual functioning. Despite the considerable research indicating that drawings provide a very poor estimate of intelligence (Aikman, Belter, & Finch, 1990; Scott, 1981), interest in their use with children has continued, and estimates of intelligence based on children's drawings are still reported.

In addition to attempts to estimate intellectual functioning from children's drawings, several individuals have proposed that drawings provide information about the individual's personality functioning. Machover (1949) felt that drawings illustrated the individual's conflicts, anxieties, impulses, and compensations. These drawings were regarded as "projections" of the individual. According to Cummings (1986), projective drawings serve several functions:

1. To allow nonverbal children to express themselves, that is, graphic communication between the child and psychologist through the use of symbols.
2. To gain an understanding of a child's inner con-

flicts, fears, interactions with family members, and perceptions of others.
3. To understand the child from a psychodynamic perspective....
4. To generate hypotheses and serve as a springboard for further evaluation. (Cummings, 1986, p. 202)

A variety of drawing procedures have been used with children, and a complete review of all of these is beyond the scope of the current chapter. We will present an overview of the techniques that appear to have widespread use.

The Draw-A-Person technique is probably the most widely used projective drawing. The child is simply presented a piece of blank white paper and a pencil and is asked to draw a picture of a whole person. Several authors have provided various interpretive strategies for approaching this test. Machover (1949) generated a number of interpretive hypotheses based on her observations of adolescents and adults. She felt that various aspects of the drawings were of particular importance, such as the size and placement of the figure, the line quality, the stance of the figure, the facial expression, erasures, and shading. She believed that each of these signs has interpretive significance and provides some insight into the personality functioning of the individual. A similar system has been suggested by Hammer (1958).

Cummings (1986) has discussed the difficulty of investigating test-retest reliability with human figure drawings. One major issue is whether drawings are state or trait measures of functioning. If they are state measures, minor variations in mood could result in vastly different drawings. In addition, the question of whether the total number of indicators should be the important measure or whether the presence or absence of a particular indicator is the major concern has resulted in a number of conflicting results. It seems clear that certain general characteristics of children's drawings are reliable. However, whether specific indicators are reliable is questionable.

Machover's and Hammer's systems of interpretation have received considerable clinical attention and appear to be a part of the approach most clinicians use in their interpretation of children's drawings. For example, it is generally assumed that the size of the drawing is related to self-concept. According to this assumption, a small drawing suggests a poor self-concept. However, there appear to be limited data to support the notion that self-concept is related to the size of the drawing (Prytula, Phelps, & Morrissey, 1978). However, it has been found that children with conduct disorder produce larger drawings than do neurotic children (McHugh, 1966); and depressed girls, but not depressed boys, draw smaller figures than nondepressed subjects (Prytula & Leigh, 1972). However, Holmes and Wiederholt (1982) failed to find any relationship between self-report of depression and the size of drawings.

The issue of body image being reflected in human figure drawings has received considerable attention. The basic assumption of the body image hypothesis is that when the individual is asked to draw a picture, the subject produces a picture that represents himself or herself. In a review of the literature, Swenson (1957) found little evidence to support this hypothesis. However, Cummings (1986) has suggested that the hypothesis is more complicated than it initially appears. After reviewing much of the available research, he concluded that the research suggests some disruption of body image in handicapped individuals but that the type of handicap may not necessarily be reflected directly in the nature of the drawing. For example, obese children draw more stick figures and obtain lower development scores than nonobese children. However, they draw fewer obese figures than do children of normal weight (Nathan, 1973).

Another variable that has received a great deal of attention is the sex of the figure drawn. Machover (1949) originally hypothesized that drawing a figure of the opposite sex first suggested a sexual-identification problem. It is true that individuals do tend to draw the same-sex figure most of the time (Dickson, Saylor, & Finch, 1990), but whether or not drawing a member of the opposite sex first reflects sexual-identification problems or not is another issue. Several studies have found that boys who exhibit cross-gender behaviors are more likely to draw female figures first (Green, Fuller, & Rutley, 1972; Skilbeck, Bates, & Bentler, 1975). Despite these results being statistically significant, the proportions were not that large and are probably of limited clinical utility. In addition, there are some indications that sociological factors are very important in the sex of the figure drawn and that, as sexual stereotypes change, so does the sex of first figure drawn (Teglasi, 1980).

Koppitz (1968) has developed a different series of emotional indicators in children's drawings of human figures. She demonstrated good reliability with this scoring system. In contrast to other systems, Koppitz has recommended that rather than taking each of these indicators as a sign of a particular difficulty, the total number of the indicators present should be examined. In fact, she cautions against using any of the indicators in isolation. Her data suggest that when the number of indicators between normal and emotionally disturbed children is compared, the difference is significant. However, there are no indications that specific types of disturbances can be identified. We suggest that a test's ability to differentiate emotionally disturbed from normal children is only the first step in establishing the validity of the test. Additional work is needed with Koppitz's scoring system to determine its potential usefulness. It does have the advantage of being more objective than the other systems and may hold some potential.

Another variation of drawings that has enjoyed clinical use is the House-Tree-Person technique (Buck, 1948). In this technique, the subject was originally given a four-page booklet, with each page being 7 × 8½ inches. Apparently, Buck used this format because of availability of paper in that size at the facility where he worked. Most clinicians use separate sheets of paper, and Bieliauskas and Farragher (1983) have found that the size of the paper does not matter. The individual is first asked to draw a house on the first page. Next, a tree is requested on the second page, and then a person on the third page. Finally a person of the opposite sex is drawn on the fourth page. A standard set of questions is asked about each picture. In a separate session, this process is repeated with crayons, and the individual is allowed to select different colors for the drawings.

Relatively limited research data are available on the House-Tree-Person technique. The available data indicate that reliability of the technique is adequate (Marzolf & Kirchner, 1970). However, the findings that have been reported to support the test's validity have generally been disappointing (Cummings, 1986). Although statistically significant relationships between the House-Tree-Person and other construct measures have been reported, the magnitude of the relationships between the measures that were significant was small and probably of limited clinical utility.

Burns and Kaufman (1970) introduced the Kinetic Family Drawing (KFD) as a means of determining the individual's perception of family functioning. In this test, the individual is asked to draw a picture of everyone in his or her family doing something. The subject is instructed to draw complete figures as opposed to stick figures and to include himself or herself. The examiner asks who each of the figures is and what each are doing. Burns and Kaufman (1970) present numerous case examples to demonstrate how the various actions, styles, and symbols emerge in the kinetic drawings of family members. In addition, the more traditional aspects of the drawings, such as omissions, locations, erasures, and so on are examined. Interpretation of the KFDs is highly subjective, and the authors did not provide scoring criteria. Several other authors have introduced more objective scoring methods for the KFD that appear to have fairly good interrater reliability but limited test-retest reliability (Cummings, 1986). Furthermore, there is limited validity data to support the use of the KFD as an indication of family functioning (Brannigan, Schofield, & Holtz, 1982), and Cummings has concluded that "it would be inappropriate to rely heavily on the present version" (Cummings, 1986, p. 228).

Despite wide clinical appeal and use, limited data support the use of drawings to make interpretations about personality functioning. There is no means of interpreting drawings that results in consistently valid information about the individual's functioning. This conclusion has led some to suggest that the use of projective drawings is unethical (Martin, 1983). From a purely objective point of view, this position is difficult to dispute. We suggest that drawings are an easy entry into formal testing and enable the examiner to begin the testing process in a very nonthreatening fashion. For this reason, the drawings are useful and will probably be retained in most evaluations. Drawing techniques also provide rich clinical information, which lends itself to subjective, qualitative interpretation. However, beyond this use, there are insufficient data to support the use of drawing techniques in an objective fashion.

RORSCHACH TEST

Some understanding of the history of the Rorschach test must be gained before it can be discussed here. The work of Herman Rorschach on the use of ink blots as an aid in understanding patients was prematurely halted because of his untimely death. As a result of his death and the lack of clear leadership in the development of this procedure, considerable divergence in the use of the test developed. From the very beginning, the Rorschach was controversial. In fact, the attacks on the Rorschach made shortly after its publication sound remarkably like those made today. According to Ellenberger (1954), Dr. Rorschach was attacked on one side for his methodology and statistics, and on the other side for assuming that a test could "ever seize and comprehend the human personality" (p. 97).

Within the United States, five very different systems or approaches to the Rorschach evolved (Exner, 1969). These systems varied greatly as to their emphasis on psychometric standards and the importance of normative data. At one extreme was Samuel Beck, who was trained in the United States with a commitment to scientific rigor and the development of normative data. At the other end of the continuum was Bruno Klopfer, who was educated in Europe and was much more phenomenologically oriented. For Klopfer, the overemphasis on norms and psychometrics seemed to miss the more relevant clinical features of the test. The differences between Beck's approach to the Rorschach and Klopfer's was complicated by their lack of willingness to compromise or discuss their positions with each other.

Exner (1969) provides a detailed discussion of the differences between the Klopfer and Beck systems as well as those of Piotrowski, Hertz, and Rapaport and Schafer. Each of the systems developed as a result of the various interests of the persons involved. A detailed discussion of their similarities and differences is beyond the scope of this chapter. Interested readers should consult Exner (1969). However, some understanding of the differences is necessary. Exner suggested that "if a hypothetical continuum were drawn, placing the tenets of behaviorism on the far right and those of the more subjective phenomenology on the far left, the basic premises of each of the five systems can be evaluated along such a line" (Exner, 1969, p. 8). Figure 15.1 presents such a line, with each system placed on the continuum.

As a result of these five different systems, the data from the studies have been considerably difficult to compare. The differences between these systems are not minor, and they are in no way interchangeable. As Exner (1969) pointed out, it would have been easier to compare the systems and recognize their differences if they had developed completely independently. However, there was some transfer from one system to another. Unfortunately, these incidents of transfer were not necessarily complete, and there are similar terms and symbols within the various systems that have different criteria for scoring. The result has been an extremely confusing situation that has led many to question the usefulness of the Rorschach.

As an example of how minor variations in procedures and definitions can affect the data obtained, we will examine the simplest of variables—the total number of responses. Klopfer followed Rorschach's original instructions and presented each card with the standard administration question: "What might this be?" This was followed by encouragement if the subject provided only one response to the first card. On the other hand, Beck's instructions request the subject to "Tell me everything that you can see" and provides encouragement for each of the first five cards if only one response is provided. This minor variation in procedures results in a significant difference in the number of responses given (Exner, 1974). Consequently, any attempt to compare data across systems results in a lack of consistent findings.

Given the differences between the systems and the lack of consistency of data obtained from one system to another, difficulties with reliability and validity were inevitable. Furthermore, Exner and Exner (1972) surveyed a large sample of Rorschach users and found results with major implications for the psychometric properties of the Rorschach. Slightly less than 25% of persons using the Rorschach did not score it at all. Of those scoring the test, 75% had evolved their own scoring system, which was a mixture of the various systems. As a result of these individual variations in scoring and procedures, there appeared to exist not one Rorschach test, nor five, but perhaps as many as one for each individual clinician who used the test.

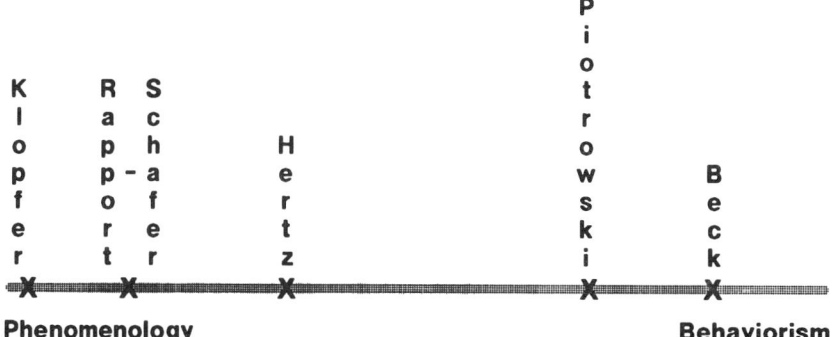

Figure 15.1. Representation of basic premises of five major Rorschach systems. Adopted from Exner (1969).

In addition to the diversity of the various systems, another issue of relevance to the current status of the Rorschach must be addressed. This issue has to do with how to determine the validity of the Rorschach. Despite the numerous scores and ratios obtained from the Rorschach, very few single scores mean anything in and of themselves. It is only when the scores are examined within the context of the entire record that they can be accurately interpreted. This need to consider a single score within the context of the entire text has been ignored in much of the research. Most attempts to study the validity of the Rorschach have taken one or two scores or ratios and attempted to correlate them with some specific behavior or rating on another scale. The Rorschach was never intended to be used in this manner, but the frequently obtained negative results have been used to demonstrate the lack of validity of the Rorschach. As Blatt (1975) has stated, many studies have failed to support the use of the Rorschach because the investigators have employed the test scores without any understanding of the assumptions and interpretive rationale of the test.

One final source of difficulty in evaluating the current status of the Rorschach comes from the nature of the scores and ratios obtained. Many of these scores are far from normally distributed, and the indiscriminate application of typical statistical techniques results in meaningless results. For example, a single Texture response was given by 79% of subjects in a large nonpatient sample (Exner, 1986). Thus, if a Texture response is absent or occurs more than once in a given Rorschach record, it is an unusual event and may have some interpretive implications. This type of distribution simply does not lend itself to parametric statistics. Unfortunately, much of the research in the area has tended to ignore this factor.

As a result of these difficulties Exner and his colleagues (Exner, 1978; Exner & Weiner, 1982) have developed the Comprehensive System for the Rorschach. This system evolved from Exner's earlier work describing the five major systems used in the United States (Exner, 1969). The Comprehensive System was developed by Exner and the Rorschach Research Foundation by taking those features of the five existing systems that were supported by firm empirical data. For example, an acceptable interrater reliability was required. Large samples of normative data were collected to determine the reliability of different scoring criteria and to evaluate the existing Rorschach literature.

The Comprehensive System has been widely accepted and is currently the most widely employed system in the United States. However, it has not been unanimously endorsed by all who use the Rorschach. Many psychoanalytically oriented psychologists argue that the Rorschach and personality cannot be reduced to ratios and scores. This group prefers to employ the "conceptual approach" to using the Rorschach test. This approach is probably more closely aligned with what most psychologists regard as a true projective approach. Advocates of the conceptual approach believe that the valid use of the Rorschach requires both a foundation in the test and a coherent theory of personality. According to Sugarman (1990), personality theory serves the following function in testing:

1. *Organization.* Theory serves to translate test findings into constructs within the theory to provide the examiner with a more complete understanding of the dynamics of the patient.
2. *Integration.* Theory serves to synthesize data and to resolve apparent paradoxes in the data. By the use of theory, the examiner can resolve apparently contradictory information by accepting that which is most consistent with the theory.
3. *Clarification.* Theory aids the examiner when the data are incomplete. Through theory, the examiner is better able to answer the referral questions by helping to fill in the gaps in the data.
4. *Prediction.* Theory aids the examiner in making predictions about the patient's behavior, since the test data provide only signs and general trends. Through the use of theory, the examiner is in a position to predict behavior, because the theory provides a more complete understanding of the person than the simple signs in the test data.

McCully (1989) and many conceptualists have argued that normative data are meaningless because a unique experience or thought cannot be standardized. Consequently, the conceptual approaches tend to focus more on the uniqueness of the individual rather than on how the individual differs from the "average" or "norm." However, the advocates of the conceptual approach do not accept the notion that this is an unscientific approach. McCully states that science is interested in discovery and validation. From the conceptual approach, discovery is the focus of the testing rather than validation. The conceptualists are interested in discovering the unique aspects of the individual, and consequently, the notion of norms is meaningless. For those who would argue that such an approach is unscientific, Jaffee (1990) has argued that such critics view science too narrowly. Science is composed of more than statistical significance, and it is difficult to rely solely on statistical analysis without losing important information about the individual. The conceptual approach is validated through the repeated observations and validation of specifically derived hypotheses with individual patients. In actuality, the conceptual approach sounds very similar to the arguments made by the early operant theorists in their approach to understanding behavior.

The conceptual approach is in contrast to the "structural approach" exemplified by Exner (1986). The term "structural" is probably an oversimplification but comes from Exner's contention that the variables on the structural summary (a summary sheet of the various scores and ratios) of the Rorschach are the most valid and reliable of the variables and should be the starting point of the test interpretation. Table 15–1, p. 233, presents a copy of the latest structural summary sheet for the Comprehensive System.

Exner is atheoretical in his approach to the Rorschach and tends to be more closely aligned with the traditional "psychometric" approaches to testing such as has been used with the Minnesota Multiphasic Personality Inventory. As previously mentioned, Exner has provided extensive data on the reliability and validity of the Rorschach as well as normative data for a wide variety of populations. Interpretation begins by comparing the individual's scores on the various ratios to the scores obtained by the normative samples. By this comparison, the clinician is able to determine how the patient differs from or is similar to the nonpatient and patient samples. With this list of differences in mind, the clinician is in a better position to describe the patient and to support that description with objective data. The clinician is also less likely to be led astray by the subjective interpretation of a single response.

Since there are many potential starting points for analyzing the data in the structural summary, Exner (1990) has provided a strategy for approaching the structural summary. A series of decision rules have been established, and the variables have been grouped into clusters that seem to be related. In this manner, analysis of the data is a structured approach that ensures that the clinician attends to the most significant information for that individual first, and then moves to more peripheral features of the data. This structural approach also emphasizes the analysis of specific variables and ratios in the context of the entire record in relation to the other pieces of data. This type of logic and the systematic nature of this approach are likely to appeal to many clinicians who have been uncomfortable with the more "freewheeling" approach that many clinicians use with the Rorschach. However, it is the very approach that others are likely to object to as being too mechanical.

In working with the Comprehensive System for the Rorschach, we are struck by the similarities that exist between its scoring and the various systems that have been developed for coding behavior. Scoring of individual responses is very similar to coding of verbal behaviors. The examiner uses various categories to code the responses of the subject. With regard to intercoder reliability, the problem of site drift is as much a problem for coding Rorschach responses as it is for any behavioral coding system. In our work with the Rorschach, we have been able to establish good intercoder reliability but have had to work hard to ensure that our scores are consistent with those given by other users of the test in other sites. This is a major concern for the average user of the Rorschach, who may be consistent with himself or herself in coding responses, but may deviate significantly from others using the same coding system.

Despite the many problems and difficulties the Rorschach has experienced, it continues to enjoy considerable popularity among clinicians. In addition, an examination of the last several years of the *Journal of Personality Assessment* indicates that considerable research is being conducted with the Rorschach. In examining this research, we were struck by how many of the same problems are appearing that have been mentioned as problems with previous research in the area. For example, Belter, Lipovsky, and Finch (1989) examined the relationship between self-reported self-concept and the Ego-Centricity Index from the Rorschach structural summary, which is reportedly related to self-concept. In this study, we compared one variable from the Rorschach with another measure from a different test. This type of variable-specific study is necessary but falls short of the reported richness of the Rorschach record. Before the Rorschach can obtain acceptance by the scientific community of psychologists, more appropriate methods of addressing its validity need to be developed. The test is simply too complex for current methodology, and frequently the scores do not lend themselves to available methodology.

SUMMARY

In this chapter, we reviewed the history and current status of the primary projective techniques employed with children. Given the nature of projective tech-

Table 15-1. STRUCTURAL SUMMARY

LOCATION FEATURES	DETERMINANTS BLENDS	DETERMINANTS SINGLE	CONTENTS	APPROACH SUMMARY CARD:	APPROACH SUMMARY LOCATIONS:
Zf =			H =		
ZSum =		M =	(H) =	I:	
ZEst =		FM =	Hd =	II:	
		m =	(Hd) =	III:	
		FC =	Hx =	IV:	
W =		CF =	A =	V:	
(Wv =)		C =	(A) =	VI:	
D =		Cn =	Ad =	VII:	
Dd =		FC' =	(Ad) =	VIII:	
S =		C'F =	An =	IX:	
		C' =	Art =	X:	
DQ		FT =	Ay =		
.... (FQ−)		TF =	Bl =		Special Scorings
+ = ( )		T =	Bt =		Lvl-1 Lvl-2
o = ( )		FV =	Cg =	DV =	x1 x2
v/+ = ( )		VF =	Cl =	INC =	x2 x4
v = ( )		V =	Ex =	DR =	x3 x6
		FY =	Fd =	FAB =	x4 x7
		YF =	Fi =	ALOG =	x5
	Form Quality	Y =	Ge =	CON =	x7
FQx FQf MQual SQx		Fr =	Hh =		
		rF =	Ls =	Raw Sum6 =	
+ = + = + = + =		FD =	Na =	Wgtd Sum6 =	
o = o = o = o =		F =	Sc =		
u = u = u = u =			Sx =	AB = CP =	
− = − = − = − =			Xy =	AG = MOR =	
none = none = none =		(2) =	Idio =	CFB = PER =	
				COP = PSV =	

RATIOS, PERCENTAGES, AND DERIVATIONS

R =	L =		*AFFECT*		*INTERPERSONAL*
			FC:CF+C = :		COP = AG =
EB = :	EA =	EBPer =	Pure C =		Food =
eb = :	es =	D =	Afr =		Isolate/R =
	Adj es =	Adj D =	S =		H:(H)+Hd+(Hd) =
			Blends:R = :		(H)+(Hd):(A)+(Ad) = :
FM =	C' =	T =	CP =		H+A:Hd+Ad = :
m =	V =	Y =			
			MEDIATION	*PROCESSING*	*SELF PERCEPTION*
IDEATION		Sum6 =	P =	Zf =	3r+(2)/R =
a:p = :		Lvl-2 =	X+% =	Zd =	Fr+rF =
$M^a:M^p$ = :		WSum6 =	F+% =	W:D:Dd = : :	FD =
2AB+(Art+Ay) =		M none =	X−% =	W:M = :	An+Xy =
M− =			S−% =	DQ+ =	MOR =
			Xu% =	DQv =	

☐ SCZI =   ☐ DEPI =   ☐ CDI =   ☐ S-Con =   ☐ HVI =   ☐ OBS =

niques, founded in theories about unconscious internal processes, it is difficult to apply standard scientific method to the study of their reliability and validity. This has been at the crux of the debate between proponents and opponents of projective techniques.

The conceptual approach to the use of projective techniques is based in theories about the individual. In this approach, analysis of the projective data is usually a subjective and qualitative process that is specific to the individual being evaluated, as well as the individual examiner. This is not necessarily invalid, but it does pose problems of demonstrating reliability across different individuals and examiners. Rather than concluding that projective techniques are invalid, we regard this as a challenge to develop innovative methods to evaluate the reliability and validity of projective techniques.

The structural approach to projective techniques represents an effort to meet that challenge. This approach is exemplified by the Roberts Apperception Test for Children (McArthur & Roberts, 1982), the Apperceptive Personality Test (Karp, Holmstrom, & Silber, 1989), and the Comprehensive System for the Rorschach (Exner, 1986). The structural approach emphasizes reliability of coding responses obtained from a given individual, as the foundation for establishing the validity of the test. After such consistency has been established, the meaning and validity of the derived scores can be assessed. The need for further research of this nature on the projective techniques that are commonly used with children and adolescents is apparent.

We advocate an approach to the use of projective techniques with children and adolescents that integrates the conceptual approach with the structural approach. By integrating multiple types and sources of data, such an approach yields rich information about the individual. Hypotheses generated can be evaluated in the context of the entire set of assessment data, with information from different sources available to support conclusions derived.

REFERENCES

Aaron, N. S. (1967). Some personality differences between asthmatics, allergic and normal children. *Journal of Clinical Psychology, 23*, 336–340.

Aikman, K., Belter, R., & Finch, A. J., Jr. (1990). Human figure drawings: Validity in assessing intellectual level and academic achievement. Manuscript submitted for publication.

Arnold, M. (1949). A demonstration analysis of the TAT in a clinical setting. *Journal of Abnormal and Social Psychology, 44*, 97–111.

Aron, B. (1949). *A manual for analysis of the Thematic Apperception Test: A method and technique for personality research*. Berkeley, CA: Berg.

Bellak, L. (1975). *The TAT, CAT, and SAT in clinical use* (3rd ed.). New York: Grune & Stratton.

Bellak, L., & Bellak, S. (1949). *The children's apperception test*. New York: C.P.S. Company.

Belter, R., Lipovsky, J., & Finch, A. (1989). Rorschach egocentricity index and self-concept in children and adolescent. *Journal of Personality Assessment, 53*, 783–789.

Bieliauskas, V., & Farragher, J. (1983). The effect of the drawing sheet on the H-T-P IQ scores. *Journal of Clinical Psychology, 39*, 1033–1034.

Blatt, S. (1975). The validity of projective techniques and their clinical and research contributions. *Journal of Personality Assessment, 39*, 327–343.

Brannigan, G., Schofield, J., & Holtz, R. (1982). Family drawings as measures of interpersonal distance. *Journal of Social Psychology, 117*, 155–156.

Buck, J. (1948). The H-T-P technique, a qualitative and quantitative method. *Journal of Clinical Psychology, 4*, 317–396.

Burns, R., & Kaufman, S. (1970). *Kinetic Family Drawings (K-F-D): An introduction to understanding children through kinetic drawings*. New York: Brunner/Mazel.

Chandler, L., Shermis, M., & Lempert, M. (1989). *Psychology in the schools, 26*, 47–54.

Cummings, J. (1986). Projective Drawings. In H. Knoff (Ed.), *The assessment of child and adolescent personality*. New York: Guilford Press.

Dana, R. (1959). Proposal for objective scoring of the TAT [Monograph]. *Perceptual and Motor Skills, 10*, 27–43.

Dana, R. (1985). Thematic Apperception Test (TAT). In C. S. Newmark (Ed.). *Major psychological assessment instruments*. Boston: Allyn & Bacon.

Davids, A., & Rosenblatt, D. (1958). Use of the TAT in assessment of alienation. *Journal of Projective Techniques, 24*, 137–143.

Dickson, J., Saylor, C., & Finch, A. J., Jr. (1990). Personality factors, family structure, and sex of drawn figure on the Draw-A-Person Test. *Journal of Personality Assessment, 55*, 362–366.

Ellenberger, H. (1954). *Bulletin of the Menninger Clinic. 18*, 173–219. Reprinted in A. M. O'Roark & J. E. Exner (Eds.). *History and directory: Society of personality assessment*. Hillsdale, NJ: Lawrence Erlbaum Associates.

Exner, J. (1969). *The Rorschach systems*. New York: Grune & Stratton.

Exner, J. (1974). *The Rorschach: A comprehensive system* (Vol. 1). New York: John Wiley & Sons.

Exner, J. (1978). *The Rorschach: A comprehensive system* (Vol. 2). New York: John Wiley & Sons.

Exner, J. (1986). *The Rorschach: A comprehensive system* (Vol. 2) (2nd ed.). New York: John Wiley & Sons.

Exner, J. E. (1990). *Alumni Newsletter*. Asheville, NC: Rorschach Workshops.

Exner, J., & Exner, D. (1972). How clinicians use the Rorschach. *Journal of Personality Assessment, 36*, 403–408.

Exner, J. E., & Weiner, I. B. (1982). *The Rorschach: A comprehensive system. Vol. 3. Assessment of children and adolescents*. New York: John Wiley & Sons.

Fine, R. (1955). A scoring scheme for the TAT and other verbal projective techniques. *Journal of Projective Techniques, 19*, 306–309.

Frank, L. (1939). Projective methods for the study of personality. *Journal of Psychology, 8*, 389–413.

Freud, S. (1894). The anxiety neurosis. *Collected papers* (Vol. 1). London: Hogarth Press, 1953, 76–106.

Garfield, S., & Eron, L. (1948). Interpreting mood and activity in TAT stories. *Journal of Abnormal and Social Psychology, 43,* 338–345.

Goodenough, F. L. (1926). *Measurement of intelligence by drawings.* New York: Harcourt, Brace, & World.

Green, R., Fuller, M., & Rutley, B. (1972). It-Scale for children and Draw-A-Person test. *Journal of Personality Assessment, 36,* 349–352.

Hafner, A. J., & Kaplan, A. M. (1960). Hostility content analysis of the Rorschach and TAT. *Journal of Projective Techniques, 24,* 137–143.

Hammer, E. (1958). *The clinical application of projective drawings.* Springfield, IL: Charles C Thomas.

Hartman, A. (1970). A basic TAT set. *Journal of Projective Techniques and Personality Assessment, 34,* 391–396.

Haworth, M. (1966). *The CAT: Facts and Fantasy.* New York: Grune & Stratton.

Henry, W. (1956). *The analysis of fantasy.* New York: John Wiley & Sons.

Holmes, C., & Wiederholt, J. (1982). Depression and figure size on the Draw-A-Person test. *Perceptual and Motor Skills, 55,* 825–826.

Holmstrom, R., Silber, D., & Karp, S. (1990). Development of the Apperception Personality Test. *Journal of Personality Assessment, 54* (1&2), 252–264.

Holt, R. (1951). The Thematic Apperception Test. In H. Anderson & C. Anderson (Eds.), *An introduction to projective techniques* (pp. 181–229). Englewood Cliffs, NJ: Prentice-Hall.

Jaffee, L. S. (1990). The empirical foundations of psychoanalytic approaches to psychological testing. *Journal of Personality Assessment, 55,* 746–755.

Karp, S., Holmstrom, R., & Silber, D. (1989). *Apperceptive personality test manual.* Chicago: International Diagnostic Systems.

Keiser, R. E., & Prather, E. N. (1990). What is the TAT? A review of ten years of research. *Journal of Personality Assessment, 55,* 800–803.

Koppitz, E. (1968). *Psychological evaluation of children's human figure drawings.* New York: Grune & Stratton.

Lawton, M. J. (1966). Animal and Human CATs with a school sample. *Journal of Projective Techniques and Personality Assessment, 30,* 243–246.

Lubin, B., Larsen, R., & Matarazzo, J. (1984). Patterns of psychological test usage in the United States: 1935–1982. *American Psychologist, 39,* 1984.

Machover, K. (1949). *Personality projection in the drawing of the human figure.* Springfield, IL: Charles C Thomas.

Martin, R. (1983). The ethical issues in the use and interpretation of the Draw-A-Person test and other similar projective procedures. *The School Psychologist, 38*(6), 8.

Marzolf, S., & Kirchner, J. (1970). Characteristics of House-Tree-Person drawings by college men and women. *Journal of Projective Techniques and Personality Assessment, 34,* 138–145.

McArthur, D. (1976). *A comparison of the stimulus influence of three thematic projective techniques with children.* Unpublished doctoral dissertation, California School of Professional Psychology, 1976.

McArthur, D., & Roberts, G. (1982). *Roberts apperception test for children: Manual.* Los Angeles: Western Psychological Services.

McClelland, D. C., Atikson, J. W., Clark, R. A., & Lowell, E. L. (1953). *The achievement motive.* New York: Appleton-Century-Crofts.

McCully, R. S. (1989). Personal communication.

McHugh, A. (1966). Children's figure drawings in neurotic and conduct disturbances. *Journal of Clinical Psychology, 22,* 219–221.

Murray, H. (1938). *Explorations in personality.* New York: Oxford University Press.

Murray, H. (1943). *Thematic apperception test.* Cambridge, MA: Harvard College.

Myler, B., Rosenkrantz, A., & Holmes, G. (1972). A comparison of the TAT, CAT, and CAT-H among second grade girls. *Journal of Projective Techniques and Personality Assessment, 36,* 440–444.

Nathan, S. (1973). Body image in chronically obese children as reflected in figure drawings. *Journal of Personality Assessment, 37,* 456–463.

Neman, R., Brown, T., & Sells, S. (1973). Language and adjustment scales for the Thematic Apperception Test for children 6–11 years. *Vital and Health Statistics, Series 2, 58,* 1–70.

Neman, R., Neman, J., & Sells, S. (1974). Language and adjustment scales for the Thematic Apperception Test for youths 12–17. *Vital and Health Statistics, Series, 2, 62,* 1–84.

Obrzut, J., & Boliek, C. (1986). Thematic approaches to personality assessment with children and adolescents. In H. Knoff (Ed.), *The assessment of child and adolescent personality.* New York: Guilford Press.

Pine, F. (1960). A manual rating drive content in the Thematic Apperception Test. *Journal of Projective Techniques, 24,* 32–45.

Polyson, J., Norris, D., & Ott, E. (1985). The recent decline in TAT research. *Professional Psychology: Research and Practice, 16,* 26–28.

Prytula, R., & Leigh, G. (1972). Absolute and relative figure drawing size in institutionalized orphans. *Journal of Clinical Psychology, 28,* 377–379.

Prytula, R., Phelps, M., & Morrissey, E. (1978). Figure drawing size as a reflection of self-concept or self-esteem. *Journal of Clinical Psychology, 34,* 207–214.

Ritzler, B., Sharkey, K., & Chudy, J. (1980). A comprehensive projective alternative to the TAT. *Journal of Personality Assessment, 44,* 358–362.

Rotter, J. (1946). Thematic apperception tests: Suggestions for administration and interpretation. *Journal of Personality, 15,* 70–92.

Scott, L. (1981). Measuring intelligence with the Goodenough-Harris drawing test. *Psychological Bulletin, 89,* 483–505.

Sharkey, K., & Ritzler, B. (1985). Comparing diagnostic

validity of the TAT and a new picture projective test. *Journal of Personality Assessment, 49,* 406–412.

Skilbeck, W., Bates, J., & Bentler, P. (1975). Human figure drawings of gender-problem boys. *Journal of Abnormal Child Psychology, 3,* 191–199.

Stein, M. (1955). *The thematic apperception test: An introductory manual for its clinical use with adults* (2nd ed.). Reading, MA: Addison-Wesley.

Sugarman, A. (1990). *Where's the beef? Putting personality back in personality assessment.* Paper presented at the Annual Meeting of the Society of Personality Assessment. San Diego, California.

Swenson, C. (1957). Empirical evaluations of human figure drawings. *Psychological Bulletin, 54,* 431–466.

Teglasi, H. (1980). Acceptance of the traditional female role and sex of first person drawn on the Draw-A-Person Test. *Perceptual and Motor Skills, 51,* 267–271.

Tomkins, S. (1947). *The Thematic Apperception Test: The theory and techniques of interpretation.* New York: Grune & Stratton.

Tuma, J., & Pratt, J. (1982). Clinical child psychology practice and training: A survey. *Journal of Clinical Child Psychology, 11,* 27–34.

Wyatt, F. (1947). The scoring and analysis of the Thematic Apperception Test. *Journal of Psychology, 24,* 319–330.

PART III

ASSESSMENT OF SPECIFIC POPULATIONS

EDITORS' COMMENTS

In part III of this book, each of the 12 chapters focuses on the strategies used to assess a specific population. In order to provide consistency and cross-chapter comparisons, each chapter follows an identical format. After initial description of the disorder, sections highlight multimodal assessment, and include a case illustration, the implications for treatment, and a summary of the state of the art. The empirical support for use of specific strategies for each population is provided if available. Although the final word is not yet in on all aspects of assessment, it is clear from the authors' reviews that the field has become increasingly empirical, that it is sensitive to the important diagnostic considerations, and that there is a trend toward very comprehensive evaluations (with attention to behavioral, cognitive, and physiological systems, as well as reliance on outside informants).

In chapter 16, Strauss notes that additional research will be required to establish the validity of assessment techniques used with *anxiety disorders*. In chapter 17, Curry and Craighead argue that improvements in the assessment of childhood *depression* will follow the better understanding of the cognitive and interpersonal factors contributing to that disorder. In chapter 18, Rapport underscores the importance of making diagnostic appraisals of *attention deficit disorder* on the basis of multiple scores and types of information, given the complexity of this disorder. In chapter 19, Kazdin shows how checklists for parents and teachers that assess the multiple dimensions of *conduct disorders* can be used to identify targets for treatment. In chapter 20, Sallee documents the progress made in the last few years in reliably assessing *tics and Tourette Syndrome*. Aman, Hammer, and Rojahn, in chapter 21, focus on the multiple problems (i.e., dual diagnosis) that warrant assessment in children suffering from *mental retardation*. Similarly, in chapter 22, Marcus and Schopler underscore the need for comprehensiveness in evaluating the child with *pervasive developmental disorder*. In chapter 23, Johnson and Hinkle review the comprehensive assessments that are available for *obesity* in children. In chapter 24 on other *eating disorders*, Garner and Parker consider the clinical interview, the semi-structured interview, self-reports, behavioral observation, and self-monitoring. In chapter 25, Williamson, Savin, and Gleaves point out that for pediatric *headache*, a medical evaluation should precede behavioral assessment to rule out non-psychological etiologies. Also, other psychological causes of headache, such as anxiety and depression, must be ruled out. In chapter 26, Russo, Lehn, and Berde document how it is possible to measure *pain* in children along several dimensions. And finally, in chapter 27, Ammerman reviews the numerous strategies designed to assess *physical abuse and neglect* in children.

CHAPTER 16

ANXIETY DISORDERS

Cyd C. Strauss

Historically, empirical research investigating anxiety in childhood has focused on subclinical fears and specific phobias in nonclinic samples. Conclusions based on extensive research in nonclinic samples were that anxiety in childhood is age and stage specific, is transient, and is not associated with long-term negative effects (Barrios, Hartmann, & Shigetomi, 1981). With the advent of the *Diagnostic and Statistical Manual of Mental Disorders—Third Edition and Revised Version* (DSM-III; DSM-III-R) (American Psychiatric Association, 1980, 1987), research efforts subsequently shifted to clinical populations of children with anxiety disorders. The findings of initial investigations examining DSM-III–identified anxious youngsters indicated that anxiety in children can indeed be severe relative to developmental norms, can be enduring, and can be associated with serious forms of impairment (Brent, Kalas, Edelbrock, Costello, Dulcan, & Conover, 1986; Last, Hersen, Kazdin, Finkelstein, & Strauss, 1987; Strauss, Lahey, Frick, Frame, & Hynd, 1988; Strauss, Last, Hersen, & Kazdin, 1988).

These latter findings underscore the need for further empirical investigations of anxiety problems in childhood and adolescence to extend our understanding of the manifestation, development, prognosis, assessment, and treatment of anxiety in children. This chapter reviews the full range of assessment techniques that have been used to measure anxiety in children. In addition, an illustrative case example and implications for treatment are discussed.

DESCRIPTION OF THE DISORDERS

DSM-III and DSM-III-R (American Psychiatric Association, 1980, 1987) identify three anxiety disorder subtypes that arise in childhood and adolescence: separation anxiety, overanxious, and avoidant disorders. Each anxiety disorder subtype is characterized by intense subjective distress and is accompanied by maladaptive patterns of cognition and behavior. The specific focus of the anxiety or fear, however, varies for each anxiety disorder subtype. The primary feature of separation anxiety disorder is excessive distress displayed upon separation from home or a major attachment figure (usually the parents). Overanxious disorder is characterized by anxiety that is not focused on a particular object or situation, but instead is generalized across multiple situations and events. The hallmark of overanxious disorder is excessive and inappropriate worry about future events (Strauss, Lease, Last, & Francis, 1988). Finally, children with avoidant disorder demonstrate excessive fearfulness and avoidance of social interactions with unfamiliar persons.

In addition to these anxiety disorders typical of childhood, children may also be diagnosed using the DSM classification system as having any of the adult anxiety diagnoses, including generalized anxiety disorder, panic disorder, phobic disorders, obsessive-compulsive disorder, and posttraumatic stress disorder. Briefly, generalized anxiety disorder is characterized by excessive worrying for 6 months or longer, as well as symptoms of motor tension, autonomic hyperactivity, and vigilance and scanning when anxious. In panic disorder, the youngster experiences unexpected and sudden attacks of intense anxiety and sympathetic arousal. Phobic disorders include agoraphobia (i.e., fear of being in situations from which escape might be difficult or in which help may be unavailable in case of a panic attack), social phobia (i.e., fearfulness and avoidance of social situations involving possible scrutiny by others or humiliation), and simple phobia (i.e., excessive fearfulness and avoidance of specific objects or situations, other than those related to agoraphobia and social phobia). In obsessive-compulsive disorder, the person experiences recurrent and distressing thoughts or urges to engage in repetitive and irrational behaviors that create considerable anxiety when resisted. Finally, the essential feature of posttraumatic stress disorder is the development of characteristic anxiety symptoms following a psychologically distressing event that is outside the range of usual human experiences (e.g., serious threat to one's life).

The study of the *prevalence of anxiety* in childhood has focused primarily on subclinical fears and school phobia rather than on the anxiety disorder subtypes described in DSM. Findings from a large set of studies have suggested that prevalence of excessive fears or anxiety in children ranges from 1.7%, in a study assessing the rate of school phobia in a school population (Kennedy, 1965), to 16% in a study of 5-to-8-year-old children based on teacher descriptions of fearfulness (Werry & Quay, 1971). Most typically, however, prevalence of intense anxiety has been found to be about 7% or 8% in children (Agras, Sylvester, & Oliveau, 1969; Earls, 1980; Graziano & DeGiovanni, 1979). Anderson, Williams, McGee, and Silva (1987) conducted the first and only study yet available on prevalence of childhood disorders defined in DSM-III in a general population sample. They examined prevalence of DSM-III disorders in 792 children aged 11 years in New Zealand using child interviews, and parent and teacher questionnaires. Findings showed that separation anxiety disorder (rate of 3.5%) was among the most common disorders in this sample and that social phobia (0.9%) was one of the most infrequently diagnosed disorders. Overanxious disorder (2.9%) and simple phobia (2.4%) had intermediate prevalence. Unfortunately, the generalizability of these data to children in the United States remains questionable, because of cultural differences that may exist.

Studies examining gender differences have fairly consistently demonstrated that girls tend to report anxiety more commonly than do boys (e.g., Croake & Knox, 1973; Lapouse & Monk, 1959). Similarly, girls with separation anxiety disorder and those with avoidant disorder outnumber boys with these disorders in clinic samples (Francis, Last, & Strauss, 1990; Last et al., 1987). On the other hand, the referral rate of boys and girls with overanxious disorder has been found to be comparable (Strauss et al., 1988). When higher rates of anxiety are observed in females, it is unknown whether this is a true gender difference or is primarily attributable to the greater willingness of girls to reveal fearfulness than boys (Graziano, DeGiovanni, & Garcia, 1979).

Age has also been shown to be related to anxiety in children. In their review of the literature, Graziano et al. (1979) noted general decline from young childhood to adolescence in the number of fears reported, as well as in the percentage of youngsters reporting one or more fears. However, some studies have found that the number of fears peaks between the ages of 9 and 11 (e.g., Chazan, 1962; MacFarlane, Allen, & Honzik, 1954). Recent studies of developmental trends in clinic samples of DSM-diagnosed youngsters have revealed that separation anxiety tends to occur more frequently in younger children, overanxious and avoidant disorders are equally prevalent in pre- and postpubertal children, and social phobias are most common in adolescents (Francis et al., 1990; Strauss & Last, 1989; Strauss, Lease et al., 1988).

Several studies have evaluated the relationship between *socioeconomic status* (SES) and anxiety in children, although findings have been somewhat inconsistent. Some studies report a higher number of fears in low-SES children (e.g., Croake & Knox, 1973; Lapouse & Monk, 1959), whereas other investigations do not obtain a differential rate of fears among different SES groups (e.g., Richman, Stevenson, & Graham, 1982). Children referred for clinical services with separation anxiety disorder most commonly come from families of lower SES (Last et al., 1987). In contrast, families of overanxious children tend to be of middle to higher SES (Last et al., 1987). Finally, equal numbers of clinically diagnosed avoidant disorder children appear to be from middle- to upper-SES families as from lower-SES families (Francis et al., 1990).

MULTIMODAL ASSESSMENT

Numerous methods of assessing anxiety in children have been devised, including use of structured clinical interviews, self-report inventories, parent and teacher questionnaires, direct observations, and physiological measures. Although initial research efforts were devoted to the development of adequate self-report measures to assess anxiety in children, more recent studies have examined the utility of semistructured interviews to evaluate anxiety. A description of the most widely employed and potentially useful assessment methods follows.

Structured interviews

Several structured or semistructured clinical interviews have been developed to determine the presence and severity of psychopathology in children and adolescents. In particular, the Diagnostic Interview Schedule for Children (DISC) (Costello, Edelbrock, Kalas, Dulcan, & Klaric, 1984), the Diagnostic Interview for Children and Adolescents (DICA) (Herjanic & Reich, 1982), the Schedule for Affective Disorders and Schizophrenia for School-Age Children (K-SADS) (Puig-Antich, Orvaschel, Tabrizi, & Chambers, 1978), the Child Assessment Schedule (CAS) (Hodges, Kline, Stern, Cytryn, & McKnew, 1982), and the Interview Schedule for Children (ISC) (Kovacs, 1983) all assess the major diagnostic categories in childhood and adolescence, including anxiety disorders. Most recently, two new semistructured interviews were devised specifically to assess anxiety in childhood and adolescence: (1) the Anxiety Disorders Interview Schedule for Children-Child and Parent versions (ADIS-C and ADIS-P) (Silverman & Nelles, 1988), and (2) the Children's Anxiety Evaluation Form (CAEF) (Hoehn-Saric, Maisami, & Wiegand, 1987).

Although initial findings from studies of the reliability of DSM-III childhood anxiety diagnoses derived from semistructured interviews were discouraging (e.g., Chambers et al., 1985; Costello et al., 1984), recent evidence suggests that anxiety disorders can indeed be assessed reliably in children and adolescents through the use of semistructured interviews. In one study, Last and her colleagues (Last, 1987; Last et al., 1987) employed a short-interval test-retest paradigm (interviews performed by separate interviewers in the morning and afternoon) to evaluate the reliability of DSM-III anxiety disorder diagnoses using the ISC in a sample of 41 anxiety disordered youngsters between the ages of 6 and 17. They obtained high interrater agreement (kappa = .84) for the overall category anxiety disorders of childhood or adolescence. Moreover, good concordance between raters was demonstrated for all childhood anxiety disorder subtypes: separation anxiety disorder, .79; overanxious disorder, .81; and avoidant disorder, .64. Silverman and Nelles (1988) also reported moderate to high agreement among clinicians in a study evaluating the reliability of the ADIS for Children, a semistructured interview for 6-to-18-year-old youngsters modeled after the ADIS used in diagnosing anxiety disorders in adults (DiNardo, O'Brien, Barlow, Waddel, & Blanchard, 1983). The ADIS for Children is comprised of questions that correspond to childhood and adult anxiety disorders contained in DSM-III and DSM-III-R, with items assessing situational and cognitive cues for anxiety, intensity of anxiety, extent of avoidance, precipitating events, and history of the problem. In this initial investigation examining the ADIS for Children, pairs of independent clinicians administered the ADIS to 51 6-through-18-year-old children and their mothers. Primary and secondary DSM-III-R diagnoses were assigned based on either child reports only, parent interview data only, or a combination of child and parent information. High interrater agreement was obtained for the overall category of anxiety disorders of childhood and adolescence using child ($k = .84$) and parent ($k = .83$) data, as well as when composite diagnoses based on both informants ($k = .78$) were employed. Furthermore, k values for the specific anxiety disorder subcategories identified in this sample (i.e., simple phobia, school phobia, overanxious disorder) were found to be adequate, with the exception of overanxious disorder diagnoses derived from the child information alone. Overall, these preliminary reliability data are promising; however, further examination of the reliability of other specific anxiety disorder subtypes and the validity of this interview schedule still is needed.

The reliability and validity of an alternative semistructured clinical interview for assessing anxiety in children, the CAEF, has been evaluated in a study by Hoehn-Saric et al. (1987). The CAEF does not correspond directly to the DSM classification system and instead gathers information more generally related to the history, symptoms, and observable signs of anxiety. Subjects in this study were 63 children between 7 and 17 years of age who were admitted to a child and adolescent psychiatric inpatient unit with a range of psychiatric problems. Child data were obtained using several measures: the CAEF administered to children only, the State-Trait Anxiety Inventory for Children (STAIC) (Spielberger, 1973), and the Revised Children's Manifest Anxiety Scale (RCMAS) (Reynolds & Richmond, 1978). Interrater reliability for the total CAEF anxiety score was found to be high ($r = .81$; $n = 15$). CAEF scores correlated significantly with the trait subscale scores of the STAIC and RCMAS ratings as well. Moreover, the discriminative validity of the CAEF was supported, in that the CAEF differentiated patients independently diagnosed on discharge from the inpatient unit with anxiety disorders from those with oppositional, conduct, and dysthymic disorders. These initial data provided preliminary support for the utility of this measure for assessing anxiety in children. However, data derived from the CAEF are somewhat limited because of the instrument's exclusive focus on child reports (i.e., parent information is not obtained) and because of the lack of correspondence of CAEF information to a syndrome-oriented classification scheme, such as DSM-III and DSM-III-R (Silverman & Nelles, 1988).

Finally, Hodges, McKnew, Burbach, and Roebuck (1987) presented interesting data examining the diagnostic concordance between two semistructured interviews—the CAS and the K-SADS—in an outpatient sample using lay interviewers. These researchers administered both interview schedules to a sample of 30 7-to-16-year-old children within a 32-hour time period. DSM-III diagnoses were assigned on the basis of parent and child responses using a computer algorithm (i.e., no clinical judgment was used in determining child diagnoses). A small subgroup of the sample met diagnostic criteria for the overall category of anxiety disorders of childhood or adolescence, ranging from $n = 3$ to $n = 14$, depending on the informants and the interview schedules used in judging diagnoses. Findings revealed low to moderate concordance between the CAS and K-SADS for anxiety diagnoses, depending on the source of information. There was very poor concordance between the two interviews when based on the child interview alone or when a consensus from both parent and child was used in diagnosing anxiety disorders. On the other hand, when diagnoses were generated from parent information alone or either parent or child interview data, k coefficients fell in the moderate range (.51 and .54, respectively). Conclusions based on these findings are tentative, however, because of the small number of anxiety disordered children studied and the use of lay interviewers in determining diagnoses, as was noted by the authors. This innovative study, however, provides a good model for evaluating the correspondence among the various (and growing number of) semistructured interviews now being used to examine anxiety and other forms of psychopathology in children. It also begins to address the issue of poor concordance typically obtained between parent and child in their reports of anxiety symptoms using structured interviews (Edelbrock, Costello, Dulcan, Conover, & Kalas, 1986; Herjanic & Reich, 1982).

In sum, empirical investigations evaluating the usefulness of semistructured interviews have demonstrated that anxiety can be assessed reliably by independent diagnosticians. However, initial studies investigating the reliability of reports of anxiety symptoms and syndromes over time using interview schedules have generally not been favorable (Chambers et al., 1985; Costello et al., 1984). In addition, poor agreement between parents and children in descriptions and reports of anxiety symptoms have typically been found through the use of structured interviews (Edelbrock et al., 1986; Herjanic & Reich, 1982), with children tending to report more anxiety symptoms than parents. Of course, this latter finding may reflect children's greater awareness of and sensitivity to internal emotional states than parents, rather than a lack of reliability of this assessment instrument. Further study of the reliability and validity of anxiety symptoms and diagnoses using the interview formats that currently show the most promise (i.e., ADIS for Children, CAEF, and ISC) clearly is needed to establish the utility of this method of assessment, although initial data generally have been positive.

Self-Report Measures

Reports by children concerning their own anxiety symptomatology have been viewed as essential in the assessment of anxiety and fearfulness, because of the covert nature of this form of psychopathology. Self-report instruments have been used widely both clinically and empirically to evaluate general levels of anxiety and specific fears in children. Despite their wide acceptance and use, self-report measures have several features that limit the conclusions that can be derived from them. In particular, children sometimes are unwilling to reveal negative characteristics about themselves and instead present a favorable description that underestimates their levels of anxiety (Glennon & Weisz, 1978). Moreover, items contained in most measures do not identify the specific situations that induce anxiety (Barrios et al., 1981). Finally, empirical studies researching the psychometric properties of many scales have been few in number (Barrios et al., 1981). Nonetheless, self-report instruments appear to provide a useful initial step in identifying children with elevated levels of anxiety from the large samples of children (e.g., in school settings), because the instruments are efficient and inexpensive to administer and normative data are available for comparison with large groups of youngsters.

Several self-report inventories have been developed to identify anxious children and to measure the effectiveness of interventions for anxiety. The Children's Manifest Anxiety Scale-Revised (RCMAS) (Reynolds & Richmond, 1978) is one of the most widely employed and researched instruments. This 37-item scale has been shown to have adequate construct (Reynolds & Richmond, 1978), concurrent (Reynolds, 1980), content (Reynolds & Richmond, 1978), and predictive (Reynolds, 1981) validity. In addition, national normative and reliability data have been obtained for the RCMAS in a large sample of children (Reynolds & Paget, 1982). Three factors of the RCMAS assess various aspects of anxiety in children: physiological, worry and oversensitivity, and difficulties with concentration. Recent studies have evaluated the correspondence between scores derived from the RCMAS and DSM-III anxiety disorder diagnoses. First, Mattison and Bagnato (1987) assessed the ability of this measure to differentiate boys aged 8 to 12 years old diagnosed with overanxious, dysthymic, and attention deficit disorders. Although these authors found that boys with DSM-III diagnoses of overanxious disorder showed elevations on the worry and oversensitivity as well as the physiological subscale scores of the RCMAS relative to boys in the two other diagnostic categories, these differences on the RCMAS were not statistically significant. However, the combined use of cutoff scores for the RCMAS and parent-completed Child Behavior Checklist (Achenbach & Edelbrock, 1983) successfully distinguished overanxious boys with 70% accuracy from boys with dysthymia or attention deficit disorder. On the other hand, Hoehn-Saric et al. (1987) found that the RCMAS failed to differentiate inpatient children with anxiety disorders from children with other psychiatric diagnoses. However, the anxiety disorder group in this latter study was small ($n = 10$), the group was comprised of children primarily diagnosed with separation anxiety disorder, and only the total RCMAS score was employed rather than factor scores. It may be that the RCMAS corresponds mainly to the childhood anxiety disorder of overanxious disorder, rather than other anxiety disorder subtypes.

A second self-report measure, the State-Trait Anxiety Inventory for Children (STAIC) (Spielberger, 1973), is commonly used to evaluate global anxiety in children that varies across situations (state subscale) and anxiety that is stable across time and situations (trait subscale). However, studies generally have failed to support the validity of the state-trait distinction in children (Johnson & Melamed, 1979). On the other hand, high split-half reliabilities have been reported for both scales of the STAIC (Morris & Kratochwill, 1983).

A third commonly employed self-report questionnaire is the Fear Survey Schedule for Children (FSSC) (Scherer & Nakamura, 1968), which assesses the number and intensity of specific fears in children. Children rate their degree of fearfulness on a 5-point scale for each of the 80 items, which represent specific objects or situations. A factor analysis yielded the following factors for this measure: fear of failure or criticism, major fears (e.g., fire, sight of blood), minor fears, (e.g., travel), medical fears, fear of death, fear of the dark, home or school fears, and miscellaneous fears. Investigations of the psychometric properties of the FSSC have been limited to reports of high internal consistency and a moderate relationship with another self-report measure of anxiety (Scherer & Nakamura, 1968). Subsequently, Ollendick (1983) provided data supporting the internal consistency, test-retest reliability, and the convergent and discriminative validity of a slightly modified version of the Fear Survey Schedule for Children (FSSC-R). Last, Francis and Strauss (1989) presented data demonstrating the ability of particular items contained in the FSSC-R to differentiate subtypes of anxiety disorders in children: overanxious disorder, separation anxiety disorder, and school phobia.

Evaluation of the cognitions of anxious children using self-report measures is an interesting new area of study (Barrios et al., 1981; Francis, 1988). The value of assessing cognitions lies in the proposed relationship between cognitions and the acquisition and maintenance of anxiety. There have been various approaches to assessing cognitions in children, including measurement of thoughts in vivo, beliefs, locus of control, attributions, expectancy, self-statements, and imagery (Kendall & Korgeski, 1979). Self-report instruments have been the primary means of obtaining these descriptions of children's cognitions. To date, the empirical evaluation of cognitions in anxious children has been limited mainly to nonclinic samples of test-anxious and socially withdrawn, fearful children (see Francis, 1988). For example, Zatz and Chassin (1983) compared the cognitions of 294 fifth- and sixth-grade children who were divided into high test-anxious, moderate test-anxious, and low test-anxious groups. Results supported the hypothesis that test anxiety is associated with maladaptive cognitions, in that high test-anxious children endorsed significantly more task-inhibiting thoughts (i.e., negative evaluation and off-task thoughts) than either moderate or low test-anxious children. Similarly, moderately test-anxious youngsters reported significantly more task-inhibiting thoughts than low test-anxious children. In contrast, low test-anxious children endorsed significantly more task-facilitating thoughts, including positive evaluation of their performance and on-task cognitions, than children in the other two groups.

These data provide preliminary support for the application of the cognitive model in anxious children. Nonetheless, considerably more research is needed in clinic samples of children with a broad range of anxiety disorders to establish the relationship between anxiety and maladaptive cognitions in children. In addition, evaluation of other types of cognitive errors using alternative self-report inventories (e.g., the Children's Negative Cognitive Error Questionnaire) (Leitenberg, Yost, & Carroll-Wilson, 1986; Harter, 1981) is suggested.

Parent and Teacher Checklists

Parent and teacher ratings have not been used extensively to assess anxiety in children. Ratings by teachers and parents have only rarely been implemented by clinicians or researchers because of the presumption that parents and teachers are unaware of, insensitive to, or highly tolerant of internal states of children (Edelbrock, 1985). Nonetheless, parent and teacher checklists provide an efficient means of initially assessing a wide range of problem areas. Normative data available for these rating scales also allow comparison with the functioning of same-aged peers to determine the level of behavioral deviance of particular behaviors. In addition, parent and teacher perceptions are considered particularly important because they most often are responsible for initiating referral for treatment services and for providing feedback regarding treatment progress.

Numerous rating scales are available that contain an anxiety or withdrawal dimension, including the Conners Teacher Rating Scale (Conners, 1969), the Child Behavior Checklist (CBCL), (Achenbach & Edelbrock, 1983), and the Revised Behavior Problem Checklist (RBPC) (Quay & Peterson, 1983). The reliability and validity of these checklists have been strongly supported by an extensive literature researching the various rating scales (see Quay, 1986).

In particular, recent research indicates that parent and teacher ratings can be a valuable and efficient means of identifying anxiety in children (Edelbrock, 1985; Strauss, Frame, & Forehand, 1987). Edelbrock (1985) provided support for the validity of employing the Teachers' Report Form of the CBCL (TRF) (Edelbrock & Achenbach, 1984) to assess child anxiety. A large group of clinically referred children with high teacher ratings on the TRF was compared to nonanxious clinic children on a range of behavioral correlates. Findings revealed that teacher-rated anxious children also were viewed as being less happy, as showing a higher prevalence and severity of somatic complaints, and as demonstrating more problematic peer relations than nonanxious clinic children.

Strauss et al. (1987) also presented data that supported the utility of the RBPC completed by teachers to measure anxiety in children. In this study, anxious children were selected through the use of the RBPC and compared to nonanxious children on independent measures of adjustment. From a sample of 325 second-through-fifth graders, 24 were identified who received high anxiety-withdrawal teacher ratings on the RBPC (i.e., 2 standard deviations above the mean or greater for a normal sample). When contrasted with children with low RBPC anxiety-withdrawal subscale ratings, teacher-identified anxious children were found to demonstrate a broad range of psychosocial difficulties. More specifically, anxious-withdrawn children showed impairment in peer relations and in levels of depression, self-esteem, attention, school performance, and social behavior relative to nonanxious children. These data lend support for use of the RBPC teacher rating scale to identify with extreme levels of anxiety.

These investigations present preliminary evidence that teachers are aware of anxiety in children and can be helpful in identifying those with high levels of anxiety relative to classmates. Further research examining the utility of parent and teacher checklists in assessing anxiety may enhance the early identification of children at risk to develop serious forms of anxiety disorders.

Direct Observations

Despite the advantages of observational methods to assess anxiety in children, this assessment approach has not commonly been used in clinical settings, nor has it been researched extensively. Observational data can be obtained reliably, are not influenced by biasing factors such as social desirability and poor recall, and can provide information that may not be accessible through alternative assessment methods, such as antecedents, consequences, and setting variables. On the other hand, observational procedures are typically expensive to use.

The most commonly used direct-observation procedure for assessing anxiety in children is the Behavioral Avoidance Test (BAT) (Lang & Lazovik, 1963). This observational approach involves instructing the child to approach the feared object or situation. The child's latency to respond, distance traveled toward the object, and time spent handling the feared object or remaining in the phobic situation are recorded. This procedure has been employed to assess children's fears of dogs (Bandura, Grusec, & Menlove, 1967), darkness (Kelley, 1976), physical examinations (Freeman, Roy, & Hemmick, 1976), water (Lewis, 1974), and snakes (Kornhaber & Schroeder, 1975). Despite such various applications of the BAT in examining children's fearful reactions, several features of this approach currently limit its usefulness (Barrios et al., 1981). As noted by Barrios et al. (1981), the BAT has not been standardized in terms of types of instructions provided and number of tasks presented. Kelley (1976) has shown that variations in instructions and demand characteristics can significantly influence children's approach responses. In addition, reliability and validity of the BAT as an assessment device for children have not been studied sufficiently.

A second type of observational approach involves use of observer rating scales to record overt anxious mannerisms and behaviors in anxiety-provoking situations. Several rating scales have been developed to observe anxiety in specific situations or settings, such as reactions to surgery (Melamed & Siegal, 1975), dental treatment (Melamed, Yurcheson, Fleece, Hutcherson, & Hawes, 1978), public speaking (Paul, 1966), peer interactions (O'Connor, 1969), and hospitalization (Vernon, Foley, & Schulman, 1967). Actual behaviors observed vary depending on the context in which the child is placed, but include crying, stuttering, trembling hands, physical or verbal complaints, clinging, and a quivering voice. Generally, reliability and validity data concerning these coding systems are quite promising, although studies evaluating psychometric properties have been few in number. A comprehensive and detailed observational coding system for observing anxiety in preschool children was developed by Glennon and Weisz (1978). Many of the anxious behaviors included in this observational coding system are applicable to older children as well and could be adapted for assessing anxiety in alternative populations and settings.

Physiological Measures

Physiological measurement of childhood has been largely overlooked until very recently. Initial evaluation of this approach to assessment produced inconsistent findings. Several studies demonstrated that heart rate and electrodermal changes can be assessed reliably and are related to the presentation of fearful stimuli in children (Melamed et al., 1978; Stricker & Howitt, 1965). On the other hand, numerous studies have failed to find significant correlations between physiological states and other indices of anxiety, such as self-reports of fearfulness (Darley & Katz, 1973; Kutina & Fischer, 1977; Sternbach, 1962).

The most recent studies, however, support use of physiological measures to evaluate anxiety in children and adolescents. First, Matthews, Manuck, and Saab (1986) examined cardiovascular responses of adolescents during a naturally occurring stressor: a required 5-minute presentation in a high school English class. Twenty-five tenth graders were divided into anxious and nonanxious groups based on their scores on the trait anxiety scale of the State-Trait Personality Inventory (Spielberger, Jacobs, Russell, & Crane, 1983). Findings revealed that anxious students exhibited elevated systolic blood pressure and heart rate responses to the stress of giving a speech, whereas nonanxious students did not show such differences. These results were considered tentative, however, given the small sample size and the uniqueness of the sample.

Beidel (1988) subsequently conducted a study comparing the psychophysiological responses of low and high test-anxious youngsters during two social-evaluative laboratory tasks: a timed vocabulary test and an oral reading session. The Test Anxiety Scale for Children (TASC) (Sarason, Davidson, Lighthall, & Waite, 1958) was used initially to select children with high and low levels of test anxiety from an original sample of 83 third-through sixth-grade students. Structured interviews then were conducted with children scoring in the high and low ranges on the TASC to determine presence of DSM-III childhood psychiatric disorders in the two groups. Twenty-five children were confirmed by interview to be test anxious, with 60% also meeting diagnostic criteria for concurrent anxiety disorders. Autonomic measures obtained every 2 minutes during baseline and the two tasks revealed that test-anxious children had significantly larger heart rate changes than their nonanxious peers. There were no differences between test-anxious and nonanxious children on systolic and diastolic blood pressure, however, during the two tasks.

The findings from these latter two investigations provide preliminary evidence that physiological measures of anxiety in children are valid and correspond to other methods of identification of anxiety (i.e., interviews and self reports). In addition, these data indicate that physiological indices may provide important information concerning patterns of responding in stressful situations that may not have been uncovered with alternative modes of assessment. Ultimately, physiological measurement may prove useful in developing new treatment strategies and detecting responsivity to intervention in anxious children. Additional research studying the utility of physiological assessments with clinically referred anxious youngsters, obtained in alternative social-evaluative situations and studied concurrently with self-report and behavioral measures, would be particularly useful.

Overview

In terms of future practices in evaluating anxiety in children, a multimethod approach to assessment is recommended at this time, because of the absence of studies evaluating and comparing the validity of the various strategies. Reports obtained from parents, teachers, and the children themselves via structured interviews, checklists, and self-report measures can be combined with direct observations of anxious or avoidance behaviors and physiological measurement of autonomic arousal in the identification of anxiety, selection of treatment approaches, and measurement of treatment progress.

CASE ILLUSTRATION

Jeremy is a 9-year-old boy referred to an outpatient anxiety clinic for children and adolescents because of problems with separation anxiety and reluctance to attend school. Jeremy resides with both natural parents and his 12-year-old sister.

The initial evaluation consisted of parent and child semistructured interviews using the ISC, parent and teacher questionnaires, self-report measures of anxiety, and a behavioral avoidance test. First, information obtained from both Jeremy and his mother using the ISC revealed that he met DSM-III-R criteria for separation anxiety disorder. Specifically, he displayed each of the following symptoms: (a) excessive worries that mother may become ill and die; (b) overconcern that he will be kidnapped; (c) anxiety associated with school attendance and frequent school refusal stemming from reluctance to be apart from his mother; (d) refusal to sleep away from home; (e) extreme reluctance to be apart from mother while at home, to the extent that he could not separate even while mother showered; (f) somatic complaints in anticipation of separation from mother; and (g) sadness and distress while separated from mother. These symptoms reportedly were present for a 15-month period prior to referral by Jeremy's school for treatment.

In addition to separation anxiety disorder, Jeremy demonstrated problems with dysthymia that appeared to be secondary to anxiety symptomatology. In particular, Jeremy and his mother reported that he had reduced appetite with significant weight loss, difficulty falling asleep, and intermittent suicidal thoughts during the year before referral. He did not meet diagnostic criteria for major depression.

In addition to the diagnostic interview, Jeremy completed several self-report measures. Included were the RCMAS, the STAIC, and the Children's Depression Inventory (CDI) (Kovacs, 1981). His responses on self-report inventories confirmed information obtained from the interviews. On the RCMAS, Jeremy reported elevated levels of worry and oversensitivity (score of 9) relative to norms for same-age peers. Similarly, his scores on the state (29) and trait (47) anxiety subscales of the STAIC were high. Finally, Jeremy's CDI score of 23 revealed significant depressive symptomatology.

Parents and teachers also provided descriptions of Jeremy's internalizing behavior on the CBCL. Jeremy's t-scores (parent version, 75; teacher version, 82) also suggested clinical levels of internalizing problems relative to peers his age.

Finally, behavioral observations were made of Jeremy's ability to separate from his mother in three situations: going to school, remaining in the waiting room while his mother was in the clinic office with the therapist, and playing at a neighbor's house while the mother was at home. Jeremy was able to attend school fully but reported a high level of anxiety while in the school setting (rating of 8 on a 10-point rating scale). While in the clinic setting, Jeremy was able to sit in the waiting room for 1 minute without his mother. His rating of anxiety in this situation was 7. Jeremy completely refused to go play at a friend's house, reporting an anxiety level of 10.

IMPLICATIONS FOR TREATMENT

Assessment of anxiety in children and adolescents has implications for the treatment of anxiety. The relationship between each assessment approach and the selection of a treatment procedure has not been studied extensively in the research literature, however, so firm conclusions await the results of additional research. Nonetheless, a *preliminary* discussion of the implications of each of the assessment methods discussed above will be provided.

Data gathered from semistructured child and parent interviews provide diagnostic information that theoretically can be useful in developing a specific treatment plan. Empirical work on treatment of each childhood anxiety disorder subtype, however, has lagged behind research on classification, descriptions of each subtype, and assessment of anxiety. Clinical descriptions of treatment of children diagnosed with separation anxiety disorder versus those with overanxious disorder suggest that different strategies are effective for treating these two disorders. In particular, graduated exposure to separation situations with cognitive coping strategies has been used to treat separation anxiety. Alternatively, a multimethod treatment approach has been recommended for overanxious disorder, including cognitive restructuring to alter maladaptive cognitive patterns and relaxation training to reduce general levels of tension. Further research clearly is needed to evaluate the relative utility of these approaches and to determine whether identification of distinct subtypes does indeed have implications for selection of treatment.

Self-report questionnaires (e.g., RCMAS) and parent-and teacher-rated checklists are useful primarily in determining a need for treatment, rather than in selecting a specific treatment strategy. These forms of assessment can be utilized as a first step to identify children from among large populations of children (e.g., pediatric samples, school settings) who display elevated levels of anxiety relative to normative data. Although these approaches may produce false positives because of factors such as acquiescence, inflation of the severity of anxiety symptoms, and reports of transient feelings of anxiety in children who generally do not experience excessive levels of anxiety (see Reynolds, in press), readministration of questionnaires, the use of follow-up interviews by professionals, or both can be implemented to confirm the need for intervention. These forms of assessment are not especially useful in selecting specific treatment approaches, however, since they assess anxiety globally.

Direct observations of anxious and avoidance behaviors can be useful in developing a treatment strategy. In particular, avoidance of particular situations and stimuli suggests that a graduated exposure procedure (as in systematic desensitization) (see Morris & Kratochwill, 1983) or flooding approach can be used to overcome anxiety. That is, the client can be exposed directly to the feared stimuli because they have been identified specifically. Observational data can also be used to identify consequences of anxious or avoidance behavior that may be serving to maintain such behavior. Operant approaches, such as extinction of anxious behaviors or positive reinforcement of approach behaviors may then be useful in such cases.

Assessment of cognitions associated with anxiety has implications for whether a cognitive-behavioral component should be included in a treatment package. If maladaptive thoughts are found to give rise to anxious feelings, then treatment aimed at modifying thought patterns seems appropriate. However, if cognitive errors simply are sequelae of feeling anxious, then cognitive interventions seem less important. Study of the temporal relationship between thoughts and anxiety clearly is needed to clarify this issue further. Nonetheless, several cognitive-behavioral treatment approaches have been developed to modify maladaptive thoughts that are believed to underlie or maintain anxiety (see Morris & Kratochwill, 1983). The few studies evaluating the effectiveness of cognitive approaches in treating fearful children have provided tentative evidence supporting their utility (Ross, 1981; Graziano et al., 1979).

Finally, physiological measurement is instructive in determining whether treatment components aimed at somatic symptoms would be useful. Most notably, progressive relaxation training (Jacobsen, 1938) can be employed successfully to alleviate somatic symptoms.

Overall, research conducted to date suggests that behavioral and cognitive-behavioral treatments can be used successfully to treat anxiety in childhood. The relationship between information obtained from assessment methods needs to be more directly related to selection of treatment, however.

SUMMARY

This chapter describes recent advances in the assessment of anxiety in children and adolescents. Assessment techniques that have been employed to measure anxiety include structured interviews, self-report instruments, parent and teacher checklists, direct observations, and physiological measures. Structured interviews have been used increasingly to assess anxiety, because they have been found to be reliable in evaluating anxiety. More research is needed, however, to establish the validity of structured interviews. Self-report inventories and parent-teacher checklists are useful in the initial identification of children with elevated levels of anxiety, because of their efficiency and the availability of normative data for comparison purposes. Finally, physiological and observational data add an important adjunct to a comprehensive evaluation of anxiety. Direct observations allow for measurement of antecedents and consequences of anxious behavior, the degree of avoidance of anxiety-inducing situations, and overt anxious mannerisms. Physiological measures permit direct examination of an individual's autonomic reaction to various stimuli, which may not always correspond to the individual's report of anxiety. It is recommended that a comprehensive evaluation of anxiety incorporate multiple informants using several modalities, to assess fully behavioral, physiological, and cognitive aspects of anxiety. Finally, more research is needed to establish the validity and utility of specific assessment techniques to evaluate anxiety.

REFERENCES

Achenbach, T. M., & Edelbrock, C. S. (1983). Taxonomic issues in child psychopathology. In T. H. Ollendick & M. Hersen (Eds.), *Handbook of child psychopathology.* New York: Plenum Press.

Agras, S., Sylvester, D., & Oliveau, C. (1969). The epidemiology of common fears and phobia. *Comprehensive Psychiatry, 10,* 151–156.

American Psychiatric Association. (1980). *Diagnostic and statistical manual for mental disorders: (Third ed.).* Washington, DC: Author.

American Psychiatric Association. (1987). *Diagnostic and statistical manual for mental disorders: (Third ed.—Revised).* Washington, DC: Author.

Anderson, J. C., Williams, S., McGee, R., & Silva, P. A. (1987). DSM-III disorders in preadolescent children. *Archives of General Psychiatry, 44,* 69–76.

Bandura, A., Grusec, J., & Menlove, F. (1967). Vicarious extinction of avoidance behavior. *Journal of Personality and Social Psychology, 5,* 16–23.

Barrios, B. A., Hartmann, D. P., & Shigetomi, C. (1981). Fears and anxieties in children. In E. J. Mash & L. G. Terdal (Eds.), *Behavioral assessment of childhood disorders* (pp. 259–304). New York: Guilford Press.

Beidel, D. C. (1988). Psychophysiological assessment of anxious emotional states in children. *Journal of Abnormal Psychology, 97,* 80–82.

Brent, D. A., Kalas, R., Edelbrock, C., Costello, A. J., Dulcan, M. K., & Conover, N. (1986). Psychopathology and its relationship to suicidal ideation in childhood and adolescence. *Journal of the American Academy of Child Psychiatry, 25,* 666–673.

Chambers, W. J., Puig-Antich, J., Hirsch, M., Paez, P., Abrosini, P. J., Tabrizi, M. A., & Davies, M. (1985). The assessment of affective disorders in children and adolescents by semistructured interviews: Test-retest reliability of the K-SADS-P. *Archives of General Psychiatry, 42,* 696–702.

Chazan, M. (1962). School phobia. *British Journal of Educational Psychology, 32,* 200–217.

Conners, C. K. (1969). A teacher rating scale for use in drug studies with children. *American Journal of Psychiatry, 126,* 884–888.

Costello, A. J., Edelbrock, C., Kalas, R., Dulcan, M. K., & Klaric, S. H. (1984). *Development and testing of the NIMH Diagnostic Interview Schedule for Children (DISC) in a clinic population: Final Report.* Rockville, MD: Center for Epidemiological Studies, NIMH.

Croake, J. W., & Knox, F. H. (1973). The changing nature of children's fears. *Child Study Journal, 3,* 91–105.

Darley, S., & Katz, I. (1973). Heart rate changes in children as a function of test versus game instructions and test anxiety. *Child Development, 44,* 784–789.

DiNardo, P. A., O'Brien, G. T., Barlow, D. H., Waddel, M. T., & Blanchard, E. B. (1983). Reliability of DSM-III anxiety disorder categories using a new structured interview. *Archives of General Psychiatry, 40,* 1070–1074.

Earls, F. (1980). Prevalence of behavior problems in three-year-old children. A cross-national replication. *Archives of General Psychiatry, 37,* 1153–1157.

Edelbrock, C. (1985). *Teachers' perceptions of childhood anxiety and school adjustment.* Paper presented at a conference for "Anxiety Disorders in Children: Implications for School Adjustment" Cape Cod, MA.

Edelbrock, C., & Achenbach, T. M. (1984). The teacher version of the Child Behavior Profile: I. Boys aged 6–11. *Journal of Consulting and Clinical Psychology, 52,* 207–217.

Edelbrock, C., Costello, A. J., Dulcan, M. K., Conover, N. C., & Kalas, R. (1986). Parent-child agreement on child psychiatric symptoms assessed via structured interview. *Journal of Child Psychology and Psychiatry, 27,* 181–190.

Francis, G. (1988). Assessing cognitions in anxious children. *Behavior Modification, 12,* 267–280.

Francis, G., Last, C. G., & Strauss, C. C. (1990). Avoidant

disorder of childhood or adolescence: A preliminary study on 25 cases. Submitted for publication.

Freeman, B. J., Roy, R. R., & Hemmick, S. (1976). Extinction of a phobia of physical examination in a 7-year-old mentally retarded boy: A case study. *Behaviour Research and Therapy, 14*, 63–64.

Glennon, B., & Weisz, J. R. (1978). An observational approach to the assessment of anxiety in young children. *Journal of Consulting and Clinical Psychology, 46*, 1246–1257.

Graziano, A., & DeGiovanni, I. S. (1979). The clinical significance of childhood phobias: A note on the proportion of child-clinical referrals for the treatment of children's fears. *Behaviour Research and Therapy, 17*, 161–162.

Graziano, A., DeGiovanni, I. S., & Garcia, K. (1979). Behavioral treatment of children's fears: A review. *Psychological Bulletin, 86*, 804–830.

Harter, S. (1981). A new self-report scale of intrinsic versus extrinsic orientation in the classroom: Motivational and informational components. *Developmental Psychology, 17*, 300–312.

Herjanic, B., & Reich, W. (1982). Development of a structured psychiatric interview for children (DICA): Agreement between child and parent on individual symptoms. *Journal of Abnormal Child Psychology, 10*, 307–324.

Hodges, K., Kline, J., Stern, L., Cytryn, L., & McKnew, D. (1982). The development of a child assessment interview for research and clinical use. *Journal of Abnormal Child Psychology, 10*, 173–189.

Hodges, K., McKnew, D., Burbach, D. J., & Roebuck, L. (1987). Diagnostic concordance between the Child Assessment Schedule (CAS) and the Schedule for Affective Disorders and Schizophrenia for School-age Children (K-SADS) in an outpatient sample using lay interviewers. *American Academy of Child and Adolescent Psychiatry, 26*, 654–661.

Hoehn-Saric, E., Maisami, M., & Wiegand, D. (1987). Measurement of anxiety in children and adolescents using semistructured interviews. *American Academy of Child and Adolescent Psychiatry, 26*, 541–545.

Jacobsen, F. (1938). *Progressive relaxation*. Chicago, Illinois: University of Chicago Press.

Johnson, S. B., & Melamed, B. G. (1979). Assessment and treatment of children's fears. In B. B. Lahey & A. E. Kazdin (Eds.) *Advances in clinical child psychology* (Vol. 2, pp. 108–139). New York: Plenum Press.

Kelley, C. K. (1976). Play desensitization of fear of darkness in preschool children. *Behaviour Research and Therapy, 14*, 79–81.

Kendall, P. C., & Korgeski, G. P. (1979). Assessment and cognitive-behavioral interventions. *Cognitive Therapy and Research, 3*, 1–21.

Kennedy, W. A. (1965). School phobia: Rapid treatment of fifty cases. *Journal of Abnormal Psychology, 70*, 285–289.

Kornhaber, R., & Schroeder, H. (1975). Importance of model similarity on extinction of avoidance behavior in children. *Journal of Consulting and Clinical Psychology, 43*, 601–607.

Kovacs, M. (1981). Rating scales to assess depression in school-aged children. *Acta Paedopsychiatrica, 46*, 305–315.

Kovacs, M. (1983). The Interview Schedule for Children (ISC): Interrater and parent-child agreement. Unpublished manuscript. University of Pittsburgh, Pittsburgh.

Kutina, J., & Fischer, J. (1977). Anxiety, heart rate and their interrelation with mental stress in school children. *Activitas Nervos Superior, 19*, 89–95.

Lang, P. J., & Lazovik, A. D. (1963). Experimental desensitization of a phobia. *Journal of Abnormal and Social Psychology, 66*, 519–525.

Lapouse, R., & Monk, M. A. (1959). Fears and worries in a representative sample of children. *American Journal of Orthopsychiatry, 29*, 803–818.

Last, C. G. (1987). Developmental considerations. In C. G. Last & M. Hersen (Eds.), *Issues in diagnostic research*. New York: Plenum Press.

Last, C. G., Francis, G., Hersen, M., Kazdin, A. E., & Strauss, C. C. (1987). Separation anxiety and school phobia: A comparison using DSM-III criteria. *American Journal of Psychiatry, 144*, 653–657.

Last, C. G., Francis, G., & Strauss, C. C. (1989). Assessing fears in anxiety-disordered children with the Revised Fear Survey Schedule for Children (FSSC-R). *Journal of Clinical Child Psychology, 18*, 137–141.

Last, C. G., Hersen, M., Kazdin, A. E., Finkelstein, R., & Strauss, C. C. (1987). Comparison of DSM-III separation anxiety and overanxious disorders: Demographic characteristics and patterns of comorbidity. *Journal of the American Academy of Child Psychiatry, 26*, 527–531.

Leitenberg, H. Yost, L. W., & Carroll-Wilson, M. (1986). Negative cognitive errors in children: Questionnaire development, normative data, and comparisons between children with and without self-reported symptoms of depression, low self-esteem, and evaluation anxiety. *Journal of Consulting and Clinical Psychology, 54*, 528–536.

Lewis, S. (1974). A comparison of behavior therapy techniques in the reduction of fearful avoidance behavior. *Behavior Therapy, 5*, 648–655.

MacFarlane, J. W., Allen, L., & Honzik, M. P. (1954). *A developmental study of the behavior problems of normal children between twenty-one months and fourteen years*. Berkeley: University of California Press.

Matthews, K. A., Manuck, S. B., & Saab, P. G., (1986). Cardiovascular responses of adolescents during a naturally occurring stressor and their behavioral and psychophysiological predictors. *Psychophysiology, 23*, 198–209.

Mattison, R. E., & Bagnato, S. J. (1987). Empirical measurement of overanxious disorder in boys 8 to 12 years old. *Journal of the American Academy of Child and Adolescent Psychiatry, 26,* 536–540.

Melamed, B. G., & Siegal, L. J. (1975). Reduction of anxiety in children facing hospitalization and surgery by use of filmed modeling. *Journal of Consulting and Clinical Psychology, 43,* 511–521.

Melamed, B. G., Yurcheson, R., Fleece, E. L., Hutcherson, S., & Hawes, R. (1978). Effects of film modeling on the reduction of anxiety-related behaviors in individuals varying in levels of previous experience in the stress situation. *Journal of Consulting and Clinical Psychology, 46,* 1357–1367.

Morris, R. J., & Kratochwill, T. R. (1983). *Treating children's fears and phobias.* New York: Pergamon Press.

O'Connor, R. D. (1969). Modification of social withdrawal through symbolic modeling. *Journal of Applied Behavior Analysis, 2,* 15–22.

Ollendick, T. H. (1983). Reliability and validity of the Revised Fear Survey Schedule for Children (FSSC-R). *Behaviour Research and Therapy, 21,* 685–692.

Paul, G. L. (1966). *Insight vs. desensitization in psychotherapy.* Stanford, CA: Stanford University Press.

Puig-Antich, J., Orvaschel, H., Tabrizi, R. N., & Chambers, W. J. (1978). Schedule for affective disorders and schizophrenia for school-age children (K-SADS). New York: New York State Psychiatric Institute.

Quay, H. C. (1986). Classification. In H. C. Quay & J. S. Werry (Eds.), *Psychopathological disorders of childhood* (3rd ed., pp. 1–34). New York: Wiley.

Quay, H. C., & Peterson, D. R. (1983). Interim manual for the Revised Behavior Problem Checklist. Coral Gables, FL: University of Miami.

Reynolds, C. R. (1980). Concurrent validity of "what I think and feel": The revised children's manifest anxiety scale. *Journal of Consulting and Clinical Psychology, 48,* 774–775.

Reynolds, C. R. (1981). Long-term stability of scores on the Revised Children's Anxiety Scale. *Perceptual and Motor Skills, 53,* 702.

Reynolds, C. R., & Paget, K. D. (1982). National normative and reliability data for the Revised Children's Manifest Anxiety Scale. Paper presented at the annual meeting of the National Association of School Psychologists, Toronto, Canada.

Reynolds, C. R., & Richmond, B. O. (1978). Factor structure and construct validity of "What I think and feel": The revised children's manifest anxiety scale (RCMAS). *Journal of Personality Assessment, 43,* 281–283.

Richman, N., Stevenson, J., & Graham, P. (1982). Prevalence of behaviour problems in 3-year-old children: An epidemiological study in a London borough. *Journal of Child Psychology and Psychiatry, 16,* 272–287.

Ross, A. O. (1981). Child behavior therapy. *Principles, procedures, and empirical basis* (pp. 251–289). New York: John Wiley & Sons.

Sarason, S. B., Davidson, K. S., Lighthall, F. F., & Waite, R. R. (1958). A test anxiety scale for children. *Child Development, 29,* 105–113.

Scherer, M. W., & Nakamura, C. Y. (1968). A fear survey schedule for children (FSS-FC): A factor analytic comparison with manifest anxiety. *Behaviour Research and Therapy, 6,* 173–182.

Silverman, W. K., & Nelles, W. B. (1988). The anxiety disorders interview schedule for children. *Journal of the American Academy of Child and Adolescent Psychiatry, 27,* 772–778.

Spielberger, C. D. (1973). *Manual for the state-trait anxiety inventory for children.* Palo Alto: Consulting Psychologists Press.

Spielberger, C. D., Jacobs, G., Russell, S., & Crane, R. S. (1983). Assessment of anger. The state-trait anger scale. In J. N. Butcher & C. D. Spielberger (Eds.), *Advances in personality assessment* (Vol. 2, pp. 159–187). New Jersey: Lawrence Erlbaum Associates.

Sternbach, R. (1962). Assessing differential autonomic patterns in emotions. *Journal of Psychosomatic Research, 6,* 87.

Strauss, C. C., Frame, C. L., & Forehand, R. L. (1987). Psychosocial impairment associated with anxiety in children. *Journal of Clinical Child Psychology, 16,* 235–239.

Strauss, C. C., Lahey, B. B., Frick, P., Frame, C. L., & Hynd, G. W. (1988). Peer social status of children with anxiety disorders. *Journal of Consulting and Clinical Psychology, 56,* 137–141.

Strauss, C. C., & Last, C. G. (1989). Phobic disorders in childhood and adolescence. Unpublished manuscript.

Strauss, C. C., Last, C. G., Hersen, M., & Kazdin, A. E. (1988). Association between anxiety and depression in children and adolescents with anxiety disorders. *Journal of Abnormal Child Psychology, 15,* 57–68.

Strauss, C. C., Lease, C. A., Last, C. G., & Francis, G. (1988). Developmental differences between children and adolescents with overanxious disorder. *Journal of Abnormal Child Psychology, 16,* 433–443.

Stricker, G., & Howitt, J. (1965). Physiological recording during simulated dental appointments. *New York State Dental Journal, 31,* 204–213.

Vernon, D., Foley, J. L., & Schulman, J. L. (1967). Effect of mother-child separation and birth order on young children's responses to two potentially stressful experiences. *Journal of Personality and Social Psychology, 5,* 162–174.

Werry, J. S., & Quay, H. C. (1971). The prevalence of behavior symptoms in younger elementary school children. *American Journal of Orthopsychiatry, 41,* 136–143.

Zatz, S., & Chassin, L. (1983). Cognitions of test-anxious children. *Journal of Consulting and Clinical Psychology, 51,* 526–534.

CHAPTER 17

DEPRESSION

John F. Curry
W. Edward Craighead

Recognition of the existence of depression among children and adolescents has resulted in an enormous increase in interest on this topic. Conceptual advances regarding depression among this age group have been accompanied by parallel advances in psychopathology and assessment research, although advances in intervention and prevention procedures have lagged. The purpose of this chapter is to provide a review and critique of the instruments that have been developed to assess depression among children and adolescents.

It is now generally accepted that about 3% of children and adolescents meet the criteria for a DSM-III diagnosis of major depression, with the incidence being slightly higher among older adolescents and slightly lower among younger individuals (Craighead & Curry, in press). The disorder appears to become more isomorphic with adult depression as adolescents mature toward young adulthood. Within the DSM-III-R classification system, children and adolescents may receive more than one diagnosis, and most depressed individuals do so with anxiety and conduct disorder or oppositional disorder being the most frequently comorbid diagnoses. All of these factors must be considered when one assesses children and adolescents for presence of a mood disorder.

DESCRIPTION OF THE DISORDER

Both DSM-III and DSM-III-R list three nonbipolar depressive disorders (APA, 1987): (1) major depression; (2) dysthymia; and (3) adjustment disorder with depressed mood. Major depression is a full syndrome episode lasting at least 2 weeks, marked by persistent depressed mood (or irritable mood in children and adolescents) or significant loss of interest or pleasure in usual activities. In addition, at least five symptoms (including one of the preceding) must be present nearly every day. These symptoms may include significant weight or appetite loss or gain; insomnia or hypersomnia; psychomotor agitation or retardation; fatigue or loss of energy; feelings of worthlessness or excessive guilt; loss of ability to think, concentrate, or make decisions; recurrent thoughts of death or suicide, or a suicide plan or attempt.

Dysthymia is a less severe form of depression. Depressed or irritable mood must be present most of the time, on more days than not, for at least 1 year. This must be accompanied by at least two symptoms while depressed: poor or excessive appetite; insomnia or hypersomnia; fatigue; low self-esteem; concentration difficulties, or hopelessness. An adjustment disorder is, by definition, a reaction to an identifiable stressor, marked predominantly (in this case) by depressed mood, but lasting no more than 6 months and not meeting criteria for a major episode.

MULTIMODAL ASSESSMENT

In their review of the then recently emerging measures of childhood and adolescent depression, Kazdin and Petti (1982) noted that, although parent ratings, peer nomination, and projective tests had been employed, the most commonly used measures were clinical interviews and self-report scales. This observation is as accurate now as it was then. Structured or semistructured interviews have also been widely used in research on diagnosed depressive disorders. Both interviews and self-report scales have been used as well to measure current severity of symptomatology (syndromal depression). In the following sections, we review these two methods for the assessment of depression. We then more briefly review findings on alternative assessment methods, including behavioral observations, clinician rating scales, sociometric measures, and psychological tests. A brief review of biological measures is included, but a full assessment of their current utility is beyond the scope of this chapter.

THE CLINICAL INTERVIEW

The development of structured interviews paralleled the shift toward use of explicit criteria for defining psychiatric disorders. Development of structured interview procedures was motivated in part by dissatisfaction with the diagnostic unreliability of unstructured clinical interviews. Most applications of structured interviewing have been in research projects, but some interviews were designed for both clinical and research purposes (e.g., the Child Assessment Schedule; see Hodges, 1987). In addition, studies have begun to examine the utility of structured interviews in clinical settings (Carlson, Kashani, Thomas, Vaidya, & Daniel, 1987), and other studies report on their use as part of a clinical data-collection procedure (Curry & Craighead, 1990).

In this section we review the interviews most frequently used in published research reports for diagnosis of depressive disorders (more general reviews of structured diagnostic interviews are available: Edelbrock & Costello, 1988a; Angold, 1988; Gutterman, O'Brien, & Young, 1987). These interviews tend to be revised fairly frequently, to reflect results of psychometric research and to accommodate changes in diagnostic criteria. Moderate to extensive interview-specific training is required before any of these instruments are used.

Each interview's format, procedure, and time frame for diagnoses is described. The focus then shifts to the psychometric properties of the interview. Finally, the issue of parent-child concordance for these interviews is reviewed. We discuss two highly structured interviews in which the wording of each item is to be followed exactly as written, and three semistructured interviews that allow clinicians to rephrase, probe, and inquire until they can evaluate presence and severity of a symptom.

Highly Structured Diagnostic Interviews

Diagnostic Interview for Children and Adolescents (DICA)

The DICA is a highly structured interview that covers interpersonal relationships, academic and social functioning, and symptomatology in children and adolescents age 6 and older (Herjanic & Reich, 1982). Clinicians or lay interviewers can be trained in its use. It has parallel forms administered by separate interviewers to a parent (DICA-P) and the child (DICA-C). The earliest version of the DICA yielded ICD-9 diagnoses, but the revised version, completed in 1981, yields DSM-III diagnoses (Welner, Reich, Herjanic, Jung, & Amado, 1987). The time frame for questioning is the present, but past symptomatology is inquired about in older children (Gutterman et al., 1987).

Interrater reliability on symptoms averaged 85% agreement in small, early studies (Herjanic & Reich, 1982). Welner et al. (1987) recently reported test-retest reliability for the DICA-C in a sample of 27 inpatients ages 7 through 17, who were interviewed twice within a 1- to 7-day period shortly after admission. Kappa coefficients of diagnostic concordance were high for affective disorder ($\kappa = .90$) and other categories (Attention Deficit, Conduct, Oppositional, and Anxiety Disorders—κ's between .76 and 1.00).

Parent-child agreement has been problematic for the DICA as well as for other measures. Early studies with a sample of 307 6- to-16-year-olds and their mothers (Herjanic & Reich, 1982; Reich, Herjanic, Welner, & Gandhy, 1982) demonstrated moderately high levels of mother-child agreement ($\kappa \geq .50$) for only 16 of 168 symptom questions, including none of the depression items. Agreement was best on items measuring observable, concrete behaviors. Children reported more worried, anxious, and depressed feelings than did their mothers. Using either the ICD-9 or the Feighner criteria diagnoses generated by a computer algorithm, the Kappa for mother-child concordance was only .36 for depression and was highest (.58) for antisocial personality. Probable overdiagnosis of depression was suggested by the finding that 53% of the sample met criteria. The authors noted the lack of symptom duration and severity criteria in this earlier version of the DICA as a possible cause of such a high rate of affective diagnosis. A more recent study (Welner et al., 1987) with 84 consecutive outpatient children and their mothers showed considerably higher diagnostic concordance for DSM-III affective disorder ($\kappa = .63$). However, Sylvester and her colleagues (1987), studying nonreferred children from normal and at-risk families, found poor agreement between parent and child on presence of major depression ($\kappa = .11$), suggesting that findings may be influenced by sample characteristics.

Validity of the DICA was first studied by evaluating its ability to discriminate between psychiatric and pediatric referrals (Herjanic & Campbell, 1977). As Edelbrock and Costello (1988b) noted, discrimination between the two groups in that study was rather weak, with much overlap on symptom scores. Two recent studies have tested DICA diagnoses against external diagnostic criteria. Welner et al. (1987) compared DICA-C diagnoses at admission to diagnoses at final discharge for 27 inpatient children and adolescents. Agreement for affective disorder was moderate ($\kappa = .52$). Kappa scores for attention deficit and conduct disorder were at a similar level ($\kappa = .50$ and .43, respectively), but agreement for anxiety disorder and adjustment disorder did not exceed a chance level. The DICA gave more diagnoses per patient than did the clinician. Carlson, Kashani, Thomas, Vaidya, and Daniel (1987) compared DICA-C and DICA-P interviews to a best-estimate diagnosis for 30 8- to 12-year-old inpatients. The best-estimate diagnosis was formulated by two child psychiatrists who were not informed of DICA results. Agreement was moderate for affective diagnoses ($\kappa = .48$ for DICA-C; $\kappa = .43$ for DICA-P). The structured interviews again overdiagnosed affective disorder.

In summary, for assessment of depressive disorder, the DICA has shown good test-retest reliability. Parent-child concordance has been weak, except in one small study of a referred sample. Validity, when compared to expert diagnosis, appears moderate for depression, but all studies that have addressed the issue find that the DICA overdiagnose depression compared to clinicians.

Diagnostic Interview Schedule for Children (DISC)

The DISC, a highly structured interview for children ages 6 through 18, was developed for epidemiological research purposes by several investigators under contract to the National Institute of Mental Health. Most research has been conducted with the version written by Costello and his colleagues (Costello et al., 1984), but additional research on a subsequent revision is continuing (Gutterman et al., 1987). Clinicians or lay interviewers can be trained in use of the DISC. It has parallel parent (DISC-P) and child (DISC-C) forms that are administered by separate interviewers. The time frame for most items is the past year. DSM diagnoses are generated by computer algorithm, and 27 symptom complex scores assess domains of psychopathology. Edelbrock and Costello (1988a) note that the DISC-C usually takes 40 to 60 minutes, while the DISC-P takes approximately 60 to 70 minutes to complete.

Costello et al. (1984) reported interrater reliability on symptom scores based on 10 videotaped child interviews coded by three lay interviewers. High reliability was demonstrated (Pearson's rs ranged from .94 to 1.00). An extensive study of test-retest reliability was conducted with interviews repeated at a median of 9 days. Reliability of diagnoses based on parent interviews ($n = 243$) was moderately high ($\kappa \geq .50$ for attention deficit, conduct disorder, oppositional disorder, overanxious disorder, and major depression) and just below this point for dysthymia and separation anxiety (κ's = .49 and .48, respectively). Enuresis, substance abuse, and schizophrenia showed high reliability ($\kappa \geq .79$). Based on child interviews ($n = 242$), test-retest reliability was low, with Kappa values for major depression, dysthymia, conduct, and attention deficit disorder in the range from .41 to .47. Symptom area reliabilities were also higher for DISC-P (mean intraclass correlation coefficient = .75) than for DISC-C (mean ICC = .62) (Edelbrock, Costello, Dulcan, Kalas, & Conover, 1985). Total DISC-C symptom score ICCs were very reliable for adolescents (ICC = .81) but declined with younger children (ICC = .55, ages 10–13, and ICC = .39 for ages 6–9). Reliability was higher for behavior and conduct problems (ICC = .75) than for affective and neurotic problems (ICC = .59). Total symptom score reliabilities were higher for

DISC-P than for DISC-C, particularly in younger children (ICC = .90 for 6–9-year-olds, .78 for 10–13-year-olds, and .80 for 14–18-year-olds). Depression reliability was moderately high across all three age groups with the DISC-P (ICC's .75 to .83).

Parent-child agreement of the DISC was assessed with 299 children ages 6 through 18 years and their parents (Edelbrock, Costello, Dulcan, Conover, & Kalas, 1986). Parent-child agreement was moderate for scales measuring behavior and conduct problems (mean Pearson $r = .42$ for 10 scales), but low for scales measuring affective or neurotic problems (mean r .19 for 16 scales; $r = .25$ for depression). Average symptom scale agreement was best (but only moderate) for adolescents and parents ($r = .35$) and poor for younger age groups ($r = .27$, ages 10–13; $r = .10$ ages 6–9). As had been found in earlier studies of the DICA, parents reported more behavior problems than did children, while children reported more affective or neurotic problems.

Three studies have addressed the validity of the DISC. Costello, Edelbrock, and Costello (1985) found DISC-P symptom complex scores higher in a psychiatric referral group than in a pediatric referral group in all areas except fears, phobias, and obsessions/compulsions. Significantly more of the psychiatric sample met criteria for a severe DSM-III diagnosis, but the specificity of the interview declined markedly if mild diagnoses were used as criteria. The DISC-C also discriminated between groups at the level of total symptoms and on all but four symptom complex scores. Classification accuracy for severe diagnoses was not as good as that of the DISC-P, and there were no differences between psychiatric and pediatric referrals in the total number of mild diagnoses. Correlation of DISC-P and DISC-C total symptom scores with parent-completed Child Behavior Checklist (CBCL) total behavior problem scores showed a similar pattern. Convergent validity was much higher for DISC-P than for DISC-C (Pearson $r = .72$ and .71 for pediatric and psychiatric referrals, respectively, for DISC-P, but only .29 and .14 for DISC-C). The authors concluded that results supported the discriminant validity of the DISC-P at the level of symptoms and severe diagnoses, but not for mild or moderate levels of diagnoses. The validity of the DISC-C was considerably weaker.

Edelbrock and Costello (1988b) examined convergent validity of DISC-P diagnoses and parent-completed CBCL scale scores with 270 youngsters aged 6 through 16 and their parents. In general, on these measures of parent-reported problems, internalizing diagnoses from the DISC-P were associated with internalizing scales for the CBCL, while externalizing diagnoses were associated with externalizing CBCL scales. Regarding depression diagnoses, major depression and dysthymic disorder were associated with elevated depressed/withdrawal scale scores for adolescent girls, Depressed and Social withdrawal scale scores for boys and girls ages 6 through 11, and Uncommunicative scale scores for boys 6 through 11 and 12 through 16. However, many children who met DISC-P criteria for dysthymic disorder had low scores on the CBCL Depression scale, which led the authors to conclude that the diagnostic criteria for this disorder were too lenient for children.

In the third validity study, DISC diagnoses from an epidemiological sample were compared to diagnoses based on a clinician-administered Schedule for Affective Disorders and Schizophrenia for School-Age Children (K-SADS) (Cohen, O'Connor, Lewis, Velez, & Malachowski, 1987). Agreement was low for diagnoses of major depression. Lack of correspondence on these two scales may reflect limitations in reliabilities of both scales, and may not just demonstrate a low validity from the DISC.

Finally, Breslau (1987) compared DISC results based on original interviewer coding to results based on clinician editing of subject responses to highly structured questions about obsessions, compulsions, and delusions. She found high rates of initial false positive responses apparently based on interviewer lack of familiarity with these rare symptoms. She recommended modifying the structured interview assessment of such symptoms by using explanations and questions and providing examples of symptoms. This modification would move highly structured interviews in the direction of the more flexible, semistructured instruments, described next.

In summary, for assessment of depressive symptoms and diagnosis, test-retest reliability of the DISC-P is moderately high and that of the DISC-C is adequate only for adolescents. Parent-child concordance for depressive symptoms is modest above age 10, but lower than the concordance levels for behavior disorder symptoms. Validity of the DISC-P depression diagnoses compared to parent-completed checklist scores is supported, and the DISC-P has discriminant validity for symptoms and severe diagnoses, but diagnoses at the mild level may be too lenient. Limited support is evident for the validity of the DISC administered to the child alone.

Semistructured Diagnostic Interviews

Interview Schedule for Children (ISC)

The ISC was developed by Kovacs (1985a) for use in longitudinal research on childhood depression. It is oriented toward clinical assessment of symptom presence and severity through sets of questions used by the clinician to elucidate and check the child's responses. It is to be used from ages 8 to 17. The parent is interviewed first about the child, and then the child is interviewed. Two forms exist: one for initial evaluation and one for follow-up. In addition to symptoms of affective and other psychopathology, the ISC covers mental status, clinical signs, clinical impressions, and selected developmental milestones. Extensive interview-specific training is required, and research with the ISC has used a consensus group conference rather than computer algorithms to determine diagnoses.

Kovacs (1985a) reported that the initial parent ISC usually requires 1½ to 2½ hours, with the child ISC requiring 45 to 90 minutes. The time frame covered by the ISC is 6 months for behavioral items and 2 weeks for affective, cognitive, and vegetative symptom items. Evaluation of onset and duration of the child's symptom and disorder is based primarily upon the semistructured interview with the parent (Kovacs, 1985a). Examples of symptoms are given, and probes are used to ensure that the verbal interaction enables the interviewer to determine clinical significance of the symptoms.

Relatively few psychometric data are available on the ISC. Interrater reliability was assessed by Kovacs (1985a) on a sample of 35 school-aged children. Independent ratings by two clinicians were analyzed by intraclass correlation coefficient (ICC); the mean ICC for symptom ratings was .89. As Edelbrock and Costello (1988) noted, test-retest reliability and formal validity studies of the ISC have not been completed. However, validity is somewhat supported by the instrument's utility in longitudinal research on childhood depression (Kovacs et al., 1984a, 1984b).

Child Assessment Schedule (CAS)

The CAS was developed by Hodges and her associates in 1978 for the assessment of current psychological disorder (Hodges, McKnew, Cytryn, et al., 1982). It was modeled after traditional clinical interviews with children, and it was designed to be used for both clinical and research purposes. It contained 75 semistructured questions in content areas and 53 observational items to be completed by the clinician. The time required for the interview was about 45 minutes. Revisions in 1983 and 1985 included additional symptom items, questions about onset and duration of symptomatology, a parallel parent version of the interview (P-CAS), and diagnostic algorithms to correspond to DSM-III categories. Although the original CAS was administered to the child only, the authors of the interview recognized that diagnostic formulations require additional information from other sources (Hodges, Kline, Stern, Cytryn, & McKnew, 1982). Although most research with the CAS has been conducted with children, the instrument can be used with adolescents. However, certain adolescent diagnostic categories are screened rather than fully assessed by the CAS (e.g., eating disorders).

The CAS has received more extensive psychometric evaluation than other semistructured diagnostic interviews (summarized in Hodges, 1987). Interrater reliability with 53 videotaped interviews was .90 (Pearson r) for total symptom score, and ranged from .59 for "worries" to .84 for "somatic complaints" across content areas. For mood symptoms, reliability was .82 (Hodges et al., 1982). In a Dutch epidemiological study (Verhulst et al., 1985), interrater reliability for 20 interviewer-observer pair cases yielded an overall ICC of .94 for total pathology and .74 for mood.

Test-retest reliability with a sample of 32 child psychiatry inpatients interviewed twice over an average of 5 days was high ($\kappa > .70$) for diagnoses of conduct disorder, major depression, and dysthymia, and moderate ($\kappa = .56$) for separation anxiety. Dimensional symptom scores for major depression and dysthymia were also highly reliable (Pearson $r = .89$ and $= .86$, respectively) (Hodges, Cools, & McKnew, 1989).

Concurrent and discriminant validity of the CAS has been demonstrated in several studies. CAS total symptom scores have been found to correlate significantly with psychiatrists' global clinical ratings and parent-completed CBCLs (Hodges et al., 1982; Verhulst et al., 1985). Significant correlations between CAS symptom complex scores for attention deficit with hyperactivity, conduct disorder, and depression were obtained with corresponding CBCL narrow-band scales (.44, .50, and .51, respectively; Hodges et al., 1982). Recent data indicate a strong relationship between a diagnosis of MDD and the three primary depressive factors of the Children's Depression Inventory (Hodges & Craighead, in press).

Diagnoses of conduct disorder and affective disorder based on the CAS showed moderate to high levels of agreement with diagnoses of the same disorders based on the Schedule for Affective Disorders and Schizophrenia for School Age Children when both instruments were administered by lay interviewers within 1 to 2 days (Hodges, McKnew, Burbach, & Roebuck, 1987). Indices of agreement based on parent interviews were higher than those based on child interviews (for affective disorders, parent interview $\kappa = .75$; child interview $\kappa = .52$). Anxiety diagnoses showed lower levels of agreement.

Discriminant validity is supported by findings that CAS total symptom scores and eight of nine symptom complex scores (including depression) discriminate among child inpatients, outpatients, and controls. More CAS scales than CBCL scales significantly discriminated between all three groups (Hodges et al., 1982).

Hodges, Gorden, and Lennon (in press) studied 48 child psychiatry inpatients and primary caretakers with the parallel child and parent versions of the CAS. Moderately high parent-child agreement was found for the dimensional diagnosis-related scale measuring conduct disorder ($r = .63$) and moderately high agreement for attention deficit disorder ($r = .47$), major depression ($r = .46$), and dysthymia ($r = .45$). As has been found with more structured instruments, parents reported more behavioral symptoms than children; children reported more anxiety and somatic symptoms.

In summary, the CAS has good reliability for the clinical assessment of children, particularly for conduct and affective disorders. Data supporting convergent validity of CAS depressive diagnoses have also been generated, and the interview discriminates well between child psychiatric inpatients, outpatients, and controls.

Schedule for Affective Disorders and Schizophrenia for School Age Children (K-SADS)

The K-SADS was developed by Puig-Antich and Chambers (1978) for use in the study of affective disorders in children and adolescents. The Present Episode version assesses severity of symptomatology at its worst during the present episode and during the past week (K-SADS-P). A version for assessment of past episodes or current episodes, which rates presence of symptoms but not severity, has also been developed (K-SADS-E) (Orvaschel, Puig-Antich, Chambers, Tabrizi, & Johnson, 1982). Both versions assess affective, anxiety, conduct, and psychotic symptoms, and both include a brief set of observational ratings. The interview yields diagnoses based on Research Diagnostic Criteria or on DSM-III or DSM-III-R.

In the administration of the K-SADS, the parent is interviewed first to establish onset, duration, and chronicity of the child's problems. The semistructured interview for severity of each symptom is then conducted. The child is subsequently interviewed separately following a similar sequence. The same interviewer conducts both parent and child interviews and completes a final summary rating, taking into account all available information. In some cases, a brief joint interview with parent and child may be used to clarify discrepancies. Approximately 1 hour is required for administration of the parent interview, and an additional hour is required for the child interview. Because the purpose of the K-SADS is to enable a clinician to rate the significance and severity of symptoms, the question format is not rigidly determined; thus, clinically sophisticated interviewers are required.

Test-retest reliability of the K-SADS-P was assessed in a clinical sample of 52 youngsters aged 6–17, who were reinterviewed within 72 hours (Chambers, Puig-Antich, Hirsch, Paez, Ambrosini, Tabrizi, & Davies, 1985). The mean intraclass correlation coefficient for 14 symptoms of major depressive disorder was .60. Only pathological guilt and impaired concentration were unreliable (ICC $< .50$). Correlations between ratings based on the child interview and clinicians' final summary ratings were higher than those between parent and summary ratings. Test-retest reliability of four depression summary scales ranged from .67 to .81 (Pearson r), with internal consistency (Cronbach's *alpha*) ranging from .68 to .84. Test-retest reliability of diagnoses was somewhat surprisingly higher for nonmajor depression ($\kappa = .70$) than for major depression ($\kappa = .54$). Mean reliability of 11 conduct disorder items was in a range similar to that of the depression items (ICC = .67) with excessive fighting and pathological lying failing to be adequately reliable (ICC $< .40$). A summary conduct disorder scale has good test-retest reliability ($r = .74$) and internal consistency (alpha = .86), and the diagnosis showed acceptable test-retest reliability ($\kappa = .63$).

Findings for reliabilities of anxiety symptoms, scales, and diagnosis were too low to meet acceptable criteria, with the exception of the symptomatic rating of separation anxiety.

Orvaschel and her colleagues retrospectively reassessed 17 children with the K-SADS-E; these children had been previously assessed (up to 24 months earlier) with the K-SADS-P. Sixteen subjects were given the same primary diagnosis on both instruments. A trend toward underreporting of past symptoms, however, was noted, and this particularly affected secondary diagnoses. In a departure from the usual K-SADS procedure, Weissman et al. (1987) conducted independent parent and child interviews with 220 children of depressed and normal parents. Concordance for categorical diagnoses was generally poor. Although concordance for major depression was best in the age range of 10–13 ($\kappa = .47$) and was higher for boys than for girls, overall concordance between parent and child was problematic for this interview as well as for those previously reviewed.

Ambrosini, Metz, Prabrucki, and Lee (1989) recently reported videotape interrater reliability on a small sample of 25 youngsters, for a revised K-SADS-P that yields DSM-III-R diagnoses. Categorical diagnoses showed high reliability of this type ($\kappa \geq .75$) for depression, oppositional, attention-deficit problems, and anxiety symptoms other than simple phobia. Dimensional scale scores for depression, anxiety, and oppositional problems were also highly reliable (ICC $\geq .85$).

Validity of the K-SADS for affective disorders is supported by its content, which focuses heavily upon affective symptoms. Construct validity is supported by studies of cognitive correlates of depression in children and adolescents (McCauley, Mitchell, Burke, & Moss, 1988) where hypothesized associated cognitive factors have been significantly related to depression diagnosed using the K-SADS. Concurrent validity is also supported by high concordance for diagnoses of conduct or affective disorders based on the K-SADS and the CAS in a study of 30 outpatient children (Hodges, McKnew, Burbach, & Roebuck, 1987). Finally, Carlson et al. (1987) tested K-SADS-P and DICA diagnoses generated for 30 children upon admission to an inpatient unit, against final postdischarge best-estimate diagnoses. K-SADS diagnoses of conduct disorder, affective disorder, and attention deficit disorder showed moderately high validity ($\kappa > .55$). Anxiety diagnoses failed to attain this level of agreement. Overall, agreement of K-SADS diagnoses with best estimate was 70%, and overdiagnosis with the semistructured interview was the major problem contributing to diagnostic disagreement.

Comment

Assessment of depression in children and adolescents should include interviews with the parent and child to determine presence and severity of core symptoms. For clinical samples, semistructured interviews have the advantage of flexibility and clinical judgment about significance of reported symptoms. However, no single instrument can be considered a "gold standard" for defining depression at this time. Numerous issues related to psychometric properties of interview schedules, and to alternate methods of combining data from different sources, remain to be addressed in clinical research. For routine clinical use, current interview schedules offer the advantage of more comprehensive symptomatic assessment than traditional clinical interviews. Proper use of semistructured interviews requires clinical sensitivity and empathy and is not a mechanical or automated process (Young, O'Brien, Gutterman, & Cohen, 1987).

SELF-REPORT INSTRUMENTS

Self-rating scales have long been used in the assessment of severity and change in adult depression. The need for standardized, economical measures of severity and change in child and adolescent depression has led to development of several self-report instruments. Only those scales with published psychometric properties will be discussed in this section. They include Children's Depression Inventory (CDI), Children's Depression Scale (CDS), Depression Self-Rating Scale (DSRS), Center for Epidemiological Studies Depression Scale for Children (CES-DC), and the Beck Depression Inventory BDI).

Children's Depression Inventory (CDI)

The CDI continues to be the most widely used self-report measure of childhood depression (Kazdin, 1981). Developed by Kovacs (Kovacs & Beck, 1977; Kovacs, 1985b) as a downward extension of the Beck Depression Inventory, the CDI has 27 items, each consisting of three statements about a particular depressive symptom. One statement reflects minimal or no severity (scored 0), one moderate (scored 1), and one more severe (scored 2). Total scores range from 0 to 54. The time frame for reporting is the past 2 weeks. The CDI has been rated as the easiest self-report depression measure to read, requiring only a third-grade level of proficiency (Berndt, Schwartz, & Kaiser, 1983).

Reliability studies reported by Kovacs and subsequent normative research with 1,252 8-to-16-year-olds (Smucker, Craighead, Craighead, & Green, 1986) showed high internal consistency (coefficient *alpha* .70 to .86). One-month test-retest reliability was only .43 (Pearson *r*) for a small sample of diabetic youngsters (Kovacs, 1985b). Saylor, Finch, Spirito, and Bennett (1984), however, found that 1-week test-retest reliability was much higher for emotionally disturbed children ($r = .87$) than for normal controls ($r = .38$), and Smucker and colleagues found 1-year test-retest stability was higher for early adolescent girls ($r = .69$) than for boys ($r = .41$).

Extensive normative data are available for the CDI. Finch, Saylor, and Edwards (1985) reported a mean of 9.65 (standard deviation 7.30) for 1,463 students in the second through the eighth grades. Very small gender and grade effects were found. An overall mean of 9.05 (standard deviation = 7.04) was obtained in the large study by Smucker and colleagues. These findings are consistent with norms reported by Kovacs (1985a) based on a Canadian sample of 860 8-to-14-year-olds (mean = 9.3, SD = 7.3). With 534 psychiatrically hospitalized 6-to-17-year-olds, Nelson and colleagues (1987) found that the mean CDI score was 12.69.

Concurrent validity of the CDI is supported by high positive correlations with self-reported anxiety and negative correlations with self-esteem (Craighead & Green, in press; Kovacs, 1985b; McCauley et al., 1988; Saylor, Finch, Furey, Baskin, & Kelly, 1984). The CDI total score is significantly negatively correlated with the composite score for internal, stable, and global attributions for positive events (Curry & Craighead, 1990; McCauley et al., 1988) and significantly positively correlated with hopelessness for negative events (McCauley et al., 1988) and depressive cognitive distortions (Haley, Fine, Marriage, Moretti, and Freeman, 1985). High-CDI scorers are more external in locus of control (Doerfler, Felner, Rowlison, Raley, & Evans, 1988), less assertive, more withdrawn, and have poorer academic achievement than low-CDI scorers (Strauss, Forehand, Frame, & Smith, 1984).

Discriminant validity of the CDI has been problematic. Using a multitrait-multimethod matrix, Saylor, Finch, Furey, et al. (1984) compared self-report to peer and teacher measures of depression and anger. Method variance was approximately double the magnitude of trait variance. Boys' CDI scores correlated with peer ratings but not teacher ratings of depression, while the reverse was true for girls. Likewise, Kazdin and his colleagues (Kazdin, Esveldt-Dawson, Unis, & Rancurello, 1983) found that measures of depression and hostility completed by the same rater (parent or child) corresponded highly, but that measures of child depression across parent and child were not highly correlated.

Kazdin, Colbus, and Rodgers (1986) found that CDI scores, as well as other self- or parent-report measures of depression, were significantly higher in inpatient children with diagnosed depressive disorders than in matched nondepressed controls. However, magnitude of the difference was small, and sensitivity and specificity of a recommended cutoff value of 19 were very limited (25% and 75%, respectively). More recently, Kazdin (1989) reported a low rate of overlapping diagnosis in children identified as "depressed" on the basis of three sources: self-report CDI, parent-report CDI, or clinician-completed diagnoses.

Several studies have failed to detect group differences in CDI scores between depressed and nondepressed psychiatric controls (Nelson, Politano, Finch, Wendel, & Mayhall, 1987; Saylor, Finch, Spirito, and Bennett, 1984). Carey, Faulstich, Gresham, Ruggiero, and Enyart (1987) found that only CDI items measuring depressed affect discriminated depressed, conduct disordered, and normal 9-to-17-year-olds, and only 44% of cases were correctly classified.

Other studies have found that CDI scores are higher in depressed than in nondepressed psychiatrically disturbed youngsters (Lobovits & Handal, 1985; Marriage, Fine, Moretti, & Haley, 1986). Curry and Craighead (1990) found that adolescent inpatients with major depression had higher CDI scores than inpatients with no major or minor depressive disorder. Such mixed results on the discriminant validity of the CDI may be attributable to subject factors, including age and defensiveness of the children, and severity of depressed state, and to methodological factors including how children with secondary depressive diagnoses and minor depressive diagnoses are grouped for data analyses.

Smucker and Craighead (1990) recently reported a factor analysis of the CDI for 2,790 children in grades 3 through 9 from public schools. The five factors were I, dysphoric mood; II, acting out; III, loss of personal and social interest; IV, self-deprecation; and V, vegetative symptoms. Hodges and Craighead (in press) recently reported that factors I, III, and IV were related to major depression among inpatient depressives ages 6–13, while factor II was related to acting out, and factor V was related to overanxious disorder. They recommend the use of the combined scores for Smucker and Craighead's factors I, III, and IV as a better measure of depression severity than the CDI total score.

In summary, findings do suggest that, although the CDI is a reliable measure of current distress and depressive symptomatology, it cannot be used alone as a measure of diagnosed depressive disorder. It may best be used as a measure of severity of depression among groups diagnosed with a depressive disorder or as a screening measure to identify individuals who might be interviewed to determine whether they meet criteria for a depressive diagnosis.

Children's Depression Scale (CDS)

The CDS is a 66-item scale, with 48 depressive and 18 positive items that yield two separate scores. The depressive scale has five subscales: affective responses, social problems, self-esteem, preoccupation with sickness or death, and guilt. A parallel form of parents or teachers (CDS-Adult) is available. The original CDS had each item printed on a card. Cards were then sorted into one of five boxes rating how "wrong" to how "right" the item statment was in a description of the subject. Subsequently, a questionnaire format has been developed and used.

Tisher and Lang (1983) reported that overall internal consistency of the scale was high (coefficient alpha = .92), with subscale internal consistency ranging from .54 to .77. Test-retest reliability correlation for sixty 9-to-13-year-old children tested twice over 7 to 10 days was .74 for both the depression and the positive scales.

Initial validity work contrasted severe school refusers ($n = 40$), non-school-refusing outpatients ($n = 19$), and normal controls ($n = 37$), and showed significant group differences. Review of studies of six samples (Tisher & Lang, 1983) showed that girls usually scored higher than boys. Normative mean scores were more variable than has been found with the CDI, possibly because the samples were considerably smaller than those on which CDI norms have been based. Haley, Fine, Marriage, Moretti, and Freeman (1985) found CDS scores associated with cognitive distortions characteristic of depression. Rotundo and Hensley (1985) tested concurrent and discriminant validity of the CDS with 60 clinical and 24 normal adolescents. CDS depression scores correlated highly with CDI scores ($r = .84$), and both scales discriminated between clinical and normal subjects, and between depressed and nondepressed clinical subjects. The CDS-A completed by parents also discriminated between these diagnostic groups. The CDS, but not the CDS-A, also discriminated between depressed and sad (not depressed) clinical subjects. Based on mean CDS scores of their depressed and nondepressed subjects, Rotundo and Hensley found that the original normative data published by Lang and Tisher (1978) overidentified severe depression, and they argued for use of a higher threshold. This study further corroborated the high internal consistency of the CDS, but factor analysis did not support its hypothesized subscale structure.

Kazdin (1987) tested the validity of the CDS with 185 child psychiatry inpatients, ages 7–12. High internal consistency, significant correlations with hopelessness, low self-esteem, and CDI scores were found. Both CDS depressive and positive scales differed between diagnosed depressed and nondepressed youngsters. By contrast, CDI total score did not differentiate between these groups. The CDS-A completed by parents was somewhat superior to CDS completed by the children in this group discrimination, despite nearly total lack of correlation between depression scores on the CDS and CDS-A ($r = .04$). The principal difference between the findings of Rotundo and Hensley (1985) and those of Kazdin (i.e., the relatively greater discriminating power of child vs. parent forms of the CDS) may be attributable to factors such as age of subjects or severity of self-reported depression.

In summary, the CDS has strong internal consistency and appears to discriminate well between depressed and nondepressed clinic children or adolescents. To date, however, comparatively few studies have tested this type of validity. A major limitation of this scale is lack of a large normative base.

Depression Self-Rating Scale (DSRS)

The DSRS was developed by Birleson (1981). It contains 18 items measuring cognitive, behavioral, and affective symptoms of depression, which discriminated between depressed and nondepressed prepubertal children. Internal consistency (split-half) was .86, and test-retest reliability with 20 residential-treatment-center children was .80. Each item is rated absent, sometimes present, or always present (scale of 0 to 2). Therefore, unlike the CDI, the DSRS does not require children with limited attention span or mental age to make comparative judgments among statements reflecting levels of symptom severity. In addition, the DSRS is the shortest of the available depression self-report scales.

Asarnow and Carlson (1985) administered the DSRS to 82 child psychiatry inpatients who were independently diagnosed as depressed or not depressed by DSM-III criteria based on K-SADS-E interviews. This study demonstrated acceptable internal consistency of the DSRS ($\alpha = .73$), significant concurrent validity assessed through correlation with the CDI on a subsample of 24 children ($r = .81$), and significant discrimination between diagnosed depressed and nondepressed subjects on the DSRS. A cutoff score of 13, originally proposed by Birleson, had a sensitivity of 64% and specificity of 88% in Asarnow and Carlson's sample. Thirteen of 39 depressed children were not identified by the DSRS, but only 5 of 43 nondepressed children were falsely identified as depressed. The authors suggest that denial of depression led some depressed children to obtain spuriously low scores on this self-report measure, a consideration that needs to be taken into account in the clinical practice of assessing childhood and adolescent depression.

In summary, limited data are available on the psychometric properties of the DSRS. Normative data and further validation with outpatient samples are required. The preliminary findings are encouraging.

Center for Epidemiological Studies Depressive Scale for Children (CES-DC)

The CES-DC (Weissman, Orvaschel, & Podian, 1980) contains 20 items rated for accuracy of self-description on a scale from 0 to 3. Two recent studies have addressed its psychometric properties. Faulstich, Carey, Ruggiero, Enyart, and Gresham (1986) studied the CES-CD with 148 child and adolescent psychiatric inpatients. Two-week test-retest reliability on a subsample of 78 was moderate ($r = .51$), and internal consistency for the whole sample was high (*alpha = .84*). When broken down into child and adolescent subsamples, internal consistency was high in both groups, but test-retest reliability was extremely poor for children ($r = .12$). A moderate correlation with the CDI was obtained for adolescents ($r = .61$), and no significant correlation with the CDI was obtained for children ($r = .03$). At neither age did CES-CD scores differentiate subjects with clinical diagnoses of depression from nondepressed subjects. However, diagnoses in this study were not formalized or tested for reliability.

Doerfler, Felner, Rowlison, Raley, and Evans (1988) administered the CES-CD and other scales to 1,207 children in grades 4 to 12. No significant grade, gender, or race effects were found. CES-CD and CDI scores were moderately correlated ($r = .58$). Neither CES-CD nor CDI showed strong correlations with teacher or parent ratings or mood problems. The cutoff score of 16, previously used by Weissman et al. (1980) to identify depressed children, was found to be much too low in this sample, in which it classified 46% of the subjects as depressed.

In summary, evidence to support the use of the CES-CD is currently weak, especially with younger samples.

Beck Depression Inventory

Beck and his colleagues (Beck, Ward, Mendelson, Mock, & Erbaugh, 1961) developed this 21-item self-report measure of depression, which is widely used in research and clinical practice with adults. Each item consists of four statements describing varying degrees of severity of a depressive symptom, and the respondent chooses the statement that most accurately reflects the self over the past week. Total scores range from 0 to 63. Scores above 16 are considered indicative of moderate to more severe depression.

Kaplan, Hong, and Weinhold (1984) studied 385 adolescents ages 11–18. Overall BDI mean score was 6.00 (SD = 5.8). Scores were higher in older subjects and in subjects with lower socioeconomic status. Moderate to severe depression occurred in 8.6% of subjects. Teri (1982) studied 568 adolescents ages 14–17. The mean score was 8.47 (SD = 8.03). Scores were not related to age within this senior high school sample, and gender effects occurred only when comparing extreme high vs. low scores. There were more females in the high group.

Internal consistency of the BDI is high for normal adolescents (alpha = .87) (Teri, 1982) and for psychiatrically hospitalized adolescents (alpha = .86—Barrera and Garrison-Jones, 1988; alpha = .79—Strober, Green, & Carlson, 1981b). Test-retest reliability over 5 days in the latter study was high in adolescents with major depression ($r = .74$), but only moderate in those with other diagnoses ($r = .51$).

Concurrent validity of the BDI is supported by correlation with a psychiatrist's global rating of depression ($r = .69$) (Strober, Green, & Carlson, 1981b), and with the Child Assessment Schedule (CAS) depression scores for clinical ($r = .49$) and normal ($r = .73$) samples (Barrera & Garrison-Jones, 1988). Its discriminant validity is supported by lack of correlation with CAS conduct disorder or anxiety disorder scales in a clinical sample, and significant but low correlations with these scales in a normal sample (Barrera & Garrison-Jones, 1988). Strober and colleagues (1981b) found that the recommended cutoff score of 16 correctly classified 81% of inpatient subjects diagnosed by SADS interviews as depressed or not depressed. Barrera and Garrison-Jones found that the same cutoff score correctly classified 93% of 49 normal adolescents diagnosed by CAS interviews as depressed or not depressed. However, a cutoff as low as 11 was required to classify correctly just 65% of hospitalized adolescents in this study. This may reflect guardedness of defensiveness in endorsing symptomatology among the hospitalized youths.

In summary, the BDI can be used as a screening instrument and as a measure of depressive severity with adolescents. Its estimated reading level is high, however (grades 6–8) (Berndt, Schwartz, & Kaiser, 1983), and the item on loss of libido is rarely endorsed by adolescents (Kaplan, Hong, & Weinhold, 1984; Barrera & Garrison-Jones, 1988). An advantage of using the BDI is increased direct comparability between adolescent and adult studies.

CLINICAL RATING SCALES

Although considered a standard component of the assessment of adult depression, clinician-completed rating scales have received limited investigation in the study of child and adolescent depression. Such scales combined advantages of an interactive interview and a behavioral observation and occupy a medium range of specificity between global clinical ratings and specific behavioral observations. Because of their relative brevity, some clinician rating scales could be used with self-report scales to assess change over time through repeated measures. Two rating scales are reviewed here: the Hamilton Rating Scale for Depression (HRSD) (Hamilton, 1960) and the Children's Depression Rating Scale (CDRS) (Poznanski, Cook, & Carroll, 1979).

Hamilton Rating Scale For Depression (HRSD)

This scale is the most commonly used clinician-completed measure of depressive severity with adults (Hurt, Friedman, Clarkin, Corn, & Aronoff, 1982). It had 21 items in its original form (Hamilton, 1960). Seventeen-item and eighteen-item versions have also been used with adolescents, but the literature is extremely limited (Hurt et al., 1982; Robbins, Alessi, Colfer, & Yanchyshyn, 1985). Hurt et al. (1982) found interrater reliability based on a joint interview of 19 adolescent inpatients to be .90 or above for the HRSD. Robbins et al. (1985) compared 17-item HRSD ratings by two child psychiatrists based on joint interviews of 81 adolescent inpatients to self-reported depression on the Carroll Self-Rating-Scale (Carroll, Feinberg, Smouse, Rawson, & Greden, 1981), which assesses the same 17 symptoms. In adult inpatients, these two instruments are highly correlated ($r = .80$; Carroll et al., 1981). In the adolescent sample, the HRSD again showed interrater reliability of .90, but correlation with CSRS was only .56. Overall CSRS scores exceeded HRSD scores. However, on certain definitive symptoms, clinician ratings were higher, and low correlations were particularly striking for these symptoms: depressed mood ($r = .30$) and anhedonia ($r = .26$). Findings suggested that depressed adolescents may be more direct in reporting insomnia and somatic complaints than in reporting mood and pleasure. Yanchyshyn and Robbins (1983) found that both the HRSD and the CSRS discriminated between adolescent inpatients and normal controls. Although the HRSD and similar scales appear to have promising utility in studies with adolescents, further work on stability, internal consistency, and discriminant validity should now be pursued.

Children's Depression Rating Scale (CDRS)

The CDRS, developed by Poznanski, Cook, and Carroll (1979) requires approximately 20 minutes to complete, and it yields ratings in 15 categories for children 6 through 12 years old. A revised version with 17 items was published in 1984 (Poznanski, Grossman, Buchsbaum, Banegas, Freeman, & Gibbons, 1984). Interrater reliability was high for the original CDRS with pediatric patients ($r = .96$) (Poznanski, Cook, & Carroll, 1979) and with other psychiatric inpatients ($r = .80$) (Poznanski, Cook, Carroll, & Corzo, 1983). Concurrent validity was supported by correlations with psychiatrists' global depression ratings ($r = .89$ and $= .75$) in these two types of samples. For the CDRS-R, correlation with global depression ratings was high in an outpatient psychiatric sample ($r = .87$), and test-retest reliability over 2 weeks was also high ($r = .86$), although it may have been inflated by use of the same clinician at each time. Children diagnosed as depressed scored significantly higher than those not so diagnosed (Poznanski et al., 1984). Mokros, Poznanski, Grossman, and Freeman (1987) found that CDRS-R scores based on child interview were higher than those based on parent interview for depressed mood, suicidal ideation, and sleep problems, while the reverse was true for social withdrawal and somatic complaints in a large ($n = 110$) nonclinical school sample. With children referred to an affective disorders clinic ($n = 34$), however, overall summary scores were higher when based on parent than on child interviews. Therefore, parent-child concordance and clinical status appear to affect clinician ratings just as they do self-report and interview measures of depression.

OBJECTIVE AND PROJECTIVE PSYCHOLOGICAL TESTS

Although traditional psychological tests, such as the Minnesota Multiphasic Personality Inventory (MMPI) and the Rorschach obviously antedate the formulation of phenomenological criteria for depressive disorders and were not designed to provide DSM-III diagnoses, both instruments measure constructs that are theoretically related to depressed mood or disorder. A limited body of recent literature has evaluated such tests in relation to depression in adolescents.

Adolescent inpatients with an MMPI high point on Scale 2 (depression), compared to inpatients with other high-point codes, were seen by nurses as seclusive, tearful, lacking in energy, and by therapists as motivated, self-critical, introspective, and overcontrolled (Archer, Gordon, Gianetti, & Singles, 1988). Two studies examining MMPI Scale 2 differences as a function of clinical depression diagnoses, however, reported conflicting results (Archer & Gordon, 1988; Lupovsky, Finch, & Belter, 1989).

Rorschach studies of adolescents (Archer & Gordon, 1988; Lupovsky et al., 1989) found the Depression Index (Exner, 1986) unrelated to depression diagnosis. The Index correlated very moderately with self-reported depression on the MMPI, as did frequency of morbid content responses. The sum of all shading responses differed significantly between diagnosed depressed and nondepressed adolescents, although both groups averaged less than one such response.

Considerably more research is needed with quantified projective test scores before conclusions can be drawn about the types of psychological processes they may measure in depressed adolescents. Although there is little theoretical reason to expect them to detect DSM-III-R diagnostic group differences, they may be sensitive to inner experiences associated with depression that are not readily assessed by more direct measures.

TEACHER RATINGS, PEER RATINGS AND DIRECT OBSERVATIONS

Hoier and Kerr (1988) recently reviewed these extrafamilial sources of information for assessment of childhood depression. Their review of six studies using various teacher rating forms concluded that teachers tend to agree with peers regarding who is depressed, but not with parents or with the children themselves. A variety of problems may account for the relative insensitivity of teacher ratings to childhood depression, including lack of sufficiently extensive observational opportunities, lack of scales specifically designed to facilitate teacher observations of depressive behavior, and the relatively greater prominence of externalizing as compared with internalizing problems in the classroom setting. At present, teacher ratings may yield important information about qualitative aspects of a particular child's depression, but they do not constitute a major source of diagnostic information, as they do, for example, for attention deficit and other externalizing disorders.

PARENT-REPORT INSTRUMENTS

A comprehensive review of broad-based parent checklists is beyond the scope of this chapter. Several commonly used checklists, however, include scales to measure childhood or adolescent depression. These include the Child Behavior Checklist (CBCL) (Achenbach, 1978), the Behavior Problem Checklist (BPC) (Quay & Peterson, 1979) (recently revised), and the Personality Inventory for Children (PIC) (Wirt, Lachar, Klinedinst, & Seat, 1977). Kazdin and Heidish (1984) compared CBCL depression and internalizing scales and BPC personality problems scales to clinical diagnoses of major depression for 113 inpatient boys, using a cutoff point of 1 standard deviation above the mean. The two CBCL scales showed high sensitivity (>88%), but very poor specificity (<20%). Therefore, although few depressed children were missed by these scales, many children not diagnosed as depressed scored high on these scales. The BPC scale had lower sensitivity (61%) but higher specificity (45%). Lobovits and Handal (1985) compared PIC depression scores to clinical diagnoses of major depression in 50 outpatient children. Eleven were depressed. Using a PIC-depression score 2 standard deviations above the mean as a cutoff, there was only one false negative (91% sensitivity) but 13 false positives (66% specificity). Edelbrock and Costello (1988) also reported significant convergence between parent-based child diagnoses and associated CBCL scale scores. All of these studies are limited by lack of full independence between parent ratings and the process of diagnostic formulation.

A major problem has been low levels of concordance between parents and children across various methods of reporting child depression (Kazdin,

French, Unis, & Esveldt-Dawson, 1983; Moretti, Fine, Haley, & Marriage, 1985). To date, the reasons for this phenomenon are not well understood. It may be influenced by factors such as age and cognitive status of the child, severity of depression in child or parent, relative salience of depression and comorbid conditions, and quality of the parent-child relationship. Further research on the phenomenon is needed to provide guidelines for combining and evaluating information from these different sources.

BIOLOGICAL MARKERS

Puig-Antich (1986) reviewed the status of several psychobiological markers for depression in children and adolescents. These include sleep EEG, growth hormone secretion, and the dexamethasone suppression test (DST). It is beyond the scope of this chapter to review these proposed markers. The most extensively studied marker has been the DST. Findings have been complicated by lack of an acceptable "gold standard" (clinical diagnosis) against which to measure the test, inconsistent adherence to exclusion criteria, and technical problems related to the timing of the test with inpatients (Carroll, 1985). A task force of the American Psychiatric Association (1987) reviewed the status of the DST, concluding that its sensitivity is modest in adult major depression (about 40% to 50%), but higher in severe forms of the disorder. Specificity was found to vary in relation to disorders that often need to be differentiated from major affective disorder. Conditions leading to false positive results were outlined. The Task Force concluded that, at present, the test has limited clinical utility, but appropriate use in certain clinical situations may be helpful and continued research is warranted.

CASE ILLUSTRATION

B.P. was a 13-year-old adolescent who was admitted to an adolescent inpatient psychiatry program after outpatient intervention had been insufficient to resolve her problems of missing classes or entire days of school, depressed mood, multiple somatic complaints, and conflictual relationships with family and peers. Assessment of possible depression, anxiety disorder, and learning difficulties was conducted. The latter possibility was ruled out by results of intelligence and achievement tests.

The assessment protocol included a version of the K-SADS-E that has been used with adolescent inpatients. Both mother and child were interviewed. In addition, an HRSD was completed by B.P.'s diagnostic interviewer, and B.P. completed the CDI and the Rorschach. Medical evaluation included the DST.

Both parent and adolescent K-SADS-E interviews indicated current major depression. Mother reported that B.P. also had past episodes of major depression, although B.P. described these as brief dysthymic periods. Current symptoms included weight loss, insomnia, fatigue, mild agitation, and concentration difficulties. Symptoms of separation anxiety were present, and other symptoms of this disorder had been present in the past. However, neither current nor past episodes met criteria for diagnosis of that disorder. The interviews were negative for mania, psychotic symptoms, panic or other anxiety disorders, attention deficit, or conduct disorder.

On the CDI, B.P. obtained a score of 26, indicating a high level of current depressive symptomatology. The HRSD was 16. The DST was also abnormal in her case, which was interpreted as confirming a depressive disorder. Projective testing with the Rorschach (Exner system) showed indices of morbid ideation, self-critical introspection, and an elevated isolation index. There was no projective test evidence of difficulties with perceptual accuracy or thought processes.

Treatment implications of the assessment included psychotherapeutic focusing on self-critical thinking and on isolating, socially withdrawn behavior. Group psychotherapy was used as a modality in which B.P. could become more aware of those cognitive and behavioral patterns and could practice alternative responses through role-playing and direct in-group interactions. The primary diagnosis given was major depression. As an empirical trial, B.P. was given tricyclic antidepressant medication, which indication for specific treatment for depression is the lack of empirical data on treatment outcomes. For adult depression, three major treatment approaches have been supported by outcome research: (1) tricyclic antidepressant medication, (2) cognitive behavior therapy, and (3) interpersonal psychotherapy (Craighead, Evans, & Robins, in press). To date, none of these approaches has been demonstrated to have generalized effectiveness in the treatment of childhood or adolescent depression. Puig-Antich, Ryan, and Rabinovich (1985) noted unexpectedly high placebo response rates in studies of imipramine with children and adolescents with major depression, so this medication was no more effective than a pill placebo with these subjects. Further research with antidepressant medications, including investigation of nontricyclics, is indicated to determine which depressed youngsters would be likely to benefit from medications.

Interpersonal psychotherapy for depression has not

been evaluated in controlled studies with children or adolescents. Three controlled studies of cognitive behavior therapy (Stark, Reynolds, & Kaslow, 1987; Reynolds & Coats, 1986; Lewinsohn, Hops, Williams, Clarke, & Andrews, 1987) indicate that such treatments are superior to wait-list control conditions in reducing childhood and adolescent depression. Considerably more research is needed to determine specific indications for and limitations of cognitive behavioral interventions for depression in young people.

In summary, future research focused on clarification of the psychopathology of depression and on the outcomes of well-defined interventions is needed to move beyond the present limitations in selection of treatment modalities for childhood and adolescent depression. At present, treatment choice must be guided not only by assessment of diagnosis, severity of depression, and possible concurrent disorders, but also by an individualized clinical formulation. Current assessment methods do permit monitoring of response to treatment through repeated measurements of the presence and severity of depression.

SUMMARY

At present, assessment of childhood and adolescent depression should include interviews with parent and with the child or adolescent, as well as a self-report rating of severity of depression.

Clinical rating scales and parent rating scales may provide useful supplementary data. Biological markers may eventually be of wide clinical utility, but presently they are of more limited clinical value. No "gold standards" exist in the form of specific instruments suited to general clinical purposes. As Costello and Angold (1988) noted, the choice of what rating scale to use must follow from the purpose of the assessment (screening, assessment of severity, assessment of change), and characteristics of the child to be assessed. Likewise, use of a particular interview will depend on the coverage of disorders in that instrument, the purpose of assessment, and the ease of the procedure for parent and child. Implementation of formal diagnostic interviews in clinical settings is a relatively new and not-well-researched development. As the cognitive and interpersonal psychopathology of childhood and adolescent depression is more completely understood, assessment instruments for diagnosis will, in all likelihood, be supplemented by techniques to assess specific cognitive and interpersonal processes to be addressed in treatment.

REFERENCES

Achenbach, T. M. (1978). The Child Behavior Profile: I. Boys aged 6–11. *Journal of Consulting and Clinical Psychology, 46*, 478–488.

Ambrosini, P. J., Metz, C., Prabrucki, K., & Lee, J. (1989). Videotape reliability of the third revised edition of the K-SADS. *Journal of the American Academy of Child and Adolescent Psychiatry, 28*, 723–728.

American Psychiatric Association. (1987). *Diagnostic and statistical manual of mental disorders*, 3rd ed. revised. Washington, DC: Author.

Angold, A. (1988). Structured assessments of psychopathology in children and adolescents. To appear in C. Thompson (Ed.), *Structured assessments in psychiatry*.

APA Task Force on Laboratory Tests in Psychiatry (1987). The dexamethasone suppression test: An overview of its current status in psychiatry. *American Journal of Psychiatry, 144*, 1253–1262.

Archer, R. P., & Gordon, R. A. (1988). MMPI and Rorschach indices of schizophrenic and depressive diagnoses among adolescent inpatients. *Journal of Personality Assessment, 52*, 276–287.

Archer, R. P., Gordon, R. A., Giannetti, R. A., & Singles, J. M. (1988). MMPI scale clinical correlates for adolescent inpatients. *Journal of Personality Assessment, 52*, 707–731.

Asarnow, J. R., & Carlson, G. A. (1985). Depression self-rating scale: Utility with child psychiatric inpatients. *Journal of Consulting and Clinical Psychology, 53*, 491–499.

Barrera, M., & Garrison-Jones, C. V. (1988). Properties of the Beck Depression Inventory as a screening instrument for adolescent depression. *Journal of Abnormal Child Psychology, 16*(3), 263–273.

Beck, A., Ward, C., Mendelson, M., Mock, J., & Erbaugh, J. (1961). An inventory for measuring depression. *Archives of General Psychiatry, 4*, 53–63.

Berndt, D. J., Schwartz, S., & Kaiser, C. F. (1983). Readability of self-report depression inventories. *Journal of Consulting and Clinical Psychology, 51*, 627–628.

Birleson, P. (1981). The validity of depressive disorder in childhood and the development of a self-rating scale. *Journal of Child Psychology and Psychiatry, 22*, 73–88.

Breslau, N. (1987). Inquiring about the bizarre: False positives in Diagnostic Interview Schedule for Children (DISC) ascertain of obsessions, compulsions, and psychotic symptoms. *Journal of the American Academy of Child and Adolescent Psychiatry, 26*, 639–644.

Carey, M. P., Faulstich, M. E., Gresham, F. M., Ruggiero, L., & Enyart, P. (1987). Children's depression inventory: Construct and discriminant validity across clinical and nonreferred (control) populations. *Journal of Consulting and Clinical Psychology, 55*, 755–761.

Carlson, G. A., Kashani, J. H., Thomas, M. D. F., Vaidya, A., & Daniel, A. E. (1987). Comparison of two structured interviews on a psychiatrically hospitalized population of children. *Journal of the American Academy of Child and Adolescent Psychiatry, 26,* 645–648.

Carroll, B. J. (1985). Dexamethasone suppression test: A review of contemporary confusion. *Journal of Clinical Psychiatry, 46,* 13–24.

Carroll, B. J., Feinberg, M., Smouse, P. E., Rawson, S. G., & Greden, J. F. (1981). The Carroll Rating Scale for Depression: I. Development, reliability and validation. *British Journal of Psychiatry, 138,* 194–200.

Chambers, W. J., Puig-Antich, J., Hirsch, M., Paez, P., Ambrosini, P. J., Tabrizi, M. A., & Davies, M. (1985). The assessment of affective disorders in children and adolescents by semistructured interview: Test-retest reliability of the Schedule for Affective Disorders and Schizophrenia for school-age children, present episode version. *Archives of General Psychiatry, 42,* 696–702.

Cohen, P., O'Connor, P., Lewis, S., Velez, C. N., & Malachowski, B. (1987). Comparison of DISC and K-SADS-P Interviews of an epidemiological sample. *Journal of the American Academy of Child and Adolescent Psychiatry, 26,* 662–667.

Costello, E. J., & Angold, A. (1988). Scales to assess child and adolescent depression: Checklists, screens, and nets. *Journal of the American Academy of Child and Adolescent Psychiatry, 27,* 726–737.

Costello, E. J., Edelbrock, C. S., & Costello, A. J. (1985). Validity of the NIMH diagnostic interview schedule for children: A comparison between psychiatric and pediatric referrals. *Journal of Abnormal and Child Psychology, 13,* 579–595.

Costello, A. J., Edelbrock, C. S., Dulcan, M. K., Kulas, R., & Klaric, S. R. (1984). *Development and testing of the NIMH Diagnostic Interview Schedule for Children in a clinic population.* First report (Contract No. REP-DB-81-0027). Rockville, MD: Center for Epidemiological Studies, National Institute of Mental Health.

Craighead, L. W., & Green, B. J. (in press). The relationship between depression and sex-typed personality characteristics in adolescents. *Journal of Youth and Adolescence.*

Craighead, W. E., & Curry, J. F. (in press). Depression in children and adolescents. In L. W. Craighead, W. E. Craighead, A. E. Kazdin, & M. J. Mahoney (Eds.), *Cognitive-behavioral interventions.* New York: Pergamon Press.

Craighead, W. E., Evans, D. D., & Robins, C. J. (in press). Unipolar depression. In S. M. Turner, K. S. Calhoun, & H. E. Adams (Eds.), *Handbook of clinical behavior therapy* (2nd ed.). New York: John Wiley & Sons.

Curry, J. F., & Craighead, W. E. (1990). Attributional style in clinically depressed and conduct disordered adolescents. *Journal of Consulting and Clinical Psychology, 58,* 109–115.

Doerfler, L. A., Felner, R. D., Rowlison, R. T., Raley, P. A., & Evans, E. (1988). Depression in children and adolescents: A comparative analysis of the utility and construct validity of two assessment measures. *Journal of Consulting and Clinical Psychology, 56,* 769–772.

Edelbrock, C., & Costello, A. J. (1988a). Structured psychiatric interviews for children. In M. Rutter, A. H. Tuma, and I. S. Lann (Eds.), *Assessment and diagnosis in child psychopathology.* New York: Guilford Press.

Edelbrock, C., & Costello, A. J. (1988b). Convergence between statistically derived behavior problem syndromes and child psychiatric diagnoses. *Journal of Abnormal Child Psychology, 16,* 219–232.

Edelbrock, C., Costello, A.J., Dulcan, M. K., Conover, N. C., & Kalas, R. (1986). Parent-child agreement on child psychiatric symptoms assessed via structured interview. *Journal of Child Psychology and Psychiatry, 27,* 181–190.

Edelbrock, C., Costello, A. J., Dulcan, M. K., Kalas, R., & Conover, N. C. (1985). Age differences in the reliability of the psychiatric interview of the child. *Child Development, 56,* 265–275.

Exner, J. (1986). *The Rorschach: A comprehensive system, Vol. 1,* (2nd Ed.). New York: Wiley.

Faulstich, M. E., Carey, M. P., Ruggiero, L., Enyart, P., & Gresham, F. (1986). Assessment of depression in childhood and adolescence: An evaluation of the Center for Epidemiological Studies Depression Scales for Children (CES-DC). *American Journal of Psychiatry, 143,* 1024–1027.

Finch, A. J., Saylor, C. F., & Edwards, G. L. (1985). Children's Depression Inventory: Sex and grade norms for normal children. *Journal of Consulting and Clinical Psychology, 53,* 424–425.

Gutterman, E. M., O'Brien, J. D., & Young, J. G. (1987). Structured diagnostic interviews for children and adolescents: Current status and future directions. *Journal of the American Academy of Child and Adolescent Psychiatry, 26,* 621–630.

Haley, G. M. T., Fine, S., Marriage, K., Moretti, M. M., & Freeman, R. J. (1985). Cognitive bias and depression in psychiatrically disturbed children and adolescents. *Journal of Consulting and Clinical Psychology, 53,* 535–537.

Hamilton, M. (1960). A rating scale for depression. *Journal of Neurology, Neurosurgery, and Psychiatry, 23,* 56–62.

Helsel, W. J., & Matson, J. L. (1984). The assessment of depression in children: The internal structure of the Child Depression Inventory (CDI). *Behavior Research and Therapy, 22,* 289–298.

Herjanic, B., & Campbell, U. (1977). Differentiating psychiatrically disturbed children on the basis of a structured interview. *Journal of Abnormal Child Psychology, 5,* 127–134.

Herjanic, B., & Reich, W. (1982). Development of a structured psychiatric interview for children: Agreement between child and parent on individual symptoms. *Journal of Abnormal Child Psychology, 10,* 307–324.

Hodges, K. (1987). Assessing children with a clinical research interview: The Child Assessment Schedule. In R.

J. Prinz (Ed.), *Advances in behavioral assessment of children and families* (Vol. 3) (pp. 203–233). Greenwich, CT: JAI Press.

Hodges, K., Cools, J., & McKnew, D. (1989). Test-retest reliability of a clinical research interview for children: The Child Assessment Schedule. *Psychological Assessment: A Journal of Consulting and Clinical Psychology, 1*, 317–322.

Hodges, K., & Craighead, W. E. (in press). Relationship of Children's Depression Inventory factors to diagnosed depression. *Psychological Assessment: A Journal of Consulting and Clinical Psychology.*

Hodges, K., Gordon, Y., & Lennon, M. P. (in press). Parent-child agreement on symptoms assessed via a clinical research interview for children: The Child Assessment Schedule. *Journal of Child Psychology and Psychiatry.*

Hodges, K., Kline, J., Stern, L., Cytryn, L., & McKnew, D. (1982). The development of a child assessment schedule for research and clinical use. *Journal of Abnormal Child Psychology, 10*, 173–189.

Hodges, K., McKnew, D., Burbach, D. J., & Roebuck, L. (1987). Diagnostic concordance between the Child Assessment Schedule (CAS) and the Schedule for Affective Disorders and Schizophrenia for School-age Children (K-SADS) in an outpatient sample using lay interviewers. *Journal of the American Academy of Child Psychiatry, 26*, 654–661.

Hodges, K., McKnew, D., Cytryn, L., Stern, L., & Kline, J. (1982). The Child Assessment Schedule (CAS) diagnostic interview: A report on reliability and validity. *Journal of the American Academy of Child Psychiatry, 21*, 468–473.

Hodges, K., Siegel, L. J., Mullins, L., & Griffin, N. (1983). Factor analysis of the Children's Depression Inventory. *Psychological Reports, 53*, 759–763.

Hoier, T. S., & Kerr, M. M. (1988). Extrafamilial information sources in the study of childhood depression. *Journal of the American Academy of Child and Adolescent Psychiatry 27*, 21–33.

Hurt, S. W., Friedman, R. C., Clarkin, J., Corn, R., & Aronoff, M. S. (1982). Rating the severity of depressive symptoms in adolescents and young adult. *Comprehensive Psychiatry, 23*, 263–270.

Kaplan, S. L., Hong, G. K., & Weinhold, C. (1984). Epidemiology of depressive symptomatology in adolescents. *Journal of the American Academy of Child Psychiatry, 23*, 91–98.

Kazdin, A. E. (1981). Assessment techniques for childhood depression. *Journal of the American Academy of Child Psychiatry, 20*, 358–375.

Kazdin, A. E. (1987). Children's Depression Scale: Validation with child psychiatric inpatients. *Journal of Child Psychology and Psychiatry, 28*, 29–41.

Kazdin, A. E. (1989). Identifying depression in children: A comparison of alternative selection criteria. *Journal of Abnormal Child Psychology, 17*, 437–454.

Kazdin, A. E., Colbus, D., & Rodgers, A. (1986). Assessment of depression and diagnosis of depressive disorder among psychiatrically disturbed children. *Journal of Abnormal Child Psychology, 14*, 499–515.

Kazdin, A. E., Esveldt-Dawson, K., Unis, A., & Rancurello, M. D. (1983). Child and parent evaluations of depression and aggression in psychiatric inpatient children. *Journal of Abnormal Child Psychology, 11*, 401–413.

Kazdin, A. E., French, N. H., Unis, A. S., & Esveldt-Dawson, K. (1983). Assessment of childhood depression: Correspondence of child and parent ratings. *Journal of the American Academy of Child Psychiatry, 22*, 157–164.

Kazdin, A. E., & Heidish, I. E. (1984). Convergence of clinically derived diagnoses and parent checklists among inpatient children. *Journal of Abnormal Child Psychology, 12*, 421–436.

Kazdin, A. E., & Petti, T. (1982). Self-report and interview measures of childhood and adolescent depression. *Journal of Child Psychology and Psychiatry, 23*, 437–457.

Kovacs, M. (1985a). The Interview Schedule for Children. *Psychopharmacology Bulletin, 21*, 991–994.

Kovacs, M. (1985b). The Children's Depression Inventory. *Psychopharmacology Bulletin, 21*, 995–998.

Kovacs, M., & Beck, A. T. (1977). An empirical clinical approach toward a definition of childhood depression. In J. G. Schulterbrantt and A. Raskin (Eds.), *Depression in childhood: Diagnosis, treatment, and conceptual models*. New York: Raven Press.

Kovacs, M., Feinberg, T. L., Crouse-Novak, M. A., Paulauskas, S. L., & Finkelstein, R. (1984a). Depressive disorders in children: I. A longitudinal prospective study of characteristics and recovery. *Archives of General Psychiatry, 41*, 229–237.

Kovacs, M., Feinberg, T. L., Crouse-Novak, M. A., Paulauskas, S. L., & Finkelstein, R. (1984b). Depressive disorders in children: II. A longitudinal study of the risk for a subsequent major depression. *Archives of General Psychiatry, 41*, 643–649.

Lang, M., & Tisher, M. (1978). Children's Depression Scale. *Australian Council for Educational Research*, Melbourne.

Lefkowitz, M. M., & Tesing, E. P. (1980). Assessment of childhood depression. *Journal of Consulting and Clinical Psychology, 48*, 43–50.

Lewinsohn, P. M., Hops, H., Williams, J. A., Clarke, G. N., & Andrews, J. A. (October, 1987). Cognitive-behavioral treatment for depressed adolescents. Presented at the Annual Meeting of the American Academy of Child and Adolescent Psychiatry, Washington, DC.

Lobovits, D. A., & Handal, P. J. (1985). Childhood depression: Prevalence using DSM-III criteria and validity of parent and child depression scales. *Journal of Pediatric Psychology, 10*, 45–54.

Lupovsky, J. A., Finch, A. J., & Belter, R. W. (1989). Assessment of depression in adolescents: Objective and projective measures. *Journal of Personality Assessment, 53*, 449–458.

Marriage, K., Fine, S., Moretti, M., & Haley, G. (1986). Relationship between depression and conduct disorder in children and adolescents. *Journal of the American Academy of Child Psychiatry, 25*, 687–691.

McCauley, E., Mitchell, J. R., Burke, P., & Moss, S. (1988). Cognitive attributes of depression in children and adolescents. *Journal of Consulting and Clinical Psychology, 56*, 903–908.

Mokros, H. B., Poznanski, E., Grossman, J. A., & Freeman, L. N. (1987). A comparison of child and parent ratings of depression for normal and clinically referred children. *Journal of Child Psychology and Psychiatry, 28*, 613–627.

Moretti, M. M., Fine, S., Haley, G., & Marriage, K. (1985). Childhood and adolescent depression: Child-report versus parent-report information. *Journal of the American Academy of Child Psychiatry, 24*, 298–302.

Nelson, W. M., Politano, P. M., Finch, A. J., Wendel, N., & Mayhall, C. A. (1987). Children's Depression Inventory: Normative data and utility with emotionally disturbed children. *Journal of the American Academy of Child and Adolescent Psychiatry, 26*, 43–48.

Orvaschel, H., Puig-Antich, J., Chambers, W., Tabrizi, M. A., & Johnson, R. (1982). Retrospective assessment of prepubertal major depression with the Kiddie-SADS-E. *Journal of the American Academy of Child Psychiatry, 21*, 392–397.

Poznanski, E. O., Cook, S. C., & Carroll, B. J. (1979). A depression rating scale for children. *Pediatrics, 64*, 442–450.

Poznanski, E. O., Cook, S. C., Carroll, B. J., & Corzo, H. (1983). Use of the Children's Depression Rating Scale in an inpatient psychiatric population. *Journal of Clinical Psychiatry, 44*, 200–203.

Poznanski, E. O., Grossman, J. A., Buchsbaum, Y., Banegas, M., Freeman, L., & Gibbons, R. (1984). Preliminary studies of the reliability and validity of the Children's Depression Rating Scale. *Journal of the American Academy of Child Psychiatry, 23*, 191–197.

Puig-Antich, J. (1986). Psychobiological markers: Effects of age and puberty. In M. Rutter, C. Izard, & P. Read (Eds.), *Depression in young people* (pp. 381–382). New York: Guilford Press.

Puig-Antich, J., & Chambers, W. (1978). *The Schedule for Affective Disorders and Schizophrenia for School-Aged Children (K-SADS)*. New York: New York State Psychiatric Institute.

Puig-Antich, J., Ryan, N., & Rabinovich, H. (1985). Affective disorders in childhood and adolescence. In J. M. Weiner (Ed.), *Diagnosis and psychopharmacology of childhood and adolescent disorders* (pp. 151–177). New York: John Wiley & Sons.

Quay, H. C., & Peterson, D. R. (1979). *Manual for the Behavior Problem Checklist*. Unpublished manuscript. University of Miami and Rutgers State University.

Reich, W., Herjanic, B., Welner, Z., & Gandhy, P. R. (1982). Development of a structured psychiatric interview for children: Agreement on diagnosis comparing child and parent interviews. *Journal of Abnormal Child Psychology, 10*, 325–336.

Reynolds, W. M., & Coats, K. I. (1986). A comparison of cognitive-behavioral therapy and relaxation training for the treatment of depression in adolescents. *Journal of Consulting and Clinical Psychology, 54*, 653–660.

Robbins, D. R., Alessi, N. E., Colfer, M. V., & Yanchyshyn, G. W. (1985). Use of the Hamilton Rating Scale for Depression and the Carroll Self-rating Scale in Adolescents. *Psychiatry Research, 14*, 123–129.

Robbins, D. R., Alessi, N. E., Yanchyshyn, G. W., & Colfer, W. (1983). Psychodynamic and characterological heterogeneity among adolescents with major depressive disorders. *Journal of the American Academy of Child Psychiatry, 22*, 487–491.

Rotundo, N., & Hensley, V. R. (1985). The Children's Depression Scale: A study of its validity. *Journal of Child Psychology and Psychiatry, 26*, 917–927.

Saylor, C. F., Finch, A. J., Furey, W., Baskin, C. H., & Kelly, M. M. (1984). Construct validity for measures of childhood depression: Application of multitrait-multimethod methodology. *Journal of Consulting and Clinical Psychology, 52*, 977–985.

Saylor, C. F., Finch, A. J., Spirito, A., & Bennett, B. (1984). The Children's Depression Inventory: A systematic evaluation of psychometric properties. *Journal of Consulting and Clinical Psychology, 52*, 955–967.

Smucker, M. R., & Craighead, W. E. (1990). *Factor analysis of the Children's Depression Inventory*. Unpublished manuscript. Available from W. E. Craighead, Ph.D., Department of Psychiatry, Box 3270, Duke University Medical Center, Durham, NC, 27710.

Smucker, M. R., Craighead, W. E., Craighead, L. W., & Green, B. J. (1986). Normative and reliability data for the Children's Depression Inventory. *Journal of Abnormal Child Psychology, 14*, 25–39.

Stark, K. D., Reynolds, W. M., & Kaslow, N. J. (1987). A comparison of the relative efficacy of self-control therapy and a behavioral problem-solving therapy for depression in children. *Journal of Abnormal Child Psychology, 15*, 91–113.

Strauss, C. C., Forehand, R., Frame, C., & Smith, K. (1984). Characteristics of children with extreme scores in the Children's Depression Inventory. *Journal of Clinical Child Psychology, 13*, 227–231.

Strober, M. G., Green, J., & Carlson, G. A. (1981a). Phenomenology and subtypes of major depressive disorders in adolescents. *Journal of Affective Disorders, 3*, 277–290.

Strober, M. G., Green, J., & Carlson, G. (1981b). Utility of the Beck Depression Inventory with psychiatrically hospitalized adolescents. *Journal of Consulting and Clinical Psychology, 49*, 482–483.

Sylvester, C. E., Hyde, T. S., & Reichler, R. J. (1987). The

Diagnostic Interview for Children and Personality Inventory for children in studies of children at risk for anxiety disorders or depression. *Journal of the American Academy of Child and Adolescent Psychiatry, 26,* 668–675.

Teri, L. (1982). The use of the Beck Depression Inventory with adolescents. *Journal of Abnormal Child Psychology, 10,* 277–284.

Tisher, M., & Lang, M. (1983). The Children's Depression Scale: Review and further developments. In D. Cantwell & G. Carlson (Eds.), *Affective disorders in childhood and adolescence.* Jamaica, New York: Spectrum Press.

Verhulst, F. C., Berden, G. F. M. G., & Sanders-Woudstra, J. A. R. (1985). Mental health in Dutch children: (II). The prevalence of psychiatric disorder and relationship between measures. *Acta Psychiatrica Scandinavica, 324,* 1–45.

Weissman, M., Orvaschel, H., & Podian, N. (1980). Children's symptom and social functioning: Self-report scales. *Journal of Nervous and Mental Disease, 168,* 736–740.

Weissman, M. M., Wickramaratne, P., Warner, V., John, K., Prusoff, B. A., Merikangas, K. R., & Gammon, G. D. (1987). Assessing psychiatric disorders in children. *Archives of General Psychiatry, 44,* 747–753.

Welner, Z., Reich, W., Herjanic, B., Jung, K. G., & Amado, H. (1987). Reliability, validity, and parent-child agreement studies of the diagnostic interview for children and adolescents (DICA). *Journal of the American Academy of Child and Adolescent Psychiatry, 26,* 649–653.

Wirt, R. D., Lachar, D., Klinedinst, J. K., & Seat, P. D. (1977). *Multidimensional description of child personality: A manual for the Personality Inventory for Children.* Los Angeles: Western Psychological Services.

Yanchyshyn, G. W., & Robbins, D. R. (1983). The assessment of depression in normal adolescents: A comparison study. *Canadian Journal of Psychiatry, 28,* 522–526.

Young, J. G., O'Brien, J. D., Gutterman, E. M., & Cohen, P. (1987). Structured diagnostic interviews for children and adolescents. *Journal of the American Academy of Child and Adolescent Psychiatry, 26,* 611–612.

CHAPTER 18

ATTENTION DEFICIT HYPERACTIVITY DISORDER

Mark D. Rapport

Attention deficit hyperactivity disorder (ADHD) is a complex and chronic disorder of brain, behavior, and development whose behavioral and cognitive consequences pervade multiple areas of functioning. There is no known cure. Although the cause of ADHD remains unknown, current thinking suggests that a primary component of the disorder involves the regulatory processes of the brain—that is, the brain's ability to regulate itself appropriately (which includes both the initiation *and* inhibition of behavior and activity) on an ongoing basis and under a range of normally occurring circumstances and conditions (Conners & Wells, 1986; Douglas, 1988; Kinsbourne, 1984). Thus, individuals with ADHD experience a wide range of behavioral, cognitive, and interpersonal difficulties. The extent to which these difficulties are manifested are influenced by factors such as what the individual is asked to do or not to do, for how long, and the prevailing environmental conditions (see Douglas, 1988; Rapport, 1983; and Whalen & Henker, 1985, for reviews). Abilities related to these broad areas of dysfunction also appear to vary within and across days. Although children with ADHD can exhibit improved behavior and performance under certain incentive, threat, and punishment conditions, they lack the ability to do so *consistently* over extended periods of time. Instead, they must rely on others to provide them with the necessary external (behavioral) and internal (medication) mechanisms for which to regulate their behavior.

Clinical assessment of children with ADHD has changed substantially over the past decade. These changes may be attributed to several factors—some relevant to an increased understanding of the clinical manifestations and treatment of the disorder, and others to the proliferation of recently designed clinical instruments, techniques, and procedures. Despite these advances, creation of a standardized assessment battery for diagnosing or monitoring treatment effects in children with ADHD has not been realized to date. This situation exists largely because of the complex, multifaceted nature of the disorder and the resulting difficulties in reaching consensual agreement as to both (a) strategy and (b) what should be measured or included during the assessment process. Various instruments have nevertheless been developed and borrowed from other fields to assess the ADHD child's attention, cognitive functioning, impulsiveness, and related areas of dysfunction. The rationale for, development, use, and criticisms of these instruments are discussed throughout the chapter, as are various issues relevant to the assessment of children with ADHD.

In the first section of the chapter, the clinical manifestations associated with ADHD as well as the most recent diagnostic criteria are described. The second section addresses the multitude of empirically based assessment techniques and instruments as they apply to both the diagnosis and treatment of children with ADHD. The following two sections include a case presentation and description of treatment that highlight the importance of multimodal clinical assessment for the individual. A brief summary is provided at the end of the chapter, in which speculations regarding the future of assessment and treatment of ADHD are presented.

CLINICAL DESCRIPTION OF THE DISORDER

Subjective clinical descriptions of children with ADHD have remained remarkably similar over the past century, whereas periodic changes have occurred in the formal Diagnostic and Statistical Manual of Mental Disorders (DSM) nomenclature. The evolution from "Hyperkinetic Reaction of Childhood" described in *Diagnostic and Statistical Manual of Mental Disorders,* Second Edition (DSM-II; American Psychiatric Association, 1968) to "Attention Deficit Disorder with or without Hyperactivity" (ADDH) in DSM-III (Third edition; APA, 1980), to its current moniker, "Attention-Deficit Hyperactivity Disorder" (ADHD) in DSM-III-R (Third Edition—Revised; APA, 1987) reflect numerous changes and advances in the field. The concept of minimal brain damage or dysfunction has been replaced with the more benign but nebulous concept of attentional dysfunction, because of the unproven assumptions of the former and increasing empirical support for the latter. The recognition of overactivity as a necessary core component has been in (ADD with H) and out (ADD without H) of favor over the years. Having weathered the storm, it continues to be considered a prominent and necessary feature of the disorder. "Impulsivity" was recognized as a core component of the disorder in DSM-III because "much of the difficulty that hyperactive children get into is not necessarily because of their lack of attention, but because of the aversive, disruptive behaviors that accompany this inattentive pattern" (Gittelman, 1988, p. 15). It has since been relegated to less prominent status in the recent DSM-III-R nomenclature, in part because of difficulties separating the construct from "inattention" in factor analytic studies (Carlson & Rapport, 1989; Hinshaw, 1987).

Other changes initiated between the earlier DSM-II (APA, 1968) and more recent DSM-III-R (APA, 1987) versions reflect and emphasize the developmental nature, chronic course, and behavioral pattern associated with the disorder. The result is an emerging model of biopsychosocial dysfunction whose impact is to affect multiple modalities (sensory, motor, auditory, perceptual) and domains (cognitive, behavioral, interpersonal, affective). Attempts to improve the reliability of clinical diagnosis have also been made. Subjective clinical descriptions of symptoms have given way to more precise behavioral definitions and observations. Inclusion of differential and exclusionary criteria also portend improved clinical judgment.

Current Diagnostic Criteria and Essential Features of the Disorder

The DSM-III-R (APA, 1987) diagnostic criteria for ADHD are presented in Table 18–1. According to the criteria, a child must exhibit any 8 of the 14 symptoms or behaviors listed under the "A" criterion. The essential features of the disorder include developmentally inappropriate levels of inattention, impulsiveness, and hyperactivity (similar to DSM-III criteria) to varying degrees, with additional emphasis in DSM-III-R placed on the developmental or age-specific nature associated with the clinical picture.

Diagnostic criteria are presently arranged in "descending order of discriminating power based on DSM-III-R field trials" rather than by core clinical symptoms of inattention, impulsivity, and hyperactivity, as described in the earlier DSM-III version. This change represents an important conceptual shift from a monothetic—wherein a diagnosis is made only in those exhibiting behaviors characteristic of each of the three primary core areas of the disorder—to a polythetic phenotypic category schema. No single characteristic is presently essential or sufficient for group membership, and members having the greatest number of shared characteristics or clinical features are grouped together. One result of redefining formal membership criteria in this fashion will be to broaden the diagnostic net, resulting in a more heterogeneous population of children that may satisfy diagnostic criteria for ADHD than for ADDH. A second result is provocative. Although it would be difficult not to include items from each of the three areas of hyperactivity, inattention, and impulsivity with the eight items required by current rules, it is possible to arrive at a diagnosis of ADHD in a child who exhibits signs of hyperactivity and impulsiveness but few or no signs of attentional problems (Newcorn et al., 1989).

Table 18-1. Diagnostic Criteria for Attention-Deficit Hyperactivity Disorder (ADHD)

Note: Consider a criterion met only if the behavior is considerably more frequent than that of most people of the same mental age.

A. A disturbance of at least 6 months, during which at least eight of the following are present:
   1. often fidgets with hands or feet or squirms in seat (in adolescents may be limited to subjective feelings of restlessness)
   2. has difficulty remaining seated when required to do so
   3. is easily distracted by extraneous stimuli
   4. has difficulty awaiting turn in games or group situations
   5. often blurts out answers to questions before they have been completed
   6. has difficulty following through on instructions from others (not due to oppositional behavior or failure of comprehension), e.g., fails to finish chores
   7. has difficulty sustaining attention in tasks or play activities
   8. often shifts from one uncompleted activity to another
   9. has difficulty playing quietly
   10. often talks excessively
   11. often interrupts or intrudes on others, e.g., butts into other children's games
   12. often does not seem to listen to what is being said to him or her
   13. often loses things necessary for tasks or activities at school or at home (e.g., toys, pencils, books, assignments)
   14. often engages in physically dangerous activities without considering possible consequences (not for the purpose of thrill-seeking), e.g., runs into street without looking
B. Onset before the age of 7.
C. Does not meet the criteria for a Pervasive Developmental Disorder.

Criteria for severity of attention deficit hyperactivity disorder:
Mild: Few, if any, symptoms in excess of those required to make the diagnosis and only minimal impairment in school and social functioning.

Moderate: Symptoms or functional impairment intermediate between "mild" and "severe."

Severe: Many symptoms in excess of those required to make the diagnosis and significant and pervasive impairment in functioning at home and school and with peers.

Note: From American Psychiatric Association: *Diagnostic and statistical manual of mental disorders, third edition, revised.* Washington, DC, American Psychiatric Association, 1987. Reprinted by permission.

Secondary Features of the Disorder

Aside from the primary clinical descriptions provided in DSM-III-R, a variety of associated symptoms or behaviors are reported in children with ADHD. Many of these symptoms or patterns of behavior are reported early in the developmental course of the disorder and may thus represent less prominent features of the disorder. These include affective volatility, lability of mood, temper tantrums, low frustration tolerance, social disinhibition, cognitive impairment with associated learning disability, and perceptual motor difficulties (Barkley, 1981; Rapport et al., 1987, 1988). Other aspects of disturbance or behavioral difficulties may be secondary to or direct and indirect consequences of the disorder. For example, disturbed peer and interpersonal relationships, academic underachievement, school failure, decreased self-esteem, depressed mood, and conduct problems are characteristic of many children with ADHD (Barkley, 1981; Rapport, 1987; Whalen & Henker, 1985). The presence or absence of attendant aggressive or conduct features is especially important and may be of both diagnostic and prognostic value (Hinshaw, 1987; Lahey et al., 1988; Loney, 1987; Loney & Milich, 1982; Stewart, DeBlois, & Cummings, 1980).

MULTIMODAL ASSESSMENT

A chief role of behavioral assessment is the identification of prominent behavioral or social, cognitive, affective, and physical signs and symptoms in the individual. Information obtained may be used subsequently to formulate initial diagnosis, select and evaluate response to treatment, and in some cases portend long-term outcome. The complexity and multifaceted nature of ADHD eludes facile efforts at clarification and measurement. Broad-based behavioral and sensory domains are affected in the disorder. Many areas of dysfunction are apparent only under certain environmental conditions or situations (Douglas, 1988; Kinsbourne, 1984; Rapport, 1983; Whalen & Henker, 1985). To complicate matters, children with ADHD frequently exhibit an inconsistent pattern of deficits from day to day, even when tasks and other parameters are held constant. This phenomenon has been observed in both field and highly controlled laboratory settings (Kinsbourne, 1984; Rapport, in press), to the dismay of researchers and clinicians alike.

Eliciting information from single sources and limiting or relying exclusively on certain types of information to determine diagnosis of ADHD results in a high rate of misidentified cases. A careful, thorough evaluation that assesses multiple modalities, relies on multiple informants, and incorporates a variety of instruments and methods is preferred. It is equally important to gain an experienced clinical understanding of ADHD phenomenology and its "consistently inconsistent" behavioral and cognitive manifestations. We are seeking to identify a developmental and aberrant pattern of behavior that is perceived as overtly disruptive to others and that interferes with the individual's ability to (a) achieve academically, (b) attend *consistently* to select environmental stimuli, (c) regulate, and especially inhibit, behavioral and cognitive functioning in accordance with rules and situational demands, and (d) experience positive regard from usual environmental sources, including interpersonal relationships that, in turn, contribute to development of self-esteem and adaptive functioning.

Overview

A review of several structured and semistructured psychiatric interviews and popularly used behavioral rating scales and checklists is presented in the first two parts of this section. Aside from the handful of small *n* and uncontrolled case studies, the use of self-report and self-monitoring instruments has been confined primarily to assessing treatment emergent effects (e.g., side effect scales) and co-occurring symptomatology (e.g., self-report depression and anxiety scales) in children with ADHD. Readers interested in the use of such specialty instruments can find detailed discussions throughout this book and elsewhere (see Mash & Terdal, 1981; and entire issue of *Psychopharmacology Bulletin*, 1985. *Vol.* 21, No. 4).

A rationale for and description of direct behavioral observational methods and procedures are presented in the third part of this section. A few of the more robust procedures and methods, which have proven useful for the dual purposes of differential diagnosis and monitoring treatment effects, are featured. Coverage of social skills deficits and use of sociometric ratings for assessment purposes are not included here because of the breadth and diversity of available instruments and degree of elaboration required for adequate presentation. Detailed, extensive coverage as well as current reviews of these instruments for use with ADHD children are available from several sources (Barkley, 1981; Hops & Greenwood, 1981; Milich & Landau, 1982; Pelham & Bender, 1982).

The role of traditional psychoeducational testing for identifying core deficits or patterns of responding is discussed and critiqued in the fourth part of this section. This is followed by a summary presentation on neuropsychological and cognitive assessment instruments and techniques.

Standardized Interviews

The suggested practice of using a standardized interview format as a clinical diagnostic tool, and the recognition that parents and children frequently disagree regarding both the occurrence and severity of child dysfunction have been credited to the pioneering work of Rutter and Graham (1968). Development of structured and semistructured psychiatric interviews suitable for use with children and adolescents, however, did not become popular until the publication of the DSM-III (APA, 1980), with its more specific diagnostic criteria. The relative merits and specific advantages associated with their use have been outlined and reviewed (Saghir, 1971; Spitzer, 1983; Weinstein, Stone, Noam, Grimes, & Schwab-Stone, 1989). Chief among them are their potential to reduce or minimize different sources of error variance that are internal (e.g., interviewer's behavior, training, and personal or professional biases) or external (e.g., informant and source discrepancies) to the interview (Weinstein et al., 1989; Weissman et al., 1987). Structured and semistructured interviews also provide clinicians with a reliable method by which to probe, clarify, and facilitate the reporting of specific aspects of behavior and symptomatology (including history) that may be overlooked during the course of an unstructured clinical interview (Gammon et al., 1983; Rutter & Shaffer, 1980) yet are relevant to treatment (Achenbach & Edelbrock, 1978; Helzer et al., 1985; Quay & Quay, 1965). Finally, the increased uniformity by which clinicians derive diagnoses and its impact on the establishment of an empirical data base for heuristic and clinical purposes may be realized.

Structured Interviews

The Diagnostic Interview for Children and Adolescents (DICA) (Herjanic & Campbell, 1977; Herjanic & Reich, 1982) and the Diagnostic Interview Schedule for Children (DISC) (Costello, Edelbrock, Kalas, Kessler, & Klaric, 1984) are the two most popularly used structured psychiatric interviews suitable for assessing children with ADHD. Total interview time ranges from 60 to 90 minutes, and the total number of items ranges from approximately 260 to 310 items for both interviews. Both instruments assess the major disruptive disorders of childhood as well as Axis I disorders, are suitable for interviewing children between 6 and 16 or 17 years of age, and may be administered by either a clinician or a trained lay interviewer. It should be noted, however, that at least one study has reported poor agreement between the structured interviews conducted by lay interviewers and clinical interviews conducted by psychiatrists (Anthony et al., 1985), whereas those conducted by psychiatrists and psychologists have not been found to differ (Wittchen, Semler, & von Zerssen, 1985).

Computer scoring and separate versions for interviewing parents and children are available for both the DICA and DISC; however, no standardized method for aggregating parent and child interview information is provided presently. Primary psychometric properties have been established for both instruments. Reliability between parent and children for expressed symptomatology tends to improve with increasing age of the child.

Semistructured Interviews

The semistructured interviews allow the interviewer more flexibility with regard to probing and follow-up questioning than do the structured interviews. Most also require that expressed symptomatology be quantified using severity ratings, as opposed to a present-absent or yes-no format. The tradeoff is that the increased reliance on clinical acumen for appropriate probing, follow-up questioning, and symptom quantification necessitates administration by a trained and experienced clinician who is familiar with childhood psychopathology and DSM-III diagnostic criteria.

The three most popularly used semistructured interviews for assessing child psychopathology include the Children's Assessment Schedule (CAS) (Hodges, McKnew, Cytryn, Stern, & Klein, 1982), the Kiddie-SADS (K-SADS) (Chambers et al., 1985; Puig-Antich & Chambers, 1978), and the Interview Schedule for Children (ISC) (Kovacs, 1982). Total interview time ranges from 45 to 120 minutes, and total number of items ranges from 128 to just over 200 for the CAS, K-SADS, and ISC. All three instruments have established psychometric properties, are suitable for interviewing children between 6 and 17 years of age, and assess all major DSM-III Axis I disorders pertinent to childhood, with the exception of the K-SADS. The epidemiologic version (K-SADS-E) (Orvaschel et al., 1982) must be used to assess items relevant to ADHD, and there is no assessment of Oppositional Defiant Disorder on the earlier version. Separate parent and child versions and computer scoring are available for all three interviews, whereas the K-SADS alone allows for an item-by-item summary rating based on clinical judgment and information obtained during the parent-child interviews.

Use of Interviews for Diagnosing Children with ADHD

Only one study was located that compared structured to semistructured interviews with regard to assessment of children with ADHD. Low to moderate concordance was found when comparing structured (DICA) and semistructured (Kiddie SADS) interviews to best-estimate diagnosis in assessing DSM-III axis I disorders in a child psychiatry inpatient population (Carlson, Kashani, Thomas, Vaidya, & Daniel, 1987). *Kappa* estimates (controlling for base rate) for both interviews fell within the modest to poor range for reliability. Although the sensitivity (true positive rate) of both interviews for identifying ADHD symptomatology in particular was high (i.e., between 0.75 and 1.0), specificity rates (true negatives) were unacceptably low (0.22) for the DICA. As might be expected, the primary source of confusion was in differenting ADHD from the other two disruptive behavior disorders—conduct disorder (CD) and oppositional disorder (OD).

Sensitivity (true positives) and specificity (true negatives) rates have been used in most validation studies to estimate the probability that certain symptoms are present given the presence of a particular disorder (diagnosed positive), or absent given the absence of a disorder (diagnosed negative), respectively. For diagnostic decision-making purposes, however, clinicians may be more interested in knowing the reverse: the likelihood that a particular disorder is or is not present given the presence or absence of a particular symptom or set of symptoms. That is, which symptoms or behaviors, reported as present or absent in a child's history or current repertoire, are most useful for determining diagnosis? The statistics that address this question are referred to as positive predictive power (PPP) and negative predictive power

(NPP), respectively (Dawes, 1986; Widiger, Hurt, Frances, Clarkin, & Gilmore, 1984) and indicate the utility of specific symptoms as inclusionary (PPP) and exclusionary (NPP) criteria for a particular diagnosis. The information these statistics yield may be especially valuable when attempting to assign appropriate diagnosis to children within the DSM-III-R "disruptive behavior disorders" category, because of the overlap and covariation in symptomatology among children with ADHD and CD (Hinshaw, 1987).

A single study was located that examined the relative value of different symptoms, elicited during the course of a structured psychiatric interview (DISC-P), in differentiating children with ADDH from those with CD (Milich, Widiger, & Landau, 1987). Optimal *inclusion* criteria for identifying ADDH consisted of four (of 16 possible) DSM-III items: "can't sit still," "restless sleeper," "games unfinished," and "runs around" (i.e., specificity and PPP rates for these items ranged from 0.86 to 0.92 and from 0.76 to 0.79, respectively). Unfortunately, the items occurred with relatively low frequency (base rate range = 0.17–0.28) and had low sensitivity (range = 0.25–0.40) in the referral sample studied, thus limiting their potential usefulness as exclusionary criteria for the disorder. Only one DSM-III symptom was found to be useful as an exclusionary criterion: "easily distracted." It occurred frequently (base rate = .80), it was a commonly found symptom in the ADDH children studied (sensitivity rate = .95), and its absence suggested that ADHD was not present (NPP = .87). The relatively low specificity (0.36) and PPP rates (0.62) reported, however, indicate that the presence of this symptom was not specific to a diagnosis of ADDH. It was associated with other disorders of childhood, as might be expected, thus prohibiting its usefulness as a two-way pathognomic.

Interview Information: Other

Standard questions regarding a child's developmental, medical, neuropsychiatric, behavioral, and educational history are included in most structured and semistructured interviews. These factors should be explored, in combination with information relevant to family history, leisure activities, peer relations, behavior at and away from home, and treatment history, to determine whether and how they contribute to the presenting clinical picture. Most of this information must be derived from the parent interview, as young children are notoriously poor historians regarding their early development, and frequently minimize or are unaware of their behavioral and educational difficulties.

A routine physical examination should be scheduled to assess for the presence of physical and sexual characteristics that may be associated with sex-linked genetic disorders and to rule out hearing and vision impairment as causal or contributing factors to a child's attentional or behavioral symptoms. Although much has been written on the subject of minor physical anomalies, their presence has not proven to be sufficiently useful to qualify them as marker variables for identifying children at risk for ADHD (Firestone & Prabhu, 1983; Shaywitz, 1982). In a similar vein, the results of neurological examination of children with ADHD are usually normal and unrevealing; however, inclusion of certain aspects of a neuromaturational examination is recommended (Shaywitz, Shaywitz, McGraw, & Groll, 1984).

Comment

Overall, clinical and semistructured interviews usually employ more questioning and allow for more probing than do the structured interviews. As a result, they frequently yield more information relevant to differential diagnosis. In either case, the use of and time required for both types of interviews is easily justified for both clinical training and diagnostic decision-making purposes. Much as a pilot needs to read off the preflight checklist before every flight despite having flown for thousands of hours, clinicians and their patients benefit similarly by taking the time to review symptoms and patterns of behavior in a systematic fashion. Clinicians should be astutely aware, however, of both the individual and collective shortcomings inherent to interviews (see Edelbrock & Costello, 1984; Orvaschel, 1985; Shrout, Spitzer, & Fleiss, 1987; Rosenberger & Lewine, 1982; Weinstein et al., 1989; Weissman et al., 1987). With respect to ADHD, both types of interviews used alone tend to overdiagnose "caseness" in general, resulting in an inflated rate of false positive diagnoses. Continued difficulty with differential diagnosis for the disruptive class of childhood disorders will also be experienced (i.e., differentiating ADHD, CD and OD from one another). Much of this is because of efforts at applying quantitative measurements to categorical diagnoses. As a result, additional information relevant to diagnosis must be obtained from other sources such as rating scales, historical or school records, direct observations of behavior, psychoeducational testing, and neurocognitive assessment techniques as discussed below.

Checklists and Rating Forms

Behavioral checklists and rating scales play a prominent role in assessing children with ADHD. They serve as an important source of information concerning a child's behavior in different settings, how it is judged by significant others, and the extent to which it deviates from age- and gender-related norms. For some instruments, the information obtained contributes to the diagnostic process, whereas the value of others lies in their detection of and sensitivity to treatment effects. Numerous publications have been devoted in recent years to reviewing the major scales and checklists (Barkley, 1987; Achenbach, 1985; Mash & Terdal, 1981). Others have focused on discussing how they are used in diagnosing ADHD (Achenbach, 1987; Barkley, 1981; Barkley & Edelbrock, 1987; Conners, 1987; Edelbrock, Costello, & Kessler, 1984; Shaywitz & Shaywitz, 1988), and still others, their usefulness in child psychopharmacology (Conners & Barkley, 1985). Extensive reviews regarding the limitations inherent to rating scales and checklists have also been presented (Barkley, 1987; Ross & Ross, 1982; Sandberg, Rutter, & Taylor, 1978).

The most popularly used instruments for assessing children with ADHD are presented in Table 18-2. Descriptions and critiques of these instruments, as well as detailed information relevant to their development, inherent psychometric properties, length, factor structure, and general characteristics have been discussed (see Barkley, 1987).

Broad-band Rating Scales and Checklists

The usefulness of scales that assess both broad- and narrow-band dimensions of child psychopathology is their ability to provide a means by which to compare children with expected, normative levels of developmentally and gender appropriate behavior. If present, the severity or deviance of ADHD symptomatology can be assessed in particular, and the presence or pattern of more generalized psychopathological dysfunction documented. This has become increasingly important in recent years because of the converging evidence that hyperactivity (Lahey, Green, & Forehand, 1980), aggression (Loney & Milich, 1982), conduct disturbance (Trites & Laprade, 1983), and academic or cognitive functioning (August & Garfinkel, 1989) may be associated with a different course, unique blend of behavioral disturbance, and prognosis (Hinshaw, 1987; Shaywitz & Shaywitz, 1988). Several of the instruments listed in Table 18-2 fall within this category: The Child Behavior Checklist (CBC) (Achenbach & Edelbrock, 1983), the Conners Parent Symptom Questionnaire (Conners, 1970) and revised edition (Goyette, Conners, & Ulrich, 1978), the Conners Teacher Rating Scale (Conners, 1969) and revised edition (Goyette et al., 1978), the Revised Behavior Problem Checklist (Quay & Peterson, 1983), the Personality Inventory for Children (PIC) (Lachar, 1982), and the Yale Children's Inventory (YCI) (Shaywitz, Schnell, Shaywitz, & Towle, 1986). The CBC is currently the most widely used of the broad-band instruments, and its covergence with

Table 18-2. Broad-band and Narrow-band Rating Scales and Checklists for Assessing Children with ADHD

Broad-Band Rating Scales and Checklists:
   Child Behavior Checklist (CBC)
   Conners Parent Symptom Questionnaire—Revised (CPSQ-R)
   Conners Teacher Rating Scale—Revised (CTRS-R)
   Personality Inventory for Children (PIC)
   Revised Behavior Problem Checklist (BPC-R)
   Yale Children's Inventory (YCI)

Narrow-Band Rating Scales and Checklists:
   Abbreviated Conners Teacher Rating Scale (ACTRS)
   ADD-H Comprehensive Teacher Rating Scale (ACTeRS)
   Children's Learning Profile (CLP)
   Home Situations Questionnaire (HSQ)
   IOWA Conners Teacher Rating Scale (IOWA-ACTRS)
   School Situations Questionnaire (SSQ)
   Teacher Self-Control Rating Scale (TSCRS)
   Werry-Weiss-Peters Activity Scale (WWPAS)

DSM-III diagnoses (and specifically ADDH) derived using structured interviews has been reported on recently by Edelbrock & Costello (1988).

Narrow-band Rating Scales and Checklists

The usefulness of other scales and checklists lies in their ability to assess specific aspects and dimensions of behavioral dysfunction in children with ADHD. For example, the Werry-Weiss-Peters Activity Scale (WWPAS) (Routh, Schroeder & O'Tuama, 1974), a 22-item questionnaire completed by parents, assesses the child's behavior across six different activities or settings (i.e., meals, television, homework, play, sleep, and public places). Most questions are related to gross motor overactivity, impulsiveness, and disruptiveness to others. The Home Situations Questionnaire (HSQ) and School Situations Questionnaire (SSQ) are similar in that they require the parent and teacher to indicate the existence and severity of problems across different situations (Barkley & Edelbrock, 1987). An advantage of these two scales is that, aside from providing information regarding whether behavioral dysfunction is pervasive and generalized or setting or situation specific, they are potentially prescription-sensitive instruments. That is, they provide quantifiable information regarding specific types of problems that may be targeted for intervention and used subsequently as outcome measures.

The ADDH Comprehensive Teacher Rating Scale (ACTeRS) (Ullmann, Sleator, & Sprague, 1985), Teacher Self-Control Rating Scale (TSCRS) (Humphrey, 1982), Abbreviated Conners Teacher Rating Scale (ACTRS) (Conners & Barkley, 1985; Goyette et al., 1978), IOWA Conners (Loney & Milich, 1982), and Children's Learning Profile (CLP) (DuPaul, Rapport, & Perriello, 1989) are instruments commonly used for assessing the behavior of children with ADHD in academic settings.

The ACTeRS is completed by a child's classroom teacher, has age- and gender-related norms, and assesses behavior across four factors: attention, overactivity, oppositional behavior, and social competence. A profile summary sheet is also available and can be used to facilitate visual comparison with normative data, as well as to compare changes across different treatment conditions. The ACTeRS has been shown to differentiate children with ADHD from normals and from those with learning disabilities, and it is sensitive in detecting both overall (Ullmann & Sleator, 1985; Rapport, DuPaul, Stoner, & Jones, 1986a) and between-dose medication effects (Rapport et al., 1987).

The TSCRS is a relatively new but welcome addition to the field because of its external validity (i.e., directly established association with direct observations of children's behavior in school) and provision of normative information relevant to children's self-control. The scale yields two factors that are highly relevant to the functioning of children with ADHD: cognitive-personal and behavioral-interpersonal self-control. The TSCRS can be helpful in quantifying the "impulsivity" dimension in children with ADHD and in differentiating these children from those who are reading disabled but not hyperactive (Brown & Wynne, 1984). The scale has also proven to be one of the most sensitive classroom instruments for detecting overall and between-dose methylphenidate (MPH) effects (Rapport, 1990; Rapport et al., 1988).

The ACTRS continues to be one of the most popularly used teacher rating scales for screening children with ADHD. Its 10 items were selected from the lengthier teacher version and considered initially as a "hyperkinesis index." Conners considers "psychopathology index" a more accurate term (Conners & Barkley, 1985, p. 810), as the scale includes several items relevant to aggression and overactivity. The ACTRS continues to be one of the most frequently used weekly teacher rating scales for monitoring psychostimulant effects and tends to yield a dose-response profile pattern nearly identical to that obtained from direct observational measures of attention and academic performance (Rapport, 1990). In a related vein, several investigators have opted to use the IOWA Conners when separate factor scores for conduct disturbance (aggression) and inattention-overactivity (IO) dimensions are desired (Loney & Milich, 1982). The IOWA Conners IO subscale has been shown to be related to several measures of hyperactivity and inattention (Milich & Fitzgerald, 1985) and classroom academic performance (Atkins, Pelham, & Licht, 1989), whereas the aggression subscale tends to be associated with behaviors such as talking back to the teacher or inappropriately in class, and physical aggression with peers (Milich & Fitzgerald, 1985). These findings may have implications for both identifying subtypes of children with ADHD as well as for monitoring treatment effects.

The CLP is a newly developed and normed classroom rating scale (see Table 18–3) that yields information relevant to four factors: academic performance, impulsiveness, learning ability, and attentional disturbance; the latter is associated with certain clinical states, daydreaming or constricted attention (e.g., seizure disorders, Asperger syndrome, or "overfocused" phenomena caused by a child's medi-

Table 18-3. Children's Learning Profile

Student _____ Date _____

Age _____ Grade _____ Teacher _____

For each of the items below, please estimate the above student's performance over the **PAST WEEK**. For each item, please circle **one** choice only.

1. Estimate the percentage of written math work <u>completed</u> (regardless of accuracy) relative to classmates.	0-49% 1	50-69% 2	70-79% 3	80-89% 4	90-100% 5
2. Estimate the percentage of written language arts work <u>completed</u> (regardless of accuracy) relative to classmates.	0-49% 1	50-69% 2	70-79% 3	80-89% 4	90-100% 5
3. Estimate the <u>accuracy</u> of completed written math work (i.e., percent correct of work done).	0-64% 1	65-69% 2	70-79% 3	80-89% 4	90-100% 5
4. Estimate the <u>accuracy</u> of completed written language arts work (i.e., percent correct of work done).	0-64% 1	65-69% 2	70-79% 3	80-89% 4	90-100% 5
5. How consistent has the quality of this child's academic work been over the past week?	Consistently Poor 1	More Poor Than Successful 2	Variable 3	More Successful Than Poor 4	Consistently Successful 5
6. How frequently does the student accurately follow teacher instructions and/or class discussion during <u>large-group</u> (e.g., whole class) instruction?	Never 1	Rarely 2	Sometimes 3	Often 4	Very Often 5
7. How frequently does the student accurately follow teacher instructions and/or class discussion during <u>small-group</u> (e.g. reading group) instruction?	Never 1	Rarely 2	Sometimes 3	Often 4	Very Often 5
8. How quickly does this child learn new material (i.e., pick up novel concepts)?	Very Slow 1	Slow 2	Average 3	Quickly 4	Very Quickly 5
9. What is the quality or neatness of this child's handwriting?	Poor 1	Fair 2	Average 3	Above Average 4	Excellent 5
10. What is the quality of this child's reading skills?	Poor 1	Fair 2	Average 3	Above Average 4	Excellent 5

				Above	
11. What is the quality of this child's speaking skills?	Poor 1	Fair 2	Average 3	Average 4	Excellent 5
12. How often does the child complete written work in a careless, hasty fashion?	Never 1	Rarely 2	Sometimes 3	Often 4	Very Often 5
13. How frequently does the child take more time to complete work than his/her classmates?	Never 1	Rarely 2	Sometimes 3	Often 4	Very Often 5
14. How often is the child able to pay attention without you prompting him/her?	Never 1	Rarely 2	Sometimes 3	Often 4	Very Often 5
15. How frequently does this child require your assistance to accurately complete his/her academic work?	Never 1	Rarely 2	Sometimes 3	Often 4	Very Often 5
16. How often does the child begin written work prior to understanding the directions?	Never 1	Rarely 2	Sometimes 3	Often 4	Very Often 5
17. How frequently does this child have difficulty recalling material from a previous day's lessons?	Never 1	Rarely 2	Sometimes 3	Often 4	Very Often 5
18. How often does the child appear to be staring excessively or "spaced out"?	Never 1	Rarely 2	Sometimes 3	Often 4	Very Often 5
19. How often does the child appear withdrawn or tend to lack an emotional response in a social situation?	Never 1	Rarely 2	Sometimes 3	Often 4	Very Often 5

Note: Reprinted by permission from DuPaul, G.J., Rapport, M.D., & Perriello, L.M. (1990). *Teacher Ratings of Academic Performance: The Development of the Children's Learning Profile.* Department of Psychiatry, University of Massachusetts Medical Center. Unpublished Manuscript.

cation status). Separate percentages may also be calculated for mathematics and language arts to derive an academic efficiency score (AES), which represents the weekly percentage of academic assignments completed correctly. The reasons for developing this scale were to provide a standardized instrument for assessing children's academic performance that could be compared with age and gender norms across the primary grades (1–6), and that could be used as an outcome measure to reflect changes in classroom functioning (DuPaul et al., 1989).

Comment

Broad-band rating scales and checklists are used primarily during the initial screening or diagnostic process, whereas the strength of the narrow-band scales lies in their quantification of very specific types of dysfunction that are usually more relevant to setting or situational characteristics associated with ADHD. Most instruments were created for somewhat different purposes, and each has its own strengths and limitations (see Barkley, 1987). It is also important to keep in mind that the convergence of child psychiatric diagnoses and behavior problems quantified by checklists and rating scales is in its infancy. At present, it is recommended that both parent and teacher ratings be used as integral components of a diagnostic battery, keeping in mind that the latter are better for discriminating between ADHD and other disorders of childhood. Whenever possible, information should be obtained from both sources and used in tandem to maximize diagnostic sensitivity and specificity.

The question remains whether child psychopathology should be viewed as a quantitative deviation from normal or as a discrete entity that is best described by categorical diagnosis (Achenbach, 1980; Edelbrock & Costello, 1988). The convergence of psychiatric diagnoses and behavior problems quantified by checklists and ratings scales should be questioned and not assumed. That is, no parent or teacher rating scale can be used by itself with any degree of confidence to make a clinical diagnosis of ADHD. Instrument selection depends on several factors and must be determined by the specific interests and needs of the individual investigator or clinician. All of the narrow-band instruments described have proven useful for measuring outcome in children with ADHD. Their ability to detect medication states and correspondence with classroom academic performance under different dosage conditions, however, is far from monolithic and must be considered separately if used for these purposes (Rapport, 1990).

Classroom Behavior and Direct Observations

In school and without treatment, the behavior of children with ADHD may be described as "consistently inconsistent." Most experience problems in at least four primary areas: maintaining attention or staying on task, completing academic assignments *correctly* on a regular basis, peer and interpersonal relationships, and difficulties with learning and memory. Learning and memory difficulties are especially handicapping under conditions involving complex tasks that require use and generation of careful, logical search strategies and perceptual analysis (Douglas, 1988).

The impulsivity component of the disorder tends to interact with and pervade other areas of disturbance. For example, children with ADHD frequently pay attention, but to what *other* children are doing in the classroom. They speak out of turn and initiate actions that are inconsistent with and disruptive to ongoing classroom activities. They begin academic assignments before receiving or fully understanding instructions. They often vacillate between not attempting assignments and rushing through them without regard for correctness. Most children with ADHD are also quite sociable but tend to overwhelm their peers with their unbridled enthusiasm and intrusiveness. They experience great difficulty in paying attention during slow-moving activities that require waiting and taking turns; preferring activities that are limited to small groups of children and that are relatively "active" by comparison.

Direct observations of children with ADHD have focused traditionally on two central aspects of their behavior: school functioning and personal or interpersonal interactions and relationships. Observations of school functioning usually center on providing detailed information regarding the ADHD child's overt behavior while in the classroom, as well as behavioral signs that the child is experiencing difficulties with covert functioning in areas related to academic efficiency and learning performance.

Information derived from rating and classroom coding instruments range from straightforward data regarding time spent on task and academic efficiency (Rapport, Stoner, DuPaul, Birmingham, & Tucker, 1985a; Rapport et al., 1986a, 1988), to relatively complex information obtained using multicategory ratings of conduct (Abikoff, Gittelman-Klein, & Klein, 1977; Atkins et al., 1989). The former are used primarily as outcome measures and to study treatment effects, whereas the complex, multifaceted coding instruments are used more for heuristic purposes.

Direct observations of interpersonal interactions are used typically to facilitate and clarify the nature of deficiencies in parent-child, teacher-child, and child-child relationships, and in recent years, as treatment outcome measures (Barkley, Fisher, Newby, & Breen, 1988; Landau & Milich, 1988; Pelham & Milich, 1984; Whalen, Henker, Collins, McAuliffe, & Vaux, 1979). Most necessitate the use of relatively sophisticated coding instruments. As such, they require extensive training to achieve acceptable interrater reliability. Aside from their heuristic value for studying interactional patterns, they represent one of the few methods by which to capture and evaluate the dynamic interplay between antecedent and consequent events in the interpersonal behavior of children with ADHD. The more popular instruments for assessing the interactions between ADHD children and significant others include the Response-Class Matrix (Mash & Barkley, 1987; Mash, Terdal, & Anderson, 1973), the Parent-Child Interaction Code (Barkley et al., 1988; Forehand & McMahon, 1981), and the Parent-Adolescent Interaction Coding System (Robin, 1981).

Direct observations with their high face validity are considered a "luxury" source for rich and often revealing information. Their use is highly recommended for monitoring psychostimulant treatment effects, as existing teacher rating scales are specific to measuring *reductions in disruptive behavior,* which may or may not coincide with *increases in academic performance.* Clinical phenomena associated with psychostimulant treatment, such as "overfocused" states and resulting loss of cognitive efficiency (Kinsbourne, 1984), may consequently go undetected. In these situations, it is important to obtain information regarding a child's weekly academic performance, as well as collecting indirect indices of learning such as test scores in various subject areas.

Intellectual and Achievement Testing

Psychometric testing is an integral and necessary part of a diagnostic evaluation for children presenting with ADHD symptomatology, as recent estimates suggest that greater than 50% of these children have learning or achievement deficiencies (McGee & Share, 1988). Information relevant to the child's overall intellectual functioning and academic achievement are used to discern not only the general level of cognitive functioning, but to elucidate specific and overall patterns of strength and weakness that may be related to classroom functioning. Testing also allows for a fuller understanding of the range of attentional deficits, their impact on cognitive performance and academic achievement, and the opportunity to observe the child directly in a one-to-one situation.

Comparisons between ability and level of achievement are also essential to ascertain whether learning disabilities are present, and if so, whether they are primary or secondary to ADHD phenomena. Whether or not a child is eligible for special assistance by resource room instructors, or in more serious cases, special education classroom placement for partial or full-day instruction, depends in most states on an ability-achievement discrepancy formula (which varies from state to state). Although legislative action is being proposed to remedy the problem, children presently diagnosed as ADHD (without LD) do not fall under the national learning disability (LD) guidelines for special instruction eligibility. As a result, they must qualify for an "emotionally disturbed" (ED) categorization until the "failure model" materializes and the child falls behind to a significant enough degree to qualify for LD services. The behavioral sequelae of ADHD, misdiagnosis, and inadequate classroom instruction that often result in an ED classification, contribute to the self-fulfilling prophecy of disordered behavior that justifies continued placement. Other children with ADHD never quality for services despite their arduous and continuous struggle with the educational process.

The Wechsler Intelligence Scales for Children—Revised (WISC-R) test battery is currently the most popular instrument for assessing children's intelligence, because of its relatively broad survey of verbal and performance repertoires. With respect to overall intellectual functioning, no compelling evidence to date indicates that children with ADHD differ in any significant fashion from normals (Campbell, Douglas, & Morgenstern, 1971; Douglas, 1988; Loney, 1974). Recent evidence suggests, however, that performance on certain aspects of neuropsychological functioning may decrease as a function of increasing age in children with hyperactive and inattention problems (Massman, Nussbaum, & Bigler, 1988).

A relatively ubiquitous misconception is that the subscales that comprise the "freedom from distractability" factor (i.e., arithmetic, coding, and digit span subscales), or including the information subscale, the "ACID" profile (Kaufman, 1975), are pathognomonic to children with ADHD. Difficulties with attention, concentration, and alertness are characteristic of most major disorders of childhood, including the developmental disabilities and academic skills (learning disabilities) disorders. As such, these profile patterns have not been shown to be associated with a "specific" diagnosis and should neither be relied upon nor expected as confirmatory or exclusionary evidence for the presence or absence of ADHD. Similarly, neither significant discrepancies between verbal and performance scales (Henry & Wittman, 1981) nor the presence of inter- or intrasubscale scatter (Kaufman, 1981) has proven particularly useful in the differential diagnosis of children with ADHD or other learning disorders.

Caution should also be observed when interpreting the results of group-administered intelligence batteries. Their results are frequently gross underestimates of intellectual functioning in children with ADHD, as to a lesser extent, are individually administered instruments. Not unexpectedly, the inattention and impulsivity components inherent to the disorder may interfere with test performance to the extent that they result in an incomplete and inaccurate evaluation of a child's knowledge and level of achievement.

Academic achievement tests are routinely incorporated as part of a psychoeducational battery, because of the prevalance *and* depth of academic achievement problems associated with ADHD that cannot be explained by lower intellect or chronological age (Cantwell & Satterfield, 1978). Standardized test scores for reading, arithmetic, and writing skills may be obtained from any number of instruments, such as the Woodcock-Johnson Psychoeducational Battery, the Peabody Individual Achievement Test, the Wide Range Achievement Test, and more recently, the Kaufman (K-TEA) battery. More analytical assessment of these areas are often warranted for purposes of developing curricula interventions and may be accomplished by using measures that yield specific, more detailed information regarding a particular topic area (e.g., Key Math).

Neurocognitive Assessment

Because ADHD represents a constellation of behavioral and cognitive deficits, a relatively wide range of clinic-administered instruments are being used in an attempt to capture and assess various aspects of the disorder. Renewed and growing interest in neurocognitive instruments may be attributed to two factors. The first is their potential for unraveling some of the diagnostic dilemmas inherent to ADHD in particular and child psychopathology in general. The second is their demonstrated sensitivity and usefulness in monitoring and assessing treatment effects. Presentation in this section is limited to discussing the most popularly used instruments, and the overriding emphasis is on their ability to monitor psychostimulant treatment effects.

The three neurcognitive instruments used most often for assessing and monitoring treatment effects in children with ADHD include the Continuous Performance Test (CPT), the Matching Familiar Figures Test (MFFT), and the Paired Associates Learning Task (PAL).

Continuous Performance Test: CPT

The CPT (Rosvold, Mirsky, Sarason, Bransome, & Beck, 1956) is the most frequently used laboratory-based measure for identifying attentional deficiencies in children with ADHD, with both manual and computerized versions available (Conners, 1985). The CPT is designed to detect momentary lapses of attention and yields two dependent measures: omission and commission errors, indicative of attentional and impulsivity problems, respectively (Sostek, Buchsbaum, & Rapoport, 1980). Children with ADHD typically make fewer detections (i.e., omission errors) and more incorrect responses (i.e., commission errors) to presented stimuli compared to normal children (Sykes, Douglas, & Morgenstern, 1973).

The three primary models of the CPT listed in hierarchical order of difficulty from easiest to most difficult are the "X" version, the "BX" version, and the "double-letter" version (Klorman, Salzman, & Borgstedt, 1988a). In all versions, the child views a visual display on which single alphabetic or numeric characters appear for a relatively brief period of time (usually ranging from milliseconds to a few seconds depending on the model) in random, unpredictable order.

In the "X" version, the child's task is to watch for the occurrence of a designated target letter that remains the same throughout the entire test, usually the letter X, and to respond immediately and only to the designated target—usually by pushing a button, lifting one's hand off of a lever, or clicking a switch mechanism.

The "BX" version is more difficult and places a greater memory load on the child. In this version, the child is instructed to respond to a letter such as X only when it is immediately preceded by a different designated letter, such as B. Thus, vigilance as well as increased discrimination among target stimuli are required for correct performance.

The "double-letter" version (Friedman, Vaughan, & Erlenmeyer-Kimling, 1978) is by far the most demanding of the three CPT models. It requires the child to respond to any letter that repeats itself immediately during the test. Thus, unlike the "X" and "BX" models, in which responding is limited to identifying a single (e.g., if X, then respond) or designated combination of letters (e.g., if B is immediately followed by X, then respond) that remain the same throughout the task, all presented letters in the "double" version represent potential target combinations and must be attended to and evaluated for response appropriateness.

Aside from understanding the fundamental differences between the three most basic CPT models, it is important to stress that many other parameters associated with the task, such as the number of targets presented and total test time, directly influence children's performance, and hence, the sensitivity of the task (Chee, Logan, Schachar, Lindsay, & Wachsmuth, 1989; Klorman et al., 1989b; Davies & Parasuraman, 1981). Investigations using the low-cognitive-demand models of the CPT (e.g., the "X" version) have found few or no differenes in performance between children with ADHD and normal or clinical-control children (Werry, Reeves, & Elkind, 1987; Schachar, Logan, Wachsmuth, & Chajczyk, 1988) and a relative insensitivity in detecting psychostimulant effects (Rapport et al., 1986a, 1987). Similar results have been obtained using the more demanding versions of the CPT under conditions in which total test duration is too brief or the stimulus presentation-response interval is too long. Thus, most versions of the CPT currently in use cannot be relied upon to differentiate children with ADHD from those with other disorders, nor is deficient CPT performance requisite for a diagnosis of ADHD.

Matching Familiar Figures Test: MFFT

The MFFT was developed by Kagan and colleagues (Kagan, Day, Albert, & Phillips, 1964) and is considered a clinic-based index of cognitive tempo and impulsivity in children with regard to visual problem solving. It should be noted, however, that some researchers have suggested that the MFFT is not a pure measure of impulsivity and that other variables, such as attention, motivation, and intelligence, may influence test scores (Douglas, 1988; Milich & Kramer, 1984).

In administering the MFFT, children are shown a target stimulus picture and required to select the one correct match from six similar pictures presented below the target. The entire test consists of 12 trials and yields two primary measures: incorrect identifications (errors) and response latency (i.e., the mean time between the presentation of the target and matching stimuli and the child's initial response for all 12 trials). Parallel forms of the MFFT are constructed when the test is to be used for repeated measurement.

Children with ADHD usually make more errors and take less time to consider alternatives before selecting a match (i.e., exhibit faster response latencies) than do normal children (Rapport, Tucker, DuPaul, Merlo, & Stoner, 1986b). Thus, their basic cognitive style as it applies to solving visually presented problems with minimal external structure is characteristically found to be "fast-inaccurate" or impulsive. The MFFT error score is usually regarded as a more reliable (Brown & Quay, 1977; Quay & Brown, 1980) and drug-sensitive (Brown & Sleator, 1979; Rapport, DuPaul, Stoner, Birmingham, & Masse, 1985b; Rapport et al., 1988) measure than MFFT response latency. In recent studies, however, neither MFFT error nor latency scores were useful in differentiating children with ADHD from other clinical controls (Werry et al., 1987). These findings suggest that cognitive impulsivity with respect to visual problem solving may be associated with the general class of disruptive disorders, as opposed to ADHD in particular.

Paired Associate Learning: PAL

The PAL task is considered a "high-level" or "effortful" task because of its complexity and performance demands (Hasher & Zachs, 1979; Weiss & Laties, 1962), which in turn, are thought to be related to classroom learning. In administering the PAL task, the child is shown a series of stimulus pictures consisting of familiar animals (on cards or by slide projector) and told that each one belongs in a specific zoo, designated by a digit (e.g., zoo number 1, 2, 3...). List length varies (usually between 6 and 14 paired associations) and is established according to a child's age and ability (Swanson, Sandman, Deutsch, & Baren, 1983). Recently developed versions have been developed for computer administration and involve learning associations between letters (usually bi-grams or tri-grams) and numerals for a predesignated time period. Following the initial presentation of paired associations, the child's task is to verbally or manually (depending on the format used) match each animal with its appropriate zoo number (or bi-grams with numerals) until either two perfect recitations are made or 10 trials are administered.

The primary dependent variable used in previous studies has been either (a) the total number of correctly learned paired associations over 10 trials; or (b) a percentage correct score, calculated by dividing the number of correct identifications by the number of total possible correct identifications, then multiplying by 100. In a recent study, however, it was shown that the number of trials required to reach criterion performance (i.e., perfect or near-perfect recall of all associations) may be an equally important variable to monitor, especially in children who have partially mastered the learning of paired associations (Rapport, Quinn, DuPaul, Quinn, & Kelly, 1989).

Thus far, the PAL task has been shown to differentiate children with ADHD from normals (Douglas, 1988), but not from other clinically relevant controls. Elucidation of how and what degree of PAL performance is a function of overall intelligence and its relationship to various learning disabilities in children awaits further empirical study. Despite its touted sensitivity to *overall* (i.e., active vs. inactive medication conditions) psychostimulant effects (Swanson, 1985, 1988), the traditional PAL task has been shown to be relatively insensitive to *between-dose* effects (Rapport, in press; Rapport et al., 1985a). Moreover, many children who exhibit behavioral improvement as a result of stimulant therapy *do not* show a corresponding improvement in their ability to learn paired associations.

MPH Effects: Relationship Between Clinic-Based Measures and Direct Observations of Classroom Functioning

My colleagues and I completed a series of studies over the past 8 years that examined the relationship between direct observations of children's classroom functioning and performance on clinic-based measures of vigilance (Rapport et al., 1986a, 1987), cognitive tempo (Rapport et al., 1988), and paired associate learning (Rapport et al., 1985a, in press). As detailed elsewhere (Rapport, 1990), the results suggest that the most frequently used clinic-based measures for assessing MPH effects in children with ADHD (i.e., CPT, MFFT, and PAL) are relatively insensitive to dosage manipulations and do not reflect the type or complexity of behavior required to function in normal elementary school classrooms.

Figure 18.1 was drawn to facilitate visual comparison between children's performance on the three clinic-based measures and direct observations of their attention (on task) and academic efficiency (i.e., AES, or the percentage of academic assignments completed correctly) in the classroom. It shows the percentage of improvement possible from baseline conditions, keeping in mind that order of MPH dose was randomized and counterbalanced. Values were obtained by converting the range of change possible for each dependent measure to standard (T) scores, and calculating the percentage of change associated with each dose condition relative to baseline. Converting scores in this manner not only places all dependent measures on the same scale for comparison purposes, but also equates for differences in the degree or range

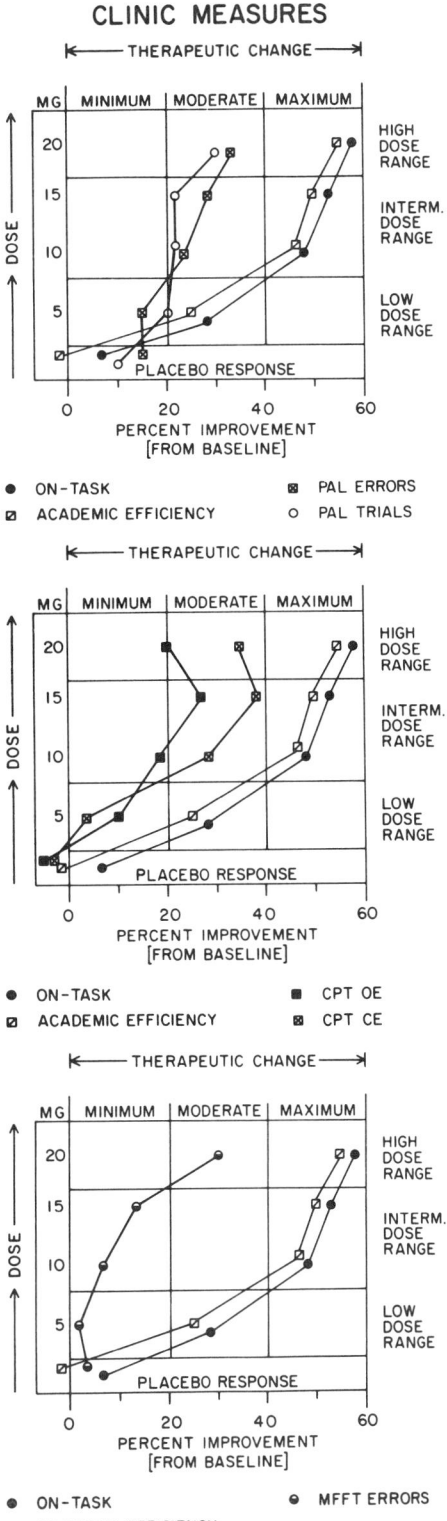

Figure 18.1. The mean percentage of improvement possible on each dependent measure relative to baseline conditions depicted as dose-response curves and expressed as standard (T) scores for the clinic (MFFT errors, CPT omission and commission errors, and PAL trials and errors) and classroom observational (on-task and AES) measures. Improvement on all dependent variables is indicated by left-to-right movement on the horizontal axis. Dose is shown on the vertical axis. Therapeutic "windows" highlight Dose X Change effects.

of change possible across measures. For example, the variable "on-task" ranges from 0% to 100%, as defined in our studies, whereas the total number of possible CPT omission errors range from 0 to 45 and Paired Associate Learning (PAL) trials range from 1 to 10.

Inspection of Figure 18.1 suggests that two reasons for the apparent insensitivity of the clinic measures involve (1) practice or placebo effects, and (2) a failure to differentiate between the low-, intermediate, and high-dose conditions. Changes caused by placebo or practice effects can be evaluated by inspecting the rectangular boxes labeled "placebo response" shown at the bottom of each of the three miniplots. Greater susceptibility to placebo or practice effects are incurred as scores progress from left to right on the abscissa. Thus, two of the variables, PAL trials and errors, evidence approximately 10% and 16% of their total change from baseline performance conditions under placebo (see top plot in Figure 18.1). Other variables, such as CPT omission and commission errors (see middle plot in Figure 18.1), show an opposite effect and worsen under placebo conditions as indicated by their movement from right to left of the "0" line in the bottom left-hand corner of the figure (Note: CPT omission and commission errors actually show a worsening effect of 14% and 48%, respectively, but could not be plotted as such because of practical considerations in constructing the graph). The information obtained for PAL and CPT suggest that both show an undesirable degree of instability from baseline to placebo testing conditions, but for different reasons. This finding is in keeping with our clinical experience. Children appear to improve on the PAL with repeated practice and worsen on the CPT over time under no-medication conditions.

The dose-response curves shown in the three miniplots in Figure 18.1 also suggest that none of the clinic-based measures (with the exception of CPT commission errors) evidence the degree of change from baseline conditions compared to direct observation measures of children's in vivo academic functioning. That is, most are limited to a change of approximately 20% to 30% from baseline, whereas classroom variables evidence between 50% and 65% of their total possible change under drug compared to baseline conditions.

The shape and placement of the curves are also informative and indicate that one of the most serious problems with the clinic-based measures is their failure to differentiate between low- and high-dose conditions. This is shown by the preponderance of dose X change data points falling within a single therapeutic range (minimum or intermediate) on the figure. It is also interesting to note that the two clinic-based measures that require learning or problem solving (PAL and MFFT) begin to move from a left (minimum change) to right (intermediate change) position on the figure as a function of increasing dose, similar to the classroom variables on task and AES. Conversely, the dose-response curves for both CPT omission and commission errors begin to retreat toward baseline levels of functioning under high-dose conditions. This finding suggests that the degree of change possible (from baseline conditions) evidenced on a particular task or measure may be inversely related to MPH dose, with low-level cognitive demand tasks showing maximal improvement under low-dose conditions and high-level cognitive demand tasks (see Vyse & Rapport, 1989) manifesting optimal improvement under high-dose conditions—the exact opposite of currently held beliefs regarding dosage and cognitive functioning in children.

The construction of a clinic-based battery that might complement traditional methods of titrating MPH in children has not been realized to data. None of the clinic-based instruments described in this chapter can be recommended individually or collectively for purposes of titrating MPH in children. Aside from the limitations associated with the tests themselves (see Rapport, 1990), many of the discrepancies between clinic and classroom measures are related to setting and demand characteristics. In contrast to the highly controlled clinic or laboratory environment, elementary school classrooms contain many children who engage simultaneously in multiple activities and tasks that are rarely limited to dimensions of vigilance, visually matching pictures, or learning associations with constant feedback regarding correctness of response. The relationship between performance on experimental tasks or paradigms and classroom behavior and learning will probably occur to the extent that the former begin to approximate the complex and multifaceted dimensions of the latter.

CASE STUDY AND IMPLICATIONS FOR TREATMENT

Joe is an 8½-year-old boy with a history of multiple behavioral problems. These ranged from seemingly endless and frenzied energy, which often resulted in destruction of household belongings, to severe temper tantrums in school and chronic violation of rules. Joe's parents reported and their child's pediatrician confirmed a chronic and worsening history of hyperactivity (excessive gross motor activity), destructive behavior, short attention span with poor concentration, difficulty following verbal directions, low frustration tolerance, extreme impulsiveness, poor peer and interpersonal relationships, frequent fighting, and conduct disturbance, the latter of which included repeated lying, stealing money from home and from classmates with minimal or no confrontation, running away from school, disobedience to and disregard for authority, violation of rules at home and in school, and setting fires. Joe's parents had continually discounted the importance of these reports, preferring to believe that little boys should be given the chance to "express themselves."

Joe had been recommended by the Committee on Special Education for a special education (ED) classroom placement in the middle of the first grade because of the problems described above, in addition to his volatile, and increasingly oppositional and destructive behavior. He remained in a regular classroom for the remainder of the year, however, because his parents refused the recommendation and the notion that their son experienced "emotional" problems. Behavioral difficulties continued and worsened during the course of second and third grade, with nearly daily fighting with peers, continued classroom functioning well below estimated potential, and frequent suspensions from school. Following an incident in which Joe exposed himself to several female peers, the school informed his parents that they were recommending to the committee on special education that Joe be placed in a residential setting. During the school meeting, it was agreed upon by the school and Joe's parents to postpone the recommendation for residential placement and that they could jointly seek an inpatient psychiatric evaluation.

Admission for Inpatient Care

On admission, Joe was a well-developed, slightly chubby boy who was loud and talkative and considered his hospitalization a "joke." He denied having behavioral problems, insisting that he was usually blamed unfairly or misunderstood by others. He denied depressed mood, suicidal ideation, anger, hallucinatory phenomena, and appeared to have no signs of delusional thought. His mood and affect were euthymic and broad, respectively. Speech was relevant and normal in content, tone, and rate, but difficult to comprehend at times. Within the first few hours of admission, Joe punched his roommate, kicked another child, assaulted a staff member, and required physical restraint.

Initial admission workup revealed no abnormalities in his routine blood chemistry or EKG. An EEG showed some spike and wave formation but was read by the pediatric neurologist as within normal limits for his age. Audiologic screen revealed a mild hearing loss bilaterally, which was consitent with a chronic serious otitis media. Developmental history obtained revealed that Joe was precocious regarding motor milestones, but somewhat delayed in his acquisition and production of language. Family history was positive for the "tri-opathy" of alcoholism, hyperactivity, and antisocial personality in the father, alcoholism in the maternal grandfather, depression in both the mother and her sister, and hyperactivity in both maternal siblings.

Clinical Interview, Checklist and Rating Scales Scores

Both the patient and his mother were administered the Kiddie-SADS-E (epidemiologic version) semi-structured interview. Summary ratings (which included information derived from the parent completed, Werry-Weiss-Peters Activity Scale and Stony Brook Checklist) indicated the presence of ADHD and conduct disorder (solitary-aggressive). Mood disturbance was also noted, albeit insufficient to warrant a clinical diagnosis.

The Child Behavior Checklist (CBC), IOWA Conners, Teacher Self-Control Rating Scale (TSCRS), the Stony Brook Checklist (DSM-III-R symptom checklist using a Likert-type format), and the ADD-H Comprehensive Teacher Rating Scale (ACTeRS) were completed by Joe's classroom teacher. The CBC showed significant elevations, which were primarily limited to the externalizing domain. School performance and adaptive functioning were low as expected, and t scores of between 2.0 and 2.5 SD above the mean were obtained for the narrow-band problem scales of Unpopular, Inattentive, Aggressive, and Nervous-overactive. The remaining scales were in concurrence and indicated a highly inattentive, aggressive, impulsive, overly active child with disturbed conduct and impaired peer and interpersonal relations.

Psychometric, Neurocognitive Assessment

Psychometric testing revealed that Joe had a full-scale IQ of 93 (average range), with a verbal and performance IQ of 82 (low average range) and 107 (average range), respectively. During testing, Joe was easily frustrated, highly impulsive in his approach to tasks, and motorically overactive throughout the sessions. His efforts and resulting scores were somewhat improved on the more stimulating tasks. Although his strengths were clearly in the nonverbal area, his achievement in reading was significantly lower than expected based on his verbal IQ. Speech and language evaluation revealed a serious speech impediment, without significant impairment in receptive or expressive language.

Neurocognitive testing revealed a pattern characterized by inattention, poor concentration, extreme impulsivity, and impaired performance on tests of both short- and long-term memory.

Formulation of Clinical Diagnosis and Implications for Treatment

The "best estimate" method was used to derive the following clinical diagnoses using DSM-III-R criteria:

Axis I: Attention-deficit hyperactivity disorder Conduct disorder, solitary aggressive type Functional enuresis (nocturnal), secondary type
Axis II: Developmental articulation disorder Developmental reading disorder
Axis III: Mild hearing loss secondary to chronic serious otitis media

A multimodal treatment approach was used during the course of Joe's hospitalization to include highly structured behavioral milieu (see Rapport, Pataki, & Carlson, in press), a combined regimen of methylphenidate and desipramine, child management training, and family therapy. Small, structured special education placement, continued behavioral and medical therapy, family therapy, and an eventual referral to child protective services were made upon discharge.

SUMMARY

Assessment of children with ADHD has undergone a mercuric evolution over the past two decades. Significant changes in both clinical technique and instrumentation bode well for the field, and reflect an increased understanding of the nature of ADHD, as well as a growing emphasis on the development of relatively sophisticated measures for heuristic and outcome purposes. Continued emphasis on diagnosis, probably growth in development of computerized instruments that measure constructs such as inattention and impulsivity, as well as behavioral dimensions relevant to learning and cognitive performance are expected in the near future. Practical concerns ranging from mandates for documentation and accountability from health providers to increasing exigencies for utilization of instrumentation that can be applied in office and field settings by practitioners, exist presently and will continue to influence the field of assessment.

Unfortunately, the already burgeoning armamentarium of manual and computerized instruments established for assessment purposes has surpassed what little regulatory ability the system has for monitoring their claims. This situation, may in turn, lead to an unwanted proliferation of "snake oil" measures and remedies reminiscent of the curative claims of dietary regimens for ADHD of yesteryear. It is incumbent upon the individual users of newly developed assessment instruments to apply the same clinical standards and demands for methodological rigor as are described currently under APA guidelines and principles of test construction.

Attempts to identify the "core components" of the disorder (namely, inattention, impulsiveness, and hyperactivity) by means of laboratory (clinic-based) and field studies have produced inconsistent, often equivocal, and largely discouraging results. It may be naive, however, to expect that a complex disorder of brain, behavior, and development will yield itself to facile attempts at diagnostic dissection made with teacher rating scales or laboratory instruments. This viewpoint takes on additional significance if factors hypothesized to be associated with ADHD were related to an underlying central defect in self-regulation (Douglas, 1988; Kinsbourne, 1984), an imbalance between or dysregulation of the behavioral inhibition and reward systems that underlie learning (Quay, 1988), or deficiencies in functional or structural control mechanisms related to efficient allocation of control over one's own behavior (Sergeant, 1988). Each of these current theoretical positions would posit that the myriad of behavioral and cognitive sequelae associated with ADHD should pervade disparate areas of children's behavior and performance across different modalities, situations, and settings. A host of other factors would also be expected to affect differentially the ADHD child's behavior or susceptibility to these factors (see Douglas, 1988; Kinsbourne, 1984; and Rapport, 1983, for reviews).

Differential diagnosis will remain problematic with regard to the disruptive disorders until we increase our knowledge and understanding of the phenomenology, clinical course, outcome, and exclusionary criteria associated with the various psychopathological disorders of childhood. It is unlikely that a unitary set of symptoms will be pathognomonic of any of the disruptive disorders or that an absolute validity standard will be found for identifying "caseness." Erstwhile, it is recommended that practitioners formulate diagnosis based on multiple sources and types of information as described herein, using what has been popularly termed the best-estimate method (Leckman, Sholomskas, Thompson, Belanger, & Weissman, 1982).

REFERENCES

Abikoff, H., Gittelman-Klein, R., & Klein, D. F. (1977). A replication of validity. *Journal of Consulting and Clinical Psychology, 48,* 555-565.

Achenbach, T. M. (1980). DSM-III in light of empirical research on the classification of child psychopathology. *Journal of the American Academy of Child Psychiatry, 19,* 395-412.

Achenbach, T. M. (1985). *Assessment and Taxonomy of Child and Adolescent Psychopathology.* Beverly Hills, CA: Sage.

Achenbach, T. M. (1987). How is a parent rating scale used in the diagnosis of attention deficit disorder? In J. Loney (Ed.), *The young hyperactive child: Answers to questions about diagnosis, prognosis, and treatment* (pp. 19-32). New York: Haworth Press.

Achenbach, T. M., & Edelbrock, C. S. (1978). The classification of child psychopathology: A review and analysis of empirical efforts. *Psychological Bulletin, 85,* 1275-1301.

Achenbach, T. M., & Edelbrock, C. S. (1983). *Manual for the child behavior checklist and revised child behavior profile.* Burlington, VT: T. M. Achenbach.

American Psychiatric Association. (1968). *Diagnostic and statistical manual of mental disorders* (2nd ed.). Washington, DC: Author.

American Psychiatric Association. (1980). *Diagnostic and statistical manual of mental disorders* (3rd. ed.). Washington, DC: Author.

American Psychiatric Association. (1987). *Diagnostic and statistical manual of mental disorders* (3rd. ed., rev.). Washington, DC: Author.

Anthony, J. C., Folstein, M., Romanoski, A. J., Von Korff, M. R., Nestadt, G. N., Chahal, R., Merchant, A., Brown, C. H., Shapiro, S., Kramer, M., & Gruenberg, E. M. (1985). Comparison of the lay Diagnostic Interview Schedule and a standardized psychiatric diagnosis: Experience in eastern Baltimore. *Archives of General Psychiatry, 42,* 667-675.

Atkins, M. S., Pelham, W. E., & Licht, M. H. (1989). The differential validity of teacher ratings of inattention/overactivity and aggression. *Journal of Abnormal Child Psychology, 17,* 423-435.

August, C. J., & Garfinkel, B. D. (1989). Behavioral and cognitive subtypes of ADHD. *Journal of the American Academy of Child and Adolescent Psychiatry, 28,* 739-748.

Barkley, R. A. (1981). *Hyperactive children: A handbook for diagnosis and treatment.* New York: Guilford Press.

Barkley, R. A. (1987). Child behavior rating scales and checklists. In M. Rutter, A. Tuma, & I. S. Lann (Eds.), *Assessment and diagnosis in child psychopathology* (pp. 113-155). New York: Guilford Press.

Barkley, R. A., & Edelbrock, C. (1987). Assessing situational variation in children's problem behaviors: The home and school situations questionnaires. In R. J. Prinz (Ed.), *Advances in Behavioral Assessment of Children and Families* (Vol. 3, pp. 157-176). Greenwich, CT: JAI Press.

Barkley, R. A., Fisher, M., Newby, R., & Breen, M. (1988). Development of a multi-method clinical protocol for assessing stimulant drug responses in ADHD children. *Journal of Clinical Child Psychology, 17,* 14-24.

Brown, R. T., & Quay, L. C. (1977). Reflection-impulsivity in normal and behavior disorder children. *Journal of Abnormal Child Psychology, 4,* 457-461.

Brown, R. T., & Sleator, E. K. (1979). Methylphenidate in hyperkinetic children: Differences in dose effects on impulsive behavior. *Pediatrics, 64,* 408-411.

Brown, R. T., & Wynne, M. E. (1984). Attentional characteristics and teachers ratings in hyperactive, reading disabled, and normal boys. *Journal of Clinical Child Psychology, 13,* 38-43.

Campbell, S. B., Douglas, V. I., & Morgenstern, G. (1971). Cognitive styles in hyperactive children and the effect of methylphenidate. *Journal of Child Psychology and Psychiatry and Allied Disciplines, 18,* 239-249.

Cantwell, D. P., & Satterfield, J. H. (1978). The prevalence of academic underachievement in hyperactive children. *Journal of Pediatric Psychology, 3,* 168-171.

Carlson, G. A., Kashani, J. H., Thomas, M., Vaidya, A., & Daniel, A. E. (1987). Comparison of two structured interviews on a psychiatrically hospitalized population of children. *Journal of the American Academy of Child and Adolescent Psychiatry, 26,* 645-648.

Carlson, G. A., & Rapport, M. D. (1989). Diagnostic classification issues in attention deficit disorder. *Psychiatry Annals, 19,* 576-583.

Chambers, W. J., Puig-Antich, J., Hirsch, M., Paez, P., Ambrosini, P. J., Tabrizi, A., Davies, M. (1985). The assessment of affective disorders in children and adolescents by a semi-structured interview. *Archives of General Psychiatry, 42,* 696-702.

Chee, P., Logan, G., Schachar, R., Lindsay, P., & Wachsmuth, R. (1989). Effects of event rate and display time on sustained attention in hyperactive, normal, and control children. *Journal of Abnormal Child Psychology, 17,* 371–391.

Conners, C. K. (1969). A teacher rating scale for use in drug studies with children. *American Journal of Psychiatry, 126,* 152–156.

Conners, C. K. (1970). Symptom patterns in hyperkinetic, neurotic and normal children. *Child Development, 41,* 667–682.

Conners, C. K. (1985). The computerized continuous performance test. *Psychopharmacology Bulletin, 21,* 891–892.

Conners, C. K. (1987). How is a teacher rating scale used in the diagnosis of attention deficit disorder? In J. Loney (Ed.), *The young hyperactive child: Answers to questions about diagnosis, prognosis, and treatment* (pp. 33–52). New York: Haworth Press.

Conners, C. K., & Barkley, R. A. (1985). Rating scales and checklists for child psychopharmacology. *Psychopharmacology Bulletin, 21,* 809–843.

Conners, C. K., & Wells, K. C. (1986). Hyperkinetic children: A neuropsychosocial approach. In A. E. Kazdin (Ed.), *Developmental Clinical Psychology and Psychiatry* (Vol. 7). Beverly Hills, CA: Sage Publications.

Costello, A., Edelbrock, C., Kalas, R., Kessler, M., & Klaric, S. (1984). *NIMH Diagnostic Interview Schedule for Children (DISC)*. Rockville, MD: National Institute of Mental Health.

Davies, D. R., & Parasuraman, R. (1981). *The psychology of vigilance.* New York: Academic Press.

Dawes, R. M. (1986). Representative thinking in clinical judgment. *Clinical Psychology Review, 26,* 422–441.

Douglas, V. I. (1988). Cognitive deficits in children with attention deficit disorder with hyperactivity. In L. M. Bloomingdale & J. A. Sergeant (Eds.), *Attention deficit disorder: Criteria, cognition, intervention* (pp. 65–81). New York: Pergamon Press.

DePaul, G. J., Rapport, M. D., & Perriello, L. M. (1989). Teacher ratings of academic performance: The development of the Children's Learning Profile. Unpublished manuscript.

Edelbrock, C., & Costello, A. J. (1984). Structured psychiatric interviews for children and adolescents. In G. Goldstein & M. Hersen (Eds.), *Handbook of psychological assessment* (pp. 276–290). New York: Pergamon Press.

Edelbrock, C., & Costello, A. J. (1988). Convergence between statistically derived behavior problem syndromes and child psychiatric diagnoses. *Journal of Abnormal Child Psychology, 16,* 219–231.

Edelbrock, C., Costello, A. J., & Kessler, M. D. (1984). Empirical corroboration of the attention deficit disorder. *Journal of the American Academy of Child and Adolescent Psychiatry, 23,* 285–290.

Firestone, P., & Prabhu A. N. (1983). Minor physical anomalies and obstetrical complications: Their relationship to hyperactive, psychoneurotic and normal children and their families. *Journal of Abnormal Child Psychology, 11,* 207–216.

Forehand, R., & McMahon, R. (1981). *Helping the noncompliant child: A clinician's guide to parent training.* New York: Guilford Press.

Friedman, D., Vaughan, H., & Erlenmeyer-Kimling, L. (1978). Task related cortical potentials in children in two kinds of vigilance tasks. In D. A. Otto (Ed.), *Multidisciplinary perspectives in event-related brain potential research* (pp. 309–313). Washington, DC: U.S. Government Printing Office.

Gammon, G. D., Rothblum, J. K., Mullen, K., Tischler, G. L., & Weissman, M. M. (1983). Use of a structured diagnostic interview to identify bipolar disorder in adolescent inpatients: Frequency and manifestations of the disorder. *American Journal of Psychiatry, 140,* 543–547.

Gittelman, R. (1988). The assessment of hyperactivity: The DSM-III approach. In L. M. Bloomingdale & J. Sergeant (Eds.), *Attention Deficit Disorder: Criteria, cognitive, intervention* (pp. 9–28). New York: Pergamon Press.

Goyette, C. J., Conners, C. K., & Ulrich, R. F. (1978). Normative data on revised Conners Parent and Teacher Rating Scales. *Journal of Abnormal Child Psychology, 6,* 221–236.

Hasher, L., & Zachs, R. T. (1979). Automatic and effortful processing in memory. *Journal of Experimental Psychology, 108,* 356–388.

Helzer, J. E., Robins, L. N., McEvoy, L. T., Spitznagel, E. L., Stoltzman, R. K., Farmer, A., & Brockington, I. F. (1985). A comparison of clinical and Diagnostic Interview Schedule diagnoses: Physician reexamination of lay interviewed cases in the general population. *Archives of General Psychiatry, 42,* 657–666.

Henry, S. A., & Wittman, R. D. (1981). Diagnostic implications of Bannatyne's recategorized WISC-R scores for identifying learning disabled children. *Journal of Learning Disabilities, 14,* 517–520.

Herjanic, B., & Campbell, W. (1977). Differentiating psychiatrically disturbed children on the basis of a structured interview. *Journal of Abnormal Child Psychology, 5,* 127–134.

Herjanic, B., & Reich, W. (1982). Development of a structured psychiatric interview for children: Agreement between child and parent on individual symptoms. *Journal of Abnormal Child Psychology, 10,* 307–324.

Hinshaw, S. P. (1987). On the distinction between attentional deficits/hyperactivity and conduct problems/aggression in child psychopathology. *Psychological Bulletin, 101,* 443–463.

Hodges, K., McKnew, D., Cytryn, L., Stern, L., & Kline, J. (1982). The Child Assessment Schedule (CAS) diagnostic interview: A report on reliability and validity. *Journal of the American Academy of Child Psychiatry, 21,* 468–473.

Hops, H., & Greenwood, C. R. (1981). Social skill deficits. In E. J. Mash and L. G. Terdal (Eds.), *Behavioral assessment of childhood disorders* (pp. 347–394). New York: Guilford Press.

Humphrey, L. L. (1982). Children's and teacher's perspectives on children's self-control: The development of two scales. *Journal of Clinical and Consulting Psychology, 50,* 624–633.

Kagan, J., Day, D., Albert, J., & Phillips, W. (1964). Information processing in the child: Significance of analytic and reflective attitudes. *Psychological Monographs, 78,* 1.

Kaufman, A. S. (1975). Factor analysis of the WISC-R at 11 age levels between ½ and 16½ years. *Journal of Consulting and Clinical Psychology, 43,* 135–147.

Kaufman, A. (1981). The WISC-R and learning disabilities assessment: State of the art. *Journal of Learning Disabilities, 14,* 520–526.

Kinsbourne, M. (1984). Beyond attention deficit: Search for the disorder in ADD. In L. Bloomingdale (Ed.), *Attention deficit disorder: Diagnostic, cognitive, and therapeutic understanding* (pp. 133–162). New York: Spectrum Publications.

Klorman, R., Crumaghim, J. T., Coons, H. W., Peloquin, L., Strauss, J., Lewine, J. D., Borgstedt, A. D., & Goldstein, M. G. (1988b). The contributions of event-related potentials to understanding effffects of stimulants on information processing in attention deficit disorder. In L. M. Bloomingdale & J. Sergeant (Eds.), *Attention deficit disorder: Criteria, cognitive, intervention* (pp. 199–218). New York: Pergamon Press.

Klorman, R., Salzman, L. F., & Borgstedt, A. D. (1988a). Brain event related potentials in evaluation of cognitive deficits in attention deficit disorder and outcome of stimulant therapy. In L. M. Bloomingdale (Ed.), *Attention deficit disorder: New research in attention, treatment, and psychopharmacology* (pp. 49–80). New York: Pergamon Press.

Kovacs, M. (1982). *The longitudinal study of child and adolescent psychopathology: I. The semi-structured psychiatric Interview Schedule for Children (ISC)*. Unpublished manuscript, Western Psychiatric Institute.

Lachar, D. (1982). *Personalilty Inventory for Children (PIC). Revised format manual supplement*. Los Angeles: Western Psychological Services.

Lahey, B. B., Green, K. D., & Forehand, R. (1980). On the independence of ratings of hyperactivity, conduct problems, and attention deficits in children: A multiple regression analysis. *Journal of Consulting and Clinical Psychology, 48,* 566–574.

Lahey, B. B., Piacentini, J. C., McBurnett, K., Stone, P., Hartdagen, S., Hynd, G. (1988). Psychopathology in the parents of children with conduct disorder and hyperactivity. *Journal of the American Academy of Child and Adolescent Psychiatry, 27,* 163–170.

Landau, S., & Milich, R. (1988). Social communication patterns of attention-deficit-disordered boys. *Journal of Abnormal Child Psychology, 16,* 69–81.

Leckman, J. F., Sholomskas, D., Thompson, W. D., Belanger, A., Weissman, M. M. (1982). Best estimate of lifetime psychiatric diagnosis: A methodological study. *Archives of General Psychiatry, 39,* 879–883.

Loney, J. (1974). The intellectual functioning of hyperactive elementary school boys: A cross-sectional investigation. *American Journal of Orthopsychiatry, 44,* 754–762.

Loney, J. (1987). Hyperactivity and aggression in the diagnosis of attention deficit disorder. In B. B. Lahey & A. E. Kazdin (Eds.), *Advances in Clinical Child Psychology* (pp. 99–135). New York: Plenum Press.

Loney, J., & Milich, R. S. (1982). Hyperactivity, inattention, and aggression in clinical practice. In M. Wolraich & D. Routh (Eds.), *Advances in Developmental and Behavioral Pediatrics* (Vol. 2, pp. 113–147). Greenwich, CT: JAI Press.

Mash, E. J., & Barkley, R. A. (1987). Assessment of family interaction with the Response-Class Matrix. In R. Prinz (Ed.), *Advances in behavioral assessment of children and families* (Vol. 2, pp. 29–67). Greenwich, CT: JAI Press.

Mash, E. G., & Terdal, L. G. (1981). *Behavioral assessment of childhood disorders*. New York: Guilford.

Mash, E. G., Terdal, L. G., & Anderson, K. (1973). The Response-Class Matrix: A procedure for recording parent-child interactions. *Journal of Consulting and Clinical Psychology, 40,* 163–164.

McGee, R., & Share, D. L. (1988). Attention deficit disorder-hyperactivity and academic failure: Which comes first and what should be treated? *Journal of the American Academy of Child and Adolescent Psychiatry, 27,* 318–325.

Milich, R., & Fitzgerald, G. (1985). Validation of inattention/overactivity and aggression ratings with classroom observations. *Journal of Consulting and Clinical Psychology, 53,* 139–140.

Milich, R., & Kramer, J. (1984). Reflections on impulsivity: An empirical investigation of impulsivity as a construct. *Advances in Learning and Behavioral Disabilities, 3,* 57–94.

Milich, R., & Landau S. (1982). Socialization and peer relations in hyperactive children. In K. D. Gadow & I. Bialer (Eds.), *Advances in learning and behavioral disabilities* (Vol. 1, pp. 283–339). Greenwich, CT: JAI Press.

Milich, R., Widiger, T. A., & Landau, S. (1987). Differential diagnosis of attention deficit and conduct disorders using conditional probabilities. *Journal of Consulting and Clinical Psychology, 55,* 762–767.

Newcorn, J. H., Jalperin, J. M., Healey, J. M., O'Brien, J. D., Pascualvaca, D. M., Wolf, L. E., Morganstein, A., Sharma, V., & Young, J. G. (1989). Are ADDH and ADHD the same or different? *Journal of the American Academy of Child and Adolescent Psychiatry, 28,* 734–738.

Orvaschel, H. (1985). Psychiatric interviews suitable for use in research with children and adolescents. *Psychopharmacology Bulletin, 21,* 737–745.

Orvaschel, H., Puig-Antich, J., Chambers, W., Tabrizi, M. A., & Johnson, R. (1982). Retrospective assessment of prepubertal major depression with the Kiddie-SADS-E. *Journal of the American Academy of Child and Adolescent Psychiatry, 21,* 392–397.

Pelham, W. E., & Bender, M. E. (1982). Peer relationships in hyperactive children: Description and treatment. In K. Gadow & E. Biale (Eds.), *Advances in Learning and Behavioral Disabilities* (pp. 365–436). New York: JAI Press.

Pelham, W. E., & Milich, R. (1984). Peer relations in children with hyperactivity/attention deficit disorder. *Journal of Learning Disabilities, 17*, 560–567.

Puig-Antich, J., & Chambers, W. (1978). *The Schedule for Affective Disorders and Schizophrenia for School-Aged Children.* New York: New York State Psychiatric Institute.

Quay, H. C. (1988). Attention Deficit Disorder and the behavioral inhibition system: The relevance of the neuropsychological theory of Jeffrey A. Gray. In L. M. Bloomingdale & J. Sergeant (Eds.), *Attention Deficit Disorder: Criteria, cognitive, intervention* (pp. 117–125). New York: Pergamon Press.

Quay, H. C., & Peterson, D. R. (1983). *Interim manual for the revised behavior problem checklist.* University of Miami. Unpublished manuscript.

Quay, H. C., & Quay, L. C. (1965). Behavior problems in early adolescence. *Child Development, 36*, 215–220.

Quay, L. C., & Brown, R. T. (1980). Hyperactivity and normal children and the error, latency and double median split scoring procedures of the Matching Familiar Figures Test. *Journal of School Psychology, 18*, 12–15.

Rapport, M. D. (1983). Attention deficit disorder with hyperactivity: Critical treatment parameters and their application in applied outcome research. In M. Hersen, R. Eisler, & P. Miller (Eds.), *Progress in Behavior Modification* (pp. 219–298). New York: Academic Press.

Rapport, M. D. (1987). Attention deficit disorder with hyperactivity. In M. Hersen & V. B. Van Hasselt (Eds.), *Behavior therapy with children and adolescents: A clinical approach* (pp. 325–361). New York: John Wiley & Sons.

Rapport, M. D. (1990). Controlled studies of the effects of psychostimulants on children's functioning in clinic and classroom settings. In K. Conners & M. Kinsbourne (Eds.), *Attention Deficit Hyperactivity Disorder* (pp. 77–111). Germany, MMV Medizin Verlag Munchen.

Rapport, M. D., DuPaul, J. G., Stoner, G., Birmingham, B. K., & Masse, G. (1985b). Attention deficit disorder with hyperactivity: Differential effects of methylphenidate on impulsivity. *Pediatrics, 76*, 938–943.

Rapport, M. D., DuPaul, G. J., Stoner, G., & Jones, J. T. (1986a). Comparing classroom and clinic measures of attention deficit disorder: Differential, idiosyncratic, and dose-response effects of methylphenidate. *Journal of Consulting and Clinical Psychology, 54*, 334–341.

Rapport, M. D., Jones, J. T., DuPaul, G. J., Kelly, K. L., Gardner, M. J., Tucker, S. B., & Shea, M. S. (1987). Attention deficit disorder and methylphenidate: Group and single-subject analyses of dose effects on attention in clinic and classroom settings. *Journal of Clinical Child Psychology, 16*, 329–338.

Rapport, M. D., Pataki, C. S., & Carlson, G. A. (in press). Attention deficit hyperactivity disorder. In V. B. Van Hasselt & D. Kolko (Eds.), *Inpatient behavior therapy for children and adolescents.* New York: Plenum Press.

Rapport, M. D., Quinn, S. O., DuPaul, G. J., Quinn, E. P., & Kelly, K. L. (1989). Attention deficit disorder with hyperactivity and methylphenidate: The effects of dose and mastery level on children's learning performance. *Journal of Abnormal Child Psychology, 17*, 669–689.

Rapport, M. D., Stoner, G., DuPaul, G. J., Birmingham, B. K., & Tucker, S. (1985a). Methylphenidate in hyperactive children: Differential effects of dose on academic, learning, and social behavior. *Journal of Abnormal Child Psychology, 13*, 227–244.

Rapport, M. D., Stoner, G., DuPaul, G. J., Kelly, K. L., Tucker, S. B., & Schoeler, T. (1988). Attention deficit disorder and methylphenidate: A multilevel analysis of dose-response effects on children's impulsivity across settings. *American Academy of Child and Adolescent Psychiatry, 27*, 60–69.

Rapport, M. D., Tucker, S. B., DuPaul, G. J., Merlo, M., & Stoner, G. (1986b). Hyperactivity and frustration: The influence of control over and size of rewards in delaying gratification. *Journal of Abnormal and Child Psychology, 14*, 191–204.

Robin, A. L. (1981). A controlled evaluation of problem-solving communication training with parent-adolescent conflict. *Behavior Therapy, 12*, 593–609.

Rosenberger, P., & Lewine, R. (1982). Conceptual issues in the choice of a structured psychiatric interview. *Comprehensive Psychiatry, 23*, 116–123.

Ross, D. M., & Ross, S. A. (1982). *Hyperactivity: Theory, research, and action* (2nd ed.). New York: John Wiley & Sons.

Rosvold, H. E., Mirsky, A. F., Sarason, I., Bransome, E. D., & Beck, L. H. (1956). A continuous performance test of brain damage. *Journal of Clinical and Consulting Psychology, 20*, 343–350.

Routh, D. K., Schroeder, C. S., & O'Tuama, L. (1974). Development of activity level in children. *Developmental Psychology, 10*, 163–168.

Rutter, M., & Graham, P. (1968). The reliability and validity of the psychiatric assessment of the child: I. Interview with the child. *British Journal of Psychiatry, 114*, 563–579.

Rutter, M., & Shaffer, D. (1980). DSM-III: A step forward or back in terms of the classification of child psychiatric disorders? *Journal of the American Academy of Child Psychiatry, 19*, 371–394.

Saghir, M. T. (1971). A comparison of some aspects of structured and unstructured psychiatric interviews. *American Journal of Psychiatry, 128*, 72–76.

Sandberg, S. T., Rutter, M., & Taylor, E. (1978). Hyperkinetic disorder in psychiatric clinic attenders. *Developmental Medicine and Child Neurology, 20*, 279–299.

Schachar, R., Logan, G., Wachsmuth, R., & Chajczyk, D. (1988). Attaining and maintaining preparation: A comparison of attention in hyperactive, normal and disturbed control children. *Journal of Abnormal Child Psychology, 16,* 361–378.

Sergeant, J. (1988). From DSM-III attentional deficit disorder to functional defects. In L. M. Bloomingdale & J. Sergeant (Eds.), *Attention deficit disorder: Criteria, cognition, intervention* (pp. 183–198). New York: Pergamon Press.

Shaywitz, S. E. (1982). Assessment of brain function in clinical pediatric research: Behavioral and biological strategies. *Schizophrenia Bulletin, 8,* 205–235.

Shaywitz, S. E., Schnell, C., Shaywitz, B. A., & Towle, V. R. (1986). Yale Children's Inventory (YCI): An instrument to assess children with attentional deficits and learning disabilities I. Scale development and psychometric properties. *Journal of Abnormal Child Psychology, 14,* 347–364.

Shaywitz, S. E., & Shaywitz, B. E. (1988). Attention deficit disorder: Current perspectives. In J. F. Kavanagh & T. J. Truss (Eds.), *Learning disabilities: Proceedings of the national conference* (pp. 369–523). Maryland: York Press.

Shaywitz, S. E., Shaywitz, B. E., McGraw, K., & Groll, S. (1984). Current status of the neuromaturational examination as an index of learning disability. *Journal of Pediatrics, 104,* 819–825.

Shrout, P. E., Spitzer, R. L., & Fleiss, J. L. (1987). Quantification of agreement in psychiatric diagnosis revisited. *Archives of General Psychiatry, 44,* 172–177.

Sostek, A. J., Buchsbaum, M. D., & Rapoport, J. L. (1980). Effects of amphetamine on vigilance performance in normal and hyperactive children. *Journal of Abnormal Child Psychology, 8,* 491–500.

Spitzer, R. L. (1983). Psychiatric diagnosis: Are clinicians still necessary? *Comprehensive Psychiatry, 24,* 399–411.

Stewart, M. A., deBlois, C. S., & Cummings, C. (1980). Psychiatric disorder in the parents of hyperactive boys and those with conduct disorder. *Journal of Child Psychology and Psychiatry, 21,* 283–292.

Swanson, J. M. (1985). Measures of cognitive functioning appropriate for use in pediatric pharmacological research studies. *Psychopharmacology Bulletin, 21,* 887–890.

Swanson, J. M. (1988). What do psychopharmacological studies tell us about information processing deficits in ADDH? In L. M. Bloomingdale & J. Sergeant (Eds.), *Attention deficit disorder: Criteria, cognitive, intervention* (pp. 97–115). New York: Pergamon Press.

Swanson, J. M., Sandman, C. A., Deutsch, C., & Baren, M. (1983). Methylphenidate hydrochloride given with or before breakfast: I. Behavioral, cognitive, and electrophysiological effects. *Pediatrics, 72,* 49–55.

Sykes, D. J., Douglas, V. I., & Morgenstern, G. (1973). Sustained attention in hyperactive children. *Journal of Child Psychology and Psychiatry, 14,* 213–220.

Trites, R. L., & Laprade, K. (1983). Evidence for an independent syndrome of hyperactivity. *Journal of Child Psychology and Psychiatry, 24,* 573–586.

Ullmann, R. K., & Sleator, E. K. (1985). Attention deficit disorder children with or without hyperactivity: Which behaviors are helped by stimulants? *Clinical Pediatrics, 24,* 547–551.

Ullmann, R. K., Sleator, E. K., & Sprague, R. L. (1985). Introduction to the use of ACTeRS. *Psychopharmacology Bulletin, 21,* 915–920.

Vyse, S. A., & Rapport, M. D. (1989). The effects of methylphenidate on learning in children with ADDH: The stimulus equivalence paradigm. *Journal of Clinical and Consulting Psychology, 57,* 425–435.

Weinstein, S. R., Stone, K., Noam, G. G., Grimes, K., & Schwab-Stone, M. (1989). Comparison of DISC with clinicians' DSM-III diagnoses in psychiatric inpatients. *Journal of the American Academy of Child and Adolescent Psychiatry, 28,* 53–60.

Weiss, B., & Laties, V. G. (1962). Enhancement of human performance by caffeine and the amphetamines. *Pharmacological Review, 14,* 1–36.

Weissman, M. M., Wickramaratne, P., Warner, V., John, K., Prusoff, B. A., Merikangas, K. R., & Gammon, G. D. (1987). Assessing psychiatric disorders in children. *Archives of General Psychiatry, 44,* 747–753.

Werry, J. S., Reeves, J. C., & Elkind, G. S. (1987). Attention deficit, conduct, oppositional and anxiety disorders in children: III. Laboratory differences. *Journal of Abnormal Child Psychology, 15,* 409–428.

Whalen, C. K., & Henker, B. (1985). The social worlds of hyperactivity (ADDH) children. *Clinical Psychology Review, 5,* 447–478.

Whalen, C. K., Henker, B., Collins, B. E., McAuliffe, S., & Vaux, A. (1979). Peer interaction in a structured communication task: Comparisons of normal and hyperactive boys and of methylphenidate (Ritalin) and placebo effects. *Child Development, 50,* 388–401.

Widiger, R. A, Hurt, S. W., Frances, A., Clarkin, J. F., & Gilmore, M. (1984). Diagnostic efficiency and DSM-III. *Archives of General Psychiatry, 41,* 1005–1012.

Wittchen, H. U., Semler, G., & von Zerssen, D. (1985). A comparison of two diagnostic methods: Clinical ICD diagnoses vs. DSM-III and Research Diagnostic Criteria using the Diagnostic Interview Schedule (version 2). *Archives of General Psychiatry, 42,* 677–684.

CHAPTER 19

CONDUCT DISORDER

Alan E. Kazdin

Antisocial behavior in childhood includes a variety of acts, such as fighting, destroying property, stealing, lying, and running away. These behaviors occur in varying degrees over the course of normal development (Achenbach & Edelbrock, 1981; MacFarlane, Allen, & Honzik, 1954). For most children, antisocial behaviors diminish over time, do not interfere with everyday functioning, and do not appear to have untoward consequences in adulthood. However, for a significant number of children, these behaviors are relatively extreme and do not attenuate over the course of childhood.

DESCRIPTION OF THE DISORDER

Conduct disorder refers to instances when the children or adolescents evince a *pattern of antisocial behavior,* when there is *significant impairment* in everyday functioning at home or school, or when the behaviors are *regarded as unmanageable by significant others* (see Kazdin, 1987). Thus, the term *conduct disorder* is reserved for antisocial behavior that is clinically significant and clearly beyond the realm of normal functioning.

As conduct disorder emerges, a wide range of consequences are evident, including disruptive relations with parents, teachers, and peers, poor school performance, and efforts to intervene in ways that themselves may be disruptive (e.g., transfer to new classrooms, schools, and neighborhoods). Clinically severe antisocial behavior is likely to bring the youth into contact with various social agencies. Mental health services (clinics, hospitals) and the criminal justice system (police, courts) are the major sources of contact for youths whose behaviors are identified as severe. Within the educational system, special services, teachers, and classes are often provided to manage such children on a daily basis.

The purpose of this chapter is to discuss the assessment of conduct disorder. Current assessment modalities, specific measures, and interpretive issues that emerge from their use are presented. The nature of the disorder and the utility of selected measures are illustrated with a case study.

Completion of this research was supported by a Research Scientist Development Award (MH00353) and by a grant (MH35408) from the National Institute of Mental Health.

Central Features

The overriding feature of conduct disorder is a persistent pattern of behavior in which the rights of others and age-appropriate social norms are violated. Isolated acts of physical aggression, destruction of property, stealing, and fire setting are sufficiently severe to warrant concern and attention in their own right. Although these behaviors may occur in isolation, several of these are likely to appear together as a constellation or syndrome.

Antisocial behavior that is clinically severe, interferes with functioning in everyday life, and entails several symptoms that co-occur is recognized in contemporary diagnosis as a specific disorder, referred to as Conduct Disorder. (For present purposes, conduct disorder is used to refer to clinically severe levels of antisocial behavior. Conduct Disorder, as a proper noun, refers specifically to the diagnostic category, as defined by DSM-III-R [American Psychiatric Association, 1987]). In the Diagnostic and Statistical Manual of Mental Disorders (DSM-III-R) (American Psychiatric Association, 1987), the diagnosis is reached if the child or adolescent shows any three of the following symptoms:

1. stealing without confrontation of a victim
2. running away
3. lying
4. deliberate fire setting
5. truancy
6. breaking into someone's house, building, or car
7. destroying property
8. cruelty to animals
9. forced sexual activity of another person
10. use of a weapon
11. often initiating fights
12. stealing with confrontation of a victim
13. physical cruelty to people

The symptoms must be present for at least 6 months for the diagnosis to apply. Any given individual is not likely to show all of the symptoms specified in the diagnostic criteria. However, the symptoms reflect core features of the disorder.

Associated Features

The core features of conduct disorder do not convey the full scope of impairment of children and adolescents who meet the diagnostic criteria. Apart from the antisocial, aggressive, and defiant behaviors, there are several correlates or associated features as well. Among alternative symptoms among antisocial children, those related to *hyperactivity* have been the most frequently identified. These symptoms include excessive motor activity, restlessness, impulsiveness, and inattentiveness. Several other behaviors have been identified as problematic among antisocial youths, such as noncompliance, boisterousness, showing off, and blaming others (Quay, 1986). Many of these appear to be relatively mild forms of obstreperous behavior in comparison to aggression, theft, vandalism, or other acts that invoke damage to persons or property.

Children with conduct disorder are also likely to suffer from *academic deficiencies,* as reflected in achievement level, grades, and specific skill areas, especially reading (e.g., Ledingham & Schwartzman, 1984; Sturge, 1982). Such children are often seen by their teachers as uninterested in school, unenthusiastic toward academic pursuits, and careless in their work (Glueck & Glueck, 1950). They are more likely to be left behind in grades and to end their schooling sooner than their peers matched in age, socioeconomic status, and other demographic variables (Bachman, Johnston, & O'Malley, 1978; Glueck & Glueck, 1968). The core symptoms of the dysfunction appear to begin a sequence of events that foster continued dysfunction. Thus, failure to complete homework and possible truancy or lying are likely to decrease the attention of teachers to aid the student. Consequently, the initial dysfunctions at school are likely to portend further deterioration.

Poor interpersonal relations are likely to correlate with antisocial behavior. Children high in aggressiveness or other antisocial behaviors are rejected by their peers and show poor social skills (e.g., Behar & Stewart, 1982; Carlson, Lahey, & Neeper, 1984). Such youths are socially ineffective in their interactions with an array of adults (e.g., parents, teachers, community members). Specifically, antisocial youths are less likely to defer to adult authority, to show politeness, and to promote further positive interactions (Freedman et al., 1978; Gaffney & McFall, 1981).

The correlates of antisocial behavior involve not only overt behaviors but also a variety of *cognitive and attributional processes*. Antisocial youths are deficient in cognitive problem-solving skills that underlie social interaction (Dodge, 1985; Kendall & Braswell, 1985). For example, such youths are more likely than their peers to interpret gestures of others as hostile and are less able to identify solutions to interpersonal problem situations and to take the perspective of others.

Parent and Family Features

A variety of parent and family characteristics are associated with conduct disorder. Parents of antisocial youths are more likely to suffer from various psychiatric disorders than are parents of children in the general population (Rutter, Tizard, & Whitmore 1970). Criminal behavior and alcoholism, particularly of the father, are two of the stronger and more consistently demonstrated parental characteristics of youths with severe antisocial behavior (Robins, 1966; Rutter & Giller, 1983; West, 1982).

Several features related to the interaction of parents with their children characterize families of conduct-disordered youths. Parent disciplinary practices and attitudes have been especially well studied. Parents of conduct-disordered youths tend to be harsh in their attitudes and disciplinary practices with their children (e.g., Farrington, 1978; Glueck & Glueck, 1968; McCord, McCord, & Howard, 1961). These children are more likely than nonreferred children and clinical referrals without antisocial behavior to be victims of child abuse and to be in homes where spouse abuse is evident (Behar & Stewart, 1982; Lewis, Shanok, Pincus, & Glaser, 1979). Lax, erratic, and inconsistent discipline practices for a given parent and between the parents also characterize families of children with conduct disorder. For example, severity of punishment on the part of the father and lax discipline on the part of the mother have been implicated in delinquent behavior (Glueck & Glueck, 1950; McCord et al., 1959). When parents are consistent in their discipline practices, even if they are punitive, children are less likely to be at risk for antisocial behavior (McCord, McCord, & Zola, 1959).

Parents of antisocial children are more likely to give commands to their children, to reward deviant behavior directly through attention and compliance, and to ignore or provide aversive consequences for prosocial behavior (see Patterson, 1982). Fine-grained analyses of parent-child interaction suggest that antisocial behavior, particularly aggression, is systematically, albeit unwittingly, trained in the homes of antisocial children.

Supervision of the child, as another aspect of parent-child contact, has been frequently implicated in conduct disorder (Glueck & Glueck, 1968; Goldstein, 1984; Robins, 1966). Parents of antisocial or delinquent children are less likely to monitor their children's whereabouts, to make arrangements for their care when they are temporarily away from the home, or to provide rules in the home stating where the children can go and when they must return home (Wilson, 1980).

Dysfunctional family relations are manifest in several ways. Parents of antisocial youths, compared with parents of normal youths, show less acceptance of their children, less warmth, affection, and emotional support, and report less attachment (Loeber & Dishion, 1983; McCord et al., 1959; West & Farrington, 1973). At the level of family relations, less supportive and more defensive communications among family members, less participation in activities as a family, and more clear dominance of one family member are also evident (Alexander, 1973; Hanson, Henggeler, Haefele, & Rodick, 1984; West & Farrington, 1973). In addition, unhappy marital relations, interpersonal conflict, and aggression characterize the parental relations of delinquent and antisocial children (see Hetherington & Martin, 1979; Rutter & Giller, 1983). Whether or not the parents are separated or divorced, it is the extent of discord that is associated with antisocial behavior and childhood dysfunction.

The present discussion does not exhaust the range of characteristics of parents and families of conduct-disordered youths. Other characteristics such as mental retardation of the parent, early marriage of the parents, lack of parent interest in the child's school performance, and lack of participation of the family in religious or recreational activities have been found as well (Glueck & Glueck, 1968; Wadsworth, 1979). Many of the factors come in "packages." For example, family size, overcrowding, poor housing, poor parental supervision, parent criminality, and marital discord are likely to be related. Thus, although research often can identify the influence of individual components, in practice they are invariably intertwined.

ASSESSMENT OF THE DISORDER

The diverse features of conduct disorder are germane to assessment and treatment decisions. The central characteristics of the child's dysfunction need to be carefully delineated. At the same time, associated features (e.g., hyperactivity, school performance) and contextual factors (e.g., parent psychopathology, child-rearing practices) make relevant an extremely broad set of constructs each with manifold measurement strategies. The present discussion focuses on assessment of child antisocial behavior to convey progress and prospects within this domain.

Aggression, a key symptom of conduct disorder, has been the subject of research in diverse areas of research (e.g., social and developmental psychology). In these areas, multiple assessment procedures and laboratory paradigms to measure aggression have emerged. This discussion examines major modalities available and in use for the assessment of clinical dysfunction among children who are identified or referred for treatment.

Alternative Modalities and Measures

Several measures developed specifically to assess antisocial behavior, and their salient characteristics are enumerated in Table 19-1. A few measures are highlighted for illustrative purposes.

Self-Report Measures

Self-report measures are frequently used in clinical work with adult patient samples. There is a greater reticence in relying on self-report in children and adolescents. Children occasionally underestimate the presence and severity of their symptoms when parallel information is obtained from other sources (Kazdin, French, Unis, & Esveldt-Dawson, 1983; Orvaschel et al., 1982). Underreporting of antisocial behaviors might be expected because children may not perceive their behaviors as unusual or problematic, or they may hide the behaviors from adults to avoid punishment. Actually, antisocial behaviors have been readily identified through self-report (Herjanic & Reich, 1982). Indeed, information regarding antisocial behaviors are often more readily reported by children and adolescents than by others or by institutional records

Table 19-1. Selected Measures of Antisocial Behaviors for Children and Adolescents

MEASURE	RESPONSE FORMAT	AGE[a] RANGE	SPECIAL FEATURES
Self-Report			
Children's Action Tendency Scale (Deluty, 1979)	30 items in forced-choice format, child selects what he or she would do in interpersonal situations	6–15 yrs	Scores for response dimensions: aggressiveness, assertiveness, and submissiveness
Adolescent Antisocial Self-Report Behavior Checklist (Kulik, Stein, & Sarbin, 1968)	52 items, each of which is rated by the child on a 5-point scale (from never to very often).	Adolescence	The measure samples a broad range of behaviors from mild misbehavior to serious antisocial acts. The items load four factors: delinquency, drug usage, parental defiance, and assaultiveness.
Self-Report Delinquency Scale (Elliott & Ageton, 1980)	47 items that measure frequency with which individual has performed offences included in the Uniform Crime Reports. Responses provide frequency with which behavior was performed over the last year.	11–21 yrs	Measure has been developed as part of the National Youth Survey, an extensive longitudinal study of delinquent behavior, alcohol and drug use, and related problems in American youths.
Minnesota Multiphasic Personality Inventory Scales (Lefkowitz, Eron, Walder & Huesmann, 1977)	True-false items derived from Scales F (test-taking attitude), 4 (psychopathic deviate and 9 (hypomania) are summed to yield an aggression/delinquency score.	Adolescence	Part of more general measure that assesses multiple areas of psychopathology.
Interview for Aggression[b] (Kazdin & Esveldt-Dawson, 1986)	Semistructured interview, 30 items pertaining to aggression such as getting into fights, starting arguments. Each item rated on a 5-point scale for severity and a 3-scale for duration.	6–13 yrs	Yields scores for severity, duration, and total (severity + duration) aggression. Separate factors assess overt and covert behaviors.

Table 19-1. Continued

MEASURE	RESPONSE FORMAT	AGE[a] RANGE	SPECIAL FEATURES
Children's Hostility Inventory[b] (Kazdin, Rodgers, Colbus, & Siegel, 1987)	38 true-false statements assessing different facets of aggression and hostility.	6-13 yrs	Derived from Buss-Durke Hostility Guilt Inventory. A priori subscales cover from that scale comprise factors that relate to overt acts (aggression) and aggressive thoughts and feelings (hostility)
Reports of Others			
Eyberg Child Behavior Inventory (Eyberg & Robinson, 1983a)	36 items rated on 1 to 7 point scale for frequency and whether the behavior is a problem.	2-17 yrs	Designed to measure wide range of conduct problems in the home.
Sutter-Eyberg Student Behavior Inventory (Funderburk & Eyberg, 1989)	36 items identical in format but not content to the Eyberg Child Behavior Inventory	2-17 yrs	Measures a range of conduct problem behaviors at school.
Peer Nomination of Aggression (Lefkowitz et al., 1977)	Items that ask children to nominate others who show the characteristics (e.g., "Who starts a fight over nothing"?)	3rd through 13th grade	Items reflect the child's reputation among peers regarding overall aggression Different versions of peer nominations have been used.
Direct Observations			
Adolescent Antisocial Behavior Checklist (Curtiss, et al., 1983)	57 items to measure antisocial behavior during hospitalization. Behaviors are rated as having occurred or not based on staff observations.	Adolescence	The items can be scored using different sets of subscales; one set focuses on the form of the problem (e.g., physical vs. verbal harm); another set focuses on the objects of aggression (e.g., toward self, others, property). Different versions are available and differ in scoring.
Family Interaction Coding System (Reid, 1978)	Direct observational system to measure occurrence or nonoccurrence of 29 specific parent-child behaviors in the home. Each behavior is scored within small intervals for an hour each day for a period of several days.	3-12 yrs	Individual behaviors are observed but usually summarized with a total aversive behavior score. The general procedure can be adopted using some or all of the behaviors of the FICS
Parent Daily Report (Chamberlain & Reid, 1987)	Parents identify symptoms of antisocial behavior. After symptoms are identified, the parent is called daily for several days. Each day the parent is asked if each behavior has or has not occurred in previous 24-hr. period.	3-12 yrs	Measure does not reflect a standardized set of items but rather refers more to an assessment approach for collecting data on behaviors at home.

[a] The age ranges are tentative and are derived from age of cases reported rather than inherent restrictions of the measure.
[b] This measure has separate versions: (1) a self-report measure for children, and (2) a parent-report measure to evaluate children's behavior.

(e.g., Elliott & Ageton, 1980; Williams & Gold, 1972). The validity has been attested to by studies showing that self-reported antisocial behaviors predict subsequent arrest and convictions, as well as educational, employment, and marital adjustment (e.g., Bachman et al., 1978; Farrington, 1984).

Relatively few self-report measures of conduct problems are available (see Table 1). Among those listed, no single measure enjoys widespread use or has been the focus of large-scale psychometric research. As an illustration, the Children's Action Tendency (CATS) (Deluty, 1979) presents 13 situations to the child that reflect conflict situations. The child is asked how he or she would respond among alternative answers presented in a forced-choice format. The responses, and the eventual scores they comprise, reflect aggression, assertiveness, and submissiveness. The aggressiveness scale directly reflects characteristics of conduct disorder. This subscale has been shown to possess adequate internal consistency and test-retest reliability (over 4 months). Validity evidence has been derived from demonstrations that CAT aggressiveness correlates with teacher and peer measures of the same construct, differentiates aggressive from nonaggressive schoolchildren, and reflects change after treatment of antisocial behavior (e.g., Deluty, 1979, 1983; Groot & Prins, 1989; Kazdin, Bass, Siegel, & Thomas 1989). Notwithstanding the initial evidence in behalf of the measure, the CATS is not in widespread use. Further work is needed to provide larger scale evaluation of normative data and to examine the measure in relation to other strategies to assess antisocial behavior.

Reports of Significant Others

Reports of significant others (parents, teachers, therapists) are the most widely used measures of childhood disorders in general. As an assessment modality, measures completed by significant others have major advantages. Many rating scales are available that can be completed relatively quickly and can cover a wide range of symptom areas (see Barkley, 1988). There may be a partial bias in the types of conduct problems that rating scales can assess. Behaviors such as testing, fighting, yelling, arguing, and other overt acts are likely to be easily detected by parents and teachers. More covert acts, such as stealing, substance abuse, and gang behavior, may be more difficult to detect. Parents are the most frequently relied upon source of information because they usually are readily available, are knowledgeable about the child's behavior over time and across situations, and usually play a central role in the referral of children for treatment.

Measures completed by significant others have received more attention than self-report measures. A prime example is the frequently used and extensively evaluated Eyberg Child Behavior Inventory (ECBI) (Eyberg & Robinson, 1983a; Robinson, Eyberg, & Ross, 1980). The measure is used to assess child behavior problems that parents report at home. Sample items include verbally fighting with friends one's own age, refusing to do chores when asked, poor table manners, and yelling or screaming. Most of the items reflect refusal and other oppositional behaviors that are annoying to parents, rather than serious antisocial acts, although there are exceptions (e.g., stealing, destroying objects). Each item is rated by the parent as to whether it is a problem (yes, no) and how often it occurs (Likert scale: 1=never, 7=always). The measure yields two scores that reflect the number of problems (items endorsed affirmatively) and the intensity of the problem (total score of the Likert scale scores summed for all items).

The ECBI stands apart from other measures devoted to conduct problems by virtue of the scope of available evidence. The measure has been used in studies to evaluate the instrument and concurrent validity of other measures, to characterize child dysfunction and family adjustment, and to evaluate alternative treatments. Psychometric evaluation has indicated that the ECBI has adequate reliability (e.g., internal consistency and test-retest reliability) and validity (e.g., criterion, convergent, and discriminant) (Boggs, Eyberg, & Reynolds, in press; Eyberg & Robinson, 1983a; Robinson et al., 1980; Eyberg & Ross, 1978). Also, the measure reflects change associated with treatment of conduct problems (e.g., Eyberg & Robinson, 1982; Webster-Stratton, Kolpacoff, & Hollinsworth, 1988). Normative data are also available for children and adolescents (Eyberg & Robinson, 1983a; Robinson et al., 1980), including recent data spanning grades 1 through 12 (Burns & Patterson, in press). Clearly, among available measures for antisocial behavior, the measure has achieved substantial attention.

Teacher evaluations of child behavior also play a role in identification of conduct disorder. Teachers observe children for protracted amounts of time and across a wide range of situations (e.g., structured vs. unstructured classroom activities, academic, social and recreational settings). Moreover, the teacher can evaluate children in the context of their peers. A given child's departure from his or her peers provides a perspective that may not be available to parents.

As an illustration, the Sutter-Eyberg Student Behavior Inventory (SESBI) (Funderburk & Eyberg, 1989) has been developed as a teacher rating scale to assess conduct problems at school. The measure closely parallels the ECBI in items and scoring format. However, several items were modified or replaced to reflect behavior at school (e.g., makes noises in class, sasses teacher, demands teacher attention). As with the ECBI, the behaviors tend to focus on annoying problems rather than the more severe forms of antisocial acts. The measure has been subjected to considerable psychometric evaluation with nonreferred and clinic samples. Data recently reported have demonstrated internal consistency, test-retest reliability (1 and 3 weeks), interrater reliability, and convergent validity with ratings completed by others (Funderburk, Eyberg, & Behar, 1989; Ladish, Sosna, Warner, & Burns, 1989; Schaughency et al., 1989). The close relation to the ECBI and the relative ease with which each is administered make the SESBI attractive for school assessment of conduct problems.

Antisocial behavior is often included in multidimensional rating scales completed by parents and teachers. The measures include diverse symptom areas designed to cover a broad spectrum of dysfunctions, one or more of which address antisocial behavior (e.g., aggression, delinquency). Typically these scales present a large number of items that the parent or teacher rates in terms of presence or absence or severity of dysfunction. The measures do not focus primarily on antisocial behavior and hence are not included in Table 1. However, the measures warrant mention because of their breadth and level of development.

The Child Behavior Checklist (CBCL) (Achenbach & Edelbrock, 1983) exemplifies this type of instrument in which parents complete items to convey characteristics of their children. There are separate versions of the measure for parents, teachers, and children for different age groups spanning 2–16 years of age. The most commonly used version is the parent form, which includes 118 items that refer to behavior problems, each of which is rated on a 3-point scale (0 = not true, 2 = very or often true). Three sample items related to conduct disorder include cruelty, bullying, or meanness to others; argues a lot; sets fires. The scale yields several different factors or constellations of symptoms including aggression, delinquency, hyperactivity, anxiety, depression, uncommunicativeness, schizophrenia, and others. The scale has been evaluated separately for boys and girls in different age groups from nonclinic samples. Consequently, with the CBCL, one can evaluate an individual child's standing relative to same-age and same-gender peers who have not been referred for treatment. Many other rating scales and checklists have been administered to parents. Prominent examples include the Revised Behavior Problem Checklist (Quay & Peterson, 1983), the Parent Symptom Questionnaire (Conners, 1970), the Louisville Behavior Checklist (Miller, 1984), the Institute for Juvenile Research Behavior Checklist (Lessing, Williams, & Revelle, 1981), and the Personality Inventory for Children (Wirt, Lachar, Klindinst, & Seat, 1977).

Several multidimensional scales are also available for teachers. These measures do not differ in structure or format. Indeed, many scales such as the Revised Behavior Problem Checklist have been administered to parents, teachers, and other adults (e.g., clinic staff). For several measures, parallel forms exist for teacher and parents. Examples include the CBCL-Teacher Report Form (Achenbach & Edelbrock, 1983), the Conners Teachers Questionnaire (Conners, 1969), and the School Behavior Checklist (Miller, 1972), which are parallel to forms mentioned above for parents.

As an assessment modality, multidimensional parent and teacher rating scales have been widely used. Their value derives from sampling a wide spectrum of symptom areas and from their ease of administration. Considerable data have been generated on their use and psychometric properties (reliability and validity). Also, normative data are available for many measures that permit comparison of clinic and nonclinic samples and variations in symptom areas as a function of age, gender, social class, and other subject or demographic variables.

Peer Evaluations

Ratings by peers are worth distinguishing even though peers qualify as "significant others." Also, peer measures reflect an assessment methodology that departs from the rating scales used for parent and teacher assessments. Peer-based measures usually consist of different ways of soliciting peer nominations of persons who evince particular characteristics such as aggressiveness (e.g., Banta & Walder, 1961; Pekarik et al., 1976). For example, peers may be asked to nominate children in class to answer such questions as "Who gets into most fights?" or "Who starts a fight over nothing?" (Huesmann, Lefkowitz,

& Eron, 1978; Lochman & Lampron, 1985). A child's score usually is the proportion of nominations in which he or she has been selected. The consensus of the peer group is likely to reflect consistencies in performance and stable characteristics. Indeed, elementary school peer evaluations of aggressive behavior correlate with antisocial behavior years later (Huesmann et al., 1984; Tremblay, LeBlanc, & Schwartzman, 1988).

Peer sociometric ratings are often used to assess such characteristics as popularity, likeability, acceptance, rejection, and social competence. Such characteristics are quite relevant given the difficulties in each of these areas that antisocial children usually evince. Peer evaluations of social dimensions are correlated with independent evaluations of adjustment. Although the perspective of peers is clearly unique and important, the clinical utility of peer ratings is limited. The measures have enjoyed use in situations in which one has access to a peer group, such as in a classroom. Studies of antisocial behavior and intervention projects in school settings have been able to utilize peer-based measures.

Direct Observation

The youth's specific behaviors at home, at school, or at a clinic can be observed directly. The key ingredients of direct observations are defining behavior carefully, identifying the situations in which behavior will be observed, using trained observers to record the behaviors, and ensuring that behavior is observed accurately and reliably. The requirements for direct observation vary as a function of the complexity of the assessment procedures. Several observation systems are available (e.g., Eyberg & Robinson, 1983b; Forehand & McMahon, 1981; Patterson, 1982; Wahler, House, & Stambaugh, 1976). They differ in the specific behavioral codes for various conduct problems, the setting in which they are usually completed (e.g., home, clinic, school), and the extent to which the situation and tasks are structured for the parent and child (e.g., specific tasks such as playing a game, or everyday interaction) (see Reid, Baldwin, Patterson, & Dishion, 1988). Typically, a given measure has been designed for one setting such as the home or clinic. However, the codes can be adapted for use across settings. In each situation, highly trained observers usually are required to observe behavior.

An advantage of direct observations is that they provide samples of the actual frequency or occurrences of particular antisocial or prosocial behaviors. Direct observations have their own liabilities. Many behaviors, especially covert acts (theft, drug use, fire setting, sexual promiscuity), are not readily observed directly. Also, when behaviors are observed directly and obtrusively, the act of observation can influence their performance. Nevertheless, observations contribute unique information by sampling behavior directly.

As an illustration of direct observational methods, the Family Interaction Coding System (FICS) warrants special mention (Patterson, 1982). The FICS has been used to record behaviors of antisocial children as they interact with their parents and siblings at home (Patterson et al., 1975; Reid, 1978). More specifically, the measure is designed to assess aggressive behaviors and the antecedents and consequences (family interactions) with which they are associated. Among direct observation systems, the FICS is relatively elaborate. Twenty-nine different behaviors are coded by observers as present or absent in each of several brief time intervals (e.g., 30 seconds) over a period of approximately 1 hour. Prosocial and deviant child behaviors (e.g., complying with requests, attacking someone, yelling) and parent behaviors (e.g., providing approval, playing with the child, humiliating the child) are included.

The FICS has several important requirements. To begin with, observers must be carefully trained and monitored closely to ensure that the codes are scored reliably. In addition, the situations in which observers complete their assessment need to be partially controlled to limit the variability in the setting. For example, when the FICS is used in the home, families are instructed to remain in a small number of rooms during the period in which observations are obtained and not to watch television or to make outgoing phone calls, all of which help observers score child-parent interactions.

The FICS and other observational systems, beyond those included in Table 1, have been used in several studies (see McMahon & Forehand, 1988; Reid et al., 1988). However, individual measures have been largely restricted to specific research programs. The methods are somewhat complex, require well-trained observers, and are not easily disseminated for widespread use. Direct observational systems need not involve such well-developed and formalized systems as the FICS. Occasionally observational codes are devised for individual cases to observe one or more behaviors at home or at school (see Kazdin, 1989a). With relatively simple definitions and only one or a few codes, parents and teachers can be used in place of trained observers. The ease of implementation in such cases, relative to more complex systems, bears a commensurate reduction in the scope of information. The more complex codes evaluate multiple child behaviors and usually provide information about parent-child interchanges; more simplified codes tend to focus on one or two target behaviors of the child.

Not all observational procedures that include multiple behaviors of the child require trained observers at home. A unique measure designed to assess behaviors at home is the Parent Daily Report (PDR) (Patterson, 1982; Chamberlain & Reid, 1987). This measure is completed by the parent who is called each day for a period covering several days (e.g., 6–10 days). Each day a list of conduct problem behaviors is reviewed with the parent. The parent is asked whether any of several behaviors has occurred in the preceding 24-hour period. From the replies, two scores usually are delineated: namely, the total number of conduct problem behaviors and the total number of target behaviors. The total behavior score is the sum of the behaviors that were noted to have occurred that day. The target behavior score is the sum of occurrences of a subset of the behaviors that the parents previously identified as problematic.

The PDR embraces advantages of direct observations, including specification of the behaviors and observations restricted to a specific time period. Also, the measure samples behaviors in everyday situations without artificial constraints that direct observations by observers can impose. Finally, the PDR can assess low-rate behaviors (stealing, fire setting) that are less likely to be evident in the usual observational system. Yet, the measure relies on impressions and is not invariably based on what actually occurred. Correspondence between what the parent says the child did and what the child has actually done may vary widely.

The PDR has been shown to be reliable as reflected in measures in interjudge (caller) agreement, internal consistency, and test-retest reliability (over periods of 2–4 weeks). The measure correlates moderately with direct observations (FICS) and reflects change associated with interventions designed to reduce antisocial behavior (Chamberlain & Reid, 1987; Kazdin et al., 1989; Patterson, 1982; Webster-Stratton et al., 1988). Some data are available on normative samples to facilitate interpretation of the results (Chamberlain & Reid, 1987). Low interparent agreement, varied and occasionally low correlations with direct observations, and different conclusions for total behavior versus target behavior scores raise ambiguities with the measure. Also, at this point, the measure has not been standardized; different versions are in use varying in the number and content of behavioral categories (see Chamberlain & Reid, 1987; McMahon & Forehand, 1988). As such, the measure refers more to a procedure than to a specific scale.

Institutional and Societal Records

Evaluation of antisocial youths frequently relies on institutional records such as school attendance, grades, graduation, school suspensions and expulsions, contact with the police, or arrest records. Institutional records are exceedingly important because they represent socially significant measures of the impact of the problem. Alternative governmental agencies at the state and national level monitor such events as the number of juvenile arrests or juvenile court cases. Such information can plot important social trends and facilitate decision making about allocation of resources and services for a particular problem.

There are many problems with institutional and societal records as a measure of antisocial behavior. Most antisocial and delinquent acts are not observed or recorded. In fact, research has suggested that 9 of 10 illegal acts are not detected or not acted on officially (Empey, 1982). This conclusion has been supported by studies that ask children and adolescents to report on their delinquent and antisocial behaviors (Elliott & Ageton, 1980; Williams & Gold, 1972). Official records can greatly underestimate the occurrence of antisocial behaviors because of imperfect and often discretionary recording of the act on some archival record. Nevertheless, institutional records are critical measures for the evaluation of antisocial behavior. Antisocial behavior by its very nature often leaves its mark on society (e.g., vandalism, fire setting, crime statistics). Institutional records have been used to measure the behavior of juveniles and to evaluate interventions designed to reduce antisocial behavior (e.g., Kirigin et al., 1982; Offord et al., 1985).

Projective Techniques

Projective tests present ambiguous or relatively unstructured material to the child. Responses are considered to reflect underlying psychological processes depending on the specific assessment device and the theoretical position from which the device or scoring system has been derived. Several different measures have been used to examine constructs directly relevant to conduct disorder including aggression, anger, and hostility, as well as psychic processes such as defense mechanisms, ego development, and fantasy though which these constructs may be manifest. Prominent among the measures are the Rorschach, Thematic Apperception Test or Children's Apperception Test, Figure Drawings, and others (Lochman, 1984). Individual measures often include a number of scoring systems and stimuli configurations (e.g., subsets of TATs cards). Reviews and critiques have questioned the validity of such measures and the unclear relation of projective test performance to overt antisocial acts (e.g., Gittelman, 1980; Lochman, 1984). Research can be cited that demonstrates that alternative projective tests distinguish aggressive from nonaggressive individuals or correlate significantly with other measures of antisocial behavior (e.g., Purcell, 1956; Koppitz, 1966). However, as an assessment modality, projective techniques do not enjoy widespread use for conduct disorders. Infrequent use may be due in part to fact that the measures by design do not attempt to access directly the core phenomenological symptoms of the disorder and do not aid in achieving a psychiatric diagnosis based on current phenomenological approaches.

Multimodal Assessment

Each of the modalities cited has its own strengths, methodological weaknesses, and sources of bias. For example, parent evaluations of deviant child behavior provide an obviously important and unique perspective given that parents usually are in an excellent position to comment on the child's functioning. Yet, parent ratings of child deviance are influenced by parent psychopathology, stress, and marital discord (e.g., Forehand, Lautenschlager, Faust, & Graziano, 1986; Mash & Johnston, 1983). Also, parents occasionally fail to detect problems identified through child report or direct observation. Similarly, direct observation reflects performance of a particular behavior free from the global judgments and recollections of parents and teachers. Yet, critical behaviors of interest may be too low in frequency, covert, or performed when observers are not present. Hence, direct observation may miss many behaviors of interest.

No single measure has been shown to assess the multiple facets of dysfunction that conduct disorder reflects. Consequently, the assessment of conduct disorder needs to include multiple measures that encompass different methods of assessment (e.g., interviews, direct observations), perspectives (e.g., child, parent, teacher), domains (e.g., affect, cognition, behavior), and settings (at home, at school, in the community). The importance of multichannel assessment strategies is also accentuated by findings on several substantive methodological and substantive questions about child performance.

Cross-situational Performance

Children with conduct problems are likely to evince dysfunction across diverse situations such as home and school. Assessment of child behavior in one of these settings cannot be assumed to represent performance in other settings. For example, in a treatment study with antisocial children, ratings of child behavior were obtained from parents and teachers to assess a broad range of symptoms at home and at school (Kazdin et al., 1989). Correlations before treatment indicated that total symptom scores at home (Child Behavior Checklist) and at school (School Behavior Checklist) were not significantly correlated ($r = .08$). This rather low correlation suggests considerable specificity of performance for conduct problem behavior or large discrepancies in the perspectives of parents and teachers. After treatment, pre- to posttreatment change at home was significantly correlated with change at school ($r = .26, p < .05$). Although improvements in performance in one setting were related to improvements in the other setting, the magnitude of the correlation is low. These data as well as other studies indicate the relative independence in level of conduct problems and other dysfunctions across different settings (Achenbach, McConaughy, & Howell, 1987; Kazdin, 1989b; Kazdin & Bass, 1988). Thus, multimodal assessment is essential to characterize performance across different settings.

Symptoms and Prosocial Functioning

The impetus for seeking evaluation or treatment usually is the presence of maladaptive, disturbing, or disruptive behaviors. Naturally, the effects of treatment are measured by the extent to which the problems identified at the outset of treatment are reduced when treatment is completed. Often, assessment includes other symptom areas to see whether treatment reduces dysfunction in other domains than those initially identified as problematic. The reduction of symptoms is obviously central to the evaluation of outcome.

In addition to symptom reduction, it is important to assess prosocial functioning or adaptive skills of the child. Prosocial functioning refers to the presence of positive adaptive behaviors and experiences such as participating in social activities, socially interacting, and making friends. With children and adolescents, adjustment may depend heavily on the positive adaptive behaviors or skills, given the significance of the peer group and prosocial experiences outside the home.

Reducing symptoms no doubt can improve a child's functioning. Yet, the overlap of symptom reduction and positive prosocial functioning may not be great (Kazdin, 1989b; Kazdin et al., 1989). For example, in the latter study parents rated antisocial children on the CBCL, which yielded scores for overall symptoms (total behavior problems) and prosocial functioning (total social competence). Scores on this measure were correlated significantly, and, as would be expected, negatively ($r = -.31; p < .001$). The magnitude of the correlation is relatively low, indicating approximately 9% shared variance. Changes in symptoms and prosocial functioning from pre- to posttreatment also showed a very low correlation ($r = -.17$, ns). Similar findings were evident when symptoms and prosocial functioning were examined at school. Thus, reductions in symptoms were not strongly associated with improvements in prosocial functioning.

These findings suggest that *anti*social behavior is not merely the opposite of *pro*social behavior. Thus, multiple measures are essential to examine the positive adaptive functioning of children as well as target symptoms of interest. In the case of treatment evaluation, such assessment may be particularly critical. Quite possibly, treatments that appear equally effective in reducing symptoms may vary in the extent to which they promote and develop prosocial behaviors. In addition, for children whose symptom reduction is equivalent, the prognosis may vary as a function of prosocial behaviors evident at treatment outcome. For these reasons, assessment of prosocial behavior remains important.

Method Variance

The assessment of childhood disorders has shown that method factors can contribute quite significantly to the information yielded. The role of the rater (child, parent) has received special attention (e.g., Achenbach et al., 1987). Results have shown across diverse areas of functioning that measures of the same construct (e.g., aggression, depression) completed by different raters often show low-magnitude correlations (e.g., Kazdin, Esveldt-Dawson, Unis, & Rancurello, 1983; Kazdin, French, & Unis, 1983; Kazdin, French, Unis, & Esveldt-Dawson, 1983). Measures that are completed by the same rater, even if of different constructs, occasionally correlate as highly as or more highly than measures of the same construct by different raters. Multimethod multitrait evaluations indicate that both the trait (construct) variance and method variance contribute to the results (Kazdin, Esveldt-Dawson, Unis, & Rancurello, 1983; Reynolds et al., 1985; Wolfe et al., 1987). The strong method component indicates that conclusions reached about performance with one method of assessment may differ from those reached in relation to another measure. The contribution of raters as one method factor is yet another reason to include multiple methods of assessment.

CASE ILLUSTRATION

Background

The nature of conduct disorder and the information provided by alternative assessment modalities can be better conveyed by the case of an 11-year-old boy named Rick, who lived at home with his mother, stepfather, three younger brothers, and a half-sister. He attended regular elementary school and was in the sixth grade at the time of referral. He was referred for treatment because he was unmanageable at home and at school. At home, his mother reported that he was increasingly oppositional and angry. When he did not get his own way, he was verbally abusive to his mother. He also took things from his mother, stepfather, and siblings, including personal belongings (e.g., jewelry) and money. When he was mad, he engaged in behaviors that varied in severity from pouring his mother's cosmetics all over her room to setting small fires at home.

At school, he had a history of disruptive behavior. In his last few years of school, he was reported as disruptive, rowdy, and out of his seat. He was critical of friends and became isolated from other children. He constantly fought with peers and as a result was suspended many times. His most recent incident was physically grabbing his teacher when he was mad at her. He grabbed and kicked her and was immediately expelled. He entered another school and immediately began fighting and verbally abusing peers and teachers. By the third day, he was suspended. The lack of control of Rick's behavior at school was the primary precipitant for referral.

Academically, Rick's performance at school was remarkable. He was able to read when he entered kindergarten. Although his mother had helped him, she reports that he sought out books and struggled to learn to read on his own. In the first and second grades, his grades were excellent, consisting of primarily As and Bs. Psychological testing indicated that his intelligence was well above the normal range (Full-Scale IQ = 122 on the Wechsler Intelligence Scale for Children—Revised). Because of his academic performance, particularly in his early school years, he was placed on a waiting list for a gifted class. However, his disruptive and aggressive behavior began to lead to frequent suspensions and lower grades. By the third and fourth grade, he was obtaining Bs and Cs and was in frequent trouble at school.

There are several background events relevant to this case. Rick's mother was married when she was 16 years old and gave birth to him about 4 months later. The mother and father experienced great financial difficulties throughout their marriage. They lived with relatives and often moved to live with other relatives as relations became strained. Within the first 6 years of marriage, they had four children. Two of the children were unplanned and said to be "unwanted." After 7 years of marriage and a number of separations, Rick's mother and father were divorced. The mother remarried and had another child with her new husband. Rick's biological father also remarried and lived nearby. Rick saw his biological father about once a month. He reported not caring for his biological father because they were never together. However, he reported being close to his stepfather. He wished to be adopted by his stepfather, but the biological father objected.

Initial Evaluation and Assessment

At the initial appointment, the child and parents were interviewed separately by a psychiatrist and social worker. The purpose was to learn about Rick's history and current functioning and pertinent parent and family information. Based on these interviews, and in consultation with the parents, the recommendation was made to admit Rick to a child psychiatric inpatient unit for a brief period where treatment might by initiated. The facility to which Rick was admitted was a children's inpatient unit that houses 22 children at any one time. The children (ages 5–13) were admitted for acute disorders, including highly aggressive and destructive behavior, suicidal or homicidal ideation or behavior, and deteriorating family conditions.

When Rick, his mother, and stepfather came to the hospital, they received a brief tour of the children's unit. They also completed several measures at this time. The parents and child were interviewed to provide a more intensive evaluation of Rick's functioning at home and at school. A semistructured diagnostic interview (Schedule for Affective Disorders and Schizophrenia for School-Age Children) was administered. The measure samples the full range of symptoms and can be used to provide a psychiatric diagnosis based on DSM-III criteria. DSM-III criteria were invoked because DSM-III-R criteria were not yet available at the time of Rick's admission to the hospital. On the basis of the interview, Rick received the diagnosis of Conduct Disorder.

In addition to the interview with the child and parents, other measures were administered to evaluate Rick's functioning. Rick's mother completed the Child Behavior Checklist (CBCL), as highlighted earlier. Apart from scales for several symptom areas, the measure includes broader scales to characterize type of dysfunction more generally. The total behavior problem score includes the full spectrum of symptoms and hence reflects an overall summary of a broad range of symptoms. In addition to the behavior problem scales, the CBCL includes three positive social behavior scales participation in activities, interactions with others, and academic progress at school. These scales together yield a total social competence score, which summarizes the child's overall prosocial functioning.

To evaluate Rick's performance at school, the School Behavior Checklist (SBCL) (Miller, 1977) was sent to his teacher. The measure includes 96 items, each of which is rated as true or false. The measure includes six scales, including low need achievement (underachievement, low motivation), aggression (fighting), anxiety (fearful), academic disability (poor academic skills), hostile isolation (holding grudges, not respecting others' belongings), and extraversion (self-centered, attracting attention). A summary score is provided by the total disability scale, which includes all of the symptoms of the six scales. The SBCL also includes five items the teacher rates on a 9-point Likert scale: the child's intellectual ability, academic skills, and performance, emotional adjustment, and personal appeal. These ratings can be summed to provide a global rating of school adjustment.

The CBCL and SBCL were selected to evaluate Rick's current functioning and changes over time. First, the measures sample a broad range of dysfunction. Antisocial behaviors were the reason for referral. However, it is also important to examine a much larger set of symptoms that may be evident. Second, the measures evaluate prosocial behavior. The CBCL includes three social competence scales and an overall social competence summary scale. The SBCL includes the overall rating of school adjustment. Finally, both the SBCL and CBCL have been extensively evaluated with large samples of children at different ages. Scores can be discussed in relation to normative levels of performance among nonreferred ("normal") children.

Overview of Treatment

The treatment program consisted of individual cognitive-behavior therapy referred to as Problem-Solving Skill Training. This technique focuses on the child's cognitive processes (perceptions, self-statements, attributions, and problem-solving skills) that are presumed to underlie maladaptive behavior. The processes refer to the child's appraisals of the situation, anticipated reactions of others, and self-statements in response to particular events. The focus of treatment was to alter how Rick approached interpersonal situations in which he had been aggressive and disruptive (see Kazdin, Esveldt-Dawson, French, & Unis, 1987). The treatment began while Rick was in the hospital. After about 7 weeks, Rich was discharged. Treatment continued on an outpatient basis with one session per week. Rick received a total of 20 individual sessions of PSST. During hospitalization and prior to discharge, Rick's mother and stepfather visited the hospital and met with the therapist. The therapist explained the goals and procedures used in treatment and provided some hints to describe how they might help Rick use the procedures at home.

Posttreatment and Follow-up

Three weeks treatment were completed, the CBCL was mailed home, and the SBCL was mailed to Rick's teacher. The instructions were to complete the measure to describe Rick's behavior and to return the materials in a return, stamped envelope. This same procedure was followed 1 year later so that both posttreatment and 1-year follow-up data were available to evaluate the case. The CBCL and SBCL both yield scores for overall symptoms that cover the full range of problems. These scores are referred to as total behavior problems (CBCL) and total disability (SBCL). Figure 19-1 plots these scores for Rick at each of the three assessment periods. In addition, the figure includes the upper level of scores that have been obtained from studies of boys approximately the same age as Rick. This level reflects that point in the normative range that discriminates clinic from nonreferred (normative) samples (see Achenbach & Edelbrock, 1983). Ideally, treatment would place Rick well within the normative range for level of deviance at home and at school (below the horizontal line in the figure).

As evident in the upper panel, Rick was well above the normal range in level of symptoms at home before and immediately after treatment. Immediately after treatment, his behavior had not really changed. At the 1-year follow-up, his behavior had declined but re-

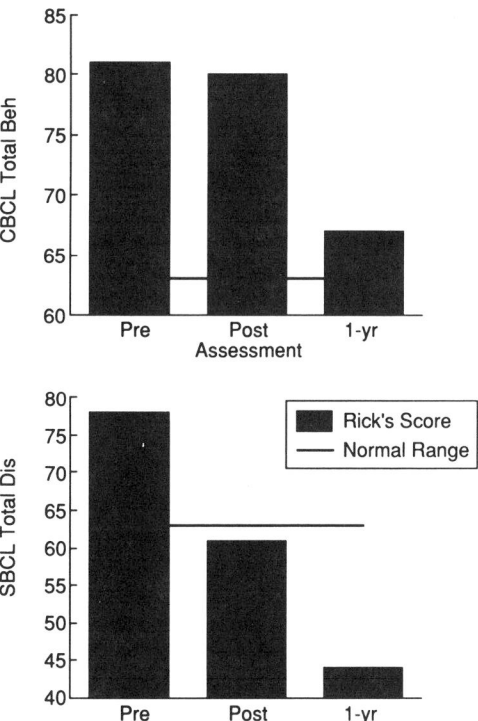

Figure 19-1. Total symptom scores for Rick on the CBCL (Total Behavior Problems-upper panel) and SBCL (Total Disability-lower panel) before (Pre) and after (Post) treatment and 1 year later (Follow-up). The CBCL and SBCL reflect home and school functioning, respectively. Reductions in scores on both measures reflect improvements. The horizontal line reflects the upper limit of the nonclinical "normal" range of boys within the same age range.

mained above the normative level. As for performance at school (lower panel), Rick was well above the normative level of deviance at pretreatment. After treatment and continuing to the 1-year follow-up, his deviant behavior declined and fell within the normative range. Rick's prosocial behaviors were also assessed by the CBCL. Prior to treatment, Rick was within the normal range for overall social competence on the CBCL. Thus, low prosocial functioning often evident with conduct disorder was not a problem at the inception of treatment. Over the course of treatment and follow-up, there were no clear changes; he continued to perform well within the normal range.

The improvements convey that there were changes. One cannot without further information and experimental controls state that the treatment was responsible for these changes. It is possible that Rick would have improved as a function of time because of his own maturation, the period of separation from his parents, changes in teachers, or a host of other factors. The reason for the change cannot be determined here.

The case at best provides somewhat mixed results. The data suggest that behavior at home remained a problem, although social functioning improved markedly. The case is rather typical in terms of the type of behavior that is evident and, given the current state of knowledge, what one can expect from treatment (Kazdin, 1985). Conduct disorder remains an extremely serious clinical problem. The fact that change occurs in cases like Rick's generates considerable optimism. Yet, at best, treatment did not return his behavior to normative levels, suggesting that a great deal more needs to be learned about the treatment and methods for its effective application.

Functional Analysis

The case of Rick illustrates several facets of conduct disorder and the need to assess multiple domains of functioning. By itself, the notion of multiple measures does not provide a helpful way of integrating assessment strategies and making selection decisions. A useful framework to integrate current measures is that of a behavioral or functional analytic approach (Kanfer & Saslow, 1969). The approach is posed here to organize current assessment strategies for antisocial behavior, rather than to argue for a substantive position with regard to etiology or treatment of conduct disorder.

A behavioral analytic approach examines the: *stimuli* (S), *organism* (O) or individual child, the *responses* (R), the *contingencies* (K), and the *consequences* (C) of behavior. The stimuli refer to possible antecedent events for conduct disorder (e.g., severe abuse at home, exposure to marital violence between parents); the organism refers to those factors within the individual that may affect behavior (e.g., maladaptive cognitive processes in interpersonal situations, limited coping skills); the responses refer to those observed behaviors that serve as the focus of assessment and treatment (e.g., aggressive acts toward others, tantrums, noncompliance); the contingencies refer to the relationships (e.g., various reinforcement schedules) between behaviors and antecedent and consequent events in the environment (e.g., child-parent and child-peer interactions associated with, preceding, and resulting from the manifestation of aggressive behavior); and the consequences refer to the specific events (e.g., reinforcing, punishing, or absence of consequences) that follow behavior (e.g., social contacts with others). The S-O-R-K-C model points to different aspects of conduct disorder and the context in which they emerge that may be relevant for assessment.

From the standpoint of a functional analytic model, current measures of conduct disorder clearly focus on the response (R) or behavioral domain. The core features of the disorder entail disturbing behaviors. Understandably, self-, parent-, and teacher ratings as well as other modalities emphasize behavior. In contrast, relatively little attention focuses on characteristics within the individual (or O portions of the S-O-R-K-C analysis). Such measures might focus on affective or cognitive underpinnings and correlates of antisocial behavior. Selected parent-report measures (Children's Hostility Inventory) and projective tests (Thematic Apperception Test) address this focus. Measures of other constructs such as anger are also available to address this domain (e.g., Finch & Eastman, 1983). Measures of characteristics of the individual may be viewed as particularly critical if the conceptualization of dysfunction entails internalized constructs (e.g., cognitive processes) and if the treatment (e.g., anger control training) is designed to effect change through altering of such processes.

Other dimensions of the S-O-R-K-C model include the stimuli (*S*), contingencies (*K*), and consequences (*C*). These are routinely addressed in direct observational coding systems. Behavioral models emphasize the importance of these components in the emergence, daily performance, and escalation of antisocial behavior (e.g., Patterson, 1982; Wahler & Dumas, 1986). Thus, the measures of overt behavior include interactions in which parent and child exchanges and child responses to antecedents (commands, instructions) and specific contingencies (praise or attention after aggressive or nonaggressive behavior) are assessed. Intervention programs such as parent management training are directed toward altering the S, R, K, and C components of the model, much less than the O component, and focus assessment toward these components.

Selecting Measures of Conduct Disorder

The nature of conduct disorder has important implications for the selection of alternative assessment strategies. The characteristics of dysfunction can be translated into assessment guidelines. To begin, it is useful to use measures that are designed specifically to dimensionalize antisocial behavior. These measures typically cover a broad range of conduct problems and provide an overall measure of severity. Available measures reflect a range of severity from mild to moderate conduct problems (e.g., Eyberg Child Behavior Inventory), symptoms of Conduct Disorder (e.g., Interview for Antisocial Behavior), and delinquent behaviors that reflect law violations (e.g., Self-Report Delinquency Scale). In addition, individual items can be perused and culled as an individualized subscale for the child to identify salient antisocial behaviors that might serve as primary targets for treatment.

Second, conduct disorder is associated with dysfunctions in diverse domains. The child is likely to show impairment in symptoms beyond antisocial behavior (e.g., hyperactivity), academic performance, and across multiple settings (home, school). The breadth could be used to advance a diverse and prohibitively large assessment battery. As a general guideline, multidimensional scales (e.g., CBCL) are useful to characterize the range of symptom areas and also can be readily administered to different raters to sample performance in different settings.

Third, measurement of prosocial functioning is important. Conduct-disordered children usually evince maladaptive social behaviors. Reductions of symptoms and antisocial acts in relation to others is not necessarily reflected in positive social interaction. Assessment and treatment may address positive skills and adjustment of the child in his or her relations with peers and adults.

Fourth, evaluation of the child is enhanced greatly by normative data. Antisocial behaviors vary widely in nonclinic samples over the course of development. Interpretation of a child's functioning is facilitated by a developmental baseline derived from performance of peers of the same age and sex. Many standardized scales (e.g., CBCL) have considerable normative data that facilitate interpretation of an individual child's scores. Other scales, noted earlier, designed to assess antisocial behavior (e.g., ECBI, PDR) have normative data, although it is less well elaborated than the data available for multidimensional scales. Understanding of the child can be greatly enhanced by the inclusion of measures with normative data. Also, the use of normative levels of performance may be of interest to evaluate the impact and clinical significance of treatment.

Fifth, the context in which the child is embedded may be critical to assess. Of particular interest are parent and family characteristics because they bear on the long-term prognosis of dysfunction (Kazdin, 1987). For example, parent psychopathology, marital discord, and abusive child-rearing practices are relevant for understanding the child. The range of parent and family factors that relate to child antisocial behavior is vast. Assessment of contextual factors may be dictated by the model of treatment as in the case of parent management training where parent-child interaction is assessed directly. In this instance, the context is considered to be a central mechanism that contributes directly to antisocial behavior.

Sixth, in treatment it is useful to assess those components considered to mediate therapeutic change. Already mentioned in this context was the role of parent-child interaction in parent management training. In parent training, changes in the interaction patterns are considered to be responsible for change and hence represent a critical area of assessment. With other treatments (e.g., cognitively based interventions), one may wish to assess the specific processes to see if they are being altered as expected in treatment.

Finally, most assessment is designed to be conducted on one or two occasions. Before and after treatment are obviously logical assessment occasions. However, assessment on more than these occasions has much to offer. It is useful to see during the course of treatment whether changes are evident in critical areas of child functioning. The information provides important feedback about whether treatment efforts need to be intensified, whether new treatments are needed, and whether a given area of functioning has not been altered.

SUMMARY

Conduct disorder represents a significant clinical and social problem. As a disorder, the symptoms are relatively clear because they involve rather concrete behaviors. Many assessment devices are available to measure aspects of antisocial behavior. Few measures specific to antisocial behavior are well developed. Great attention has been accorded direct observational systems. Diverse systems capture critical facets of family interaction and reflect changes in parents and children. For clinical use, such measures are not readily feasible because of the need to send observers to other settings or to train observers to assess functioning at the clinic. Interpretation of such measures is also difficult because the codes vary across measures, and normative data are not widely available for specific coding systems.

Checklists for parents and teachers that assess multiple dimensions and include antisocial behavior and delinquency are readily available. Their standardization, availability for different raters and settings, and normative data base makes their use quite feasible and well advised. For the individual child, data from broad checklists, whether from multidimensional scales or measures of antisocial behavior, can be scrutinized to identify salient target symptoms (items). These can then be evaluated separately from and in addition to the overall scores of the measure.

REFERENCES

Achenbach, T. M., & Edelbrock, C. S. (1981). Behavioral problems and competencies reported by parents of normal and disturbed children aged four through sixteen. *Monographs of the Society for Research in Child Development, 46* (188).

Achenbach, T. M., & Edelbrock, C. S. (1983). *Manual for the Child Behavior Checklist and Revised Child Behavior Profile*. Burlington, VT: University Associates in Psychiatry.

Achenbach, T. M., McConaughy, S. H., & Howell, C. T. (1987). Child/adolescent behavioral and emotional problems: Implications of cross-informant correlations for situational specificity. *Psychological Bulletin, 101,* 213–232.

Alexander, J. F. (1973). Defensive and supportive communications in normal and deviant families. *Journal of Consulting and Clinical Psychology, 40,* 223–231.

American Psychiatric Association. (1987). *Diagnostic and statistical manual of mental disorders* (3rd ed.—Revised). Washington, DC: Author.

Bachman, J. G., Johnston, L. D., & O'Malley, P. M. (1978). Delinquent behavior linked to educational attainment and post-high school experiences. In L. Otten (Ed.), *Colloquium on the correlates of crime and the determinants of criminal behavior* (pp. 1–43). Arlington, VA: MITRE Corp.

Banta, T. J., & Walder, L. O. (1961). Discriminant validity of a peer-rating measure. *Psychological Reports, 9,* 573–582.

Barkley, R. A. (1988). Child behavior rating scales and checklists. In M. Rutter, A. H. Tuma, & I. S. Lann (Eds.), *Assessment and diagnosis in child psychopathology* (pp. 113–155). New York: Guilford Press.

Behar, D., & Stewart, M. A. (1982). Aggressive conduct disorder of children. *Acta Psychiatrica Scandinavica, 65,* 210–220.

Boggs, S. R., Eyberg, S., & Reynolds, L. A. (in press). Concurrent validity of the Eyberg Child Behavior Inventory. *Journal of Clinical Child Psychology*.

Burns, G. L., & Patterson, D. R. (in press). New standardization data on the Eyberg Child Behavior Inventory. *Psychological Assessment*.

Carlson, C. L., Lahey, B. B., & Neeper, R. (1984). Peer assessment of the social behavior of accepted, rejected, and neglected children. *Journal of Abnormal Child Psychology, 12,* 189–198.

Chamberlain, P., & Reid, J. B. (1987). Parent observation and report of child symptoms. *Behavioral Assessment, 9,* 97–109.

Conners, C. K. (1969). A teacher rating scale for use in drug studies with children. *American Journal of Psychiatry, 126,* 884–888.

Conners, C. K. (1970). Symptom patterns in hyperkinetic, neurotic, and normal children. *Child Development, 41,* 667–682.

Curtiss, G., Rosenthal, R. H., Marohn, R. C., Ostrov, E., Offer, D., & Trujillo, J. (1983). Measuring delinquent behavior in inpatient treatment settings; Revision and validation of the Adolescent Antisocial Behavior Checklist. *Journal of the American Academy of Child Psychiatry, 22,* 5:459–466.

Deluty, R. H. (1979). Children's Action Tendency Scale: A self-report measure of aggressiveness, assertiveness, and submissiveness in children. *Journal of Consulting and Clinical Psychology, 47,* 1061–1071.

Deluty, R. H. (1983). Children's evaluations of aggressive, assertive, and submissive responses. *Journal of Clinical Child Psychology, 12,* 124–129.

Dodge, K. A. (1985). Attributional bias in aggressive children. In P. C. Kendall (Ed.), *Advances in cognitive-behavioral research and therapy* (Vol. 4, pp. 73–110). Orlando, FL: Academic Press.

Elliott, D. S., & Ageton, S. S. (1980). Reconciling race and class differences in self-reported and official estimates of delinquency. *American Sociological Review, 45,* 95–110.

Empey, L. T. (1982). *American delinquency: Its meaning and construction*. Homewood, IL: Dorsey Press.

Eyberg, S. M., & Robinson, E. A. (1982). Parent-child interaction training: Effects of family functioning. *Journal of Clinical Child Psychology, 11,* 130–137.

Eyberg, S. M., & Robinson, E. A. (1983a). Conduct problem behavior: Standardization of a behavioral rating scale with adolescents. *Journal of Clinical Child Psychology, 12,* 347–354.

Eyberg, S. M., & Robinson, E. A. (1983b). Dyadic Parent-child Interaction Coding System: A manual. *Psychological Documents, 13,* 24 (No. 2582).

Eyberg, S. M., & Ross, A. W. (1978). Assessment of child behavior problems: The validation of a new inventory. *Journal of Clinical Child Psychology, 7,* 113–116.

Farrington, D. P. (1978). The family backgrounds of aggressive youths. In L. A. Hersov, M. Berger, & D. Shaffer (Ed.), *Aggression and anti-social behaviour in childhood and adolescence.* Oxford: Pergamon Press.

Farrington, D. P. (1984). Measuring the natural history of delinquency and crime. In R. A. Glow (Ed.), *Advances in the behavioral measurement of children* (Vol. 1). Greenwich, CT: JAI Press.

Finch, Jr., A. J., & Eastman, E. S. (1983). A multimethod approach to measuring anger in children. *Journal of Psychology, 55–60.*

Forehand, R., Lautenschlager, G. J., Faust, J., & Graziano, W. G. (1986). Parent perceptions and parent-child interactions in clinic-referred children: A preliminary investigation of the effects of maternal depressive moods. *Behaviour Research and Therapy, 24,* 73–75.

Forehand, R., & McMahon, R. J. (1981). *Helping the noncompliant child: A clinician's guide to parent training.* New York: Guilford Press.

Freedman, B. J., Rosenthal, L., Donahoe, C. P., Schlundt, D. G., & McFall, R. (1978). A social-behavioral analysis of skills deficits in delinquent and nondelinquent adolescent boys. *Journal of Consulting and Clinical Psychology, 46,* 1448–1462.

Funderburk, B. W., & Eyberg, S. M. (1989). Psychometric characteristics of the Sutter-Eyberg Student Behavior Inventory: A school behavior rating scale for use with preschool children. *Behavioral Assessment, 11,* 297–313.

Funderburk, B. W., Eyberg, S. M., & Behar, L. (1989, August). *Psychometric properties of the SESBI with high-SES Preschoolers.* Presented at the Meeting of the American Psychological Association, New Orleans, LA.

Gaffney, L. R., & McFall, R. M. (1981). A comparison of social skills in delinquent and nondelinquent adolescent girls using a behavioral role-playing inventory. *Journal of Consulting and Clinical Psychology, 49,* 959–967.

Gittelman, R. (1980). The role of psychological tests for differential diagnosis in child psychiatry. *Journal of the American Academy of Child Psychiatry, 19,* 413–438.

Glueck, S., & Glueck, E. (1950). *Unravelling juvenile delinquency.* Cambridge, MA: Harvard University Press.

Glueck, S., & Glueck, E. (1968). *Delinquents and nondelinquents in perspective.* Cambridge, MA: Harvard University Press.

Goldstein, H. S. (1984). Parental composition, supervision, and conduct problems in youths 12 to 17 years old. *Journal of the American Academy of Child Psychiatry, 23,* 679–684.

Groot, M., & Prins, P. (1989). Children's social behavior: Reliability and concurrent validity of two self-report measures. *Journal of Psychopathology and Behavioral Assessment, 11,* 195–207.

Hanson, C. L., Henggeler, S. W., Haefele, W. F., & Rodick, J. D. (1984). Demographic, individual, and family relationship correlates of serious and repeated crime among adolescents and their siblings. *Journal of Consulting and Clinical Psychology, 52,* 528–538.

Herjanic, B., & Reich, W. (1982). Development of a structured psychiatric interview for children: Agreement between child and parent on individual symptoms. *Journal of Abnormal Child Psychology, 10,* 307–324.

Hetherington, E. M., & Martin, B. (1979). Family interaction. In H. C. Quay & J. S. Werry (Eds.), *Psychopathological disorders of childhood* (2nd ed.). New York: John Wiley & Sons.

Huesmann, L. R., Eron, L. D., Lefkowitz, M. M., & Walder, L. O. (1984). Stability of aggression over time and generations. *Developmental Psychology, 20,* 1120–1134.

Huesmann, L. R., Lefkowitz, M. M., Eron, L. D. (1978). Sum of MMPI Scales F, 4, and 9 as a measure of aggression. *Journal of Consulting and Clinical Psychology, 46,* 1071–1078.

Kanfer, F. H., & Saslow, G. (1969). Behavioral diagnosis. In C. M. Franks (Ed.). *Behavior therapy: Appraisal and status* (pp. 417–444). New York: McGraw-Hill.

Kazdin, A. E. (1985). *Treatment of antisocial behavior in children and adolescents.* Homewood, IL: Dorsey Press.

Kazdin, A. E. (1987). *Conduct disorder in childhood and adolescence.* Newbury Park, CA: Sage Publications.

Kazdin, A. E. (1989a). *Behavior modification in applied settings* (4th ed.). Pacific Grove, CA: Brooks/Cole.

Kazdin, A. E. (1989b). Hospitalization of antisocial children: Clinical course, follow-up status, and predictors of outcome. *Advances in Behaviour Research and Therapy, 11,* 1–67.

Kazdin, A. E., & Bass, D. (1988). Parent, teacher, and hospital staff evaluations of severely disturbed children. *American Journal of Orthopsychiatry, 58,* 512–523.

Kazdin, A. E., Bass, D., Siegel, T., & Thomas, C. (1989). Cognitive-behavioral treatment and relationship therapy in the treatment of children referred for antisocial behavior. *Journal of Consulting and Clinical Psychology, 57,* 522–535.

Kazdin, A. E., & Esveldt-Dawson, K. (1986). The Interview for Antisocial Behavior: Psychometric characteristics and concurrent validity with child psychiatric inpatients. *Journal of Psychopathology and Behavioral Assessment, 8,* 289–303.

Kazdin, A. E., Esveldt-Dawson, K., French, N. H., & Unis, A. S. (1987). Problem-solving skills training and relationship therapy in the treatment of antisocial child behavior. *Journal of Consulting and Clinical Psychology, 55,* 76–85.

Kazdin, A. E., Esveldt-Dawson, K., Unis, A. S., & Rancurello, M. D. (1983). Child and parent evaluations of depression and aggression in psychiatric inpatient children. *Journal of Abnormal Child Psychology, 11,* 401–413.

Kazdin, A. E., French, N. H., & Unis, A. S. (1983). Child,

mother, and father evaluations of depression in psychiatric inpatient children. *Journal of Abnormal Child Psychology, 11,* 167–180.

Kazdin, A. E., French, N. H., Unis, A. S., & Esveldt-Dawson, K. (1983). Assessment of childhood depression: Correspondence of child and parent ratings. *Journal of the American Academy of Child Psychiatry, 22,* 157–164.

Kazdin, A. E., Rodgers, A., Colbus, D., & Siegel, T. (1987). Children's Hostility Inventory: Measurement of aggression and hostility in psychiatric inpatient children. *Journal of Clinical Child Psychology, 16,* 320–328.

Kendall, P. C., & Braswell, L. (1985). *Cognitive-behavioral therapy for impulsive children.* New York: Guilford Press.

Kirigin, K. A., Braukmann, C. J., Atwater, J. D., & Wolf, M. M. (1982). An evaluation of teaching-family (Achievement Place) group homes for juvenile offenders. *Journal of Applied Behavior Analysis, 15,* 1–16.

Koppitz, E. M. (1966). Emotional indicators on human figure drawings of shy and aggressive children. *Journal of Clinical Psychology, 22,* 466–469.

Kulik, J. A., Stein, K. B., & Sarbin, T. R. (1968). Dimensions and patterns of adolescent antisocial behavior. *Journal of Consulting and Clinical Psychology, 32,* 375–382.

Ladish, C., Sosna, T. D., Warner, D., & Burns, G. L. (1989, August). *Psychometric properties of the Sutter-Eyberg Student Behavior Inventory in a preschool sample.* Presented at the Meeting of the American Psychological Association, New Orleans, LA.

Ledingham, J. E., & Schwartzman, A. E. (1984). A 3-year follow-up of aggressive and withdrawn behavior in childhood: Preliminary findings. *Journal of Abnormal Child Psychology, 12,* 157–168.

Lefkowitz, M. M., Eron, L. D., Walder, L. O., & Huesmann, L. R. (1977). *Growing up to be violent: A longitudinal study of the development of aggression.* New York: Pergamon Press.

Lessing, E. E., Williams, V., & Revelle, W. (1981). Parallel forms of the IJR Behavior Checklist for parents, teachers, and clinicians. *Journal of Consulting and Clinical Psychology, 49,* 34–50.

Lewis, D. O., Shanok, S. S., Pincus, J. H., & Glaser, G. H. (1979). Violent juvenile delinquents: Psychiatric, neurological, psychological, and abuse factors. *Journal of the American Academy of Child Psychiatry, 18,* 307–319.

Lochman, J. E. (1984) Psychological characteristics and assessment of aggressive adolescents. In C. Keith (Ed.), *The aggressive adolescent: A clinical perspective* (pp. 17–62). New York: Free Press.

Lochman, J. E., & Lampron, L. B. (1985). The usefulness of peer ratings of aggression and social acceptance in the identification of behavioral and subjective difficulties in aggressive boys. *Journal of Applied Developmental Psychology, 6,* 187–198.

Loeber, R., & Dishion, T. J. (1983). Early predictors of male delinquency: A review. *Psychological Bulletin, 94,* 68–99.

McCord, W., McCord, J., & Howard, A. (1961). Familial correlates of aggression in nondelinquent male children. *Journal of Abnormal and Social Psychology, 62,* 79–93.

McCord, W., McCord, J., & Zola, I. K. (1959). *Origins of crime.* New York: Columbia University Press.

MacFarlane, J. W., Allen, L., & Honzik, M. P. (1954). *A developmental study of the behavior problems of normal children between 21 months and 14 years.* Berkeley, CA: University of California Press.

McMahon, R. J., & Forehand, R. (1988). Conduct disorders. In E. J. Mash & L. G. Terdal (Eds.), *Behavioral assessment of childhood disorders* (2nd ed., pp. 105–153). New York: Guilford Press.

Mash, E. J., & Johnston, C. (1983). Parental perceptions of child behavior problems, parenting self-esteem, and mothers' reported stress in younger and older hyperactive and normal children. *Journal of Consulting and Clinical Psychology, 51,* 86–99.

Miller, L. C. (1972). School Behavior Checklist: An inventory of deviant behavior for elementary school children. *Journal of Consulting and Clinical Psychology, 38,* 138–144.

Miller, L. C. (1977). *School Behavior Checklist manual.* Los Angeles: Western Psychological Services.

Miller, L. C. (1984). *Louisville Behavior checklist manual.* Los Angeles: Western Psychological Services.

Offord, D. R., Jones, M. B., Graham, A., Poushinsky, M., Stenerson, P., Stenerson, P., & Weaver, L. (1985). *Community skill-development programs for children: Rationale and steps in implementation.* Canada: Canadian Parks and Recreation Program.

Orvaschel, H., Puig-Antich, J. Chambers, W. J., Tabrizi, M. A., & Johnson, R. (1982). Retrospective assessment of prepubertal major depression with the Kiddie-SADS-E. *Journal of the American Academy of Child Psychiatry, 21,* 392–397.

Ostrov, E., Marohn, R. C., Offer, D., Curtiss, G., & Feczko, M. (1980). The Adolescent Antisocial Behavior Check List. *Journal of Clinical Psychology, 36,* 594–601.

Patterson, G. R. (1982). *Coercive family process.* Eugene, OR: Castalia.

Patterson, G. R., Reid, J. B., Jones, R. R., & Conger, R. W. (1975). *A social learning approach to family intervention* (Vol. 1). Eugee, OR: Castalia.

Pekarik, E. G., Prinz, R. J., Liebert, D. E., Weintraub, S., & Neale, J. M. (1976). The Pupil Evaluation Inventory: A sociometric technique for assessing children's social behavior. *Journal of Abnormal Child Psychology, 4,* 83–97.

Purcell, K. (1956). The TAT and antisocial behavior. *Journal of Consulting Psychology, 20,* 449–456.

Quay, H. C. (1986). Conduct disorders. In H. C. Quay & J. S. Werry (Eds.), *Psychopathological disorders of child-*

hood (3rd ed., pp. 35–72). New York: John Wiley & Sons.

Quay, H. C., & Peterson, D. R. (1983). *Interim manual for the Revised Behavior Problem Checklist,* Unpublished manuscript. University of Miami, Coral Gables, FL.

Reid, J. B. (Ed.). (1978). *A social learning approach to family intervention* (Vol. 2), *Observation in home settings.* Eugene, OR: Castalia Press.

Reid, J. B., Baldwin, D. V., Patterson, G. R., & Dishion, T. J. (1988). Observations in the assessment of childhood disorders. In M. Rutter, A. H. Tuma, & I. S. Lann (Eds.), *Assessment and diagnosis in child psychopathology* (pp. 156–195). New York: Guilford Press.

Reynolds, W. M., Anderson, G., & Bartell, N. (1985). Measuring depression in children: A multi-method assessment investigation. *Journal of Abnormal Child Psychology, 13,* 513–526.

Robins, L. N. (1966). *Deviant children grown up.* Baltimore: Williams & Wilkins.

Robinson, E. A., Eyberg, S. M., & Ross, A. W. (1980). The standardization of an inventory of child conduct problem behaviors. *Journal of Clinical Child Psychology, 9,* 22–28.

Rutter, M., & Giller, H. (1983). *Juvenile delinquency: Trends and perspectives.* New York: Penguin Books.

Rutter, M., Tizard, J., & Whitmore, K. (Eds.). (1970). *Education, health and behaviour.* London: Longmans.

Schaughency, E. A., Hurley, L. K., Yano, K. E., Seeley, J., & Talarico, B. (1989, August). *Psychometric properties of the SESBI with clinic-referred children.* Presented at the Meeting of the American Psychological Association, New Orleans, LA.

Sturge, C. (1982). Reading retardation and antisocial behaviour. *Journal of Child Psychology and Psychiatry, 23* 21–31.

Tremblay, R. E., LeBlanc, M., & Schwartzmann, A. (1988). The predictive power of first-grade peer and teacher ratings of behavior: Sex differences in antisocial behavior and personality at adolescents. *Journal of Abnormal Child Psychology, 16,* 571–583.

Wadsworth, M. (1979). *Roots of delinquency: Infancy, adolescence and crime.* New York: Barnes & Noble.

Wahler, R. G., & Dumas, J. E. (1986). Maintenance factors in coercive mother-child interactions: The compliance and predictability hypotheses. *Journal of Applied Behavior Analysis, 19,* 13–22.

Wahler, R. G., House, A. E., & Stambaugh, E. E. (1976). *Ecological assessment of child problem behavior: A clinical package for home, school, and institutional settings.* New York: Pergamon Press.

Webster-Stratton, C., Kolpacoff, M., & Hollinsworth, T. (1988). Self-administered videotape therapy for families with conduct problem children: Comparison with two cost-effective treatments and a control group. *Journal of Consulting and Clinical Psychology, 57,* 558–566.

West, D. J. (1982). *Delinquency: Its roots, careers and prospects.* Cambridge, MA: Harvard University Press.

West, D. J., & Farrington, D. P. (1973). *Who becomes delinquent?* London: Heinemann Educational Books.

Williams, J. R., & Gold, M. (1972). From delinquent behavior to official delinquency. *Social Problems, 20,* 209–229.

Wilson, H. (1980). Parental supervision: A neglected aspect of delinquency. *British Journal of Criminology, 20,* 203–235.

Wirt, R. D., Lachar, D., Klinedinst, J. K., & Seat, P. D. (1977). *Multidimensional description of child personality: A manual for the Personality Inventory for Children.* Los Angeles: Western Psychological Services.

Wolfe, V. V., Finch, A. J. Jr., Saylor, C. F., Blount, R. L., Pallmeyer, T. P., & Carek, D. J. (1987). Negative affectivity in children: A multitrait-multimethod investigation. *Journal of Consulting and Clinical Psychology, 55,* 245–250.

CHAPTER 20

TICS AND TOURETTE'S DISORDER

Floyd R. Sallee

DESCRIPTION OF THE DISORDER

Tics are the most common movement disorder of childhood. The prevalence of tics is estimated at 5% to 18% of school-age children between the ages of 6 and 16 (Achenbach & Edelbrock, 1981; Lapouse & Monk, 1964; Rutter, Yule, Berger, Yule, Morton, & Bagley 1974). The task of the clinician is to determine when tics are likely to be self-limited, as in transient tic disorder, or part of a more progressive and debilitating syndrome. Tourette's disorder, commonly called Tourette's syndrome (TS), is a severe form of tic disorder, characterized by involuntary movements (motor tics) and involuntary vocalizations (phonic tics). Frequently the signs and symptoms of TS range from infrequent movements and sounds that are barely detectable or easily camouflaged to dramatic and disabling tic symptoms. Patients frequently consciously try to suppress their tic symptoms and can do so for a period of a few minutes to a few hours. This makes the assessment of tic symptoms in these patients a challenge. Once considered a rare disorder, new evidence from population studies indicate that prevalence of TS in children under age 17 is approximately 3 per 10,000 (Caine, McBride, Chiverton, Bamford, Rediess & Shiao, 1988; King & Ollendick, 1984). Principal features of TS are the presence of repetitive motor and phonic tics, although behavioral and mental symptoms frequently are present and perhaps are etiologically related. Associated symptoms include obsessive thoughts and compulsive behaviors, irritability and mood lability, attentional problems, impulsivity, motor hyperactivity, and specific learning disabilities. These associated features are frequently found in those children referred for clinical evaluation. Comprehensive evaluation of suspected TS in patients should include both a complete neurological and psychiatric examination, with more specialized assessments for those patients with associated features. No pathophysiologic factors have yet been identified in the etiology of TS, although genetic factors may play a role in a subset of patients suffering from TS (Pauls & Leckman, 1986). There is no definitive diagnostic test other than a careful clinical evaluation with diagnosis based solely on observable signs and symptoms.

Tic Phenomenology

Tics are sudden, repetitive, stereotyped movements that are brief and rapid and may involve multiple muscle groups. Tics occur at random intervals and can be voluntarily suppressed for varying periods of time. Some patients describe premonitory sensory urges for which tics are voluntarily performed to relieve the urge. Tics in general tend to be exacerbated by several factors, including stress, fatigue, or underlying medical illness. Tics can also be triggered by environmental stimuli and over varying periods of time wax and wane in severity and change anatomical location.

Clinical characteristics of Tourette's disorder described in patients from around the world have shown concurrence in age of onset, male-to-female ratio, and tic symptom spectrum. Typical age on onset is 7 years, with eye tics being the most common first symptom (eye rolling, eye blinking, or wide eye opening) in 20% to 53% of patients (Bruun, 1988a&b; Nomura & Segawa, 1982). Next most common tics are reported as either facial (grimacing, nose twitching, or licking movements) or vocal tics (sniffing, throat clearing, grunting, or coughing). Vocal tics often lead to investigations for allergy, upper respiratory infections, sinusitis, or other ENT abnormalities. Whole body tics such as body rocking, pelvic thrusting, shutters, or diaphragmatic tics may also be encountered in a significant number of patients (Lees, Robertson, Trimble, & Murray, 1984). Coprolalia is the most dramatic of the vocal tics. It is the spontaneous interruption of speech flow with various obscenities with no obvious provoking cause. Coprolalia is not necessary for the diagnosis of Tourette's disorder, nor is it pathognomonic, as it can be present in other neurological disorders. Other unusual symptoms of copropraxia, echolalia, or echopraxia are present in most patient series with varying frequency. Self-abusive tics such as hitting oneself or lip biting (significant enough to inflict damage) are present in 5% to 13% of patients (Comings & Comings, 1985; Bruun, 1988a&b). Complicated movements or unusual repetitive behaviors, such as touching of objects or body parts or smelling of hands or of objects, can take on a compulsive quality as patients often report an internal driven quality to perform these behaviors. Symptoms do tend to progress in TS as the patient enters adolescence, with amelioration of symptoms in late adolescence or adult life (Erenberg, Cruse, Rothner, & Rothner, 1987).

Associated Psychiatric Symptomatology

Psychiatric and learning disorders have been seen in association with Tourette's disorder with attention deficit disorder, hyperactivity disorder (ADHD) and obsessive-compulsive disorder (OCD) being most frequently encountered. Comings & Comings (1984, 1985) report that in 250 cases of TS, ADHD is present in 54%. In the more severely disordered TS patients, the incidence of concurrent ADHD increases to 70%–80%. Even in very mild cases of Tourette's disorder, the incidence of ADHD is 7 to 8 times that of the general population. Learning disabilities have been suggested in a large proportion of patients, but it is undetermined whether these exist in the absence of ADHD. Hagin and Kugler (1988) report a series of Tourette-disordered patients that have lower-than-expected school achievement in mathematics and reading comprehension. Frankel, Cummings, Robertson, Trimble, Hill, and Benson (1986) found an incidence of OCD in adult Tourette-disordered patients of 51%, using an inventory derived from the Leyton Obsessional Inventory (LOI) (Cooper, 1970). An epidemiologic study of 431 patients diagnosed with Tourette's disorder commissioned by the Ohio Tourette's Syndrome Association found a point prevalence of 74% for OCD at sometime during their illness (Stefl, 1983). In children, Grad, Pelcovitz, Olson, Matthews, and Grad (1987) found that 7 of 25 patients with average age of 11.1 years met criteria for OCD based on the child version of the LOI (Berg, Rapoport, & Flament, 1986). Stefl (1983) found a high incidence of aggression, hostility, and depression in a sample of Tourette's patients in addition to obsessive-compulsive behavior.

DSM-III-R Diagnosis

Transient tic disorder is a disorder of childhood in which stress is said to play a predominant role in the etiology. The main characteristic that separates transient tics from TS is the duration criteria that tics should persist for no longer than 12 consecutive months. In some children, transient tics may recur over several years, but tics tend to be mild and not to persist for longer than a few weeks or months. Chronic motor or vocal tic disorder is stable in its symptomatology with tics that persist either in the same anatomic location or with the same phenomenology. Patients display either vocal or motor tics, but not both, and limited motor tics are by far more common. Family studies suggest that this disorder is 2 to 3 times more prevalent than TS (Comings, Comings, Devor, & Cloninger, 1984). Family genetic studies support an etiologic relationship between chronic motor tic disorder and TS (Pauls, Kruger, Leckman, Cohen, & Kidd, 1984; Pauls & Leckman, 1986).

A diagnosis of Tourette's disorder is clearly delineated in the DSM-III-R diagnostic criteria, but assessment of the durational criteria is sometimes difficult. Both multiple motor and one or more vocal tics must be present for some time during the illness, although not necessarily concurrently, and tics must occur many times per day, nearly every day, or intermittently throughout a period of more than 1 year. The anatomic location number, frequency, and complexity of tics are noted to change over time, and the onset must be before age 21. Furthermore, the occurrence of tics should not be exclusively during psychoactive substance intoxication or as a result of known central nervous system disease such as Huntington's chorea or postviral encephalitis (see Table 20-1).

MULTIMODAL ASSESSMENT

Tics are difficult to objectively quantify reliably because of their heterogeneous presentation (simple eye blinks and grunts must be measured along with copropraxia and coprolalia). Complicating assessment is the tendency for symptoms to wax and wane irrespective of treatments of interventions. Can the clinician be sure that this month's shoulder shrug is equivalent to last week's grunt? Presence of partial volitional control and the tendency in most patients to suppress tics when observed, post additional obstacles to assessment of symptoms. Goetz, Tanner, Wilson, and Shannon (1987a) found that in the 30 patients studied, motor tics recorded with the examiner present is 27% of that recorded in the absence of an examiner. For seven of these patients with flagrant tics, no observable tics were noted with the examiner present.

Clinical Interview

The anatomical location, number, frequency, intensity, complexity, and degree of disruption associated with motor and phonic tics should be documented by the clinician. The age of onset should be noted along with associated stressors and toxic insults such as stimulant medications. Clinicians should delineate the course of tics over the past year and over the past several months prior to presentation. Assessment should substantiate clinical waxing and waning of the disorder, duration of severe tic symptoms, and factors associated with exacerbation or improvement. Does the patient recognize sensory urges or mental phenomena associated with tics? Do external stimuli provoke or trigger tic symptoms? What impact on the individual's self-esteem, social adaptation, or academic performance do tic symptoms have? Finally, an assess-

Table 20-1. Etiology of Tics

IDIOPATHIC
Transient tic disorder
Chronic motor or vocal tic disorder
Tourette's disorder
"SECONDARY" TICS
Postencephalitic
Postrheumatic chorea
Head injury
Carbon monoxide poisoning
Neuroacanthocytosis
Drug-induced (stimulants, levodopa, neuroleptics ("tardive Tourette"), carbamazepine, phenytoin, phenobarb)

ment should be made of risk to self-injury as a result of the presence of tics. Such findings will serve as a record of tic symptom severity at the time of initial presentation and for documentation of impairment associated with motor and phonic tic phenomena. Associated behavioral phenomenon should be assessed in addition to tics. These include the presence or absence of obsessive-compulsive symptoms and behaviors such as simple rituals, and full-fledged OCD. Does the patient have attentional problems, mood lability, or irritability, and is an affective disturbance also present? How does the patient get along with family and friends? What is his or her premorbid history and adjustment before tic onset? What are the life events associated with onset and exacerbation of tic symptoms, stability of family life, coping skills, and social support available to the patient? A genetic family history should be taken about other relatives or family members who have unusual movement problems or obsessive-compulsive behaviors. Finally, past medical or developmental history that may be relevant to the presence of tics, such as prenatal birth history, developmental delays, medication exposures, and injuries. If the patient has not had a thorough neurologic exam prior to presentation, this should be done with an assessment of soft neurologic signs and presence or absence of EEG abnormalities or brain structural problems. If the patient has been on medication for tic symptoms, note response to medication, adequate length of trials, and exacerbation due to medication treatment. In addition, assessment of school status and presence or absence of learning disabilities and adequacy of school placement is pertinent.

Neurologic Examination

Motor tics are very characteristic and rarely confused with other forms of hyperkinetic movement disorders. Both clonic and tonic tics occur, but most often tics are brief and are of the clonic variety. Clonic tics can sometimes be confused with myoclonus and chorea. Tonic tics may be confused with dystonic movements. Buccal-lingual tics can be problematic in TS patients who have been exposed to neuroleptics, as it is difficult to readily distinguish these movements from neuroleptic-induced dyskinesias. Tics often involve ocular movements that are rare in other types of dyskinesias. Characteristics of abruptness, suppressibility, and the influence of stress or relaxation on movements should help the clinician make the determination that a tic is present. Most other dyskinesias are continuous and not abrupt and cannot be readily suppressed for long time periods. Stress can exacerbate tics as well as other dyskinesias; however, tics are characteristically increased during periods of relaxation as well. A careful neurologic workup should be done so as not to miss metabolic conditions or Wilson's disease, which may produce tremors that can be confused with tics.

Upon neurologic examination, minor motor asymmetries (e.g., unilateral impairment of rapid alternating movements, increased tone on one side) are found in half of TS patients (Sweet, Solomon, Wayne, Shapiro, & Shapiro, 1973). In 12% to 38% of patients, EEG abnormalities exist but they are rarely epileptiform and are most often reported as nonspecific slowing (Bergen, Tanner, & Wilson, 1982). Neuroimaging of TS patients has also been nonspecific with reports of asymmetrical lateral ventricles or prominent cortical sulci (Caparulo, Cohen, Rothman, Young, Katz, Shaywitz, & Shaywitz, 1981; Lees et al., 1984). At present, in the absence of localizing findings on neurologic examination, an EEG and CT scan are not routinely performed in the evaluation of TS.

Assessment Instruments

Assessment tools are critical in the evaluation of TS. In clinical practice, these instruments document the course of illness and monitor the waxing and waning of symptoms in treatment. These assessment tools were initially developed for research strategies to determine outcome in drug treatment studies (Goetz, Tanner, Wilson, Carroll, Como, & Shannon, 1987b; Leckman, Walkup, Riddle, & Cohen, 1987) or to do epidemiological research (Stefl, 1983). The two strategies presently employed to quantitate tic symptoms in an objective fashion rely either on the microanalysis of a timed sample of tic behavior, as in the method of Shapiro and Shapiro (1984) or Tanner, Goetz, & Klawans (1982), or by the use of subjective clinical ratings after review of a patient's symptoms and history (Harcherick, Leckman, Detlor, & Cohen, 1984). The reader is referred to two excellent reviews of the rating scales used in TS assessment that are described here briefly (Leckman, Towbin, Ort, & Cohen, 1988; Shapiro, Shapiro, Young, & Feinberg, 1988). Unfortunately, many of the rating scales currently employed in research settings are cumbersome and not easily adapted to clinical practice. Furthermore, the various assessment tools do not have widespread use across centers, so validation across centers and in different clinical settings has not been done.

Parental and Self-Reports

Systematic collection of self-report data was the first strategy employed in the assessment of TS. While patients and their parents may be unskilled at detecting tics, they have an advantage over the clinician of frequent samplings across multiple settings. Structured parental and self-report instruments have been used in epidemiologic, genetic, and longitudinal studies. The Tourette's Syndrome Questionnaire (TSQ) (Jagger, Prusoff, Cohen, Kidd, Carbonari, & John, 1982) systematically obtains historical information such as developmental history, course of tic behavior, and effect of TS on the individual. The Tourette's Syndrome Symptom List (Cohen, Leckman, & Shaywitz, 1984) quantitates daily and weekly ratings of tic behaviors by asking the respondent to identify and estimate the frequency and disruption of tics and associated behavioral symptoms. Adjunctive symptoms of inattention, impulsivity, and motoric hyperactivity are best delineated by relevant scales such as the Conners Parent Questionnaire (Goyette, Conners, & Ulrich, 1978) or Child Behavior Checklist and Profile (Achenbach & Edelbrock, 1983). Obsessive-compulsive symptoms can be quantitated on the Leyton Obsessional Inventory-Child Version (Berg et al., 1986).

Clinician Observer Assessment

Clinician observer methods employ the skill of the clinician to determine the nuances of tic symptoms and can, with varying degrees of success, ask for a judgment concerning impairment as a result of the tics noted. The Tourette's Symptom Severity Scale (TSSS) developed by Shapiro and Shapiro (1984) and the Tourette's Syndrome Global Scale (TSGS) (Harcherick et al., 1984) are examples of this approach. The TSSS asks the clinician five questions: How many tics are there? Are the tics noticeable to others? Do the tics elicit comments? Is the patient considered odd or bizarre? Do the tics interfere with functioning? The ratings for the five items are summed, resulting in a single score for severity. This severity rating correlates well with tic counts done by trained clinicians ($r = 0.61$), and with global ratings of clinical improvement (0.72), with good test-retest reliability (Shapiro & Shapiro, 1984). The TSSS has a reported internal consistency reliability of 0.82, but interrater reliabilities are unreported. Most recently the TSSS has been used to evaluate potent pharmacologic treatments such as pimozide and haloperidol (Shapiro et al., 1989).

The TSGS is a multidimensional scale not only of TS symptoms, but of behavioral symptoms as well, while incorporating a social functioning determination. There are eight rated dimensions that are summed into an overall global score. The scale ranges from 0 (no symptoms) to 100 (severe nonstop incapacitating TS symptoms). The TSGS has a tic domain with four dimensions (simple motor tics, complex motor tics, simple phonic tics, complex phonic tics) and a social functioning domain with three dimensions (behavioral problems, motor restlessness, school or occupational dysfunctioning). Because of the two domains and the scoring properties, the TSGS potentially can weight the social and behavioral scales out of proportion to the tic symptom scales (Harcherick et al., 1984). Using this scale, one can have the same score whether tics are relatively mild but behavior and school functioning severely impaired (perhaps due to concomitant ADHD) as a patient with good school functioning but severe motor tics and coprolalia. Internal consistency in the tic symptom dimension is good (intraclass correlation = 0.71) and agreement of raters in the global score is excellent ($r = 0.89$) despite the wide diversity of symptom dimensions. The global severity as measured by the TSGS has been compared to ratings on the Children's Global Assessment Scale (CGAS) (Shaffer, Gould, Brasic, Ambrosini, Fisher, Bird, & Aluwahlia, 1983) and the TSSS with interclass correlations across raters above 0.76 (Leckman, Towbin, Ort, & Cohen, 1988).

Recently a new clinician-rated scale of tic severity, the Yale Global Tic Severity Scale (YGTSS), has been developed (Leckman et al., 1989) The YGTSS provides an evaluation of the number, frequency, intensity, complexity and interference of motor and phonic symptoms. This semistructured interview gathers information on the specific character and anatomical location of tics during the course of a 1-week interval before assessment, then the clinician is asked to rate the severity of the tics along five separate dimensions. The YGTSS is a second-generation instrument derived from the earlier TSGS but focuses only on tic behaviors without attempting to assess a broader range of maladaptive behaviors or academic performance. The YGTSS has two subscale scores of motor and phonic tics, which are shown to be internally consistent. Moreover, factor analyses have shown that the items of the YGTSS can be recombined into categories that were identical to the a priori motor and phonic subscales. The scale has demonstrated good to excellent interrater reliability except for motor tic intensity measures. There is close agreement between the TGTSS and the TSGS and the TS-CGI and Shapiro's TSSS scales but not with the ADHD-CGI.

Videotaped Assessment

Goetz et al. (1987a) have developed a videotape rating scale that could be adapted clinically for routine assessment of tic symptoms. The advantage of such a method is that it obviates the subjective quantification of symptoms and can provide an objective measure of severity. Their method utilizes short, videotaped recordings and measures five tic variables including number of body areas affected, frequency of motor tics and vocalizations, and severity of motor tics and vocalizations. Scores for motor tics (body area, frequency, severity) showed significant intercorrelation as did scores for vocal tics, but much weaker correlations exist between motor and vocal tics. The scale has been tested for interrater reliability and temporal stability and correlates well with global clinical scales used to assess changes over prolonged time periods. Moderate correlation was found by Goetz et al. (1987a) between their motor scores and that of the motor subscale of the subjective TSGS rating scale. The videotaped ratings accurately detected improvement in tic symptoms with neuroleptic treatment, suggesting that this method could be used to follow patients in therapy. The videotaped method has been used by Goetz et al. (1987b) to follow clinical treatment outcome in a study of clonidine treatment of Tourette disorder. Drawbacks to videotaping include the need for expensive and cumbersome equipment and the need to edit tapes so that scoring can be unbiased. The videotaped ratings seem least adaptable to a clinical setting where "blind" and unbiased review frequently cannot be obtained.

Assessment tools that are quick and reliable with broad general applicability across clinical settings are needed in the management of TS. Recently, an attempt has been made to integrate several strategies and rating scales into a single "Unified Rating Scale" (TSURS), sponsored by the Tourette Syndrome Association, Inc. The TSURS consists of six parts embracing symptom checklists, historical ratings, examiner rating, tic counts, overall impairment ratings, and a global disability rating. It is an amalgam of parts of several scales, including the YGTSS, STSS, Children's Global Assessment Scale (CGAS) (Shaffer, Gould, Brasic, Ambrosini, Fisher, Bird, & Aluwahlia, 1983) and has been empirically shown to be useful in TS assessment (Peter Como, personal communication).

CASE ILLUSTRATION

Mark is a 10-year-old white male who presents to the clinic with an 18-month history of "grunting spells." In the 3 months prior to presentation, he has experienced the onset of eye blinking and jerking of the head to the right. His parents complain of his low frustration tolerance at school and his fighting with his older brother at home. His grades normally have been superior, but in the month prior to presentation they have deteriorated. He is attending a rural elementary school and is in the fourth grade. His teacher describes him as having good peer relationships and good social adjustment, but that he appears frustrated with his schoolwork and frequently bursts into tears in the classroom. The teacher reports that she has seen few tics in the classroom. His parents state that Mark has a "short fuse" and frequently fights with his brother and calls his mother names. They report that his tics are worse when he comes home from school, and he frequently grunts continuously and shakes his head as he is relaxing watching television. He had been previously evaluated by his pediatrician who did not witness any abnormal movements in the office and who told the parents that their child was probably "nervous" and that he would "grow out of it."

Mark is the product of a normal, full-term delivery with no evidence of toxic insult or birth trauma. His development was normal, with appropriate milestones attained, and speech was apparent at age 18 months. No family history of tics is present, although father has some mild obsessive-compulsive symptomatology.

Psychoeducational assessment was performed that included a Weschsler Intelligence Scale for Children—Revised, Peabody Individual Achievement Test, Wide Range Achievement Test, Gray Oral Reading Test, Developmental Test of Visual Motor Integration, and a Slingerland Screening Test for Identifying Children with Specific Language Disability. The WISC-R revealed a full-scale IQ of 115, with both verbal and performance scores in the high average range. Academic achievement was assessed as being either at grade level or above.

Neurologic examination revealed a slightly obese child with no obvious neurological abnormality except for the presence of bilateral ocular tics with a frequency of four to five per minute and a head jerk to the right with a frequency of two per minute. No vocal tics were noted during the examination. An EEG was obtained that revealed a nonspecific dysrhythmia.

A formal tic rating scale (Tourette's Symptom Global Scale) was administered after a review of the patient's history and neurological examination and a score of 26/100 was obtained, indicating a moderate level of TS symptomatology. A Tourette's Syndrome Symptom List (TSSL) given to parents to rate the week prior to presentation at the clinic confirmed the clinician's rating of symptomatology. Additional clinical information was obtained from parents and teacher using the Child Behavior Checklist Parent and Teacher Versions (Achenbach & Edelbrock, 1983, 1986).

Mental status examination revealed an anxious and distraught 10-year-old whose self-perception was that he was going crazy: "I try to stop my habits but I can't." His thought pattern and stream of consciousness revealed no abnormality. He was not depressed. He was not hypermotoric and did not have any difficulty sustaining attention.

A diagnosis of Tourette's disorder was made and both diagnosis and prognosis were explained to the patient and family. Both patient and family were informed about treatment options and pharmacotherapy was selected as the primary treatment. Treatment was initiated with a low dose of neuroleptic, haloperidol 1 mg per day and increased over the course of several weeks to 6 mg per day. Mark's tics were controlled, resulting in a 70% reduction from baseline. Subsequent to treatment, the patient developed a severe school phobia and depression manifesting itself in sleep disturbance and social withdrawal accompanied by school failure, as he missed 83 of 180 days for the academic year. He was withdrawn from the neuroleptic, and within 2 weeks his school phobia and depression resolved, but reemergence of severe trunkal and facial tics was evident. After failure of combined treatment with antidepressant and the neuroleptic he was withdrawn from all medication and treated with clonidine 0.1 mg three times a day alone. Both tics and depressive symptoms ameliorated with clonidine treatment, and at 6-month follow-up Mark was found to be doing well at school, with minimal tic symptoms.

CASE DISCUSSION

Frequently teachers and other observers in settings associated with social consequences for the child observe no tics or reduced frequencies of tics. The same can be said of the pediatrician who reassured Mark's parents that because no tics were observed in his office, the child could not have a problem. The determination of Mark's impairment in this case rested on the use of a clinician rating scale with supporting evidence from a symptom self-report. The rating of Mark's tic impairment in the moderate range could be a function of the TSGS that factored in Mark's behavioral problems and recent poor academic performance. Assessment tools that count symptoms only or frequency of tics would miss this important aspect of impairment. Fortunately, in this case, behavioral symptoms were assessed at baseline so that when a medication trial resulted in further impairment in this dimension, it was detected. School phobia (Mikkelsen, Detlor, & Cohen, 1981; Linet, 1985) and dysphoria (Bruun, 1988) are frequent side effects of neuroleptic treatment in TS patients, and adequate pretreatment baselines covering a wide range of behavior and functioning are necessary for detection.

IMPLICATIONS FOR TREATMENT

Self-monitoring is frequently used in TS studies as a method of gathering data on tic frequency in the child's natural environment. Motor and phonic tics are most likely to occur at home in an environment where the child feels comfortable and where he is least afraid of embarrassment or ridicule. Rarely have tic counts been employed in a natural setting, and so patients are asked to use wrist counters or notebooks or to fill out daily questionnaires for a specified period of time. This procedure alone seems to reduce tic frequency. Four case study reports document this effect of self-monitoring and have used it as a treatment (Billings, 1978; Hutzell et al., 1974; Ollendick, 1981; Thomas et al., 1971). Furthermore, these improvements were shown to be maintained at 1-year follow-up (Hutzell et al., 1974; Ollendick, 1981). Therefore, careful assessment of the clinician focuses the patient's awareness and seemingly promotes an effort to diminish symptoms.

Behavioral treatments have capitalized on the very observable nature of tics and the ability of patients to control symptoms for various periods of time. Techniques of massed negative practice, contingency management, and relaxation training rely heavily on the accurate and ongoing assessment of treatment outcome documented on either direct observation or videotaping of sessions. Behavioral treatment research in this area has used within-subject designs exclusively, with no group studies to demonstrate generalizability (Azrin & Peterson, 1988). While this research approach most closely approximates the clinical situation, it has contributed to the lack of enthusiasm for behavioral treatments in favor of pharmacotherapy.

Accurate assessment of symptom severity has profound implications for treatment. A risk-benefit determination must utilize the assessment information prior to a decision to treat. This is particularly true with regard to pharmacotherapy, as neuroleptic medications are frequently employed. Pharmacological interventions are the most widely used in TS, and more than 70% of patients have a history of pharmacotherapy (Stefl, 1983). Patients who have mild symptoms or for whom tics do not constitute a major disruption of lifestyle or functioning frequently receive no intervention. Transient tic diagnoses and a substantial number of patients with chronic motor tic disorder do not receive neuroleptics. Supportive counseling and observation for these patients may be all that is needed. Neuroleptic drug treatment has many short- and long-term risks, not the least of which is the tendency to produce movement and psychiatric disorders de novo. A careful and complete assessment of associated behavioral symptomatology at the beginning of treatment will prove invaluable if the outcome of psychopharmacologic intervention is the production of increased psychopathology, as in the case illustration.

Many inherent characteristics of pharmacologic intervention with neuroleptics makes assessment critical to their judicious use and for optimal clinical results. Due to the long biologic half-life of neuroleptics, therapeutic trials are often many weeks in duration, necessitating the use of stable measures and demanding test-retest reliability. Outcome variables such as tic frequency may differ from academic achievement so that a dose of neuroleptic that is optimal for the former goal is detrimental to the latter (Shapiro, Shapiro, Young & Feinberg, 1988). Having multidimensional flexibility of ongoing assessment measures such as in the YGTSS or the TSGS is preferable to unidimensional tic counts in this regard.

Unidimensional assessment prematurely narrows the focus of treatment and overlooks the broad range of symptomatology that is characteristic of this neuropsychiatric disorder. Many patients with TS have a "short fuse" or exhibit aggression more easily with less inhibition than others. The patient feels often out of control both in a physical sense with regard to tics but also in a psychological sense with angry, hostile emotions and actions directed frequently at family members. This was illustrated in the case of "Mark," who frequently could not define the source of his frustration or anger. Tic symptoms and aggressive behaviors are frequently performed at home with the family producing guilt and anxiety in the patient and frustration in the parents. The symptoms of TS are as bewildering to the family as they are to the patient himself. The patient's ability to withhold or to control symptoms makes the appearance of symptoms seem to be a willful act. Frequently individual or family therapy is warranted to help patients and their families cope. Multimodal assessment in such complex and difficult cases can be invaluable.

The symptoms of TS are frequently perceived by the community as "bad" or rude behavior that necessitates intervention with a range of support systems in the school and community at large. Assessment of school functioning from an academic and social perspective can be a useful aid to the clinician in promoting a good treatment outcome and for defusing punitive action from school personnel for TS symptomatology.

SUMMARY

Much progress has been made over the last 5 years in the assessment of TS, primarily because of the development of reliable and repeatable measures such as the TSSS, the TSGS, and the YGTSS. The advantage of such measures is that they can be easily adapted for treatment management and for patient follow-up. The disadvantage of these global measures is that they force the examiner to integrate disparate features of the syndrome that may fluctuate widely over the assessment period of interest. Strategies to combine successful rating scales and assessment tools into a unified approach holds promise for accurate determinations of the symptomatology in TS.

The assessment of the child in the natural environment has not been a major feature of the pharmacotherapeutic research in TS. Given the tendency for symptoms to be quite variable across settings, naturalistic observational data should be included as part of the assessment procedure. From self-monitoring information, we know that the frequency of tics decreases with this approach. Research addressing the self-monitoring phenomenon may shed light on the mechanisms underlying this interaction between tic awareness and suppression.

Assessment of associated psychiatric symptoms such as obsessive-compulsive and attention deficit symptoms in patients with TS has opened the possibility that TS may be part of a larger family of disorders of which tics is one manifestation. TS appears to be genetically related to chronic motor tic disorder and possibly to OCD (Pauls & Leckman, 1986). Careful assessment of patients and their families should integrate this information with the possible goal of giving genetic counseling according to familial loading. Multigenerational family history assessment should provide a data base for more sophisticated research using genetic linkage analysis and DNA recombinant techniques (Kurlan, Behar, Medred, Shoulson, Pauls, & Kidd, 1987).

REFERENCES

Achenbach, T. M., & Edelbrock, C. S. (1981). Behavioral problems and competencies reported by parents of normal and disturbed children aged four through sixteen. *Monographs of the Society for Research in Child Development, 46.*

Achenbach, T. M., & Edelbrock, C. S. (1983). *Manual for the Revised Child Behavior Checklist and Profile.* Burlington, VT: University Associates in Psychiatry.

Achenbach, T. M., & Edelbrock, C. S. (1986). *Manual for the Teacher's Report Form and Teacher Version of the Child Behavior Profile.* Burlington, VT: University Associates in Psychiatry.

Azrin, N. H., & Peterson, A. L. (1988). Behavior therapy for Tourette's syndrome and tic disorders. In D. J. Cohen, R. D. Bruun, & J. F. Leckman (Eds.), *Tourette's Syndrome and Tic Disorders: Clinical Understanding and Treatment* (pp. 238–255). New York: John Wiley & Sons.

Berg, C. J., Rapoport, J. L., & Flament, M. F. (1986). The Leyton Obsessional Inventory-Child Version. *Journal of the American Academy of Child Psychiatry, 25,* 84–92.

Bergen, D., Tanner, C. M., & Wilson, R. (1982). The electroencephalogram in Tourette syndrome. *Annals of Neurology, 11,* 638–641.

Billings, A. (1978). Self-monitoring in the treatment of tics: A single-subject analysis. *Journal of Behavior Therapy & Experimental Psychiatry, 9,* 339–342.

Bruun, R. D. (1988a). The natural history of Tourette's Syndrome. In D. J. Cohen, R. D. Bruun, & J. F. Leckman (Eds.), *Tourette's Syndrome and Tic Disorders: Clinical understanding and treatment* (pp. 22–39). New York: John Wiley & Sons.

Bruun, R. D. (1988b). Subtle and underrecognized side effects of neuroleptic treatment in children with Tourette's disorder. *American Journal of Psychiatry, 145,* 621–624.

Caine, E. O., McBride, M. C., Chiverton, P., Bamford, K. A., Rediess, S., & Shiao, J. (1988). Tourette's syndrome in Monroe County School children. *Neurology, 38,* 472–475.

Caparulo, B. K., Cohen, D. J., Rothman, S. L., Young, D. G., Katz, J. D., Shaywitz, S. E., & Shaywitz, B. A. (1981). Computed tomographic brain scanning in children with developmental neuropsychiatric disorders. *Journal of the American Academy of Child Psychiatry, 20,* 388–357.

Cohen, D. J., Leckman, J. F., & Shaywitz, B. A. (1984). The Tourette Syndrome and other tics. In D. Shaffer, A. A. Ehrhardt, & L. Greenhill (Eds.), *The clinical guide to child psychiatry.* New York: Free Press.

Cooper, J. (1970). The Letyon obsessional inventory. *Psychological Medicine, 1,* 48–64.

Comings, D. E., & Comings, B. G. (1984). Tourette's syndrome and attention deficit disorder with hyperactivity: Are they genetically related? *Journal of the American Academy of Child Psychiatry, 23,* 138–146.

Comings, D. E., & Comings, B. G. (1985). Tourette syndrome: Clinical and psychological aspects of 250 cases. *American Journal of Human Genetics, 37,* 435–450.

Comings, D. E., Comings, B. G., Devor, E. J., & Cloninger, C. R. (1984). Detection of major gene for Gilles de la Tourette Syndrome. *American Journal of Human Genetics, 36,* 586–600.

Erenberg, G., Cruse, R. P., Rothner, D. O., & Rothner, A. D. (1987). The natural history of Tourette's syndrome: A follow-up study. *Annals of Neurology, 22,* 383–385.

Frankel, M., Cummings, J. L., Robertson, M. M., Trimble, M. R., Hill, M. A., & Benson, D. F. (1986). Obsessions and compulsions in Gilles de la Tourette's syndrome. *Neurology, 36,* 378–382.

Goetz, C. G., Tanner, C. M., Wilson, R. S., & Shannon, K. M. (1987a). A rating scale for Gilles de la Tourette's syndrome: Description, reliability, and validity data. *Neurology, 37,* 1542–1544.

Goetz, C. G., Tanner, C. M., Wilson, R. S., Carroll, V. S., Como, P. G., & Shannon, K. M. (1987b). Clonidine and Gilles de la Tourette's Syndrome: Double-Blind study using objective rating methods. *Annals of Neurology, 21,* 307–310.

Goyette, C. H., Conners, C. K., & Ulrich, R. F. (1978). Normative data on revised Conners Parent and Teacher Rating Scales. *Journal of Abnormal Child Psychology, 6,* 221–236.

Grad, L. R., Pelcovitz, D., Olson, M., Matthews, M., & Grad, G. (1987). Obsessive-compulsive symptomatology in children with Tourette's syndrome. *Journal of the American Academy of Child Psychiatry, 26,* 69–74.

Hagin, R. A., & Kugler, J. (1988). School problems associated with Tourette's syndrome. In D. J. Cohen, R. D. Bruun, & J. F. Leckman (Eds.), *Tourette's Syndrome and Tic Disorders: Clinical understanding and treatment* (pp. 224–236). New York: John Wiley & Sons.

Harcherick, D. F., Leckman, J. F., Detlor, J. & Cohen D. J. (1984). A new instrument for clinical studies of Tourette's syndrome. *Journal of the American Academy of Child Psychiatry, 23,* 153–160.

Hutzell, R. R., Platzek, D., & Logue, P. E. (1974). Control of symptoms of Gilles de la Tourette's syndrome by self-monitoring. *Journal of Behavior Therapy & Experimental Psychiatry, 5,* 71–76.

Jagger, J., Prusoff, B. A., Cohen, D. J., Kidd, K. K., Carbonari, C. M., & John, K. (1982). The epidemiology of Tourette's syndrome. *Schizophrenia Bulletin, 8,* 267–278.

King, A. C., & Ollendick, T. H. (1984). Gilles de la Tourette Disorder: A review. *Journal of Clinical Child Psychology, 13,* 2–9.

Kurlan, R., Behar, J., Medved, L., Shoulson, I., Behar, J., Pauls, D. L., & Kidd, K. K. (1987). Severity of Tourette's syndrome in one large kindred: Significance for determination of disease prevalence rate. *Archives of Neurology, 44,* 268–269.

Lapouse, T., & Monk, M. A. (1964). Behavior deviations in a representative sample of children: Variation between sex, age, race, social class, and family size. *American Journal of Orthopsychiatry, 34,* 436–446.

Leckman, J. F., Walkup, J. T., Riddle, M. A., & Cohen, D. J. (1987). Tic Disorders, In H. Y. Meltzer, W. Bunney, J. Coyle, J. David, I. Kopin, C. Schuster, R. Shader, & G. Simpson (Eds.), *Psychopharmacology, the third generation of progress.* New York: Raven Press.

Leckman, J. F., Towbin, K. E., Ort, S. I., & Cohen, D. J. (1988). Clinical assessment of tic disorder severity. In D. J. Cohen, R. D. Bruun, & J. F. Leckman (Eds.), *Tourette's Syndrome and Tic Disorders: Clinical understanding and treatment* (pp. 56–78). New York: John Wiley & Sons.

Leckman, J. F., Riddle, M. A., Hardin, M. T., Ort, S., Swartz, K. L., Stevenson, J., & Cohen, D. J. (1989). *Journal of the American Academy of Child and Adolescent Psychiatry, 28,* 566–573.

Lees, A. J., Robertson, M., Trimble, M. R., & Murray, N. M. F. (1984). A clinical study of Gilles de la Tourette's syndrome in the United Kingdom. *Journal of Neurology, Neurosurgery, and Psychiatry, 47,* 1–8.

Linet, L. S. (1985). Tourette syndrome, pimozide, and school phobia: Neuroleptic separation anxiety syndrome. *American Journal of Psychiatry, 142,* 613–615.

Mikkelsen, E. J., Detlor, J., & Cohen, D. J. (1981). School avoidance and social phobia triggered by haloperidol in patients with Tourette disorder. *American Journal of Psychiatry, 138,* 1572–1576.

Nomura, Y., & Segawa, M. (1982). Tourette syndrome in Oriental children: Clinical and pathophysiological considerations. In A. J. Friedhoff & T. N. Chase (Eds.), *Gilles de la Tourette Syndrome.* New York: Raven Press.

Ollendick, T. H. (1981). Self-monitoring and self-administered overcorrection: The modification of nervous tics in children. *Behavior Modification, 5,* 75–84.

Pauls, D. L., Kruger, S. D., Leckman, J. F., Cohen, D. J., & Kidd, K. K. (1984). The risk of Tourette Syndrome and chronic multiple tics among relatives of Tourette Syndrome patients obtained by direct interview. *Journal of the American Academy of Child Psychiatry, 23,* 134–137.

Pauls, D. L., & Leckman, J. F. (1986). The inheritance of Gilles de la Tourette syndrome and associated behaviors: Evidence for an autosomal dominant transmission. *New England Journal of Medicine, 315,* 993–997.

Rutter, M., Yule, W., Berger, M., Yule, B., Morton, J., & Bagley, C. (1974). Children of West Indian immigrants-I. Rates of behavioral deviance and psychiatric disorder. *Journal of Child Psychology & Psychiatry, 15,* 241–262.

Shaffer, D., Gould, M. S., Brasic, J., Ambrosini, P., Fisher, P., Bird, H., & Aluwahlia, S. (1983). A children's global assessment scale (CGAS). *Archives of General Psychiatry, 40,* 1228–1231.

Shapiro, A. K., & Shapiro, E. (1984). Controlled study of pimozide vs. placebo in Tourette's syndrome. *Journal of the American Academy of Child Psychiatry, 23,* 161–173.

Shapiro, A. K., Shapiro, E., Young, J. G., & Feinberg, T. E. (1988). *Gilles de la Tourette Syndrome.* New York: Raven Press.

Shapiro, E., Shapiro, A. K., Fulop, G., Hubbard, M., Mandeli, J., Nordlie, J., & Phillips, R. A. (1989). Controlled study of haloperidol, pimozide, and placebo for the treatment of Gilles de la Tourette's Syndrome. *Archives of General Psychiatry, 46,* 722–730.

Stefl, M. E. (1983). *The Ohio Tourette study.* Cincinnati: University of Cincinnati: School of Planning.

Sweet, R. D., Solomon, G. E., Wayne, H. L., Shapiro, E., & Shapiro, A. K. (1973). Neurological features of Gilles de la Tourette's syndrome. *Journal of Neurology, Neurosurgery, & Psychiatry, 36,* 1–9.

Tanner, C. M., Goetz, G. G., & Klawans, H. L. (1982). Cholinergic mechanisms in Tourette syndrome. *Neurology, 32,* 1315–1317.

Thomas, E. J., Abrams, K. S., & Johnson, J. B. (1971). Self-monitoring and reciprocal inhibition in the modification of multiple tics on Gilles de la Tourette's syndrome. *Journal of Behavior Therapy & Experimental Psychiatry, 2,* 159–171.

CHAPTER 21

MENTAL RETARDATION

Michael G. Aman
David Hammer
Johannes Rojahn

DESCRIPTION OF THE DISORDER

One point that cannot be made too forcefully is that mental retardation does not constitute a disorder or a single condition but is instead a common set of symptoms that applies to a myriad of clinical conditions. Today the most widely accepted definition of mental retardation is that put forth by the American Association on Mental Retardation and adopted by other schemes such as the third edition of The Diagnostic and Statistical Manual of Mental Disorders (DSM-III) (American Psychiatric Association, 1987) and the International Classification of Diseases, ninth revision (ICD-9) (Seltzer, 1983).

The American Association on Mental Retardation (AAMR) definition requires that a person meet three criteria to qualify as being mentally retarded (Grossman, 1983). First, a child must fall 2 or more standard deviations below the mean on one of the individually administered IQ tests. The AAMR specifically mentions the Wechsler and the Stanford Binet Scales as ideal general-purpose scales, and the Cattel, the Kuhlmann-Binet, and the Bayley infant scales as being suitable for infants or severely retarded children (Grossman, 1977).

The second component of the AAMR definition of mental retardation is that the child must show deficits in adaptive behavior relative to the standards of personal independence and social responsibility expected of him/her relative to his or her age and culture (Grossman, 1983). The AAMD Adaptive Behavior Scales (Nihira, Foster, Shellhaas, & Leland, 1974) and the Vineland Adaptive Behavior Scales (Sparrow, Balla, & Cicchetti, 1984) are the most commonly used instruments for estimating level of adaptive behavior, although clinical judgment may also play a significant role in determining level of adaptive behavior (Grossman, 1983).

Depending upon the child's age, different standards tend to be applied in assessing adaptive behavior. For example, during infancy and early childhood, sensory motor skills, communication skills, self-help skills,

---

Work on this chapter was supported by grants from the United States Office of Human Development Services (grant 07 DD 0270/16) and the Maternal and Child Health Service (Training Project 922) awarded to the Nisonger Center for Mental Retardation and Developmental Disabilities, Ohio State University.

and socialization are emphasized. During childhood and early adolescence, basic academic skills, appropriate reasoning and judgment, and social skills are stressed, and during late adolescence and adult life, vocational and social responsibilities are taken most heavily into account (Grossman, 1983). The requirement of adaptive behavior deficits in the definition tends to make the condition more exclusive. Thus, to be diagnosed as having mental retardation, a child must have an IQ that falls 2 standard deviations below the mean, *and* he or she must also show deficits in adaptive behavior. Although the demonstration of deficits in adaptive behavior is specifically required for a diagnosis of mental retardation to be applied, serious questions have been raised about the extent to which this criterion is actually observed both in clinical practice and in mental retardation research (e.g., Smith & Polloway, 1979).

The third criterion for an individual to be diagnosed as mentally retarded is that the deficits must be manifested during the developmental period, specifically by 18 years of age. It is important to note that this three-part definition (deficits in intellectual functioning and adaptive behavior, manifested during the developmental period) posits nothing about the etiology of the condition and is based solely upon description of the individual's current behavior.

It is common practice to classify persons with mental retardation in terms of degree of functional handicap, and this is determined by the number of standard deviations below the mean that the individual scores. For example, using the Wechsler scales, the various functional levels and their respective IQ scores are as follows: mild, 55–69; moderate, 40–54; severe, 25–39; and profound, 0–24 (Seltzer, 1983).

Exclusionary Criteria and Confounding Factors

There is really only one exclusionary criterion insofar as mental retardation is concerned, and that is age. If the intellectual and adaptive deficits appear after the developmental period (defined as 0 to 18 years), the condition is designated as dementia. However, there is a variety of organic and environmental factors that can greatly complicate establishing whether a child has mental retardation. For example, presence of a severe sensory impairment, such as blindness or deafness, can not only complicate the process of obtaining a legitimate estimate of IQ performance, but it may also raise the issue of whether the child had sufficient opportunity to profit from the usual learning experiences to justify comparison with norm-referenced tests. Similar issues may also arise in the case of children reared in impoverished environments. Likewise, severe emotional and behavioral disturbance may confound attempts to obtain a reliable estimate of IQ level. Finally, there have been reports of drug interference with cognitive and neurological functioning, especially with certain anticonvulsant drugs (e.g., Cordes, 1973; Logan & Freeman, 1969; Vallarta, Bell, & Reichert, 1974). Such effects may or may not be reversible, and they are particularly problematic in the case of mentally retarded individuals, because the signs and symptoms of drug intoxication (e.g., ataxia, confusion, slurred speech) may be confused with symptoms commonly encountered in this population.

Prevalence of Mental Retardation

Many workers have set the prevalence of mental retardation in the general population at approximately 3%. However, this is based on a one-dimensional conceptualization of mental retardation defined solely in terms of IQ. This figure of 3% is derived from a 2 standard deviation cutoff, and it assumes that IQ is more or less normally distributed. Given the two-criterion definition of mental retardation, most authorities have adopted a figure around 1% (see Baroff, 1986). Mercer (1973), who conducted an epidemiological study in Riverside, California, found a prevalence of 9.7 per 1,000 persons (i.e., 0.97%), who had a deficit in both adaptive behavior and IQ (defined as less than 70).

It is well known that the prevalence of mental retardation varies with age, and the highest rates are found during the school years, when the child's intellectual deficit would be expected to create the most difficulty in adapting to the demands of the classroom. It is also well established that lower socioeconomic class is associated with a higher prevalence of mental retardation. Baroff (1986) cites one study that showed that children from the lowest social class had a rate of mental retardation almost 13 times higher than children from the upper three social classes. This reflects on a major cause of mental retardation, to be discussed later, that is determined in part by the genetic pool inherited by the child but also in large part by an impoverished, hostile, and often chaotic environment.

Baroff (1983) feels that the majority of persons with moderate through profound mental retardation will require supportive services throughout much of their lives, whereas the large majority of those with mild mental retardation (IQ 55–69) will not. Based on their need for services, Baroff presents figures suggesting that approximately 50% of those administratively classified as mentally retarded will have mild mental retardation, 30% will have moderate retardation, 15% severe retardation, and 5% profound retardation.

ETIOLOGY

Introduction

The causes of mental retardation may exist singly, but often they occur as a complex interplay of biological, sociocultural, and psychological factors. Figure 21-1, taken from Garrard and Richmond (1965), depicts this situation. Experiential factors are depicted both in the sociocultural and the psychological sectors of the figure. As represented by the arrows, a given factor not only has an impact within its own domain, but it often tends to have a secondary, perpetuating effect in the adjacent domains. Indeed, psychological and sociocultural factors frequently serve as the setting events for the various biological factors to have an effect. To provide a concrete example, the impact of maternal illness (e.g., toxoplasmosis [a biological factor]) may be accentuated by reduced access to optimal health care (a socioeconomic stressor) and subsequent poor infant-maternal interactions (a psychological factor). Based on the data from numerous epidemiological population studies of risk factors, Baumeister (in press) has observed that biological causes often tend to be minor etiological factors in themselves, but, when combined with stressors from the psychological and sociocultural categories, their combined impact is usually much more serious. The

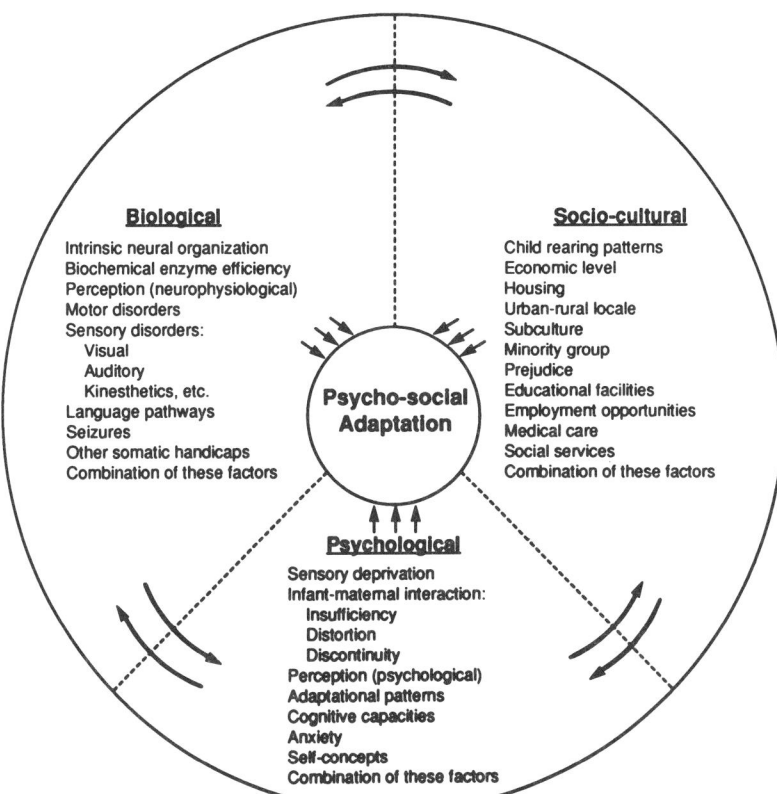

Figure 21-1. Conceptual scheme showing the impact of biological, sociocultural, and psychological influences and their interrelationships as causal factors of mental retadation. Reprinted by permission of the publisher from S. D. Garrard and J. B. Richmond (1965). Mental retardation without biological manifestations. In C. H. Carter (Ed.), *Medical aspects of mental retardation*, (pp. 32–78). Springfield, IL: Charles C. Thomas.

important thing to realize at this stage is that seldom do factors from these domains act in total isolation.

In the following pages, we attempt to review some of the better recognized specific etiological factors associated with mental retardation. In preparing this material, we relied heavily on excellent reviews by Baroff (1986), Kolb and Brodie, (1982), Oliphant, Geiger-Parker, and Gundell (1985), Szymanski and Crocker (1985), and Taft and Cohen (1977). The interested reader may wish to consult these sources for fuller discussions of individual factors. We have adopted the approach of several authors, (e.g., Kolb & Brodie, 1982) of classifying etiological factors in terms of temporal impact as follows: (a) prior to birth, (b) at the time of birth, and (c) after birth. However, although it is convenient and instructive to consider these factors singly, it is important to remember that most exert their effects in a complex matrix of forces as depicted in Figure 21-1.

Prenatal Causes

As suggested by Oliphant et al. (1985), these can be grouped as organic conditions, environmentally determined conditions, and socially determined conditions.

Organic Conditions

Genetic abnormalities. Four forms of inheritance are of interest here: namely dominant traits, recessive traits, polygenic conditions that require the presence of several different genes to produce the condition, and spontaneous mutations. To inherit a recessive disorder, the child must inherit a recessive gene from each parent. Both parents are ordinarily unaffected and the probability of any given child receiving both recessive genes is 1 in 4. Some examples of recessive genetic disorders associated with mental retardation include phenylketonuria (PKU), galactosemia, Tay-Sachs disease, Hurler syndrome, and Lesch-Nyhan syndrome. With the exception of Lesch-Nyhan syndrome, these are autosomal (non-sex-linked) disorders. Lesch-Nyhan syndrome is only manifested in males by virtue of the fact that the recessive sex-linked gene is carried on the X chromosome. Phenylketonuria is a well-understood disorder causing the deficiency of an enzyme, phenylalanine hydroxylase, which results in a marked elevation of phenylalanine and its metabolites. These are toxic to the CNS, and, if the child is not maintained on a low-phenylalanine diet, they can produce brain damage resulting in severe mental retardation, often in combination with seizures and eczema. Lesch-Nyhan syndrome is a rare disorder of purine metabolism that results in the buildup of large amounts of uric acid. Its most prominent features are mental retardation, often in association with cerebral palsy, and the presence of compulsive self-mutilative behavior.

In the case of dominant inheritance, the disorder is likely to appear in successive generations with one parent affected and with each child having a 50% chance of inheriting the condition (Baroff, 1986). Examples of disorders associated with mental retardation that are or can be transmitted by a dominant gene include tuberous sclerosis and neurofibromatosis. Tuberous sclerosis is a disorder often characterized by the presence of seizures, adenoma sebaceum (a benign neoplasm of epithelial tissue occurring on the face), white skin lesions, and mental retardation.

A number of reviews have classified such disorders of metabolism, not by mode of inheritance, but by metabolic pathway affected (e.g., Kolb & Brodie, 1982; Taft & Cohen, 1977). Among the genetic biochemical disorders associated with abnormal amino acid levels are the following: phenylketonuria, maple syrup urine disease, tyrosinemia, Hartnup disease, and isoveric acidemia. The lipid storage diseases (lipidoses) include Hurler disease, Nieman Pick disease, and Tay-Sachs disease. The disorders of carbohydrate metabolism include galactosemia and glycogen storage disease.

Polygenic inheritance refers to the *cumulative* or additive effects caused by the interaction of genes at more than one locus on the chromosome. Polygenic inheritance allows for a wide range of expression insofar as the inheritance of a trait is concerned (Baroff, 1986). Polygenic characteristics might determine a number of traits that can take on a range of values such as height or athletic ability. Likewise, within limits, intelligence has been suggested to be determined by polygenic inheritance (Baroff, 1986). In discussing this notion, Baroff introduces the concept of "reaction range," an idea that attempts to relate heredity and environment. Using this concept, polygenic inheritance is seen as placing constraints on the development of IQ, whereas the environment is seen as modifying IQ within those constraints.

Chromosomal abnormalities. This section is heavily reliant upon an excellent discussion by Baroff (1986), and the interested reader may wish to consult his text for a fuller treatment of the topic. The normal complement of chromosomes in human beings is 46, with 23 each derived from the sperm and the egg. Chromosomal abnormalities associated with mental retardation are caused by at least one chromosome, a missing chromosome, or a missing part of a chromosome. Down syndrome is the most common diagnosable form of mental retardation, occurring with a frequency of about one in 700 live births (Baroff, 1986). Three variations of Down syndrome exist. In trisomy, all cells have 47 chromosomes, there being an extra chromosome 21. This is caused by a failure of one pair of chromosomes to separate at the miotic stage of cell division, with the result that the fertilized egg has an extra, or 47th, chromosome. In translocation Down syndrome, the disorder is caused by a major portion of chromosome 21 being attached to another, usually chromosome 14. In mosaicism, some cells have the normal compliment of 46, whereas others have 47 chromosomes, and such individuals may vary from apparently unaffected to having the typical physical presentation of Down syndrome (Baroff, 1986). Baroff notes that the trisomy 21 variant accounts for about 92% of cases of Down syndrome, whereas translocations and mosaicism account for 5 and 3%, respectively. It is well established that the risk of having a Down syndrome infant increases with maternal age, the risk increasing quite markedly after the mother reaches an age in the upper 30s. The IQ levels attained in Down syndrome can differ widely.

Because of the prevalence of Down syndrome (8–10%) of mentally retarded individuals), it is worth mentioning some of the more prominent physical signs and symptoms. Down syndrome is frequently characterized by retarded growth, flatness of the face, prominent epicanthal folds (resulting in the former designation of "mongolism"), small rounded ears, fissured and thickened tongue, hypotonia, transverse crease in the palms, broad hands and feet, and defects in the heart, lungs, and eyes. The latter result in a high death rate in the first year of life, but between ages 5 and 50 years life expectancy is similar to that in the normal population. In terms of their profile of abilities, Down syndrome children appear to have greatest difficulty with speech, verbal communication, and fine motor coordination, whereas their gross motor skills are often a relative strength (Baroff, 1986).

There are also several chromosomal disorders associated with mental retardation involving extra or missing sex chromosomes. These include Klinefelter's syndrome (XXY) (in which the male offspring possesses an extra X chromosome), XYY syndrome (in which an extra Y chromosome is present), XXX syndrome (in which the female has an extra X chromosome), and Turner's syndrome (XO) (in which the affected female is missing an X chromosome, there being 45 chromosomes in total) (see Baroff, 1986).

One syndrome that has received substantial attention in recent years is the Fragile X syndrome. A number of epidemiological surveys of mental retardation have noted an excess of males over females, and because of this a sex-linked mode of inheritance was postulated (see de la Cruz, 1985). The syndrome is named after an abnormality in the long arm of the X chromosome that can be observed when these chromosomes are specially treated for analysis (de la Cruz, 1985). Fragile X syndrome tends to occur largely in males, and in males its most prominent symptoms include enlarged testes, long ears, and mental retardation of variable severity. Fragile X is one of the more common specific (diagnosable) forms of mental retardation; it is outnumbered only by Down syndrome among the chromosomal abnormalities and has an estimated prevalence of 1 in 2,000 males (de la Cruz, 1985).

Congenital infections and maternal diseases. These include a multitude of diseases that can be transmitted either in utero or during delivery to the fetus via the mother. Several viruses if contracted by the mother and transmitted to the fetus can cause mental retardation. These include rubella (German measles), cytomegalic inclusion body disease (the most common viral cause of mental retardation), and mumps. If contracted during the first trimester of pregnancy, the effects of rubella can be devastating to the fetus, with severe mental retardation and a variety of physical disorders ensuing. Other maternal infections that can permanently adversely affect the offspring include toxoplasmosis, herpes, human immunodeficiency virus, and syphilis.

Maternal diabetes, especially if uncontrolled, can cause excessive or retarded growth, which may be associated with congenital abnormalities (Oliphant et al., 1985). Finally, toxemia is a metabolic disorder of unknown origin that occurs during pregnancy and is characterized by hypertension, edema, and albuminuria (protein in the urine). It can be diagnosed only after the 20th week of gestation and can affect the fetus's brain, heart, kidney, and liver (Oliphant et al., 1985).

Environmental Conditions

These include a variety of substances or conditions that, if applied to the fetus in utero, can have long-term adverse affects, including mental retardation. Some of the better known toxins include lead, mercury, exposure to radiation, and certain of the illicit drugs. A number of drugs given for therapeutic reasons, such as warfarin and phenytoin (Dilantin), are capable of causing birth defects as well. Alcohol consumed by the mother appears to pose a threat to the well-being of the fetus. According to Baroff (1986), the fetal alcohol syndrome occurs in approximately 1–2 of every 1,000 births, a rate commensurate with Down syndrome. Furthermore, the earliest period of pregnancy, up to 6 weeks, appears to carry the greatest risk for developing fetal alcohol syndrome, and the prospective mother may not even realize she is pregnant during this time!

Finally, the last "environmental" condition actually relates to the health status of the mother—which shows how arbitrary classification systems tend to be. This situation, called "maternal PKU," involves normal IQ mothers who themselves were successfully treated for PKU when young with a low-phenylalanine diet. Unless the diet is reinstituted for such women before becoming pregnant, they will unwittingly subject their offspring to toxic phenylalanine levels, with the likelihood that the offspring will be severely retarded. It is perhaps ironic that a genetic disorder, successfully treated in the mother, can lead to a serious environmental hazard for the child (Oliphant et al., 1985).

Thus there is a myriad of possible causes that can occur antenatally and result in mental retardation. Kolb and Brodie (1982) note that, of diagnosable conditions, 50%–65% of such cases arise from poorly understood factors existing prior to birth.

Perinatal Causes

Baroff (1986) provides an excellent summary of factors that at the time of birth can lead to mental retardation and other serious handicaps. According to Baroff, a variety of assaults at the time of birth can result in neurological injury, which may later be manifested as cerebral palsy, deafness, or mental retardation. The two most common perinatal causes of subsequent problems are prematurity and low birthweight. Traditionally, prematurity is defined as birth before 38 weeks of gestation or having a birthweight less than 2,500 grams (5½ pounds). Baroff reports that 7%–10% of all births are premature and that the major causes include maternal health problems, dietary insufficiency, heavy cigarette smoking, and extreme maternal age (under 18 and over 35 years).

Because the premature neonate enters the world with underdeveloped organ systems, it is more susceptible to a variety of problems, such as oxygen deprivation and brain hemorrhage due to structural weakness of the blood vessels (Baroff, 1986). Low birthweight is also associated with prematurity, but the full-term infant who is born small for gestational age is also at risk for a variety of problems. Physical trauma caused by malpresentation of the fetus or disproportion between the infant's head and the pelvis of the mother can result in physical trauma and intracranial hemorrhage, which in turn can cause motor abnormalities, seizures, and mental retardation. Asphyxia is another perinatal factor sometimes associated with subsequent mental retardation, and it may be due to premature separation of the placenta, prolapse of the umbilical cord, anesthesia, or obstruction of the airways (Baroff, 1986; Kolb & Brodie, 1982). Finally, large birthweight (often associated with maternal diabetes) and herpes transmitted from mother to infant at the time of birth are further complications that can lead to mental retardation.

Postnatal Causes

Kolb and Brodie (1982) estimate that 25% to 30% of cases of mental retardation stem from causes after birth. Of all the etiological factors occurring after birth, encephalitis (inflammation of the brain) and meningitis (inflammation of the brain's covering membranes) are the most frequently occurring (Kolb & Brodie, 1982). Other physical causes include (but are not limited to) head trauma (from automobile and other accidents), toxemia, poisons and toxins such as lead and carbon monoxide, malnutrition, cerebrovascular accidents, and degenerative diseases (Taft & Cohen, 1977).

Probably the most important postnatal cause of mental retardation is at the same time one of the most difficult to quantify, namely psychosocial deprivation. This is often characterized by poverty, a chaotic living environment, family instability, inadequate caregiving, and an emphasis on day-to-day survival rather than on social, academic, and cultural stimulation. Because of the preponderance of persons so affected, we discuss psychosocial mental retardation below.

Psychosocial Mental Retardation

This term was preceeded by "cultural-familial" retardation, which is perhaps more descriptive. According to Baroff (1986), approximately half of the offspring of mentally retarded parents, if reared by those parents, will also be retarded. Psychosocial retardation is a presumptive diagnosis whose existence hinges on the presence of the following: (a) retarded intellectual functioning and adaptive behavior; (b) a history of mental retardation in the family; (c) no demonstrable organic cause; and (d) impoverished background, with poor housing, undernutrition, inadequate medical care, and a general lack of healthy stimulation (Aman & Schroeder, 1990). Psychosocial retardation is often first identified at school age when the child is confronted with a set of demands that he or she is ill equipped to meet. Unlike organically determined mental retardation, which is more or less associated with all functional levels, psychosocial retardation tends to be confined to mild levels of handicap.

Psychosocial mental retardation defies easy categorization by the etiological classification system presented previously. Teenage pregnancies are a commonly associated feature, and poor prenatal medical care and poor nutrition are also commonplace. Obstetric complications, prematurity, and low birthweight are often associated with psychosocial retardation. Finally, poor medical care and nutrition, exposure to toxins, physical trauma, family instability, and inappropriate caretakers are all frequently associated features (Szymanski & Crocker, 1985). Owing to the tendency for psychosocial retardation to run in families, a polygenic mode of inheritance is commonly regarded to be a possible causal factor. However, other organic, social, and economic factors are also seen to operate before, during, and after birth. Social and environmental forces are especially conspicuous, and they appear to interact with and accentuate the impact of any organic factors. Thus, the most prevalent form of mental retardation is seen to result from a complex blend of social, psychological, and organic factors.

CORRELATES OF MENTAL RETARDATION

Other than the two components specified in the definition of mental retardation, there are no invariable correlates of intellectual handicap. Short stature is a frequent nonspecific finding (Taft & Cohen, 1977) as are the occasional presence of dysmorphic facial features or other anomalies. However, these are usually of no functional significance except for the fact that they may help further to stigmatize an already handicapped population. Cerebral palsy is sometimes associated with mental retardation and, obviously, this would need to be taken into account in any assessment and treatment program. Baroff (1986) has presented data suggesting that the rates of blindness and deafness among persons with mental retardation exceed those in the general population by ratios of 30 to 1 and 20 to 1, respectively. Epilepsy is found much more commonly among mentally retarded persons than in the general population, and it also tends to increase as severity of mental retardation worsens. A number of surveys have suggested that 20% to 35% of institutionalized retarded populations may have epilepsy, and among institutionalized profoundly retarded persons the rate sometimes approaches 50% (Pond, 1979). A number of behavioral and emotional problems are more prevalent among mentally retarded individuals than in the general population. Foremost among these are stereotypic behavior, self-injurious behavior, hyperactivity, aggression, and destructive behavior. Such behavior and emotional problems are the subject of the following section. Finally, it should be noted that, although the various correlates cited here are statistically associated with mental retardation, they are in no sense invariable or necessarily even common traits. As noted at the opening of this chapter, diversity tends to be the rule in mental retardation, and that is also true of these so-called correlates.

PSYCHOPATHOLOGY AND BEHAVIORAL PROBLEMS IN MENTAL RETARDATION

Dual Diagnosis

"Dual diagnosis' refers to the presence of both mental retardation and concomitant mental illness. Prevalence figures differ widely depending upon age, residential setting, and functional level, but several studies have suggested that between 15% and 30% of mentally retarded persons have a psychiatric condition (Jacobson, 1982; Menolascino, Levitas, & Greiner, 1986). Others report lower rates (e.g., Bruininks, Hill, & Morreau, 1988), although it is clear that the frequencies observed are still several times those existing in the general population. It has been demonstrated in a number of surveys that individuals with mental retardation display the full range of psychiatric disorders seen in the nonretarded population (Menolascino, et al., 1986; Sovner, 1986), although there may be differences in the relative rates of occurrence of various disorders. Likewise it is possible that some qualitatively distinct psychiatric conditions (e.g., a self-injurious behavioral syndrome) may occur in mental retardation that do not occur in the general population (Menolascino et al., 1986; Webster, 1970). It is unclear what the reasons are for such inflated rates of psychopathology, although various workers have suggested that the following may place mentally retarded persons at increased risk: (a) increased psychosocial stress due to the person's handicap, (b) relative inability to understand the demands of the culture, (c) major handicaps secondary to central nervous system impairments, (d) impaired ability to express needs, and (e) impaired or atypical personality defenses (Menolascino et al., 1986).

The presence of mental retardation, especially severe and profound retardation, can often make it very difficult to establish accurately and reliably the existence of a psychiatric condition. Reid (1983) has discussed a number of common impediments to dual diagnosis. First, some behaviors, which would be abnormal in the general population (e.g., stereotypy, echolalia) may be developmentally appropriate in persons of low mental age. Second, the lack of language or the existence of overly concrete language may make it extremely difficult to determine the presence of some symptoms such as hallucinations, delusions, depressed affect, and so forth. Another phenomenon that has led to the apparent underdiagnosis of psychiatric conditions among retarded persons is that of "diagnostic overshadowing." This refers to a tendency among mental health professionals to overlook emotional disorders when they accompany mental retardation or to conceptualize them as part of the mental retardation when in fact they exemplify a personality or behavior disorder (Reiss, Levitan, & Szysko, 1982). Thus, it is clear that psychiatric disorders (dual diagnoses) do frequently occur among mentally retarded persons, but there are a number of factors that make their assessment very difficult. This is the topic of considerable research at present and it is hoped that the prevalences, presentations, and treatments of psychiatric disorders in this population will be much better understood in the not-too-distant future.

Major Behavioral Problems

A large proportion of people with mental retardation are prone to develop at some point in their lives maladaptive behavior or behavior problems. Such behavior problems have been found to impede adjustment to the community and to jeopardize attempts to provide a normalized lifestyle under nonrestrictive living conditions. They are also related to admission to restrictive institutions and readmission after failure in the community. Therefore, treatment or prevention of behavior problems is a prime target of applied research.

Jacobson (1982) reported that, in the New York Mentally Retarded/Developmentally Disabled population of over 30,000 persons, the three most prevalent behavior problems were aggression with a 10.9% prevalence rate, self-injurious behavior (8.2%), and destruction (4.3%). More recent data on these three types of behavior for the child and adolescent population are presented in Figure 21-2. The information was obtained with the Developmental Disabilities Profile (Policy and Planning Office, 1986) on a sample of 3,341 children and adolescents with mental retardation receiving relevant services from the state of New York. The data in this figure reflect behaviors that were rated as occurring at least once a week. Other commonly occurring behavior problems that do not appear in the figure include stereotypic (repetitive non-goal-directed) movements, hyperactivity, and repetitive vocal utterances.

Across all age groups up to 21 years, aggression and self-injury occurred in 11.1% of the sample, and destructive behavior in 9.7%. These data are relevant to those individuals receiving services in New York state and therefore are not necessarily representative of the entire population with mental retardation. Nevertheless, interesting characteristics can be observed. For the most part, the proportion of individuals with problem behaviors increases with lower levels of functioning, particularly among adolescents (13 to 21 years of age).

MULTIMODAL ASSESSMENT OF MENTAL RETARDATION

The concept of multimodal assessment emphasizes the variety of behavioral modalities that make up human behavior, such as gross motor, physiological, emotional, and cognitive behavior. Each one of these modalities may have to be considered in a given situation, and they require different approaches to measurement. Some of the principal approaches for assessing mentally retarded children and adolescents are discussed in the following pages.

Direct Observation

Direct systematic observation is probably the most widely used form of data collection in applied research with children having mental retardation. Its popularity

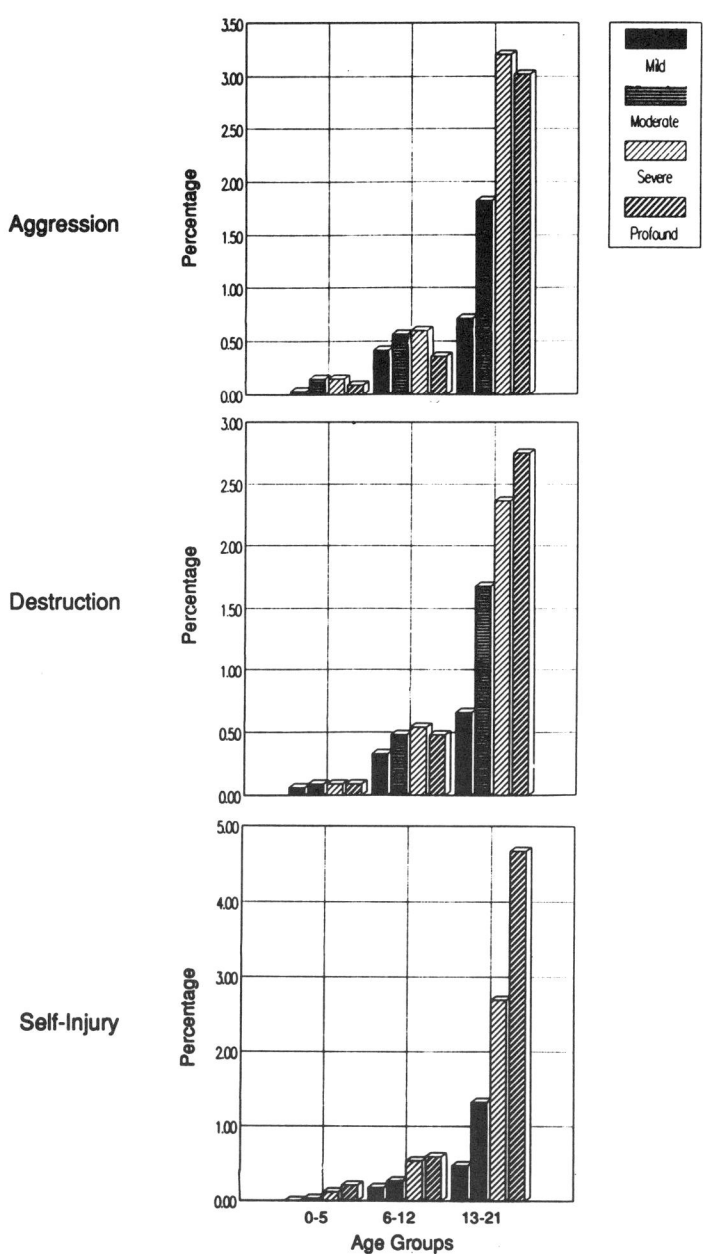

Figure 21-2. Percentage of individuals who exhibit aggressive, destructive, and self-injurious behavior at least once per week. These cases were identified among 3,341 children and adolescents with mental retardation in the State of New York (Policy and Planning Office, 1986). We are grateful to John W. Jacobson from the Policy and Planning Office of the New York State Office of Mental Retardation and Developmental Disabilities for making these data available.

is probably due to the fact that it does not require prerequisite skills on the part of the observed individual. In the clinical setting, observation systems are usually developed for each individual case. Development of individual observation systems requires many decisions: (a) which behaviors should be targeted, (b) how they should be defined, (c) what setting may elicit the behavior of interest, (d) what activities the subject should be engaged in, (e) what time of day would be most appropriate, (f) how often and how long the client should be observed, and (g) which recording method should be chosen.

There are many ways to describe different observation systems. One way is to describe them by the parameters they measure (response frequency recording, response duration recording, etc.). Another way is to divide them by their sampling approach. Systematic behavior observation is always based on a two-level sampling decision: First, it has to be determined when during the day the observations should be scheduled. This will depend on what the most relevant times are for a given case. The second decision pertains to the data-collection method within the observation period. We can distinguish between (a) time sampling procedures or (b) continuous observation procedures. The most straightforward procedure is to observe continuously throughout the observation period, such that the entire time period is "sampled." However, for practical purposes, this is seldom possible. In time sampling procedures, smaller time units are sampled from within the observation period, with observation intervals alternating with nonobservation intervals. Issues related to this type of data collection are discussed in the following sections.

Discontinuous Recording Strategies (Time Sampling)

Interval recording (modified frequency time sampling). Interval recording consists of alternating observation intervals and recording intervals. A simple timing device is used to signal the beginning of each interval, and events are recorded as having occurred or not during the previous observation interval. Observation intervals usually range between 5 and 30 seconds; recording intervals may be equally long or, for efficiency, may be of briefer duration.

Two subtypes of interval recording exist, different in terms of how a scorable response is defined. In partial-interval time sampling, the response has to occur only during a portion of the interval, whereas in whole-interval sampling the response must be present during the whole interval. Powell, Martindale, and Kulp (1975) demonstrated that the partial-interval method tends to overestimate the actual response occurrence, whereas the whole-interval method tends to underestimate it. Generally speaking, accuracy improves with increases in the number of observation intervals.

Momentary time sampling (discontinuous probe-time sampling). With this method, the observer scans the subject after certain, equally long intervals for a brief period, checking whether a specified response occurred at that moment or not. The nonobservational intervals are usually fixed, and the length of the observation is often specified more precisely, such as "2 seconds." Momentary time sampling is appropriate for behaviors in which the child is typically engaged for considerable periods (e.g., engaging in a task or in stereotyped body rocking) rather than brief behavior events (e.g., facial tics, eye blinks). A good example from the literature is a study by Doke and Risley (1972) in which it was determined whether the activity schedule or the availability of materials in certain areas affected the presence of children in various locations of a preschool.

Continuous Recording Strategies

There are several forms of data collection that are typically used in a continuous fashion. The simplest procedure is probably *frequency recording,* wherein the number of occurrences of a given behavior are counted within a given period. Frequency data are particularly useful for discrete and brief behavioral events (e.g., aggressive attacks, head banging). Paper and pencil or inexpensive counters are the only prerequisite materials.

Duration recording measures the amount of time a person spends in a particular activity, such as attending to a specific task, continuous body rocking, or the time it takes to get dressed. A simple stopwatch usually suffices for observing single behaviors. With more complex analyses, involving multiple behaviors, more sophisticated recording devices are needed.

In *continuous recording* each onset and termination of a given behavior is recorded in real time as they occur. In addition to frequency and duration, the resulting information includes temporal structures, such as patterns of occurrence, interresponse times, and latencies. The natural tradeoff is the sheer amount of work involved in data collection and the equipment requirement. However, the completeness of the data enables a large variety of options to be considered for statistical analysis.

In *trial recording,* both the dependent and the independent variables are observed and recorded. This type of recording is often used in training on stimulus discrimination, such as word-recognition tasks. The independent variable is a discrete trial (e.g., teacher prompts the child with a cue card), and the dependent variable is the child's response. The response is typically recorded either as having occurred or not, as correct/incorrect, or as complete/incomplete. Error responses can be classified as omission and commission errors. Independent variables are recorded for occurrences, whether they were presented appropriately, and whether the appropriate error correction procedures were used (e.g., Karsh, Repp, & Lenz, 1990).

The principal purpose of *interaction recording* is to record the interaction between two or more persons. Recording is paced by behaviors rather than by time intervals. The resulting record contains interaction chains that can be analyzed for functional relationships between the people of interest. Interaction recording has been used a great deal in research on families of developmentally delayed children and children with behavior problems (Forehand & McMahon, 1981).

Occasionally, *subject location* can be a response measure. For instance, Doke and Risley (1972) used group participation in different play activity areas of a preschool as a dependent measure of activity preference, while Routh, Schroeder, and O'Tuama (1974) developed an objective measure of children's activity levels on the basis of locomotion in an activity room.

Adaptive Behavior Scales

The assessment of adaptive behavior in persons with mental retardation plays an important role in both the diagnosis of the disorder and its ongoing habilitation process. As noted earlier in the chapter, a significant deficit in the ability of a person to behave in such a way as to meet the natural and social demands of his or her environment is one of the defining criteria for the diagnosis of mental retardation. The adaptive behavior assessment can also be of use to the clinician and other professionals in identifying a person's behavioral strengths and weaknesses, provide for a comparison of the person's behavior across different environments or stimulus conditions (e.g., home vs. school), and provide a relatively uniform and objective method of evaluation for ongoing educational and intervention programs. Sattler (1988, p. 376) cautions that adaptive behavior scores typically reflect a complex interaction of factors related to the scale itself, the child being rated, the informant who is providing the information for the rating, the examiner who is taking that information, the setting in which the behavior is being observed and reported, and the reasons for the evaluation. Such influences should be kept in mind when interpreting the adaptive behavior scores, and prudent clinical judgment should be applied. Most adaptive behavior scales require an informant such as a parent, teacher, mental health worker, or other direct care staff person (usually relatively naive to the assessment procedures and their standards) to provide detailed information regarding an individual's behavior. Such reports are often subjective and open to potential bias and distortions. In fact, it is relatively common to find parents providing relatively higher ratings of overall adaptive behavior on their child than the teacher's rating of that child (Shaw, Hammer, & Leland, in press).

The range of behavior rated in most adaptive behavior scales covers a broader range of behavior under a number of domains or subscales than most mental health professionals are accustomed to assessing. For example, in the DSM-III-R (American Psychiatric Association, 1987) a single rating is made of adaptive functioning level on Axis V (Global Assessment of Functioning Scale) focusing primarily upon social relations and school or occupational functioning. Adaptive behavior scales, by contrast, have the individual rated on numerous specific categories of behavior that cover a broader range of life functions, including such things as the ability to travel independently in the community, motor skills, communication ability, the use of number and time concepts, and various personal and social responsibility functions, as well as those areas evaluated in the DSM-III-R. Adaptive behavior scales also often include an assessment of a broad range of maladaptive behaviors.

A recent study by Sullivan, Vitello, and Foster (1988) used direct behavioral observation methodology to evaluate the adaptive behavior of adults with mental retardation as they moved into a community group home living environment from a more institutional-based residence. Six men with moderate mental retardation were evaluated over a 6-month period. The observations indicated that a major change in adaptive behavior took place in the areas of personal and domestic living skills, while their abilities in interpersonal and social development remained relatively stable. This was believed to be primarily related to the men's poor communication ability and limited interaction outside the home but within the community itself. This type of more in-depth direct observation of adaptive behavior in assessment is apparently more useful than the adaptive behavior scales in providing information regarding the relationship between the observed adaptive behavior abilities and the environmental context in which they occur. It would appear to be a much more useful process in the development of specific habilitation goals and strategies, but for finan-

AAMD Adaptive Behavior Scale

The AAMD Adaptive Behavior Scale (ABS) (Nihira, Foster, Shellhaas, & Leland, 1974) provides a rating of both adaptive and maladaptive behaviors in persons with mental retardation, developmental disabilities, and serious emotional maladjustment. The scale was normed on approximately 4,000 persons with mental retardation, ages 3 through 69 years, living in 68 different institutions across the United States. Adaptive behaviors are assessed in Part I of the ABS, which includes 10 behavioral domains, including the following: Independent Functioning; Physical Development; Economic Activity; Language Development; Number and Time Concepts; Domestic Activity; Vocational Activity; Self Direction; Personal Responsibility; and Socialization. In Part II of the ABS, maladaptive behaviors related to the domains of personality and behavior disorders are evaluated. The AAMD Adaptive Behavior Scale—School Edition (ABS-SE) (Lambert, Windmiller, Tharinger, & Cole, 1981) is also available for school personnel to provide adaptive behavior ratings of children and adolescents in the school environment. This scale is quite similar to the ABS, except that certain domains on both the adaptive and maladaptive sections, which are typically not observable in the school environment (e.g., domestic activity), have been eliminated from the school version of the rating scale.

The ABS is generally considered to be a clinically useful instrument in the evaluation and tracking of adaptive behavior for a given individual. Sattler (1988, pp. 378–382) notes that there appears to be limited evidence of reliability and validity for the scale. The major clinical strength of this instrument appears to be that it provides a profile of an individual's strengths and weaknesses in adaptive behavior across the various domains, which may be helpful in the development of individual habilitative plans. There are even more serious concerns in the area of standardization and validity regarding the ABS-SE and, therefore, it should be used with caution in the classification of children. However, it may be helpful in determining strengths and weaknesses also.

Vineland Adaptive Behavior Scales

The Vineland Adaptive Behavior Scales (VABS) (Sparrow et al., 1984) is probably the most frequently used measure of adaptive behavior in handicapped and nonhandicapped individuals. They were normed on age groups from birth through age 18 years, inclusive. The VABS is a relatively recent revision of the earlier Vineland Social Maturity Scale published by Doll in 1953. Three different versions of the VABS are provided, including the Survey Form (297 items), the Expanded Form (577) items), and the Classroom Edition (244 items). Each version of the VABS includes four general domains of adaptive behavior: Communication, which assesses receptive, expressive, and written communication skills; Daily Living Skills, which assesses personal living habits, performance of domestic activities, and actions in the community; Socialization, which assesses interpersonal interactions in play, use of leisure time, and responsibility and sensitivity to others; and Motor Skills, which assesses gross and fine motor activity. The Survey and Expanded forms of the VABS also include a domain that evaluates maladaptive behaviors. The VABS provides the examiner with a composite adaptive behavior score and scores for each of the four domains. The four domain scores vary considerably across age groups (Silverstein, 1986) and therefore should be interpreted with caution; this is especially true for mentally retarded individuals. As reported in the VABS manual, the standardization sample of 3,000 individuals for each form of the scale appears to be adequate, and in fact, much better than average. Median, split-half, and test-retest reliability scores all fall in a range from .83 to .97 across the four domains and the composite, which suggests good reliability of the VABS. However, interrater reliability on the Survey and Expanded forms ranges from .62 to .75, underscoring the importance of selecting informants who have good knowledge of the individual being rated and who are familiar with the scale and its use. The manual points out that variables related to race, ethnic group, community size, and region of the United States had little or no effect on the composite score of the standardization sample. There was, however, up to a 5-point difference on average between males and females, with females being rated higher, and as much as an 8-point higher rating for children of more highly educated parents. Overall, the VABS appears to be a potentially useful assessment device. However, the problems with inconsistent standard deviations across the age groups may make this a difficult instrument to use in research involving comparisons across age groups or in longitudinal comparisons of the same individuals.

Client Development Evaluation Record (CDER)

The Client Development Evaluation Record (CDER) (California Department of Developmental Services, 1986) is a standardized, 66-item informant rating instrument that is a short derivative of the widely used AAMD Adaptive Behavior Scale. It is a state-mandated instrument for mentally retarded persons receiving services from the state of California. The items were grouped a priori into six domains: motor, independent living, social, emotional, cognitive, and communication. Harris, Eyman, and Mayeda (1982) found adequate levels of interrater reliability for virtually all of these items (median correlation of .82, with 60 of the 66 items above .65). Concurrent validity, which was assessed by correlating the CDER with two other scales, ranged between .50 to .88 (Arias, Ito, & Takagi, 1983).

Behavior Development Survey

The Behavior Development Survey (UCLA Mental Retardation Research Center, 1979) is also a derivative of the ABS. It was designed as a short adaptive behavior assessment instrument. The Behavior Development Survey can be completed by trained professionals or by people without special training. It contains a total of 62 items for rating observable behaviors that constitute three domains of daily living skills and two maladaptive behavior domains; additionally, information on important client characteristics is collected.

Behavior Inventory for Rating Development

The Behavior Inventory for Rating Development (BIRD) (Sparrow & Cicchetti, 1984) is a 68-item instrument encompassing five a priori domains of adaptive behavior: communication, physical skills, self-help skills, self-control, and social skills. Factor analysis suggested that four of these subscales were interpretable in terms of subscale classification. Maladaptive behavior items are contained in two of the subscales. The BIRD has since been superseded by the Vineland Adaptive Behavior Scales, which were based in part on the BIRD.

Minnesota Developmental Programming System (MDPS) Behavior Scales Revised

The Behavior Scales Revised (Bock & Weatherman, 1979) are part of the MDPS, which is an elaborate package for assessment and programming. The scales are designed to provide information about behavioral competencies that can be used for individual program planning and for improvement of service delivery. Two versions are available, one for higher functioning and one for lower functioning individuals. The version for the higher functioning clients has 18 domains with 20 behavior statements each, whereas that for the lower functioning persons consists of four domains with 20 items. Items are scored in terms of whether the individual produces a given behavior 100%, more than 50%, less than 50%, or 0% of the time. The MDPS behavior scales have undergone extensive field tests and revisions, and, in fact, have been adopted by several states. Several types of reliability, and item, Rasch, and validity analyses have been performed, suggesting generally good psychometric properties.

Developmental Disabilities Profile

The Developmental Disabilities Profile (DDP) was developed at the State of New York Office of Mental Retardation and Developmental Disabilities for administrative functions such as program planning, and determination of eligibility for state services (Policy and Planning Office, 1986). It has undergone intense field testing, and a wealth of information on psychometric properties is available, although unfortunately, it is mainly in unpublished form. Generally speaking, these data indicate good psychometric characteristics overall.

IQ Tests

The reader wishing to obtain a thorough discussion of these tests (as well as a number of other assessment instruments) is referred to an outstanding text by Sattler (1988); useful discussions are also found in Morgenstern (1983) and Taylor (1984). As with most other clinical populations, the Wechsler intelligence scales and the Stanford-Binet Intelligence Scale are the mainstays of intelligence assessment in mental retardation. The Wechsler Preschool and Primary Scale of Intelligence (WPPSI) was introduced by Wechsler in 1967. It covers children between ages 4 and 6½ years, and it comprises 11 subscales. The Wechsler Intelligence Scale for Children—Revised (WISC-R) was published in 1974 by Wechsler. It was developed for children in the age range of 6 years to 16 years 11 months and comprises 12 subtests. Both the

WPPSI and the WISC-R provide Verbal, Performance, and Full-Scale IQs. The Stanford-Binet Intelligence Scale, Fourth Edition (Stanford-Binet: FE) is a recent revision that was made available in 1986 (Thorndike, Hagen, & Sattler, 1986).

All three of these are excellent tests with extremely good standardization, very good reliability and validity, and good administration guidelines and test materials (Sattler, 1988). The Wechsler scales are based on a view of intelligence as made up of multifaceted abilities, rather than a single entity (Taylor, 1984). In contrast, the Stanford-Binet reflects a conceptualization of intelligence as a general factor, and it taps a variety of tasks that stress manipulative and visual skills at younger ages, but it increasingly emphasizes verbal and abstract reasoning abilities at older levels (Morgenstern, 1983). The principal weakness of the WPPSI and WISC-R, insofar as the assessment of mental retardation is concerned, is that they have limited floors, with 45 and 40 defining the lower possible IQ limits, respectively (Sattler, 1988). Thus, these would not be satisfactory instruments if severe or profound mental retardation were suspected, and the McCarthey Scales of Children's Abilities may be more suitable in such youngsters. The major limitation with the Stanford-Binet:FE is that it lacks a consistent battery of subtests throughout the range of ages assessed (Sattler, 1988).

As noted in the etiology section, the assessment of children for mental retardation can be complicated by the presence of hearing impairment, visual impairment, motor problems (e.g., cerebral palsy), and speech problems. Additionally, the need to assess children at a very young age may pose problems with the tests discussed so far, particularly with the Wechsler scales. In the case of children with visual impairments, Sattler (1988), suggests that the Wechsler scales and the Stanford-Binet: FE (especially the verbal items) can be used so long as the visual handicap is not too severe. Sattler recommends the Hays-Binet, the Perkins-Binet and the Blind Learning Aptitude Test if the child is blind or has a severe visual handicap. For children with hearing impairments, verbally based items should be avoided and suitable performance tests from the WPPSI, WISC-R, and Stanford Binet: FE can be used if the impairment is not too severe. Supplemental tests recommended by Sattler include the Ontario School Ability Examination, the Leiter International Performance Scale, the Hiskey Nebraska Test of Learning Aptitude, Ravens Progressive Matrices, the nonverbal portions of the Illinois Test of Psycholinguistic Abilities, and possibly the Goodenough Harris Draw a Person Test. Special modifications for deaf children can include the addition of printed or signed words, pantomimes, demonstration, and manual prompting (Sattler, 1988).

Children with motor problems may be at a particular disadvantage with timed performance tests (Sattler, 1988). Possible supplemental tests for such children include the Leiter International Performance Scale, Ravens Progressive Matrices, the Pictorial Test of Intelligence, and the Columbia Mental Maturity Test. In general, performance tests are recommended for children with speech and language handicaps or for those from non-English-speaking homes. Sattler suggests that Ravens Progressive Matrices, the Leiter International Performance Scales, the Pictorial Test of Intelligence, the Columbia Mental Maturity Scale, and the Hiskey-Nebraska Test of Learning Aptitude may be useful specialized measures in such children. Finally, for the assessment of very young children, the following tests may prove particularly helpful: Bayley Scales of Infant Development (2 months to 2½ years), Gesell Developmental Schedule (4 weeks to 6 years), Cattel Infant Intelligence Test (2 to 30 months), the Pictorial Test of Intelligence (3 to 8 years), and the Columbia Mental Maturity Scale (3½ to 9 years).

This treatment of tests for assessing children who are mentally retarded with additional handicaps is necessarily limited by space considerations. The interested reader requiring a more thorough treatment is referred to one of the authoritative texts, such as that by Sattler (1988).

Behavior Rating Scales

Scales used for assessing the behavior of persons with mental retardation have been extensively reviewed elsewhere (Aman, in press; Aman & White, 1986), and the interested reader may want to consult those sources. Rating scales have two primary functions: (a) to select and classify individuals for clinical or research purposes and (b) to assess the effects of various forms of intervention. In theory, there is no reason why a rating scale cannot be used for both of these functions, although that has not been the case so far with most instruments used to assess children and adults with mental retardation. In the following discussion, we describe some of the scales typically used for diagnostic purposes and the assessment of treatment effects.

Reiss Screen for Maladaptive Behavior

The Reiss Screen for Maladaptive Behavior (Reiss, 1988) is a 36-item informant measure for dual diagnosis intended for use with adolescents and adults. Each item refers to a psychiatric symptom. Factor analysis from a national sample yielded seven clinically meaningful factors: (1) Aggressive Behavior, (2) Psychosis, (3) Paranoia, (4) Depression (Behavioral Signs), (5) Depression (Physical Signs), (6) Dependent Personality Disorder, and (7) Avoidant Disorder. Subsequently an eighth subscale, the Autism scale, was added to the screen. The Reiss Screen was developed to detect the presence of a possible psychiatric disorder and was not intended to provide a specific diagnosis, although the various subscales would probably be helpful in this respect. The Reiss Screen has been relatively well researched in terms of its psychometric properties, which appear to be generally good (Aman, 1989a).

Aberrant Behavior Checklist

The Aberrant Behavior Checklist (ABC) (Aman, Singh, Stewart, & Field, 1985a) is an empirically-derived scale that was developed to assess treatment effects, especially those of pharmacotherapy. Its 58 items score into five subscales as follows: (I) Irritability, Agitation, Crying, (II) Lethargy, Social Withdrawal, (III) Stereotypic Behavior, (IV) Hyperactivity, Noncompliance, and (V) Inappropriate Speech. Considerable research has been done on the psychometric characteristics of the ABC, which appear to be satisfactory to good (Aman, Singh, Stewart, & Field, 1985b). The factor structure of the instrument has been assessed in three countries and been found to be remarkably consistent (Aman, 1989a). In recent years the ABC has probably become the most widely used rating instrument for assessing clinical effects in drug studies.

Emotional Disorders Rating Scale for Developmental Disabilities

The Emotional Disorders Rating Scale for Developmental Disabilities (Feinstein, Kamner, Barrett, & Tylenda, 1988) was developed for children and adolescents with developmental disabilities. It consists of 59 items intended to assess emotional symptoms in eight subscales developed on an a priori basis. The items were chosen to conform to current diagnostic criteria in the DSM-III for affective disorders. The subscales are labeled

1. irritability,
2. anxiety,
3. hostility/anger,
4. psychomoter retardation,
5. depressive mood,
6. somative/vegetative,
7. elated/manic, and
8. sleep disturbance.

Unfortunately, there is presently a dearth of data in relation to this instrument's psychometric characteristics, so that its appropriate place in the assessment of children with mental retardation is yet to be determined.

Behavior Problems Inventory

The Behavior Problems Inventory (BPI) (Rojahn, Polster, Mulick, & Wisniewski, in press) was primarily developed to assess the presence and severity of various forms of self-injurious behavior (SIB). It comprises 29 specific maladaptive behaviors: 15 types of SIB, 5 stereotypic behaviors, and 9 aggressive behavior topographies. Each of these items has an operational definition that is used by the raters to determine whether a given behavior qualifies as self-injurious, stereotypic, or aggressive behavior. The BPI was used for SIB surveys in West Germany on an institutionalized population (Rojahn, 1984), and a noninstitutionalized population (Rojahn, 1986), and in a group of nonambulatory institutionalized profoundly retarded subjects (Mulick, Dura, Rasnake, & Wisniewski, 1988). The data from Mulick et al. (1988) suggest that high rater agreement levels can be obtained with the BPI.

Prout-Strohmer Assessment System

The Prout-Strohmer Assessment System (PSAS) (Prout & Strohmer, 1989; Strohmer & Prout, 1989) is a two-component multitrait, multimethod assessment instrument for emotional and behavioral problems in the adolescent and adult population with mild and borderline retardation. The Prout-Strohmer Personality Inventory (PSPI) is a self-report instrument that consists of 162 items. The Strohmer-Prout Behavior Rating Scale (SPBRS) is administered to caregivers familiar with the individual, such as a psychologist, teacher, or rehabilitation counselor. Twelve clinical scales that fall into two broad-based factors, Internalizing and Externalizing, comprise a total of 135 items.

There are several scales that will not be described in detail because of space limitations. The Psychopathology Instrument for Mentally Retarded Adults (PIMRA) (Senatore, Matson, & Kazdin, 1985) is an instrument designed to assist in arriving at an appropriate psychiatric diagnosis in mentally retarded adults with mental illness. The Behavior Disturbance Scale is an empirically derived tool that appears to be useful for assessing problem behavior in adolescents and adults with mental retardation (Leudar, Fraser, & Jeeves, 1984). The Conners Parent and Teacher Rating Scales (Conners, 1969, 1970) and the Parent Teacher Questionnaire (Goyette, Conners, & Ulrich, 1978) have all been used a great deal for assessing children of normal IQ, although validity and sensitivity in mentally retarded children becomes increasingly questionable as the severity of the handicap increases. The Fairview Problem Behavior Checklist, reported by Barron and Sandman (1983), may prove to be a useful instrument for descriptive purposes, although it is much lengthier than most checklists. Other instruments that may be useful for assessing children and adolescents with mental retardation have been described by Aman (in press), Aman and White (1986), and in a special issue of *Psychopharmacology Bulletin* specifically devoted to a review of available rating scales for children (Special Issue, 1985).

Other Methods

Functional Taxonomy Scales

Functional analysis is a principal objective of behavioral assessment. To obtain this information through experimental manipulations as suggested by Iwata, Dorsey, Slifer, Bauman, and Richman (1982) is seldom feasible in clinical reality, and often this information is obtained through interviews and informal observations. Two instruments were recently introduced to enable such motivational information to be collected: (1) The *Contingency Analysis Questionnaire (CAQ)* (Wieseler, Hansler, Chamberlain, & Thompson, 1985) is a staff-administered survey instrument with six items to determine the most common consequences of SIB. Each item has to be rated on a 4-point frequency scale; (2) the *Motivation Assessment Scale (MAS)* (Durand & Crimmins, 1988) has 16 items scored on a 7-point Likert scale. Four items each are geared to address four motivating conditions: social attention, escape from aversive situations, sensory consequences, and tangible rewards. Durand and Crimmins reported high interrater and test-retest reliabilities and very good concurrent validity with analog baselines. However, in an independent analysis of the MAS, Sturmey (1989) found the instrument's psychometric properties to be much weaker.

Permanent Product Measures

In addition to systematic and direct behavior observation, other data-collection methods are also available. Permanent product measures involve a determination of work output, such as the number of correctly assembled pieces in a task or the number of correctly solved math problems. The advantage of using such measurement is that it is relatively inexpensive, objective, and socially valid.

Automated Recording

This represents another facet of behavioral assessment. A wide variety of biometric measurement techniques has been used in research in mental retardation. For instance, single plane accelerometers (Lewis et al., 1984) and photosensitive devices, based on the interruption of a light beam directed at a photosensor (Hollis, 1978) can be used to record stereotypic movements. Stabilimetric cushions (Christensen, 1975) and pressure-sensitive mats (Campbell et al., 1982) have been employed to assess movement in drug studies. Automated devices are also used to measure the application of the independent variable in treatment studies (e.g., number of aversive stimuli delivered; Foxx, McMorrow, Rendleman, & Bittle, 1986). An advantage of automated measurement is that it can measure parameters of behaviors that elude the eye of the human observer, that it is generally less expensive than a human observer, and it can be very reliable, objective, and accurate. However, achieving satisfactory content and criterion validity are often a problem. Furthermore, these devices are rather inflexible in that they can measure only very specific kinds of response characteristics.

Self-Monitoring

Self-monitoring refers to an assessment technique in which the client is asked to monitor and record his or her own behavior. Obviously, this process of self-observation and recording requires some preliminary skills and understanding and is more popular with clients of normal intelligence. However, a few successful attempts have been made to have children with mild to moderate mental retardation monitor their own behavior. For instance, Shapiro, McGonigle, and Ollendick (1980) were able to show that children with mild mental retardation would assess their own disruptive and on-task behavior accurately. Evidently, self-monitoring is not only an assessment method. It has been shown to affect the observed behavior, thereby introducing a possible bias in the data. Therefore, from an assessment perspective, self-monitoring is suspect and has to be validated by other, nonbiased data (see chapter 9).

CASE ILLUSTRATION

The following is a case illustration of behavioral assessment techniques as they are often applied in addressing severe behavior problems found in persons with mental retardation. In this example, the client was determined to have a "dual diagnosis" of both profound mental retardation and a significant emotional disturbance. The behavioral assessment procedures helped us to define and verify multiple structural and functional environmental factors that covaried with the cross-situational rates of severe self-injurious behaviors. As is common with comprehensive evaluations for persons with mental retardation, the behavioral assessment was done in conjunction with an interdesciplinary team including the disciplines of psychology, psychiatry, pediatrics, social work, neurology, and special education. As a result, specific behavioral management and therapy recommendations were derived for reducing problem behaviors and increasing more adaptive social behaviors.

Referral

Patty, a 7-year-old girl, was referred for interdisciplinary evaluation of severe and extremely high frequency self-injurious behavior. A behavioral assessment was requested to assist in planning a treatment program to decrease self-injury and increase adaptive skills.

History

By her father's report, Patty did not achieve developmental milestones at the expected ages in infancy (e.g., she walked around 14 months but had developed no expressive language and was not toilet trained). By the age of 1 year, she was noted to spend much of her time rocking on her hands and knees and to be socially unresponsive and difficult to console. Patty was diagnosed as "developmentally delayed" and was self-injurious by age 2, and at age 3 she was placed in temporary foster care because of her parents' inability to manage her self-injury. Evaluations conducted at that time revealed a markedly abnormal CAT scan (including calcifications of both grey and white matter and other features suggestive of a prenatal encephalitis) and severe-to-profound mental retardation.

Patty's medication history included trials of thioridazine (Mellaril) at age 3 and age 5 (in an attempt to reduce self-injury) which reportedly were unsuccessful. A trial of methylphenidate (Ritalin) was conducted at age 5 also, and this apparently worsened Patty's behavior.

For the past 3 years, Patty has resided at a group home. Patty's father takes her home for visits infrequently because of his inability to manage her self-injury at home, but he remains closely involved in decisions about her care and treatment.

One year prior to this evaluation, a study of Patty's self-injury and potential treatment approaches at another clinic resulted in recommendations for a treatment program consisting of intensive monitoring of Patty's behavior, a mild aversive contingent upon self-injury (staff were to push Patty's hands down and say "No!") and consistent prompting and reinforcing alternative behaviors including communicative gestures, self-feeding, and so on. Group home and school staff members reported that the recommended program required essentially one-on-one staffing for Patty and that funding for this level of staffing was available only for a 1-month period. This resulted in rather inconsistent application of the program over time.

Sources of Information

Sources of information included (a) chart review, (b) parent interview, (c) group home and school staff interview, (d) structured observation and videotape analysis, and (e) cognitive and adaptive behavior evaluations.

Behavioral Interview

An interview was conducted with Patty's father, group home staff, and Patty's special education teacher. There was relative agreement among all parties regarding Patty's status. At this time, Patty's self-injury included a range of topographies, several of which routinely resulted in tissue damage (i.e., bruising, open sores). Patty exhibited head banging (against tables and floors), face slapping and punching, hair pulling, pinching and scratching, and "bouncing" (sitting down very forcefully on a chair or floor). Patty wore a protective helmet for most of the day. However, this did not prevent tissue damage caused by face punching, hair pulling, and pinching or scratching. Reportedly, Patty's behavior was interfering with the implementation of essentially all habilitative goals proposed by her group home and by her school. It also limited her access to activities outside these settings, most notably visits with her father.

Interview questions regarding the common antecedent and consequent characteristics of Patty's self-injurious behavior (SIB) suggested that (1) the level of demand; (2) presence of a familiar adult, unfamiliar adult, or no adult; (3) access to preferred activities and stimulation; (4) and use of a mild aversive condition (putting her hands down and saying "No!") contingent upon self-injury were all variables to be considered for direct observational assessment.

The SIB was described as likely to occur with mild to extreme intensity (tissue damage) in all situations. Episodes of SIB usually lasted 10 to 30 minutes, but in extreme cases could last up to 3 hours.

Behavioral Observations

An evaluation of the impact of the following variables was conducted: (a) level of demand; (b) presence of a familiar adult, unfamiliar adult, or no adult; (c) access to preferred activities or stimulation; and (d) use of a mild aversive condition (putting her hands down and saying "No!") contingent upon self-injury. In general, Patty engaged in all of the self-injurious behaviors mentioned above at an extremely high rate. In addition, she exhibited aerophagia and pica (of paper, lint, etc.). Patty cried at a high rate as well, and both self-injury and crying were elicited by even minor stressors (e.g., adult adjusting how Patty was sitting in their lap). Patty was frequently noncompliant with minor task demands (e.g., expressed by throwing items) and occasionally attempted to bite adults.

The most remarkable features of Patty's self-injury are illustrated in Figure 21-3 and were as follows:

1. The topography of her self-injury was hierarchically organized. That is, she tended to exhibit pinching (and crying) first, followed by hair pulling and face hitting, followed by head banging in a highly predictable sequence. Patty's behavior progressed through the hierarchy if there was no environmental response to behavior occurring early in the sequence.

2. Patty's self-injury appeared to function in two major ways. First, it appeared to serve as a means for her to make requests (for attention, for an adult to get something for her, etc.) and second, as a means of escaping and avoiding unpleasant situations. These are both essentially communicative functions. For example, Patty was noted to self-injure when an adult momentarily stopped a game that she liked (as a signal for the adult to continue), when an adult was present in the room but not interacting with her (as a signal for the person to interact), or when Patty was prompted to manipulate blocks of other toys (when a demand was introduced), etc.

3. Structurally, Patty's rate of self-injury was lowest when she was provided with nearly constant physical contact with an adult, was provided with a range of preferred stimuli (e.g., vibratory stimulation, tactile) and no performance demands whatsoever were made. Self-injury occurred during 46% of these intervals; however, 70% of this self-injury consisted of low-intensity neck pinching. Under these circumstances, she also exhibited a very low rate of crying (crying occurred during 0% of these intervals) and demonstrated a much greater degree of social responsivity (smiling and initiating contact with the adult).

In contrast, Patty's rates of self-injury and crying were highest when she was presented with structured demands. Self-injury occurred during 45% to 100% of teaching intervals (and included the full range of topographies described above). Crying occurred during 90% to 100% of teaching intervals. When Patty was left alone or when she could see an adult who was not interacting with her, her rates were high as well, with self-injury (all topographies displayed) during 65% of intervals and crying during 60%.

4. In short probe sessions, a "hands down" contingency appeared to have some utility in reducing the rate of self-injury. The contingency had no effect when her rate was already low (in a no-demand situation): 20% without and 30% with the contingency. When her rate originated at high levels, the contingency did appear to bring the rate down (90% of intervals without the contingency to 45% with the contingency). She demonstrated some tendency to "substitute" aggression and oppositional behavior for self-injury when self-injury was blocked by the hands-down procedure.

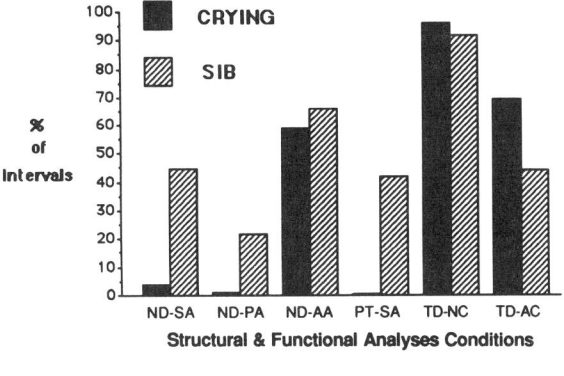

Figure 21-3. Rates of self-injurious behavior (SIB) and crying across various stimulus and consequence conditions during a clinic assessment.

5. Patty's insistence on being in close contact with an adult seemed to have some characteristics of a pattern of self-restraint. That is, at times she appeared to use her contact with the adult (particularly holding onto the adult's hands with both of hers and wrapping the adult's arm around her) as a means of preventing herself from engaging in self-injury.

6. Patty evidenced a clear recognition of familiar adults and demonstrated some reduction in overall agitation and crying in the presence of her father or another very familiar caretaker. Nevertheless, self-injury was still quite high in the presence of all adults.

DSM III-R Diagnosis

Axis I: 310.10—Organic personality disorder
311.00—Depressive disorder (NOS)
307.30—Stereotypy/habit disorder (Self-injurious behavior)
307.52—Pica

Axis II: 318.20—Profound mental retardation

Axis III: Postencephalitic syndrome
Chronic undernutrition
Chronic superficial skin infection (secondary to self-injury)

Axis IV: Severity of psychosocial stressors: 3—Moderate: Changes in level and intensity of staffing and programming

Axis V: Global assessment of functioning: 10—Persistent severe self-injury, profound delays in all adaptive skills.

Intervention Recommendations

1. The intensity and rate of Patty's self-injury and the degree to which it restricted her from profiting from habilitative services dictated that an intensive treatment protocol be designed and implemented. The complexity, seriousness, and chronic nature of her behavior suggested that extensive staff training and ongoing behavioral consultation would be required to implement, monitor, and calibrate such a protocol.

2. A deceleration program for Patty's self-injury was judged most likely to be successful if it incorporated the following features:

(a) Begin with implementation by *one* staff member with whom Patty spent much of her time and with whom she already had a good relationship (practically this meant one person at the group home and one person at school).

This would provide a high degree of consistency to the program in its early stages and provide Patty with a reinforcing and predictable attachment figure. Additional people who interacted with Patty (including her father) were to be introduced to the program gradually as Patty's behavior improved.

(b) Include aggressive teaching of alternative and incompatible behaviors. For example, these were to include prompting and reinforcing gestures, teaching Patty to manipulate sources of preferred stimulation on her own, etc.

(c) Gradually introduce increased demands (as Patty's behavior improved in low-demand situations) to increase her time spent in learning situations and to "un-teach" Patty's use of self-injury to escape from minor demands.

BEHAVIORAL MANAGEMENT

Behavior Modification

Behavior modification techniques are probably the most widely used treatment modalities in the mentally retarded population of all age groups. There are numerous excellent textbooks that can be highly recommended for the interested reader not already familiar with those procedures (e.g., Cooper, Heron, & Heward, 1987; Kazdin, 1984). The treatment literature on problem behaviors in children and adolescents with mental retardation is ample and rapidly growing. We can, therefore, only briefly sketch the basic strategies of behavior modification. There are two basic approaches of treating problem behaviors with behavior modification techniques. One can either directly reduce problem behavior by changing its controlling stimuli, or one can strengthen appropriate behavior and build new behavioral skills, hoping that they will indirectly contribute to the reduction of the problem behavior. These two approaches are not incompatible and, in fact, are often applied in combination.

Strengthening Appropriate Behaviors and Teaching New Skills

Mental retardation is characterized by the lack of age-appropriate skills and behaviors. Building new behavior is therefore an essential task for behavioral programming strategies. Indeed, teaching appropriate behavior and adjustment skills is considered a most effective form of prevention and treatment of maladaptive behavior (Carr & Durand, 1985). Teaching new competencies or skills usually begins with a task analysis, which entails breaking down that new skill into small, successive, trainable components. It further requires a schedule of reinforcement for correct responding, a plan of how to deal with incorrect responding (ignore, redirect, or punish), and a strategy of building the new skill (shaping and fading, chaining, or trial-and-error). To strenghten existing appropriate behaviors that could compete with the inappropriate target behavior, therapists use reinforcement schedules, such as differential reinforcement of other behavior (DRO), or differential reinforcement of incompatible behavior (DRI). In DRO, the subject is rewarded for periods of time in which the target behavior is not exhibited (also called "omission training"). In DRI the client has to fulfill a dual requirement to receive a reinforcer. Reinforcers are delivered only for periods of time in which the target behavior does not occur, but also a specified behavior that is incompatible with the target behavior must be emitted as well.

Directly Decreasing the Target Behavior

Direct reduction of a behavior can be achieved by punishment or extinction. Punishment is defined by two conditions. The first condition—which is usually the one people think about—is the delivery of an "aversive" stimulus contingent upon the target behavior. The second condition, which has to be present for the procedure to qualify as punishment, has to do with its effect on the behavior: It has to reduce its probability of future occurrence. In other words, punishment is defined by its *function* on behavior, and *not* by its intuitively assumed "aversiveness."

As a result of a major debate over the appropriateness of using punishment with mentally retarded persons, researchers have begun to investigate boundary conditions for its use. For instance, relatively unobtrusive yet effective punishers have been developed, such as facial and visual screening. Visual screening involves the therapist covering the eyes of the child with the palm of his or her hand following the occurrence of a target behavior; facial screening uses a biblike object to cover the client's face. A review of the literature suggests that contingent screening can be an effective and easy-to-implement treatment procedure. It has been employed with a large variety of individuals and behaviors, but, given a certain likelihood that a client will try to avoid screening by struggling, it seems to be more practical with younger age groups (Rojahn & Marshburn, in press). Another relatively noninvasive punishment is the interruption-redirection procedure, in which the target behavior is interrupted by verbal or physical instruction and the child's behavior is redirected to a desirable activity.

Extinction refers to the withholding of reinforcement of the target behavior. While extinction is a useful strategy for the prevention of maladaptive behavior, it is a relatively weak treatment method when used alone. It usually acts very slowly, which is seldom clinically feasible. With less serious behavior, it is frequently combined with differential reinforcement procedures such as DRO or DRI.

Pharmacological Treatments

This topic is well covered in two recent texts exclusively devoted to drug therapy of persons with mental retardation (Aman & Singh, 1988a; Gadow & Poling, 1988). The most compelling and rational case to be made for psychotropic drugs in mental retardation is among those with true psychiatric conditions, or dual diagnosis. Unfortunately, however, there is only a small handful of studies in this field examining the major psychotropic drugs in well-established disorders, and many of these are poorly controlled (Aman, 1987). It is reasonable to expect that psychotropic drugs will prove effective for the same psychiatric conditions as those for which they have an established place in the nonretarded population. However, for the most part this still needs to be established empirically, and the major challenge appears to be reaching consensus on markers of psychiatric disorders in this population.

Self-injurious behavior (SIB) is a serious behavior problem that is often treated pharmacologically. In general, most psychotropic drugs have not been demonstrated to be effective in diminishing SIB. Indications for a therapeutic effect are strongest for thioridazane (Mellaril), lithium carbonate, and possibly the opiate antagonists, such as naltrexone (Trexan) (Aman, 1990; Farber, 1987; Singh & Millichamp, 1985). Psychotropic drugs are also commonly used for a variety of acting-out problems, such as aggressive or destructive behavior, hyperactivity, screaming and shouting, and stereotypic behavior. The most commonly used drugs to manage such behaviors are the neuroleptics, such as thioridazine and haloperidol. The data on clinical efficacy are mixed and appear to depend in part on dose, choice of drug, subject selection, and so forth. There is some evidence of reductions in target behaviors, although it is not always clear whether this is a specific clinical effect or whether it results from a general suppression of *all* behavior (Aman, 1987; Schroeder, 1988). The cerebral stimulants (e.g., methylphenidate [Ritalin] and dextroamphetamine [Dexedrine]) are commonly used to treat hyperactivity in nonretarded children. Views differ on this, but the stimulants appear to be the most effective in hyperactive children who are the least impaired functionally, whereas their effectiveness in severely/profoundly retarded children appears to be very limited (Aman, 1982; Aman, Marks, Turbott, Wilsher, & Merry, in press; Aman & Singh, in press).

The indications for other types of psychotropic drugs (other than in specific psychiatric disorders) also appear to be limited in mental retardation. Lithium may have some role in managing aggressive and self-injurious behavior (Chandler, Gualtieri, & Fahs, 1988). Anxiolytic drugs have not been researched for their most reasonable indication, namely anxiety-based problems, and they appear ineffective or possibly even counterproductive in acting-out behaviors (Chandler et al., 1988). Finally, beyond their probable place for managing clinical depression in this population, the antidepressant drugs are essentially unresearched and have no established role in treating acting-out behaviors (Chandler et al., 1988).

Other Treatments

From time to time, various combinations of vitamins and minerals, usually in megadoses, have been recommended for managing behavioral or learning problems. Thus far, none of these has been shown to be effective in children having developmental disabilities (Aman & Singh, 1988b, in press).

SUMMARY

To recapitulate, mental retardation is defined by the presence of significantly subaverage IQ, marked deficits in adaptive behavior, and appearance within the developmental period (< 18 years). The prevalence of mental retardation varies over the life span, but its overall prevalence is thought to be about 1% of the population. The etiology of mental retardation is seldom simple and often involves a complex interplay of biological, sociocultural, and psychological factors. Etiological factors are often divided according to time and classified as those occurring prior to birth, and after birth. Prenatal causes include genetic abnormalities; chromosomal abnormalities; congenital infections and maternal diseases; and environmental conditions brought about by toxins, drugs, and alcohol. The most common perinatal causes include prematurity; low birthweight; physical trauma and hemorrhage; asphyxia; and large birthweight. Postnatal causes include encephalitis, meningitis, head trauma, toxemia, malnutrition, cerebrovascular accidents, and (perhaps most notably) psychosocial deprivation. Factors associated with mental retardation may include short stature, dysmorphic facial features, cerebral palsy, significant visual and hearing handicaps, epilepsy, and increased rates of behavioral and emotional problems.

The term *dual diagnosis* in this field refers to the presence of mental retardation in conjunction with a psychiatric condition. The presence of severe and profound mental retardation greatly complicates the process of establishing the presence of a psychiatric disorder. Nevertheless, some writers maintain that as many as 15% to 30% of mentally retarded persons could qualify as having a dual diagnosis. A variety of behavior problems are also commonly reported among children with mental retardation. Foremost among these are aggression, self-injurious behavior, and destructive behavior, but stereotypic behavior, hyperactivity, and repetitive vocal utterances are also commonly observed.

The variety of human behavior together with problems in assessing many children with mental retardation make a multimodal approach to assessment very desirable. Some of the most common modes of assessment in mental retardation include direct observation, the use of adaptive behavior scales, IQ tests, and behavior rating scales. Direct observation is very flexible and can include a wide array of continuous and discontinuous recording strategies. Several of the most popular adaptive behavior scales, IQ tests, and behavior rating scales were described. Special impairments (e.g., hearing, visual, motor, and speech handicaps) can affect these measures, often necessitating appropriate adjustments or caution in their use and interpretation.

A case illustration was presented in which a young girl presented with severe self-injurious behavior, crying, noncompliance, and biting others. Professionals from several disciplines were engaged in the assessment of this child who had marked behavioral, psychiatric, and physical problems. The child's SIB was found to have the functional roles of communicating requests and avoiding certain situations, leading to a coherent set of recommendations for intervention. Finally, the chapter concluded with a discussion of two common modes of therapy, namely behavioral management and pharmacotherapy.

In conclusion, mental retardation is a field with a heavy commitment to collecting objective and standardized data for assessing problem behaviors and formulating decisions. The existence of functional handicaps, often in combination with sensory and physical problems, has demanded a certain amount of creativity and has necessitated a wide array of assessment techniques. Furthermore, the frequent occurrence of numerous other difficulties and handicaps coexisting with behavior problems means that optimal assessment will often require the input of professionals from several disciplines.

REFERENCES

Aman, M. G. (1982). Stimulant drug effects in developmental disorders and hyperactivity: Toward a resolution of disparate findings. *Journal of Autism and Developmental Disorders, 12*, 385–398.

Aman, M. G. (1987). Guest editorial. Overview of pharmacotherapy: Current status and future directions. *Journal of Mental Deficiency Research, 31*, 121–130.

Aman, M. G. (in press). *Assessing psychopathology and behavior problems in persons with mental retardation. A review of available instruments*. Washington, DC: Department of Health and Human Services.

Aman, M. G. (1990). *Efficacy of psychotropic drugs for reducing self-injurious behavior in the developmental disabilities*. Manuscript submitted for publication. Ohio State University.

Aman, M. G., Marks, R. E., Turbott, S. H., Wilsher, C. P., & Merry, S. N. (in press). Clinical effects of methylphenidate and thioridazine in intellectually subaverage children. *Journal of the American Academy of Child and Adolescent Psychiatry*.

Aman, M. G., & Schroeder, S. R. (1990). Specific learning disorders and mental retardation. In B. Tonge, G. D. Burrows, & J. S. Werry (Eds.), *Handbook of studies on child psychiatry* (pp. 209–224). Amsterdam: Elsevier Science Publishers.

Aman, M. G., & Singh, N. N. (Eds.) (1988a). *Psychopharmacology of the developmental disabilities*. New York: Springer-Verlag.

Aman, M. G., & Singh, N. N. (1988b). Vitamin, mineral, and dietary treatments. In M. G. Aman & N. N. Singh (Eds.), *Psychopharmacology of the developmental disabilities* (pp. 168–196). New York: Springer-Verlag.

Aman, M. G., & Singh, N. N. (in press). Pharmacological intervention—An update. To appear in J. L. Matson and J. A. Mulick (Eds.), *Handbook of mental retardation* (2nd ed.). New York: Pergamon Press.

Aman, M. G., Singh, N. N., Stewart, A. W., & Field, C. J. (1985a). The Aberrant Behavior Checklist: A behavior

rating scale for the assessment of treatment effects. *American Journal on Mental Deficiency, 89,* 485–491.
Aman, M. G., Singh, N. N., Stewart, A. W., & Field, C. J. (1985b). Psychometric characteristics of the Aberrant Behavior Checklist. *American Journal on Mental Deficiency, 89,* 492–502.
Aman, M. G., & White, A. J. (1986). Measures of drug change in mental retardation. In K. Gadow (Ed.), *Advanced in learning and behavioral disabilities* (pp. 157–202). Greenwich, CT: JAI Press.
American Psychiatric Association (1987). *Diagnostic and statistical manual of mental disorders, third edition, revised.* Washington, DC: Author.
Arias, M., Ito, E., & Takagi, N. (1983). Concurrent validity of the Client Development and Evaluation Report. In T. Ford, A. B. Silverstein, & A. L. Fluharty (Eds.), *Pacific State Archives, VII.* Los Angeles: University of California at Los Angeles.
Baroff, G. S. (1986). *Mental retardation: Nature, cause and management* (2nd ed.). New York: John Wiley & Sons.
Barron, J., & Sandman, C. A. (1983). Relationship of sedative-hypnotic response to self-injurious behavior and stereotypy by mentally retarded clients. *American Journal of Mental Deficiency, 88,* 177–186.
Baumeister, A. A., Dotecki, P. R., & Dupstas, F. D. (in press). The new morbidity. In S. A. Garcia & R. Batey (Ed.), *Current perspectives in psychological, legal, and ethical issues. Volume I: Children and families.* Greenwich, CT: JAI Press.
Bock, W. H., & Weatherman, R. F. (1979). *The assessment of behavioral competence of developmentally disabled individuals: The MDPS.* Minneapolis: University of Minnesota, College of Education, Department of Educational Administration.
Bruininks, R. H., Hill, B. K., & Morreau, L. E. (1988). Prevalence and implications of maladaptive behaviors and dual diagnosis in residential and other service programs. In J. A. Stark, F. J. Menolascino, M. H. Albarelli, & V. C. Gray (eds.), *Mental retardation and mental health: Classification, diagnosis, treatment, services.* (pp. 3–29). New York: Springer-Verlag.
California Department of Developmental Services (1986). *Client Development Evaluation Report.* Sacramento, CA: Author.
Campbell, M., Anderson, L. T., Small, A. M., Perry, R., Green, W., & Caplan, R. (1982). The effects of haloperidol on learning and behavior in autistic children. *Journal of Autism and Developmental Disorders, 12,* 167–175.
Carr, E. G., & Durand, V. M. (1985). Reducing behavior problems through functional communication training. *Journal of Applied Behavior Analysis, 18,* 111–126.
Chandler, M., Gualtieri, C. T., & Fahs, J. J. (1988). Other psychotropic drugs: Stimulants, antidepressants, the anxiolytics, and lithium. In M. G. Aman & N. N. Singh (Eds.), *Psychopharmacology of the developmental disabilities* (pp. 119–145). New York: Springer-Verlag.
Christensen, D. E. (1975). Effects of combining methylphenidate and classroom token systems in modifying hyperactive behavior. *American Journal of Mental Deficiency, 80,* 266–276.
Conners, C. K. (1969). A teacher rating scale for use in drug studies with children. *American Journal of Psychiatry, 126,* 884–888.
Conners, C. K. (1970). Symptom patterns in hyperactive, neurotic, and normal children. *Child Development, 41,* 667–682.
Cooper, J. O., Heron, T. E., & Heward, J. L. (1987). *Applied behavior analysis.* Columbus, OH: Charles Merrill.
Cordes, C. K. (1973). Chronic drug intoxication causing pseudoretardation in a young child. *Journal of the American Academy of Child Psychiatry, 12,* 215–222.
de la Cruz, F. F. (1985). Fragile X syndrome. *American Journal of Mental Deficiency, 90,* 119–123.
Doke, L. A., & Risley, T. R. (1972). The organization of day-care environments: Required vs. optional activities. *Journal of Applied Behavior Analysis, 5,* 405–9.
Doll, E. (1953). *A manual of social competence: A manual for the Vineland Social Maturity Scale.* Minneapolis: Educational Test Bureau.
Durand, V. M., & Crimmins, D. B. (1988). Identifying the variables maintaining self-injurious behavior. *Journal of Autism and Developmental Disorders, 18,* 99–117.
Farber, J. M. (1987). Psychopharmacology of self-injurious behavior in the mentally retarded. *Journal of the American Academy of Child and Adolescent Psychiatry, 26,* 296–302.
Feinstein, C., Kaminer, Y., Barrett, R. B., & Tylenda, B. (1988). The assessment of mood and affect in developmentally disabled children and adolescents: The Emotional Disorders Rating Scale. *Research in Developmental Disabilities, 9,* 109–121.
Forehand, R. L., & McMahon, R. J. (1981). *Helping the noncompliant child.* New York: Guilford Press.
Foxx, R. M., McMorrow, M. J., Rendleman, L., & Bittle, R. G. (1986). Increasing staff accountability in shock programs: Simple and inexpensive shock device modifications. *Behavior Therapy, 17,* 187–189.
Gadow, K. D., & Poling, A. D. (1988). *Pharmacotherapy and mental retardation.* Boston: College-Hill Press.
Garrard, S. D., & Richmond, J. B. (1965). Mental retardation without biological manifestations. In C. H. Carter (Ed.), *Medical aspects of mental retardation* (pp. 32–72). Springfield, IL: Charles C Thomas.
Goyette, C. H., Conners, C. K., & Ulrich, R. F. (1978). Normative data on revised Conners parent and teacher scales. *Journal of Abnormal Child Psychology, 6,* 221–236.
Grossman, H. J. (1977). *Manual on terminology and classification in mental retardation* (1973 rev.). Washington: American Association on Mental Deficiency.
Harris, C. W., Eyman, R. K., & Mayeda, T. (1982). *An interrater reliability study of the Client Development Evaluation Report.* Los Angeles, CA: University of

California, Los Angeles, Mental Retardation Research Center.

Hollis, J. (1978). Analysis of rocking behavior. In C. E. Meyers (Ed.), *Quality of life in severaly and profoundly retarded mentally retarded people: Research foundations for improvement* (pp. 1–53). Washington, DC: AAMD.

Iwata, B. A., Dorsey, M. F., Slifer, K. J., Baumann, K. E., & Richman, G. S. (1982). Toward a functional analysis of self-injury. *Analysis and Intervention in Developmental Disabilities, 2,* 3–20.

Jacobson, J. W. (1982). Problem behavior and psychiatric impairment in a developmentally disabled population I: Behavior frequency. *Applied Research in Mental Retardation, 3,* 121–139.

Karsh, K. G., Repp, A. C., & Lenz, M. W. (1990). A comparison of the task demonstration model and the standard prompting hierarchy in teaching word identification to persons with moderate retardation. *Research in Developmental Disabilities, 11,* 395–410.

Kazdin, A. E. (1984). *Behavior modification in applied settings* (3rd ed.). Homewood, IL: Dorsey.

Kolb, L. C., & Brodie, H. K. H. (1982) Mental retardation. In L. C. Kolb & H. K. H. Brodie, *Modern Clinical Psychiatry* (10th ed.) (pp. 715–744). Philadelphia: W. B. Saunders.

Lambert, N. M., Windmiller, M., Tharinger, D., & Cole, L. J. (1981). *AAMD Adaptive Behavior Scale—School Edition*. Monterey, CA: McGraw-Hill.

Leudar, I., Fraser, W. I., & Jeeves, M. A. (1984). Behaviour disturbance and mental handicap: Typology and longitudinal trends. *Psychological Medicine, 14,* 923–935.

Lewis, M., MacLean, W. E., Bryson-Brockman, W., Arendt, R., Beck, B., Fidler, P. S., & Baumeister, A. A. (1984). Time series analysis of stereotypes movements: Relationships of body-rocking to cardiac activity. *American Journal of Mental Deficiency, 89,* 287–294.

Logan, W. J., & Freeman, J. M. (1969). Pseudodegenerative diseases due to diphenylhydantoin intoxication. *Archives of Neurology, 21,* 631–637.

Menolascino, F. J., Levitas, A., & Greiner, C. (1986). The Nature and types of mental illness in the mentally retarded. *Psychopharmacology Bulletin, 22,* 1060–1071.

Mercer, J. R. (1973). *Labeling the mentally retarded*. Berkeley: University of California.

Morgenstern, M. (1983). Standard intelligence tests and related assessment techniques. In J. L. Matson & J. A. Mulick (Eds.), *Handbook of mental retardation* (pp. 201–214). New York: Pergamon Press.

Mulick, J. A., Dura, J. R., Rasnake, L. K., & Wisniewski, K. (1988, May). *Self-injurious behavior and stereotypy in nonambulatory children with profound mental retardation*. Poster presented at the 2nd Annual North Coast Regional Conference of the Society of Pediatric Psychology, Worthington, Ohio.

Nihira, K., Foster, R., Shellhaas, M., & Leland, H. (1974). *AAMD adaptive behavior scale* (rev. ed.). Washington, DC: American Association on Mental Deficiency.

Oliphant, P. S., Geiger-Parker, B., & Gundell, G. W. (1985). *Programs for preventing the causes of mental retardation*. New Brunswick, NJ: Summerset Press.

Policy and Planning Office (1986). *The Developmental Disabilities Profile—Final Report*. Albany, NY: New York State Office of Mental Retardation and Developmental Disabilities.

Pond, D. (1979). Epilepsy and mental retardation. In M. Craft (Ed.), *Tredgold's mental retardation* (12th ed.) (pp. 331–345). London: Bailliere Tindall.

Powell, J., Martindale, B., & Kulp, D. (1975). An evaluation of time-sample measures of behavior. *Journal of Applied Behavior Analysis, 8,* 436–496.

Prout, H. T., & Strohmer, D. C. (1989). *Prout-Strohmer Personality Inventory manual*. Schenectady, NY: Genium Publishing Corporation.

Reid, A. H. (1983). Psychiatry of mental handicap: A review. *Journal of The Royal Society of Medicine, 76,* 587–592.

Reiss, S. (1988). *Test manual for the Reiss Screen for Maladaptive Behavior*. Orland Park, IL: International Diagnostic Systems.

Reiss, S., Levitan, G., & Szyszko, J. (1982). Emotional disturbance and mental retardation: Diagnostic overshadowing. *American Journal of Mental Deficiency, 86,* 567–574.

Rojahn, J. (1984). Self-injurious behavior in institutionalized, severely/profoundly retarded adults—Prevalence and staff agreement. *Journal of Behavioral Assessment, 6,* 13–27.

Rojahn, J. (1986). Self-injurious and stereotypic behavior of noninstitutionalized mentally retarded people: Prevalence and classification. *American Journal of Mental Deficiency, 91,* 268–276.

Rojahn, J. & Marshburn, E. (in press). Facial screening and visual occlusion. In J. Luiselli, J. M. Matson, & N. N. Singh (Eds.), *Assessment, analysis, and treatment of self-injury*. New York: Springer.

Rojahn, J., Polster, L. M., Mulick, J. A., & Wisniewski, J. T. (in press). Reliability of the Behavior Problem Inventory. *Journal of the Multihandicapped Person*.

Routh, D. K., Schroeder, C. S., & O'Tuama, L. A. (1974). Development of activity level in children. *Developmental Psychology, 10,* 163–168.

Sattler, J. M. (1988). *Assessment of children* (3rd ed.). San Diego: Author.

Schroeder, S. R. (1988). Neuroleptic medications for persons with developmental disabilities. In M. G. Aman and N. N. Singh (Eds.), *Psychopharmacology of the developmental disabilities* (pp. 82–100). New York: Springer-Verlag.

Seltzer, G. B. (1983). Systems of classification. In J. L. Matson & J. A. Mulick (Eds.) *Handbook of mental retardation* (pp. 143–156). New York: Pergamon Press.

Senatore, V., Matson, J. L., & Kazdin, A. E. (1985). An inventory to assess psychopathology of mentally retarded adults. *American Journal of Mental Deficiency, 89,* 459–466.

Shapiro, E. S., McGonigle, J. J., & Ollendick, T. H. (1980). An analysis of self-assessment and self-reinforcement in a self-managed token economy with mentally retarded children. *Applied Research in Mental Retardation, 1,* 227–240.

Shaw, J., Hammer, D., and Leland, H. (in press). Adaptive behavior of delayed preschool children: Parent versus teacher ratings. *Mental Retardation.*

Silverstein, A. B. (1986). Nonstandard standard scores on the Vineland Adaptive Behavior Scales: A cautionary note. *American Journal of Mental Deficiency, 91,* 1–4.

Singh, N. N., & Millichamp, C. J. (1985). Pharmacological treatment of self-injurious behavior in mentally retarded persons. *Journal of Autism and Developmental Disorders, 15,* 257–267.

Smith, J. D., & Polloway, E. A. (1979). The dimension of adaptive behavior in mental retardation research: An analysis of recent practices. *American Journal of Mental Deficiency, 84,* 203–206.

Sovner, R. (1986). Limiting factors in the use of DSM-III criteria with mentally ill/mentally retarded persons. *Psychopharmacology Bulletin, 22,* 1055–1059.

Sparrow, S. S., & Cicchetti, D. V. (1984). The behavior inventory for rating development (BIRD): Assessment of reliability and factorial validity. *Applied Research in Mental Retardation, 5,* 219–231.

Sparrow, S. S., Balla, D. A., & Cicchetti, D. V. (1984). *Vineland Adaptive Behavior Scales.* Circle Pines, MN: American Guidance Service.

Special Issue (1985). Rating scales and assessment instruments for use in pediatric psychopharmacology research. *Psychopharmacology Bulletin, 21,* 713–1125.

Stack, J. G. (1984). Interrater reliability of the adaptive behavior scale with environmental effects controlled. *American Journal of Mental Deficiency, 88,* 396–400.

Strohmer, D. C., & Prout, H. T. (1989). *Strohmer-Prout Behavior Rating Scale manual.* Schenectady, NY: Genium Publishing Corporation.

Sturmey, P. (1989, September). The Motivation Assessment Scale: Report of poor psychometric properties. In J. Rojahn (Chair), *Behavior Modification Research in Mental Retardation.* Symposium conducted at the meeting of the 19th Annual Congress of the European Association of Behavior Therapy, Vienna.

Sullivan, C. C., Vitello, S. J., & Foster, W. (1988). Adaptive behavior of adults with mental retardation in a group home: An intensive case study group. *Education and Training in Mental Retardation, 23,* 76–81.

Szymanski, L. S., & Crocker, A. C. (1985). Mental retardation. In H. I. Kaplan & B. J. Srdock (Eds.), *Comprehensive textbook of psychiatry IV,* Vol. 2 (pp. 1635–1671). Baltimore: Williams & Wilkins.

Taft, L. T., & Cohen, H. J. (1977). Mental retardation. In A. M. Rudolph (Ed.), *Pediatrics* (16th ed., pp. 1767–1779). New York: Appleton, Century, Crofts.

Taylor, R. L. (1984). *Assessment of exceptional students: Educational and psychological procedures.* Englewood Cliffs, NJ: Prentice-Hall.

Thorndike, R. L., Hagen, E. P., & Sattler, J. M. (1986). *Guide for administering and scoring the Stanford-Binet Intelligence Scale: Fourth Edition.* Chicago: Riverside.

UCLA Mental Retardation Research Center (1979). *Behavior Development Survey. User's manual.* Unpublished manuscript, University of California, Los Angeles, Neuropsychiatric Institute Research Group at Lanterman State Hospital, Pomona, CA.

Vallarta, J. M., Bell, D. B., & Reichert, A. (1974). Progressive encephalopathy due to chronic hydantoin intoxication. *American Journal of Diseases of Children, 128,* 27–34.

Webster, T. G. (1970). Unique aspects of emotional development in mentally retarded children. In F. J. Menolascino (Ed.), *Psychiatric approaches to mental retardation* (pp. 3–54). New York: Basic Books.

Wechsler, D. (1967). *Manual for the Wechsler Preschool and Primary Scale of Intelligence.* San Antonio: The Psychological Corporation.

Wechsler, D. (1974). *Manual for the Wechsler Intelligence Scale for Children—Revised.* San Antonio: The Psychological Corporation.

Wieseler, N. A., Hanslen, R. H., Chamberlain, T. P., & Thompson, T. (1985). Functional taxonomy of stereotypic and self-injurious behavior. *Mental Retardation, 23,* 230–234.

CHAPTER 22

PERVASIVE DEVELOPMENTAL DISORDERS

Lee M. Marcus
Eric Schopler

DESCRIPTION OF THE DISORDER

Introduction

In this chapter we describe concepts, methods, and techniques for the assessment of children and adolescents with pervasive developmental disorders, especially those diagnosed as having autism. The past two decades have witnessed a dramatic shift in the understanding and treatment of these severely disabling developmental conditions (Coleman & Gillberg, 1985; DeMyer, Hingten, & Jackson, 1981; Schopler, 1987), with the current emphasis on the search for biological etiologies on the one hand, and practical approaches to helping families and children on the other. Along with the discussion of assessment strategies, this chapter reviews current efforts to translate such data into effective interventions.

Current Nosology

Currently, the two major classification systems used for the formal diagnosis of autism and pervasive developmental disorders are the Diagnostic and Statistical Manual III-Revised or DSM-III-R (American Psychiatric Association, 1987) and the International Classification of Diseases or ICD-10 (World Health Organization, 1987). Development of the PDD classification in DSM-III-R represented a significant attempt to both simplify this category of childhood disorders and provide highly specific behavioral descriptors. Simplification was achieved by reducing the category to two: autistic disorder (AD) and pervasive developmental disorder not otherwise specified (PDDNOS). Both conditions include three major areas of symptomatology: qualitative impairment in social reciprocity; qualitative impairment in communication, language, and symbolic (imaginative) development; and markedly restricted repertoire of activities or interests. From a possible total of 16 behaviorally defined characteristics, at least 8 were needed to make a diagnosis of autism, with a minimum of 2 from the social area and 1 from the other two areas. Individuals who meet some but not the requisite number of characteristics from this list are called PDDNOS. Although an improvement from the earlier DSM-III system, which lacked sufficient precision and carried the problematic diagnosis of childhood onset pervasive development disorder, the revised PDD can be criticized for a certain arbitrariness in the selection of the behavioral criteria and examples and the "magic" number of eight for a diagnosis of autism. The auxiliary category of PDDNOS is intended for those individuals who meet some but not a sufficient number of behavioral criteria for AD, yet who do not meet diagnostic criteria for any other childhood disorder. PDDNOS tends in practice to be avoided because of the ambiguous information it conveys to parents, teachers, and others involved in the care of the handicapped child. On the other hand, Autistic Disorder may be underutilized because of the strictness of the 8-of-16 rule for classification. There is also the question of whether PDDNOS represents a cluster of unrelated disorders or the mild end of autism. Research on the efficacy of the DSM-III-R system is needed to sort out these and other issues related to accurate diagnosis.

ICD-10 has the similar umbrella classification of Pervasive Development Disorders, but it differs in several ways: age of onset (defined by some delay or abnormal functioning language, social or play behavior before age 3) is a criterion; use of the term *childhood autism* instead of *autistic disorder;* less emphasis on illustrative examples; different wording and emphases on behavioral criteria; and use of separate classifications instead of PDDNOS, including Asperger's syndrome, Rett syndrome, and Atypical Autism. While there is still no consensus among professionals on the uniqueness of these disorders separate from autism, especially regarding Asperger's syndrome (Volkmar & Cohen, 1988), specification of criteria of these related conditions appears more constructive than the "wastebasket" approach of a PDDNOS.

Apart from the more formal diagnostic classification systems of DSM-III-R and ICD-10, researchers and clinicians have emphasized different aspects of the disorder of autism as being primarily or secondary as well as what characteristics should constitute the basic elements that define the condition. Kanner's original formulation focused on the social-affective deficit: the failure of the child to develop interpersonal relatedness as the primary problem in autism (Kanner, 1943). Later, the autistic child's problems in language and communication (Schopler & Mesibov, 1985) and cognitive disabilities (Rutter, 1983) were viewed as fundamental and the basis for the social dysfunctions. Disturbances in sensory functioning and the presence of unusual motility patterns also have had proponents emphasizing the importance of these deficits in defining autism (Ornitz, 1989). More recently, the field has appeared to come full circle, returning to Kanner's hypothesis that autism is first and foremost a disturbance in the child's ability to relate to others (Mundy & Sigman, 1989; Rutter & Schopler, 1988). Other deficits, such as communication and cognition, are now interpreted as deriving from this basic impairment (considered biological in origin) in social-affective understanding and expression.

Primary and Secondary Features

There is currently a consensus that the primary features of PDD/autism include delayed and deviant development in social reciprocity and relatedness, delayed and deviant development and use of language and communication, and unusual responsiveness to the environment (a category that includes deviant sensory responses, restricted interests, and ritualistic, perseverative behaviors and need for sameness and difficulties reacting to change). It is recognized that there can be variability in the expression of these different characteristics along a continuum of severity and qualitative impairment. Within and across these domains, individuals can vary in the intensity of delay and deviancy. For example, one youngster may be extremely aloof with virtually no communicative skills but may be only mildly affected by change or have few atypical sensory responses. Another youngster may have some social interests and ability to communicate but may show obsessive preoccupations and markedly restricted play interests. Both children would meet the criteria of PDD or autism, yet present different diagnostic profiles. A brief review of these major criteria follows.

Impairments in Social Functioning

Autistic children demonstrate a wide variety of problems in social development, markedly discrepant for what is expected for both chronological and developmental age. These problems include poor eye contact or eye-to-eye gaze, rare seeking of comfort, lack of shared enjoyment with others, inadequate response to others' emotions, and failure to develop peer relationships that involve mutual sharing of interests and activities. Many, but certainly not all, autistic children are aloof and distant, especially when young, but some attempt to socially engage with others, although they lack the necessary understanding of social rules and the give-and-take of reciprocal interactions. Lack of initiation is a significant aspect to the social problems, since many children are responsive to the attention and intrusions of adults. Not all components of social development are universally deficient, since attachment to a primary caretaker seems adequate for many children (Mundy & Sigman, 1989), but the consistency, timing, and complexity of social and emotional relatedness are always inadequate. As autistic children grow older, social interests increase, including the desire for peer friendships as well as other "normal" experiences such as dating or getting married. But social skills lag well behind social interests and, even with the higher ability autistic adults, obvious peculiarities and awkward behaviors remain (Mesibov, 1983).

Impairments in Communicative Functioning

Autistic individuals suffer from multiple problems in speech, language, and communication. Although the current research emphasis is on the pragmatic deficits in autistic language (Watson, Lord, Schaffer, & Schopler, 1989; Wetherby, 1986), abnormalities in other aspects of speech and language are also characteristic. Approximately half of autistic persons lack any meaningful speech (i.e., they are essentially mute). The other half appear to be evenly split among those with limited speech: perhaps two- to-three-word phrases mixed with delayed or immediate echolalia and used in relatively few contexts. Those with more advanced speech and language usually have some problems with syntax and complex sentence structures, have a tendency to use idiosyncratic words or phrases, have a limited range of topics or content, and show abnormalities in the rhythm, intonation, and rate of speech. Thus, there is a continuum in the speech and language dysfunctions, varying across developmental levels.

In addition to the problems already noted, autistic persons show serious deficits in three areas (deficits that may be the most significant in distinguishing their disorder from nonautistic mentally retarded and aphasic individuals). Included are deficits in verbal comprehension, nonverbal communication, and, as mentioned earlier, pragmatic language or language used for social communicative purposes. Problems in receptive language or comprehension are difficult to identify because of the multiplicity of cues in the environment that an individual can use, but it appears that from the very early years, autistic children fail to identify communicative signals: first the social and nonverbal ones, later verbal and symbolic ones (Lord, 1985). They do poorly on standardized tests involving receptive language, and it is likely that many of the difficult behavior problems parents and teachers face is the result of the disability in adequately interpreting language used in everyday situations.

Problems in nonverbal communication include the delays and deviances in the use of pointing, gesturing, and miming as means of compensating for lack of speech. Autistic children typically do not use facial expressions to communicate; their vocalizations often lack meaning, except perhaps to their parents, who have learned to interpret the idiosyncratic patterns (Hermelin & O'Conner, 1985). Even when an autistic child does use some basic gesture communication, it tends to not be coordinated with a gaze at the other person and lacks a social emphasis.

Problems in pragmatic language are manifested in the inability of the autistic child to fully understand the two-way nature of social communication. Conversations tend to be limited and restricted to perseverative themes or a one-sided recounting of a special interest. There is a failure to take the other person's perspective, to listen attentively, and respond on the basis of what is needed to sustain the give-and-take of a communicative interaction. There may be frequent interruptions or poorly timed comments. In brief, although on standardized measures of language expression and knowledge, the higher level autistic person may show relatively intact skills, the ability to make use of this language for successful communicative interchanges is deficient.

Unusual Interests, Repetitive, and Stereotyped Behaviors

This broad category encompasses Kanner's original hallmark characteristic of obsessive preoccupation with sameness as well as a variety of ritualistic and repetitive behaviors that are both motoric and cognitive (e.g., obsessive thought). Also subsumed here is the deficit in symbolic and imaginative play. The developmental continuum is relevant in that the more mentally handicapped individuals are likely to engage in sensorimotor-type perseverative actions with objects, such as excessive touching, staring, licking, or banging. With more able autistic children, ritualistic behavior is elaborated upon and rudimentary symbolic play is seen. However, much play lacks variety and spontaneity and often is a direct copy of what the child has observed. Motor stereotypies, such as body whirling, hand and arm flapping, and varying degrees of self-injurious behaviors, fall into this domain. Rigid and compulsive adherence to routines and marked distress over minor environmental changes characterize the behavior patterns as well as specific attachments to unusual objects.

Associated Features

Several additional characteristics are often associated with autism and PDD but are not part of the formal definition. These are important for consideration in the assessment process and programmatic planning.

Irregularities in Development and Learning

Most autistic persons have some degree of mental retardation (DeMyer, 1979; Schopler, 1983). In terms of global mental retardation, approximately 70% to 75% fall into the mild, moderate, or severe-profound range, but even among those who test out higher, most have some measured cognitive functioning that can be considered retarded in development. What tends to distinguish nonautistic and autistic mentally retarded individuals is the unevenness and irregularities in cognitive and developmental abilities. Relative strengths, including normal and above-normal skills, typically lie in visual-motor, visual spatial, and rote memory areas, as well as fine and gross motor skills. However, there are weaknesses in language, abstract reasoning, numerical concepts, and sequential thinking. In a learning situation these also reflect poor organization, memory for ordinary events, problems with auditory processing and generalization, and change. Autistic children tend to be distractible, have short attention spans (especially for language-related tasks), and organize themselves poorly in time and space. Attentional problems can take the form of overfocusing—that is, excessive preoccupation with details or irrelevant stimuli to the exclusion of more essential stimuli, such as attending to distant sounds and ignoring speech.

Neurobiological Problems

A variety of medical conditions have been associated with autism and can affect development and the manifestations of the disorder. Most notable are the presence of seizures that have been documented in approximately 20% to 30% of the cases with autism, many of which first appear only in adolescence (Coleman & Gillberg, 1985). A variety of biologic conditions have been documented, including congenital rubella, tuberous sclerosis, certain viral infections, abnormalities in purine metabolism and intestinal absorption, phenylketonuria, and cerebellum function (Courchesne, Yeung-Courchesne, Press, Hesselink, & Jernigan, 1988; Coleman & Gillberg, 1985). Neurochemical factors, such as those involving the dopaminergic and serotonergic systems, have been implicated (Volkmar & Anderson, 1989) as have perinatal events and genetic factors such as Fragile X syndrome (Gillberg & Wallstrom, 1985). Autism can be associated with the sensory impairments of deafness and blindness, although making an accurate differential diagnosis can be difficult. Autistic individuals often have gross and fine motor and sensorimotor integrative problems (DeMyer, 1979; Watson & Marcus, 1988), even though these skill areas usually are more advanced than cognitive and language abilities.

Behavior Problems

This final category of associated features is included as a reminder that the often troublesome and interfering problems in behavior, such as severe tantrums, aggressive outbursts, and noncompliance are best understood as the result of the autistic person's struggle to cope with the various deficits described. Although sometimes the main target of an intervention program, these behavioral problems should be viewed as markers of cognitive, communicative, social-affective, and perceptual inadequacies. This approach requires that the focus of intervention be on the teaching of skills that can lead to improved competencies and a subsequent reduction in behavioral difficulties.

MULTIMODAL ASSESSMENT

For this section, multiaxial evaluation is the framework for the umbrella category of multimodal assessment. A multiaxial system is one in which various domains or axes are classified separately. It provides a richer and more complete picture of important sources of information obtained in an evaluation than a uniaxial system. Cantwell and Baker (1988) noted several advantages of the multiaxial approach: It has the potential to provide a rich description of a child in terms of such factors as family functioning, intelligence, presence or absence of developmental disorders, all of which may predict outcome to treatment better than a single diagnostic label. It can be helpful in a multidiscipline setting, especially where pervasive developmental disorders are assessed. The coding of multiple domains may prevent the oversight of some important clinical issue of a case. And from a research perspective, it can allow the recognition of associations between particular disorders and environmental or biological factors.

The World Health Organization has long been interested in the use of multiaxial classification for the description and coding of disorders of childhood (Sartorius, 1976; Schopler & Rutter, 1978). The five axes of DSM-III-R include psychiatric diagnosis (Axis I), personality disorders and developmental disorders (Axis II), physical and medical factors (Axis III), psychosocial stressors (Axis IV) and intellectual functioning (Axis V). At Division TEACCH, the North Carolina statewide treatment, education, research and training program for autistic and related communication-handicapped children, adolescents, and adults (Schopler, 1987), a multiaxial approach has been used in the evaluation of such persons (Marcus, Bristol, & Schopler, 1989). This process includes a developmental/psychoeducational assessment of the child (Schopler, Reichler, Bashford, Lansing, & Marcus, 1990), psychological assessment, detailed parent interviewing including assessment of adaptive functioning, and a medical screening. This integrated and multiperspective approach generates comprehensive data on diagnosis, intellectual and adaptive functioning, motor, language, and social functioning, behavioral problems, medical factors, family functioning and school or community factors. The data are sufficiently detailed and objective to be organized into dimensions or axes that both overlaps with and extends beyond the DSM-III-R system. The TEACCH multiaxial evaluation methodology serves as the framework for the various procedures described in this section on multimodal assessment.

Diagnostic Instruments

Diagnosis is an essential first step in the assessment and treatment process in autism and PDD. It is helpful in establishing the major dimensions of the problem being studied, differentiating essential features of the disorder from similar but other fundamentally distinct conditions, providing a general direction for education and treatment, and gauging future potential for an individual. Although the purposes of diagnosis can vary for research or sociopolitical purposes (Schopler & Rutter, 1978), its thoughtful use and application can aid decision making in the clinic or school setting. However, as emphasized later in this section, diagnosis is only the initial step in the process of program planning. Assessment expands and enriches the process by examining individual strengths and weaknesses, highlighting learning styles, and evaluating the relevant contexts in which the individual functions: home, school, or work, and the community. Its major goal is to provide the information that will form the basis of an intervention plan for the autistic individual, family, and community service providers.

Although there is general consensus on the major criteria for autism, there are significant differences among instruments designed to assess the presence or degree of autism in individuals. These instruments tend to reflect the theoretical and research emphasis of their authors. Parks (1983, 1988) and Morgan (1988) have reviewed the strengths and weaknesses of these various measures, and the reader should refer to their reports for more detailed summaries. In this chapter we focus on one instrument: the Childhood Autism Rating Scale (CARS) (Schopler, Reichler, & Renner, 1986), tested and developed within the TEACCH program over the past two decades.

Childhood Autism Rating Scale

The CARS has been a clinically useful and practical procedure that aids in the screening for children with autism and related developmental disorders. Like any single test, it should not be used by itself in making the diagnosis, but can be integrated effectively into the total assessment process. The CARS can be applied in several settings and is based on varying sources of information, including direct observation of a developmental or psychological testing situation, parent interview, and observation in home or school setting. Relatively untrained and inexperienced professionals have been shown to be reliable raters after a 1-hour training session, although, of course, like any instrument, extensive experience is highly desirable in increasing the clinical meaningfulness of its use in applied settings. A valued feature of the CARS is the clarity and descriptiveness of its specific subscales. It is less concerned with theoretical constructs than meaningful, observable behaviors shown to be associated with autism. It can be used as part of a comprehensive multidiscipline evaluation or by a psychologist, educator, or other consultant observing a child in a classroom or community setting where a screening is needed.

The CARS consists of 15 subscales that are rated along a 7-point continuum having 4 anchor points, with specific descriptions and examples of behaviors. The continuum ranges from normal to severely abnormal and is based on a combination of peculiarity, intensity, and frequency of the behavior assessed. The subscales include relating to people, imitation, emotional response, body use, object use, adaptation to change, visual response, listening response, taste, smell, touch response and use, fear or nervousness, verbal communication, nonverbal communication, activity level, consistency of intellectual response, and general impression. Separate ratings on each of these subscales are scored and summed for a total that results in one of three classifications: not autistic (15–29.5), mildly to moderately autistic (30–36.5), and severely autistic (37 and over). Recently the cutoff for autism has been lowered to 28 for adults based on an analysis of diagnostic data within the TEACCH program for older autistic persons (Van Bourgondien & Mesibov, 1989). The CARS now has been used with more than 2,000 cases within the TEACCH program and has demonstrated good interrater reliability. Validity with independent judgments of clinical diagnosis has also been reported (Schopler et al., 1986), but as yet no empirical studies of discriminant validity or the relationship of the CARS to other diagnostic systems have been reported. Parks (1988) concluded that the CARS is a useful device for widespread screening because of its empirical basis and the relative ease with which it can be learned without extensive staff training for a wide variety of settings. Morgan (1988) similarly concluded that the CARS emerged as the strongest of the current scales in terms of demonstrated psychometric properties.

Other Measures

Four other systems that have been described in the literature and available on either a research or clinical basis for many years include the Diagnostic Checklist for Behavior-Disturbed—Children E-2 (Rimland, 1971), the Behavior Rating Instrument for Autistic and Atypical Children (BRIAAC) (Ruttenburg, Kalish, Wenar, & Wolf, 1977), the Behavior Observation System (BOS) (Freeman, Ritvo, & Schroth, 1984), and Autism Behavior Checklist (ABC) (Krug, Arick, & Almond, 1979). These are briefly described. For more information, the reader should consult the manuals of the instruments or Parks (1983, 1988), Morgan (1988), and Short and Marcus (1987) for critical reviews.

The E-2 is based on parental responses to 80 multiple-choice questions concerning the early development and functioning of their child, in particular social interactions, speech, reaction to stimuli, intelligence, family information, and psychological development. Plus and minus scores are added, and a cutoff of +20 is considered diagnostic of autism. The E-2 seems to be highly selective of classic Kanner-syndrome cases.

The BRIAAC consists of eight scales scored on a 10-point continuum from severe autism to behavior similar to a normally developing 3½-to-4½-year-old. The scales include relationship to adults, communication, drive for mastery, vocalization and expressive speech, sound and speech reception, social responsiveness, body movement, and psychobiological development. The main usefulness of the BRIAAC appears to be in evaluating treatment effectiveness (Parks, 1988).

The BOS has been primarily a research tool relying on objective behavioral observation of specifically defined behaviors. Originally consisting of 67 items, a current version (Freeman et al., 1984) has been reduced to 24 items. Because the conditions of observation are highly specific as are the various stimuli presented during the evaluation, this measure is of less practical utility to the clinician.

The ABC is the first component of the Autism Screening Instrument for Educational Planning (ASIEP) (Krug et al., 1979). It consists of 57 behaviors derived from various sources, such as Rimland's Form E-2, Creak's (1964) criteria, and BRIAAC items. Items are weighted based on significance for discriminating autism and total scores in five different areas (sensory, relating, body and object use, language, and social and self help). An overall total also is obtained. The developers of the scale have reported success in using the ABC to discriminate autistic from other disabled children, but questions about its reliability and validity have been raised by Parks (1983, 1988).

ADOS and ADI

Reliability and validity data have recently been reported on two instruments that appear to be useful for both clinical and research purposes. The Autistic Diagnostic Observation Schedule (ADOS) (Lord, Rutter, Goode, Heemsbergen, Jordan, Mawhood, & Schopler, 1989) and the Autistic Diagnostic Interview (ADI) (LeCouteur, Rutter, Lord, Rios, Robertson, Holdgrafer, & McLennan, 1989) derive from the most current understanding of autism and is based on the assessment of social, communicative, play, and interest functioning. The ADOS consists of a number of tasks designed to elicit social, communicative, and symbolic thinking skills using both structured and unstructured tasks and a flexible and clinically interactive approach. The scale is standardized for subjects with an estimated mental age of 3 years and older. There are nine components to the observational assessment, such as a puzzle-type construction task to observe help seeking and social interactive behavior, an unstructured make-believe play situation with a set of toy objects, and a larger poster picture of a complex scene to assess the child's ability to describe activities. Ratings of expected and atypical behaviors are very explicit and easily codable. In addition to the structured tasks and ratings obtained from direct observation, there is a global set of ratings that can be used in helping to determine the diagnosis.

The ADI is described as a standardized investigator-based assessment instrument. It is designed to be used with the principal caregiver and it covers the lifetime of range of behaviors relevant to the differential diagnosis of autism and PDD in individuals of any chronological age from 5 years to early adulthood, and with any mental age from 2 years on. The standardized history taking begins with questioning on when and how the parents first became aware that something was wrong and on key developmental milestones. It covers the child's behavior during the first 5 years of life and then shifts to current behavior. The scale attempts to specify qualitative impairments and deviance rather than just delays in the three major areas focused on: social reciprocity; communication and language; and repetitive, restricted, and stereotyped behaviors. A unique feature is the interviewing format, which requires the interviewer to obtain detailed descriptions of actual behaviors that can be coded on a carefully specified rating system. In a preliminary study, a diagnostic algorithm was derived using ICD-10 criteria. Apparently there are plans to develop a simplified version for clinical use.

The ADOS and ADI represent a promising direction that combined a sophisticated synthesis of research and clinical knowledge of autism. Both should become a valuable addition to the field of diagnostic instruments.

Developmental-Educational Assessment

Establishment of the diagnosis is only one part of the total evaluation process. Individualized and comprehensive assessment of developmental and functional skills across contexts provides the foundation on which to build an effective intervention program. Because autism has been recognized as a disorder of development rather than as an emotional or psychiatric condition, it is important to assess the skills of these children developmentally to understand to what extent and how they differ from comparably aged normally developing children. In addition to the framework of delays and deviancies from expected development, the assessment should take an educational perspective: That is, the current most consistently effective intervention for autistic individuals is structured teaching in both individual and group environments (Schopler & Olley, 1982). These twin approaches of development and education form the core for the integrated assessment necessary for program planning. This section describes an instrument, the Psychoeducational Profile-Revised (PEP-R) (Schopler et al., 1990), developed within the TEACCH program (Schopler, 1987) that illustrates how a single assessment tool can facilitate this process.

Psychoeducational Profile-Revised (PEP-R)

The PEP-R is the recent revision of the Psychoeducational Profile (Schopler & Reichler, 1979), which was designed to fill a gap in assessment methods with autistic children. Standardized tests were thought to lead to inadequate performance or "untestability" (Marcus & Baker, 1986) because of excessive language demands and task instructions that are overly rigid for these children. The characteristics of the original PEP and the new PEP-R that have overcome problems of testability include reduced language comprehension and expression requirements on nonverbal items, flexibility in administration in terms of both sequence of item presentation and task instructions, encouragement to structure the testing situation to enhance performance, and a scoring system that includes partial credit for "emerging" performance on an item (not just the pass and fail scores of most tests).

At this point, it is useful to briefly review those factors that have contributed to problems in testability and how the PEP-R enables the examiner to successfully deal with them. Baker (1983) and Marcus and Baker (1986) have discussed the interplay between the handicaps of the disorder of autism and the demands of the testing situation that interfere with adequate test performance. These problems include: (a) severe communication deficits that may not be recognized by the examiner who uses a high level of language and fails to provide alternative or supplementary cues, resulting in nonresponsiveness or negative reactions; (b) deficits in social understanding and relating to people, which makes the usual means of establishing rapport ineffective, interferes with following basic rules such as sitting and waiting, and may frustrate the examiner not experienced with minimally responsive children; (c) attention, organization, and perceptual problems that result in a wide range of potentially disruptive behaviors when expectations are too high and structure is lacking; and (d) motivational deficits such as lack of interest in social praise or preference for unusual sensory stimuli or abnormally strong attachment to an object. In addition, inappropriate test selection (e.g., verbally loaded intelligence test for a nonverbal child) exacerbates these problems.

Strategies to deal effectively with these problems embodied in the PEP-R include (a) flexibility in test administration (e.g., altering sequences of test items so that stressful language items are balanced by more enjoyable visual-motor tasks); (b) establishing an appropriate structure (e.g., clear rules, work and play areas, a box in which to put completed items); (c) alternative methods of communication (e.g., use of dramatic gestures, exaggerated affect, manual prompts or other concrete visual aids); (d) increasing motivation (e.g., use of naturally rewarding contingencies, such as access to a favorite object, break from the test to go to the play area, physical play); and (e) handling attentional and atypical behaviors by simplifying a task, presenting test materials at the moment when the child attends, interrupting perseverative behaviors, and repetition of test instructions.

The PEP-R was compiled to meet the increased demands for appropriate assessment of younger preschool and lower functioning children with autism and other developmental disorders. It is designed for use with children functioning at or below the preschool range and within the chronological age range of 6 months to 7 years. For older children who are still preadolescent, the PEP-R can still provide useful information when at least some developmental skills fall below the first grade level. Children whose skills are at that level or higher are usually able to take more traditional cognitive tests.

The test is divided into two sections: one that assesses developmental functions and the other identified unusual or atypical behaviors. The developmental functions include imitation, perception, fine motor, gross motor, eye-hand integration, cognitive verbal, and cognitive performance. Behavioral areas assessed involved relating and affect, play and interest in materials, sensory responses, and language (all of which are areas associated with the characteristics of autism).

There are 131 developmental items, not all of which are administered to every child depending on functioning level. Each of these is scored as a pass, fail, or emerge, the latter category reflecting partial or incomplete mastery of the task. For example, on an item requiring tapping a call bell twice in imitation of the examiner, an emerge would be scored if either the child tapped only once or repeatedly or if he or she tapped twice after several demonstrations. The purpose of the emerge score is to identify potential skills suitable for a teaching program and to provide some evidence that, even if the child is not achieving at an age-appropriate developmental level, that he or she is showing a number of beginning skills. Items that are passed are summed within each function area, and that score is marked on a developmental scale profile. Each function score has an age-equivalent score and the completed profile that reflects the unevenness of the skill pattern of the child. A total developmental score and age equivalent are also derived and can be converted into a ratio developmental quotient, as the need arises. Along with the flexible test administration and separation of language items from other function areas noted earlier, the PEP-R has test materials that are concrete and interesting to even the severely impaired child. Successes are possible for all children because of the wide range of developmental levels covered by the test items (e.g., social baby games and visual tracking of movement at the lowest level to reading, with comprehension at the upper level).

There are 43 behavioral abnormality items, most of which are scored on the basis of general observations across the entire test session (which normally lasts approximately 1½ hours). Each item is rated as appropriate, mildly abnormal, or severely abnormal. An example of an item in the Relating and Affect domain is "seeks help from the examiner." An appropriate rating is made if the child asks or gestures for help appropriately; a severe rating is scored if the child never asks or gestures for help when needed or requests help excessively. An example of an item in the Language area is "spontaneous communication." This is scored only for verbal children, and an appropriate rating is given if the child uses a variety of functional, spontaneous language responses to communicate ideas or ask questions; a severe rating is given if the child does not use any spontaneous, functional, relevant communication, or dwells on one subject in a perseverative and inappropriate manner. Items scored as either mild or severe are marked on a circular graph providing a visual display of the amount and degree of behavioral abnormality.

Once the PEP-R assessment is completed and the scores charted on the two profiles, information is obtained that helps with specifying problems and characteristics associated with a diagnois of autism, overall level of developmental functioning, patterns of strengths and weaknesses, strategies that might be used to enhance learning potential and behavioral functioning, and emerging areas that should be targeted for educational programming. Although by itself the PEP-R is not a substitute for assessments in other areas, it does provide a cross-sectional perspective that encompasses most of the domains relevant for a thorough multidiscipline evaluation.

AAPEP

Educational assessment of older autistic persons has only recently been a concern to professionals. Developmental issues become less important as the child moves into adolescence, at least in terms of age levels and normative reference groups. While it is still relevant to understand the cognitive, social, and communicative delays from a developmental perspective, the functionality or applicability of existing skills to meaningful everyday situations assumes prominence as the reference for success. The upward extension of the PEP into adolescence and adulthood is the Adolescent and Adult Psychoeducational Profile (AAPEP) (Mesibov, Schopler, Schaffer, & Landrus, 1988), designed as a criterion-referenced instrument for moderately to severely handicapped persons with autism. Success on the various parts of the test are considered predictive of good adjustment to supervised vocational and residential settings. The AAPEP assesses functioning in six different areas: vocational skills, independent functioning, leisure skills, vocational behavior, functional communication, and interpersonal behaviors. Like the PEP-R, the AAPEP has the three ratings of pass, fail, and emerge for each of the items. An innovative feature is that the test measures these functional skills across three environments with separate scales: Direct Observation scale, a set of tasks administered by a clinician or evaluator; Work/School scale, an inventory of skills completed through interview with the teacher or staff person in the work setting; and Home scale, a similar inventory geared to the home setting and completed by interview with the primary caretakers. Performance across settings allows for a profile of strengths and weaknesses in different environments as well as the pattern across functions within an environment. Program goals and specific teaching and training activities can be developed from the analysis of the assessment data.

Intellectual-Adaptive Assessment

Traditional, standardized cognitive and adaptive tests are also relevant for a comprehensive assessment of autistic individuals. As noted earlier, a factor in the testability problem with autistic children was the selection of language-loaded IQ tests, such as the Stanford-Binet (Terman & Merrill, 1960). Research has repeatedly shown that most autistic children suffer from mental retardation. The majority of these children have at least moderate mental retardation (Schopler, 1983). Even among the 25% to 30% not mentally retarded, many, if not most, of this group have significant cognitive and communicative impairments that limit performance on at least some parts of standardized intelligence tests. With young preschool autistic children, the Binet or Wechsler Scales (Wechsler, 1974), K-ABC (Kaufman & Kaufman, 1983), or McCarthy (1972) are rarely appropriate. Appropriate alternatives, depending on level of functioning, are the Bayley Scales of Infant Development (Bayley, 1969), Merrill-Palmer Scales of Mental Tests (Statsman, 1948), or Leiter International Performance Scale (Leiter, 1969). These measures tend to emphasize the autistic child's strengths of visual motor, visual discrimination, matching, and sorting skills, or drop down to low enough developmental levels to better tap the child's abilities.

A somewhat higher percentage of school-age and older children and adolescents can be reliably tested on the higher level, verbally demanding tests, although some minor modifications may be required to make sure the task instructions are understood. Subtest analysis can be helpful to identify cognitive abilities and disabilities, especially on the Wechsler Scales. Research has highlighted a profile of higher Performance and Verbal IQs and relative strengths on subtests of Block Design and Object Assembly, with weaknesses on Comprehension, Picture Arrangement, and Coding (Rutter, 1978). Picture and Verbal Absurdities and Problem-Solving on the Stanford-Binet also seem to differentiate high-level autistic persons from normal individuals (Rumsey & Hamburger, 1988). Marcus and Baker (1986) and Short and Marcus (1987) provide detailed critical reviews of intelligence tests used with autistic children.

It is important to get an assessment of adaptive functioning, and the Vineland Adaptive Behavior Scales (Sparrow, Balla & Cicchetti, 1984) adequately serve this purpose. Typically, autistic individuals do more poorly on adaptive than on cognitive measures of functioning. This appears to be especially true for normal-IQ persons whose adaptive skills may fall into the mildly to moderately deficient range, with weakness in the Socialization domain. It is then not surprising to note that this individual, while having the intellectual capability to be independent and achieve successfully, requires a supervised or semisupervised living and vocational situation.

Communication and Language Assessment

Recent developments in the understanding of the basic problems in autism have underscored the centrality of the communicative rather than the semantic, syntactic, or speech aspects of language (Watson et al., 1989; Wetherby, 1986). An appropriate assessment of language must be broader than the usual measures of receptive and expressive language, and one must examine various functions, forms, intent, and situations in which communication occurs. Still, it is important not to overlook knowledge of words and language content so that standardized tests can be useful.

Formal testing, informal and observational assessment, and parental interviews are helpful strategies for assessing language and communication skills. Since the language impairments of autistic children are typically severe, measures that cover the preschool range are more likely to yield accurate findings. The more useful scales include the Sequenced Inventory of Communication Development (Hedrick, Prather, & Tobin, 1975), which covers expressive and receptive skills from 4 months to 4 years; the Reynell Developmental Language Scales (Reynell, 1978), which measures receptive and expressive language skills of children from 1 to 7 years; and the Peabody Picture Vocabulary Test, Revised edition (Dunn & Dunn, 1981), a satisfactory measure of single-word receptive vocabulary.

A number of investigators have reported procedures for assessing communication skills utilizing natural settings and involving multiple sources of information. Although, as with social assessment, no formal, standardized instruments yet exist, these methods are based on empirical data and sound conceptual frameworks. Prizant (1988) lists three basic strategies: interviewing caregivers and significant others, use of a checklist for communication inventories for on-line observations, and behavior sampling and/or formal assessments. A major purpose is to derive a social-communicative profile identifying developmental levels, primary obstacles in communication, and communicative needs. He describes four assessment dimensions of communicative functions:

1. repertoire of communicative functions such as regulating another's behavior and engaging in social interaction;
2. degree of intentionality for each function;
3. variety and sophistication of communicative means for each function such as gestural and vocal modality; and
4. reciprocity of communication such as the ability to participate in turn-taking interactions and ability to elaborate on topics based on conventional meaning.

The TEACCH Communication Curriculum (Watson et al., 1989) is a recent effort to develop an assessment system as a basis for programming. The assessment process uses three tools: a communication sample, an interview on parent observations and priorities, and a goal priorities worksheet. The program is built around several factors: (a) communicative intent: that is, not only whether the child's behavior can be interpreted, but also whether the child intends for a behavior to communicate something to another; (b) purposes of functions, such as requesting, rejecting, seeking or giving information, expressing feelings, or participating in social and communicative routines; (c) means of communication through motoric action, vocalizations or gestures, pictures, or printed words; (d) content of communication or the type and range of concepts the child uses. For verbal children, the content might involve range of vocabulary and semantic categories represented by that vocabulary such as objects, actions, and locations; (e) use of communication in relation to context such as persons and situations and its generalizability.

This system is just one of the newer, productive approaches to assess communication abilities. It may lead to clarification of this fundamental problem in autism and to constructive intervention programs. In addressing the pragmatic aspects of language, this type of assessment process is conceptually and strategically linked to the next dimension or axis of the multiaxial process: social assessment.

Social Assessment

Current clinical and research investigations have pointed to a social-affective component as the basis of autism (Hobson, 1989), returning to Kanner's original conceptualization. Although the exact nature and precise biological cause of the social dysfunction are yet to be determined, there is little doubt about the lifelong social impairment faced by autistic individuals regardless of level of functioning. Despite this recognition, interestingly, methods for assessment are generally informal (ad hoc or based on a research protocol). There are problems in definition and addressing the boundaries and scope of what is social behavior. Social dysfunctions include deficits in judgment, lack of empathy, difficulties in reciprocity, communicative impairments, inappropriate behavior, noncompliance, rejection or avoidance of peers, intrusiveness, withdrawn behavior, failure to seek or give comfort, role-taking deficiencies, and many other characteristics. Social behavior has to be defined and observed across multiple settings, and the developmental perspective has to be considered.

It is useful to have some defined framework or structure to guide the assessment process. Olley (1986) described one such potentially valuable framework designed for use in the school setting. In this model, developmental social skills and prerequisites are defined. Prerequisites to social development include proximity (distance from others, facing proper direction, and the right location); interfering behavior or use of body (e.g., inappropriate use of toys, strong attachments to objects, body stereotypies); and adaption to change (e.g., insistence on rituals or sameness). Components to social development include looking, parallel play, social responses such as simple imitation games, social interactions such as turn-taking, imitation of social interaction, and reciprocal interaction, the most complex form of social interaction. Social behavior is then examined in various contexts: play or leisure such as schoolyard or playroom; eating such as snacktime and school cafeteria; community settings such as library or church; structured time such as desk work or independent classroom work; and travel or transition from place to place, such as movement about the room or using public transportation.

The PEP-R (Schopler et al., 1990) described earlier uses observational information to assess social behaviors in the areas of relating and affect displayed during interaction. The ADOS (Lord et al., 1989) provides several unstructured and structured situations to assess social reciprocity, turn-taking, and affective responses in the clinical setting. Information from a detailed parent interview is a necessary supplement to direct observations. The Vineland Adaptive Behavior Scales (Sparrow et al., 1984) provide formal data based on interview information regarding several aspects of social behavior. The ADI (LeCouteur et al., 1989) also is a standardized interview format yielding highly specific information on many aspects of social functioning.

Related to issues of the evaluation of social behavior is behavioral assessment. Powers (1988) reviews goals and methods of such assessment for individuals with autism. Essentially these are quite similar to those used with other handicapping conditions. Basic goals include identification of target behaviors, determining controlling variables, development and implementation of a treatment plan, and evaluation of treatment effects. Multiple sources of data and multiple methods of data collection are recommended, with emphasis on precise description of behaviors targeted for intervention, environmental or organismic control over behavior, and deemphasis on inference. In the context of social aspects of autism, behavioral assessment basically is concerned with identifying two classes of problems: interfering, disruptive behaviors is need of reduction (e.g., aggression, self-stimulation) and behaviors in need of being increased (e.g., social interaction, play with peers). Traditionally, behavioral approaches have been relatively unconcerned with intervening variables, such as the developmental levels or unique deficits, but there has been a more recent effort to incorporate and integrate knowledge of the cognitive and communicative bases of autism into the behavioral framework (Hart, 1985).

Family Assessment

An important component in the total assessment process is the family perspective, especially that of the parents. As has been indicated throughout this chapter, parents are an important source of information for understanding how a child behaves, plays, learns, and communicates in his natural environment. The TEACCH Communication and Social Curriculums (Olley, 1986; Watson et al., 1989) have a specific role for parents in the data collection process as does the Autistic Diagnostic Interview (LeCouteur et al., 1989). The family assessment process also lays the groundwork for future collaboration with the parents by determining their concerns and needs. The importance of parent involvement in evaluation and treatment cannot be emphasized enough. It has been repeatedly demonstrated that only through ongoing, direct, and meaningful coordination of intervention efforts with families that the lives of autistic individuals can be maximally enhanced (Marcus & Schopler, 1987).

At TEACCH, parents are involved in the evaluation process from the outset: that is, from the time of referral when they are contacted and their concerns are first identified. Prior to the evaluation, a detailed history form, which includes developmental and medical information as well as a behavior checklist, is completed along with an open-ended questionnaire that allows the parents to describe a typical day with their child, their main concerns, what is most distressing and gratifying about the child, and goals and hopes for the future. The parent interview is semistructured, covering relevant areas and allowing sufficient time to air feelings and sources of worry and frustration. Specific areas reviewed include behavioral problems, communication skills, play skills, relationships with others (including siblings), daily living skills, and information about informal or formal support networks. The Vineland ABS (Sparrow et al., 1984) and the ADI (LeCouteur et al., 1989) help provide a framework within which the clinical interview is conducted. At the conclusion of the interview, the clinician should have a clear picture of the family and its relationship to their handicapped child, its worries and hopes, what resources are available, what stressors aside from having a handicapped child are present, and what treatment recommendations for the family should be made. A good interview will better prepare the family for the diagnostic and assessment information that is later presented at an interpretive conference.

Harris (1988) discusses the relevance of understanding the family's developmental status within the life cycle in helping to assess the overall impact of the autistic child on the family. In her model, along with a family interview, systematic observation of the child and various subgroups of the family (as well as the family as a unit) and selected paper-and-pencil tests that measure adaptation to stress and perception of family functioning (Holroyd, 1974) further clarify patterns and dynamics important for intervention.

Medical Assessment

Although the main focus of this chapter is on developmental and behavioral factors in the assessment of autistic persons, careful evaluation of medical aspects is also needed. Comprehensive information on these factors can be found in Coleman and Gillberg (1985) and Schopler and Mesibov (1987). Three areas should be covered in this assessment: factors related to possible etiology such as chromosome abnormalities, disorders of metabolism, and gestational disorders; neurological status, in particular evaluating the possibility of seizures and motor functioning; and general health status, including the current quality of medical and dental care. Normal health problems may easily be overlooked because of the inability of the child to communicate about pain and discomfort. If an initial screening and examination suggest the possibility of a genetic, biochemical, or neurological problem, further laboratory tests should be considered. It is our experience that such tests should not be done arbitrarily or routinely, but only if indicated by evidence from interview and observation. Others recommend that comprehensive laboratory studies be done as part of an initial systematic medical examination (DeMyer, 1979). The medical assessment also can evaluate the potential role of medications in the treatment of the child. Any such intervention necessitates careful collection of baseline data, effects of the drug treatment, monitoring of side effects, and ongoing laboratory studies, as required for the particular medication.

IMPLICATIONS FOR TREATMENT

Translating assessment information into treatment planning involves five components: integrating and interpreting results for parents and community program staffs, developing an individualized program for the child or adolescent, defining and determining curriculum areas, collaborating with parents as cotherapists, and collaborating with schools and other community agencies. Each of these is briefly discussed.

Integration and Interpretation of Results

The goal of the diagnostic evaluation should be to answer as fully and candidly as possible the concerns and questions of the family and referring agency. Some questions may be broad, such as What is the cause of the problem or What is the diagnosis, or more specific, How can the parents improve the child's play skills? Integration involves pulling together the diverse sources of information around a specific set of issues and questions, including diagnosis, level of development, strengths and weaknesses, and unique behavioral, social, and biomedical features. The process flows better if it is issue or problem focused rather than discipline focused. Each team member should contribute his or her findings to a complete understanding of the essential concerns raised by the parents and others involved with the case. The interpretive conference should deal candidly and sensitively with these concerns and allow the parents to articulate their ideas in the ensuing discussion. Intervention with autistic persons is a lifelong enterprise and the foundation for dialog is laid in the discussions that follow the initial assessment.

Developing an Individualized Program

The heterogeneity among autistic children and adolescents necessitates a highly individualized approach to program planning. There are certain common elements, of course, across individuals, but the pattern of strengths and weaknesses in cognition, problem-solving, communication, social skills, and motor abilities, along with unique learning styles means that goals, methods and activities must be specifically designed for each child (Schopler & Olley, 1982). One youngster may need an object-exchange system for communication training; another may be learning advanced conversational skills. One child may be relatively independent in self-help, while another needs considerable prompting in most areas of self-care. One child may learn from modeling and demonstration, while another needs intensive intrusion and multiple repetitions. The multimodal assessment data provide the basis for developing the treatment goals and strategies. However, assessment is an ongoing process, and good teaching and intervention should include reevaluation and rethinking of the initial findings.

Curriculum Areas

Relevant components for a curriculum for autistic students include independent work behaviors, social skills, communication skills, functional academics, and self-help. These areas overlap, of course, but can be planned separately and relate to the assessment procedures described earlier. These components cover the various domains considered typically deficient in most autistic children and adolescents and are relevant for successful adjustment and adaptation in the future. With the younger child, there is more emphasis on play, self-help, preacademics, and normalizing social experiences. With the older autistic adolescent, greater emphasis is placed on the functionality of potential work-related and academic skills, functional communication, and appropriate social and leisure-recreational behavior.

Collaboration with Parents

Helping parents with their autistic child starts with the diagnostic evaluation and continues throughout the early childhood, latency, adolescent, and adult years (Marcus & Schopler, 1987). The nature and intensity of parent involvement may change as others take greater responsibility for direct service, but the parent perspective always must be considered in any treatment decision. During the preschool years, parents' motivation for teaching their child is at its highest (Schopler, Mesibov, Shigley & Bashford, 1984) and therapists should take advantage of the situation by enlisting them as co-therapists. During the school years, parent and teacher communication is critical for generalizing success across settings, preventing or dealing with behavior problems, and determining appropriate education goals. Parents also need to be involved in the transitional planning from school to work and from their own home to an alternative residential facility. Parents are the ones who have the lifelong responsibility, who ultimately have to bridge the gaps across service agencies, and plan for future settings. Professionals have to recognize this and do whatever is needed to support such families.

School and Community Programming

The primary setting in which individualized educational programming and curriculae are carried out is the school classroom. As children mature the emphasis shifts from a developmental to a functional approach and the environment in which teaching takes place becomes more community-based (Van Bourgondien & Mesibov, 1989). Assessment data need to be translated into the settings in which the intervention will occur. For a beginning younger student, goals typically involve learning basic rules and routines, becoming integrated into a group situation, and developing fundamental communication, problem-solving, and social skills in line with appropriate expectations. With older students, learning to work in a variety of contexts for long periods of time, self-directedness, and prevocational and vocational skills become the focus of attention. Students need to use their skills in nonclassroom environments within the school, such as the library or cafeteria, and in the community, such as the grocery stores and recreational areas.

CLINICAL CASE ILLUSTRATION

The following case illustrates the main points discussed earlier in the chapter. It is based on an evaluation in the TEACCH program of a preschooler, but the approaches and strategies are applicable across all ages.

Background Information

John is a 3-to-7-year-old referred to TEACCH to help clarify the diagnosis, provide support for the parents, and consultation support for his normal preschool program. Classroom observations by the referring psychologist noted problems in communication and lack of social peer interaction. Parental concerns included John's lack of affection and interest in social interaction, delayed language, unusual sensitivity, and their uncertainty over how to discipline, knowing what is wrong and why, and finding ways to help him. They were very anxious to get started with TEACCH because of their worry that time was passing and John was not developing.

Assessments

Results from the various assessment procedures are briefly summarized.

Diagnostic Summary

Based on observations during the PEP-R, a completion of the CARS, and school and home reports, a diagnosis of autism was made. Autistic characteristics noted were impaired relating skills and resistance to intrusion, inconsistent and noncommunicative language, and limited interests and minimal play skills. In addition, he showed a typically uneven profile, with strong visual memory and weak cognitive and abstract skills. His CARS score was 35, which placed him in the moderately autistic range. Relating to people, imitation, emotional expression, and communication were items scored in the more severe range; activity level and sensory responses were considered less significant.

Development-educational Summary

On the PEP-R, John scored at approximately the 2-year level, with a significantly scattered pattern of strengths and weaknesses. He did not pass any imitation items, although he showed a beginning understanding of this process and had three emerges (e.g., tapped the call bell repeatedly). Fine and gross motor and eye-hand integration skills fell in the 1¾-year to 2½-year levels. He neither passed nor obtained any emerging score on the Cognitive Performance items, but he did pass one item and had four emerging scores on the Cognitive Verbal items. He was able to name nine letters and a few numbers and to identify a few pictures. Despite this higher ability to name letters and numbers, John showed relatively little abstraction ability or language concepts.

Intellectual-adaptive Summary

The Bayley Scales of Infant Development was given and his overall age score was at the 17-to-18-month level. Since John was chronologically above the 30-month upper level for this test, no formal IQ score was derived, but the approximate 1½ year level suggested functioning in the moderately mentally retarded range. He did some imitating with objects (e.g., stirring with a spoon) and did best on the visual-motor items of the pegboard and simple formboard. He failed early language and social items. On the Vineland ABS (with his parents as informants), John obtained an Adaptive Behavior Composite of 57 and an age equivalent of 1 to 9 years.

Communication and Social Assessment Summary

At home, John was described as being able to carry out a familiar request and understanding language in the context of daily routines. Expressively at home, he talks often, sometimes to himself, occasionally to tell his parents something. During testing he spoke spontaneously a number of times. There were some meaningful requests (e.g., "get car," "I am hungry"). Often he named what he saw: pictures and objects, numbers and letters, as if delighted with the naming of things. But he seemed unconcerned as to whether anyone was listening. His receptive language was hard to judge because he did not follow the directions of showing or giving something to the examiner. Socially, he was initially quite distant and his emotional expression was very subdued and uncomfortable in social interactions. His interests were oriented toward objects. In a free play situation, he paced about, shuffling some picture cards in his hands and talking to himself in jargon-type speech, preoccupied and oblivious to the examiner. By contrast, he was responsive to physical roughhousing play, seemingly genuine in his laughter and apparently enjoying this type of interaction. At home, he plays with his sister in physically active games, loves to swing and climb, and plays with rolling a ball back and forth. Behavior problems involve getting upset, during which time he cries, tries to butt his mother with his head, or scratch her face; he also throws things down when angered, which also is a school problem. He would become upset if his parents were to take away father's shoes and ties, which he likes to collect from the closet.

Medical Summary

Pregnancy and birth history were uncomplicated as newborn period was normal. General health was considered satisfactory, with some recurring ear infections. Sleep and diet were also satisfactory. Physical examination indicated some characteristic suggestive of possible Fragile X (large head, prominent ears) and a Fragile X karyotyping was suggested although not strongly recommended because of the presence of just a few signs.

Family Assessment Summary

John's family was described as close and highly involved with child care and very gentle in their approach to raising children. They were intelligent and wanted to be able to understand all aspects of child development, particularly as it applied to John's special needs. An earlier evaluation that had raised the possibility of autism and mental retardation had come as a shock. They were not defensive about these diagnoses but were confused about how they applied to John. They used wit and humor to describe their observations of him, but underlying this style was a clearly painful disappointment and worry, which they admit and state is handled through humor. Both parents were highly motivated to become involved in teaching John at home and working with the school staff.

Conference Summary

The first part of the parent interpretive conference clarified the diagnosis of autism, recognizing that John did not fit all the characteristics found in books but did meet the major criteria and showed a mild to moderate degree of autism: limited social relating skills; delayed language and minimal use of this for communication purposes; a tendency to play with one object or one activity for overly long periods of time to the exclusion of other choices or imaginative play; and an uneven development of skills, such as unusual memory for songs and spatial memory. His problems with organization and attention and significant delay in development were also reviewed. The parents stated their confusion over whether the problem was due to a lack of skill or lack of interest, an issue that might be assessed over an extended period with teaching sessions. Although eager to teach their child, the parents were concerned about giving equal time to their daughter. They were told that since both children are getting excellent attention and care, the important consideration was spending the time with John in a more productive, active teaching way. The conference also dealt with issues about appropriate expectations and how to deal with John like other children, but recognizing his unique needs.

Intervention: Parents as Cotherapists

The parents came to the clinic for biweekly home teaching sessions over a 4-month period. The goals for the initial sessions included teaching a predictable work-play routine to improve his organization, attending, and task completion, as well as his responsiveness to another's directions, to further assess and develop receptive language, including following simple directions, and to develop an understanding of social reciprocity by focusing at a concrete level. Teaching strategies involved alternating an activity first by having John do it according to the direction of the therapist or parent, then allowing him to use his preferred approach; helping him extensively to get through an activity properly; keeping the activities very short and making sure he was successful; and keeping language very simple, using single words more than phrases. Example of activities included pegboards, stacking blocks, Tinker Toy® construction, object sorting, and finding objects in a shoe box with a picture book to help cue him. These activities and goals were gradually accomplished and more complex ones added. An 18-month follow-up evaluation indicated that John had made a year's progress and had improved in a number of autistic behaviors. Along with the home teaching, his parents also worked on behavior problems and reported a significant decrease in tantrums.

Intervention: School

John continued to attend the regular preschool with normal peers for approximately a year following his evaluation. Although he was benefiting somewhat from the standard developmental curriculum and peer relationships, it became increasingly apparent, even with recognition by the staff of his deficits and extensive consultation, that he needed a more tightly structured preschool classroom. His parents decided to enroll him in a specialized preschool class for autistic children housed in a regular elementary school, with opportunities for mainstreaming with normal kindergarten children. His social behavior in school improved, as did his organization and attention and ability to learn the developmentally based curriculum. In addition, the parents worked very closely with the teacher, and this link between the TEACCH center, home, and classroom helped facilitate John's learning potential.

SUMMARY

The comprehensive assessment of children and adolescents with autism and other pervasive developmental disorders is an essential first step to clarification of the major problems faced by the individual and the family. In this chapter, we discussed a variety of strategies and techniques that can be used effectively by the clinician, either individually or as part of a team. Although there are still a number of unresolved issues in establishing the nature and boundaries of autism and PDD, there is considerable knowledge available for professionals to draw upon in carrying out a careful, useful evaluation. By making an accurate diagnosis and assessing skills and weaknesses across and within areas of functioning, the clinician can facilitate the development of a treatment program that will enable the child and family to have as productive and meaningful a life as possible.

REFERENCES

American Psychiatric Association. (1987). *Diagnostic and statistical manual of mental disorders-DSM-III* (3rd ed., rev.). Washington, DC: Author.

Baker, A. F. (1983). Psychological assessment of autistic children *Clinical Psychology Review, 3,* 41–59.

Bayley, N. (1969). *Bayley Scales of Infant Development.* New York: Psychological Corporation.

Cantwell, D. P., & Baker, L. (1988). Multiaxial diagnostic approaches. In E. Schopler & G. B. Mesibov (Eds.), *Diagnosis and assessment in autism* (pp. 111–122). New York: Plenum Press.

Coleman, M., & Gillberg, C. (1985). *The biology of the autistic syndrome.* New York: Praeger.

Courchesne, E., Yeung-Courchesne, R., Press, G. A., Hesselink, J. R., & Jernigan, T. L. (1988). Hypoplasia of cerebellar vermal lobules VI and VII in autism. *New England Journal of Medicine, 318,* 1349–1354.

Creak, M. (1964). Schizophrenic syndrome in childhood: Further progress report of a working party (April, 1964). *Developmental Medicine and Child Neurology, 6,* 530–535.

DeMyer, M. K. (1979). *Parents and children in autism.* New York: John Wiley & Sons.

DeMyer, M. K., Hingtgen, J. N., & Jackson, R. K. (1981). Infantile autism reviewed. *Schizophrenia Bulletin, 7,* 388–445.

Dunn, L., & Dunn, L. (1981). *Peabody Picture Vocabulary Test—Revised.* Circle Pines, MN: American Guidance Service.

Freeman, B. J., Ritvo, E. R., & Schroth, P. (1984). Behavior assessment of the syndrome of autism: Behavior Observation System. *Journal of the American Academy of Child Psychiatry, 23,* 588–594.

Gillberg, C., & Wahlstrom, J. (1985). Chromosome abnormalities in infantile autism and other childhood psychoses: A population study of 66 cases. *Developmental Medicine and Child Neurology, 27,* 293–304.

Harris, S. (1988). Family assessment in autism. In E. Schopler & G. B. Mesibov (Eds.), *Diagnosis and assessment in autism* (pp. 199–210). New York: Plenum Press.

Hart, B. (1985). Naturalistic training techniques. In S. Warren & A. Rogers-Warren (Eds.), *Teaching functional language* (pp. 63–88). Baltimore: University Park Press.

Hedrick, D. L., Prather, E. M., & Tobin, A. R. (1975). *Sequenced Inventory for Communication Development.* Seattle: University of Washington Press.

Hermelin, B., & O'Connor, N. (1985). Logico-affective states and non-verbal language. In E. Schopler & G. B. Mesibov (Eds.), *Communication problems in autism* (pp. 283–310). New York: Plenum Press.

Hobson, R. P. (1989). Beyond cognition: A theory of autism. In G. Dawson (Ed.), *Autism: Nature, diagnosis, and treatment* (pp. 22–48). New York: Guilford Press.

Holroyd, J. (1974). The questionnaire on resources and stress: An instrument to measure family response to a handicapped member. *Journal of Community Psychology, 2,* 92–94.

Kanner, L. (1943). Autistic disturbances of affective contact. *Nervous Child, 2,* 217–250.

Kaufman, A. S., & Kaufman, N. L. (1983). *Kaufman Assessment Battery for Children.* Circle Pines, MN: American Guidance Service.

Krug, D. A., Arick, J. R., & Almond, P. J. (1979). *Autism Screening Instrument for Educational Planning.* Portland, OR: ASIEP Educational Co.

LeCouteur, A., Rutter, M., Lord, C., Rios, P., Robertson, S., Holdgrafer, M., & McLennan, J. (1989). Autism Diagnostic Interview: A standardized investigator-based instrument. *Journal of Autism and Developmental Disorders, 19,* 363–387.

Leiter, R. G. (1969). *Leiter International Performance Scale.* Los Angeles: Western Psychological Services.

Lord, C. (1985). Autism and the comprehension of language. In E. Schopler & G. B. Mesibov (Eds.), *Communication problems in autism* (pp. 257–310). New York: Plenum Press.

Lord, C. Rutter, M., Goode, S., Heemsbergen, J., Jordan, H., Mawhood, L., & Schopler, E. (1989). *Journal of Autism and Developmental Disorders, 19,* 185–212.

Marcus, L. M., & Baker, A. F. (1986). Assessment of autistic children. In R. J. Simeonsson (Ed.), *Psychological assessment of special children* (pp. 279-304). Boston: Allyn and Bacon.

Marcus, L. M., Bristol, M. M., & Schopler, E. (1989). *A multiaxial approach in the evaluation of autistic children.* Paper presented at the Regional Congress of the World Federation of Societies of Biological Psychiatry, Jerusalem.

Marcus, L. M., & Schopler, E. (1987). Working with families: A developmental perspective. In D. Cohen, A. Donnellan, & R. Paul (Eds.), *Handbook of autism and atypical development* (pp. 499-512). New York: John Wiley & Sons.

McCarthy, D. (1972). *Manual for the McCarthy Scales of Children's Abilities.* New York: Psychological Corporation.

Mesibov, G. B. (1983). Current perspectives and issues in autism and adolescence. In E. Schopler & G. B. Mesibov (Eds.), *Autism in adolescents and adults* (pp. 37-53). New York: Plenum Press.

Mesibov, G. B., Schopler, E., Schaffer, B., & Landrus, R. (1988). *Individualized assessment and treatment for autistic and developmentally disabled children. Vol. 4. Adolescent and adult psychoeducational profile (AAPEP).* Austin, TX: Pro-Ed.

Morgan, S. (1988). Diagnostic assessment of autism: A review of objective scales. *Journal of Psychoeducational Assessment, 6,* 139-151.

Mundy, P., & Sigman, M. (1989). Specifying the nature of the social impairment in autism. In G. Dawson (Ed.), *Autism: Nature, diagnosis, and treatment* (pp. 3-21). New York: Guilford Press.

Olley, J. (1986). The TEACCH curriculum for teaching social behavior to children with autism. In E. Schopler & G. B. Mesibov (Eds.), *Social behavior in autism* (pp. 351-373). New York: Plenum Press.

Ornitz, E. (1989). Autism at the interface between sensory and information processing. In G. Dawson (Ed.), *Autism: Nature, diagnosis, and treatment* (pp. 174-207). New York: Guilford Press.

Parks, S. L. (1983). The assessment of autistic children: A selective review of available instruments. *Journal of Autism and Developmental Disorders, 13,* 255-267.

Parks, S. L. (1988). Psychometric instruments available for the assessment of autistic children. In E. Schopler & G. B. Mesibov (Eds.), *Diagnosis and assessment in autism* (pp. 123-136). New York: Plenum Press.

Powers, M. D. (1988). Behavioral assessment of autism.

Prizant, B. M. *(1988) Communication in preschool autistic children.* Paper presented at the TEACCH Conference on Preschool Issues in Autism, Chapel Hill, NC.

Prizant, B. M. (1988). *Communication in preschool autistic children.* Paper presented at TEACCH Conference on Preschool Issues in Autism.

Reynell, J. K. (1978). *Reynell Developmental Language Scales, Revised Edition.* Windsor, England: NFER/Nelson.

Rimland, B. (1971). The differentiation of childhood psychoses: an analysis of checklists for 2,218 psychotic children. *Journal of Autism and Childhood Schizophrenia, 1,* 161-174.

Rumsey, J. M., & Hamburger, S. D. (1988). Neuropsychological findings in high-functioning men with infantile autism, residual state. *Journal of Clinical and Experimental Neuropsychology, 10,* 201-221.

Ruttenburg, B. A., Kalish, B. I., Wenar, C., & Wolf, E. G. (1977). *Behavior rating instrument for autistic and other atypical children* (rev. ed.). Philadelphia: Developmental Center for Autistic Children.

Rutter, M. (1978). Diagnosis and definition of childhood autism. *Journal of Autism and Developmental Disorders, 8,* 139-161.

Rutter, M. (1983). Cognitive deficits in the pathogenesis of autism. *Journal of Child Psychology and Psychiatry, 24,* 513-531.

Rutter, M., & Schopler, E. (1988). Autism and pervasive developmental disorders: Concepts and diagnostic issues. In E. Schopler & G. B. Mesibov (Eds.), *Diagnosis and assessment in autism* (pp. 15-36). New York: Plenum Press.

Sartorius, N. V. (1976). Classification: An international perspective. *Psychiatric Annals, 6,* 24-35.

Schopler, E. (1983). New developments in the definition and diagnosis of autism. In B. B. Lahey & A. E. Kazdin (Eds.), *Advances in clinical child psychology, Vol. 6* (pp. 93-127). New York: Plenum Press.

Schopler, E. (1987). Specific and nonspecific factors in the effectiveness of a treatment system. *American Psychologist, 42,* 376-383.

Schopler, E., & Mesibov, G. B. (Eds.). (1985). *Communication problems in autism.* New York: Plenum Press.

Schopler, E., & Mesibov, G. B. (Eds.). (1987). *Neurobiological issues in autism.* New York: Plenum Press.

Schopler, E., Mesibov, G. B., Shigley, R. H., & Bashford, A. (1984). Helping autistic children through their parents: The TEACCH Model. In E. Schopler & G. B. Mesibov (Eds.), *The effects of autism on the family* (pp. 65-81). New York: Plenum Press.

Schopler, E., & Olley, J. G. (1982). Comprehensive educational services for autistic children: The TEACCH model. In C. R. Reynolds & T. B. Gutkin (Eds.), *Handbook of school psychology* (pp. 626-643). New York: John Wiley & Sons.

Schopler, E., & Reichler, R. J. (1979). *Individualized assessment and treatment for autistic and developmentally disabled children. Vol. I. Psychoeducational profile.* Austin, TX: Pro-Ed.

Schopler, E., Reichler, R. J., Bashford, A., Lansing, M. D., & Marcus, L. M. (1990). *Individualized assessment and treatment for autistic and developmentally disabled children. Vol. I. Psychoeducational profile-revised.* Austin, TX: Pro-Ed.

Schopler, E., Reichler, R. J., & Renner, B. R. (1986). *The Childhood Autism Rating Scale.* Los Angeles: Western Psychological Services.

Schopler, E., & Rutter, M. (1978). Subgroups vary with selection purpose. In M. Rutter & E. Schopler (Eds.), *Autism: A reappraisal of concepts and treatment* (pp. 507–517). New York: Plenum Press.

Short, A., & Marcus, L. (1987). Psychoeducational evaluation of autistic children and adolescents. In S. S. Strichart & P. Lazarus (Eds.) *Psychoeducational evaluation of school-aged children with low-incidence disorders* (pp. 155–180). Orlando, FL: Grune & Stratton.

Sparrow, S. S., Balla, D. A., & Cicchetti, D. V. (1984). *Vineland Adaptive Behavior Scales*. Circle Pines, MN: American Guidance Service.

Stutsman, R. (1948). *Merrill-Palmer Scale of Mental Tests*. Los Angeles: Western Psychological Services.

Terman, L. M., & Merrill, M. A. (1960). *Stanford-Binet Intelligence Scale*. Boston: Houghton-Mifflin.

Van Bourgondien, M. E., & Mesibov, G. B. (1989). Diagnosis and treatment of adolescents and adults with autism. In G. Dawson (Ed.), *Autism: Nature, diagnosis, and treatment* (pp. 367–385). New York: Guilford Press.

Volkmar, F. R., & Anderson, G. M. (1989). Neurochemical perspectives on infantile autism. In G. Dawson (Ed.), *Autism: Nature, diagnosis, and treatment* (pp. 208–224). New York: Guilford Press.

Volkmar, F. R., & Cohen, D. J. (1988) Classification and diagnosis of childhood autism. In E. Schopler & G. B. Mesibov (Eds.), *Diagnosis and assessment in autism* (pp. 71–89). New York: Plenum Press.

Watson, L., Lord, C., Schaffer, B., & Schopler, E. (1989). *Teaching spontaneous communication to autistic and developmentally handicapped children*. New York: Irvington.

Watson, L., and Marcus, L. M. (1988). Diagnosis and assessment of pre-school children. In E. Schopler and G. Mesibov (Eds.), *Diagnosis and assessment in autism* (pp. 271–301). New York: Plenum Press.

Wechsler, D. (1974). *Wechsler Intelligence Scale for Children—Revised*. New York: Psychological Corporation.

Wetherby, A. M. (1986). Ontogeny of communicative functions in autism. *Journal of Autism and Developmental Disorders, 15*, 295–315.

World Health Organization. (1987). *ICD-10 1986 Draft* (Chap. V, categories F80-F99: Mental, behavioural and developmental disorders). Geneva, Switzerland: World Health Organization.

CHAPTER 23

OBESITY

William G. Johnson
Linda K. Hinkle

DESCRIPTION OF THE DISORDER

Child and adolescent obesity is widely recognized as a significant public health problem. The current interest in overweight children and adolescents has arisen in part as a result of information that documents the increasing prevalence of obesity in children, its persistent developmental course, and its untoward consequences. While estimates of the prevalence of obesity in children range from 10% to 30%, the majority of studies report that approximately 20% of children and adolescents are obese (Kirschenbaum, 1987). Unfortunately, prevalence of obesity in children and adolescents appears to be increasing significantly. Over a 15-year period, Gortmaker and colleagues observed increases of more than 50% in 6- to 11-year-old children and of almost 40% in a 12- to 17-year-old group (Gortmaker, Deitz, Sobol, & Wehler, 1987).

Most studies also suggest that children do not outgrow the obese condition. Seventy-five percent of obese boys and 72% of obese girls 10 to 13 years of age become obese adults, compared to 11% of thin children of the same age (Abraham & Nordsieck, 1960). According to Stunkard and Burt (1967), the average obese child has a 28-to-1 chance of being an overweight adult. There is one exception to the finding of the persistence of obesity in children (Poskitt & Cole, 1977). The presence of obesity in infancy is related to high remission rates. When the obese condition continues into middle and late childhood, however, persistence into adolescence and adulthood is typical (Shear, Freedman, Burke, Harsha, Webber, & Bereman, 1988).

Obesity is associated with adverse consequences that are both physical and psychological. Physically, attention has been devoted primarily to the increased risk of heart disease. Obesity is strongly associated with elevated cholesterol, which increases the risk for heart disease, and this problem is now widely recognized as beginning in the early and middle childhood years. Two large-scale studies of children and adolescents, namely, the Muscatine and the Bogalusa studies, have documented these adverse physical consequences of obesity in children and adolescents with specific reference to cholesterol.

Approximately 25% of children in the Muscatine Study had total cholesterol values over 200 mg/dl, which is the level generally considered clinically significant. The presence of obesity was higher in the older children. Five percent of 6- to 9-year-old and 8 percent of 14- to 18-year-old children were 30%

heavier than the median of the same length-age-sex reference group (Lauer, Connor, Leaverton, Reiter, & Clarke, 1975).

An objective of the Bogalusa study was to document the early development of heart disease as it relates to obesity (Berenson et al., 1982). In this study, a significant correlation between high cholesterol levels and overweight, which was more pronounced in white children, was observed. Also, older children demonstrated a positive correlation between obesity and levels of low-density lipoprotein (LDL), which is a type of cholesterol associated with coronary heart disease. Additionally, blood lipids or fat levels displayed a close tracking over the years with LDL cholesterol showing a .6 correlation over a 5-year span. Weight also tracked closely over the years. Specifically, children who were initially ranked in the upper 25% of weight relative to their peers continued to be ranked in this upper quartile.

An interesting feature of the Bogalusa Study was the attempt to relate dietary intake to obesity and cholesterol. The investigators noted a progressive impact of diet and other behavioral-environmental variables on the development of cardiovascular risk with increasing age. Interestingly, the intake of complex carbohydrates was inversely related to these risk variables.

In a follow-up to this earlier report, Shear et al. (1988) examined weight changes in 5- to 14-year-old children from 1973 to 1984. Over this 11-year time frame, the prevalence of overweight increased from 15% in 1973–1974 to 24% in 1984–1985. The authors attribute these weight changes primarily to the time spent in nonphysical activity and not to an increase in caloric intake. Based upon data from these and other studies, Morrison and Glueck (1981) conclude that children and adolescents with significant risks for heart disease became high-risk adults. In addition to these physical consequences, obese children and adolescents often suffer psychologically. Overweight children are typically evaluated negatively by their peers and suffer poor self-image (Brownell & Stunkard, 1980). Moreover, onset of obesity in childhood has been associated with poor response to weight-reduction efforts (Johnson & Corrigan, 1987). In summary, the pervasive nature of obesity, its persistence into adulthood, and the adverse health and psychological correlates clearly establish obesity as a significant public health problem. A comprehensive approach to assessment is necessary to elucidate the multiple etiologies of obesity and to aid in the evaluation of interventions for weight control.

MULTIMODAL ASSESSMENT

The many facets of child and adolescent obesity and its clinical management call for the assessment of a variety of factors in addition to weight. This argument for a broad-based, multimodal assessment recognizes that targets in the treatment of obesity are behavior changes that mediate weight and not weight, per se. Important targets for change during a 15- to-20-week treatment program, then, are specific behaviors and cognitions that mediate weight loss. Examples of these behavioral targets include activity, eating habits, nutrition, family atmosphere and structure, and cognitions and attributions related to the causes and treatments of obesity. Other important measures, such as body composition, metabolic processes based upon blood and urine samples, and measures of aerobic capacity, can provide valuable information on overall health status.

Determinations of Obesity

There are many formal methods to determine the extent of obesity, and we shall review the most popular procedures, which are based upon weight and body composition. These methods vary in their usefulness for determining the extent of obesity and tracking the progress of treatment.

Weight Tables and Related Indices

One of the first questions facing researchers and clinicians is the appropriate selection of patients. For children and adolescents, body weight is the most common indicator of obesity, just as it is with adults. For adults, body weight is compared to an ideal or desirable weight based upon actuary and mortality tables. For children and adolescents, however, the determination of obesity is most often based upon weight that is compared to a peer reference group similar in gender, age, and height. Here, obesity is defined as a body weight for a given gender, age, and height that exceeds a certain percentile and suggestions range from the 70th to the 90th percentile for the identification of obesity. Table 23-1 presents weights for girls and boys respectively adapted from Berhman and Vaughan (1983).

The second approach to classifying obesity is based upon ideal or desirable weights by age and height for both boys and girls. Typically, weights that are 20% or greater than these ideal values are considered

Table 23-1. Cutoff Weights (in pounds) for Obese Boys and Girls in the 75th, 90th, and 95th Percentiles

AGE (IN YEARS)	GIRLS: PERCENTILES			BOYS: PERCENTILES		
	75TH	90TH	95TH	75TH	90TH	95TH
6.0	47.25	52.75	56.75	49.50	53.50	58.00
7.0	53.25	60.50	65.50	55.00	60.25	66.50
8.0	61.50	70.75	76.50	61.50	68.50	76.00
9.0	71.50	83.00	89.50	69.25	78.50	87.75
10.0	82.75	96.25	104.00	78.50	90.00	99.75
11.0	94.50	110.25	119.00	89.00	102.75	113.50
12.0	106.00	123.50	134.00	101.00	116.25	128.00
13.0	116.75	135.50	148.25	114.25	130.25	143.25
14.0	125.75	145.50	161.00	128.50	144.50	159.00
15.0	133.00	153.25	171.50	142.75	158.50	174.50
16.0	137.25	158.00	178.50	155.00	172.00	188.75
17.0	138.75	159.50	181.75	163.50	184.25	201.25
18.0	138.50	159.25	181.75	167.75	195.00	211.00

Note: From *Nelson textbook of pediatrics* (12th ed., pp. 30-31) by R. E. Behrman and V. C. Vaughan, III, 1983, Philadelphia, PA: W. B. Saunders. Copyright 1983 by W. B. Saunders. Adapted by permission.

obese. Tables 23-2 and 23-3 present values proposed by the World Health Organization.

In addition to these normative classifications, several ratios have been constructed using weight and height. For adults, the body mass index (BMI) is the most widely used index. The formula for BMI is

$$\text{BMI} = \frac{\text{weight (kg)}}{\text{height (m}^2\text{)}}$$

Berenson and colleagues have found another ratio, namely the ponderal index (PI), to be highly related to risk factors such as cholesterol in children. The formula for PI is

$$\text{PI} = \frac{\text{weight (kg)}}{\text{height (m}^2\text{)}}$$

The weight-length index (WLI) has been suggested as the most accurate measure of weight while correcting for height and weight of a child's reference group (DuRant & Linder, 1981). The formula for WLI is

$$\text{WLI} = \frac{\text{actual weight}}{\text{actual height}} \div \frac{\text{50th percentile weight expected by age}}{\text{50th percentile height expected by age}} \times 100$$

DuRant and Linder (1981) indicate that the normal range in WLI for children falls between 90 and 100.

Children scoring between 110 and 119 should be classified as overweight, and those greater than 120 as obese.

While the WLI corrects for height, it may not adequately correct for growth in height and the concomitant weight gain from lean body mass over the course of a weight-reduction program that may last up to 6 months. Accordingly, Kirschenbaum (1988) recommends adjusting for the increase in height and its effect on lean body weight.

Treatment success in weight-reduction programs is in part related to longer duration of active intervention (Perri, 1987). For programs lasting up to 6 months with regular follow-up sessions, the AW formula may be particularly useful.

Measures of Body Composition

The aforementioned measures and indices assess the extent of obesity based primarily upon excess weight. While the BMI, PMI, and WLI provide corrections for weight gain due to height, these indices do not estimate the lean and fat weight of the body. Knowing, for example, that a child's weight is 30% over an ideal weight or in the 90th percentile when compared to a reference group is important; however, such excess weight by itself provides no information on the child's fat and lean body mass. It is not unusual for male adolescents to exceed the weight standards for obesity when their excess weight is primarily lean muscle and not fat. The use of weight, then, as a criterion for obesity is flawed because it includes lean

Table 23-2. Ideal Body Weights for Boys (in pounds)

HEIGHT (IN INCHES)	AGE (IN YEARS)												
	6	7	8	9	10	11	12	13	14	15	16	17	18
38	33												
39	34												
40	35												
41	37	37											
42	38	38	38										
43	38	41	40										
44	43	43	43										
45	45	45	45	45									
46	47	48	47	47									
47	49	50	49	49	49								
48	52	52	52	52	52								
49	54	54	54	54	54	54							
50		57	57	57	57	57	57						
51		60	60	60	60	60	60						
52		62	63	63	63	63	63	63					
53			66	66	65	65	67	67					
54			68	68	69	68	69	69	70				
55			71	71	72	72	72	73	73				
56				75	75	76	76	77	77	78			
57				78	79	80	80	82	82	82			
58					82	83	84	84	85	85			
59					86	87	87	88	88	89	89		
60						90	91	92	93	94	96		
61						94	95	96	97	98	101	105	
62						99	100	101	103	103	107	111	116
63							106	105	107	108	111	115	120
64							109	110	111	113	115	119	124
65								114	116	118	120	125	129
66								117	121	123	126	129	132
67									127	127	131	134	136
68									131	132	135	139	141
69									135	136	138	141	144
70									140	142	143	145	147
71										146	147	148	150
72										149	152	154	156
73										153	156	159	161

Source: *Meaning change in the nutritional status: Guidelines for assessing the nutritional impact of supplementary feeding programmes for vulnerable groups.* Geneva, Switzerland, World Health Organization, 1983.

body mass (e.g., muscle, bone, and vital organs) in addition to fat.

There are several methods of measuring body composition and thereby of estimating the amount of weight that is fat. These methods include hydrostatic weighing, K-40 counting, anthropometry, and the more recent extensions of ultrasound and computer-assisted tomography (see Buskirk, 1987; Roche, 1985). One of the most widely researched and accurate methods for estimating body fat, when compared to actual chemical analyses of human cadavers, is hydrostatic weighing. Hydrostatic weighing is also referred to as densitometry, and it is based on the fact that lean body mass, which consists primarily of bone and muscle, is more dense than water, whereas fat is less so. Therefore, given two adolescents of equal weight, one with a high percentage of body fat will weigh less underwater than one with a low percentage of body fat. In this procedure the difference between an individual's weight underwater and out of water determines body density. The percentage of body fat is then computed using one of several equations, the most common of which is the Siri equation (see McArdle, Katch, & Katch, 1986, pp. 490–496). Hydrostatic weighing is cumbersome in terms of subject compliance, equipment, and the necessity for

Table 23-3. Ideal Body Weights for Girls (in pounds)

HEIGHT (IN INCHES)	AGE (IN YEARS)												
	6	7	8	9	10	11	12	13	14	15	16	17	18
39	34												
40	35	35											
41	37	37											
42	38	38											
43	40	40	40										
44	42	42	42										
45	45	44	45										
46	47	46	47	47	47								
47	50	50	49	50	50								
48	51	52	52	52	52	52							
49	53	53	54	55	55	56							
50		56	57	58	58	60	60						
51		59	60	60	61	62	62						
52		63	63	63	64	64	66						
53			66	67	67	67	68	70					
54			68	70	70	71	71	73					
55				73	74	74	75	77	78				
56				76	78	78	79	80	84				
57					81	82	82	84	89	93			
58					84	87	86	88	93	96	100		
59					87	91	90	93	97	101	104	105	
60						95	96	97	101	105	108	109	111
61						97	101	101	105	108	112	113	114
62							105	106	108	112	114	115	116
63							110	111	112	115	116	118	118
64							114	115	117	118	120	121	122
65								120	120	121	124	125	126
66								124	125	126	128	128	131
67								127	129	131	133	133	134
68									131	133	134	136	138
69									133	135	136	138	140
70									134	136	138	140	141

Source: *Meaning change in the nutritional status: Guidelines for assessing the nutritional impact of supplementary feeding programmes for vulnerable groups.* Geneva, Switzerland, World Health Organization, 1983.

subjects to exhale while being totally submerged underwater. Also the procedure has not been studied with children and adolescents.

Total body electrical conductivity (TBEC) is a recent development in the measurement of body composition. TBEC is based on the greater hydration and concentration of electrolytes in lean as opposed to fat tissue. Accordingly, lean tissue is a better conductor of electricity than adipose tissue. The actual measurement is accomplished by passing a subject through a chamber that contains an electromagnetic field. The TBEC procedure has been validated in both animal and human studies, with correlations above .90 with cadaver samples and hydrostatic weighing (Harrison, 1987). While the procedure is simple and safe, takes only a few minutes, and holds great promise, the cost for a TBEC unit ranges from $75,000 to $100,000, making it impractical for routine clinical use. As with hydrostatic weighing, TBEC has not been validated with children and adolescents. However, the principles upon which TBEC is based appear to allow for a more straightforward application to children than hydrostatic weighing. Furthermore, the actual measurement operations are decidedly in favor of TBEC.

Skinfold measures represent perhaps the most appropriate alternative to determine body composition for the researcher and practicing clinician alike. These measures can provide inexpensive, quick, and accurate estimates of the extent of body fat and its distribution. Estimates of body fat based upon skinfold measures also correlate well with those obtained with hydrostatic weighing, with values of .83 to .89 reported (Pollock & Jackson, 1980). If only one measure is taken, several investigators recommend the triceps skinfold for its high degree of association with other measures of body fat; its high interrater reliability; and its ease, simplicity, and unobtrusiveness (e.g., Seltzer & Mayer, 1967). Pollock, Wilmore, and Fox (1981) provide a thorough discussion of the measurement technique and tables to estimate total body fat.

Use of skinfold measures is based upon the assumption that most body fat lies just below the surface of the skin and can be measured from various external sites. Equations and tables for estimating total body fat are usually based upon the sum of measures taken from three to seven sites. These estimates of body fat have been developed on men and women ranging in age from 18 to 55 years, with none yet available for younger children. In contrast to specific estimates for adults of the percent of body fat, norms for children are available based upon age and gender. One popular reference population is that of the National Health and Nutrition Examination Surveys I and II (NHANES) conducted from 1970 through 1973 and from 1975 through 1980 (Gortmaker, Dietz, Sobol, & Wehler, 1987). Table 23-4 provides norms by age and gender for skinfold values at the 75th and 90th percentiles.

Cautions in Using Skinfold Measures

Burkinshaw, Jones, and Kruppwicz (1973) evaluated observer errors in measuring skinfold thickness by both trained and untrained observers. They also varied the specificity of sites by comparing marked and unmarked locations. When the sites were marked, the values of observers were in close agreement. When the sites were not marked, however, those observers who had less experience reported values that were approximately 2 mm higher than those obtained by experienced observers. Johnson and Stalonas (1977) studied within- and between-observer agreement of skinfold measures. Within-observer correlations over time approximated .90; between-observer correlations ranged from .67 to .90.

While encouraging, these studies suggest several precautions. Observers should receive training in obtaining skinfold measures by an experienced teacher. Training must be conducted on persons varying in weight and should occur until measures at each site are ideally within 2 mm in the lean and 4 mm in the obese when compared to measures taken by an experienced observer. Additionally, skinfold measures may be less sensitive than balance-bar scale measures of weight over 1 to 3 weeks. Measures should be obtained over at least three sites, and the same observer should perform the measures throughout the program.

Body circumference measures may be even more easily accomplished than skinfold thickness and require only a tape measure. With young adults (average age 19+ yrs) Katch and McArdle (1973) found that arm, abdomen, forearm, and thigh circumferences were as accurate as skinfolds in predicting body

Table 23-4. Eighty-fifth Percentile Cutoff Values for Triceps Skinfold for Obese Children

BOYS		GIRLS	
AGE (IN YEARS)	85TH PERCENTILE	AGE (IN YEARS)	85TH PERCENTILE
6.0	12.0	6.0	13.0
7.0	12.0	7.0	14.0
8.0	12.0	8.0	12.0
9.0	15.0	9.0	14.0
10.0	15.0	10.0	15.0
11.0	17.0	11.0	18.0
12.0	19.0	12.0	20.0
13.0	18.0	13.0	20.0
14.0	18.0	14.0	20.0
15.0	20.0	15.0	22.0
16.0	19.0	16.0	23.0
17.0	14.0	17.0	23.0

Notes
From *Childhood obesity* (p 27) by M. Winick (Ed.) (1975), New York: John Wiley & Sons. Copyright 1975 by John Wiley & Sons. Adapted by permission.
Skinfold measured in millimeters.

density measured by hydrostatic weighing. While norms are not available for children and adolescents, changes in circumference measures are of considerable clinical merit and are inherently interesting to patients. In summary, the current literature indicates that skinfold and body circumference measures appear to be the most satisfactory indices of obesity in terms of reliability, ease of measurement, relationship to other estimates of body fat, such as hydrostatic weighing, and independence from height. Also, it is not unusual to find minimal weight loss during the initial phase of a program in which exercise is an important intervention, yet to observe larger changes in skinfolds and body circumference measures. Taken together, skinfold and circumference measures can provide valuable information to complement balance-bar weight measures.

Physical Measures of Health

Improvements in overall health are expected as a result of participation in a weight-control program. In fact, many adolescents and children are now referred by physicians to weight-control programs not only because they are overweight, but also because they display some abnormal measure of overall health, such as high cholesterol, blood pressure, or glucose. There are several laboratory tests that give information about an individual's physical health. Under supervision of a physician, samples of blood and urine can provide valuable information on metabolism and levels of electrolytes, cholesterol, vitamins, and nutrients. These tests are often organized in groups such as PDP (Primary Diagnostic Panel) and SMAC (Standard Medical Automated Chemistry). Other sources of important information include blood pressure and heart rate.

It is important for clinicians to form collaborative relationships with primary-care physicians and to require each patient to undergo a complete physical examination, with blood and urine tests prior to undertaking a weight-reduction project. For the most part, these tests are more sensitive to malnourishment and malnutrition. Therefore, they may be limited in the type of information that is directly applicable to overweight children and adolescents who are overnourished, but their importance in general health screening cannot be ignored.

The emphasis of the physical evaluation is on those medical conditions that are associated with overweight. As with adults, the two most frequent medical conditons associated with obesity in children and adolescents are elevations in risk factors for heart disease and diabetes. Both the Muscatine and Bogalusa studies have documented that coronary heart disease begins early in life. For example, in the Muscatine Study, approximately 25% of the children had cholesterol values over 200 mg/dl, with almost 10% above 220 mg/dl. Children, however, rarely suffer heart attacks or other precursors such as angina, thus making the search for risk factors more important.

Cholesterol is essential for human function, and it is manufactured by the liver as well as obtained from dietary sources. Cholesterol values are usually contained in what is referred to as a lipid profile. Although there are finer determinations, the lipid or cholesterol profile is divided into total cholesterol (T-chol), high-density lipoproteins (HDL), low-density lipoproteins (LDL), and triglycerides. High T-chol is related to an increased risk for coronary heart disease, high LDL levels are associated with increased risk of coronary heart disease, and high HDL levels are associated with a lower risk. T-chol levels of 175 mg/dl or higher, LDL levels of 115 or higher, and HDL levels of 40 or below should be cause for concern.

Diabetes is also a medical problem linked with obesity. The diabetic condition occurs when glucose cannot be properly utilized by cells for energy. There are two major types of diabetes: Type I (insulin-dependent) and Type II (non-insulin-dependent). The latter accounts for over 90% of all cases and is strongly associated with obesity. In Type II diabetes, insulin is secreted by the pancreas but cannot facilitate the entry of glucose into the cell because of the presence of fat cells. Such insulin resistance results in hyperglycemia and over time contributes to heart, kidney, eye, and nerve disease. While Type II diabetes is more common in adults, its possible development in obese children should be routinely screened by assessing for hyperglycemia or glucosuria.

Measures of Physical Fitness and Activity

Increased attention has been directed at inactivity in general and television viewing in particular for its role in the development and maintenance of obesity in children. Dietz (1983), for example, concludes, on the basis of a longitudinal study, that television viewing is related to the onset of obesity and that children who watch more television are likely to be fatter than those who watch less. Also, Tucker (1986) found that among high school students, light viewers were more physically fit and active than moderate and heavy television viewers.

Physical Fitness

Evaluations of physical fitness can differ in the type of performance being measured and the method by which it is measured. Testing of physical fitness can include flexibility, strength, and endurance measures. Because they reflect the ability to process oxygen, endurance or aerobic measures are most important in the assessment of the fitness of the obese, and they are often used in conjunction with measures of cardiovascular function. Direct measures of physical fitness are obtained by determining how well a child can perform oxygen-utilizing work over a period of time. The most exact index of physical fitness is the body's maximum oxygen uptake, or VO_2 max. In this method, inhaled and expired gases (e.g., oxygen, and carbon dioxide) are measured from a mouthpiece or helmet while the subject is exercising continuously on a treadmill, rowing machine, or stationary cycle. The device may be too cumbersome for children but perhaps better tolerated by older adolescents.

More practical measures for practitioners include submaximal physical fitness measures that are related to VO_2 max. One of the most popular has been the Harvard Step Test and its variations. This procedure involves having children step up and down for a fixed period of time at a given cadence on a step of a standard height. Measures of pulse are taken prior to, immediately after, and at 1-minute intervals during the recovery period. The exercise phase can run from 2 to 5 minutes, and the level of fitness is related to how quickly the heart rate recovers. Working with children and adolescents, Johnson and colleagues (Johnson, Hinkle, Smith, Cox, & Pagac, 1990) used a four-count step sequence onto an 8-inch stand at a rate of 24 steps per minute for 2 minutes. Heart rate was recorded before the test, immediately following the 2-minutes of stepping, and again at 1 and 2 minutes. Children exposed to an exercise intervention displayed lower heart rate levels than those receiving dietary treatment. While most of the work with step-tests have been with adults and college students (see McArdle, Katch, Pechar, Jacobson, & Ruck, 1972), Montoye (1975) provides norms for boys and girls.

Another practical and easy to implement procedure for measuring fitness is a fixed timed distance walk-run in which children cover as much ground as possible during a 12-minute period. The total distance covered is correlated with VO_2 max.

Physical Activity

A number of different methods have been used to measure physical activity. Some of the measures are identical to those used to measure physical fitness such as oxygen uptake and heart rate (see Saris, 1986; Seliger, Trefny, Bartunkova, & Paver, 1974).

Another biological measurement procedure for estimating levels of physical activity is a doubly labeled water technique. This technique requires that the subject drink a glass of water and provide a urine sample. It allows for estimating CO_2 production and energy expenditure using stable isotopes. As Saris (1986) points out, the technique is promising because it may be more accurate than common field techniques and more practical than other biological procedures such as oxygen uptake. It is, however, costly and requires specialized equipment (i.e., a mass spectrometer). In addition, it provides only a summary of energy expenditure for the observation period (optimal length = 3 to 14 days) and gives no information about changes in energy utilization over that period.

Motion sensors are also used to estimate levels of physical activity. Pedometers record acceleration and deceleration of the waist in the vertical direction. Pedometers, however, are not the movement counters of choice because they tend to be unreliable and give no information about different intensity levels (Saris, 1986). Actometers and accelerometers record both movements and their intensity and are preferable to pedometers (Saris, 1986). An electronic single-plane accelerometer has been used with preschool children and found to yield moderate to high correlations with all-day observations of physical activity, particularly for older, female, and overweight children (Klesges & Klesges, 1987).

A questionnaire measuring activity levels that can be administered several times during the course of a weight-reduction program has been developed by Johnson and Johnson (1989). In a preliminary study, this measure has been shown to be related to lung capacity. In this study, children who were more active had greater lung capacity than those who were less active.

Another method of measuring of physical activity is via self-monitoring. Subjects can be given a list of activities such as that provided in Table 23-5, which are divided into low, moderate, and high aerobic potential based on the number of calories expended per minute of time. Subjects record the amount of time spent in each activity.

Increased validity may be obtained by dividing each

Table 23-5. Exercise/Calorie Expenditure List

Light Exercise (4 calories per minute)
  Dancing (slow)
  Gardening (light)
  Golf
  Table tennis
  Softball
  Volleyball
  Bowling
  Canoeing
  Horseshoes
  Lawn mowing (power)
  Horseback riding
  Bicycling (5 mph)
  Walking (3 mph)
  Downhill Skiing

Moderate Exercise (7 calories per minute)
  Badminton
  Dancing (fast)
  Calisthenics (moderate)
  Cycling (9.5 mph)
  Gardening (heavy)
  Stationary cycling (moderate)
  Swimming (30 yards per minute)
  Tennis
  Walking (4.5 mph)
  Ice skating, roller skating, cross country skiing

Heavy Exercise (10 calories per minute)
  Calisthenics (fast)
  Ice skating or roller skating
  Rowing a boat
  Climbing stairs (up and down)
  Cycling (12 mph)
  Handball, paddleball, squash
  Jogging
  Skipping rope
  Stationary cycling (quick)
  Stationary jogging
  Swimming (40 yards per minute)
  Basketball

Note: From *Weight no longer* (p. 54) by W. G. Johnson & P. M. Stalonas, Jr., (1981), Gretna, LA: Pelican.

day into functional components and having the child record activity within each component, rather than considering the day as a whole (Baranowski et al., 1984). Personal interviews may also be used to clarify and improve the reliability of self-monitoring data (e.g., Seliger et al., 1974).

The last measure of physical activity is the observation of children's activity throughout the day or during selected times or activities (e.g., recess). Klesges and colleagues (Klesges et al., 1984) developed the Fargo Activity Time-Sampling Survey (FATS), which is an observational procedure assessing children's physical activity and parental interactions with the child related to physical activity. This system uses an interval time-sampling method to code children's behavior, the intensity of the behavior, and interactions. Klesges et al. (1984) found acceptable levels of interrater and test-retest reliability as well as evidence of convergent validity with preschoolers. Further validation studies are needed before FATS is applicable to older children. Hovell, Bursick, Sharkey, and McClure (1978) also constructed an observational system for third to sixth graders at recess, which utilizes intensity ratings of activity for the upper and lower body separately every 5 seconds for 5 minutes.

Dietary Intake

Dietary intake in general and fat intake in particular are receiving renewed attention for their role in obesity. An evolving data base on dietary fat underscores the necessity of targeting and evaluating dietary intake in weight-control programs. Dietary intake is measured primarily by self-report and observational measures, and most of the research has focused on the accuracy of these measures of food intake.

Self-report Measures

One of the most common measures of dietary intake is the 24-hour recall. A trained interviewer (typically a dietitian) reviews with the child or the parent what the child has eaten in the previous 24 hours. Recall is sometimes facilitated by dividing the day into discrete time periods and by using visual aids such as food models (e.g., Frank, Berenson, & Webber, 1978). Dietary intake is then classified according to the purpose of the assessment as meals or snacks or according to nutritional quantity or quality. The 24-hour recall has been criticized because of the possibility of inaccurate reporting due to memory bias, a social desirability response set, and the fact that one day of dietary intake may not be representative. In addition, if parents are providing the recall information, they may not be aware of everything their child has eaten, particularly outside the home (McDonald, Brun, & Esserman, 1981).

Axelson (1984) studied the 24-hour recall by comparing two recalls obtained 7 to 12 months apart from 340 ninth graders and found a significant difference between the first and second recalls without any intervention. This study demonstrates changes in 24-hour recalls over time and also shows the need for inclusion of a control group when using 24-hour recall as a dependent measure in a research treatment program.

Another method of assessing dietary intake is for children or their parents to complete food diaries in which all food intake over a specified time period (e.g., a few days to several weeks) is recorded. Food diaries are most helpful if completed immediately after eating, as they then avoid the memory problems associated with 24-hour recall. In addition, if parents or children record situational and emotional factors surrounding eating, food diaries can be useful in evaluating the multiple antecedents of eating. Schlundt (1989) has recently developed a self-monitoring analyses system (SMAS), which provides such an evaluation of eating behavior. Table 23-6 provides an example of the recording form, which is 14

Table 23-6. Food Diary

Time _____ A.M./P.M.   Date _____/_____/_____

Day (Mo$_1$ Tu$_2$ We$_3$ Th$_4$ Fr$_5$ Sa$_6$ Su$_7$)

Meal (breakfast$_1$ lunch$_2$ dinner$_3$ snack$_4$)

Place (home$_1$ work$_2$ restaurant$_3$ other$_4$)

People (family$_1$ friend$_2$ alone$_3$ other$_4$)

Mood (very negative$_1$ negative$_2$ neutral$_3$ positive$_4$ very positive$_5$)

Hunger (very hungry$_1$ moderately hungry$_2$ neutral$_3$ not hungry$_4$ full$_5$)

Junk Food (yes$_1$ no$_2$)

Overeat (yes$_1$ no$_2$)

Food	Amount	Calories

Total Calories _____

Exercise (yes$_1$ no$_2$) Minutes _____   Type _____

Subscript numbers used for computer data entry.
Note: From D. G. Schlundt (1989), *Assessment of eating behavior in bulimia nervosa: The self monitoring analysis systems*. In W. G. Johnson (Ed.), Advances in eating disorders, Vol. I (p. 31). Greenwich CT: JAI Press.

cm × 10.5 cm and is easily carried on one's person.

Food diaries may also be used to compute nutritional composition of the diet. Estimates of the dietary intake in the United States consistently report values of fat intake at 45%, and the American Heart Association and several government agencies recommend reducing fat intake to no more than 30% of the diet. There are several methods for identifying the nutritional composition of dietary intake. One relatively simple procedure is the color-coding system developed by Epstein and Squires (1988) in which foods are classified according to their composition and caloric value as red, yellow, or green. Using a self-monitoring form, foods can be coded as R Y, or G for red, yellow, or green. Epstein and Squires (1988) provide a list of R, Y, and G foods for dairy, grain, fruit-vegetable, and protein groups, yet the criteria for inclusion in one group or another are not specified. Johnson and colleagues (Johnson et al., 1990) developed a list similar to Epstein and Squires' (1988) based on the following criteria: *red:* fat = > 30%/serving, calories = > 200 kcal/serving, sodium = > 300 mg/serving, or cholesterol > 100 mg/serving: *yellow*: fat = 11–30%/serving, calories = 101–200 kcal/serving, sodium = 101–300 mg/serving, or cholesterol = 51–100 mg/serving; *green:* fat = < 11%/serving, calories = < 101/serving, sodium = < 101 mg/serving, *and* cholesterol < 50 mg/serving. In an attempt to determine the intake of these foods, approximately 200 foods in each category (R,Y,G) are listed in the Foods Survey. The child or parents indicate whether the foods were eaten during the past week. Like similar surveys, the Foods Survey has merit in determining the proportion of intake that is categorized as red, yellow, or green, and Johnson et al. (1990) documented changes in these proportions as a result of participation in a weight-reduction program. However, there are no psychometric data available on this instrument.

Another procedure for identifying the nutrient composition in the diet is to use one of the available computer software packages. For example, with the Food Processor (ESHA Research, 1987) each food eaten is coded and the codes are entered into the computer by meal or intake. This program can then generate an analysis of the macro- and micronutrient content of the diet and compare the values with RDAs. While these data are extraordinarily useful, the process of coding each food and data entry is time-consuming.

A major problem with food diaries is compliance. The response cost associated with complete and accurate recording of dietary intake is high. Moreover, food diaries share with the 24-hour recall a susceptibility to response bias. In addition, young children may lack the requisite cognitive and writing skills for correct recording, and so parents must assist them or perform the recordings themselves.

There are ways that may make the recordings easier and more accurate. Baranowski et al. (1986) studied the accuracy of four different methods of collecting food diaries. Food diaries used in the study varied in two ways: The children recorded the whole day or a segment of the day, and the forms either did or did not include pictures of the food items. These forms were validated by observation of eating behavior for 2 days. The authors found a high level (83%) of agreement between the children's self-report and observers' records of consumption. They observed no evidence for beneficial effects of segmented days, pictures, learning, or parental assistance with the forms. The authors recommended the whole-day forms with pictures because these elicited the fewest problems in form completion. Although this study is enecouraging about the use of food diaries, the food diary forms were different from those typically employed, in that children tallied the frequency of consumption of various categories of foods rather than freely recording food eaten and portion sizes. Therefore, caloric intake could not be calculated through use of this form. As the authors point out, the frequency format may be particularly useful when an obesity treatment program emphasizes food substitution rather than portion and calorie changes.

A social desirability response set can also be a problem with food diaries. This influence may be more pronounced when there is no provision for actual external monitoring by parents or when record completion leads to some reinforcing consequence. Given the wealth of data potentially available from food diaries, efforts should be made to decrease their associated problems.

Another means of assessing dietary intake is via checklists of various types of food groups. Here, children or parents are asked to check foods consumed and the frequency of their comsumption. For example, McDonald et al. (1981) had children indicate a consumption frequency for 40 common foods and beverages to test the effects of a school nutrition education program. From the list, they computed four food variety indices and five food avoidance indices. In another study, Sabry, Ford, Roberts, and Wardlaw (1974) employed a Food Frequency Questionnaire with mothers of 49 children (ages 18 to 48 months).

The mothers responded to detailed questions about the frequency of consumption of various foods in six food groups. Although the Food Frequency Questionnaire was shown to yield acceptable coefficients for scale replicability, no relationship was found between scores on this questionnaire and foods recorded on 3-day food diaries. This highlights the major problem with checklists: They may be inaccurate because of memory biases and because of response biases such as social desirability. In addition, when foods are presented in a summary fashion, there is a risk that relevant foods will be missed or that the respondents will not classify foods according to the investigator's taxonomy. It is to their credit that Sabry et al. (1974) assessed the reliability and validity of their checklist; many checklists lack basic psychometric properties.

While recognizing the many problems associated with the various self-report measures, Stunkard and Waxman (1981) note that the obese appear to be as reliable as the nonobese in recording dietary intake, and that their study of three obese and three normal-size children yielded a close correspondence between reported and actual food intake.

Observational Measures

There are two types of observational measures of dietary intake: those obtained in a laboratory and those obtained in a naturalistic setting. Laboratory measures generally involve a test meal. Children are brought into the laboratory, offered a variety of foods, and what they choose to eat is considered an example of their eating elsewhere. For example, the Behavioral Eating Test (BET) was designed to be a nonreactive behavioral assessment technique for food and beverage consumption (Wilson & Jeffrey, 1985). In the BET procedure, foods and beverages are served to subjects in transparent cups placed on a tray. High-nutrition and low-nutrition foods are divided equally among the cups and interspersed randomly on the tray. Children are left alone with the foods for a predetermined period of time after instructions to taste the foods so they can say what they think of them. Unobtrusive observations are then made of children's eating behavior.

There are problems with the psychometric properties of the BET. The authors acknowledge that individual food scores have only moderate test-retest stability. This limits the BET's ability to predict eating behavior in general reliably. The authors point out that, to find consistent patterns in dietary intake, it may be necessary to test subjects over a period of days. This repeated testing limits the advantage of laboratory measures over other types of observational measures and highlights the major problem with these measures: the fact that eating on one occasion in the laboratory may not generalize to eating in naturalistic settings.

Another example of a laboratory measure of eating behavior is found in a study by Karpowitz and Zeis (1975) in which subjects were observed while waiting alone in a waiting room with a bowl of candy. Obese subjects participating in a treatment program snacked significantly less often than obese subjects who were not in treatment; however, there were no significant differences between these groups in *amounts* eaten or between obese and nonobese subjects. Clayton and Hovel (1985) validated a role-played measure of snack selection with elementary school students. Subjects participated in a snack period before and after nutrition education. For half of these snack periods, students selected and ate snacks. For the remaining periods, subjects selected the snacks they would prefer from pictures of foods. Although the researchers found a high interrater reliability for both measures, correlations between snack and picture selections were small, thereby undermining the validity of the role-play snack procedure. As Wilson and Jeffrey (1985) point out, laboratory measures of dietary intake may be considered part of a multicomponent assessment package of dietary intake but should not be used as the sole measure of eating behavior.

Observations of dietary intake in naturalistic settings may have fewer problems with generalizability than assessments in the laboratory, but they are much more time-intensive and, if obtrusive, can have reactive effects on eating behavior. Various techniques for observing dietary intake in naturalistic settings have been described. For example, Wilson (1974) described following children and recording all of their dietary intake for an entire day. Waxman and Stunkard (1980) used a similar procedure within a family context and found that the obese children ate more food and at a faster rate than did their nonobese controls. Although naturalistic observation may be a more valid technique than others, it is often impractical because of its time demands.

Assessing Body Image

Obese children have been shown to have more distorted perceptions of their bodies and to be more dissatisfied with their bodies than normal-weight children (Mendelson & White, 1985; Zakin, Blyth, &

Simmons, 1984). The assessment of body image in childhood obesity, then, is important to determine whether body image disturbance may be contributing to the maintenance of excess weight, whether body image may become distorted as a function of weight loss, and to identify unrealistic expectations for weight loss. If body image is found to be dysfunctional, it should probably be a treatment target as it is with anorexia and bulimia nervosa (Schlundt & Johnson, 1990). Body image disturbances are typically categorized as faulty perceptions of bodily size (body size distortion) or dissatisfaction with perceived appearance (body dissatisfaction: cf. Cash & Brown, 1987).

Body Size Distortion

Measures of perceptual distortion include estimates of body part size and imaging techniques. Body size estimates request subjects to estimate the size of various body parts such as the head, chest, waist, abdomen, and thighs. For example, Kreitler and Kreitler (1986) used a Body Size Estimation method in which subjects from preschool age through adulthood estimated the size of 10 body parts by distances between their fingers or hands. Distortion scores were then computed between subjects' size estimations and acutal sizes. Two-week test-retest and interrater reliability coefficients for size estimates ranges from .93 to .98. A common computation from a body part size estimation procedure is the body perception index (BPI) (BPI = perceived size/real size $\times$ 100). The BPIs for each body part may be averaged to yield a composite BPI.

Another method of assessing body size distortion is through imaging techniques. These techniques have subjects estimate body size while viewing their own or others' images. For example, Gardner, Martinez, and their colleagues (Gardner, Martinez, & Espinoza, 1987; Gardner, Martinez, & Sandoval, 1987) have conducted studies in which the body images of obese and normal-weight subjects were measured using a video monitor. Subjects adjusted the size of their own image on the monitor until it matched their perception. They also rated images of themselves as too heavy or too thin. The authors used a signal-detection analysis to evaluate results of this later task. Distorting image techniques have been underutilized with obese children and adolescents and need to be validated with this age group.

Barrios has developed an innovative technique, the body image detection device (BIDD), to assess body image. The BIDD consists of templates placed atop an overhead projection so as to produce bands of light on a wall 8 feet away. The widths of the bands are adjusted by moving the templates. Subjects are asked to estimate the width of various body parts (e.g., face, hips, waist, thighs) to correspond to the width of the projected beam of light. In preliminary studies with non-eating-disordered, normal-size, and bulimic college women, the BIDD displays sound psychometric properties and may have merit in studies with obese children and adolescents (Barrios, Ruff, & York, 1989).

Body Dissatisfaction

Body dissatisfacton in children has been measured using a variety of self-report questionnaires, such as the *Body Cathexis Scale* (Secord & Jourard, 1953), the *Body Experience Scale* (Rierdan, Koff, & Stubbs, 1987), and the *Body-Esteem Scale* (Mendelson & White, 1982, 1985). In addition, children sometimes are asked to give a single rating of themselves as overweight, underweight, or about the right weight (Kaplan, Busner, & Pollack, 1988; Levinson, Powell, & Steelman, 1986).

Silhouettes are also used to measure body dissatisfaction in children. In this method, children choose from a collection of silhouettes, ranging from extremely lean to extremely obese, the one that best reflects their ideal and current sizes. The discrepancy between ideal and current choices is used as an index of dissatisfaction (see Schlundt & Johnson, 1990).

When assessing body image, it is important to include measures of both perceptual disturbance and body dissatisfaction. In addition, it is often useful to determine whether perceptual distortions and body dissatisfaction are limited to self-judgments or generalize to ratings of others and inanimate objects.

Self-Report Instruments of Eating Behavior

Although there are numerous self-report instruments that are useful for overweight adults, few have been shown to be developmentally appropriate for children and adolescents. Examples of instruments that are useful with obese adults include the *Revised Restraint Scale* (Herman, 1978), the *Three-Factor Eating Questionnaire* (Stunkard & Messick, 1985), the *Binge-Eating Scale* (Gormally, Black, Datson, & Rardin, 1982), and the *Dieter's Inventory of Eating Temptations* (Schlundt, 1988). More research is needed to develop scales measuring eating behavior in children and adolescents. Kagan and Squires (1984) began to develop two such scales for adolescents. The *Concern Over Weight and Dieting Scale* is a 14-item inventory measuring weight concerns and dieting behavior. The *Compulsive Eating Scale* is an eight-item instrument measuring uncontrollable eating. Although these scales have yielded fair to good levels of internal consistency and there is some evidence of concurrent validity, no normative data or test-retest reliability information are available. Further establishment of the psychometric properties of these instruments is needed before they are widely used.

Also, Perry, Griffin, and Murray (1985) describe the assessment component of the Minnesota Heart Health program, a communitywide project targeting smoking, eating, exercise, and hypertension. Prior to designing interventions in the schools, several *Needs Assessment Surveys* were constructed that measured eating and exercise patterns, food preparation and shopping, and environmental opportunities and barriers to healthful eating and exercise. The authors provide examples of the surveys and the responses of more than 1,000 students in grades 4 through 11. They acknowledge, however, the lack of psychometric analyses.

Although most studies have shown obese individuals to be free from significant psychopathology, some overweight children and adolescents have severe levels of depression and anxiety that may actually be caused by the problems associated with being overweight and dieting (see Wadden & Stunkard, 1985, for review). Therefore, investigators and clinicians may want to employ a measure of depression appropriate for obese children, such as the *Children's Depression Inventory* (Kovacs, 1980/81).

A problem frequently encountered by overweight participants is controlling inappropriate eating in social situations. Under such circumstances, children may not be effectively assertive in dealing with requests of peers and family to eat at particular times or to eat certain foods that are high in calories. Accordingly, weight-control programs should make provisions to teach their participants assertion skills (see Kirschenbaum, Johnson, & Stalonas, 1987). An appropriate model for assessing social skills in eating situations is provided by Gross and Johnson (1981) in their work on developing social coping skills in children with diabetes. The *Diabetes Assertiveness Test* is a role-play measure consisting of problem situations frequently encountered by preadolescent diabetics.

In their research, Gross and colleagues (Gross, Johnson, Wildman, & Mullet, 1981) trained children with diabetes over problem social situations in eye contact, duration of speech, appropriateness of verbalization, and affect. Generalization was also trained by the parents at home, and the trained social coping skills were assessed in both laboratory and naturalistic settings. It is this latter aspect of the study that is particularly promising in the assessment of progress for child and adolescent weight-control participants. Generalization was tested in a local restaurant as the child ordered and the waiter repeatedly prompted them to buy high-calorie selections. Such a measure could easily be constructed for use with children in weight-control programs.

The Family Context of Childhood Obesity

The past several years have seen increasing attention devoted to the role of families in the development, perpetuation, and treatment of child and adolescent obesity. There are two distinct lines of studies investigating the family context of child and adolescent obesity. One area of investigation has emanated from family systems theory and therapy. These studies are largely impressionistic and typically limit their methodology to case reports and descriptive studies using self-report questionnaires surveying family structure and function. Examples of instruments used in these studies include the Family Environment Scale (FES) (Moos, 1974), the Family Inventory of Resource Management (FIRM) McCubbin, Comeau, & Harkins, 1981), and the FACES (Olson, Portner, & Levee, 1985), to name a few of the most popular.

In contrast to this literature are studies employing more objective methods designed to explore the myriad of variables within the family context that influence obesity. Within this framework, the influence of parents and the family on childhood obesity can be considered from genetic, in utero, and early developmental perspectives. Recent studies by Stunkard and colleagues (Stunkard et al., 1986) suggest a definite role for genetics. A major finding of this study is that the weight of adopted children was correlated with that of their biological parents but not their adoptive parents. While the adoptees may not have lived with their adopted families for a sufficient period, and other studies have not found such a degree of heritability as that of Stunkard et al. (1986), the strength of the data supporting a genetic input cannot be denied. Accordingly, the weight status of a child's parents as well as their associated eating and activity habits should be assessed for their impact on the child.

The biological impact on obesity underscores an area of research on in utero fetal development that is not at this point represented in the obesity literature. Here, the scope of potential influences on the development of child obesity include maternal nutrition, emotionality, and substance use as well as variables emanating from the child and their interactions with those of the mother.

Observations by Agras (1988) also highlight the impact of biological variables and are important for their potential role in the early identification of infants at risk for obesity. Specificlly, a form of the "obese eating style" of rapid eating with less mastication found in many studies with children and adults was present in the sucking behavior of infants. Moreover, a robust sucking style evident by 4 weeks of age was correlated with skinfold measures at 1 and 2 years of age. Agras suggests that this vigorous sucking style may be the behavioral expression of a genetic trait for obesity. Such an eating style may also serve as a precursor to adult binge eating. While the difficulty of measuring sucking behavior in infancy may be impractical, research efforts will no doubt identify a more feasible method and perhaps identify other behaviors and assessment strategies in attempts to interfere with any genetic or early experiential predisposition towards obesity.

The influence of experience within the family context is also powerful on the emerging eating and activity habits of children. These influences consists of direct experiences with food and activity as well as communications, modeling, and expectancies of the parents. One dramatic example of parental influence on eating behavior is provided by Waxman and Stunkard (1980), who found that mothers served their obese sons larger meals than the son's nonobese brothers. Also, regarding physical activity, Klesges and colleagues (Klesges, Coates, Holzer, Moldenhauer, Woolfrey, & Vollmer, 1983) found that parental encouragement to be active or inactive were correspondingly positively or negatively correlated with the observed physical activity of the children. Klesges and Hanson (1988) summarize evidence that indicates that family conflict and overdependence and parental characteristics such as depression are related to child obesity. The assessment of these family and personal attributes can be accomplished by the measures of family functioning mentioned above, standard personality tests (e.g., MMPI) and interviews and home observations.

The assessment of family influences on obesity can also include direct observations of family members as they interact at mealtime or in the consulting room. Humphrey (1989) has developed a procedure for such observations using Benjamin's coding system. While her work has been with families in which a member has anorexia or bulimia nervosa, this method is readily applicable to the obese.

CASE ILLUSTRATIONS

The following cases were selected from the files of a weight control program for children and adolescents (Johnson et al., 1990). These two children are representative of the 28 who completed a 14-week program.

Case 1

RE is an 8-year-old white female who was 57.5 inches tall and weighed 111 pounds at the initiation of the project. She had no physical complaints, and a physical examination by her physician was unremarkable except for her obesity. During the screening session she reported frequent after-school snacking and a low level of physical activity. She had dieted in the past by trying to reduce sugary snacks, but she was not successful. RE wanted to lose weight in order to be healthier. A standard assessment included measures taken prior to, during, and after completing a 14-week, cognitive-behavioral program that emphasized diet and exercise interventions. The results are presented in Table 23-7.

Case 2

BJ is a 12-year-old-boy in the seventh grade who was 62 inches tall and weighed 160 pounds at the initiation of the project. With the exception of a minor skin rash, he had no physical problems. Overweight, diabetes, high blood pressure, and heart disease are common problems in BJ's family. His father and both sets of grandparents are, or were, obese, as are a number of uncles and aunts. There have been several deaths due to heart disease.

BJ ate substantially large meals prior to his participation in the program. For breakfast he would eat a sugary cereal, whole milk, and several doughnuts. For lunch at school, he ate a sandwich of luncheon meat with potato chips and pickles. His favorite afternoon snacks were chocolate candy, cookies, or ice cream. For dinner, BJ ate a large portion of meat, a vegetable,

Table 23-7. Scores on Assessment Measures

	EXERCISE 1ST WEEK		EXERCISE + NUTRITION 8TH WEEK	15TH WEEK
Weight (lb)	111		107	99
Body Fat (Sum of 4 sites in mm)	89		70	62
Lipid Profile (mg/dl)				
T-Chol	166		169	136
HDL	57		47	53
LDL	98		104	74
ACTIVITY SURVEY (hours/week)	Pre	Post		
high	0	13		
medium	3	8		
low	30	20		
FOODS SURVEY (number eaten past week)	Pre	Post		
Green foods	30	35		
Yellow foods	15	15		
Red foods	32	13		
Compulsive Eating Scale	14	12		
Self-Concept Scale	86	91		
Depression Self-Rating Scale	5	1		
Rosenberg Self-Esteem	30	38		
Heart Rate (bpm)				
resting	70	72		
1 min after 2 min of exercise	119	105		

It is clear from this data that RE was significantly overweight, ate too many red foods, and was physically inactive. During the course of the program, she made major changes in her eating behavior and her activity level. These changes resulted in a reduction of 12 pounds, a substantial decrease in her lipid profile, improved cardiovascular functioning, and a more positive self-concept.

and potatoes, which were usually french fires. He always had an evening snack of candy or ice cream.

BJ was very inactive. He had never participated in organized sports programs and spent most of his leisure time watching television and playing video games. During the screening, BJ stated that he did not know why he was overweight, but that he would like to lose 40 to 50 pounds to feel better and so that other kids would not tease him. The results of the screening are shown in Table 23-8.

SUMMARY

The literature on child and adolescent obesity points to a number of associated problems, including the prospect of persistence of obesity into the adult years, an increased risk for physical problems, the most prominent of which is cardiovascular disease, and compromised psychological adjustment among others. Targets of intervention in the treatment of obesity are behavioral, cognitive, and physical variables and the social-environmental milieu in which they operate. These variables become the prime focus of assessment, with weight maintaining an important yet subordinate role. Determination of the nature and extent of obesity can vary from the sole use of weight to measures of skinfolds, body circumference, and even the more sophisticated densitometry and TBEC. Cardiovascular and other risk factors associated with obesity, such as cholesterol levels and blood glucose, can be routinely evaluated and do provide important feedback during treatment. The assessment of eating behavior, fitness, physical activity, and familial influences can also be accomplished according to specific clinical and research requirements. These requirements, in turn, dictate the nature and level of variable measurement. The clinician or researcher can select from a variety of self-report measures, observational coding schemes, and electronic, telemetric, and gas analyzing devices—all of which differ in their psycho-

Table 23-8. BJ's scores on the assessment measures

	1ST WEEK		8TH WEEK	15TH WEEK
Weight (lb)	160		158	141
Body Fat (Sum of 4 sites in mm)	124.5		98	80
Lipid Profile (mg/dl)				
T-Chol	142		157	126
HDL	43		55	43
LDL	92		94	75
ACTIVITY SURVEY (hours/week)	Pre	Post		
high	0	3		
medium	6	11		
low	13	20		
FOODS SURVEY (number eaten past week)	Pre	Post		
Green foods	29	30		
Yellow foods	19	29		
Red foods	39	24		
Compulsive Eating Scale	18		14	
Self-Concept Scale	80		77	
Depression Self-Rating Scale	6		5	
Rosenberg Self-Esteem	31		38	
Heart Rate (bpm)				
resting	84		78	
1 min after 2 min of exercise	84		78	

BJ lost 19 pounds over the course of the program as a result of changes in his eating and activity. While he continued to eat far too many red foods, he was able to limit his snacking to a piece of fruit each day. BJ also became more physically active in after-school games and organized sports. He rode his bicycle regularly, jumped on a trampoline, and joined a soccer team. Like RE, his lipid profile improved significantly.

metric properties and their applicability with children and adolescents. While the focus of this chapter is assessment techniques, research strategies for the identification of variables implicated in the development of obesity as well as its prevention and treatment should be articulated. One area that has all but been neglected in the assessment of child and adolescent obesity is that of motivation for treatment. All too often, children are presented for a treatment screening session by their parents, and the child expresses little knowledge of why he or she is being screened, and even less interest in weight control. It is important for clinicians and researchers alike to inform both child and parent together the nature of the program and what will be expected along the way.

REFERENCES

Abraham, S., & Nordsieck, M. (1960). Relationship of excess weight in children and adults. *Public Health Reports, 25,* 263–273.

Agras, W. S. (1988). Does early eating behavior influence later adiposity? In N.A. Krasnegor, G. D. Gave, and K. N. Kretchsmer (Eds.), *Childhood obesity: A biobehavioral perspective* (pp. 49–66). Caldwell, NJ: Telford Press.

Axelson, J. M. (1984). Repeated measurements in evaluation. *Journal of Nutrition Education, 16,* 12–14.

Baranowski, T., Dworkin, R. J., Cieslik, C. J., Hooks, P., Clearman, D. R., Ray, L., Dunn, J. K., & Nader, P. R. (1984). Reliability and validity of self report of aerobic activity: Family health project. *Research Quarterly for Exercise and Sport, 55,* 309–317.

Baranowski, T., Henske, J., Dworkin, R., Clearman, P., et al. (1986). The accuracy of children's self reports of diet: Family health project. *Journal of American Diet Association, 86,* 1381–1385.

Barrios, B. A., Ruff, G., & York, C. (1989). Bulimia and body image: Assessment and explication of a promising construct. In W. G. Johnson (Ed.), *Advances in eating disorders: Vol. 2. Bulimia nervosa: Perspectives on clinical research and therapy* (pp. 67–89). Greenwich CT: JAI Press.

Behrman, R. E., & Vaughan, V. C. (1983). *Nelson textbook of pediatrics: 12th Ed.* (pp. 30–31). Philadelphia, PA: W. B. Saunders.

Berenson, G. S., Frank, G. C., Hunter, S. M., Srinivasan, S. R., Voors, A. W., & Webber, L. S. (1982). Cardiovascular risk factors in children. *American Journal of Children, 136,* 855–862.

Brownell, K. D., & Stunkard, A. J. (1980). Behavioral treatment for obese children and adolescents. In A. J. Stunkard (Ed.), *Obesity* (pp. 415–437). Philadelphia: W. B. Saunders.

Burkinshaw, L., Jones, R. M., & Kruppwicz, D. W. (1973). Observer error in skinfold thickness measurements. *Human Biology, 45,* 273–279.

Buskirk, E. R. (1987). The 1986 C. H. McCloy research lecture body composition analysis: The past, present and future. *Research Quarterly, 58,* 1–10.

Cash, T. F., & Brown, T. A. (1987). Body image in anorexia nervosa and bulimia nervosa. *Behavior Modification, 11,* 487–521.

Clayton, B., & Hovell, M. F. (1985). The validity of a role-played measure of student's snack selections. *Education & Treatment of Children, 8,* 229–238.

Dietz, W. H. (1983). Childhood obesity: Susceptibility, cause, and management. *Journal of Pediatrics, 103,* 676–685.

DuRant, R. H., & Linder, C. W. (1981). An evaluation of five indexes of relative body weight for use with children. *Journal of American Diet Association, 78,* 35–41.

Elizabeth Stewart Hands & Associates (ESHA) Research (1987). *The food processor II.* Salem, OR: Author.

Epstein, L. H., & Squires, S. (1988). *The stop-light diet for children: An eight-week program for parents and children.* Boston: Little, Brown.

Frank, G. C., Berenson, G. S., & Webber, L. S. 1978). Dietary studies and the relationship of diet to cardiovascular disease risk factor variables in 10-year-old children—The Bogalusa Heart Study. *The American Journal of Clinical Nutrition, 31,* 328–340.

Gardner, R. M., Martinez, R., & Espinoza, T. (1987). Psychophysical Measurement of body image of self and others in obese subjects. *Journal of Social Behavior and Personality, 2,* 205–217.

Gardner, R. M., Martinez, R., & Sandoval, Y. (1987). Obesity and body image: An evaluation of sensory and non-sensory components. *Psychological Medicine, 17,* 927–932.

Gormally, J., Black, D., Datson, S., & Rardin, D. (1982). The assessment of binge eating severity among obese persons. *Addictive Behaviors 7,* 47–55.

Gortmaker, S. L., Dietz, W. H., Sobol, A. M., & Wehler, C. A. (1987). Increasing pediatric obesity in the United States. *American Journal of Diseases of Children, 141,* 535–540.

Gross, A. M., & Johnson, W. G. (1981). The diabetes assertiveness test: A measure of social coping skills in pre-adolescent diabetics. *The Diabetes Educator, 7,* 26–27.

Gross, A., Johnson, W. G., Wildman, H. E., & Mullet N. (1981). Coping skills training with insulin-dependent preadolescent diabetics. *Child Behavior Therapy, 3,* 141–153.

Harrison, G. G. (1987). The measurement of total body Electrical Conductivity. *Human Biology, 59,* 311–317.

Herman, C. P. (1978). Restrained eating. *Psychiatric Clinics of North America, 1,* 593–607.

Hovell, M. D., Bursick, J. H., Sharkey, R., & McClure, J. (1978). An evaluation of elementary students' voluntary physical activity during recess. *Research Quarterly, 49,* 460–474.

Humphrey, L. L. (1989). Is there a casual link between disturbed family processes and eating disorders? In W. G. Johnson (Ed.), *Advances in eating disorders: Vol. 2. Bulimia nervosa: Perspectives on clinical research and therapy* (pp. 119–136). Greenwich, CT: JAI.

Johnson, W. G., & Corrigan, S. A. (1987). Innovative treatment approaches to bulimia nervosa. *Behavior Modification, 11,* 373–388.

Johnson, W. G., Hinkle, L., Smith, S., Cox, S., & Pagac, S. (1990). Dietary and exercise interventions for child and adolescent obesity. Poster to be presented at the Society of Behavioral Medicines's Eleventh Annual Scientific Session. Chicago, IL.

Johnson, W. G., & Johnson, W. G. (1989). Reported aerobic activity and lung capacity. Unpublished manuscript.

Johnson, W. G., & Stalonas, P. (1977). Measuring skinfold thickness—A cautionary note. *Addictive Behaviors, 2,* 105–107.

Kagan, D. M., & Squires, R. L. (1984). Eating disorders among adolescents: Patterns and prevalence. *Adolescence, 19,* 15–29.

Kaplan, S. L., Busner, J., & Pollack, S. (1988). Perceived weight, actual weight, and depressive symptoms in a general adolescent sample. *International Journal of Eating Disorders, 7,* 107–113.

Karpowitz, D. H., & Zeus, F. R. (1975). Personality and behavior differences of obese and nonobese adolescents. *Journal of Consulting and Clinical Psychology, 43,* 886–891.

Katch, F. I., & McArdle, W. D. (1973). Prediction of body density from simple anthropometric measurements in college-age men and women. *Human Biology, 45,* 445–454.

Kirschenbaum, D. S. (1988). Adjusted weight measure for children. In M. Hersen & A. S. Bellack (Eds.), *Dictionary of behavioral assessment techniques* (pp. 11–13). New York: Pergamon Press.

Kirschenbaum, D. S. (1987). Elements of Success of the treatment of childhood and adolescent obesity. In W. G. Johnson (Ed.), *Advances in eating disorders: Vol. 1. Treating and preventing obesity* (pp. 235–251). Greenwich CT: JAI Press.

Kirschenbaum, D. S., Harris, E. S., & Tomarken, A. J. (1984). Effects of parental involvement in behavioral weight loss therapy for preadolescents. *Behavior Therapy, 15*, 485–500.

Kirschenbaum, D. S., Johnson, W. G., & Stalonas, P. M., Jr. (1987). *Treating childhood and adolescent obesity.* New York: Pergamon Press.

Klesges, L. M., & Klesges, R. C. (1987). The assessment of children's physical activity: A comparison of methods. *Medicine and Science in Sports and Exercise, 19*, 511–517.

Klesges, R. C., Coates, T. J., Holzer, B., Moldenhaur, L. M., Woolfrey, J., & Vollmer, J. (1983). Parental influences on children's eating behavior. *Journal of Applied Behavior Analysis, 16*, 371–378.

Klesges, R. C., Coates, T. J., Moldenbaun, L. M., Klesges, L. M., Holzer, B., Gustawson, J., & Barnes, J. (1984). The FATS: and observational system for assessing physical activity in children and associated parent behavior. *Behavioral Assessment, 6*, 333–345.

Klesges, R. C., & Hanson, C. L. (1988). Determining environmental causes and correlates. In N. A. Krasnegor, G. D. Grave, & N. Kretchner (Eds.), *Childhood obesity: A biobehavioral perspective* (pp. 89–118). Caldwell, NJ: Telford Press.

Kovacs, M. (1980/81). Rating scales to assess depression in school-aged children. *Acta Paedopsychiatrica, 46*, 305–315.

Kreitler, S., & Kreitler, H. (1986). Body image: The dimension of size. *Genetic, Social, and General Psychology Monographs, 114*, 7–32.

Lauer, R. M., Connor, W. E., Leaverton, P. E., Reiter, M. A., & Clarke, W. R. (1975). Coronary heart disease risk factors in school children: The Muscatine study. *The Journal of Pediatrics, 86*, 697–706.

Levinson, R., Powell, B., & Steelman, L. C. (1986). Social location, significant others and body image among adolescents. *Social Psychology Quarterly, 49*, 330–337.

McArdle, W. D., Katch, F. I., & Katch, V. L. (1986). Common techniques for assessing body composition. *Exercise physiology: Energy, nutrition,* and *human performance, 2nd ed.* (pp. 490–496). Philadelphia: Lea and Feliger.

McArdle, W. D., Katch, F. I., Pechar, G. S., Jacobsen, L., & Ruck, S. (1972). Reliability and interrelationships between maximal oxygen intake, physical work capacity and step-test scores in college women. *Medicine Science Sports, 4*, 182–186.

McCubbin, H. I., Comeau, J. K., & Harkins, J. A. (1981). *Family inventory of resources for management.* St. Paul, MN: Family Social Science.

McDonald, W. F., Brun, J. K., & Esserman, J. (1981). In-home interviews measure positive effect of a school nutrition program. *Journal of Nutrition Education, 13*, 140–144.

Mendelson, B. K., & White, D. R. (1982). Relation between body-esteem and self-esteem of obese and normal children. *Perceptual and Motor Skills, 54*, 899–905.

Mendelson, B. K., & White, D. R. (1985). Development of self-body esteem in overweight youngsters. *Developmental Psychology, 21*, 90–96.

Montoye, H. J. (1975). *Physical activity and health: An epidenuolgic study of an entire community.* Englewood Cliffs, NJ: Prentice-Hall.

Mooe, R. H. (1974). *Family environment scale.* Palo Alto, CA: Consulting Psychologists Press.

Morrison, J. A., & Glueck, C. J. (1981). Pediatric risk factors for adult coronary heart disease: Primary atherosclerosis prevention. *Cardiovascular Reviews & Reports, 2*, 1269–1276, 1279–1281.

Olson, D. H., Portner, J., & Lavee, Y. (1985). *Family adaptability and cohesion evaluation scale.* St. Paul, MN: Family Social Science.

Perri, M. G., (1987). Maintenance strategies for the management of obesity. In W. G. Johnson (Ed.), *Advances in eating disorders. Vol. I. Treating and preventing obesity* (pp. 177–194). Greewich, CT: JAI Press.

Perry, C. L., Griffin, G., & Murray, D. M. (1985). Assessing needs for youth health promotion. *Preventive Medicine, 14*, 379–393.

Pollock, M. L. & Jackson, A. S. (1980). Measurement of cardiorespiratory fitness and body composition in the clinical setting. *Comprehensive Therapy, 6*, 12–18.

Pollock, M. L., Wilmore, J. W., & Fox, S. (1981). Exercise in health and disease evaluation: Prescription for prevention and rehabilitation. In *Medical screening and evaluation* (pp. 205–229). Philadelphia: W.B. Saunders.

Poskitt, E. M. E., & Cole, T. J. (1977). Do fat babies stay fat? *British Medical Journal, 1*, 7–9.

Rierdan, J., Koff, E., & Stubbs, M. L. (1987). Depressive symptomatology and body image in adolescent girls. *Journal of Early Adolescence, 7*, 205–216.

Roche, A. F. (Ed.) (1985). Body composition assessments in youth and adults. *Report of the Sixth Ross Conference on Medical Research.* Columbus, OH: Ross Laboratories.

Sabry, J. H., Ford, D. Y., Roberts, M. L., & Wardlaw, J. M. (1974). Evaluation techniques for use with children's diets. *Journal of Nutrition Education, 6*, 52–56.

Saris, W. M. (1986). Habitual physical activity in children: Methodology and findings in health and disease. *Medicine and Science in Sports and Exercise, 18*, 253–263.

Schlundt, D. G. (1988). Dieter's Inventory of Eating Temptations. In M. Hersen & A. S. Bellack (Eds.), *Dictionary of behavioral assessment techniques* (pp. 177–178). New York: Pergamon Press.

Schlundt, D. G. (1988). Self-monitoring analysis system. *Dictionary of Behavioral Assessment Techniques* (pp. 399–401). New York: Pergamon Press.

Schlundt, D. G. (1989). Assessment of rating behavior in bulimia nervosa: The self-monitoring analysis system. In W. G. Johnson (Ed.), *Advances in eating disorders, Vol 2. Bulimia nervosa: perspectives on clinical research and therapy* (pp. 1–43). Greenwich, CT: JAI Press.

Schlundt, D. G., & Johnson, W. G. (1990). Eating disorders: *Assessment and treatment.* Boston, MA: Allyn and Bacon.

Secord, P. F., & Jourard, S. M. (1953). The appraisal of body-cathexis: Body-cathexis and the self. *Journal of Consulting Psychology, 17*, 343–347.

Seliger, V., Trefny, Z., Bartunkova, S., & Paver, M. (1974). The habitual activity and physical fitness of 12 year old boys. *Acta Paediatrica Belgica, 28*, 54–59.

Seltzer, C. C., & Mayer, J. (1967). Greater reliability of the triceps skin fold over the subscapuler skin fold as an index of obesity. *The American Journal of Clinical Nutrition. 20*, 950–953.

Shear, C. L., Freedman, D. S., Burke, G. L., Harsha, D. W., Webber, L. S., & Berenson, G. S. (1988). Secular trends of obesity in early life: The Bolgalusa Heart Study. *American Journal of Public Health, 78*, 75–77.

Stunkard, A. J., & Burt, V. (1967). Obesity and body image: II. Age of disturbances in the body image. *American Journal of Psychiatry, 123*, 1443–1447.

Stunkard, A. J., & Messick, S. (1985). The three-factor eating questionnaire to measure dietary restraint, disinhibition and hunger. *Journal of Psychological Research, 29*, 71–83.

Stunkard, A. J., Sorensen, T. I. A., Hanis, C., Teasdale, T. W., Charkraborty, R., Schull, W. J., & Schulsinger, R. (1986). An adoption study of human obesity. *The New England Journal of Medicine, 314*, 193–198.

Stunkard, A. J., & Waxman, M. (1981). Accuracy of self-reports of food intake. *Journal of American Diet Association, 79*, 547–551.

Tucker, L. A. (1986). The relationship of television viewing to physical fitness and obesity. *Adolescence, 21*, 797–806.

Wadden, T. A., & Stunkard, A. J. (1985). Social and psychological consequences of obesity. *Annals of Internal Medicine, 103*, 1062–1067.

Waxman, M., & Stunkard, A. (1980). Caloric intake and expenditure of obese boys. *Journal of Pediatrics, 96*, 187–193.

Wilson, C. S. (1974). Child following: A technique for learning food and nutrient intakes. *Journal of Tropical Pediatrics and Environmental Child Health, 20*, 9–14.

Wilson, G. L. & Jeffrey, D. B. (1985). Behavioral eating test. In M. Hersen & A.S. Bellack (Eds.), *Dictionary of behavioral assessment techniques* (pp 66). New York: Pergamon Press.

Wilson, G. L., & Jeffrey, D. B. (1981). Body mass index. In M. Hersen & A.S. Bellack (Eds.), *Dictionary of behavioral assessment techniques* (pp. 84–85). New York: Pergamon Press.

Zakin, D. F., Blyth, D. A., & Simmons, R. G. (1984). Physical attractiveness as a medicator of the impact of early pubertal changes for girls. *Journal of Youth and Adolescence, 13*, 439–450.

CHAPTER 24

EATING DISORDERS

David M. Garner
Peggy Parker

DESCRIPTION OF THE DISORDERS

Anorexia nervosa and bulimia nervosa are disorders characterized by morbid overconcern with weight and shape leading to extreme and often dangerous weight-control behaviors. The clinical features and related psychopathology of both of these distinct diagnostic entities are well documented and widely accepted (Anderson, 1985; Beumont, George, & Smart, 1976; Dally & Gomez, 1979; Fairburn, 1985; Garfinkel & Garner, 1982; Garner & Garfinkel, 1980; Johnson & Connors, 1987; Palmer, 1979; Russell, 1970; Strober, 1980). According to these reviews, both disorders are conceptualized as final common pathways that derive from a range of potential predisposing factors. Moreover, they have a variety of associated psychological symptoms that may, or may not, have etiological significance but, in either case, contribute to the heterogeneity in the disorder on presentation. Finally, both anorexia nervosa and bulimia nervosa result in potentially serious physical and psychological sequelae that may not only perpetuate the eating disorder but may also cloud the assessment picture.

There has been a dramatic increase in the number of eating disorder cases identified among women, and to a lesser degree among men, in recent years (cf. Leichner & Gertler, 1988). This, at least in part, may be due to unrealistic social pressures on women to diet to conform to current standards of attractiveness (Garner, Garfinkel, Schwartz, & Thompson, 1980). The cultural norms related to thinness and weight control are so widely accepted in their extreme that the attitudes and behaviors required for a diagnosis of either anorexia nervosa or bulimia nervosa have been found to be widely accepted by the public as neither uncommon nor abnormal (Huon, Brown, & Morris, 1988).

It has also been noted that the psychological features of the eating disordered patient population may have undergone subtle changes over time (Russell, 1985). Although anorexia nervosa was once believed to be a disorder of higher socioeconomic classes, recent evidence suggests that is has become more common in the middle and lower social classes (Gowers & McMahon, 1989). Eating disorders are still most common in adolescence, but cases have been reported in children (Fosson, Knibbs, Bryant-Waugh, & Lask, 1987; Maloney, McGuire, & Daniels, 1988) and in older adults (Kellett, Trimble, & Thorley, 1976).

The heterogeneity of the patient population and diversity of theoretical and clinical opinion render the assessment process for anorexia nervosa and bulimia nervosa a complex and multifaceted task. In addition, assessment involves a dynamic process, as it influences the course of treatment. Moreover, reassessment is ongoing during treatment. There exists no universally accepted or standardized assessment protocol for eating disorders; however, descriptive refinements along with advances in the understanding of diagnostic, etiological, and treatment considerations have resulted in tremendous improvements in the technology of assessment. The primary aim of this chapter is to provide a multimodal framework for assessing the aspects of eating disorders that are relevant to treatment and research.

Anorexia Nervosa

Anorexia nervosa is characterized by self-imposed starvation to the point of emaciation and an intense drive for thinness or fear of becoming fat. This may be expressed as distortions about one's body size or as extreme dissatisfaction with one's own size or shape. The following diagnostic criteria represent refinements based upon recent conceptual and empirical advancements (cf. Garner & Garfinkel, 1988):

DSM-III-R Diagnostic Criteria for Anorexia Nervosa

1. Refusal to maintain body weight over a minimal normal weight for age and height, e.g., weight loss leading to maintenance of body weight 15% below that expected; or failure to make expected weight gain during a period of growth, leading to body weight 15% below that expected.
2. Intense fear of gaining weight or becoming fat, even though underweight.
3. Disturbance in the way in which one's body weight, size, or shape is experienced, e.g., the person claims to "feel fat" even when emaciated, believes that one area of the body is "too fat" even when obviously underweight.
4. In females, absence of at least three consecutive menstrual cycles when otherwise expected to occur (primary or secondary amenorrhea). (A woman is considered to have amenorrhea if her periods occur only following hormone [e.g., estrogen] administration.)

DSM-III-R Diagnostic Criteria for Bulimia Nervosa

1. Recurrent episodes of binge eating (rapid consumption of a large amount of food in a discrete period of time).
2. A feeling of lack of control over eating during the eating binges.
3. The person regularly engages in self-induced vomiting, use of laxatives or diuretics, strict dieting or fasting, or vigorous exercise to prevent weight gain.
4. A minimum average of two binge eating episodes per week for at least 3 months.
5. Persistent overconcern with body weight and shape.

These and theoretically compatible criteria proposed by Russell (1970) specifically require presence of self-induced weight loss or absence of weight gain during normal growth as well as extreme overconcern about weight and shape. Failure to gain expected weight during normal growth and development is particularly relevant to diagnosis in younger age groups, in which body weight loss is not as extreme and failure to maintain growth is a more common occurrence. In pediatric cases it is particularly important to establish the deliberate intent of weight loss through self-starvation to distinguish anorexia nervosa from childhood syndromes with different etiologies (Jaffe & Singer, 1989).

Binge eating occurs in approximately 50% of anorexia nervosa cases and has led to the identification of two subgroups of patients. The restricting type, in which a suboptimal body weight is maintained through rigid control of eating, has been differentiated from the bulimic type, in which strict dieting is punctuated by episodes of bingeing, typically occurring along with purging behaviors (Beumont et al., 1976; Casper, Eckert, Halmi, Goldberg, & Davis, 1980; Strober, Salkin, Burroughs, & Morrell, 1982). Bulimic anorexics have been found to be more similar to bulimia nervosa patients than to those with restricting anorexia nervosa. However, the differentiation between subgroups based on bingeing may be overly simplistic, since there appears to be more psychological variability within than between such diagnostic groups (Garner, Garfinkel, & O'Shaughnessy, 1985a).

Bulimia Nervosa

Russell (1979) proposed the term *bulimia nervosa* to define a syndrome that shares many features in common with anorexia nervosa, perhaps the most important of which is "morbid fear of fatness." Other key features of bulimia nervosa are the powerful and intractable urges to overeat that invariably lead to bouts of binge eating followed by inordinate attempts to control weight through self-induced vomiting, laxative abuse, fasting, vigorous exercise, and other behaviors with similar intent (Fairburn & Cooper, 1984). While bulimia nervosa may be distinguished from anorexia nervosa in terms of absolute weight, it is evident that patients may move between the different eating disorder syndromes at different points in time (Vandereycken & Pierloot, 1983).

The term *bulimia nervosa* was adopted in the recent DSM-III-R diagnostic criteria (APA, 1987). These criteria represent a significant improvement over the vague and overinclusive criteria for "bulimia" (APA, 1980). The DSM-III criteria originally excluded the diagnosis of bulimia nervosa if anorexia nervosa was present, rendering the issued of amount of weight loss the key element in differential diagnosis between the syndromes. Currently, diagnosis of both disorders is indicated when bulimic symptoms are evident in conjunction with diagnostic criteria for anorexia nervosa (APA, 1987). Diagnosis of bulimia nervosa, like anorexia nervosa, assumes the presence of "persistent overconcern with body shape and weight" (APA, 1987, p. 68) The similarities noted between the bulimic subgroup of anorexia nervosa patients and those meeting diagnostic criteria for bulimia nervosa (as well as certain ambiguities in the DSM-III-R criteria) have led to various recommendations for further research and diagnostic refinement of the eating disorders (cf., Fairburn, 1987; Garner, Shafer, & Rosen, 1991).

Prior to the designation of bulimia nervosa as a distinct syndrome, bulimic behaviors had typically been reported in connection with obesity (Stunkard, 1959), and recent reports have confirmed that binge eating is common in obese individuals presenting for weight-loss treatment (Marcus & Wing, 1987; Hudson et al., 1988). Thus, symptoms of binge eating can occur at any point along the weight continuum and appear to be accompanied by similar concerns about weight and shape.

MULTIMODAL ASSESSMENT

The aim of this section is to delineate aspects of the assessment that are specifically pertinent to eating disorders. Clearly, this framework presupposes that the clinician has broad technical competence in assessment and that data gathered in evaluating the eating-disordered patient are *added to* the base of information obtained in a general assessment. As indicated earlier, anorexia nervosa and bulimia nervosa may be conceptualized as multidetermined disorders that occur with a range of predisposing, precipitating, and maintaining factors. In this sense, there is broad overlap between both disorders, as their etiology and course derive from an interplay between the same broad set of background issues related to the individual, family, and culture. Thorough assessment requires a comprehensive understanding of the common themes as well as the potential variability in these factors as they come to be expressed in the individual patient.

The initial interview involves an analysis of a particular patient's history, present level of psychosocial functioning, severity of the eating disorder, complications, and motivation for change. Treatment options grow out of the clinical picture derived through this process. A critical part of the assessment involves careful attention to both the salient psychological issues as well as the impact of biological changes induced by disturbed eating and weight loss (see Foreyt & McGavin, 1988; Garner, Rockert, Olmsted, Johnson, & Coscina, 1985c; Mitchell, 1986).

Reasons for Seeking Treatment

Although it may seem obvious that inquiry should be made about the reasons for initiation of treatment or consultation, it is of particular significance for the eating-disordered patient. It has been observed often for both anorexia nervosa and bulimia nervosa that many of the core symptoms are "ego-syntonic," in that the patient views them as positive and even necessary for her well-being (Garner & Bemis, 1982). The secretive nature of self-induced vomiting and other weight-losing behaviors and the denial of weight loss may thwart attempts at accurate assessment. Often the patient has sought treatment under duress at the insistence of someone else. Adolescents and younger children are almost invariably brought to the consultation or treatment interview by their parents. In these cases, the clinician may be viewed by the patient as an unwelcome agent of the parents. In other cases, treatment may be self-initiated because of a recognition that eating symptoms reflect underlying emotional problems. Most often the motivation is a mixture of these two factors. Determination of the reason or reasons for seeking treatment sets the stage for developing rapport and a therapeutic alliance involving at least two key elements. The first is to make it clear to the identified patient that the possibility of meaningful treatment must involve exploration and resolution of issues that are truly relevant to her (i.e., treatment cannot simply involve carrying out the objectives of weight gain or the elimination of weight-control behaviors that disturb others more than her). The second element involves helping parents and the patient conceptualize the problem in a manner that reduces guilt that may stem from the overly simplistic assumption that the disorder is caused by "poor parenting," malicious intent on anyone's part, or some other naive understanding that may have developed from a variety of sources. Specific strategies for promoting motivation for treatment have been described elsewhere and are relevant to the assessment process (Garner & Bemis, 1982, 1985; Garner, Garfinkel, & Bemis, 1982a). To the degree that information obtained in assessment interviews is derived from the patient's own report, issues of motivation and a trusting therapeutic relationship cannot be overemphasized.

Typical Versus Atypical Eating Disorders in Young Children

It is generally believed that anorexia nervosa and bulimia nervosa are rare in young children and that most prepubertal cases only superficially resemble typical eating disorders (Jaffe & Singer, 1989). Atypical eating disorders in young children usually present with one or more of the symptoms of weight loss, refusal to eat normal amounts of food, phobic food aversions, ritualistic and other bizarre eating habits, depression, and significant associated psychopathology, as well as family conflict. Such children do not display the fear of fatness and overconcern for weight and shape seen in typical eating disorders (Jaffe & Singer, 1989). In terms of signs and symptoms, genuine eating disorders do not have fundamentally different presentations in children, adolescents, or adults. Thus, for the purpose of the foregoing discussion, it can be assumed that descriptions and etiological formulations may apply to patients who present at any age. Although the potential range of information gathered during an assessment is similar regardless of the patient's age, there are important differences in the manner in which assessments are performed with younger and older patients.

Format of the Assessment Interview

When assessments are being performed on young patients who are living at home, it is advisable that all members of the family participate in the evaluation. Sometimes it is impractical or clinically unnecessary for the siblings to be part of an initial assessment; however, in some instances, they may be very important members in subsequent meetings. When the eating disorder occurs in an older patient, it is preferable to see the individual alone for all or at least part of the initial assessment. Many times patients are reluctant to share information regarding their eating symptoms in the presence of their parents or spouse, but they will reveal details in an individual meeting. The decisions regarding whether or not to perform the assessment and subsequent treatment with the individual alone or to include the spouse, current family members, or the members of the family of origin must depend on the specific clinical issues that are pertinent to the given case (Vandereycken, Kog, & Vanderlinden, 1989).

Detailed Weight History

A thorough weight history provides important information about the nature and temporal sequence of events as they relate to the patient's struggle with weight. It also is a relatively nonthreatening area for early discussion that allows for the development of rapport. Moreover, asking about details of the patient's weight and concurrent events provides the interviewer with an initial picture of her understanding of factors that may be responsible for the development of the eating disorder. In most cases, it is preferable for the weight history to be elicited in an individual interview, since details related to weight may have highly personal significance to the patient. With younger patients, it may be necessary or even desirable to obtain such information in an interview involving both the parents and the child. Within this context, it is important to be mindful of the fact that weight has probably become an emotionally charged topic within the family. Beginning with when the patient first reached current height and weight, a detailed account of significant weight changes are elicited through the use of questioning. Specific probes may be required to clearly ascertain the following key features: (a) current weight, (b) highest and lowest premorbid weights, (c) details of weight fluctuations during the period between the onset of the eating disorder and the present, (d) weight at which regular menstrual periods ceased, if this has occurred, (e) the patient's desired or preferred weight, and (f) weight that the patient believes would be attained in the absence of conscious control of weight.

Preliminary information derived from the weight history can serve as a base from which to initiate questions about the meaning of weight and shape to the patient. Because self-worth is perceived as dependent on the attainment and maintenance of a low body weight, the patient may not view her beliefs and attitudes in relation to weight and dieting behaviors as dysfunctional and thus, may withdraw if she perceives that these core beliefs are being confronted and challenged (Garner & Bemis, 1982).

Overconcern for Weight and Shape

Directly flowing from an assessment of weight history is the evaluation of the nature and intensity of the patient's overconcern with weight and shape (Fairburn & Garner, 1986). It is the magnitude of the overconcern about weight and shape and the lengths that the individual is willing to go in the interests of weight control that distinguishes one who is merely dissatisfied with weight and shape from another who meets the criteria for a clinical eating disorder. Nevertheless, it is vital that the assessment be performed with a clear appreciation of the general imperatives for thinness and abhorrence for fatness that confront women in our culture. The suggestion that the patient suffers from "overconcern" about weight and shape may at times seem insensitive to the enormous daily pressures for thinness that challenge women. The fashion industry, movies, magazines, and television persistently bombard the public with role models for women whose gaunt shape is idealized. Acknowledging the tremendous magnitude of these cultural pressures and how they undoubtedly affect most women may be helpful in diminishing defensiveness on the part of some patients. Patients and their family members often begin with an overly simplistic interpretation of the eating disorder (occasionally reinforced by others) as denoting personal culpability. At the same time, an overly zealous attack on the mistaken assumption that thinness is a valid framework for evaluation of self-worth may be interpreted by the patient as a direct assault on her current value system, and this may sabotage further assessment and treatment efforts.

Specific questions regarding weight and shape not only provide valuable information on this topic but also reveal the more general belief structure and conceptual style of the patient. Specific probes may include the following: (a) If you could change your weight, what would your desired weight be? (b) How important is it for you to achieve this weight? (c) How would your life change if you achieved it? (d) If by gaining 5 pounds you could recover from your eating disorder, would you gain the weight? (e) How does your assessment of yourself change as your weight goes up? (f) How do you think others view your self-worth at different weights? (g) Would you be able to stop weighing yourself for a week? Through this type of questioning, the meaning of weight and shape and the intensity of the patient's convictions can be explored. Standardized and more systematic structured interview methods for gathering information related to weight, shape, and body image are described later.

Dieting and Weight Losing Behaviors

Intensity of dieting efforts and types of weight-losing behaviors employed should be assessed in an initial interview. A dieting history should pinpoint when dieting first began and the different methods that have been used to reduce or control weight. Many patients have followed a wide range of commercial diets, and some have developed their eating disorder following participation in commercial or hospital weight-loss programs. Some patients report that their intense dieting efforts began following weight loss due to illness. Specific questions should be asked about self-induced vomiting, including (a) Has self-induced vomiting ever been used to control weight? (b) If so, when did it begin? Why was it discontinued? How is vomiting induced? (c) What was the monthly, weekly, or daily frequency at its worst? When was this, what was the patient's body weight at the time, and had it been ascending or descending at the time? What were the psychosocial circumstances surrounding this period in time? (d) Has the course been fluctuating or rather consistent? If fluctuating, what are highest and lowest points like in terms of frequency and associated affective state and interpersonal circumstances? (e) Is the patient currently engaging in self-induced vomiting, and what is the average weekly frequency during the past 3 months? (f) What is the longest period of time since the eating disorder began that the patient has been able to avoid self-induced vomiting? What were the circumstances? (g) How has self-induced vomiting interfered with interpersonal relationships and employment? (h) Is self-induced vomiting ever experienced as pleasurable? (i) Are any other affective states or changes in consciousness consistently associated with vomiting (i.e., anger, sadness, clouded sensorium)? (j) What does the patient think would happen if vomiting were inhibited for a week?

Similar questions should be asked regarding other weight-controlling behaviors such as laxative and diuretic abuse, diet pills or other drugs to control appetite, use of emetics, chewing and spitting food out before swallowing, prolonged fasting, and vigorous exercise for the explicit purpose of controlling body weight. Some diabetic patients manipulate their insulin levels to control weight (Rodin, Silberstein, & Striegel-Moore, 1985). Occasionally, patients on thyroxin alter their dosage to control their weight (Garfinkel & Garner, 1982). Many of these behaviors have obvious, serious health consequences and require a detailed medical evaluation. Mitchell et al. (1985) found that in a group of 275 bulimic patients presenting for treatment, 84% induced vomiting, 47% took laxatives, and 25% used diuretics one or more times per week. Careful evaluation of the presence, duration, and severity of these symptoms is important in the assessment protocol to determine the most appropriate treatment. These questions should be asked of patients who fall into the "restricting" anorexia nervosa subtype, since about 20% of them engage in self-induced vomiting and other behaviors that are more common in bulimic patients (Garfinkel & Garner, 1982).

Binge Eating

Binge eating, "rapid consumption of a large amount of food in a discrete period of time" (APA, 1987), is recognized as a key symptom in bulimia nervosa and occurs in about 50% of patients presenting with anorexia nervosa (Casper et al., 1980). However, the definition, measurement, and relative significance of this behavior has not yet been designated. In part, this may be attributed to the ambiguity associated with determining the quantity of food required to define a "binge episode." While quantitative evaluation of binge eating according to specific guidelines has been advocated (Fairburn, 1987; Katzman & Wolchik, 1984), there is little agreement on the exact amount of food that differentiates a binge from the amount of food that would fall within the boundaries of normal consumption. Patients describe their behavior as "binge eating" even when small or relatively normal amounts of food have actually been consumed (Rosen, Leitenberg, Fisher, & Khazam, 1986; Rossiter & Agras, 1990).

It may be argued that the most clinically relevant issues in determining whether eating qualifies as a "binge episode" relate to the patient's experience of loss of control of eating regardless of the actual number of calories consumed (Garner et al., 1991). Nevertheless, there is a subset of patients who do not perceive their binge episodes as "out of their control" but instead describe them as carefully preplanned or calculated behaviors. The sense of control over bingeing may be directly related to an awareness that vomiting of the unwanted calories will quickly follow the binge episode. In some cases, bingeing and vomiting may be associated with secondary gain in that it may serve a specific function in certain interpersonal relationships.

Inquiries about the frequency and duration of symptoms of bingeing and vomiting are essential in determining the severity of the disorder and assessing the need for medical consultation. In gathering information pertaining to the history, frequency, and duration of bingeing and vomiting episodes, it is important to begin to look for repetitive themes within a functional analytic framework. Questions should be directed toward identifying the degree of dietary restriction or weight suppression that might account for the symptoms, as well as antecedent and consequent mood states, interpersonal situations, other important events, or cognitions that directly precede or follow bingeing and vomiting.

Assessment of binge eating should attempt to answer the following questions: (a) Is binge eating a current problem? (b) At what age did binge eating begin, and when did it begin occurring on a regular basis? (c) Did it begin following a period of strict dieting? (d) What is the frequency and duration of binge episodes in the past 3 months? (e) What is the longest period of time without binge eating once it began on a regular basis, and what were the circumstances surrounding this respite? (f) How much food is eaten in a typical binge? What is the most and least consumed during a binge? (g) Is binge eating accompanied by feeling out of control? Do you feel that you can stop once a binge has started? Do you feel that you could prevent a binge from starting in the first place? Do you plan binges ahead of time? (h) How much distress does bingeing create? Do you ever find bingeing pleasurable? (i) Does bingeing become worse with mood changes, particularly depression? What is your mood like before, during, and after a binge? (j) Does bingeing become worse during premenstrual days? (k)

What are typical "binge foods" or "forbidden foods" that lead to a binge, and what foods can be eaten without leading to a binge? (l) Would you continue to binge if you could not purge? (m) Are there particular settings, times of the day, or social interactions that are associated with a binge? (n) What feelings and behaviors result from bingeing (e.g., anxiety, guilt, shame, fatigue, and social withdrawal).

Physical and Psychological Complications

A medical evaluation of patients with eating disorders may be necessary to identify or rule out physical complications of starvation or those associated with certain extreme weight-losing behaviors. Occasionally, a medical evaluation will be necessary to determine whether weight loss has been precipitated by an underlying physical disorder. Certain features, such as hypotension, hypothermia, bradycardia, and overall reduced metabolic rate, are common symptoms of starvation and may be evident in anorexia nervosa. Self-induced vomiting and purgative abuse may cause various symptoms or abnormalities, such as weakness, muscle cramping, edema, constipation, cardiac arrhythmias, and paresthesia. Additionally, general fatigue, constipation, depression, various neurological abnormalities, kidney and cardiac disturbances, swollen salivary glands, electrolyte disturbances, dental deterioration, finger clubbing or swelling, edema, and dehydration have been reported (Fairburn, 1985; Garner et al., 1985a; Mitchell, 1986). Amenorrhea is required for anorexia nervosa and occurs in some cases of bulimia nervosa. Information should be collected on current complications as well as those that have appeared over the course of the eating disorder.

The effects of the eating disorder on interpersonal, scholastic, vocational, and personal functioning should be carefully assessed. The degree to which the eating disorder interferes with these areas of performance may be important considerations in determining the patient's motivation for change and potential for functioning.

Hospitalization is not required in most cases of bulimia nervosa, the exceptions being individuals who are experiencing refractory bingeing and vomiting that is unresponsive to outpatient treatment, those with physical complications caused by electrolyte disturbance, abuse of emetics or other drugs, or those who are at serious risk for self-harm. Hospitalization is necessary more often in anorexia nervosa than in bulimia nervosa cases to promote renutrition as well as to manage complications (Andersen, 1985; Garfinkel & Garner, 1982). The presence and severity of depressive symptoms should be assessed and the possibility of suicidal ideation explored (Crisp, 1980; Hatsukami, Mitchell, Eckert, & Pyle, 1986).

Individual, familial, and sociocultural background factors separately and in combination have been implicated in the development of anorexia nervosa and bulimia nervosa. These background factors have formed the basis for different theoretical approaches to eating disorders that have resulted in treatment orientations that may be characterized as primarily behavioral, cognitive-behavioral, educational, psychodynamic, and family systems in focus. Full discussion of the range of determinants and the psychological orientations that they represent is far beyond the scope of the current chapter and are reviewed elsewhere (Garfinkel & Garner, 1982; Garner & Garfinkel, 1985; Johnson & Connors, 1987; Vandereycken et al., 1989). There is the tendency to perform assessments from a specific theoretical orientation, and while adhering to a particular model has certain advantages, we would encourage the assessing clinician to adopt a multidimensional perspective of eating disorders that allows for the integration of a range of potentially relevant theoretical principles (Garner, Garfinkel, & Irvine, 1986).

Bruch (1962, 1973) was one of the first theorists to provide an integrated developmental model for eating disorders. She attributed anorexia nervosa to core deficits reflected in body size misperception, interoceptive disturbances, and an overwhelming sense of personal ineffectiveness (Bruch, 1962). These deficits in self-awareness were accompanied by feelings of worthlessness, anxiety, and confusion over various aspects of bodily functioning.

Bruch's early formulations related to conceptual deficits have been translated into the language of cognitive-behavioral psychology with practical recommendations for treatment (Garner & Bemis, 1982, 1985; Garner, 1986, 1988; Guidano & Liotti, 1983). The beliefs that anorexia nervosa patients have regarding food, weight, and their bodies have been linked to more fundamental disturbances in their individual meaning systems and those that have been likely fostered by their family of origin. Guidano and Liotti (1983) suggest the operation of "deep cognitive structures" associated with "personal identity" (p. 299) in some eating-disordered patients. Similarly, Beck's (1976) notions of "reasoning errors" and "underlying assumptions" have been applied to eating-disordered patients to describe different levels of meaning systems that organize different levels of behavior and thinking (Fairburn, 1985; Garner, 1986; Garner & Bemis, 1982, 1985; Garner & Rosen, 1990). For example, eating-disordered patients may infer self-worth in terms of weight and shape as part of a more general proclivity for judging themselves and others by rigid and literal performance standards. During adolescence and early adulthood, weight and dieting become a concrete means of superimposing structure and control in an increasingly complex world. In the course of the development of the eating disorder, control over bodily shape and weight become overvalued symbols of personal identity and autonomy that serve to organize the individual in relation to other aspects of life functioning.

Often the weight history of the patient during adolescence reveals shifts in attitudes and behaviors in conjunction with some life change or significant life event. Assessment of potential sources of familial distress, recent changes occurring in the family, (e.g., loss, separation, illness, divorce) along with a history of eating disorders in parents and siblings may provide insights into potential precipitants of an eating disorder. Some clinicians have postulated that the manifestation of the eating disorder reflects the patient's attempts to divert attention away from deeply rooted familial distress and conflict (Humphrey & Stern, 1988). Identification of psychological themes related to adaptation to the separation-individuation process may reveal inordinate fears on the part of the child, the parents, or both. These often are indicated by enmeshed and overprotective interactional patterns or poor definition of interpersonal boundaries that have been identified by family theorists (cf. Vandereycken et al., 1989). In some cases, there has been parental disregard or lack of sensitivity to the child's actual needs, which has left her unprepared to deal with demands of autonomy and self-mastery (Bruch, 1973). Another common theme is the patient's repudiation of her wish for interpersonal closeness and nurturance in pursuit of more socially valued traits of mastery and competence. Still another relates to basic deficits is self-definition and tension regulation that have given rise to bingeing, vomiting, and dietary restriction (Goodsitt, 1985). Finally, for various reasons, some families have difficulties in direct expression of emotions of anger, depression, anxiety, or tenderness that have made the behavioral symptoms surrounding the eating disorder a more acceptable form of conveying feeling states. In a review of familial contributions to eating disorders, Strober and Humphrey (1987) note a number of characteristic family topologies but emphasize the wide range of individual differences both between and within patient groups in stressing the etiologically complex nature of eating disorders. These authors hypothesized an interaction between genetic factors and family environments that negatively affect the development of self-esteem and self-efficacy. The following checklist summarizes several important areas that need to be assessed in the initial or in early interviews:

Clinical Interview Checklist

1. Demographic features and treatment history
2. Body weight and weight history
   a. Current weight and height
   b. Weight range at current height
      i. Highest and lowest weight
      ii. Highest stable weight prior to disorder onset
      iii. Chronology of weight changes year by year
3. Weight-controlling behavior (frequency, intensity, duration)
   a. Dieting, fasting
   b. Vomiting
   c. Spitting food
   d. Exercise
   e. Substance abuse to control weight
      • Laxatives   • Amphetamines
      • Diuretics   • Cocaine
      • Emetics   • Alcohol
4. Binge eating and eating behavior
   a. Frequency of binge eating over past 3 months (note fluctuations and longest period of abstinence)
   b. "Binge foods" (foods eaten and those that trigger episodes)
   c. Typical times and settings for binge eating
   d. Mood before, during, and after episodes
   e. Experience of loss of control
   f. Description of eating
      • Intake when adhering to restrictive dieting
      • Intake when violating restrictive pattern
      • Estimated caloric intake when adhering to restrictive pattern
      • Specific dietary "rules"
5. Attitudes toward weight and shape
   a. Level of disparagement (whole body and specific regions)
   b. Misperceptions of shape

c. Hypothetical question: "If gaining 5 pounds would eliminate all symptoms, could you tolerate the gain?" What effect would the gain have on mood and self-esteem?
d. Frequency of weighings, weight preoccupations, intrusive thoughts about weight, response to weighing
e. Perception of others' attitudes about patient's weight
6. Physical symptoms (see Mitchell, 1986)
   - cardiac arrhythmias
   - bradycardia
   - yellowing of skin
   - dry, cracking skin
   - lanugo
   - salivary gland swelling
   - amenorrhea
   - dental decalcification
   - electrolyte disturbances: dehydration, weakness, tetany
   - alternations in gastric emptying
   - vague abdominal pain, bloating, swelling
   - dental cavities due to acid from vomiting
   - hypotension
   - edema
   - hypoglycemia
   - hand calluses from vomiting
   - constipation
   - anemia
   - hypothermia
7. Psychological and interpersonal
Cover all standard assessment areas with particular emphasis on depression, substance abuse, impulse control, sexual abuse, vocational capacity, and quality of interpersonal and family relationships. Specific psychological themes that have been identified in eating disorders should be explored to determine their relevance.

Predisposing Factors

While certain core features may be common to many eating-disordered patients, individual differences in premorbid personality and levels of psychological functioning contribute to major differences in the manifestation of key symptoms. Moreover, it may not be apparent from the initial assessment whether psychological distress, cognitive impairment, and behavioral symptoms reported by anorexic and bulimic patients signal fundamental emotional disturbance or are secondary elaborations resulting from weight loss and chaotic dietary patterns. Symptoms such as poor concentration, lability of mood, depressive features, obsessional thinking, irritability, difficulties with decision making, impulsivity, and social withdrawal have been identified in human semistarvation studies (cf. Garner et al., 1985c). Many of these and other symptoms that may initially appear to reflect fundamental psychological deficits (e.g., "borderline traits," severe depression) ameliorate quickly with the reduction of binge-vomiting episodes (Fairburn, Cooper, Kirk, & O'Connor, 1985; Garner et al., 1990) or weight gain. Greater confidence that these symptoms reflect primary disturbances comes from determining whether they were evident before the onset of the eating disorder. Relying on convergent reports about the patient's psychological picture before the development of the eating disorder may provide relevant information in this regard. Perhaps the best assessment tool is speed of treatment response, since it provides information regarding resistance to change as well as an indication of symptom improvement in response to more consistent eating patterns and weight restoration. The assumption that certain symptoms reflect personality disturbance is weakened if these symptoms resolve relatively quickly in response to treatment.

ASSESSMENT TECHNIQUES

Various approaches to information gathering have been developed for eating disorders, including standard clinical interviews, semistructured interviews, behavioral observation, standardized self-report measures, symptom checklists, clinical rating scales, self-monitoring procedures, and standardized test meals. There are three broad areas of focus in the assessment process:

1. assessment of specific symptom areas that allow the diagnosis of the eating disorder,
2. measurement of other attitudes or behaviors characteristic of eating disorders,
3. identification and measurement of associated psychological and personality features indicative of overall functioning.

The assessment and evaluation process usually begins with a detailed clinical interview in which information pertinent to the content areas outlined earlier are carefully explored. It is important that the format and style of the initial or early interviews be aimed at the development of a sense of openness and trust between the patient and the assessing clinician.

This is of paramount importance for eating-disordered patients, who may assume that the goal of assessment and treatment is fundamentally to convince them to abandon symptoms that are viewed by them as functional, necessary, or even desirable. The structure, format, style, and potential motivational problems to be considered in the initial interview need not be addressed here because these issues are discussed in detail elsewhere (Fairburn, 1982, 1985; Foreyt & McGavin, 1988; Garner, 1988; Garner et al., 1982a; Garner & Bemis, 1982; Garner & Davis, 1986; Williamson, 1990). Clinical and background information may be supplemented by a number of nonstandardized symptom checklists that have been developed, including the Bulimia Interview Form (Walsh & Gladis, 1985), the Eating Disorders Questionnaire (Mitchell et al., 1985), the Eating Disorder Inventory Checklist (EDI-SC, Garner, 1991), and the Diagnostic Survey for Eating Disorders (Johnson, 1985). Incorporating items pertinent to demographic, familial, and weight history elements with direct questions about food-related attitudes and behaviors, these instruments are intended to be used in conjunction with interview data.

Semistructured Interview

The development of standardized, semistructured clinical interviews designed to evaluate the eating disorders represents a major advancement in the field (Cooper & Fairburn, 1987; Palmer, Christie, Cordle, Davies, & Kenrick, 1987). The semistructured interview has the advantage of allowing the clinician to achieve greater precision in distinguishing concerns about weight and shape that are of clinical proportions from those that may not be indicative of a formal eating disorder. The Eating Disorder Examination (EDE) (Cooper & Fairburn, 1987) was designed to measure the clinical features and specific psychopathology in anorexia nervosa and bulimia nervosa, with a focus on the personal importance attached to weight and shape. The EDE is comprised of 62 items geared towards the assessment of the patient's present and recent level of functioning; thus, the items are to be answered in relation to a temporal span of the previous 4 weeks. The EDE involves the assessment of behavioral and attitudinal features of eating disorders. It depends on clinical judgments by the interviewer; thus, training and some skill and knowledge about eating disorders is required. It takes approximately 1 hour to administer. The Clinical Eating Disorder Rating Instrument (CEDRI) (Palmer et al., 1987) is a 31-item clinical rating scale for the evaluation of three symptom areas (i.e., behavioral patterns, attitudes, and other symptoms such as depression and poor self-esteem) that are commonly observed in eating disorders. Two preliminary studies with the CEDRI indicate that it has satisfactory interrater reliability (Palmer et al., 1987).

Self-Report Measures

Self-report measures provide an efficient means of obtaining information for clinical and research purposes. While self-report measures should never be used as the sole basis for diagnostic and treatment decisions, they do provide the advantages of economy in administration and scoring. They also minimize interviewer bias and other potential threats to validity that stem from responses being derived from the interaction between the interviewer and the subject.

Various instruments have been introduced to measure eating disorder symptoms, and two that have been widely used in clinical and research settings are the Eating Attitudes Test (EAT) (Garner & Garfinkel, 1979; Garner, Olmsted, Bohr, & Garfinkel, 1982b) and the Eating Disorder Inventory (EDI) (Garner, 1991; Garner, Olmsted, & Polivy, 1983). The EAT was specifically designed to provide a standardized self-report measure of symptoms of anorexia nervosa and is equally useful for bulimia nervosa (Garner, Olmsted, & Garfinkel, 1985b). The 26-item instrument provides factor scores for dieting, bulimia and food preoccupation, and oral control.

The EDI is a self-report measure that was developed to identify psychological, attitudinal, and behavioral traits common in anorexia nervosa and bulimia nervosa. The original EDI was comprised of three subscales assessing attitudes and behaviors concerning eating, weight, and shape (Drive for Thinness, Bulimia, Body Dissatisfaction), and five subscales tapping more general organizing constructs or psychological traits clinically relevant to eating disorders (Ineffectiveness, Perfection, Interpersonal Distrust, Interoceptive Awareness, Maturity Fears). A new version (EDI-2) retains the original 64 items of the original measure and adds 27 additional items to form three new subscales (i.e., Aseticism, Impulse Regulation, and Social Insecurity) (cf. Garner, 1991). The EDI was developed on the premise, shared by a growing number of clinicians and researchers, that eating disorders are multidetermined and multidimensional. In clinical settings, the EDI may be useful in determining severity of disturbance compared to norms and clinical themes that are relevant to treatment planning. In research studies of nonclinical samples, the EDI and the EAT have been used as the initial stage of a two-stage screening process in which subjects with high scores are interviewed to determine whether they meet diagnostic criteria for an eating disorder. These tests have also been used in patient samples as measures of clinical state and response to treatment. It is important to make the distinction between the formal diagnosis of an eating disorder and the assessment of severity of symptomatology that is associated with an eating disorder. Just as it would be improper to diagnose a major affective disorder with the Beck Depression Inventory, it is unacceptable to "diagnose" eating disorders with the EDI or any other self-report, paper and pencil test. The most appropriate method for deriving a diagnosis is a clinical interview designed to determine if an individual meets all of the criteria corresponding to a recognized classification system.

A number of other self-report instruments have been developed to assess symptoms of eating disorders. The SCANS (Screening Instrument for Identifying Individuals at Risk of Developing Anorexia Nervosa or Bulimia Nervosa) was proposed by Slade and Dewey (1986) to provide scores corresponding to constructs conceived of as "setting conditions" for eating disorders. Smith and Thelen (1984) developed the "Bulimia Test," which is a 32-item multiple-choice scale based upon the DSM-III diagnostic criteria for bulimia (APA, 1980). Self-reports of binge eating or purging behaviors have also been measured by the Binge Scale (Hawkins & Clement, 1980), the Compulsive Eating Scale (Dunn & Ondercin, 1981), and the Binge Eating Scale (Gormally, Black, Daston, & Rardin, 1982). Since the revised diagnostic criteria for bulimia nervosa (APA, 1987) have refined and narrowed the range of "binge-eaters" who would meet diagnostic criteria for this eating disorder, interpretation of results from these instruments should be approached with caution.

Body Image

Body image is integral to eating disorders, and different measures have been employed in a vast number of studies (cf. Garner, Garfinkel, & Bonato, 1987b). Disturbances in body image may be manifested in a number of different ways. They can take the form of gross unhappiness with body fat, intense dissatisfaction with body weight, loathing of specific regions of the body, or actual misperception of body size (Garner et al., 1987b). These attitudes or perceptions are usually accompanied by the corollary conviction that rigid self-control over eating, body weight, and body shape are absolutely necessary for personal happiness and well-being. The fact that patients express such intense distress about their weight or shape at a statistically normal or subnormal weight is the aspect of eating disorders that has made them particularly perplexing to most clinicians.

Operational measures of "body image" have either been aimed at size estimation or attitudes toward weight and shape. The fact that studies of size estimation find that size overestimation is neither uniform nor unique to eating disorders has led to criticisms of size estimation as a measure of body image disturbance in eating disorders (Hsu, 1982). Measures of body dissatisfaction have earned greater acceptance because they are more clearly tied to the manifest psychopathology of the eating disorders; however, there are patients who do not display high scores on standardized measures (i.e., particularly those who are emaciated), and body dissatisfaction is certainly not unique to eating disorder patients (cf. Garner et al., 1987b). Nevertheless, measures of body dissatisfaction and other parameters of body image have clinical utility with anorexia nervosa and bulimia nervosa patients and are unquestionably of theoretical interest in these syndromes.

General Measures of Psychopathology

Complete psychiatric assessment of eating-disordered patients should include measures of personality functioning, psychological distress, depression, anxiety, family functioning, history of sexual abuse, self-esteem, social and vocational adaptation, and impulse-related features may be relevant to the development and maintenance of these syndromes. Careful assessment of these related areas is important in confirming Axis II diagnoses and in treatment planning. As indicated earlier, reassessment during the course of treatment is desirable because it may provide a more meaningful picture of personality dimensions that endure once the acute symptoms of the eating disorder are resolved.

Behavioral Observation and Self-Monitoring

Direct behavioral observation of target behaviors of the eating disorders has the advantage of minimizing the patient's potential reporting bias. Ordman and Kirschenbaum (1985) and Rosen et al. (1986) have recommended the use of standardized test meals in the assessment of eating behavior in bulimia nervosa and have argued that this may provide a valid picture of symptom severity and response to treatment. Self-monitoring has been recommended as a component of most cognitive-behavioral and other successful treatments for bulimia nervosa (cf. Garner, Fairburn, & Davis, 1987a; Williamson, 1990). There have been differences in the content areas of self-monitoring in different treatment programs, with some focusing on recording all food and liquids consumed on a daily basis and others centering on situational or emotional precipitant of binge eating episodes.

CASE ILLUSTRATION

Char is a 12-year-old female who is an only child and lives with her parents in a middle-class urban area. She was referred by her family physician for an assessment following weight loss during the preceding 6 months from 100 pounds to 75 pounds. She had lost approximately 5 pounds in the 10 days prior to the assessment interview. Char complained that she had felt depressed over the past year and indicated that she did not understand why everyone was so concerned about her weight. Her parents were distressed because Char had become increasingly withdrawn and would not eat with the family. Their attempts to prod her into eating had been met with increasing resistance, with fights around mealtime becoming the norm. Char was first interviewed alone and then with her parents. She then completed a self-report assessment battery that included the EDI, the EAT, the Beck Depression Inventory (Beck, Ward, Mendelson, Mock, & Erbaugh, 1961), the SCL-90 (Derogatis, 1977), the Family Assessment Measure (Skinner, Santa-Barbara, & Steinhauer, 1983), and the Rosenberg Self-Esteem Measure (Rosenberg, 1965).

Specific questions concerning weight history indicated that Char had been of average weight compared to her peers during most of grade school and had precipitately gained about 10 pounds over the 3 months before attaining her highest weight of 100 pounds. At this time, she reported becoming increasingly self-conscious and concerned about "being too fat," which led to marked restriction of her food intake. Her health-conscious parents were initially supportive of her weight-loss efforts and praised her resolve in dieting. The assessment interview clarified that although mild depression predated Char's weight loss, her mood had become significantly worse in recent months. She did not report binge eating or purging, and this was consistent with her parents' observations. She indicated that although her mood and concentration were poor, she was not willing to gain weight, because her accomplishment in this area had provided her with the only positive feelings that she had experienced in many months.

The interview with the parents revealed that they considered the family bonds to be extremely close. They were terrified that Char was going to continue to waste away, and they felt incapable of managing her at home. They revealed that they had been experiencing serious marital problems related to the mother's increasing involvement in her career in real estate sales. The heightened conflicts between the parents had preceded Char's weight loss and these had been set aside because of the emergent weight loss.

Psychometric evaluation indicated that Char had scores at or above the 85th percentile for eating-disorder patients on the Drive for Thinness, Ineffectiveness, and Maturity Fears subscales of the EDI. She displayed moderate depression on the BDI and the depression scale of the SCL-90. The scores on the FAM suggested that the areas of affective expression and affective involvement were sources of conflict within the family.

Implications for Treatment

Hospitalization was recommended to interrupt the weight loss and to provide renutrition. The inpatient weight goal of 100 pounds was established with the expectation that Char would continue to gain weight at a rate that would put her back on the weight-growth curve that had been interrupted with the onset of her disorder. Char was initially resistant to the suggestion of hospitalization and reluctantly accepted the plan at her parents' insistence. The rationale provided was that she had anorexia nervosa, that this was a serious condition, and that she was unlikely to make adequate progress at home. It was also emphasized that the most important goal of hospitalization was to help her feel better about herself. To even understand the relevant issues, potential starvation-related symptoms had to be separated from other more fundamental psychological or family issues that may have become dormant during the past few months of weight loss. Several tentative and purposely simplified hypotheses were shared with the family regarding possible psychological functions that Char's weight loss could have served in their situation. Weight loss could have provided a boost to Char's self-confidence at a time of growing self-doubt. It may have deflected the parents' attention away from potentially serious conflicts that were evident before Char's weight loss. The symptoms may have subdued more general maturational fears that Char or her parents may have experienced consistent with the observation that weight loss may result in a general developmental arrest (Crisp, 1980). By providing this array of explanations, it was emphasized that treatment was not just focused on weight restoration but also on helping the family and Char to solve other psychological issues that were relevant. By not insisting on the validity of any one hypothesis, the family was stimulated to accept the general idea of psychological mediating factors without having to confront at this particular time the implications of any one interpretation. The timing of Char's weight loss corresponding to a period of heightened family conflict, Char's age, the elevated Maturity Fears EDI subscale score, and the apparent difficulties in the family around affective expression provided support for the tentative hypothesis that the eating disorder was providing Char and the family with a means of avoiding potentially distressing developmental demands that are very much a part of adolescence. Individual therapy was recommended for Char to help her address her fears of weight gain and to deal with emergent concerns related to self-esteem, self-awareness, and developmental themes (Garner, 1988; Garner et al., 1982a; Garner & Bemis, 1985). It was suggested that the parents meet with a therapist to address the sources of conflict that were apparent just before Char's weight loss, with the possibility that Char could participate in meetings if this became appropriate. Considerable effort was made to coordinate the inpatient and outpatient management to reduce the likelihood of readmission.

SUMMARY

An overview of a multimodal assessment framework for eating disorders has been presented. Three broad areas of evaluation were described:

1. assessment of specific symptom areas that allow the diagnosis of an eating disorder,
2. measurement of other attitudes or behaviors characteristic of eating disorders,
3. identification and measurement of associated psychological and personality features indicative of overall functioning.

Specific recommendations were made for evaluating body weight, attitudes toward weight and shape, bingeing, purging, weight-losing behaviors, psychological and physical complications, psychological disturbance, social adjustment, and family functioning.

A range of assessment methods was reviewed, including the clinical interview, the semistructured interview, self-report measures, behavioral observation, and self-monitoring. These areas of assessment and methods are minimal guidelines that should be reapplied throughout the course of treatment.

REFERENCES

American Psychiatric Association. (1980). *Diagnostic and statistical manual of mental disorders* (3rd ed.). Washington, DC: Author.

American Psychiatric Association. (1987). *Diagnostic and statistical manual of mental disorders* (3rd ed., rev.). Washington, DC: Author.

Andersen, A. E. (1985). *Practical comprehensive treatment of anorexia nervosa and bulimia*. Baltimore, MD: Johns Hopkins Press.

Beck, A. T. (1976). *Cognitive therapy and the emotional disorders*. New York: International Universities Press.

Beck, A. T., Ward, C. H., Mendelson, M., Mock, J., & Erbaugh, J. (1961). An inventory for measuring depression. *Archives of General Psychiatry, 4*, 561–571.

Beumont, P. J. V., George, G. C. W., & Smart, D. E. (1976). "Dieters" and "vomiters and purgers" in anorexia nervosa. *Psychological Medicine, 6*, 617–622.

Bruch, H. (1962). Perceptual and conceptual disturbances in anorexia nervosa. *Psychosomatic Medicine, 24*, 187–194.

Bruch, H. (1973). *Eating disorders: Obesity, anorexia nervosa and the person within*. New York: Basic Books.

Casper, R. C., Eckert, E. D., Halmi, K. A., Goldberg, S. C., & Davis, J. M. (1980). Bulimia. Its incidence and clinical importance in patients with anorexia nervosa. *Archives of General Psychiatry, 37*, 1030–1034.

Cooper, Z., & Fairburn, C. G. (1987). The Eating Disorder Examination: A semi-structured interview for the assessment of the specific psychopathology of eating disorders. *International Journal of Eating Disorders, 6*, 1–8.

Crisp, A. H. (1980). *Anorexia nervosa*. New York: Grune & Stratton.

Dally, P. J., & Gomez, J. (1979). *Anorexia nervosa*. London: William Heinemann.

Derogatis, L. R. (1977). *SCL-90-R administration, scoring and procedures manual—II*. Towson, MD: Clinical Psychometric Research.

Dunn, P. K., & Ondercin, P. (1981). Personality variables related to compulsive eating in college women. *Journal of Clinical Psychology, 37*, 43–49.

Fairburn, C. G. (1982). Binge-eating and its management. *British Journal of Psychiatry, 141*, 631–633.

Fairburn, C. G. (1985). Cognitive-behavioral treatment for bulimia. In D. M. Garner & P. E. Garfinkel (Eds.), *Handbook of psychotherapy for anorexia nervosa and bulimia* (pp. 160–192). New York: Guilford Press.

Fairburn, C. G. (1987). The definition of bulimia nervosa: Guidelines for clinicians and research workers. *Annals of Behavioral Medicine, 9,* 3–7.

Fairburn, C. G., & Cooper, P. J. (1984). The clinical features of bulimia nervosa. *British Journal of Psychiatry, 144,* 238–246.

Fairburn, C. G., Cooper, P. J., Kirk, J., O'Connor, M. (1985). The significance of the neurotic symptoms of bulimia nervosa. *Journal of Psychiatric Research, 19,* 135–140.

Fairburn, C. G., & Garner, D. M. (1986). The diagnosis of bulimia nervosa. *International Journal of Eating Disorders, 5,* 403–419.

Foreyt, J. P., & McGavin, J. K. (1988). Anorexia nervosa and bulimia. In E. J. Marsh & L. G. Tudal (Eds.), *Behavioral assessment of childhood disorders* (pp. 776–805). New York: Guilford Press.

Fosson, A., Knibbs, J., Bryant-Waugh, R., & Lask, B. (1987). Early onset anorexia nervosa. *Archives of Disease in Childhood, 62,* 114–118.

Garfinkel, P. E., & Garner, D. M. (1982). *Anorexia nervosa: A multidimensional perspective.* New York: Brunner/Mazel.

Garner, D. M. (1986). Cognitive therapy for bulimia nervosa. *Annals of Adolescent Psychiatry, 13,* 358–390.

Garner, D. M. (1988). Anorexia nervosa. In M. Hersen & C. G. Last (Eds.), *Child behavior therapy casebook* (pp. 263–276). New York: Plenum Press.

Garner, D. M. (1991). *The eating disorder inventory manual.* Odessa, FL: Psychological Assessment Resources.

Garner, D. M., & Bemis, K. M. (1982). A cognitive-behavioral approach to anorexia nervosa. *Cognitive Therapy and Research, 6,* 123–150.

Garner, D. M., & Bemis, K. M. (1985). Cognitive therapy for anorexia nervosa. In D. M. Garner & P. E. Garfinkel (Eds.), *Handbook of psychotherapy for anorexia nervosa and bulimia* (pp. 107–146). New York: Guilford Press.

Garner, D. M., & Davis, R. (1986). The clinical assessment of anorexia nervosa and bulimia nervosa. In P. A. Keller & L. Ritt (Eds.), *Innovations in clinical practice: A source book* (pp. 5–28). Sarasota, FL: Professional Resource Exchange.

Garner, D. M., Fairburn, C. G., & Davis, R. (1987a). Cognitive-behavioral treatment of bulimia nervosa: A critical appraisal. *Behavior Modification, 11,* 398–431.

Garner, D. M., & Garfinkel, P. E. (1979). The Eating Attitudes Test: An index of the symptoms of anorexia nervosa. *Psychological Medicine, 9,* 273–279.

Garner, D. M., & Garfinkel, P. E. (1980). Socio-cultural factors in the development of anorexia nervosa. *Psychological Medicine, 10,* 647–656.

Garner, D. M., & Garfinkel, P. E. (1985). *Handbook of psychotherapy for anorexia nervosa and bulimia.* New York: Guilford Press.

Garner, D. M., & Garfinkel, P. E. (1988). *Diagnostic issues in anorexia nervosa and bulimia nervosa.* New York: Brunner/Mazel.

Garner, D. M., Garfinkel, P. E., & Bemis, K. M. (1982a). A multidimensional psychotherapy for anorexia nervosa. *International Journal of Eating Disorders, 1,* 3–46.

Garner, D. M., Garfinkel, P. E., & Bonato, D. (1987b). Body image measurement in eating disorders. In G. A. Fava & T. N. Wise (Eds.), *Advances in psychosomatic medicine* (pp. 119–133). Basel: Karger.

Garner, D. M., Garfinkel, P. E., & Irvine, M. J. (1986). Integration and sequencing of treatment approaches for eating disorders. *Psychotherapy and Psychosomatics, 46,* 67–75.

Garner, D. M., Garfinkel, P. E., & O'Shaughnessy, M. (1985a). The validity of the distinction between bulimia with and without anorexia nervosa. *American Journal of Psychiatry, 142,* 581–587.

Garner, D. M., Garfinkel, P. E., Schwartz, D. M., & Thompson, M. M. (1980). Cultural expectations of thinness in women. *Psychological Reports, 47,* 483–491.

Garner, D. M., Olmsted, M. P., Bohr, Y., & Garfinkel, P. E. (1982b). The Eating Attitudes Test: Psychometric features and clinical correlates. *Psychological Medicine, 12,* 871–878.

Garner, D. M., Olmsted, M. P., & Garfinkel, P. E. (1985b). Similarities among bulimic groups selected by different weights and weight histories. *Journal of Psychiatric Research, 19,* 129–134.

Garner, D. M., Olmsted, M. P., & Polivy, J. (1983). The Eating Disorder Inventory: A measure of cognitive-behavioral dimensions of anorexia nervosa and bulimia. In P. L. Darby, P. E. Garfinkel, D. M. Garner, & D. V. Coscina (Eds.), *Anorexia nervosa: Recent developments in research* (pp. 173–184). New York: Alan R. Liss.

Garner, D. M., Rockert, W., Olmsted, M. P., Johnson, C. L., & Coscina, D. V. (1985c). Psychoeducational principles in the treatment of bulimia and anorexia nervosa. In D. M. Garner & P. E. Garfinkel (Eds.), *Handbook of psychotherapy for anorexia nervosa and bulimia* (pp. 513–572). New York: Guilford Press.

Garner, D. M., & Rosen, L. W. (1990). Anorexia nervosa and bulimia nervosa. In A. S. Bellack, M. Hersen, & A. E. Kazdin (Eds.), *International handbook of behavior modification and therapy* (pp. 805–817). New York: Plenum Press.

Garner, D. M., Shafer, C. L., & Rosen, L. W. (1991). Critical appraisal of the DSM-III-R diagnostic criteria for eating disorders. In S. R. Hooper, G. W. Hynd, & R. E. Mattison (Eds.), *Child psychopathology. Diagnostic criteria and clinical assessment* (pp. 261–303). Hillsdale, NJ: Lawrence Erlbaum Associates.

Goodsitt, A. (1985). Self psychology and the treatment of anorexia nervosa. In D. M. Garner & P. E. Garfinkel

(Eds.), *Handbook of psychotherapy for anorexia nervosa and bulimia* (pp. 55–84). New York: Guilford Press.

Gormally, J., Black, S., Daston, S., & Rardin, D. (1982). The assessment of binge eating severity among obese persons. *Addictive Behavior, 7,* 47–55.

Gowers, S., & McMahon, J. B. (1989). Social class and prognosis in anorexia nervosa. *International Journal of Eating Disorders, 8,* 105–110.

Guidano, V. F., & Liotti, G. (1983). *Cognitive processes and emotional disorders: A structural approach to psychotherapy.* New York: Guilford Press.

Hatsukami, D., Mitchell, J. E., Eckert, E. D., & Pyle, R. (1986). Characteristics of patients with bulimia only, bulimia with affective disorder, and bulimia with substance abuse problems. *Addictive Behaviors, 11,* 399–406.

Hawkins, R. C., II, & Clement, P. F. (1980). Development and construct validation of a self-report measure of binge-eating tendencies. *Addictive Behaviors, 7,* 435–439.

Hsu, L. K. G. (1982). Is there a disturbance in body image in anorexia nervosa? *International Journal of Eating Disorders, 2,* 11–20.

Hudson, J. I., Pope, H. G., Wurtman, J., Yurgelun-Todd, D., Mark, S., & Rosenthal, N. E. (1988). Bulimia in obese individuals: Relationship to normal-weight bulimia. *Journal of Nervous and Mental Disease, 176,* 144–152.

Humphrey, L. L., & Stern, S. (1988). Object relations and the family system in bulimia. *Journal of Marital and Family Therapy, 14,* 337–350.

Huon, G. F., Brown, L., & Morris, S. (1988). Lay beliefs about disordered eating. *International Journal of Eating Disorders, 7,* 239–252.

Jaffe, A. C., & Singer, L. T. (1989). Atypical eating disorders in young children. *International Journal of Eating Disorders, 8,* 575–582.

Johnson, C. (1985). Initial consultation for patients with bulimia and anorexia nervosa. In D. M. Garner & P. E. Garfinkel (Eds.), *Handbook of psychotherapy for anorexia nervosa and bulimia* (pp. 19–51). New York: Guilford Press.

Johnson, C., & Connors, M. E. (1987). Treatment of bulimia: A review. In P. J. V. Beaumont, G. D. Burrows, & R. C. Casper (Eds.), *Handbook of eating disorders Part 1: Anorexia and bulimia nervosa* (pp. 299–317). New York: Elsevier.

Katzman, M. A., & Wolchik, S. A. (1984). Bulimia and binge eating in college women: A comparison of personality and behavioral characteristics. *Journal of Consulting and Clinical Psychology, 52,* 423–428.

Kellett, J., Trimble, M., & Thorley, A. (1976). Anorexia nervosa after the menopause. *British Journal of Psychiatry, 128,* 555–558.

Leichner, P., & Gertler, A. (1988). Prevalence and incidence studies of anorexia nervosa. In B. J. Blinder, B. F. Chaitin, & R. S. Goldstein (Eds.), *The eating disorders* (pp. 131–149). New York: PMA Publishing.

Maloney, M. J., McGuire, J. B., & Daniels, S. R. (1988). Reliability testing of a children's version of the Eating Attitudes Test. *Journal of the American Academy of Child and Adolescent Psychiatry, 27,* 541–543.

Marcus, M. D., & Wing, R. R. (1987). Binge eating among the obese. *Annals of Behavioral Medicine, 9,* 23–27.

Mitchell, J. E. (1986). Anorexia nervosa: Medical and physiological aspects. In K. D. Brownell & J. P. Foreyt (Eds.), *Handbook of eating disorders* (pp. 247–265). New York: Basic Books.

Mitchell, J. E., Hatsukami, D., Goff, G., Pyle, R. L., Eckert, E. D., & Davis, L. E. (1985). Intensive outpatient group treatment for bulimia. In D. M. Garner & P. E. Garfinkel (Eds.), *Handbook of psychotherapy for anorexia nervosa and bulimia* (pp. 240–256). New York: Guilford Press.

Ordman, A. M., & Kirschenbaum, D. S. (1985). Cognitive-behavioral therapy for bulimia: An initial outcome study. *Journal of Consulting and Clinical Psychology, 53,* 305–313.

Palmer, R. L. (1979). The dietary chaos syndrome: A useful new term? *British Journal of Medical Psychology, 52,* 187–190.

Palmer, R., Christie, M., Cordle, C., Davies, D., & Kenrick, J. (1987). The Clinical Eating Disorder Rating Instrument (CEDRI): A preliminary description. *International Journal of Eating Disorders, 6,* 9–16.

Rodin, J., Silberstein, L., & Striegel-Moore, R. (1985). Women and weight: A normative discontent. In T. B. Sonderegger (Ed.), *Nebraska symposium on motivation, 1984: Psychology and gender* (pp. 267–307). Lincoln: University of Nebraska Press.

Rosen, J. C., Leitenberg, H., Fisher, C., & Khazam, C. (1986). Binge-eating episodes in bulimia nervosa: The amount of type of food consumed. *International Journal of Eating Disorders, 5,* 255–267.

Rossiter, E. M., & Agras, W. S. (1990). An empirical test of the DSM-III-R defnition of binge. *International Journal of Eating Disorders, 9,* 513–518.

Rosenberg, M. (1965). *Society and the adolescent self-image.* Princeton, NJ: Princeton University Press.

Russell, G. F. M. (1970). Anorexia nervosa: Its identity as an illness and its treatment. In J. H. Price (Ed.), *Modern trends in psychological medicine,* Vol. 2 (pp. 131–164). London: Butterworths.

Russell, G. F. M. (1979). Bulimia nervosa: An ominous variant of anorexia nervosa. *Psychological Medicine, 9,* 429–448.

Russell, G. F. M. (1985). The changing nature of anorexia nervosa: An introduction to the conference. *Journal of Psychiatric Research, 19,* 101–109.

Skinner, H. A., Santa-Barbara, J., & Steinhauer, P. D. (1983). The family assessment measure. *Canadian Journal of Mental Health, 2,* 91–105.

Slade, P. D., & Dewey, M. E. (1986). Development and preliminary validation of SCANS: A screening instrument for identifying individuals at risk of developing anorexia and bulimia nervosa. *International Journal of Eating Disorders, 5,* 517–536.

Smith, M. C., & Thelen, M. H. (1984). Development and validation of a test for bulimia. *Journal of Consulting and Clinical Psychology, 52,* 863–872.

Strober, M. (1980). Personality and symptomatological features in young, nonchronic anorexia nervosa patients. *Journal of Psychosomatic Research, 24,* 353–359.

Strober, M., & Humphrey, L. L. (1987). Familial contributions to the etiology and course of anorexia nervosa and bulimia. *Journal of Consulting and Clinical Psychology, 55,* 654–659.

Strober, M., Salkin, B., Burroughs, J., & Morrell, W. (1982). Validity of the bulimia-restrictor distinction in anorexia nervosa: Parental personality characteristics and family psychiatric morbidity. *The Journal of Nervous and Mental Disease, 170,* 345–351.

Stunkard, A. J. (1959). Eating patterns and obesity. *Psychiatric Quarterly, 33,* 284–295.

Vandereycken, W., Kog, E., & Vanderlinden, J. (1989). *The family approach to eating disorders.* New York: PMA Publishing Corp.

Vandereycken, W., & Pierloot, R. (1983). The significance of subclassification in anorexia nervosa: A comparative study of clinical features in 141 patients. *Psychological Medicine, 13,* 543–549.

Walsh, B. T., & Gladis, M. (1985). Bulimia Interview Form. *Psychopharmacology Bulletin, 21*(3), 1017–1023.

Williamson, D. A. (1990). *Assessment of eating disorders: Obesity, anorexia, and bulimia nervosa.* New York: Pergamon Press.

CHAPTER 25

HEADACHES

Donald A. Williamson
Suzanne M. Savin
David H. Gleaves

DESCRIPTION OF THE DISORDERS

Headache is a symptom reported in the majority of children and adolescents (Bille, 1962; Sillanpae, 1983). Historically, headache has been treated medically through the use of analgesic medications, tranquilizers, muscle relaxants, and other methods (Williamson & Waggoner, 1986). In children, it is generally inadvisable to use these types of medications on a long-term basis. In recent years, a diversity of nonpharmacological treatment approaches have been developed for headaches in adults (Williamson & Waggoner, 1986). Recently, these treatment methods have been tested with children and adolescents and have been found to be quite effective (Labbé, 1988).

With the development of psychological treatment approaches, psychological assessment approaches have also evolved. This chapter summarizes the primary methods for evaluating headaches in children. Descriptions of migraine and muscle-contraction headache, the most common types of headache in children, are provided. Finally, case presentations for both types of headache are presented to illustrate the clinical application of these assessment procedures.

Migraine Headaches

Migraine and migraine variants may be the most frightening types of headaches that children experience (Moe, 1978). They can be easily confused with other conditions. The Ad Hoc Committee on Classification of Headache (1962) described migraines as recurrent types of headache, widely varied in intensity, frequency, and duration. There is usually throbbing pain, which is often localized on one side of the head. Before the actual headache, a patient may report a variety of prodromal symptoms, including scotoma, photosensitivity, vertigo, syncope, sweating, nausea, and paresthesia of the face and hands.

Migraines are generally classified into one of four types: classic migraine, common migraine, cluster headache, and complicated migraine. Classic migraines are characterized by a distinct aura of prodrome and unilateral pain. Common prodromal symptoms include flashing lights, vertigo, abdominal pain, blurred vision, scotomata, and paresthesia of the face and hands (Shinner & D'Souza, 1981; Williamson, 1981). Gascon (1984) indicated that expression of classic migraine is more frequent in adolescence than in preadolescence. However, it may also be the case that young children simply have trouble recognizing and describing prodromal symptoms (Iezzi & Neeper, 1987).

Common migraines are not preceded by a well-defined aura and are generally more diffuse. The headaches are often accompanied by nausea, vomiting, and a general feeling of being unwell (Brown, 1977). Common migraines generally last longer than classic migraines. Often the headache ends with the child falling asleep (Shinner & D'Souza, 1981). Common migraines are the most frequent type experienced by children. Jay and Tomasi (1981) reported that 78% of 54 pediatric patients seen for migraines were diagnosed as having common migraine.

Cluster headaches are characterized by attacks of unilateral intense pain over the eye and forehead, generally with flushing and watering of the eyes and nose. Attacks generally last about an hour and occur in clusters (Diamond & Dalessio, 1982). For example, a person may not have a headache for months and then experience three to five headaches during a 2-week period. Cluster headaches are rarely seen in children.

In some cases of migraine, transient neurological deficits are experienced with the headaches. Though rare, these forms of complicated migraine are believed to be more common in children than in adults. Common types of complicated migraine are hemiplegic, ophthalmoplegic, and basilar artery migraines. Acute confusional state and the Alice in Wonderland syndrome (Shinner & D'Souza, 1981) may occur along with neurological symptoms, including aphasia, paresthesia, eye pain, and a variety of visual disturbances (Williamson, Davis, & Kelley, 1989).

In children, there are several paroxysmal disturbances believed to be migraine variants that do not involve head pain. Included in this group are recurrent abdominal pain, cyclic vomiting, and paroxysmal tachycardia (Bille, 1962). These disturbances may alternate with migraine attacks or may be replaced by migraines in later life (Hoelscher & Lichstein, 1984).

Many environmental factors can trigger a migraine, including anxiety, and in many persons, specific allergies. Children often report their headaches as being precipitated by such factors as fatigue, bright lights, foods with tyramine, stress, or use of certain drugs.

Numerous differences between child and adult migraineurs have been noted in the literature. Traditionally it was thought that children, in contrast to adults, were less likely to experience prodromal symptoms and unilateral pain (Prensky & Sommer, 1979). However, Passchier and Bonke (1985) assessed migraine symptomatology in more than 2,000 children and found that the majority of the subjects reported experiencing unilateral pain. Children's headaches are often less intense and of shorter duration than those of adults; however, children's headaches may occur more frequently (Trued, 1974). The headaches of older children more closely resemble those experienced by adults.

Very often, children's migraine headaches are accompanied by gastrointestinal problems, including nausea, vomiting, and/or abdominal pain (MacDonald, 1986). Prensky and Sommer (1979) found that more than 70% of their sample reported at least one of these symptoms occurring in conjunction with the migraine headache.

The incidence of childhood migraine has been found to vary, depending upon the age group being studied. The youngest reported case of migraine headaches was in an 18-month-old child (Selby & Lance, 1960). Bille (1962), in studying 8,993 schoolchildren, found the incidence to be 2.5% for ages 7 through 9, 4.6% for ages 10 through 12, and 5.3% for ages 13 through 15. Deubner (1979) studied an older age group and found the incidence of migraine to be 9% for ages 15 through 17. The sex ratio has also been found to vary with age. Prior to age 11, males predominate; however as age increases, an increasing percentage of migraine sufferers are female (Brown, 1977). By age 15, approximately 60% are female (Bille, 1962), which approaches the estimates that 67% to 75% of adult migraineurs are woman (Waters & O'Connor, 1975).

Pathophysiology

Research concerning the physiological basis of migraine has focused predominantly on migraine during adulthood. There is general agreement that the biological basis of migraine is probably similar across ages. Therefore, the following discussion does not distinguish between studies of adult and childhood migraine.

Wolff and colleagues (summarized in Wolff, 1963) were the first medical scientists to systematically study the pathophysiology of migraine. Through a series of studies, they were able to document that the prodromal symptoms of classic migraine were associated with intracranial vasoconstriction and that the headache phase was associated with extracranial vasodilation. Recognizing that these vascular changes could not fully account for the excruciating pain of migraine, they also studied biochemical changes associated with migraine. These studies found that tissues surrounding distended extracranial arteries accumulated neurokinins, which were postulated to decrease pain threshold. The net result of these vascular and biochemical changes was severe throbbing pain. According to this vascular theory of migraine, the neurological symptoms during the preheadache phase are caused by reduced blood flow (and thereby reduced oxygen, glucose, etc.) in certain regions of the brain. Research using modern, sophisticated methodology for measuring regional cerebral blood flow has supported these observations for classic migraine but not for common migraine (Olesen, 1984).

Williamson (1981) integrated this vascular theory of migraine into a more complete psychophysiological model of migraine. This model proposed that any event or substance (e.g., alcohol, nicotine) that was vasoactive could precipitate a migraine in individuals who were genetically susceptible to migraine attacks. The implications of this model are that (a) migraines are likely to have multicausality, even in the same individual, (b) stress and strong emotions are likely to be common antecedents of migraine attacks, and (c) treatment planning must be preceded by careful documentation of life events associated with migraine attacks. This latter point is addressed in more detail when assessment strategies are discussed.

As research on migraine has progressed, it has become apparent that migraine headaches may be a heterogeneous syndrome. In particular, evidence is accumulating that classic and common migraine may have separate biological bases (Bruyn & Ferrari, 1988; Olesen, 1984). Also, there is some evidence suggesting a neurophysiological basis for migraine (Raskin, 1988; Spierings, 1988). In general there is a growing consensus that there may be more than one pathophysiological process by which children and adults develop the symptoms of migraine. At this time, however, no widely accepted theory or set of theories has been proposed. Therefore, most treatments are based upon the earlier vascular theories of migraine (Williamson, 1981; Williamson & Waggoner, 1986).

Muscle Contraction Headache

While the majority of the medical and psychological literature focuses on childhood migraine, the most common type of childhood headache is the tension headache, or muscle contraction headache (MCH). The two terms are generally used interchangeably in the literature. The Ad Hoc Committee on the Classification of Headache (1962) described muscle contraction headache as an ache or sensation of tightness, pressure, or constriction. Muscle contraction headaches vary in intensity, frequency, and duration, but can be quite long-lasting. In the medical literature, MCH is referred to as functional, meaning without organic cause of structural change and implying causation by psychological factors (Labbé, 1988). Generally physical findings are minimal and may include tenderness of the cervical muscles and occipital scalp. Frontal tenderness may also occur but is less common (Lavigne, Schulein, & Hahn, 1986).

Tension headaches are generally described as a dull, steady ache located in the suboccipital or forehead area of the head. The headache may be described as caplike with a band of pressure or tightness around the head. The pain is usually bilateral and is not accompanied by prodromal symptoms. The discomfort of muscle contraction headaches generally develops as the day progresses, and generally does not occur at night or in the morning as migraines often do (Golden, 1982). The pain of MCH may range from mild to severe, and in severe cases the headache may occur daily.

Stress is the primary psychological factor thought to cause MCH. Some authors have described children with muscle contraction headaches as perfectionistic, achievement oriented, and tense, but these reports have generally been anecdotal (Meloff, 1982). Some authors also speculate that the severity of the headache may reflect the intensity of the stressful event (Ferry, 1972), but research supporting this claim is lacking.

While muscle contraction headaches are more common in women than men, with children the prevalence appears to be equal for both sexes (Thompson, 1980). As with migraine, however, headaches may be more problematic for females as age increases. The prevalence of MCH in children also does not approach the frequency of occurrence in adults and may be more common in the adolescent than in the preadolescent child (MacDonald, 1986).

The relative infrequency of MCH may reflect a lessor prevalence of MCH in children or may reflect parental recognition of the type of headache and a lack of concern (Labbé, 1988). The symptoms of MCH are generally not as alarming as the symptoms of migraine. Another problem in determining the incidence of MCH is that many studies report the incidence of childhood migraine headaches, and then group all remaining types of head pain into a nonmigrainous headache category. Bille (1962) reported that 54% of children reported nonmigrainous headaches, which included tension headaches. Similarly, Sillanpae (1983) did not separate muscle contraction headaches from other types but found that 69% of the sample reported at least one headache during the past year. The prevalence of headache among older children was greater than that of younger children. Approximately 76% of the students who reported having a headache in the previous year reported experiencing no more than one headache per month. Thus, headaches occurred infrequently in the majority of those who experienced headaches.

Unfortunately, a wide variety of conditions can be included under the title of nonmigrainous headaches. Moe (1978) described several conditions that can cause childhood headaches. In addition to muscle contraction and migraine headaches, he noted headaches arising from disorders of the eyes, ears, nose, or teeth; hypertension, anemia or hypoglycemia; neck problems; or trauma. Future research should attempt to determine the prevalence specifically of muscle contraction headache in children and adolescents.

Pathophysiology

Wolff and colleagues (Wolff, 1963) first described the physiological basis of MCH as (a) sustained contraction of the muscles of the scalp, face, shoulders, and neck, and (b) vasoconstriction of the nutrient arteries supplying blood to these muscles. Wolff theorized that stress was the primary cause of both the muscular tension and vasoconstriction. Recent tests of this prediction using psychophysiological methods have yielded mixed results (e.g., Andrasik, Blanchard, Arena, Saunders, & Baron, 1982; Cohen, Williamson, Monguillot, Hutchinson, Gottlieb, & Waters, 1983). At present, these is convincing evidence that the etiology of MCH involves more than simple, sustained contraction of facial muscles.

Pertaining to adult MCH subjects, Holroyd and Andrasik (1978) proposed that these patients are generally deficient in the skills for coping with stress. They designed a very effective cognitive treatment program based upon this conceptualization. No tests of this cognitive explanation for MCH in children have been published.

An alternative psychological explanation for MCH is that of operant conditioning. Epstein and Cinciripini (1980) were among the first to note that reporting headache often leads to positive outcomes such as sympathy and relief from work. Theoretically, reports of headache could be reinforced, leading to a chronic pain condition similar to that described by Fordyce (1976). This possibility is especially problematic in young children, in whom somatic complaints are often inadvertently reinforced by adults. A single-case experiment reported by Ramsden, Friedman, and Williamson (1983) illustrates this point. In this case, a 6-year-old child was found to report pain only at school and other situations where reporting headache resulted in relief from responsibilities. Treatment using contingency management procedures to reinforce "healthy" behavior and extinguish "pain" behavior was very successful.

Based upon these conceptualizations of tension headache, the diagnostic evaluation should assess both stress-related explanations of tension headache and more operant explanations. The case formulation can then lead directly to a treatment plan based upon either a stress reduction of operant framework.

Combined or Mixed Headaches

Some children may experience both migraine and muscle contraction headaches. Some may have discrete headaches of the two types. Others report attacks that contain symptoms of both migraine and tension headaches. The pathophysiology of this type of headache is thought to be a combination of the physiological changes associated with migraine and tension headaches (Williamson, Ruggiero, & Davis, 1985). This category of headache in children has received very little empirical attention.

ASSESSMENT OF HEADACHE

Medical Examination

In the assessment of pediatric headache, the first step is a thorough medical examination. Medical evaluation is required to rule out other medical problems that may cause head pain.

Headache is a common symptom of temporomandibular joint dysfunction, as well as infections of the intracranial structures, such as meningitis, encephalitis, and brain abscess. Infections of the teeth, ears, and paranasal sinuses may also lead to headache. In a study of 150 children referred to pediatric neurologists for chronic headache, 10% were found to have headache secondary to sinusitis (Faleck, Rothner, Erenberg, & Cruse, 1988). The presence of toxins such as lead, carbon monoxide, and excessive vitamin administration may also lead to headache, because of increased cranial pressure (Atkinson, 1976).

Neurological dysfunction is also a common cause of headache. Of headache patients treated by pediatric neurologists, approximately 5% to 13% are found to have headache secondary to neurological problems such as hematomas, tumors, and cranial neuralgias (Koch & Melchior, 1969).

Migraine headache has been associated with epilepsy (Camfield, Metrokos, & Andermann, 1978) and with cerebral arteriovenous malformation, typically involving laterally placed hemispheric vessels (Atkinson, 1976). Because of the association of migraine with these medical disorders, medical diagnosis is essential for the development of an appropriate treatment plan.

Diagnostic Interview

The behavioral interview is the most frequently used method in the assessment of childhood headache (Hoelscher & Lichstein, 1984). The interview allows the clinician to gather information on headache characteristics, and antecedents and consequences of head pain. Typically, both the child and parents are interviewed.

Headache characteristics that should be assessed include headache location, duration, the severity and quality of head pain, headache frequency, and degree of incapacitation experienced during head pain. Associated factors, such as the presence of aura, nausea, vomiting, or sleep disturbances, should also be evaluated. Parents should be questioned regarding family history of migraine as a possible predisposing factor. The child and parents should also be questioned about the presence of dizziness, vertigo, or motion sickness during headache or headache-free periods, as these symptoms have been highly associated with migraine (Barabas, Mathews, & Ferrari, 1983).

Also important is the identification of antecedents of head pain. Commonly reported antecedents of migraine include psychological and physical stressors. Bille (1962) reported that 50% of all migraine attacks were precipitated by school demands or conflicts at home. Physical stressors implicated in the initiation of migraine include physical exertion, eye strain, fatigue, and hunger (Bille, 1962). Stress has also been proposed as a factor in the development of muscle contraction headache. If physical or psychological stressors appear to be associated with headache onset, these sources of stress can be monitored to determine whether they predict headache.

Consequences of head pain should be identified to determine whether operant factors are maintaining headache reports (Williamson, Davis, & Kelley, 1989). For example, a child's report of head pain may result in an excuse from school or attention from significant others. If stressful situations precipitate headache onset, the child may learn to escape these situations by reporting head pain and may thus receive reinforcement for headache onset.

The child's self-report provides the clinician with important information about headache conditions. However, the reliability of children's self-report is uncertain. Children may lack the vocabulary to accurately describe their head pain. They may be unaware of or unable to specify antecedents and consequences of headache, such as physical and psychological stress. In addition, children are highly suggestible and may report headache symptoms that are not actually present in order to please the examiner. The clinician must avoid the use of leading questions when interviewing a child about headache characteristics. Because of these factors, interview of parents as well as teachers and significant others is essential to corroborate children's reports and ensure the reliability of the information obtained.

Visual Analog Scales

A potentially useful adjunct to the diagnostic interview may be the visual analog scale, which is a type of cross-modality matching procedure. Cross-modality matching procedure is a method by which individuals adjust the strength of one perception (such as brightness of light) to match the perceived strength of another dimension, such as pain. Cross-modality matching procedures may be well suited as measures of pain severity for children, because they do not require children to understand numbers or terms describing severity of pain (McGrath, 1987).

Visual analog scales (VAS) use the adjustment of the length of a line to represent the strength of a perception. Such scales have been demonstrated to be reliable and valid measures of adult pain, and VAS-related numerical estimates have been found to have properties of a ratio scale (Price, McGrath, Rafii, & Buckingham, 1983).

A series of studies have examined children's ability to use VAS to measure dimensions of several types of pain (McGrath, DeVeber, & Hearn, 1985). Children over 5 years of age were able to use VAS in a valid and reliable manner to describe their pain perceptions. Visual analog scales offer a practical means of measuring various dimensions of childhood pain. One proposed application of visual analog scales is to incorporate them into pain diaries so that children can rate the severity and affect associated with incidence of pain (McGrath, 1987).

Self-Report Inventories

Few questionnaires have been developed for the assessment of headache in children. Questionnaires developed for adult headache sufferers are not appropriate for assessment of childhood headache, because of the use of vocabulary that may be difficult for children to understand (Labbé, Williamson, & Southard, 1985).

Three questionnaires have been designed for the evaluation of childhood headache. Leviton, Slack, Masek, Bana, and Graham (1984) developed a computerized "interview" of headache symptomatology and associated problems. No data on the reliability and validity of the procedure were reported, so its utility as a method of headache assessment is uncertain.

A second study examined the utility of the Childhood Headache Questionnaire (CHQ) (see Table 25-1) with a sample of child migraineurs (Labbé et al., 1985). Responses to this 40-item questionnaire were highly correlated with self-monitoring data collected over the following month. In addition, children's self-report correlated significantly with their parents' report on 19 of 33 symptom descriptors.

A third questionnaire that has been tested is the Headache Symptom Questionnaire—Revised (HSQ-R) (Mindell & Andrasik, 1987). The responses of children and their parents to this questionnaire were generally highly correlated; in addition, the questionnaire accurately classified 66.2% of migraine, MCH, and combined migraine-muscle contraction headache. The percentage of agreement obtained by the HSQ-R was comparable to the diagnostic agreement found by independent diagnostic interviews.

Presently, the CHQ and HSQ-R are the only two questionnaires that have demonstrated validity. The CHQ was validated on a small number of subjects ($n = 28$). Neither the CHQ nor the HSQ-R has demonstrated test-retest reliability. Further validation and development of questionnaires assessing childhood headache are clearly needed.

Self-Monitoring Procedures

Self-monitoring provides a means of checking the validity of the information obtained from diagnostic interviews and questionnaires. The most frequently employed method for self-monitoring headache activity is the headache diary (Labbé et al., 1985; Williamson, Ruggiero, & Davis, 1985).

Evidence suggests that the headache diary provides a more reliable and accurate measure of headache activity than global self-report inventories or diagnostic interviews. Andrasik, Burke, Attanasio, and Rosenblum (1985) found that during the interview, children and parents overstated the incidence of headaches as compared to their self-monitoring data. Agreement between interview and self-monitoring improved as a function of self-monitoring during treatment. Richardson, McGrath, Cunningham, and Humphreys (1983) also found good agreement between child self-monitoring ratings and parent ratings using the headache diary.

Data collected through self-monitoring reflects variations and patterns in headache activity and are sensitive to treatment effects (Lichstein, Hoelscher, Nickel, & Hoon, 1983). Use of the headache diary can reveal symptom patterns that are not evident from interview and questionnaire data. For example, Joffe, Bakal, and Kagonov (1983) reviewed the headache diaries of 47 children diagnosed as having MCH, migraine, or mixed headache. Diaries included a list of symptoms characteristic of both migraine and MCH, which the children checked during a headache. Results showed that children endorsed symptoms of both MCH and migraine. Both categories of symptoms were observed to increase in frequency with increasingly problematic or lengthy headaches.

The accuracy of the data obtained from the headache diary depends on prompt monitoring of headache activity as it occurs, rather than relying on memory. To ensure the effective use of the headache diary, it is important to train the child in accurate self-monitoring of headache activity. In addition, some children will require prompting from parents, as well as reinforcement, to complete the headache diary.

Direct Behavioral Observation

In addition to self-report, self-monitoring, and interview, other methods can be used to obtain data about headache activity. Parents, teachers, and significant others can observe the child headache sufferer and record the number of verbal reports of head pain, frequency and amount of headache medication consumed, amount of time spent in bed, and the incidence of headache-associated symptoms such as vomiting (Hoelscher & Lichstein, 1984).

Table 25-1. Childhood Headache Questionnaire

Child's Name _____ Date _____

Parent's Name _____

DIRECTIONS: Read each question carefully and then circle the answer which is the most correct for you (or your child). The five possible answers are defined as follows: Always; occurs without exception; Usually; occurs on most occasions with infrequent exceptions; Sometimes; occurs approximately half the time; Infrequently; occurs only once in a great while; Never; absolutely does not occur and never has.

		NEVER	RARELY	SOMETIMES	USUALLY	ALWAYS
1.	I wake up with a headache.	1	2	3	4	5
2.	My headache ends within 1 hour.	1	2	3	4	5
3.	My headache ends within 4 hours.	1	2	3	4	5
4.	My headache ends within 8 hours.	1	2	3	4	5
5.	My headache ends within 12 hours.	1	2	3	4	5
6.	My headache ends within 24 hours.	1	2	3	4	5
7.	My headache is worse at the end of the working day.	1	2	3	4	5
8.	My headache is throbbing or pulsating.	1	2	3	4	5
9.	My headache feels like a tightness or an external pressure around my head.	1	2	3	4	5
10.	My headache feels like an internal pressure.	1	2	3	4	5
11.	My headache begins on the left-hand side of my head.	1	2	3	4	5
12.	My headache begins on the right-hand side of my head.	1	2	3	4	5
13.	My headache begins behind my eye(s).	1	2	3	4	5
14.	My headache begins behind my temple and/or forehead.	1	2	3	4	5
15.	My headache begins in the back of my head.	1	2	3	4	5
16.	When I have a headache I hurt over my entire head.	1	2	3	4	5
17.	When I get a headache I have visual changes like seeing stars, blind spots, wavy lines, or double vision.	1	2	3	4	5
18.	Some parts of my body becomes numb before my headache begins.	1	2	3	4	5
19.	My headache gets worse if I cough, strain or lift objects.	1	2	3	4	5
20.	My headache begins in my neck or shoulders.	1	2	3	4	5
21.	My headache is better if I can loosen up my neck muscles.	1	2	3	4	5
22.	Aspirin, Anacin, Bufferin, Excredrin, BC, Alka-Seltzer, or other nonprescription pain medications relieve my headache.	1	2	3	4	5
23.	My head hurts all the time.	1	2	3	4	5
24.	I take a prescribed medication to prevent a full-blown attack of a headache.	1	2	3	4	5
25.	My headache starts during periods of relaxation or rest.	1	2	3	4	5
26.	My headache begins after exercise.	1	2	3	4	5
27.	I have nausea with my headache.	1	2	3	4	5
28.	I have nausea and vomiting with my headache.	1	2	3	4	5
29.	A headache wakes me up from my sleep.	1	2	3	4	5
30.	My headache delays me from going to sleep.	1	2	3	4	5
31.	Strong sunlight triggers my headache.	1	2	3	4	5
32.	During a headache, I am sensitive to sounds, sunlight, or artificial light.	1	2	3	4	5

Table 25-1. *Continued*

	NEVER	RARELY	SOMETIMES	USUALLY	ALWAYS
33. I have warning signs that a headache is coming.	1	2	3	4	5
34. My headache occurs when I am under pressure.	1	2	3	4	5
35. I have dizziness *before* my headaches.	1	2	3	4	5
36. During a headache, I have blind spots in my vision.	1	2	3	4	5
37. After a headache, there are areas of my head that are sensitive to touch.	1	2	3	4	5
38. My headache begins early in the morning and worsens as the day continues.	1	2	3	4	5
39. My headache is located near the area where my jaw connects to the skull (near the ear or temple).	1	2	3	4	5
40. I notice (or have been told) that I grind my teeth or clinch my jaws together.	1	2	3	4	5

Observation of the child's headache related behavior serves several functions: It provides validation for the child's self-report of headache activity and it reflects the degree of incapacitation experienced by the child. To date, no research has compared headache monitoring done by children with social validation measures such as behavioral observation. However, research on the relationship between adult patients' headache diaries and ratings made by significant others has indicated that the two highly correlated (Blanchard, Andrasik, Neff, Jurish, & O'Keefe, 1981).

Behavioral observation of headache activity in children is an area that deserves further study. The use of behavioral observation offers a potentially important means of gauging the social significance of both head pain and of improved functioning resulting from treatment (Hoelscher & Lichstein, 1984).

Assessment of Other Problems

In the evaluation of headache in children, the possibility that headache may be secondary to psychological distress must also be considered. Anxiety and depression have been found to be more pronounced in child headache patients than in children without headache. Cunningham et al. (1987) found that child migraineurs reported more symptoms of anxiety and internalizing behavior problems than a comparison group of pain-free children. However, when the amount of pain experienced by the children was statistically controlled, the only variable differentiating migraineurs from other children was number of somatic complaints.

Andrasik et al. (1988) compared child migraineurs with nonheadache peer controls on several standardized measures of anxiety and depression. Child migraineurs received higher scores on all scales measuring depression, while adolescent migraineurs also received higher scores on measures of trait anxiety than the control group. The authors of both studies suggest that the psychological differences found in migraineurs are most likely a *consequence* of having to live with unpredictable attacks of pain, rather than factors that predispose to migraine (Andrasik et al., 1988; Cunningham et al., 1987). Because of the correlational nature of these studies, alternative explanations cannot be ruled out.

The presence of anxiety and depression should be assessed during evaluation of child headache. If anxiety or depression is present, the clinician must decide whether affective disturbance or headache is the primary problem.

CASE ILLUSTRATIONS

Case 1: Migraine Headache

Janet first presented for assessment of headache at age 14. She was referred by her family doctor. He had diagnosed her headaches as classic migraine. She described her head pain as very intense and throbbing. Headaches generally lasted several hours and were preceded by a clearly defined aura. These prodromal symptoms were described as beginning with visual abnormalities, usually bright flashing lights and occasionally "blank spots" in her visual field. When these blind spots were noted, she feared having a "very bad headache." After the visual abnormalities began, she then experienced a feeling of numbness in her right hand and fingers that often spread up her right arm. These warning signs usually preceded the headache by about 30 to 60 minutes. Janet's mother confirmed this description of events. Once the headache began, it was usually localized on one side of the head, mostly on the left side near the temple region. During the headache she usually felt very nauseous, often vomiting to the point of dehydration. After the headache, she noted that her scalp was very tender for several days. Her family physician had treated her using antiemetics for the vomiting and analgesic medication for the pain. She was referred because he did not wish to use long-term pharmacological interventions until psychological approaches were attempted.

Self-monitoring and responses to the Childhood Headache Questionnaire by Janet and her mother confirmed the information obtained during interview. Four weeks of self-monitoring showed that she had experienced five headaches in one month. The mean duration of headaches was 4 hours. All were described as very intense and throbbing. Vomiting accompanied four of the five headaches. The headaches occurred at home and at school, and on the weekends and weekdays. There was no apparent relationship between stressful life events or foods consumed. Psychological testing suggested that Janet was intelligent and oriented toward achievement. No significant personality or family problems were evident.

Based upon these data, it was concluded that Janet was a rather straightforward case of classic migraine. No single antecedent to headache could be established. Also, the finding that headaches were incapacitating and occurred in all settings argued against an operant explanation for her pain. From this case formulation, a trial of autogenic feedback training (Labbé & Williamson, 1984) was recommended.

Case 2: Muscle Contraction Headaches

Steven was 16 years old at the time of referral. He was referred by a social worker who had sent Steven's family for family therapy. Steven was the oldest of four children. His parents were married but were experiencing considerable marital distress. His father, Chris, was described as being very critical and authoritarian. His mother, Sarah, was described as very dependent and submissive.

Steven had been seen by his family physician for complaints of daily headache. The physician could find no organic basis for the head pain and recommended psychological evaluation. Steven described his head pain as a dull constant ache around his entire head and in his neck and shoulders. The headaches generally started during the middle of the day and persisted into the evening. Over-the-counter analgesics helped relieve the pain, but he often took five to six aspirins (or the equivalent) per day. Nausea and vomiting were never reported. Also, no prodromal symptoms were noted. Self-monitoring for 3 weeks indicated that Steven seldom awakened with a headache, but reported at least mild head pain during most of the day. Headache ratings were seldom indicative of severe, incapacitating pain. He and his parents reported that he often left class because of headaches and sometimes escaped household responsibilities because of headaches. Sarah noted that she also had frequent headaches and suggested that perhaps it was an inherited medical problem.

Analysis of the family environment showed that the father, Chris, held very high standards for the children. He was a chemical engineer and was quite perfectionistic. Sarah was a housewife with few outside activities. Their marital problems stemmed from frequent arguments related to the "messiness of the house" and Sarah's unwillingness to find work. They were experiencing considerable financial difficulties because of a failed business 2 years earlier. Steven was described as a tense child who tried to please his father but could not make exceptional grades. Also, he was not particularly athletic, which was a disappointment to his father, who had been a star high school football player. When Steven was scolded by his father, he turned to his mother, who attempted to moderate his emotional reactions. A younger brother, James, had recently rebelled against his parents and had been caught stealing and using drugs. This sequence of events had led the family to seek therapy with the social worker.

In contrast to the first case, this case was complicated by significant psychosocial factors. Based upon Steven's description of headache symptoms, it was probable that he was experiencing chronic MCH. The most likely cause of these headaches was the stress of his family environment. Also, there was a high probability of operant factors determining the extent of Steven's pain reports. His family environment supported passive means of dealing with stress and conflict. Headache reports clearly were a passive behavior that yielded relief from responsibilities and avoidance of criticism. Steven's mother apparently modeled this type of behavior, which undoubtedly influenced Steven.

Based upon this formulation, Steven was trained in stress management, problem solving, and assertion. Also, family therapy was continued to modify the dysfunctional relationships among all family members. This therapy was conducted through consultation with the social worker.

IMPLICATIONS FOR TREATMENT

Migraine

Treatment of headaches can generally be grouped into either medical or behavioral approaches. For childhood migraines, pharmacologic treatment is most common. In a review of the medical literature, Shinner and D'Souza (1981) concluded that previous research, although generally uncontrolled, supported the effectiveness of both prophylactic and abortive medications in treating child migraine. However, many physicians have expressed concern over the use of pharmacological treatments with children, because of concerns of drug habituation and eventual dependency, and occasional side effects of certain medications (Hoelscher & Lichstein, 1984). Such concerns have provided strong rationale for the development of effective nonpharmacological treatments.

With adults, a variety of behavioral treatments have been evaluated and found to be effective in treating migraines, including skin-temperature biofeedback (Blanchard et al., 1982), relaxation training (Williamson et al., 1984), and cephallic VMR biofeedback (Bild & Adams, 1980).

In studies with children and adolescents, skin-temperature biofeedback and relaxation training have been the most thoroughly studied interventions. Several case reports and single case experiments using skin-temperature biofeedback and autogenic training (called autogenic feedback training) have reported significant decreases in headache activity at the end of treatment (Diamond & Franklin, 1975; Andrasik, Blanchard, Edlund, & Rosenblum, 1982; Labbé & Williamson, 1983).

Recently, several controlled outcome studies have validated the effectiveness of autogenic feedback and relaxation training with children and adolescents (Labbé & Williamson, 1984; Richter et al., 1986; Fentress, Masek, Mehegan, & Benson, 1986; Blanchard & Andrasik, 1985; Wisnieski, Genshaft, Mulick, Coury, & Hammer, 1988; Larsson & Melin, 1986). Relaxation training has been found to have good maintenance at 3-to-4 year follow-up (Larsson & Melin, 1989). Cognitive restructuring has also been found to be effective, although only one study has examined its use (Richter et al., 1986).

Muscle Contraction Headaches

The first step of medical management of MCH is reassurance to the patient that no serious medical problem exists (Thompson, 1980). Pharmacological treatments most commonly involve symptomatic treatment such as pain medication. Local anesthetic blocks or hypnotic medications with muscle relaxant properties are rarely used with children or adolescents.

Several studies on the behavioral treatment of tension headaches have been reported. Three case studies (Andrasik, Blanchard, Edlund, & Attanasio, 1983; Andrasik, Blanchard, Attanasio, & Burke, 1982), two uncontrolled group studies (Waranch & Keenan, 1985; Werder & Sargent, 1984), and two controlled group studies (Wisniewski et al., 1988; Larsson & Melin, 1986) have all reported positive results. Relaxation training and electromyogram biofeedback have been the main approaches evaluated. Larsson and Melin (1989) recently reported follow-up of 3 to 4 years and found mean headache reductions of 85%. In both controlled outcome studies, combined migraine and tension headache samples were used, and thus the subjects were not a homogeneous sample. The method of treatment in these studies was relaxation training. EMG biofeedback has yet to be evaluated in a controlled outcome study with childhood MCH sufferers. Also, the relative effectiveness of relaxation training and EMG biofeedback has yet to be evaluated.

Operant Factors

In cases in which the beneficial consequences of head pain complaints serve to maintain the complaints and pain behavior, contingency management may be the appropriate treatment approach. Such operant factors may play a role in both migraine and tension headaches. In one study of a 6-year-old child with migraines, Ramsden, Friedman, and Williamson (1983) reported a substantial reduction in head pain reports when a contingency management approach was taken to treatment. Similar results were found in single case studies by Lake (1981) and Yen and McIntire (1971). These data suggest that contingency management may be an effective intervention when it is determined that operant factors play a large role in the maintenance of head pain complaints.

Other Problems with Headache

As was mentioned earlier, frequently headaches in children are accompanied by other problems such as depression and anxiety. While these problems may often be the result of living with intense, unpredictable pain, there may also be cases in which the secondary problems may be serious enough to demand primary attention or in which the headaches are actually secondary in nature. In such cases, anxiety or depression should be the primary focus of treatment. (See Matson and Carey [1988] for a discussion of treatment approaches for childhood depression, and Krotochwill, Acardie, and Morris [1988] for anxiety treatment approaches.)

SUMMARY

Psychological assessment and treatment procedures for pediatric headache have been developed over the past 10 years. At present, the treatment literature is much more well developed than the assessment literature. However, both are sufficiently established to recommend clinical usage in children with migraine and muscle contraction headache.

When evaluating pediatric headache, a thorough medical evaluation is a necessary first step. Behavioral assessment of the interaction between the child's headaches and his or her environment is the second step. The third step should rule out other psychological causes of headache, such as anxiety and depression. From this evaluation, proper medical or psychological treatment can be prescribed.

REFERENCES

Ad Hoc Committee on Classification of Headache (1962). Classification of headache. *Journal of the American Medical Association, 179,* 717–718.

Andrasik, F., Blanchard, E. B., Arena, J. G., Saunders, N. L., & Baron, K. D. (1982). Psychophysiology of recurrent headache: Methodological issues and new empirical findings. *Behavior Therapy, 13,* 407–429.

Andrasik, F., Blanchard, E. B., Attanasio, V., & Burke, E. E. (1982, March). *Progressive muscle relaxation training as a treatment for childhood headache.* Paper presented at the meeting of the Biofeedback Society of America, Chicago, March.

Andrasik, F., Blanchard, E. B., Edlund, S. R., & Attanasio, V. (1983). EMG biofeedback treatment of a child with muscle contraction headache. *American Journal of Clinical Biofeedback, 6,* 96–102.

Andrasik, F., Blanchard, E. B., Edlund, S. R., & Rosenblum, E. L. (1982). Biofeedback treatment of childhood vascular headache. *Child and Family Behavior Therapy, 4,* 13–23.

Andrasik, F., Burke, E. J., Attanasio, V., & Rosenblum, E. L. (1985). Child, parent, and physician reports of a child's headache pain: Relationship prior to and following treatment. *Headache, 25,* 421–425.

Andrasik, F., Kabela, E., Quinn, S., Attanasio, V., Blanchard, E. B., & Rosenblum, E. L. (1988). Psychological functioning of children who have recurrent migraine. *Pain, 34,* 43–52.

Atkinson, R. A. (1976). Headaches in children. In O. Appenzeller (Ed.), *Pathogenesis and treatment of headache.* New York: Spectrum.

Barabas, G., Mathews, W. S., & Ferrari, M. (1983). Childhood migraine and motion sickness. *Pediatrics, 12,* 188–190.

Bild, R., & Adams, H. E. (1980). Modification of migraine headaches by cephalic blood volume pulse and EMB biofeedback. *Journal of Consulting and Clinical Psychology, 48,* 51–57.

Bille, B. (1962). Migraine in school children. *Acta Paediatrica, 51* (Suppl. 136), 14–151.

Blanchard, E. B., & Andrasik, F. (1985). *Management of chronic headaches: A psychological approach.* New York: Pergamon Press.

Blanchard, E. B., Andrasik, F., Neff, D. F., Arena, J. G., Ahles, T. A., Jurish, S. E., Pallmeyer, T. P., Saunders, N. L., Teders, S. J., Barron, T. P., & Rodichock, L. D. (1982). Biofeedback and relaxation training with three kinds of headache: Treatment effects and their prediction. *Journal of Consulting and Clinical Psychology, 30,* 562–575.

Blanchard, E. B., Andrasik, F., Neff, D. F., Jurish, S. E., & O'Keefe, D. M. (1981). Social validation of the headache diary. *Behavior Therapy, 12,* 711–715.

Brown, J. K. (1977). Migraine and migraine equivalents in children. *Developmental Medicine and Child Neurology, 19,* 683–692.

Bruyn, G. W., & Ferrari, M. D. (1988). The biochemistry of migraine. In F. C. Rose (Ed.), *The management of headache* (pp. 47–67). New York: Raven Press.

Camfield, R. P., Metrakos, K., & Andermann, F. (1978). Basilar migraine, seizures, and severe epileptiform EEG abnormalities: A relatively benign syndrome in adolescents. *Neurology, 28,* 584–588.

Cohen, R. A., Williamson, D. A., Monguillot, J. E., Hutchinson, P. C., Gottlieb, J., & Waters, W. F. (1983). Psychophysiological response patterns in vascular and muscle contraction headaches. *Journal of Behavioral Medicine, 6,* 93–107.

Cunningham, S. J., McGrath, P. J., Ferguson, H. B., Humphreys, P., D'Astous, J., Latter, J., Goodman, J. T., & Firestone, P. (1987). Personality and behavioral characteristics in pediatric migraine. *Headache, 27,* 16–20

Deubner, D. C. (1979). An epidemiologic study of migraine and headache in 16-20 year olds. *Headache, 17,* 173–180.

Diamond, S., & Dalessio, D. J. (1982). *The practicing physicians approach to headache*. Baltimore: Williams & Wilkins.

Diamond, S., & Franklin, M. (1975). Autogenic training with biofeedback in the treatment of children with migraine. In W. Luth & F. Antonelli (Eds.), *Therapy in Psychosomatic Medicine, Proceedings of the 3rd Congress of the International College of Psychosomatic Medicine*, Rome.

Epstein, L. H., & Cinciripini, P. M. (1980). Behavioral control of tension headaches. In J. M. Ferguson & C. B. Taylor (Eds.), *The comprehensive handbook of behavioral medicine*, Vol. 2 (pp. 229–240). New York: SP Medical & Scientific Books.

Faleck, H., Rothner, A. D., Erenberg, G., & Cruse, R. P. (1988). Headache and subacute sinusitis in children and adolescents. *Headache, 28*, 96–98.

Fentress, D. W., Masek, B. J., Mehegan, J. E., & Benson, H. (1986). Biofeedback and relaxation-response training in the treatment of pediatric migraine. *Journal of Developmental Medicine and Child Neurology, 28*, 139–146.

Ferry, P. C. (1972). Diagnostic and office management of headaches in children. *Clinical Pediatrics, 11*, 195–200.

Fordyce, W. F. (1976). *Behavioral methods for chronic pain and illness*. St. Louis: C V Mosby.

Gascon, G. C. (1984). Chronic and recurrent headaches in children. *Pediatric clinics of North America, 31*, 1027–1051.

Golden, G. S. (1982). The child with migraines. *Developmental and Behavioral Pediatrics, 3*, 639–642.

Hoelscher, T. J., & Lichstein, K. L. (1984). Behavioral assessment and treatment of child migraine: Implications for clinical research and practice. *Headache, 24*, 94–103.

Holroyd, K. A., & Andrasik, F. (1978). Coping and the self-control of chronic tension headache. *Journal of Consulting and Clinical Psychology, 46*, 1036–1045.

Iezzi, A., & Neeper, R. (1987). Selected Chronic physiological disorders, II: Gastrointestinal, headache, and seizure disorders. In C. L. Frame & J. L. Matson (Eds.), *Handbook of assessment in childhood psychopathology* (pp. 433–460). New York: Plenum Press.

Jay, G. W., & Tomasi, L. G. (1981). Pediatric headaches: A one year retrospective analysis. *Headache, 21*, 5–9.

Joffe, R., Bakal, D. A., & Kagonov, T. (1983). A self observation study of headache symptoms in children. *Headache, 23*, 20–25.

Koch, C., & Melchior, J. C. (1969). Headache in children. *Danish Medical Bulletin, 16*, 109–114.

Kratochwill, T. R., Acardi, A., & Morris, R. J. (1988). Anxiety and phobias: Psychological therapies. In J. L. Matson (Ed.), *Handbook of treatment approaches in childhood psychopathology*. New York: Plenum Press.

Labbé, E. E. (1988). Childhood muscle contraction headache: Current issues in assessment and treatment. *Headache, 28*, 430–434.

Labbé, E. E., & Williamson, D. A. (1983). Temperature biofeedback in the treatment of children with migraine headaches. *Journal of Pediatric Psychology, 8*, 317–326.

Labbé, E. E., & Williamson, D. A. (1984). Treatment of childhood migraine using autogenic feedback training. *Journal of Consulting and Clinical Psychology, 52*, 968–976.

Labbé, E. E., Williamson, D. A., & Southard, D. R. (1985). Reliability and validity of children's reports of migraine headache symptoms. *Journal of Psychopathology and Behavioral Assessment, 7*, 375–383.

Lake, A. E. (1981). Behavioral assessment considerations in the management of headache. *Headache, 21*, 170–178.

Larsson, B., & Melin, L. (1986). Chronic headaches in adolescents: Treatment in a school setting with relaxation training as compared with information-contact and self-registration. *Pain, 25*, 325–336.

Larsson, B., & Melin, L. (1989). Followup on behavioral treatment of recurrent headache in adolescents. *Headache, 29*, 249–253.

Lavigne, J. V., Schulein, M. G., & Hahn, V. S. (1986). Psychological aspects of painful medical conditions in children: II. Personality factors, family characteristics and treatment. *Pain, 27*, 147–169.

Leviton, A., Slack, W. V., Masek, B., Bana, D., & Graham, J. R. (1984). A computerized behavioral assessment for children with headaches. *Headache, 24*, 182–185.

Lichstein, K. L., Hoelscher, T. J., Nickel, R., & Hoon, P. W. (1983). An integrated blood volume pulse biofeedback system for migraine treatment. *Biofeedback and Self Regulation, 8*, 127–134.

MacDonald, J. T. (1986). Childhood migraine: Differential diagnosis and treatment. *Postgraduate Medicine, 80*, 301–304.

Matson, J. L., & Carey, M. (1988). Depression: Psychological therapies. In J. L. Matson (Ed.), *Handbook of treatment approaches in childhood psychopathology*. New York: Plenum Press.

McGrath, P. A. (1987). An assessment of children's pain: A review of behavioral, physiological and direct scaling techniques. *Pain, 31*, 147–176.

McGrath, P. A., DeVeber, L. L., & Hearn, M. T. (1985). Multidimensional pain assessment in children. In H. L. Fields, R. Dubner, & F. Cervero (Eds.), *Advances in pain research and therapy* (Vol. 9). New York: Raven Press.

Meloff, K. L. (1982). Headaches in children. *Postgraduate Medicine, 72*, 195–202.

Mindell, J. A., & Andrasik, F. (1987). Headache classification and factor analysis with a pediatric population. *Headache, 27*, 96–101.

Moe, P. G. (1978). Headaches in children: Meeting the challenge of management. *Postgraduate Medicine, 63*, 169–174.

Olesen, J. (1984). Vascular aspects of migraine pathophysiology. In F. C. Rose (Ed.), *The management of headache* (pp. 39–46). New York: Raven Press.

Passchier, J., & Bonke, B. (1985). Migraine symptoms in

school children: What is the best diagnostic characteristic for migraine? *Headache, 10,* 139–143.

Prensky, A. L., & Sommer, D. (1979). Diagnosis and treatment of migraine in children. *Neurology, 29,* 506–510.

Price, D. D., McGrath, P. A., Rafii, A., & Buchingham, B. (1983). The validation of visual analogue scales as ratio scale measures for chronic and experimental pain. *Pain, 17,* 45–56.

Ramsden, R., Friedman, B. A., & Williamson, D. A. (1983). Treatment of childhood headache reports with contingency management procedures. *Journal of Clinical Child Psychology, 12,* 202–206.

Raskin, N. H. (1988). On the origin of head pain. *Headache, 28,* 254–257.

Richardson, G. M., McGrath, P. J., Cunningham, S. J., & Humphreys, P. (1983). Validity of the headache diary for children. *Headache, 23,* 184–187.

Richter, I. L., McGrath, P. L., Humphreys, P. J., Firestone, P., & Keene, D. (1986). Cognitive and relaxation treatment of paediatric migraine. *Pain, 25,* 195–203.

Selby, G., & Lance, J. W. (1960). Observations on 500 cases of migraine and allied vascular headache. *Journal of Neurology, Neurosurgery, and Psychiatry, 23,* 23–32.

Shinner, S., & D'Souza, B. J. (1981). The diagnosis and management of headaches in children. *Pediatric Clinics of North America, 29,* 79–93.

Sillanpae, M. (1983). Prevalence of headache in prepuberty. *Headache, 21,* 10–14.

Spierings, E. L. H. (1988). Recent advances in the understanding of migraine. *Headache, 28,* 655–658.

Thompson, J. A. (1980). Diagnosis and treatment of headaches in the pediatric patient. *Current Problems in Pediatrics, 10,* 5–52.

Trued, S. (1974). Migraines in childhood. *Journal of the American Medical Women's Association, 29,* 78–86.

Waranch, R. H., & Keenan, D. H. (1985). Behavioral treatment of children with recurrent headaches. *Journal of Behavioral and Experimental Psychiatry, 18,* 31–38.

Waters, W. E., & O'Connor, P. J. (1975). Prevalence of migraine. *Journal of Neurology, Neurosurgery, and Psychiatry, 38,* 613–616.

Werder, D. D., & Sargent, J. D. (1984). A study of childhood headache using biofeedback as a treatment alternative. *Headache, 24,* 122–126.

Williamson, D. A. (1981). Behavioral treatment of migraine and muscle-contraction headaches. Outcome and theoretical explanation. In M. Hersen, R. M. Eisler, & P. M. Miller (Eds.), *Progress in Behavioral Modification* (Vol. 11, pp. 163–201). New York: Academic Press.

Williamson, D. A., Davis, C. J., & Kelley, M. L. (1989). Headaches in children. In T. H. Ollendick and M. Hersen (Eds.), *Handbook of child psychopathology.* New York: Plenum Press.

Williamson, D. A., Monguillot, J. E., Jarrell, M. P., Cohen, R. A., Pratt, J. M., & Blouin, D. C. (1984). Relaxation for the treatment of headache. Controlled evaluation of two group programs. *Behavior Modification, 8,* 497–424.

Williamson, D. A., Ruggiero, L., & Davis, C. J. (1985). Headache. In M. Hersen & A. S. Bellack (Eds.), *Handbook of clinical behavior therapy with adults.* New York: Plenum Press.

Williamson, D. A., & Waggoner, C. D. (1986). Psychophysiological Disorders. In M. Hersen (Ed.), *Pharmacological and behavioral treatment: An integrative approach* (pp. 312–341). New York: John Wiley & Sons.

Wisniewski, J. J., Genshaft, J. L., Mulick, J. A., Coury, D. L., & Hammer, D. (1988). Relaxation therapy and compliance in the treatment of adolescent headache. *Headache, 28,* 612–617.

Wolff, H. G. (1963). *Headache and other head pain.* London and New York: Oxford University Press.

Yen, S., & McIntire, R. W. (1971). Operant therapy for constant headache complaint: A simple response-cost approach. *Psychological Reports, 28,* 267–270.

CHAPTER 26

PAIN

Dennis C. Russo
Beate M. Lehn
Charles B. Berde

DESCRIPTION OF THE PROBLEM

Human beings are born with the capacity to experience pain. Pain is a universal and basic experience. Unpleasant, painful experiences are often unavoidable events in the life of a child, and pain in children can originate from a variety of sources. A healthy child experiences pain as part of routinely scheduled immunizations; infants frequently undergo heel pricks for diagnostic purposes. Painful scratches and sprains are common consequences of enthusiastic participation in sports activities. Ear infections are one of the most common painful ailments in children. The extent to which children and adolescents of all ages experience pain has seemingly not been fully acknowledged. Most of the research on pain assessment and pain management has been focused on adult patients, whereas the study of the pediatric pain has been relatively neglected.

In 1977, Eland and Anderson reviewed the medical research literature on pain between 1970 to 1975. Of the 1,380 articles they reviewed, less than 3% dealt with pediatric pain issues. In standard pediatric textbooks (e.g., Avery & First, 1989) reference to pain is made in the context of different disorders in which pain is a presenting symptom, but detailed information about the topic as a specific problem is missing. This is even more surprising if one considers that pediatricians are confronted with painful conditions in their young patients on a daily basis.

Pain experiences derive from a multiplicity of sources in the growing child. The distinction of four primary categories to classify pain in children and their demographics illustrates the clinical significance and broad population impact of the problem (Varni, Katz, & Dash, 1982):

1. *Acute pain following injuries and trauma.* An estimated 22,000 children die yearly from injuries, and the number of children treated medically for injuries is more than 1,000 times higher (Feldman, Rosser, & McGrath, 1987). Home accidents are today one of the leading cause of painful morbidity and mortality in the United States in childhood.

2. *Recurrent pain syndromes of unknown etiology.* Complaints of recurrent headaches, abdominal pain, and limb pain are extremely common in childhood, although data about prevalence and incidence tend to vary somewhat. For school-age children, incidence rates between 7% and 30% have been reported, with headaches occurring most frequently. According to

Bille (1962), 75% of children younger than 15 years of age had suffered from headaches. In the sample of Oster and Nielson (1972), 20.6% of the children indicated having headaches, 15.5% growing pains, and 12.3% episodes of abdominal pain. The pain is often so severe as to interfere substantially with regular school attendance and social activities. Frequently, these recurrent pain syndromes are not confined to childhood years, but the symptoms are likely to persist into adulthood. Studies on the long-term prognosis of recurrent pain, for example, show that a third of the children will continue to complain about abdominal pain in later life (Apley & Hale, 1973; Christensen & Mortensen, 1975).

3. *Pain occurring in the context of a well-defined physical disorder.* With advances in medical care has come increased incidence of chronic illness of great duration and painful morbidity. For example, a high percentage of children diagnosed with cancer suffer from pain that relate either to the disease itself or to the diagnostic or treatment regimen. Whereas most studies have focused on the management of pain due to procedures, only recently have attempts been made to develop guidelines for treatment of pain related to the progression of the disease.

In juvenile rheumatoid arthritis, the most common connective tissue disease in children, severe pain in numerous joints occurring in conjunction with swelling and heat are characteristic symptoms (Cassidy, 1982). The prevalence of the disorder, including all different subtypes, has been estimated to be 250,000 American children with a yearly incidence of 1.1 cases per 1,000 school-age children (Schaller, 1984). The prognosis is poor for a large percentage of these children. Between 10% and 50% of the children, depending on the type of arthritis, will experience symptoms in later life of increasing severity. Blood disorders like hemophilia and sickle-cell disease are other examples for painful conditions in childhood that affect a significant number of children. The pain associated with these diseases often makes treatment on an emergency basis necessary. Presently, a condition called "Reflex Sympathetic Dystrophy" (RSD), which had previously been described only in the adult population, is gaining increasing recognition in children and adolescents. Our initial experience with a multidisciplinary pediatric pain treatment team showed that during the first 6 months, 15 patients were diagnosed with RSD of the 110 patients who were evaluated (Berde, Lacoutre, Masek, Sethna, & Shannon, 1987). The severity of the presented symptoms was often comparable to those described in adult patients (Greipp & Thomas, 1989).

4. *Pain related to medical procedures.* Painful, invasive medical procedures performed for either diagnostic or treatment purposes seem to be among the most critical events for children during hospitalizations. Whereas the majority of the research on the impact of disease and hospitalizations on children has focused on such variables as age, the unfamiliarity of the environment, separation from the family or premorbid adjustment of a child, a study by Saylor, Pallmeyer, Finch, Eason, Trieber, and Folger (1987) identified the number of physical stressors as the most significant predictor of psychological distress and adjustment following the hospitalization. These stressors can range from venipunctures and intramuscular injections to more invasive and potentially dangerous procedures, such as lumbar punctures and bone marrow aspirations. Bone marrow aspirations are among the most traumatic and painful procedures for pediatric patients with leukemia, the procedure must be undergone routinely to test for the presence of cancer cells in the marrow. Although some local anesthetic agent is administered during the procedure, this often relieves only the superficial pain component, and the child still experiences the more intense pain resulting from the suctioning of the marrow. Because pharmacological interventions accomplish only partial pain relief, pediatric psychologists have been consulted to alleviate children's distress during these medical procedures by teaching them a variety of cognitive-behavioral techniques for pain management (Chapman & Turner, 1986; Jay, Elliot, Katz, & Siegel, 1987; Jay, 1988).

These examples and demographics illustrate that pediatric pain problems are not a rare, exotic phenomenon experienced only by a few children, but are extremely common everyday problems in pediatric practice. This increased awareness of both acute and chronic pain problems in children has led to a rapid increase in the number of publications, ranging from original articles, review articles, to books solely devoted to pediatric pain (Berde, Sethna & Anand, 1989; Karoly, 1988; McGrath, 1990; McGrath & Unruh, 1987; Ross & Ross, 1988; Zeltzer, 1989). The founding of a section on pediatric pain within the International Association for the Study of Pain and conferences dealing exclusively with pediatric pain issues have also occurred (Greipp & Thomas, 1989).

In this chapter, we present some of the dilemmas in the management of pediatric pain problems and relate these to fundamental assessment and measurement problems of pain in children. In our review of recent advances of pain assessment in children, we focus our attention on behavioral and self-report measures. Assuming that the developmental level of a child affects his or her report of pain and behavior, we make reference to those developmental changes. We discuss the large number of assessment instruments now available to various health professionals, with emphasis on their utility and criteria of reliability and validity. Finally, we argue that the greatest challenge in pediatric pain assessment still consists of the integration of behavioral, self-report, and biomedical data (Russo, Bird, & Masek, 1980).

Definition of Pain and Dimensions of Assessment

Although pain is a common phenomenon, it is one of the most difficult constructs to define and measure. Today the definition of pain developed by the International Association for the Study of Pain (IASP) in 1979 is widely accepted despite several weaknesses. The official definition states that "pain is an unpleasant, sensory and emotional experience associated with actual or potential tissue damage, or described in terms of such damage." Pain is always subjective. Each individual learns the application of the word through experiences related to injury in early life. This definition alludes to pain as a multidimensional construct composed of sensory and emotional facets. Applying this definition means that all pain assessment needs to be multidimensional to reflect these different aspects of pain.

The sensory component refers to the noxious stimulus that in most cases signals the actual or potential tissue damage. The sensory component includes information about the character of the pain (e.g., dull, throbbing, burning), its location, duration, or intensity and the affective-motivational dimension of the pain experience. Emotional and aversive aspects of perception lead to behaviors that attempt to avoid or potentially reduce the pain producing stimulus.

Discussions of the utility of the IASP definition, in particular with regard to pediatric pain problems, suggest several important issues. First, accepting pain as a subjective experience suggests that it might best be assessed by self-report measures that seem most feasible with adult patients. In the pediatric setting, this strategy poses an immediate dilemma for the caretaker, who is asked to assess pain in newborns, infants, or younger children, whose language abilities are either not yet developed or who might have a limited and highly idiosyncratic understanding of pain-related questions.

Second, it seems important to conceptualize the sensory and emotional component of the pain construct as separate, alluding to the fact that it is possible to have a painful sensation in the absence of nociception, as in patients with phantom pain. Alternatively, the definition captures the case that nociception can be documented but might not be perceived as pain under certain circumstances, as in the classic example of the soldier being wounded in combat without having awareness of the pain until he finds help (Beecher, 1957). While the definition reflects a view of pain as being modulated by both emotional factors and the learning history of the individual, especially past experiences within the context of the family or situational factors, the relationship between these factors is not sufficiently clarified. Difficulties in separating the different aspects of pain experience become obvious in the clinical situation.

Some of these methodological problems inherent in the definition become even more pronounced in the study of pediatric pain. For example, the problem of clearly distinguishing the behavioral manifestations of anxiety and pain in children has become a focal point of discussion for many investigators (Beyer & Knapp, 1986; Lavigne, Schulein, & Hahn, 1986). Katz, Kellerman, and Siegel (1980) see pain and anxiety so closely related in reality that they suggest introducing the term *behavioral distress"* to incorporate both aspects.

Third, in the absence of adequate physical findings to account for the pain or its intensity, a clinician applying the IASP definition must be cautioned against prematurely diagnosing the presenting pain problem as "psychogenic" or, according to the DSM III R classification, as a "somatoform pain disorder," unless a number of other features are present. This notion seems to be a particularly important contribution to the discussion of pain in children because adults tend to question whether a child's pain report is accurate and tend to underestimate the intensity of the pain, as suggested by the data on insufficient medication practices following surgery (Beyer, De Good, Ashley, & Russell, 1983; Lamaire, D'Herouville, Piquard-Gauvain, & Flamant, 1987). In addition, Karoly (1988) comments that "the IASP definition of pain remains strongly medical . . . and focuses perhaps too much on the short-term aspects of adaption." Further elaboration on the difference between acute and chronic pain problems would be helpful, as would a stronger reference to developmental aspects that goes beyond the mere mentioning of the importance of childhood learning experience for the acquisition of verbal descriptors for pain.

Using the IASP as a working definition clearly implies that the ideal assessment of pediatric pain can be accomplished only by using an interdisciplinary, multidimensional, and comprehensive approach, combining self-report, behavioral, cognitive, socioenvironmental, medical and biological parameters (Varni, 1983). Karoly (1988) points out that assessment has a broad range of meanings to different disciplines. Within a strictly biomedical model, assessment would exclusively focus on biological parameters with the goal of diagnosing the underlying organic pathology accounting for the presenting symptoms. Since the shift from this classic biomedical model to a more complex biopsychosocial model of health and illness (Russo, 1986), the purpose of assessment has been redefined accordingly. Applying this changed model of health and illness requires consideration of a child's underlying medical disorder, the cognitive and emotional state of the child, the child's developmental level, his or her family system, as well as the child's physical and social care environment (Russo, Hamada, & Marques, 1988). The pediatric health psychologist who works in a multidisciplinary pain treatment team will likely be asked to provide information about appropriate targets for intervention than to classify or categorize symptoms. This focus on assessing the modifiability of behaviors and symptoms and determining the optimal level(s) at which to intervene implies that such treatment-related assessment will exceed a simple listing of a child's psychological characteristics or description of the child's psychopathology but that it will be directed towards the identification of strengths and weaknesses at each level of the system.

Impact of Assessment Difficulties

Accurate assessment of pain is the basis for clinical decision making about when to intervene to relieve pain and how to evaluate the efficacy of whatever intervention method was used: pharmacological, psychological or behavioral. Clinically, these assessment difficulties account in part for the undertreatment of peri-, and postoperative pain in children compared to adult patients (Schechter, Allen, & Hanson, 1986). In a review of 40 papers describing thoracotomies, the most common surgical procedure in the preterm neonate, Anand and Aynsley-Green (1985) found that 76% of them received no or only minimal anesthesia.

Marked differences in the management of postoperative pain in adults and children have also been described. Physicians tend to prescribe smaller doses (on a mg/kg basis) to children; often, dosages are below the recommended levels and are consequently subtherapeutic (Burokas, 1985). Children are also more likely to receive less potent drugs (Bush, Hombeck, & Cockrell, 1989). Mather and Mackie (1983) documented, in a chart review of 170 pediatric patients, that in 40% of the cases the primary drugs ordered were not often given, and non-narcotic medications were substituted for narcotic analgesics. Following cardiac surgery, Beyer et al. (1983) found a significant age-related differences between the amount of analgesics prescribed and the actual amounts given. Children received 30%, unlike adults, who received 70% of prescribed doses. Inadequate management of pain occurring during burn debridement was documented by Perry and Heidrich (1982).

It is not unusual for children to receive no analgesics postoperatively, although orders were initially written. This was true for almost 50% of the 25 children ages of 4 through 8 years studied by Eland and Anderson (1977) and for more than 10% of children following major cardiac procedures (Beyer et al., 1983). The prescription of narcotic drugs seems to be age-related, with younger children being less likely to receive narcotics than older children.

These available data show consistent differences in assumptions about and the management of pain in children and adult patients. Besides the lack of appropriate pain measurement instruments, Eland and Anderson (1977) identified several misconceptions and erroneous beliefs that further explain the undermanagement in pediatric patients:

- Because an immature nervous system (lack of myelinization, immature cerebral cortex in newborns, or incomplete synaptogenesis with pain paths), children experience pain less intensely than adults
- Children recover more quickly
- It is dangerous to administer analgesics or anesthetics for two reasons: the greater risk of addiction in children and adverse effects of narcotics (e.g., respiratory depression)
- Children are unable to communicate the characteristics of their pain (such as localization, intensity or quality) reliably, and often have no memory for painful experiences.

Whether these "old nurses' tales" are still alive has been questioned by some researchers. Schechter and Allen (1986) approached pediatricians, family practitioners, and surgeons and showed that 75% of the total sample felt that children experience adultlike pain by age 2. Differences in opinions were significantly related to physicians' specialty and age with pediatricians, younger physicians being more likely to agree that children experience adultlike pain at a younger age and being more willing to use narcotics for younger children. Fear of adverse side effects from the use of narcotics was reported by many physicians as an important concern limiting a liberal prescribing practice. Recently, a study surveyed attitudes of pediatric anaesthetists towards pain perception and pain treatment in children under the age of 1 month (Purcell-Jones, Dormon, & Sumner, 1988). The results indicate that some of these misconceptions have been corrected but that physicians still feel reluctant to actually prescribe opoids in this age group. Although 100% of the responding physicians agreed that infants (1–3 months) experience pain, only 2% always prescribe post-operative opoids in the neonatal and newborn age group. The willingness to use narcotics increases dramatically with age.

It appears that misinformation about properties of narcotics are common among physicians. A survey of 102 house officers in a teaching hospital (Marks & Sachar, 1973) revealed that risk of addiction and duration of narcotics were frequently overestimated, and the effective dose was underestimated. The writing of PRN (pro re nata) orders has been suggested as an additional factor related to the conservative treatment of pain in children (Bush, in press). This practice should allow for more individualized pain management; however, PRN orders are often interpreted by nurses as meaning "as little as possible" (Cohen, 1980). That PRN orders characteristically result in very low drug delivery and fail to be tailored to the need of each individual child was again confirmed by a study of Bush et al. (1989). Their analysis indicated that the clinical decision making about the use of analgesics in children may be influenced by other factors as well; while estimated painfulness and seriousness of the procedures were significantly related to medication prescription, only seriousness ratings were consistent predictors of analgesics actually delivered. The authors did not find age-dependent medicating practices, suggesting that generalized beliefs regarding pain in children may function as guidelines for clinical practice. However, existence of such beliefs or myths has been questioned by several researchers. McGrath, Vair, McGrath, Unruh, and Schnurr (1984) and Hodson (1984) found nurses to be better educated about pain issues in children than previously reported in the literature. This is consistent with findings by Jeans (1984). She found that childrens' postoperative pain was treated in a way comparable to that of adults.

These results are difficult to evaluate, because many studies are based solely on retrospective chart reviews and lack information about the actual pain relief accomplished by the provided medication. In this context, it is important to consider that postoperative pain in adults is frequently poorly managed and that a large percentage of these patients experience significant amounts of pain (Angell, 1982). Some studies have been criticized for not operationalizing parameters for adequate analgesia and their reliance on retrospective self-report of patients.

In attempting to summarize the current status of our discussion about medication practices in children, one might conclude that some new studies indicate a slow shift in attitudes about pediatric pain. However, it seems that the behavior of physicians and nurses responsible for the delivery of anesthesia and postoperative pain management still lags behind these cognitive changes. It is predictable that the increased knowledge about safety of analgesics and their pharmokinetics, and growing knowledge base about mechanism of pain control in neonates, infants, and children will further promote better pain management in this group. It would exceed the scope of this chapter to review the new literature on these topics.

Even in light of increased knowledge about the biology of pain and new treatment modalities, we believe that improvements in pain management are crucially linked to the development of reliable and valid methods for pain measurement in children. The accurate and comprehensive assessment of pain is a prerequisite to decide which intervention or combination of methods, including pharmacological or behavioral approaches, is most useful to the patient. Clinical application of assessment is hampered by at least several factors:

1. Assessment techniques applied with adult patients are often not suitable for children. This is particularly true for the administration of self-report measures. Given the limited or nonexistent verbal abilities of the young child to communicate pain, self-report measures are selectively applicable with children. Even if verbal descriptors are used, it has been questioned whether children interpret words like "hurt" or "pain" in the same manner as adults.

2. Behavioral measures have been advocated as the alternative approach to self-report procedures. Although a variety of behaviors have been proposed as indicators of pain in children, the meaning of a certain behavior might be ambiguous and difficult to interpret. The crying of a toddler after surgery may reflect postoperative pain, fear from being in an unfamiliar

environment, or loneliness. In addition, some young children tend to withdraw when in pain and may not show any obvious signs of distress. They may lie still in bed and become unusually quiet because they hurt too much to move or are afraid to complain of pain because they are frightened to get another injection for pain medication. In this case, the untrained observer will see no overt behaviors that indicate pain in this child, and may assume that the child is comfortable or may interpret the behavior of the child as adaptive coping with pain (Mather & Mackie, 1983).

3. The integration of data from different sources remains one of the greatest challenges in the assessment of pain in children. It is not uncommon to find little consistency and little correlation between self-report and observational data of pain intensity. Whether to attribute such findings to methodological weaknesses of the used instruments or to value them as meaningful information is another topic of discussion. Another level of complexity is added when the goal is to accomplish a comprehensive assessment of pain that includes biomedical data, psychosocial and behavioral findings.

MULTIMODAL ASSESSMENT

Behavioral Component of Pain

Many investigators of pain have emphasized the central importance of the behavioral component for the understanding of pain (Beecher, 1957; Fordyce, 1976). They draw attention to the fact that a person has to emit certain behaviors that are interpreted by an observer as a response to an internal, painful sensation in order to assess the quality and intensity of pain. Many researchers in pediatrics have further argued that recording of children's overt pain behaviors is associated with numerous advantages. First, it circumvents the problem of determining whether certain self-report measures are actually accurate and whether measures are age-appropriate for a given child. Second, behavioral observations are, besides the measurement of physiologic parameters, the only other avenue to assess pain in neonates, infants, and young children. Compared to verbalizations of pain, it has also been argued that behavioral expressions of pain are less subject to influences resulting from different learning experiences or different cultural backgrounds. Some believe that behavioral expressions are the more immediate responses to pain and therefore are regarded as the more reliable indicator of discomfort. In contrast, verbal descriptions of pain might be more easily distorted. Within a behavioral framework, the rigor of behavioral assessment compared to self-report measures has traditionally been underscored. While some of these assumptions may seem to be questionable, we believe that researchers as well as clinicians will find behavioral measures of pain most valuable because they are independent from the verbal abilities of a child and the child's cooperation.

Many studies have shown that children's pain behavior changes as they grow older and their behavioral repertoire broadens. An infant's response to a heel stick might consist of a diffuse body movement accompanied by crying and certain facial expressions. A toddler is more likely to show a more directed response towards a similar painful stimulation by protecting the affected body part. With an adolescent, verbal expression of discomfort and more subtle signs of pain like increased muscle rigidity will probably prevail, whereas a crying response might be less often observed. Having these developmental changes in mind, crying of an adolescent will be judged differently from that of an infant, considering which other forms of pain related behaviors might be in his or her repertoire.

Thus, this developmental trend towards greater behavioral complexity is mirrored in the type of behavioral indicators of pain chosen for different age groups. Pain assessment in infants in largely dependent on the analysis of the crying response, facial expressions and body movements following noxious stimulation. Physiological changes might be monitored simultaneously to validate behavioral observations in the preverbal child. The older child will express discomfort through a greater variety of behaviors; consequently behavioral measures and scales designed for this age group are composed of more categories and frequently include verbal complaints of pain.

Infants

Because both pain cries and physical configurations can be detected in neonates starting with birth, these behaviors can be considered as the most immediate reflections of pain and pain perception, unmodified by past experiences or learning, in newborns.

Crying. It seems that the infant's crying following noxious stimulation has been most widely used as possible indicator of pain in this age group. According to a biosocial model of crying by Lester (1984), the infant's vocalizations are instrumental to the child's survival by engaging the care givers and communicating different biological states to them. Crying mostly reflects aversive states such as hunger, fear, anger, soiled or wet diapers, or boredom. Research efforts have focused on identification of psychoacoustic properties that are discriminative for differential modes of crying. Up to 11 acoustical attributes of infant cries have been isolated, including latency from stimulus, pitch, duration, melody, or number of cry cycles (Wasz-Hockert, Lind, Vuorenkoski, Partanen & Valaane, 1968). Three variables—the length of the cry, its phonation, and its frequency—seem to be most predictive of the type of cry (Barr, Kramer, Leduc, Boisjoly, McVey, & Pless, 1987). For example, the initial acute pain cry has been characterized as being long, intense, high-pitched with a falling melody (fundamental frequency).

Use of sound spectrography and sophisticated analysis have produced more complex descriptions of acoustical attributes of pain cries (Golub & Corwin, 1985; Johnston & Strada, 1986). These precise measures indicate that the pain cry signals not only the presence or absence of pain, but that the cry signal changes with the intensity of the painful stimulations (Porter, Miller, and Marshall, 1986). Intensity of the infant's response is in part state-dependent. Infants who were sleeping before a heel lance cried later than alert infants (Grunau & Craig, 1987). The same study revealed that boys had a shorter latency and cried significantly more cry cycles compared to girls. In addition, it has been shown that duration of vocalizations shortens with increasing age of the child when comparing infants between 12 and 24 months with younger ones.

In the clinical situation, it is often not practical to conduct such elaborate analysis. Thus, it is equally important to establish the ability of caretakers or trained listeners to understand the meaning of a cry signal and to accurately differentiate different biological states of the infant (Dunn, 1977). Findings in this area are inconsistent. In a study by Muller, Hollien, and Murry (1974), mothers frequently mistook startle or pain cries for hunger cries. It is difficult to draw final conclusions from these studies, because some raters have been placed in an artificial situation, which puts them at a disadvantage compared to the natural circumstances. When subjects are asked to listen to audiotaped recordings of cries, they lack additional information from other nonverbal channels, such as the facial expressions accompanying the cry, and other situational clues.

Facial expression. Some researchers claim that facial expressions in infants after a painful stimulation are a more uniform and less variable response than pain cries (Johnston & Strada, 1986). Similar to the investigations on pain-related crying, efforts have been oriented towards identifying a specific configuration of facial movements associated with pain. Two coding systems have been applied to study such patterns: the maximally discriminative facial movement coding system (MAX) (Izard, Huebner, Resser, McGiness, & Dougherty, 1980) and the facial action coding system (FACS) (Eckman & Friesen, 1978). Both systems are well-established methods derived from the study of nonverbal communication of human emotions. To provide reliable and valid information, they should be used by trained observers.

According to studies based on these coding systems, an infant in pain will probably show the following features: lowered eyebrows, broadened nasal root, an angular and squarish mouth, and tightly closed eyes (Grunau & Craig, 1987; Johnston & Strada, 1986). Other indicators, such as taut tongue, lip position, and mouth stretch have been included in the analysis and seem relevant to distinguish the infants' reactions dependent on sleep or awake state. Quiet, awake infants show stronger responses to heel lance than quietly sleeping infants. Taut tongue and stretch mouth signs are significantly more often found in awake infants. Izard et al. (1980) examined the infants' reactions to needle injections and described an interesting developmental shift. They found that the typical facial configuration indicating pain were seen especially clearly in infants less than 4.4 months of age. Toward the end of the second year of life, facial expressions reflecting anger expression become increasingly more noticeable. The expression of anger was particularly long lasting in children who were difficult to soothe compared to those who responded quicker to their mother comforting. This observation is especially relevant because it underlines the early importance of the social context in which pain behavior occurs and how pain behavior communicates the emotional aspect of the pain experience (Craig, Grunau, & Branson, 1988).

Body movements. Several studies have documented that noxious stimulation elicits general, diffuse body movements involving the whole torso and limbs in infants during their first month of life. During the neuromuscular maturation of the infant, this generalized response is, in subsequent months, replaced by a more directed, specific reflex withdrawal to the stimulus, which is often accompanied by an attempt to visually focus on the stimulated body area (McGraw 1945; Owens, 1986). Infants 12 months and older will also try to touch the affected body part after they have received a painful pinprick. Observation of 124 normal-term neonates after a pinprick in the lower extremity showed that the motor response is two-phasic, resulting first in a flexion and then an adduction of the upper and lower limbs (Rich, Marshall, & Volpe, 1974).

In conjunction with the facial expression and vocalization, the monitoring of body movements will add information and help to validate the assessment of pain in infants. In clinical settings however, infants might be restrained because the health care professional anticipates a strong behavioral response which might interfere with a procedure. Anand, Sippell, and Aynsley-Green (1987a) commented on another limitation of behavioral observation in the context of pain assessment of neonates undergoing surgery. The newborns ability to express discomfort behaviorally can be blocked by muscle relaxants and further restricted through ventilation during a procedure. In such a case, assessment of the infant's pain is limited to a monitoring of physiological changes (see "Physiological Component" section).

An attempt to combine information about the pain cry, facial expressions, and body movements of an infant following heel lance has been proposed by Franck (1986). This technique has not been used in a clinical context, but promises to provide a precise and integrated measure of an infant's response to pain.

Children and Adolescents

Children's behavioral responses to pain stimuli become more complex as they develop. Certain behaviors like diffuse vocal protest or crying decrease in older children, whereas other behaviors like verbal request for emotional support become more prominent with improving verbal abilities of the child. Observational rating systems encompassing multiple behavioral categories reflect this broader spectrum of behavioral responses. The clinician can choose today from a variety of observational scales that are often very specific to a clinical and age population and are linked to a defined procedure. We will review some of the most commonly used scales with regard to these specific applications.

The reactions of young oncology patients undergoing bone marrow aspirations and lumbar punctures have been studied repeatedly using the Procedure Behavior Rating Scale (PBRS) established by Katz and colleagues (1980) and its modified version: the Observational Scale of Behavioral Distress (OSBD), by Jay, Ozolins, Elliott, and Caldwell (1983). Katz et al. (1980) had initially sought to develop a rating scale that would be a reliable measure of anxiety occurring during 4 different stages of the treatment procedure. Of the originally chosen 25 behavioral categories, 13 were found to be discriminative of children who were rated by the nurses as highly anxious or less anxious. Because of the before-mentioned difficulty in separating behavioral expressions of pain and anxiety, the authors suggest that the behaviors observed are global indicators of the children's distress. Comparing three different age groups, children younger than 6.4 years, 6.4 to 9.11 years, and older patients between 10.0 and 17.9 years of age, the authors found that the rating scale in sensitive towards developmental changes in pain behavior. Younger children tended to react more strongly to the procedure and exhibited a greater variety of behaviors than older children. In the youngest age group, crying, screaming, the need to be physically restrained, and verbal expressions of pain were the most common behavioral categories. School-age children usually no longer required physical restraint, and an increase in verbalizations was described. Children in the oldest group displayed their distress, besides verbal expressions, predominantly through increased muscle rigidity. This category includes behaviors like clenched fists, white knuckles, gritted teeth, clenched jaw, wrinkled brow, contracted limbs, and overall body stiffness. Good interrater reliability for the scale has been reported with coefficients above 0.85 and its validity has been demonstrated as well.

Jay and Elliot (1984) proposed two major methodological modifications to the PBRS concerning the observation intervals and the incorporation of a way to reflect the intensity of each behavior displayed during a certain time interval. In the OSBD, occurrence of the distress behaviors are recorded continuously in 15-second intervals rather than over the total length of an observed procedure. Second, a weighting system was introduced so that the intensity of each behavior is taken into account. Despite this increase in sophistication of the scale, the expected increase in validity was not documented. Jay and her coworkers mention that more time is needed to train observers in the use of the OSBD compared to the PBRS. In light of the good reliability and validity of both measures, it is not surprising that they have been frequently applied, as well, to other stressful medical situations, such as during injections and during proctoscopy (Gonzalez, Routh, Saab, Armstrong, Shifman, Guerra, & Fawcett, 1989; Rasnake & Linscheid, 1989; van Aken, van Lieshout, Katz, & Heezen, 1989).

Some cultural differences may also exist. A study of cultural differences in the behavioral expression of distress during bone marrow aspirations revealed no differences in the overall distress score. Differences were found though in the behaviors during specific phases of the treatment (van Aken et al., 1989). Children from America demonstrated more anticipatory distress than Dutch children. This and other minor differences were less robust than the developmental and phases differences. Previous findings about the decrease of overall behavioral distress during the BMA procedure with age and an increase in muscle rigidity were confirmed. The largest changes in behavior were seen in the younger age group between the ages 2 and 6 years and were related to the preparatory and the recovery phase. The phase during which the actual puncture occurs was associated with the highest distress reactions.

LeBaron and Zeltzer (1984) argued that the both behavioral checklists are age biased and developed a shorter eight-category observational rating scale, The Procedure Behavior Check List (PBCL). The scale consists of items that are identical or similar to those found in the PBRS by Katz et al. (1980), with one important modification. To correct for the different expression of distress in adolescents, LeBaron and Zeltzer (1984) added two categories "flinching" and "groaning," which are more prominent in this age group. After adjusting the scale for these two categories, the authors concluded that both age groups experienced an equal amount of pain and anxiety. The self-reports provided by the children and adolescents were consistent with this assumption. The patients' self-ratings of anxiety and pain, as well as subjective ratings of anxiety and pain by the observers, were significantly correlated with the observational data based on the PBCL.

To document distress of younger children, mainly in the age range between 18 months and 7 years, the Frankl Behavior Rating Scale was modified by Shaw and Routh (1982). The 5-point scale includes categorization of behaviors as (1) definitely positive, pronounced exhibition of overt positive behavior, (3) neutral, absence of overt negative or positive behaviors and (5) definitely negative, pronounced exhibition of negative behavior. No further operational definitions of the different categories are supplied. Interrater reliability can be considered satisfactory with coefficients between .60 to .93, and a median of .91 (Broome & Endsley, 1989; Gonzalez et al., 1989). Moderate, significant correlation between the Frankl ratings and the OSBD have been reported in the study by Gonzalez et al. (1989) studying the reactions of children undergoing injections. The Frankl Behavior Rating Scale might serve as an easy-to-administer, easy-to-score alternative method to assess a child's distress in an aversive medical situation of short duration.

To assess postoperative pain in children, McGrath, Johnson, Goodman, Schillinger, Dunn, and Chapman (1985) developed The Children's Hospital of Eastern Ontario pain scale (CHEOPS). The following six aspects of pain behavior compose the scale: vocalizations, facial expression, child's verbal behavior, torso position, touch behavior, and leg position. The observer has to make judgments about the presence or absence, as well as the intensity of the behaviors. For example, the observer can distinguish between six different states for the torso position, including categories like neutral or at rest, shifting, tense, shivering, upright, or restrained. Conversely, three options are available to characterize the facial expressions of a child: composed, grimace, and smiling. Ratings are made in a time sampling method once every 30 seconds, divided into five-second observation and 25-second recording time. According to a number of studies, the CHEOPS is a valid and reliable measure for postoperative pain in children which can be applied with children aged 1 to 7 years (Beyer, McGrath, & Berde, in press). Two other measures of postoperative pain proposed by Broadman and colleagues (1987, 1988) and by Attia, Amiel-Tison, Mayer, Shnider, and Barrier (1987) are applicable to infants as well.

Several investigators have cautioned against use behavioral measures as the sole indicator of pain in children because of numerous methodological problems. The difficulty of discriminating between the behavioral expressions of pain and anxiety continues to be one of the major limitations in the use of observational scales. Recently, Gauvain-Piquard, Rodary, Rezvani, and Lemerle (1987) attempted to address this issue by using a factorial correspondence analysis to clarify the relationship between items measuring pain, depression, and anxiety in young children aged 2 through 6 years, in a pediatric oncology unit. Of the two factors identified, the first one accounted for 51% of the variance. Pain and depression items contributed to the first factor, whereas items indicating anxious behaviors were identified with the second axis explaining about 13% to 14% of the total variance. These preliminary findings underscore the necessity to consider other correlated variables in the behavioral assessment of pain. The variables to be considered may be highly specific to the population studied. The study by Gauvain-Piquard et al. (1987) illustrates that behavioral expression of pain is not independent from the affective state of the child. It is well known that depression can be an emotional sequelae of a life-threatening illness like cancer. The role of depression as a modulating variable in the experience of pain has been discussed for other patient populations.

Beyer, McGrath, and Berde (in press) have suggested use of the term "behavioral inhibition" to explain discrepancies between the behavioral manifestation of pain and pain intensity experienced. The authors cite examples of when such a generalized reduction in behavioral output in children might lead the observer to misjudge how much pain a child is actually experiencing. Some children might have learned to associate their complaining of pain with getting an injection and therefore deny any pain and avoid showing it to avoid "shots"; others will avoid any movement and try to lie as still as possible, not because they are pain free, but because movements increase their pain as in children following lateral thoracotomies. Postoperatively, an adolescent might suppress any overt signs of pain and behave in a manner consistent with a stoic self-image. The earlier increase in behavioral control and decrease of emotional outburst during medical procedures that has been consistently documented for adolescents could be another example of behavioral inhibition. Older children and adolescents, who have learned to deal with other stressors in a socially more acceptable form, may adopt such strategies in this situation. One could hypothesize that more adaptive and mature coping strategies might get positively reinforced by adult figures interacting with the child, whereas others may get systematically ignored (Craig, 1983).

In addition, Craig et al. (1988) link the drop of overt pain expression in children at about 7 years of age to developmental progression so that these cognitive changes account for more cooperative behavior. In a clinical context, it is relevant to further understand the variables that might counteract such a behavioral inhibition. Beyer et al. (1983) speculate that display of behavioral distress might be more pronounced when the intensity of pain exceeds a certain threshold or when intense emotions are evoked by a given situation. An observation in the study by van Aken et al. (1989) is consistent with this explanation. The display of anticipatory distress behavior prior to a BMA declined earlier for boys than girls, but this increased degree of behavioral control could not be maintained during the much more threatening and painful puncture that followed the waiting period. Increased arousal and pain associated with the first ambulation of a child after surgery or during chest therapy might lead to a similiar disinhibition of pain behavior.

Parental presence might be another important modifying factor of children's display pain behavior. Although the debate about these effects has been quite controversial and nonconclusive, there is increasing evidence that the caretaker's presence might in fact be related to behavioral disinhibition during medical stress conditions. Two methodologically similar studies (Gross, Stern, Levin, Dale & Wojnilower, 1983; Shaw & Routh, 1982) revealed that children cried more and were rated as more aroused during venipunctures and immunizations when the mothers were present. A subsequent, well-designed study by Gonzalez et al. (1989) confirmed these results and specified them with regard to age. The behavioral disinhibitory effect of the parental presence was exclusively documented for the older children but not found for the younger children. The authors explain these findings using a behavioral paradigm stating that mothers might be a discriminative stimulus for exhibiting distress during this stressful situation. The behavior of the older children in this sample can be interpreted as a meaningful attempt to elicit emotional support from their parents. Put in the same situation with a stranger, the child may be more likely to suppress such behaviors because the child has no expectancies based on previous interactions with this person.

In the light of these issues, it appears that observations of overt pain behavior under some circumstances might not be an accurate measure for the intensity of pain a child is experiencing. When behavioral scales fail to detect changes in pain intensity, self-report measures might indeed provide a more valid reflection of the child's condition (Beyer et al., 1983).

Most of these reviewed behavioral measures are based on the assumption that there is a systematic relationship between display of behavioral distress and the degree of pain experienced. An additional hidden assumption refers to the notion that the behaviors observed are associated with tissue damage or nociception. Such a view is associated with a biomedical disease model of pain in which pain is viewed as a symptom of an underlying organic disease. This conceptualization of pain seems especially relevant to understand acute pain problems.

Fordyce (1976, 1988) is probably the single most influential figure in answering this question and further differentiates this notion in proposing a theory about the importance of learned behaviors for the development and maintenance of chronic pain problems. He stated that pain behaviors might occur for many reasons and that they might be only loosely related to documented tissue damage and nociception. According to Fordyce, pain behavior is not simply the function of nociception, but is changed by external contingencies and a number of cognitive factors such as cognitive labeling or anticipation of suffering when pain persists and chronicity is reached. Therefore, observing pain behavior may provide little or no information about the presence of nociception or its magnitude. Within this framework, he proposes a distinction between nociception and pain as signal systems and suffering and pain behavior as responses or output systems. He defines nociception and pain as the signal system reflecting the activity of certain nerve fibers to the central nervous system in conjunction with the sensations arising from the stimulation of perceived nociception. In contrast to the signal systems, he classifies both the emotional component ("suffering") and the behavioral component ("pain behaviors") as responses or output systems. Fordyce's definition of pain behavior as "the things people do when they suffer or are in pain" highlights the communicational aspect of pain as well as the emotional dimension of this experience.

When translating this theoretical framework into the clinical situation, it means that the question "Why does this person have pain?" is most appropriate in the assessment of acute pain problems. When pain becomes chronic, which is conventionally defined after a 6-month period, asking "Why is this person emitting pain behavior?" takes into account that pain behavior is not a direct reflection of physical pathology. In Fordyce's theory of operant conditioning of pain behaviors, the assumption is made that behaviors that serve to communicate suffering to others are capable of being positively reinforced and maintained by reinforcement contingencies. According to a paradigm of operant conditioning, frequency of these behaviors is likely to increase if their occurrence is followed by positive consequences such as increased attention or by the avoidance of undesirable activities such as school or household chores. In chronic pain patients, this explains how pain behaviors can be controlled and maintained through socioenvironmental influences even after resolution of a pathological disease process or after termination of sensations arising from nerve impulses. The adaptive function of acute pain as a warning signal to trigger an orienting response to the injured body area and avoidance reaction of the harmful stimuli gets lost over time. In some cases, pain behavior might be influenced to a great extent by the prior learning history and patient expectancies and might only be marginally related to actual tissue damage.

Understanding of pain behaviors in an operant model therefore exceeds a descriptive level and addresses the functional meaning of the behaviors displayed. According to Fordyce, the term *pain behaviors* has been confined to overt and observable expressions of pain and include (1) verbal complaints of pain and suffering, (2) nonlanguage, paraverbal sounds (e.g., moans, sighs), (3) body posturing and gesturing (e.g., limping, rubbing a painful body part, grimacing), (4) display of functional limitations or impairments (e.g., reclining for excessive periods of time), and (5) behaviors designed to reduce pain such as the use of medication and use of health care providers. The first three behavioral categories have also been employed in the assessment of acute pain, the latter ones seem especially relevant in the assessment of chronic pain problems. Based on the work with adult chronic pain patients, the functional meaning of these behaviors has been seen mostly the communication of suffering to elicit responses from significant others, in gaining financial compensation such as disability, or in the avoidance of aversive activities. Research in adults as well as in children provides substantial evidence for such a notion.

Recently, behavioral scientists have elaborated possible shortcomings of such an approach. Turk and Flor (1987) draw attention to the fact that the relationship between medical status variables and pain behavior has been overlooked in the past. Some studies suggest that overt pain behaviors, such as guarding and bracing, could in fact be predicted by findings from physical examinations and the number of operations. (Keefe & Block, 1982; McDaniel, Anderson, Bradley, Young, Turner, Agudelo, & Keefe, 1986). Assuming that pain behavior in those patients is exclusively determined by the psychological or environmental factors reintroduces a dualistic model of pain as either organic or psychogenic. The lack of a well-defined medical diagnosis in a large number of chronic pain patients might discourage health care providers from seriously considering medical treatment modalities.

Recently, some chronic pain treatment programs have been criticized for not including medical treatment options into their behavioral treatment approaches (Russo, 1986). Within an exclusively operant model of pain, additional functions of pain behavior that are directly related to physical impairment or nociceptive stimulation might be overlooked. The patient's rubbing of a painful body part might be an active attempt to reduce pain rather than an effort to gain attention from others, or the avoidance of certain activities might prevent the exacerbation of symptoms (Turk & Flor, 1987). Clinically, it is often difficult to decide whether certain behaviors have already lost their adaptive function and have now gained a rather maladaptive quality in perpetuating the symptoms.

Cognitive or Self-report Component of Pain

According to Merskey's definition, pain is essentially a subjective experience, and thus self-report measures might be most suited to gain an understanding of the private dimensions of the pain experience. Feelings, self-evaluative statements, images, and the meaning of the painful sensation have all been classified as being part of the cognitive component of pain (Karoly, 1988). Self-report measures have a long tradition in the assessment of pain in adults, and their value as reliable and valid instruments has been extensively shown. A clear consensus exists between researchers that the language of self-report measures for children needs to match the level of cognitive understanding and the language skills of children in a given age range. Furthermore, it might be beneficial to employ visual information, such as pictures or drawings, to facilitate the child's comprehension of words like *pain* or *hurt*. Simple questions like "How is your pain today?" are not likely to provide any meaningful information to the clinician with younger children. For example, most 2-year-olds are still unable to indicate whether it hurts more or less or to specify the location of pain precisely when asked to do so. To assist the development of assessment tools and decision making around which self-report measures to choose with a given young patient, it is important to draw upon some normative data about the children's concepts of pain and their pain language.

When applying self-report measures with children, some of the same methodological issues mentioned in the section about behavioral measures have to be considered. Ross and Ross (1984) have investigated how the type of question and the psychological climate systematically influence the child's answers. In this study, a large cohort ($n = 994$) of 5-to-12-year-old, healthy children were interviewed about their concepts, knowledge, and language of pain. They found that the children's answers differed according to whom they directed their responses. When telling their mother, their responses were said to be consise and unemotional, but when describing the same experience to a friend, the responses were more dramatic, communicating the emotional aspect, the suffering. The most comprehensive responses were produced following the request to describe their pain to young doctors who needed to learn about children's pain. One can easily imagine that this scenario would radically change if this conversation were to take place in the physician's office with the child being frightened by the unfamiliar environment or by the sight of frightening-looking equipment. The authors also examined differences in responses to open-ended questions and checklists. Therefore, it seems crucial to be aware of these context-related variables instead of rejecting the possibility to use self-report measures as a whole. Ross et al. (1984) have developed some additional guidelines for the conduct of the interviews with children to minimize possible distorting factors.

Several studies have generated normative data on healthy children's vocabulary describing various aspects of pain experience and typical concepts of pain. This knowledge is instrumental for interviewing children about pain and facilitates the construction of age-appropriate self-report measures or questionnaires. Tesler, Savedra, Ward, Holzemer, and Wilkie (1988) compiled a list of 129 words either known to children or used by them to describe pain. Of the 958 children, ages 8 to 17, half of them used 67 words of the list, and 75% of the sample knew 115 of the 129 pain descriptors. The six most frequently used and known words across all age groups were *hurting, sore, burning, stinging, aching,* and *like a sharp knife*. Children in the lower grades 3 through 6 were found to select fewer words compared to older children; a significant sex difference revealed that girls tended to use more words and analogies compared to the boys in this sample, an observation shared by other investigators (Gaffney, 1988). Prior hospitalization did not affect selection of words. The children were also able to assign intensity value to the words they choose consistently. Children viewed words like *pinching* or *scratching* as representing low intensity, whereas *burning, shooting,* and *uncontrollable* were associated with higher intensity ratings. Words indicating higher intensity often had affective connotations.

In a similar study based on 680 children, Gaffney and Dunne (1986) showed that acquisition of a concept of pain follows a developmental progression from concrete, perceptually rooted pain descriptions in the youngest age study group (5–7-year-olds), to more abstract, generalized, and psychologically oriented views of pain in the adolescent group (11–14 year olds). These findings correspond with results on the elaboration of the more general concepts of illness in children and have often been interpreted within the framework of Piaget's theory on cognitive development (Bibace & Walsh, 1979).

Gaffney (1988) concluded that the ability of older children to describe pain in more complex terms does not simply reflect an increase vocabulary but represents a qualitative change in the cognitive structure. Children who reach the stage of formal operational thinking are able to encompass the affective, qualitative and evaluative aspects of pain like adults. This implies that adult pain self-report measures such as the McGill-Melzack Scale should be administered only to older adolescents who can comprehend the full range of verbal pain descriptors and whose general understanding of pain is comparable to that of adult patients (Melzack, 1975). According to these findings, children in the preoperational stage have concepts that are greatly discrepant with an adult view of pain. They are more likely to locate pain primarily in their head or stomach and are unable to see the relationship between pain and illness. Because the development of more elaborated concepts is a gradual process and age alone is not an indicator of the child's cognitive developmental stage, it is essential to determine for each child individually the meaning of pain. Especially when children are stressed by illness or hospitalization, they may regress in their cognitive abilities, and less developed concepts about illness and pain may reemerge.

Because of these developmental considerations, special attention has been directed toward the development of simpler verbal scales that are suitable for younger children. Furthermore, efforts have been made to determine whether some of the measures used with adults would be suitable for children as well. We will differentiate between pain intensity measures, projective and drawing methods, and more complex, multidimensional pain questionnaires, which often incorporate aspects of both categories.

Pain Intensity Measures

Jensen, Karoly, and Braver (1986) propose five criteria for judging intensity scales that can be helpful to guide the selection of a measure in the context of a particular clinical or research question: (1) ease of administration; (2) relative rate of incorrect responding; (3) sensitivity as defined by the number of available response categories; (4) sensitivity as defined by statistical power; and (5) the magnitude of the relationship between each scale and a linear combination of pain indices. For assessment of pain with pediatric patients, the age appropriateness has to be added as another criterion.

Visual analog scales (VAS) are one of the most popular measurement techniques used in adults, as well as in children. A VAS can be seen as a form of cross-modality matching procedure in which the length of a line (typically 10 cm long) represents the continuum of pain intensity. The subjects are asked to mark, on the line between the anchors "no pain" and on the other end point "very severe pain" or "pain as bad as it could be," a point that best corresponds with the amount experienced at a specified time point. The VAS is easy to administer and score. Among researchers there is no consensus with regard to the youngest age group able to use the VAS. Normally developed children over the age of 7 can probably understand the scale, although its use with younger children has also been reported (Abu-Saad & Holzemer, 1981; McGrath, 1987). To ensure the proper understanding of the VAS, it is recommended to practice with a child how to mark the scale with pain resulting from different sources such as a mosquito bite, getting an injection, falling off a bike and getting bruises being used as examples.

VAS has been shown to be sensitive to detect treatment effects (Webb, Stergios, & Rodgers, 1989; Beyer & Aradine, 1986). Research suggests that the VAS correlates well with behavioral measures and verbal pain reports (Abu-Saad, 1984). VAS has been validated as ratio scale measures for both chronic and experimental pain (Gracely, 1984; Price, McGrath, Rafii, & Buckingham, 1983). Currently, the views differ whether a horizontal or vertical display of the VAS is more reliable with children. Whereas adults clearly prefer a horizontal scale (Sriwatanakul, Kelvie, Lasagna, Calimlim, Weis, & Mehta, 1983) use of the vertical scale is recommended for younger children. In adults, it has been shown that the vertical display of the line results in greatest coefficients of variation and in slightly higher scores (Scott & Huskisson, 1979; Sriwatanakul et al., 1983). Some researchers have translated a vertical VAS into a so-called pain thermometer (Szyfelbein, Osgood, & Carr, 1985), which integrates a numerical scale (0–10 or 1–100) with the picture of a thermometer. Children point to the level that reflects their pain or they can adjust a movable part to the same level.

The Poker Chip Tool (Hester, 1979, modified by Molsberry, 1979) is an example of a numerical scale that uses concrete material rather than a paper-and-pencil approach. Children can choose among one white and four red chips to describe their pain. The white chip symbolizes no pain; four red chips stand for the "biggest hurt you could ever have." Hester (1979) reported significant correlations between the Poker Chip Tool and verbal and vocal expressions of pain. Data from Molsberry (1979) indicate convergent validity of the measure. The tool is developed for children between 4 and 7 years.

Another class of measures uses faces as stimuli to assess the intensity and affective component of pain experience in children. The happy-sad scale by McGrath, DeVeber, and Hearn (1985) consists of nine different faces depicting different emotional expressions. The child chooses the face that matches with his or her pain best. Compared with other instruments, the scale apparently measures mostly affective components of the pain experience, and to what extent sensory aspects are included remains unclear. Six pictures showing the face of one child with expressions ranging from no discomfort to display of severe discomfort are arranged parallel to a vertical numerical scalen (1–100) in the Oucher (Beyer & Knapp, 1986). The posterlike device is suitable for children between 3 and 12 years. The younger children who are not able to count to 100 use only the right side showing the pictures. In a series of studies, content, convergent, and discriminant validity of the measure have been established (Beyer & Aradine, 1986; Beyer & Aradine, 1988). Especially high correlations were found between the Poker Chip Tool and the Oucher. The authors attribute the somewhat lower correlational coefficients between the Oucher and the VAS to the fact that the use of the VAS with younger children included in their sample has not yet been sufficiently proven. The good psychometric properties of the Oucher make it a promising instrument to assess pain intensity and to document treatment effects in toddlers, as well as in older children.

Affective Meaning of Pain/Projective and Drawing Techniques

Pain drawings and projective techniques are additional tools to evaluate pain. Given how difficult it can be even for adults to communicate the character and location of pain verbally, it is not surprising that pain drawings are not only used with pediatric patients, but are also part of pain questionnaire in adults (Margolis, Chibnall, & Tait, 1988; Melzack, 1975). Drawings are typically used in three variations; patients are asked to color or shade the points where they experience pain within an outline of an human figure, to select among different colors the one that best describes the pain or to draw a picture of their pain experience. Compared to self-report measures, only sparse information about reliability or validity of these nonverbal methods is available. Although these techniques should not be viewed as means to measure pain intensity (Kurylyszyn, McGrath, Cappelli, & Humphreys, 1987), they can provide tools to evaluate the emotional meaning of the pain and the child's attitudes. In addition, drawings may serve as a valuable method to engage children in conversations about previous painful experiences and their ability to cope with these situations. A recent study by Savedra, Tesler, Ward, Holzemer, and Wilkie (1987) further suggests that color scales are best liked by children across a wide age range (8–17 years).

The few studies investigating pain drawings in children have documented a clear color preferences for pain descriptions: children choose red and black most frequently to indicate pain in general, regardless of intensity (Eland & Anderson, 1977; Jeans, 1983; Scott, 1978; Unruh, McGrath, Cunningham, & Humphreys, 1983). The Eland Color Tool gives children the opportunity to construct their own color scale choosing among eight colors to represent increasing pain intensity (Eland & Anderson, 1977). Then the child is asked to color different areas within a human figure in a way that it best corresponds with his or her pain experience.

Besides consideration of color, valuable information can be derived from the content of children's pain drawings. Unruh et al. (1983) suggested a categorical system to classify children's drawings. Drawings were grouped into five categories: (1) recipient of the pain; (2) agent in relieving pain; (3) emotion due to pain; (4) location of pain; (5) nonspecific representation of pain. Their study showed no significant developmental or sex differences with regard to the use of these categories. It is noteworthy that children's drawings frequently contain information about the way the child is attempting to cope with pain. Of the 109 children suffering from recurrent migraine headaches or chronic musculoskeletal pain participating in the project, only one child portrayed himself taking medicine. Applying pressure, being quiet, or sleeping were the most frequently seen coping strategies. Despite the fact that pain drawings have not been analyzed in a formal way, it is apparent that information concerning emotional impact of the pain on the child and the spontaneously occurring coping strategies of a child can facilitate treatment planning.

Two projective scales have been published that both use cartoons for pain assessment. Eland (1974) showed five cartoons showing a dog in various painful situations (e.g., in a neutral position, hurting different body parts) to hospitalized children. The children were able to distinguish the neutral situation from the painful situation. The attempts to rank order the situation were only consistent for individual children but not for the whole group. The Pediatric Pain Inventory (Lollar, Smits, & Patterson, 1982) might be the more promising tool because it uses 24 pictures showing a human figure in potentially pain-evoking situations. Situations from four different settings are part of the Inventory: medical (e.g., getting a shot, receiving stitches or having a cast put on), psychosocial (e.g., getting scolded by a policeman, striking out in a baseball game), recreation (e.g., being hit by a baseball, dropping a bowling ball on the foot), activities of daily living (e.g., closing a finger in a door, pulling off a Band-Aid). Children are asked a set of questions addressing the responsibility for the situation presented, whether the person in the picture needed help, who would help, and what action should be taken. Ratings of pain intensity and duration were also obtained. The Inventory has so far been tested only with healthy children. In this sample, it became apparent that the children's responses were in part influenced by their own pain experience. Having little experience with pain was associated with higher pain ratings. Other age differences and differences in responses to pictures from the four settings were described by the test constructers. The authors provide no information about administration time. Compared with the dog cartoons, the PPI uses a much broader spectrum of situations that seem to be more closely related to the child's own experiences. One might conclude that until the psychometric properties of these projective techniques are more rigorously evaluated, it remains unclear under what circumstances they can be applied.

Multifaceted Pain Questionnaires

Most of the instruments reviewed previously are unidimensional mostly oriented to assess pain intensity. The Varni/Thompson Pediatric Pain Questionnaire (PPQ) and the Children's Comprehensive Pain Questionnaire (CCPQ) have been designed to facilitate assessment in children with recurrent and chronic pain conditions. Both instruments are similar in that they combine information about pain intensity, the sensory dimensions of the child's pain, with the affective and evaluative aspects. Both questionnaires have been constructed to be sensitive to cognitive developmental considerations.

The PPQ (Varni & Thompson, 1985) has been modeled after the McGill Pain Questionnaire (Melzack, 1975). The PPQ consists of a child, adolescent, and parent form to address possible differences in the patient's and parent's perception of the pain problem and to allow for cross-validation of the child's reporting of pain. The child form of the PPQ uses visual analog scales that are anchored with verbal descriptors and happy and sad faces for pain intensity ratings; a listing of pain descriptors helps to assess the child's pain vocabulary and to elicit information about the quality of the pain experience; color-coded scale in conjunction with the outline of a child's figure, available for boys and girls separately, are included to assess the intensity and location of pain. The parent form addresses the child's and family pain history, as well as questions regarding symptomatology, previous and current treatments, and situational or emotional factors that might be related to changes in symptomatology. The PPQ also provides information about the functional impairment of the child due to pain and includes questions to assess the impact the child's pain has had on the family. In a modified version, functional status measures have been added. High correlations between child, parent, and physician pain scores were found in a study investigating families who had children with juvenile rheumatoid arthritis (Thompson, Varni, & Hanson, 1987). The study suggested that children as young as 5 years of age are able to communicate central aspects of their pain experience using the PPQ.

The Children's Comprehensive Pain Questionnaire (McGrath, 1990) combines generate and supplied-format questions, VAS, and affective facial scales.

The CCPQ should be administered by a trained interviewer; some parts such as the child's pain history are obtained from the parent, but the majority of the questions are directed toward the child. The questionnaire further provides information not only about possible triggering factors for pain episodes the child has identified, but also about the efforts of the child to reduce the pain associated with estimates about how effective different interventions have been in the past. The description of the parent's and sibling's reactions to the child during painful episodes might indicate whether some of the behaviors have become controlled by external contingencies. The CCPQ has been evaluated with children between 4 and 16 years.

Both questionnaires can serve as ways to gather information about a child's pain experience in a comprehensive and systematic manner. Both questionnaires provide the researcher and clinician with a practical format for how to structure interviews with children who suffer from recurrent or chronic pain problems.

Coping Strategies

Within a contextual assessment model, a primary goal is to determine the person's cognitive and behavioral style in approaching stressful events and to identify possible strengths and weaknesses in the person's repertoire that could be further developed or modified if found to be dysfunctional. How people cope with pain and illness-related experiences like hospitalizations and surgical procedures has become the paradigm to explore differences in coping both in adults and children. Coping has been defined by Lazarus and Folkman (1984) as "constantly changing cognitive and behavioral efforts to manage specific external/and or internal demands that are appraised as taxing or exceeding the resources of a person." Rather than conceptualizing differences in coping styles as personality traits, coping is now considered process-oriented and a temporally and situationally specific process (Tunks & Bellissimo, 1988). Difficulties in consistently predicting a person's coping across situations or times have supported this notion. Therefore, assessment of coping strategies has to include information about situational variables, the nature of the stressor eliciting coping and inclusion of a time component. For example, in children it has been reported that young children react very strongly to painful procedures such as venipunctures and injections, which are relatively short-term and highly salient stressors (Peterson, 1989).

Despite the host of conceptual and methodological problems that are magnified due to developmental issues, Peterson (1989) found the construct to be of heuristic value in classifying coping strategies along a dimension of active versus avoidant. Active coping is characterized through behaviors such as seeking information about the stressor, focusing one's attention on the source of the stress, actively asking questions about a stressful event. Burstein and Meichenbaum (1979) used play observations to describe children anticipating hospitalization as active copers who choose medically relevant toys rather than neutral one. In contrast, children with more avoidant strategies tend to turn their attention away from the stressor, and to use strategies such as denial or displacement.

As the definition by Lazarus and Folkman (1984) states, all efforts to manage stress are subsumed under coping. While coping should therefore not be confounded with outcome on a conceptual level, some research findings show that children who use more active coping strategies are likely to report less anxiety dealing with fear-provoking medical encounters, to be more cooperative, and to have a higher tolerance for pain than children who avoided information (Siegel, 1981; Burstein & Meichenbaum, 1979). Active coping has been shown to be associated with lower distress prior to a blood test and with better recovery after surgery (Peterson & Toler, 1986). In the adult literature, further evidence is found that a passive coping style was correlated with greater functional impairment, higher levels of depression, and disease activity in chronic pain patients suffering from rheumatoid arthritis (Brown & Nicassio, 1987).

That coping strategies change over time and may be influenced by learning and repeated exposure to a stressful situation was recently shown by Smith, Ackerson, and Blotcky (1989). After assessing the preferred coping style of children scheduled for bone marrow aspirations, they were assigned to four different experimental groups. It was postulated that children would benefit most from behavioral intervention for anxiety reduction when it was consistent with their preferred coping style. Whereas the main hypothesis could only be partially supported, the study generated an unexpected finding pointing to the importance of chronicity of the illness and amount of prior experiences as other factors influencing coping. Children in the initial phase of their cancer treatment tended to repress, minimize, and avoid information, whereas participants who actively sought information had been diagnosed for a longer time and had experienced more procedures.

Investigating coping strategies in children has often been directly related to clinical decision-making (e.g., to determine the usefulness of programs preparing children for hospitalizations or to teach children coping strategies that are thought to enhance their adjustment to stress). Comparatively less is known about the repertoire of coping strategies in healthy children as it occurs spontaneously. Brown, O'Keefe, Sanders, and Baker (1986) asked 487 students from different schools between the ages of 8 to 18 to describe their reactions during four potentially stressful events in a questionnaire format. One hypothetical situation included getting an injection at the dentist's office. Based on all responses, the authors chose a somewhat unusual distinction between coping strategies, implying a positive outcome and catastrophizing strategies as those that magnify the potential threat of the situation for the person. Only 37% of the children were classified as copers, reporting predominantly coping strategies such as positive self-talk, attention diversion by thinking of something else, relaxation, or thought stopping. Positive self-talk was more often part of the cognitive repertoire than thought stopping, a technique reported by only a few students. Older children made use of a larger number of coping strategies. Comparatively more children were identified as catastophizers, dwelling on negative aspects of the situation; their number decreased with age: 79% of the 8-to-9-year-old children and 54% of the 16-to-18-year-old students fell into the category of catastrophizers. Typical strategies included focusing on the negative aspects of the dental situation and their own emotional reactions ("I am afraid"; "This hurts"; "I hate shots"); thinking about escape or avoidance; being concerned about an unlikely consequence; or focusing on negative aspects of the dentist. A similar low rate of spontaneously occurring coping strategies was reported by Ross and Ross (1984). It is questionable whether the children's actual behavior in these stressful situations would be identical with their written statements about their coping strategies in these hypothetical situations. This might be especially relevant for the younger children studied.

LeBaron, Zeltzer, and Fanurik (1989) explored self-initiated coping strategies used by 37 children, 6-to-12 years of age, who participated in a cold pressor experiment. Focusing on cognitive coping strategies, the children's responses were grouped into five general categories: (1) nonimagery distraction (e.g., counting squares in the ceiling; trying not to think about pain); (2) imagery (e.g., related to the situation: swimming in cold water or unrelated to situation: playing with dolls); (3) concentrating on sensory aspects of the present experience (e.g., water going up and down the arm); (4) concentrating on mechanical aspects of the present experience (e.g., on giving of ratings, equipment); (5) no mental activity was reported. Imagery and concentration on sensory aspects were spontaneously used by 35% of the children vs. 34% of the interviewed children and were the two most common coping strategies. Overall, the majority of the children reported an active way to cope with the discomfort; only 6% did not describe any strategy. Use of different coping strategies was not associated with differences in the reported pain. The authors noted that three boys with unusually low pain ratings were described by their mothers as having a high tolerance for pain in general. High pain ratings in one child were associated with dramatic descriptions of the sensations that could be classified as catastrophizing following Brown et al. (1986). In seven other children who had equally high pain ratings, an interesting discrepancy between affect and reported discomfort was observed. This impression fitted with parental reports that these children had a tendency to overreact to minor painful events such as bruises or small cuts. Because it was a major objective of the investigators to design the experimental situation in a nonthreatening manner minimizing stress and anxiety, one could speculate that rate of self-initiated coping strategies might be lower under more stressful circumstances when the stressor become more threatening and anxiety might be interfering wih accessing all coping strategies available to a person. The increased number of children (11% compared to 6%) who were apparently not using any coping strategy under the second experimental condition with lowered water temperature could be seen as evidence of such a trend. Compared with other studies using written statements, LeBaron et al. (1989) were able to elicit a greater number of coping responses available to a higher percentage of children. Differences in relation to other studies probably result from methodological problems and different assessment strategies.

The fact that even in a healthy sample, many children attempt to cope with stressful events by focusing primarily on negative aspects of the situation and by expressing negative affect raises interesting research and clinical issues. Adult pain patients are consistently characterized as being depressive, displaying negative affect (as hostility), and expressing attitudes of hopelessness and helplessness. A considerable controversy exists about the relationship between depression and chronic pain.

Recent research on coping styles in children suggests that maladaptive coping strategies can be present in early childhood and that they will be activated when they are adults coping with chronic pain. Second, one could ask how experience and learning history is different for children using more adaptive or problematic coping styles. In this context, a study by Dunn-Geier, McGrath, Rourke, Latter, and D'Astous (1986) hints at how children's attempts to deal with pain might be influenced by parent-child interactions. Within a group of adolescents with chronic benign intractable pain, the distinction between copers and noncopers was made according to the degree of functional impairment operationalized as school absence caused by the pain problem. Copers regularly attended school; noncopers missed an average of 14.7 days over a 2-month period. Mother–child interactions were recorded while the adolescent engaged in 15 minutes of physical exercises. Noncoping adolescents engaged in more negative behaviors, reported more pain to their mothers, and tended to be offtask more often than copers. In addition, their mothers alternated between discouragement and encouragement when interacting with their children. They seemed to be more actively involved during the task and were seen as overprotective in this pain-oriented situation. Because the study concentrated on behavioral differences in the parental behavior, it remains to be asked whether the child's typical coping strategies in dealing with pain resemble those used by the parent in a similar situation. This question is especially pertinent when children grow up in families in which one or more caretakers have a history of a chronic illness or pain problem.

Recommendations for the Use of Coping Strategies

Although the literature is currently inconclusive about the occurrence of different coping strategies in different populations, we feel that the assessment of coping strategies in a child with pain should be taken into account for planning treatment intervention. The use and elaboration of strategies that are already in the child's repertoire facilitates learning and helps to establish rapport with the child. Such an approach is not only therapeutically favorable but also promises to be quite powerful considering that the technique used by most children spontaneously, imagery (LeBaron, et al., 1989), has been identified as the single most effective cognitive coping strategy for altering pain perception (Fernandez & Turk, 1989).

As indicated by the reviewed research, coping strategies can be assessed through behavioral observation, interview methods, and self-report. Recently, Spirito, Stark, and Williams (1988) published a 10-item checklist (Kidcope) covering both cognitive and behavioral cognitive coping strategies. The following categories are included: distraction, social isolation, cognitive restructuring, self-blame, blaming others, problem-solving, emotional regulation, wishful thinking, social support and resignation. Data for both healthy and pediatric patients are now available (Stark, Spirito, Williams, & Guevremont, 1989). Because the instrument has been designed to be applicable to a wide range of pediatric problems, it remains to be seen whether it is specific enough to provide a profile of coping in children with pain and whether it captures developmental shifts.

Intense efforts to construct self-report measures for pain assessment in children have produced a significant number of available instruments. Research in this area suggests that these measures provide reliable and valid quantitative data on children's subjective pain experience. There is increasing evidence that children older than 6 or 7 years are well able to quantify somatic symptoms, such as pain, nausea, or vomiting, in a meaningful way through the use of rating scales (Zeltzer, LeBaron, Richie, Reed, Schoolfield, & Prihoda, 1988). The availability of rating scales with good psychometric properties enables the clinician and researcher to optimize pain assessment in children by combining observational data and patient self-report. How to interpret discrepancies between these two sources of information remains a challenge. Under certain circumstances, self-reports might even provide a more accurate picture of the patient's condition than behavioral measures. For example, Beyer, McGrath, & Berde (in press) compared the CHEOPS, the Oucher and a variant of a color and hurt thermometer, an Analogue Chromatic Continuous scale, when used with 3-to-7-year-old children postoperatively after major orthopedic, general, or urological surgeries. The authors found evidence that the two self-report measures mirrored the postoperative course of these children more precisely than the observational scale. In contrast, the profile in the CHEOPS, the observational scale appeared rather flat, suggesting little discomfort. Such results show that the sole reliance on behavioral measures might be misleading and result in continuing underestimation of a child's pain.

Physiological Component of Pain

A number of physiological measures, such as cardiovascular changes, respiratory, and hormonal-metabolic parameters have been recorded to assess pain in children. So far, no single, objective physiological indicator of the pain experience has not been identified. This is related to the fact that these physiological changes are not unique to painful stimulation. An increase in heart rate is a rather nonspecific response of the body to stress, and therefore such a change does not necessarily reflect an increase in pain intensity. Another limitation is the tendency of most of these measures to habituate over time, and repeated measurements are influenced by these trends. Despite these limitations, monitoring of physiological changes has been employed successfully to compare effectiveness of different analgesic treatments during and after invasive procedures. Physiological measures of pain have been used mainly in infants and young children and have been integrated with behavioral measures.

Cardiorespiratory Changes

Systematic changes in heart rate, respiration, transcutaneous oxygen, and palmar sweating have been documented for infants undergoing painful procedures such as circumcision or heel lancing. During these procedures, the typically occurring heart rate acceleration and increases in blood pressure was decreased or eliminated for infants who received local anesthesia during these procedures compared to a control group of neonates who were given a pacifer (Williamson & Williamson, 1983). Significant differences were also found in the level of transcutaneous oxygen, whereas respiratory changes did not prove to be a sensitive measure. Decreases in transcutaneous oxygen level have been observed during surgical procedures and during awake intubation of neonates, which can be controlled through administration of local analgesia (Clifton, Graham, Hatton, 1986). Harpin and Rutter (1982) reported significant increases in palmar sweating in infants undergoing heel stick procedures that were reversible after the end of the procedure.

For three physiological parameters—heart rate, blood pressures, and palmar sweating—good correlations with behavioral indicators of distress have been reported (Jay & Elliott, 1984; Melamed & Siegel, 1980). Because of great variability of these parameters and technical difficulties in measuring them accurately, it is not surprising that some studies did not confirm these findings.

Hormonal-Metabolic Changes

Increased study in the area of hormonal metabolic changes has produced a new avenue for pain assessment. For example, in a series of studies, Anand and his collegues found evidence that the inadequate treatment of pain in neonates results in a massive stress response detectable in significant changes of hormonal and metabolic parameters. A large number of studies has consistently documented a marked release of cathecholamines, cortisol, aldosterone and other corticosteroids, growth hormone, glucagen in neonates undergoing surgery (Anand & Aynsley-Green, 1985). Such neontal stress responses often persisted for more than 24 hours after the surgery. In subsequent randomized controlled studies, Anand, Sippell, and Aynsley-Green (1987b) reported that the stress response could be significantly inhibited by the administration of potent anesthesia during surgery. Additional work in this area is critically needed to challenge long-held, and often incorrect assumptions about pain in children.

On a more basic biochemical level, a new avenue of research has focused on internally mediated pain management mechanisms. The relationship between changes in β-endorphin levels and other measures of pain is currently not clear. In older children, increases in plasma concentration of β-endorphin level in the cerebrospinal fluid were associated with decreased pain ratings in burned children during debridement procedures (Szyfelbein et al., 1985). In contrast, Katz et al. (1982) found the plasma concentrations to be moderately correlated with behavioral ratings performed by the nurses during lumbar punctures, but not with the patient's self-reports. McGrath and Unruh (1987) attribute these contrasting findings to differences in the study designs. Further research in this area may elucidate the contribution of endorphins and similar substances in pain genesis and amelioration.

IMPLICATIONS FOR TREATMENT

Patients with acute, recurrent, or chronic pain problems often share a feeling of helplessness and a sense of little control over the painful event. This is often due to the belief that pain has only a physiological dimension. This leads many patients and parents to assume that pain is only ammenable to pharmacologic interventions. Consequently, the information that pain experience can be affected by a person's behavior, emotional state, and situational factors is often met with some initial disbelief.

We believe that it is crucial to pursue both medical and psychological evaluation together early in the diagnostic process, thereby communicating to the patient the notion that pain can in fact be influenced by a number of factors. This information later serves as a rationale to explain why different treatment modalities might be considered for the pain, ranging from medical and pharmacological to nonpharmacological behavioral interventions. Taking such an approach also helps to overcome the focus on simply determining the degree of organic pathology and allows a more balanced integration of psychological explanations of the pain problem. Patients and their families may perceive this as the physician questioning the existence of their pain experience entirely and feel blamed for exaggerating or making up the problem. To prevent this and establish a trustful therapeutic relationship it is essential to give the patient the opportunity to describe his or her pain experience in detail and to avoid moving too fast into exploring other issues, such as family dynamics, that might appear unrelated to the patient's pain. In this phase of the treatment, it is our goal to reassure the patient that we see the pain problem as real and acknowledge the difficulties in coping with the situation both for the individual and the family. This seems particularly important for the assessment of pain in children, because adult caregivers tend to assume that children are less accurate and capable in reporting their pain. By providing developmentally appropriate child-centered assessment instruments, we reinforce the notion that the child or adolescent has credibility and is capable of providing meaningful information about his or her experiences. This will facilitate acceptance of the idea that the child can play an active role in the treatment course.

We consider it equally important to highlight the role of the parents in supporting their child's adaptive coping with pain. Asking about the impact of the pain problem on other family members, about changes in the routine of daily activities in the family, or about pain experiences of the parents and their strategies to deal with painful episodes will open the discussion about the role of the parent's in the management of the child's pain. The younger the child, the more likely it is that the parent will not only be the primary source of information about the child's symptoms and behavior, but will also assume a more active role in the treatment. It often appears that parents feel quite frustrated and overwhelmed when their child is in pain, and they feel insecure as to how to intervene effectively. Based on the assessment of the parental responses to the child's expression of pain, we develop strategies that help parents to enhance their competencies in supporting their child and reduce the likelihood that they will teach or unintentionally reinforce maladaptive responses to painful experiences.

By applying a multidimensional approach to the assessment and treatment of pain and by ensuring the patient's and parental understanding of this rationale, we aim to enhance the feeling of controllability over the pain experience and a motivation for change.

CASE STUDY

Maria, a 15-year-old promising gymnast, had fallen off of a balance beam during practice, badly spraining her left ankle. After consultation with an orthopedist, X-rays, and the placement of a soft cast to immobolize the joint, she was assured that the sprain would heal quickly and that she could return to her sport in several weeks. She was advised to rest as much as possible and to interrupt any activity should the pain increase.

Four months later, Maria and her parents arrived in our office. Despite medical assurances that the sprain had completely healed, she had for the past 3 months experienced excruciating, burning pain in the ankle, reported coldness and numbness, and was clearly angry about the lack of successful treatment she had received at the hands of several specialists. Her parents reported that she spent much time in her room, upset and ambivalent about her return to sports. The parents, themselves athletes, put a great deal of pressure on Maria to excel. This had predated the accident, as Maria's performance had been lacking and she had expressed thoughts of "being more like the other kids" and dropping out of gymnastics. The parents reported that she had become increasingly isolative, moody, and anxious, and her pain always appeared worse during these periods. The parents brought to us copies of Maria's medical records, showing good healing of the sprain and no further complications. They were clearly upset over the doctor's impression that the pain is "all in her head."

During our initial evaluation, Maria remained quiet for most of the time. Repeatedly, when a question was directed to Maria, her mother was quick to jump in and provide an answer for her. She stated that her daughter had become increasingly frustrated with telling her story to different experts and with having to answer the same questions over and over again. Maria's descriptions of her pain were rather vague. She was unable to identify any aggravating factors. She explained that the only measure that would provide some relief from the pain was sleeping.

It became apparent that Maria had adopted a passive and hopeless attitude about her pain problem. We explained to the family that it is crucial for Maria to actively participate in the diagnostic and treatment process. Therefore, we underscored the importance of gaining further information about the history of the pain problem and the current status from Maria herself. We asked her to complete the adolescent form of the Pediatric Pain Questionnaire, and the parents filled out the Parent Form. In addition, we requested Maria to keep a pain diary monitoring the pain intensity using a visual analog scale over the course of the day during defined times. She was to briefly indicate the activity she was involved in and to note how she tried to cope with the pain.

During the next visit, we decided to spend time with Maria alone, reviewing her pain diary and the PPQ. It became obvious that the questionnaire had enabled Maria to give much more specific information about her pain condition than in the interview with the parents present. Maria had left out a couple of questions in the PPQ and she made critical remarks about how the questions were stated. We used this as an opportunity to understand her viewpoint better and further explored the meaning of these questions to her. Following this discussion, she talked more openly about her anger towards her mother, who inquired frequently about her pain and advised her to rest. We learned that Maria had missed a considerable amount of time at school and that she worried about not being promoted to the next grade. The PPQ also revealed that Maria's responsibilities at home had decreased since the onset of her pain (e.g., she was no longer required to do her share of household chores). Maria reported with some surprise that the pain diary made her aware that her pain was not at the same level throughout the day as she had stated during our first meeting. The pain was most likely to be moderate during morning hours, intensifying in the evenings. She noticed that talking to her girlfriend on the phone had distracted her from the pain, as well as listening to her favorite music with headphones. Consistent with the parental report, Maria's entries in her diary suggested that at times when she felt anxious and depressed her pain appeared to be worse. Interestingly, her mother rated Maria's pain as less intense than the patient did.

Maria was also seen by the anesthesiologist from the Pain Treatment Service. After a review of her medical history, a physical examination, and laboratory studies to rule out rheumatologic or vascular diseases had been performed, the diagnosis of Reflex Sympathetic Dystrophy was made. Results from a diagnostic lumbar sympathetic nerve block with a local anesthetic were consistent with this diagnosis.

Applying the traditional, purely psychological approach, one might have concluded from Maria's initial presentation that her pain problem was a manifestation of the conflict with her parents about her future as an athlete. This formulation might have focused on the fact that Maria's independence-seeking wishes were blocked by the strong parental investment in her sports career, leading to anxiety regarding her relationship with peers and suppressed anger towards her parents. Although these issues were certainly relevant to the case, this approach would have neglected the physiological dimension of Maria's pain condition. However, this part was of critical importance for the further treatment planning. Pharmacologic and physical interventions, such as electrical nerve stimulation and nerve blocks, which would not have been considered otherwise, were used in conjunction with behavioral and cognitive methods, resulting in a significant reduction of pain and a return to more normal activities for this patient.

SUMMARY

A growing body of research on pain in children supports the notion that children of all ages share the capacity to experience pain and to communicate this experience to others. Like adults, children describe pain as an unpleasant sensory and emotional experience. Despite the subjective nature of the pain experience, it is evident that it is possible to measure pain along these dimensions. This task is difficult because the multidimensional nature of pain.

In assessing pain in pediatric patients, another dimension has to be considered: the cognitive-developmental level of the child. The child's ability to communicate pain verbally and nonverbally depends on the age and developmental level of the child. Therefore, choosing an age-appropriate assessment strategy should be guided by the knowledge of these developmental changes in pain behavior and changes in their understanding of pain.

With infants and young children who have not yet developed verbal communication skills, pain assessment has to rely on behavioral measures and physiological indicators of pain. Both behavioral and physiological measures are ambiguous and difficult to interpret. While the difficulty of discriminating the pain and anxiety component in these measures presents methodological problems, self-report measures are an important additional avenue to gain information about a child's experience of pain. The emerging literature suggests that at a very early age, children are able to use visual analog scales and other self-report scales to quantify their pain experience. The majority of these self-report scales are unidimensional and measure solely intensity. To capture other dimensions of the pain experience such as the meaning ascribed to the affective aspects of pain, projective techniques or clinical interviews can be used.

Today, clinicians and researchers can decide among a multitude of measures and how to use them conjunctively. Yet, information is lacking on how to integrate data from different sources, especially in those cases when the findings are contradictory or inconclusive. The most typical constellation is the one in which the patient's pain behavior seems to be exaggerated in light of only minimal or no findings suggesting organic pathology. Fortunately, more sophisticated biomedical assessment methods are now available to establish the nature and extent of pathology and to determine the patient's degree of physcial impairment. Using these new technologies might reduce the number of patients who would have been falsely diagnosed with a "psychogenic pain disorder" because no organic pathology was found that could account for the pain. Despite these advances in biomedical procedures, for some patients the discrepancies between "objective" physical findings and subjective pain experience and disability will remain.

Regardless of whether organic pathology can be diagnosed or not, an accurate assessment of pain is the prerequisite to the development and the evaluation of more effective pain management in children. When attempting to identify appropriate targets for intervention, it is necessary to consider additional factors that influence the experience of pain and the ways of coping with pain: the nature of pain as acute or chronic, whether pain results from trauma, illness, or medical procedures; previous experiences with painful events; and to which extent the pain is perceived by the individual as controllable. The experience of pain and ways of coping with pain are also influenced by a number of additional factors that need to be considered: the meaning ascribed to the pain. In assessing pain in pediatric patients, the cognitive-developmental level of the child becomes an additional dimension.

Most importantly, it appears that pain in children has become the object of study in its own right. The burgeoning literature that we have reviewed suggests a growing complexity and sophistication in the studies conducted and increasing interdisciplinary application and cooperation in treatment of pediatric pain.

REFERENCES

Abu-Saad, H. (1984). Assessing children's responses to pain. *Pain, 19,* 63–171.

Abu-Saad, H., & Holzemer, W. (1981). Measuring children's self-assessment of pain. *Issues in Comprehensive Nursing, 5,* 337–349.

van Aken, M. A. G., van Lieshout, C. F. M., Katz, E. R., & Heezen, T. J. M. (1989). Development of behavioral distress in reaction to acute pain in two cultures. *Journal of Pediatric Psychology, 14,* 421–432.

Anand, K. J. S., & Aynsley-Green, A. (1985). Metabolic and endocrine effects of surgical ligation of patent ductus arteriosus in the human preterm neonate: Are there implications for further improvement of postoperative outcome? *Mod. Probl. Paediatr., 23,* 143–157.

Anand, K. J. S., Sippell, W. G., & Aynsley-Green, A. (1987a). Randomized trial of fentanyl anaesthesia in preterm babies undergoing surgery: Effects on the stress response. *Lancet, i,* 62–65.

Anand, K. J. S., Sippell, W. G., & Aynsley-Green, A. (1987b). Does the newborn infant require anaesthesia during surgery? Answers from a randomized trial of halothane anaesthesia. *Vth World Congress on Pain,* Hamburg. Pain suppl. *4,* S451.

Angell, M. (1982). The quality of mercy. *New England Journal of Medicine, 306,* 98–99.

Apley, J., & Hale, B. (1973). Children with recurrent abdominal pain: How do they grow up? *British Medical Journal, 3,* 7–9.

Attia, J., Amiel-Tison, C., Mayer, M., Shnider, S., & Barrier, G. (1987). Measurement of postoperative pain and narcotic administration in infants using a new clinical scoring system. *Anesthesiology, 67,* A532.

Avery, M. E., & First, L. R. (1989). *Pediatric medicine.* Baltimore: Williams & Wilkins.

Barr, R. G., Kramer, M. S., Leduc, D. G., Boisjoly, C., McVey, L., & Pless, I. B. (1987). Validation of a parental diary of infant cry/fuss behavior by a 24-hour voice-activated infant recording (VAR) system. Unpublished manuscript.

Beecher, H. K. (1957). The measurement of pain. *Pharmacology Review, 9,* 59–209.

Berde, C. B., Lacouture, P. G., Masek, B. J., Sethna, N. F., & Shannon, M. (1987). Initial experience with a multidisciplinary pain treatment service. *Pain,* Suppl. *4,* S99.

Berde, C. B., Sethna, N. F., & Anand, K. J. S. (1989).

Pediatric pain management. In Gregory (Ed.), *Pediatric anesthesia* (pp. 679–727). New York: Livingstone.

Beyer, J. E., & Aradine, C. R. (1986). Content validity of an instrument to measure young children's perceptions of the intensity of their pain. *Journal of Pediatric Nursing, 1*, 386–395.

Beyer, J. E., & Aradine, C. R. (1988). The convergent and discriminant validity of a self-report measure of pain intensity for children. *Children's Health Care, 16*, 274–282.

Beyer, J. E., DeGood, D. E., Ashley, L. C., & Russell, G. A. (1983). Patterns of postoperative anagesic use with adults and children following cardiac surgery. *Pain, 17*, 71–81.

Beyer, J. E., & Knapp, T. (1986). Methodological issues in the measurement of children's pain. *Children's Health Care, 14*, 233–241.

Beyer, J. E., McGrath, P. J., & Berde, C. B. (in press). Discordance between self-report and behavior pain measures in 3–7 year old following surgery. *Journal of Pain and Symptom Management*.

Bibace, R., & Walsh, M. E. (1979). Developmental stages of children's conceptualizations of illness. In G. C. Stone, F. Cohen, & N. E. Adler (Eds.), *Health psychology: A handbook* (pp. 285–301). San Francisco: Jossey & Bass.

Bille, B. (1962). Migraine in school children. *Acta paediatrica Scandinavica, 51*, Suppl., 1–151.

Broadman, L., Hannallah, R., Belman, A., Elder, P., Ruttimann, U., & Epstein, B. (1987). Post-circumcision pain: A prospective evaluation of subcutaneous ring block of the penis. *Anesthesiology, 67*, 399–402.

Broadman, L., Rice, L., & Hannallah, R. (1988). Evaluation of an objective pain scale for infants and children. *Regional Anesthesia, 13*(1S), 45.

Broome, M. E., & Endsley, R. (1989). Parent and child behavior during immunization. *Pain, 37*, 85–92.

Brown, G. K., & Nicassio, P. M. (1987). Development of a questionnaire for the assessment of active and passive coping strategies in chronic pain patients. *Pain, 31*, 53–64.

Brown, J. M., O'Keefe, J., Sanders, S. H., & Baker, B. (1986). Developmental changes in children's cognition to stressful and painful situations. *Journal of Pediatric Psychology, 11*, 343–357.

Burokas, L. (1985). Factors affecting nurses' decisions to medicate pediatric patients after surgery. *Heart and Lung, 14*, 373–376.

Burstein, S., & Meichenbaum, D. (1979). The work of worrying in children undergoing surgery. *Journal of Abnormal Child Psychology, 7*, 121–132.

Bush, J. P., Holmbeck, G. N., & Cockrell, J. L. (1989). Pattern of PRN Analgesic drug administration in children following elective surgery. *Journal of Pediatric Psychology, 14*, 449–462.

Bush, J. P. (in press). Understanding pediatric pain: a developmental perspective. In: T.W. Miller (Ed.), *Chronic pain: Issues in health care management*, Vol. 2 (pp. 1121–1167). Madison, CT: International Universities.

Cassidy, J. T. (1982). Definition and classification of rheumatic diseases in children. In: J. T. Cassidy (Ed.), *Textbook of pediatric rheumatology* (pp. 1–13). New York: John Wiley & Sons.

Chapman, C. R., & Turner, J. A. (1986). Psychological control of acute pain in medical settings. *Journal of Pain and Symptom Management, 1*, 9–20.

Christensen, M. F., & Mortensen, O. (1975). Long-term prognosis in children with recurrent abdominal pain. *Archives of Diseases in Children, 50*, 110–114.

Clifton, R. K., Graham, F. K., & Hatton, H. M. (1968). Newborn heart-rate response and response habituation as a function of stimulus duration. *Journal of Experimental Child Psychology, 6*, 265–278.

Cohen, F. L. (1980). Postsurgical pain relief: Patients' status and nurses' medication choices. *Pain, 9*, 265–274.

Craig, K. D. (1983). Modeling and social learning factors in chronic pain. In J. J. Bonica (Ed.), *Advances in pain research and therapy*, Vol. 5. New York: Raven Press.

Craig, K. D., Grunau, R. V. E., & Branson, S. M. (1988). Age-related aspects of pain in children (pp. 317–328). In R. Dubner, G. F. Gebhardt & M. R. Bond (Eds.), *Proceedings of the Fifth World Congress on Pain*. Amsterdam: Elsevier.

Dunn, J. (1977). *Distress and Discomfort*. Cambridge, MA: Harvard University Press.

Dunn-Geier, B. J., McGrath, P. J., Rourke, B. P., Latter, J., & D'Astous, J. (1986). Adolescent chronic pain: The ability to cope, *Pain, 26*, 23–32.

Eckman, K., & Friesen, W. V. (1978). *The Facial Action Coding System (FACS)*. Palo Alto, CA: Consulting Psychology Press.

Eland, J. M., & Anderson, J. E. (1977). The Experience of pain in children. In: A. Jacox (Ed.). *Pain: a source book for nurses and other professionals* (pp. 453–473). Boston: Little, Brown.

Feldman, W., Rosser, W., & McGrath, P. (1987). *Primary medical care of children and adolescents*. New York: Oxford University Press.

Fernandez, E., & Turk, D. C. (1989). The utility of cognitive coping strategies for altering pain perception: A meta-analysis. *Pain, 38*, 123–135.

Fordyce, W. E. (1976). *Behavioral methods for chronic pain and illness*. St. Louis: C V Mosby.

Fordyce, W. E. (1988). Pain and suffering. A reappraisal. *American Psychologist, 43*, 4, 276–283.

Franck, L. S. (1986). A new method to quantitatively describe pain behavior in infants. *Nursing Research, 35*, 28–31.

Gaffney, A. (1988). How children describe pain: A study of words and analogies used by 5–14-year-olds. In R. Dubner, G. F. Gebhart, & M. R. Bond (Eds.), *Proceed-*

ings of the Fifth World Congress of Pain (pp. 341–347). Amsterdam: Elsevier.

Gaffney, A., & Dunne, E. A. (1986). Developmental aspects of children's definitions of pain. *Pain, 26*, 105–117.

Gauvain-Piquard, A., Rodary, C., Rezvani, A., & Lemerle. J. (1987). Pain in children aged 2–6 years: A new observational rating scale elaborated in a pediatric oncology unit—Preliminary report. *Pain, 31*, 177–188.

Golub, H. L., & Corwin, M. J. (1985). A physioacoustic model of the infant cry (pp. 59–82). In B. M. Lester and C. F. Z. Boukydis (Eds.), *Infant crying: Theoretical and research perspectives.* New York: Plenum Press.

Gonzalez, J. C., Routh, D. K., Saab, P. G., Armstrong, F. D., Shifman, L., Guerra, E., & Fawcett, N. (1989). Effects of parent presence on children's reactions to injections: Behavioral, physiological, and subjective aspects. *Journal of Pediatric Psychology, 14*, 3, 449–462.

Gracely, R. H. (1984). Subjective quantification of pain perception (pp. 371–387). In B. Bromm (Ed.), *Pain measurement in Man. Neurophysiological correlates of pain.* Amsterdam: Elsevier.

Greipp, M., & Thomas, A. (1989). Reflex sympathetic dystrophy pain in children. Abstracts (p. 31). *First European Conference on Pain in Children.* Maastricht, Netherlands.

Gross, A. M., Stern, R. M., Levin, R. B., Dale, J., & Wojnilower, D. A. (1983). The effect of mother-child separation on the behavior of children experiencing a diagnostic medical procedure. *Journal of Consulting and Clinical Psychology, 51*, 783–785.

Grunau, R. V. E., & Craig, K. D. (1987). Pain expression in neonates: Facial action and cry. *Pain, 28*, 395–410.

Harpin, V. A., & Rutter, N. (1982). Development of emotional sweating in the newborn infant. *Archives of Disease in Childhood, 57*, 691–695.

Hester, N. (1979). The preoperational child's reaction to immunizations. *Nursing Research, 28*, 250–254.

Hodson, C. J. (1984). Assessing and managing pain in children and adults from a nursing perspective. Master's thesis, Yale University, New Haven, CT.

Izard, C. E., Huebner, R. R., Resser, D., McGiness, G. C., & Dougherty, L. M. (1980). The infants ability to produce discrete emotional expressions. *Developmental Psychology, 16*, 132–140.

Jay, S. M. (1988). Invasive medical procedures. Psychological intervention and assessment. In D. K. Routh (Ed.), *Handbook of Pediatric Psychology* (pp. 401–425). New York: Guilford Press.

Jay, S. M., & Elliott, C. H. (1984). Behavioral observation scale for measuring children's distress: The effects of increased methodological rigor. *Journal of Consulting and Clinical Psychology, 52*, 6, 1106–1107.

Jay, S. M., Elliott, C. H., Katz, E., & Siegel, S. E. (1987). Cognitive-behavioral and pharmacologic interventions for children's distress during painful medical procedures. *Journal of Consulting and Clinical Psychology, 55*, 6, 860–865.

Jay, S. M., Ozolins, M., Elliott, C. H., & Caldwell, S. (1983). Assessment of children's distress during painful medical procedures. *Health Psychology, 2*, 133–147.

Jeans, M. E. (1983). Pain in children: A neglected area. In P. Firestone, P. J. McGrath, & W. Feldman (Eds.), *Advances in Behavioral Medicine for Children and Adolescents* (pp. 23–38). Hillsdale, NJ: Lawrence Erlbaum Associates.

Jeans, M. E. (1984). Pain in children. Breakfast session. *4th World Congress on Pain*, Seattle, WA.

Jensen, M. P., Karoly, P., & Braver S. (1986). The measurement of clinical pain intensity: a comparison of six methods. *Pain, 27*, 117–126.

Johnston, C. C., & Strada, M. E. (1986). Acute pain response in infants: a multidimensional description. *Pain, 24*, 373–382.

Karoly, K. (1988). Pain Assessment in children I. Concepts and measurement strategies. In K. Karoly (Ed.). *Handbook of Child Health Assessment. Biopsychosocial perspectives.* New York: John Wiley & Sons.

Katz, E. R., Kellerman, J., & Siegel, S. E. (1980). Behavioral distress in children with cancer undergoing medical procedures: developmental considerations. *Journal of Consulting and Clinical Psychology, 48*, 356–365.

Keefe, F. J., & Block, A. R. (1982). Development of an observation method for assessing pain behavior in chronic low back pain patients. *Behavior Therapy, 13*, 363–375.

Kurylyszyn, N., McGrath, P. J., Cappelli, M., & Humphreys, P. (1987). Children's drawings: What can they tell us about intensity of pain? *Clinical Journal of Pain, 2*, 155–158.

Lavigne, J. L., Schulein, M. J., & Hahn, Y. S. (1986). Psychological aspects of painful medical conditions in children. I. Developmental aspects and assessment. *Pain, 27*, 133–146.

Lazarus, R. S., & Folkman, S. (1984). *Stress, appraisal and coping* (pp. 141–142). New York: Springer.

LeBaron, L., & Zeltzer, L. (1984). Assessment of acute pain and anxiety in children and adolescents by self-reports, observer reports, and a behavioral checklist. *Journal of Consulting and Clinical Psychology, 52*, 729–738.

LeBaron, L. Zeltzer, L., & Fanurik, D. (1989). An investigation of cold pressor pain in children (part I). *Pain, 37*, 161–171.

Lemaire, F., D'Herouville, A., Piquard-Gauvain, A., & Flamant, F. (1987). Painful procedures in children: Pain evaluation by the child himself. *Pain.* Suppl. 4, S98.

Lester, B. M. (1984). A biosocial model of infant crying. In L. P. Lipsitt (Ed.), *Advances in infancy research*, Vol. 3, (pp. 167–212). Norwood, NJ: Ablex.

Lollar, D. J., Smits, S. J., & Patterson, D. L. (1982). Assessment of pediatric pain: An empirical perspective. *Journal of Pediatric Psychology, 7*, 267–277.

Margolis, R. B., Chibnall, J. T., & Tait, R. C. (1988). Test-retest reliability of the pain drawing instrument. *Pain, 33*, 49–51.

Marks, R. M., & Sachar, E. J. (1973). Undertreatment of medical inpatients with narcotic analgesics. *Annals of Internal Medicine, 78*, 173–181.

Mather, L., & Mackie, J. (1983). The incidence of postoperative pain in children. *Pain, 15*, 271–282.

McDaniel, L. K., Anderson, K. O., Bradley, L. A., Young, L. D., Turner, R. A., Agudelo, C. A., & Keefe, F. J. (1986). Development of an observation method for assessing pain behavior in rheumatoid arthritis patients. *Pain, 24*, 165–184.

McGrath, P. A. (1987). An assessment of children's pain: a review of behavioral, physiological and direct scaling techniques. *Pain, 31*, 147–176.

McGrath, P. A. (1990). *Pain in children. Nature, assessment and treatment*. New York: Guilford Press.

McGrath, P. A., deVeber, L. L., & Hearn, M. T. (1985). Multidimensional pain assessment in children. In H. L. Fields, R. Dubner, F. Cervoro (Eds.), *Advances in pain research and therapy* (pp. 387–393). New York: Raven.

McGrath, P. A., Johnson, G., Goodman, J. T., Schillinger, J., Dunn, J., & Chapman, J. (1985). The CHEOPS: A behavioral scale to measure post-operative pain in children. In H. L. Fields, R. Dubner & F. Cervero (Eds.), *Advances in pain research and therapy* (pp. 395–402). New York: Raven.

McGrath, P. J., Vair, C., McGrath, M., Unruh, E., & Schnurr, R. (1984). Pediatric nurses' perception of pain experienced by children and adults. *Nursing Papers, 16*, 34–39.

McGrath, P. J., & Unruh, A. M. (1987). *Pain in children and adolescents*. Amsterdam: Elsevier.

McGraw, M. B. (1945). *The neuromuscular maturation of the human infant*. New York: Hafner.

Melamed, B. G., & Siegel, L. J. (Eds.). (1980). *Behavioral medicine*, Vol. 6. *Practical applications in health care*. New York: Springer.

Mersky, H. (1979). Pain terms: A list with definitions and notes on usage: recommended by the IASP Subcommittee on Taxonomy. *Pain, 6*, 249.

Melzack, R. (1975). The McGill Pain Questionnaire: major properties and scoring methods. *Pain, 1*, 277–299.

Melzack, R. (Ed.). (1983). *Pain measurement and assessment*. New York: Raven Press.

Milling, L. S., Shaw, W. J., & Durniat, K. (1989). Behavioral management of chronic back pain in children and adolescents. In M. C. Roberts & C. E. Walker (Eds.), *Casebook of child and pediatric psychology* (pp. 380–403). New York: Guilford Press.

Muller, E., Hollien, H., & Murry, T. (1974). Perceptual responses to infant crying: Identification of cry types. *Journal of Child Language, 1*, 89–95.

Molsberry, D. (1979). Young children's subjective quantifications of pain following surgery. Unpublished master's thesis. University of Iowa, Iowa City.

Oster, J., & Nielsen, A. (1972). Growing pains: A clinical investigation of a school population. *Acta paeditrica scandinavica, 61*, 329–334.

Owens, M. E. (1986). Assessment of infant pain in the clinical settings. *Journal of Pain Symptom Management, 1*, 29–31.

Perry, S., & Heidrich, G. (1982). Management of pain during debridement: A survey of U. S. burn units. *Pain, 13*, 267–280.

Peterson, L. (1989). Coping by children undergoing stressful medical procedures: Some conceptual, methodological and therapeutic issues. *Journal of Consulting and Clinical Psychology, 57*, 380–387.

Peterson, L., & Toler, S. M. (1986). An information seeking disposition in child surgery patients. *Health Psychology, 5*, 343–358.

Porter, F. L., Miller, R. H., & Marshall, R. E. (1986). Neonatal pain cries: Effect of circumcision on acoustic features and perceived urgency. *Child Development, 57*, 790–802.

Price, D. D., McGrath, P. A., Rafii, A., & Buckingham, B. (1983). The validation of visual analogue scales for chronic and experimental pain. *Pain, 17*, 45–56.

Purcell-Jones, G., Dormon, F., & Sumner, E. (1988). Paediatric anaesthetists' perceptions of neonatal and infant pain. *Pain, 33*, 181–187.

Rasnake, L. K., & Linscheid, T. R. (1989). Anxiety reduction in children receiving medical care: Developmental considerations. *Developmental and Behavioral Pediatrics, 10*, 169–175.

Rich, E. C., Marshall, R. E., & Volpe, J. J. (1974). The normal neonatal response to pinprick. *Developmental Medicine and Child Neurology, 16*, 432–434.

Ross, D. M., & Ross, S. A. (1984). Childhood pain: The school-aged child's viewpoint. *Pain, 20*, 179–191.

Ross, D. M., & Ross, S. A. (1988). *Childhood pain: current issues, research, and management*. Baltimore: Urban & Schwarzenberg.

Russo, D. C. (1986). Chronicity and normalcy as the psychological basis for reseach and treatment in chronic disease in children. In N. Krasnegor, J. Aresteh & M. Cataldo (Eds.), *Child health behavior. A behavioral pediatrics perspective* (pp. 521–536). New York: John Wiley & Sons.

Russo, D. C., Bird, B. L., & Masek, B. J. (1980). Assessment issues in behavioral medicine. *Behavioral Assessment, 2*, 1–18.

Russo, D. C., Hamada, R. S., & Marques, D. (1988). Linking assessment and treatment in pediatric health psychology. In K. Karoly (Ed.), *Handbook of child health assessment. Biopsychosocial perspectives* (pp. 30–52). New York: John Wiley & Sons.

Savedra, M., Tesler, M., Ward, J., Holzemer, W., & Wilkie, D. (1987). Children's preference for pain intensity scales. *Pain*, Suppl. 4, S234.

Saylor, C. F., Pallmeyer, T. P., Finch, Jr., A. J., Eason, L., Trieber, F., & Folger, C. (1987). Predictors of psychological distress in hospitalized children. *Journal American Academy Child Adolescent Psychiatry, 26*, 232–236.

Schaller, J. G. (1984). Chronic childhood arthritis and the spondylarthropathies. In A. Calin (Ed.), *Spondylarthropathies* (pp. 187–208). New York: Grune & Stratton.

Schechter, N. L., & Allen, D. A. (1986). Physicians' attitudes toward pain in children. *Developmental and Behavioral Pediatrics, 7*, 350–353.

Schechter, N. L., Allen, D. A., & Hanson, K. (1986). Status of pediatric pain control: A comparison of hospital analgesic usage in children and adults. *Pediatrics, 77*, 11–15.

Scott, R. (1978). It hurts red: A preliminary study of children's perception of pain. *Perceptual and Motor Skills, 47*, 787–791.

Scott, J., & Huskisson, E. C. (1979). Vertical and horizontal visual analogue scales. *Annals of the Rheumatic Diseases, 38*, 560–567.

Shaw, E. G., & Routh, D. K. (1982). Effect of mother presence on the children's reaction to aversive procedures. *Journal of Pediatric Psychology, 7*, 33–42.

Siegel, L. J. (1981). Naturalistic study of coping strategies in children facing medical strategies. Paper presented at the meeting of the Southeastern Psychological Association, Atlanta, GA.

Smith, K. E., Ackerson, J. D., & Blotcky, A. D. (1989). Reducing stress during invasive medical procedures: Relating behavioral interventions with preferred coping style. *Journal of Pediatric Psychology, 14*, 405–420.

Spirito, A., Stark, L., & Williams, C. (1988). Development of brief coping checklist for use in pediatric populations. *Journal of Pediatric Psychology, 13*, 555–574.

Sriwatanakul, K., Kelvie, W., Lasagna, L., Calimlim, J. F., Weis, O. F., & Mehta, G. (1983). Studies with different types of visual analog scales for measurement of pain. *Clinical Pharmacology Therapy, 34*, 234–239.

Stark, L., Spirito, A., Williams, C., & Guevremont, D. (1989). Common problems and coping strategies. I: Findings with normal adolescents. *Journal of Abnormal Child Psychology, 17*, 203–212.

Szyfelbein, S. K., Osgood, P. F., & Carr, D. B. (1985). The assessment of pain and plasma beta-endorphin immunoactivity in burned children. *Pain, 22*, 173–182.

Tesler, M., Savedra, M., Ward, J. A., Holzemer, W. L., & Wilkie, D. (1988). Children's language of pain (pp. 348–352). In R. Dubner, G. F. Gebhart, & M. R. Bond (Eds.), *Proceedings of the Fifth World Congress of Pain*. Amsterdam: Elsevier.

Thompson, K. L., Varni, J. W., & Hanson, V. (1987). Comprehensive assessment of pain in juvenile rheumatoid arthritis. *Journal of Pediatric Psychology, 12*, 241–255.

Tunks, E., & Bellissimo, A. (1988). Coping with the coping concept: A brief comment. *Pain, 34*, 171–174.

Turk, D. C., & Flor, H. (1987). Pain > pain behaviors: the utility and limitations of the pain behavior construct. *Pain, 31*, 277–295.

Unruh, A., McGrath, P. J., Cunningham, S. J., & Humphreys, P. (1983). Children's drawings of pain. *Pain, 17*, 385–392.

Varni, J. W. (1983). *Clinical behavioral pediatrics: An interdisciplinary biobehavioral approach*. New York: Pergamon Press.

Varni, J. W., Katz, E. R., & Dash, J. (1982). Behavioral and neurochemical aspects of pediatric pain. In D. C. Russo & J. W. Varni (Eds.), *Behavioral pediatrics: Research and practice* (pp. 177–224). New York: Plenum Press.

Varni, J. W., Thompson, K. L., & Hanson, V. (1987). The Varni/Thompson Pediatric Pain Questionnaire: Chronic musculoskeletal pain in juvenile rheumatoid arthritis. *Pain, 28*, 27–38.

Wasz-Hockert, O., Lind, J., Vuorenkoski, V., Partanen, T., & Valaane, E. (1968). The infant cry: A spectographic and auditory analysis. *Clinical Developmental Medicine, 29*, 9–42.

Webb, C. J., Stergios, D. A., & Rodgers, B. M. (1989). Patient-controlled analgesia as postoperative treatment for children. *Journal of Pediatric Nursing, 4*, 162–171.

Williamson, P. S., & Williamson, M. L. (1983). Physiologic stress reduction by a local anesthetic during newborn circumcision. *Pediatrics, 71*, 36–40.

Zeltzer, L. K. (Ed.). (1989). Pediatric pain: Diagnosis, assessment, and management. *Pediatrician, 16*, 1–2.

Zeltzer, L. K., LeBaron, S., Richie, D. M., Reed, D., Schoolfield, J., & Prihoda, T. J. (1988). Can children understand and use a rating scale to quantify somatic symptoms? Assessment and vomiting as a model. *Journal of Consulting and Clinical Psychology, 56*, 567–572.

CHAPTER 27

PHYSICAL ABUSE AND NEGLECT

Robert T. Ammerman

DESCRIPTION OF THE PROBLEMS

It is a sign of the dramatically increased awareness of child maltreatment that a chapter of this kind is included in a book on child psychopathology. Retrospective studies of child and adult patient populations attest to the widespread occurrence of child abuse and neglect in clinical samples (Ammerman, Hersen, Van Hasselt, McGonigle, & Lubetsky, 1989; Monane, Leichter, & Lewis, 1984). Moreover, the association between child maltreatment and psychopathology is robust (see review by Ammerman, Cassisi, Hersen, & Van Hasselt, 1986). Abused and neglected children exhibit a variety of behavioral and emotional disturbances, including aggressiveness (Hoffman-Plotkin & Twentyman, 1984), depression (Kazdin, Moser, Colbus, & Bell, 1985), low self-esteem (Green, 1978), and social withdrawal (Bousha & Twentyman, 1984). The likelihood of a clinician seeing a child with a current or past history of maltreatment is great.

It is imperative, therefore, that all practitioners who work with children be familiar with the available assessment techniques and intervention approaches for abuse and neglect.

Accurate statistics on the incidence and prevalence of maltreatment have eluded epidemiologists. In large part, this is because of the almost insurmountable difficulties in arriving at a universal consensus for an operational definition of abuse and neglect. Child maltreatment is inextricably embedded in cultural and community values and perspectives. Starr, Dubowitz, and Bush (1990) point out that there are four factors that influence criteria of maltreatment (see also Garbarino & Gilliam, 1980). These are (1) intentionality, (2) effect of the act on the child, (3) society's value judgment regarding the act, and (4) the standard employed by society in making the judgment. Garbarino (1990) further notes that community standards of adequate child care are continually changing, thus precluding establishment of a durable definition of

---

Preparation of this paper was facilitated in part by grants from the Vira I. Heinz Endowment and the National Institute on Disabilities and Rehabilitation Research (No. G008720109). However, the opinions presented herein do not necessarily reflect the position of policy of these agencies and no official endorsement should be inferred.

abuse and neglect. Confusion over operational definitions has greatly contributed to the sometimes conflicting findings reported in the literature, as well as to the impediments faced in delineating the etiology and consequences of maltreatment.

Despite these shortcomings, several large-scale epidemiological studies have been conducted that have attempted to ascertain the incidence and prevalence of abuse and neglect. In their thorough review of the epidemiology of maltreatment, Starr et al. (1990) describe five levels of population samples examined in epidemiological investigations (NCCAN, 1988): (a) cases reported to child protective services; (b) maltreated children referred to other agencies with investigative powers (e.g., police); (c) cases detected by noninvestigative service agencies (e.g., hospitals, schools); (d) cases recognized by laypeople; and (e) unidentified cases. Children represented in levels 2 through 4 may not come to the attention of child protective service agencies. Separate examination of these disparate samples yields divergent findings about the incidence and prevalence of abuse and neglect.

One of the most comprehensive epidemiological investigations is the National Incidence Study conducted in 1986 (NCCAN, 1988). This study examined the incidence of child maltreatment in levels 1 through 3. Results indicated that more than 1.5 million children (25 per 1,000 children in the population) suffered physical abuse, sexual abuse, neglect, or psychological abuse. It is likely that these data underestimate the true incidence of maltreatment given the omission of levels 4 and 5. However, this represents one of the most thorough surveys of its kind and is an indispensable source of information on the incidence of child abuse and neglect. (For a more in-depth discussion of the epidemiology of child maltreatment, see Starr et al., 1990).

The tragedy of child maltreatment is reflected in the numerous dysfunctional elements exhibited by abused and neglected children and their families. (This chapter examines the literature on child physical abuse and neglect. The word *maltreatment* is used to encompass these phenomena. Sexual abuse and psychological maltreatment, per se, are not considered directly, although some of the assessment strategies described are also applicable for these populations.) As previously mentioned, the child is likely to display symptoms of internalizing or externalizing behavior disorders. These may occur in conjunction with the physical sequelae of maltreatment, such as broken bones, internal organ injuries, and brain damage (see Briggs, 1991). Parental perpetrators, too, evince symptoms of maladjustment. Maltreating parents have been found to exhibit low self-esteem (Lahey, Conger, Atkeson, & Treiber, 1984), be socially isolated (Salzinger, Kaplan, & Artemyeff, 1983), have poor parenting skills (Trickett & Kuczynski, 1986), have unrealistic expectations regarding child behavior (Rosenberg & Reppucci, 1983), and have greater perceived life stress (Mash, Johnston, & Kovitz, 1983) when contrasted to their nonabusing counterparts. Neglectful parents, in turn, are described as isolated, lonely, immature, and withdrawn (Polansky, Ammons, & Gaudin, 1985). Furthermore, maltreating parents and their children have inadequate social relationships. Neglectful families are characterized by a paucity of parent-child interactions (Bousha & Twentyman, 1984). Abusive parents, on the other hand, have a greater proportion of negative to positive interactions with their children than nonabusive parents (see Wolfe, 1987).

In summary, these findings demonstrate that families engaged in child abuse and neglect exhibit pervasive maladjustment. Indeed, maltreatment is best conceptualized as a symptom of broader family disturbance. Specific acts of abuse and neglect combine with other aspects of family disturbance to negatively affect the child's development. Thus, in the case of child abuse and neglect, assessment and treatment *must* be multimodal and comprehensive to encompass the variety of possible dysfunctions.

MULTIMODAL ASSESSMENT

Child abuse and neglect are complex constructs with numerous psychosocial correlates and predictors. Because any one or a combination of contributing factors may be present, the goals of a multimodal assessment are to identify etiological and maintaining variables or effects of maltreatment that should be targeted for intervention (see Ammerman, 1989; Walker, Bonner, & Kaufman, 1988). Unfortunately, the assessment process is impeded by the fact that abuse and neglect are socially undesirable and usually private acts. As a result, they are rarely available for direct observation and careful scrutiny. It is for this reason that the assessment of maltreatment typically relies upon indirect measures of a variety of areas of individual and family functioning (Wolfe & Bordeau, 1987).

Before examining specific assessment procedures, it is useful to briefly review current etiological models of abuse and neglect. The multimodal assessment of maltreatment stems directly from these models. They are noteworthy in their rejection of unidimensional explanations and emphasis on the fact that abuse and neglect arise from the (often unique) interaction of several causative variables.

Theoretical Overview

Describing the processes by which abuse and neglect develop and are maintained has proven to be a difficult task. No single parent, child, or situational factor is consistently associated with maltreatment. Therefore, multivariate models have understandably gained in favor as research on child abuse and neglect has progressed. Earlier conceptualizations proposed single factor explanations for maltreatment. For example, the Psychopathology Model (e.g., Steele & Pollock, 1968) posited that parental psychopathology (i.e., personality disorder, psychosis) was the primary cause of mistreatment. Recent research, however, has failed to identify severe psychopathology in most abusive parents (see Wolfe, 1985). The Social-Cultural model, on the other hand, implicates societal causes (poverty, unemployment, educational disadvantage) in maltreatment. There is compelling evidence that socioeconomic stress is a major contributor to abuse and neglect (e.g., Garbarino, 1976). However, the multidimensional nature of maltreatment defies such relatively simplistic etiological models.

The dynamic interactions between causative variables are reflected in more recent theoretical proposals (see Ammerman, 1990). The Ecological Model describes four levels of influence that work together to bring about maltreatment (Belsky, 1980). These levels are the ontogenetic (e.g., parental IQ), microsystem (e.g., marital distress), exosystem (e.g., unemployment), and macrosystem (e.g., societal acceptance of corporal punishment). Cicchetti and Rizley (1981) expanded this conceptualization in their Transactional Model of maltreatment. As with the Ecological Model, the Transactional Model underscores the importance of multiple variables in the etiology of abuse and neglect. The authors further delineate potentiating factors (those that increase the probability of maltreatment) and compensatory factors (those that decrease the likelihood of abuse or neglect). These factors, in turn, are categorized as enduring (i.e., they cannot be changed, such as past history of maltreatment or parental IQ) or transient (i.e., temporary situations or states, such as unemployment). The Transitional Model (Wolfe, 1987), on the other hand, proposes a continuum of parenting in which abuse is viewed as an extreme form of deviant parent–child interaction. Specifically, the family moves through three stages reflecting the increased likelihood of engaging in violent conflict. At each stage, destabilizing and compensatory elements merge together to propel or prevent advancement to the next stage.

Format of Assessment

As evidenced by the aforementioned theoretical formulations, it is imperative that the assessment of abuse and neglect consider several areas of individual and family functioning. Moreover, within each unit of measurement (i.e., individual, dyadic, family), numerous domains (e.g., psychopathology, social adjustment, parenting) are of interest to the clinician. Behavioral, cognitive, and affective elements need to be evaluated. All of these may differentially play a role in family dysfunction in general, and abuse and neglect in particular.

Ideally, an assessment consists of an observation of all family members in the natural home environment. Circumstances, however, often preclude such an arrangement. In some cases, child protective service agencies will have removed the perpetrator or the child from the home before their referral for treatment. Also, perpetrators may be especially defensive and reluctant to permit more intrusive assessment procedures. Logistical considerations may further prohibit direct observational assessments.

In the absence of (or in addition to) a thorough home assessment, the clinician should evaluate the family using a combination of approaches. Self-report instruments, in-office observations, interviews, and psychometric measures completed by others (e.g., teachers) are all critical components of a multimodal assessment. No single type of assessment approach is satisfactory in isolation in that each has limitations. For example, self-report indices are subject to negative biases in abusive mothers (Reid, Kavanagh, & Baldwin, 1987). Interviews are prone to distortion and confabulation. Simulated in-office observations can be so removed from the natural environment that they fail to elicit the parent-child interactional patterns that are of greatest interest. Taken together, these shortcomings in specific assessment techniques highlight the need for multiple measures and approaches in abuse and neglect.

There are three foci of assessment in evaluating child abuse and neglect: the perpetrator, the child victim, and the family. Of these, assessment of the perpetrator is most critical in stopping maltreatment and reducing the likelihood of recidivism. Interactions between family members are also important in identifying coercive patterns that may contribute to the escalation of conflict and eventual violence. Family functioning must also be considered within the social and cultural contexts that may predispose the family to maltreatment (e.g., poverty, sanctioning of punitive disciplinary methods). Finally, the child requires careful evaluation. Because the effects of maltreatment vary considerably in terms of type, extent, and severity (see Ammerman et al., 1986; Friedrich & Einbender, 1983), it is probable that the child will require remedial intervention.

The assessment of parent, child, and family functioning is discussed in the following sections. Table 27-1 presents some of the measures and techniques often used in the multimodal assessment of abuse and neglect. These are drawn from both the clinical and research literature. This is not an exhaustive list of the possible measures for maltreatment. On the contrary, the heterogeneous clinical manifestations of abuse and neglect necessitate a broad, flexible, and creative approach to assessment. Rather, the strategies described herein are meant to be representative of the many clinical and research assessment approaches for abuse and neglect.

Assessment of Parents

Although there are several contributing factors to maltreatment, often working concurrently, the perpetrator (most often the parent) is the primary focus of clinical attention. It is through intervention with the parent that abuse and neglect will ultimately be remediated, and adequate care of the child carried out. Thus, parental assessment is of paramount importance in treatment planning. There are seven broad areas of parental functioning that warrant examination: parental knowledge and attitudes, stress, parenting practices and adequacy of care, anger responsivity, social functioning, problem-solving skills, and psychopathology. Each of these is considered in turn.

Parenting Knowledge and Attitudes

Parental attitudes about child-rearing and knowledge of specific parenting practices and normal child development are crucial assessment components. Such measures assist in identifying particular skills deficits, as well as attributions that facilitate violent responses to parent-child conflict. The Knowledge of Behavioral Principles as Applied to Children (KBPAC) (O'Dell, Tarler-Benlolo, & Flynn, 1979) is an excellent measure of parental knowledge of the use of reinforcement, extinction, and punishment. It contains 50 descriptions of problem behaviors in children followed by four possible solutions, one of which is endorsed by the respondent. An advantage of the KBPAC is that it is a rather difficult test (mean in one sample was 24.4, SD = 11.75; see O'Dell, 1988), thus allowing for a wide variability in obtained scores. Its psychometric properties are good, and it is well suited for use with maltreating parents (Kelly, 1983).

The Michigan Screening Profile of Parenting (MSPP) (Helfer, Schneider, & Hoffmeister, 1977) evaluates parenting attitudes and child-rearing problems. It contains 50 items that are summarized in five subscales: relationship with parents, emotional needs met, dealing with others, expectations of children, and coping. Although this instrument is not used as extensively as it once was (as reflected in the recent literature), it remains a good example of a parent screening measure. The MSPP has given way to the rapid proliferation of assessment methods examining more circumscribed aspects of parenting.

The Parent Opinion Questionnaire (POQ) (Twentyman, Plotkin, Dodge, & Rohrbeck, 1981) is an 80-item instrument measuring parental views of the appropriateness of expectations for child behavior. It yields six subscales: self-care, family responsibility and care of siblings, help and affection to parents, leaving children alone, proper behavior and feelings, and punishment. The Parenting Sense of Competence Scale (PSOCS) (Gibaud-Wallston & Wandersman, 1978), on the other hand, taps parental self-esteem and confidence in the parenting role. It consists of 17 items that are endorsed using a 7-point scale (1 = strongly agree, 7 = strongly disagree). Factor analysis has identified two categories in this measure: satisfaction and efficacy (Johnston & Mash, 1989). Summary scores are subsequently derived for the total and the two factors.

Stress

Stress has consistently been implicated in child maltreatment (see Straus, 1980). There is some evidence to suggest that parents who engage in abuse and neglect do not necessarily experience more stressful events than their nonmaltreating counterparts. Rather, they *perceive* these events to be more stressful (Rosenberg & Reppucci, 1983). The assessment of stress is

Table 27-1. Selected list of commonly used measures in the assessment of child abuse and neglect.

MEASURES	AUTHOR(S)	RESPONDENT	TYPE OF ASSESSMENT	AREA EXAMINED
Parental Knowledge and Attitudes				
Knowledge of Behavior Principles as Applied to Children	O'Dell, Tarler-Benlolu, & Flynn, 1979	Parent	Self-report	Parenting knowledge
Michigan Screening Profile of Parenting	Helfer, Schneider, & Hoffmeister, 1977	Parent	Self-report	Parenting attitudes
Parent Opinion Questionnaire	Twentyman, Plotkin, Dodge, & Rohrbeck, 1981	Parent	Self-report	Parenting expectations
Parenting Sense of Competence Scale	Gibaud-Wallston & Wandersman, 1978	Parent	Self-report	Parenting self-efficacy
Stress				
Parenting Stress Index	Abidin, 1986	Parent	Self-report	Parenting stress
Questionnaire on Resources and Stress	Holroyd, 1974	Parent	Self-report	Stress (special-needs children)
Schedule of Recent Experience	Holmes & Rahe, 1967	Parent	Self-report	Stressful life events
Parenting Practices and Adequacy of Care				
Home Observation for Measurement of the Environment Inventory	Caldwell & Bradley, 1984	Parent(s)	Home observation	Adequacy of resources
Maternal History Interview	Altemeier, Vietze, Sherrod, Sandler, Falsey, & O'Connor, 1979	Mother	Interview	Factors associated with maltreatment
Child Abuse and Neglect Interview Schedule	Ammerman, Hersen, & Van Hasselt, 1988b	Parent	Interview	Disciplinary practices and related factors
Checklist for Living Environments to Assess Neglect	Watson-Perczel, Lutzker, Greene, & McGimpsey, 1988	Home	Observation	Adequacy of home cleanliness
Home Accident Prevention Inventory	Tertinger, Greene, & Lutzker, 1984	Home	Observation	Adequacy of home safety
Anger Responsivity				
Novaco Provocation Inventory	Novaco, 1975	Parent	Self-report	Anger responsivity
MacMillan-Olson-Hansen Anger Control Scale	MacMillan, Olson, & Hansen, 1988b	Parent	Self-report	Anger responsivity to child misbehavior
Physiological Arousal	Frodi & Lamb, 1980; Friedrich, Tyler, & Clark, 1985	Parent	Psychophysiological measurements	Reactivity to child behaviors and characteristics
Social Functioning				
Social Network Interview	Salzinger, Kaplan, & Artemyeff, 1983	Parent	Interview	Social network
Social Provisions Scale	Russell, & Cutrona, 1984	Parent	Self-report	Adequacy of social network
Interpersonal Support Evaluation List	Cohen, Mermelstein, Kamarck, & Hoberman, 1985	Parent	Self-report	Social support
Problem-Solving Skills				
Parent Problem-Solving Instrument	Wasik, Bryant, & Fishbein, 1980	Parent	Self-report	Problem-solving skills
Parental Problem-	Hansen, Pallotta,	Parent	Self-report	Problem-solving skills

MEASURES	AUTHOR(S)	RESPONDENT	TYPE OF ASSESSMENT	AREA EXAMINED
Solving Measure	Tishelman, Conaway, & MacMillan, in press			
Home Simulation Assessment	MacMillan, Olson, & Hansen, 1988a	Parent	Analogue simulated observation	Responses to deviant child misbehavior (adult confederate)
Psychopathology				
Child Abuse Potential Inventory	Milner, 1986	Parent	Self-report	Risk for child abuse
Minnesota Multiphasic Personality Inventory	Hathway & McKinley, 1940	Parent	Self-report	Parental psychopathology
Symptom Checklist-90-Revised	Derogatis, 1983	Parent	Self-report	Parental psychopathology
Beck Depression Inventory	Beck, Ward, Mendelsohn, Mock, & Erbaugh, 1961	Parent	Self-report	Parental depression
State-Trait Anxiety Inventory	Spielberger, Gorsuch, & Lushene, 1970	Parent	Self-report	Parental anxiety
Child Adjustment				
Eyberg Child Behavior	Eyberg & Ross, 1978	Parent	Other report	Parent perceptions of child behavior problems
Child Behavior Checklist	Achenbach & Edelbrock, 1983	Parent or teacher	Other report	Child psychopathology and behavior problems
Vineland Adaptive Behavior Scales—Revised	Sparrow, Balla, & Cicchetti, 1984	Parent or teacher	Other report	Child developmental functioning
Family Interactions				
Family Interaction Coding System	Patterson, Ray, Shaw, & Cobb, 1969	Family	Observation	Family interaction patterns
Fagot Interactive Behavior Code	Fagot & Hagan, 1986	Family	Observation	Family interaction patterns
Measure of Maternal Stimulation	Dietrich, Starr, & Kaplan, 1980	Mother and infant	Observation	Quality of maternal stimulation

particularly relevant given that abusive and neglectful parents exhibit poor coping skills (Egeland, Breitenbucher, & Rosenberg, 1980).

One of the most useful measures of parental stress is the Parenting Stress Index (PSI) (Abidin, 1986). The PSI is a carefully developed and especially comprehensive instrument examining stress related to parenting as well as other sources. It is comprised of 126 items that reflect stress associated with the parent-child relationship, and child, parent, and situational characteristics. Scale scores are derived reflecting total stress, life stress during the past year, child domain (adaptability, acceptability, demandingness, mood, distractibility/hyperactivity, reinforces parent), and parent domain (depression, attachment, restriction of role, sense of competence, social isolation, relationship with spouse, and parent health). Normative percentile rankings are available for comparison.

The Questionnaire on Resources and Stress (QRS) (Holroyd, 1974) is a good instrument to evaluate perceived stress in parents of children with disabilities. Because this measure was standardized using children with handicapping conditions, it has greater validity for use with this special population (its utility with multihandicapped children, however, is unclear). Indeed, parents of disabled children routinely obtain elevated scores on self-report indices of stress that were originally developed for nonhandicapped children. Thus, the QRS provides a good basis of comparing stress within disabled populations. The QRS is composed of true-false items. Scale scores are derived that reflect parent-family problems, pessimism, child characteristics, and physical participation. There are shorter versions of the QRS (Friedrich, Greenberg, & Crnic, 1983; Salisbury, 1986) which correlate highly with the longer form.

Measures of overall stress or the occurrence of significant life stressors are a useful adjunct to the examining parenting stress. The PSI contains a life stress subscale. Numerous instruments derived from life stress research can also be employed. The Schedule of Recent Experience (SRE) (Holmes & Rahe, 1967) is one of the most widely used measures of this type. However, numerous other options are available (see Dohrenwend & Dohrenwend, 1981).

Parenting Practices and Adequacy of Care

Because of the private nature of abuse and neglect, indirect methods are needed to examine specific parenting behaviors. In general, there are four strategies that can be used to this end: (1) observation of interactions in the home, (2) observation of simulated interactions in the laboratory or clinic, (3) evaluation of the home environment through observation, and (4) parent interview. The first two approaches are discussed in the section entitled "Family Interactions."

The Home Observation for Measurement of the Environmental Inventory (HOME) (Caldwell & Bradley, 1984) has been utilized in measuring the adequacy of care and stimulation provided to the child by parents. A trained rater enters the home while the child is awake and rates the occurrence or absence of certain situations or family procedures. Items that are unclear are clarified in a brief discussion with parents. There are three versions of the HOME based on age (birth to 3 years old, 3 to 6 years old, and 6 to 10 years old). The number of items ranges from 42 to 59, depending upon the form used, and a variety of subscales are derived reflecting specific aspects of the home environment (e.g., emotional and verbal responsivity of the parent, organizational of physical and temporal environment, warmth and affection, academic stimulation, growth fostering materials, and experiences). The HOME has excellent reliability characteristics and correlates highly with IQ and language development.

Altemeier and his colleagues (Altemeier, O'Connor, Vietze, Sandler, & Sherrod, 1984; Altemeier, Vietze, Sherrod, Sandler, Falsey, & O'Connor, 1979) developed the Maternal History Interview (MHI), a structured interview designed to identify high-risk prenatal mothers. The MHI examines such areas as the mother's childhood nurture, self-image, support available from others, parenting philosophy, attitude about current pregnancy, general health-related problems (e.g., substance abuse), stress, and knowledge and expectations regarding child development. The MHI was constructed based upon retrospective studies of factors related to child abuse. It has a high interrater agreement and is modestly predictive of future mistreatment (Altemeier et al., 1984).

The Child Abuse and Neglect Interview Schedule (CANIS) (Ammerman, Hersen, & Van Hasselt, 1988b) is a semistructured interview that is administered to the parent to derive information about disciplinary practices and related factors. It is approximately 45 minutes in length and is divided into seven sections: demographics, family situations, child care, child behavior problems and disciplinary practices, past history of family violence, sexual abuse, and parent history. An advantage of the CANIS is that it yields information about many aspects of maltreatment, including the use of harsh physical punishment, psychological mistreatment, sexual abuse, and child observation of spouse battering. In its nascent stage (Ammerman, Hersen, & Lubetsky, 1988a), psychometric data on the CANIS are as yet unavailable.

Project 12-Ways (Lutzker & Rice, 1984) has produced two observation instruments suitable for use with neglectful parents. The Checklist for Living Environments to Assess Neglect (CLEAN) (Watson-Perczel, Lutzker, Greene, & McGimpsey, 1988) is used to examine cleanliness in the home. Specific areas in each room are rated according to presence of dirt or organic matter, the number of clothes or linens in contact with the area, and the number of nonclothing items or nonorganic matter touching the area. This measure has excellent reliability characteristics and has been found to be sensitive to changes in cleaning practices following a home cleanliness intervention (Watson-Perczel et al., 1988). Likewise, the Home Accident Prevention Inventory (HAPI) (Tertinger, Greene, & Lutzker, 1984) is used to evaluate home safety in neglectful families. Presence or absence of hazardous items is rated by a home observer involving fire and electrical, suffocation by ingested objects, suffocation by mechanical objects, firearms, and solid and liquid poisons. Both of these measures add considerably to the assessment of neglect.

Anger Responsivity

There is convincing evidence that many abusive parents exhibit high levels of anger reactivity (see Frodi, 1981). It is hypothesized that these parents have difficulty recognizing physiological cues of anger and are more likely to "explode" in response to conflict (Kelly, 1983; Walker et al., 1988). Several measures are available to assess anger responsivity. The Novaco Provocation Inventory (NPI) (Novaco, 1975), originally developed for anger-reactive individuals in general, has also been used with abusive parents. It consists of 80 items reflecting a variety of anger-provoking situations. Respondents endorse each item using a 5-point scale indicating level of anger arousal (1 = very little, 5 = very much). Factor analytic studies have consistently found three factors in the NPI: injustice/unfairness, frustration/clumsiness, and physical affronts (see Novaco, 1988).

MacMillan, Olson, and Hansen (1988b) developed an anger responsivity inventory specifically designed for abusive parents. The MacMillan-Olson-Hansen Anger Control Scale is comprised of 50 child-related problem situations. Each item is endorsed using a 5-point scale reflecting degree of anger evoked. Preliminary research supports the reliability and validity of this measure (MacMillan et al., 1988b).

Clinicians can also monitor physiological reactivity directly. Although this approach has almost exclusively been employed for research purposes (due to equipment needs and logistical difficulties), it has some potential for clinical screening. Frodi and her colleagues (Frodi, 1981) have demonstrated that abusive parents exhibit negative physiological reactions to both crying and positive social behaviors in premature infants. Friedrich, Tyler, and Clark (1985) also used measures of skin conductance, heart rate, and finger blood volume to assess abusive parents' reactions to infant cries. In addition, Wolfe, Fairbank, Kelly, and Bradlyn (1983) monitored physiological reactivity in abusive parents who watched videotapes of child behavioral transgressions.

Social Functioning

Social problems are a common feature of child abuse. There is evidence to suggest that abusive parents have fewer social contacts and more restricted social networks than their nonabusive peers (Salzinger et al., 1983). Likewise, some abusive parents indicate a dissatisfaction with their social network, independent of its size.

Salzinger et al. (1983) developed an especially thorough structured interview designed to measure the size and nature of abusive parents' social networks. The interview, which lasts from 1 to 1½ hours in duration, evaluates social contacts in the following areas: home subnetwork, close family outside the home, distant family outside the home, close and best personal friends, work connections, school connections, neighbors, organizational connections, other friends or acquaintances, and professional caretakers. The parent is asked about the frequency of social contacts and the interconnectedness among contacts. Data are derived from the interview reflecting size and frequency of contacts, as well as interconnectedness (i.e., insularity). Interrater agreement for the interview is high, ranging from 62% to 100%.

The Social Provisions Scale (SPS) (Russell & Cutrona, 1984) provides an excellent summary of the individual's satisfaction with his or her social support system. It contains 24 items that are endorsed using a 7-point scale reflecting the extent to which the statement reflects their social network (1 = not at all true, 7 = completely true). The SPS examines six areas: attachment, social integration, opportunity for nurturance, reassurance of worth, reliable alliance, and guidance. This measure has been widely used in research on social support in general, and it demonstrates good psychometric properties (Cutrona, 1982). The Interpersonal Support Evaluation List (ISEL) (Cohen, Mermelstein, Kamarck, & Hoberman, 1985) also asks the respondent to evaluate adequacy of solid support. It examines the following four constructs: tangible support, appraisal support, self-esteem support, and belonging support.

Problem-Solving Skills

Abusive and neglectful parents often display deficits in problem-solving skills, particularly those involving child situations. The Parent Problem-Solving Instrument (PPSI) (Wasik, Bryant, & Fishbein, 1980, cited in Azar, Robinson, Hekimian, & Twentyman, 1984) contains 10 child problem situations. Parents are asked to generate solutions to these problems, and responses are scored for number of items in which a solution is given, total number of solutions, number of items on which more than one solution is offered, number of solutions in which elaboration occurs, and total number of content categories used. Azar et al. (1984) found deficits in abusive parents when compared with nonabusive parents on this measure.

Hansen, Pallotta, Tishelman, Conaway, and MacMillan (1989) developed a problem-solving assessment measure that examines both child-related and other types of problematic situations. The Parental Problem-Solving Measure (PPSM) subsumes five areas: child behavior and child management, anger and stress control, financial, child care resources, and interpersonal problems. Responses are rated for number and effectiveness of solutions. There is both a 25-item (Hansen et al., 1989) and a 15-item (Smith, Conaway, Smith, & Hansen, 1988) version of the PPSM, both of which have adequate psychometric characteristics (see Hansen & MacMillan, 1990).

The Home Simulation Assessment (HSA) (MacMillan, Olson, & Hansen, 1988a) is a broad measure of parenting behavior that encompasses problem-solving approaches, child management skills, and anger responsivity. The procedure for the HAS consists of presenting parents with 10 child-related problems, and asking them to "do their best" in prompting an adult confederate (playing the role of child) to complete the task. The confederate acts out a "deviant" script of responses dependent upon each of four parental behaviors: instructions, prediscipline warnings, initiation of time-out, and maintenance of time-out. The confederate is prompted by a clinician observing the interaction via a one-way mirror using a bug-in-the-ear device. Parental behaviors are recorded and rated for correctness of interactions and responses.

Psychopathology

One of the most important measures in the parental assessment of maltreatment is the Child Abuse Potential Inventory (CAPI) (Milner, 1986). The CAPI is used primarily as a screening instrument in conjunction with other assessment strategies (Milner, 1986). However, it yields valuable information for already identified abusive parents. Specifically, the CAPI is composed of 160 statements that are endorsed by the respondent as true or false. Items reflect a variety of child-related issues and personality characteristics. Scale scores are derived comprising child abuse risk, distress, rigidity, unhappiness, problems with child or self, problems with family, and problems with others. In addition, validity scales are provided (fake-good, fake-bad, random responding) to determine profile accuracy. The CAPI reliably distinguishes between abusive and nonabusive parents (Milner, Gold, & Wimberley, 1986), and displays excellent internal reliability and construct validity characteristics.

There are many psychometrically sound instruments available to assess psychopathology, deviant personality characteristics, and specific psychiatric disorders. In the area of child maltreatment, some of the more commonly used measures are the Minnesota Multiphasic Personality Inventory (MMPI) (Hathaway & McKinley, 1940), the Symptom Checklist-90-Revised (SCL-90-R) (Derogatis, 1983), the Beck Depression Inventory (BDI) (Beck, Ward, Mendelsohn, Mock, & Erbaugh, 1961), and the State-Trait Anxiety Inventory (STAI) (Spielberger, Gorsuch, & Lushene, 1970). (The reader is referred to Goldstein & Hersen [1990] for an expanded discussion of psychological assessment in general). The original MMPI is one of the most widely studied measures of its kind. It consists of 566 true-false items and yields standardized scores for 4 validity scales (cannot say, lie, infrequent, correction) and 10 clinical scales (hypochondriasis, depression, hysteria, psychopathic deviate, masculinity-femininity, paranoia, psychasthenia, schizophrenia, hypomania, social introversion). It is most useful as a general screening measure of psychopathology. Although the MMPI-2 is now available, the bulk of the research has been done with the original MMPI. The SCL-90-R, on the other hand, provides information on specific symptomatology that can be used in diagnosing psychiatric disorders. This measure consists of 90 symptoms that are endorsed on a 5-point scale of distress (0 = not at all, 4 = extremely). Standardized scores are yielded on the following scales: somatic, obsessive-compulsive, interpersonal sensitivity, depression, anxiety, hostility, phobia, paranoia, and psychosis.

The BDI is one of the most commonly employed indices of depression. It is comprised of 21 depressive symptoms that are endorsed using a 4-point scale reflecting a hierarchical increase in intensity. Finally, the STAI permits the assessment of state anxiety (how the respondent feels now) and trait anxiety (how the respondent feels generally). For each type of anxiety, the individual completes 20 items listing subjective anxiety symptoms. These are endorsed using a 4-point rating of severity (1 = not at all, 4 = very much so).

Child Adjustment

The goals of child assessment are twofold. First, because the consequences of child maltreatment are often disruptive and pervasive, it is necessary to identify targets for possible remediation. And second, some difficult-to-manage children may contribute indirectly to the escalation of parent-child conflict through provocative behavior. Recognition of such problems is crucial for treatment planning.

The assessment of childhood psychopathology relies heavily on the report of parents or others involved with the education or care of the child. The Eyberg Child Behavior Inventory (ECBI) (Eyberg & Ross, 1978), for example, is comprised of 36 items indicating different forms of behavioral disturbance. Two scales are derived that denote those behaviors the parents find difficult to manage (problem score) and sum of the occurrence of problem behaviors (intensity). The Child Behavior Checklist (CBCL) (Achenbach & Edelbrock, 1983) provides information on social functioning and psychopathology in children. There are forms for parents, teachers, and older children (i.e., Youth Self-Report Form). Similarly, there are separate forms available depending upon age and gender. Normative data are available from both clinic and nonclinic samples to provide a comparison. Scale scores are derived reflecting such areas as school performance, schizoid, hyperactive, anxious, and depressed. Finally, the Vineland Adaptive Behavior Scales-Revised (Sparrow, Balla, & Cicchetti, 1984) is a measure of functional ability in childhood through adulthood. It is administered in interview format to parents or to someone who knows the child well. Information is provided via standardized scores on communication, daily living skills, socialization, and motor skills, among others.

Very few self-report measures are available for child victims of maltreatment. This is due, in part, to the relative nascence of this area. Future research should address this issue.

Family Interactions

The research literature is replete with observational studies of maltreating parents and their children (e.g., Mash et al., 1983; Reid, Patterson, & Loeber, 1982; Trickett & Kuczynski, 1986). These investigations provide detailed accounts of specific interactive patterns and frequencies of these behaviors that might contribute to mistreatment. Indeed, child abuse is fundamentally an interactive phenomenon, and remedial interventions are ultimately focused on altering maladaptive patterns that promote violence. Studies of family interactions involve observation either in the home or in the laboratory. Because maltreatment is private, abusive and neglectful acts are rarely directly observed in these investigations, although patterns of interaction that facilitate maltreatment are often displayed. In some studies, parents, and children are asked to interact in the laboratory while performing a difficult or demanding task (e.g., Ammerman, 1988; Mash et al., 1983). This approach is often more successful in eliciting behaviors of interest than simple requests to "play together." Unfortunately, systematic observations and codings of interactions are quite cumbersome. They require trained raters, sometimes necessitate the use of expensive coding machinery, and often entail sophisticated statistical analyses. From a clinical perspective, however, it is extremely useful to observe the parent and child (and other family members) before developing a treatment plan.

The coding systems used in observational research vary considerably in terms of focus and complexity. Most of them focus on specific overt behaviors and therefore are limited in rating more subtle aspects of family interactions, such as affect (Wolfe & Bordeau, 1987). The Family Interaction Coding System (FICS) (Patterson, Ray, Shaw, & Cobb, 1969; Reid, 1978) is widely used in observational research with dysfunctional families. It consists of 29 codes reflecting verbal and nonverbal elements of communication (e.g., noncompliance, disapproval, ignore, physical negative, physical positive). The Interactive Behavior Code (IBC) (Fagot & Hagen, 1986) was especially developed for evaluating parent-child interactions. It is comprised of a variety of child behavior (e.g., talk, help/initiate, normative play) and parent response (e.g., comment favorably, positive physical, directive) codes. It is especially posited for sequential as well as frequency analyses. Other systems, such as the Measure of Maternal Stimulation (MMS) (Dietrich, Starr, & Kaplan, 1980), are appropriate for mother-infant interactions. (See Wolfe & Bordeau [1987] for a continued discussion of observational rating approaches.)

CASE ILLUSTRATION

Jane T. was a 26-year-old single black female who was referred to the Child Assessment and Management Project (CAMP). CAMP is an ongoing assessment and treatment program for maltreating parents of handicapped children conducted by the John Merck Program for Developmentally Disabled Children, Western Psychiatric Institute and Clinic, University of Pittsburgh School of Medicine in collaboration with the Western Pennsylvania School for Blind Children. Her son, Jason, was a 9-year-old boy undergoing his second hospitalization for behavior problems. Ms. T. was a high school graduate, had never been employed, and received public assistance.

Jason was referred to the John Merck Program by his school for increased aggression, motoric overactivity, destructiveness, and noncompliance. His mother denied that these problems occurred at home. Jason received diagnoses of attention deficit-hyperactivity disorder, oppositional defiant disorder, severe mental retardation, infantile autism, and pica.

Ms. T. had prior experience with child protective services. When Jason was 5, she was observed striking him across the face. This led to a child abuse report, which was substantiated. At that point, Jason was hospitalized for the first time, and foster care was considered following discharge. This was, however, subsequently rejected by the treatment team, and Jason returned home. Several months prior to Jason's second hospitalization, Ms. T. reported using daily physical punishment at home. Since then, however, she reported ignoring his misbehavior, which resulted in increased behavior problems at school.

Ms. T. was interviewed clinically and evaluated with the Child Abuse and Neglect Interview Schedule. It was evident that she had few social contacts and received no help or assistance in caring for Jason. Indeed, she had a history of social isolation and few friends. She stated that she did not intervene in her child's disruptive behaviors, noting that "It is easier to let him have his own way." As previously noted, she relied heavily on physical punishment as a means of discipline. As a child, she was disciplined by her own mother frequently, and often with a belt. It was evident from the interview that Ms. T. was suffering from depression. Her affect was dysphoric, she reported a low energy level, difficulty concentrating, episodes of crying, poor sleep, anhedonia, and hopelessness. Onset of her depression corresponded with her ignoring of Jason's behavior problems. She further stated that she objected to Jason's most recent hospitalization. On the whole, she was uncooperative in participating in unit activities, such as group parent training, and frequently missed her appointments with social workers. Following discharge, she was inconsistent in giving Jason his medication (Imipramine). Her failure to correctly administer his medication resulted in a report of neglect to her child protective service worker.

While Jason was in the hospital, Ms. T. participated in the assessment phase of the CAMP. This involved administration of a variety of assessment measures examining such areas of functioning as psychopathology, child abuse potential, distress, and child behavior problems. The assessment measures used and the obtained scores are presented in Table 27-2. Most striking are Ms. T.'s elevated scores on measures of psychopathology. For example, she obtained a 29 on the Beck Depression Inventory, placing her in the upper end of moderate depression. Likewise, on the SCL-90-R, she obtained t-scores of greater than 70 on the following subscales: interpersonal sensitivity, depression, anxiety, hostility, phobia, paranoia, and psychosis. She obtained a WAIS-R equivalent of 84 on the Shipley Institute of Living Scale, although it is probable that this score is somewhat lower than her true intellectual functioning, because of suspected depression. Similarly, her score of 11 correct on the Knowledge Behavioral Principles as Applied to Children is quite low, but this too may have been influenced by her depressive symptomatology. Deviant scores were also obtained on the Child Abuse Potential Inventory and the Novaco Provocation Inventory (for comparison, mean = ranges from 230 to 255, SD is approximately 45; see Novaco, 1988). The Parenting Stress Index is also significantly elevated. Interestingly, her life stress score is at the fifth percentile, suggesting that her obtained scores in other areas are typical of her day-to-day life. Results from the Social Provision Scale indicate that Ms. T. is satisfied with the adequacy of her social network. This is contrary to what was revealed in the interview. Finally, the Aberrant Behavior Checklist highlights the severe behavior problems exhibited by Jason.

In some ways, this case is atypical. Psychopathology is more prominent in Ms. T. than with most other abusive parents. This fact underscores the need to screen for serious psychopathology. In other respects, Ms. T. has much in common with abusive and neglectful parents. She has limited knowledge of child disciplinary skills, perceives herself as experiencing a great deal of stress from multiple sources, has a high degree of anger reactivity, and has a difficult-to-manage child. These assessment results confirm the need for a comprehensive battery examining several areas of functioning. In terms of treatment planning, it was decided to target Ms. T.'s depression before implementing parent training and training in coping with stress. Unfortunately, consistent with her past history, Ms. T. was noncompliant with treatment suggestions and refused to be evaluated for pharmacotherapy.

IMPLICATIONS FOR TREATMENT

As the multimodal assessment of maltreatment yields data on several areas of dysfunction, it follows that the treatment of abuse and neglect must use multiple components and interventions. No single treatment is appropriate for all families, although some interventions (i.e., child management training) have wide applicability for abusive parents (see Ammerman, 1989). Project 12-Ways, an intervention program for maltreating families, emphasizes the individual tailoring of treatment for each family

Table 27-2. Summative and scale scores for assessment measures administered to Jane T.

MEASURE	SCORE
Child Abuse Potential Inventory	
Abuse	366 (elevated)
Distress	248 (elevated)
Rigidity	54 (elevated)
Unhappiness	25 (elevated)
Problems with Child/Self	18 (elevated)
Problems with Family	0 (normal)
Problems with Others	21 (elevated)
Shipley Institute of Living Scale	
WAIS-R Equivalent	84
Beck Depression Inventory	29
Symptom Checklist-90-Revised (*t*-scores)	
Somatic	48
Obsessive-Compulsive	66
Interpersonal Sensitivity	81
Depression	75
Anxiety	72
Hostility	72
Phobia	70
Paranoia	81
Psychosis	81
Parenting Stress Index	
Total Stress	312 (95th percentile)
Child Domain	145 (+99th percentile)
Adaptability	28 (80th percentile)
Acceptability	15 (80th percentile)
Demandingness	33 (+99th percentile)
Mood	14 (95th percentile)
Distractability/Hyperactivity	43 (+99th percentile)
Reinforces Parent	12 (90th percentile)
Parent Domain	167 (95th percentile)
Depression	28 (95th percentile)
Attachment	11 (35th percentile)
Restriction of Role	33 (+99th percentile)
Sense of Competence	36 (90th percentile)
Social Isolation	14 (70th percentile)
Relationship with Spouse	25 (95th percentile)
Parent Health	20 (99th percentile)
Life Stress	6 (5th percentile)
Knowledge of Behavioral Principles as Applied to Children	11
Novaco Provocation Inventory	322
Wolpe-Lazarus Assertion Inventory	13
Aberrant Behavior Checklist	
Irritability	28
Lethargy	15
Stereotype	5
Hyperactivity	41
Excessive Speech	0
Social Provisions Scale	
Attachment	12
Social Integration	14
Opportunity of Nurturance	9
Reassurance of Worth	15
Reliable Alliance	15
Guidance	15

based on a comprehensive ecobehavioral assessment (Lutzker & Rice, 1984). Likewise, Ammerman et al. (1988a) employ a multicomponent behavioral package for maltreating parents of handicapped children in which components (e.g., child management training, stress-reduction training, leisure skills training) are selected on the basis of a careful pretreatment assessment.

The Transactional and Transitional Models of maltreatment have much to offer in establishing guidelines for intervention. Both theoretical formulations stipulate compensatory and destabilizing variables, respectively, that prevent or protect the family from engaging in maltreatment. One goal of a multimodal assessment, therefore, is to recognize strengths in the family that can be maximized and used to deter recidivism. The Transactional Model also delineates transient and durable factors that influence maltreatment. The clinician must be aware of those elements that cannot be changed, such as low parental IQ or history of mistreatment. Treatment should take these into account, and modifications may need to be made to address these issues or to work around family limitations. Finally, the Transitional Model, which postulates three levels of parenting that progressively increase the probability of abuse, suggests that treatment will differ depending upon at what stage the family is functioning. Relatively nonintrusive and psychoeducational interventions are appropriate at early stages, whereas more intensive treatments are appropriate at early stages, whereas more intensive treatments are required for later stages.

The many contexts of maltreatment must also be considered. The abusive or neglectful parent and his or her child behave within a family system, a community, and society. Individual interventions may fail if family variables interfere with progress. Similarly, some psychological interventions may have little chance of success in the face of extreme poverty and poor living conditions. Thus, treatment should be implemented concurrently with social service interventions. Both of these approaches, however, have inherent limitations, and it must be recognized that circumstance may make it extremely difficult to treat some families.

Use of standardized assessment measures, too, are of limited utility. They do not replace sound clinical judgment. For example, some aspects of maltreatment are not readily accessible to formal assessment procedures. Included are the degree of intent attributed to the child by the parent in specific behavioral transgressions, other parental cognitive variables that facilitate aggression, the affective tone of the parent-child relationship, and the existence of psychological mistreatment.

The complexity of abuse and neglect is underscored by the chronicity of the problem. Maltreating parents, particularly those who have engaged in severe abuse and neglect, will need to be followed for an extended period of time. Short-term interventions are unlikely to bring about significant and lasting change. Rather, the family should often be seen intermittently for years following a more intensive treatment period.

SUMMARY

The widespread prevalence of maltreatment attests to the need for clinicians to be familiar with appropriate assessment procedures. Abuse and neglect are multifactor phenomena that require a comprehensive multimodal assessment approach. Strategies available include observational, self-report, report by others, and interview procedures. Measurement is needed for such diverse areas as parenting, parental psychopathology, anger reactivity, social functioning, and child behavior problems. As a result of this kind of assessment, treatment targets are identified and interventions can be individually tailored. Repeated application of selected instruments, in turn, allows for the monitoring of treatment progress over the extended period in which these families need to be seen.

REFERENCES

Abidin, R. R. (1986). *Parenting Stress Index* (2nd ed.). Charlottesville, VA: Pediatric Psychology Press.

Achenbach, T., & Edelbrock, C. (1983). *The Child Behavior Checklist-Revised*. Burlington, VT: Queen City Printers.

Altemeier, W. A., O'Connor, S., Vietze, P., Sandler, H., & Sherrod, K. (1984). Prediction of child abuse: A prospective study of feasibility. *Child Abuse and Neglect, 8*, 393–400.

Altemeier, W. A., Vietze, P., Sherrod, K., Sandler, H., Falsey, S., & O'Connor, S. (1979). Prediction of child maltreatment during pregnancy. *Journal of the American Academy of Child Psychiatry, 18*, 205–218.

Ammerman, R. T. (1988). Prevention of mother-child problems in families with young multihandicapped children. *International Journal of Rehabilitation Research, 11*, 416–417.

Ammerman, R. T. (1989). Child abuse and neglect. In M. Hersen (Ed.), *Innovations in child behavior therapy* (pp. 353–394). New York: Springer.

Ammerman, R. T. (1990). Etiological models of child

maltreatment: A behavioral perspective. *Behavior Modification, 14*, 230–254.
Ammerman, R. T., Cassisi, J. E., Hersen, M., & Van Hasselt, V. B. (1986). Consequences of physical abuse and neglect in children. *Clinical Psychology Review, 6*, 291–310.
Ammerman, R. T., Hersen, M., & Lubetsky, M. J. (1988a). Assessment and treatment of abuse and neglect in multihandicapped children and adolescents. *International Journal of Rehabilitation Research, 11*, 313–314.
Ammerman, R. T., Hersen, M., & Van Hasselt, V. B. (1988b). *The Child Abuse and Neglect Interview Schedule (CANIS)*. Unpublished instrument, Western Pennsylvania School for Blind Children, Pittsburgh.
Ammerman, R. T., Hersen, M., Van Hasselt, V. B., McGonigle, J. J., & Lubetsky, M. (1989). Abuse and neglect in psychiatrically hospitalized multihandicapped children. *Child Abuse and Neglect, 13*, 335–343.
Azar, S. T., Robinson, D. R., Hekimian, E., & Twentyman, C. T. (1984). Unrealistic expectations and problem-solving ability in maltreating and comparison mothers. *Journal of Consulting and Clinical Psychology, 52*, 687–691.
Beck, A. T., Ward, C. H., Mendelsohn, M., Mock, J., & Erbaugh, J. (1961). An inventory for measuring depression. *Archives of General Psychiatry, 4*, 561–571.
Belsky, J. (1980). Child maltreatment: An ecological integration. *American Psychologist, 35*, 320–335.
Bousha, D. M., & Twentyman, C. T. (1984). Mother-child interactional style in abuse, neglect, and control groups: Naturalistic observations in the home. *Child Development, 93*, 106–114.
Briggs, S. E. (1991). Medical issues with child victims of family violence. In R. T. Ammerman & M. Hersen (Eds.), *Case studies in family violence* (pp. 87–96). New York: Plenum Press.
Caldwell, B., & Bradley, R. (1984). *Home observation for measurement of the environment*. New York: Dorsey Press.
Cicchetti, D., & Rizley, R. (1981). Developmental perspectives on the etiology, intergenerational transmission, and sequelae of child maltreatment. *New Directions for Child Development, 11*, 31–55.
Cohen, S., Mermelstein, R., Kamarck, T., & Hoberman, H. M. (1985). Measuring the functional components of social support. In I. G. Sarason & B. R. Sarason (Eds.), *Social support: Theory, research, and applications* (pp. 73–94). The Hague, Holland: Martinus Nijhoff.
Cutrona, C. E. (1982). Transition to college: Loneliness and the process of social adjustment. In L. A. Peplau & D. Perlman (Eds.), *Loneliness: A sourcebook of current research, theory, and, therapy*. New York: John Wiley & Sons.
Derogatis, L. R. (1983). *SCL-90-R Administration, Scoring, and Procedure Manual*. Baltimore, MD: Clinical Psychometric Research.
Dietrich, K. N., Starr, R. H., & Kaplan, M. G. (1980). Maternal stimulation and care of abused infants. In T. M. Field, S. Goldberg, D. Stern, & A. M. Sostek (Eds.), *High-risk infants and children: Adult and peer interactions* (pp. 25–41). New York: Academic Press.
Dohrenwend, B. S., & Dohrenwend, B. P. (Eds.). (1981). *Stressful life events and their contexts*. New York: Prodist.
Egeland, B., Breitenbucher, M., & Rosenberg, D. (1980). Prospective study of significance of etiology of child abuse. *Journal of Consulting and Clinical Psychology, 48*, 195–205.
Eyberg, S. M., & Ross, A. W. (1978). Assessment of child behavior problems: The validation of a new inventory. *Journal of Clinical Child Psychology, 7*, 113–116.
Fagot, B. I., & Hagan, R. (1986). *Training manual for the Fagot Interactive Code*. Unpublished manuscript, University of Oregon, Eugene.
Friedrich, W. N., & Einbender, A. J. (1983). The abused child: A psychological review. *Journal of Clinical Child Psychology, 12*, 244–256.
Freidrich, W. N., Greenberg, M. T., & Crnic, K. (1983). A short-form of the Questionnaire on Resources and Stress. *American Journal of Mental Deficiency, 88*, 41–48.
Friedrich, W. N., Tyler, J. D., & Clark, J. A. (1985). Personality and psychophysiological variables in abusive, neglectful, and low-income control mothers. *Journal of Nervous and Mental Disease, 173*, 449–460.
Frodi, A. M. (1981). Contribution of infant characteristics to child abuse. *American Journal of Mental Deficiency, 85*, 341–349.
Frodi, A. M., & Lamb, M. E. (1980). Child abusers' responses to infant smiles and cries. *Child Development, 51*, 238–241.
Garbarino, J. (1976). A preliminary study of some ecological correlates of child abuse: The impact of socioeconomic stress on mothers. *Child Development, 47*, 178–185.
Garbarino, J. (1990). Future directions. In R. T. Ammerman & M. Hersen (Eds.), *Children at risk: An evaluation of factors contributing to child abuse and neglect* (pp. 291–298). New York: Plenum Press.
Garbarino, J., & Gilliam, G. (1980). *Understanding abusive families*. Lexington, MA: Lexington Books.
Gibaud-Wallston, J., & Wandersman, L. P. (1978, August). *Development and utility of the Parenting Sense of Competence Scale*. Paper presented at the meeting of the American Psychological Association, Toronto, Canada.
Goldstein, G. R., & Hersen, M. (Eds.). (1990). *Handbook of psychological assessment* (2nd ed.). New York: Pergamon Press.
Green, A. H. (1978). Psychopathology of abused children. *Journal of the American Academy of Child Psychiatry, 17*, 92–103.
Hansen, D. J., & MacMillan, V. M. (1990). Behavioral assessment of child abusive and neglectful families:

Recent developments and current issues. *Behavior Modification, 14*, 255–278.

Hansen, D. J., Pallotta, G. M., Tishelman, A. C., Conaway, L. P., & MacMillan, V. M. (1989). Parental problem-solving skills and child behavior problems: A comparison of physically abusive, neglectful, clinic, and community families. *Journal of Family Violence, 4*, 353–368.

Hathaway, S. R., & McKinley, J. C. (1940). A multiphasic personality schedule (Minnesota): Construction of the schedule. *Journal of Psychology, 10*, 249–254.

Helfer, R., Schneider, C., & Hoffmeister, J. (1977). *Manual for the use of the Michigan Screening Profile of Parenting.* East Lansing, MI: Department of Human Development, Michigan State University.

Hoffman-Plotkin, D., & Twentyman, C. T. (1984). A multimodal assessment of behavioral and cognitive deficits in abused and neglected preschoolers. *Child Development, 55*, 794–802.

Holmes, T. H., & Rahe, R. (1967). *Schedule of recent experience (SRE).* Seattle, WA: School of Medicine, University of Washington.

Holroyd, J. (1974). The Questionnaire on Resources and Stress: An instrument to measure family response to a handicapped family member. *Journal of Community Psychology, 2*, 92–94.

Johnston, C., & Mash, E. J. (1989). A measure of parenting satisfaction and efficacy. *Journal of Clinical Child Psychology, 18*, 167–175.

Kazdin, A. E., Moser, J., Colbus, D., & Bell, R. (1985). Depressive symptoms among physically abused and psychiatrically disturbed children. *Journal of Consulting and Clinical Psychology, 94*, 298–307.

Kelly, J. A. (1983). *Treating child abusive families: Intervention based on skills-training principles.* New York: Plenum Press.

Lahey, B. B., Conger, R. D., Atkeson, B. M., & Treiber, F. A. (1984). Parenting behavior and emotional status of physically abusive mothers. *Journal of Consulting and Clinical Psychology, 52*, 1062–1071.

Lutzker, J. R., & Rice, J. M. (1984). Project 12-Ways: Measuring outcome of a large in-home service for treatment and prevention of child abuse and neglect. *Child Abuse and Neglect, 8*, 519–524.

MacMillan, V. M. Olson, R. L., & Hansen, D. J. (1988a, November). *Low and high stress analogue assessment of parent training/stress minimization package with physically abusive parents.* Paper presented at the meeting of the Association for the Advancement of Behavior Therapy, New York.

MacMillan, V. M., Olson, R. L., & Hansen, D. J. (1988b, November). *The development of an anger inventory for use with maltreating parents.* Paper presented at the meeting of the Association for the Advancement of Behavior Therapy, New York.

Mash, E. J., Johnston, C., & Kovitz, K. (1983). A comparison of the mother-child interactions of physically abused and non-abused children during play and task situations. *Journal of Clinical Child Psychology, 12*, 337–346.

Milner, J. S. (1986). *The Child Abuse Potential Inventory manual* (2nd ed). Webster, NC: Psytec.

Milner, J. S., Gold, R. G., & Wimberley, R. C. (1986). Prediction and explanation of child abuse: Cross-validation of the Child Abuse Potential Inventory. *Journal of Consulting and Clinical Psychology, 54*, 865–866.

Monane, M., Leichter, D., & Lewis, D. O. (1984). Physical abuse in psychiatrically hospitalized children and adolescents. *Journal of the American Academy of Child Psychiatry, 23*, 653–658.

National Center on Child Abuse and Neglect. (1988). *Study findings: Study of national incidence and prevalence of child abuse and neglect: 1988.* Washington, DC: U.S. Department of Health and Human Services.

Novaco, R. W. (1975). *Anger control: The development and evaluation of an experimental treatment.* Lexington, MA: D.C. Heath.

Novaco, R. W. (1988). Novaco Provocation Inventory. In M. Hersen & A. S. Bellack (Eds.), *Dictionary of behavioral assessment techniques* (pp. 315–317). New York: Pergamon Press.

O'Dell, S. L. (1988). Instrument to Measure Knowledge of Behavioral Principles as Applied to Children. In M. Hersen & A. S. Bellack (Eds.), *Dictionary of behavioral assessment techniques* (pp. 258–260 New York: Pergamon Press.

O'Dell, S. L., Tarler-Benlolo, L., & Flynn, J. M. (1979). An instrument to measure knowledge of behavioral principles as applied to children. *Journal of Behavior Therapy and Experimental Psychiatry, 10*, 29–34.

Patterson, G. R., Ray, R. S., Shaw, D. A., & Cobb, J. A. (1969). *Manual for coding of family interactions. 1969 revision. NPAS document #01234.*

Polansky, N. A., Ammons, P. W., & Gaudin, J. M. (1985). Loneliness and isolation in child neglect. *Social Casework: The Journal of Contemporary Social Work, 66*, 38–47.

Reid, J. B. (Ed.). (1978). *A social learning approach to family intervention*, Vol. 2. Eugene, OR: Castalia.

Reid, J. B., Kavanagh, K., & Baldwin, D. V. (1987). Abusive parents' perceptions of child problem behaviors: An example of parental bias. *Journal of Abnormal Child Psychology, 15*, 457–466.

Reid, J. B., Patterson, G. R., & Loeber, R. (1982). The abused child: Victim, instigator, or innocent bystander? *Nebraska Symposium on Motivation, 29*, 47–68.

Rosenberg, M. S., & Reppucci, N. D. (1983). Abusive mothers: Perceptions of their own and their children's behavior. *Journal of Consulting and Clinical Psychology, 51*, 674–682.

Russell, D., & Cutrona, C. E. (1984). *The Social Provisions Scale.* Unpublished manuscript, University of Iowa, College of Medicine, Iowa City, IA.

Salisbury, C. (1986). Adaptation of the Questionnaire on Resources and Stress-Short Form. *American Journal of Mental Deficiency, 90*, 456–459.

Salzinger, S., Kaplan, S., & Artemyeff, C. (1983). Mothers' personal social networks and child maltreatment. *Journal of Abnormal Psychology, 92*, 68–76.

Smith, J. M., Conaway, R. L., Smith, G. M., & Hansen, D. J. (1988, November). *Evaluation of a problem-solving measure for use with physically abusive and neglectful parents.* Paper presented at the Association for the Advancement of Behavior Therapy Convention, New York.

Sparrow, S. S., Balla, D. A., & Cicchetti, D. V. (1984). *The Vineland Adaptive Behavior Scales* (rev.). Circle Pines, MN: American Guidance Service.

Spielberger, C. D., Gorsuch, R. L., & Lushene, R. E. (1970). *Manual for the State-Trait Anxiety Inventory.* Palo Alto, CA: Consulting Psychologists Press.

Starr, R. H., Jr., Dubowitz, H., & Bush, B. A. (1990). The epidemiology of child maltreatment. In R. T. Ammerman & M. Hersen (Eds.), *Children at risk: Evaluation of factors contributing to child abuse and neglect* (pp. 23–53). New York: Plenum Press.

Steele, B. J., & Pollock, C. (1968). A psychiatric study of parents who abuse infants and small children. In R. Helfer & C. H. Kempe (Eds.), *The battered child* (pp. 89–133). Chicago: University of Chicago Press.

Straus, M. A. (1980). Stress and child abuse. In C. H. Kempe and R. E. Helfer (Eds.), *The battered child* (3rd ed.) (pp. 86–102). Chicago: University of Chicago Press.

Tertinger, D. A., Greene, B. V., & Lutzker, J. R. (1984). Home safety: Development and validation of one component of an ecobehavioral treatment program for abused and neglected children. *Journal of Applied Behavior Analysis, 17*, 159–174.

Trickett, P. K., & Kuczynski, L. (1986). Children's misbehaviors and parental discipline strategies in abusive and nonabusive families. *Developmental Psychology, 22*, 115–123.

Twentyman, C. T., Plotkin, R., Dodge, D., & Rohrbeck, C. A. (1981, November). *Inappropriate expectations of parents who maltreat their children.* Paper presented at the 15th Annual Convention of the Association for Advancement of Behavior Therapy, Toronto, Canada.

Walker, C. E., Bonner, B. L., & Kaufman, K. L. (1988). *The physically and sexually abused child: Evaluation and treatment.* New York: Pergamon Press.

Watson-Perczel, M., Lutzker, J. R., Greene, B. F., & McGimpsey, B. J. (1988). Assessment and modification of home cleanliness among families adjudicated for child neglect. *Behavior Modification, 12*, 57–81.

Wolfe, D. A. (1985). Child abusive parents: An empirical review and analysis. *Psychological Bulletin, 97*, 462–482.

Wolfe, D. A. (1987). *Child abuse: Implications for child development and psychopathology.* Newbury Park, CA: Sage Publications.

Wolfe, D. A., & Bordeau, P. A. (1987). Current issues in the assessment of abusive and neglectful parent-child relationships. *Behavioral Assessment, 9*, 271–290.

Wolfe, D. A., Fairbank, J., Kelly, J. A., & Bradlyn, A. S. (1983). Child abusive parents' physiological responses to stressful and nonstressful behavior in children. *Behavioral Assessment, 5*, 363–371.

AFTERWORD

EDITORS' COMMENTS ABOUT THE FIELD'S PROGRESS AND FUTURE

In this large, multiauthored handbook we have endeavored to provide the reader with an understanding of what child and adolescent assessment is like in the 1990s. In so doing, we were astounded by the vast advances that have taken place since we were graduate students in clinical psychology in the early 1960s (MH) and late 1960s (THO). At that time, life was rather simple: This field was much narrower. Indeed, the sheer number of assessment devices and strategies that are now available can appear most confusing to the neophyte assessor. As we will comment upon later, the development of so many new strategies may actually prove to be a double-edged sword.

Probably the healthiest development in assessing child and adolescent psychopathology is the broadened approach to the problem. Not only are the acrimonious debates of yesteryear between opposing theoretical camps virtually nonexistent, but there is the increasing recognition that the best assessment is one that is conducted at multilevels with multiple foci. Thus, professionals with diverse training and resultant expertise may be required to complete such an assessment. The medical evaluation may be carried out by a neurologist, the intellectual and neuropsychological evaluation by a pediatric neuropsychologist, the behavioral assessment by a child behavior therapist, and the physiological assessment by a psychophysiologist. All cases, of course, will not require such comprehensive attention, but the availability of this kind of expertise when required and the current openness to multidisciplinary consultation make the assessment enterprise exciting and challenging in the 1990s. Computerization, imaging techniques, and improved technology, as well as improved psychometric strategies and interviewing techniques, all have contributed to the enhanced sophistication of assessing children and adolescents.

Increased emphasis in DSM-III and DSM-III-R on childhood and adolescent nosology coupled with developments of semistructured and structured interviewing techniques have made the diagnostic process more respectable and to some extent more scientific. Also, those practitioners who previously denounced the value of psychiatric classification in children and adolescents now can see how the DSM is able to serve as a superordinate system that is not incompatible with the idiographic analysis done by behavioral asssessors. Furthermore, the critical developmental and neuropsychological features in making an accurate diagnostic appraisal of children and adolescents finally has received the attention in the literature that they both obviously deserve. Thus, arriving at a diagnosis for a given child or adolescent now is much more than simply attaching a label that irrevocably follows him or her into adulthood.

Let us now consider areas in the field of child and adolescent assessment where further developments and refinements are warranted. In so doing, we will go back to our comments about the virtual explosion of new assessment devices and why we have labeled this phenomenon as a double-edged sword. Our greatest concerns, of course, are over the psychometric properties of many of these new assessment strategies. With the academic pressure to publish, many have appeared somewhat prematurely, given that appropriate normative data, internal consistency, reliability, and validity are not terribly well established. Use of these devices, then, will have limited utility from a cross-study comparison standpoint. Indeed, we argue that the field will be better served if there are fewer strategies developed, but that are well-conceptualized, carefully crafted, and then studied psychometrically with assiduous care.

As already noted throughout the book and the Afterword, the development of semistructured and structured interview schedules have helped to improve the diagnostic process. However, since many of these schedules were developed for field studies, their clinical value may not be translated automatically. Indeed, it is quite clear that patients with distinct etiologies may eventuate with the same diagnostic label because of like symptomatology. However, in arriving at a viable treatment approach, the context in which symptomatology appears requires a similarly careful evaluation. Thus, the individual behavioral analysis of the historical and current determinants of psychopathology will be most critical in devising treatment strategies that will have some degree of permanence. That is, we believe that identification and modification of the unique determinants of psychopathology should result in the most cost-effective and parsimonious treatment approaches.

Again with respect to the relationship of assessment to treatment, much work remains to be accomplished. Unfortunately, psychotherapeutics and pharmacotherapeutics have not yet attained a level of sophistication where it is possible to match the right treatment to the right assessment. But ultimately this should be the goal of the comprehensive assessment. Assessment is not to be conducted as an academic assessment in vacuo; to the contrary, its goal is to link the data uncovered by the assessment to the most efficacious remedial regime. Perhaps progress for this latter goal will be seen in the decade of the 1990s.

Author Index

Aaron, N. S., 225, 234
Abate, F., 191
Abidin, R. R., 443, 444, 451
Abikoff, H. A., 85, 96, 279, 287
Abraham, S., 364, 380
Abrams, K. S., 320
Abrosini, P. J., 248
Abu-Saad, H., 425, 434
Acardi, A., 410, 411
Achenbach, T. M., 3, 12, 21, 24, 28, 31, 34, 36, 37, 67, 73, 79, 82, 83, 84, 85, 86, 87, 88, 89, 93, 115, 116, 243, 244, 248, 262, 264, 272, 275, 279, 287, 292, 298, 301, 302, 304, 307, 311, 314, 316, 318, 444, 448, 451
Ackerman, A., 124, 127, 130, 138
Ackerson, J. D., 428, 438
Ad Hoc Committee on Classification of Headache, 400, 402, 410
Adams, H. E., 409, 410
Adams, R. D., 27, 39, 42, 49
Adams, T. W., 137
Adelman, H. S., 11, 12
Adkins, D. C., 100, 107, 116
Ageton, S. S., 295, 297, 300, 307

Agras, S., 240, 248
Agras, W. S., 378, 380, 389, 398
Agudelo, C. A., 423, 437
Ahles, T. A., 410
Aicardi, J., 49
Aikman, K., 227, 234
Albert, J., 107, 119, 282, 289
Alessi, N. E., 37, 261, 267
Alexander, J., 143, 162
Alexander, J. F., 294, 307
Alford, H. F., 131, 138
Allen, A., 8, 12
Allen, D. A., 416, 438
Allen, J. C., 49
Allen, L., 240, 249, 292, 309
Allison, R., 197, 207
Allport, G. W., 149, 162
Almond, P. J., 351, 361
Alpert, B. S., 184, 190
Alster, B., 100, 121
Altemeier, W. A., 443, 445, 451
Althaus, M., 73, 81
Altman, E., 166, 176
Altman, J., 126, 137

Aluwahlia, S., 315, 316, 320
Amado, H., 36, 40, 74, 81, 252, 268
Aman, M. D., 87, 93, 94
Aman, M. G., 327, 334, 335, 336, 341, 342, 343
Amatora, M., 102, 116
Ambrosini, P. J., 34, 36, 37, 38, 39, 77, 78, 79, 80, 256, 257, 264, 265, 287, 315, 320
American Educ Research Assn, 54, 61, 194, 205
American Psychiatric Assn, 27, 31, 37, 54, 61, 65, 66, 79, 85, 94, 116, 239, 248, 263, 264, 270, 272, 287, 293, 307, 321, 331, 343, 346, 361, 386, 389, 394, 396
American Psychological Assn, 170, 176, 194, 205
Amiel-Tison, C., 421, 434
Ammerman, R. T., 439, 440, 441, 442, 443, 445, 448, 449, 451, 452
Ammons, P. W., 440, 453
Anand, K. J. S., 414, 416, 420, 431, 434
Anastasi, A., 84, 85, 94, 157, 162, 170, 176, 192, 194, 202, 205
Andermann, F., 404, 410
Andersen, A. E., 384, 390, 396
Anderson, G., 122, 310
Anderson, G. M., 349, 363
Anderson, J. C., 33, 37, 240, 248
Anderson, J. E., 413, 416, 426, 435
Anderson, K., 279, 289
Anderson, K. O., 423, 437
Anderson, L. T., 343
Andrasik, F., 183, 189, 403, 405, 407, 409, 410, 411
Andreasen, N. C., 28, 35, 37, 39
Andrews, J. A., 264, 266
Angell, M., 417, 434
Angleitner, A., 98, 116
Angold, A., 36, 37, 78, 79, 252, 264, 265
Anthony, J. C., 273, 287
APA Task Force on Lab Test in Psychiatry, 264
Apley, J., 414, 434
Apter, A., 78, 79
Aradine, C. R., 425, 426, 435
Archer, R. P., 103, 117, 262, 264
Arena, J. G., 182, 183, 184, 185, 191, 403, 410
Arendt, R., 344
Arias, M., 333, 343
Arick, J. R., 351, 361
Aries, P., 3, 12
Armentano, M., 29, 37
Armstrong, F. D., 421, 436
Arnold, M., 225, 234
Aron, B., 225, 234
Aronoff, M. S., 261, 266

Arrington, R. E., 150, 162
Artemyeff, C., 440, 443, 454
Ary, D. V., 175, 178
Asarnow, J. R., 166, 176, 259, 264
Ascione, F. R., 141, 144, 147, 149, 162
Asher, S. R., 114, 117, 165, 166, 167, 168, 169, 170, 171, 172, 173, 175, 176, 178
Ashley, L. C., 415, 435
Atikson, J. W., 225, 235
Atkeson, B. M., 440, 453
Atkins, M. S., 85, 94, 170, 177, 276, 279, 287
Atkinson, R. A., 403, 404, 410
Attansio, V., 405, 409, 410
Attia, J., 421, 434
Attie, I., 112, 117
Atwater, J. D., 309
Atwood, R., 107, 117
August, C J., 275, 287
Autor, S., 29, 37
Avery, M. E., 413, 434
Axelrod, H. C., 100, 121
Axelson, J. M., 372, 380
Aynsley-Green, A., 416, 420, 431, 434
Azar, S. T., 446, 452
Azrin, N. H., 317, 318

Babigian, H., 8, 12
Bachman, J. G., 293, 297, 307
Baer, D. M., 15, 24
Bagley, C., 311, 320
Bagnato, S. J., 243, 249
Bailey, J. A., 169, 176
Baisel, E. J., 184, 191
Bakal, D. A., 405, 411
Baker, A. F., 354, 361, 362
Baker, B., 429, 435
Baker, L., 30, 38, 349, 352, 361
Bakker, D. J., 209, 223
Baldwin, D. V., 299, 310, 441, 453
Balla, D. A., 321, 345, 354, 363, 444, 448, 454
Ballard, K. D., 130, 136
Ballif, B. L., 100, 107, 116
Bamford, K. A., 311, 319
Bana, D., 405, 411
Bandura, A., 5, 11, 12, 17, 19, 24, 115, 117, 245, 248
Banegas, M., 261, 267
Banta, T. J., 298, 307
Barabas, G., 404, 410
Barabasz, A. F., 187, 188, 189
Baranowski, T., 372, 374, 380
Baren, M., 282, 291

Barkley, R. A., 16, 20, 24, 82, 83, 84, 86, 89, 90, 91, 94, 143, 163, 186, 190, 271, 272, 275, 276, 278, 279, 287, 288, 289, 297, 307
Barlow, D. H., 241, 248
Barnes, J., 382
Baroff, G. S., 322, 324, 325, 326, 327, 343
Baron, K. D., 403, 410
Barr, R. G., 419, 434
Barrera, M., 260, 261, 264
Barrett, C. L., 10, 13, 110, 120
Barrett, R. B., 335, 343
Barrett, R. P., 9, 14
Barrier, G., 421, 434
Barrios, B. A., 140, 142, 144, 148, 149, 156, 157, 159, 162, 243, 245, 248, 376, 380
Barron, J., 336, 343
Barron, T. P., 410
Bartell, N. P., 111, 117, 122, 310
Bartko, J. J., 67, 79
Bartlett, D. P., 141, 164
Barton, E. J., 141, 144, 147, 149, 162
Bartunkova, S., 371, 383
Bashford, A., 350, 358, 362
Baskin, C. H., 258, 267
Bass, D., 297, 301, 308
Bastien, R., 11, 12
Bates, J., 228, 236
Batshw, M. L., 47, 49
Bauer, D., 10, 12
Bauernfeind, R. H., 103, 121
Bauman, R., 147, 164
Baumann, K. E., 336, 344
Baumeister, A. A., 343, 344
Baxter, E. D., 101, 117
Bayley, N., 354, 361
Bays, K., 183, 190
Beck, A. T., 257, 260, 264, 266, 390, 395, 396, 444, 447, 452
Beck, B., 203, 207, 344
Beck, L. H., 281, 290
Beck, S., 82, 89, 94, 96, 99, 117, 172, 177
Beecher, H. K., 415, 418, 434
Beegle, G. P., 137
Behar, D., 293, 294, 307
Behar, J., 318, 319
Behar, L., 298, 308
Behrman, R. E., 365, 381
Beidel, D., 185, 186, 188, 189
Beidel, D. C., 245, 248
Beitchman, J. H., 99, 115, 117
Belanger, A., 35, 39, 287, 289
Bell, D. B., 322, 345

Bell, H. M., 101, 117
Bell, R., 439, 453
Bell, W. E., 45, 46, 49
Bell-Dolan, D. J., 140, 162, 168, 176
Bellack, A. S., 5, 13, 131, 136, 145, 164, 187, 191
Bellak, L., 225, 226, 234
Bellak, S., 226, 234
Bellissimo, A., 428, 438
Bellman, M., 20, 24
Belman, A., 435
Belsky, J., 441, 452
Belter, R. W., 113, 117, 227, 232, 234, 262, 266
Bem, D. J., 8, 12
Bemis, K. M., 386, 387, 390, 391, 392, 396, 397
Bender, M. E., 272, 290
Benoit, M., 86, 96
Bennett, B., 258, 267
Benson, D. F., 312, 319
Benson, H., 409, 411
Bentler, P. M., 107, 121, 228, 236
Berde, C. B., 414, 422, 430, 434, 435
Berden, G., 73, 81
Berden, G. F. M. G., 268
Berenson, G. S., 364, 365, 372, 381, 383
Berg, B., 107, 119
Berg, C. J., 110, 117, 118, 312, 314, 318
Berg, C. Z., 38
Berg, I., 10, 12
Bergen, D., 314, 319
Berger, M., 18, 22, 24, 311, 320
Berk, R. A., 156, 162
Berkler, M. S., 147, 164
Berler, E. S., 168, 176
Bernard, B. A., 185, 191
Berndt, D. J., 257, 261, 264
Bernreuter, R. G., 101, 117
Bernstein, D. A., 182, 190
Bersheid, E., 172, 176
Bersoff, D. N., 58, 61
Bertucci, M., 151, 162
Beumont, P. J. V., 384, 385, 396
Beyer, J. E., 415, 416, 421, 422, 425, 426, 430, 435
Bialer, I., 90, 95, 113, 117
Bibace, R., 425, 435
Biederman, J., 29, 37
Biederman, M., 32, 39
Bieliauskas, V., 229, 234
Bigler, E. D., 215, 217, 223, 280, 289
Bijou, S. W., 3, 12, 15, 24
Bild, R., 409, 410

Bille, B., 400, 401, 402, 404, 410, 414, 435
Billings, A., 317, 319
Birch, H. G., 19, 25
Bird, B. L., 187, 189, 415, 437
Bird, H. R., 26, 33, 37, 315, 316, 320
Birleson, P., 259, 264
Birmingham, B. K., 279, 282, 290
Bittle, R. G., 336, 343
Black, D., 376, 381
Black, S., 394, 398
Blagg, N., 23, 24
Blanchard, E. B., 183, 189, 241, 248, 403, 407, 409, 410
Blatt, S., 231, 234
Bleuler, E., 37
Blevings, G., 183, 190
Blick, D. W., 124, 132, 136
Block, A. R., 423, 436
Blom, W., 49
Bloninger, C. R., 38
Blotcky, A. D., 428, 438
Blouin, A. G., 89, 90, 94, 96
Blouin, D. C., 185, 191, 412
Blount, R. L., 310
Blum, G., 52, 61
Blyth, D. A., 375, 383
Bock, W. H., 333, 343
Boggs, S. R., 297, 307
Bohr, Y., 112, 119, 393, 397
Boice, R., 148, 149, 162
Boisjoly, C., 419, 434
Boliek, C., 226, 235
Boll, T. J., 215, 219, 222
Bolstad, O. D., 128, 137, 150, 163
Bonato, D., 394, 397
Bonke, B., 401, 411
Bonner, B. L., 440, 454
Bonney, M. E., 169, 176
Bordeau, P. A., 440, 448, 454
Borgstedt, A. D., 289
Boring, F. W., 184, 190
Bousha, D. M., 74, 79, 439, 440, 452
Bower, E. M., 168, 176
Boykin, R. A., 138, 219
Bradley, L. A., 423, 437
Bradley, R., 443, 445, 452
Bradlyn, A. S., 446, 454
Brannigan, G., 229, 234
Bransome, E. D., 281, 290
Branson, S. M., 419, 435
Brasic, J., 315, 316, 320
Braswell, L., 293, 309

Braud, L. W., 186, 187, 189
Braud, W. G., 186, 189
Braukmann, C. J., 149, 162, 309
Braver, S., 425, 436
Breen, M., 279, 287
Breitenbucher, M., 444, 452
Brennan, R. L., 157, 162
Brent, D., 33, 38, 75, 80
Brent, D. A., 239, 248
Breslau, N., 34, 36, 37, 254, 264
Brigden, R. L., 101, 117
Briggs, S. E., 440, 452
Brinza, S. R., 112, 122
Bristol, M. M., 350, 362
Broadman, L., 421, 435
Brockington, I. F., 288
Broden, M., 130, 136
Brodie, H. K. H., 324, 326, 344
Brooks-Gunn, J., 112, 117
Broome, M. E., 421, 435
Browder, D. M., 126, 138
Brown, C. H., 287
Brown, F. J., 3, 12, 36, 38, 101, 117
Brown, G. K., 428, 435
Brown, J. K., 401, 410
Brown, J. M., 429, 435
Brown, L., 177, 384, 398
Brown, L. L., 176
Brown, L. P., 119
Brown, R., 65, 80
Brown, R. T., 276, 282, 287, 290
Brown, T., 225, 235
Brown, T. A., 376, 381
Brownell, K. D., 365, 381
Brubakk, A. M., 49
Bruch, H., 390, 391, 396
Bruininks, R. H., 327, 343
Brun, J. K., 372, 382
Brusilow, S., 49
Brusoff, B., 39
Bruun, R. D., 312, 317, 319
Bruyn, G. W., 402, 410
Bryant, B. R., 177
Bryant-Waugh, R., 384, 397
Bryson-Brockman, W., 344
Buchingham, B., 404, 412
Buchsbaum, M. D., 281, 291
Buchsbaum, Y., 261, 267
Buck, J., 229, 234
Buckingham, B., 425, 437
Bugental, B. D., 11, 12
Bukowski, W. M., 169, 173, 174, 178

Bunney, E. E., 38
Bunney, W. E., Jr., 28, 38
Burbach, D. J., 73, 80, 241, 249, 257, 266
Burchinal, L. G., 100, 117
Burge, D. A., 140, 162
Burgess, N., 126, 134, 138
Burk, J. P., 34, 35, 38
Burke, E. E., 409, 410
Burke, E. J., 405, 410
Burke, G. L., 364, 383
Burke, P., 257, 267
Burkinshaw, L., 369, 381
Burks, B. S., 100, 117
Burland, S., 105, 120
Burns, B. J., 33, 38
Burns, E., 176
Burns, G. L., 297, 298, 307, 309
Burns, R., 229, 234
Burokas, L., 416, 435
Buros, O. K., 116, 117
Burroughs, J., 385, 399
Bursick, J. H., 372, 381
Burstein, S., 428, 435
Bursuck, W. D., 172, 176
Burt, V., 364, 383
Burton, B. K., 49
Bush, B. A., 439, 454
Bush, J. P., 416, 417, 435
Busk, P. L., 169, 176
Buskirk, E. R., 367, 381
Busner, J., 376, 381
Butkus, M., 112, 120

Cady, V. M., 100, 117
Caine, E. O., 311, 319
Cairns, R. B., 83, 94, 141, 162
Caldwell, B., 443, 445, 452
Caldwell, S., 148, 163, 420, 436
California Dept of Developmental Services, 333, 343
Calimlim, J. F., 425, 438
Calkins, R. P., 9, 13
Cameron, R., 105, 120
Camfield, R. P., 404, 410
Campbell, C., 126, 137
Campbell, D. T., 86, 94
Campbell, M., 336, 343
Campbell, S. B., 280, 287
Campbell, U., 253, 265
Campbell, W., 272, 288
Campos, J. J., 184, 191
Canino, G., 33, 37

Cann, H. M., 49
Cantwell, D. P., 19, 24, 30, 38, 281, 287, 349, 361
Caparulo, B. K., 314, 319
Caplan, R., 343
Cappelli, M., 426, 436
Caputo, J., 84, 96
Carbonari, C. M., 314, 319
Carek, D. J., 310
Carey, M., 410, 411
Carey, M. P., 258, 260, 264, 265
Carlson, C. L., 293, 307
Carlson, G. A., 252, 253, 257, 259, 260, 264, 267, 270, 273, 286, 287, 290
Carlson, G. C., 28, 39, 77, 79, 91, 96
Carlson, S., 115, 117
Carpenter, W. T., Jr., 67, 79
Carr, D. B., 426, 438
Carr, E. G., 340, 343
Carroll, B. J., 261, 263, 265, 267
Carroll, I. L., 196, 206
Carroll, J. J., 105, 117
Carroll, V. S., 314, 319
Carroll-Wilson, M., 5, 13, 244, 249
Carstens, C. B., 129, 138
Carvajal, H., 199, 205
Casat, C. D., 110, 118
Cash, T. F., 376, 381
Casper, R. C., 385, 389, 396
Cassidy, J. T., 414, 435
Cassisi, J. E., 439, 452
Castenada, A., 109, 117, 185, 189
Cataldo, M. F., 187, 189
Cattell, M. D., 115, 117
Cattell, R. B., 103, 115, 117, 118, 196, 198, 206
Caviness, V. S., 211, 222
Cerny, J. A., 6, 14
Chahal, R., 287
Chajczyk, D., 282, 291
Chamberlain, P., 296, 300, 307
Chamberlain, T. P., 336, 345
Chambers, W. J., 36, 38, 65, 77, 78, 79, 81, 241, 248, 250, 256, 265, 267, 273, 287, 289, 290, 309
Chandler, L., 226, 234
Chandler, M., 341, 343
Chapman, C. R., 414, 435
Chapman, J., 421, 437
Charkraborty, R., 383
Charlesworth, R., 8, 13
Chassin, L., 109, 123, 244, 250
Chazan, M., 240, 248

Chee, P., 281, 287
Cheiken, M., 153, 163
Chess, S., 19, 25
Chestnut, E. C., 38
Chibnall, J. T., 426, 437
Childers, P., 18, 24
Chiverton, P., 311, 319
Christ, M. A., 85, 96
Christensen, D. E., 336, 343
Christensen, M. F., 414, 435
Christiansen, B. A., 108, 118
Christie, D. J., 134, 136
Christie, M., 393, 398
Chudy, J., 225, 235
Cicchetti, D. V., 18, 24, 321, 333, 345, 354, 363, 441, 444, 448, 452, 454
Cieslik, C. J., 380
Ciminero, A. R., 3, 9, 20, 21, 24
Cinciripini, P. M., 403, 411
Clarizio, H., 30, 38
Clark, E., 111, 119, 135, 137, 202, 205
Clark, J. A., 443, 446, 452
Clark, R. A., 225, 235
Clark, W. W., 101, 123
Clarke, G. N., 264, 266
Clarke, W. R., 365, 382
Clarkin, J. F., 261, 266, 273, 291
Clayton, B., 375, 381
Clayton, G. A., 199, 206
Clearman, D. R., 380
Clearman, P., 380
Clegg, M., 115, 117
Clement, P. F., 394, 398
Clifton, R. K., 184, 189, 431, 435
Cloninger, C. R., 31, 38, 74, 80, 312, 319
Coates, T. J., 378, 382
Coats, K. I., 111, 121, 264, 267
Cobb, J. A., 444, 448, 453
Cockrell, J. L., 416, 435
Cogan, E. A., 118
Cohen, A. S., 170, 176
Cohen, D. J., 28, 39, 312, 314, 315, 317, 319, 320, 347, 363
Cohen, F. L., 417, 435
Cohen, H. J., 324, 326, 327, 345
Cohen, J., 80
Cohen, L. H., 107, 122
Cohen, M. N., 86, 97
Cohen, P., 67, 77, 78, 80, 254, 257, 265, 268
Cohen, R. A., 403, 410, 412
Cohen, S., 443, 446, 452
Coie, J. D., 11, 12, 166, 167, 171, 172, 173, 176

Colbus, D., 112, 120, 258, 266, 296, 309, 439, 453
Cole, C. L., 126, 129, 137
Cole, L. J., 332, 344
Cole, N. S., 55, 61
Cole, T. J., 364, 382
Coleman, M., 346, 349, 357, 361
Colfer, M. V., 261, 267
Colligan, R. C., 103, 118
Collins, B. E., 279, 291
Comeau, J. K., 377, 382
Comings, B. G., 312, 319
Comings, D. E., 312, 319
Como, P. G., 314, 315, 319
Compas, B. E., 11, 12, 107, 118
Conaway, L. P., 444, 446, 453
Conaway, R. L., 447, 454
Cone, J. D., 7, 8, 12, 140, 153, 156, 157, 162
Conger, A., 166, 169, 176
Conger, R. D., 440, 453
Conger, R. W., 309
Connell, J. P., 113, 118
Conners, C. K., 83, 84, 86, 89, 90, 91, 94, 95, 244, 248, 269, 275, 276, 281, 288, 298, 307, 314, 319, 336, 343
Conners, M. E., 384, 390, 398
Connolly, A. J., 199, 205
Connor, W. E., 365, 382
Conover, N. C., 35, 36, 38, 67, 76, 80, 89, 91, 94, 239, 241, 248, 253, 254, 265
Cook, S. C., 261, 267
Cool, V. A., 199, 206
Cools, J., 73, 79, 80, 255, 266
Coons, H. W., 289
Cooper, J., 312, 319
Cooper, J. O., 340, 343
Cooper, P. J., 386, 392, 398
Cooper, Z., 393, 396
Coopersmith, S., 114, 118
Coppotelli, H., 176
Cordes, C. K., 322, 343
Cordle, C., 393, 398
Corn, R., 261, 266
Cornblatt, B., 28, 38
Cornell, E. L., 118
Corradini, A., 99, 117
Corrigan, S. A., 365, 381
Corwin, M. J., 419, 436
Coryell, W., 35, 37
Corzo, H., 261, 267
Coscina, D. V., 386, 397
Costa, F. M., 107, 118

Costello, A. J., 16, 24, 33, 38, 66, 67, 75, 76, 80, 86, 89, 94, 239, 241, 248, 252, 253, 254, 255, 262, 265, 273, 274, 275, 276, 279, 288
Costello, E. J., 33, 35, 36, 38, 75, 76, 80, 88, 94, 254, 264, 265
Courchesne, E., 349, 361
Courthial, A., 100, 118
Coury, D. L., 409, 412
Cowan, E. A., 101, 118
Cowen, E. L., 8, 12, 119
Cox, S., 371, 381
Coxe, W. W., 118
Coyette, C. H., 319
Craig, K. D., 419, 422, 435, 436
Craighead, L. W., 111, 122, 257, 258, 265, 267
Craighead, W. E., 111, 122, 141, 163, 183, 190, 251, 252, 255, 257, 258, 263, 265, 266, 267
Crandall, V. C., 105, 113, 118
Crandall, V. J., 118
Crane, R. S., 245, 250
Crawford, J. J., 170, 177
Creak, M., 351, 361
Crimmins, D. B., 336, 343
Crisp, A. H., 390, 396
Crnic, K., 445, 452
Croake, J. W., 240, 248
Crocker, A. C., 324, 327, 345
Cronbach, L. J., 84, 94, 140, 157, 162, 170, 176, 199, 205
Croughan, J., 65, 81
Crouse, T. R., 137
Crouse-Novak, M. A., 30, 38, 39, 81, 266
Crowe, R. R., 28, 38
Crowne, D. P., 105, 118
Crumaghim, J. T., 289
Cruse, R. P., 312, 319, 403, 411
Cummings, C., 271, 291
Cummings, J., 227, 228, 229, 234
Cummings, J. L., 312, 319
Cunningham, C. E., 187, 189
Cunningham, S. J., 405, 407, 410, 412, 426, 438
Curry, J. F., 251, 252, 258, 265
Curtiss, G., 296, 307, 309
Curtona, C. E., 114, 122, 443, 446, 452, 453
Cytryn, L., 73, 80, 88, 95, 241, 249, 255, 266, 273, 288

D'Astous, J., 410, 430, 435
D'Herouville, A., 415, 436
D'Huyvetters, K. K., 126, 138
D'Souza, B. J., 400, 401, 409, 412
Dabbs, J. M., 184, 189, 190

Dale, J., 422, 436
Dalessio, D. J., 401, 411
Dally, P. J., 384, 396
Dana, R., 225, 234
Dancer, D. D., 149, 162
Dandes, S. K., 109, 120
Daniel, A., 77, 79
Daniel, A. E., 252, 253, 264, 273, 287
Daniels, S. R., 384, 398
Daniels-Beirness, T., 170, 172, 178
Danquah, S. A., 186, 189
Darley, S., 245, 248
Das, J. P., 194, 207
Dash, J., 413, 438
Daston, S., 394, 398
Datson, D., 376, 381
Davids, A., 225, 234
Davidson, K. S., 109, 122, 245, 250
Davies, D. R., 281, 288, 393, 398
Davies, M., 30, 36, 38, 80, 81, 117, 248, 256, 265, 287
Davis, C. J., 401, 403, 404, 405, 412
Davis, C. M., 182, 191
Davis, G. C., 34, 36, 37
Davis, G. E., 107, 118
Davis, H., 84, 85, 95
Davis, J. M., 385, 396
Davis, L. E., 398
Davis, R., 393, 395, 397
Davison, L. A., 214, 215, 223
Dawes, R. M., 274, 288
Dawson, M. E., 186, 191
Day, D., 107, 119, 282, 289
de la Cruz, F. F., 325, 343
Deardorff, P., 109, 118
DeBauche, B. A., 38
deBlois, C. S., 271, 291
DeGiovanni, I. S., 240, 249
DeGood, D. E., 415, 435
DeGroot, J., 85, 95
Delaney, E. A., 198, 205
Delugack, J. D., 172, 176
Deluty, R. H., 108, 118, 295, 297, 307
DeMaster, B., 152, 153, 162
DeMelio, L., 33, 38
DeMyer, M. K., 346, 349, 357, 361
Dennis, M., 212, 222
DePaul, G. J., 288
Derogatis, L. R., 395, 396, 444, 447, 452
Detlor, J., 314, 317, 319, 320
Deubner, D. C., 401, 410
Deuerstein, R. F., 205

Deutsch, C., 282, 291
Devany, J., 128, 131, 138
deVeber, L. L., 404, 411, 426, 437
Devor, E. J., 312, 319
Dewey, M. E., 394, 399
Dezanteux, C. A., 46, 49
Diament, C., 150, 153, 163, 164
Diamond, S., 401, 409, 411
Dibble, E., 38, 40
Dickson, J., 228, 234
Diener, C. I., 113, 118
Dietiker, K. E., 110, 122
Dietrich, K. N., 444, 448, 452
Dietz, A., 150, 163
Dietz, W. H., 364, 369, 370, 381
Dilsaver, S. C., 37
DiNardo, P. A., 241, 248
Dinswiddle, R., 46, 49
Dion, K. K., 172, 176
Dishion, T. J., 294, 299, 309, 310
Dixon, H., 35, 40
Dobes, R. W., 143, 163
Dodge, D., 442, 443, 454
Dodge, K. A., 172, 173, 176, 293, 307
Doerfler, L. A., 258, 260, 265
Dohrenwend, B. P., 445, 452
Dohrenwend, B. S., 445, 452
Doke, L. A., 330, 331, 343
Doleys, D. M., 20, 24
Doll, E., 343
Dollinger, S. J., 11, 13
Donahoe, C. P., 308
Donovan, J. E., 107, 118
Dormon, F., 417, 437
Dorsey, M. F., 336, 344
Dotan, N., 197, 207
Dotecki, P. R., 343
Dougherty, L. M., 419, 436
Douglas, V. I., 269, 271, 279, 280, 281, 282, 286, 287, 288, 291
Downing, M., 107, 122
Drabman, R. S., 3, 9, 12, 129, 138
Dragnus, J. G., 141, 164
Driscoll, P. F., 49
Drucker, A. J., 102, 121
DuBose, R. F., 168, 170, 178
Dubowitz, H., 439, 454
Duckro, P. N., 186, 189
Duke, M. P., 113, 121
Dulcan, M. K., 33, 35, 36, 38, 66, 67, 75, 76, 80, 239, 241, 248, 253, 254, 265
Dumas, J. E., 305, 310

Dunn, J. K., 380, 419, 421, 435, 437
Dunn, L., 355, 361
Dunn, P. K., 394, 396
Dunn-Geier, B. J., 430, 435
Dunne, E. A., 425, 436
DuPaul, J. G., 276, 278, 279, 282, 290
Dupstas, F. D., 343
Dura, J. R., 335, 344
Durand, V. M., 336, 340, 343
DuRant, R. H., 366, 381
Durniat, K., 437
Dweck, C. S., 113, 118
Dworkin, R. J., 380
Dygdon, J. A., 165, 166, 169, 171, 176

Earls, F., 74, 75, 80, 84, 89, 95, 240, 248
Earls, L. J., 28, 38
Eason, L., 414, 438
Eastman, E. S., 305, 308
Eber, H. W., 103, 118
Eberhart, S., 197, 206
Eckert, E. D., 385, 390, 396, 398
Eckman, K., 419, 435
Edelberg, R., 184, 189
Edelbrock, C. S., 9, 13, 16, 21, 24, 31, 33, 35, 36, 37, 38, 67, 73, 75, 76, 79, 80, 82, 83, 84, 85, 86, 87, 88, 89, 90, 91, 93, 94, 96, 115, 116, 141, 162, 239, 241, 243, 244, 248, 252, 253, 254, 255, 262, 265, 272, 273, 274, 275, 276, 279, 287, 292, 298, 304, 307, 311, 314, 316, 318, 444, 448, 451
Edelbrock, L. S., 66, 80
Edelsohn, G. A., 81
Edgell, D., 210, 223
Edlund, S. R., 409, 410
Edwards, C. D., 109, 122
Edwards, G. L., 258, 265
Edwards, K. L., 215, 223
Egeland, B., 444, 452
Einbender, A. J., 442, 452
Eisenberg, L., 142, 164
Eland, J. M., 413, 416, 426, 427, 435
Elder, P., 435
Eldridge, R., 49
Elizabeth Stewart Hands & Assoc, 374, 381
Elkind, G. S., 31, 40, 282, 291
Ellenberger, H., 229, 234
Elliot, W. R., 11, 14
Elliott, C., 148, 163
Elliott, C. H., 414, 420, 431, 436
Elliott, D. S., 295, 297, 300, 307
Elliott, S. N., 165, 172, 177

Emery, R. E., 85, 94
Empey, L. T., 300, 307
Endicott, J., 27, 31, 35, 37, 39, 65, 80
Endsley, R., 421, 435
Enyart, P., 258, 260, 264, 265
Epstein, B., 435
Epstein, H. T., 212, 222
Epstein, L. H., 129, 136, 374, 381, 403, 411
Epstein, S., 99, 118
Epstein, W. B., 149, 163
Erbaugh, J., 260, 264, 395, 396, 444, 447, 452
Erenberg, G., 312, 319, 403, 411
Erickson, M. T., 150, 151, 164
Erlenmeyer-Kimling, L., 28, 38, 281, 288
Eron, L. D., 225, 235, 295, 299, 308, 309
Espinoza, T., 376, 381
Esserman, J., 372, 382
Esveldt-Dawson, K., 36, 38, 85, 86, 89, 90, 92, 93, 95, 112, 120, 258, 263, 266, 295, 302, 304, 308, 309
Evans, D. D., 263, 265
Evans, E., 258, 260, 265
Evans, I. M., 3, 5, 7, 9, 13
Everson, M., 81
Exner, D., 230, 234
Exner, J. E., 99, 118, 229, 230, 231, 232, 234, 262, 265
Eyberg, S. M., 92, 94, 96, 296, 297, 298, 299, 307, 308, 310, 444, 447, 452
Eyman, R. K., 333, 343
Eysenck, H. J., 18, 24, 115, 118
Eysenck, S. B. G., 18, 24, 115, 118

Fabricant, R., 49
Fagot, B. I., 444, 448, 452
Fahs, J. J., 341, 343
Fairbank, J., 446, 454
Fairburn, C. G., 384, 386, 389, 390, 391, 392, 393, 395, 396
Faleck, H., 403, 411
Falsey, S., 443, 445, 451
Fantie, B., 210, 212, 223
Fantuzzo, J. W., 124, 132, 133, 137
Fanurik, D., 429, 436
Farber, J. M., 341, 343
Farmer, A., 288
Farragher, J., 229, 234
Farrington, D. P., 294, 297, 308, 310
Fassler, D., 187, 189
Faulstich, M. E., 185, 191, 258, 260, 264, 265
Faust, J., 301, 308
Fawcett, N., 421, 436

Feczko, M., 309
Feighner, J. P., 27, 31, 38, 74, 80
Feinberg, M., 265
Feinberg, T. E., 314, 318, 320
Feinberg, T. L., 30, 38, 39, 81, 261, 266
Feinstein, C., 335, 343
Feldman, W., 413, 435
Felner, R. D., 258, 260, 265
Fenichel, G. M., 44, 45, 48, 49
Fentress, D. W., 409, 411
Ferguson, H., 90, 96
Ferguson, H. B., 410
Fernandez, E., 430, 435
Ferrari, M. D., 402, 404, 410
Ferry, P. C., 402, 411
Feuerstein, M. J., 181, 182, 185, 190
Feuerstein, R. F., 196, 205
Fidler, P. S., 344
Field, C. J., 335, 342, 343
Finch, A. J., Jr., 108, 109, 110, 111, 113, 117, 118, 120, 227, 228, 232, 234, 258, 262, 265, 266, 267, 305, 308, 310, 414, 438
Fine, R., 225, 234
Fine, S., 36, 38, 39, 258, 259, 263, 265, 267
Finkelstein, R., 30, 34, 39, 76, 81, 239, 249, 266
Finley, W. W., 187, 189
Firestone, P., 274, 288, 410, 412
First, L. R., 413, 434
Fischer, J., 185, 190, 245, 249
Fisher, C., 389, 398
Fisher, K. W., 105, 118
Fisher, M., 279, 287
Fisher, P., 66, 81, 315, 316, 320
Fisk, J. L., 209, 223
Fiske, D. W., 86, 94
Fitch, P., 65, 80
Fitzgerald, G., 276, 289
Fitzpatrick, J., 35, 40, 87, 94
Fixsen, D. L., 124, 136
Flamant, F., 415, 436
Flamant, M. E., 38
Flament, M. F., 110, 117, 118, 312, 318
Flaugher, R. L., 196, 205
Flavell, J. H., 105, 119
Fleece, E. L., 245, 250
Fleiss, J. L., 274, 291
Fletcher, J. M., 219, 220, 222, 223
Flor, H., 423, 424, 438
Flynn, J. M., 442, 443, 453
Foa, D., 22, 24
Foley, J. L., 245, 250
Folger, C., 414, 438

Folkman, S., 428, 436
Folstein, M., 287
Ford, D. Y., 374, 382
Ford, L. H., 105, 109
Ford, R. C., 169, 176
Fordyce, W. E., 418, 423, 435
Fordyce, W. F., 403, 411
Forehand, R. L., 85, 90, 95, 96, 172, 177, 178, 244, 250, 258, 267, 275, 280, 288, 289, 299, 300, 301, 308, 309, 331, 343
Foreyt, J. P., 386, 393, 397
Forlano, G., 100, 101, 121
Forness, S., 166, 178
Forrest v Ansbach, 58, 61
Forsythe, C. J., 107, 118
Fosson, A., 384, 397
Foster, R., 321, 332, 344
Foster, S. L., 140, 143, 144, 147, 149, 150, 151, 153, 156, 162, 163, 167, 168, 172, 176
Foster, W., 331, 345
Fourqurean, J. M., 197, 206
Fowler, S. A., 135, 136
Fox, J. E., 109, 119
Fox, N. A., 184, 191
Fox, S., 369, 382
Foxx, R. M., 336, 343
Frame, C. L., 87, 95, 166, 178, 239, 244, 250, 258, 267
Frances, A., 273, 291
Francis, G., 34, 39, 180, 191, 240, 241, 243, 244, 248, 249, 250
Franck, L. S., 420, 435
Frank, G. C., 372, 381
Frank, L., 224, 234
Frankel, M., 312, 319
Franklin, M., 409, 411
Franzini, L., 128, 137
Frary, P. B., 9, 14, 21, 25
Frary, R., 183, 191
Fraser, W. I., 336, 344
Frederiksen, L. W., 129, 136
Fredrikson, M., 183, 189
Freedman, B. J., 293, 308
Freedman, D. S., 364, 383
Freeman, B. J., 245, 249, 351, 361
Freeman, J. M., 322, 344
Freeman, L. N., 36, 39, 261, 267
Freeman, R. J., 258, 259, 265
Freitas, J. L., 128, 129, 130, 137
French, N. H., 36, 38, 85, 92, 93, 95, 112, 120, 263, 266, 295, 302, 304, 308, 309
Frentz, C., 172, 177

Freud, S., 224, 235
Frick, P., 239, 250
Frick, P. J., 85, 86, 95, 96, 166, 178
Frick, T., 156, 162
Friedland-Bandes, R., 11, 12
Friedman, B. A., 403, 409, 412
Friedman, D., 281, 288
Friedman, E. G., 48, 49
Friedman, R. C., 261, 266
Friedrich, W. N., 442, 443, 445, 446, 452
Friesen, W. V., 419, 435
Frodi, A. M., 443, 445, 446, 452
Froham, P. E., 140, 164
Fuchs, D., 131, 136
Fuchs, L. S., 131, 136
Fuller, G. B., 101, 119
Fuller, M., 228, 235
Fulop, G., 320
Funderburke, B. W., 92, 94, 296, 298, 308
Furey, W., 258, 267
Furman, W., 10, 13

Gaddes, W., 217, 223
Gadow, K. D., 85, 94, 341, 343
Gaffney, A., 424, 425, 436
Gaffney, L. R., 293, 308
Gajar, A., 136
Galaburda, A. M., 211, 222
Galante, R., 22, 24
Gall, C., 212, 222
Gammon, G. D., 35, 36, 37, 40, 79, 268, 272, 288, 291
Gandhy, P. R., 74, 81, 252, 267
Garbarino, J., 439, 441, 452
Garber, J., 19, 20, 21, 22, 24, 141, 142, 162
Garcia, K., 240, 249
Gardner, B., 100, 117
Gardner, M. J., 290
Gardner, R. A., 212, 222
Gardner, R. M., 376, 381
Gardner, W. I., 126, 129, 137
Garfield, S., 225, 235
Garfinkel, B. D., 275, 287
Garfinkel, P. E., 112, 119, 384, 385, 387, 389, 390, 393, 394, 397
Garfinkle, B. D., 90, 95
Garmezy, N., 18, 24
Garner, D. M., 112, 119, 384, 385, 386, 387, 389, 390, 391, 392, 393, 394, 395, 396, 397
Garrard, S. D., 323, 343
Garrison, W. T., 84, 89, 95
Garrison-Jones, C. V., 260, 261, 264

Gascon, G. C., 400, 411
Gatsonis, C., 34, 39
Gaudin, J. M., 440, 453
Gauvain-Piquard, A., 421, 422, 436
Gdowski, C. L., 75, 81, 112, 120
Geiger-Parker, B., 324, 344
Gelb, R., 166, 177
Gelder, M. G., 10, 13
Gelfand, D. M., 5, 13, 15, 25, 143, 147, 156, 162
Geller, B., 36, 38
Genshaft, J. L., 409, 412
George, G. C. W., 384, 396
Gerber, J., 199, 205
Gershon, E. S., 28, 38, 40
Gertler, A., 384, 398
Geschwind, N., 211, 222
Giannetti, R. A., 262, 264
Gibaud-Wallston, J., 442, 443, 452
Gibbons, R., 261, 267
Gibson, E. J., 184, 189
Giebenhain, J., 148, 162
Gillberg, C., 346, 349, 357, 361
Giller, H., 294, 310
Gilliam, G., 439, 452
Gillis, J. S., 109, 119
Gilmore, M., 273, 291
Gioia, P., 81
Gittelman, R., 270, 288, 301, 308
Gittelman-Klein, R., 279, 287
Gladis, M., 393, 399
Glarizio, H., 38
Glaser, G. H., 294, 309
Glazer, J. A., 8, 13
Glennon, B., 243, 245, 249
Gleser, G. C., 157, 162
Glick, J., 148, 163
Glow, P. H., 90, 95
Glow, R. A., 90, 95
Glueck, C. J., 365, 382
Glueck, E., 293, 294, 308
Glueck, S., 293, 294, 308
Glutting, J. J., 199, 206
Glynn, T., 130, 136
Goetz, C. G., 313, 314, 315, 319, 320
Goff, G., 398
Goh, D. S., 101, 119
Gold, M., 107, 117, 297, 300, 310
Gold, R. G., 447, 453
Goldberg, L. R., 102, 119
Goldberg, S. C., 385, 396
Golden, C. J., 197, 207, 214, 218, 219, 222
Golden, G. S., 402, 411

Golden, L. R., 38
Golden, M. M., 169, 178
Golden, R. R., 28, 38
Goldfried, M. R., 4, 13
Goldman, M. S., 108, 118
Goldstein, G. R., 447, 452
Goldstein, H. S., 294, 308
Goldstein, I. B., 182, 189
Goldstein, K., 208, 222
Goldstein, M. G., 289
Golub, H. L., 419, 436
Gomez, J., 384, 396
Gonzalez, J. C., 421, 422, 436
Goode, S., 351, 361
Goodenough, F. L., 227, 235
Goodman, J. T., 410, 421, 437
Goodsitt, A., 391, 397
Gordon, R. A., 262, 264
Gordon, Y., 73, 80, 256, 266
Gormally, J., 376, 381, 394, 398
Gorman, J. M., 188, 191
Gorsuch, R. L., 444, 447, 454
Gortmaker, S. L., 364, 369, 381
Gotlib, I., 166, 176
Gottfried, A. E., 107, 119
Gottlieb, J., 166, 177, 403, 410
Gottman, J. M., 140, 162, 167, 177
Gough, H. G., 103, 119
Gould, M. S., 33, 37, 315, 316, 320
Gowers, D., 384, 398
Goyette, C. H., 83, 90, 91, 95, 314, 319, 336, 343
Goyette, C. J., 275, 276, 288
Gracely, R. H., 425, 436
Grad, G., 312, 319
Grad, L. R., 312, 319
Graham, A., 309
Graham, F. K., 184, 189, 431, 435
Graham, J. R., 405, 411
Graham, P., 240, 250, 272, 290
Graham, P. J., 20, 25, 73, 81
Gramling, S., 181, 182, 183, 191
Graves, A. W., 111, 122, 133, 137
Graziano, A. M., 10, 13, 240, 247, 249
Graziano, W. G., 301, 308
Greden, J. F., 261, 265
Green, A. H., 439, 452
Green, B. F., 52, 61, 144, 163
Green, B. J., 111, 122, 257, 258, 265, 267
Green, C. J., 115, 120
Green, J., 260, 267
Green, J. A., 83, 94, 141, 162

Green, K. D., 90, 95, 172, 177, 275, 289
Green, R., 228, 235
Green, W., 343
Greenbaum, R., 89, 91, 94
Greenberg, M. T., 445, 452
Greene, B. F., 443, 445, 454
Greene, B. V., 443, 445, 454
Greenfield, N. S., 183, 189
Greenspan, S. I., 65, 80
Greenwood, C. R., 272, 288
Gregg, N. B., 196, 207
Gregory, J., 186, 189
Greiner, C., 327, 344
Greipp, M., 414, 436
Greist, D. L., 85, 96
Greist, J. H., 112, 122
Gresham, F. M., 8, 13, 165, 166, 167, 170, 171, 172, 177, 178, 258, 260, 264, 265
Griffin, G., 377, 382
Griffin, N., 266
Grimes, K., 75, 81, 272, 291
Groll, S., 274, 291
Gronlund, N. E., 168, 177
Groot, M., 297, 308
Gross, A. M., 108, 123, 377, 381, 422, 436
Grossman, H. J., 321, 322, 343
Grossman, J. A., 36, 39, 261, 267
Grove, T., 197, 207
Gruber, A. B., 49
Gruen, W., 103, 118
Gruenberg, E. M., 287
Grunau, R. V. E., 419, 435, 436
Grusec, J., 245, 248
Gruson, L., 105, 120
Gualtieri, C. T., 341, 343
Guardino, M., 85, 96
Guare, J. C., 119
Guerra, E., 421, 436
Guevremont, D., 430, 438
Guidano, V. F., 390, 398
Guilford, J. P., 102, 119
Guion, R. M., 52, 61
Gullone, E., 183, 190
Gundell, G. W., 324, 344
Guroff, J. J., 28, 38, 40
Gustawson, J., 382
Gutterman, E. M., 252, 253, 257, 265, 268
Guttman, H. A., 149, 163
Guyer, C. G., 187, 189
Guyer, N. P., 187, 189
Guze, S. B., 27, 31, 38, 39, 80

Habelow, W., 29, 37
Haddad, F. A., 196, 206
Haefele, W. F., 294, 308
Haesly, R. R., 184, 190
Hafner, A. J., 225, 235
Hagan, R., 444, 448, 452
Hagberg, B., 48, 49
Hagborg, W. J., 87, 95
Hagen, E. P., 194, 207, 334, 345
Hagin, R. A., 312, 319
Hahn, V. S., 402, 411
Hahn, Y. S., 415, 436
Hale, B., 414, 434
Haley, G. M. T., 36, 38, 39, 258, 259, 263, 265, 267
Hall, R. V., 130, 136
Hallahan, D. P., 129, 132, 133, 134, 137, 138
Haller, D. L., 104, 120
Halmi, K. A., 385, 396
Hamada, R. S., 416, 437
Hamburger, S. D., 354, 362
Hamilton, D. I., 180, 190
Hamilton, M., 112, 119, 261, 265
Hamlett, C. L., 131, 136
Hamlett, K., 73, 80
Hammen, C. L., 131, 137
Hammer, D., 331, 345, 409, 412
Hammer, E., 228, 235
Hammes, R. R., 174, 177
Hammill, D. D., 176, 177
Hamovit, J., 28, 38, 40
Hampe, E., 10, 13, 110, 120
Hampstead, W. J., 187, 189
Handal, P. J., 258, 262, 266
Hanis, C., 383
Hannallah, R., 435
Hansen, D. J., 443, 444, 446, 447, 452, 453, 454
Hanslen, R. H., 336, 345
Hanson, C. L., 294, 308, 378, 382
Hanson, K., 416, 438
Hanson, V., 427, 438
Harari, H., 172, 178
Harcherick, D. F., 314, 315, 319
Hardin, M. T., 319
Hare, R. D., 183, 190
Harkins, J. A., 377, 382
Harpin, V. A., 431, 436
Harrell, A. V., 108, 119
Harris, C. W., 333, 343
Harris, E. S., 382
Harris, F. C., 150, 163

Harris, J. C., 89, 95
Harris, K. R., 133, 137
Harris, S., 357, 361
Harrison, G. G., 368, 381
Harrison, P. L., 193, 194, 195, 202, 203, 206
Harsha, D. W., 364, 383
Hart, B., 356, 361
Hart, J., 183, 190
Hartdagen, S., 86, 95, 289
Harter, S., 105, 114, 119, 249
Hartlage, L. C., 219, 223
Hartman, A., 225, 235
Hartmann, D. P., 5, 13, 15, 25, 140, 141, 142, 143, 144, 147, 148, 149, 150, 152, 153, 156, 157, 159, 162, 163, 248
Hartshorne, H., 168, 170, 177
Hartup, W. W., 8, 13
Hartwig, S. S., 199, 206
Hasher, L., 282, 288
Hassett, J., 182, 183, 190
Hastings, J. E., 186, 190
Hathaway, S. R., 103, 119, 444, 447, 453
Hatsukami, D., 390, 398
Hatton, H. M., 431, 435
Hawes, R. R., 148, 163, 245, 250
Hawkes, G. R., 100, 117
Hawkins, C. R., II, 394, 398
Hawkins, R. P., 7, 12, 143, 163
Haworth, M., 226, 235
Hay, L. R., 128, 129, 131, 138
Hay, W. M., 129, 138
Hayes, S. C., 7, 13
Haynes, S. N., 129, 137, 146, 148, 149, 150, 152, 163, 188, 190
Hayvren, M., 175, 177
Healey, J. M., 289
Hearn, M. T., 404, 411, 426, 437
Hedley, J., 152, 163
Hedrick, D. L., 355, 361
Heemsbergen, J., 351, 361
Heezen, T. J. M., 421, 434
Heiby, E., 148, 163
Heidish, I. E., 86, 95, 262, 266
Heidrich, G., 416, 437
Hekimian, E., 446, 452
Helfer, R., 442, 443, 453
Helms, P., 46, 49
Helsel, W. J., 93, 95, 96, 265
Helton, G. B., 139
Helzer, J. E., 65, 81, 272, 288
Hemmick, S., 245, 249

Hendrickson, J. M., 132, 137
Henggeler, S. W., 294, 308
Henker, B., 11, 12, 166, 178, 269, 271, 279, 291
Henry, D., 187, 190
Henry, S. A., 280, 288
Henry, W., 225, 235
Henske, J., 380
Hensley, V. R., 259, 267
Herjanic, B., 35, 36, 38, 40, 65, 73, 80, 81, 241, 249, 252, 253, 265, 267, 268, 272, 288, 295, 308
Herjanic, M., 36, 38, 65, 80
Herman, C. P., 376, 381
Hermecz, D. A., 188, 190
Hermelin, B., 348, 361
Heron, T. E., 340, 343
Hersen, M., 3, 4, 5, 13, 14, 34, 39, 76, 81, 110, 122, 140, 145, 164, 180, 181, 187, 188, 191, 239, 249, 250, 439, 443, 445, 447, 452
Hersh, R. H., 166, 177
Herzbergen, S. D., 113, 119
Hesselbrock, V., 184, 190
Hesselink, J. R., 349, 361
Hester, N., 426, 436
Hetherington, E. M., 294, 308
Heward, J. L., 340, 343
Hewes, P., 199, 205
Hidalgo, J., 33, 38
Higa, W. R., 9, 13
Hightower, A. D., 115, 119
Hill, B. K., 327, 343
Hill, M. A., 312, 319
Hingtgen, J. N., 346, 361
Hinkle, L., 371, 381
Hinshaw, S. P., 270, 271, 274, 275, 288
Hirsch, M., 36, 38, 79, 248, 256, 265, 287
Hiss, M., 134, 136
Hobbs, N., 55, 61
Hoberman, H. M., 443, 446, 452
Hobson, R. P., 355, 361
Hodge, G. K., 113, 120
Hodges, K., 68, 73, 77, 79, 80, 88, 95, 241, 249, 252, 255, 256, 257, 258, 265, 266, 273, 288
Hodges, V. K., 65, 80
Hodgson, R., 188, 190
Hodson, C. J., 436
Hoehn-Saric, E., 241, 243, 249
Hoelscher, T. J., 401, 404, 405, 407, 409, 411
Hoffman-Plotkin, D., 439, 453
Hoffmeister, J., 442, 443, 453
Hoge, S. K., 29, 37

Hoier, T. S., 7, 12, 262, 266
Holdgrafer, M., 351, 361
Hollien, H., 419, 437
Hollinsworth, T., 297, 310
Hollis, J., 336, 344
Hollon, S. D., 5, 13
Holmbeck, G. N., 416, 435
Holmes, C., 228, 235
Holmes, F. B., 3, 13
Holmes, G., 226, 235
Holmes, T. H., 443, 445, 453
Holmstrom, R., 225, 226, 227, 234, 235
Holroyd, J., 357, 361, 443, 444, 453
Holroyd, K. A., 403, 411
Holt, R., 225, 235
Holtz, R., 229, 234
Holzemer, W. L., 424, 425, 426, 434, 437, 438
Holzer, B., 378, 382
Hong, G. K., 260, 261, 266
Honzik, M. P., 240, 249, 292, 309
Hood, C., 197, 206
Hooks, P., 380
Hoon, P. W., 405, 411
Hopkins, T. F., 198, 205
Hops, H., 9, 13, 264, 266, 272, 288
Horn, J. L., 196, 198, 206
Horn, W. F., 149, 150, 152, 163
House, A., 131, 138
House, A. E., 299, 310
Houston, B. K., 109, 119
Hovell, M. D., 372, 381
Hovell, M. F., 375, 381
Howard, A., 294, 309
Howard, K. L., 114, 121
Howell, C. T., 34, 36, 37, 67, 79, 83, 84, 93, 116, 301, 307
Howell, K. W., 128, 130, 137
Howitt, J., 245, 250
Hsu, L. K. G., 394, 398
Hubbard, M., 320
Hubner, J. J., 115, 122
Hudson, J. I., 386, 398
Huebner, R. R., 419, 436
Huertas-Goldman, S., 33, 37
Huesmann, L. R., 295, 298, 299, 308, 309
Hughes, A., 187, 190
Hughes, C. A., 132, 137
Hughes, H., 187, 190
Humphrey, L. L., 107, 119, 276, 288, 378, 381, 391, 398, 399
Humphreys, P. J., 405, 410, 412, 426, 436, 438
Humphries, S., 21, 25

Hunter, S. M., 381
Hunter, W., 81
Huntzinger, R. M., 10, 14
Huon, G. F., 384, 398
Hurley, L. K., 310
Hurt, S. W., 261, 266, 274, 291
Husek, T., 118
Huskisson, E. C., 426, 438
Huston, M., 151, 162
Hutcherson, S., 245, 250
Hutchinson, P. C., 403, 410
Hutzell, R. R., 317, 319
Hyde, T., 74, 81, 267
Hymel, S., 114, 117, 165, 167, 168, 169, 170, 171, 175, 176, 177
Hynd, G. W., 86, 95, 166, 178, 219, 223, 239, 250, 289

Iacuone, R., 183, 190
Iezzi, A., 401, 411
Irvine, M. J., 390, 397
Irwin, C. P., 22, 25
Ito, E., 333, 343
Ivens, C., 36, 38
Iwata, B. A., 336, 344
Iyenger, S., 39
Izard, C. E., 22, 25, 419, 436
Izzo, L. D., 8, 12

Jackson, A. S., 369, 382
Jackson, R. K., 346, 361
Jacob, T., 107, 119
Jacobs, G., 245, 250
Jacobsen, B., 28, 38
Jacobsen, F., 247, 249
Jacobsen, L., 371, 382
Jacobson, J., 166, 177
Jacobson, J. W., 327, 328, 344
Jacobson, N. S., 140, 163
Jaffe, A. C., 385, 387, 398
Jaffee, L. S., 231, 235
Jagger, J., 314, 319
Jalperin, J. M., 289
Janes, C. L., 184, 190
Jarrell, M. P., 412
Jarrett, R. B., 7, 13
Jastak Associates, 202, 203, 206
Jastak, S., 199, 202, 206
Jay, G. W., 401, 411
Jay, S. M., 148, 163, 414, 419, 431, 436
Jeans, M. E., 417, 426, 436
Jeeves, M. A., 336, 344

Jeffrey, D. B., 375, 383
Jensen, A., 197, 206
Jensen, M. P., 425, 436
Jensen, P. S., 84, 85, 95
Jenson, W. R., 111, 119, 135, 137
Jernigan, T. L., 349, 361
Jessor, R., 107, 118, 119
Jessor, S. L., 107, 119
Joffe, R., 405, 411
John, K., 35, 36, 37, 40, 79, 268, 291, 314, 319
Johns, E., 115, 117
Johnson, C., 384, 390, 393, 398
Johnson, C. L., 386, 397
Johnson, G., 421, 437
Johnson, J. B., 320
Johnson, J. E., 184, 189
Johnson, J. H., 107, 110, 114, 119
Johnson, P. A., 184, 190
Johnson, R., 184, 190, 256, 267, 309
Johnson, S. B., 84, 96, 186, 190, 243, 249
Johnson, S. M., 128, 137, 150, 163
Johnson, W. G., 365, 369, 371, 374, 376, 377, 378, 381, 382
Johnston, C., 170, 177, 293, 309, 440, 442, 453
Johnston, C. C., 419, 436
Johnston, C. L., 85, 88, 90, 95
Johnston, H. F., 110, 119
Johnston, J. O., 114, 122
Johnston, L. D., 301, 307
Jones, H. E., 190
Jones, J. T., 276, 290
Jones, M. B., 309
Jones, M. C., 3, 13, 180, 184, 190
Jones, R. M., 369, 381
Jones, R. R., 309
Jordan, H., 351, 361
Jourard, S. M., 376, 383
Julilano, J. M., 196, 206
Jung, K. G., 35, 40, 74, 75, 80, 81, 252, 268
Jurish, S. E., 405, 410

Kabela, E., 410
Kagan, D. M., 377, 381
Kagan, J., 107, 119, 282, 289
Kagonov, T., 405, 411
Kahn, J. S., 111, 119
Kaiser, C. F., 257, 261, 264
Kala, R., 35, 36, 38, 76, 80
Kalas, I. R., 67, 80
Kalas, R., 66, 80, 239, 241, 248, 253, 254, 265, 273, 288
Kessler, M. D., 288

Kalikow, K., 38
Kalish, B. I., 351, 362
Kallman, W. M., 181, 182, 185, 190
Kamarck, T., 443, 446, 452
Kaminer, Y., 335, 343
Kamphaus, R. W., 197, 198, 199, 206, 207
Kandel, D. B., 30, 38
Kane, J. S., 177
Kanfer, F. H., 4, 6, 13, 128, 129, 130, 131, 137, 180, 190, 305, 308
Kanner, L., 347, 361
Kanowitz, J., 153, 163
Kanter, W. R., 48, 49
Kapadia, E. S., 124, 132, 133, 137
Kaplan, A. M., 225, 235
Kaplan, M. G., 448, 452
Kaplan, S. L., 260, 261, 266, 376, 381, 440, 443, 444, 454
Karin, D., 49
Karoly, K., 414, 415, 416, 424, 436
Karoly, P., 425, 436
Karp, S., 225, 226, 227, 234, 235
Karpowitz, D. H., 375, 381
Karsh, K. G., 331, 344
Kashani, J. H., 34, 35, 38, 68, 73, 74, 77, 79, 80, 252, 253, 264, 273, 287
Kaslow, N. J., 111, 122, 264, 267
Katch, F. I., 367, 369, 371, 381, 382
Katch, V. L., 367, 382
Katkin, E. S., 180, 190
Katkovsky, W., 105, 113, 118
Katz, E. R., 413, 414, 415, 420, 421, 431, 434, 436, 438
Katz, I., 245, 248
Katz, J. D., 314, 319
Katzman, M. A., 389, 398
Kauffman, J. M., 133, 137
Kaufman, A. S., 192, 193, 194, 195, 196, 197, 198, 199, 205, 206, 280, 289, 354, 361
Kaufman, K. L., 440, 454
Kaufman, N. L., 194, 197, 198, 199, 201, 206, 354, 361
Kaufman, S., 229, 234
Kavanagh, K., 441, 453
Kazdin, A. E., 10, 13, 34, 36, 38, 39, 76, 81, 85, 86, 89, 90, 92, 93, 95, 110, 112, 120, 122, 140, 141, 142, 147, 148, 149, 151, 163, 239, 249, 250, 252, 257, 258, 259, 262, 266, 292, 295, 296, 297, 299, 301, 302, 304, 305, 306, 308, 309, 336, 340, 344, 345, 439, 453
Keane, S., 166, 176
Keefe, F. J., 423, 436, 437

Keenan, D. H., 409, 412
Keene, D., 412
Kehle, T. J., 111, 119, 135, 137
Keiser, R. E., 225, 235
Keith, T. Z., 197, 199, 206
Kellerman, J., 415, 436
Kellett, J., 384, 398
Kelley, C. K., 245, 249
Kelley, J. A., 442, 446, 453, 454
Kelley, M. L., 401, 404, 412
Kelly, K. L., 282, 290
Kelly, M. B., 147, 163
Kelly, M. M., 258, 267
Kelly, W. J., 135, 137
Kelvie, W., 425, 438
Kendall, P. C., 5, 13, 141, 142, 148, 163, 244, 249, 293, 309
Kendler, K. S., 28, 38
Kennedy, W. A., 240, 249
Kenrick, J., 393, 398
Kent, R. N., 4, 13, 150, 151, 152, 153, 163, 164
Keogh, B. K., 18, 25
Keough, T. E., 184, 190
Kerr, D., 49
Kerr, M. M., 262, 266
Kessler, M. K., 86, 89, 94, 273, 275, 288
Kety, S. S., 28, 38
Keys, N., 101, 120
Khazam, C., 389, 398
Kiburz, C. S., 135, 137
Kidd, K. K., 28, 35, 39, 40, 312, 314, 318, 319, 320
Kiesler, D. J., 142, 163
Kilby, G., 169, 178
Kilts, C., 118
King, A. C., 311, 319
King, C. A., 112, 120
King, N. J., 6, 9, 14, 15, 16, 21, 23, 25, 180, 183, 188, 190, 191
King, S. L., 89, 95
Kinsbourne, M., 269, 271, 272, 280, 286, 289
Kirchner, J., 229, 235
Kirigin, K. A., 149, 162, 300, 309
Kirk, J., 392, 397
Kirschenbaum, D. S., 364, 366, 377, 381, 382, 395, 398
Klaric, S. H., 66, 80, 241, 248, 265, 273, 288
Klass, E., 85, 96
Klawans, H. L., 314, 320
Klee, S. H., 90, 95
Klein, D. F., 273, 279, 287
Klein, R. G., 85, 93, 95, 96

Klesges, L. M., 371, 378, 382
Klesges, R. C., 371, 372, 378, 382
Kline, J., 73, 80, 241, 249, 255, 266, 288
Kline, L., 88, 95
Klinedinst, J. K., 262, 268, 298, 310
Klinefelter, D., 103, 117
Klorman, R., 281, 289
Klove, H., 217, 223
Knapp, M. L., 149, 163
Knapp, T., 415, 426, 435
Knee, D., 29, 32, 37, 39
Kneedler, R. D., 129, 132, 133, 137
Knibbs, J., 384, 397
Knights, R. M., 217, 223
Knox, F. H., 240, 248
Kobal, K., 112, 122
Koch, C., 404, 411
Koch, G. G., 67, 81
Koch, H. J., 168, 177
Koch, R., 48, 49
Koerber, T., 49
Koff, E., 376, 382
Kog, E., 387, 399
Kohn, B., 212, 222
Kolb, B., 210, 212, 223
Kolb, L. C., 324, 326, 344
Kolpacoff, M., 297, 310
Koocher, G. P., 18, 25
Koppitz, E. M., 228, 235, 301, 309
Korgeski, G. P., 244, 249
Kornhaber, R., 245, 249
Kosevsky, B. P., 129, 136
Kosiewicz, M. M., 133, 137
Koslow-Green, L., 128, 131, 138
Kovacs, M., 22, 23, 25, 30, 34, 38, 39, 65, 66, 67, 73, 76, 77, 81, 92, 95, 111, 120, 241, 246, 249, 255, 257, 258, 266, 273, 289, 377, 382
Kovitz, K., 440, 453
Kraepelin, E., 26, 39
Kramer, J., 282, 289
Kramer, M., 287
Kramer, M. S., 419, 434
Krappman, V. F., 132, 138
Kratochwill, T. R., 137, 180, 190, 243, 247, 250, 410, 411
Krehbiel, G., 172, 176, 177
Kreitler, H., 376, 382
Kreitler, S., 376, 382
Krug, D. A., 351, 361
Kruger, S. D., 312, 320
Kruidenier, B., 115, 117

Kruppwicz, D. W., 369, 381
Kuczynski, L., 440, 448, 454
Kugler, J., 312, 319
Kulik, J. A., 295, 309
Kulp, D., 330, 344
Kulp, S., 147, 164
Kunzelmann, H. D., 126, 137
Kupersmidt, J. B., 167, 172, 176
Kupietz, S., 90, 95
Kurdek, L. A., 107, 120
Kurlan, R., 318, 319
Kurylyszyn, N., 426, 436
Kutina, J., 185, 190, 245, 249

Labbe, E. E., 400, 402, 405, 408, 409, 411
Lachar, D., 75, 81, 262, 268, 275, 289, 298, 310
Lacouture, P. G., 414, 434
Ladd, G. W., 115, 123, 166, 167, 171, 172, 175, 177
Ladish, C., 298, 309
LaGreca, A. M., 99, 109, 120, 166, 177
Lahey, B. B., 84, 85, 86, 87, 90, 95, 96, 150, 163, 166, 178, 239, 250, 271, 275, 289, 293, 307, 440, 453
Lake, A. E., 409, 411
Lamb, M. E., 443, 452
Lambert, N. M., 55, 61, 332, 344
Lamparski, D., 145, 164, 187, 191
Lampron, L. B., 299, 309
Lance, J. W., 401, 412
Landau, S., 169, 178, 272, 274, 279, 289
Landis, J. R., 67, 81
Landrus, R., 354, 362
Lang, M., 259, 266, 268
Lang, P. J., 6, 13, 180, 183, 186, 188, 190, 245, 249
Langhorne, J. E., 91, 95
Langlois, J. H., 171, 172, 178
Lansing, M. D., 350, 362
Lapan, R., 107, 120
Lapouse, R., 240, 249
Lapouse, T., 311, 319
Laprade, K., 90, 96, 275, 291
Larry P. v Riles, 55, 61
Larsen, P. D., 49
Larsen, R., 225, 235
Larsson, B., 409, 411
Lasagna, L., 425, 438
Laseg, M., 78, 79
Lashley, K. S., 208, 223
Lask, B., 384, 397

Last C. G., 28, 34, 39, 76, 77, 81, 93, 95, 110, 120, 122, 239, 240, 241, 248, 249
Laties, V. G., 282, 291
Latter, J., 410, 430, 435
Lauer, R. M., 365, 382
Lautenschlager, G. J., 301, 308
Lavee, Y., 107, 121, 377, 382
Lavigne, J. L., 415, 436
Lavigne, J. V., 402, 411
Lawler, E. E., 177
Lawton, M. J., 226, 235
Lazarus, A. A., 180, 190
Lazarus, R. S., 428, 436
Lazovik, A. D., 245, 249
Leark, R. A., 197, 207
Lease, C. A., 240, 250
Leaverton, P. E., 365, 382
LeBaron, L., 421, 429, 430, 436
LeBaron, S., 113, 120, 123, 430, 438
LeBlanc, M., 299, 310
Leckman, J. F., 28, 38, 39, 40, 287, 289, 311, 312, 314, 315, 318, 319, 320
LeCouteur, A., 351, 356, 357, 361
Ledingham, J. E., 293, 309
Leduc, D. G., 419, 434
Lee, J., 78, 79, 257, 264
Lees, A. J., 312, 314, 319
Lefkowitz, M. M., 166, 177, 266, 295, 296, 298, 308, 309
Leibert, D. E., 166, 178
Leichner, P., 384, 398
Leichter, D., 439, 453
Leigh, G., 228, 235
Leitenberg, H., 5, 13, 244, 249, 389, 398
Leiter, R. G., 354, 361
Leland, H., 321, 331, 332, 344, 345
Lemaire, F., 415, 436
Lemanek, K. L., 99, 105
Lemerle, J., 421, 436
Lempert, M., 226, 234
Lennon, M. P., 73, 80, 256, 266
Lenz, M. W., 331, 344
Lepper, M. R., 131, 138
Lerner, R. M., 141, 163
Lessing, E. E., 298, 309
Lester, B. M., 418, 436
Leudar, I., 336, 344
Leventhal, H., 184, 189
Levin, R. B., 422, 436
Levinson, R., 376, 382
Levitan, G., 328, 344
Levitas, A., 327, 344, 405, 411

Levitt, E. E., 142, 163
Levy, H. L., 47, 49
Levy, S. M., 137
Lewandowski, L. J., 200, 201, 206
Lewin, L., 9, 13
Lewine, J. D., 289
Lewine, R., 274, 290
Lewinsohn, P. M., 177, 264, 266
Lewis, D. O., 294, 309, 439, 453
Lewis, M., 336, 344
Lewis, S., 67, 77, 80, 245, 249, 254, 265
Lezak, M. D., 219, 223
Libert, J., 177
Lichstein, K. L., 401, 404, 405, 407, 409, 411
Licht, M. H., 85, 94, 276, 287
Liebert, D. E., 309
Liebert, R. M., 185, 190
Lighthall, F. F., 109, 122, 245, 250
Lind, J., 419, 438
Linder, C. W., 366, 381
Lindsay, P., 281, 287
Linet, L. S., 317, 320
Link, H. C., 102, 120
Linn, R. T., 113, 120
Linney, J. A., 113, 119
Linnoila, M., 118
Linscheid, T. R., 421, 437
Liotti, G., 390, 398
Lipinski, D. P., 129, 137, 138
Lipovsky, J. A., 110, 118, 232, 234
Lippman, W., 51, 61
Lipsedge, M., 10, 12
Litrownik, A. J., 128, 129, 130, 137
Little, B. C., 191
Lloyd, J. W., 128, 129, 132, 133, 137
Loar, L., 86, 89, 90, 95
Lobovits, D. A., 258, 262, 266
Lochman, J. E., 299, 301, 309
Loeber, R., 8, 13, 30, 39, 294, 309, 448, 453
Loevinger, J., 99, 120
Loftus, J. J., 100, 121
Logan, G., 281, 282, 287, 291
Logan, W. J., 322, 344
Logue, P. E., 319
Lollar, D. J., 427, 436
London, M., 179
Loney, J., 84, 91, 95, 96, 271, 275, 276, 280, 289
Loofbourow, G. C., 101, 120
Lord, C., 348, 351, 356, 361, 363
Lore, R. K., 184, 190
Lotyczewski, B. S., 119

Lourie, R., 65, 81
Loven, M. D., 150, 152, 164
Lowe, M., 87, 94
Lowe, T., 36, 39
Lowell, E. L., 225, 235
Lozanoff, B., 134, 136
Lubetsky, M. J., 439, 445, 452
Lubin, B., 225, 235
Lueptow, L., 174, 177
Lupin, M. N., 186, 189
Lupovsky, J. A., 262, 266
Luria, A. R., 196, 206, 215
Lushene, R. E., 109, 122, 444, 447, 454
Lutzker, J. R., 443, 445, 451, 453, 454
Lynch, G. W., 90, 96, 212, 222
Lynn, R., 183, 190

Mabe, P. A., 105, 120
Mabee, W. S., 133, 138
MacDonald, J. T., 401, 402, 411
Mace, F. C., 126, 137
MacFarlane, J. W., 240, 249, 292, 309
Machover, K., 228, 235
Mackie, J., 416, 418, 437
MacLean, W. E., 344
MacMillan, D., 166, 178
MacMillan, V. M., 443, 444, 446, 452, 453
Madden, N. M., 166, 172, 177
Mahoney, M. J., 127, 137
Mahrolin, D., 143, 163
Maisami, M., 241, 249
Majovski, L. V., 210, 223
Malachowski, B., 67, 77, 80, 254, 265
Maller, J. B., 100, 121, 168, 177
Maloney, M. J., 384, 398
Mamunes, P., 49
Mandeli, J., 320
Manuck, S. B., 245, 249
March, J. S., 110, 119
Marcus, L. M., 349, 350, 351, 352, 354, 356, 358, 362, 363
Marcus, M. D., 386, 398
Margolis, R. B., 426, 437
Mark, S., 398
Marks, I. M., 10, 12, 13
Marks, P. A., 104, 120
Marks, R. E., 341, 342
Marks, R. M., 417, 437
Markwardt, F. C., 199, 202, 206
Marlowe, D., 105, 118
Marohn, R. C., 307, 309
Marques, D., 416, 437

Marriage, K., 36, 38, 39, 258, 259, 263, 265, 267
Marshall, H. R., 9, 13
Marshall, K. J., 129, 132, 133, 137
Marshall, R. E., 419, 420, 437
Marshburn, E., 340, 344
Martin, B., 294, 308
Martin, H. G., 102, 119
Martin, R., 229, 235
Martindale, A., 147, 164
Martindale, B., 147, 164, 330, 344
Martinez, R., 376, 381
Marzolf, S., 229, 235
Masek, B. J., 405, 409, 411, 414, 415, 434, 437
Mash, E. J., 3, 4, 5, 6, 7, 9, 13, 82, 83, 84, 85, 88, 90, 95, 96, 140, 143, 152, 163, 181, 188, 190, 272, 275, 279, 289, 301, 309, 440, 442, 448, 453
Masse, G., 282, 290
Massman, P. J., 280, 289
Master, L. S., 174, 177
Matalon, R., 49
Matarazzo, J., 225, 235
Mather, L., 416, 418, 437
Mathews, E., 100, 120
Mathews, W. S., 404, 410
Matson, J. L., 11, 14, 93, 95, 96, 265, 336, 345, 410, 411
Matthew, D. J., 46, 49
Matthews, K. A., 245, 249
Matthews, M., 312, 319
Mattison, R. E., 243, 249
Mawhood, L., 351, 361
May, M. A., 168, 177
Mayeda, T., 333, 343
Mayer, G. R., 5, 14
Mayer, J., 10, 14, 369, 383
Mayer, M., 421, 434
Mayhall, C. A., 111, 120, 258, 267
McArdle, W. D., 367, 369, 371, 381, 382
McArthur, D., 225, 226, 234, 235
McAuliffe, S., 279, 291
McBride, M. C., 311, 319
McBurnett, K., 86, 95, 289
McCaffrey, L. G., 168, 178
McCandless, B. R., 9, 13, 109, 117, 185, 189
McCarthy, D., 354, 362
McCauley, E., 257, 258, 267
McClellan, M. C., 118
McClelland, D. C., 225, 235
McClure, J., 372, 381
McConaughy, S. H., 34, 36, 37, 67, 79, 83, 84, 93, 116, 301, 307

McConnell, S. R., 167, 169, 170, 171, 172, 177
McCord, J., 294, 309
McCord, W., 294, 309
McCormick, W. F., 45, 46, 49
McCubbin, H. I., 107, 120, 377, 382
McCully, R. S., 231, 235
McCurdy, B. L., 124, 135, 137
McDaniel, L. K., 423, 437
McDavid, J. W., 172, 178
McDonald, W. F., 372, 374, 382
McEvoy, L. T., 288
McFall, R. M., 7, 13, 131, 137, 166, 178, 293, 308
McFarlane, A. C., 22, 25
McGavin, J. K., 386, 393, 397
McGee, R., 33, 37, 240, 248, 280, 289
McGimpsey, B. J., 443, 445, 454
McGiness, G. C., 419, 436
McGonigle, J. J., 125, 138, 337, 345, 439, 452
McGrath, M., 437
McGrath, P., 413, 435
McGrath, P. A., 404, 405, 411, 412, 414, 417, 421, 425, 426, 427, 437
McGrath, P. J., 405, 410, 412, 414, 417, 421, 422, 425, 426, 430, 431, 435, 436, 438
McGrath, P. L., 412
McGrath, T., 21, 25
McGraw, K., 274, 291
McGraw, M. B., 420, 437
McGuire, J. B., 384, 398
McGuire, R., 10, 12
McHugh, A., 228, 235
McIntire, R. W., 409, 412
McIntosh, J. A., 113, 117
McKinley, J. C., 444, 447, 453
McKinley, J. D., 103, 119
McKnew, D., 73, 80, 88, 95, 241, 249, 255, 257, 266, 273, 288
McLaughlin, T. F., 125, 126, 132, 133, 134, 137, 138
McLean, J. E., 197, 206
McLennan, J., 351, 361
McMahon, J. B., 384, 398
McMahon, R. J., 82, 84, 85, 96, 280, 288, 299, 300, 308, 309, 331, 343
McMorrow, M. J., 336, 343
McNamara, J. R., 150, 164
McReynolds, P., 4, 13
McVey, L., 419, 434
Meagher, R. B., 115, 120
Medred, L., 318, 319
Meehl, P. E., 170, 176

Mehegan, J. E., 409, 411
Mehrens, W. A., 197, 206
Mehta, G., 425, 438
Meichenbaum, D., 5, 13, 105, 120, 428, 435
Melamed, B. G., 148, 163, 183, 184, 186, 187, 188, 190, 243, 245, 249, 250, 431, 437
Melchior, J. C., 404, 411
Melin, L., 409, 411
Mellstrom, B., 118
Meloff, K. L., 402, 411
Melzack, R., 425, 426, 427, 437
Mendelsohn, M., 444, 447, 452
Mendelson, B. K., 375, 376, 382
Mendelson, M., 260, 264, 395, 396
Menkes, J. H., 44, 45, 46, 49
Menlove, F., 245, 248
Menolascino, F. J., 327, 328, 344
Mercer, J. R., 322, 344
Merchant, A., 287
Merikangas, K. R., 35, 36, 37, 40, 79, 268, 291
Merlo, M., 282, 290
Mermelstein, R., 443, 446, 452
Merrill, K. H., 206
Merrill, M. A., 354, 363
Merritt, H. H., 27, 39
Merry, S. N., 341, 342
Mersky, H., 437
Mesibov, G. B., 347, 348, 351, 354, 357, 358, 362, 363
Messer, S. B., 113, 120
Messick, S., 157, 164, 194, 206, 376, 383
Methven, R. J., 35, 40
Metrakos, K., 404, 410
Metz, C., 34, 37, 78, 79, 257, 264
Meyers, A. W., 183, 190
Michelson, L., 108, 120
Mikkelsen, E. J., 317, 320
Milich, R. S., 84, 91, 95, 96, 169, 170, 178, 271, 272, 274, 275, 276, 279, 282, 289, 290
Miller, G., 193, 206
Miller, K. L., 111, 113, 114, 122
Miller, L. C., 10, 13, 110, 120, 298, 303, 309
Miller, M. D., 38
Miller, N. E., 180, 190
Miller, P. M., 129, 136
Miller, R. H., 419, 437
Miller, S. R., 135, 137
Millichamp, C. J., 341, 345
Milling, L. S., 437
Millon, T., 115, 120
Milner, J. S., 444, 447, 453
Mindell, J. A., 405, 411

Mirsky, A. F., 281, 290
Mischel, W., 4, 5, 8, 13, 113, 120
Mitchell, J. E., 386, 389, 390, 392, 393, 398
Mitchell, J. R., 257, 267
Mitts, B., 130, 136
Mize, J., 167, 177
Mock, J., 260, 264, 395, 396, 444, 447, 452
Moe, P. G., 400, 403, 411
Mokros, H. B., 36, 39, 261, 267
Moldenhaur, L. M., 378, 382
Molfese, D. L., 211, 223
Molloy, G., 180, 190
Molsberry, D., 426, 437
Monane, M., 439, 453
Monguillot, J. E., 403, 410, 412
Monk, M. A., 240, 249, 311, 319
Montgomery, L. E., 109, 118
Montoye, H. J., 371, 382
Montuori, J., 109, 122
Moore, B. S., 127, 137
Moore, D., 114, 120
Moore, S. G., 168, 178
Moos, B. S., 107, 120
Moos, R. H., 107, 120, 377, 382
Moreno, J. L., 178
Moretti, M. M., 36, 39, 258, 259, 263, 265, 267
Morgan, D. P., 128, 132, 138
Morgan, S., 350, 351, 362
Morganstein, A., 289
Morgenstern, G., 280, 281, 287, 291
Morgenstern, M., 333, 334, 344
Morreau, L. E., 327, 343
Morrell, W., 385, 399
Morris, L. W., 185, 190
Morris, R. J., 243, 247, 250, 410, 411
Morris, R. M., 180, 190
Morris, S., 384, 398
Morrison, G. M., 166, 178
Morrison, J. A., 365, 382
Morrissey, E., 228, 235
Morrow, L. W., 135, 137
Morrow, M. C., 184, 190
Mortensen, O., 414, 435
Morton, J., 311, 320
Moscosa, M., 33, 37
Moser, J., 439, 453
Moses, T., 78, 79
Moss, S., 257, 267
Moura, N. G. M., 127, 137
Moxley, R., 133, 139
Mueller, S. A., 174, 177
Mulick, J. A., 335, 344, 409, 412

Mullen, K., 288
Muller, E., 419, 437
Mullet, N., 377, 381
Mullins, L., 266
Mundy, P., 347, 348, 362
Munir, K. A., 29, 37
Munir, M. B., 32, 39
Munoz, R., 38, 80
Murphy, J. K., 184, 190
Murphy, P. M., 188, 191
Murray, D. M., 377, 382
Murray, E. N., 180, 190
Murray, H., 224, 225, 235
Murray, N. M. F., 312, 319
Murry, T., 419, 437
Myerberg, D., 49
Myler, B., 226, 235

Nader, P. R., 380
Nagle, R. J., 166, 177
Naglieri, J. A., 194, 197, 207
Nakamura, C. Y., 9, 14, 110, 122, 243, 250
Nanda, H., 157, 162
Nathan, S., 228, 235
National Center on Child Abuse and Neglect, 440, 453
National Council on Measurement in Education, 54, 61, 194, 205
Nay, W. R., 84, 96, 144, 151, 164
Neale, J. M., 166, 178, 309
Neeper, R., 293, 307, 401, 411
Neff, D. F., 405, 410
Neisser, U., 196, 207
Nelles, W. B., 241, 250
Nelson, B., 39
Nelson, K. A., 36, 38
Nelson, R. O., 3, 7, 9, 13, 93, 96, 126, 128, 129, 130, 131, 134, 135, 137, 138
Nelson, W. M., 108, 111, 113, 120, 258, 267
Neman, J., 225, 235
Neman, R., 225, 235
Nestadt, G. N., 287
Newby, R., 279, 287
Newcomb, A. F., 169, 173, 174, 178
Newcomb, M. D., 107, 121
Newcorn, J. H., 270, 289
Nicassio, P. M., 428, 435
Nickel, R., 405, 411
Nielsen, A., 414, 437
Nietzel, M. T., 182, 190
Nihira, K., 321, 332, 344
Niman, C. A., 187, 189

Noam, G. G., 75, 81, 272, 291
Noble, H., 110, 120
Nomura, Y., 312, 320
Nordlie, J., 320
Nordsieck, M., 364, 380
Norris, D., 225, 235
Northway, M. L., 169, 178
Norwood, J. A., 217, 223
Novaco, R. W., 443, 445, 453
Novak, C. G., 199, 206
Nowicki, S., 113, 121
Noyes, R., 28, 38
Nunnally, J., 141, 157, 164
Nurnberger, J. I., 38
Nussbaum, N. L., 215, 217, 223, 280, 289

O'Brien, G. T., 241, 248
O'Brien, J. D., 252, 257, 265, 268, 289
O'Connor, M., 392, 397
O'Connor, N., 348, 361
O'Connor, P., 67, 77, 80, 254, 265
O'Connor, P. J., 401, 412
O'Connor, R. D., 245, 250
O'Connor, S., 443, 445, 451
O'Dell, S. L., 149, 162, 164, 442, 443, 453
O'Gorman, J. G., 183, 191
O'Keefe, D. M., 405, 410
O'Keefe, J., 429, 435
O'Leary, K. D., 84, 85, 94, 96, 150, 153, 163, 164
O'Malley, P. M., 293, 307
O'Shaughnessy, M., 385, 397
O'Tuama, L. A., 276, 290, 331, 344
Obrzut, J., 226, 235
Oden, S., 166, 169, 178
Odom, S. L., 167, 168, 169, 170, 171, 172, 177, 178
Offer, D., 114, 121, 307, 309
Offord, D. R., 300, 309
Offord, K. P., 104, 118
Olesen, J., 402, 411
Oliphant, P. S., 324, 325, 326, 344
Oliveau, C., 240, 248
Ollendick, T. H., 3, 4, 5, 6, 7, 8, 9, 10, 11, 12, 13, 14, 15, 16, 21, 23, 25, 109, 110, 121, 122, 125, 130, 138, 140, 143, 164, 180, 181, 183, 188, 190, 191, 243, 250, 311, 317, 319, 320, 337, 345
Olley, J. G., 352, 356, 358, 362
Ollier, K., 21, 25, 183, 190
Olmstead, M. P., 112, 119, 386, 393, 397
Olson, D. H., 107, 121, 377, 382

Olson, M., 312, 319
Olson, R. L., 443, 444, 446, 447, 453
Olweus, D., 8, 10, 14
Ondercin, P., 394, 396
Opipari, L., 112, 120
Opitz, J. M., 43, 49
Ordman, A. M., 395, 398
Ornitz, E., 347, 362
Ort, S. I., 314, 315, 319
Orvaschel, H., 28, 34, 35, 36, 38, 39, 40, 68, 74, 78, 79, 80, 81, 90, 97, 241, 250, 256, 260, 267, 268, 273, 274, 289, 295, 309
Orvin, G. H., 103, 117
Osgood, P. F., 426, 438
Oster, J., 414, 437
Ostrov, E., 114, 121, 307, 309
Ott, E., 225, 235
Owens, M. E., 420, 437
Ozolins, M., 148, 163, 420, 436

Pachman, J. S., 129, 138
Pack, P. L., 168, 178
Padian, N., 36, 39, 40, 90, 97
Paez, P., 79, 248, 256, 265, 287
Paez, R., 36, 38
Pagac, S., 371, 381
Pagan, A., 33, 37
Paget, K. D., 243, 250
Palermo, D. S., 109, 117, 185, 189
Pallmeyer, T. P., 310, 410, 414, 438
Pallotta, G. M., 443, 446, 453
Palmer, R. L., 384, 393, 398
Pancoast, D. L., 103, 117
Papay, J. P., 109, 121
Papillo, J. F., 188, 191
Parasuraman, R., 281, 288
Parker, J. B., 166, 172, 178
Parks, S. L., 350, 351, 362
Parsons, B. V., 143, 162
Parsons, G. M., 183, 191
Parsons, J. E., 9, 14
Partanen, T., 419, 438
Pascualvaca, D. M., 289
PASE v Hannon, 55, 61
Passchier, J., 401, 411
Pataki, C. S., 85, 91, 96, 286, 290
Patterson, D. G., 100, 121
Patterson, D. L., 427, 436
Patterson, D. R., 297, 307
Patterson, G. J., 131, 138
Patterson, G. R., 16, 25, 142, 143, 164, 294, 299, 300, 305, 309, 310, 444, 448, 453

Patton, M. J., 107, 120
Paul, G. L., 245, 250
Paulauskas, S. L., 30, 34, 39, 81, 266
Pauls, D. L., 28, 38, 39, 40, 311, 312, 318, 319, 320
Paver, M., 371, 383
Paykel, E. S., 31, 39
Pechar, G. S., 371, 382
Pederson, A., 8, 12
Peery, J. C., 173, 178
Pekarik, E. G., 166, 169, 170, 178, 298, 309
Pelcovitz, D., 312, 319
Pelham, W. E., 85, 94, 170, 177, 272, 276, 279, 287, 290
Peloquin, L., 289
Pennington, B. F., 11, 12
Peplau, L. A., 114, 122
Perloff, E., 151, 162
Perri, M. G., 366, 382
Perriello, L. M., 276, 288
Perry, C. L., 377, 382
Perry, R., 343
Perry, S., 416, 437
Peterson, A. L., 317, 318
Peterson, D. R., 86, 87, 96, 173, 178, 244, 250, 262, 267, 275, 290, 298, 310
Peterson, G. L., 131, 138
Peterson, L., 428, 437
Peterson, R. F., 3, 12
Petti, T. A., 85, 95, 252, 266
Pezzuti, K. A., 113, 118
Pfohl, B., 28, 39
Phelps, M., 228, 235
Philips, W., 282, 289
Phillips, E. L., 124, 136
Phillips, L., 141, 164
Phillips, R. A., 320
Phillips, W., 107, 119
Piacentini, J. C., 66, 81, 85, 86, 87, 95, 96, 289
Piaget, J., 121
Pierce, K. A., 169, 176
Pierloot, R., 386, 399
Piers, E. V., 114, 121
Piersel, W. C., 125, 127, 130, 131, 138
Pike, R., 114, 119
Pincus, J. H., 294, 309
Pine, F., 225, 235
Pintner, R., 100, 101, 121
Piquard-Gauvain, A., 415, 436
Platzek, D., 319
Pless, I. B., 419, 434
Plotkin, R., 442, 443, 454
Podian, N., 260, 268

Polansky, N. A., 440, 453
Policansky, S., 22, 25
Policy and Planning Office, 328, 333, 344
Poling, A. D., 341, 343
Politano, P. M., 111, 120, 258, 267
Polivy, J., 112, 119, 393, 397
Pollack, S., 369, 376, 381
Pollock, C., 441, 454
Pollock, M. L., 30, 39, 81, 382
Polloway, E. A., 133, 138, 322, 345
Polster, L. M., 335, 344
Polyson, J., 225, 235
Pond, D., 327, 344
Pope, H. G., 398
Porges, S. W., 184, 191
Porter, F. L., 419, 437
Portner, J., 107, 121, 377, 382
Poskitt, E. M. E., 364, 382
Poteat, G. M., 196, 207
Pottebaum, S. M., 197, 199, 206
Poushinsky, M., 309
Powell, B., 376, 382
Powell, J., 147, 164, 330, 344
Powell, M., 168, 170, 178
Powers, M. D., 356, 362
Poznanski, E. O., 36, 39, 261, 267
Prabhu, A. N., 274, 288
Prabrucki, K., 36, 37, 78, 79, 257, 264
Prather, E. M., 355, 361
Prather, E. N., 225, 235
Pratt, B. M., 118
Pratt, J., 224, 236
Pratt, J. M., 412
Prensky, A. L., 401, 412
Press, G. A., 349, 361
Price, D. D., 404, 412, 425, 437
Price, D. T., 38
Prihoda, T. J., 113, 123, 430, 438
Prins, P., 297, 308
Prinz, R. J., 166, 178, 309
Prizant, B. M., 355, 362
Prout, H. T., 335, 344, 345
Prusoff, B. A., 35, 36, 37, 39, 40, 79, 268, 291, 314, 319
Prytula, R., 228, 235
Puig-Antich, J., 36, 38, 39, 65, 79, 81, 241, 248, 250, 256, 263, 265, 267, 273, 287, 289, 290, 309
Purcell, K., 186, 189, 301, 309
Purcell-Jones, G., 417, 437
Putallaz, M., 172, 178
Pyle, R. L., 390, 398

Quay, H. C., 86, 87, 96, 140, 164, 173, 178, 240, 244, 250, 262, 267, 272, 275, 282, 286, 287, 290, 293, 298, 309, 310
Quinn, E. P., 282, 290
Quinn, S. O., 282, 290, 410

Rabinovich, H., 39, 263, 267
Rachlin, H., 138
Rachman, S., 188, 190
Raczynski, J. M., 191
Radencich, M. C., 200, 207
Rafii, A., 404, 412, 425, 437
Rahe, R., 443, 445, 453
Rajaratnam, N., 157, 162
Rakoff, V., 149, 163
Raley, P. A., 258, 260, 265
Raman, S., 115, 117
Ramos, O., 49
Ramsden, R., 403, 409, 412
Rancurello, M. D., 85, 86, 90, 92, 93, 94, 95, 258, 266, 302, 308
Rapin, I., 48, 49, 50
Rapoport, J. L., 38, 39, 86, 96, 110, 113, 117, 118, 119, 281, 291, 312, 318
Rapport, M. D., 91, 96, 269, 270, 271, 272, 276, 279, 282, 283, 285, 286, 287, 288, 290, 291
Rardin, D., 376, 381, 394, 398
Raskin, A., 112, 120
Raskin, N. H., 402, 412
Rasnake, L. K., 335, 344, 421, 437
Ratcliff, K., 65, 81
Rawson, S. G., 261, 265
Ray, L., 380
Ray, R. S., 444, 448, 453
Ray, W. J., 182, 191
Raymond, K. I., 93, 96
Rayner, R., 3, 14
Read, P. B., 22, 25
Rediess, S., 311, 319
Reed, D., 113, 123, 430, 438
Reed, H. B. C., 217, 223
Reed, M. L., 86, 89, 96
Reeves, J. C., 31, 40, 282, 291
Rehm, L. P., 36, 38
Reich, T., 37
Reich, W., 35, 40, 74, 75, 80, 81, 241, 249, 252, 265, 267, 268, 272, 288, 295, 308
Reichert, A., 322, 345
Reichler, R. J., 74, 81, 267, 350, 352, 362
Reid, A. H., 328, 344
Reid, J. B., 296, 299, 300, 307, 309, 310, 441, 448, 453

Reid, J. C., 34, 35, 38, 68, 80, 152, 162
Reid, N., 202, 207
Reifler, J. P., 89, 95
Reiss, S., 328, 335, 344
Reitan, R. M., 214, 215, 216, 217, 223
Reiter, M. A., 365, 382
Reiter, S. M., 133, 138
Rekers, G. A., 10, 14
Remmers, H. H., 102, 103, 121
Rendleman, L., 336, 343
Renner, B. R., 350, 362
Renshaw, P. D., 114, 117
Repp, A. C., 147, 164, 331, 344
Repp, C. F., 147, 164
Reppucci, N. D., 440, 442, 453
Reschley, D. J., 172, 177
Reschly, D. J., 166, 178
Resser, D., 419, 436
Revelle, W., 298, 309
Reynell, J. K., 355, 362
Reynolds, C. R., 109, 121, 192, 193, 194, 197, 198, 199, 200, 202, 205, 206, 207, 242, 243, 250
Reynolds, L. A., 297, 307
Reynolds, W. M., 98, 99, 106, 107, 110, 111, 112, 113, 114, 115, 116, 117, 121, 122, 123, 264, 267, 302, 310
Rezvani, A., 421, 436
Rhode, G., 128, 132, 138
Ribera, J., 33, 37
Riccardi, V. M., 48, 50
Rice, J. M., 35, 37, 445, 451, 453
Rice, L., 435
Rich, E. C., 420, 437
Richards, C., 34, 39
Richardson, G. M., 405, 412
Richie, D. M., 113, 123, 430, 438
Richman, G. S., 336, 344
Richman, N., 73, 81, 240, 250
Richmond, B. O., 109, 121, 242, 243, 250
Richmond, J. B., 323, 343
Richter, I. L., 409, 412
Rickard, K. M., 85, 96, 172, 178
Riddle, M. A., 314, 319
Rie, H. E., 3, 14
Rieger, R. E., 65, 81
Rierdan, J., 376, 382
Rimland, B., 351, 362
Rios, P., 351, 361
Risley, T. R., 330, 331, 343
Risser, A., 210, 223
Ritchey, W. L., 168, 176

Ritvo, E. R., 351, 361
Ritzler, B., 225, 235
Rizley, R., 441, 452
Robbins, D. R., 37, 261, 267, 268
Roberts, D. M., 147, 164
Roberts, F., 200, 207
Roberts, G., 226, 234, 235
Roberts, M. A., 84, 96
Roberts, M. L., 374, 382
Roberts, R. N., 134, 138
Robertson, M. M., 312, 319
Robertson, S., 351, 361
Robertson, S. J., 129, 138
Robin, A. L., 143, 162, 280, 290
Robins, C. J., 263, 265
Robins, E., 27, 29, 31, 38, 39, 65, 80
Robins, L. N., 39, 65, 81, 288, 294, 310
Robinson, D. R., 39, 446, 452
Robinson, E. A., 92, 94, 96, 296, 297, 299, 307, 310
Roche, A. F., 367, 382
Rockert, W., 386, 397
Rockinson, R., 147, 164
Rodary, C., 421, 436
Rodgers, A., 112, 120, 258, 266, 296, 309
Rodgers, B. M., 425, 438
Rodichock, L. D., 410
Rodick, J. D., 294, 308
Rodin, J., 389, 398
Rodriguez, A., 142, 164
Rodriguez, M., 142, 164
Roebuck, L., 73, 80, 241, 249, 257, 266
Roehling, P. V., 108, 118
Roff, M., 169, 178
Rogers, C. R., 100, 122
Rogers, T. R., 108, 118
Rohrbeck, C. A., 119, 442, 443, 454
Roistacher, R. C., 168, 178
Rojahn, J., 335, 341, 344
Romanczyk, R. G., 153, 164
Romano, B. A., 93, 96
Romanoski, A. J., 287
Rooney, K. J., 133, 134, 138
Rosen, L. W., 386, 389, 390, 395, 397
Rosenberg, D., 444, 452
Rosenberg, L. A., 89, 95
Rosenberg, M., 114, 122, 395, 398
Rosenberg, M. S., 440, 442, 453
Rosenberg, R. P., 89, 96
Rosenberg, T., 68, 80
Rosenberger, P., 274, 290
Rosenblatt, D., 225, 234

Rosenblum, E. L., 405, 409, 410
Rosenblum, N. D., 145, 164, 187, 191
Rosenkrantz, A., 226, 235
Rosenthal, B. L., 199, 207
Rosenthal, D., 28, 38
Rosenthal, L., 308
Rosenthal, N. E., 398
Rosenthal, R. H., 307
Rosman, B. L., 107, 119
Ross, A. O., 143, 164, 247, 250
Ross, A. W., 92, 94, 96, 297, 308, 310, 444, 447, 452
Ross, D. M., 90, 96, 275, 290, 414, 424, 429, 437
Ross, J., 9, 14
Ross, S. A., 90, 96, 275, 290, 414, 424, 429, 437
Rosser, W., 413, 435
Rossiter, E. M., 389, 398
Rosvold, H. E., 281, 290
Rotatori, A. F., 93, 96
Rothbaum, F., 105, 122
Rothblum, J. K., 288
Rothman, S. L., 314, 319
Rothner, A. D., 312, 319, 403, 411
Rothner, D. O., 312, 319
Rotter, J., 225, 235
Rotundo, N., 259, 267
Rourke, B. P., 430, 435
Rourke, R. P., 209, 210, 212, 217, 220, 223
Routh, D. K., 276, 290, 331, 344, 421, 422, 436, 438
Rowe, P., 125, 130, 135, 139
Rowland, K. M., 179
Rowlison, R. T., 258, 260, 265
Roy, R. R., 245, 249
Rozensky, R. H., 131, 136, 138
Rubin, B. M., 105, 118
Rubin, K. H., 170, 172, 178
Rubio-Stipec, M., 33, 37
Ruck, S., 371, 382
Rudel, R. G., 212, 223
Ruebush, B. K., 109, 122
Rueda, R., 128, 137
Ruff, G., 376, 380
Ruggiero, L., 258, 260, 264, 265, 403, 405, 412
Rump, E. E., 90, 95
Rumsey, J. M., 354, 362
Runyon, D. K., 74, 81
Ruple, D. N., 9, 14
Russell, D., 114, 122, 443, 446, 453
Russell, G. A., 415, 435
Russell, G. F. M., 384, 385, 398

Russell, R. L., 182, 190
Russell, S., 245, 250
Russo, D. C., 415, 416, 424, 437
Rutherford, R. B., 128, 137
Rutley, B., 228, 235
Ruttenburg, B. A., 351, 362
Rutter, M., 3, 14, 15, 17, 18, 19, 20, 21, 22, 25, 79, 81, 142, 164, 272, 275, 290, 291, 294, 310, 311, 320, 347, 350, 351, 354, 361, 362
Rutter, N., 431, 436
Ruttimann, U., 435
Ryan, N., 39, 263, 267
Rydall, M. R., 110, 122

Saab, P. G., 245, 249, 421, 436
Sabry, J. H., 374, 375, 382
Sachar, E. J., 417, 437
Sackville-West, L., 126, 138, 314
Saghir, M. T., 272, 290
Sagotsky, G., 131, 138
Salisbury, C., 445, 454
Salkin, B., 385, 399
Salzberg, C. L., 137
Salzinger, S., 440, 443, 446, 454
Salzman, L. F., 289
Sanchez-Lacay, A., 33, 37
Sandberg, S. T., 275, 291
Sanders, S. H., 429, 435
Sanders-Woudstra, J. A. R., 268
Sandler, H., 443, 445, 451
Sandman, C. A., 282, 291, 336, 343
Sandoval, J., 196, 207
Sandoval, Y., 376, 381
Santa-Barbara, J., 395, 398
Santogrossi, D., 166, 177
Santostefano, S., 18, 25
Sapona, R., 132, 133, 137
Sapp, G. L., 199, 206
Sarason, I., 281, 290
Sarason, S. B., 109, 122, 245, 250
Sarbin, T. R., 295, 309
Sargent, J. D., 409, 412
Saris, W. M., 371, 382
Sartorius, N. V., 350, 362
Saslow, G., 4, 6, 13, 180, 190, 305, 308
Satterfield, J. H., 186, 191, 281, 287
Sattler, J. M., 194, 195, 196, 199, 207, 214, 219, 223, 331, 332, 333, 334, 344, 345
Satz, P., 220, 223
Saunders, N. L., 403, 410
Saunders, W., 68, 73, 80

Savedra, M., 424, 426, 437, 438
Saylor, C. F., 113, 117, 228, 234, 258, 265, 267, 310, 414, 438
Scanlon, E. M., 7, 14, 109, 122
Sceery, W., 38, 118
Schachar, R., 21, 25, 281, 282, 287, 291
Schafer, I. A., 49
Schaffer, B., 348, 354, 362, 363
Schaller, J. G., 414, 438
Schaughency, E. A., 84, 85, 87, 95, 96, 297, 310
Schechter, N. L., 416, 438
Schectman, A., 142, 164
Scherer, M. W., 9, 14, 110, 122, 243, 250
Schillinger, J., 421, 437
Schloss, C. N., 136
Schloss, P. J., 136
Schlundt, D. C., 172, 176
Schlundt, D. G., 308, 373, 376, 382
Schmidt, C. R., 12, 14
Schneider, C., 442, 443, 453
Schnell, C., 275, 291
Schnurr, P., 29, 39
Schnurr, R., 417, 437
Schocken, I., 172, 176
Schoeler, T., 290
Schofield, J., 229, 234
Schoolfield, J., 113, 123, 430, 438
Schopler, E., 346, 347, 348, 349, 350, 351, 352, 354, 356, 357, 358, 361, 362, 363
Schroeder, C. S., 276, 290, 331, 344
Schroeder, H., 245, 249
Schroeder, S. R., 327, 341, 342, 344
Schroth, P., 351, 361
Schulein, M. G., 402, 411
Schulein, M. J., 415, 436
Schull, W. J., 383
Schulman, J. L., 245, 250
Schulsinger, F., 28, 38
Schulsinger, R., 383
Schultz, K., 186, 189
Schultz, N. R., 114, 120
Schumaker, J. B., 149, 162
Schuster, S., 183, 190
Schwab-Stone, M., 66, 75, 81, 272, 291
Schwartz, A. N., 184, 191
Schwartz, D. M., 384, 397
Schwartz, J. A., 131, 136
Schwartz, M. S., 20, 24
Schwartz, S., 257, 261, 264
Schwartzman, A. E., 292, 299, 309, 310
Scott, L., 227, 235
Scott, R., 426, 438

Seat, P. D., 262, 268, 298, 310
Secord, P. F., 376, 383
Seeley, J., 310
Seeman, W., 104, 120
Segalowitz, S. J., 211, 223
Segawa, M., 312, 320
Seidman, E., 113, 119
Selby, G., 401, 412
Seliger, V., 371, 372, 383
Sells, B., 169, 178
Sells, S., 225, 235
Selman, R. L., 105, 122
Seltz, M., 214, 215, 216, 217, 223
Seltzer, C. C., 369, 383
Seltzer, G. B., 321, 322, 344
Semler, G., 273, 291
Semmel, M. I., 156, 162, 166, 177
Senatore, V., 336, 345
Sergeant, J., 286, 291
Sesman, M., 33, 37
Sethna, N. F., 414, 434
Severson, H. H., 175, 178
Shafer, C. L., 386, 397
Shaffer, D., 19, 20, 22, 25, 38, 66, 75, 81, 272, 290, 315, 316, 320
Shannon, K. M., 313, 314, 319
Shannon, M., 414, 434
Shanok, S. S., 294, 309
Shapiro, A. K., 314, 315, 318, 320
Shapiro, E., 314, 315, 318, 320
Shapiro, E. G., 197, 207
Shapiro, E. S., 9, 14, 124, 125, 126, 127, 128, 129, 130, 131, 135, 137, 138, 337, 345
Shapiro, S., 287
Shapiro, S. B., 169, 178
Share, D. L., 280, 289
Sharkey, K., 225, 235
Sharkey, R., 372, 381
Sharma, V., 289
Sharpley, C. F., 183, 191
Shavelson, R. J., 115, 122
Shaw, D. A., 444, 448, 453
Shaw, E. G., 421, 422, 438
Shaw, J., 331, 345
Shaw, K., 109, 120
Shaw, W. J., 437
Shaywitz, B. A., 314, 319
Shaywitz, B. E., 274, 275, 291
Shaywitz, S. E., 274, 275, 291, 314, 319
Shea, M. S., 290
Shear, C. L., 364, 365, 383
Shellhaas, M., 321, 332, 344

Sherick, R. B., 112, 120
Shermis, M., 226, 234
Sherrod, K., 443, 445, 451
Shiao, J., 311, 319
Shifman, L., 421, 436
Shigetomi, C., 248
Shigley, R. H., 358, 362
Shimberg, B., 102, 121
Shinebourne, E. A., 184, 185, 191
Shinner, S., 400, 401, 409, 412
Shnider, S., 421, 434
Sholomskas, D., 287, 289
Short, A., 351, 354, 363
Shoulson, I., 318, 319
Shrout, P. E., 274, 291
Shuller, D. Y., 150, 164
Shulman, J. L., 169, 176
Siegal, L. J., 148, 163, 184, 187, 190, 245, 250, 266, 428, 431, 437, 438
Siegel, S. E., 414, 415, 436
Siegel, T., 296, 297, 308, 309
Sigal, J. J., 149, 163
Sigman, M., 347, 348, 362
Silber, D., 225, 226, 227, 234, 235
Silberstein, L., 389, 398
Sillanpae, M., 400, 403, 412
Silva, P. A., 33, 37, 240, 248
Silverman, W. K., 241, 250
Silverstein, A. B., 195, 207, 332, 345
Simmons, J. E., 65, 81
Simmons, R. G., 376, 383
Simon, S. J., 129, 138
Singer, L. T., 385, 387, 398
Singh, N. N., 335, 341, 342, 343, 345
Singles, J. M., 262, 264
Singleton, L. C., 168, 170, 172, 176, 178
Sippell, W. G., 420, 431, 434
Skaer, M., 118
Skilbeck, W., 228, 236
Skinner, H. A., 395, 398
Slack, D. L., 147, 164
Slack, W. V., 405, 411
Slade, P. D., 394, 399
Slavin, R. E., 166, 172, 177
Slawson, J., 100, 122
Sleator, E. K., 86, 91, 96, 97, 276, 282, 287, 291
Slifer, K. J., 336, 344
Slyman, D., 28, 38
Small, A. M., 343
Smart, D. E., 384, 396
Smith, A., 21, 25
Smith, D. W., 43, 44, 50

Smith, E., 75, 80
Smith, G. M., 447, 454
Smith, G. T., 108, 118
Smith, J. D., 322, 345
Smith, J. M., 447, 454
Smith, K., 258, 267
Smith, K. E., 428, 438
Smith, M. C., 112, 122, 394, 399
Smith, S., 371, 381
Smits, S. J., 427, 436
Smouse, P. E., 261, 265
Smucker, M. R., 111, 122, 257, 258, 267
Snider, V., 138
Snowden, L. R., 106, 122
Snyder, T. J., 197, 207
Sobel, M., 169, 178
Sobol, A. M., 364, 369, 381
Solomon, G. E., 314, 320
Solomon, H. C., 27, 39
Somes, G. S., 184, 190
Sommer, D., 401, 412
Sorensen, T. I. A., 383
Sosna, T. D., 298, 309
Sostek, A. J., 281, 291
Southard, D. R., 405, 411
Sovner, R., 327, 345
Sparrow, S. S., 321, 332, 333, 345, 354, 356, 357, 363, 444, 448, 454
Spates, C. R., 131, 138
Spatz, K. C., 114, 122
Special Issue, 336, 345
Spector, R. M., 149, 163
Sperry, R. W., 196, 207
Spielberger, C. D., 73, 81, 108, 109, 121, 122, 242, 243, 245, 250, 444, 447, 454
Spierings, E. L. H., 402, 412
Spies, T., 27, 39
Spinell, A. P., 119
Spirito, A., 258, 267, 430, 438
Spitzer, R. L., 27, 31, 39, 65, 66, 79, 80, 81, 272, 274, 291
Spitznagel, E. L., 288
Sprafkin, J., 85, 94
Sprague, R. L., 84, 86, 90, 91, 97, 276, 291
Spreen, O., 210, 217, 223
Spruill, J., 198, 199, 203, 207
Squires, R. L., 377, 381
Squires, S., 374, 381
Srinivasan, S. R., 381
Sriwatanakul, K., 425, 426, 438
Sroufe, L. A., 3, 14, 18, 19, 22, 25
St. James-Roberts, I., 212, 223

Staats, A. W., 17, 25
Stack, J. G., 345
Stalonas, P., 369, 377, 381, 382
Stambaugh, E. E., 299, 310
Standley, J., 187, 189
Stanton, G. C., 115, 122
Stark, K. D., 99, 107, 111, 122, 264, 267
Stark, L., 430, 438
Starr, R. H., 439, 440, 444, 448, 452, 454
Steele, B. J., 441, 454
Steelman, L. C., 376, 382
Stefl, M. E., 312, 314, 317, 320
Stein, D. M., 112, 122
Stein, K. B., 295, 309
Stein, M., 225, 236
Steinhauer, P. D., 395, 398
Stenerson, P., 309
Stergios, D. A., 425, 438
Stern, J., 184, 190
Stern, J. A., 184, 190
Stern, L., 73, 80, 88, 95, 241, 249, 255, 266, 273, 288
Stern, R. M., 182, 183, 185, 188, 191, 422, 436
Stern, S., 391, 398
Sternbach, R. D., 183, 189, 245, 250
Stevenson, J., 73, 81, 240, 250, 319
Steward, M. S., 105, 117
Stewart, A. W., 335, 342, 343
Stewart, M. A., 271, 291, 293, 294, 307
Stockdale, D. F., 184, 190
Stoltzman, R. K., 288
Stone, K., 75, 81, 272, 291
Stone, P., 289
Stone, W. L., 99, 105, 109, 120, 122
Stoner, G., 276, 279, 282, 290
Strada, M. E., 419, 436
Strang, J. D., 209, 223
Straus, M. A., 442, 454
Strauss, C. C., 28, 34, 39, 76, 81, 87, 95, 110, 122, 166, 178, 239, 240, 243, 244, 248, 249, 250, 258, 267
Strauss, J., 289
Stricker, G., 245, 250
Strickland, B. R., 113, 120
Striegel-Moore, R., 389, 398
Strober, M. G., 28, 39, 260, 267, 384, 385, 391, 399
Strohmer, D. C., 335, 344, 345
Stubbs, M. L., 376, 382
Studwell, P., 133, 139
Stunkard, A. J., 364, 365, 375, 376, 377, 378, 381, 383, 386, 399

Sturge, C., 293, 310
Sturgis, E. T., 181, 182, 183, 184, 185, 191
Sturmey, P., 336, 345
Stutsman, R., 354, 363
Sugai, G., 125, 130, 135, 139
Sugarman, A., 231, 236
Sullivan, C. C., 331, 345
Sulzer-Azaroff, B., 5, 14
Sumner, E., 417, 437
Sundberg, N. D., 98, 106, 122
Sutter, J., 92, 96
Swanson, J. M., 282, 291
Swartz, K. L., 319
Swearingen, E. M., 107, 122
Swedo, S. S., 39
Sweet, R. D., 314, 320
Swenson, C., 228, 236
Sykes, D. J., 281, 291
Sylvester, C., 74, 81, 267
Sylvester, D., 240, 248
Szyfelbein, S. K., 426, 431, 438
Szymanski, L. S., 324, 327, 345
Szyszko, J., 328, 344

Tabrizi, A., 287
Tabrizi, M. A., 36, 38, 80, 248, 256, 265, 267, 289, 309
Tabrizi, R. N., 241, 250
Taft, L. T., 324, 326, 327, 345
Taft, R., 149, 164
Tait, R. C., 426, 437
Takagi, N., 333, 343
Talarico, B., 310
Tanner, C. M., 313, 314, 319, 320
Targum, S. D., 38
Tarler-Benlolo, L., 442, 443, 453
Tarter, R. E., 215, 223
Tatsuoka, M. M., 103, 118
Taylor, A. R., 172, 176
Taylor, E., 275, 291
Taylor, H. G., 208, 219, 220, 223
Taylor, R., 107, 117
Taylor, R. L., 333, 334, 345
Teasdale, T. W., 383
Teders, S. J., 410
Teglasi, H., 228, 236
Telzrow, C. F., 219, 223
Tennenbaum, D. L., 107, 119
Terdal, L. G., 3, 4, 5, 6, 7, 9, 13, 82, 83, 84, 96, 140, 163, 181, 188, 190, 272, 275, 279, 289
Teri, L., 260, 268
Terman, L. M., 198, 207, 354, 363

Tertinger, D. A., 443, 445, 454
Tesing, E. P., 266
Tesler, M., 424, 426, 437, 438
Teslow, C. J., 101, 119
Test, D. W., 124, 132, 136
Testiny, E., 166, 177
Tharinger, D., 332, 344
Thelen, M. H., 11, 13, 112, 122, 394, 399
Thomas, A., 19, 25, 414, 436
Thomas, C., 297, 308
Thomas, E. J., 317, 320
Thomas, M., 77, 79, 273, 287
Thomas, M. D. F., 252, 253, 264
Thompson, A. E., 107, 120
Thompson, C. K., 136
Thompson, G. G., 168, 170, 178
Thompson, J. A., 402, 409, 412
Thompson, K. L., 427, 438
Thompson, M. M., 384, 397
Thompson, R., 73, 80
Thompson, T., 336, 345
Thompson, W. D., 35, 39, 40, 287, 289
Thorley, A., 384, 398
Thorndike, R. L., 194, 198, 199, 207, 334, 345
Thorp, R. G., 9, 13
Thorpe, L. P., 101, 123
Thurstone, L. L., 102, 122
Tiegs, E. W., 101, 122
Tillinh, H., 184, 191
Tinsley, B. R., 168, 170, 176
Tinsley, H. E. A., 156, 164
Tischler, G. L., 288
Tishelman, A. C., 444, 446, 453
Tisher, M., 259, 266, 268
Tizard, J., 15, 21, 22, 25, 294, 310
Tobin, A. R., 355, 361
Toler, S. M., 428, 437
Tomarken, A. J., 382
Tomasi, L. G., 401, 411
Tomkins, S., 225, 236
Towbin, K. E., 28, 39, 314, 315, 319
Towle, V. R., 275, 291
Towne, W. S., 215, 223
Traylor, J., 84, 85, 95
Trefny, Z., 371, 383
Treiber, F. A., 105, 120, 440, 453
Tremblay, R. E., 299, 310
Trickett, P. K., 440, 448, 454
Trieber, F., 414, 438
Trimble, M. R., 312, 319, 384, 398
Trites, R. L., 90, 96, 275, 291
Trost, M. A., 8, 12

Trued, S., 401, 412
Truhlicka, M., 132, 138
Trujillo, J., 307
Tschechtelin, M. A., 102, 123
Tsui, E., 21, 25
Tucker, L. A., 370, 383
Tucker, S. B., 279, 282, 290
Tuma, J., 224, 236
Tunks, E., 428, 438
Tuokko, H., 210, 223
Tupper, D., 210, 223
Turbott, S. H., 341, 342
Turk, D. C., 423, 424, 430, 435, 438
Turner, J. A., 414, 435
Turner, R. A., 423, 437
Tusushima, W. T., 215, 223
Twentyman, C. T., 152, 162, 439, 440, 442, 443, 446, 452, 453, 454
Tyano, S., 78, 79
Tylenda, B., 335, 343
Tyler, J. D., 443, 446, 452

UCLA Mental Retardation Research Center, 333, 345
Ullman, D. G., 86, 94
Ullman, R. K., 86, 89, 91, 96, 97
Ullmann, R. K., 276, 291
Ulrich, R. F., 83, 90, 95, 275, 288, 314, 319, 336, 343
Unis, A. S., 36, 38, 85, 86, 92, 93, 95, 112, 120, 258, 263, 266, 295, 302, 304, 308, 309
Unruh, A. M., 414, 426, 431, 437, 438
Unruh, E., 417, 437
Updegraff, R., 168, 178

Vaidya, A., 77, 79, 252, 253, 264, 273, 287
Vaillant, G. E., 29, 39
Vair, C., 417, 437
Valaane, E., 419, 438
Valencia, R. R., 196, 207
Vallarta, J. M., 322, 345
van Aken, M. A. G., 421, 422, 434
Van Bourgondien, M. E., 351, 358, 363
Van Eerdewegh, M., 38
Van Hasselt, V. B., 145, 164, 187, 188, 191, 439, 443, 445, 452
van Lieshouat, C. F. M., 421, 434
Van Tassel, E. A., 170, 176
Vandereycken, W., 386, 387, 390, 391, 399
Vanderlinden, J., 387, 399
Varni, J. W., 181, 191, 413, 416, 427, 438
Vaughan, H., 281, 288

Vaughan, V. C., 365, 381
Vaughn, B. E., 170, 171, 172, 178
Vaux, A., 279, 291
Veldman, D., 166, 177
Velez, C., 67, 77, 80, 254, 265
Venables, P. H., 184, 185, 191
Verhulst, F. C., 73, 81, 255, 268
Vernon, D., 245, 250
Victor, M., 42, 49
Vietze, P., 443, 445, 451
Vitello, S. J., 331, 345
Volkmar, F. R., 347, 349, 363
Vollmer, J., 378, 382
Volpe, J. J., 420, 437
Von Korff, M. R., 287
von Zerssen, D., 273, 291
Voors, A. W., 381
Vosk, B., 172, 177, 178
Vuorenkoski, V., 419, 438
Vyse, S. A., 284, 291

Waber, L., 49
Wachsmuth, R., 281, 282, 287, 291
Waddel, M. T., 241, 248
Wadden, T. A., 377, 383
Wade, T. C., 127, 137
Wadsworth, M., 294, 310
Waggoner, C. D., 400, 402, 412
Wagner, B. M., 107, 118
Wahler, R. G., 299, 305, 310
Wahlstrom, J., 349, 361
Waite, R. R., 109, 122, 245, 250
Walder, L. O., 295, 298, 307, 308, 309
Walk, R. D., 184, 189
Walker, C. E., 440, 446, 454
Walker, H. M., 166, 177
Walker, J., 86, 95
Walkup, J. T., 314, 319
Wall, S. M., 133, 139
Walsh, B. T., 393, 399
Walsh, M. E., 425, 435
Walsh, M. L., 11, 13
Wampold, B. E., 135, 137
Wandersman, L. P., 442, 443, 452
Wansley, R. A., 187, 189
Waranch, R. H., 409, 412
Ward, C. H., 260, 264, 395, 396, 444, 447, 452
Ward, J. A., 424, 426, 437, 438
Wardlaw, J. M., 374, 382
Warham, J. E., 36, 38
Warner, D., 298, 309

Warner, V., 35, 36, 37, 40, 79, 268, 291
Warrenteltz, R. B., 137
Wasik, B. H., 150, 152, 164
Wasz-Hockert, O., 419, 438
Waternaux, C., 29, 37
Waters, E., 170, 178
Waters, J., 87, 94
Waters, W. E., 401, 412
Waters, W. F., 185, 191, 403, 410
Watson, J. B., 3, 14
Watson, L., 348, 349, 355, 356, 363
Watson, P. J., 139
Watson-Perczel, M., 443, 445, 454
Waxler, C. Z., 149, 164
Waxman, M., 375, 378, 383
Wayne, H. L., 314, 320
Weatherman, R. F., 333, 343
Weaver, K. A., 199, 205
Weaver, L., 309
Webb, C. J., 425, 438
Webber, L. S., 364, 372, 381, 383
Webster, J. S., 129, 136
Webster, T. G., 328, 345
Webster-Stratton, C., 297, 300, 310
Wechsler, D., 194, 207, 345, 354, 363
Wehler, C. A., 364, 369, 381
Weiner, I. B., 99, 118, 231, 234
Weinhold, C., 260, 261, 266
Weinstein, S. R., 75, 81, 272, 274, 291
Weintraub, S., 166, 178, 309
Weis, O. F., 425, 438
Weismann, M. M., 79
Weiss, B., 282, 291
Weiss, D. J., 156, 164
Weiss, R. L., 140, 164
Weissman, M., 257, 260, 268
Weissman, M. M., 28, 35, 36, 37, 39, 40, 90, 97, 272, 274, 287, 288, 289, 291
Weisz, J. R., 105, 122, 243, 245, 249
Wells, K., 85, 96, 269, 288
Welner, Z., 35, 40, 74, 81, 252, 253, 267, 268
Welsh, J. M., 132, 138
Wenar, C., 351, 362
Wendel, N., 111, 120, 252, 258, 267
Wender, P. H., 28, 38, 191
Wenger, M. A., 188, 191
Werder, D. D., 409, 412
Werry, J. S., 31, 35, 40, 84, 86, 87, 90, 93, 94, 97, 140, 164, 240, 250, 282, 291
West, B. J., 126, 137
West, D. J., 294, 310
Wetherby, A. M., 348, 355, 363

Whalen, C. K., 11, 12, 166, 178, 269, 271, 279, 291
Wheatt, T., 36, 38, 65, 80
Wheeler, V. A., 114, 115, 117, 123
Whitaker, A., 38, 117, 118
White, A. J., 334, 336, 343
White, D. R., 375, 376, 382
White, J. L., 103, 117
White, L. J., 199, 206
Whitmore, K., 15, 21, 22, 25, 294, 310
Whitten, P., 169, 178
Wick, P., 109, 120
Wicker, A. W., 174, 178
Wickramaratne, P., 35, 36, 37, 40, 79, 268, 291
Wicks, J., 66, 81
Widiger, R. A., 274, 291
Widiger, T. A., 274, 289
Wiederholt, J., 228, 235
Wiegand, D., 241, 249
Wierzbicki, M., 92, 93, 97
Wieseler, N. A., 336, 345
Wiggins, J. S., 98, 116, 169, 179
Wigley, V., 22, 24
Wilder, J., 183, 191
Wildman, B. G., 150, 151, 152, 164
Wildman, H. E., 377, 381
Wilkie, D., 424, 426, 437, 438
Wilkinson, G. S., 199, 202, 206
Willey, E. S., 184, 190
Williams, C., 430, 438
Williams, C. L., 142, 163
Williams, J. A., 264, 266
Williams, J. B. W., 27, 39
Williams, J. R., 297, 300, 310
Williams, R. S., 19, 22, 25, 211, 222
Williams, S., 33, 37, 240, 248
Williams, V., 298, 309
Williamson, D. A., 185, 191, 393, 395, 399, 400, 401, 402, 403, 404, 405, 408, 409, 410, 411, 412
Williamson, M. L., 431, 438
Williamson, P. S., 431, 438
Willingham, W. W., 179
Willis, W. G., 219, 223
Willner, A. G., 149, 162
Wilmore, J. W., 369, 382
Wilsher, C. P., 341, 342
Wilson, B. C., 212, 214, 215, 223
Wilson, C. S., 375, 383
Wilson, G. L., 375, 383
Wilson, H., 294, 310
Wilson, R. S., 313, 314, 319

Wilson, T. D., 104, 123
Wimberley, R. C., 447, 453
Wimmer, M., 18, 24
Winder, C. L., 169, 179
Windmiller, M., 332, 344
Wine, J. D., 145, 148, 164
Wineman, E. W., 184, 191
Wing, R. R., 386, 398
Winokur, G., 27, 38, 80
Winsburg, B., 90, 95
Wirt, R. D., 262, 268, 298, 310
Wirtz, P. W., 108, 119
Wisniewski, J. J., 409, 412
Wisniewski, J. T., 335, 344
Wisniewski, K., 335, 344
Wittchen, H. U., 273, 291
Wittman, R. D., 280, 288
Wojnilower, D. A., 108, 123, 422, 436
Wolchik, S. A., 389, 398
Wolf, E. G., 351, 362
Wolf, L. E., 289
Wolf, M. M., 10, 14, 124, 136, 149, 162, 171, 179, 309
Wolfe, D. A., 440, 441, 446, 448, 454
Wolfe, V. V., 302, 310
Wolff, H. G., 401, 403, 412
Wolff, S., 18, 25
Woo-Sam, J. M., 196, 207
Wood, D. D., 140, 141, 143, 144, 147, 149, 150, 152, 153, 156, 163
Wood, R., 108, 120
Woodbury, M., 33, 37
Woodcock, R. W., 199, 207
Woodruff, R. A., 31, 38, 80
Woolfrey, J., 378, 382
Workman, E. A., 139
Worland, J., 184, 190
World Health Organization, 346, 363
Worthington, C. F., 200, 207
Wright, H. F., 147, 164
Wuensch, K. L., 196, 207
Wurtman, J., 398
Wyatt, F., 225, 236
Wynne, M. E., 276, 287

Xenakis, S. N., 84, 85, 95

Yanchyshyn, G. W., 261, 267, 268
Yano, K. E., 310
Yarrow, M. R., 149, 164
Yates, E., 38
Yen, S., 409, 412

Yeung-Courchesne, R., 349, 361
York, C., 376, 380
Yost, L. W., 5, 13, 244, 249
Young, D. G., 319
Young, J. G., 252, 257, 265, 268, 289, 314, 318, 320
Young, K. R., 128, 132, 138
Young, L. D., 423, 437
Yule, B., 311, 320
Yule, W., 9, 14, 15, 19, 20, 21, 22, 24, 25, 311, 320
Yurcheson, R., 245, 250
Yurgelun-Todd, D., 398

Zachs, R. T., 282, 288
Zahn, T. P., 186, 191
Zahner, G. E. P., 28, 39
Zaichkowsky, L. B., 187, 188, 191
Zaichkowsky, L. D., 187, 188, 191
Zakin, D. F., 375, 383
Zammuto, R. F., 179
Zatz, S., 109, 123, 244, 250
Zeichner, A., 181, 182, 191
Zeiss, A., 113, 120
Zeiss, R., 113, 120
Zeitlin, H., 29, 31, 40
Zeltzer, L. K., 113, 120, 123, 414, 421, 429, 430, 436, 438
Zeus, F. R., 375, 381
Zimmerman, I. L., 196, 207
Zimmerman, W. S., 102, 119
Zola, I. K., 294, 309

Subject Index

Anxiety Disorders, 239–250
  description of, 239–241
    generalized anxiety disorder, 240
    obsessive-compulsive disorder, 240
    overanxious and avoidant disorders, 239, 240
    panic disorder, 240
    phobic disorders, 240
    post-traumatic stress disorder, 240
  multimodal assessment, 241–246
    direct observations, 245
      anxiety-provoking scales, 245
      Behavioral Avoidance Test (BAT), 245
    implications for treatment, 247
    parent and teacher checklists, 244, 245
      Conners Teacher Rating Scale, 244
      Revised Behavior Problem Checklist (CBCL), 244
      Teachers' Report Form of the CBCL (TRF), 244
    physiological measures, 245, 246
    self-report measures, 242, 243, 244
      Child Behavior Checklist, 243
      Children's Manifest Anxiety Scale-Revised (RCMAS), 243
      Children's Negative Cognitive Error Questionnaire, 244
      Fear Survey Schedule for Children (FSSC), 243
      Fear Survey Schedule for Children Revised (FSSC-R), 243
      State-Trait Anxiety Inventory for Children (STAIC), 243
    structured interviews, 241, 242
      Anxiety Disorders Interview Schedule for Children-Child and Parent versions (ADIS-C and ADIS-P), 241
      Child Assessment Schedule (CAS), 241
      Children's Anxiety Evaluation Form (CAEF), 241
      Diagnostic Interview for Children and Adolescents (DICA), 241
      Diagnostic Interview Schedule for Children (DISC), 241
      Interview Schedule for Children (ISC), 241
      Schedule for Affective Disorders and Schizophrenia for School-Age Children (K-SADS), 241

Attention Deficit Hyperactivity Disorder (ADHD), 269–291
  clinical description of, 270
    classroom behavior and direct observations, 279
      Parent-Adolescent Interaction Coding System, 280
      Response-Class Matrix, 279
    current diagnostic criteria and essential features, 270
    intellectual and achievement testing, 280
      Kaufman battery (K-TEA), 281
      learning disability, 280
      Peabody Individual Achievement Test, 281
      Wide Range Achievement Test
      Woodcock-Johnson Psychoeducational Battery, 281
    neurocognitive assessment, 281
      case studies, 284, 285, 286
      Continuous Performance Test (CPT), 281, 282, 284
      Matching Familiar Figures Test (MFFT), 281, 284
      Paired Associates Learning Task (PAL), 281, 284
        "BX" version, 281
        "double-letter" version, 281
        "X" version, 281
    secondary features, 271
  multimodal assessment, 271–286
    overview, 272
    standardized interviews, 272
      broad-band rating scales, 275
        Child Behavior Checklist, 275
        Conners Parent Symptom Questionnaire-Revised (CPSQ-R), 275
        Conners Teachers Rating Scale-Revised (CTRS-R), 275
        Personality Inventory for Children (PIC), 175
        Revised Behavior Problem Checklist (BPC-R), 275
        Yale Children's Inventory (YCI), 275
      narrow-band rating scales and checklists, 275
        Abbreviated Conners Teacher Rating Scale (ACTRS), 275, 276
        ADD-H Comprehensive Teacher Rating Scale (ACTeRS), 275, 276
        Children's Learning Profile (CLP), 275–278
        Home Situations Questionnaire (HSQ), 275, 276
        IOWA Conners Teacher Rating Scale (IOWA-ACTRS), 275, 276
        School Situations Questionnaire (HSQ), 275, 276
        Teacher Self-Control Rating Scale (TSCRS), 275, 276
        Werry-Weiss-Peters Activity Scale (WWPAS), 275, 276
      semistructured interviews, 273
        Children's Assessment Schedule (CAS), 273
        Interview Schedule for Children, (ISC), 273
        Kiddie-SADS (K-SADS), 273
      structured interviews, 272, 273
        Diagnostic Interview for Children (DISC), 273
        Diagnostic Interview for Children and Adolescents (DICA), 272
      use of interviews for diagnosing children with ADHD, 273
        Child Behavior Checklist (CBC), 275
        Conners Parent Symptom Questionnaire, 275
        Conners Teacher Rating Scale, 275
        Personality Inventory for Children (PIC),
        Revised Behavior Problem Checklist, 275
        Yale Children's Inventory (YCI), 275

Behavioral Assessment, 3–14
  characteristics, 5–11
    developmental and normative comparisons, 9–11
      Fear Survey Schedule for Children, 9
      generalizations, 10–11
    empirically validated measures, 5, 7–9
    multimethod approach, 5–7
    S-O-R-K-C, 6–7
  role of the child and adolescent, 11–12

Checklists and Rating Scales, 82–97
  advantages of, 82–83
  assumptions underlying use, 83–84
  individual rating scales, 86–93
    broad-band scales, 86–89
      Child Behavior Checklist, (CBCL), 86, 87–89
      Revised Behavior Problem Checklist (RBPC), 86–87
    narrow-band scales, 89–93

SUBJECT INDEX

ADD-H Comprehensive Teacher Rating
  Scale (ACTeRS), 91–92
Children's Depression Inventory (Parent
  Version) (CDI-P), 92–93
Conners Abbreviated Rating Scale, 91
Conners Parent Rating Scale, 89–90
Conners Rating Scales, 89
Conners Teacher Rating Scale, 90–91
Eyberg Child Behavior Inventory (ECBI),
  92
Matson Evaluation of Social Skills
  (MESSY), 93
psychometric considerations, 84–86
  reliability, 84–85
    interrater agreement, 84–85
  validity, 85–86
    Gadow-Sprafkin Stony Brook Child
      Psychiatric Checklist
    New York Disruptive Behavior Scales
    SNAP Rating Scale for hyperactivity
Conduct Disorder, 292–310
  description of, 292
    associated features, 293–294
      academic deficiencies, 293
      cognitive and attributional processes, 293
      hyperactivity, 293
      poor interpersonal relations, 29
    central features, 293
    parent and family features, 294
  assessment of, 294–302
    cross-situational performance, 301
    direct observation, 299–300
    institutional and societal records, 300
    method variance, 302
    peer evaluations, 298–299
    projective techniques, 200–301
    reports of significant others, 297–298
    self-report measures, 295–297
    symptoms and prosocial functioning, 301–302

Depression, 251–268
  biological markers, 263
    dexamethasone suppression test (DST), 263
    EEG, 263
    growth hormone secretion, 263
  case illustration, 263, 264
  clinical interview, 252
    highly structured diagnostic interviews,
      252–255

Child Behavior Checklist (CBCL), 254
Diagnostic Interview for Children and
  Adolescents (DICA), 252
Diagnostic Interview for Children and
  Adolescents (DICA-C), 252
Diagnostic Interview for Children and
  Adolescents (DICA-P), 252
Schedule for Affective Disorders and
  Schizophrenia for School-Age Children
  (K-SADS), 254
semistructured diagnostic interviews, 255
  Child Assessment Schedule (CAS), 255
  Children's Depression Inventory, 255
  Interview Schedule for Children, 255
  Schedule for Affective Disorders and
    Schizophrenia for School Age Children
    (K-SADS), 254, 256
clinical rating scales, 261, 262
  Children's Depression Rating Scale (CDRS),
    261
  Hamilton Rating Scale for Depression
    (HRSD), 261
  Carrol Self Rating Scale, 261
description of, 251
  adjustment disorder with depressed mood, 251
  dysthymia, 251
  major depression, 251
multimodal assessment, 252
objective and projective psychological tests, 262
  Minnesota Multiphasic Personality Inventory
    (MMPI), 262
parent-report instruments, 262
  Behavior Problem Checklist (BPC), 262
  Child Behavior Checklist (CBLC), 262
  Personality Inventory for Children (PIC), 262
self-report instruments, 257–261
  Beck Depression Inventory, 260
  Child Assessment Schedule (CAS), 260
  Center for Epidemiological Studies Depressive
    Scale for Children (CES-DC), 260
  Children's Depression Inventory (CDI), 257,
    258
  Children's Depression Scale (CDS), 259
  Depression Self-Rating Scale, 259
teacher ratings, peer ratings, and direct
  observations, 262
Developmental Considerations, 15–25
  assessment, 16
  implications for behavioral assessment, 20–23
    age-related problems, 22
    cognitive level, 22–23

screening questionnaires, 20–22
    Child Behavior Checklist (CBCL), 21
    Fear Survey Schedule for Children Revised, 21
    Rutter Behavior Rating Scales (B-Scale), 21–22
perspective, 16–18
psychopathology, 18–20
    theories, 18–19

Diagnostic Issues, 26–40
  comorbidity, 31–34
  family psychiatric history, 28–29
  informant variance, 34–37
    assessment methodology, 35–36
    patient characteristics, 36
    reporter characteristics, 36–37
    symptom content, 36
  stability, 29–31
  validity and reliability, 26–28

Diagnostic and Statistical Manual of Mental Disorders—Third Edition, 31, 65, 67, 74–76, 85, 239, 240–243, 246, 251–254, 259, 270, 272–274, 276, 303, 321, 346–347, 386

Diagnostic and Statistical Manual of Mental Disorders—Third Edition, Revised, 19, 23, 27–28, 66, 74, 85, 186, 239, 241–242, 246, 251, 257, 270–271, 285–286, 293, 303, 331, 346–347, 350, 386

Direct Observation, 140–164
  aims, 140, 141
  construction, 141–149
    collecting the observations, 146–148
    developmental considerations, 141, 142
    scoring the responses, 148
    selecting the observers, 148, 149
    selecting the setting, 144–146
    specifying the domain, 142–144
  definition, 141
  implementation, 149–155
    gaining permission, 149, 150
    training and monitoring observers, 150–155
      application, 151
      education, 150
      evaluation, 151
      orientation, 150
      recalibration, 152, 153
      termination, 153
      troubleshooting, 153–155
  interpretation, 155–158
    accuracy model, 157, 158
    client-referenced approach, 156
    criterion-referenced approach, 156
    generalizability model, 157
    norm-referenced approach, 156, 157
    psychometric model, 157
  selection, 158–162
    considerations, 159–160
      backdrop, 160
      network, 160
      nomen, 159
      observers, 159, 160
      scoring key, 160
      settings, 159
      subjects, 159
      window, 159

Eating Disorders, 384–399
  anorexia nervosa, 384–399
  bulimia nervosa, 384–399
    multimodal assessment, 386–395
    clinical interview checklist, 391–392

Headaches, 400–412
  assessment of, 403–407
    diagnostic interview, 404
    direct behavioral observation, 405
    medical examination, 403–404
    other problems, 407, 410
    self-monitoring procedures, 405
    self-report inventories, 405
      Childhood Headache Questionnaire (CHQ), 405
      Headache Symptom Questionnaire—Revised (HSQ-R), 405
      visual analog scales (VAS), 404–405
  description of, 400–403
    combined or mixed, 403
    migraine, 400–402
    muscle contraction, 402–403
  implications for treatment, 409–410

Intellectual and Achievement Testing, 192–207
  a philosophy of intelligent testing, 193, 194
  major contemporary measures of achievement, 199
    case study, 203–205
    Kaufman Test of Educational Achievement (K-TEA), 199–201
    Peabody Individual Achievement Test-Revised (PIAT-R), 201–202
    Wide Range Achievement Test-Revised (WRAT-R), 202–203
  major contemporary measures of intelligence, 194

psychometric properties of individual intelligence
and achievement measures, 194–199
    Kaufman Assessment Battery for Children
        (K-ABC), 196–198
    Stanford-Binet Intelligence Scale: Fourth
        Edition (S-BIV), 198–199
    Wechsler Intelligence Scale for Children—
        Revised (WISC-R)
Interviewing, 65–81
    Child Assessment Schedule (CAS), 65–66,
        68–74
    Diagnostic Interview for Children and
        Adolescents (DICA), 65–66, 74–75
    Diagnostic Interview Schedule for Children
        (DISC), 66, 75–76
    Interview Schedule for Children (ISC), 65–66,
        76–77
    overview of psychometric issues, 67–68
    Schedule for Affective Disorders and
        Schizophrenia for School-Aged Children
        (K-SADS), 64–66, 77–79

Mental Retardation, 321–345
    behavioral management, 340–341
        behavior modification 340–341
        pharmacological treatments, 341
    correlates of, 327
    description of, 321–323
    etiology of, 323–327
        perinatal causes, 326
        postnatal causes, 326–327
            psychosocial, 326–327
        prenatal causes, 324–326
            environmental conditions, 325–326
            organic conditions, 324–325
                chromosomal abnormalities, 324–325
                congenital infections and maternal
                    diseases, 325
                genetic abnormalities, 324
    multimodal assessment of, 328–337
        adaptive behavior scales, 331–333
            AAMD Adaptive Behavior Scale, 332
            Behavior Development Survey, 333
            Behavior Inventory for Rating Development
                (BIRD), 333
            Developmental Disabilities Profile (DDP),
                333
            Client Development Evaluation Record
                (CDER), 333
            Minnesota Developmental Programming
                System (MDPS) Behavior Scales
                Revised, 333

            Vineland Adaptive Behavior Scales, 332
        behavior rating scales, 334–336
            Aberrant Behavior Checklist (ABC), 335
            Behavior Disturbance Scale, 336
            Behavior Problems Inventory (BPI), 335
            Conners Parent and Teacher Rating Scales,
                336
            Emotional Disorders Rating Scale for
                Developmental Disabilities, 335
            Fairview Problem Behavior Checklist, 336
            other, 336–337
            Prout-Strohmer Assessment System (PSAS),
                335–336
            Psychopathology Instrument for Mentally
                Retarded Adults (PIMRA), 336
            Psychopharmacology Bulletin (Special
                Issue, 1985), 336
            Reiss Screen for Maladaptive Behavior, 335
            Teacher Questionnaire, 336
        direct observation, 328–331
            continuous recording strategies, 330–331
            discontinuous recording strategies, 330
        IQ Tests, 333–334
            impaired testing, 334
            Stanford-Binet Intelligence Scale (4th Ed.),
                334
            Wechsler Preschool and Primary Scale of
                Intelligence (WPPSI), 333–334
            Wechsler Intelligence Scale for Children -
                Revised (WISC-R), 333–334
    psychopathology and behavioral problems,
        327–328
    dual diagnosis, 327–328

Neurological Assessment, 41–50
    development, 43–49
        gray matter disorders, 48–49
            mitochondrial encephalopathies, 49
            neuronal ceroid lipofuscinosis, 49
            Rett syndrome, 48–49
        metabolic disease, 46–47
            aminoacidurias, 47
                homocystinuria, 47
                maple syrup urine disease, 47
                phenylketonuria, 47
            mucopolysaccharidosis, 48
                Hunter's syndrome, 48
                Sanfilippo disease, 48
            neurocutaneous syndromes, 48
                neurofibromatosis, 48
                tuberous sclerosis, 48
        progressive encephalopathy, 46

static encephalopathy, 43-46
  brain malformations, 44
  chromosomal disorders, 43-44
    Down syndrome, 43
    Fragile X syndrome, 43-44
  congenital infection, 44
  fetal development, 44-45
  infection, 45-46
  intraventricular hemorrhage, 45
  perinatal asphyxia, 45
  Reye's syndrome, 46
  white matter disorders, 48
    adrenoleukodystrophy, 48
    Alexander's disease, 48
    Canavan's disease, 48
    Krabbe disease, 48
    metachromatic leukodystrophy, 48
    Pelizaeus-Merzbacher disease, 48
  urea cycle disorders, 47
Neuropsychological Assessment, 208-223
  assessment process, 212-213
    content, 213
    context, 213-214
      McCarthy Scales of Children's Abilities, 214
    parameters, 213
      phases of assessment, 213
    stability of neurocognitive capacity, 214
    strategy, 214
      Halstead-Reitan Battery, 214, 215
      Luria-Nebraska Battery for Children, 214, 215
      Luria-Nebraska Neuropsychological Battery (LNNB), 215
  coverage, 221-222
    abstract reasoning, 221
    attention, 221
    executive processes, 221, 222
    language, 221
    learning and memory, 221
    motor capacity, 221
    sensory-perceptual capacity, 221
    visuospatial capacity, 221
  distinctions, 209-210
  goals, 219-221
    developmental perspective, 220, 221
      remarks, 220, 221
    psychoeducational, 219
    treatment directed, 220
  Halstead-Reitan Neuropsychological Battery, 215-219

Halstead-Reitan Battery for Children, 214, 215, 217
Luria-Nebraska Neuropsychological Battery for Children, 218, 219
  remarks, 219
Reitan-Indiana Battery for Children, 217-218
scoring and interpretation, 217, 218
neurodevelopmental perspective, 210-212

Obesity, 364-383
  description of, 364-365
  multimodal assessment, 365-378
    assessing body image, 375-376
      Body Cathexis Scale, 376
      Body-Esteem Scale, 376
      Body Experience Scale, 376
      body image detection device (BIDD), 376
      body perception index (BPI), 376
      body size estimation, 376
    determinations of, 365-370
      measures of body composition, 367-370
        skinfold measures, 368-369
        total body electrical conductivity (TBEC), 368-369
      weight tables and related indices, 365-366
        body mass index, 366
        ponderal index, 366
        weight-length index, 366
    dietary intake, 372-375
      observational measures, 375
        Behavioral Eating Test (BET), 375
      self-report measures, 372-375
        Food Frequency Questionnaire, 374-375
        Food Processor, 374
        Foods Survey, 374
        Self-Monitoring Analyses System (SMAS), 373
    family context, 377-378
      FACES, 377
      Family Environment Scale, (FES), 377
      Family Inventory of Resource Management, 377
    measures of physical fitness and activity 370-372
    physical measures of health, 370
    self-report instruments, 376-377
      Binge-Eating Scale, 376
      Children's Depression Inventory, 377
      Compulsive Eating Scale, 377
      Concern Over Weight and Dieting Scale, 377
      Diabetes Assertiveness Test, 377

Dieter's Inventory of Eating Temptations, 376
Needs Assessment Surveys, 377
Revised Restraint Scale, 376
Three-Factor Eating Questionnaire, 376

Pain, 413–438
  description of, 413–418
    assessment difficulties, 416–418
    definition of, 415–416
      International Association for the Study of Pain (IASP), 415
    implications for treatment, 431–432
    multimodal assessment, 418–431
      affective meaning of pain, 426–427
        Eland Color Tool, 426
      behavioral component of pain, 418–424
        Children's Hospital of Eastern Ontario pain scale (CHEOPS), 421
        facial action coding system (FACS), 419
        Frankl Behavior Rating Scale, 421
        maximally discriminative facial movement coding system (MAX), 419
        Observational Scale of Behavioral Distress (OSBD), 420–421
        Procedure Behavior Check List (PBCL), 421
        Procedure Behavior Rating Scale (PBRS), 420
      cognitive/self report component, 424–425
      coping strategies, 428–430
      multifaceted pain questionnaires, 427–428
        Children's Comprehensive Pain Questionnaire (CCPQ), 427–428
        Varni/Thompson Pediatric Pain Questionnaire (PPQ), 427–428
      pain intensity measures, 425–426
        visual analog scales (VAS), 425–426.
        See also, Headaches.
      psychological components, 431
    primary categories, 413–415
Peer-Referenced Assessment Strategies, 165–179
  classification of sociometric types
    social impact, 173, 174
      amiable, 173
      isolated, 173
      popular, 173
      rejected, 173
    social preference, 173, 174
  correlates of peer-referenced assessment, 171–173
    behavioral, 172, 173
    nonbehavioral, 171, 172
  definitions, 165, 166
    purpose and use, 166
  ethical issues, 174–176
    child permission, 174, 175
    parental permission, 174
    use of negative peer nominations, 175
  methodologies, 167–169
    mixed assessment, 169
      Friendship Rating Scale, 169
      Peer Nomination Inventory, 169
      Peer Perception Inventory, 169
      Pupil Evaluation Inventory (PEI), 169
    paired comparisons, 168
    peer assessment, 168, 169
      Class Play technique, 169
      Guess Who? Test, 168
      Shapiro Sociometric Role Assignment Test (SSRAT), 169
    peer nominations, 167
    peer ratings, 168
  psychometric characteristics, 169, 170
    reliability, 169, 170
  social competence, 166, 167
    definitions of, 166, 167
  validity of peer-referenced assessment, 170, 171
    construct validity, 170, 171
    social validity, 171
Pervasive Developmental Disorders, 346–363
  description of, 346–349
  multimodal assessment, 349–357
    communication and language assessment, 355
      Peabody Picture Vocabulary Test - Revised, 355
      Reynell Developmental Language Scales, 355
      Sequenced Inventory of Communication Development, 355
      TEACCH Communication Curriculum, 355
    developmental-educational assessment, 352–354
      Adult Psychoeducational Profile (AAPEP), 354
      Psychoeducational Profile (PEP), 352–353
      Psychoeducational Profile - Revised (PEP-R), 352–354
    diagnostic instruments, 350–352
      Autism Behavior Checklist (ABC), 351
      Autistic Diagnostic Interview (ADI), 351

Autistic Diagnostic Observation Schedule (ADOS), 351
Behavior Observation System (BOS), 351
Behavior Rating Instrument for Autistic and Atypical Children (BRIAAC), 351
Childhood Autism Rating Scale (CARS), 350–351
Diagnostic Checklist for Behavior-Disturbed Children—E-2, 351
family assessment, 356–357
    Autistic Diagnostic Interview (ADI), 356–357
    TEACCH Communication and Social Curriculums, 356
    Vineland Adaptive Behavior Scale, 357
intellectual-adaptive assessment, 354–355
    Bayley Scales of Infant Development, 354
    Binet or Wechsler Scales
    K-Autism Behavior Checklist (K-ABC), 354
    Leiter International Performance Scale, 354
    Merrill-Palmer Scales of Mental Tests, 354
    Stanford-Binet, 354
    Vineland Adaptive Behavior Scales, 354
medical assessment, 357
social assessment, 355–356
    Autistic Diagnostic Observation Schedule (ADOS), 356
    Psychoeducational Profile - Revised (PEP-R), 356
treatment planning, 357–358
Physical Abuse and Neglect, 439–454
description of, 439–440
implications for treatment, 449–451
multimodal assessment, 440–448
    format of, 441–442
    of parents, 442–448
        Beck Depression Inventory (BDI), 447
        Checklist for Living Environments to Assess Neglect (CLEAN), 445
        Child Abuse and Neglect Interview Schedule (CANIS), 445
        Child Abuse Potential Inventory (CAPI), 447
        Child Assessment and Management Project (CAMP), 448
        Child Behavior Checklist (CBCL), 448
        Eyberg Child Behavior Inventory (ECBI), 447
        Family Interaction Coding System (FICS), 448
        Home Accident Prevention Inventory (HAPI), 445
        Home Observation for Measurement of the Environmental Inventory (HOME), 445
        Home Simulation Assessment (HSA), 447
        Interactive Behavior Code (IBC), 448
        Interpersonal Support Evaluation List (ISEL), 446
        Knowledge of Behavioral Principles as Applied to Children (KBPAC), 442
        MacMillan-Olson-Hansen Anger Control Scale, 446
        Maternal History Interview (MHI), 445
        Measure of Maternal Stimulation (MMS), 448
        Michigan Screening Profile of Parenting (MSPP), 442
        Minnesota Multiphasic Personality Inventory (MMPI), 447
        Novaco Provocation Inventory (NPI), 446
        Parent Opinion Questionnaire (POQ), 442
        Parent Problem-Solving Instrument (PPSI), 446
        Parental Problem-Solving Measure (PPSM), 446
        Parenting Sense of Competence Scale (PSOCS), 442
        Parenting Stress Index (PSI), 444
        Questionnaire on Resources and Stress, (QRS), 444
        Schedule of Recent Experience (SRE), 445
        Social Provisions Scale (SPS), 446
        State-Trait Anxiety Inventory (STAI), 447
        Symptom Checklist-90-Revised (SCL-90-R), 447
        Vineland Adaptive Behavior Scales-Revised, 447
Physiological Assessment, 180–191
applications, 186–188
developmental factors, 183–185
instrumentation and measures, 181–183
reliability and validity, 185, 186
response fractionation, 188, 189
Projective Techniques, 224–236
apperception techniques, 225–227
    Children's Apperception Test, 226
    Roberts Apperception Test for Children (RATC), 226, 227
    APT Questionnaire booklet, 227
    Thematic Apperception Test (TAT), 225, 226, 227

SUBJECT INDEX

drawing techniques, 227–229
  Draw-A-Person, 228
  House-Tree-Person, 229
  Kinetic Family Drawing (KFD), 229
Rorschach Test, 229–234
  Comprehensive System for the Rorschach, 231, 232
  Ego-Centricity Index, 232
  Minnesota Multiphasic Personality Inventory, 103, 232
Psychological Assessment, ethical issues in, 51–61
  advocacy against misuse of tests, 57–60
    consent, 58–59
    obsolescence, 59
    ownership, 59–60
  basic psychometric concepts, 52–54
    key terms, 52–53
      reliability, 52
      sources of error, 53
      validity, 52
        construct, 52–53
        content, 52
        criterion-related, 53
    problems, 53–54
      Detrimental School Function Test (DSFT), 53
  guiding principles, 60–61
    Standards for Educational and Psychological Testing, 60–61
  revised standards (Standards for Educational and Psychological Testing), 54–57
    operating procedures, 54–55
      Childhood Reading Achievement Profile, 54
    test bias, 55–56
    user competence, 56–57
      Rorschach Inkblots, 53
      Wechsler Intelligence Scale for Children-Revised, 53

Self-Monitoring, 124–139
  applications of, 132–136
    self-monitoring of academic behaviors, 132, 133
      academic accuracy, 134
      academic productivity, 133, 134
      on-task behavior, 132, 133
    social behaviors, 134–136
      disruptive behavior, 134, 135
      inappropriate verbalizations, 135
      social skills, 135, 136
  methodology, 124–129
    considerations, 126–128
    devices used, 126
    types of behaviors, 124, 125
      complexity, 125
      objectivity, 124, 125
      number of behaviors, 125
    types of data, 125, 126
      frequency counting, 125
      narrative descriptions, 125, 126
      time sampling, 125
    variables affecting the accuracy of, 128, 129
      awareness, 128
      nature of the recording device, 129
      other variables, 129
      training and reinforcement, 129
      valence of target behavior, 129
  reactivity, 129–131
    explanation of, 130
    variables affecting, 130, 131
      goals, reinforcement and feedback, 130, 131
      motivation for behavior change, 130, 131
      presence and nature of the recording device, 130
      timing of self-recording, 130, 131
      training in accurate recording, 130, 131
      valence of target behavior, 130
  relationship between accuracy and reactivity, 131, 132
Self-Report Methodology, 98–123
  assessment methodology, 98–100
  broad-bandwidth measures, 115
    Adolescent Psychopathology Scale, 116
    California Psychological Inventory (CPI), 103, 115
    Child Rating Scale, 115
    Children's Self-Report Psychiatric Rating Scale [a.k.a. Children's Self-Report Scale (CSRS)], 115
    Eysenck Personality Inventory, 115
    Eysenck Personality Questionnaire, 115
    High School Personality Questionnaire (HSPQ), 103, 115
    Millon Adolescent Personality Inventory (MAPI), 115
    Minnesota Multiphasic Personality Inventory (MMPI), 103, 115, 232
    Youth Self-Report (YSR), 116
  historical excursion, 100–104
    Adjustment Inventory, 101
    Adjustment Questionnaire, 102

Analytic Personality Test Battery, 103
Aspects of Personality Inventory (API), 101
Baxter Child Personality Test, 101
Cady Modification of the Personal Data Sheet, 100
California Psychological Inventory (CPI), 103, 115
California Test of Personality (CTP), 101
Child Personality Scale, 102
Cowen Adolescent Personality Schedule, 101
Institute for Personality and Ability Testing (IPAT), 103
  Children's Personality Questionnaire, 103
  Early School Personality Questionnaire, 103
  IPAR Anxiety Scale, 103
  IPAT Contact Personality Factor Test, 103
  IPAT High School Personality Questionnaire (HSPQ), 103, 115
  IPAT Music Preference Test of Personality, 103
  IPAT Neurotic Personality Factor Test, 103
Minnesota Multiphasic Personality Inventory (MMPI), 103, 115, 232
Personal Index, 101
Personality Adjustment Inventory, 100
Personality Inventory, 101
Personality Inventory for Children, 101
Personality Quotient Test, 102
Personality Rating Scale, 102
Pupil Portraits, 100
School Inventory, 101
Sixteen Personality Factor Questionnaire (16 PFQ), 103
Student Form of Bell's Adjustment Inventory, 103
Test of Personality Adjustment, 100
Thurstone Temperament Schedule (TTS), 102
SRA Youth Inventory, 102
STS Junior Inventory, 103
STS Youth Inventory, 103
Woodoworth's Personal Data Sheet, 100
issues and assumptions, 104–106
  developmental issues, 104
  psychometric qualities, 105
  self-disclosure, 105
  social desirability, 105
overview, 106, 107
selection of child and adolescent self-report measures, 107–115
  achievement motivation, 107
    Children's Academic Intrinsic Motivation Inventory (CAIMI), 107

alcoholism, 108
  Adolescent Drinking Index (ADI), 108
  Alcohol Expectancy Questionnaire-Adolescent Form (AEQ-A), 108
anger, assertiveness, and aggression, 108, 109
  Children's Action Tendency Scale (CATS), 108
  Children's Assertive Behavior Scale (CABS), 108
  Children's Assertiveness Inventory (CAI), 109
  Children's Inventory of Anger (CIA), 108
  State Trait Anger Expression Inventory (STAXI), 108
anxiety and related disorders, 109, 110
  Child Anxiety Scale (CAS), 109
  Children's Cognitive Assessment Questionnaire, 109
  Children's Fear Survey Schedule (CFSS), 110
  Children's Manifest Anxiety Scale, 109
  Cognitive and Somatic State Anxiety Inventory, 109
  Cognitive and Somatic Trait Anxiety Inventory, 109
  Fear Survey Schedule for Children (FSSC), 110
  Fear Survey Schedule for Children - Revised (FSSC-R), 110
  Leyton Obsessional Inventory - Child Version, 110
  Louisville Fear Survey Schedule, 110
  Revised Children's Manifest Anxiety Scale (RCMAS), 109
  Social Anxiety Scale for Children (SASC), 109
  State-Trait Anxiety Inventory for Children (STAIC), 109
  Test Anxiety Scale for Children, 109
depression and related domains, 110–112
  Children's Depression Inventory (CDI), 111
  Hamilton Depression Rating Scale, 112
  Hopelessness Scale for Children (HSC), 112
  Pleasure Scale for Children, 112
  Reynolds Adolescent Depression Scale (RADS), 111
  Reynolds Child Depression Scale (RCDS), 111
  Suicidal Behaviors Interview, 112
  Suicidal Ideation Questionnaire (SIQ), 112
eating disorders, 112
  Anorexia-Bulimia Inventory (ABI), 112

Bulimia Test (BULIT), 112
Eating Attitudes Test (EAT), 112
Eating Disorders Inventory, 112
locus of control, 113, 114
   Bialer-Cromwell Children's Locus of Control Scale, 113
   Children's Nowicki-Strickland Internal-External Control Scale (CNS-IE), 113
   Intellectual Achievement Responsibility Questionnaire (IAR), 113
   Mastery Orientation Inventory (MOI), 114
   Multidimensional Measure of Children's Perceptions of Control, 113
   Preschool and Primary Nowicki-Strickland Internal-External Control Scale (PPNS-IE), 113
   Stanford Preschool Internal-External Scale (SPIES), 113
loneliness, 114
   UCLA Loneliness Scale, 114
pain and health-related somatic symptoms, 112, 113
   faces scale, 113
   "Oucher" scale, 113
   pain thermometer, 113
self-concept, 114, 115
   Academic Self-Concept Scale, 115
   Academic Self-Concept Scale - High School Version, 115
   Children's Self-Efficacy for Peer Interaction Scale (CSPI), 115
   Coopersmith Self-Esteem Inventory (SEI), 114
   Offer Self-Image Questionnaire for Adolescents, 114
   Perceived Competency Scale for Children (PCSC), 114
   Piers-Harris Children's Self-Concept Scale, 114
   Rosenberg Self-Esteem Scale (RSES), 114
   Self-Perception Profile for Adolescents, 114

Tics and Tourette's Disorder, 311–320
  case illustration, 316–318
  description of, 311–313
    associated psychiatric symptomatology, 312
    DSM-III-R diagnosis, 312–313
  multimodal assessment, 313–316
    assessment instruments, 314–316
      clinician observer assessment
        Children's Global Assessment Scale (CGAS), 315
        Tourette's Symptom Severity Scale (TSSS), 315
        Tourette's Syndrome Global Scale (TSGS), 315
        Yale Global Tic Severity Scale (YGTSS), 315
      parental and self-reports, 314
        Child Behavior Checklist and Profile, 314
        Conners Parent Questionnaire, 314
        Leyton Obsessional Inventory-Child Version, 314
        Tourette's Syndrome Questionnaire (TSQ), 314
        Tourette's Syndrome Symptom List, 314
      videotaped assessment, 315–316
  clinical interview, 313
  neurologic examination, 314
  tic phenomenology, 311–312

ABOUT THE EDITORS AND CONTRIBUTORS

ABOUT THE EDITORS

Thomas H. Ollendick, Ph.D., is currently professor of psychology and director of clinical training at Virginia Polytechnic Institute and State University. He has coauthored or coedited several books, including *Clinical Behavior Therapy with Children*, *Handbook of Child Psychopathology*, *Child Behavioral Assessment: Principles and Procedures*, *Enhancing Children's Social Skills*, and *Children's Phobias: A Behavioural Perspective*. A fellow of APA's Division 12, he is president of APA's Section on Clinical Child Psychology and serves on the Board of Directors of the Association for Advancement of Behavior Therapy and the Council of University Directors of Clinical Psychology.

Michel Hersen, Ph.D., is professor of psychiatry and psychology at the University of Pittsburgh School of Medicine. Past president of the Association for Advancement of Behavior Therapy, he has coauthored and coedited over 80 books, including *Single Case Experimental Designs*. He has also published more than 170 scientific journal articles and is coeditor of several psychological journals, including *Behavior Modification*, *Clinical Psychology Review*, *Journal of Anxiety Disorders*, *Journal of Family Violence*, and *Journal of the Multihandicapped Person*. He is coeditor of *Progress in Behavior Modification* and associate editor of *Addictive Behaviors*. Dr. Hersen is the recipient of many research grants from the National Institute of Mental Health, the Department of Education, the National Institute of Disabilities and Rehabilitation Research, and the March of Dimes Birth Defects Foundation.

ABOUT THE CONTRIBUTORS

Michael A. Alexander, M.D., is a clinical associate professor of pediatrics at the University of Pittsburgh. He is a diplomate of both the American Board of Pediatrics and the American Board of Physical Medicine and Rehabilitation. He has published in several areas relevant to the rehabilitation of infants and children. His research interests include outcome studies and the application of technological advances to children.

Cathy L. Alpert, Ph.D., is a research assistant professor of special education at Peabody College of

Vanderbilt University. Her major research interests include incidental language teaching strategies and social interaction training for young handicapped children. She has conducted studies on training parents and teachers to apply incidental teaching procedures with language-delayed children and currently is investigating the effectiveness of incidental teaching procedures for training handicapped children to communicate using a nonvocal communication mode. She has published chapters and articles on language development and language-related intervention and assessment strategies.

Michael Aman, Ph.D., is associate professor of psychology and psychiatry at The Ohio State University and director of research at The Nisonger Center for Mental Retardation and Developmental Disabilities. His areas of research interest include psychopharmacology in mental retardation and childhood disorders, psychopathology and behavior problems in mental retardation, and specific learning disabilities. He is a co-editor of the standardized rating scale for assessing treatment effects (the Aberrant Behavior Checklist), coeditor of a text on psychopharmacology in the developmental disabilities, and the author of a monograph reviewing available instruments for assessing behavior disorders in mental retardation.

Paul J. Ambrosini, M.D., is associate professor of psychiatry and director of Child Outpatient Services in the Division of Child Psychiatry at the Medical College of Pennsylvania, Eastern Pennsylvania Psychiatric Institute. His major research interests are in affective disorders in children and adolescents, as well as biological correlates and pharmacotherapy of depression. He has published in the areas of pediatric affective disorders, structured psychiatric interviewing, and psychiatric nosology.

Robert T. Ammerman, Ph.D., is supervisor, Department of Research and Clinical Psychology at the Western Pennsylvania School for Blind Children. He also is assistant professor of psychiatry and lecturer in psychology at the University of Pittsburgh. His research interests include child maltreatment, abuse and neglect in handicapped children, family adjustment, and child behavior therapy.

Billy A. Barrios, Ph.D., is associate professor of psychology at the University of Mississippi. He has served as associate editor for the journal *Behavioral Assessment* and editorial board member for the journal *Behavior Therapy* and the *Journal of Consulting and Clinical Psychology*. He spends much of his time developing and evaluating realistic clinical assessment procedures.

Roberta E. Bauer, M.D., is a developmental pediatrician with Pediatric and Neonatal Associates of Pittsburgh, Pennsylvania. After fellowships in Child Development and in Pediatric Rehabilitation at Children's Hospital of Pittsburgh and D. T. Watson Rehabilitation Hospital, respectively, she served as a staff pediatrician and medical director of the Infant and Development Program at D. T. Watson, as medical consultant to the Early Childhood Therapies Program at Allegheny General Hospital, and as a clinical instructor in pediatrics and staff pediatrician to the Cerebral Palsy Clinic at Children's Hospital of Pittsburgh and the state cerebral palsy clinics in Western Pennsylvania. She is presently actcive in the Neonatal ICU and High Risk Infant Follow-up Clinic at West Penn Hospital where her interests are promoting health parenting and optimal development of families.

Ronald W. Belter, Ph.D., is assistant professor in the Department of Psychiatry and Behavioral Sciences at the Medical University of South Carolina in Charleston. He is actively involved in research, teaching, and service with adolescents and children. He has published in the area of children's ability to give consent for treatment and in the area of child and adolescent assessment.

Charles B. Berde, M.D., Ph.D., is director of the Pain Treatment Service at the Children's Hospital in Boston and assistant professor of anesthesia at the Harvard Medical School. He has published numerous articles on pain in children, its medical management, and the development of new methods for its treatment.

Christine L. Cole, Ph.D., is assistant professor of school psychology at Lehigh University and a behavioral consultant to Centennial School, an approved private school for students with severe behavior disorders. Her major research interests include self-management intervention strategies and social interaction training for children with behavioral/emotional difficulties. She has recently conducted studies evaluating the generalization effects of self-monitoring in the classroom and the effects of program-wide social skills training on students with severe behavior disorders. Dr. Cole has coauthored numerous chapters and articles on self-management and other behavioral assessment and intervention techniques.

W. Edward Craighead, Ph.D., is professor in the Department of Psychiatry at Duke University Medical Center. He is director of clinical research and of the outpatient clinic in the Duke University Medical Center Affective Disorders Program. He has served as president of the Association for Advancement of Behavior Therapy, on the board of directors of Division 12 of American Psychological Association, and the Board of the Council of University Directors of Clinical Psychology. He is currently the editor of *Behavior Therapy*. He is the coauthor/editor of several books, book chapters, and articles. Most of his research and clinical work are focused on affective disorders.

John F. Curry, Ph.D., is associate professor in the Department of Psychiatry at Duke University Medical Center, and a diplomate in Clinical Psychology of the American Board of Professional Psychology. He is director of the Clinical Child and Adolescent Psychology Laboratory and directs psychological services and research for the Adolescent Inpatient Psychiatry Program. He is a consulting editor for the *Journal of Pediatric Psychology* and for the *Journal of Clinical Child Psychology*. He is author of numerous articles and chapters. His research is focused on affective and behavioral disorders of adolescence.

A. J Finch, Jr., Ph.D., is professor in the Department of Psychiatry and Behavioral Science at the Medical University of South Carolina in Charleston. He is a diplomate in clinical psychology of the American Board of Professional Psychology and a fellow of the American Psychological Association and the Society for Personality Assessment. He has published extensively in the area of child psychopathology and assessment.

David M. Garner, Ph.D., is professor of psychiatry at Michigan State University and the director of research for the eating disorders program. He was a scholar of the Medical Research Council of Canada from 1980 to 1985 and the recipient of a Research Associate Award from the Ontario Mental Health Foundation from 1965 to 1988. His primary research interests in the area of eating disorders are diagnosis, pathogenesis, prognosis, psychotherapy outcome, and the development of assessment materials.

David H. Gleaves, M.A., is a doctoral candidate in clinical psychology at Louisiana State University. He has published several papers related to eating disorders and behavioral medicine. His primary clinical interests concern psychological assessment of adults and behavior therapy for obesity.

Frank M. Gresham, Ph.D., is professor and director of the Combined Program in Clinical and School Psychology at Hofstra University. He is a fellow of the American Psychological Association and serves on numerous editorial boards of journals in psychology and education. His major research interest is social skills assessment and training with children and adolescents. He is coauthor of the *Social Skills Rating System*, a norm-referenced, multirater system for assessing social skills for children and adolescents ages 3 to 18.

David Hammer, Ph.D., is adjunct assistant professor of psychology at The Ohio State University and director of the Behavior Pediatrics Clinic at the Nisonger Center for Mental Retardation and Developmental Disabilities. Special clinical, training, and research interests include behavioral pediatric disorders and behavior therapy with children and families, including children with severe behavior problems and dual diagnoses.

Linda K. Hinkle, Ph.D., is assistant professor of psychology at Edinboro University of Pennsylvania. She completed a residency in clinical psychology at the University of Mississippi Medical Center/Veterans Affairs Medical Center, and earned her Ph.D. from Purdue University in 1989. She is active in clinical work and research related to eating disorders and obesity.

Kay Hodges, Ph.D., is professor of psychology and director of clinical training at Eastern Michigan University. She is a diplomate in clinical psychology, awarded by the American Board of Professional Psychology, and a fellow in the American Psychological Association. She has published in several areas, including assessment of children, childhood depression, and psychosomatic illness in children. She was formally on the faculty of the medical schools at the University of Missouri at Columbia and Duke University.

Toshinori Ishikuma, Ph.D., is assistant professor of psychology at the University of Tsukuba, Japan. He served as a teaching assistant to Dr. Alan S. Kaufman at the University of Alabama and a lecturer of School Psychology at San Diego State University. He has published chapters and articles in the areas of cross-cultural assessment and Rational-Emotive Therapy (RET).

William G. Johnson, Ph.D., is professor at the University of Mississippi Medical Center. He has published over fifty scientific articles and several books on eating behavior and the treatment of eating disorders. Dr. Johnson is a diplomate in clinical psychology, American Broad of Professional Psychology, and a fellow in Divisions 12 and 38 of the American Psychological Association. A sports enthusiast, he is a marathon runner and triathlete.

Alan S. Kaufman, Ph.D., is research professor at the University of Alabama, where he trains school psycholgists in assessment techniques. A fellow of four APA divisions and member of eight editorial boards, he is author of *Intelligent Testing with the WISC-R* and *Assessing Adolescent and Adult Intelligence*. He has coauthored, with his wife Nadeen, several intelligence and achievement tests for American Guidance Service, including the Kaufman Assessment Battery for Children (K-ABC), Kaufman Test of Educational Achievement (K-TEA), and the forthcoming Kaufman Adolescent and Adult Intelligence Test (KAIT).

Alan E. Kazdin, Ph.D., is professor of psychology and professor in the Child Study Center at Yale University. He received his Ph.D. at Northwestern University (1970). His primary areas of research are the assessment, diagnosis, and treatment of childhood disorders, particularly depression and antisocial behavior in children, and in processes and outcome of child therapy. He has been editor of the *Journal of Consulting and Clinical Psychology* and currently is editor of *Psychological Assessment*. He has been a fellow of the Center for Advanced Study in the Behavioral Sciences and is a fellow of APA in Divisions 5 (Evaluation, Measurement, and Statistics), 12 (Clinical Psychology), and 25 (the Experimental Analysis of Behavior).

Neville John King, Ph.D., is senior lecturer in the faculty of education at Monash University. He has published extensively in several areas relevant to child behavioral assessment. Currently he is researching childhood fears and anxiety disorders, and is the senior author of *Children's Phobias: A Behavioral Perspective*.

Gerald P. Koocher, Ph.D., is chief psychologist at Boston's Children's Hospital and Judge Baker Children's Center, and associate professor of psychology at Harvard Medical School. He is a diplomate of the American Board of Professional Psychology in both clinical and forensic psychology. He has served on both the APA Ethics Committee and the Massachusetts Board of Registration in Psychology. In addition, he is the author of numerous publications dealing with topics in pediatric psychology, clinical child psychology, and forensic issues. His books include: *Ethics in Psychology* and *Children, Ethics, and the Law*.

Beate M. Lehn, Dipl. Psych., provides pediatric psychology services at the Dr. vonHaunersches Kinderspital in Munich, Germany. Her research interests are in the area of psychological factors in childhood pain.

Steven G. Little, Ph.D., is assistant professor of school and clinical psychology at Hofstra University. His major research interests include child behavior therapy within an educational context and school consultation.

Lee M. Marcus, Ph.D., is associate professor of psychology and psychiatry and clinical director, Chapel Hill TEACCH Center, Department of Psychiatry, University of North Carolina School of Medicine in Chapel Hill, North Carolina. Dr. Marcus also is the director of psychology training in the Department. He is author of many chapters in textbooks on the topic of diagnosis and assessment in autism and is currently involved in research in this area.

Helen Orvaschel, Ph.D., is associate professor of psychiatry and director of child psychology in the Division of Child Psychiatry at the Medical College of Pennsylvania, Eastern Pennsylvania Psychiatric Institute. Her major research interests are in risk factors that contribute to the development of child and adolescent affective disorders. She has published in the areas of psychiatric assessment, psychiatric epidemiology, and children at risk for depression.

Peggy Parker, M.A., is a doctoral candidate in counseling psychology at Michigan State University. She has a special interest in eating disorders and eating behavior in athletes.

Dennis C. Russo, Ph.D., is director of behavioral and pediatric programming for the New Medico Head Injury System. He holds a joint appointment as associate professor of psychology at the Harvard Medical School. Dr. Russo is a fellow of the American Psychological Association and the Society of Behavioral Medicine. He has published numerous books and articles in pediatric psychology.

Floyd R. Sallee, M.D., Ph.D., is assistant professor of psychiatry at the Medical University of South Carolina (MUSC), where he is engaged in teaching and research in the field of child psychiatry. He is director of the Tic and Tourette Program at MUSC and is investigating the pharmacotherapeutic treatment of Tourette Syndrome. He is also director of the molecular neuropharmacology laboratory in the department of psychiatry and is presently investigating dopamine receptor ontogeny.

Suzanne M. Savin, M.A., holds a master's degree in clinical psychology from Louisiana State University. Her major research and clinical interests relate to eating disorders.

Eric Schopler, Ph.D., is professor of psychology and psychiatry, director, Division for Treatment and Education of Autistic and related Communication handicapped Children (TEACCH) at the University of North Carolina School of Medicine, Chapel Hill. He is the author of numerous texts, chapters in texts, and articles in the field. He is editor of the *Journal of Autism and Developmental Disorders* and is editorially involved with six other related professional journals. Among his advisory activities is his involvement with the Work Group to revise the *Diagnostic and Statistical Manual of Mental Disorders* (DSM-III-R).

Edward S. Shapiro, Ph.D., is professor and director of the school psychology program at Lehigh University. He has published several articles and book chapters in the areas of curriculum-based assessment, behavioral assessment, behavioral interventions, and self-management with persons with developmental disabilities. Dr. Shapiro has published three books, his most recent entitled *Academic Skills Problems: Direct Assessment and Intervention*. He is also editor of *School Psychology Review*, official journal of the National Association of School Psychologists, having served as one of the associate editors since 1985.

Gregory T. Slomka, Ph.D., is a consulting neuropsychologist at the Allegheny Neuropsychiatric Institute, Oakdale, Pennsylvania, and Allegheny General Hospital, Pittsburgh, Pennsylvania. His principal research interests are focused in the area of developmental neuropsychology. He has published articles and chapters pertinent to the assessment of children and adults with neurodevelopmental disorders.

Cyd Strauss, Ph.D., is clinical assistant professor in the Department of Psychiatry at the University of Florida. She also holds positions as clinical director of The Fear and Anxiety Clinic in the Department of Clinical and Health Psychology at the University of Florida and as co-director at the Center for Children and Families in Gainesville, Florida. She specializes in the area of childhood anxiety disorders and has published numerous articles and chapters in her area of specialization.

Ralph Tarter, Ph.D., is professor of psychiatry and neurology, University of Pittsburgh School of Medicine and director of the Center for Education and Drug Abuse Research. He has authored or coauthored seven books and over 150 articles in the field of neuropsychology, alcoholism, drug abuse, and children at risk.

Janet B. Teodori, M.D., received her medical degree from the University Pennsylvania in 1981. Until 1989 she was assistant professor of psychiatry, pediatrics, and neurology at the University of Pittsburgh School of Medicine, Western Psychiatric Institute and Clinic, Pittsburgh, Pennsylvania.

Donald A. Williamson, Ph.D., is professor in the Department of Psychology at Louisiana State University. He is also director of the Psychological Services Center. He has published extensively in the areas of behavioral medicine, behavior therapy, and eating disorders.

William Yule, Ph.D., is professor of applied child psychology at the University of London, Institute of Psychiatry, and head of clinical psychology services for the Bethlem Royal and Maudsley Hospital. He has a long-standing interest in the epidemiology of children's disorders and has done research and published in the area of reading disability, behavior modification in the classroom, the effect of lead on children's development, school refusal, fears, and most recently post-traumatic stress disorder in children.

Janice Zeman, M.S., is a graduate student in clinical psychology at Vanderbilt University. She completed a predoctoral internship in clinical child psychology at Duke University Medical Center.

General Psychology Series

Editors: **Arnold P. Goldstein,** Syracuse University
Leonard Krasner, Stanford University & SUNY at Stony Brook

Vol. 1. WOLPE—*The Practice of Behavior Therapy, Fourth Edition*
Vol. 2. MAGOON et al.—*Mental Health Counselors at Work**
Vol. 3. McDANIEL—*Physical Disability and Human Behavior, Second Edition**
Vol. 4. KAPLAN et al.—*The Structural Approach in Psychological Testing*
Vol. 5. LaFAUCI & RICHTER—*Team Teaching at the College Level**
Vol. 6. PEPINSKY—*People and Information**
Vol. 7. SIEGMAN & POPE—*Studies in Dyadic Communication*
Vol. 8. JOHNSON—*Existential Man: The Challenge of Psychotherapy*
Vol. 9. TAYLOR—*Climate for Creativity*
Vol. 10. RICKARD—*Behavioral Intervention in Human Problems**
Vol. 14. GOLDSTEIN—*Psychotherapeutic Attraction*
Vol. 15. HALPERN—*Survival: Black/White*
Vol. 16. SALZINGER & FELDMAN—*Studies in Verbal Behavior: An Empirical Approach*
Vol. 19. LIBERMAN—*A Guide to Behavioral Analysis and Therapy*
Vol. 22. PEPINSKY & PATTON—*The Psychological Experiment: A Practical Accomplishment**
Vol. 23. YOUNG—*New Sources of Self**
Vol. 24. WATSON—*Child Behavior Modification: A Manual for Teachers, Nurses and Parents**
Vol. 25. NEWBOLD—*The Psychiatric Programming of People: Neo-Behavioral Orthomolecular Psychiatry*
Vol. 26. ROSSI—*Dreams and the Growth of Personality: Expanding Awareness in Psychotherapy**
Vol. 27. O'LEARY & O'LEARY—*Classroom Management: The Successful Use of Behavior Modification, Section Edition*
Vol. 28. FELDMAN—*College and Student: Selected Readings in the Social Psychology of Higher Education*
Vol. 29. ASHEM & POSER—*Adaptive Learning: Behavior Modification with Children*
Vol. 30. BURCK et al.—*Counseling and Accountability: Methods and Critique**
Vol. 31. FREDERIKSEN et al.—*Prediction of Organizational Behavior*
Vol. 32. CATTELL—*A New Morality from Science: Beyondism*
Vol. 33. WEINER—*Personality: The Human Potential*
Vol. 34. LIEBERT & SPRAFKIN—*The Early Window: Effects of Television on Children and Youth, Third Edition*
Vol. 35. COHEN et al.—*Psych City: A Simulated Community*

*Out of print.

Vol. 36. GRAZIANO—*Child Without Tomorrow*
Vol. 37. MORRIS—*Perspectives in Abnormal Behavior*
Vol. 38. BALLER—*Bed Wetting: Origins and Treatment**
Vol. 40. KAHN, CAMERON & GRIFFIN—*Methods and Evaluation in Clinical and Counseling Psychology*
Vol. 41. SEGALL—*Human Behavior and Public Policy: A Political Psychology*
Vol. 42. FAIRWEATHER et al.—*Creating Change in Mental Health Organizations*
Vol. 43. KATZ & ZLUTNICK—*Behavior Therapy and Health Care: Principles and Applications*
Vol. 44. EVANS & CLAIBORN—*Mental Health Issues and the Urban Poor*
Vol. 46. BARBER, SPANOS & CHAVES—*Hypnosis, Imagination and Human Potentialities*
Vol. 47. POPE—*The Mental Health Interview: Research and Application*
Vol. 48. PELTON—*The Psychology of Nonviolence**
Vol. 49. COLBY—*Artificial Paranoia—A Computer Simulation of Paranoid Processes*
Vol. 50. GELFAND & HARTMANN—*Child Behavior Analysis and Therapy, Second Edition*
Vol. 51. WOLPE—*Theme and Variations: A Behavior Therapy Casebook**
Vol. 52. KANFER & GOLDSTEIN—*Helping People Change: A Textbook of Methods, Fourth Edition*
Vol. 53. DANZIGER—*Interpersonal Communication**
Vol. 55. GOLDSTEIN & STEIN—*Prescriptive Psychotherapies*
Vol. 56. BARLOW & HERSEN—*Single-Case Experimental Designs: Strategies for Studying Behavior Changes, Second Edition*
Vol. 57. MONAHAN—*Community Mental Health and the Criminal Justice System*
Vol. 58. WAHLER, HOUSE & STAMBAUGH—*Ecological Assessment of Child Problem Behavior: A Clinical Package for Home, School and Institutional Settings*
Vol. 59. MAGARO—*The Construction of Madness: Emerging Conceptions and Interventions into the Psychotic Process*
Vol. 60. MILLER—*Behavioral Treatment of Alcoholism**
Vol. 61. FOREYT—*Behavioral Treatments of Obesity*
Vol. 62. WANDERSMAN, POPPEN & RICKS—*Humanism and Behaviorism: Dialogue and Growth*
Vol. 63. NIETZEL, WINETT, MACDONALD & DAVIDSON—*Behavioral Approaches to Community Psychology*
Vol. 64. FISHER & GOCHROS—*Handbook of Behavior Therapy with Sexual Problems*. Vol. I: *General Procedures*. Vol. II: *Approaches to Specific Problems**
Vol. 65. BELLACK & HERSEN—*Behavioral Assessment: A Practical Handbook, Third Edition*
Vol. 66. LEFKOWITZ, ERON, WALDER & HUESMANN—*Growing Up to Be Violent: A Longitudinal Study of the Development of Aggression*
Vol. 67. BARBER—*Pitfalls in Human Research: Ten Pivotal Points*
Vol. 68. SILVERMAN—*The Human Subject in the Psychological Laboratory*
Vol. 69. FAIRWEATHER & TORNATZKY—*Experimental Methods for Social Policy Research**
Vol. 70. GURMAN & RAZIN—*Effective Psychotherapy: A Handbook of Research**
Vol. 71. MOSES & BYHAM—*Applying the Assessment Center Method*

Vol. 72.   GOLDSTEIN—*Prescriptions for Child Mental Health and Education*
Vol. 73.   KEAT—*Multimodal Therapy with Children*
Vol. 74.   SHERMAN—*Personality: Inquiry & Application*
Vol. 75.   GATCHEL & PRICE—*Clinical Applications of Biofeedback: Appraisal and Status*
Vol. 76.   CATALANO—*Health, Behavior and the Community: An Ecological Perspective*
Vol. 77.   NIETZEL—*Crime and Its Modification: A Social Learning Perspective*
Vol. 78.   GOLDSTEIN, HOYER & MONTI—*Police and the Elderly*
Vol. 79.   MIRON & GOLDSTEIN—*Hostage*
Vol. 80.   GOLDSTEIN et al.—*Police Crisis Intervention*
Vol. 81.   UPPER & CAUTELA—*Covert Conditioning*
Vol. 82.   MORELL—*Program Evaluation in Social Research*
Vol. 83.   TEGER—*Too Much Invested to Quit*
Vol. 84.   MONJAN & GASSNER—*Critical Issues in Competency-Based Education*
Vol. 85.   KRASNER—*Environmental Design and Human Behavior: A Psychology of the Individual in Society*
Vol. 86.   TAMIR—*Communication and the Aging Process: Interaction Throughout the Life Cycle*
Vol. 87.   WEBSTER, KONSTANTAREAS, OXMAN & MACK—*Autism: New Directions in Research and Education*
Vol. 89.   CARTLEDGE & MILBURN—*Teaching Social Skills to Children: Innovative Approaches, Second Edition*
Vol. 90.   SARBIN & MANCUSO—*Schizophrenia—Medical Diagnosis or Moral Verdict?**
Vol. 91.   RATHJEN & FOREYT—*Social Competence: Interventions for Children and Adults*
Vol. 92.   VAN DE RIET, KORB & GORRELL—*Gestalt Therapy: An Introduction*
Vol. 93.   MARSELLA & PEDERSEN—*Cross-Cultural Counseling and Psychotherapy*
Vol. 94.   BRISLIN—*Cross-Cultural Encounters: Face-to-Face Interaction*
Vol. 95.   SCHWARTZ & JOHNSON—*Psychopathology of Childhood: A Clinical-Experimental Approach, Second Edition*
Vol. 96.   HEILBRUN—*Human Sex-Role Behavior*
Vol. 97.   DAVIDSON, KOCH, LEWIS & WRESINSKI—*Evaluation Strategies in Criminal Justice*
Vol. 98.   GOLDSTEIN, CARR, DAVIDSON & WEHR—*In Response to Aggression: Methods of Control and Prosocial Alternatives*
Vol. 99.   GOLDSTEIN—*Psychological Skill Training: The Structured Learning Technique*
Vol. 100. WALKER—*Clinical Practice of Psychology: A Guide for Mental Health Professionals*
Vol. 101. ANCHIN & KIESLER—*Handbook of Interpersonal Psychotherapy*
Vol. 102. GELLER, WINETT & EVERETT—*Preserving the Environment: New Strategies for Behavior Change*
Vol. 103. JENKINS—*The Psychology of the Afro-American: A Humanistic Approach*
Vol. 104. APTER—*Troubled Children/Troubled Systems*
Vol. 105. BRENNER—*The Effective Psychotherapist: Conclusions from Practice and Research*

Vol. 106. KAROLY & KANFER—*Self-Management and Behavior Change: From Theory to Practice**

Vol. 107. O'BRIEN, DICKSON & ROSOW—*Industrial Behavior Modification: A Management Handbook*

Vol. 108. AMABILE & STUBBS—*Psychological Research in the Classroom: Issues for Educators and Researchers**

Vol. 109. WARREN—*Auditory Perception: A New Synthesis**

Vol. 110. DiMATTEO & DiNICOLA—*Achieving Patient Compliance: The Psychology of the Medical Practitioner's Role*

Vol. 111. CONOLEY & CONOLEY—*School Consultation: A Guide to Practice and Training*

Vol. 112. PAPAJOHN—*Intensive Behavior Therapy: The Behavioral Treatment of Complex Emotional Disorders*

Vol. 113. KAROLY, STEFFEN & O'GRADY—*Child Health Psychology: Concepts and Issues*

Vol. 114. MORRIS & KRATOCHWILL—*Treating Children's Fears and Phobias: A Behavioral Approach*

Vol. 115. GOLDSTEIN & SEGALL—*Aggression in Global Perspective*

Vol. 116. LANDIS & BRISLIN—*Handbook of Intercultural Training*

Vol. 117. FARBER—*Stress and Burnout in the Human Service Professions*

Vol. 118. BEUTLER—*Eclectic Psychotherapy: A Systematic Approach*

Vol. 119. HARRIS—*Families of the Developmentally Disabled: A Guide to Behavioral Interventions*

Vol. 120. HERSEN, KAZDIN & BELLACK—*The Clinical Psychology Handbook, Second Edition*

Vol. 121. MATSON & MULICK—*Handbook of Mental Retardation, Second Edition*

Vol. 122. FELNER, JASON, MORITSUGU & FARBER—*Preventive Psychology: Theory, Research and Practice*

Vol. 123. CENTER FOR RESEARCH ON AGGRESSION—*Prevention and Control of Aggression*

Vol. 124. KRATOCHWILL & MORRIS—*The Practice of Child Therapy, Second Edition*

Vol. 125. VARNI—*Clinical Behavioral Pediatrics: An Interdisciplinary Biobehavioral Approach*

Vol. 126. RAMIREZ—*Psychology of the Americas: Mestizo Perspectives on Personality and Mental Health*

Vol. 127. LEWINSOHN & TERI—*Clinical Geropsychology: New Directions in Assessment and Treatment*

Vol. 128. BARLOW, HAYES & NELSON—*The Scientist Practitioner: Research and Accountability in Clinical and Educational Settings*

Vol. 129. OLLENDICK & HERSEN—*Child Behavioral Assessment: Principles and Procedures*

Vol. 130. BELLACK & HERSEN—*Research Methods in Clinical Psychology*

Vol. 131. GOLDSTEIN & HERSEN—*Handbook of Psychological Assessment, Second Edition*

Vol. 132. BELLACK & HERSEN—*Dictionary of Behavior Therapy Techniques*

Vol. 133. COOK—*Psychological Androgyny*

Vol. 134. DREW & HARDMAN—*Designing and Conducting Behavioral Research*

Vol. 135. APTER & GOLDSTEIN—*Youth Violence: Programs and Prospects*

Vol. 136. HOLZMAN & TURK—*Pain Management: A Handbook of Psychological Treatment Approaches*

Vol. 137. MORRIS & BLATT—*Special Education: Research and Trends*
Vol. 138. JOHNSON, RASBURY & SIEGEL—*Approaches to Child Treatment: Introduction to Theory, Research and Practice*
Vol. 139. RYBASH, HOYER & ROODIN—*Adult Cognition and Aging: Developmental Changes in Processing, Knowing and Thinking*
Vol. 140. WIELKIEWICZ—*Behavior Management in the Schools: Principles and Procedures*
Vol. 141. PLAS—*Systems Psychology in the Schools*
Vol. 142. VAN HASSELT & HERSEN—*Handbook of Adolescent Psychology*
Vol. 143. BRASSARD, GERMAIN & HART—*Psychological Maltreatment of Children and Youth*
Vol. 144. HERSHENSON & POWER—*Mental Health Counseling: Theory and Practice*
Vol. 145. GOLDSTEIN & KRASNER—*Modern Applied Psychology*
Vol. 146. CARSTENSEN & EDELSTEIN—*Handbook of Clinical Gerontology*
Vol. 147. HERSEN & BELLACK—*Dictionary of Behavioral Assessment Techniques*
Vol. 148. VAN HASSELT, STRAIN & HERSEN—*Handbook of Developmental and Physical Disabilities*
Vol. 149. BLECHMAN & BROWNELL—*Handbook of Behavioral Medicine for Women*
Vol. 150. MAHER & ZINS—*Psychoeducational Interventions in Schools: Methods and Procedures for Enhancing Student Competence*
Vol. 151. LAST & HERSEN—*Handbook of Anxiety Disorders*
Vol. 152. KAZDIN—*Child Psychotherapy: Developing and Identifying Effective Treatments*
Vol. 153. RUSSELL—*Stress Management for Chronic Disease*
Vol. 154. HUGHES—*Cognitive Behavior Therapy with Children in Schools*
Vol. 155. HIGGINBOTHAM, WEST & FORSYTH—*Psychotherapy and Behavior Change: Social, Cultural and Methodological Perspectives*
Vol. 156. WINETT, KING & ALTMAN—*Health Psychology and Public Health: An Integrative Approach*
Vol. 157. HESTER & MILLER—*Handbook of Alcoholism Treatment Approaches: Effective Alternatives*
Vol. 158. WHITE—*The Troubled Adolescent*
Vol. 159. HOWES—*The Psychology of Human Cognition: Mainstream and Genevan Traditions*
Vol. 160. SEGALL, DASEN, BERRY & POORTINGA—*Human Behavior in Global Perspective: An Introduction to Cross-Cultural Psychology*
Vol. 161. HERSEN & LAST—*Handbook of Child and Adult Psychopathology: A Longitudinal Perspective*
Vol. 162. SNYDER & FORSYTH—*Handbook of Social and Clinical Psychology: The Health Perspective*
Vol. 163. JOHNSON & GOLDMAN—*Developmental Assessment in Clinical Child Psychology: A Handbook*
Vol. 164. MARTIN—*Handbook of Behavior Therapy and Psychological Science: An Integrative Approach*
Vol. 165. WINIARSKI—*Aids-Related Psychotherapy*
Vol. 166. LIBERMAN—*Handbook of Psychiatric Rehabilitation*
Vol. 167. OLLENDICK & HERSEN—*Handbook of Child and Adolescent Assessment*
Vol. 168. HAYNES—*Models of Causality in Psychopathology: Toward Dynamic, Synthetic, and Nonlinear Models of Behavior Disorders*